UNDERSTANDING THE GREATEST WAR CAMPAIGN EVER CONCEIVED

(Clarity from the Book of Proverbs and How to Win)

The Rich, Poor, Needy, Prudent, Witness, Wise, Counselor, Neighbor

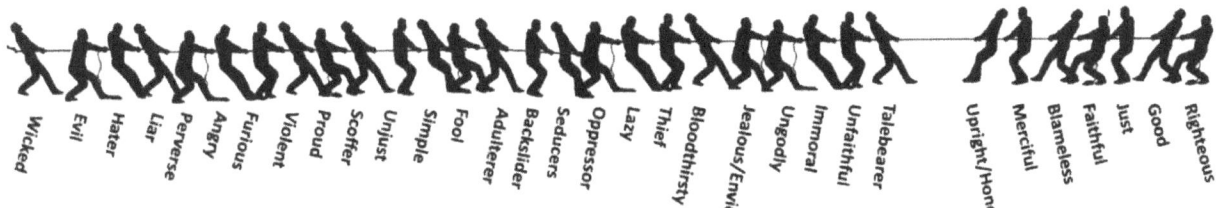

Wicked, Evil, Hater, Liar, Perverse, Angry, Furious, Violent, Proud, Scoffer, Unjust, Simple, Fool, Adulterer, Backslider, Seducers, Oppressor, Lazy, Thief, Bloodthirsty, Jealous/Envious, Ungodly, Immoral, Unfaithful, Talebearer, Upright/Honorable, Merciful, Blameless, Faithful, Just, Good, Righteous

By: Joseph J. Frazier
Colonel, U.S. Army (Retired)

Copyright ©2018 by Colonel Joseph J. Frazier, U.S Army (Ret.)

All rights reserved. This book or any portion thereof may not be reproduced or used in any manner whatsoever without the expressed written permission of the publisher except for the use of brief quotations such as in a book review, church bulleting, sermons, or marketing purposes.

First Edition: March 2019; Revised July 2019; January 2021

Mastering the Positive, LLC
Chesapeake, VA. 23322
www.masteringthepositive.com

Unless otherwise indicated, all Scripture quotations are from:
The New King James Version (NKJV). Nashville, TN: Thomas Nelson Publishers, 1982

Additionally, all statement cited from the apostles will only be done so by their names. The title of "apostle" will not accompany these men's name as it commonly accepted who the apostles are. This includes Peter, James, John, and Andrew; Philip and Thomas; Bartholomew and Matthew; James the son of Alphaeus and Simon the Zealot; and Judas the son of James (Acts 1:13); Matthias (Acts 1:26); and Paul (Acts 9:3-18).

Copyright © 2019 Joseph J. Frazier

All right reserved.

ISBN: 978-0-578-21318-7
ISBN-13:

"We know that we are of God, and the whole world lies under the sway of the wicked one"

~ 1 John 5:19

"...whose minds the god of this age has blinded, who do not believe, lest the light of the gospel of the glory of Christ, who is the image of God, should shine on them"

~ 2 Corinthians 4:4

"For we do not wrestle against flesh and blood, but against principalities, against powers, against the rulers of the darkness of this age, against spiritual hosts of wickedness in the heavenly places."

~ Ephesians 6:12 ~

"And if it seems evil to you to serve the Lord, choose for yourselves this day whom you will serve, whether the gods which your fathers served that were on the other side of the River, or the gods of the Amorites, in whose land you dwell. But as for me and my house, we will serve the Lord."

~ Joshua 24:15

This is a Natural Crisis

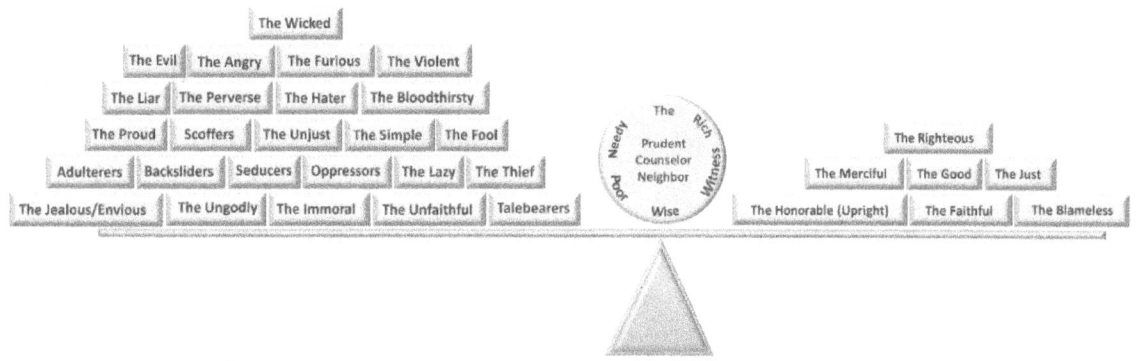

Figure 1: The War Campaign Scale

~ TABLE OF CONTENTS ~

Preface 6

Chapter I: Introduction 9

Chapter II: A Biblical Perspective of the War Campaign 26

Chapter III: The Dilemma and Results 31

Chapter IV: Introducing the Attributes and Their Roles 45

Chapter V: The Negative Attributes   49

1.	The Wicked	53
2.	The Evil	66
3.	The Perverse	84
4.	The Talebearer	89
5.	The Unfaithful	93
6.	The Immoral	105
7.	The Ungodly	117
8.	The Jealous/Envious	123
9.	The Thief	132
10.	The Lazy	141
11.	The Oppressor	150
12.	The Seducer	160
13.	The Backslider/Transgressor	169
14.	The Adulterer	175
15.	The Fool	188
16.	The Simple	198
17.	The Unjust	202
18.	The Scoffer	208
19.	The Proud	213
20.	The Hater	223
21.	The Liar	240
22.	The Angry	257
23.	The Furious	264
24.	The Violent	269
25.	The Bloodthirsty	283

Chapter VI: The Positive Attributes — 301

    1. The Merciful 308
    2. The Just 330
    3. The Upright/Honorable 348
    4. The Blameless 363
    5. The Good 375
    6. The Faithful 420
    7. The Righteous 449

Chapter VII: The Harvest — 488

    1. The Neighbor 492
    2. The Counselor 500
    3. The Witness 508
    4. The Prudent 515
    5. The Wise 524
    6. The Needy 539
    7. The Poor 545
    8. The Rich 560

Chapter VIII: What Happens in the Harvest When the Influences of the Attributes are Allowed? 584

Chapter IX: Why Identification of the Attributes is Critical for Winning the War Campaign? 599

      Strife 603

      Calamity 610

Chapter X: Is God's Calamity Occurring in the World Today? 648

Chapter XI: A View of the Spiritual Battlefield and the Complicated Nature of Spiritual Warfare 735

Chapter XII: Understanding Christ's Church and its Critical Role on the Spiritual Battlefield 752

Chapter XIII: What Christ's Church Bring to the Positive Forces of the War Campaign 788

Chapter XIV: Conclusion: A Call for Leaders 806

~ PREFACE ~

"Every day, we are all engaged in battles and skirmishes as part of a greater spiritual war. Our very survival depends on our knowledge of the true enemy."

~ Colonel Joseph J. Frazier, U.S. Army (Retired)

This book is dedicated to everyone who truly understands the meaning of fighting the "good fight." That is to say, fighting for the things that are just, pure, lovely, of good report, virtuous, and praiseworthy (Philippians 4:8). It is written as a rallying call for true leadership; leaders willing to open their eyes to truth and speak out on injustice wherever and in whatever form it is found. Leaders who understand strategy and can see the strategic maneuvering of forces that are willing to destroy the things of this world that are wholesome, decent, and civil - for their own gain. Leaders that understand Paul's statement, *"…this I pray, that your love may abound still more and more in knowledge and all discernment, that you may approve the things that are excellent, that you may be sincere and without offense till the day of Christ, being filled with the fruits of righteousness which are by Jesus Christ, to the glory and praise of God"* (Philippians 1:9-11). This book is about a lost dimension of leadership. It is the dimension that writers of leadership books refuse to take on. Mostly because of their lack of understanding of this dimension and partly out of fear of the politically correct secular and religious academic communities. For this dimension of leadership revolves around a complete *"walk by faith, not by sight"* (2 Corinthians 5:7) discipline only understood by a transformed mind (Romans 12:2). It is the spiritual dimension of leadership.

You see, the world is engaged in the greatest war campaign ever devised. It is a war fought on the spiritual level as well as the physical level across all of humanity. It is war so complicated in its execution that its comprehension is out of reach for most people and they are swept away as collateral damage by the war. It is a war controlled by unseen forces that revealed themselves as human behaviors, attitudes, and verbal responses. Purely through the power of influence, these forces manipulate the human mind; the center of cognitive thoughts, logic, and reason, to influence decisions and choices toward good or bad and right or wrong. But only leaders who understand the spiritual dimension of leadership can resolve the complicated issues unleashed in this campaign. This is not science fiction. It is an active presence of spiritual warfare that the world no longer understands. Why? Because most of humanity has lost the ability of "discernment"; the ability to understand "right" from "wrong" and "good" from "evil" on the spiritual level. This book explains this lost ability and the reason why it is lost in detail. This book will help one connect the dots between spiritual and physical warfare.

For now, try to understand that this campaign has a leader; a superior strategist with ambitious goals. Furthermore, this leader controls the greatest military ever organized. The leader of this military operates from a place of obscurity while his forces operate worldwide to strategically maneuver towards a final decisive battle. In fact, the war campaign's intensity has increased for centuries, but distractors have strategically obstructed humanity from seeing the war's true devastation and destruction. The Bible confirms these distractors as earthly wars and rumors of wars (Matthew 24:6; Mark 13:7), the cares of this world, the deceitfulness of riches, the desires for other things, and the pleasures of life (Matthew 13:22; Mark 4:18; Luke 8:14).

This book exposes how these distractors combine to disguise how every act of violence, negative thought, and hateful word interconnects to form the foundation of spiritual warfare. One will learn how every negative act strategically furthers the advancement of the war campaign while positive behaviors seek to counter their effects. The negative force's strategy and these distractors work together to keep the masses of humanity confused, frustrated, afraid, divided, and in chaos as civility deteriorates in society and worldwide. I hope this has whet your appetite.

My goal is to present a reality that many secular and religious groups desire to filter, change, or keep hidden. My primary objective is to clearly identify what spiritual warfare is. You see, I have invested years of study trying to unravel this campaign. God knows it has not been an easy task. However, it has been a worthy task. Even King Solomon of the Bible, took on this task as he faithfully recorded that he set his, "*...heart to seek and search out by wisdom concerning all that is done under heaven; this burdensome task God has given to the sons of man, by which they may be exercised*" (Ecclesiastes 1:13). Now, I offer what I have learned from this "*burdensome task*" with confidence. I have tried to write this book from a layman's view of the Bible without the aid of commentaries, men's interpretation of every Biblical word, or theological lexicons of Hebrew, Greek, or other study aides. Thus, I present this book as a leader fighting a battle providing direction to his soldiers – clear and concise.

This book analyzes the issues of this world to reveal the unseen forces that are actually driving them. It takes a critical look at what the religious and secular world misunderstands about good and evil and provides clarity. I believe that both good and evil are competing opponents of a great war campaign that began years beyond humanity's memory. It is a war that results from a "natural crisis" within man himself when knowledge and discernment are discarded out of ignorance. **Figure 1** on page 3 of this book provides an illustration of the scale on which the competing forces of the war balance. In the middle of the scale are the resources these forces compete for. This book will explain this scale in detail and the knowledge will expose a Truth that will help one survive the war campaign.

This book explains what I have learned through years of research. I believe God Himself provided mankind a source document that explains the war campaign and spiritual warfare in its totality. Yes, I am referring to the Bible in which the Psalmist stated, "*Your word is a lamp to my feet and a light to my path*" (Psalm 119:105). To my knowledge, this Book is the only ancient writing that proclaims that God, "*...desires all men to be saved and to come to the knowledge of the truth*" (1 Timothy 2:4). Based on my personal experiences in life, I believe that there is a Truth for the existence of all things. When Jesus proclaimed, "*If you abide in My word, you are My disciples indeed. And you shall know the truth, and the truth shall make you free*" (John 8:31-32), He laid out that Truth in His Gospel message. However, a brilliantly conceived and orchestrated war campaign developed by another master strategist has distorted and hidden this Truth from the public. If you will keep reading, I promise that you will discover some fascinating things that you may have never considered in your lifetime. In addition, I will show you the answer to the world's problems and demonstrate that there is a solution. I am not saying the solution is simple, but I am saying that there is a solution if one is willing to listen.

Here is an appetizer for what one will learn from this book. In spiritual warfare, just like physical warfare, one can never expect to defeat an enemy if he or she does not know who the enemy is. To defeat one's enemy, one must know:

- Who or what is the enemy
- What are his or her capabilities
- What motivates him or her to fight

Without a knowledge of these key elements, there is no hope for defeating an anonymous enemy. The world today, as from times beyond man's memory, is engaged in a fight with an anonymous adversary simply because most of humanity has rejected what can be known.

Without further delay, I would like to thank all my family and extended family for their support and interest in this book. I have spent countless hours pondering, studying, and writing this book, but the time has been worth it. Much of my time was preoccupied with thoughts that I hasten to capture on paper before distractors attempted to consume them. I never realized the reality of the war campaign's tactics until I sat down to pen something good, wholesome, and true. To my immediate family, although my time away has been long, I believe God will and has already rewarded and cared for you in my time of mental and physical absence. We have never suffered times of need and the Lord has provided at every opportunity. To my wife Allegra, I personally thank her with all my heart because the Lord knew the right match for me as my helpmate. The Bible records, "*He who finds a wife finds a good thing, and obtains favor from the Lord*" (Proverbs 18:22). I can truly attest to the Truth of this proverb. To Mariah, Joseph, and Jetera, I pray that each of you will always "*Draw near to God and He will draw near to you...*" (James 4:8). Your mom and I have given you our best. You are now responsible adults facing the war campaign on your own. To our granddaughters Kianna and Koi, we will continue to pray that you are reared, "*...up in the training and admonition of the Lord...*" (Ephesians 6:4) in this sinful world. Finally, to my entire church family and all my friends, I pray this book will help you in some way understand the common trials of life that we all experience and how to overcome them.

Joseph (J.J.) Frazier
COL, U.S. Army (Ret)
"A soldier in Christ"
joseph.frazier909@gmail.com

First Edition
First Printing – Feb 2019

CHAPTER I: INTRODUCTION

"...and the whole world lies under the sway of the wicked one"
~ 1 John 5:19

For years, I grieved over the senseless crime and violence strangling societies worldwide. Television, radio, newspapers, and social media outlets constantly broadcast the overwhelming evidence of societal chaos on an hourly basis. During my thirty years of service in the United States Army, I had the opportunity to study many Great War campaigns in the superb archives of the libraries at the Army War College in Pennsylvania and the Joint Forces Staff College in Virginia. These were wars that cost the lives of untold millions of people. Wars like the Vietnam War and Vo Nguyen Giap; the Invasion of Northern Germany by Gustavus Adolphus; the campaign against the Byzantine Empire; Frederick the Great's defense of Prussia during the Seven Years War; the conquest of Gaul by Caesar; the march across the Alps by Hannibal; the Mongol Invasion of China; the Defeat of the Third Coalition by Napoleon, World Wars I and II, and even America's great Civil War. I have physically participated in war as a soldier involved in the Gulf War of Desert Shield/Desert Storm. I can personally attest that war is the execution of violence on many levels that impacts local communities up to the national level. I have known war, peace, and even natural calamities in my lifetime. And yet, all these pales in comparison to the war campaign I hope to expose one to in this book. The war campaign I am writing about includes all the campaigns mentioned above, as well as battles on streets in our hometowns between citizens, police, and governments. Even acts of terrorism at any level are part of this war campaign. Mankind simply has not learned to perceive the local activities as part of a greater campaign because of the loss of <u>discernment</u> in the world. The scale on which spiritual warfare occurs is so vast that one cannot perceive it in its totality. **Figure 2** captures this great but overlooked truth. But to be even more precise, for every conflict there are leaders involved that are influenced by negative attributes who desire evil things and all of their followers support them. In opposition, there

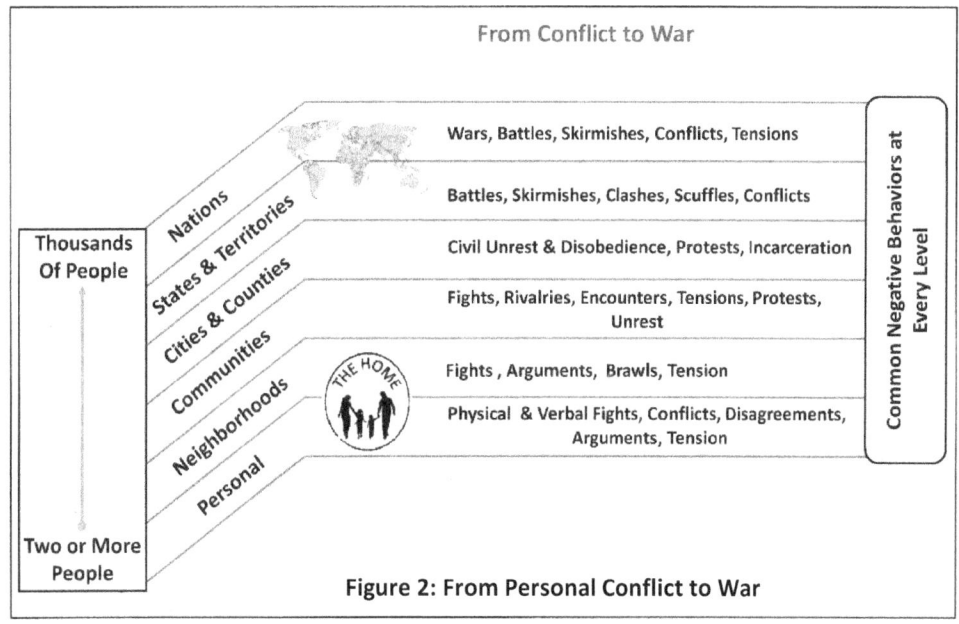

Figure 2: From Personal Conflict to War

are leaders influenced by positive attributes who actively resist evil and their followers support them in the common cause. The result from this interplay is war or conflict. Hence, this book will explain that terms such as wicked, evil, good, bad, right and wrong have far greater meanings than one may have ever imagined. Moreover, one will come to understand that there is more to war and conflict than what one can physically see. Thus, it is extremely important to resist the redefining of God's terms by anyone who claims superior knowledge or by virtue of their position in life. God's terms are divinely designed to expose the adversary whereas man's redefined terms are design to disguise the adversary.

I have always known in my heart that there had to be more to life than what my physical eyes could see or my senses perceive. I prayed for understanding. Somewhere along the way, I was taught that I should pray and if I were sincere in my prayers, God would help me understand. Today with certainty, I can say I understand. My true education started as I understood the reason for <u>discernment</u>. Once I understood <u>discernment</u>, I then understood the importance of knowing what was good, acceptable, and the perfect will of God. In the best words that I can find to share this knowledge, I offer the fruit of my research and what I believe is the wisdom contained in God's Word about spiritual warfare, the war campaign, and its solution. One will see that God used men, influenced by His Holy Spirit, to document the history and cause of the campaign. An example that best describes what fuels the war is a rhizome; a continuously growing horizontal underground stem which puts out lateral shoots and adventitious roots at intervals. The War Campaign itself is like a rhizome that stemmed from a singular root long ago. Today, it continues to spread unnoticed. Like a poorly managed weed, it stifles and destroys everything in its path. **Figure 3** illustrates the spread of the rhizome.

You see, I learned that it takes more than logic, reason, and critical thinking to understand the campaign that engulfs the world. Paul documented, *"Now we have received, not the spirit of the world, but the Spirit who is from God, that we might know the things that have been freely given to us by God. These things we also speak, not in words which man's wisdom teaches but which the Holy Spirit teaches, comparing spiritual things with spiritual. But the natural man does not receive the things of the Spirit of God, for they are foolishness to him; nor can he know them, because they are spiritually discerned"* (1 Corinthians 2:12-14). In other words, God provided a Spirit that helped

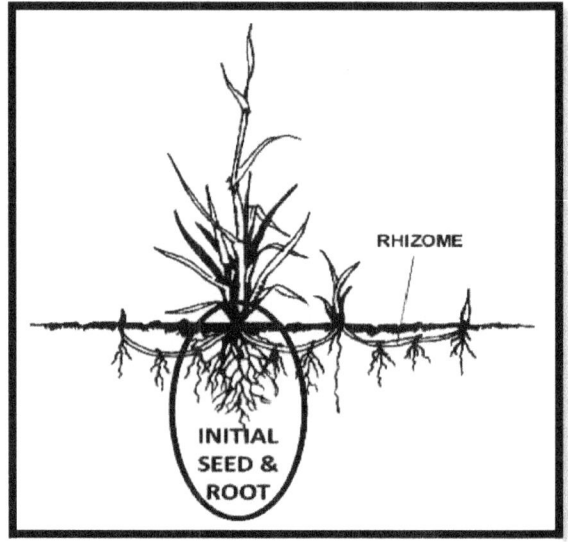

Figure 3: The Spread of a Rhizome

specific men document His Holy Word. Within their documentation, they recorded the pathway to God and the campaign that would attempt to prevent this knowledge from being accepted or even told. However, <u>discernment</u> provided the key for understanding the things that were written. Over time, most of mankind lost their ability to <u>discern</u> what is good, acceptable, and the perfect will of God. This happened because many, *"...who were once enlightened, and have tasted the heavenly gift, and have become partakers of the Holy Spirit, and have tasted the good word of God and the powers of the age to come...*" (Hebrews 6:4-5) turned their backs to God and stopped teaching the Truth. This began many millenniums ago and beyond the memories of anyone that came before you and me. Until mankind regains this wisdom, worldly chaos will prevail and increase. The problems of today are not what they seem. To see the truth behind the problems, one must acquire a new lens to see things for what they truly are. This new lens can only come through the process that I have called "Biblical Transformational Thinking" or BTT for brevity. I will refer to this way of thinking as BTT from here forward.

BTT was described by a man named Paul who committed himself to God and wrote to the world, "*...do not be conformed to this world, but be transformed by the renewing of your mind, that you may prove what is that good and acceptable and perfect will of God*" (Romans 12:2). Paul and other Bible writers identified the idea of transforming the mind and how to achieve it. This book documents this wisdom. For it is transformational thinking that allows <u>discernment</u> to take root in one's spiritual heart which influences the mind.

To set the stage for what one can expect to read about in this book, there are three major themes. The first and primary theme covers spiritual warfare and the war campaign engulfing the entire world. The second theme defines BTT and explains how it works. The final theme explains *<u>discernment</u>* and its necessity to survive spiritual warfare. All three themes are inextricably connected and this book explains the interaction of these three themes in detail. One will not read about people in our society today, nor will one find current world events linked to Biblical references. I have resisted this temptation. Yes, these types of worldly comparisons are popular by religious authors, but this book only allows God's Word to speak on its own merits. Why? Because Solomon documented, "*That which has been is what will be, that which is done is what will be done, and there is nothing new under the sun*" (Ecclesiastes 1:9). One will learn that human behavior has not changed since the beginning of time and the real answers needed for understanding the world's condition and human behavior are found in God's Word. God's Word identified the ancient spiritual forces that were involved in the war campaign but long forgotten by countless generations. These forces influence the choices we now see manifested in every person's behavior and attitude today. This is the truth behind what drives one's conduct and behavior and either starts conflict or sows the seeds of peace. This Truth is steadfast and will continue until the war campaign ends. However, the negative forces of the campaign execute an active strategy to stifle this Truth through spiritual warfare each generation. Solomon understood this from the Spirit of wisdom and documented for our learning that, "*There is no remembrance of former things, nor will there be any remembrance of things that are to come by those who will come after*" (Ecclesiastes 1:11). Although there is no remembrance, one has God's Word to learn from as a secure record of Truth. God's Word was the answer to the Roman governor of Judaea, Pontius Pilate's question when he asked, "*What is truth?*" (John 18: 38). This book analyzes the "truth" which provides the key to <u>discerning</u> things that are "right" and "wrong." So, let me begin by providing a general understanding of BTT, the war campaign, and <u>discernment</u>.

First, BTT is a process that helps one look beyond the physical things of life to see the spiritual stimuli behind them. These stimuli are the instigators of human behaviors. This may sound scary, but I assure you that it is not. I will explain this in detail and you will be amazed at what the Bible contains that is rarely taught. The fact is, Paul identified transformational thinking when he wrote, "*And do not be conformed to this world, but be transformed by the renewing of your mind, that you may prove what is that good and acceptable and perfect will of God*" (Romans 12:2). This form of thinking is above all the methods of thinking created by mankind. One must reach for a higher level of thinking to resolve the issues created by spiritual warfare.

For centuries, elements of transformational thinking have been proposed and ignored. However, no one has provided this way of thinking from the overall perspective of the war campaign that I propose until now. You see, my perspective comes from a document that is now rarely consulted by leaders who desire to find solutions to societal issues. Yes, that document is the Bible. I am simply providing a format from a military strategist point of view, of how I believe God intended all - who claim the name Christian - to look at the world and the spiritual fight that is unfolding worldwide. I pray my clarity will work for you. But only you can decide when you have had enough of the world's chaos and desire to try something that works. When one reaches this point, only then will one be ready to entertain the solution for which your spiritual heart already knows exist. God gave us an answer for peace and world maintenance thousands of years ago. It is man's dismissal of God's answer that has placed the world in the condition it is in now. I ask that you give me an opportunity to explain. **Figure 4** depicts transformational thinking against worldly though; that is, everything involved in the thinking described in James 3:14-16 of the Biblical record.

In physical warfare, one must understand that it is hard to fight an enemy if one has no clue who the enemy is. This same principle applies in spiritual warfare. Thus, whether physical or spiritual, both forms of war are complicated, messy, and full of deception. Warfare cannot be understood in a soundbite. There are

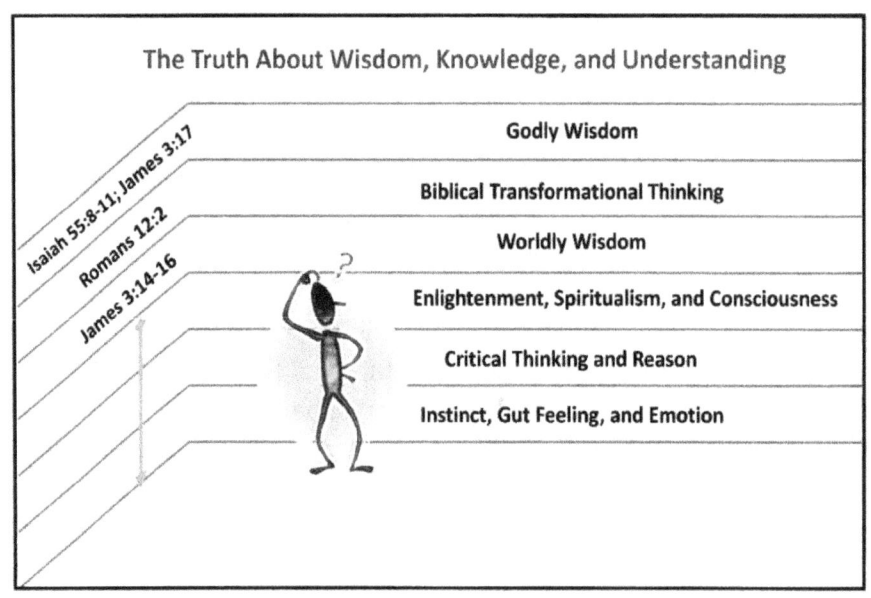

Figure 4: The Truth About Wisdom, Knowledge, and Understanding

no cliff-notes, summaries, or briefs that can explain the flashpoint that eventually ignites into what is defined as war. Moreover, every war is different because time, circumstance, and ingenuity causes battles to evolve. Only through study, wisdom, and experience can one decipher warfare and all its volatility and violence. For warfare does not start all by itself. People influenced by negative stimuli start wars and blindly fight to maintain them. Meanwhile, the people engaged in the physical fight, sideline supporters, and the people who become collateral damage, all simply focus on the bloodshed, violence, and destruction. Typically during the entire effort, the factors that influenced the original people who started the war from the beginning, gets overlooked or lost in the chaos. The key for true resolution of the war rest in understanding the initial influences that began the war. In other words, something influenced the choices and decisions the people made that initially started the war. It is that "something" that this book identifies. For what is always overlooked are the common stimuli that drove the behaviors before the initial conflict started. When Jesus, moments before His cruel death, stated "*Father, forgive them, for they do not know what they do*" (Luke 23:34), He confirmed the existence of the "something" behind His murderers' behavior. The people who orchestrated His horrible death, to include the Roman government, were all influenced by unseen negative forces foretold in the ancient writings of the Old Testament Bible. These same people were accountable for rejecting Jesus' Word and listening to the wrong voice. They lacked <u>discernment</u>. This book explains spiritual warfare through the lens of physical warfare. Hence, the thoroughness of this book.

This book explains that in physical warfare, two or more opposing forces face off with each other while strategically maneuvering their forces to weaken and destroy the opposing force. The game of chess; a game purely based on strategy, is the ultimate expression of the war concept (**Figure 5**). Just like physical warfare, both sides of the spiritual war have a leader. On one side is Jesus of the New Testament and His followers. Jesus the Commander said, "*For I have not spoken on My own authority; but the Father who sent Me gave Me a command, what I should say and what I should speak*" (John 12:49). Jesus identified the opposing leader in the war campaign when He told the nation of Israel's leadership, "*You are of your father the devil, and the desires of your father you want to do. He was a murderer from the beginning, and does not stand in the

Figure 5: The War Campaign and the Chess Game

truth, because there is no truth in him. When he speaks a lie, he speaks from his own resources, for he is a liar and the father of it*" (John 8:44). This leader is also identified as the ruler of this world in John 12:31 and the god of this age in 2 Corinthian 4:4. This identification is crucial for understanding the power and capabilities at his disposal. For this leader has used his resources to mislead and confused generations of people as to which side Christ leads in the war campaign. This strategic move is confirmed where the Bible documents, "*For such are false apostles, deceitful workers, transforming themselves into apostles of Christ. And no wonder! For Satan himself transforms himself into an angel of light. Therefore it is no great thing if his ministers also transform themselves into ministers of righteousness, whose end will be according to their works*" (2 Corinthians 11:13-15). And because of this great Truth, like the game of chess, the war campaign has many winners and losers.

Unlike the game of chess, the war campaign claims more than just pieces on a board; it cost people their souls. Death in the war campaign is the ultimate defeat. In the game of chess, stalemates and compromises are acceptable. But in spiritual warfare, the adversary's goal is complete destruction of the opposing force. Jesus stated, "...*do not fear those who **kill** the body but cannot **kill** the soul. But rather fear Him who is able to destroy both soul and body in hell*" (Matthew 10:28). Hence, in spiritual warfare there is no stalemate or compromise. This war is a win or lose war. So, playing by the rules of engagement become extremely critical for everyone with the positive attributes. For this reason, Christians understand that one never engages Satan in open ground combat as the religious community advocates. Satan wears many faces. He leads his side while at the same time, masquerading as a friend on the opposite side of the war. He even claims Christ while all along, spreading doubt, heresies, and division from within the ranks. Christians understand that the Gospel of peace (Romans 10:15) must be taken to individual homes where Truth can be taught and lasting relationships are established. This setting offers the only real opportunity in the campaign for spiritual hearts to hear the Truth, be converted, and commit to a life in Christ. The religious community does not understand this Truth. When this community stands shoulder to shoulder with secular society in defiance of a perceived wrong, both communities now engage in spiritual warfare that challenges Satan in open combat. This is a no-win scenario for both communities. For the religious community specifically, compromise is the only possible option as this community strives to maintain its friendship with its worldly counterpart. Unfortunately, this union cannot succeed because it is unable to uncover the root cause of the problem. For in this union, the application of earthly wisdom will take precedence over God's Word. The spiritual solution for peace that the Gospel brings will be lost to compromise. God does not compromise.

The war campaign thrives on a long-established strategy. The strategy consists of smaller sustained but decisive battles. These battles keep mankind preoccupied and God's Truth hidden. The negative forces produce "fog"; a blanket of deceit, lies, partial truths, and distractions, all designed to keep one from hearing or focusing on the actual content of the Bible. Fog is a "ruse" in physical warfare. A ruse is a tactic designed to deceive and turn the tide of warfare in the favor of the opposing side. The negative forces produce the fog to hide their intentions and maintain confusion across the spiritual battlefield. For the positive forces, Jesus stated, "*I am the way, the truth, and the life...*" (John 14:6). For the negative forces Satan simply traverses the battlefield "*...seeking whom he may devour*" (1 Peter 5:8). Today, many people are lost in the fog of the campaign as depicted by **Figure 6**. But people who hear Jesus' voice through His Gospel gain the opportunity to rise above the fog and clearly see the battlefield for what it is. God spiritually saves these people when they are obedient to his complete Word. However, for those who

Figure 6: Lost in the Fog of Spiritual Warfare

reject Jesus's Word, He said "*...Every plant which My heavenly Father has not planted will be uprooted. Let them alone. They are blind leaders of the blind. And if the blind leads the blind, both will fall into a ditch*" (Matthews 15:13-14). Historically, every physical war has supported the war campaign described in this book. Thus, this book will reveal hundreds of strategies employed by the negative forces to keep people from knowing the Truth of the real war and what is at stake. To counter these strategies, I have included "pearls of wisdom" directly from the Biblical record that show how to overcome the negative forces. I call them "pearls of wisdom" because they contain the essential Word of God for understanding spiritual warfare and they provide the clarity for seeing that the war campaign itself is all about deception and division.

Only God knows when spiritual warfare and the war campaign began. Solomon noted, "*As you do not know what is the way of the wind, or how the bones grow in the womb of her who is with child, so you do not know the works of God who makes everything*" (Ecclesiastes 11:5). One's only clue comes from a statement in the Biblical record documenting, "*And war broke out in heaven: Michael and his angels fought with the dragon; and the dragon and his angels fought, but they did not prevail, nor was a place found for them in heaven any longer. So the great dragon was cast out, that serpent of old, called the Devil and Satan, who deceives the whole world; he was cast to the earth, and his angels were cast out with him*" (Revelations 12:7-9). One can know that Satan and his negative forces continued the war campaign on earth because the Biblical record documented, "*My people are destroyed for lack of knowledge. Because you have rejected knowledge...*" (Hosea 4:6). But the Bible also makes clear that God is in control. Even the apostles gathered and said in a unified prayer documented in Acts 4:24-28:

> "*Lord, You are God, who made heaven and earth and the sea, and all that is in them, who by the mouth of Your servant David have said:*
>
>> '*Why did the nations rage, and the people plot vain things? The kings of the earth took their stand, and the rulers were gathered together against the Lord and against His Christ.*'
>
> "*For truly against Your holy Servant Jesus, whom You anointed, both Herod and Pontius Pilate, with the Gentiles and the people of Israel, were gathered together to do whatever Your hand and Your purpose determined before to be done*"

This war continues to this very day. In fact, because of spiritual warfare, an important fact has been lost to history. The fact is, before the existence of any world religion, there was one God. If a religion began after Adam and Eve, it was destroyed along with all the other **wickedness** during the flood of Noah's day recorded in Genesis 6:5-8. Therefore, BTT allows one to see that any world religion developed from strategies perpetrated by the negative attributes after the flood and after God dispersed people across the face of the earth with the destruction of the tower of Babel (Genesis 11). But in the beginning, God only had one path, one faith, and one religious way for mankind. His Word reveals this truth that's been hidden in the fog of the war campaign.

Now before I provide the full perspective of the campaign, I would like you to consider a Biblical perspective of the human design. This perspective will set the stage for everything to follow in the pages of this book. By understanding the human design, one can understand what one is up against from birth to death. It is from this perspective that I believe one can understand the full concept behind the war campaign that all people involuntarily participate in each day. The Bible is key for this understanding. Remember I said that hidden from the average person's eyes is the fact that physical warfare is complicated, noisy, bloody, costly, and very confusing. More amazing than this, spiritual warfare is even more brutal. Why? Where physical war may cost the lives of thousands of people in a confined space over a period of time, spiritual warfare kills millions of people in undefined geographies for generations and cost them their souls. Physical war affects one's mind and leaves physical scars on one's body. Spiritual war affects one's spiritual heart and permeates one's entire body with unseen effects. I submit for your consideration that not all the societal issues that cause people to fight each other are rooted in the things that sociologists, psychologists, and psychiatrists have led the world to believe. There is more to the story than the scientific community's prognosticators and psychoanalysts can see or measure. Physical issues leading to confrontations begin when the carnal side of a person reacts from the influences of unseen forces within one's inner spirit because of spiritual conflict. The manifestation of the spiritual conflict is the outward demonstration of negative behaviors, thoughts, and words. Within humanity, a war between forces that are antithetical to the mind is occurring. This war continues until one becomes aware of another part of his or her existence. This other part is one's inner spirit and soul. Acknowledgment of this human design is the only way to begin understanding peace, contentment, and one's true interaction in a community. The carnal side of humanity always reacts and responds to spiritual impulses. This happens because of the ignorance found in the carnal side of a person that prevents him or her from recognizing the true nature of the adversary. To rebuff the adversary, one's inner spirit requires education, training, and discipline. Without these three items, one blindly stabs in the dark for solutions. This truth is part of the key for understanding the war campaign.

From the very beginning of creation, God composed man of flesh, blood, spirit and a soul. Mankind has always focused on the carnal side to respond to satisfying the physical stimuli of life. That is, he or she relies on the brain to think, reason, and to decipher things; the eyes to see, the tongue to taste, the ears to hear, the nose to smell, the skin to protect vital organs, the heart to pump life sustaining blood, the bones to keep one upright, etc.... Damage to the flesh allows the body to bleed and it can cease functioning. Of course, death is dependent on the severity of injury. With a major wound, bodily systems and processes can cease and a person can die. Yes, medical and scientific advances can prolong life, but eventually death occurs. As important as this information is, it is not the more important point of this book. What is more important is the other side of man – the inner spirit and the soul.

A critical objective of the negative forces of the war campaign is getting people to dismiss the idea of the spirit and soul. Even some people who profess to believe in God have fallen for this deception. The Holy Spirit provided the apostles with an understanding for making the connection between the inner spirit of man and the Spirit of God. Paul documented, *"Now we have received, not the spirit of the world, but the Spirit who is from God, that we might know the things that have been freely given to us by God. These things we also speak, not in words which man's wisdom teaches but which the Holy Spirit teaches, comparing spiritual things with spiritual. But the natural man does not receive the things of the Spirit of God, for they are foolishness to him; nor can he know them, because they are spiritually discerned"* (1 Corinthians 2:12-14). In fact, the very Bible itself documents that *"...the flesh lusts against the Spirit, and the Spirit against the flesh; and these are contrary to one another, so that you do not do the things that you wish"* (Galatians 5:17). This verse explains that without God in one's life, the natural man or flesh will do things contrary to the will of God. This is why many people want to do what is right but find themselves doing just the opposite. They dismiss the role of the human spirit and soul and they lack the understanding of how both play in the affairs of their lives. This dismissal and lack of understanding should shame the religious community. Both situations allow for the perpetuation of the scientific community's false claim that life is merely a physical existence. The responsibility for correctly teaching on the role of the spirit and soul belongs to both the Christian and religious communities. However, the vast amount of false teachings from the religious community has overshadowed the correct teachings from the Christian community. Hence, false teaching on this subject has diminished the significance of the spirit and soul in the affairs of every human's life. Instead, self-gratification of the flesh dominates. In fact, self-gratification has permeated the religious community so much that it reflects in religious leader's lifestyles, attire, and the worship facility. Moreover, it has become part of the fabric for resolving spiritual matters over God's Word. Hence, non-believers and even many believers, never learn that damage can occur to the inner spirit. They never learn that, when damage occurs to man's inner spirit, one's carnal side attempts to blindly relieve an unseen pain. Without understanding the source of the pain, the flesh becomes discontented and dissatisfied with life. As the carnal side seeks remedies, the remedies themselves become internal torment leading first to spiritual death, and then to physical death. No one sees the spirit. Therefore, repairing it requires knowledge from its originating source. This is where BTT comes in. This type of thinking is the only source for repairing the spirit. Allow me to provide the source of this information since it may be foreign to many of the readers of this book.

When God created us, the Bible documented, *"And the Lord God formed man of the dust of the ground, and breathed into his nostrils the breath of life; and man became a living being"* (Genesis 2:7). The psalmist recognized the wonderful works of God when he stated, *"You formed my inward parts; You covered me in my mother's womb. I will praise You, for I am fearfully and wonderfully made; marvelous are Your works, and that my soul knows very well. My frame was not hidden from You, when I was made in secret, and skillfully wrought in the lowest parts of the earth. Your eyes saw my substance, being yet unformed. And in Your book they all were written,*
the days fashioned for me, when as yet there were none of them" (Psalm 139:13-16). From these facts forward, the Bible recorded that God created a living being of flesh, blood, soul, and spirit. **Figure** 7 provides a graphic illustration of the four key components of mankind. One must understand that the flesh of one's body includes the brain, the heart, the bones, and everything made of human tissue. Our blood is represented by the graphic of the human heart.

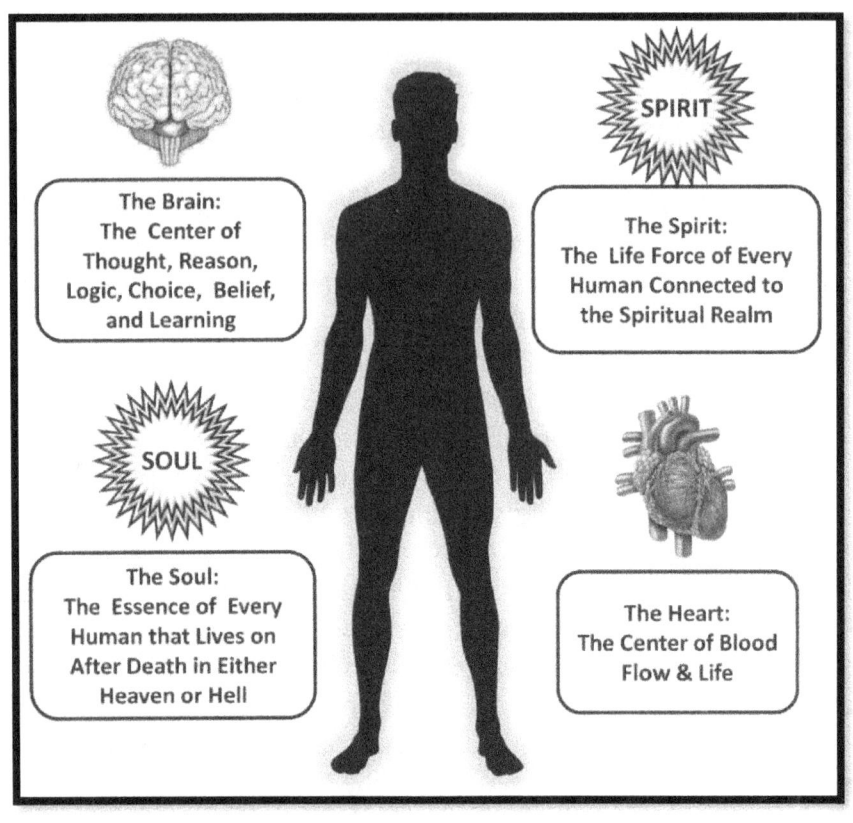

Figure 7: The Key Components of Man

But all these things deteriorate overtime with age. But the spirit and soul does not. One can refresh one's spirit with God's Word. The Holy Spirit revealed through Paul that, *"Therefore we do not lose heart. Even though our outward man is perishing, yet the inward man is being renewed day by day"* (2 Corinthians 4:16).

With this thought, Table 1 below documents pearls of wisdom that one can study on one's own time that illustrates various wisdom about the flesh, blood, spirit, and soul. The Bible documents:

"Whoever guards his mouth and tongue keeps his soul from troubles" (Proverbs 21:23)	*"But there is a spirit in man, and the breath of the Almighty gives him understanding"* (Job 32:8)	*"You shall love the Lord your God with all your heart, with all your soul, and with all your strength"* (Deuteronomy 6:5)
"...flesh and blood cannot inherit the kingdom of God; nor does corruption inherit incorruption" (1 Corinthians 15:50)	*"The law of the Lord is perfect, converting the soul; the testimony of the Lord is sure, making wise the simple..."* (Psalm 19:7)	*"You who love the Lord, hate evil! He preserves the souls of His saints; He delivers them out of the hand of the wicked"* (Psalm 97:10)
"He who keeps the commandment keeps his soul, but he who is careless of his ways will die" (Proverbs 19:16)	*"...it is not good for a soul to be without knowledge, and he sins who hastens with his feet"* (Proverbs 19:2)	*"He who gets wisdom loves his own soul; He who keeps understanding will find good"* (Proverbs 19:8)
"Whoever commits adultery with a woman lacks understanding; he who does so	*"For the life of the flesh is in the blood, and I have given it to you upon the altar to make atonement for your*	*"...Thus says the Lord, who stretches out the heavens, lays the foundation of the earth, and forms the spirit*

destroys his own soul" (Proverbs 6:32)	*souls; for it is the blood that makes atonement for the soul.'"* (Leviticus 17:11)	*of man within him..."* (Zechariah 12:1)
"And do not fear those who kill the body but cannot kill the soul. But rather fear Him who is able to destroy both soul and body in hell" (Matthew 10:28)	*"Jesus said to him, "You shall love the Lord your God with all your heart, with all your soul, and with all your mind"* (Matthew 22:37)	*"Watch and pray, lest you enter into temptation. The spirit indeed is willing, but the flesh is weak"* (Matthew 26:41; Mark 14:38)
"...Walk in the Spirit, and you shall not fulfill the lust of the flesh. For the flesh lusts against the Spirit, and the Spirit against the flesh; and these are contrary to one another, so that you do not do the things that you wish" (Galatians 5:16, 17)	*"For we do not wrestle against flesh and blood, but against principalities, against powers, against the rulers of the darkness of this age, against spiritual hosts of wickedness in the heavenly places"* (Ephesians 6:12)	*"...for it is the life of all flesh. Its blood sustains its life. Therefore I said to the children of Israel, 'You shall not eat the blood of any flesh, for the life of all flesh is its blood. Whoever eats it shall be cut off.'"* (Leviticus 17:14)
"...abstain from fleshly lusts which war against the soul..." (1 Peter 2:11)	*"The spirit of a man will sustain him in sickness, but who can bear a broken spirit?"* (Proverbs 18:14)	*"The spirit of a man is the lamp of the LORD searching all the inner depths of his heart"* (Proverbs 20:27)

Table 1: Additional Wisdom on the Components of Man

These few scriptures in Table 1 represent a sample of the vast Biblical documentation that God has provided for one to understand His creation. One should take away from these scriptures that mankind is more than just flesh and blood. Humans have a soul and a spirit that play a major role between the earthly and spiritual realms. It takes all four elements working together for one's life to be complete. BTT allows one to see that one's inner spirit engages with spiritual things. Jesus even told His disciples, *"It is the Spirit who gives life; the flesh profits nothing. The words that I speak to you are spirit, and they are life. But there are some of you who do not believe...."* (John 6:63-64). The negative forces of the war campaign consume everyone who dismisses this vital information. How? The carnal side of man is deceived and distracted by the manifestation of negative behaviors that emanate from negative spiritual forces. BTT opens one's eyes to this truth. When one reads the Bible for oneself, one begins to see this truth. By the end of this book, one will understand how God opens one's eyes to His Truth. Moreover, if one places his or her trust in God, believes what He has documented, and remains obedient to His word, one can survive the spiritual war encompassing the world.

There is one other thing within the inner spirit of man. There exists a spiritual heart. The Biblical record refers to the heart of man all the time but, one must allow BTT to discern when the writers speak of the heart as the physical heart, the physical mind, or the spiritual heart. This <u>discernment</u> is very important because the spiritual heart plays a critical role in the war campaign. The spiritual heart highlights the complexity of God's creations and the need for a greater understanding of the inner spirit. Here are just a few Biblical references to inform one about the spiritual heart. It is real; do not overlook this. The Biblical record documents:

- The Lord said to Solomon: "*As for you, my son Solomon, know the God of your father, and serve Him with a loyal **heart** and with a willing **mind**; for the Lord searches all **hearts** and understands all the intent of the thoughts. If you seek Him, He will be found by you; but if you forsake Him, He will cast you off forever*" (1 Chronicles 28:9)

- David documented in the Psalms: "*Oh, let the wickedness of the wicked come to an end, but establish the just; for the righteous God tests the **hearts** and **minds***" (Psalm 7:9), and "*Examine me, O Lord, and prove me; try my **mind** and my **heart***" (Psalm 26:2), "*Thus my **heart** was grieved, and I was vexed in my **mind***" (Psalm 73:21)

- The prophet Jeremiah mentioned it while pleading his case against the wicked: "*But, O Lord of hosts, You who judge righteously, testing the **mind** and the **heart**, let me see Your vengeance on them, for to You I have revealed my cause*" (Jeremiah 11:20; see also Jeremiah 20:12 and Jeremiah 31:33)

- Jesus said: "*You shall love the Lord your God with all your **heart**, with all your soul, and with all your **mind**. This is the first and great commandment*" (Matthew 22:37-38; see also Mark 12:30 and Luke 10:27)

- Paul wrote to the church of Philippi: "*...and the peace of God, which surpasses all understanding, will guard your **hearts** and **minds** through Christ Jesus*" (Philippians 4:7)

- Paul, speaking of God's plan of salvation for the Jews, stated: "*For this is the covenant that I will make with the house of Israel after those days, says the Lord: I will put My laws in their **mind** and write them on their **hearts**; and I will be their God, and they shall be My people*" (Hebrews 8:10)

Clearly one can see this spiritual heart can be loyal, searched, tested, examined, grieved, judged, loved, guarded, and written on. The fleshy heart does none of these; it simply pumps blood throughout the body. Moreover, the context of the scriptures distinguishes the human mind from the spiritual heart. BTT allows one to see that learning about the spiritual heart takes a little study, but it is critical to understand the difference between it and the physical heart and mind; for the spiritual heart plays a major role in baptism as described in the Bible. I will discuss this in detail and its relationship to the war campaign in Chapter X of this book. For now, try to understand that baptism allows Christ to coexist in one's spiritual heart to help one navigate life's journey in preparation for eternal life, **if** one is obedient and faithful to God's Word. Paul documented, "*The Spirit Himself bears witness with our spirit that we are children of God, and if children, then heirs—heirs of God and joint heirs with Christ, if indeed we suffer with Him, that we may also be glorified together*" (Romans 8:16-17). The journey with Christ is difficult and suffering often occurs for following Christ's path. Why? Because the negative attributes hate one's positive choice on the spiritual battlefield. Most people reject this difficult path. But this book will explain how true baptism places one in a state to overcome the influences of the negative attributes that mock this journey. Paul provided information on this idea when he documented, "*For as many of you as were baptized into Christ have put on Christ*" (Galatians 3:27). From this statement, he further prayed that God, "*...would grant you,* *according to the riches of His glory, to be strengthened with might through His Spirit in the inner man, that Christ may dwell in your hearts through faith; that you, being rooted and grounded in love, may be able to comprehend with all the saints what is the width and length and depth and height—to know the love of Christ which passes knowledge; that you may be filled with all the fullness of God*" (Ephesians 3:16-19). It is the fullness of God that gives the inner spirit of man the ability to resist and defeat the negative forces in spiritual warfare.

It is vitally important to understand that you are more than just flesh and blood. You are a spiritual being as well. It is also vitally important for one to understand that the inner spirit can be educated, fed to remain healthy, and controlled. Solomon documented, "*He who is slow to anger is better than the mighty, and he who <u>rules his spirit</u> than he who takes a city*" (Proverbs 16:32). Moreover, one's inner spirit can get sick, weak, disoriented, and become destructive when not fed properly. This is exactly why the spiritual side of man must stay connected to God. People are initially fed on the milk of God's Word because of spiritual warfare. But eventually, they must mature to the meat of His Word to grow spiritually according to 1 Peter 2:2 and Hebrews 5:12- 13. Paul even told the early Christians, "*I fed you with milk and not with solid food; for until now you were not able to receive it, and even now you are still not able; for you are still carnal. For where there are envy, strife, and divisions among you, are you not carnal and behaving like mere men?*" (1 Corinthians 3:2-3). BTT allows one to see that without God's Word, <u>*strife*</u> and rebellion will cripple the carnal side of man permanently. Hence, Paul documented, "*...if you live according to the flesh you will die; but if by the Spirit you put to death the deeds of the body, you will live. For as many as are led by the Spirit of God, these are sons of God*" (Romans 8:13-14). Paul explained that one's inner spirit is strengthened by the Holy Spirit through knowledge and obedience to God's Word. This provides the defense against the negative forces that would influence one's behavior in the war campaign. With this defense, he further documented that "*There is therefore now no condemnation to those who are in Christ Jesus, who do not walk according to the flesh, but according to the Spirit. For the law of the Spirit of life in Christ Jesus has made me free from the law of sin and death*" (Romans 8:1-2). The indwelling Spirit of Jesus strengthens one's inner spirit. Jesus said Himself that "*It is the Spirit who gives life; the flesh profits nothing. The words that I speak to you are spirit, and they are life. But there are some of you who do not believe." For Jesus knew from the beginning who they were who did not believe, and who would betray Him*" (John 6:63-64). What Jesus said about betrayal did not only apply to Judas, it spiritually applies to everyone who learns His Word and then turns his or her back on it. It applies to **false** teachers and entire religious communities. Moreover, this applies to Christians who were once in the Lord's church and fell to the **deception** of spiritual warfare. These Christians are in a state of apostasy. Paul documented this sad state when he wrote, "*For it is impossible for those who were once enlightened, and have tasted the heavenly gift, and have become partakers of the Holy Spirit, and have tasted the good word of God and the powers of the age to come, if they fall away, to renew them again to repentance, since they crucify again for themselves the Son of God, and put Him to an open shame*" (Hebrews 6:4-6). These things stated thus far are a glimpse into the complex nature of the war campaign and spiritual warfare.

Finally, there is the issue of <u>*discernment*</u>. <u>*Discernment*</u> is a spiritual element that allows one to differentiate between things that are **good** or **evil** and **right** or **wrong**. It is a divine key for unraveling and understanding the entire war campaign. This spiritual key has been lost for generations and the negative attributes strive every day to keep it hidden through the confusion of life's daily battles. Paul wrote, "*But the natural man does not receive the things of the Spirit of God, for they are foolishness to him; nor can he know them, because they are spiritually discerned*" (1 Corinthians 2:14). One can read that Solomon clearly asked the Lord for this spiritual key and most students of the Bible are familiar with his request. Solomon asked the Lord "*...give to Your servant an understanding heart to judge Your people, that I may discern between good and evil. For who is able to judge this great people of Yours?*" (1 Kings 3:9). The Lord responded, "*...Because you have asked this thing, and have not asked long life for yourself, nor have asked riches for yourself, nor have asked the life of your enemies, but have asked for yourself understanding to discern justice...*" (1 Kings 3:11). He gave Solomon what he asked for and much more. However, Solomon was not the first to have this ability. A few examples before him included:

Who	What Is Documented
Joseph	After Joseph interpreted the Egyptian Pharaoh's dream in Genesis 41:25-32, Joseph suggested that the Pharaoh, "*...select a discerning and wise man, and set him over the land of Egypt*" (Genesis 41:33) to manage the kingdom's resources during the times of plenty and the times of famine. The Pharaoh agreed and said to Joseph, "*...Inasmuch as God has shown you all this, there is no one as discerning and wise as you*" (Genesis 41:39). Pharaoh promoted Joseph and set him over all the land of Egypt according to Genesis 41:41.
David	Joab used a woman to lift the heart of David from the grief he had over his son Absalom who had fled to Geshur according to 2 Samuel 13: 37-39. Joab told the woman what to say. After she stated, "*...The word of my lord the king will now be comforting; for as the angel of God, so is my lord the king in discerning good and evil. And may the Lord your God be with you*" (2 Samuel 14:17), David discerned there was more to the woman behind her actions and words. He asked the woman, "*...Is the hand of Joab with you in all this?*" And the woman answered and said, "*As you live, my lord the king, no one can turn to the right hand or to the left from anything that my lord the king has spoken. For your servant Joab commanded me, and he put all these words in the mouth of your maidservant*" (2 Samuel 14:19).

Table 2: The Spirit of *Discernment* Working in Joseph and David

In fact, Moses was instructed by the Lord to tell the children of Israel that, "*...you shall take no bribe, for a bribe blinds the discerning and perverts the words of the righteous*" (Exodus 23:8). So, the element of *discernment* was available to many others. In fact, Solomon confirmed this when he documented:

- "*Yes, if you cry out for discernment, and lift up your voice for understanding, if you seek her as silver, and search for her as for hidden treasures; then you will understand the fear of the Lord, and find the knowledge of God*" (Proverbs 2:3-5)

- "*Folly is joy to him who is destitute of discernment, but a man of understanding walks uprightly*" (Proverbs 15:21)

- "*...rebuke one who has understanding, and he will <u>discern</u> knowledge*" (Proverbs 19:25)

- "*Whoever keeps the law is a <u>discerning</u> son...*" (Proverbs 28:7)

- "*He who keeps his command will experience nothing harmful; and a wise man's heart <u>discerns</u> both time and judgment, because for every matter there is a time and judgment, though the misery of man increases greatly. For he does not know what will happen; so who can tell him when it will occur?*" (Ecclesiastes 8:5-7)

Initially, teaching the people about the element of <u>discernment</u> was the responsibility of the Levitical priest. The Biblical record documented that the prophet Ezekiel stated from the Lord, "*...they shall teach My people the difference between the holy and the unholy, and cause them to <u>discern</u> between the unclean and the clean. In controversy they shall stand as judges, and judge it according to My judgments. They shall keep My laws and My statutes in all My appointed meetings, and they shall hallow My Sabbaths*" (Ezekiel 44:23-24). When the priests stopped teaching as the Lord commanded, the people chose their own paths. In the Book of Judges, it recorded a time when "*...everyone did what was right in his own eyes*" (Judges 21:25). Their choice allowed the negative forces of the campaign to tip the balance of the war. Over time, whole cities lost the element of <u>discernment</u> as priests strayed from the truth. The Book of Jonah provides an example of this as the Lord said to Jonah, "*...should I not pity Nineveh, that great city, in which are more than one hundred and twenty thousand persons who cannot <u>discern</u> between their right hand and their left—and much livestock?*" (Jonah 4:11). Later, the prophet Malachi would document a prophecy about <u>discernment</u> that would apply to Christians today. He documented from the Lord, "*They shall be Mine,*" says the Lord of hosts, "*On the day that I make them My jewels. And I will spare them as a man spares his own son who serves him.*" Then you shall again <u>discern</u> between the righteous and the wicked, between one who serves God and one who does not serve Him*" (Malachi 3:17-18). Malachi's prophecy applied to the era of Christians; not to the Jews that fought against Jesus' ministry as He walked the earth. One can know this truth because Jesus,

- ...told the Pharisees and Sadducees who asked Him to show them a sign from heaven, said "*When it is evening you say, 'It will be fair weather, for the sky is red'; and in the morning, 'It will be foul weather today, for the sky is red and threatening.' Hypocrites! You know how to <u>discern</u> the face of the sky, but you cannot <u>discern</u> the signs of the times. A wicked and adulterous generation seeks after a sign, and no sign shall be given to it except the sign of the prophet Jonah.*" And He left them and departed" (Matthew 16:2-4)

- ...told the multitude, "*Whenever you see a cloud rising out of the west, immediately you say, 'A shower is coming'; and so it is. And when you see the south wind blow, you say, 'There will be hot weather'; and there is. Hypocrites! You can <u>discern</u> the face of the sky and of the earth, but how is it you do not <u>discern</u> this time?*" (Luke 12:54-56)

BTT allows one to see that the Jewish leadership did not teach the truth about _discernment_. In fact, Jesus even referred to the Jewish leadership as "*blind guides*" in Matthew 23:16; and verse 24. But after Jesus' death, His apostles began teaching the Gospel which included teachings on _discernment_. To ensure the church in its infancy had the ability to survive the negative forces of the war campaign, the Holy Spirit gave some people the ability to _discern_ the difference between **clean** and **unclean spirits**. These are the positive and negative attributes of this book. The Biblical record documented, "*...to another the working of miracles, to another prophecy, to another _discerning_ of spirits, to another different kinds of tongues, to another the interpretation of tongues*" (1 Corinthians 12:10). This ability, along with the others, was necessary to get the Lord's church firmly rooted in a place where Judaism, paganism, and Satan were dominant. It is my contention for the war campaign, people in Christ's church that are committed and obedient, still have the opportunity to gain the element of _discernment_ as they mature in Christ. Now there are many people in Christ's church who never gain the element of _discernment_ because of their lack of commitment and obedience. _Discernment_ cannot be achieved without one's total commitment and obedience to God's Holy Word.

To close out this discussion on the element of _discernment_, here are just a few pearls of wisdom that the Holy Spirit revealed to Paul. Paul documented these for one's survival during spiritual warfare and the war campaign. He wrote:

- Concerning the communion commanded for Christians to observe every Lord's day: "*For he who eats and drinks in an unworthy manner eats and drinks judgment to himself, not _discerning_ the Lord's body*" (1 Corinthians 11:29)

- To the Lord church established in Philippi and one's example to this very day, Paul prayed "*...this I pray, that your love may abound still more and more in knowledge and all _discernment_, that you may approve the things that are excellent, that you may be sincere and without offense till the day of Christ, being filled with the fruits of righteousness which are by Jesus Christ, to the glory and praise of God*" (Philippians 1:9-11)

- A fact about the Word of God: "*For the word of God is living and powerful, and sharper than any two-edged sword, piercing even to the division of soul and spirit, and of joints and marrow, and is a _discerner_ of the thoughts and intents of the heart*" (Hebrews 4:12)

- A fact about learning the Word of God: "*But solid food belongs to those who are of full age, that is, those who by reason of use have their senses exercised to _discern_ both good and evil*" (Hebrews 5:14)

Now the element of _discernment_ is not the only spiritual element involved in the war campaign. One will learn that the positive and negative attributes employ a host of spiritual elements across the spiritual battle field. These elements will be identified in the chapters with their specific attribute. With that said, allow me to offer a disclaimer about what I believe. It is very important to me to Biblically document everything that I write in this book. I treat the Bible with the utmost respect and I sincerely believe the message contained in the Bible is from the inspired Word of God. I believe with all my heart, mind and soul that, "*All Scripture is given by inspiration of God, and is profitable for doctrine, for reproof, for correction, for instruction in righteousness, that the man of God may be complete, thoroughly equipped for every good work*" (2 Timothy 3:16-17). For this reason, it is my personal decision to refer to the Bible as the "Biblical record." This terminology formally illustrates that the Bible is God's **binding authority** given to the world. For those who accuse me or any member of Christ' church of being legalistic, we are guilty. The psalmist even wrote, "*Open my eyes, that I may see Wondrous things from Your law*" (Psalm 119:18).

Now with the Bible serving as God's **binding authority**, my stance also includes God's _grace_. However, this book will explain the true application of God's _grace_; a subject ***false*** teachers have twisted in spiritual warfare. Hence, under the new covenant, which does not delete the education from the old covenant, Paul documented that Christians are a people, "*...of the new covenant, not of the letter but of the Spirit; for the letter kills, but the Spirit gives life*" (2 Corinthians 3:6). The Biblical record terminology documents that God's divine authority is greater than any legally binding document ever to exist. This term places emphasis on the fact that the Bible is the world's information resource Book from God and it provides mankind, "*...all things that pertain to life and godliness...*" (2 Peter 1:3). Therefore, I will capitalize the term "Biblical record" and other related terms to show my respect for His word. I believe society's low regard for the Bible and its message partially comes from the way religious groups and writers have handled the Bible itself over the years. Treating the Bible as just another book on a table or shelf contradicts the act of claiming the Bible contains God's Word – the Highest Authority! If one truly believes the Bible contains God's inspired Word, then it should be treated with dignity and respect. For me, any other treatment of the Bible results in a denigration of its content. For who would willfully throw an oyster in the trash if they knew it had a pearl inside? But this is how many treat the Bible. This contradiction has aided the negative attributes in their advancement of spiritual warfare. The negative attributes influence people to point out the inconsistency of the believer's physical treatment of the Bible and stance on God's Word in it. Secular society has even convinced people that the Scriptures are no more than an ancient text with no application for a modern, evolving, and progressive people. Enlightenment is the new truth. The Old Testament, Jesus' teachings, and His parables, only serve as religious stories. I reject this. Studying the complete Bible helps one to understand his or her direction in life. Moreover, "*...whatever things were written before were written for our learning, that we through the patience and comfort of the Scriptures might have hope*" (Romans 15:4). The complete Bible gives one an understanding of life. Without it, one will lose hope for oneself and all of humanity. By studying it, one learns that, "*...we were saved in this hope, but hope that is seen is not hope; for why does one still hope for what he sees? But if we hope for what we do not see, we eagerly wait for it with perseverance*" (Romans 8:24-25). Further, the Bible helps one to develop "***faith***". The Bible documents, "*...**faith** is the substance of things hoped for, the evidence of things not seen*" (Hebrews 11:1). Therefore, the Bible must be treated as the "Book of books" and regain a place of honor in our homes, society, and even in the church. So, when one sees the terms "Bible", "Biblical" record, or other references to God's Word capitalized in this book, know that it is not a mistake but my honor and respect for God and His inspired Word.

CHAPTER II: A Biblical Perspective of the War Campaign

"For we do not wrestle against flesh and blood, but against principalities, against powers, against the rulers of the darkness of this age, against spiritual hosts of wickedness in the heavenly places"

~ Ephesians 6:12

Consider this for a moment. Each day in this world, heinous and incomprehensible acts of wickedness, evil, and perversion occur. These acts are either in the conception stage, in progress, or wrapping up. For many people, taking a human life is no different from killing an animal for sport. For others, the lack of respect for any form of flesh defies both reason and understanding. Although from time to time, one sees random acts of kindness, but wickedness, evil, and perverse acts appear to dominate. The sanctity of the home and community often unravels under the weight of these acts. Many of the elderly live in <u>*fear*</u> and the young revolt to "experience life", creating a complicated dynamic within many households. Even more painful is the fact that many of the world's children become unwilling participants of actions and behaviors that increasingly corrupts their innocence. Caring parents and adults used to shelter children from the issues of the world. However, now worldly issues bleed into homes through technology, social media, and unconstrained experimentation in educational institutions at all levels. Hence, the moral foundation of the home stays under constant assault and many children can only see a future of hopelessness. Sadly, the things that once served as cornerstones of truth, nobility, justice, purity, love, good report, virtuosity, and praiseworthiness, are now being twisted to be bad or false. The Lord warned of this **evil** to come and the Biblical record documented it. He had the prophet Isaiah warn the nation of Israel, *"Woe to those who call evil good, and good evil; who put darkness for light, and light for darkness; who put bitter for sweet, and sweet for bitter!"* (Isaiah 5:20).

One would think in a world rich in academia, counselors, psychologists, psychiatrists and mental wellness professionals, that there would be more solutions to manage the deteriorating human condition. One should ask why are the levels of social chaos growing today instead of decreasing? Or maybe one would think with thousands of churches, televangelists, and religious social media outlets broadcasting diverse messages twenty-four hours a day, social interactions would improve instead of decline. But none of these have had an impact on the overall condition of the home, the community, or even society. In fact, just the opposite is true. Peace remains elusive while both chaos and depression rule. Worldwide tensions, turmoil, violence, and death have increased among communities. Issues over race, money, sexual identity, politics, judicial paralysis, and an inability to <u>discern</u> right from wrong have added to the social moray. This book will expose how false teachers have permeated echelons of these communities and validate Peter's writing in the Bible. Peter documented that, *"...there were also false prophets among the people, even as there will be false teachers among you, who will secretly bring in destructive heresies, even denying the Lord who bought them, and bring on themselves swift destruction. And many will follow their destructive ways, because of whom the way of truth will be blasphemed. By covetousness they will exploit you with deceptive words; for a long time their judgment has not been idle, and their destruction does not slumber*" (2 Peter 2:1-3). From the religious community, to academia, and the mental health profession, false teachers embedded themselves in the fabric of society to bring destructive philosophies rooted in the ancient doctrines of the negative attributes of the war campaign.

To cope, many people resort to abusing illegal and prescription drugs and alcohol. Others create fantasy lives for their escape by engaging with virtual images or acts of immorality and pornography. Often, these coping activities lead to increased divorce rates, children born out of wedlock, and the destruction of the family unit. The legal system, hijacked by dishonorable and corrupt people, further compromises the family unit. People corrupted during their own childhood begin serving as judges, lawyers, and other law-making or enforcing entities as adults and add to the problem. **Figure 8** illustrates the negative forces of spiritual warfare that attempt to compromise people and their families. Their compromised and uncorrected lifestyles automatically lead them down paths that support other people just as compromised as they are. This group suffers from spiritual ignorance. They proudly display their error through biased decisions based on favoritism, partiality, and bribery. These are the people of Romans 1:28-32

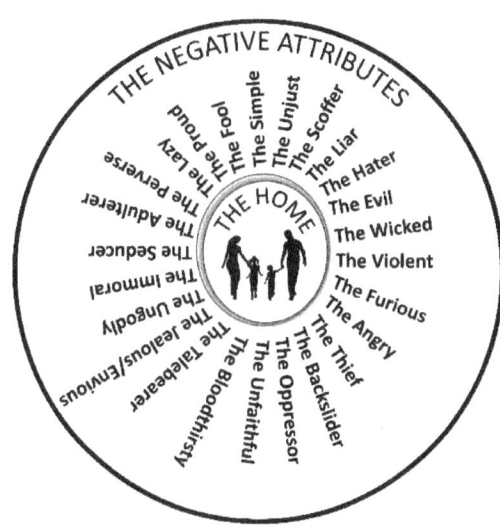

Figure 8: Negative Forces Surrounding Man and Woman

"*...who not only do the same but also approve of those who practice them*".

In response to the chaos, the wealthy and wicked capitalize on the instability. Prison construction skyrockets. When <u>discernment</u> is lost, even the innocent is imprisoned or charged with bogus crimes. Like the guilty, even after their time is served, the weight of the penalties of incarceration causes many people to return to the failed system. This happens because of inadequate rehabilitation programs, improper spiritual counseling, and minimal opportunities to start afresh. Moreover, discreet records are filed and shared on people freed from prison. In the age of automation, these records take on a virtual life of their own. They affect job and educational opportunities, credit, and other financial needs indefinitely. These same records contain legal jargon intentionally crafted to ensure the financial stability of the people maintaining the failed system. People requiring interpretation or counsel on their legal records feed the owners of the failed system financially upon each request for support. Except for the wealthy and privileged, these records are nearly impossible to expunge, and they prevent the average person from ever recovering from this system. The result is a perpetual cast system that grows from the steady injections of laws and complicated forms governed by legal interpretations. People caught in this system often can never overcome it, let alone understand it. By design, this system is complicated, financially taxing, and creates a legal yoke that locks both the innocent and the guilty to societal shackles nearly impossible to break. BTT allows one to see that all of this is part of the war campaign. During the war campaign, the failed system creates a revolving judicial door that serves the financial pockets of the wealthy and wicked leaving most of the population disenfranchised and skeptical of the law.

Yet, there is another group of people unknowingly supporting this failed system. This is the group that professes to know God but falsely teaches His word. These are the ministers, false teachers, and scholars that compromise the religious community. They mishandle and pervert God's Word for personal gain according to Titus 1:11. These are men and women described in 2 Corinthians 11:13-15 who masquerade as ministers of righteousness while all along removing the ancient boundaries and landmarks according to Proverbs 22:28 and 23:10. Instead of comparing spiritual things to spiritual, based on the Holy Spirit's direction given in 1st Corinthians 2:13, these individuals use their own wisdom to compare spiritual things to carnal things. Their earthly concoctions espoused as wisdom, creates a perversion of God's Word that never helps the hearer leave their sinful state. Whole families are led astray as God's Word is replaced by inspirational stories preached by motivational speakers, life coaches, and church CEOs. Many families never recover. The hearer of these false teachers remains just as compromised as the teacher who delivered the words. Teaching God's Word out of context to satisfy the hearer's worldly desires and passions compromise the teachers. Equally, hearers who accept the teacher's false teachings are compromise. The Biblical record documented, *"For the time will come when they will not endure sound doctrine, but according to their own desires, because they have itching ears, they will heap up for themselves teachers; and they will turn their ears away from the truth, and be turned aside to fables"* (2 Timothy 4:3-4). They may be able to change their condition and hear the truth if their conscience is not seared shut according to 1 Timothy 4:2. But sadly, most of these hearers turn away from God's Word and the teachers fall by their own pride. This book reveals how unseen forces influence the religious community.

This community often unknowingly follows ancient creeds. The prophet Jeremiah documented from the Lord, *"...An astonishing and horrible thing has been committed in the land: The prophets prophesy falsely, and the priests rule by their own power; and My people love to have it so..."* (Jeremiah 5:30-31). Titus 1:10-11 and 1 Timothy 6:3-5, in the New Testament documents this same behavior. Then and now, God's Word is overshadowed by false teaching. Sadly, these same teachers have crafted elaborate forms of religious activities to support their form of worship. They give their followers entertainment. This entertainment is not authorized in the Bible. With entertainment, God's Word takes a backseat to man's wisdom. Ministers and false teachers sprinkle God's Word in portions of their messages simply to stimulate the hearer's ears. The hearer's mind gets stimulated emotionally, while the spiritual heart remains untouched. This means the hearer's life remains unchanged and their mental state and behavior remains compromised. It takes BTT for one to take God's Word from the Bible and apply it. Without the understanding and application of God's Word, a person, their home, community and society simply continues to spiral out of control. Unknowingly, everyone mentioned above plays a role in the war campaign. They validate Solomon's proverb that states, *"There is a generation that curses its father, and does not bless its mother. There is a generation that is pure in its own eyes, yet is not washed from its filthiness. There is a generation—oh, how lofty are their eyes! And their eyelids are lifted up. There is a generation whose teeth are like swords, and whose fangs are like knives, to devour the poor from off the earth, and the needy from among men"* (Proverbs 30:11-14). These generations of people cause chaos in society and leaves whole communities confused and in an uproar. This book and BTT will demonstrate that the religious community is influenced by the negative forces of the campaign. Their efforts are not "Christian" at all, and they have nothing to do with "Christianity" or following Christ. All along, many people from these same generations attend worship services to a "god" religiously. In fact for our example, it was Jesus Himself who addressed the religious community of His day. He ask them, "*Why do you not understand My speech? ...*" (John 8:43). Then He went on to tell them, "*...Because you are not able to listen to My word. You are of your father the devil, and the desires of your father you want to do. He was a murderer from the beginning, and does not stand in the truth, because there is no truth in him. When he speaks a lie, he speaks from his own resources, for he is a liar and the father of it. But because I tell the truth, you do not believe Me*" (John 8:43-45).

As bad as all of this may sound, there is hope and an answer. The Bible tells one that the increasing violence and chaos stemming from the singular root problem, as documented in **Figure 3** earlier in this book, is spiritual sickness. It continues to grow because of the removal of God and His Word from every aspect of human affairs. Thus, by using an opposite strategy, chaos and violence can be reversed. Remember, the Biblical record documents "*For whatever things were written before were written for our learning, that we through the patience and comfort of the Scriptures might have hope*" (Romans 15:4). One can read about the upheavals of nations of people provided in clear black and white text. Just as King Asa was told, "*...the Lord is with you while you are with Him. If you seek Him, He will be found by you; but if you forsake Him, He will forsake you*" (2 Chronicles 15:2), and "*For the eyes of the Lord run to and fro throughout the whole earth, to show Himself strong on behalf of those whose heart is loyal to Him...*" (2 Chronicles 16:9), the same applies to all life today.

The Spirit of wisdom told Solomon, "*He who is slow to anger is better than the mighty, and he who rules his spirit than he who takes a city*" (Proverbs 16:32). People's lack of control of their inner spirit causes worldly problems. This book documents this truth. Instead of people ruling their inner spirit by the influence of positive attributes, they have allowed their inner spirits to be influenced by a host of negative attributes which are driving their behaviors out of control. One must remember, without the proper feeding of one's spirit, one will only react to the overwhelming number of negative attributes that influence human behavior from the spiritual realm. These influences cause mankind to stumble. Worse yet, when one's inner spirit becomes consumed by the influences of the powerful negative forces, they can literally drive one's carnal side out of control to the point of depression and finally suicide. This is the real but unfortunate aspect of the greatest war campaign ever conceived.

BTT allows one to protect one's self in the campaign. BTT provides one the clarity for seeing the real issues behind all the distractors placed in one's path. This book addresses BTT using examples from the Biblical record and the solutions for resolving those issues. It explains why so much negativism prevails. This book offers, through the application of BTT, methods for resolving issues in homes, workplaces, communities, cities, and nations. As one reads this book, consider **Figure 9**. This graphic depicts the physical principle of time and distance. Earlier in my education, I learned that if a person attempted to travel a straight distance to a far-off destination but got one degree off, over time, that person would miss the intended destination. If one applies this principle mathematically and one is off course by just one degree, after 100 yards one will be off from his or her intended destination by 5.2 feet and after a mile by 92.2 feet. The farther one goes without making a course correction, the farther one moves away from the intended destination. One degree makes a difference. This same physical principle is true with one's spiritual walk. God has given the world instructions to follow. When man changes them, each small compromise matters. One's destination to God will be totally missed. This happens during spiritual warfare because the negative attributes continuously feed false information into the campaign that clouds one's course correction and the pathway to salvation. The net result is a missed opportunity for heaven. When one gets distracted, one may not know one is off course by even a degree. In physical war, this distraction is the fog of the war and one can find himself or herself in an ambush. I will cover this in detail later in the book. In the spiritual war, one misses heaven because of the deceitfulness of riches (Matthew 13:22), the cares of this world, the desires for other things (Mark 4:18-19), and the pleasures of life (Luke 8:14) that choke the word of God from one's life. These very things are the ambushes of the negative attributes in spiritual warfare. Please do not be deceived.

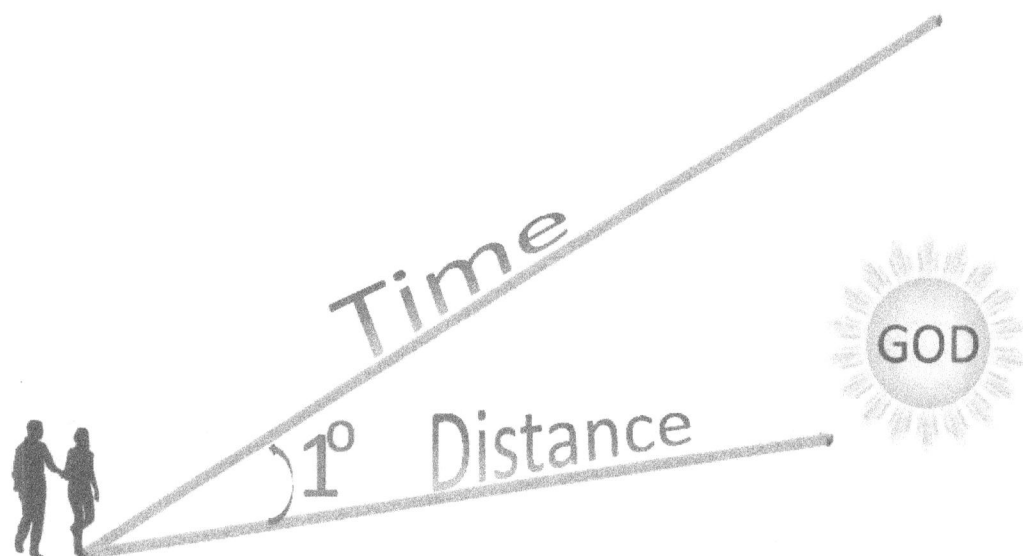

Figure 9: The Law of Time & Distance

CHAPTER III: The Dilemma and Results

"And you He made alive, who were dead in trespasses and sins, in which you once walked according to the course of this world, according to the prince of the power of the air, the spirit who now works in the sons of disobedience, among whom also we all once conducted ourselves in the lusts of our flesh, fulfilling the desires of the flesh and of the mind, and were by nature children of wrath, just as the others."

~ Ephesians 2:1-3 ~

To understand spiritual warfare, the war campaign, and BTT, I would like to take you to the writings of a Biblical character named Solomon. Solomon's documentation provided the foundation for this book. You see, several thousand years ago, he faced a breakdown in society when he inherited his father's kingdom. The kingdom was vast and reached across the known world of that day. His father was King David and his mother was Bathsheba. You can read about them in your Bible in the Books of 1st Samuel, 1st and 2nd Kings, and 1st and 2nd Chronicles. Their lives were as interesting as the life of Solomon. However, my focus is on Solomon and his request of God.

When Solomon assumed the throne, he became the wealthiest man in the world and had untold honor and fame. But none of this was important compared to what he gained from his actual request of God. It was this request and God's response that I share with you. You see, God's timeless response provided Solomon the means to maintain peace, resolve conflicts, and ensure that his kingdom nation served as a positive light in a world plagued by darkness. God still offers the same solution today. God shared with Solomon the spiritual attributes that can influence people and ultimately determine the balance of peace and chaos on earth. In addition to the attributes, the Spirit of wisdom revealed categories in which people exist. One must understand that the attributes influence the categories to the right or left of the war campaign. The categories can go tilt in the direction of the positive or negative side of the war. More importantly, from what he learned from the Spirit of wisdom, Solomon achieved BTT well before Paul identified the concept in the New Testament.

I will share some background on Solomon that led up to his request. If one opens the Bible, to the First Book of the Kings, one can read how Solomon became a king in 1 Kings 1:28-40. In Chapter 3 of this book, because Solomon loved the Lord and walked in the statues of his father David according to 1 Kings 3:3, the Lord appeared to him in a dream one night and said, "*Ask! What shall I give you?*" (1 Kings 3:5). Solomon humbled himself before the Lord and said, "*Now, O Lord my God, You have made Your servant king instead of my father David, but I am a little child; I do not know how to go out or come in. And Your servant is in the midst of Your people whom You have chosen, a great people, too numerous to be numbered or counted. Therefore give to Your servant an understanding heart to judge Your people that I may <u>discern</u> between good and evil. For who is able to judge this great people of Yours?*" (1 Kings 3:7-9).

Look closely at Solomon's request. It was very simple, sincere, and honest. The idea expressed from Solomon's youthful heart came from profound wisdom. The Lord responded and the Bible documented in 1 Kings 3: 10-14 the following:

> *"The speech pleased the Lord, that Solomon had asked this thing. Then God said to him: "Because you have asked this thing, and have not asked long life for yourself, nor have asked riches for yourself, nor have asked the life of your enemies, but have asked for yourself understanding to <u>discern</u> justice, behold, I have done according to your words; see, I have given you a wise and understanding heart, so that there has not been anyone like you before you, nor shall any like you arise after you. And I have also given you what you have not asked: both riches and honor, so that there shall not be anyone like you among the kings all your days. So if you walk in My ways, to keep My statutes and My commandments, as your father David walked, then I will lengthen your days."*

Solomon's request for <u>*discernment*</u> between good and evil, and God's response to his request, provides the foundation of this book. I want you to know upfront, the Lord's response came with a condition. The condition was that everything He granted would only remain valid if *"you walk in My ways, to keep My statutes and My commandments, as your father David walked, then I will lengthen your days."* There are two important points here. First, God used a condition clause and He continues to use one today. **False** teachers teach that God will show His favor to unrepentant people. They even want one to believe that a person can say anything, do anything, and even act ungodly, and God will hear their prayers or save them. Both of these teachings are ***false***. These teachings are strategies from the negative attributes to keep people lost in the fog of the campaign. God saves a person based on His condition which is obedience to His word. One will come to this truth by reading this book. The second point is like the first. What God showed to Solomon is applicable today. But only if one accepts the condition to be obedient to God's Word. BTT allows one to see the condition clause clearly and everything afterwards.

Solomon's request of God was clearly for something that he knew he could not get from the knowledge of his world. If one can accept this point, then it will be easier to accept the answer that Solomon received. Remember, Solomon's answer came from a superior Spiritual Being. Untaught and spiritually immature people contest this fact alone. God granted Solomon access to Him through a "spirit." That is right. The Lord granted Solomon access to the Spirit of wisdom. In the Book of Isaiah in chapter 11:2, the prophet Isaiah spoke of the Spirit of wisdom, along with other spirits that exist. Isaiah documented the existence of the Spirit of the Lord, the Spirit of wisdom and understanding, the Spirit of counsel and might, and the Spirit of knowledge and of the fear of the Lord.

Before I go any further, let me make something perfectly clear. I am not advocating that by asking God for wisdom that you will be able to have a conversation with the Spirit of wisdom. This would be false teaching. However, I agree that if you sincerely ask God for wisdom, He will grant your request through the study of His Holy Word – that is, the Bible. For God gives His wisdom, "*...to all liberally and without reproach...*" (James 1:5) and His word is "*...living and *powerful, and sharper than any two-edged sword, piercing even to the division of soul and spirit, and of joints and marrow, and is a <u>discerner</u> of the thoughts and intents of the heart*" (Hebrews 4:12). The Lord also said, "*For as the rain comes down, and the snow from heaven, and do not return there, but water the earth, and make it bring forth and bud, that it may give seed to the sower and bread to the eater, so shall My word be that goes forth from My mouth; it shall not return to Me void, but it shall accomplish what I please, and it shall prosper in the thing for which I sent it*" (Isaiah 55:11). The words documented in our Bible today, from the Old and New Testaments, are inspired and God-breathed. These written words speak to one's spiritual heart and mind, **if** one is prepared to listen. But, when I emphasize what the Spirit says to you and me throughout this book, it is always from the context of God's Word through the Holy Scriptures as they apply to you and me. I am expressing this point to ensure that all readers understand that I do not believe, nor do I imply, that God speaks directly to His creation today. God only speaks through His inspired Word. I know this contradicts many religious leaders and ***false*** teachers today but either their claim is ***false*** or the Bible is ***false***. The Bible documents, *Certainly not! Indeed, let God be true but every man a liar. As it is written: "That You may be justified in Your words, and may overcome when you are judged*" (Romans 2:4). The Bible documents that God told Jesus' disciples, "*...This is My beloved Son, in whom I am well pleased. Hear Him!*" (Matthew 17:5). Further, the Hebrew writer decisively wrote, "*God, who at various times and in various ways spoke in time past to the fathers by the prophets, has in these last days spoken to us by His Son, whom He has appointed heir of all things, through whom also He made the worlds...*" (Hebrews 1:1-2). It gets no clearer than this. No one else today is given authority to speak on matters of salvation separate from what Jesus provided from God Himself. This means that any message that one claims came directly from God to him or her in a dream, vision, or otherwise, is a contradiction of the Bible. The truth is, these claims are no more than ***false*** statements and part of the strategy employed by the negative attributes during spiritual warfare. Jesus spent years teaching His disciples what God wanted them to deliver to us today. However, ***false*** teachers hijacked Jesus' teaching. The Biblical record documented that this would occur many years prior to His coming. Given this information, I chose to follow God's Holy Word only; not man, academia, or commentaries. Also, there are curses that come with the misuse of God's Word. Paul wrote, "*...there are some who trouble you and want to pervert the gospel of Christ. But even if we, or an angel from heaven, preach any other gospel to you than what we have preached to you, let him be accursed. As we have said before, so now I say again, if anyone preaches any other gospel to you than what you have received, let him be accursed*" (Galatians 1:7-9). For context, Paul was talking about the Jews who were confusing some of the early Christians by adding acts of Judaism to the Gospel. Paul condemned this. However, this is applicable today because some are mixing some of the teachings of the Mosaic Law with Christianity. Still others mix religious or pagan beliefs with the Gospel of Jesus Christ. After Jesus' death and resurrection, He became the meditator between God and man alone according to 1 Timothy 2:5. Paul documented, "*For there is one God and one Mediator between God and men, the Man Christ Jesus...*" Thus, once again it is documented no man, woman, or hierarchical organization is authorized to stand between you and God outside of Jesus Christ. Other influences from the negative forces of the campaign have caused man to teach otherwise. This book demonstrates that this false teaching is part of the strategy of the greatest war campaign ever conceived. God's written Word, supported by the Holy Spirit, divinely speaks to one's inner spirit by His design. The message is the same for all. Flee from anyone that teaches otherwise. I take this charge seriously, and I pray you will see this through the information that follows.

Once again, this book offers clarification of what the Lord told Solomon through the Spirit of wisdom. Solomon penned this wisdom in the Book of the Proverbs. According to 1 Kings 4:29-33, *"And God gave Solomon wisdom and exceedingly great understanding, and largeness of heart like the sand on the seashore... He spoke three thousand proverbs, and his songs were one thousand and five. Also he spoke of trees, from the cedar tree of Lebanon even to the hyssop that springs out of the wall; he spoke also of animals, of birds, of creeping things, and of fish"*. But please understand, although God made wisdom available to Solomon, he still had to work at what he learned. I make this point to refute people who falsely claim that Solomon received everything from God with no exerted effort on Solomon's part. This is false. Solomon documented himself, *"And I set my heart to seek and search out by wisdom concerning all that is done under heaven; this <u>burdensome</u> task God has given to the sons of man, by which they may be exercised"* (Ecclesiastes 1:13). From Solomon's own statement, one can see that his education was burdensome and required mental exercises. In other words, gaining spiritual wisdom and understanding is not easy and nor is grasping the complexity of the war campaign. God expects everyone to engage in this mental exercise. The exercise is a God given task that trains the physical mind to handle <u>*discernment*</u>. From Solomon's writings, there is more than enough information for understanding the attributes and war campaign revealed by the Spirit of wisdom. From the Book of Proverbs, this book analyzes the information to provide clarity of Solomon's work. Too many people have ignored the truth behind Solomon's wisdom for far too long. Consequently, wickedness, evil, perversion, and violence have taken the lead through the influence of unethical people around the world. Through this book, I hope to empower readers with God's answer to Solomon by which he survived the war campaign. Solomon achieved BTT through the process of spiritual maturity and studying God's Word.

Here is what one can expect to find in this book. When the Lord granted Solomon <u>*discernment*</u> between good and evil, I believe Solomon learned about the **clean** and **unclean spirits** involved in spiritual warfare. These are the spirits that I refer to as "positive and negative attributes" in this book. Solomon learned and documented the existence of at least thirty-two distinguishable attributes that could <u>influence</u> one's behavior. There are other attributes in the Bible. However, these thirty-two are enough to illustrate the war campaign. BTT allows one to see that once Solomon understood the operation of these attributes, he was then able to see beyond the physical presence of a man or woman and see what was influencing their actual behavior. This is <u>*discernment*</u>. In other words, he could see the spirits of the spiritual realm that influenced people's behavior. Wisdom gave him the understanding that people could only be influenced based on their own desires. Because of people's desire at a given time, i.e. love, greed, or even hate, people would manipulate events based on the influence they allow in their inner spirits. This influence and the manipulation of behaviors are what causes the ebbs and flow in the war campaign. Please understand that these spirits cannot force themselves on anyone. One must open one's mind to their influences. I say this because, these spirits are not demons. The Biblical record documented that demons had their own time and place. Demons were active during the first century and could overtake one's physical body. When Jesus walked the earth, demons made their physical presence known. During this period, demons and the miracles that removed them confirmed Christ's deity. Jesus gave the apostles miraculous gifts to confirm God's Word and Himself as deity. The Biblical record documented that Jesus said, "*And these signs will follow those who believe: In My name they will cast out demons; they will speak with new tongues; they will take up serpents; and if they drink anything deadly, it will by no means hurt them; they will lay hands on the sick, and they will recover." So then, after the Lord had spoken to them, He was received up into heaven, and sat down at the right hand of God. And they went out and preached everywhere, the Lord working with them and confirming the word through the accompanying signs*" (Mark 16:17-20; see also Hebrews 2:3-4). Part of the miraculous gifts included the ability to remove demons and their activities. As Christ's church became functional, and as the last apostle passed away, the miraculous gifts were no longer needed as Paul wrote, "*Love never fails. But whether there are prophecies, they will fail; whether there are tongues, they will cease; whether there is knowledge, it will vanish away. For we know in part and we prophesy in part. But when that which is perfect has come, then that which is in part will be done away*" (1 Corinthians 13:8-10). God's Word is perfect and a perfect man, Jesus Christ, delivered it on earth. BTT allows one to see that Jesus came to earth (John 1:10-11; 14); His Word was given (John 17:7-8), His church was established (Acts 2:47; Acts 11:26), and His Word is now preserved in written form called the Bible (Revelation 22:18-19). James documented God's Word as the perfect law of liberty when he wrote, "*So speak and so do as those who will be judged by the law of liberty*" (James 2:12; see also James 1:25). Thus, the role of demon possession, miraculous gifts, and the need for speaking in tongues, all ceased after the confirmation of Christ's deity, the delivery of His Word, and the death of His last apostle. However, the influence of the **clean** and **unclean spirits** remained because they were part of the fabric of God's divine creation to provide one with choices and to make freewill an undeniable truth. This is not to say one cannot conjure up demons using demonic magic, witchcraft, or sorcery. But one must remember, the Biblical record condemns these actions. There are people who "*sacrifice and fellowship with demons*" (1 Corinthians 10:20) and "*give heed to deceiving spirits and doctrines of demons*" (1 Timothy 4:1) in the world today whose souls are lost in spiritual warfare because they exercise demonic options. However, demons are not active in the way that many portray them today. Thus, to keep down any confusion, I refer to the thirty-two **clean** and **unclean spirits** as positive and negative "attributes" respectively. For the Bible documents, "*...since the creation of the world His **invisible attributes** are clearly seen, being understood by the things that are made, even His eternal power and Godhead, so that they are without excuse...*" (Romans 1:20). Thus, the term "attributes" is more palatable to audiences new to the Bible and the spiritually immature.

    Also consider the fact that one sees idiosyncrasies in people all the time. These idiosyncrasies are often brushed off as quirks that are weird or sometimes even crazy until the idiosyncrasy matures and something significant happens. Everyone throws around terms like "wicked", "evil", "good", and "righteous" while never once considering their ancient origins. However, this book offers a response for these terms and common idiosyncrasies often ignored.

    Now, it is true that Jesus removed both demons and negative attributes from the lives of the people that believed in Him and His mission. For example, the Bible documented that, "*...certain women who had been healed of **evil** spirits and infirmities—Mary called Magdalene,* *out of whom had come seven demons, and Joanna the wife of Chuza, Herod's steward, and Susanna, and many others who provided for Him from their substance"* (Luke 8:2-3). Please notice that this scripture documents Jesus' authority over both demons and spirits. Other examples include:

*"Also a multitude gathered from the surrounding cities to Jerusalem, bringing sick people and those who were tormented by **unclean spirits**, and they were all healed"* (Acts 5:16)	*"...as well as those who were tormented with **unclean spirits**. And they were healed"* (Luke 6:18)	*"And the **unclean spirits**, whenever they saw Him, fell down before Him and cried out, saying, "You are the Son of God"* (Mark 3:11)
*"And at once Jesus gave them permission. Then the **unclean spirits** went out and entered the swine (there were about two thousand); and the herd ran violently down the steep place into the sea, and drowned in the sea"* (Mark 5:13)	*"Then they were all amazed, so that they questioned among themselves, saying, "What is this? What new doctrine is this? For with authority He commands even the **unclean spirits**, and they obey Him"* (Mark 1:27)	*"And when He had called His twelve disciples to Him, He gave them power over **unclean spirits**, to cast them out, and to heal all kinds of sickness and all kinds of disease"* (Matthew 10:1; Mark 6:7)
*"Then they were all amazed and spoke among themselves, saying, "What a word this is! For with authority and power He commands the **unclean spirits**, and they come out"* (Luke 4:36)	*"For **unclean spirits**, crying with a loud voice, came out of many who were possessed; and many who were paralyzed and lame were healed"* (Acts 8:7)	*"And I saw three **unclean spirits** like frogs coming out of the mouth of the dragon, out of the mouth of the beast, and out of the mouth of the false prophet"* (Revelation 16:13)

Table 3: Examples of *Unclean Spirits*

In fact, as Jesus prepared the disciples for their mission, He explained to them that *"When an **unclean spirit** goes out of a man, he goes through dry places, seeking rest, and finds none. Then he says, 'I will return to my house from which I came.' And when he comes, he finds it empty, swept, and put in order. Then he goes and takes with him seven other spirits more wicked than himself, and they enter and dwell there; and the last state of that man is worse than the first. So shall it also be with this wicked generation"* (Matthew 12:43-45). This is significant information about one's adversary and explains why a good defense is necessary in spiritual warfare. Paul documented that during the establishment of the early church, there were people capable of *"...discerning of spirits..."* (1 Corinthians 12:10). I submit that these may have been people who could <u>discern</u> between the influences of the positive and negative attributes influencing a person down to the precise influencing spirit. Furthermore, before the first written Bible, these were people who could <u>discern</u> right and wrong immediately during the establishment of the early church. Without this ability, the negative forces of the war campaign could hinder the early church by influencing weaker members. The element of <u>discernment</u> protected the confirming of God's Word until His people's spiritually matured.

Today, the element of _discernment_ is no longer a special gift for select people. With God's written word, every Christian can acquire the element _discernment_. It comes by studying God's Word, maturity and obedience. Studying His Word is essential for surviving the spiritual warfare. Spiritual maturity is the discipline of the inner spirit and carnal mind which allows the understanding of spiritual things.

What is significant about all the attributes is their life span. These attributes existed before the foundations of the world were formed. Only God knows when the attributes came into existence. However, the Biblical record gives one a hint of their age in the Book of Revelation. Here the Bible documented, *"And war broke out in heaven: Michael and his angels fought with the dragon; and the dragon and his angels fought, but they did not prevail, nor was a place found for them in heaven any longer. So the great dragon was cast out, that serpent of old, called the Devil and Satan, who deceives the whole world; he was cast to the earth, and his angels were cast out with him"* (Revelation 12:7-9). No one can say when this war took place. However, what is clear is that the leader of the negative forces of the war campaign started his role in the war long ago. Even Jesus gave His disciples a hint of this when He shared with them, *"I saw Satan fall like lightning from the heavens"* (Luke 10:18). This information also suggests that the negative attributes have ancient knowledge that is immense and universal which makes them capable of influencing all races, nationalities, and genders. Thus, their influences impact every nation on earth and every generation. As I break down each attribute by chapter, one will be amazed at what the Spirit of wisdom revealed to Solomon. An example of Solomon's earliest knowledge of the attributes and their applications occurred with two women who were fighting over a child. Please read this in 1 Kings 3:16-28. The example demonstrated Solomon's ability to _discern_ right and wrong. The situation leading up to Solomon's actions illustrated the influences of the positive and negative attributes manifested through the behaviors of the two women. The positive attributes clearly influenced one woman. The other woman, influenced by the negative attributes, was ready to murder an innocent child.

Each of the chapters on the attributes will begin first by subject with the information revealed by the Spirit of wisdom to Solomon. Separating the subjects from the Hebrew writers' use of parallelism and comparisons will provide the clarity needed for critical thinking about the attributes. Although I have strived to maintain the original poetry, some of the sentence structures may read a little funny. You will understand these minor quirks as you get to them. It is the separation of each subject that results in 32 attributes. The separated subjects will help one easily understand what Solomon learned. This same method is used to documents the eight categories.

The thirty-two attributes, along with any derivative of their names, are the behavioral representations found, seen, and observed in people. An example is the **good** attribute. Just as you can find **good** in a person, so can you find **goodness** in a person or observe the **good** of a person. In any form, the **good** attribute is present, and the term is generally the same in all its uses. One will also learn from this idea that the Lord's wisdom imbedded in these attributes transcends time. Thus, each attribute's influence is as applicable today as it was in the days of Adam and Eve. After each subject is extracted from the Book of Proverbs, the rest of the chapter will explore examples and supporting information from the rest of the Old and New Testament of the Biblical record. This exercise through the rest of the Biblical record will provide a greater level of clarity for each attribute.

With each chapter, the specific attribute under discussion will be in **bolded** and *italicized* text and Scriptural references will have *italicized* text within quotation marks. People within the eight categories will simply have **bolded** text. Although I provide the Scriptural reference in this book, I still encourage one not to rely on me, but to fact check my work for one's self. To illustrate what I have said, here are two examples. Solomon learned that "***Wise** people store up knowledge, but the mouth of the **foolish** is near destruction*" (Proverbs 10:14) and "*A **wise** man fears and departs from evil, but a **fool** rages and is self-confident*" (Proverbs 14:16). From these scriptures, one can see the parallelism between the "***wise***" and the "***fool***." In my book, the ***wise*** and any comment about them will reside in a section dedicated solely to the people in the ***wise*** category. Likewise, comments about the "***fool***" will be treated the same in its own section among the attributes. Thus, all thirty-two attributes and the eight categories will have their own dedicated section in the book along with the wisdom expressed by the Lord, thoughts expressed by the Spirit of wisdom to Solomon, or other contributors to the Book of Proverbs such as King Lemuel and Agur. So, taking the two examples provided above, one can expect to see in their respective sections of the book, a statement that may read: The Spirit of wisdom revealed to Solomon that, "***Wise** people store up knowledge…*" (Proverbs 10:14) and He further revealed that, "*A **wise** man fears and departs from evil…*" (Proverbs 14:16). Unless the reference about the "***fool***" is critical for understanding the proverb itself, its reference will be removed. The ***fool*** attribute example would follow the same format as the people in the ***wise*** category in its own chapter.

Before getting into the attributes, one needs to understand that the positive and negative attributes reside on paths that people choose for themselves. As one reads the chapters in this book, this subject will invariably come up. The Lord in His thoroughness wanted Solomon to understand an important thing about life itself.

- God gave mankind life and that life is only for a short time
- During one's life, each person chooses a path to walk on
- There are only two paths; no alternate path exist
- Everyone makes a choice willingly or unwillingly
- Life ends and there is a Day of Judgement

This wisdom of the two paths documents the nexus of the spiritual war and the physical world. Solomon explained the way of wisdom to his son in Proverbs 4:10-13, and about the good and evil paths. **Figure 10** illustrates this path for which Solomon said, "*Do not enter the path of the wicked, and do not walk in the way of evil. Avoid it, do not travel on it; turn away from it and pass on. For they do not sleep unless they have done evil; and their sleep is taken away unless they make someone fall. For they eat the bread of wickedness, and drink the wine of violence. But the path of the just is like the shining sun, that shines ever brighter unto the perfect day. The way of the wicked is like darkness; they do not know what makes them stumble*" (Proverbs 4:14-19). From Solomon's comment, one can see two paths in life and the entire Biblical record provides the facts of what these paths contain. Since Solomon started with the path of darkness, so will I. Proverbs 4:19 and Matthew 7:13 identified this path. Solomon wrote, "*…The way of the wicked is like darkness; they do not know what makes them stumble*" (Proverbs 4:19). And Jesus taught, "*Enter by the narrow gate; for wide is the gate and broad is the way that leads to destruction, and there are many who go in by it…*" (Matthew 7:13). One can see that the bad path is full of negative behaviors, thoughts, words, and deeds. It reflects the large number of negative elements used from the arsenal of the negative attributes to trap and enslave the innocent, simple, and unwise. Moreover, this path contains everything necessary to entice people that are unaware of the spiritual war surrounding them. This path even employs deceptive tools to ensnare those with positive attributes. Thus, Paul wrote, "*For many walk, of whom I have told you often, and now tell you even weeping, that they are the enemies of the cross of Christ: whose end is destruction, whose god is their belly, and whose glory is in their shame—who set their mind on earthly things*" (Philippians 3:18-19). Thus, God identified what resides along the path of darkness for humanity. Moreover, one must remember the Bible documents that God, "*…reveals deep and secret things; He knows what is in the darkness, and light dwells with Him*" (Daniel 2:22).

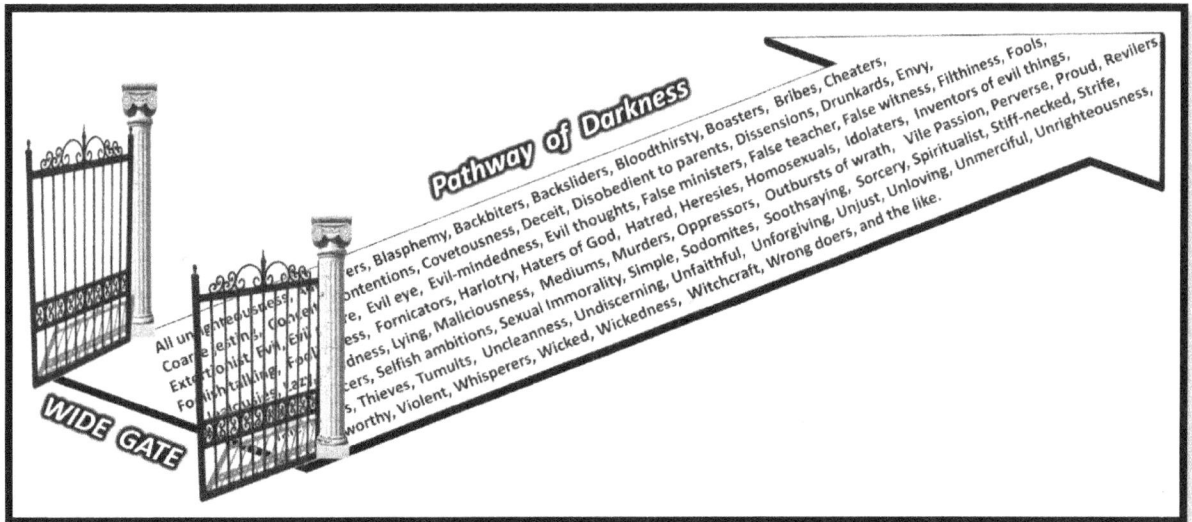

Figure 10: The Path of Darkness or "The Bad Path"

Figure 11 illustrates the ***good*** path, the path of the ***just*** (Proverbs 4:18), the way of **righteousness** in the midst of the paths of justice (Proverbs 8:20), and the narrow gate (Matthew 7:14). On this path are the things that Paul identified when he wrote, *"...the fruit of the Spirit is love, joy, peace, longsuffering, kindness, goodness, faithfulness, gentleness, self-*

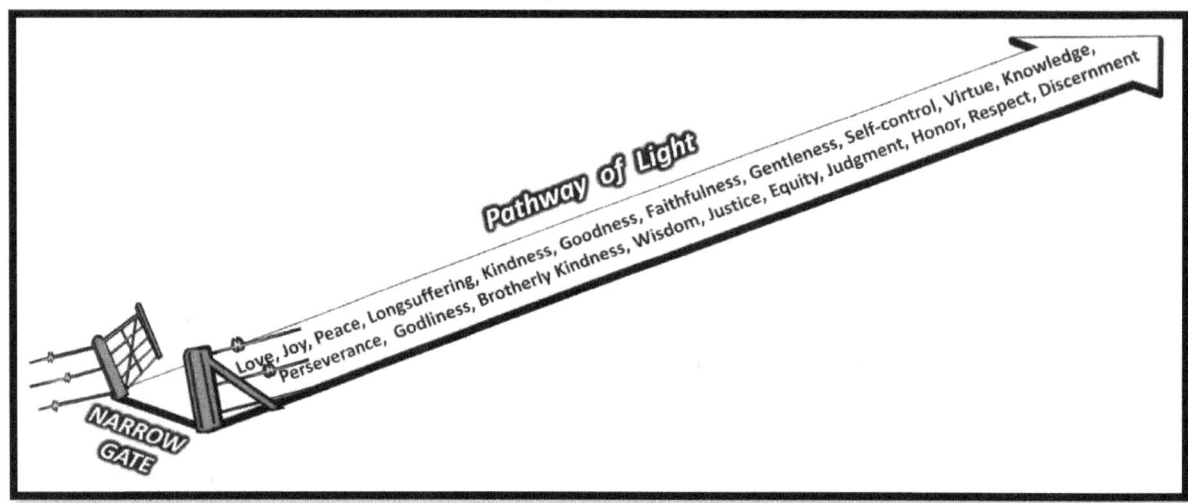

Figure 11: The Path of Light or "The Good Path"

control. Against such there is no law. And those who are Christ's have crucified the flesh with its passions and desires. If we live in the Spirit, let us also walk in the Spirit" (Galatians 5:23-25). When one walks this path, he or she commits to a life of faith, virtue, knowledge, self-control, and display godliness, brotherly kindness, and love (2 Peter 1:5-11). They are obedient to God's Word and trust in His Holy standard. They understand Paul's writings which say, *"Finally, brethren, whatever things are true, whatever things are noble, whatever things are just, whatever things are pure, whatever things are lovely, whatever things are of good report, if there is any virtue and if there is anything praiseworthy—meditate on these things"* (Philippians 4:8) and *"And whatever you do in word or deed, do all in the name of the Lord Jesus, giving thanks to God the Father through Him"* (Colossians 3:17). People on this path allow their inner spirits to be influenced by this small numbers of positive attributes. For BTT helps one to understand that a few good things from the Lord are more than enough to combat the numerous influences of the negative attributes.

Moreover, people on this path know what is at stake in spiritual warfare and the war campaign. They understand, believe, and accept Jesus statement when asked *"Lord, are there few who are saved?"* (Luke 13:22). Jesus responded in Luke 13:23-30 with the following Truth:

> *"Strive to enter through the narrow gate, for many, I say to you, will seek to enter and will not be able. When once the Master of the house has risen up and shut the door, and you begin to stand outside and knock at the door, saying, 'Lord, Lord, open for us,' and He will answer and say to you, 'I do not know you, where you are from,' then you will begin to say, 'We ate and drank in Your presence, and You taught in our streets.' But He will say, 'I tell you I do not know you, where you are from. Depart from Me, all you*

workers of iniquity.' There will be weeping and gnashing of teeth, when you see Abraham and Isaac and Jacob and all the prophets in the kingdom of God, and yourselves thrust out. They will come from the east and the west, from the north and the south, and sit down in the kingdom of God. And indeed there are last who will be first, and there are first who will be last."

The two paths of life are not separated by some spiritual medium. One must not think that once he or she is on the good path, one is safe and can never fall off. These two thoughts constitute false doctrines. Here is what Solomon learned and the Bible documents. It looks like **Figure 12** which illustrates the good and bad paths together.

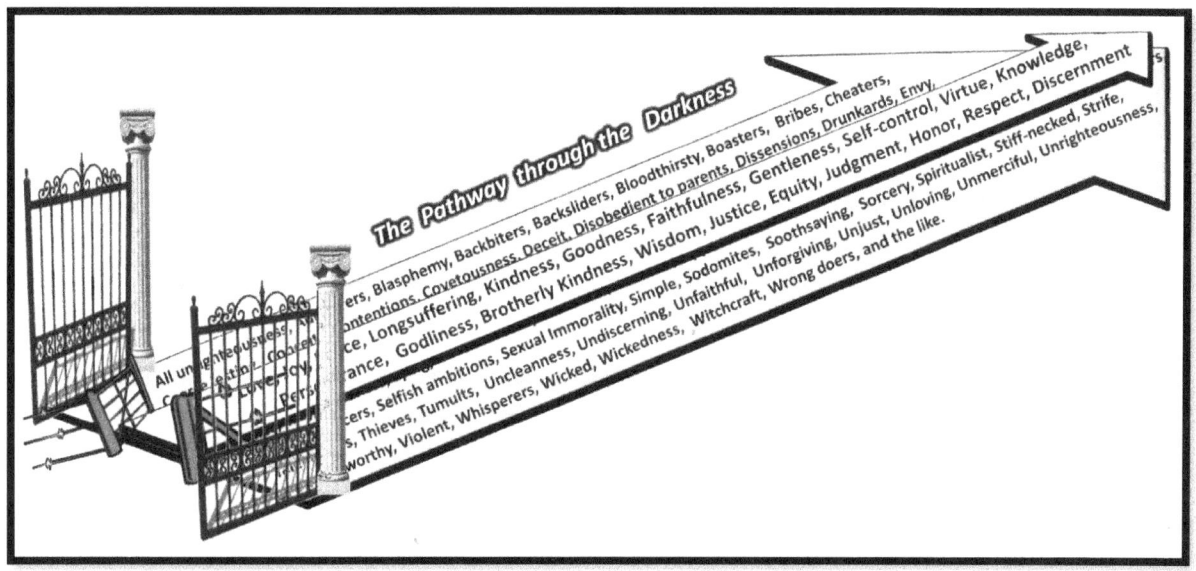

Figure 12: The Interaction of the Good and Bad

The negative attributes surround people on the good path every day. It is much like Lot who was living in the city of Sodom and the Bible documented, *"…righteous Lot, who was oppressed by the filthy conduct of the wicked (for that righteous man, dwelling among them, tormented his righteous soul from day to day by seeing and hearing their lawless deeds) …"* (2 Peter 7-8). The same negative attributes surround Christians every day. This is why the Lord provides His people the Bible; a living road map to navigate the pathway of darkness, and a virtual description of the spiritual warfare and the war campaign. The Bible provides every Christian directives for behavior, obedience to God's Word, and spiritual nourishment. Hence, Paul by inspiration of the Holy Spirit wrote, *"…having these promises, beloved, let us cleanse ourselves from all filthiness of the flesh and spirit, perfecting holiness in the fear of God"* (2 Corinthians 7:1).

Now this is contrary to a popular belief, that a Christian can mimic the world in any form and still be of Christ at the same time. In fact, the Biblical record documents, *"For the grace of God that brings salvation has appeared to all men, teaching us that, denying ungodliness and worldly lusts, we should live soberly, righteously, and godly in the present age, looking for the blessed hope and glorious appearing of our great God and Savior Jesus Christ, who gave*

Himself for us, that He might redeem us from every lawless deed and purify for Himself His own special people, zealous for good works" (Titus 2:11-14). One must choose. Paul wrote, *"...be imitators of God as dear children. And walk in love, as Christ also has loved us and given Himself for us, an offering and a sacrifice to God for a sweet-smelling aroma"* (Ephesians 5:1-2). BTT helps one to see God's Word teaches one how to imitate Christ. James even documented, *"Does a spring send forth fresh water and bitter from the same opening? Can a fig tree, my brethren, bear olives, or a grapevine bear figs? Thus no spring yields both salt water and fresh"* (James 3:11-12). One simply cannot have life both ways. Christians must come to grips with these statements to survive the war campaign:

- *"Then Jesus said to those Jews who believed Him, "If you abide in My word, you are My disciples indeed. And you shall know the truth, and the truth shall make you free"* (John 8:31-32)

- *"Wash yourselves, make yourselves clean; put away the evil of your doings from before My eyes. Cease to do evil, learn to do good; seek justice, rebuke the oppressor; defend the fatherless, plead for the widow"* (Isaiah 1:16-17)

- *"He has shown you, O man, what is good; and what does the LORD require of you but to do justly, to love mercy, and to walk humbly with your God?"* (Micah 6:8)

- *"For the grace of God that brings salvation has appeared to all men, teaching us that, denying ungodliness and worldly lusts, we should live soberly, righteously, and godly in the present age..."* (Titus 2:11-12)

Remember, even when Jesus taught His disciples the Truth that they were to deliver to the world, He did not take them out of the world. He prayed for them and all the believers who would come after them because the task set before them was difficult. Look at what Jesus prayed to God as recorded in John 17:13-21.

> *"But now I come to You, and these things I speak in the world, that they may have My joy fulfilled in themselves. I have given them Your word; and the world has hated them because they are not of the world, just as I am not of the world. <u>I do not pray that You should take them out of the world, but that You should keep them from the evil one</u>. They are not of the world, just as I am not of the world. Sanctify them by Your truth. Your word is truth. As You sent Me into the world, I also have sent them into the world. And for their sakes I sanctify Myself, that they also may be sanctified by the truth. I do not pray for these alone, but also for those who will believe in Me through their word; that they all may be one, as You, Father, are in Me, and I in You; that they also may be one in Us, that the world may believe that You sent Me."*

The disciples, and everyone then and today who accepts the Truth of the Gospel, is required to remain engaged in the war campaign and teach others. This fact demands that one must prepare for the campaign. I write this as a follower of Christ and a former soldier in the military. Preparation is critical and necessary. More importantly in today's world and as the campaign intensifies, preparation is vital for survival. Paul validated this argument for preparation when he wrote Ephesians 6:10-18. He documented:

> *"Finally, my brethren, be strong in the Lord and in the power of His might. Put on the whole armor of God, that you may be able to stand against the wiles of the devil. For we do not wrestle against flesh and blood, but against principalities, against powers, against the rulers of the darkness of this age, against spiritual hosts of wickedness in the heavenly places. Therefore take up the whole armor of God, that you may be able to withstand in the evil day, and having done all, to stand. Stand therefore, having girded your waist with truth, having put on the breastplate of righteousness, and having shod your feet with the preparation of the gospel of peace; above all, taking the shield of faith with which you will be able to quench all the fiery darts of the wicked one. And take the helmet of salvation, and the sword of the Spirit, which is the word of God; praying always with all prayer and supplication in the Spirit, being watchful to this end with all perseverance and supplication for all the saints—"*

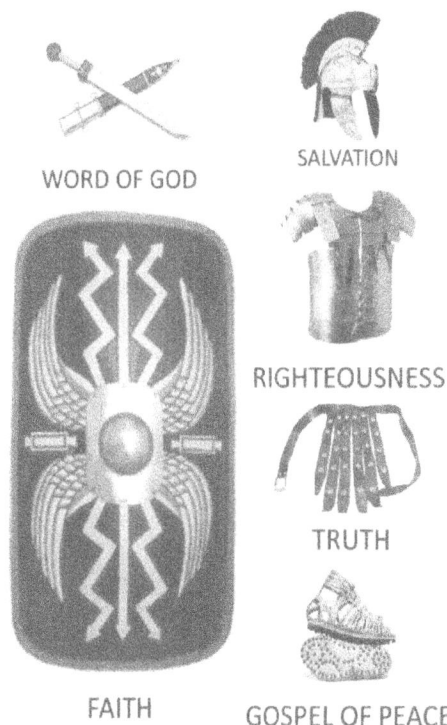

Figure 13: The Tools of Spiritual Warfare

Figure 13 illustrates the images of the tools of spiritual warfare that Paul described. Paul's comments above did not teach that one should arm oneself with weapons for physical warfare. No! The Holy Spirit specifically inspired him to document, *"For though we walk in the flesh, we do not war according to the flesh. For the weapons of our warfare are not carnal but mighty in God for pulling down strongholds, casting down arguments and every high thing that exalts itself against the knowledge of God, bringing every thought into captivity to the obedience of Christ, and being ready to punish all disobedience when your obedience is fulfilled"* (2 Corinthians 10:3-6). He documented the spiritual tools needed for fighting the unseen spiritual war that began long ago. He described the tools in physical terms because 1st Century Christians could readily identify the oppressive Roman military tools of war. The 1st Century Christians and Jews alike could immediately understand Paul and correlate the power of these spiritual tools to the tools of the Roman warfighting machine. Make no mistake, the tools that Paul described are the mightiest tools ever conceived.

Paul understood spiritual warfare and the war campaign. His documentation provided the insight into the struggle between the carnal and spiritual side of man. In fact, he wrote, *"For the flesh lusts against the Spirit, and the Spirit against the flesh; and these are contrary to one another, so that you do not do the things that you wish"* (Galatians 5:17). See, when the Spirit of Christ joins one's inner spirit, war occurs as the Spirit of Christ helps one to resist evil. When the influences of the negative attributes manifest themselves in a person, that person partakes in sin. Thus, Paul wrote, *"Walk in the Spirit, and you shall not fulfill the lust of the flesh"* (Galatians 5:16). He also documented, *"For if you live according to the flesh you will die; but if by the Spirit you put to death the deeds of the body, you will live. For as many as are led by the Spirit of God, these are sons of God"* (Romans 8:13-14). Having Jesus in one's life is the only way for one to have hope in staying on the right path. Knowing God's Word is the only defense in the war campaign.

God wants strong Christian warriors on the spiritual battlefield. Paul documented, *"...my brethren, be strong in the Lord and in the power of His might"* (Ephesians 6:10). How does one gain *"His might"*? The Bible documents, *"I can do all things through Christ who strengthens me"* (Philippians 4:13). Jesus Christ is the answer. I hope what one has learned thus far has helped one to understand the importance of <u>discernment</u>. The spiritual war is real. Understanding it, and the positive and negative forces involved, is one's only hope for salvation through the chaos of the war campaign. When we stand before God – whether we believe in Him or not, two things will be true. The Bible documents, *"...it is written: "As I live, says the Lord, every knee shall bow to Me, and every tongue shall confess to God"* (Romans 14:11) and *"...there is no creature hidden from His sight, but all things are naked and open to the eyes of Him to whom we must give account"* (Hebrews 4:12-13).

CHAPTER IV: Introducing the Attributes and Their Roles

"All Scripture is given by inspiration of God, and is profitable for doctrine, for reproof, for correction, for instruction in righteousness, that the man of God may be complete, thoroughly equipped for every good work"

~ 2 Timothy 3:16- 17

To fully understand the war campaign, one must have the details. The adversary intentionally makes the campaign complicated to hide the details; in this case, his intentions and objectives. This is basic strategy and often referred to as fog. For this reason, I will begin with the negative attributes which will provide an understanding of the complete thinking of the adversary. I will follow the negative attributes with a breakdown of the positive attributes; the force that counters the negative forces. After one has gained an appreciation for the role of the positive and negative attributes, I will then provide eight categories of people and show how the attributes influence them to either side of the war campaign. The people of the eight categories strengthen either side of the war campaign with the resources for the earthly fight. This amazing documentation of the categories of people will bring clarity to the campaign unrealized by most people. Finally, I will show how the elements of strife and calamity impact the overall campaign. By the end of this book, one will be able to examine where one stands in relation to the ongoing campaign. **Figure 14** provides a global perspective of all the attributes and the categories of people involved in the war campaign. The campaign balances on a divine scale. This book will provide as much information as possible for one to have a complete understanding of each attribute and the categories of people. The book's size reflects this truth

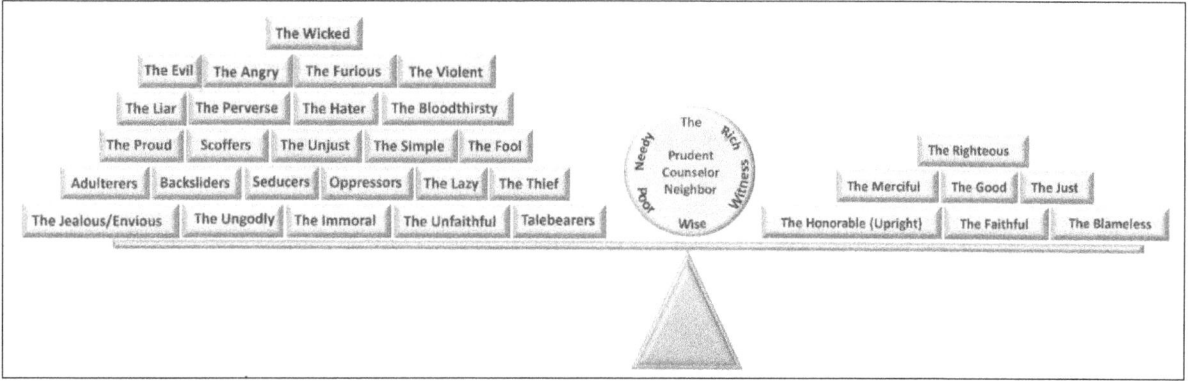

Figure 14: The War Campaign Scale

as I have taken no shortcuts to explain this complicated war. Just as physical war and the flashpoint that started it is complicated, so is the spiritual war. Thus, to fully understand the campaign, which began with Adam, Eve and the serpent in the Garden of Eden, one must have all the information available.

This book documents that every man and woman will experience the fight represented in this war. It depicts the confrontation and fighting that occurs between unseen positive and negative forces. The results of their confrontation influence one's life through behaviors. These attributes naturally spar with each other over right and wrong. Neither side desires to give up ground. Thus, both sides use their influence to manipulate people, identified in the categories in **Figure 14**, to expand their presence. This natural contention for the center tips the war campaign's balance towards one side or the other. If it is not clear at this point, this will all become clear by the end of the book. If it helps as we study each of the attributes, consider people that you know or have known and then consider their outward behavior, attitude, or action. The reality is, one will realize that the people considered, were or are travelling on the good or bad path of life just like you and me. Remember, there are other attributes and categories identified in the Biblical record, but I am only dealing with the ones identified mostly from the Book of Proverbs.

Now when one considers the positive attributes in **Figure 14**, it is easy to get focused on their small numbers. Do not worry. One will learn that when the Lord is involved, one's battle is already won. However, there is a correlation between the number of attributes and the number of people who actually have them. In other words, the huge number of Christians reported by many religious and secular outlets is false. The large numbers are part of the deception strategy used by the negative forces in the war to create a false sense of security. The larger numbers cause a misrepresentation of who God's people really are and breeds the influence of the lazy attribute, as well as the inclusion of other negative attributes from the campaign. God's people; the faithful, dedicated and obedient people, have always been in small numbers. The Old Testament of the Biblical record confirms this fact from the unchanging Word of God. Even Moses understood this fact when he told the children of Israel, *"The Lord did not set His love on you nor choose you because you were more in number than any other people, for you were the least of all peoples; but because the Lord loves you, and because He would keep the oath which He swore to your fathers, the Lord has brought you out with a mighty hand, and redeemed you from the house of bondage, from the hand of Pharaoh king of Egypt. Therefore know that the Lord your God, He is God, the faithful God who keeps covenant and mercy for a thousand generations with those who love Him and keep His commandments..."* (Deuteronomy 7:7-9). I will cover this fact in more detail in the Chapter X as I discuss God's calamity on the world today. For now, consider these three examples from the Old Testament written for our learning. The Biblical record documented:

- The Lord said: *"You will chase your enemies, and they shall fall by the sword before you. Five of you shall chase a hundred, and a hundred of you shall put ten thousand to flight; your enemies shall fall by the sword before you. For I will look on you favorably and make you fruitful, multiply you and confirm My covenant with you"* (Leviticus 26:7-9)

- Moses recorded: *"How could one chase a thousand, and two put ten thousand to flight, unless their Rock had sold them, and the Lord had surrendered them? For their rock is not like our Rock, even our enemies themselves being judges"* (Deuteronomy 32:30-31)

- Joshua recorded: *"For the Lord has driven out from before you great and strong nations; but as for you, no one has been able to stand against you to this day. One man of you shall chase a thousand, for the Lord your God is He who fights for you, as He promised you. Therefore take careful heed to yourselves, that you love the Lord your God*" (Joshua 23:9-11)

Here is the most critical piece of wisdom one can have when it comes to the number of people influenced by the positive attributes; that is, "*...the solid foundation of God stands, having this seal: "The Lord knows those who are His," and, "Let everyone who names the name of Christ depart from iniquity*"" (2 Timothy 2:19). When we get to the positive attributes in this book, one will understand who belongs to the Lord.

Just as Solomon identified the attributes of the war campaign, Paul documented the war more directly when he wrote "*For we do not wrestle against flesh and blood, but against principalities, against powers, against the rulers of the darkness of this age, against spiritual hosts of wickedness in the heavenly places*" (Ephesians 6:12). These principalities, powers, rulers of the darkness of this age, and spiritual hosts of wickedness are currently in the driver's seat. The influences of the negative attributes are causing irrational and unnatural behaviors in people as they unleash a torrent of sinful thoughts into society. The Truth of the Gospel counters these influences. **Figure 15** labeled "*The Struggle Between **Good** Versus **Evil***" illustrates the war between the attributes first documented by Solomon. The illustration visually depicts the struggle between spiritual influences that war within the inner spirit of man. It is an unseen "tug of war" between the carnal and the spirit that cannot be avoided and today has been sorely misunderstood.

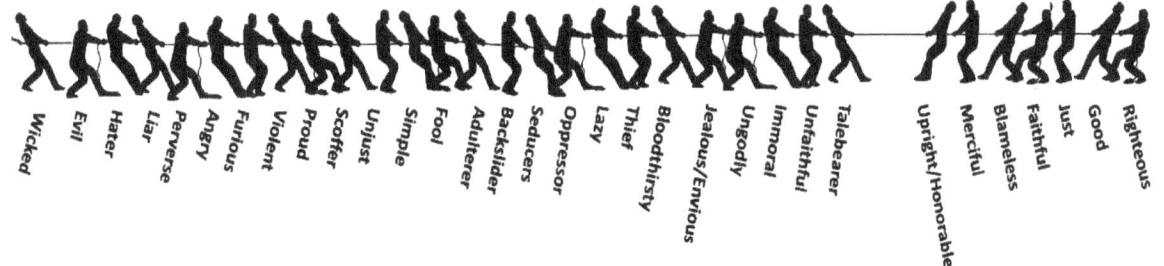

Figure 15: The Struggle Between Good and Evil

Earthly laws have no authority over the attribute's influences over the behaviors of mankind. A person can have multiple attributes influencing his or her behavior at any given time. But regardless of whether a person has one or multiple attributes influencing their actions, that person can never have a mix of both the positive and negative attributes at the same time. This requires BTT to accept and <u>discernment</u> to understand. One must see that the positive and negative attributes are diametrically opposed to each other. So, when an individual has one or more negative attribute, that person walks on the negative path of life (see **Figure 10**). That person's only option for redemption is repentance and conversion to the positive path of life (see **Figure 11**). Conversely, a person with one or more positive attribute walks on the positive path of life (see **Figure 11**). However, if this person takes on even one of the negative attributes and retains it, he or she is compromised. They spiritually stumble over to the negative path. This person can only return by repenting. The act of repentance is thoroughly documented in this book in a later chapter. When one is truly walking in the light of Christ on the positive path, one influenced by the positive attributes can always recognize others influenced by the other attributes. If not, one's <u>discernment</u> is skewed. One needs to self-examine their faith and spiritual walk. Paul documents this fact as he wrote, "*Examine yourselves as to whether you are in the faith. Test yourselves. Do you not know yourselves, that Jesus Christ is in you?—unless indeed you are disqualified*" (2 Corinthians 13:5). Starting within themselves, people influenced by the positive attributes must seek out deception and purge the influence of any negative attributes. This is a hard truth, but it is also a small glimpse into BTT, not worldly logic. God said, "*For My thoughts are not your thoughts, nor are your ways My ways," says the Lord*" (Isaiah 55:8). You see, with God, there is no "in-between." BTT allows one to see that it is hard for one who left the positive path to return. The longer one walks on the negative path, the harder it is to get off. This is explained in the Book of Hebrew where the writer documented, "*For it is impossible for those who were once enlightened, and have tasted the heavenly gift, and have become partakers of the Holy Spirit, and have tasted the good word of God and the powers of the age to come, if they fall away, to renew them again to repentance, since they crucify again for themselves the Son of God, and put Him to an open shame*" (Hebrews 6:4-6). However, for now understand that in the war campaign, a reason for not seeing this truth is part of the negative attribute's strategy.

Once again, the thirty-two positive and negative attributes influence people in the eight categories to swing them to either side of the campaign. These categories are depicted in **Figure 16**. These categories are the world's population. I call this group the "Harvest" just like Jesus said to His disciples, "*…The harvest truly is plentiful, but the laborers are few*" (Matthew 9:37). When Jesus spoke of the harvest, He may have referred to the people of these categories to give His disciples a visual of the war campaign. BTT allows one to see that the people of these categories supply the physical resources and support to the campaign.

Figure 16: The Harvest

The physical resources and support provided are manpower, finances, logistics, maintenance, guidance and instruction, and consistent leadership. The behavior and actions of every single person makes a difference in the campaign and, from time to time, alters the balance of the spiritual war. As one reads the chapters dedicated to these categories, their roles will become very clear. More importantly, the Biblical examples of the people in each category will help one understand where one might fit in the war campaign. Then a decision must be made if one finds himself or herself on the negative side of the war. Unfortunately, the more Jesus and the Bible are pushed out or compromised in society, the harder it becomes for one to see the right path to take. The negative attributes will cloud the pathway with multiple options.

With this said, let me introduce the attributes of the war campaign. Remember, there are other attributes, but these are the ones most prominent in Solomon's writings. Please enjoy the learning experience.

CHAPTER V:

The Negative Attributes

"All the nations will be gathered before Him, and He will separate them one from another, as a shepherd divides his sheep from the goats. And He will set the sheep on His right hand, but the goats on the left."

~ Matthew 25:32-34

INTRODUCTION

"Beloved, do not believe every spirit, but test the spirits, whether they are of God; because many false prophets have gone out into the world"

~ 1 John 4:1

The negative attributes account for all the negative issues that exist in the world going back to the dawn of creation. Their influences on mankind has caused individuals to do heinous and perverted crimes, caused homes to fail, destroyed communities, and even caused nations to revolt against nations. They can accomplish their influences by overwhelming and overtaking the spirit of the inner man. Because one cannot see his or her inner spirit, the connection between the spirit and the attributes is difficult to conceive. The secular community struggles because it has no knowledge of the inner spirit while the religious community struggles because it lacks <u>discernment</u>. Millennia's of false teaching have created religious communities that lacks spiritual maturity and denies the inner spirit's role in one's life. Regardless of the reason, both communities are lost in the war campaign. However, there remains a remnant of people who actively search God's Word against the world's wisdom. They follow the path of the Bereans in Acts 17:11 who, *"...were more fair-minded than those in Thessalonica, in that they received the word with all readiness, and searched the Scriptures daily to find out whether these things were so."* Without an active search of God's Word and obedience to it, one cannot see the negative forces causing whole communities to fail.

BTT allows one to see that God did not create mankind and then leave it without knowledge of the inner spirit. God provided man His written Word and expected him to use and follow it. However, as man rejects God's Word, the negative attributes, infused with ancient knowledge, fills the void. What is paramount to understand about these negative attributes is that their goal is simply to keep mankind separated from God. In fact, the negative attributes first hinder and then attempt to destroy anything positive that comes from God. One will see this in Chapter VI on the positive attributes. **Figure 17** illustrates the negative attributes surrounding every family and influencing every person individually. Their first objective is to destroy homes. Since the beginning of time, strong homes have served as the centers of learning about God; secure places where generations passed down God's Truth. But over time, the negative attributes eroded the unity of the family unit using influences that inspired negative behaviors, attitudes, and words in weaker members of the household. This strategy served to hinder or prevent God's Word among the entire household while

Figure 17: The Negative Attributes Attacking the Home

covertly promoting dissension and rebellion within the family. This is all part of the grand strategy of the negative forces of the war campaign.

As one reads about each negative attribute, one will gain information that may be overwhelming at first. However, given some critical thought, one will gain an appreciation for the truth documented on each attribute. Moreover, one will gain a wisdom unmatched by anything else one has read or heard of in religious and secular outlets. I will begin this chapter of the book with the ***wicked*** attribute. The influences of this attribute serve as the kingpin of all the other negative attributes since the Biblical record documents that, "*...we do not wrestle against flesh and blood, but against principalities, against powers, against the rulers of the darkness of this age, against spiritual hosts of **wickedness** in the heavenly places*" (Ephesians 6:12). This attribute serves as a catalyst for all the ills produced on the negative side of the campaign and it empowers the rest of the negative attributes. **Figure 18** illustrates the sphere of influence for the ***wicked*** attribute. Once it acquires the services of the evil, hater, liar, and scoffer attributes, its span of control becomes easier through schemes, manipulation, deception, and fraud. However, what is most disturbing about the wicked attribute is when it influences a leader who has a great impact on society. One will learn that when a leader allows the influence of this attribute and is in charge, it is the unseen and unnoticed things that occur that cause the greater damage. As wicked leaders draw attention to themselves, his or her supporters are free to alter boundaries established on godly principles. World history is replete with examples of nation's failure when the wicked are in charge.

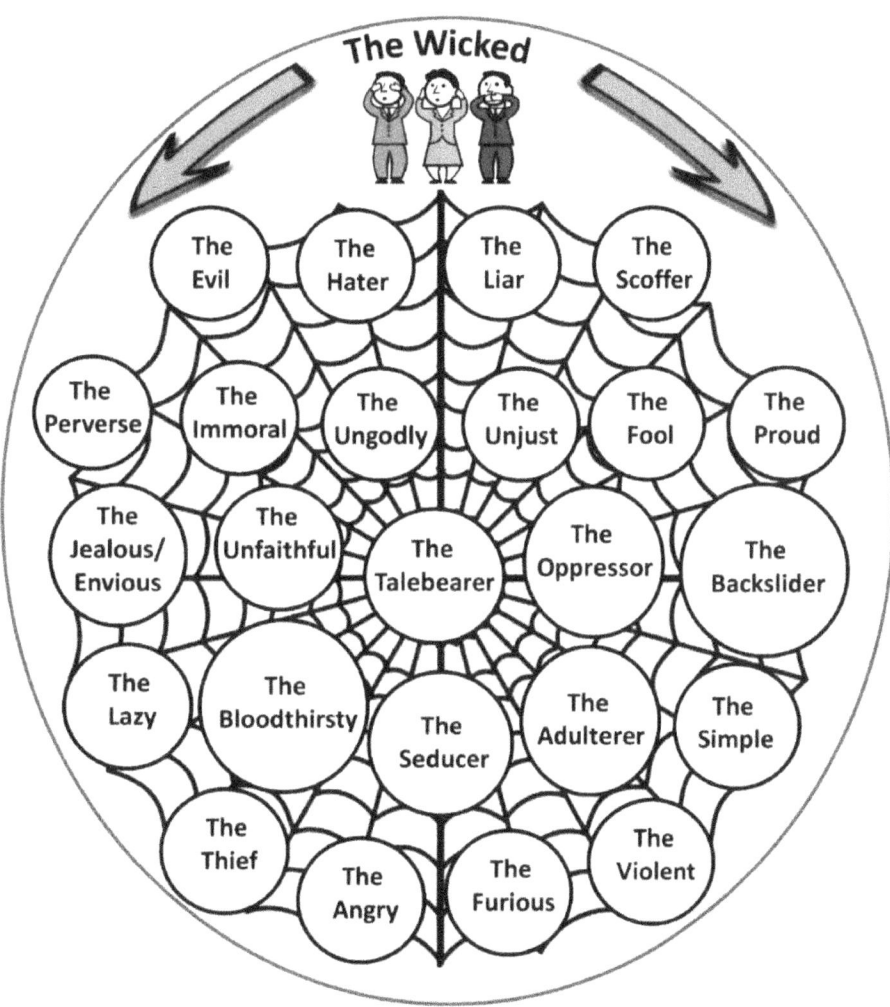

Figure 18: The Wicked Attribute's Sphere of Influence

Moreover, when Christians and good people alike keep silent, chaos is the only expectation for

51

a nation's people. This highlights a goal and strategy of the negative forces of the war campaign; to silence the voices of the positive forces.

The ***Wicked* attribute**: One influenced by this attribute sees no truth, hears no truth, and speaks no truth. The influence of this attribute causes one to reject all authority but his or her own. In addition, the influence of this attribute causes one to scheme, plot, and create elaborate snares for others. This is the attribute that influences one to think evil of or creates suspicion about another person's character, motives, or actions. It is the master ***unclean spirit*** of planting the element of <u>doubt</u> in 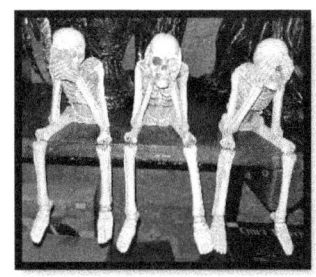 one's inner spirit. This element will be fully discussed later. One with the ***wicked*** attribute displays characteristics that are directly opposite of one with the righteous attribute – they lack honor, show no mercy, are unjust, not good, faithless, and the cause for blame. This person is amoral because the attribute influences them to be unethical and they are willing to sacrifice anyone and everyone for personal gain. One influenced by this attribute instigates strife using suggestions or random thoughts with no form of facts in order to gain traction for deploying deviant schemes. The influence of this attribute will covertly convince others that their truth is superior to all others. Unlike any other attribute, this attribute is the master of cultivating "group think"; the practice of thinking or making decisions as a group in a way that discourages creativity or individual responsibility. Thus, when the ***wicked*** are in charge, the people they lead make irrational and dysfunctional decisions. Alternate or dissenting viewpoints are suppressed by the supporters of the ***wicked*** while isolationism covertly leads the group down destructive paths. This attribute is a master manipulator of God's Word. It uses worldly wisdom to craft deceptive networks of social, political, and psychological advantage. This is the attribute that questions the wisdom of God (Proverbs 21:30), moves ancient landmarks (Proverbs 23:10), and teaches relativism (James 3:15). Nothing is sacred to this attribute. The attribute deceptively convinces its host that there are other paths to God despite Biblical writings that state the opposite. This is the principle attribute that calls, "*evil good, and good evil; who put darkness for light, and light for darkness; who put bitter for sweet, and sweet for bitter!*" (Isaiah 5:20). Unfortunately, anyone who knowingly or unknowingly follows this attribute's schemes can fall in the category of people of whom Paul stated, "*…who, knowing the righteous judgment of God, that those who practice such things are deserving of death, not only do the same but also approve of those who practice them*" (Romans 1:32). Please understand, the influence of the ***wicked*** attribute is beyond powerful. One who allows the influence of this attribute can become the negative forces ultimate warrior on the spiritual battlefield because of their ability to rapidly think, scheme, lie, deceive, and manipulate others. In fact, this attribute's schemes can even take down one with the righteous attribute who momentarily drops his or her guard. The Biblical record documented this fact through the prophet Ezekiel when he recorded from the Lord, "*But when a righteous man turns away from his righteousness and commits iniquity, and does according to all the abominations that the **wicked** man does, shall he live? All the righteousness which he has done shall not be remembered; because of the unfaithfulness of which he is guilty and the sin which he has committed, because of them he shall die*" (Ezekiel 18:24). If the righteous can fall on the spiritual battlefield, consider how much strength is required of people with smaller measures of the other positive attributes against the adversary.

BTT allows one to see that the influence of the **wicked** and liar attributes is spiritually joined at the hip. One who allows this combination will use his or her influence to advance **wicked** agendas, schemes, and plans across the full spectrum of the spiritual battlefield. Thus, this attribute pulls one influenced by the evil attribute close to its side as a companion. The Spirit of wisdom told Solomon that "*the **wicked** covet the catch of evil men...*" (Proverbs 12:12). But the attribute still requires all the other negative attributes to carry out its schemes. Wisdom told Solomon that, "*The way of the **wicked** is an abomination to the LORD...*" (Proverbs 15:9), and "*The thoughts of the **wicked** are an abomination to the LORD...*" (Proverbs 15:26). One can clearly see, the Lord has no regard for one that allows the influence of the **wicked** attribute. In fact, Wisdom even revealed that "*The soul of the **wicked** desires evil...*" (Proverbs 21:10) which emphasizes how deep this attribute penetrates one's body. Hence, Solomon documented, "*Do not enter the path of the **wicked**, and do not walk in the way of evil. Avoid it, do not travel on it; turn away from it and pass on. For they do not sleep unless they have done evil; and their sleep is taken away unless they make someone fall. For they eat the bread of **wickedness**, and drink the wine of violence. But the path of the just is like the shining sun, that shines ever brighter unto the perfect day. The way of the **wicked** is like darkness; they do not know what makes them stumble*" (Proverbs 4:14-19). This truth sets the tone for all that will follow about the influence of the **wicked** attribute.

The Spirit of wisdom informed Solomon that, "*These six things the LORD hates, yes, seven are an abomination to Him: A proud look, a lying tongue, hands that shed innocent blood, a heart that devises **wicked** plans, feet that are swift in running to evil, a false witness who speaks lies, and one who sows discord among brethren*" (Proverbs 6:16-19). Using still stronger language, the Spirit of wisdom revealed to Solomon that, "*...the heart of the **wicked** is worth little*" (Proverbs 10:20), that "*...violence covers the mouth of the **wicked***" (Proverbs 10:6 and 10:11), and that the "*... lips of the righteous know what is acceptable, but the mouth of the **wicked** what is perverse*" (Proverbs 10:32). Further, Solomon learned that, "*...the mouth of the **wicked** pours forth evil*" (Proverbs 15:28) and it "*...devours iniquity*" (Proverbs 19:28). The Spirit of wisdom even revealed to him that, "*A **wicked** man accepts a bribe behind the back to pervert the ways of justice*" (Proverbs 17:23). For this attribute, nothing is off limits for the right price. Hence, people influenced by this attribute will sacrifice anyone if it will make them successful or get them what they want. Solomon also learned that people influenced by the **wicked** attribute suffer from a self-inflicted paranoia. They are constantly looking over their shoulders. They fear that someone is always watching them and therefore trust no one. Hence, the Spirit of wisdom revealed to Solomon that, "*The **wicked** flee when no one pursues...*" (Proverbs 28:1).

Further, Solomon learned a plethora of information from Wisdom to include:

"The **wicked** man does deceptive work..." (Proverbs 11:18)	"...the **wicked** will fall by his own **wickedness**" (Proverbs 11:5)	"Treasures of **wickedness** profit nothing..." (Proverbs 10:2)
"...the name of the **wicked** will rot." (Proverbs 10:7)	"...the wages of the **wicked** [leads] to sin" (Proverbs 10:16)	"...the revenue of the **wicked** is trouble" (Proverbs 15:6)

"...the counsels of the **wicked** are deceitful" (Proverbs 12:5)	"Like a roaring lion and a charging bear is a **wicked** ruler over poor people" (Proverbs 28:15)	"When the **wicked** comes, contempt comes also; and with dishonor comes reproach" (Proverbs 18:3)
"When the **wicked** are multiplied, transgression increases..." (Proverbs 29:16)	"When the **wicked** arise, men hide themselves" Proverbs 28:12 and 28:28).	"...he who is upright in the way is an abomination to the **wicked**" (Proverbs 29:27)
"Righteousness guards him whose way is blameless, but **wickedness** overthrows the sinner" (Proverbs 13:6)	"Behold, the **wicked** brings forth iniquity; yes, he conceives trouble and brings forth falsehood" (Psalms 7:14)	"Although a city is exalted by the blessing of the upright, it is overthrown by the mouth of the **wicked**" (Proverbs 11:11)
"The righteous considers the cause of the poor, but the **wicked** does not understand such knowledge" (Proverbs 29:7)	Don't show them any partiality: "It is not good to show partiality to the **wicked**, or to overthrow the righteous in judgment" (Proverbs 18:5)	Don't justify them: "He who justifies the **wicked**, and he who condemns the just, both of them alike are an abomination to the LORD" (Proverbs 17:15)
Don't call them "righteous": "He who says to the **wicked**, "You are righteous," him the people will curse; Nations will abhor him" (Proverbs 24:24)	Be extremely careful when rebuking them: "He who corrects a scoffer gets shame for himself, and he who rebukes a **wicked** man only harms himself" (Proverbs 9:7)	Learn to rebuke them correctly: "But those who rebuke the **wicked** will have delight, and a good blessing will come upon them" (Proverbs 24:25)
Don't pick them to be your friend: "The righteous should choose his friends carefully, for the way of the **wicked** leads them astray" (Proverbs 12:26)	Do as the Lord commands us: "Those who forsake the law praise the **wicked**, but such as keep the law contend with them" (Proverbs 28:4)	"A righteous man regards the life of his animal, but the tender mercies of the **wicked** are cruel" (Proverbs 12:10)

Table 4: Pearls of Wisdom about the Wicked Attribute

Wisdom also shared important lessons with Solomon that leaders need to know for dealing with the influence of the ***wicked*** attribute. Solomon documented that, "*It is an abomination for kings to commit **wickedness**, for a throne is established by righteousness*" (Proverbs 16:12). Further he documented that "*A wise king sifts out the **wicked**, and brings the threshing wheel over them*" (Proverbs 20:26). This means a leader punishes one influenced by the ***wicked*** attribute; not reward them for their ***wickedness***. Also, a wise leader "sifts" out the ***wicked*** from his presence. This means removal; not allowing one influenced by this attribute to remain in the organization. By following this strategy, Solomon documented "*Take away the **wicked** from before the king, and his throne will be established in righteousness*" (Proverbs 25:5). One should see that Solomon learned, "*If a ruler pays attention to lies, all his servants become **wicked***" (Proverbs 29:12) and that, "*When the righteous are in authority, the people rejoice; but when a **wicked** man rules, the people groan*" (Proverbs 29:2). The items in this paragraph constitute the foundation of true leadership and are applicable to everyone serving in a leadership role.

The Book of Proverb is not the only book in the Biblical record that documented sage warnings about the influences of the **wicked** attribute. David and the prophets documented the following pearls of wisdom:

*"The **wicked** watches the righteous, and seeks to slay him"* (Psalm 37:32)	*"God is a just judge, and God is angry with the **wicked** every day"* (Psalm 7:11)	*"The **wicked** plots against the just, and gnashes at him with his teeth"* (Psalm 37:12)
*"The Lord is known by the judgment He executes; the **wicked** is snared in the work of his own hands. Meditation. Selah. The **wicked** shall be turned into hell, and all the nations that forget God"* (Psalm 9:16-17)	*"The **wicked** have drawn the sword and have bent their bow, to cast down the poor and needy, to slay those who are of upright conduct. Their sword shall enter their own heart, and their bows shall be broken"* (Psalm 37:14-15)	*"No, in heart you work **wickedness**; you weigh out the violence of your hands in the earth. The **wicked** are estranged from the womb; they go astray as soon as they are born, speaking lies"* (Psalm 58:2-3)
*"Many sorrows shall be to the **wicked**; but he who trusts in the Lord, mercy shall surround him"* (Psalm 32:10)	*"...You are not a God who takes pleasure in **wickedness**, nor shall evil dwell with You"* (Psalm 5:4)	*"Why do the **wicked** renounce God? He has said in his heart, "You will not require an account"* (Psalm 10:13)
*"The **wicked** borrows and does not repay, but the righteous shows mercy and gives"* (Psalm 37:21)	*"The **wicked** prowl on every side, when vileness is exalted among the sons of men"* (Psalm 12:8)	*"Behold, the **wicked** brings forth iniquity; Yes, he conceives trouble and brings forth falsehood"* (Psalm 7:14)
*"The **wicked** in his pride persecutes the poor; let them be caught in the plots which they have devised. For the **wicked** boasts of his heart's desire; he blesses the greedy and renounces the Lord. The **wicked** in his proud countenance does not seek God; God is in none of his thoughts"* (Psalm 10:2-4)	*"... There is no fear of God before his eyes. For he flatters himself in his own eyes, when he finds out his iniquity and when he hates. The words of his mouth are **wickedness** and deceit; he has ceased to be wise and to do good. He devises **wickedness** on his bed; he sets himself in a way that is not good; he does not abhor evil"* (Psalm 36:1-4)	*"For **wickedness** burns as the fire; it shall devour the briers and thorns, and kindle in the thickets of the forest; they shall mount up like rising smoke. Through the wrath of the Lord of hosts the land is burned up, and the people shall be as fuel for the fire; no man shall spare his brother"* (Isaiah 9:18-19)
*"The **wicked** watches the righteous, and seeks to slay him"* (Psalm 37:32)	*"Salvation is far from the **wicked**, for they do not seek Your statutes"* (Psalm 119:155)	*"The Lord is righteous; He has cut in pieces the cords of the **wicked**"* (Psalm 129:4)
	*"For look! The **wicked** bend their bow, they make ready*	*"For yet a little while and the **wicked** shall be no*

	their arrow on the string, that they may shoot secretly at the upright in heart" (Psalm 11:2)	*more; indeed, you will look carefully for his place, but it shall be no more"* (Psalm 37:10)
*For the Lord loves justice, and does not forsake His saints; they are preserved forever, but the descendants of the **wicked** shall be cut off.* (Psalm 37:28) *and "...the future of the **wicked** shall be cut off"* (Psalm 37:38)	*"The righteous also shall see and fear, and shall laugh at him, saying, "Here is the man who did not make God his strength, but trusted in the abundance of his riches, and strengthened himself in his **wickedness**"* (Psalm 52:6-7)	*"The Lord tests the righteous, but the **wicked** and the one who loves violence His soul hates. Upon the **wicked** He will rain coals; fire and brimstone and a burning wind shall be the portion of their cup"* (Psalm 11:5-6)
*"He turns rivers into a wilderness, and the watersprings into dry ground; a fruitful land into barrenness, for the **wickedness** of those who dwell in it"* (Psalm 107:33-34)	*"The Lord watches over the strangers; He relieves the fatherless and widow; but the way of the **wicked** He turns upside down"* (Psalm 146:9)	*"For a day in Your courts is better than a thousand. I would rather be a doorkeeper in the house of my God than dwell in the tents of **wickedness**"* (Psalm 84:10)
*"You put away all the **wicked** of the earth like dross; therefore I love Your testimonies"* (Psalm 119:119)	*"Evil shall slay the **wicked**, and those who hate the righteous shall be condemned"* (Psalm 34:21)	*"The Lord preserves all who love Him, but all the **wicked** He will destroy"* (Psalm 145:20)
*"As the proverb of the ancients says, '**Wickedness** proceeds from the **wicked**.' But my hand shall not be against you"* (1 Samuel 24:13)	*"You who love the Lord, hate evil! He preserves the souls of His saints; He delivers them out of the hand of the **wicked**"* (Psalm 97:10)	*"The **wicked** will see it and be grieved; he will gnash his teeth and melt away; the desire of the **wicked** shall perish"* (Psalm 112:10)
*"...the scepter of **wickedness** shall not rest on the land allotted to the righteous, lest the righteous reach out their hands to iniquity"* (Psalm 125:3)	*"God shall judge the righteous and the **wicked**, for there is a time there for every purpose and for every work"* (Ecclesiastes 3:16-17)	*"Woe to the **wicked**! It shall be ill with him, for the reward of his hands shall be given him"* (Isaiah 3:11)
*"...it will not be well with the **wicked**; nor will he prolong his days, which are as a shadow, because he does not fear before God"* (Ecclesiastes 8:13)	*"Woe to men mighty at drinking wine, woe to men valiant for mixing intoxicating drink, who justify the **wicked** for a bribe, and take away justice from the righteous man!"* (Isaiah 5:22-23)	*"No one has power over the spirit to retain the spirit, and no one has power in the day of death. There is no release from that war, and **wickedness** will not deliver those who are given to it"* (Ecclesiastes 8:8)
"There is a vanity which occurs on earth, that there are just men to whom it happens according to the	*"For you have trusted in your **wickedness**; you have said, 'No one sees me'; your wisdom and your*	*"The Lord knows the thoughts of man, that they are futile. Blessed is the man whom You instruct, O Lord,*

*work of the **wicked**; again, there are **wicked** men to whom it happens according to the work of the righteous. I said that this also is vanity"* (Ecclesiastes 8:14)	*knowledge have warped you; and you have said in your heart, 'I am, and there is no one else besides me"* (Isaiah 47:10)	*and teach out of Your law, that You may give him rest from the days of adversity, until the pit is dug for the **wicked**"* (Psalm 94:11-13)
*"Let grace be shown to the **wicked**, yet he will not learn righteousness; in the land of uprightness he will deal unjustly, and will not behold the majesty of the Lord"* (Isaiah 26:10)	*"Also the schemes of the schemer are evil; he devises **wicked** plans to destroy the poor with lying words, even when the needy speaks justice"* (Isaiah 32:7)	*"A little that a righteous man has is better than the riches of many **wicked**. For the arms of the **wicked** shall be broken, but the Lord upholds the righteous"* (Psalm 37:16-17)
*"The Lord lifts up the humble; He casts the **wicked** down to the ground"* (Psalm 147:6)	*"There is no peace," says the Lord, "for the **wicked**"* (Isaiah 48:22)	*"...The Lord shall repay the evildoer according to his **wickedness**"* (2 Samuel 3:39)
*"Let the **wicked** forsake his way, and the unrighteous man his thoughts; let him return to the Lord, and He will have mercy on him; and to our God, for He will abundantly pardon"* (Isaiah 55:7)	*"But the **wicked** are like the troubled sea, when it cannot rest, whose waters cast up mire and dirt. "There is no peace," says my God, "for the **wicked**"* (Isaiah 57:20-21)	*"I will punish the world for its evil, and the **wicked** for their iniquity; I will halt the arrogance of the proud, and will lay low the haughtiness of the terrible"* (Isaiah 13:11)

Table 5: More Pearls of Wisdom about the Wicked Attribute from David and Other Prophets

God has a clear message for everyone who allows this attribute to influence his or her life. This message is not good. First, "*... to the **wicked** God says: "What right have you to declare My statutes, or take My covenant in your mouth, seeing you hate instruction and cast My words behind you? When you saw a thief, you consented with him, and have been a partaker with adulterers. You give your mouth to evil, and your tongue frames deceit. You sit and speak against your brother; you slander your own mother's son. These things you have done, and I kept silent; you thought that I was altogether like you; but I will rebuke you, and set them in order before your eyes*" (Psalm 50:16-21). If this is not clear enough, second the Biblical record documents, "*When the **wicked** spring up like grass, and when all the workers of iniquity flourish, it is that they may be destroyed forever*" (Psalm 92:7). These very Scriptures give one an understanding as to why the Psalmist prayed, "*Search me, O God, and know my heart; try me, and know my anxieties; and see if there is any **wicked** way in me, and lead me in the way everlasting*" (Psalms 139:23-24).

For our learning, the Biblical record is also replete with examples of individuals influenced by the **wicked** attribute. All one must do is read the Biblical accounts of their behavior to know why the Lord called them out as **wicked**. Some of the many examples include:

Who	What They Did
Cain	"...*Cain who was of the **wicked** one and murdered his brother. And why did he murder him? Because his works were evil and his brother's righteous*" (1 John 3:12)
The men of Sodom and Gomorrah	"...*the men of Sodom were exceedingly **wicked** and sinful against the Lord*" (Genesis 13:13), and "...*righteous Lot, who was oppressed by the filthy conduct of the **wicked** (for that righteous man, dwelling among them, tormented his righteous soul from day to day by seeing and hearing their lawless deeds) ...*" (2 Peter 2:7-8)
Er, Judah's firstborn	"...*as **wicked** in the sight of the Lord, and the Lord killed him*" (Genesis 38:6)
Potiphar's wife	Joseph said to her, "...*because you are his wife. How then can I do this great **wickedness**, and sin against God?*" (Genesis 39:9)
Pharaoh and his people	He told Moses, "...*The Lord is righteous, and my people and I are **wicked***" (Exodus 9:27)
Korah, Dathan, and Abiram (Genesis 16:24)	Moses said, "*Depart now from the tents of these **wicked** men! Touch nothing of theirs, lest you be consumed in all their sins*" (Numbers 16:26)
The nations outside the children of Israel	Moses documented, "...*it is because of the **wickedness** of these nations that the Lord is driving them out from before you....*" (Deuteronomy 9:3-5)
The children of Israel from time to time	Moses documented "*Then I took the two tablets and threw them out of my two hands and broke them before your eyes...because of all your sin which you committed in doing **wickedly** in the sight of the Lord, to provoke Him to anger*" (Deuteronomy 9:17-18)
Abimelech (he coordinated a conspiracy)	"... *God repaid the **wickedness** of Abimelech, which he had done to his father by killing his seventy brothers*" (Judges 9:56)
Perverted men in the tribe of Benjamin	"...*certain men of the city, perverted men, surrounded the house and beat on the door. They spoke to the master of the house, the old man, saying, "Bring out the man who came to your house, that we may know him carnally!" But the man, the master of the house, went out to them and said to them, "No, my brethren! I beg you, do not act so **wickedly**...*" (Judges 19:22-23)
The children of Israel demand for a king	Samuel warned "...*your **wickedness** is great, which you have done in the sight of the Lord, in asking a king for yourselves*" (1 Samuel 12:17) and "...*if you still do **wickedly**, you shall be swept away, both you and your king*" (1 Samuel 12:25)
Rechab and Baanah	David had them put to death when he said, "...*How much more, when **wicked** men have killed a righteous person in his own house on his bed? Therefore, shall I not now require his blood at your hand and remove you from the earth?" So David commanded his young men, and they executed them, cut off their hands and feet, and hanged them by the pool in Hebron. ...*" (2 Samuel 4:9-12)

Person	Reference
Nabal, Abigail's husband	David documented "...*the Lord has returned the **wickedness** of Nabal on his own head...*" (1 Samuel 25:39)
Shimei, an adversary of David	Solomon documented, "*...You know, as your heart acknowledges, all the **wickedness** that you did to my father David; therefore the Lord will return your **wickedness** on your own head*" (1 Kings 2:44)
Baal's prophets	Elijah said to the people, "*I alone am left a prophet of the Lord; but Baal's prophets are four hundred and fifty men*" (1 Kings 18:22)
Ahab and Jezebel	The Biblical documented, "*But there was no one like Ahab who sold himself to do **wickedness** in the sight of the Lord, because Jezebel his wife stirred him up...*" (1 Kings 21:25-26)
Manasseh	The Bible documented "*Because Manasseh king of Judah has done these abominations (he has acted more **wickedly** than all the Amorites who were before him, and has also made Judah sin with his idols), therefore thus says the Lord God of Israel: 'Behold, I am bringing such calamity upon Jerusalem and Judah, that whoever hears of it, both his ears will tingle'*" (2 Kings 21:11-12)
Ahaziah	The Bible documented, "*...Jehoshaphat king of Judah allied himself with Ahaziah king of Israel, who acted very **wickedly***" (2 Chronicles 20:35)
Athaliah, Ahaziah's mother	The Biblical documented, "*He also walked in the ways of the house of Ahab, for his mother advised him to do **wickedly**...*" (2 Chronicles 22:3; 24:7)
Haman	He plotted, "*...to destroy all the Jews who were throughout the whole kingdom of Ahasuerus—the people of Mordecai*" (Ester 3:6) but Queen Ester called him out when she said, "*The adversary and enemy is this **wicked** Haman...*" (Esther 7:6)
The Pharisees and Sadducees	They wanted a sign from heaven and Jesus said, "*A **wicked** and adulterous generation seeks after a sign, and no sign shall be given to it except the sign of the prophet Jonah." And He left them and departed*" (Matthew 16:4)
The Pharisees	The Pharisees: The Bible documented, "*...Jesus perceived their **wickedness**, and said, "Why do you test Me, you hypocrites?"*" (Matthew 22:18), and he also told them, "*...your inward part is full of greed and **wickedness***" (Luke 11:39)
Simon	Peter told him, "*...Repent therefore of this your **wickedness**, and pray God if perhaps the thought of your heart may be forgiven you. For I see that you are poisoned by bitterness and bound by iniquity*" (Acts 8:20-23)
The ungodly and unrighteous	"*...even as they did not like to retain God in their knowledge, God gave them over to a debased mind, to do those things which are not fitting; being filled with all unrighteousness, **sexual immorality**, **wickedness**...*" (Romans 1:28-32)
One's life before becoming a Christian	Paul documented, "*And you, who once were alienated and enemies in your mind by **wicked** works, yet now He has reconciled in the body of His flesh through death, to present you holy, and blameless, and above reproach in His sight— if indeed you continue in the faith, grounded and steadfast, and are not moved away from the hope of the gospel which you heard, which was preached to every creature under heaven...*" (Colossians 1:21-23)

Table 6: Examples of People Influenced by the Wicked Attribute

In addition to these examples, one must understand that it was because of the **wicked** attribute's influence over mankind that God destroyed all living flesh on the earth by a great flood. The Biblical record documented, "*...the Lord saw that the **wickedness** of man was great in the earth, and that every intent of the thoughts of his heart was only evil continually. And the Lord was sorry that He had made man on the earth, and He was grieved in His heart*" (Genesis 6:5-6). As one continues to read Genesis 6:13 through Genesis chapter 10, one learns that except for eight souls, God wiped man off the face of the earth. A large vessel called an "ark" carried these eight souls to safety. Their families repopulated the earth and produced the nations that exist to this very day according to Genesis 9:1; 9:13; and 10:32.

Later in the Bible, Moses documented a few things about the influence of the **wicked** attribute that the Lord commanded him to tell the children of Israel. He documented the following items that are still applicable today:

- Circulating false reports: "*You shall not circulate a false report. Do not put your hand with the **wicked** to be an unrighteous witness*" (Exodus 23:1)

- Involvement in false matters: "*Keep yourself far from a false matter; do not kill the innocent and righteous. For I will not justify the **wicked***" (Exodus 23:7)

- Prostituting one's daughter: "*Do not prostitute your daughter, to cause her to be a harlot, lest the land fall into harlotry, and the land become full of **wickedness***" (Leviticus 19:29)

- Engaging in **wicked** relationships:

    - (A): "*You shall not uncover the nakedness of a woman and her daughter, nor shall you take her son's daughter or her daughter's daughter, to uncover her nakedness. They are near of kin to her. It is **wickedness***" (Leviticus 18:17)

    - (B): "*If a man marries a woman and her mother, it is **wickedness**. They shall be burned with fire, both he and they, that there may be no **wickedness** among you*" (Leviticus 20:14)

    - (C): "*If a man takes his sister, his father's daughter or his mother's daughter, and sees her nakedness and she sees his nakedness, it is a **wicked** thing. And they shall be cut off in the sight of their people. He has uncovered his sister's nakedness. He shall bear his guilt*" (Leviticus 20:17)

- Engaging in false worship: "*If there is found among you...**wicked**...who has gone and served other gods and worshiped them, either the sun or moon or any of the host of heaven, which I have not commanded, and it is told you, and you hear of it, then you shall inquire diligently. And if it is indeed true ...that man or woman who has committed that **wicked** thing, and shall stone to death that man or woman with stones*" (Deuteronomy 17:2-5)

- Engaging in witchcraft, fortune tellers, sorcery, spells casters, mediums, spiritualist, or one who calls up the dead: "*There shall not be found among you anyone who makes* *his son or his daughter pass through the fire, or one who practices witchcraft, or a soothsayer, or one who interprets omens, or a sorcerer, or one who conjures spells, or a medium, or a spiritist, or one who calls up the dead. For all who do these things are an <u>abomination</u> to the Lord, and because of these <u>abominations</u> the Lord your God drives them out from before you*" (Deuteronomy 18:9-12)

- Judicial punishment: "*If there is a dispute between men, and they come to court, that the judges may judge them, and they justify the righteous and condemn the **wicked**, then it shall be, if the **wicked** man deserves to be beaten, that the judge will cause him to lie down and be beaten in his presence, according to his guilt, with a certain number of blows*" (Deuteronomy 25:1-2)

- Military rules: "*When the army goes out against your enemies, then keep yourself from every **wicked** thing*" (Deuteronomy 23:9)

Finally, one should know that the nation of Israel, God's chosen people, lost their status because of the influence of the **wicked** attribute. The Lord sent numerous prophets to plead with the nation to repent, to explicitly point out the nature of their sin, and to specifically identify the influence of the **wicked** attribute among them. Purely for the sake of space in this book, I will only highlight a few scriptural references where the prophets identified this attribute. The details captured in the Biblical record are remarkable and I encourage you to read each item at your convenience. Here are some of the prophets and their statements from the Lord that gave warnings about the influence of the **wicked** attribute on Israel:

The Prophet	What Was Said
Jeremiah	"*I will utter My judgments against them concerning all their **wickedness**, because they have forsaken Me, burned incense to other gods, and worshiped the works of their own hands*" (Jeremiah 1:16)
	"*Lift up your eyes to the desolate heights and see: Where have you not lain with men? By the road you have sat for them like an Arabian in the wilderness; and you have polluted the land with your harlotries and your **wickedness***" (Jeremiah 3:2)
	"*O Jerusalem, wash your heart from **wickedness**, that you may be saved. How long shall your evil thoughts lodge within you?*" (Jeremiah 4:14)
	"*Your ways and your doings have procured these things for you. This is your **wickedness**, because it is bitter, because it reaches to your heart*" (Jeremiah 4:18)
	"*Why has this people slidden back, Jerusalem, in a perpetual backsliding? They hold fast to deceit, they refuse to return. I listened and heard, but they do not speak aright. No man repented of his **wickedness**, Saying, 'What have I done?' Everyone turned to his own course, as the horse rushes into the battle*" (Jeremiah 8:5-6)
	"*The wind shall eat up all your rulers, and your lovers shall go into captivity; surely then you will be shamed and humiliated for all your **wickedness***" (Jeremiah 22:22)
	"*For both prophet and priest are profane; Yes, in My house I have found their **wickedness**,*" says the Lord*" (Jeremiah 23:11)

	*"And I have seen folly in the prophets of Samaria: They prophesied by Baal and caused My people Israel to err. Also I have seen a horrible thing in the prophets of Jerusalem: They commit adultery and walk in lies; they also strengthen the hands of evildoers, so that no one turns back from his **wickedness**. All of them are like Sodom to Me, and her inhabitants like Gomorrah"* (Jeremiah 23:13-14)
	*"However I have sent to you all My servants the prophets, rising early and sending them, saying, "Oh, do not do this abominable thing that I hate!" But they did not listen or incline their ear to turn from their **wickedness**, to burn no incense to other gods"* (Jeremiah 44:4-5)
Ezekiel	*"She has rebelled against My judgments by doing **wickedness** more than the nations, and against My statutes more than the countries that are all around her; for they have refused My judgments, and they have not walked in My statute"* (Ezekiel 5:6)
	*"And He said to me, "Go in, and see the **wicked** abominations which they are doing there"* (Ezekiel 8:9; See Ezekiel 8:5-17 for the **wicked** abominations)
	*"...with lies you have made the heart of the righteous sad, whom I have not made sad; and you have strengthened the hands of the **wicked**, so that he does not turn from his **wicked** way to save his life. Therefore you shall no longer envision futility nor practice divination; for I will deliver My people out of your hand, and you shall know that I am the Lord"* (Ezekiel 13:22-23)
	Wickedness with the Egyptians, Philistines, Assyrians, and Chaldean are called out. *"Then it was so, after all your **wickedness**—'Woe, woe to you!' says the Lord God— that you also built for yourself a shrine, and made a high place for yourself in every street. You built your high places at the head of every road, and made your beauty to be abhorred. You offered yourself to everyone who passed by, and multiplied your acts of harlotry..."How degenerate is your heart!" says the Lord God, "seeing you do all these things, the deeds of a brazen harlot"* (Ezekiel 16:23-30)
Daniel	*"Many shall be purified, made white, and refined, but the **wicked** shall do **wickedly**; and none of the wicked shall understand, but the wise shall understand"* (Daniel 12:10)
Hosea	*"When I would have healed Israel, then the iniquity of Ephraim was uncovered, and the **wickedness** of Samaria. For they have committed fraud; a thief comes in; a band of robbers takes spoil outside. They do not consider in their hearts that I remember all their **wickedness**; now their own deeds have surrounded them; they are before My face. They make a king glad with their **wickedness**, and princes with their lies"* (Hosea 7:1-3)
Joel	*"Let the nations be wakened, and come up to the Valley of Jehoshaphat; for there I will sit to judge all the surrounding nations. Put in the sickle, for the harvest is ripe. Come, go down; for the winepress is full, the vats overflow— for their **wickedness** is great"* (Joel 3:12-13)
Micah	*"And I said: "Hear now, O heads of Jacob, and you rulers of the house of Israel: Is it not for you to know justice? You who hate good and love evil; who strip the skin from My people, and the flesh from their bones..."* (Micah 3:1-2)
	*"Are there yet the treasures of **wickedness** in the house of the **wicked**, and the short measure that is an abomination? Shall I count pure those with the **wicked** scales, and with the bag of deceitful weights? For her rich men are

	full of violence, her inhabitants have spoken lies, and their tongue is deceitful in their mouth" (Micah 6:10-12)
Nahum	"*God is jealous, and the Lord avenges; the Lord avenges and is furious. The Lord will take vengeance on His adversaries, and He reserves wrath for His enemies; the Lord is slow to anger and great in power, and will not at all acquit the **wicked**. The Lord has His way in the whirlwind and in the storm, and the clouds are the dust of His feet*" (Nahum 1:2-3)
Habakkuk	"*Therefore the law is powerless, and justice never goes forth. For the **wicked** surround the righteous; therefore perverse judgment proceeds*" (Habakkuk 1:4)
Malachi	"*So now we call the proud blessed, for those who do **wickedness** are raised up; they even tempt God and go free*" (Malachi 3:15)
	"*For behold, the day is coming, burning like an oven, and all the proud, yes, all who do **wickedly** will be stubble. And the day which is coming shall burn them up,*" says the Lord of hosts, "*That will leave them neither root nor branch*" (Malachi 4:1)

Table 7: Examples from the Prophets about the Wicked Attribute

By the close of the Old Testament and the beginning of the New Testament, the influence of the **wicked** attribute was extremely active. Jesus explained, "*When an **unclean spirit** goes out of a man, he goes through dry places, seeking rest, and finds none. Then he says, 'I will return to my house from which I came.' And when he comes, he finds it empty, swept, and put in order. Then he goes and takes with him seven other spirits more **wicked** than himself, and they enter and dwell there; and the last state of that man is worse than the first. So shall it also be with this **wicked** generation*" (Matthew 12:43-45). Jesus' statement alone documented the strength of the influence of the **wicked** attribute. This attribute strengthened among the generation that Jesus walked with and it has continued to intensify to this very day. Jesus' return will end the **wicked** attribute's reign. However, people influenced by the positive attributes can make a difference in the execution of the war campaign until He returns.

Satan, the one behind the **wicked** attribute quickly attacks first-time hearers of the Gospel's Truth. The Biblical record documents that Satan snatches the Gospel message away before it reaches one's inner spirit. Jesus warned of this in the parable of the sower when He said, "*When anyone hears the word of the kingdom, and does not understand it, then the **wicked one** comes and snatches away what was sown in his heart. This is he who received seed by the wayside*" (Matthew 13:19). Now watch this. Mark and Luke are more specific about who the **wicked** one is. Mark recorded, "*The sower sows the word. And these are the ones by the wayside where the word is sown. When they hear, <u>Satan</u> comes immediately and takes away the word that was sown in their hearts*" (Mark 4:14-15). Luke further documented, "*Now the parable is this: The seed is the word of God. Those by the wayside are the ones who hear; then the <u>devil</u> comes and takes away the word out of their hearts, lest they should believe and be saved*" (Luke 8:11-12). When one considers these three Gospel writer's perspectives, BTT allows one to see that the influence of the **wicked** attribute comes directly from the same leader. Satan, the devil, and the **wicked** one are all the same person. The influence of the **wicked** attribute is the direct manifestation of Satan.

Although time and time again, Jesus demonstrated that He is the Son of God, the Pharisees and Sadducees refused to believe Him. They asked Jesus to show them a sign from heaven. You see, the **wicked** attribute influencing them sought anything usable to trap Jesus and shame Him in the eyes of the people. But Jesus simply said to them, *"A **wicked** and adulterous generation seeks after a sign, and no sign shall be given to it except the sign of the prophet Jonah." And He left them and departed"* (Matthew 16:4). There are some religious groups today that teach their members to seek and chase signs. Both teachers and followers fall in the category of the Pharisees and Sadducees of Jesus' time. In the war campaign, these same people have not heard Jesus' statement documented in Matthew 16:4 above. Like the Pharisees who attempted to trap Jesus by His words over the issue of paying taxes, then and today *"...Jesus perceived their **wickedness**, and said, "Why do you test Me, you hypocrites?"* (Matthew 22:18).

Jesus taught that the influence of the **wicked** attribute can only lodge itself in one's inner spirit if one allows it. The influence of this attribute defiles the spiritual heart of a person. Jesus told His disciples, *"...What comes out of a man, that defiles a man. For from within, out of the heart of men, proceed evil thoughts, adulteries, fornications, murders, thefts, covetousness, **wickedness**, deceit, lewdness, an evil eye, blasphemy, pride, foolishness. All these **evil** things come from within and defile a man"* (Mark 7:20-23). This is the same point Jesus drove home to the Pharisees when He told them, *"...Now you Pharisees make the outside of the cup and dish clean, but your inward part is full of greed and **wickedness**"* (Luke 11:39).

Paul documented the existence of the influence of the **wicked** attribute when he, by inspiration of the Holy Spirit, wrote that *"...we do not wrestle against flesh and blood, but against principalities, against powers, against the rulers of the darkness of this age, against spiritual hosts of **wickedness** in the heavenly places"* (Ephesians 6:12). As hard as it may be to see, it is the spiritual hosts of **wickedness** in the heavenly places that are influencing so many things on the spiritual battlefield. BTT allows one to see that these spiritual host are the influencers behind the principalities, powers, and rulers of the darkness of this age. Refer back to **Figure 18** if this is not clear. Hence, God's Word and the spiritual armor documented in Ephesians 6:14-18 is essential for standing against this attribute.

James spoke about the influence of the **wicked** attribute when he documented, *"Therefore lay aside all filthiness and overflow of **wickedness**, and receive with meekness the implanted word, which is able to save your souls"* (James 1:21). Likewise, Peter warned Christians about this attribute when he documented, *"You therefore, beloved, since you know this beforehand, beware lest you also fall from your own steadfastness, being led away with the error of the **wicked**; but grow in the grace and knowledge of our Lord and Savior Jesus Christ. To Him be the glory both now and forever. Amen"* (2 Peter 3:17-18).

Finally, John commented on the influence of the **wicked** attribute when he wrote, *"I write to you, fathers, because you have known Him who is from the beginning. I write to you, young men, because you have overcome the **wicked** one. I write to you, little children, because you have known the Father. I have written to you, fathers, because you have known Him who is from the beginning. I have written to you, young men, because you are strong, and the word of God abides in you, and you have overcome the **wicked** one"* (1 John 2:13-14). John's comment that *"...the whole world lies under the sway of the **wicked** one"* (1 John 5:18-20) is significant because it highlights the extent of the war campaign with emphasis on who is leading the earthly war. Please do not miss this important point.

The **Evil attribute**: In the worst possible terms, the influences of this attribute causes one to be morally corrupt, reprehensible, and sinful. It is so corrosive that it consumes one's thoughts and very essence. This attribute is different from the wicked attribute in that it is the executer of the thoughts and schemes of one influenced by the wicked attribute. Hence, where one influenced by the wicked attribute schemes and releases a negative idea, concept, or thought to the public or even an individual, one influenced by the *evil* attribute embraces the idea, concept, or thought and carries them out even to the extreme. But be aware, the worst-case scenario is one who has allowed both the wicked and *evil* attributes to influence their inner spirit. This is one that conceives a wicked idea and then personally implements its wickedness and *evilness*. One with this combination is a formidable adversary in the war campaign. This is especially concerning if one is influenced by this combination and engaged in matters of religious doctrine. Paul addressed this point in his statement, "*...For Satan himself transforms himself into an angel of light. Therefore it is no great thing if his ministers also transform themselves into ministers of righteousness, whose end will be according to their works*" (2 Corinthians 11:14-15).

One of the first things Solomon learned about this attribute from the Spirit of wisdom was, "*When wisdom enters your heart, and knowledge is pleasant to your soul, discretion will preserve you; understanding will keep you, to deliver you from the way of **evil**, from the man who speaks perverse things, from those who leave the paths of uprightness to walk in the ways of darkness; who rejoice in doing **evil**, and delight in the perversity of the wicked...*" (Proverbs 2:10-14). This mouthful of information clearly identifies that there is a "way of *evil*" which translates to methods and methodologies, and that one can get caught up in it; i.e. "*rejoice in doing evil, and delight in the perversity of the wicked.*" This should all sound bad because it is. This is precisely why the Spirit of wisdom revealed to Solomon that, "*The fear of the LORD is to hate **evil**; pride and arrogance and the **evil** way and the perverse mouth I hate. Counsel is mine, and sound wisdom; I am understanding, I have strength*" (Proverbs 8:13-14). BTT allows one to see that even Wisdom hates pride and arrogance and the **evil** way and the perverse mouth. She provides counsel, sound wisdom, understanding, and strength to avoid these things. In other words, Wisdom provides the resources from God to survive the negative forces of the war campaign.

Solomon learned that "*Deceit is in the heart of those who devise **evil**...*" (Proverbs 12:20). You see, ***evil's*** influence roots itself deeply within the spiritual heart and shields itself in deception. Thus, one influenced by this attribute may smile in one's face, while all along have intentions of bringing harm. Wisdom told Solomon that, "*An **evil** man seeks only rebellion...*" (Proverbs 17:11). Later he learned that, "***Evil** men do not understand justice, but those who seek the LORD understand all*" (Proverbs 28:5). Because one influenced by the *evil* attribute does not understand justice, Solomon learned that, "*An **evildoer** gives heed to false lips; a liar listens eagerly to a spiteful tongue*" (Proverbs 17:4).

If not already obvious, this attribute can unite with other negative attributes to enhance the intensity of its influence. For example, the influence of the **evil** attribute can combine with the *bloodthirsty* attribute. Solomon told his son not to partner with "sinners" to commit premeditated murder in Proverbs 1:10. He said, *"...their feet run to **evil**, and they make haste to shed blood"* (Proverbs 1:16). Within this context, the Spirit of wisdom revealed to Solomon, *"These six things the LORD hates, yes, seven are an abomination to Him: A proud look, a lying tongue, <u>hands that shed innocent blood</u>, a heart that devises wicked plans, <u>feet that are swift in running to **evil**</u>, a false witness who speaks lies, and one who sows discord among brethren"* (Proverbs 6:16-19). Solomon summarized it all by documenting, *"Ponder the path of your feet, and let all your ways be established. Do not turn to the right or the left; remove your foot from **evil**"* (Proverbs 4:26-27). Other attributes that the influence of the **evil** attribute unites with are the fool, ungodly, violent, liar, and the perverse attributes. On can see the influence of the **evil** attribute as the Spirit of wisdom revealed to Solomon, *"To do **evil** is like sport to a fool..."* (Proverbs 10:23); and *"An ungodly man digs up **evil**, and it is on his lips like a burning fire"* (Proverbs 16:27); and *"A violent man entices his neighbor, and leads him in a way that is not good. He winks his eye to devise perverse things; he purses his lips and brings about **evil**"* (Proverbs 16:29-30). Further, Solomon began to understand that the influence of the **evil** attribute flourishes for many reasons. Here are a few of the reasons. The **evil** attribute flourishes because of people who:

- Reward **evil** for good: *"Whoever rewards **evil** for good, **evil** will not depart from his house"* (Proverbs 17:13)

- Have a perverse tongue: *"He who has a deceitful heart finds no good, and he who has a perverse tongue falls into **evil**"* (Proverbs 17:20)

- Are envious or jealous: *"Do not be envious of **evil** men, nor desire to be with them; for their heart devises violence, and their lips talk of troublemaking"* (Proverbs 24:1)

- Pursue riches at the expense of everything else: *"A man with an **evil** eye hastens after riches, and does not consider that poverty will come upon him"* (Proverbs 28:22)

- Are self-wise: *"Do not be wise in your own eyes; fear the LORD and depart from **evil**. It will be health to your flesh, and strength to your bones"* (Proverbs 3:7-8).

- Pursue **evil**: *"...he who pursues **evil** pursues it to his own death"* (Proverbs 11:19). Solomon learned that, *"...trouble will come to him who seeks **evil**"* (Proverbs 11:27).

Probably one of the most important things that Solomon learned about the **evil** attribute is the fact that, *"The eyes of the LORD are in every place, keeping watch on the **evil** and the good"* (Proverbs 15:13). This knowledge should give one the assurance that God is in control. Based on all the information presented on the influence of the **evil** attribute, now consider what the rest of the Old Testament shares about this attribute.

The Old Testament documented the influence of the ***evil*** attribute well. Literally, in the first book of the Bible, one can learn how it made it entrance on the earth. The Biblical record documented that God placed this attribute on the earth in the Garden of Eden. BTT allows one to see that this attribute was imbedded in a special tree in this Garden of Eden near man. The Bible documents, "*...out of the ground the Lord God made every tree grow that is pleasant to the sight and good for food. The <u>tree of life</u> was also in the midst of the garden, and the <u>tree of the knowledge</u> of good and **evil**"* (Genesis 2:9). Placing the ***evil*** attribute in the garden provided humanity the freedom to make a choice. One must understand that this construct was an expression of God's love for humanity. This expression gave humanity the right to choose obedience to God or the freedom to listen to others. This construct is far beyond what the human mind can fathom. One can only trust in God and accept the Lord's Word documented by the prophet Isaiah who wrote, "*For as the heavens are higher than the earth, so are My ways higher than your ways, and My thoughts than your thoughts*" (Isaiah 55:9). The freedom of choice never negates the consequences that come with the choices one makes.

God demonstrated His true love by giving His creation the freedom to make choices. One can chose to love God unconditionally or one can go one's own way. However, with freedom came responsibility, accountability, and consequences. BTT allows one to see that freedom and choice mandates consequences or rewards; life or death. Without the freedom to choose, one would only perform robotic functions from a zombie-like state of mind. This is not what God desires. The Biblical record informs us that, "*...the true worshipers will worship the Father in spirit and truth; for the Father is seeking such to worship Him. God is Spirit, and those who worship Him must worship in spirit and truth*" (John 4:23-24). With that said, here is what unfolded. The Bible documented, "*And the Lord God commanded the man, saying, "Of every tree of the garden you may freely eat; but of the tree of the knowledge of good and **evil** you shall not eat, for in the day that you eat of it you shall surely die*" (Genesis 2:17). One can see within God's statement, the expression of freedom, responsibility, accountability, and consequences.

From this moment on, the influence of the ***evil*** attribute patiently waited for the opportunity to enter the inner spirits of God's creations. BTT helps one to see that another negative attribute conspired with the ***evil*** attribute to create the opportunity. The wicked attribute influenced a serpent that the Biblical record documented, "*...was more cunning than any beast of the field which the Lord God had made. And he said to the woman, "Has God indeed said, 'You shall not eat of every tree of the garden'?*" (Genesis 3:1-2). If one continues reading the Biblical record in Genesis 3:3, one will clearly see that man had taught the woman what she needed to know about responsibility, accountability, and consequences. But the cunning serpent twisted God's Word to the woman and said, "*You will not surely die. For God knows that in the day you eat of it your eyes will be opened, and you will be like God, knowing good and **evil**"* (Genesis 3:5). Thus, the Bible documented, "*...when the woman saw that the tree was good for food, that it was pleasant to the eyes, and a tree desirable to make one wise, she took of its fruit and ate. She also gave to her husband with her, and he ate. Then the eyes of both of them were opened...*" (Genesis 3:6-7). BTT helps one to see that the negative forces of the war campaign conspired together to influence the cunning serpent to deceive the first human beings of God's creation. God's command (Genesis 2:17) was violated as the influence of the ***evil*** attribute defiled the inner spirits of His perfect creation. But make no mistake, this strategic move by the negative forces of the campaign was anticipated by God. Hence, He simply enforced responsibility, accountability, and consequences which now gained a weightier role. The Biblical record documented that, "*...the Lord God said, "Behold, the man has become like one of Us, to know good and **evil**. And now, lest he put out his hand and take also of the tree of life, and eat, and live forever"— therefore the Lord God sent him out of the garden of Eden to till the ground from which he was taken. So He drove out the man; and He placed cherubim at the east of the garden of Eden, and a flaming sword which turned every way, to guard the way to the tree of life*" (Genesis 3:22-24). Notice that God did not destroy his human creation. Instead, He held them accountable for their decisions and allowed them to suffer the consequences of their behavior. God removed them from paradise to face the hardships of a new reality.

From that day forward and after the first man and women began to populate the earth with children, the influence of the ***evil*** attribute made its presence known through its influences of the generations that followed. In fact, the influence of this attribute was so strong that the Biblical record documented, "*...the Lord saw that the wickedness of man was great in the earth, and that every intent of the thoughts of his heart was only **evil** continually and the Lord was sorry that He had made man on the earth, and He was grieved in His heart*" (Genesis 6:5-6). The Lord's grief led Him to destroy His creation from the face of the earth (Genesis 6:7-8) except one man and his family. A man named Noah and his family lived through the earth's great ***calamity***. One can read the full account of Noah and how God wiped the face of the earth clean except for those He saved in an ark in Genesis Chapters 7 and 8. However, BTT allows one to see that God's actions did not destroy the ***evil*** or other negative attributes. Why? Because the attributes are spirits. However, God destroyed all flesh that allowed the attribute's influence. To this point, the Biblical record documented after the flood and after Noah and his family made a sacrifice to the Lord, that "*...the Lord smelled a soothing aroma. Then the Lord said in His heart, "I will never again curse the ground for man's sake, although the imagination of man's heart is **evil** from his youth; nor will I again destroy every living thing as I have done*" (Genesis 8:21). After this, Noah and his family repopulated the earth based on God's command found in Genesis 9:1. Meanwhile, the influence of the ***evil*** attribute, along with the other negative attributes, simply waited for another opportunity to influence someone at another time.

Moving forward in the Biblical record, a man named Lot recognized the influence of the ***evil*** attribute during the time he was escaping the destruction of Sodom and Gomorrah. The Bible recorded that Lot told two angels leading him and his family out of the city to safety, "*Indeed now, your servant has found favor in your sight, and you have increased your mercy which you have shown me by saving my life; but I cannot escape to the mountains, lest some **evil** overtake me and I die*" (Genesis 19:19). One cannot know what Lot was thinking about after God had just saved him by angels. However, I am sure whatever ***evil*** he was thinking of came from the overwhelming experience he had just witnessed.

After Lot, there were many other examples documented in the Biblical record of people influenced by the ***evil*** attribute that allows one to see how their behaviors and actions supported the negative forces of the war campaign. Instead of covering each example separately, please consider the table below. To gain a full understanding of the wide-ranging nature of the actions and behaviors behind everyone influenced by the *evil* attribute, one can read each example at one's leisure. The examples include:

Joseph's 11 brothers: Genesis 50:20; Joseph's ordeal began in Genesis Chapter 37 and his brothers are all identified in Genesis 35:22-26	Pharaoh: Exodus 5:23; He threaten Moses with *evil* in Exodus 10:10	Some of the children of Israel: Exodus 32:22; Numbers 14:27-29; Numbers 14:35
Jehoahaz: 2 Kings 23:32-34	The men of Shechem: Judges 9:57	The perverted men of Gibeah: Judges 20:13
Zimri: 1 Kings 16:11; 16:18-19	Saul: 1 Samuel 15:19; 24:17	Nabal: 1 Samuel 25:2-3
Eli's two sons, Hophni and Phinehas: 1 Samuel 2:12-17	Amnon who raped Tamar: 2 Samuel 13:12-14; 13:16	Jeroboam: 1 Kings 13:33-34; 14:9-11; 2 Kings 14:24
Rehoboam: 2 Chronicles 12:14	Judah: 1 Kings 14:22-24	Abijam: 1 Kings 15:3
Nadab: 1 Kings 15: 26	Baasha: 1 Kings 15:34; 16:7	Elah: 1 Kings 16:10
Joab: 2 Samuel 3:27	Omri: 1 Kings 16:25	Ahab: 1 Kings 16:30; 21:20
Jehoram: 2 Kings 3:2	Hazael: 2 Kings 8:12	Menahem: 2 Kings 15:18
Jehoash: 2 Kings 13:11	Jehoahaz: 2 Kings 13:2	Pekah: 2 Kings 15:28
Ahaziah: 1 Kings 22:52; 2 Kings 8:27; 2 Chronicles 22:4	Zechariah, the son of Jeroboam: 2 Kings 15:9	Pekahiah, the son of Menahem: 2 Kings 15:24
Amon: 2 Kings 21:20	Cain: 1 John 3:12	Hoshea: 2 Kings 17:2-18
Manasseh: 2 Kings 21:2; 2 Chronicles 33:2-9; 2 Kings 21:6-9	The men sent to spy out the land of promise except Joshua and Caleb: Numbers 14:36-38	Jehoiakem: 2 Kings 23:37; 2 Chronicles 36:5
Jehoiachin: 2 Kings 24:9; 2 Chronicles 36:9	Zedekiah: 2 Kings 24:19; 2 Chronicles 36:12	Eliashib, a priest: Nehemiah 13:7
Haman the Agagite: Esther 7:7; 8:3	Syria, Ephraim, and the son of Remaliah: Isaiah 7:5-6	Ishmael, the son of Nethaniah: Jeremiah 41:11
The warring kings of the North & South: Daniel 11:27	The city of Gilead: Hosea 6:8; 9:15	The Scribes: Matthew 9:4; 12:39; Luke 11:29
The Pharisees: Matthew 12:34, 35; Luke 6:45	King Herod: Luke 3:19, 20	The *evil* men from the marketplace: Acts 17:5
Some Jews in Ephesus: Acts 19:8-9	Some Jews bound by oath to kill Paul: Acts 23:12; Acts 23:14	

Table 8: Examples of the Influence of the Evil Attribute on Different People

As one can see, there are plenty of examples of people influenced by the *evil* attribute in the Biblical record. One should also consider that God gave Moses commands for the children of Israel to follow to protect them from the *evil* attribute's influence. Some of the various commands included:

Area of Concern	What Is Documented
Mobs	"*You shall not follow a crowd to do **evil**; nor shall you testify in a dispute so as to turn aside after many to pervert justice*" (Exodus 23:2)
Oaths	"*...if a person swears, speaking thoughtlessly with his lips to do **evil** or to do good, whatever it is that a man may pronounce by an oath, and he is unaware of it—when he realizes it, then he shall be guilty in any of these matters*" (Leviticus 5:4)
Idol worship	"*When you beget children and grandchildren and have grown old in the land, and act corruptly and make a carved image in the form of anything, and do **evil** in the sight of the Lord your God to provoke Him to anger, I call heaven and earth to witness against you this day, that you will soon utterly perish from the land which you cross over the Jordan to possess; you will not prolong your days in it, but will be utterly destroyed. And the Lord will scatter you among the peoples, and you will be left few in number among the nations where the Lord will drive you*" (Deuteronomy 4:25-27)
False prophets	"*...But that prophet or that dreamer of dreams shall be put to death, because he has spoken in order to turn you away from the Lord your God...to entice you from the way in which the Lord your God commanded you to walk. <u>So you shall put away the **evil** from your midst</u>*" (Deuteronomy 13:5)
Treatment of the poor	"*Beware lest there be a wicked thought in your heart, saying, 'The seventh year, the year of release, is at hand,' and your eye be **evil** against your poor brother and you give him nothing, and he cry out to the Lord against you, and <u>it become sin among you</u>*" (Deuteronomy 15:9)
Crimes deserving the death penalty	"*Whoever is deserving of death shall be put to death on the testimony of two or three witnesses; he shall not be put to death on the testimony of one witness. The hands of the witnesses shall be the first against him to put him to death, and afterward the hands of all the people. <u>So you shall put away the **evil** from among you</u>*" (Deuteronomy 17:6-7)
Disrespect for the law	"*Now the man who acts presumptuously and will not heed the priest who stands to minister there before the Lord your God, or the judge, that man shall die. <u>So you shall put away the **evil** from Israel</u>*" (Deuteronomy 17:12)
False witness	"*If a false witness rises against any man to testify against him of wrongdoing, then both men in the controversy shall stand before the Lord, before the priests and the judges who serve in those days. And the judges shall make careful inquiry, and indeed, if the witness is a false witness, who has testified falsely against his brother, then you shall do to him as he thought to have done to his brother; <u>so you shall put away the **evil** from among you</u>. And those who remain shall hear and fear, and hereafter they shall not again commit such **evil** among you*" (Deuteronomy 19:16-20)
Stubborn and rebellious children	"*And they shall say to the elders of his city, 'This son of ours is stubborn and rebellious; he will not obey our voice; he is a glutton and a drunkard.' Then all the men of his city shall stone him to death with stones; <u>so you shall put away the **evil** from among you</u>, and all Israel shall hear and fear*" (Deuteronomy 21:20-21)
Lies concerning Virginity	*If it is proven true that a women that marries a man who claimed to be a virgin lied,* "*then they shall bring out the young woman to the door of her father's house, and the men of her city shall stone her to death with stones,*

	*because she has done a disgraceful thing in Israel, to play the harlot in her father's house. So you shall put away the **evil** from among you*" (Deuteronomy 22:21)
Adultery	"*If a man is found lying with a woman married to a husband, then both of them shall die—the man that lay with the woman, and the woman; so you shall put away the **evil** from Israel*" (Deuteronomy 22:22)
Dishonest activity	"*If a young woman who is a virgin is betrothed to a husband, and a man finds her in the city and lies with her, then you shall bring them both out to the gate of that city, and you shall stone them to death with stones, the young woman because she did not cry out in the city, and the man because he humbled his neighbor's wife; so you shall put away the **evil** from among you*" (Deuteronomy 22:24)
Kidnapping	"*If a man is found kidnapping any of his brethren of the children of Israel, and mistreats him or sells him, then that kidnapper shall die; and you shall put away the **evil** from among you*" (Deuteronomy 24:7)

Table 9: Some of God's Commands Concerning the Influence of the Evil Attribute

God's commands in the areas above protected the children of Israel from the influence of the ***evil*** attribute. The children of Israel simply had to obey. One might think, as they were freed from Egyptian bondage and after all the things they witnessed from God, they would easily keep His commands. But this was far from true. The truth of the matter is that the ***evil*** attribute influenced the people in ways beyond comprehension. In fact, the influence was so strong that the Biblical record documented, "*...the Lord's anger was aroused against Israel, and He made them wander in the wilderness forty years, until all the generation that had done **evil** in the sight of the Lord was gone*" (Numbers 32:13). Further it was recorded that the Lord said, "*Surely not one of these men of this **evil** generation shall see that good land of which I swore to give to your fathers except Caleb the son of Jephunneh; he shall see it, and to him and his children I am giving the land on which he walked, because he wholly followed the Lord*" (Deuteronomy 1:35-36). Even further it was documented that the Lord said, "*Moreover your little ones and your children, who you say will be victims, who today have no knowledge of good and **evil**, they shall go in there; to them I will give it, and they shall possess it*" (Deuteronomy 1:39). One must understand that the influence of the ***evil*** attribute is so strong that it can take down generations of people if not countered with God's Word and obedience.

The Biblical record clearly documented that what the Lord instructed the children of Israel to do was for their benefit. Moses told them, "*See, I have set before you today life and good, death and **evil**...*" (Deuteronomy 30:15) and the Lord revealed their future stating, "*...And many **evils** and troubles shall befall them, so that they will say in that day, 'Have not these **evils** come upon us because our God is not among us?' And I will surely hide My face in that day because of all the **evil** which they have done, in that they have turned to other gods*" (Deuteronomy 31:17-18). You see, the Lord told Moses that the influence of the ***evil*** attribute would have its way among the children of Israel because of their stubbornness. Before he died, Moses even told the children of Israel, "*...I know that after my death you will become utterly corrupt, and turn aside from the way which I have commanded you. And **evil** will befall you in the latter days, because you will do **evil** in the sight of the Lord, to provoke Him to anger through the work of your hands*" (Deuteronomy 31:29). And guess what? Time and time again, the influence of the ***evil*** attribute devastated the Israelites. In fact, the Biblical record specifically recorded that the "*children of Israel did **evil** in the sight of the Lord*" in Judges 2:11-12; 3:7; 3:12; 4:1; 6:1; 8:33; 10:6; and 13:1 by serving Baals, Asherahs, Baal-Berith the gods of Syria, the gods of Sidon, the gods of Moab, the gods of the people of Ammon, and the gods of the Philistines; and they forsook the Lord and did not serve Him.

Allow me to reemphasize just how powerful the influence of the ***evil*** attribute is. Because of its insidious nature, like the wicked attribute, this attribute can cause righteous people to stumble and fall if they let their guard down. Two excellent examples of righteous people who stumbled by letting their guard down are King David and his son Solomon. According to 2 Samuel Chapter 11, the Biblical record documented that David had an adulterous affair with Bathsheba and then arranged to have her husband Uriah, murdered in battle. One should note that in this example, several negative attributes worked together influencing David's behavior, thoughts, and actions. The attributes included the ***evil***, wicked, adulterer, liar, and bloodthirsty attributes. The Lord sent the prophet Nathan to confront David about his behavior. After telling David a parable, and getting his reaction (2 Samuel 12:1-6), Nathan told him, "*Why have you despised the commandment of the Lord, to do **evil** in His sight? You have killed Uriah the Hittite with the sword; you have taken his wife to be your wife, and have killed him with the sword of the people of Ammon*" (2 Samuel 12:9). The influence of the ***evil*** attribute supported by other negative attributes, led David into sin with both Bathsheba and Uriah. But David repented for his stumble. However, according to 2 Samuel 12:10-18, the Lord still punished him for his actions. Afterwards, David regained favor with the Lord.

However, the influence of the ***evil*** attribute caught David a second time. The Biblical record documented, "*Now Satan stood up against Israel, and moved David to number Israel*" (1 Chronicles 17:1). Although Joab tried to stop David (2 Samuel 24:3-4), he proceeded with the headcount anyway according to 1 Chronicles 21:6. According to 1 Chronicles 21:10-12, God sent Gad the seer to confront David and gave him three choices for punishment. David was in such distress that he told Gad to ask the Lord to choose. The Lord did, and the Bible documented that, "*...the Lord sent a plague upon Israel, and seventy thousand men of Israel fell. And God sent an angel to Jerusalem to destroy it. As he was destroying, the Lord looked and relented of the disaster, and said to the angel who was destroying, "It is enough; now restrain your hand." And the angel of the Lord stood by the threshing floor of Ornan the Jebusite*" (1 Chronicles 21:14-15). When David saw the angel of the Lord, he fell on his face and the Bible documented, "*...David said to God, "Was it not I who commanded the people to be numbered? I am the one who has sinned and done **evil** indeed; but these sheep, what have they done? Let Your hand, I pray, O Lord my God, be against me and my father's house, but not against Your people that they should be plagued*" (1 Chronicles 21:17). The ***evil*** attribute led David to sin and he suffered greatly for it. Before one judge this incident and claims thousands of innocent lives were lost due to David's error, hold off. Read my chapter on God's use of calamity to purge his people of sin. There is more to this story than what meets the eye. For in the spiritual realm, the war campaign is in a high operational state when both Satan (1 Chronicles 17:1) and an angel of the Lord (1 Chronicles 21:14-15) are involved. BTT allows one to see that the people under David's leadership had also sinned.

King Solomon's battle with the influence of the **evil** attribute occurred when he experienced a lapse in <u>discernment</u> due to his sexual appetite for different women. The Biblical record documented that his passion for women led him to increase his kingdom with, "*...seven hundred wives, princesses, and three hundred concubines...*" (1 Kings 11:3). However, with his wives from foreign lands, he retained their gods and the Biblical record documented, "*...when Solomon was old, that his wives turned his heart after other gods; and his heart was not loyal to the Lord his God, as was the heart of his father David. For Solomon went after Ashtoreth the goddess of the Sidonians, and after Milcom the abomination of the Ammonites. Solomon did* **evil** *in the sight of the Lord, and did not fully follow the Lord, as did his father David*" (1 Kings 11:4-6). The influence of the **evil** attribute had its way with Solomon and the Lord raised up Hadad the Edomite, Rezon the son of Eliadah, and Solomon's own servant Jeroboam, as adversaries to humble Solomon. Because of Solomon's sin, he lost his kingdom and died having reigned in Jerusalem and over all of Israel for forty years.

Job, David, and Solomon provided a few more pearls of wisdom on the influences of the **evil** attribute. For one's learning, the Bible documented:

- Job speaking of God: "*He shall deliver you in six troubles, Yes, in seven no* **evil** *shall touch you*" (Job 5:19)

- "*...Behold, the fear of the Lord, that is wisdom, and to depart from* **evil** *is understanding*" (Job 28:28)

- "***Evil*** *shall slay the wicked, and those who hate the righteous shall be condemned*" (Psalm 34:21)

- David speaking of people with the wicked attribute: "*They encourage themselves in an* **evil** *matter; they talk of laying snares secretly; they say, "Who will see them?"* (Psalm 64:5) and "*He devises wickedness on his bed; he sets himself in a way that is not good; he does not abhor* **evil**" (Psalm 36:4)

- "*...***evildoers** *shall be cut off; but those who wait on the Lord, they shall inherit the earth*" (Psalm 37:9)

- "*The face of the Lord is against those who do* **evil**, *to cut off the remembrance of them from the earth*" (Psalm 34:16)

- "*Walk prudently when you go to the house of God; and draw near to hear rather than to give the sacrifice of fools, for they do not know that they do* **evil**" (Ecclesiastes 5:1)

- "*There is a severe* **evil** *which I have seen under the sun: Riches kept for their owner to his hurt. But those riches perish through misfortune...*" (Ecclesiastes 5:13-14)

- "*There is an* **evil** *which I have seen under the sun, and it is common among men: A man to whom God has given riches and wealth and honor, so that he lacks nothing for himself of all he desires; yet God does not give him power to eat of it, but a foreigner consumes it. This is vanity, and it is an* **evil** *affliction*" (Ecclesiastes 6:1-2)

- *"This is an **evil** in all that is done under the sun: that one thing happens to all. Truly the hearts of the sons of men are full of **evil**; madness is in their hearts while they live, and after that they go to the dead"* (Ecclesiastes 9:3)

- *"...Keep the king's commandment for the sake of your oath to God. Do not be hasty to go from his presence. Do not take your stand for an **evil** thing, for he does whatever pleases him"* (Ecclesiastes 8:2-3)

- *"...Because the sentence against an **evil** work is not executed speedily, therefore the heart of the sons of men is fully set in them to do **evil**. Though a sinner does **evil** a hundred times, and his days are prolonged, yet I surely know that it will be well with those who fear God, who fear before Him"* (Ecclesiastes 8:10-12)

- *"...The race is not to the swift, nor the battle to the strong, nor bread to the wise, nor riches to men of understanding, nor favor to men of skill; but time and chance happen to them all. For man also does not know his time: Like fish taken in a cruel net, like birds caught in a snare, so the sons of men are snared in an **evil** time, when it falls suddenly upon them"* (Ecclesiastes 9:11-12)

- *"Cast your bread upon the waters, for you will find it after many days. Give a serving to seven, and also to eight, for you do not know what **evil** will be on the earth"* (Ecclesiastes 11:1-2)

- *"Let us hear the conclusion of the whole matter: Fear God and keep His commandments, for this is man's all. For God will bring every work into judgment, including every secret thing, whether good or **evil**"* (Ecclesiastes 12:14)

Allow me to now share one of the greatest examples in the Bible about the influence of the **evil** attribute. For one's learning, the example is about the powerful influence of this attribute over the nation of Israel. The influence of the **evil** attribute was so strong that the Lord decided to destroy the nation for its refusal to repent of their grave sins and return to him. Please understand, before the Lord brought destruction, He sent numerous prophets to plead with them to repent and even identified the **evil** among them for their own clarity. There is so much documentation concerning the influence of the **evil** attribute on the nation of Israel that it would be impossible to cover every instance. Below, Table 10 will help one see the extent of the influence of the **evil** attribute on Israel as stated by the prophets. The Biblical record documented:

The Prophet	What Was Said
Isaiah	"Alas, sinful nation, a people laden with iniquity, a brood of **evildoers**, children who are corrupters! They have forsaken the Lord, they have provoked to anger the Holy One of Israel, they have turned away backward" (Isaiah 1:4)
	*"Wash yourselves, make yourselves clean; put away the **evil** of your doings from before My eyes. Cease to do **evil**, learn to do good; seek justice, rebuke the oppressor; defend the fatherless, plead for the widow"* (Isaiah 1:16-17)

	"...because their tongue and their doings are against the Lord, to provoke the eyes of His glory. The look on their countenance witnesses against them, and they declare their sin as Sodom; they do not hide it. Woe to their soul! For they have brought **evil** upon themselves" (Isaiah 3:8-9)
	"Woe to those who call **evil** good, and good **evil**; who put darkness for light, and light for darkness; who put bitter for sweet, and sweet for bitter!" (Isaiah 5:20)
	"Also the schemes of the schemer are **evil**; he devises wicked plans to destroy the poor with lying words, even when the needy speaks justice" (Isaiah 32:7)
	"The righteous perishes, and no man takes it to heart; merciful men are taken away, while no one considers that the righteous is taken away from **evil**" (Isaiah 57:1)
	"No one calls for justice, nor does any plead for truth. They trust in empty words and speak lies; they conceive **evil** and bring forth iniquity" (Isaiah 59:4)
	"Their feet run to **evil**, and they make haste to shed innocent blood; their thoughts are thoughts of iniquity; wasting and destruction are in their paths" (Isaiah 59:7)
	"...I will number you for the sword, and you shall all bow down to the slaughter; because, when I called, you did not answer; when I spoke, you did not hear, but did **evil** before My eyes, and chose that in which I do not delight" (Isaiah 65:12)
	Concerning Israel worship of false gods: The Lord said, "Show the things that are to come hereafter, that we may know that you are gods; yes, do good or do **evil**, that we may be dismayed and see it together. Indeed you are nothing, and your work is nothing; he who chooses you is an abomination" (Isaiah 41:23)
	"In transgressing and lying against the Lord, and departing from our God, speaking oppression and revolt, conceiving and uttering from the heart words of falsehood. Justice is turned back, and righteousness stands afar off; for truth is fallen in the street, and equity cannot enter. So truth fails, and he who departs from **evil** makes himself a prey. Then the Lord saw it, and it displeased Him that there was no justice" (Isaiah 59:13-15)
	"So will I choose their delusions, and bring their fears on them; because, when I called, no one answered, when I spoke they did not hear; but they did **evil** before My eyes, and chose that in which I do not delight" (Isaiah 66:4)
Jeremiah	"For My people have committed two **evils**: They have forsaken Me, the fountain of living waters, and hewn themselves cisterns—broken cisterns that can hold no water" (Jeremiah 2:13)
	"Your own wickedness will correct you, and your backslidings will rebuke you. Know therefore and see that it is an **evil** and bitter thing that you have forsaken the Lord your God, and the fear of Me is not in you, "Says the Lord God of hosts" (Jeremiah 2:19)
	"Circumcise yourselves to the Lord, and take away the foreskins of your hearts, you men of Judah and inhabitants of Jerusalem, lest My fury come forth like fire, and burn so that no one can quench it, because of the **evil** of your doings" (Jeremiah 4:4)
	"O Jerusalem, wash your heart from wickedness, that you may be saved. How long shall your **evil** thoughts lodge within you?" (Jeremiah 4:14)

	"*For My people are foolish, they have not known Me. They are silly children, and they have no understanding. They are wise to do **evil**, but to do good they have no knowledge*" (Jeremiah 4:22)
	"*For the house of Israel and the house of Judah have dealt very treacherously with Me,*" says the Lord. They have lied about the Lord, and said, "*It is not He. Neither will **evil** come upon us, nor shall we see sword or famine*" (Jeremiah 5:12)
	"*But this is what I commanded them, saying, 'Obey My voice, and I will be your God, and you shall be My people. And walk in all the ways that I have commanded you, that it may be well with you.' Yet they did not obey or incline their ear, but followed the counsels and the dictates of their **evil** hearts, and went backward and not forward*" (Jeremiah 7:23-24)
	"*...the children of Judah have done **evil** in My sight,*" says the Lord. "*They have set their abominations in the house which is called by My name, to pollute it*" (Jeremiah 7:30)
	"*And like their bow they have bent their tongues for lies. They are not valiant for the truth on the earth. For they proceed from **evil** to **evil**, and they do not know Me,*" says the Lord" (Jeremiah 9:3)
	"*This **evil** people, who refuse to hear My words, who follow the dictates of their hearts, and walk after other gods to serve them and worship them, shall be just like this sash which is profitable for nothing*" (Jeremiah 13:10)
	Israel's prophets and priest: "*... both prophet and priest are profane; Yes, in My house I have found their wickedness,*" says the Lord" (Jeremiah 23: 10-11)
	Israel's prophets and priest: "*...They commit adultery and walk in lies; they also strengthen the hands of **evildoers**, so that no one turns back from his wickedness. All of them are like Sodom to Me, and her inhabitants like Gomorrah*" (Jeremiah 23:14)
	Israel's prophets and priest: "*They continually say to those who despise Me, 'The Lord has said, "You shall have peace"'; and to everyone who walks according to the dictates of his own heart, they say, 'No **evil** shall come upon you'*" (Jeremiah 23:17)
	Israel's prophets and priest: The Lord said, "*I have not sent these prophets, yet they ran. I have not spoken to them, yet they prophesied. But if they had stood in My counsel, and had caused My people to hear My words, then they would have turned them from their **evil** way and from the **evil** of their doings*" (Jeremiah 23:21-22)
	"*...Thus says the Lord: "Behold, I am fashioning a disaster and devising a plan against you. Return now everyone from his **evil** way, and make your ways and your doings good." And they said, "That is hopeless! So we will walk according to our own plans, and we will every one obey the dictates of his **evil** heart*" (Jeremiah 18:6-12)
	"*Woe to the shepherds who destroy and scatter the sheep of My pasture!*" says the Lord. Therefore thus says the Lord God of Israel against the shepherds who feed My people: "*You have scattered My flock, driven them away, and not attended to them. Behold, I will attend to you for the **evil** of your doings,*" says the Lord" (Jeremiah 23:1-2)
Ezekiel	"*Thus says the Lord God: "Pound your fists and stamp your feet, and say, 'Alas, for all the **evil** abominations of the house of Israel! For they shall fall by the*

	sword, by famine, and by pestilence....Thus will I spend My fury upon them" (Ezekiel 6:11-12)
Micah	*"Woe to those who devise iniquity, and work out **evil** on their beds! At morning light they practice it, because it is in the power of their hand. They covet fields and take them by violence, also houses, and seize them. So they oppress a man and his house, a man and his inheritance...for this is an **evil** time"* (Micah 2:1-3)
Micah	*"...Is it not for you to know justice? You who hate good and love **evil**; who strip the skin from My people, and the flesh from their bones; who also eat the flesh of My people, flay their skin from them, break their bones, and chop them in pieces like meat for the pot, like flesh in the caldron. Then they will cry to the Lord, but He will not hear them; He will even hide His face from them at that time, because they have been **evil** in their deeds"* (Micah 3:1-4)
	*"That they may successfully do **evil** with both hands— the prince asks for gifts, the judge seeks a bribe, and the great man utters his **evil** desire; so they scheme together"* (Micah 7:3)
Habakkuk	*"Woe to him who covets **evil** gain for his house, that he may set his nest on high, that he may be delivered from the power of disaster!"* (Habakkuk 2:9)
Zechariah	*"Thus says the Lord of hosts: 'Execute true justice, show mercy and compassion everyone to his brother. Do not oppress the widow or the fatherless, the alien or the poor. Let none of you plan **evil** in his heart against his brother"* (Zechariah 7:9-10)
	*"These are the things you shall do: Speak each man the truth to his neighbor; give judgment in your gates for truth, justice, and peace; let none of you think **evil** in your heart against your neighbor; and do not love a false oath. For all these are things that I hate,' Says the Lord"* (Zechariah 8:16-17)
Malachi	*"You offer defiled food on My altar, but say, 'In what way have we defiled You?' by saying, 'The table of the Lord is contemptible.' And when you offer the blind as a sacrifice, is it not **evil**? And when you offer the lame and sick, is it not **evil**? Offer it then to your governor! Would he be pleased with you? Would he accept you favorably?' Says the Lord of hosts"* (Malachi 1:7-8)
	*"You have wearied the Lord with your words; Yet you say, "In what way have we wearied Him?" In that you say, "Everyone who does **evil** is good in the sight of the Lord, and He delights in them," Or, "Where is the God of justice?"* (Malachi 2:17)

Table 10: The Prophet's Comments About the Influence of the Evil Attribute on Israel

Surely the references captured above provide enough evidence to convince one of the extents of the ***evil*** attribute's influence on the nation of Israel. There should be no <u>doubt</u> as to the reason why the Lord destroyed the nation and rejected them as His chosen people. Israel, to this very day, has not repented. One should see the value of putting as far away from oneself as possible the influence of the ***evil*** attribute. Knowing God's Word and obeying it is the only way for this to happen. From the example of the nation of Israel, BTT allows one to see that God will destroy any nation that allows the influence of the ***evil*** attribute to dominate it.

It should be very easy for one to understand that the influence of the ***evil*** attribute transitioned to the New Testament of the Biblical record. Jesus identified the attribute up front when He said, *"Blessed are you when they revile and persecute you, and say all kinds of **evil*** *against you falsely for My sake"* (Matthew 5:11) and *"Blessed are you when men hate you, and when they exclude you, and revile you, and cast out your name as **evil**, for the Son of Man's sake"* (Luke 6:22). One should see that people influenced by the ***evil*** attribute will deflect attention away from themselves and their behavior by calling other people with positive attributes ***evil***. Just as those influenced by the wicked attribute, they will *"...call **evil** good, and good **evil**; who put darkness for light, and light for darkness; who put bitter for sweet, and sweet for bitter!"* (Isaiah 5:20). In other words, people influenced by the ***evil*** attribute will call anyone who claims Jesus ***evil*** things, hate them, and exclude them. But in truth, one can identify the real person influenced by the ***evil*** attribute by these behaviors and actions. Here are some of the things that Jesus taught for those who want to claim Him as their Lord and Savior. Hint: His words are opposite of everything that one influenced by the ***evil*** attribute would say.

*"...let your 'Yes' be 'Yes,' and your 'No,' 'No.' For whatever is more than these is from the **evil** one"* (Matthew 5:37)	*"But I tell you not to resist an **evil** person. But whoever slaps you on your right cheek, turn the other to him also"* (Matthew 5:39)	*"...love your enemies, do good, and lend, hoping for nothing in return; and your reward will be great, and you will be sons of the Most High. For He is kind to the unthankful and **evil**"* (Luke 6:35)
*"...I say to you, love your enemies, bless those who curse you, do good to those who hate you, and pray for those who spitefully use you and persecute you that you may be sons of your Father in heaven; for He makes His sun rise on the **evil** and on the good, and sends rain on the just and on the unjust"* (Matthew 5:43-45)	Praying to God: *"And do not lead us into temptation, but deliver us from the **evil** one. For Yours is the kingdom and the power and the glory forever. Amen"* (Matthew 6:13) and *"And forgive us our sins, for we also forgive everyone who is indebted to us. And do not lead us into temptation, but deliver us from the **evil** one"* (Luke 11:4)	*"For out of the heart proceed **evil** thoughts, murders, adulteries, fornications, thefts, false witness, blasphemies. These are the things which defile a man, but to eat with unwashed hands does not defile a man"* (Matthew 15:19)
*"...What comes out of a man, that defiles a man. For from within, out of the heart of men, proceed **evil** thoughts, adulteries, fornications, murders, thefts, covetousness, wickedness, deceit, lewdness, an **evil** eye, blasphemy, pride, foolishness. All these **evil** things come from within*	*"Most assuredly, I say to you, the hour is coming, and now is, when the dead will hear the voice of the Son of God; and those who hear will live...the hour is coming in which all who are in the graves will hear His voice and come forth—those who have done good, to the resurrection of life, and those who have done **evil**, to the resurrection of*	*"And this is the condemnation, that the light has come into the world, and men loved darkness rather than light, because their deeds were **evil**. For everyone practicing **evil** hates the light and does not come to the light, lest his deeds should be exposed"* (John 3:19-20)

and defile a man" (Mark 7:18-23)	*condemnation"* (John 5:25-29)	
*"The world cannot hate you, but it hates Me because I testify of it that its works are **evil**"* (John 7:7)		

Table 11: Some of Jesus' Teaching About the Influence of the Evil Attribute

After Jesus returned to heaven, He left God's Word with the apostles to teach mankind through His Gospel. Jesus taught the apostles everything necessary to teach individuals how to avoid and overcome the influence of the **evil** attribute. The apostle teachings were consistent with Jesus' teachings and therefore came from the Lord. Here are some of the pearls of wisdom from the apostles for one to sustain one's footing in the war campaign and fend off the influence of the **evil** attribute:

*"Let love be without hypocrisy. Abhor what is **evil**. Cling to what is good"* (Romans 12:9)	*"Repay no one **evil** for **evil**. Have regard for good things in the sight of all men"* (Romans 12:17)	*"Do not be overcome by **evil**, but overcome **evil** with good"* (Romans 12:21)
*"... be wise in what is good, and simple concerning **evil**"* (Romans 16:19)	*"Therefore do not let your good be spoken of as **evil**"* (Romans 14:16)	*"Beware of dogs, beware of **evil** workers, beware of the mutilation!"* (Philippians 3:2)
*"Do not destroy the work of God for the sake of food. All things indeed are pure, but it is **evil** for the man who eats with offense"* (Romans 14:20)	*"But those who are outside God judges. Therefore "put away from yourselves the **evil** person"* (1 Corinthians 5:13)	*"See that no one renders **evil** for **evil** to anyone, but always pursue what is good both for yourselves and for all"* (1 Thessalonians 5:15)
*"...rulers are not a terror to good works, but to **evil**. Do you want to be unafraid of the authority? Do what is good, and you will have praise from the same. For he is God's minister to you for good. But if you do **evil**, be afraid; for he does not bear the sword in vain; for he is God's minister, an avenger to execute wrath on him who practices **evil**"* (Romans 13:1-4)	*"Love suffers long and is kind; love does not envy; love does not parade itself, is not puffed up; does not behave rudely, does not seek its own, is not provoked, thinks no **evil**; does not rejoice in iniquity, but rejoices in the truth; bears all things, believes all things, hopes all things, endures all things"* (1 Corinthians 13:4-7)	*"Therefore put to death your members which are on the earth: fornication, uncleanness, passion, **evil** desire, and covetousness, which is idolatry. Because of these things the wrath of God is coming upon the sons of disobedience, in which you yourselves once walked when you lived in them"* (Colossians 3:5-7)
*"But **evil** men and impostors will grow worse and worse, deceiving and being deceived"* (2 Timothy 3:13)	*"Test all things; hold fast what is good. Abstain from every form of **evil**"* (1 Thessalonians 5:22)	*"Beloved, do not imitate what is **evil**, but what is good. He who does good is of God, but he who does **evil***

		has not seen God" (3 John 1:11)
*"Let all bitterness, wrath, anger, clamor, and **evil** speaking be put away from you, with all malice. And be kind to one another, tenderhearted, forgiving one another, even as God in Christ forgave you"* (Ephesians 4:31-32)	*"See then that you walk circumspectly, not as fools but as wise, redeeming the time, because the days are **evil**. Therefore do not be unwise, but understand what the will of the Lord is"* (Ephesians 5:15-17)	*"Do not be deceived: "**Evil** company corrupts good habits." Awake to righteousness, and do not sin; for some do not have the knowledge of God. I speak this to your shame"* (1 Corinthians 15:33-34)
*"Beware, brethren, lest there be in any of you an **evil** heart of unbelief in departing from the living God; but exhort one another daily, while it is called "Today," lest any of you be hardened through the deceitfulness of sin"* (Hebrews 3:12-13)	*"Likewise, exhort the young men to be sober-minded, in all things showing yourself to be a pattern of good works; in doctrine showing integrity, reverence, incorruptibility, sound speech that cannot be condemned, that one who is an opponent may be ashamed, having nothing **evil** to say of you"* (Titus 2:6-8)	*"...those who desire to be rich fall into temptation and a snare, and into many foolish and harmful lusts which drown men in destruction and perdition. For the love of money is a root of all kinds of **evil**, for which some have strayed from the faith in their greediness, and pierced themselves through with many sorrows"* (1 Timothy 6:9-10)
Speaking of the examples from the Old Testament: *"Now these things became our examples, to the intent that we should not lust after **evil** things as they also lusted"* (1 Corinthians 10:6)	*"If the Lord wills, we shall live and do this or that. But now you boast in your arrogance. All such boasting is **evil**"* (James 4:15-16)	*"Remind them to be subject to rulers and authorities, to obey, to be ready for every good work, to speak **evil** of no one, to be peaceable, gentle, showing all humility to all men"* (Titus 3:1-2)
*"But no man can tame the tongue. It is an unruly **evil**, full of deadly poison"* (James 3:8) and *"And the tongue is a fire, a world of iniquity. The tongue is so set among our members that it defiles the whole body, and sets on fire the course of nature; and it is set on fire by hell"* (James 3:6)	*"Do not speak **evil** of one another, brethren. He who speaks **evil** of a brother and judges his brother, speaks **evil** of the law and judges the law. But if you judge the law, you are not a doer of the law but a judge"* (James 4:11)	If *"...you pay attention to the one wearing the fine clothes and say to him, "You sit here in a good place," and say to the poor man, "You stand there," or, "Sit here at my footstool, have you not shown partiality among yourselves, and become judges with **evil** thoughts?"* (James 2:3-4)
*"...But if you have bitter envy and self-seeking in your hearts, do not boast and lie against the truth. This wisdom does not descend from above, but is	*"Likewise also these dreamers defile the flesh, reject authority, and speak **evil** of dignitaries...But these speak **evil** of whatever they do not know;	*"If <u>anyone</u> comes to you and does not bring this doctrine, do not receive him into your house nor greet him; for he who greets him shares in his **evil** deeds"* (2 John 1:10-11)

earthly, sensual, demonic. *For where envy and self-seeking exist, confusion and every **evil** thing are there*" (James 3:13-16)	*and whatever they know naturally, like brute beasts, in these things they corrupt themselves*" (Jude 1:8-10)	
People who walk according to the flesh in the lust of uncleanness and despise authority "*...They are presumptuous, self-willed. They are not afraid to speak **evil** of dignitaries, whereas angels, who are greater in power and might, do not bring a reviling accusation against them before the Lord. But these, like natural brute beasts made to be caught and destroyed, speak **evil** of the things they do not understand, and will utterly perish in their own corruption, and will receive the wages of unrighteousness, as those who count it pleasure to carouse in the daytime*" (2 Peter 2:10-13)	"*...be of one mind, having compassion for one another; love as brothers, be tenderhearted, be courteous; not returning **evil** for **evil** or reviling for reviling, but on the contrary blessing, knowing that you were called to this, that you may inherit a blessing. For "He who would love life and see good days, let him refrain his tongue from **evil**, and his lips from speaking deceit. Let him turn away from **evil** and do good; let him seek peace and pursue it. For the eyes of the Lord are on the righteous, and His ears are open to their prayers; but the face of the Lord is against those who do **evil***" (1 Peter 3:8-12)	For *the ungodly and unrighteous*: "*...even as they did not like to retain God in their knowledge, God gave them over to a debased mind, to do those things which are not fitting; being filled with all unrighteousness, **sexual immorality**, wickedness, covetousness, maliciousness; full of envy, murder, strife, deceit, **evil-mindedness**; they are whisperers, backbiters, haters of God, violent, proud, boasters, inventors of **evil** things, disobedient to parents, un<u>discerning</u>, untrustworthy, unloving, unforgiving, unmerciful...*" (Romans 1:28 – 31)
"*...but to those who are self-seeking and do not obey the truth, but obey unrighteousness—indignation and wrath, tribulation and anguish, on every soul of man who does **evil**, of the Jew first and also of the Greek...*" (Romans 2:8-9)	"*Therefore, laying aside all malice, all deceit, hypocrisy, envy, and all **evil** speaking, as newborn babes, desire the pure milk of the word, that you may grow thereby, if indeed you have tasted that the Lord is gracious*" (1 Peter 2:1-3)	"*...submit yourselves to every ordinance of man for the Lord's sake, whether to the king as supreme, or to governors, as to those who are sent by him for the punishment of **evildoers** and for the praise of those who do good*" (1 Peter 2:13-14)
Concerning Jesus' one Gospel: "*If anyone teaches otherwise and does not consent to wholesome words, even the words of our Lord Jesus Christ, and to the doctrine which accords with godliness, he is proud, knowing nothing, but is obsessed with disputes	"*Let no one say when he is tempted, "I am tempted by God"; for God cannot be tempted by **evil**, nor does He Himself tempt anyone. But each one is tempted when he is drawn away by his own desires and enticed. Then, when desire has conceived, it gives birth to	"*...even if you should suffer for righteousness' sake, you are blessed. "And do not be afraid of their threats, nor be troubled." But sanctify the Lord God in your hearts, and always be ready to give a defense to everyone who asks you a reason for the hope that is in you, with

*and arguments over words, from which come envy, strife, reviling, **evil** suspicions, useless wranglings of men of corrupt minds and destitute of the truth, who suppose that godliness is a means of gain. From such withdraw yourself"* (1 Timothy 6:3-5)	*sin; and sin, when it is full-grown, brings forth death"* (James 1:13-15)	*meekness and fear; having a good conscience, that when they defame you as **evildoers**, those who revile your good conduct in Christ may be ashamed. For it is better, if it is the will of God, to suffer for doing good than for doing **evil**"* (1 Peter 3:14-17)
Handling God's Word: *"…For everyone who partakes only of milk is unskilled in the word of righteousness, for he is a babe. But solid food belongs to those who are of full age, that is, those who by reason of use have their senses exercised to <u>discern</u> both good and **evil**"* (Hebrews 5:13-14)	*"…abstain from fleshly lusts which war against the soul, having your conduct honorable among the Gentiles, that when they speak against you as **evildoers**, they may, by your good works which they observe, glorify God in the day of visitation"* (1 Peter 2:11-12)	*"For we have spent enough of our past lifetime in doing the will of the Gentiles—when we walked in lewdness, lusts, drunkenness, revelries, drinking parties, and abominable idolatries. In regard to these, they think it strange that you do not run with them in the same flood of dissipation, speaking **evil** of you"* (1 Peter 4:3-4)
*"…let none of you suffer as a murderer, a thief, an **evildoer**, or as a busybody in other people's matters. Yet if anyone suffers as a Christian, let him not be ashamed, but let him glorify God in this matter"* (1 Peter 4:15-16)		

Table 12: Pearls of Wisdom Concerning the Evil Attribute

Here are a few more very important points that one must understand about the nature of the ***evil*** attribute. First, according to 2 Peter 2:9-14 (see also Jude 1:8-10), this attribute influences peoples to "*speak **evil** of dignitaries*" and to "*speak **evil** of the things they do not understand*." This behavior clearly identifies one who has the ***evil*** attribute influencing his or her inner spirit. Secondly, this attribute influences false teachers to share their teachings, often disguised as another Gospel, with others. John told Christians to be careful of these people when he documented, "*If <u>anyone</u> comes to you and does not bring this doctrine, do not receive him into your house nor greet him; for he who greets him shares in his **evil** deeds*" (2 John 1:10-11). If one has the Gospel of Jesus Christ from a reputable source, do not entertain other doctrines. This unassuming behavior provides an avenue for the influence of the ***evil*** attribute to enter one's inner spirit. Finally, John documented, "*…do not imitate what is **evil**, but what is good. He who does good is of God, but he who does **evil** has not seen God*" (3 John 1:11). Anyone imitating acts of ***evil*** has the influence of the ***evil*** attribute in their inner spirit. One can identify one with this attribute if that person is doing the "opposite" of what Peter documented in 1 Peter 3: 8-12. For one's learning, he documented:

> *"Finally, all of you be of one mind, having compassion for one another; love as brothers, be tenderhearted, be courteous; not returning **evil** for **evil** or reviling for reviling, but on the contrary blessing, knowing that you were called to this, that you may inherit a blessing. For "He who would love life and see good days, let him refrain his tongue from **evil**, and his lips from speaking deceit. Let him turn away from **evil** and do good; let him seek peace and pursue it. For the eyes of the Lord are on the righteous, and His ears are open to their prayers; but the face of the Lord is against those who do **evil**."*

The application of this Scripture is this: Anyone who perceives that they have been wronged and advocates revenging that wrong with **evil**, has the **evil** attribute influencing their inner spirit.

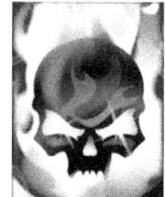

The **Perverse attribute**: The influence of this attribute causes an individual to be extremely corrupt in their behaviors, deeds, and speech in a sadistic way. It influences one toward twisted, satanic, deviant, and unnatural forms of sexual behavior. This is the attribute that leads one to experiment and become lost in the world of homosexuality, lesbianism, bestiality, pedophilia, necrophilia, fetishism, voyeurism, hyperphilia, sadism, object philia, spouse swapping activities, orgies and other similar activities. This is the attribute that influences one to become a human predator or stalker and engage in kidnapping activities. This attribute's influence is behind child pornography and sex trafficking crimes from children to adults. These behavior accounts for the countless missing persons throughout the world for abduction is a tool of this attribute. The deviant influence of this attribute not only leads one to become a predator of innocent children, but also to engage in unspeakable acts and heinous crimes against children and adults that should be sickening to the average person on either side of the campaign. Unfortunately, the end result for a child is a life of torment, self-destruction, and an inability to love. These children become highly susceptible to the future influence of the ***perverse*** attribute as they mimic behaviors of which they were exposed. In most cases, these children do not understand the consequences of their actions. Without correction, the earlier a child experiences the influence of this attribute, the harder it becomes to unhinge the attribute from their inner spirit. Although corrupted innocence is difficult to repair, it is not impossible. In spiritual warfare, the children abused by one influenced by the ***perverse*** attribute, creates a sizable force of future ***perverse*** prospects as they in turn indiscriminately harm others from positions of authority. In addition to all of the above, acts of eating human flesh (cannibalism), drinking blood, and exposing one's self publicly in sexually explicit behavior, are all part of deviant activities of the influence from the ***perverse*** attribute. Hence, this attribute is the root of debauchery. Further, when this attribute combines with the violent attribute, acts of rape, torture, molestation, and other vile behavior is perpetrate against women, children, and even men. Finally, this attribute is closely related to the immoral and ungodly attributes which have their own chapters devoted to them. Together, these attributes' influences lead people to erode boundaries of decency that support stable civil societies.

To express how far the influence of this attribute can take one down the bad path identified in **Figure 10** of this book, just consider the nation of Israel in the Old Testament of the Biblical record. The Bible documented that conditions got so bad that, *"The hands of the compassionate women have cooked their own children; they became food for them in the destruction of the daughter of my people"* (Lamentations 4:10). Because of the influence of the ***perverse*** attribute, these women's behavior became ***perverse*** and they performed ***perverted*** acts with their children. Overtime, BTT allows one to see that the practice of abortion grew out of the twisted behavior of the combined influences of the ***perverse*** and bloodthirsty attributes. Hence, the Word of God stings the inner spiritual heart of one who allows this attribute. This person will do everything in his or her power to ***pervert*** God's Word to lessen his or her internal pain. This applies to the ***perversion*** of the Gospel of Christ this very day.

The Spirit of wisdom revealed to Solomon that, *"... the **perverse** person is an abomination to the LORD..."* (Proverbs 3:32) and *"Those who are of a **perverse** heart are an abomination to the LORD..."* (Proverbs 11:20). From Wisdom's teachings, Solomon further documented that *"Thorns and snares are in the way of the **perverse**; he who guards his soul will be far from them"* (Proverbs 22:5). In other words, the actions of one influenced by the ***perverse*** attribute creates sticky situations and traps for others. One's best defense in the campaign is to stay away from one with this attribute. This defense is the best way to guard one's soul. To this end, Solomon documented that, *"A wholesome tongue is a tree of life, but **perverseness** in it breaks the spirit"* (Proverbs 15:4). BTT allows one to see that the influence of this attribute corrupt one's speech and reciprocally damages one's inner spirit. Consequently, Solomon documented that, *"He who has a deceitful heart finds no good, and he who has a **perverse** tongue falls into evil"* (Proverbs 17:20). Looking at the sum of both verses 15:4, 17:20, and 22:5, BTT allows one to see that people influenced by the ***perverse*** attribute wields a tongue that harms their own inner spirit, causes them to fall into evil, and places their souls in jeopardy. But also understand that these same people gain a deceitful heart and will find no good from their behavior.

The influence of the ***perverse*** attribute can unite with other negative attributes to intensify its influence on a person. One of the worst examples is found where Solomon documented that, *"A wicked man accepts a bribe behind the back to **pervert** the ways of justice"* (Proverbs 17:23). This union between the wicked and ***perverted*** attribute creates untold damage to the positive forces of the war campaign. It is the influence of this union that leads people to ***pervert*** the legal system and the ways of fairness among people in general. People who allow the influence of this union show an outright contempt for God. In fact, where it concerns God, Solomon would document one *"...who is **perverse** in his ways despises Him"* (Proverbs 14:2). For one to despise the Creator of the universe, one severely lacks wisdom and is a fool. However, one will die in the false security blanket provided by the influence of the ***perverse*** attribute.

The Spirit of Wisdom revealed to Solomon that the, *"...way of a guilty man is **perverse**...."* (Proverbs 21:8) and that, *"A **perverse** man sows strife..."* (Proverbs 16:28). These two important points will gain greater meaning as one gets to the chapter on strife in this book. For now, try to understand that God sees the actions of a guilty man, one who is truly guilty of violating God's commandments and laws, as ***perverse***. It does not matter what the crime is. God sees the "way" or path that the man chose as influenced by the ***perverse*** attribute. Taking the other piece of wisdom into consideration, this man more than likely sowed strife along the way. Once again, one will see this even more clearly in the chapter on strife.

Now, in the Old Testament of the Biblical record, Moses handed down laws from the Lord to keep the children of Israel away from the influence of the ***perverse*** attribute. These laws documented the negative correlation between the influence of the ***perverse*** attribute and the way of justice. This correlation demonstrates how this negative attribute impacts so many areas in the war campaign. He stated from the Lord:

- *"You shall not follow a crowd to do evil; nor shall you testify in a dispute so as to turn aside after many to **pervert** justice"* (Exodus 23:2)

- *"You shall not **pervert** the judgment of your poor in his dispute. Keep yourself far from a false matter; do not kill the innocent and righteous. For I will not justify the wicked. And you shall take no bribe, for a bribe blinds the discerning and **perverts** the words of the righteous"* (Exodus 23:6-8)

- *"You shall not **pervert** justice; you shall not show partiality, nor take a bribe, for a bribe blinds the eyes of the wise and twists the words of the righteous"* (Deuteronomy 16:19)

- *"You shall not **pervert** justice due the stranger or the fatherless, nor take a widow's garment as a pledge"* (Deuteronomy 24:17)

- *"Cursed is the one who **perverts** the justice due the stranger, the fatherless, and widow.' "And all the people shall say, 'Amen!'"* (Deuteronomy 27:19)

God hates the ***perversion*** of justice and the influence of the ***perverse*** attribute in general. Unfortunately, many well-intentioned people have ignored God's Word on this and suffered for their ***perversion*** of justice, the justice system, and aiding the negative forces of the war campaign. Here are some examples of people who allowed the influence of the ***perverse*** attribute. The influence of the ***perverse*** attribute makes one's behavior a divisive tool in the campaign that causes many on the positive side to stumble. Consider whom the Biblical record identified as having allowed the influence of the ***perverse*** attribute.

Who	**What They Did**
The children of Israel	Moses documented that, *"They have corrupted themselves; they are not His children, because of their blemish: A **perverse** and crooked generation"* (Deuteronomy 32:5)
	Moses acknowledged the Lord considered them the same when he documented, *"...He said: 'I will hide My face from them, I will see what their end will be, for they are a **perverse** generation, children in whom is no faith"* (Deuteronomy 32:20)
Balaam, a false prophet that	

practiced divination for a fee (Numbers 22:7)	The Biblical record documented, *"And the Angel of the Lord said to him, "Why have you struck your donkey these three times? Behold, I have come out to stand against you, because your way is **perverse** before Me"* (Numbers 22:32)
Joel and Abijah, Samuel sons	The Biblical record documented, *"But his sons did not walk in his ways; they turned aside after dishonest gain, took bribes, and **perverted** justice"* (1 Samuel 8:3)
The inhabitants of Sodom and Gomorrah	The Biblical record documented, the Lord had told Abraham, *"...Because the outcry against Sodom and Gomorrah is great, and because their **sin is very grave**, I will go down now and see whether they have done altogether according to the outcry against it that has come to Me; and if not, I will know"* (Genesis 18:20-21)
	When the angels arrived, and Lot took them in, the Bible documented, *"Now before they lay down, the men of the city, the men of Sodom, both old and young, all the people from every quarter, surrounded the house. And they called to Lot and said to him, "Where are the men who came to you tonight? Bring them out to us that we may know them carnally"* (Genesis 19:4-5)
The **perverted** men who are in Gibeah (Judges 20:12)	They *"committed lewdness and outrage in Israel"* (Judges 20:6) and they went after a Levite. The Bible documented *"As they were enjoying themselves, suddenly certain men of the city, **perverted** men, surrounded the house and beat on the door. They spoke to the master of the house, the old man, saying, "Bring out the man who came to your house, that we may know him carnally!"* (Judges 19:22)
Rehoboam, Solomon's son and the people of Judah	The Biblical record documented, *"...they also built for themselves high places, sacred pillars, and wooden images on every high hill and under every green tree. And there were also **perverted** persons in the land. They did according to all the abominations of the nations which the Lord had cast out before the children of Israel"* (1 Kings 14:23-24)

Table 13: Examples of People Influenced by the Perverse Attribute

There were also people who understood the nature of the ***perverse*** attribute and fought against it. King Asa of Judah was an example of one such person. The Biblical record documented that he, *"...did what was right in the eyes of the Lord, as did his father David. And he banished the **perverted** persons from the land, and removed all the idols that his fathers had made"* (1 Kings 15:11-12; 22:46). Even the Psalmist wrote, *"I will set nothing wicked before my eyes; I hate the work of those who fall away; it shall not cling to me. A **perverse** heart shall depart from me; I will not know wickedness"* (Psalm 101:3-4). The words expressed here must be one's attitude towards the influence of the ***perverse*** attribute and its influences if one wants to successfully fight in the war campaign.

The Lord sent numerous prophets to warn the nation of Israel about the influence of the ***perverse*** attribute. Here are some of the many warnings from the Lord documented in the Biblical record:

The Prophet	What Was Said
	*"Therefore thus says the Holy One of Israel: "Because you despise this word, and trust in oppression and **perversity**, and rely on them, therefore this*

Isaiah	*iniquity shall be to you like a breach ready to fall, a bulge in a high wall, whose breaking comes suddenly, in an instant"* (Isaiah 30:12-13)
	*"For your hands are defiled with blood, and your fingers with iniquity; your lips have spoken lies, your tongue has muttered **perversity**. No one calls for justice, nor does any plead for truth. They trust in empty words and speak lies; they conceive evil and bring forth iniquity"* (Isaiah 59:3-4)
Jeremiah	*"A voice was heard on the desolate heights, weeping and supplications of the children of Israel. For they have **perverted** their way; they have forgotten the Lord their God. Return, you backsliding children, and I will heal your backslidings..."* (Jeremiah 3:21-22)
	*"Thus every one of you shall say to his neighbor, and every one to his brother, 'What has the Lord answered?' and, 'What has the Lord spoken?' And the oracle of the Lord you shall mention no more. For every man's word will be his oracle, for you have **perverted** the words of the living God, the Lord of hosts, our God"* (Jeremiah 23:35-36)
Ezekiel	*"Then He said to me, "The iniquity of the house of Israel and Judah is exceedingly great, and the land is full of bloodshed, and the city full of **perversity**; for they say, 'The Lord has forsaken the land, and the Lord does not see!'"* (Ezekiel 9:9)
Amos	*"Thus says the Lord: "For three transgressions of Israel, and for four, I will not turn away its punishment, because they sell the righteous for silver, and the poor for a pair of sandals. They pant after the dust of the earth which is on the head of the poor, and **pervert** the way of the humble. A man and his father go in to the same girl, to defile My holy name"* (Amos 2:6-7)
Micah	*"Now hear this, You heads of the house of Jacob and rulers of the house of Israel, who abhor justice and **pervert** all equity..."* (Micah 3:9)
Habakkuk	*"Therefore the law is powerless, and justice never goes forth. For the wicked surround the righteous; therefore **perverse** judgment proceeds"* (Habakkuk 1:4)

Table 14: The Prophet's Warning Against the Perverse Attribute

In the New Testament of the Biblical record, the **perverse** attribute was just as prominent as in the Old Testament. The **perverse** attribute influenced the generation Jesus dealt with during His ministry. He stated, *"O faithless and **perverse** generation, how long shall I be with you? How long shall I bear with you? ..."* (Matthew 17:17; Luke 9:41). Later, because the negative forces of the war campaign came together to influence the nation of Israel to condemn Jesus, the Biblical record documented that they falsely accused Jesus of having the **perverse** attribute. They led Jesus to Pilate and falsely claimed, *"We found this fellow **perverting** the nation, and forbidding to pay taxes to Caesar, saying that He Himself is Christ, a King"* (Luke 23:2). What a twist.

After Jesus' death, the apostles began teaching the Gospel of Jesus Christ and converting Jews to Christianity. These conversions began driving out the influence of the **perverse** attribute from many Jewish communities. Peter, boldly preaching the Gospel, told the Jews to *"...Repent, and let every one of you be baptized in the name of Jesus Christ for the remission of sins; and you shall receive the gift of the Holy Spirit. For the promise is to you and to your children, and to all who are afar off, as many as the Lord our God will call." And with many other words he testified and exhorted them, saying, "Be saved from this **perverse** generation"*

(Acts 2:38-40). Acts 2:41 documented that about three thousand souls were baptized into Christ that day.

When Barnabas and Saul came to the island of Paphos, Paul had to confront a man heavily influenced by the **perverse** attribute. The Biblical record documented "*...Elymas the sorcerer (for so his name is translated) withstood them, seeking to turn the proconsul away from the faith. Then Saul, who also is called Paul, filled with the Holy Spirit, looked intently at him and said, "O full of all deceit and all fraud, you son of the devil, you enemy of all righteousness, will you not cease **perverting** the straight ways of the Lord?*" (Acts 13:8-10). Acts 13:11 documented that Paul was forced to use the authority of the Lord to blind Elymas to move him out of the way to spread the Gospel. BTT allows one to see that the **perverse** attribute's influence on Elymas was so strong that he was a stumbling block to the positive forces of the war campaign. The Lord used Paul to move Elymas out of the way. Paul's action edified the power of God; not Paul.

Paul later provided a few more pearls of wisdom for one to consider about the influence of the **perverse** attribute. He documented:

- "*For I know this, that after my departure savage wolves will come in among you, not sparing the flock. Also from among yourselves men will rise up, speaking **perverse** things, to draw away the disciples after themselves*" (Acts 20:29-30)

- "*For this reason God gave them up to vile passions. For even their women exchanged the natural use for what is against nature. Likewise also the men, leaving the natural use of the woman, burned in their lust for one another, men with men committing what is shameful, and receiving in themselves the penalty of their error which was due. And even as they did not like to retain God in their knowledge, God gave them over to a debased mind, to do those things which are not fitting; being filled with all unrighteousness,* **sexual immorality***, ...who, knowing the righteous judgment of God, that those who practice such things are deserving of death, not only do the same but also approve of those who practice them*" (Romans 1:26-32)

- To the church in Galatia he wrote, "*I marvel that you are turning away so soon from Him who called you in the grace of Christ, to a different gospel, which is not another; but there are some who trouble you and want to* **pervert** *the gospel of Christ*" (Galatians 1:6-7)

- To the church in Philippi he wrote, "*Do all things without complaining and disputing, that you may become blameless and harmless, children of God without fault in the midst of a crooked and* **perverse** *generation, among whom you shine as lights in the world, holding fast the word of life, so that I may rejoice in the day of Christ that I have not run in vain or labored in vain*" (Philippians 2:14-16)

The **Talebearer attribute**: The influence of this attributes causes one to speak on subjects that he or she knows little or nothing about. One with this attribute spreads rumors, gossip, whispers, and lies to anyone willing to listen. Interestingly, one with this attribute will spreads stories about anything just for the sake of having something to say. However, this person lacks an understanding of the fact that one influenced by this attribute aids the war campaign by creating strife among people. One influenced by this attribute lacks honor. The influence of this attribute cause people to believe they are informed, but, they and their listeners are both deceived. One influenced by the **talebearer** attribute easily subvert God's Word by unknowingly confusing Biblical matters with false beliefs, traditions, and doctrines often from pagan origins. BTT allows one to see that one influenced by the simple attribute, or people new to the Gospel of Christ, are easy prey for those influenced by the **talebearer** attribute. Today, one influenced by this attribute use the resources provided by social media, television, and radio to spread confusion and cause severe chaos across the full spectrum of the war campaign. Because of these resources, here is an important fact to understand about this **unclean spirit**: anyone who utilizes these resources to spread information they can neither corroborate or confirm is influenced by this attribute. Their actions harm the positive forces and aid the negative attributes in spiritual warfare. For one influenced by the **talebearer** attribute, the tongue is the weapon of choice. The same tongue can be is extended artificially when one uses the resources provided by social media, television, or radio. In both cases, the tongue becomes weaponized for both spiritual and physical warfare. Hence, the deceptive words of one influenced by this attribute aids all the negative attributes, generates strife and tensions among the positive and negative forces, and perverts God's Word. The **talebearer** attribute, because it breeds false information, news, gossip and wild tales, creates a more sinister influence when combined with the wicked attribute. Where the singular **unclean spirit** simply spreads false information, this combined **negative spirit** creates and spreads information with malicious intent. In other words, this combined attribute influencing one's inner spirit spreads gossip, rumors, news, and false tales with the intent to manipulate, control someone, or instigate something false. People who allow the influence of this attribute violates two key divine principles in the war campaign. First, Solomon documented *"Do not be rash with your mouth, and let not your heart utter anything hastily before God. For God is in heaven, and you on earth; therefore let your words be few"* (Ecclesiastes 5:2). Second, James documented *"So then, my beloved brethren, let every man be swift to hear, slow to speak, slow to wrath; for the wrath of man does not produce the righteousness of God"* (James 1:19-20). In other words, one better be sure he or she has the facts before committing his or her words hastily. Conspiracy theorist and speculators are associated with this negative attribute in the war campaign.

Twice, Solomon documented from the Spirit of wisdom that, *"The words of a **talebearer** are like tasty trifles, and they go down into the innermost body"* (Proverbs 18:8 and 26:22). Documenting this wisdom twice indicates its significance. In other words, one needs to understand that one influenced by the **talebearer** attributes has such a way with words that the word's attractiveness permeates the inner spirit and causes great harm. Some people get addicted to hearing the words of people influenced by the **talebearer** attribute. They literally wait anxiously to hear the latest things. Moreover, some people begin to prefer the words of people influenced by the **talebearer** attribute over of God's Word. However, there is a more sinister side to the person influenced by the **talebearer** attribute that is worthy of investigation. Solomon documented twice that, *"a **talebearer** reveals secrets"* (Proverbs 11:13 and 20:19). Consider how this impacts a leader who is attempting to develop a positive strategy against the negative forces in the war campaign. Or consider leaders influenced by this attribute that share secrets and sensitive information about others just to keep strife going among the people. Or consider people in general who establish relationships with others just to share what they learned with outsiders through loose lips. BTT allows one to clearly see that the influence of this attribute destroys relationships. This is why the Spirit of wisdom revealed two extremely important points to Solomon concerning this attribute. First Solomon documented, "*He who covers a transgression seeks love, but he who **repeats a matter** separates friends*" (Proverbs 17:9). Then he documented, "*He who goes about as a **talebearer** reveals secrets; therefore do not associate with one who flatters with his lips*" (Proverbs 20:19). In other words, these combined proverbs reveal that the words of one influenced by the **talebearer** attribute can end friendships and they employ the tool of flattery to get what they want from an unsuspecting person. In spiritual, as well as physical warfare, these proverbs reveal how a **talebearer** aids the negative forces in gaining sensitive, confidential, or personal information to harm others.

The Spirit of wisdom revealed that the influence of the **talebearer** attribute can unite with other negative attributes. An example is this attribute combining with the perverse attribute. Wisdom revealed to Solomon that, "*A perverse man sows strife, and a **whisperer** separates the best of friends*" (Proverbs 16:28). Make no mistake, one influenced by the **talebearer** attribute is also a **whisperer**. For the **talebearer** prefers not to have false or unsubstantiated information they spread come back to them. Keeping their words as low as possible is more helpful to their deceitful and perverse activities. Hence, the Spirit of wisdom ensured that Solomon understood that, "*Where there is no wood, the fire goes out; and where there is no **talebearer**, strife ceases*" (Proverbs 26:20).

One of the most important items to remember about this **unclean spirit** in spiritual warfare was summed up by Solomon in the Book of Ecclesiastes. The comment focused on keeping one's vow (*Better not to vow than to vow and not pay*) in Ecclesiastes 5:5. The application is similar with people who allow the **talebearer** attribute to influence their lips. Solomon wrote, "*Do not let your mouth cause your flesh to sin, nor say before the messenger of God that it was an error. Why should God be angry at your excuse and destroy the work of your hands? For in the multitude of dreams and many words there is also vanity. But fear God*" (Ecclesiastes 5:6-7). Do not be **deceived**.

The Old Testament of the Biblical record does not dwell on this negative attribute because it is too easy to understand. The Lord simply commanded Moses to tell the children of Israel, "*You shall not go about as a **talebearer** among your people; nor shall you take a stand against the life of your neighbor: I am the Lord*" (Leviticus 19:16). BTT allows one to see that God's Word is simple and clear. But of course, Israel ignored the Lord's commands.

The Biblical record documents the pain that people influenced by the **talebearer** attribute cause. Consider the examples of the King of Assyria and the nation of Israel. The King of Assyria attempted to take King Hezekiah's kingdom. However, he listened to people influenced by the **talebearer** attribute which changed the dynamics between him and Hezekiah. The Lord told Hezekiah, "*...Do not be afraid of the words which you have heard, with which the servants of the king of Assyria have blasphemed Me. Surely I will send a spirit upon him, and he shall hear a **rumor** and return to his own land; and I will cause him to fall by the sword in his own land*" (Isaiah 37:6-7; see also 2 King 19:7 and Isaiah 36 through 37:9). The King of Assyria received a **rumor,** returned to his kingdom and died. **Rumors** are tools of one influenced by the ***talebearer*** attribute. One should never listen to ***rumors***. Always seek the facts. In another example, the nation of Israel allowed the ***talebearer's*** words to take precedence over God's Word. The nation of Israel listened to people influenced by the ***talebearer*** attribute and they suffered the consequences of their action. Ezekiel documented, "*Disaster will come upon disaster, and **rumor** will be upon **rumor**. Then they will seek a vision from a prophet; but the law will perish from the priest, and counsel from the elders. 'The king will mourn, the prince will be clothed with desolation, and the hands of the common people will tremble. I will do to them according to their way, and according to what they deserve I will judge them; then they shall know that I am the Lord!'*" (Ezekiel 7:26-27). When one chose to listen to ***talebearers*** rather than God's Word, one suffers the consequences for his or her own actions and their choices.

The ***talebearer*** attribute found many to influence as Jesus walked the earth. Jesus said, "*For out of the abundance of the heart the mouth speaks. A good man out of the good treasure of his heart brings forth good things, and an evil man out of the evil treasure brings forth evil things. But I say to you that for every **idle word** men may speak, they will give account of it in the Day of Judgment. For by your words you will be justified, and by your words you will be condemned*" (Matthew 12:34-37). The words of one influenced by the ***talebearer*** attribute are no more than "***idle words***." One must be careful of what one says because words can sway an innocent soul away from God. ***Idle*** words used by people influenced by the negative attributes during the war campaign can send an unsuspecting soul on a journey of misery. For this reason, the Biblical record documented for one's learning:

- Do not listen to people claiming to be Christ. These are people influenced by the ***talebearer*** attribute. Jesus told His disciples, "*...Take heed that no one deceives you. For many will come in My name, saying, 'I am the Christ,' and will deceive many. And you will hear of wars and **rumors** of wars. See that you are not troubled; for all these things must come to pass, but the end is not yet*" (Matthew 24:4-6). The context of this Scripture suggests that the ***rumors*** of wars are over religious matters and one must not be deceived. This is a strategy to keep division alive.

- Be careful of philosophers, scholars, and academics. Many are influenced by the ***talebearer*** attribute and are simply trying to make a name for themselves. Paul met such people in the book of Acts when he went to the Areopagus. The Biblical record documented of the people there, "*...all the Athenians and the foreigners who were there spent their time in nothing else but **either to tell or to hear some new thing**"* (Acts 17:19-21). These individuals were ***talebearers*** with nothing better to do with their time.

- Do not take young widowed women into one's home. Paul, inspired by the Holy Spirit, warned about this. He documented that one should "*...refuse the younger widows; for when they have begun to grow wanton against Christ, they desire to marry, having condemnation because they have cast off their first faith. And besides they learn to be idle, wandering about from house to house, and not only idle but also **gossips** and **busybodies, saying things** which they ought not*" (1 Timothy 5:11-13). This is wisdom from the Lord. Communities have countless broken homes created by people who did not know or failed to hear this wisdom until it was too late.

The influence of the ***talebearer*** attribute is dangerous and exponentially increases the headcount of the negative forces engaged in the war campaign. BTT allows one to see that this attribute influences one to use their tongue to speak deceptive and despicable things. The Biblical record documented that, *"...the tongue is a little member and boasts great things. See how great a forest a little fire kindles! And the tongue is a fire, a world of iniquity. The tongue is so set among our members that it defiles the whole body, and sets on fire the course of nature; and it is set on fire by hell"* (James 3:5-6) and *"But no man can tame the tongue. It is an unruly evil, full of deadly poison"* (James 3:8). The tongue, the tool of choice of one influenced by the ***talebearer*** attribute, is one of the greatest weapons in the war campaign. The tongue of one influenced by the ***talebearer*** attribute causes serious damage even at the level of national and world affairs in the war campaign.

The **Unfaithful attribute**: The influence of this attributes causes one to be disloyal, false, fickle, inconsistent, treacherous, ***faithless***, and untrue in one's behavior, actions and deeds. This is the attribute, in spiritual warfare, that influences one to turn their back on God to pursue idols and/or worship other gods. The ***unfaithful*** attribute influences one's behavior in his or her obedience  to God's Word, church attendance, and their service and personal sacrifice within His church. This is the attribute that stunts a Christians spiritual growth and maturity in Christ. Furthermore, it is the primary attribute in the negative force's arsenal for destroying Christ's church from within on the spiritual battlefield. These points will become painfully clear by the end of this section on the ***unfaithful*** attribute. The adulterer and seducer attributes share a connection with this attribute. These attributes are discussed later in this book.

The ***unfaithful*** attribute was very prevalent during the time of Solomon. One would think that during his prosperous reign, the Lord would not have had to identify this negative attribute to Solomon. But He did. Why? Because during Solomon's reign, there was so much prosperity in the land that the people forgot their hardships of the past and they cast off the rules that God had given them to restrain their ferocious and <u>lustful</u> appetites. They pushed God, His commandments, and His laws to the side and lost the ability to <u>discern</u> right from wrong. Yes, the people grew prosperous and ***unfaithful*** with every transaction they made with the wicked nations that surrounded them. But the Spirit of wisdom revealed to Solomon that, *"... the way of the **unfaithful** is hard"* (Proverbs 13:15). Why? Wisdom revealed that one with the ***unfaithful*** attribute also has other negative attributes influencing their behavior. For instance, Wisdom told Solomon, *"... the perversity of the **unfaithful** will destroy them"* (Proverbs 11:3), and *"... the **unfaithful** will be caught by their lust"* (Proverbs 11:6), and *".... the soul of the **unfaithful** feeds on violence"* (Proverbs 13:2). Can one see the other negative attributes? These few Scriptures document the influence of the perverse, immoral, and violent attributes as they combine with the influence of the ***unfaithful*** attribute. In addition, the Spirit of wisdom revealed that prostitutes catch the eyes of one influenced by the ***unfaithful*** attribute. Solomon taught his son, *"My son, give me your heart, and let your eyes observe my ways. For a harlot is a deep pit, and a seductress is a narrow well. She also lies in wait as for a victim, increases the **unfaithful** among men"* (Proverbs 23:26-28). BTT allows one to see that the traps along the path of the war campaign are always present and the opportunities for entrapment are plentiful. The negative attributes, like the **unfaithful** attribute, makes one more susceptible to the traps when one wanders away from God's Word and is disobedient to what He has provided.

Other pearls of wisdom that the Spirit of Wisdom shared with Solomon included:

- *"Confidence in an **unfaithful** man in time of trouble is like a bad tooth and a foot out of joint"* (Proverbs 25:19)

- *"The eyes of the LORD preserve knowledge, but He overthrows the words of the **faithless**"* (Proverbs 22:12)

- *"...the wicked will be cut off from the earth, and the **unfaithful** will be uprooted from it"* (Proverbs 2:22)

- *"The wicked shall be a ransom for the righteous, and the **unfaithful** for the upright"* (Proverbs 21:18)

There is an elephant in the room, so to speak, that cannot be ignored with Solomon's behavior. For a man with *"Seven hundred wives, princes, and three hundred concubines"* according to 1 Kings 11:3, surely the influence of the **unfaithful** attribute was present with Solomon. The Bible is silent on this for his physical relationships. However, what one can know for sure of his spiritual relationship, the same Scripture documented that *"...his wives turned away his heart."* Solomon turned away from God to false gods according to 1 Kings 11:4. Thus, the **unfaithful** attribute influenced Solomon in the later years of his life.

In the Book of Exodus, one learns that the children of Israel dealt with the influence of the **unfaithful** attribute. God told Moses that He would make a covenant with them in Exodus 34:10-11. However, the covenant had a condition clause. For this was after Moses broke the first stone tablets of the Law that God had given him according to Exodus 34:1. God said, *"Take heed to yourself, lest you make a covenant with the inhabitants of the land where you are going, lest it be a snare in your midst. But you shall destroy their altars, break their sacred pillars, and cut down their wooden images (for you shall worship no other god, for the Lord, whose name is Jealous, is a jealous God), lest you make a covenant with the inhabitants of the land, and they play the harlot with their gods and make sacrifice to their gods, and one of them invites you and you eat of his sacrifice, and you take of his daughters for your sons, and his daughters play the harlot with their gods and make your sons play the harlot with their gods. You shall make no molded gods for yourselves"* (Exodus 34:12-17). God foreknew the children of Israel were going to allow the influence of the **unfaithful** attribute, but the people had the freedom to choose their path.

In the Book of Leviticus, God gave the children of Israel simple laws to follow to control the ravages of the **unfaithful** attribute. He commanded:

- *"Do not turn to **idols**, nor make for yourselves molded gods: I am the Lord your God"* (Leviticus 19:4), and

- *"You shall not make **idols** for yourselves; neither a carved image nor a sacred pillar shall you rear up for yourselves; nor shall you set up an engraved stone in your land, to bow down to it; for I am the Lord your God"* (Leviticus 26:1)

Further in Chapter 26, the Lord tells the children through Moses, *"…if they confess their iniquity and the iniquity of their fathers, with their **unfaithfulness** in which they were **unfaithful** to Me, and that they also have walked contrary to Me… if their uncircumcised hearts are humbled, and they accept their guilt— then I will remember My covenant with Jacob, and My covenant with Isaac and My covenant with Abraham…"* (Leviticus 26:40-42). BTT allows one to see that the **unfaithful** attribute ran rampant among the Israelites. But God gave them away to return to Him on His terms. Unfortunately, the Biblical record documents the Lord stating later, *"…He said: 'I will hide My face from them, I will see what their end will be, for they are a perverse generation, children in whom is **no faith**. They have provoked Me to jealousy by what is not God; They have moved Me to anger by their foolish **idols**. But I will provoke them to jealousy by those who are not a nation; I will move them to anger by a foolish nation"* (Deuteronomy 32:20-21). The Lord followed through with this pronouncement.

For the male/female relationship and the **unfaithful** attribute, the Lord simply gave Moses two specific laws to observe. First, He told Moses to teach the Israelites, *"…When a man or woman commits any sin that men commit in **unfaithfulness** against the Lord, and that person is guilty, then he shall confess the sin which he has committed. He shall make restitution for his trespass in full, plus one-fifth of it, and give it to the one he has wronged"* (Numbers 5:6-7). Thus, one can see that God meant for there to be a consequence for one who allows the influence of the **unfaithful** attribute to impact their relationship with the Lord. This command dealt primarily with commerce. The second law dealt with the relationship between a husband and wife and had a more severe consequence. For this law, the Lord gave Moses a way to handle a situation when a wife *"…goes astray and behaves **unfaithfully** toward…"* (Numbers 5:12) her husband and defiles their relationship. Numbers 5:13 spelled out the conditions surrounding the situation which included:

- Another man has laid with the wife carnally
- The act was hidden from the eyes of her husband
- The act was concealed that she has defiled herself,
- There was no witness against her and nor was she caught

If these conditions were present, the Lord gave a guarded procedure for handling the situation. The Lord's procedure applied even if the husband allowed the jealousy/envy attribute to influence him and even if the wife had not defiled herself according to Numbers 5:14. Hence, this is a situation where suspicion is present and possibly the liar attribute. Thus, the Lord involved a third party, the Levitical priest, for arbitration. In this instance, the Lord gave the Levitical priest a specific method to determine if the **unfaithful** attribute had influenced the wife. Numbers 5:16-31 described the method. I encourage one to read what the Lord put in place as it demonstrated His seriousness for dealing with the influence of the **unfaithful** attribute in a husband-wife relationship among the children of Israel.

The Psalmist also documented that the children of Israel allowed the **unfaithful** attribute to dominate their lives. He recorded, "*...they tested and provoked the Most High God, and did not keep His testimonies, but turned back and acted **unfaithfully** like their fathers; they were turned aside like a deceitful bow. For they provoked Him to anger with their high places, and moved Him to jealousy with their **carved images**. When God heard this, He was furious, and greatly abhorred Israel...*" (Psalm 78:56-59). Further the Psalmist wrote:

- "*For all the gods of the peoples are **idols**, but the Lord made the heavens*" (Psalm 96:5)

- "*Let all be put to shame who serve **carved images**, who boast of **idols**. Worship Him, all you gods*" (Psalm 97:7)

- "*Their **idols** are silver and gold, the work of men's hands*" (Psalm 115:4)

- "*The **idols** of the nations are silver and gold, the work of men's hands*" (Psalm 135:15)

Now when it comes to the **unfaithful** attribute and **idolatry**, there are many examples to review in the Biblical record. Here are just a few of them:

Idol Worshipers	**What They Did**
Laban's family	His family worshiped idols, Rachel stole and lied about her theft, Laban planned to kill Jacob for the theft according to Genesis 31. The Bible documents, "*Now Rachel had taken the household **idols**, put them in the camel's saddle, and sat on them. And Laban searched all about the tent but did not find them. And she said to her father, "Let it not displease my lord that I cannot rise before you, for the manner of women is with me." And he searched but did not find the household **idols***" (Genesis 31:34-35)
Pharaoh and the land of Egypt	Moses told the children of Israel, "...and you saw their abominations and their idols which were among them—wood and stone and silver and gold)..." (Deuteronomy 29:17)
Micah	"The man Micah had a shrine, and made an ephod and household **idols**; and he consecrated one of his sons, who became his priest" (Judges 17:5). The tribe of Dan took Micah's idols, his priest, destroyed the city of Laish, and worshipped the idols "*until the day of the captivity of the land*" according to Judges 18
The Philistines	Upon the death of Saul, "...they cut off his head and stripped off his armor, and sent word throughout the land of the Philistines, to proclaim it in the temple of their **idols** and among the people. Then they put his armor in the

	temple of the Ashtoreths, and they fastened his body to the wall of Beth Shan" (1 Samuel 31:9-10; 1 Chronicles 10:9)
Baasha and Elah	"…for all the sins of Baasha and the sins of Elah his son, by which they had sinned and by which they had made Israel sin, in provoking the Lord God of Israel to anger with their **idols**" (1 Kings 16:13)
Omri	"Omri did evil in the eyes of the Lord, and did worse than all who were before him. For he walked in all the ways of Jeroboam the son of Nebat, and in his sin by which he had made Israel sin, provoking the Lord God of Israel to anger with their **idols**" (1 Kings 16:26)
Ahab	"And he behaved very abominably in following **idols**, according to all that the Amorites had done, whom the Lord had cast out before the children of Israel" (1 Kings 21:26)
The children of Israel	"They did not destroy the peoples, concerning whom the Lord had commanded them, but they mingled with the Gentiles and learned their works; they served their **idols**, which became a snare to them. They even sacrificed their sons and their daughters to demons, and shed innocent blood, the blood of their sons and daughters, whom they sacrificed to the **idols** of Canaan; and the land was polluted with blood" (Psalm 106:34-38)
	"Also the children of Israel secretly did against the Lord their God things that were not right, and they built for themselves high places in all their cities, from watchtower to fortified city. They set up for themselves sacred pillars and wooden images on every high hill and under every green tree. There they burned incense on all the high places, like the nations whom the Lord had carried away before them; and they did wicked things to provoke the Lord to anger, for they served **idols**, of which the Lord had said to them, "You shall not do this thing" (2 Kings 17:9-12)
	"And they rejected His statutes and His covenant that He had made with their fathers, and His testimonies which He had testified against them; they followed **idols**, became **idolaters**, and went after the nations who were all around them, concerning whom the Lord had charged them that they should not do like them" (2 Kings 17:15)
Manasseh	"Because Manasseh king of Judah has done these abominations (he has acted more wickedly than all the Amorites who were before him, and has also made Judah sin with his **idols**)…" (2 Kings 21:11)
Amon	"And he did evil in the sight of the Lord, as his father Manasseh had done. So he walked in all the ways that his father had walked; and he served the **idols** that his father had served, and worshiped them" (2 Kings 21:20-21)
Jeroboam and his sons	"Then he appointed for himself priests for the high places, for the demons, and the calf **idols** which he had made" (2 Chronicles 11:15)
The leaders of Judah	"Now after the death of Jehoiada the leaders of Judah came and bowed down to the king. And the king listened to them. Therefore they left the house of the Lord God of their fathers, and served **wooden images** and **idols**; and

| | wrath came upon Judah and Jerusalem because of their trespass. Yet He sent prophets to them, to bring them back to the Lord; and they testified against them, but they would not listen" (2 Chronicles 24:17-19) |

Table 15: Examples of People Involved in Idolatry

From the time God's people were called the children of Israel to the time they became a great nation, the evidence of the influence of the **unfaithful** attribute and practice of idolatry was clear. On one's own time, I would encourage the reading of Isaiah 65:1-7 to understand this abomination to God. One will find that the Lord told these people in this reading, "*I have stretched out My hands all day long to a rebellious people, who walk in a way that is not good, according to their own thoughts; a people who provoke Me to anger continually to My face; who sacrifice in gardens, and burn incense on altars of brick; who sit among the graves, and spend the night in the tombs; who eat swine's flesh, and the broth of abominable things is in their vessels; who say, 'Keep to yourself, do not come near me, for I am holier than you!'* **These are smoke in My nostrils, a fire that burns all the day**" (Isaiah 65:2-5). In the war campaign, the Lord's Word still applies today.

Other examples of individuals that allowed the **unfaithful** attribute to influence their behavior include both King Saul and King Ahaz. King Saul lost his life because of the **unfaithful** attribute. The Biblical record documented, "*...Saul died for his **unfaithfulness** which he had committed against the Lord, because he did not keep the word of the Lord, and also because he consulted a medium for guidance*" (1 Chronicles 10:13). Saul even allowed the negative forces of the war campaign to influence him so much that the Lord took his kingdom from him. King Ahaz, on the other hand, led his kingdom into moral decay with the influence of the **unfaithful** attribute. The Biblical record documented, "*For the Lord brought Judah low because of Ahaz king of Israel, for he had encouraged moral decline in Judah and had been continually **unfaithful** to the Lord*" (2 Chronicles 28:19) and "*Now in the time of his distress King Ahaz became increasingly **unfaithful** to the Lord...*" (2 Chronicles 28:22). BTT allows one to see that if the **unfaithful** attribute reaches its full measure in one's inner spirit, its powerful influence can destroy a single home all the way up to a great nation. For Ahaz, instead of turning to God in his distress, the influence of this attribute led him deeper into **unfaithfulness** by seeking other gods. He led the nation into moral decay.

The prophet Ezekiel documented from the Lord that the **unfaithful** attribute was so widespread among the nation of Israel that other nations could see it through their behavior. He wrote, "*The Gentiles shall know that the house of Israel went into captivity for their iniquity; because they were **unfaithful** to Me, therefore I hid My face from them. I gave them into the hand of their enemies, and they all fell by the sword*" (Ezekiel 39:23). Israel, as well as all the nations outside of Israel, knew the **unfaithful** attribute had influenced their behavior.

Hence, the Lord told the prophet Ezekiel, "*Son of man, when a land sins against Me by persistent **unfaithfulness**, I will stretch out My hand against it; I will cut off its supply of bread, send famine on it, and cut off man and beast from it*" (Ezekiel 14:13). Later, the Lord said, "*Thus I will make the land desolate, because they have persisted in **unfaithfulness**,' says the Lord God*" (Ezekiel 15:8). Maybe one should consider that the Lord is doing the same thing today in nations that persistently allow the **unfaithful** attribute to thrive. Again, one can see, the ***unfaithful*** attribute is destructive personally and nationally because it is so contagious. I will speak more on this subject in Chapter IX on "Calamity."

The Lord also revealed to Ezekiel that the ***unfaithful*** attribute can take down one with the righteous attribute. Ezekiel documented, *"But when a righteous man turns away from his righteousness and commits iniquity, and does according to all the abominations that the wicked man does, shall he live? All the righteousness which he has done shall not be remembered; because of the **unfaithfulness** of which he is guilty and the sin which he has committed, because of them he shall die"* (Ezekiel 18:24). This is a powerful statement about the **unfaithful** attribute and it demonstrates this attribute's deceptive and destructive capabilities. Other warning from the prophets concerning this attribute, idols, and idol worship include:

The Prophet	What was said
Isaiah	*"O house of Jacob, come and let us walk in the light of the Lord. For You have forsaken Your people, the house of Jacob, because they are filled with eastern ways...Their land is also full of **idols**; they worship the work of their own hands, that which their own fingers have made"* (Isaiah 2:6-8)
	*"The loftiness of man shall be bowed down, and the haughtiness of men shall be brought low; the Lord alone will be exalted in that day, but the **idols** He shall utterly abolish"* (Isaiah 2:17-18)
	*"In that day a man will cast away his **idols** of silver and his **idols** of gold, which they made, each for himself to worship, to the moles and bats, to go into the clefts of the rocks, and into the crags of the rugged rocks, from the terror of the Lord and the glory of His majesty, when He arises to shake the earth mightily"* (Isaiah 2:20)
	*"As my hand has found the kingdoms of the **idols**, whose carved images excelled those of Jerusalem and Samaria, as I have done to Samaria and her **idols**, Shall I not do also to Jerusalem and her **idols**?"* (Isaiah 10:10-11)
	*"Bel bows down, Nebo stoops; their **idols** were on the beasts and on the cattle. Your carriages were heavily loaded, A burden to the weary beast. They stoop, they bow down together; they could not deliver the burden, but have themselves gone into captivity"* (Isaiah 46:1)
	*"When you cry out, let your collection of **idols** deliver you. But the wind will carry them all away, a breath will take them. But he who puts his trust in Me shall possess the land, and shall inherit My holy mountain"* (Isaiah 57:13)
	*"Truly You are God, who hide Yourself, O God of Israel, the Savior! They shall be ashamed and also disgraced, all of them; they shall go in confusion together, who are makers of **idols**"* (Isaiah 45:15-16)
Jeremiah	*"Thus says the Lord: "What injustice have your fathers found in Me, that they have gone far from Me, have followed **idols**, and have become **idolaters**?"* (Jeremiah 2:5)
	*"Listen! The voice, the cry of the daughter of my people from a far country: "Is not the Lord in Zion? Is not her King in her?" "Why have they provoked Me to anger with their carved images— With foreign **idols**?"* (Jeremiah 8:19)

	"Are there any among the **idols** of the nations that can cause rain? Or can the heavens give showers? Are You not He, O Lord our God? Therefore we will wait for You, since You have made all these" (Jeremiah 14:22)
	"And first I will repay double for their iniquity and their sin, because they have defiled My land; they have filled My inheritance with the carcasses of their detestable and abominable **idols**" (Jeremiah 16:18)
	"Because My people have forgotten Me, they have burned incense to worthless **idols**. And they have caused themselves to stumble in their ways, From the ancient paths, to walk in pathways and not on a highway, to make their land desolate and a perpetual hissing; everyone who passes by it will be astonished and shake his head" (Jeremiah 18:15)
	Judgment on Babylon and Babylonia: "*Declare among the nations, proclaim, and set up a standard; proclaim—do not conceal it— say, 'Babylon is taken, Bel is shamed. Merodach is broken in pieces; her **idols** are humiliated, her images are broken in pieces.'*" (Jeremiah 50:2)
	Judgment on the Chaldeans "*A drought is against her waters, and they will be dried up. For it is the land of carved images, and they are insane with their **idols***" (Jeremiah 50:38)
Ezekiel	"Then your altars shall be desolate, your incense altars shall be broken, and I will cast down your slain men before your **idols**. And I will lay the corpses of the children of Israel before their **idols**, and I will scatter your bones all around your altars. In all your dwelling places the cities shall be laid waste, and the high places shall be desolate, so that your altars may be laid waste and made desolate, your **idols** may be broken and made to cease, your incense altars may be cut down, and your works may be abolished" (Ezekiel 6:4-6)
	"Then those of you who escape will remember Me among the nations where they are carried captive, because I was crushed by their adulterous heart which has departed from Me, and by their eyes which play the harlot after their **idols**; they will loathe themselves for the evils which they committed in all their abominations" (Ezekiel 6:9)
	"Then you shall know that I am the Lord, when their slain are among their **idols** all around their altars, on every high hill, on all the mountaintops, under every green tree, and under every thick oak, wherever they offered sweet incense to all their **idols**" (Ezekiel 6:13)
	"So I went in and saw, and there—every sort of creeping thing, abominable beasts, and all the **idols** of the house of Israel, portrayed all around on the walls" (Ezekiel 8:10)
	"Then He said to me, "Son of man, have you seen what the elders of the house of Israel do in the dark, every man in the room of his **idols**? For they say, 'The Lord does not see us, the Lord has forsaken the land.'"" (Ezekiel 8:12)
	"Son of man, these men have set up their **idols** in their hearts, and put before them that which causes them to stumble into iniquity. Should I let Myself be inquired of at all by them? "Therefore speak to them, and say to them, 'Thus says the Lord God: "Everyone of the house of Israel who sets up his **idols** in his heart, and puts before him what causes him to stumble into iniquity, and then comes to the prophet, I the Lord will answer him who comes, according to the multitude of his **idols**, that I may seize the house of Israel by their heart, because they are all estranged from Me by their **idols**."' "Therefore say to the house of Israel, 'Thus says the Lord God: "Repent, turn away from your **idols**,

	and turn your faces away from all your abominations. For anyone of the house of Israel, or of the strangers who dwell in Israel, who separates himself from Me and sets up his **idols** in his heart and puts before him what causes him to stumble into iniquity, then comes to a prophet to inquire of him concerning Me, I the Lord will answer him by Myself" (Ezekiel 14:3-7)
	"Thus says the Lord God: "Because your filthiness was poured out and your nakedness uncovered in your harlotry with your lovers, and with all your abominable **idols**, and because of the blood of your children which you gave to them..." (Ezekiel 16:36)
	"Then I said to them, 'Each of you, throw away the abominations which are before his eyes, and do not defile yourselves with the **idols** of Egypt. I am the Lord your God.' But they rebelled against Me and would not obey Me. They did not all cast away the abominations which were before their eyes, nor did they forsake the **idols** of Egypt. Then I said, 'I will pour out My fury on them and fulfill My anger against them in the midst of the land of Egypt.'" (Ezekiel 20:7-8)
	"...because they despised My judgments and did not walk in My statutes, but profaned My Sabbaths; for their heart went after their **idols**" (Ezekiel 20:16)
	"But I said to their children in the wilderness, 'Do not walk in the statutes of your fathers, nor observe their judgments, nor defile yourselves with their **idols**" (Ezekiel 20:18)
	"...because they had not executed My judgments, but had despised My statutes, profaned My Sabbaths, and their eyes were fixed on their fathers' **idols**" (Ezekiel 20:24)
	"For when you offer your gifts and make your sons pass through the fire, you defile yourselves with all your **idols**, even to this day. So shall I be inquired of by you, O house of Israel? As I live," says the Lord God, "I will not be inquired of by you" (Ezekiel 20:31)
	"As for you, O house of Israel," thus says the Lord God: "Go, serve every one of you his **idols**—and hereafter—if you will not obey Me; but profane My holy name no more with your gifts and your **idols**" (Ezekiel 20:39)
	"Then say, 'Thus says the Lord God: "The city sheds blood in her own midst, that her time may come; and she makes **idols** within herself to defile herself. You have become guilty by the blood which you have shed, and have defiled yourself with the **idols** which you have made. You have caused your days to draw near, and have come to the end of your years; therefore I have made you a reproach to the nations, and a mockery to all countries" (Ezekiel 22:3-4)
	"...The nakedness of your harlotry shall be uncovered, both your lewdness and your harlotry. I will do these things to you because you have gone as a harlot after the Gentiles, because you have become defiled by their **idols**" (Ezekiel 23:29-30)
	"Then the word of the Lord came to me, saying: 24 "Son of man, they who inhabit those ruins in the land of Israel are saying, 'Abraham was only one, and he inherited the land. But we are many; the land has been given to us as a possession.' "Therefore say to them, 'Thus says the Lord God: "You eat meat with blood, you lift up your eyes toward your **idols**, and shed blood. Should you then possess the land?" (Ezekiel 33:23-25)
	"Moreover the word of the Lord came to me, saying: "Son of man, when the house of Israel dwelt in their own land, they defiled it by their own ways and

	*deeds; to Me their way was like the uncleanness of a woman in her customary impurity. Therefore I poured out My fury on them for the blood they had shed on the land, and for their **idols** with which they had defiled it"* (Ezekiel 36:16-18)
Ezekiel	*"And the Levites who went far from Me, when Israel went astray, who strayed away from Me after their **idols**, they shall bear their iniquity"* (Ezekiel 44:10)
	*"Because they ministered to them before their **idols** and caused the house of Israel to fall into iniquity, therefore I have raised My hand in an oath against them," says the Lord God, "that they shall bear their iniquity"* (Ezekiel 44:12)
Hosea	*"My people ask counsel from their wooden **idols**, and their staff informs them. For the spirit of harlotry has caused them to stray, and they have played the harlot against their God"* (Hosea 4:12)
	*"They set up kings, but not by Me; they made princes, but I did not acknowledge them. From their silver and gold they made **idols** for themselves— that they might be cut off"* (Hosea 8:4)
	*"Now they sin more and more, and have made for themselves molded images, **idols** of their silver, according to their skill; all of it is the work of craftsmen. They say of them, "Let the men who sacrifice kiss the calves!"* (Hosea 13:2)
Amos	*"You also carried Sikkuth your king and Chiun, your **idols**, the star of your gods, which you made for yourselves"* (Amos 5:26)
Jonah	*"Those who regard worthless **idols** forsake their own mercy"* (Jonah 2:8)
Micah	*"All her carved images shall be beaten to pieces, and all her pay as a harlot shall be burned with the fire; all her **idols** I will lay desolate, for she gathered it from the pay of a harlot, and they shall return to the pay of a harlot"* (Micah 1:7)
Habakkuk	*"What profit is the image, that its maker should carve it, the molded image, a teacher of lies, that the maker of its mold should trust in it, to make mute **idols**?"* (Habakkuk 2:18)
Zechariah	*"For the **idols** speak delusion; The diviners envision lies, and tell false dreams; they comfort in vain. Therefore the people wend their way like sheep; they are in trouble because there is no shepherd"* (Zechariah 10:2)
	*"It shall be in that day," says the Lord of hosts, "that I will cut off the names of the **idols** from the land, and they shall no longer be remembered. I will also cause the prophets and the **unclean spirit** to depart from the land"* (Zechariah 13:2)

Table 16: The Prophet's Warning to the Children of Israel

In the New Testament of the Biblical record, Jesus used the ***faithless*** term with His disciples. After they failed to heal a boy who had severe epileptic episodes, Jesus said to them, "*O **faithless** and perverse generation, how long shall I be with you? How long shall I bear with you?*" (Matthew 17:17; Mark 9:19; Luke 9:41). Their belief in the power of God was still weak. One knows this because after this incident, Jesus told His disciples "*...if you have faith as a mustard seed, you will say to this mountain, 'Move from here to there,' and it will move; and nothing will be impossible for you*" (Matthew 17:20). BTT helps one to see initially the disciple's inner spirits contained a small measure of the ***unfaithful*** attribute. For one to be ***faithless*** or to be ***unfaithful*** is a matter of degree, but these are still part of the same

unclean spirit. For the disciple's faith to grow, their inner spirits had to release the influence of ***faithlessness*** completely. This came with Jesus' teachings and obedience to His Word.

Jesus' presence caused the faithful attribute to grow. However, the negative forces of the war campaign maintained the presence of the ***unfaithful*** attribute among the Jews even though Jesus spoke with authority and provided signs, miracles, and wonders to back up His Word. This condition reemphasizes freedom of choice and the fact that even Jesus is not going to make one do something he or she chooses not to do on their own. Remember, the Jews, like everyone else, retained the right to choose regardless of what Jesus taught or what they saw from Him. The negative forces of the war campaign continues to exploit this truth to this very day. Hence, the Biblical record documented Jesus' use of the phrase, "*you of **little faith***" on numerous occasions. Jesus stated to His disciples:

- "*Now if God so clothes the grass of the field, which today is, and tomorrow is thrown into the oven, will He not much more clothe you, O you of **little faith**?*" (Matthew 6:30 and Luke 12:28)

- "*Why are you fearful, O you of **little faith**?*" *Then He arose and rebuked the winds and the sea, and there was a great calm*" (Matthew 8:23-26)

- "*...beware of the leaven of the Pharisees and the Sadducees*", He, "*...being aware of it, said to them, "O you of **little faith**, why do you reason among yourselves because you have brought no bread?*" (Matthew 16:5-8)

- "*And immediately Jesus stretched out His hand and caught him, and said to him, "O you of **little faith**, why did you* <u>doubt</u>?"" (Matthew 14:31)

The last statement made above by Jesus documented another correlation between the ***unfaithful*** attribute and the element of <u>doubt</u>. These two go hand in hand. In fact, both will fuel each other if not corrected. Jesus taught His disciples that the ***unfaithful*** attribute causes one to have <u>doubt</u> in the things that were positive, pure, and from the Lord. Jesus told His disciples about the power of the faithful attribute, the opposite spirit of the ***unfaithful*** attribute and <u>doubt</u>, in this way:

- "*...Assuredly, I say to you, if you have **faith** and do not <u>doubt</u>, you will not only do what was done to the fig tree, but also if you say to this mountain, 'Be removed and be cast into the sea,' it will be done*" (Matthew 21:21)

- "*For assuredly, I say to you, whoever says to this mountain, 'Be removed and be cast into the sea,' and does not <u>doubt</u> in his heart, but believes that those things he says will be done, he will have whatever he says*" (Mark 11:23)

- "*...Why are you troubled? And why do <u>doubts</u> arise in your hearts?*" (Luke 24:38)

The Holy Spirit inspired other writers of the Gospel to document their perspectives on the influence of the ***unfaithful*** attribute and the element of <u>doubt</u>. Paul documented, "*Do you have faith? Have it to yourself before God. Happy is he who does not condemn himself in what* *he approves. But he who doubts is condemned if he eats, because he does not eat from faith; for whatever is not from faith is sin"* (Romans 14:22-23). The element of doubt, in this context, combines with the influence of the **unfaithful** attribute to form an alliance against God's Word. When it comes to God and His relationship to the person influenced by this attribute, Paul documented, *"If we are **faithless**, He remains faithful; He cannot deny Himself"* (2 Timothy 2:13). This in no way implies that one can remain in an **unfaithful** state. It does mean that God will remain faithful whether one does or not. Because of God's stated position, one can count on Him to apply His rewards or corrective actions that He has documented in His Holy Word. Even the Spirit of wisdom told Solomon, *"Harsh discipline is for him who forsakes the way, and he who hates correction will die"* (Proverbs 15:10).

James also documented the correlation between the influence of the **unfaithful** attribute and the element of doubt. James documented that it is this combination that prevents Christians from receiving things that they have asked for from the Lord. As the **unfaithful** attribute influences one's inner spirit and the element of doubt joins it, James documented, *"...ask in faith, with no doubting, for he who doubts is like a wave of the sea driven and tossed by the wind"* (James 1:6). In other words, pure faith *"...the substance of things hoped for, the evidence of things not seen"* (Hebrews 11:1), is all one needs. The **unfaithful** attribute combined with the element of doubt, will cause one to miss out on the goodness of God. The element of doubt, working with the **unfaithful** attribute, continually increases the size of the negative forces of the war campaign across the spiritual battlefield.

There are two more important points one needs to understand about the **unfaithful** attribute and its correlation to **idolatry**. First, when one grows tired of listening to God's Word, the influence of the **unfaithful** attribute gains a foothold in one's inner spirit. This attribute then opens a spiritual door to *"works of the flesh"* of which Paul provides a list in the Book of Galatians. Interestingly, Paul's list includes **idolatry.** For the full list he states, *"...that those who practice such things will not inherit the kingdom of God"* (Galatians 5:21). Further, he would warn Christians to, *"...put to death your members which are on the earth: fornication, uncleanness, passion, evil desire, and covetousness, which is **idolatry**. Because of these things the wrath of God is coming upon the sons of disobedience, in which you yourselves once walked when you lived in them"* (Colossians 3:5-7).

Second, Christ's new covenant brought gentiles and Jews together to worship God in His name. Thus, to fight against the influence of the **unfaithful** attribute, **idols** and any practices surrounding them, had to be eradicated. Paul documented, *"What am I saying then? That an **idol** is anything, or what is offered to **idols** is anything? Rather, that the things which the Gentiles sacrifice they sacrifice to demons and not to God, and I do not want you to have fellowship with demons. You cannot drink the cup of the Lord and the cup of demons; you cannot partake of the Lord's table and of the table of demons. Or do we provoke the Lord to jealousy? Are we stronger than He?"* (1 Corinthians 10:19-22). Hence, the Holy Spirit lead the apostles to teach mightily on the subject. Here are some of the many pearls of wisdom documented to help one understand the strong and corrosive correlation between **idols** and the **unfaithful** attribute in spiritual warfare . The Bible documents:

"Now while Paul waited for them at Athens, his spirit was provoked within him when he saw that the city was given over to **idols**" (Acts 17:16)	"Little children, keep yourselves from **idols**. Amen" (1 John 5:21)	"Therefore, my beloved, flee from **idolatry**" (1 Corinthians 10:14)
"...that you abstain from things offered to **idols**, from blood, from things strangled, and from sexual immorality. If you keep yourselves from these, you will do well. Farewell" (Acts 15:29; also Acts 15:20 and Acts 21:25)	"For if anyone sees you who have knowledge eating in an **idol**'s temple, will not the conscience of him who is weak be emboldened to eat those things offered to **idols**?" (1 Corinthians 8:10)	"But if anyone says to you, "This was offered to **idols**," do not eat it for the sake of the one who told you, and for conscience' sake; for "the earth is the Lord's, and all its fullness."" (1 Corinthians 10:28)
"You know that you were Gentiles, carried away to these dumb **idols**, however you were led. Therefore I make known to you that no one speaking by the Spirit of God calls Jesus accursed, and no one can say that Jesus is Lord except by the Holy Spirit" (1 Corinthians 12:2-3)	"And what agreement has the temple of God with **idols**? For you are the temple of the living God. As God has said: "I will dwell in them and walk among them. I will be their God, and they shall be My people."" (2 Corinthians 6:16)	"Now concerning things offered to **idols**: We know that we all have knowledge. Knowledge puffs up, but love edifies... Therefore concerning the eating of things offered to **idols**, we know that an **idol** is nothing in the world, and that there is no other God but one" (1 Corinthians 8:1-4)
To the church in Ephesus, Jesus said, "*But I have a few things against you, because you have there those who hold the doctrine of Balaam, who taught Balak to put a stumbling block before the children of Israel, to eat things sacrificed to **idols**, and to commit sexual immorality*" (Revelation 2:14)	To the church in Thyatira, Jesus said, "*Nevertheless I have a few things against you, because you allow that woman Jezebel, who calls herself a prophetess, to teach and seduce My servants to commit sexual immorality and eat things sacrificed to **idols***" (Revelation 2:20)	In John's vision: "*But the rest of mankind, who were not killed by these plagues, did not repent of the works of their hands, that they should not worship demons, and **idols** of gold, silver, brass, stone, and wood, which can neither see nor hear nor walk.*" (Revelation 9:20)

Table 17: The Unfaithful Attribute and Idolatry

The **Immoral attribute**: This attribute shares a close relationship with the perverse and ungodly attributes. This attribute is the influencer of all inappropriate sexual activities and other forms of *deviant* behaviors. It is the filthiest of all the *unclean spirits* because it perpetuates a physical craving, urge, and drive to touch, see, or smell another person's body with or without their permission. Whether through pornography, peeping, of sexual harassment, the influence of the *immoral* attribute leaves countless victims harmed from the physical pain, shame, and embarrassment from the inappropriate activities. Idolatry, drug use, misused wealth, satanic practices, images of fantasy, and other negative behavioral activities enhance the influence of the ***immoral*** attribute. These enhancements cause mutations in this attribute that makes it appear to be the perverse attribute. But it is not. Hence, the element of <u>discernment</u> is extremely important when dealing with this attribute. In fact, sexual abuse falls under the influence of this attribute and overtime, it can combine with the influence of the perverse attribute. However, the root cause of sexual abuse is still the ***immoral*** attribute. Moreover, the influence of the ***immoral*** attribute will insist on blaspheming God, His name, and His Word. This behavior demonstrates a major difference between this and the perverse attribute. Although the influence of the ***immoral*** attribute leads one to sexual depravity like the perverse attribute, its influence also leads one to profess things like gender is a state of mind and sexual love has no boundaries. Hence, this attribute influences one to believe that he or she can choose their own gender regardless of God's male and female design. This belief is an affront to the Living God who made man in His own image. For the Biblical record documents, "*...God created man in His own image; in the image of God He created him; male and female He created them*" (Genesis 1:27). Remember as stated earlier, the influences of this attribute along with the perverse and ungodly attributes leads people to erode the lines of decency that support a stable civil society. Please keep reading.

Solomon taught his son about the influence of the ***immoral*** attribute by using the image of a woman involved in ***immoral*** behavior. His words were very descriptive. His choice of words gave the ***immoral*** attribute a lifelike appearance through the act of prostitution. Using the image of a woman gave the influence of the ***immoral*** attribute both form and beauty. At the same time, this image allowed Solomon to be descriptive of the attribute's deception and deadliness. Solomon explained, one would have a hard time breaking away from the idea once the allure of prostitution gripped one's inner spirit. Solomon documents in Proverbs 2:10-11 that the cure for the ***immoral*** attribute's influence is God's wisdom in one's spiritual heart, knowledge pleasant to one's soul, discretion that preserves, and understanding that keeps one safe. Solomon also documented the following information about the influence of this attribute using the image of a beautiful woman:

- Wisdom, knowledge, discretion, and understanding will, "*...deliver you from the **immoral** woman, from the seductress who flatters with her words, who forsakes the companion of her youth, and forgets the covenant of her God. For her house leads down to death, and her paths to the dead; none who go to her return, nor do they regain the paths of life...*" (Proverbs 2:16-19)

- "*...the lips of an **immoral** woman drip honey, and her mouth is smoother than oil; but in the end she is bitter as wormwood, sharp as a two-edged sword. Her feet go down to death, her steps lay hold of hell. Lest you ponder her path of life— her ways are unstable; you do not know them*" (Proverbs 5:3- 6)

- "*For why should you, my son, be enraptured by an **immoral** woman, and be embraced in the arms of a seductress?*" (Proverbs 5:20)

- *"The mouth of an **immoral** woman is a deep pit; he who is abhorred by the Lord will fall there"* (Proverbs 22:14)

Solomon ended his discussion with his son by explaining that a relationship with Wisdom would keep the influence of the ***immoral*** attribute away. He pleaded with his son to treat Wisdom as his sister and understanding as his nearest kin. He said, *"...keep my words, and treasure my commands within you. Keep my commands and live, and my law as the apple of your eye. Bind them on your fingers; write them on the tablet of your heart. Say to wisdom, "You are my sister," and call understanding your nearest kin, that they may keep you from the **immoral** woman, from the seductress who flatters with her words"* (Proverbs 7:1-5). Unfortunately, Solomon failed to heed his own advice and the influence of the ***immoral*** attribute led him to pursue ***sexually immoral*** relationships and fantasies with foreign women who led him to chase after false gods according to 1 Kings 1:1-11. In fact, the ***immoral*** attribute influenced Solomon so badly that the Biblical record documented that he, *"loved many foreign women, as well as the daughter of Pharaoh: women of the Moabites, Ammonites, Edomites, Sidonians, and Hittites— from the nations of whom the Lord had said to the children of Israel, "You shall not intermarry with them, nor they with you. Surely they will turn away your hearts after their gods." Solomon clung to these in love. And he had seven hundred wives, princesses, and three hundred concubines; and his wives turned away his heart. For it was so, when Solomon was old, that his wives turned his heart after other gods; and his heart was not loyal to the Lord his God, as was the heart of his father David"* (1 Kings 11:1-4).

In the Old Testament, the influence of the ***immoral*** attribute was among the many negative attributes leading up to the great flood documented in Genesis Chapter 6 and following. After the flood subsided and the ark came to rest, the Biblical record documented the reemergence of the ***immoral*** attribute as if it was waiting for the door of the ark to open. The Bible documented that after Noah and his family left the ark, an incident occurred. The Bible documented that *"...Noah began to be a farmer, and he planted a vineyard. Then he drank of the wine and was drunk, and became uncovered in his tent. And Ham, the father of Canaan, saw the nakedness of his father, and told his two brothers outside. But Shem and Japheth took a garment, laid it on both their shoulders, and went backward and covered the nakedness of their father. Their faces were turned away, and they did not see their father's nakedness. So Noah awoke from his wine, and knew what his younger son had done to him"* (Genesis 9:20-24).

What Ham did was an ***immoral*** act. BTT helps one to understand that prior to this situation, God had given Noah and His family instructions concerning morality. Leviticus 18:6 documents God's command. The Bible recorded, *"None of you shall approach anyone who is near of kin to him, to uncover his nakedness."* (Leviticus 18:6). Ham's correct behavior towards his father should have been the same as his brothers. That is all Ham had to do. However, the influence of the ***immoral*** attribute led him to look at his father's nakedness and go tell his brothers. The context of the Scriptures implies that Ham's motives, intentions, and thoughts were not pure.

The influence of the ***immoral*** attribute appeared within the walls of Sodom and Gomorrah. Ignore what people today teach to defend ***immorality*** in society. The fact is, the Biblical record documented, "*...the men of Sodom were **exceedingly wicked and sinful** against the Lord*" (Genesis 13:13). In this context, the ***immoral*** attribute influenced the men of Sodom in a profound way. The Lord also told Abraham, "*Because the outcry against Sodom and Gomorrah is great, and because their sin is very grave, I will go down now and see whether they have done altogether according to the outcry against it that has come to Me; and if not, I will know*" (Genesis 18:20, 21). When one reads Genesis 18:22-33 and Genesis 19:4-11, one cannot help but understand that the ***immoral*** attribute's influence dominated in these cities. This is why Jude documented, "*Sodom and Gomorrah, and the cities around them in a similar manner to these, having given themselves over to **sexual immorality** and gone after strange flesh, are set forth as an example, suffering the vengeance of eternal fire*" (Jude 1:7). The behavior in the cities was so bad that the Biblical record documented, "*...the Lord rained brimstone and fire on Sodom and Gomorrah, from the Lord out of the heavens. So He overthrew those cities, all the plain, all the inhabitants of the cities, and what grew on the ground*" (Genesis 19:24-25). In other words, just as the ***calamity*** of the great flood in Noah's day brought destruction to the human flesh, so did the ***calamity*** that rained down on Sodom and Gomorrah. The people in both cases were hopelessly influenced by the ***immoral*** and wicked attributes. BTT allows one to see that God purged the earth of their flesh. However, the negative spirits influencing their behavior moved on for another opportunity.

For one's learning, the Biblical record provided other examples of people who allowed the influence of the ***immoral*** attribute. One will notice that sometimes the attribute is implied but BTT will always allow one to see the attribute's influence clearly. Examples included:

Who	**What They Did**
The daughters of Lot	The Biblical record documented that they schemed (the wicked attribute) to get Lot drunk to lay with him and get pregnant and the Bible documented, "*...both the daughters of Lot were with child by their father. The firstborn bore a son and called his name Moab; he is the father of the Moabites to this day. And the younger, she also bore a son and called his name Ben-Ammi; he is the father of the people of Ammon to this day.*" (Genesis 19:30-38)
Shechem the son of Hamor	Shechem raped Dinah, the daughter of Leah and Jacob. The ***immoral*** attribute act influencing his behavior set off a chain reaction. The Bible documents that, "*...Shechem the son of Hamor the Hivite, prince of the country, saw her, he took her and lay with her, and **violated** her*" (Genesis 34: 1-2). Later, Shechem tried to do the right thing by marrying Dinah. However, the ***immoral*** act was done and could not be changed. Genesis 34:5-30 further documented how Shechem's ***immoral*** behavior led to his death and led other negative attributes to influence others to retaliate over his actions. Many innocent lives were lost over Shechem's behavior.
	Judah told Onan, after his brother died, to, "*Go in to your brother's wife and marry her, and raise up an heir to your brother.*" But Onan knew that the heir would not be his; and it came to pass, when he went in to his

Onan, the son of Judah	*brother's wife, that he emitted on the ground, lest he should give an heir to his brother. And the thing which he did displeased the Lord; therefore He killed him also"* (Genesis 38:6-10). Onan's behavior was **immoral**.
The children of Israel	The Biblical record documented *"and the people began to commit harlotry with the women of Moab. They invited the people to the sacrifices of their gods, and the people ate and bowed down to their gods. So Israel was joined to Baal of Peor, and the anger of the Lord was aroused against Israel"* (Numbers 25:1-3). Paul stated about their behavior, *"...nor let us commit **sexual immorality**, as some of them did, and in one day twenty-three thousand fell..."* (1 Corinthians 10:8). That's right, 2300 people fell in one day due to the influences of the **immoral** attribute.
King David (Temporarily)	He saw Bathsheba, the wife of Uriah the Hittite, from his roof bathing and observed that she was very beautiful to behold according to 1 Samuel 11:2-3. So, the Biblical record documented, *"David sent messengers, and took her; and she came to him, and he lay with her, for she was cleansed from her impurity; and she returned to her house. And the woman conceived; so she sent and told David, and said, "I am with child"* (1 Samuel 11:4-5) David's behavior was **immoral**. This attribute, combined with the wicked and bloodthirsty attributes, influenced David to murder Bathsheba husband according 1 Samuel 11:6-24.
Amnon and Jonadab	Amnon raped his sister half-sister, Tamar, using a scheme he and Jonadab concocted. The Biblical record documented that, *"...Absalom the son of David had a lovely sister, whose name was Tamar; and Amnon the son of David loved her. Amnon was so distressed over his sister Tamar that he became sick; for she was a virgin. And it was improper for Amnon to do anything to her"* (2 Samuel 13:1-2). One can read about Amnon and Jonadab's scheme in 2 Samuel 13:3-6. 2 Samuel 13:7-22 indicated that King David did not know Amnon and Jonadab's **wicked** scheme when he sent Tamar to Amnon bedside. The scheme led to Tamar's rape. As deviant behavior of the **immoral** attribute grew in Amnon, the Biblical record documented that, *"Absalom hated Amnon, because he had forced his sister Tamar"* (2 Samuel 13:22). Absalom eventually plotted and killed Amnon for revenge as documented in 2 Samuel 13:24-29
King Herod	The Biblical record documented that he had married, *"Herodias, his brother Philip's wife"* (Mark 6:17) and John the Baptist told him told him *"It is not lawful for you to have your brother's wife"* (Mark 6:18)
Herod (possibly a different one identified in Mark 6)	The Biblical record documented that this Herod, *"...arrayed in royal apparel, sat on his throne and gave an oration to them. And the people kept shouting, "The voice of a god and not of a man!" Then immediately an angel of the Lord struck him, because he did not give glory to God. And he was eaten by worms and died. But the word of God grew and multiplied"* (Acts 12:21-24)
The ungodly and unrighteous	The Biblical record documented that God, *"...gave them up to vile passions. For even their women exchanged the natural use for what is against nature. Likewise also the men, leaving the natural use of the woman, burned in their lust for one another, men with men committing what is shameful, and receiving in themselves the penalty of their error which was due. And even as they did not like to retain God in their knowledge, God gave them over to a debased mind, to do those things which are not fitting;*

	being filled with all unrighteousness, **sexual immorality**, wickedness, covetousness, maliciousness; full of envy, murder, strife, deceit, evil-mindedness; they are whisperers..." (Romans 1:26-29)
A man in the Lord's church in the church in Corinth	The Biblical record documented that Paul stated, "*It is actually reported that there is **sexual immorality** among you, and such **sexual immorality** as is not even named among the Gentiles—that a man has his father's wife!*" (1 Corinthians 5:1). Paul chastises the church for allowing **immoral** attribute to exist in the Lord's church. They were required to put the man out of the church for his behavior. Paul told them to, "*...deliver such a one to Satan for the destruction of the flesh that his spirit may be saved in the day of the Lord Jesus*" (1 Corinthians 5:5)

Table 18: Examples of People Influenced by the Immoral Attribute

The Lord told Moses of other behaviors that constituted ***immoral*** behavior. One will see the influence of the perverted and ungodly attributes in them as well. But overall, the influence of the ***immoral*** attribute causes deviant behaviors that cross the boundaries of other negative attributes to include the perverse, ungodly, bloodthirsty, etc... Because **unclean spirits** have no boundaries in the war campaign, as they see fit, they can combine with other negative attributes to fight the positive forces. Thus, Moses told the children of Israel:

"*None of you shall approach anyone who is near of kin to him, to uncover his nakedness*" (Leviticus 18:6)	"*You shall not lie with a male as with a woman. It is an abomination*" (Leviticus 18:22; 20:13)	"*The nakedness of your father's wife you shall not uncover; it is your father's nakedness*" (Leviticus 18:8; 20:11)
"*The nakedness of your sister, the daughter of your father, or the daughter of your mother, whether born at home or elsewhere, their nakedness you shall not uncover*" (Leviticus 18:9; 20:17)	"*The nakedness of your son's daughter or your daughter's daughter, their nakedness you shall not uncover; for theirs is your own nakedness*" (Leviticus 18:10)	"*The nakedness of your father's wife's daughter, begotten by your father—she is your sister—you shall not uncover her nakedness*" (Leviticus 18:11)
"*You shall not uncover the nakedness of your father's sister; she is near of kin to your father*" (Leviticus 18:12; 20:17)	"*You shall not uncover the nakedness of your mother's sister, for she is near of kin to your mother*" (Leviticus 18:13; 20:19)	"*You shall not uncover the nakedness of your father's brother. You shall not approach his wife; she is your aunt*" (Leviticus 18:14; 20:20)
"*You shall not uncover the nakedness of your daughter-in-law—she is your son's wife—you shall not uncover her nakedness*" (18:15; 20:12 Note: This is perversion)	"*You shall not uncover the nakedness of your brother's wife; it is your brother's nakedness*" (Leviticus 18:16; 20:21)	"*You shall not uncover the nakedness of a woman and her daughter, nor shall you take her son's daughter or her daughter's daughter, to uncover her nakedness. They are near of kin to her. It is wickedness*" (Leviticus 18:17)
"*Nor shall you take a woman as a rival to her	"*Also you shall not approach a woman to	"*Moreover you shall not lie carnally with your neighbor's

sister, to uncover her nakedness while the other is alive" (Leviticus 18:18)	uncover her nakedness as long as she is in her customary impurity" (Leviticus 18:19; 20:18)	wife, to defile yourself with her" (Leviticus 18:20)
"And you shall not let any of your descendants pass through the fire to Molech, nor shall you profane the name of your God: I am the Lord" (Leviticus 18:21)	"The nakedness of your father or the nakedness of your mother you shall not uncover. She is your mother; you shall not uncover her nakedness" (Leviticus 18:7)	"Nor shall you mate with any animal, to defile yourself with it. Nor shall any woman stand before an animal to mate with it. It is perversion" (Leviticus 18:23)
If a man mates with an animal, he shall surely be put to death, and you shall kill the animal. If a woman approaches any animal and mates with it, you shall kill the woman and the animal. They shall surely be put to death. Their blood is upon them." (Leviticus 20:15-16)		

Table 19: The Behavior of the Immoral Attribute Combined with Other Negative Attributes

In addition to the behaviors documented above, Leviticus 19 provided more examples of behaviors that destroy the ***morality*** of a people. When the influence of the ***immoral*** attribute combines with other negative attributes, the outcome will always be morally bad behavior. Consider the behaviors below. BTT allows one to see the influence of the ***immoral*** attribute behind each stated behaviors, actions, or deeds, along with other negative attributes. The Biblical record documented:

Turning to idols or making molded gods (Leviticus 19:4)	*Committing adultery* (Leviticus 20:10)	*Cursing one's father or his mother* (Leviticus 20:9)
Stealing, dealing falsely, lying to one another, or swearing by the Lord's name falsely (Leviticus 19:11-12)	*Cheating or robing your neighbor, cursing the deaf, or put a stumbling block before the blind* (Leviticus 19: 13-14)	*Being unjust in judgment, partial to the poor, or honor the person of the mighty (Leviticus 19:15-16)*
A man marrying a woman and her mother, it is wickedness (Leviticus 20:14)	*Allowing your livestock to breed with another kind* (Leviticus 19:19)	*Eating anything with the blood in it, practicing divination or soothsaying* (Leviticus 19:26)
Making any cuttings in your flesh for the dead, nor tattoo any marks (Leviticus 19:28)	*Prostituting your daughter, to cause her to be a harlot* (Leviticus 19:29)	*Giving regard to mediums and familiar spirits, seeking after them, to be defiled by them* (Leviticus 19:31; 20:27)

| | *Mistreating a stranger who dwells with you in your land* (Leviticus 19:33) | |

Table 20: Other Aspects of the Immoral Attribute

The children of Israel ignored God's commands even through the time they developed into a mighty nation. But so do the nations of the world today to their own peril. For during the spiritual warfare of the war campaign, a choice between good and evil will always exist. Nevertheless, the question is always, which side will one chose to serve on?

In the New Testament of the Biblical record, Jesus addressed the deviant behavior manifested by the influence of the ***immoral*** attribute within the context of a marriage between a man and a woman. Jesus stated, "*But I say to you that whoever divorces his wife for any reason except **sexual immorality** causes her to commit adultery; and whoever marries a woman who is divorced commits adultery*" (Matthew 5:32). To make this comment even clearer to the Pharisees, who later tried to test Him over Moses law on divorce, Jesus repeated God's position on the subject. Jesus told them, "…. *I say to you, whoever divorces his wife, except for **sexual immorality**, and marries another, commits adultery; and whoever marries her who is divorced commits adultery*" (Matthew 19:9). In other words, the marriage vows can only be broken for two reasons according to the Biblical record.

1. When the influence of the ***immoral*** attribute has desecrated the relationship.

2. When death takes one person away from the relationship.

In the first case, Jesus made the statement twice to clearly show the correlation between the adulterer attribute and the influence of the ***immoral*** attribute. When the influence of the adulterer attribute leads one to a sinful relationship with a third person outside the marriage, desecration of the relationship occurs when sexual contact is made. Sexual contact in this manner is one of many forms of ***sexual immorality***. The act between the two people constitutes adultery and the behavior is ***immoral***. However, the order is immaterial. For BTT allows one to see that the influence of the ***immoral*** attribute will eventually lead one to commit adultery or cause one to fall into an adulterous relationship. With both the ***immoral*** and adulterer attributes influencing one's inner spirit, the adulterer attribute will fully mature. Thus, the negative forces of the war campaign grow by one or more people who stumble from the collapse of a relationship.

BTT also allows one to see that a strong marital relationship is a cure for the influence of the ***immoral*** attribute. God's Word helps establish strong relationships. Therefore, Paul documented, "*…because of **sexual immorality**, let each man have his own wife, and let each woman have her own husband. Let the husband render to his wife the affection due her, and likewise also the wife to her husband. The wife does not have authority over her own body, but the husband does. And likewise the husband does not have authority over his own body, but the wife does. Do not deprive one another except with consent for a time, that you may give yourselves to fasting and prayer; and come together again so that Satan does not tempt* *you because of your lack of self-control*" (1 Corinthians 7:2-5). Deceptive strategies originating from negative forces within the war campaign have hijacked the teachings for creating a healthy marital relationship. Unqualified ministers, false teachers, and counselors in both religious and secular communities, covered in the sin of the ***immoral*** and adulterer attributes themselves, are destroying homes with subversive teaching. They cannot set the example of marriage God demands nor should they counsel or teach others on the subject. Consequently, these same unqualified ministers and false teachers twist God's Word to justify their own ***immoral*** behavior (Romans 1:32) and fail to teach the whole counsel of God (Acts 20:27). Their teachings result in marriages that are no more than business transactions between couples. These couples simply produce revenue for themselves and the religious organization they support. The idea that marriage serves as something holy for God's service is lost. Hence, their union only aids the negative forces of the war campaign. Why? Because a marriage not established in the foundational understanding of God's Word lacks the tools to survive spiritual warfare. BTT allows one to see the influence of the ***immoral*** attribute's desire to destroy marriages; a strategy employed to aid the negative forces of the campaign. When the influence of this attribute succeeds in destroying a marriage, the negative side of the war campaign grows exponentially by the fallout between these adults, their children, and the external families of all that were involved. Please let this soak in before going further with this attribute. The fallout that occurs from a marriage's demise strengthens the negative forces in the campaign. A failed marriage is even worse for children who are forced to pick sides between separated parents.

    BTT allows one to see that when the focus of marriage is based on God's Word, then Paul's words on marriage have more traction. Paul stated that, "*Marriage is honorable among all, and the bed undefiled; but fornicators and adulterers God will judge. Let your conduct be without covetousness; be content with such things as you have*" (Hebrews 13:4-5). One should see that when the ***immoral*** and adulterer attributes, influence one's inner spirit, the covenant relationship of a marriage will be defiled. Is this an argument for remaining single to avoid issues with the ***immoral*** attribute? Certainly not. Paul also wrote, "*...to the unmarried and to the widows: It is good for them if they remain even as I am; but <u>if they cannot exercise self-control</u>, **let them marry**. For it is better to marry than to **burn with passion**"* (1 Corinthians 7:8-9). Paul remained celibate and strong as He proclaimed the Gospel of Jesus Christ. But the deception of the influence of the ***immoral*** attribute impedes many people from remaining celibate because they lack contentment in their lives. False teacher even proclaim celibacy is impossible. But the truth is they themselves lack self-control. The guiding principle for every Christian, as it was for Paul, is that "*...the body is not for **sexual immorality** but for the Lord, and the Lord for the body*" (1 Corinthians 6:13).

    BTT also lets one see that the act of cohabitation is also an ***immoral*** relationship. No one, and especially a Christian, can expect to make it to heaven in this form of illegitimate relationship. Cohabitation's root stemmed from a strategy by the negative forces to deceive couples into consensual fornication. If one cannot exercise self-control, marriage is the only honorable option and proper Biblical education will sustain a strong relationship. Without proper Biblical education on marriage, the negative forces of the war campaign simply adds souls to their numbers. The unfortunate reality to Christians finding like-minded mates is increasingly difficult due to the decreasing numbers of Christians on the spiritual battlefield.

As for the second case, when death has taken one from the marriage relationship, Paul documented "*A wife is bound by law as long as her husband lives; but if her husband dies, she is at liberty to be married to whom she wishes, only in the Lord*" (1 Corinthians 7:39). The law spoken of here is the marriage bond she and the husband made together. However, this statement applies to both the man and woman. The spiritual bond connects them both until one pass away. Why? Because the bond is a spiritual contract signed spiritually before the eyes of God. From this spiritual union, Paul documented, "*For this reason a man shall leave his father and mother and be joined to his wife, and the two shall become one flesh*" (Ephesians 5:31). In context, the "only in the Lord" means to remarry another Christian. The reason is simple. This is the best way for two spiritually-minded people to stay focused in the spiritual war confronting them. Their maturity will aid the positive forces of the war campaign.

As one comes to grips with how the influence of the **immoral** attribute affects the bond of marriage, there is another tactic this attribute uses to inflict damage on married couples and young adults. The tactic, although seemingly subtler, is just as potent and deadly. Jesus stated, "*You have heard that it was said to those of old, 'You shall not commit adultery.' But I say to you that whoever looks at a woman to <u>lust</u> for her has already committed adultery with her in his heart*" (Matthew 5:27-28). Although I will cover the adulterer attribute as a stand-alone attribute, understand that the element of <u>lust</u> leads to **immoral** behavior. <u>Lust</u> defiles one's inner spirit. Jesus' statement deals with a deeper issue of looking at another person and <u>lusting</u> for him or her in one's imagination. BTT allows one to see that this idea includes the use of pornography. Pornography, whether it is looking at naked men, women, children, or animals in sexual acts, poses, or the like, leads one down a path of **immorality**. Look back at all the items from Leviticus 18 covered earlier with this attribute. BTT allows one to see that one who likes looking at pornography, has the influence of the **immoral** attribute lurking inside their inner spirit.

When Paul and Barnabas took the Gospel to the Gentiles, they gave them a simple decree that spoke of the **immoral** attribute. The decree stated, "*For it seemed good to the Holy Spirit, and to us, to lay upon you no greater burden than these necessary things: to abstain from things polluted by **idols**, from **sexual immorality**, from things strangled, and from blood*" (Acts 15:28, 29). BTT allows one to see that the grip of the **immoral** attribute, especially through **sexual immorality**, is so powerful that it creates some of the largest armies of resistance to the positive attributes in the war campaign. For many people seeking God's Word, the influence of the **immoral** attribute lays traps and distractions all along life's path. The internet, social media, and the entertainment industry provide multiple opportunities of entrapment for all who dismiss God's Word.

Other insights about **sexual immorality** shared by the Biblical record that the negative side of the war campaign desires one not to know are:

- Christians are to shun **sexually immoral** people in the Lord's church. Paul documented one <u>must not</u>, "*…keep company with anyone named a brother, who is **sexually immoral**, or covetous, or an idolater, or a reviler, or a drunkard, or an extortioner—not even to eat with such a person*" (1 Corinthians 5:11)

- Christians are not too practice isolationism. Paul clarified, "*Yet I certainly did not mean with the **sexually immoral** people of this world, or with the covetous, or extortioners, or idolaters, since then you would need to go out of the world*" (1 Corinthians 5:10)

- Christian have liberty but discipline takes precedence. Paul documented, "*All things are lawful for me, but all things are not helpful. All things are lawful for me, but I will not be brought under the power of any. Foods for the stomach and the stomach for foods, but God will destroy both it and them. Now the body is not for **sexual immorality** but for the Lord, and the Lord for the body*" (1 Corinthians 6:13)

- Christians are to "*Flee **sexual immorality**. Every sin that a man does is outside the body, but he who commits **sexual immorality** sins against his own body*" (1 Corinthians 6:18)

- Christians can know that "*...this is the will of God, your sanctification: that you should abstain from **sexual immorality**; that each of you should know how to possess his own vessel in sanctification and honor, not in passion of lust, like the Gentiles who do not know God...*" (1 Thessalonians 4:3-5)

- The world needs to know that "*...the cowardly, unbelieving, abominable, murderers, **sexually immoral**, sorcerers, idolaters, and all liars shall have their part in the lake which burns with fire and brimstone, which is the second death*" (Revelation 21:8) and when it comes to heaven, "*...outside are dogs and sorcerers and **sexually immoral** and murderers and idolaters, and whoever loves and practices a lie*" (Revelation 22:15)

Another topic that involves the influence of the ***immoral*** attribute is the act of prostrating or bowing down before another human being for religious reasons. God views all of mankind as equals to one another. For one to elevate oneself over another person in religious matters and expect the act of bowing in one's presence is an act of idolatry (Leviticus 19:4) and therefore, ***immoral***. With the negative forces of the war campaign influencing this behavior, eventually the strategy will lead one accepting the bow to believe that he or she is on a level equal to or greater than Jesus Christ. One sees this all the time with religious leaders who take God's Holy Word and twists it. The practice of bowing in the presence of a religious leader occurs despite the Biblical records objection to this practice. When religious leaders allow the influence of the negative attributes, they often place themselves between the people they lead and God in heaven. The influence of the ***immoral*** attribute obscures two important facts concerning this behavior. First, the Biblical record documents that "*For there is one God and one Mediator between God and men, the Man Christ Jesus...*" (1 Timothy 2:5). Second, and just as important is the fact that Jesus Christ, "*...is the blessed and only Potentate, the King of kings and Lord of lords, who alone has immortality, dwelling in unapproachable light, whom no man has seen or can see, to whom be honor and everlasting power*" (1 Timothy 6:15-16).

The Biblical record documents examples against bowing down to another of God's creations. There is Haman who desired Mordecai to bow before him. When Mordecai refused, Haman wanted all Jews of King Ahasuerus's kingdom destroyed for Mordecai's insolence according to the Book of Ester, Chapter 3:1-6. There is Daniel and his companions who did not bow down to King Nebuchadnezzar's golden **idol**. Daniel 3:1-19 documented that the **idol** represented King Nebuchadnezzar. In the Book of Acts, a situation occurred with Paul and Barnabas when they were in Lystra after healing a cripple man who had never walked. The Biblical record documented in Acts 14:11-18:

> *"...when the people saw what Paul had done, they raised their voices, saying in the Lycaonian language, "The gods have come down to us in the likeness of men!" And Barnabas they called Zeus, and Paul, Hermes, because he was the chief speaker. Then the priest of Zeus, whose temple was in front of their city, brought oxen and garlands to the gates, intending to sacrifice with the multitudes. But when the apostles Barnabas and Paul heard this, they tore their clothes and ran in among the multitude, crying out and saying, "Men, why are you doing these things? We also are men with the same nature as you, and preach to you that you should turn from these useless things to the living God..."*

Paul's example allows one to see that no one has the right to place themselves between God and His creation except Jesus Christ. God only appointed His Son. Any religious person that dismisses this divine evidence has allowed themselves to be influence by the ***immoral*** attribute and serves the negative forces of the war campaign. BTT allows one to see and hear what God said concerning this pivotal piece of wisdom. God said, *"This is My beloved Son, in whom I am well pleased. Hear Him!"* (Matthew 17:5). However, if this is not enough evidence, consider the example from the book of Revelation when, *"...the Lord God of the holy prophets sent His angel to show His servants the things which must shortly take place"* (Revelation 22:6). John documented, *"Now I, John, saw and heard these things. And when I heard and saw, I fell down to worship before the feet of the angel who showed me these things. Then he said to me, "<u>See that you do not do that</u>. For I am your fellow servant, and of your brethren the prophets, and of those who keep the words of this book. <u>Worship God</u>."* (Revelation 22:8-9). The Biblical record cannot make this wisdom any clearer.

Finally, Jesus identified the image of two congregations facing destructions because of the influence of the ***immoral*** attribute. The churches of Pergamos and Thyatira both had the ***immoral*** attribute blatantly thriving among their members. Jesus made it known that this type of behavior was unacceptable. He told the church in Pergamos, *"But I have a few things against you, because you have there those who hold the doctrine of Balaam, who taught Balak to put a stumbling block before the children of Israel, to eat things sacrificed to idols, and to commit **sexual immorality**"* (Revelation 2:14). Likewise, He told church of Thyatira, *"Nevertheless I have a few things against you, because you allow that woman Jezebel, who calls herself a prophetess, to teach and seduce My servants to commit **sexual immorality** and eat things sacrificed to idols. And I gave her time to repent of her **sexual immorality**, and she did not repent"* (Revelation 2:20-21). Both congregations were required to repent or be eternally lost. I encourage one to read these accounts. These congregations were deceived and on the wrong side of the war campaign.

The **Ungodly attribute**: The influence of this attributes causes a person to rebel against God, disrespect Him and His Authority, reject anyone speaking of Him, and deny anything documented in His Word. The influence of this attribute is closely related to the influence of the immoral and perverse attributes. One can expect the behavior of one influenced by the ***ungodly*** attribute to be contrary to any of God's laws that He has provided to establish good order, civility, and decency. In fact, it is this attribute combined with the influences of the perverse and immoral attributes that lead people to erode the lines of decency that supports civility in all societies worldwide. The influence of the ***ungodly*** attribute leads people to unite with people influenced by unrighteousness (Romans 1:18) and be "*...inventors of evil things...*" (Romans 1:30). In the war campaign, this is important to understand because it identifies the negative attribute behind people creating, pushing the distribution of, and hiding the effects of such things as weapons, alcohol, and drugs. These items, without proper education, destroy families, neighborhoods, and entire communities across the spiritual battlefield. Moreover, the Biblical record documents that people influenced by the ***ungodly*** attribute know, "*...the righteous judgment of God, that those who practice such things are deserving of death, not only do the same but also approve of those who practice them*" (Romans 1:32). Furthermore, this is the attribute whose influence leads one into all forms of idol worship. This includes the worship of other gods, humans (dead or alive), animals, material things, and angels. The unfaithful attribute influences religious communities to leave the One true God and turn to idols.

The Spirit of wisdom revealed to Solomon that, "*An **ungodly** man digs up evil, and it is on his lips like a burning fire*" (Proverbs 16:27). No one who draws the ire of one influenced by the ***ungodly*** attribute is safe. This person will dig until he or she finds something from one's past that others may exploit. But for all their efforts, the Spirit of wisdom told Solomon, "*If the righteous will be recompensed on the earth, how much more the **ungodly** and the sinner*" (Proverbs 11:31). To "*recompense*" is to reward or compensate. BTT allows one to see that if one influenced by the righteous attribute gets what they deserve from a positive standpoint, then from a negative standpoint, one with the ***ungodly*** attribute will also receive what he or she deserves. Later in this book, one will learn how God uses <u>calamity</u> in the war campaign to purge strongholds of people caught up by the influences of this and other negative attributes from among His people. Make no mistake, Wisdom clearly documents that God will punish a person who allows the influence of the ***ungodly*** attribute in their life.

BTT allows one to see that Adam and Eve behaved ***ungodly*** when they ignored God's commands and ate from the tree of good and evil according Genesis 3:1-7. One must understand that when "*...God said, "Let Us make man in Our image, according to Our likeness..."* (Genesis 1:26), He created godly people. However, they exhibited the influence of the ***ungodly*** attribute in their behavior when they considered and ate the forbidden fruit. They were punished for allowing the ***ungodly*** attribute to influence their inner spirits. This attribute modified their behavior in the garden according to Genesis 3:14-24. For their disobedience, God cast them out of the garden.

Cain also demonstrated the influence of the ***ungodly*** attribute when he pouted over his offering to God and then murdered his brother Abel according to Genesis 4:1-7. The Lord spoke to Cain and said, "*Why are you angry? And why has your countenance fallen? If you do well, will you not be accepted? And if you do not do well, sin lies at the door. And its desire is for you, but you should rule over it*" (Genesis 4:6-7). BTT allows one to see that Cain had a choice to make. However, the influence of the **ungodly** attribute clouded his thinking. One can know this because the Biblical record documented that, "*...Cain talked with Abel his brother; and it came to pass, when they were in the field, that Cain rose up against Abel his brother and killed him*" (Genesis 4:8). The **ungodly** attribute combined with several other negative attributes to influence Cain to murder his brother. Cain's behavior and action were **ungodly**.

There are countless examples of **ungodly** behavior documented in the Biblical record. The **ungodly** attribute's influence can stand alone or unite with other negative attributes to strengthen its influence. Clearly with this attribute, God shows His displeasure and His reaction is often overwhelming for man to comprehend. Consider some of the various examples where the influence of the **ungodly** attribute was clearly involved at some measure. Then consider God's providential reaction. One can study these examples on one's own time:

God's decision to destroy his first creation in Genesis 6:17	Ham's behavior in Genesis 9:22-23	The building of the tower of babel in Genesis 11:1-9
Lot's decision to go toward the cities on the plains in Genesis 13:11-13	The lifestyle of the inhabitants of Sodom and Gomorrah in Genesis Chapter 19	Esau's behavior in Genesis 25:29-34
Laban's behavior in Genesis Chapters 29-31	Shechem behavior towards Dinah in Genesis Chapter 34	Joseph's brother's behavior in Genesis Chapter 37
The children of Israel's behavior once freed from Egypt in Exodus 15:22 thru Chapter 40	The king of Egypt's plot to kill the first-born males in Exodus 1:15-17	Pharaoh's behavior throughout the plagues in Exodus Chapters 5-12
Potiphar's wife toward Joseph in Genesis 39:7-19	The profane fire of Nadab and Abihu in Leviticus 10:1-3	The behavior of an unfaithful wife in Numbers Chapter 5
The soldiers mocking of Jesus in Matthew 27:27-31	Balaam's behavior in Numbers Chapters 22-24.	The behavior of Eliphaz, Zophar, and Bildad based on Job 16:11
Herod's **ungodly** oration which cost him his life documented in Acts 12:20-23	Satan's temptation of Jesus in Matthew 4:1-11; Mark 1:12-13; Luke 4:1-13	The Pharisees accusation that Jesus was demon possessed in Matthew 12:24
The Samaritan village's rejection of Jesus, and James and John's reaction to their rejection in Luke 9:5-56	Peter confronting Jesus over His predicted death in Matthew 16:21-23; Mark 8:31-33; Luke 9:21-22	The defilement of the temple of God in Matthew 21:12-13; Mark 11:15-19; Luke 19:45-48; John 2:13-22
The Pharisees plot to trap Jesus concerning the payment of taxes in Matthew 22:15-22; Mark 12:13-17; Luke 20:20-26	Ananias and Sapphira's **ungodly** behavior as a Christian documented in Acts 5:1-10	Judas decision to betray Jesus found in Matthew 26:14-16; Mark 14:10-11; Luke 22:2-6

Those Jews who took an oath to kill Paul documented Acts 23:12-14	Jesus' trial in Matthew 26:57-68; Mark 14:53-65; Luke 22:66-71; John 18:12-14, 19-24	The Jew's ***ungodly*** behavior and reaction to Paul documented in Acts 13:44-46
The behavior of the complaining children of Israel in Numbers 11:1-10; 14:1-29; 16:1-35	Jesus rejection in His own country found in Luke 6:1-6; Matthew 13:53-58; Luke 4:16-30	Herod's beheading of John the Baptist in Matthew 14:1-12; Mark 6:14-29; Luke 9:7-9
The priests, the captain of the temple, and the Sadducees arrested Peter and John for teaching and preaching Jesus in Acts 4:1-3	The religious leadership that gathered at Jerusalem and commanded Peter and John not to speak or teach in the name of Jesus documented in Acts 4:5-18	The Jewish selection of Barabbas over Jesus in Matthew 27:15-26; Mark 15:6-15; Luke 23:13-25; John 18:39-40
Herod's massacre of innocent children in Matthew 2:16-18	The men who murdered Stephen documented in Acts 7:54-60	Saul's persecution of the church documented in Acts 8:1-3
Simon the sorcerer's ***ungodly*** behavior as a Christian documented in Acts 8:14-25, Herod's *murder* of James and arrest of Peter documented in Acts 12:1-3	The high priest and Sadducees arrested the apostles the second time only to become furious and plot to kill them according to Acts 5:17-33	The Jewish chief priest, the scrips, and the elders of the people assembly to plot to trick and kill Jesus in Matthew 26:3-4; Mark 14:1-2; Luke 22:1-2; John 11:45-53
The Jew's from Antioch and Iconium stoning of Paul documented in Acts 14:19	The ***ungodly*** behavior of Demetrius at the city of Ephesus documented in Acts 19:21-41	The Jews from Asia's ***ungodly*** behavior toward Paul documented in Acts 21:27-31
Jesus' betrayal and arrest at Gethsemane in Matthew 26:47; Mark 14:43-52; Luke 22:47-53; John 18:1-11		

Table 21: Examples of the Ungodly Attribute

These are just a few of the many examples of ***ungodly*** behavior exhibited by people who allowed the influence of the ***ungodly*** attribute. Is there overlap with this attribute and other negative attributes? Yes, because spiritual warfare is complicated, and it is often difficult to see a clear break between spiritual influences. To illustrate the point more clearly, consider an example of Cain's behavior. Cain murdered his brother while influenced by the bloodthirsty attribute. However, the angry, furious, and violent attributes also influenced his behavior prior to the bloodthirsty attribute consuming his inner spirit. Overall, in his attitude with God, the ***ungodly*** attribute influenced him. This complex interaction between the negative attributes document the complicated nature of spiritual warfare and the war campaign. But the fact is, if the ***ungodly*** attribute is not corrected with God's Word, it will provide access to the influences of other negative attributes that may lead one to eventually harm others.

The Psalmist documented three important insights concerning the influence of the ***ungodly*** attribute's attempts to lead people astray. He wrote:

- *"Blessed is the man who <u>walks not</u> in the counsel of the **ungodly**, nor stands in the path of sinners, nor sits in the seat of the scornful..."* (Psalms 1:1)

- Compared to one with the righteous attribute who will be like a tree planted by the rivers of water, *"The **ungodly** are not so, but are like the chaff which the wind drives away. Therefore the **ungodly** shall not stand in the judgment, nor sinners in the congregation of the righteous. For the Lord knows the way of the righteous, but the way of the **ungodly** shall perish"* (Psalms 1:3-6)

- Concerning people influenced by both the wicked and **ungodly** attributes: *"... my feet had almost stumbled; my steps had nearly slipped. For I was envious of the boastful, when I saw the prosperity of the wicked. For there are no pangs in their death, but their strength is firm. They are not in trouble as other men, nor are they plagued like other men. Therefore pride serves as their necklace; violence covers them like a garment. Their eyes bulge with abundance; they have more than heart could wish. They scoff and speak wickedly concerning oppression; they speak loftily. They set their mouth against the heavens, and their tongue walks through the earth. Therefore his people return here, and waters of a full cup are drained by them. And they say, "How does God know? And is there knowledge in the Most High?" Behold, these are the **ungodly**, who are always at ease; they increase in riches"* (Psalms 73:2-12)

What is most important about the last insight above is that the Psalmist shared a personal experience. People he saw influenced by the **ungodly** and wicked attributes almost caused him to sin. This pearl of wisdom is important for understanding traps laid in the war campaign. The Psalmist shared that he <u>almost </u>opened a door for the influence of the jealous/envious attribute to enter his inner spirit by watching their sinful behavior. BTT allows one to see the value of focusing on Jesus in life. For focusing on the wrong things; the negative things, will throw one off track.

In the New Testament of the Biblical record, Paul clearly addressed the influence of the **ungodly** attribute when he observed that the city of Athens was over taken by idols. In the Book of Acts, the Biblical records specifically documents that his inner spirit was provoked based on what he saw according to Acts 17:16. Paul saw Jews and gentiles worshippers in the marketplace (Acts 17:17) when he was approached by Epicurean and Stoic philosophers who wanted to know what he preached about according to Acts 17:18-19. These for philosophers took Paul to the Areopagus to speak publicly where he stated, *"Men of Athens, I perceive that in all things you are very religious; for as I was passing through and considering the objects of your worship, I even found an altar with this inscription: TO THE UNKNOWN GOD. Therefore, the One whom you worship without knowing, Him I proclaim to you..."* (Acts 17:22-23). The point is this, Paul addressed the religious communities of his day involved in **ungodly** acts of idol worship. His goal was to lead them from their religious beliefs and activity to one of Christianity where the influence of the **ungodly** attribute had no place. Likewise, Paul addressed a similar theme in Colosse concerning the worship of angels. He stated, *"Let no one cheat you of your reward, taking delight in false humility and <u>worship of angels</u>, intruding into those things which he has not seen, vainly puffed up by his fleshly mind..."* (Colossians

2:18). Please do not be **deceived**. Both the worship of idols and angels are an indicator of the influence of the **ungodly** attribute presence.

Paul provided clear identification of one who allows the influence of the **ungodly** attributes to influence their behavior. The Holy Spirit inspired him to write, *"For the wrath of God is revealed from heaven against all **ungodliness** and unrighteousness of men, who suppress the truth in unrighteousness, because what may be known of God is manifest in them, for God has shown it to them. For since the creation of the world His invisible attributes are clearly seen, being understood by the things that are made, even His eternal power and Godhead, so that they are without excuse, because, although they knew God, they did not glorify Him as God, nor were thankful, but became futile in their thoughts, and their foolish hearts were darkened"* (Romans 1:18-32). One with the **ungodly** attribute suppresses what they know of God and fights that same knowledge at every turn. During judgement, the living God will not excuse their actions. This applies to every false preacher, teacher, and atheist in the world. Moreover, God judgement applies to everyone who accepts the words of the **ungodly**. This is significant because the Biblical record documented that, *"...Christ died for the **ungodly**"* (Romans 5:6). Therefore, His judgment on the Day of Judgement will be severe and final.

For this reason, Paul told Timothy that, *"...we know that the law is good if one uses it lawfully, knowing this: that the law is not made for a righteous person, but for the lawless and insubordinate, for the **ungodly** and for sinners, for the unholy and profane, for murderers of fathers and murderers of mothers, for manslayers, for fornicators, for sodomites, for kidnappers, for liars, for perjurers, and if there is any other thing that is contrary to sound doctrine,..."* (1 Timothy 1:8-10). The Biblical record is God's Holy Law; the Old Testament for our learning (Romans 15:4) and the New Testament for our salvation (Romans 1:16). The negative attributes use spiritual warfare to distort this truth using ancient strategies. In fact, within the campaign, people influenced by the **ungodly** attribute have taken over much of religion. Paul offered this understanding when he wrote, *"For such are false apostles, deceitful workers, transforming themselves into apostles of Christ. And no wonder! For Satan himself transforms himself into an angel of light. Therefore it is no great thing if his ministers also transform themselves into ministers of righteousness, whose end will be according to their works"* (2 Corinthians 11:13-15). BTT allows one to see that there are many religious leaders who call themselves Christians while teaching coexistence with believers of all forms of unscriptural and **ungodly** practices and doctrines. This is an abomination to God. Yet, it is part of Satan's well-orchestrated strategy through spiritual warfare led by people influenced by the **ungodly** and wicked attributes.

Peter documented *"If the righteous one is scarcely saved, where will the **ungodly** and the sinner appear?"* (1 Peter 4:18; Proverbs 11:31). This statement alone should terrify people worshipping God today in facilities and organizations that some human has placed their name on and is claiming to follow Jesus Christ and His Word. BTT allows one to see that it is also an indication that these groups are contributing to the negative forces of the war campaign and spiritual warfare. The Holy Spirit revealed to Paul that one must examine oneself (1 Corinthians 11:28) to ensure that one is in the faith according to Jesus Christ's teachings. BTT allows one to see that Christ's teachings came from God (John 17:8) and the Word was not guidance to follow as some people teach. Christ's Words are commands to be carried out in *"the greatest war campaign ever conceived"*. Peter added to this point when he documented, *"...For if God did not spare the angels who sinned, but cast them down to hell and delivered them into chains of darkness, to be reserved for judgment; and did not spare the ancient world, but saved Noah, one of eight people, a preacher of righteousness, bringing in the flood on the world of the **ungodly**; and turning the cities of Sodom and Gomorrah into ashes, condemned them to destruction, making them an example to those who afterward would live **ungodly**... then the Lord knows how to deliver the godly out of temptations and to reserve the unjust under punishment for the day of judgment, and especially those who walk according to the flesh in the lust of uncleanness and despise authority. They are presumptuous, self-willed. They are not afraid to speak evil of dignitaries, whereas angels, who are greater in power and might, do not bring a reviling accusation against them before the Lord"* (2 Peter 2:4-11). Do not be deceived by the strategies of the negative forces of the war campaign. Read the Bible closely.

For people who allow the influence of the **ungodly** attribute, Peter further documented that, *"...the heavens and the earth which are now preserved by the same word, are reserved for fire until the day of judgment and perdition of **ungodly** men"* (2 Peter 3:7). Make no mistake, God has a plan for people influenced by the **ungodly** attribute. However, the ancient strategies of the negative forces fighting in the war campaign keep this truth hidden. In fact, men influenced by the **ungodly** attribute will keep the truth hidden worldwide as their deceit in religious communities is passed down each generation. Jude documented this fact when he wrote, *"For certain men have crept in unnoticed, who long ago were marked out for this condemnation, **ungodly** men, who turn the grace of our God into lewdness and deny the only Lord God and our Lord Jesus Christ"* (Jude 1:4). In fact, Jude documented that the same people influenced by the **ungodly** attribute are, *"...grumblers, complainers, walking according to their own lusts; and they mouth great swelling words, flattering people to gain advantage"* (Jude 1:16). If these men infiltrated the Lord's church, just think what happens in organizations that mimic the Lord's churches established by some man or woman's vision on the spiritual battlefield. People influenced by the **ungodly** attribute progress to leadership positions uninhibited when a church is not established and secured correctly. Thus, Jude wanted Christians to remember the very words *"...spoken before by the apostles of our Lord Jesus Christ: how they told you that there would be mockers in the last time who would walk according to their own **ungodly** lusts."* (Jude 1:17-18). From ancient times, Jude also documented that, *"...Enoch, the seventh from Adam, prophesied about these men also, saying, "Behold, the Lord comes with ten thousands of His saints, to execute judgment on all, to convict all who are **ungodly** among them of all their **ungodly** deeds which they have committed in an **ungodly** way, and of all the harsh things which **ungodly** sinners have spoken against Him"* (Jude 1:14-15). Wow! I will leave discussion of the **ungodly** attribute at this point, for it is clear this attribute's influence plays a major role in the war campaign unfolding today.

The **Jealousy/Envy attribute**: This is an *unclean spirit* with two faces; one of *jealousy* and one of *envy*. Depending on life's scenario for which one is involved, this attribute can influence one to either express both *jealousy* and *envy* at the same time, or express *jealousy* or *envy* separately. But regardless of the scenario, the influence of this attributes leads one to experience extreme negative feelings and emotions toward another person.  The combined force of this attribute causes one to have:

- *an unhappy or angry feeling of wanting to have what someone else has*

- *an unhappy or angry feeling caused by the belief that someone you love (such as your husband or wife) likes or is liked by someone else*

- *painful or resentful awareness of an advantage enjoyed by another joined with a desire to possess the same advantage*

Solomon did not document a whole lot of information about this attribute. However, from what was documented, the wisdom was strong and to the point. The Spirit of wisdom began by telling Solomon "*Do not **envy** the oppressor, and choose none of his ways; for the perverse person is an abomination to the Lord...*" (Proverbs 3:31-32). Clearly, this wisdom is a mouthful. One can see the *jealousy/envy* attribute's interaction with a person influenced by the oppressor attribute, while at the same time learn this person has deeper issues. This same person is also influenced by the perverse attribute. This combination makes the person an abomination to the Lord. For Solomon, as a leader, this is one of the most important pearls of wisdom that he could learn. Consider the impact on an organization when its leader allows the influence of the *jealousy/envy* attribute and he or she is influenced to *envy* another leader with the oppressor attribute. Should that leader begin to mimic the oppressor's ways, it would not be good. The negative forces of the war campaign would grow from all corners of the organization. This book documents the oppressor attribute in a later chapter. One will learn that its influence encourages growth among the negative attributes in the war campaign. BTT allows one to see that the *jealousy/envy* attribute's influence will put one on the wrong path of life. Further Solomon documented not to let, "*...your heart **envy** sinners, but be zealous for the fear of the Lord all the day; for surely there is a hereafter, and your hope will not be cut off*" (Proverbs 23:17-18). Should one allow this attribute to influence him or her to look upon someone in sin, and desire what that person has or is doing, then one's behavior itself is sinful. One places himself or herself in a sinful state. Make no mistake, people who allow the influence of this negative attribute are engaged in sin and therefore are sinners. One cannot allow oneself to be influenced by the *jealousy/envy* attribute to *envy* sinners. The very act makes one guilty of sin. **Envying** sinners is an active exercise of the mind that brings God's punishment. Focusing on God's Word protects one from this attribute. Be zealous for His word.

The Spirit of wisdom revealed both sides of the *jealousy/envy* attribute to Solomon. He learned that, "*Whoever commits adultery with a woman lacks understanding; he who does so destroys his own soul. Wounds and dishonor he will get, and his reproach will not be wiped* *away. For **jealousy** is a husband's fury; therefore he will not spare in the day of vengeance. He will accept no recompense, nor will he be appeased though you give many gifts"* (Proverbs 6:32-35). The influence of the ***jealousy/envy*** attribute can easily enter one's inner spirit when the husband/wife relationship is defiled by the influence of the adultery attribute. The greater problem is, once the influence of the ***jealousy/envy*** attribute is aroused, the inner spirit becomes susceptible to other negative attributes as well. Other attributes can include the evil, proud, angry, furious, and violent attributes. When these attributes take root in one's inner spirit, the bloodthirsty attribute will not be far behind. BTT allows one to see that the influence of the ***jealousy/envy*** attribute can be a destructive and disruptive force in the war campaign. This attributes success creates countless victims and increased the size of the negative forces. Religious leaders have failed to teach the truth about this on many levels. Solomon also learned:

- *"A sound heart is life to the body, but **envy** is rottenness to the bones"* (Proverbs 14:30)

- *"Wrath is cruel and anger a torrent, but who is able to stand before **jealousy**?"* (Proverbs 27:4)

From both Scriptures, one can see the detrimental effects of the influence of the ***jealousy/envy*** attribute. Its corrosive influence goes deep inside the body more so than the angry and furious attributes. One can read about these attributes at the end of this chapter. But understand that the ***jealousy/envy*** attribute's destructive nature can leave carnage and collateral damage in families worldwide. This damage includes family members that seek revenge, which through a reciprocal cycle of revenge, leads others further down the path of destruction. The influence of the ***jealousy/envy*** attribute destroys whole communities when people lack an understanding of its power. Think hard on the image of Proverbs 14:30. Rotting bones are not a pleasant picture. But that is what this attribute is like and does in one's inner spirit.

There is another aspect of the ***jealousy/envy*** attribute that one needs to see to fully appreciate the power of this attribute. That is, this attribute can bond with the element of <u>covetousness</u>. When this bonding occurs, the sinful desire to take or want more than one's share of what another person has, becomes insatiable. For example, the Spirit of wisdom revealed to Solomon that *"The desire of the lazy man kills him, for his hands refuse to labor. He <u>covets</u> greedily all day long…"* (Proverbs 21:25-26). People influenced by the lazy attribute create a great mess when they also allow the combined ***jealousy/envy*** attribute and <u>covetousness</u> element to influence their inner spirit. The result is a lazy person who refuses to work and <u>covets</u> greedily all day long. BTT helps one to see that if the element of <u>covetousness</u> is present, the influences of the ***jealousy/envy*** attribute is present too which produces a desire that eventually kills. Why? Because the two negative attributes create a conflict between the person's inner spirit and mind. This conflict creates a strong greed in one's spirit against one's mental aversion to work and earn what he or she desires. This conflict literally begins to kill the person. Eventually, the influence of the wicked or evil attributes will enter the one with this conflict to scheme a way to take what is not theirs. Possibly thinking of all these things, Solomon documented that, *"…he who hates <u>covetousness</u> will prolong his days"* (Proverbs 28:16). Why?

From the statements it is obvious. The element of _covetousness_ leads one to physically place their life in a dangerous situation. To avoid this, one must train oneself to hate _covetousness_. Jesus taught this in a principle when He said, "_...it is more blessed to give than to receive_" (Acts 20:35). One should also consider the example one sets for others when one only takes from others and never gives back or help others in need.

In addition to the **_jealousy/envy_** attribute bonding with the element of _covetousness_, the **_envy_** side of this attribute also produces the by-product "_greed_." Table 22 documents some important pearls of wisdom about this by-product. The Bible documents:

"For the wicked boasts of his heart's desire; he blesses the _greedy_ and renounces the Lord" (Psalm 10:3)	"So are the ways of everyone who is _greedy_ for gain; it takes away the life of its owners" (Proverbs 1:19)	"He who is _greedy_ for gain troubles his own house, But he who hates bribes will live" (Proverbs 15:27)
"He _covets greedily_ all day long, but the righteous gives and does not spare" (Proverbs 21:26)	"...who, being past feeling, have given themselves over to lewdness, to work all uncleanness with _greediness_" (Ephesians 4:19)	"...not given to wine, not violent, not _greedy_ for money, but gentle, not quarrelsome, not _covetous_..." (1 Timothy 3:3)
"Then the Lord said to him, "Now you Pharisees make the outside of the cup and dish clean, but your inward part is full of _greed_ and wickedness" (Luke 11:39)	"Likewise deacons must be reverent, not double-tongued, not given to much wine, not _greedy_ for money..." (1 Timothy 3:8)	"For a bishop must be blameless, as a steward of God, not self-willed, not quick-tempered, not given to wine, not violent, not _greedy_ for money..." (Titus 1:7)
"For the love of money is a root of all kinds of evil, for which some have strayed from the faith in their _greediness_, and pierced themselves through with many sorrows" (1 Timothy 6:10)	"Yes, they are greedy dogs which _never have enough_. And they are shepherds who cannot understand; they all look to their own way, every one for his _own gain_, from his own territory" (Isaiah 56:11)	"Woe to them! For they have gone in the way of Cain, have run _greedily_ in the error of Balaam for profit, and perished in the rebellion of Korah" (Jude 1:11)

Table 22: Concerning the By-Product of Greed

An excellent example in the Old Testament of the _greed_ by-product is seen in Gehazi, the servant of Elisha. After God healed Naaman of leprosy, Naaman returned to Elisha to reward him for telling him what to do. However, Elisha would not accept a reward. But the Biblical record documented, "_But Gehazi, the servant of Elisha the man of God, said, "Look, my master has spared Naaman this Syrian, while not receiving from his hands what he brought; but as the Lord lives, I will run after him and take something from him_" (2 Kings 5:20). Gehazi lied to Naaman and asked for "_a talent of silver and two changes of garments_" (2 Kings 5:22). When Gehazi returned to Elisha, he lied again about going to meet up with Naaman (2 Kings 5:25). However, Elisha knew the truth and the Bible documented that Elisha told him, "_Therefore the leprosy of Naaman shall cling to you and your descendants forever._"

And he went out from his presence leprous, as white as snow" (2 Kings 5:27). Elisha remained with the negative forces of the war campaign.

Another excellent example is provided in the New Testament with a man who was baptized into Christ (Acts 8:13) out of a life of practicing sorcery (Acts 8:9). This man was named Simon. The Bible recorded that Simon *"astonished the people of Samaria, claiming that he was someone great, to whom they all gave heed, from the least to the greatest, saying, "This man is the great power of God." And they heeded him because he had astonished them with his sorceries for a long time"* (Acts 8:9-11). Upon Simon conversion, he left the sinful practice of sorcery and negative forces behind. But the negative attributes, and especially the **envy** side of the ***jealousy/envy*** attribute patiently sought an opportunity to return to Simon. Hence, the Bible documented, *"...when Simon saw that through the laying on of the apostles' hands the Holy Spirit was given, he offered them money, saying, "Give me this power also, that anyone on whom I lay hands may receive the Holy Spirit"'* (Acts 8:18-19). But Peter, seeing that Simon was *"...poisoned by bitterness and bound by iniquity"* (Acts 8:23), scolded and rejected Simon and his offer according to Acts 8:20-22. <u>Greed</u> caused Simon to reject God and return to the negative forces of the war campaign.

Further, the Spirit of wisdom revealed to Solomon that, *"The wicked <u>covet</u> the catch of evil men..."* (Proverbs 12:12). BTT helps one to see that the ***jealousy/envy*** attribute is involved here because the influence of the evil attribute has a quality that people influenced by the wicked attribute lack. That is, while the influence of the wicked attribute aids one's ability to craft excellent schemes, often the execution skills are lacking. However, catching people influenced by the evil attribute, expands the capabilities of one influenced by the wicked attribute. Do not let this wisdom escape you. Thus, the union of the two negative attributes brought together by the influence of the ***jealousy/envy*** attribute is a serious adversary in the war campaign. This twisted cycle of negative behaviors, finding solace amongst each other, fuels the war campaign, and advances it at a rapid pace. With this said, consider what the rest of the Old Testament documented about the ***jealousy/envy*** attribute.

Beginning In the Book of Exodus, *"....Jethro, the priest of Midian, Moses' father-in-law..."* (Exodus 18:1) helped Moses by providing him some useful counsel to manage the unruly children of Israel while leading them to the Promised Land. Jethro's counsel suggested that he was familiar with the ***jealousy/envy*** attribute. He told Moses, *"Listen now to my voice; I will give you counsel, and God will be with you: Stand before God for the people, so that you may bring the difficulties to God. And you shall teach them the statutes and the laws, and show them the way in which they must walk and the work they must do. Moreover you shall select from all the people able men, such as fear God, men of truth, hating <u>covetousness</u>; and place such over them to be rulers of thousands, rulers of hundreds, rulers of fifties, and rulers of tens"* (Exodus 18:19-21). Jethro's sound counsel on organizational structure and placing honorable men in leadership positions, helped defeat the influence of the ***jealousy/envy*** attribute. Hating the element of <u>covetousness</u> defused the influence of the ***jealousy/envy*** attribute. Men with the qualities that Jethro identified provided living examples for the people and appropriate leadership to assist Moses.

The Lord gave Moses commands for the children of Israel to defeat the influence of the ***jealousy/envy*** attribute. Examples of those laws included:

- *"You shall not covet your neighbor's house; you shall not covet your neighbor's wife, nor his male servant, nor his female servant, nor his ox, nor his donkey, nor anything that is your neighbor's"* (Exodus 20:17; Deuteronomy 5:21)

- The law of **jealousy** *"This is the law of **jealousy**, when a wife, while under her husband's authority, goes astray and defiles herself, or when the spirit of **jealousy** comes upon a man, and he becomes **jealous** of his wife; then he shall stand the woman before the Lord, and the priest shall execute all this law upon her. Then the man shall be free from iniquity, but that woman shall bear her guilt"* (Numbers 5:29-31; but read Numbers 5:11-31 for the full context)

- *"You shall burn the carved images of their gods with fire; you shall not covet the silver or gold that is on them, nor take it for yourselves, lest you be snared by it; for it is an abomination to the Lord your God"* (Deuteronomy 7:25)

Conversely, the Biblical record provided some examples of people who allowed the influence of the ***jealousy/envy*** attribute in their lives. Some examples included:

Who	What They Did
Arron and Mariam	The Bible documented: *"Then Miriam and Aaron spoke against Moses because of the Ethiopian woman whom he had married; for he had married an Ethiopian woman. So they said, "Has the Lord indeed spoken only through Moses? Has He not spoken through us also?" And the Lord heard it"* (Numbers 12:1-2)
Achan the son of Carmi	The Bible documented that Achan said to Joshua, *"Indeed I have sinned against the Lord God of Israel, and this is what I have done: When I saw among the spoils a beautiful Babylonian garment, two hundred shekels of silver, and a wedge of gold weighing fifty shekels, I coveted them and took them"* (Joshua 7:20-21)
Shallum king of Judah	The Lord told Shallum, *"Yet your eyes and your heart are for nothing but your covetousness, for shedding innocent blood, and practicing oppression and violence"* (Jeremiah 22:17)
Mount Seir	The Lord told Mount Seir, *"Because you have said, 'These two nations and these two countries shall be mine, and we will possess them,' although the Lord was there, therefore, as I live," says the Lord God, "I will do according to your anger and according to the **envy** which you showed in your hatred against them; and I will make Myself known among them when I judge you"* (Ezekiel 35:10-11)
The Jews and especially Jewish leadership	The Bible documented that Pilate *"...knew that they had handed Him over because of **envy**"* (Matthew 27:18; Mark 15:10)

Table 23: Examples of People who Allowed the Influence of the Jealousy/Envy Attribute

Other contributors to the Old Testament documented the influence of the ***jealousy/envy*** attribute and the element of covetousness. The Psalmist wrote, *"Teach me, O*

Lord, the way of Your statutes, and I shall keep it to the end. Give me understanding, and I shall keep Your law; indeed, I shall observe it with my whole heart. Make me walk in the path of Your commandments, for I delight in it. Incline my heart to Your testimonies, and not to <u>covetousness</u>. Turn away my eyes from looking at worthless things, and revive me in Your way..." (Psalm 119:33-37). A darker side of the ***jealousy/envy*** attribute is expressed in the Song of Solomon as the writer documented, "*Set me as a seal upon your heart, as a seal upon your arm; for love is as strong as death, **jealousy** as cruel as the grave; its flames are flames of fire, a most vehement flame*" (Song of Solomon 8:6). The author captured the essences of the cruelty and pain brought on by the influence of the ***jealousy/envy*** attribute.

All the prophets sent by the Lord warned the nation of Israel about the ***jealousy/envy*** attribute and the element of <u>covetousness</u>. The prophets pleaded with the nation of Israel to rid themselves of this attribute and return to the Lord. Some of the warning from the Lord included:

- "*...I will stretch out My hand against the inhabitants of the land,*" *says the Lord. Because from the least of them even to the greatest of them, everyone is given to <u>covetousness</u>; and from the prophet even to the priest, everyone deals falsely*" (Jeremiah 6:10-13)

- "*Woe to those who devise iniquity, and work out evil on their beds! At morning light they practice it, because it is in the power of their hand. They <u>covet</u> fields and take them by violence, also houses, and seize them. So they oppress a man and his house, a man and his inheritance*" (Micah 2:1-2)

- "*Woe to him who <u>covets</u> evil gain for his house, that he may set his nest on high, that he may be delivered from the power of disaster! You give shameful counsel to your house, cutting off many peoples, and sin against your soul. For the stone will cry out from the wall, and the beam from the timbers will answer it*" (Habakkuk 2:9-11)

As one opens the pages of the four Gospels of the Biblical record, the transition of the ***jealousy/envy*** attribute is evident along with the element of <u>covetousness</u>. Jesus identified this combination when He stated, "*...whatever enters a man from outside cannot defile him, because it does not enter his heart but his stomach, and is eliminated, thus purifying all foods?*" And He said, "*What comes out of a man, that defiles a man. For from within, out of the heart of men, proceed evil thoughts, adulteries, fornications, murders, thefts, <u>covetousness</u>, wickedness, deceit, lewdness, an evil eye, blasphemy, pride, foolishness. All these evil things come from within and defile a man*" (Mark 7:18-23). Further, Jesus stated, "*Take heed and beware of <u>covetousness</u>, for one's life does not consist in the abundance of the things he possesses*" (Luke 12:15). Once again, that strong desire to have something that someone else has, that desire to <u>covet</u> in the inner spirit, comes because the influence of the ***jealousy/envy*** attribute is present. Directly after this statement, Jesus told the parable about the rich fool in Luke 12:16-21. BTT allows one to see that this man already had more than enough to be satisfied. But consider this. The influence of the ***jealousy/envy*** attribute did not influence this man to focus on what someone else had. This time the attribute influenced him to focus on himself and to want more of what he already had. This is a mutation of the element of <u>covetousness</u> that converts to its more sinister relative called ***greed***. The rich man's appetite grew out of control to an extreme degree. Please read the parable carefully. This man lost focus on the blessings he had and his ability to help others with his vast resources. As the negative forces of the campaign influenced this man's behavior, he became a causality in the war campaign because of wealth. God cut his life short saying, "… '*Fool! This night your soul will be required of you; then whose will those things be which you have provided?*'" (Luke 12:20)". Chapter VII on the rich category will contain more detail about this parable. One will learn how people blessed with resources will either use their resources for the positive or negative forces of the war campaign.

Matthew and Mark documented that Pontius Pilate knew that during the time of Jesus, the Jewish leaders allowed the influenced of the ***jealousy/envy*** attribute in their inner spirits. These writers documented that Pilate "*…knew that they* [the Jews] *had handed Him* [Jesus] *over because of* **envy**" (Matthew 27:18; Mark 15:10). Mark specifically called out the chief priests. BTT allows one to see the pure evil of this attribute. The ***jealousy/envy*** attribute's deceptive capability can even influence one to go against the Son of God.

Other apostles had to deal with people influenced by the ***jealousy/envy*** attribute. The Biblical record documented that when Paul took the Gospel to the people of the city of Antioch, the influence of the ***jealousy/envy*** attribute manifested itself through the Jewish believers. The Bible recorded, "*On the next Sabbath almost the whole city came together to hear the word of God. But when the Jews saw the multitudes, they were filled with* **envy**; *and contradicting and blaspheming, they opposed the things spoken by Paul*" (Acts 13:44-45). BTT helps one to see how the influence of the ***jealousy/envy*** attribute moved men to attempt to stop the spread of the Gospel. Moreover, this attribute combined with other negative attributes and influenced the Jews to contradict and blaspheme scriptural prophesies from their own religious records.

In the Book of Romans, Paul provided clarity on the behavior of people influenced by the negative attributes to include the ***jealousy/envy*** attribute. Speaking about people influenced by the ungodly and unrighteous attributes, he documented "*And even as they did not like to retain God in their knowledge, God gave them over to a debased mind, to do those things which are not fitting; being filled with all unrighteousness,* **sexual immorality**, *wickedness,* covetousness, *maliciousness; full of* **envy**, *murder, strife, deceit, evil-mindedness; they are whisperers, backbiters, haters of God, violent, proud, boasters, inventors of evil things, disobedient to parents, un*discerning, *untrustworthy, unloving, unforgiving, unmerciful; who, knowing the righteous judgment of God, that those who practice such things are deserving of death, not only do the same but also approve of those who practice them*" (Romans 1:28-32). One should look very closely at the end of Paul's statement above. It contains an indictment that directly impacts the negative forces of the war campaign. Paul documented, for people with all the negative things above, they "*…not only do the same but also approve of those who practice them.*" Hence, it is imperative to teach God's Word correctly. One cannot pick and choose portions of God's Word to teach because wisdom like that above can easily be lost. It must be the whole counsel of God (Acts 20:27). Satan uses the influence of the ***jealousy/envy*** attribute, as well as the other negative attributes, to distract one from this truth. He does not want mankind to have the Truth that God has provided.

To this end, Paul documented why teaching the whole Word of God is important. He wrote, "*... I would not have known sin except through the law. For I would not have known <u>covetousness</u> unless the law had said, "You shall not <u>covet</u>.*" (Romans 7:7). BTT helps one to understand that the entire Bible is one complete Truth. Thus, the whole Bible must all be taught; not just the "good" parts or the New Testament alone. No one can fully understand the positive and negative attributes without the complete teachings of the Biblical record. Paul offered the example of the element of <u>covetousness</u> as an example.

Further, Paul documented how the influence of the ***jealousy/envy*** attribute flourished and hurt the nation of Israel. BTT allows one to see that the Jewish's leadership knew that God had planned to expand His Word to other nations. Leaders knew their nation would no longer be God's chosen people. This message was prophesized in their old manuscripts. According to the Biblical record, Jewish leaders knew and rejected God's Word. Thus Paul, "*a Pharisee, the son of a Pharisee*" (Acts 23:6) argued that the Jews "*...have not all obeyed the gospel. For Isaiah says, "Lord, who has believed our report?" So then faith comes by hearing, and hearing by the word of God. But I say, have they not heard? Yes indeed: "Their sound has gone out to all the earth, and their words to the ends of the world." But I say, did Israel not know? First Moses says: "I will provoke you to **jealousy** by those who are not a nation, I will move you to anger by a foolish nation*" (Romans 10:16-19). Because of the influence of the ***jealousy/envy*** attribute among the nation of Israel, Paul documented, "*I say then, have they stumbled that they should fall? Certainly not! But through their fall, to provoke them to **jealousy**, salvation has come to the Gentiles*" (Romans 11:11). In other words, the Jew's rejection of Christ's message pushed the Gospel out to the Gentile nations. Christians, followers of Christ, became the new nation of nations to carry on God's Word. This was a major defeat to the ***jealousy/envy*** attribute in the war campaign and a decisive victory for the positive forces of the war. Thus, Christians cannot allow themselves to be ***deceived*** by religious leaders who claim the Jewish nation will rise again in the future. The Jewish nation's roll has passed with the coming of Jesus Christ.

There are many important pearls of wisdom that the apostles documented for Christians to protect them from the influence of the ***jealousy/envy*** attribute. Some of them, for one to take to heart to protect one's inner spirit from stumbling, are:

- "*Owe no one anything except to love one another, for he who loves another has fulfilled the law. For the commandments, "You shall not commit adultery," "You shall not murder," "You shall not steal," "You shall not bear false witness," "You shall not <u>covet</u>," and if there is any other commandment, are all summed up in this saying, namely, "You shall love your neighbor as yourself." Love does no harm to a neighbor; therefore love is the fulfillment of the law*" (Romans 13:8-10)

- "*...cast off the works of darkness, and let us put on the armor of light. Let us walk properly, as in the day, not in revelry and drunkenness, not in lewdness and lust, not in strife and **envy**. But put on the Lord Jesus Christ, and make no provision for the flesh, to fulfill its lusts*" (Romans 13:12-14)

- "*...For where there are **envy**, strife, and divisions among you, are you not carnal and behaving like mere men?*" (1 Corinthians 3:1-2)

- *"...not to keep company with sexually immoral people. Yet I certainly did not mean with the sexually immoral people of this world, or with the <u>covetous</u>, or extortioners, or idolaters, since then you would need to go out of the world. But now I have written to you not to keep company with anyone named a brother, who is sexually immoral, or <u>covetous</u>, or an idolater, or a reviler, or a drunkard, or an extortioner—not even to eat with such a person"* (1 Corinthians 5:9-12)

- *"Do you not know that the unrighteous will not inherit the kingdom of God? Do not be deceived. Neither fornicators, nor idolaters, nor adulterers, nor homosexuals, nor sodomites, nor thieves, nor <u>covetous</u>, nor drunkards, nor revilers, nor extortioners will inherit the kingdom of God"* (1 Corinthians 6:9-10)

- *"Love suffers long and is kind; love does not **envy**..."* (1 Corinthians 13:4)

- *"Now the works of the flesh are evident, which are: adultery, fornication, uncleanness, lewdness, idolatry, sorcery, hatred, contentions, **jealousies**, outbursts of wrath, selfish ambitions, dissensions, heresies, **envy**, murders, drunkenness, revelries, and the like...those who practice such things will not inherit the kingdom of God"* (Galatians 5:19-21)

- *"And those who are Christ's have crucified the flesh with its passions and desires. If we live in the Spirit, let us also walk in the Spirit. Let us not become conceited, provoking one another, **envying** one another"* (Galatians 5:24-26)

- *"But fornication and all uncleanness or <u>covetousness</u>, let it not even be named among you, as is fitting for saints; either filthiness, nor foolish talking, nor coarse jesting, which are not fitting, but rather giving of thanks. For this you know, that no fornicator, unclean person, nor <u>covetous</u> man, who is an idolater, has any inheritance in the kingdom of Christ and God. Let no one deceive you with empty words, for because of these things the wrath of God comes upon the sons of disobedience. Therefore do not be partakers with them"* (Ephesians 5:3-7)

- *"Some indeed preach Christ even from **envy** and strife, and some also from goodwill: The former preach Christ from selfish ambition, not sincerely, supposing to add affliction to my chains..."* (Philippians 1:15-16)

- *"... put to death your members which are on the earth: fornication, uncleanness, passion, evil desire, and <u>covetousness</u>, which is idolatry. Because of these things the wrath of God is coming upon the sons of disobedience, in which you yourselves once walked when you lived in them"* (Colossians 3:1-7)

- For elders of the Lord's church: *"A bishop then must be blameless, the husband of one wife, temperate, sober-minded, of good behavior, hospitable, able to teach; not given to wine, not violent, not greedy for money, but gentle, not quarrelsome, not <u>covetous</u>..."* (1 Timothy 3:2-3)

- *"If anyone teaches otherwise and does not consent to wholesome words, even the words of our Lord Jesus Christ, and to the doctrine which accords with godliness, he is proud, knowing nothing, but is obsessed with disputes and arguments over words, from which come **envy**, strife, reviling, evil suspicions, useless wranglings of men of corrupt minds and destitute of the truth, who suppose that godliness is a means of gain. From such withdraw yourself"* (1 Timothy 6:3-5)

- *"For we ourselves were also once foolish, disobedient, deceived, serving various lusts and pleasures, living in malice and **envy**, hateful and hating one another"* (Titus 3:3)

- *"Let your conduct be without covetousness; be content with such things as you have. For He Himself has said, "I will never leave you nor forsake you. So we may boldly say: "The Lord is my helper; I will not fear. What can man do to me?""* (Hebrews 13:5-6)

- *"Who is wise and understanding among you? Let him show by good conduct that his works are done in the meekness of wisdom. But if you have bitter **envy** and self-seeking in your hearts, do not boast and lie against the truth. This wisdom does not descend from above, but is earthly, sensual, demonic. For where **envy** and self-seeking exist, confusion and every evil thing are there"* (James 3:13-16)

- *"Where do wars and fights come from among you? Do they not come from your desires for pleasure that war in your members? You lust and do not have. You murder and covet and cannot obtain. You fight and war. Yet you do not have because you do not ask. You ask and do not receive, because you ask amiss, that you may spend it on your pleasures"* (James 4:1-3)

- *"Therefore, laying aside all malice, all deceit, hypocrisy, **envy**, and all evil speaking, as newborn babes, desire the pure milk of the word, that you may grow thereby, if indeed you have tasted that the Lord is gracious"* (1 Peter 2:1-3)

- False prophets and false teachers: *"… By covetousness they will exploit you with deceptive words; for a long time their judgment has not been idle, and their destruction does not slumber"* (2 Peter 2:3) and false teachers: *"…They have a heart trained in covetous practices, and are accursed children"* (2 Peter 2:14)

The **Thief attribute**: The influence of this attribute is known worldwide. Although one might think that this attribute requires very little explanation, the truth is, the Biblical record shared some insights that really require one's attention. Typically, one understands that this attribute's influence leads one to **steal** by stealth or secret; or commit a crimes called larceny. This is true. However, the Biblical record helps one to understand that all crimes influenced by the **thief** attribute must be weighed separately and an appropriate punishment rendered. But here are the Biblical facts: With this attribute, a punishment is always required, the punishment must fit the crime, and there is no "one-size-fits-all" form of punishment. God demands an appropriate judgement and level of punishment by those in authority. For a **thief's** crime can be as small as **pilfering** penny items, to **stealing** to feed his or her family, to the **white collar** crime of **embezzlement**, **money laundering**, and **tax evasion**, to

kidnapping and demanding a ***ransom***. The kleptomaniac is also found among those influenced by the ***thief*** attribute.

To understand that each situation must be weighed first, the Spirit of wisdom taught Solomon that, "*People do not despise a **thief** if he steals to satisfy himself when he is starving. Yet when he is found, he must restore sevenfold; he may have to give up all the substance of his house*" (Proverbs 6:30-31). In other words, when one is placed in position in which he or she lacks the basic staples of subsistence; i.e. food, and is starving, this situation demands a different response. Prison must not be the first and only solution for one influenced by the ***thief*** attribute in this situation. The application of compassion and mercy has a role. The reason behind the crime must be evaluated. One must render responsibility and accountability in a way that offers this person an opportunity to redeem himself or herself. If not, other negative attributes gain the opportunity to root themselves in the inner spirit of the one influenced by the ***thief*** attribute. Putting one influenced by the ***thief*** attribute to work with a suitable wage to feed him or herself, and the ability to pay back the person stolen from, is the best solution. The time spent to train a person under these circumstances may count toward the repayment. Even though the influence of the ***thief*** attribute may have led an individual down the wrong path, the initial catalyst may have been preventable. In this case, a little food and an opportunity to repay may rehabilitate an individual and save their soul. Moreover, when one influenced by the ***thief*** attribute receives genuine help one in the positive forces of the war campaign, an opportunity for conversion becomes possible.

Next, the Spirit of wisdom revealed to Solomon that, "*Whoever is a partner with a **thief** hates his own life; he swears to tell the truth, but reveals nothing*" (Proverbs 29:24). Here one should recognize that, partnering with one influenced by the ***thief*** attribute, is just as bad as one having the attribute itself. Both are in sin. Consider it this way. One that has knowledge that another person is ***stealing*** and then lies about what one knows is just as guilty as the one influenced with the ***thief*** attribute. This person does not value his or her own life when he or she can tell the truth about a matter but choose to keep silent. The Spirit of wisdom revealed that this person who essentially lies for one influenced by the ***thief*** attribute hates his or her own life. In this case, the one with the knowledge of the one influenced by the ***thief*** attribute has acquired the influence of the liar and hater attributes. These attributes are discussed in detail later in this chapter of the book. All the people now involved, the one influenced by the ***thief*** attribute and whomever partnered with him or her, are all engaged in spiritual warfare and assisting the negative forces of the war campaign. This is a sad state for everyone involved.

Finally, Agur, another contributor to the book of Proverbs, commented on the ***thief*** attribute when he prayed to the Lord, "*Two things I request of You (Deprive me not before I die): remove falsehood and lies far from me; give me neither poverty nor riches— feed me with the food allotted to me; lest I be full and deny You, and say, "Who is the Lord?" or lest I be poor and **steal**, and profane the name of my God*" (Proverbs 30:7-9). Agur's comments must be taken to heart. His comments highlight the internal conflict between one's inner spirit and one's carnal side when the influence of the ***thief*** attribute gets involved. If one allows this attribute to influence one's inner spirit, it will lead one to disrespect God in one way or another.

In another part of the Old Testament, an excellent example of one influenced by the ***thief*** attribute is seen in the behavior of a rich man named Laban. One would think, since Laban was rich, there would be no reason for him to be influenced by the ***thief*** attribute. However, the example provides a superb insight into the deceptive nature of this attribute. According to Genesis 29:1-8, a man named Jacob came to the land in which Laban resided to find a wife. Jacob met, *"...Rachel the daughter of Laban his mother's brother..."* (Genesis 29:10) and he desired to marry her. When Jacob met Laban, the Bible documented, *"...Jacob loved Rachel; so he said, "I will serve you seven years for Rachel your younger daughter." And Laban said, "It is better that I give her to you than that I should give her to another man. Stay with me." So Jacob served seven years for Rachel, and they seemed only a few days to him because of the love he had for her"* (Genesis 29:18-20). At the completion of the seven years, Laban refused to give Rachael to Jacob and instead offered him Leah, his older daughter. Although this upset Jacob, he accepted Leah as his wife, and then agreed to work another seven years for Rachael, according to Genesis 29:26-28. He also remained with Laban for an additional six years according to Genesis 29:30. During all the time, Jacob worked for Laban, Laban cheated him although the Biblical record made it clear that Laban prospered mightily according to Genesis 30:30. The ***thief*** attribute influenced Laban. He cheated Jacob for twenty years. But the ***thief*** attribute strongly made itself known when Jacob decided to leave Laban with his household. Jacob's household including two wives, his children, and livestock he obtained from Laban in a deal outlined in Genesis 30:31-43. Laban attempted to stop Jacob, but he departed anyway. Laban pursued Jacob, but the Lord intervened and told Laban in a dream, *".... Be careful that you speak to Jacob neither good nor bad"* (Genesis 31:24). Although Laban was influenced by the ***thief*** attribute, he feared God more. He relented from harming Jacob according to Genesis 31:29. BTT allows one to see that God's intervention kept the other negative attributes influencing Laban under control. BTT allows one to see that, had it not been for God's intervention, the evil, furious, violent, and even bloodthirsty attributes would have influenced Laban's behavior further down a destructive path. If one is still confused as to why Laban is identified as having the influence of the ***thief*** attribute, it may be more easily understood by Jacob's own statement when he said the following words to Laban documented in Genesis 31:36-42:

> *"...What is my trespass? What is my sin, that you have so hotly pursued me? Although you have searched all my things, what part of your household things have you found? Set it here before my brethren and your brethren, that they may judge between us both! These twenty years I have been with you; your ewes and your female goats have not miscarried their young, and I have not eaten the rams of your flock. That which was torn by beasts I did not bring to you; I bore the loss of it. <u>You required it from my hand, whether stolen by day or stolen by night</u>. There I was! In the day the drought consumed me, and the frost by night, and my sleep departed from my eyes. Thus I have been in your house twenty years; I served you fourteen years for your two daughters, and six years for your flock, <u>and you have changed my wages ten times</u>. Unless the God of my father, the God of Abraham and the Fear of Isaac, had been with me, <u>surely now you would have sent me away empty-handed</u>. God has seen my affliction and the labor of my hands, and rebuked you last night."*

If one is wondering why Laban searched Jacob's things, it is because Laban's daughter Rachael had allowed the influence of the **thief** attribute in her inner spirit. She may have been more like her father than Jacob realized. The fact was Rachael was a **thief**. The Biblical record documented that she had **stolen** Laban's family idols. The Bible recorded that "*Rachel <u>had taken</u> the household idols, put them in the camel's saddle, and sat on them. And Laban searched all about the tent but did not find them. And she said to her father, "Let it not displease my lord that I cannot rise before you, for the manner of women is with me." And he searched but did not find the household idols*" (Genesis 31:34-35). BTT allows one to see that Rachael allowed the influences of the **thief** and liar attribute as well.

The Lord gave Moses a single command to give to the children of Israel to control the influence of the **thief** attribute. The command simply stated, "*You shall not **steal***" (Exodus 20:15). However, for clarity, God followed up His command with statues that Moses delivered to the people. Here are some of the statues that Moses commanded the children of Israel to follow to regulate the punishment for one influenced by the **thief** attribute:

- "*If a man **steals** an ox or a sheep, and slaughters it or sells it, he shall restore five oxen for an ox and four sheep for a sheep*" (Exodus 22:1)

- "*If the **thief** is found breaking in, and he is struck so that he dies, there shall be no guilt for his bloodshed*" (Exodus 22:2)

- "*If a man delivers to his neighbor money or articles to keep, and it is **stolen** out of the man's house, if the **thief** is found, he shall pay double*" (Exodus 22:7)

- "*If the **thief** is not found, then the master of the house shall be brought to the judges to see whether he has put his hand into his neighbor's goods. For any kind of trespass, whether it concerns an ox, a donkey, a sheep, or clothing, or for any kind of lost thing which another claims to be his, the cause of both parties shall come before the judges; and whomever the judges condemn shall pay double to his neighbor*" (Exodus 22:8-9)

- "*If a man delivers to his neighbor a donkey, an ox, a sheep, or any animal to keep, and it dies, is hurt, or driven away, no one seeing it, then an oath of the Lord shall be between them both, that he has not put his hand into his neighbor's goods; and the owner of it shall accept that, and he shall not make it good. But if, in fact, it is **stolen** from him, he shall make restitution to the owner of it. If it is torn to pieces by a beast, then he shall bring it as evidence, and he shall not make good what was torn*" (Exodus 22:10-13)

- "*If a person sins and commits a trespass against the Lord by lying to his neighbor about what was delivered to him for safekeeping, or about a pledge, or about a **robbery**, or if he has extorted from his neighbor, or if he has found what was lost and lies concerning it, and swears falsely—in any one of these things that a man may do in which he sins: then it shall be, because he has sinned and is guilty, that he shall restore what he has **stolen**, or the thing which he has extorted, or what was delivered to him for safekeeping, or the lost thing which he found, or all that* *about which he has sworn falsely. He shall restore its full value, add one-fifth more to it, and give it to whomever it belongs..."* (Leviticus 6:2-5)

What one should see is that God's commands, laws, and statues to the people placed emphasis on the serious nature of the influence of the **thief** attribute. In fact, the Lord reiterated His command to the congregation of the children of Israel when He said, *"You shall not **steal**, nor deal falsely, nor lie to one another"* in Leviticus 19:11 and again in Deuteronomy 5:19. One should notice that there is a correlation between this attribute and the liar attribute.

Achan from the tribe of Judah, allowed himself to be influenced by the **thief** attribute. When the children of Israel took the city of Jericho, the people were given instructions, *"...by all means abstain from the accursed things, lest you become accursed when you take of the accursed things, and make the camp of Israel a curse, and trouble it. But all the silver and gold, and vessels of bronze and iron, are consecrated to the Lord; they shall come into the treasury of the Lord"* (Joshua 6:18-19). But Achan ignored God's instructions and the Biblical record documented that he, *"...took of the accursed things; so the anger of the Lord burned against the children of Israel"* (Joshua 7:1). One should notice that the Lord held the entire nation of Israel accountable for Achan's actions. The Biblical record documented in Joshua 7:10-12:

> *"So the Lord said to Joshua: "Get up! Why do you lie thus on your face? Israel has sinned, and they have also transgressed My covenant which I commanded them. For they have even taken some of the accursed things, and have both **stolen** and deceived; and they have also put it among their own stuff. Therefore the children of Israel could not stand before their enemies, but turned their backs before their enemies, because they have become doomed to destruction. Neither will I be with you anymore, unless you destroy the accursed from among you."*

Joshua had all the tribes come before him including their entire households, man by man (Joshua 7:18) only to find out Achan had **stolen** the item from the destruction of Jericho. Achan confessed to having allowed the **thief** attribute to influence his behavior (Joshua 7:20-21), and Joshua sent people to recover the items from his tent (Joshua 7:22). However, Achan's confession did not relieve him of the consequences for his behavior. The Biblical record documented in Joshua 7:22-25, the following for one's learning:

> *"So Joshua sent messengers, and they ran to the tent; and there it was, hidden in his tent, with the silver under it. And they took them from the midst of the tent, brought them to Joshua and to all the children of Israel, and laid them out before the Lord. Then Joshua, and all Israel with him, took Achan the son of Zerah, the silver, the garment, the wedge of gold, his sons, his daughters, his oxen, his donkeys, his sheep, his tent, and all that he had, and they brought them to the Valley of Achor. And Joshua said, "Why have you troubled us? The Lord will trouble you this day." So all Israel stoned him with stones; and they burned them with fire after they had stoned them with stones."*

BTT helps one to see the corruptive nature of the influence of the ***thief*** attribute. What Achan did clearly impacted him and his household. Regardless of one's thoughts about the severity of the punishment, the negative forces of the war campaign would have used Achan's situation to spread sin among God's people.

Job explained the paradox of the life of one influenced by the ***thief*** attribute. He stated, *"The tents of **robbers** prosper, and those who provoke God are secure— in what God provides by His hand"* (Job 12:6). BTT allows one to understand the paradox. The paradox is that everything in the world belongs to God. We, all of mankind, are merely caretakers of the things that God has placed on earth until we die. If the Lord blesses one with anything, and another person influenced by the ***thief*** attribute comes along and takes it, then essentially the one that ***stole*** has ***stolen*** from God. Sure, one person is out of what God gave them, but the person that took without permission has provoked God. Thus, the ***robber*** that prospered and the one who provoked God are one and the same person. The ***robber*** may feel secure in the abundance that God provided (now seen from a Biblically transformed perspective); but the ***robber*** has unknowingly placed himself in grave jeopardy. This person has joined the negative forces of the war campaign. BTT allows one to see that the influence of the ***theft*** attribute provokes God. However, in spiritual warfare, people influenced by the wicked attribute use people influence of the ***theft*** attribute to maintain strife at every level in the war campaign. The negative forces use affective strategies and methodology orchestrated through financial, economic, technological, medical, academic, professional, and judicial ***thefts***. Although the strategies and methodology seem sophisticated, the behavior behind them are still basic ***thievery*** and provokes God. He will have the last say for all who engage in this sin. For the Biblical record documents, *"...we brought nothing into this world, and it is certain we can carry nothing out"* (1 Timothy 6:7).

The Psalmist documented that people with the wicked attribute (Psalm 50:16) are supporters of people influenced by the ***thief*** attribute. He wrote, *"When you saw a **thief**, you consented with him, and have been a partaker with adulterers"* (Psalm 50:18). The Psalmist words suggest one influenced by the wicked will team with one influenced by the ***thief*** attribute. Together, their union constitutes an adulterous relationship. This is a powerful team in spiritual warfare that takes out many unsuspecting people in the fog of the war. Moreover, this powerful combination increases the negative forces by taking resources away from those in need and fueling discontent and anger throughout the spiritual battlefield of the war campaign. Discontent and anger simply add more people to the negative forces of the campaign.

Further the Psalmist wrote, *"Do not trust in oppression, nor vainly hope in **robbery**; if riches increase, do not set your heart on them"* (Psalm 62:10). With the influence of the *oppressor* attribute identified in this Scripture, one can see the act of extortion expressed. For one to rely on extortion for wealth, BTT allows one see that two primary negative attributes are involved. The influence of the ***thief*** and oppressor attributes have come together to inflict strife on people. This is a manifestation of spiritual warfare at the cruelest level. One should notice that the Psalmist contends that one should not develop a dependency on this ill-gotten wealth. If not made clear already, one will learn, that God will require an account from everyone. He will avenge those who allow the influence of the ***thief*** attribute and any other negative attribute combination, to bring harm to those on the positive attribute side of the campaign.

All the prophets warned the nation of Israel about the influence of the ***thief*** attribute. The Lord was very unhappy with His people and the way they had allowed this attribute to corrupt their nation at every level. Consider some of the things documented in the Biblical record where it concerned the ***thief*** attribute in Israel. The Biblical record documented:

The Prophet	What Was Said
Jeremiah	*"As the **thief** is ashamed when he is found out, so is the house of Israel ashamed; they and their kings and their princes, and their priests and their prophets..."* (Jeremiah 2:26)
	*"Behold, you trust in lying words that cannot profit. Will you **steal**, murder, commit adultery, swear falsely, burn incense to Baal, and walk after other gods whom you do not know, and then come and stand before Me in this house which is called by My name, and say, 'We are delivered to do all these abominations'? Has this house, which is called by My name, become a den of **thieves** in your eyes? Behold, I, even I, have seen it," says the Lord"* (Jeremiah 7:8-11)
	*"Therefore behold, I am against the prophets," says the Lord, "who **steal** My words everyone from his neighbor"* (Jeremiah 23:30)
Ezekiel	*"I will turn My face from them, and they will defile My secret place; for **robbers** shall enter it and defile it"* (Ezekiel 7:22)
	*"The people of the land have used oppressions, committed **robbery**, and mistreated the poor and needy; and they wrongfully oppress the stranger"* (Ezekiel 22:29)
Hosea	*"...There is no truth or mercy or knowledge of God in the land. By swearing and lying, killing and **stealing** and committing adultery, they break all restraint, with bloodshed upon bloodshed"* (Hosea 4:1-2)
	*"As bands of **robbers** lie in wait for a man, so the company of priests murder on the way to Shechem; surely they commit lewdness"* (Hosea 6:9)
	*"When I would have healed Israel, then the iniquity of Ephraim was uncovered, and the wickedness of Samaria. For they have committed fraud; a **thief** comes in; a band of **robbers** takes spoil outside"* (Hosea 7:1)
Amos	*"For they do not know to do right,' Says the Lord, 'Who store up violence and **robbery** in their palaces"* (Amos 3:10)
Zechariah	*"This is the curse that goes out over the face of the whole earth: 'Every **thief** shall be expelled,' according to this side of the scroll; and, 'Every perjurer shall be expelled,' according to that side of it. "I will send out the curse," says the Lord of hosts; "It shall enter the house of the **thief** and the house of the one who swears falsely by My name. It shall remain in the midst of his house and consume it, with its timber and stones"* (Zechariah 5:3-4)
Malachi	*"Will a man **rob** God? Yet you have **robbed** Me! But you say, 'In what way have we **robbed** You?' In tithes and offerings"* (Malachi 3:8)

Table 24: Some of the Prophet's Warning about the Influence of the Thief Attribute

In the New Testament of the Biblical record, Jesus spoke the same thing about the influence of the ***thief*** attribute that God told the people in latter times. When a rich young ruler confronted Jesus and asked how he could have eternal life, Jesus responded, *"...Do not **steal**..."*

(Matthew 19:18; Mark 10:19; Luke 18:20). This was obviously important. First because Jesus said it; and secondly because it is recorded three times in the Gospel for our knowledge, understanding, and acceptance. But Jesus did more teachings on the influence of the **thief** attribute as he expressed to the people that they needed to focus on heavenly things and not on the material things of the world. Some of His teachings included:

- *"Do not lay up for yourselves treasures on earth, where moth and rust destroy and where **thieves** break in and **steal**; but lay up for yourselves treasures in heaven, where neither moth nor rust destroys and where **thieves** do not break in and **steal**"* (Matthew 6:19-20)

- *"Sell what you have and give alms; provide yourselves money bags which do not grow old, a treasure in the heavens that does not fail, where no **thief** approaches nor moth destroys"* (Luke 12:33)

- Concerning preparation: *"But know this, that if the master of the house had known what hour the **thief** would come, he would have watched and not allowed his house to be broken into"* (Matthew 24:43; Luke 12:39)

- Access to Christ: *"Most assuredly, I say to you, he who does not enter the sheepfold by the door, but climbs up some other way, the same is a **thief** and a **robber**"* (John 10:1)

- *"All who ever came before Me are **thieves** and **robbers**, but the sheep did not hear them. I am the door. If anyone enters by Me, he will be saved, and will go in and out and find pasture. The **thief** does not come except to **steal**, and to kill, and to destroy. I have come that they may have life, and that they may have it more abundantly"* (John 10:8-10)

- *"For what will it profit a man if he gains the whole world, and loses his own soul?"* (Mark 8:36)

Jesus recognized that the Jews continued to allow this ancient attribute to influence their behavior even in the sacred places prepared for godly worship. Just as the prophet Jeremiah called out the Jews in Jeremiah 7:11, so did Jesus. The Bible documents that *"When He had made a whip of cords, He drove them all out of the temple, with the sheep and the oxen, and poured out the changers' money and overturned the tables. And He said to those who sold doves, "Take these things away! Do not make My Father's house a house of merchandise!"* (John 2:15-16). Further, the other Gospel writers documented that Jesus said, *"Is it not written, 'My house shall be called a house of prayer for all nations'? But you have made it a 'den of **thieves**.'"* (Mark 11:17; Matthew 21:13; Luke 19:46).

Judas Iscariot allowed the influence of the **thief** attribute in his life. This attribute literally and spiritually destroyed him. The Biblical record documented Judas falsely complained that some oil, used to anoint Jesus, was wasted. The Biblical record documented, *"This he said, not that he cared for the poor, but because he was a **thief**, and had the money box; and he used to take what was put in it"* (John 12:6). Further in the Biblical record, Judas betrayed Jesus for thirty pieces of silver (Matthew 26:15) and led the multitude to arrest Him.

Jesus asked Judas and the mob that came to arrest Him, *"...Have you come out, as against a **robber**, with swords and clubs to take Me?"* (Matthew 26:55; Mark 14:48; Luke 22:52). BTT allows one to see that although Jesus knew what Judas was doing and He wanted Judas to see it for himself. However, the wealth he obtained and the influence of the ***thief*** attribute, blinded Judas.

The Biblical record also documented another person influenced by the ***thief*** attribute with Jesus at the Praetorium. As Pilate attempted to set Jesus free, a man named Barabbas was there. The Biblical record documented, *"...Barabbas was a **robber**"* (John 18:40). The Jewish leader agitated and convinced the crowd to free Barabbas; a man influenced by the ***thief*** attribute, in exchange for the death of Jesus; an innocent man. When Jesus was convicted and crucified, the Biblical documented, *"With Him they also crucified two **robbers**, one on His right and the other on His left"* (Mark 15:27; Matthew 27:38). In all these cases, the Biblical record makes it clear that to allow the influence of the ***thief*** attribute is not good.

After Jesus' death and Paul's conversion to Christianity, Paul chastised the Jewish leadership for allowing the influence of the ***thief*** attribute in their lives. Paul argued, *"You, therefore, who teach another, do you not teach yourself? You who preach that a man should not **steal**, do you **steal**?"* (Romans 2:21). Paul understood the ways of the Pharisees for he had been one himself as documented in Acts 23:6 and Acts 26:5. Paul knew that the ***thief*** attribute influenced them to confiscate the homes of widows to increase their wealth according to Matthew 23:14; Mark 12:40; and Luke 20:47. The scribes and Pharisees had become religious ***thieves***. Later, Paul would bring together the Old and New Testament's teaching on the influence of the ***thief*** attribute when he repeated what Jesus had stated, *"For the commandments, "You shall not commit adultery," "You shall not murder," "You shall not **steal**," "You shall not bear false witness," "You shall not covet," and if there is any other commandment, are all summed up in this saying, namely, "You shall love your neighbor as yourself"* (Romans 13:9). BTT helps one to see that one will not allow the ***thief*** attribute to influence his or her behavior if one truly loves others as much as he or she loves himself or herself. People influenced by the ***thief*** attribute will ***steal*** from others whose lives have no meaning to them. This behavior is created by a blindness cause by the ***thief*** attribute's influence over one's inner spirit.

Thus, Paul wrote to the church in Ephesus, *"Let him who **stole steal** no longer, but rather let him labor, working with his hands what is good, that he may have something to give him who has need"* (Ephesians 4:28). This pearl of wisdom identifies that the influence of the ***thief*** attribute can be defeated with meaningful work. Meaningful work is good and allows one's inner spirit to be satisfied. One's life gains purpose and meaning with meaningful work. Simply to have enough to be able to help others in need is satisfying for those who understand the spiritual warfare. Thus, Peter followed up on this thought by stating to Christians, *"...let none of you suffer as a murderer, a **thief**, an evildoer, or as a busybody in other people's matters"* (1 Peter 4:15). In other words, one can overcome the pain inflicted by the influence of the ***thief*** attribute by focusing on one's relationship between oneself and God. Paul reminds us that, *"...**thieves**, nor covetous, nor drunkards, nor revilers, nor extortioners will inherit the kingdom of God"* (1 Corinthians 6:10).

The **Lazy attribute**: The influence of this attribute places a major burden on society. This attribute causes one not to be inclined to do any form of work or exertion. One with this attribute has behavior that appears to lack energy or vigor. This attribute's influence leads one into idleness, sluggishness, and shortcuts to avoid work from the time one awakes to the time one finds a place  to rest one's head. When one influenced by this attribute is forced to work, passive-aggressive behaviors are expressed in all work-related activities. Whether the activity is physical, mental, emotional, or spiritual, the influence of the *lazy* attribute does not discriminate. This person will expend great energy seeking shortcuts or alternate ways to accomplish tasks rather than simply completing the task at hand. The behavior influenced by this attribute places well defined knowledge, experience, and safety standards at risk. The influence of this attribute causes one to simply give up or quit a task that is perceived to be too hard. One influenced by this attribute squanders all learning opportunities and benefits. Squandered opportunities can even include learning information that might preserve their health, family relationships, and financial wellbeing. In fact, the influence of the *lazy* attribute will spread like a plague among people if it is allowed to persist. It leads other people to follow its deceptive ways. When the influence of the *lazy* attribute is present among workers, the workers work less than their coworkers. Their behavior instigates a perception that some people can do less work than others and still receive the same benefits. This insidious perception causes a slowdown in workplace productivity and performance. Shortcuts are taken, safety standards are violated, integrity issues increase, and the overall function of the workplace shows signs of dysfunction. Over time, this attribute's influence begins to breed animosity, strife, favoritism, and a host of other workplace issues. This is an active strategy of the negative forces of the war campaign perpetrated by the influence of the *lazy* attribute. Moreover, this strategy causes dysfunction in one's home and throughout the business world. The influence of the *lazy* attribute generates morale issues that destroys both homes and businesses when the strategy is successfully implemented. Only shrewd leaders and managers with the positive attributes will catch the negative attribute's efforts among his or her employees in time. This same principle applies to parents with *lazy* children and vice versa. Finally, this attribute is the spirit of complacency. In Christ's church, this **unclean spirit** influences people not to evangelize, visit the sick and shut-in, or participate in other related services and activities that edify the Lord.

Other negative attributes aid the *lazy* attribute through the invention of evil things (Romans 1:30), distractions such as the cares of this world, the deceitfulness of riches, the desires for other things (Mark 4:18-19), and the pleasures of life (Luke 8:14). The influence of this attribute causes more members of the Lord's church to stumble more than any other attribute. BTT allows Christians to see that there is always work to be done. Even Jesus told his disciples, "...*The harvest truly is plentiful, but the laborers are few*" (Matthew 9:37). God wants workers! Next to the unfaithful attribute, this attribute is the most detrimental to the Lord's church because it creates complacency. Complacency among God's worker allows false religious teaching to proliferate on the battlefield.

Solomon observed the behavior of a person influenced by the *lazy* attribute. He documented, "*I went by the field of the lazy man, and by the vineyard of the man devoid of understanding; and there it was, all overgrown with thorns; its surface was covered with* nettles; its stone wall was broken down. When I saw it, I considered it well; I looked on it and received instruction: A little sleep, a little slumber, a little folding of the hands to rest; so shall your poverty come like a prowler, and your need like an armed man" (Proverbs 24:30-34). Based on Solomon's observation, one can easily see how the influences of the **lazy** attribute was slowly destroying the person he observed. From this insight, Solomon stated that the one influenced by the **lazy** attribute was devoid of understanding. This person failed to see how they were a victim of the war campaign. The influence of the **lazy** attribute rendered this person useless. He squandered his blessing. He had the ability to help himself and others from the land he possessed. This person was now one that needed help. BTT allows one to see that this person's own behavior and inactivity had trapped him in a life of poverty. His inner spirit was compromised. Solomon documented more pearls of wisdom about this attribute to include:

"He who gathers in summer is a wise son; he who **sleeps** in harvest is a son who causes shame" (Proverbs 10:5)	"As vinegar to the teeth and smoke to the eyes, so is the **lazy** man to those who send him" (Proverbs 10:26)	"A **lazy** man buries his hand in the bowl, and will not so much as bring it to his mouth again" (Proverbs 19:24)
"The soul of a **lazy** man desires, and has nothing..." (Proverbs 13:4)	"In all labor there is profit, but **idle** chatter leads only to poverty" (Proverbs 14:23)	"The way of the **lazy** man is like a hedge of thorns..." (Proverbs 15:19)
"He who is **slothful** in his work is a brother to him who is a great destroyer" (Proverbs 18:9)	"**Laziness** casts one into a deep sleep, and an idle person will suffer hunger" (Proverbs 19:15)	"The **lazy** man does not roast what he took in hunting..." (Proverbs 12:27)
"The **lazy** man will not plow because of winter; he will beg during harvest and have nothing" (Proverbs 20:4)	"Do not love **sleep**, lest you come to poverty; open your eyes, and you will be satisfied with bread" (Proverbs 20:13)	"The desire of the **lazy** man kills him, for his hands refuse to labor. He covets greedily all day long..." (Proverbs 21:25, 26)
"Do not mix with winebibbers, or with gluttonous eaters of meat; for the drunkard and the glutton will come to poverty, and **drowsiness** will clothe a man with rags" (Proverbs 23:20, 21)	"As a door turns on its hinges, so does the **lazy** man on his bed" (Proverbs 26:14)	"The **lazy** man is wiser in his own eyes than seven men who can answer sensibly" (Proverbs 26:16)
"The **lazy** man buries his hand in the bowl; it wearies him to bring it back to his mouth" (Proverbs 26:15)	A Virtuous wife: "She watches over the ways of her household, and does not eat the bread of **idleness**" (Proverbs 31:27)	"Because of **laziness** the building decays, and through **idleness** of hands the house leaks" (Ecclesiastes 10:18)

Table 25: Pearls of Wisdom Concerning the Influence of the Lazy Attribute

As Solomon processed information about the influence of the **lazy** attribute that he learned from the Spirit of wisdom, he understood that he could not allow people influenced by this attribute to become a burden to his kingdom. He understood that simply feeding or allowing them free access to the wealth of his kingdom, without contributing themselves, was bad for the survival of the kingdom. Thus, Solomon documented that, "*The hand of the diligent will rule, but the **lazy** man will be put to forced labor*" (Proverbs 12:24). In other words, to combat the corrosive influence of the **lazy** attribute, able-bodied people would not be able to simply receive their livelihood from the work of others; everyone would contribute through work. This is significant spiritual wisdom. People influenced by the **lazy** attribute were forced to work. The negative forces of the war campaign want this fact struck from the Biblical record and hidden from today's eyes. However, Solomon's advice to people influenced by the **lazy** attribute was simple; he said, "*Prepare your outside work, make it fit for yourself in the field; and afterward build your house*" (Proverbs 24:27). In other words, get out there and work; rid oneself of the **lazy** attribute. Further Solomon documented, "*Do you see a man who excels in his work? He will stand before kings; he will not stand before unknown men*" (Proverbs 22:29). This is an incentive to work. Good leaders understand that acknowledgment of good work is important at every level. People laden with the influence of the negative attributes neither understand nor acknowledge this spiritual truth.

To understand the strength of the **lazy** attribute's influence over one gripped by it, Solomon documented two important insights from the Spirit of wisdom. He wrote, "*The **lazy** man says, "There is a lion outside! I shall be slain in the streets!"*" (Proverbs 22:13) and within the same context, "*The **lazy** man says, "There is a lion in the road! A fierce lion is in the streets!"*" (Proverbs 26:13). BTT allows one to see that the point of these two verses illustrates the inaction by one influenced by the **lazy** attribute. One with this attribute will see danger coming but not lift a finger to do anything about it. This includes saving themselves. Their preference is for someone else to expend their energy on the task or risk their life for theirs. This hypocrisy is a trait that runs deep inside the inner spirit of one influenced by the **lazy** attribute and causes great tension and frustration in the war campaign on both sides.

Solomon learned a lot from the Spirit of wisdom about the **lazy** attribute. In fact, he even learned that nature provided examples of what God intended for mankind concerning work. The Spirit of wisdom told Solomon to observe the behavior of the "ant." The ant provides to this very day, an example of the right attitude and behavior towards work and defeating the influence of the **lazy** attribute. Solomon documented, "*Go to the ant, you **sluggard**! Consider her ways and be wise, which, having no captain, overseer or ruler, provides her supplies in the summer, and gathers her food in the harvest. How long will you slumber, O **sluggard**? When will you rise from your sleep? A little sleep, a little slumber, a little folding of the hands to sleep— So shall your poverty come on you like a prowler, and your need like an armed man*" (Proverbs 6:6-11).

In the Old Testament of the Biblical record, the first pearl of wisdom to illustrate that God required man to work to defeat the influence of the **lazy** attribute began with Adam. When the Lord first created man, the Biblical record documented that God, "*...took the man and put him in the Garden of Eden to <u>tend</u> and <u>keep</u> it*" (Genesis 2:15). This was man's first job connected to his wellbeing, health, and happiness. However, the job became labor with man's sin when he and the woman were cast out of the garden. For the Biblical record documented when Adam and Eve were expelled, the Lord told the man, "*...Cursed is the ground for your* *sake; in <u>toil</u> you shall eat of it all the days of your life"* (Genesis 3:17). From this point on, the standard for man was set; he would labor (work) to keep from becoming **idle.**

BTT allows one to see that the influence of the ***lazy*** attribute played a role with Eve too. The time she spent with the serpent, and the time she spent contemplating whether she should or should not bite the forbidden fruit, was **idle** time. Instead of focusing on the work of the Lord, her behavior provided a victory for the negative forces of the war campaign. There are many examples in the record that make this point.

Another example is that of Cain, Adam and Eve's firstborn. The influence of the ***lazy*** attribute played a role in Cain's inability to follow God's instruction. When the Lord told Cain, *"If you do well, will you not be accepted? And if you do not do well, sin lies at the door. And its desire is for you, but you should rule over it"* (Genesis 4:7), essentially God told him to increase his efforts. However, Cain was unwilling. The ***lazy*** attribute was influencing him to seek another way. He thought he had another way by murdering his competition; his only brother, Abel. Other examples of scriptures that support the idea of work to defeat the influence of the ***lazy*** attribute include:

- God telling the children of Israel, *"Six days you shall <u>labor</u> and do all your <u>work</u>..."* (Exodus 20:9)

- *"When you eat the <u>labor of your hands</u>, you shall be happy, and it shall be well with you"* (Psalm 128:2)

- *"In all <u>labor</u> there is profit, but **idle** chatter leads only to poverty"* (Proverbs 14:23)

- *"The person who <u>labors</u>, <u>labors</u> for himself, for his hungry mouth drives him on"* (Proverbs 16:26)

- *"All things are full of <u>labor</u>; man cannot express it..."* (Ecclesiastes 1:8)

- *"Nothing is better for a man than that he should eat and drink, and that his soul should enjoy good in his <u>labor</u>. This also, I saw, was **from the hand of God**"* (Ecclesiastes 2:24); Ecclesiastes 3:13 said, *"...**it is the gift of God**"*, and Ecclesiastes 5:18 documented, *"...his <u>labor</u> in which he **toils** under the sun all the days of his life which God gives him; for **it is his heritage**."*

- *"The sleep of a <u>laboring</u> man is sweet, whether he eats little or much; but the abundance of the rich will not permit him to sleep"* (Ecclesiastes 5:12)

Moses had to deal with the influence of the ***lazy*** attribute as it influenced the children of Gad and Reuben. The Biblical record documented that Moses told them, *"Shall your brethren go to war while you **sit here**? Now why will you discourage the heart of the children of Israel from going over into the land which the Lord has given them?"* (Numbers 32:6-7). Further he told them, *"But if you do not do so, then take note, you have sinned against the Lord; and be sure your sin will find you out"* (Numbers 32:23). Fortunately, both tribes came to their senses and they helped the children of Israel. They left their families in place, crossed over the Jordan, and helped Joshua subdue the people in the land of Canaan. Afterwards, they returned to the families.

The prophet Job provided a critical insight on the Lord's view of one who allows the influence of the ***lazy*** attribute in his or her life. He documented that the Lord, "*...repays man according to his <u>work</u>, and makes man to find a reward according to his way*" (Job 34:11). This statement recognizes that the Lord blesses one according to the work he or she accomplishes in life. Notice there is no amount of work specified. However, based on the statement itself, God weighs honest work while the amount of work rest on one's shoulders. What one does, and the amount accomplished, is strictly up to the person. However, in spiritual warfare, if one does little, one's reward will be less than one who does a lot. Further, if one allows the influence of the ***lazy*** attribute into one's inner spirit, one can only expect a ***lazy*** man's reward. This is pure and simple wisdom. Hence, Solomon documented, "*...God will bring every work into judgment, including every secret thing, whether good or evil*" (Ecclesiastes 12:14). This includes every work - work done and work **sloughed** off.

The Psalmist documented that God's great mercy will judge one with the ***lazy*** attribute appropriately. He documented, "*...to You, O Lord, belongs mercy; for You render to each one according to his work*" (Psalm 62:12). BTT helps one to see that the ***lazy*** attribute must be overcome. One must engage in the many works that the Lord has sat before His creation to do. Good works are plentiful and necessary due to the effects of the war campaign. However, the deceitfulness of the negative forces use of spiritual warfare is steadily confusing good and bad works as one and the same. Discernment is critical today. Please do not be deceived.

A final point about the ***lazy*** attribute from the Old Testament is that this attribute had some involvement in Sodom and Gomorrah's destruction. The prophet Ezekiel, comparing the behavior of Jerusalem to these cities in Ezekiel 16:35-48, said from the Lord, "*Look, this was the iniquity of your sister Sodom: She and her daughter had pride, fullness of food, and abundance of **idleness**; neither did she strengthen the hand of the poor and needy. And they were haughty and committed abomination before Me; therefore I took them away as I saw fit*" (Ezekiel 16:49, 50). The ***lazy*** attribute was rampant in both Sodom and Jerusalem.

In the New Testament of the Biblical record, Jesus identified the influence of the ***lazy*** attribute among the Pharisees. They failed to put effort into understanding and teaching the whole Truth of the Old Testament prophesies. Jesus stated that they had both the evil and ***lazy*** attribute when he said to them, "*A good man out of the good treasure of his heart brings forth good things, and an evil man out of the evil treasure brings forth evil things. But I say to you that for every **idle** word men may speak, they will give account of it in the Day of Judgment. For by your words you will be justified, and by your words you will be condemned*" (Matthew 12:35-37). BTT allows one to see that this statement, although directed at the Pharisees, applies to all people in general who take shortcuts with His Word. One must invest work into understanding God's whole Word.

Jesus identified the influence of the ***lazy*** attribute using a parable. He spoke about people standing around in the marketplace when there was plenty of work to be done. I encourage one to read the whole parable in Matthew 20:1-16. It will help one understand that there is plenty of work to be found but the influence of the ***lazy*** attribute blinds one to the work available. This was the case with the people that the landowner wanted to hire to work in his vineyard according to Matthew 20:1. He hired some people right away at an agreed price. The Biblical record documented that he searched for others to work and recorded "...*about the third hour and saw others standing **idle** in the marketplace*" (Matthew 20:3). Searching for more, around the eleventh hour, he "...*found others standing **idle**, and said to them, 'Why have you been standing here **idle** all day*?" (Matthew 20:6). But look closer.

Implied in the parable, the first groups of people who chose to work, may have carried the influence of the ***lazy*** attribute with them. As the attribute matured, their work may have been impacted. The quality and quantity of work they performed may have been substandard. Hence, the landowner sought more workers from the pool that was available. But with the influence of the ***lazy*** attribute rampant among the workers, hiring more only increased the measure of the attribute in the original workers and therefore fed the negative forces that were breeding in the campaign. In the end, the work was completed, but the first people hired were dissatisfied with their pay. The first people hired received the same pay as the people hired last according to Matthew 20:10-12. BTT requires that one closely look at the situation before making any judgements. Many people view this situation and assume the landowner was not fair in his pay to the laborers. The landowner aptly stated, "*Friend, I am doing you no wrong. Did you not agree with me for a denarius? Take what is yours and go your way. I wish to give to this last man the same as to you. Is it not lawful for me to do what I wish with my own things? Or is your eye evil because I am good?*" (Matthew 20:13-15). BTT allows one to see upon closer inspection, the people hired first may have allowed the influence of the ***lazy*** attribute. This may have promoted the landowner to hire more workers. If the next workers were influenced by this attribute too, the landowner had every right to hire more. The landowner's pay was not required to be any higher or lower than the price he chose to offer. The workers chose to accept the "agreed amount". There are many applications of Jesus point on the spiritual level concerning the selection process (Matthew 20:16) and those influenced by the ***lazy*** attribute. But in the case of spiritual warfare, the parable illustrates that the influence of this attribute will lead one to do little work while expecting to gain much from his or her personal sacrifice of their time.

In another parable, Jesus compared the kingdom of heaven and a man traveling to a faraway country, while illustrating how the influence of the **lazy** attribute can have crippling effects on people. He stated that a traveler gave his servants money in the form of Roman talents, to invest while he was away. He gave one person five talents, another two, and to another one talent. The parable made it clear that each person was given an amount of talents, "...*according to his own ability*" (Matthew 25:15). The first two people, the ones given the five and two talents, were productive. But the third was not. The traveler returned expecting a yield from the investments of his money. His expectations were satisfied by the first two people, but not by the third. For the third person, after listening to his justification of ***laziness***, the traveler said, "...*You wicked and **lazy** servant, you knew that I reap where I have not sown, and gather where I have not scattered seed*" (Matthew 25:26). BTT allows one to see that just as Jesus makes an investment in each of us, a reasonable return on His investment is expected. However, if the influence of the ***lazy*** attribute is allowed in one's inner spirit, one becomes unproductive just like the third person described in Jesus' parable. Moreover, the scripture says, "*For to everyone who has, more will be given, and he will have abundance; but from him who does* *not have, even what he has will be taken away. And cast the unprofitable servant into the outer darkness. There will be weeping and gnashing of teeth*" (Mathew 25:29-30). Thus, people who work with what they are given, will receive even more. People who allow the influence of the ***lazy*** attribute, and refuse to work with what they have, will eventually lose everything.

BTT allows one to see that the influence of the ***lazy*** attribute, along with other negative attributes, will be behind the reason many people miss their opportunity for heaven. The Biblical record documented from Jesus, "*...'Depart from Me, you cursed, into the everlasting fire prepared for the devil and his angels: for I was hungry and you gave Me no food; I was thirsty and you gave Me no drink; I was a stranger and you did not take Me in, naked and you did not clothe Me, sick and in prison and you did not visit Me.' "Then they also will answer Him, saying, 'Lord, when did we see You hungry or thirsty or a stranger or naked or sick or in prison, and did not minister to You?' Then He will answer them, saying, 'Assuredly, I say to you, inasmuch as you did not do it to one of the least of these, you did not do it to Me.' And these will go away into everlasting punishment, but the righteous into eternal life*" (Matthew (25:41-46). Clearly, the influence of the ***lazy*** attribute is involved in the above situations and the negative forces of the war campaign are in full play. The influence of the ***lazy*** attribute stops one from doing what God specifically said to go and do by His Word.

Jesus shared another example of how the influence of the ***lazy*** attribute affects people in the religious community. Jesus spoke of a man robbed by thieves and left for dead. A priest and a Levite passed by and did nothing to aid the man left in this disturbing condition. Documented in Luke 10:30-37, the priest and the Levite saw the man stripped, wounded, and left half dead (Luke 25:30) but still refused to help him. The ***lazy*** attribute, along with many other negative attributes, was clearly influencing the priest and Levites's behaviors. These religious men had become pawns of the negative forces of the war campaign. BTT allows one to see that even religious people, whom one would expect to be on the positive side of the campaign, can be deceived. BTT allows one to see that the smallest measure of positive attributes will always compel a person to action in some way. This is good news. As one reads the rest of the scenario, one learns that someone influenced by the positive attributes came along and helped the fallen man in a remarkable way. The chapter on the positive attributes will go into more detail on this portion of the scenario. But please understand, the priest and the Levite were participants in spiritual warfare and aided the negative forces of the war campaign.

When Paul wrote to the church in Thessalonica, he also pushed the idea of working to defeat the influence of the ***lazy*** attribute. He wrote the church stating, "*...you also aspire to lead a quiet life, to mind your own business, and to <u>work</u> with your own hands, as we commanded you, that you may walk properly toward those who are outside, and that you may lack nothing*" (1 Thessalonians 4:11). Work keep one's focus on the good things of life and help fends off the influence of the ***lazy*** attribute. Paul even documented that he and the others traveling with him - worked. He documented, "*...nor did we eat anyone's bread free of charge, but <u>worked</u> with <u>labor</u> and <u>toil</u> night and day, that we might not be a burden to any of you, not because we do not have authority, but to make ourselves an example of how you should follow us*" (2 Thessalonians 3:8-9). Paul understood the effects of the influence of the ***lazy*** attribute and the perception it created for others. This attribute's influence on a person leads them to quickly point out the inactivity of someone else to deflect attention away from themselves. To make it even more clear to the readers of his letter, Paul wrote, *"For even when we were with you, we commanded you this: If anyone will not <u>work</u>, neither shall he eat"* (2 Thessalonians 3:10). Why? Because Paul knew there were some people already influenced by the ***lazy*** attribute. They just wanted to live off the work of others. This behavior creates many problems. Paul addressed this when he documented, *"For we hear that there are some who walk among you in a disorderly manner, <u>not working at all</u>, but are busybodies"* (2 Thessalonians 3:11). So, he told them, *"Now those who are such we command and exhort through our Lord Jesus Christ that they <u>work</u> in quietness and eat their own bread"* (2 Thessalonians 3:12). If you look at what Paul said, one can see that the influence of the ***lazy*** attribute had the effect of causing people to *"walk disorderly"* and be *"busybodies."* BTT allows one to see these effects aid the war campaign by maintaining strife, confusion, and division. The behavior also prevents the hearing of the positive attribute's message.

When Paul wrote young Timothy, he addressed the influence of the ***lazy*** attribute by some of its many behavioral trait. He addressed ***idleness*** and ***idle*** talk stating:

- *"...charge some that they teach no other doctrine, nor give heed to fables and endless genealogies, which cause disputes rather than godly edification which is in faith...some, having strayed, have turned aside to **idle** talk, desiring to be teachers of the law, understanding neither what they say nor the things which they affirm"* (1 Timothy 1:6)

- Concerning younger widows: *"...they learn to be **idle**, wandering about from house to house, and not only **idle** but also gossips and busybodies, saying things which they ought not"* (1 Timothy 5:13)

- *"O Timothy! Guard what was committed to your trust, avoiding the profane and **idle** babblings and contradictions of what is falsely called knowledge"* (1 Timothy 6:20)

- *"...shun profane and **idle** babblings, for they will increase to more ungodliness"* (2 Timothy 2:16)

When Paul wrote Titus, he documented a list of strong qualifications required of men selected to be elders in the Lord's church in Titus 1:5-9. The qualifications where necessary for defending the truth against people influenced by the ***lazy*** attribute; people who would not invest time in reading, searching, and studying God's Word. Paul wrote, *"For there are many insubordinate, both **idle** talkers and deceivers, especially those of the circumcision, whose mouths must be stopped, who subvert whole households, teaching things which they ought not, for the sake of dishonest gain"* (Titus 1:10-11). These individuals, influenced by the ***lazy*** attribute, are ones who take short cuts with God's Word, who do not invest in the study of His Word for complete understanding, and who pick and choose references to satisfy their audience's ears. Elders in the Lord's church have the tasks of stopping people influenced by the ***lazy*** attribute, who use their tongue as a tool, and attempt to hinder God's work.

Further Paul told Titus, *"This is a faithful saying, and these things I want you to affirm constantly, that those who have believed in God should be careful to maintain good <u>works</u>.*

These things are good and profitable to men" (Titus 3:8). If one immerses himself or herself in good works, one will fight off the influences of the ***lazy*** attribute. Further Paul wrote, "*And let our people also learn to maintain good <u>works</u>, to meet urgent needs, that they may not be unfruitful*" (Titus 3:14). The influence of the ***lazy*** attribute leads one to become unfruitful to the Lord. Unfruitful behavior extends to others including family, one's community, society, and life in general. In the war campaign, people influenced by the ***lazy*** attribute become massive burden on societies and nations. The negative forces of the campaign use the ***lazy*** attribute in a tactical maneuver to slow down the advances of the positive forces with people who refuse to work. Unfruitful behavior in spiritual warfare is often reflected in the work of evangelism. Positive forces are often forced to spend precious time correcting people influenced by this attribute which takes time away from work needed on the spiritual battlefield. Moreover, misguided governmental efforts designed to equalize wealth through social programs deceptively induce large communities of people to this attribute. No matter how good the intentions are, if God's principles are absent from the programs, they will fail. The negative forces of the campaign keep this fact silenced in the fog of the campaign.

BTT allows one to see another correlation between work and the ***lazy*** attribute in the words of James. Within the war campaign, the influence of the ***lazy*** attribute deceives some people within the positive forces to believe that the Lord requires no work from them as a condition to make it to heaven. James wrote, "*What does it profit, my brethren, if someone says he has faith but does not have <u>works</u>? Can faith save him? If a brother or sister is naked and destitute of daily food, and one of you says to them, "Depart in peace, be warmed and filled," but you do not give them the things which are needed for the body, what does it profit? Thus also faith by itself, if it does not have <u>works</u>, is dead*" (James 2:14-17). From the context, one can see that God does require work, along with the faith attribute, as part of one's responsibility for salvation. The influence of the ***lazy*** attribute deceives one into believing that for a person to be saved, they only need to accept God's Word in their heart. This is a deceptive strategy generated by the negative forces of the campaign to hinders the work of the positive forces and the Lord's church. BTT allows one to see that the influence of the faith attribute, discussed later in this book, shares a symbiotic relationship with work. However, one influenced by the ***lazy*** attribute cannot understand this divine relationship. Hence, one with the ***lazy*** attribute will attempt to claim the influence of the faith attribute in their life while justifying their lack of work. But people with the positive attributes know the value of the symbiotic relationship between faith and works. They will not deny or hide this truth from others. Moreover, the influence of the ***lazy*** attribute deceives one to believe that supporting secular and religious charitable organizations can substitute and satisfy God's requirements for good works. The Biblical record in no way supports this belief. Jesus said, "*And he who does not take his cross and follow after Me is not worthy of Me*" (Matthew 10:38). Taking up one cross and following Jesus is work. This work is one's personal responsibility. One cannot hand this work off to others and expect Jesus' reward. One must not allow the influence of the ***lazy*** attribute to deceive and cost one his or her opportunity for heaven. The negative forces' strategy in the war campaign is to use the influence of the ***lazy*** attribute to deceive the inner spirits of anyone and everyone who will listen.

Parents influenced by the *lazy* attribute, who refuse to expose their children to the Bible, are the greatest asset to the negative forces of the war campaign. Early exposure to the truth is vital for each generation. Children will be engaged, willingly or unwillingly, in the fight of the campaign. This fact is true for every culture in the world whether they believe in God or not. John documented that Jesus stated, "*...behold, I am coming quickly, and My reward is with Me, to give to every one according to his <u>work</u>*" (Revelation 22:12). Do not be deceived! As for Christians, God expects every Christian to do their share of work while on earth. Conversely, the influence of the *lazy* attribute works feverishly to convince them that there is always another way. Many Christians today are headed down a deceptive path because of the *lazy* attribute's influence.

The **Oppressor attribute**: This attribute influences one to spiritually and mentally burden or crush another person by abusing their authority, power, or influence over them. It is the ***unclean spirit*** that has influenced men to enslave others, to suppress women and races of people, deny equal employment and pay, and force religious beliefs on others. In spiritual warfare, the ***oppressor*** attribute ***oppresses*** either directly or indirectly. The direct mode is when one influenced by this attribute applies ***oppressive*** measures to another person by their own power. The indirect mode is when one influenced by this attribute uses another person in some established leadership hierarchy to ***oppress*** another person. The results are the same, but the latter mode protects the true ***oppressor's*** identity. Moreover, a person acting on behalf of an anonymous ***oppressor*** will often use ***oppressive*** tactics more aggressively to accomplish the true ***oppressor's*** objective. The use of the element of <u>fear</u> is an extremely aggressive tactic employed on behalf of an anonymous ***oppressor***. Fear tactics can be physical or verbal threats; which are no more than bullying, up to actual physical abuse. Gang and mafia leaders employ these tactic. But regardless of who allows the ***oppressor*** attribute, whether the one who carries out the instructions of the ***oppressor*** or the primary ***oppressor*** in anonymity, all involved in the ***oppressive*** behavior are guilty of the sin. BTT also allows one to see that this attribute has many tools in its arsenal to ***oppress*** others. Sexual and physical harassment, hazing, and verbal, mental, and physical abuse are just a few. More importantly, one needs to understand that this ancient ***unclean spirit*** cannot be controlled by earthly laws. It is a mutative attribute that influences it host to manifests itself in forms that ***oppress*** others through acts of domineering, favoritism, discrimination, and economic disparity. In spiritual warfare, this attribute inflicts devastation across the full spectrum of the spiritual battlefield in the war campaign. The ***oppressor*** attribute's objective is to eliminate an ***oppressed*** person's ability to reach for the spiritual element of "*hope*". I will discuss this element shortly. For now, understand that the ***oppressor*** attribute uses active domination, control, and <u>fear</u> tactics to keep an ***oppressed*** person bogged down in a spiritual fight. The person who allows the influence of the ***oppressor*** attribute seeks to drive the ***oppressed*** people into a spiritual hole for total control. The ***oppressor*** attribute will manifest itself as "spiritual pressure" in the form of money, bills, drugs, alcohol, bullying, responsibilities, and life. BTT allows one to see that the spiritually ***oppressed*** person, that loses hope, will eventually fall into a state of spiritual depression which leads to a spiritual paralysis. This person's behavior then becomes irrational for they cannot think clearly nor see a way out of their situation. **Figure 19** depicts this situation. BTT allows one to see set from this position of control, the ***oppressor*** attribute then influences the ***oppressed*** person to feel like he or she is alone and socially isolated while physically surrounded by a sea of people.

Now "_hope_" is a spiritual element that one's inner spirit has for something that one has asked for to occur. The Biblical record documented, "..._if we hope for what we do not see, we eagerly wait for it with perseverance_" (Romans 8:25). However, BTT allows one to see that one who allows the influence of the ***oppressor*** attribute will use unjust and excessive force to destroy the element of _hope_ in another person. In fact, BTT helps one to understand the extremely dangerous results of one with this attribute. When the influence of the ***oppressor*** attribute fully matures in one's inner spirit, it influences one to excessively bully others. Bullying pushes the person ***oppressed*** to a point

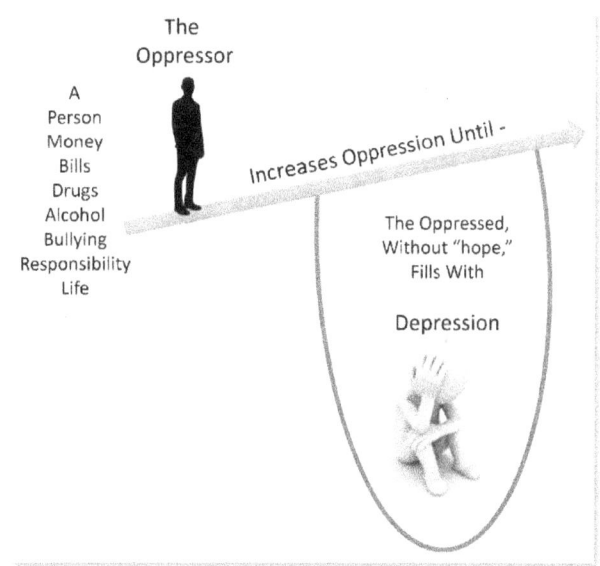

Figure 19: The Oppressors VS the Oppressed

where extreme measures must be considered for self-defense. The ***oppressed*** person, depending on their situation, may seek support from people influenced by the positive attributes. This is their best option. However, they may turn to others influenced by negative attributes to alleviate their problem. Worse yet, they may open the door for the influence of negative attributes to influence them and take matters into their own hands. Often, when negative forces influence one that is ***oppressed***, he or she retaliates. These last two options set conditions for disaster, strife, and chaos on the spiritual battlefield.

Another option available to the one ***oppressed*** involves negative behavioral activities to escape the weight imposed by one with the ***oppressor*** attribute. These activities include the use of alcohol, drugs, fantasy engagement, adulterous escapades, and the ultimate escape – suicide. When a person ***oppressed*** becomes severely depressed and loses all _hope_ and perspective of their life, he or she begins to contemplate suicide. Without God's Word, the act of suicide will occur. This is especially true among people in the younger generations who lack the maturity to weigh positive options. Without a healthy respect for God's Word, sound teaching about spiritual life and death, and the consequences of good and bad behavior, suicide rates will only increase for the youth and immature on the spiritual warfare. **Figure 20** illustrates the overall scenario. Hence, elimination of this attribute from one's inner spirit is paramount. God's Word is the key for eliminating the influence of this attribute and the strife that it brings to the spiritual battlefield. Moreover, BTT allows one to see that when a person can rationalize committing suicide, he or she has given in to the wiles of the devil (Ephesians 6:11) and the negative spiritual forces. For once the act of suicide is carried out, that person has no avenue to repent of their grave error. For as sensitive as this subject is, in the war campaign, this error is equivalent to taking an innocent life and murder even though one took their own life. This truth highlights the complexity of the war campaign and one should pay close attention to the section concerning the bloodthirsty attribute.

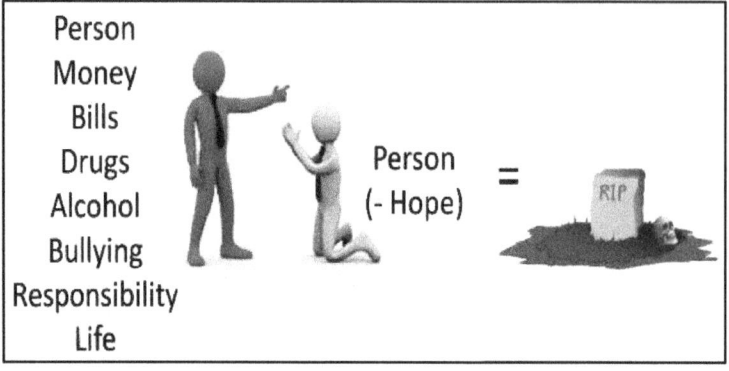

Figure 20: The Oppressor Attribute, Hope, and Death

The Spirit of wisdom revealed to Solomon that, "*A ruler who lacks understanding is a great **oppressor**...*" (Proverbs 28:16). For anyone in a leadership position, this is one of the most important pearls of wisdom that one can ever learn. If the leader or manager allows the influence of the **oppressor** attribute, just imagine what it is like at every level below his or her authority. The environment becomes toxic for everyone in the organization. BTT helps one to understand that where the influence of the **oppressor** attribute reigns, other negative attributes prosper greatly – especially the wicked and evil attributes. The world today is rampant with people influenced by the **oppressor** attribute. Moreover, the Spirit of wisdom revealed to Solomon that one should, "*...not envy the **oppressor**, and choose none of his ways; for the perverse person is an abomination to the LORD ....*" (Proverbs 3:31-32). That's right. Wisdom revealed to Solomon that one with the **oppressor** attribute also has the perverse attribute. Review the documentation presented earlier in this chapter on the perverse attribute if necessary. Consider, from the Scripture above, this person has two combined negative attributes influencing their behavior. This combination makes them also an "*abomination to the LORD.*" These are tough words of condemnation from the Spirit of wisdom that should make one tremble. So why would one want to envy someone with these negative attributes? Because they do not understand spiritual warfare and are blinded by the fog generated from the negative forces of the war campaign.

Further, the Spirit of wisdom revealed to Solomon that people influenced by the **oppressor** attribute afflict people in the poor category. Chapter VII covers the people of the poor category. Reasons vary for this phenomenon, but it is a fact of spiritual warfare. The Spirit of wisdom revealed to Solomon that "*He who **oppresses** the poor to increase his riches, and he who gives to the rich, will surely come to poverty*" (Proverbs 22:16). BTT allows one to see that in this case, one influenced by the **oppressor** attribute **oppresses** people in the poor category by taking what little resources they have from them. Why? Because in the war campaign, people in the poor category are considered easy targets who cannot afford to financially fight back. One influenced by the **oppressor** attribute harms the poor to enrich either himself or herself, or to give the resources to someone in the rich category for recognition, or for some other perverse reason. In the campaign, this behavior is rampant and a constant source of consternation, strife, and frustration that keeps people in the poor category disenfranchised. Moreover, this activity hinders masses of people from learning any of God's Truth; thereby indirectly building the negative forces of the war campaign. However, it is the last part of Wisdom's statement that most people miss because of the confusion of the war. That is, Wisdom stated that both the one influenced by the **oppressor** attribute and the one in the rich category that accepted resources from the one influenced by the **oppressor** attribute, will both "*surely come to poverty*" (Proverbs 22:16). Why? Because Wisdom also revealed to Solomon, "*Do not rob the poor because he is poor, nor* **oppress** *the afflicted at the gate; for the LORD will plead their cause, and plunder the soul of those who plunder them*" (Proverbs 22:22-23). In other words, the Lord watches out for the people in the poor category.

But one influenced by the **oppressor** attribute may also be in the poor category. Sadly, this person may **oppress** someone else that he or she feels is beneath them. This happens in many societies and cultures today as it has for thousands of years. To this, Solomon documented "*A poor man who* **oppresses** *the poor is like a driving rain which leaves no food*" (Proverbs 28:3). BTT allows one to see the tragedy of this situation. For a person in the poor category to allow the influence of the **oppressor** attribute and then **oppress** someone in the same poor state, is a tragedy of epic proportions. Both people will find nothing but pain. The poor person **oppressed** has nothing to give. So the poor **oppressor** gains nothing that can satisfy their internal inner spirit's pain. Situations like this make the person who allowed the influence of the **oppressor** attribute more susceptible to the influence of other negative attributes for satisfaction. Hence, their satisfaction may be in the form of sexual abuse and perversion on the person in the poor category. This behavior fuels the campaign with a steady source of people; the **oppressor**, the **oppressed**, and people who knew but said or did nothing to intervene. The elements of <u>fear</u> or <u>complacency</u> may have a role here, but they are not acceptable excuses. To this end, the Spirit of wisdom revealed to Solomon that, "*The poor man and the* **oppressor** *have this in common: The LORD gives light to the eyes of both*" (Proverbs 29:13). BTT allows one to see that regardless of the way things appear, the Great God of heaven is still in control of life. Whether one finds himself or herself in the poor category or allows the influence of the **oppressor** attribute, God allows each person to live their life until the judgment. This means there is no difference in the opportunity God gives for one to correct mistakes in one's life. The Lord gives everyone time and opportunity to correct mistakes while they can still see the sunlight that is common to all. However, the Spirit of wisdom still made it clear to Solomon that, "*He who* **oppresses** *the poor reproaches his Maker...*" (Proverbs 14:31). In context, this statement means that the person who allows the influenced of the **oppressor** attribute shows disapproval, disdain, or disrespect to God. It is the act of shaking one's fist at God in defiance. This act is a form of blasphemy. The Biblical record documents that this behavior will be punished. This wisdom applies regardless of one's status in life.

The Biblical record provides many examples of people influenced by the **oppressor** attribute. One of the most notorious **oppressors** found in the Biblical record was the Egyptian Pharaoh before the birth of Moses. He enslaved the children of Israel according to the Book of Exodus. The **oppressor** attribute influenced this Pharaoh so strongly that the Biblical record documented the Lord Himself heard the cry of the Israelites. Further, the Lord said, "*...I have surely seen the* **oppression** *of My people who are in Egypt, and have heard their cry because of their taskmasters, for I know their sorrows*" (Exodus 3:7). Later the Lord said, "*...Now* *therefore, behold, the cry of the children of Israel has come to Me, and I have also seen the* **oppression** *with which the Egyptians* **oppress** *them"* (Exodus 3:9). From the Israelites perspective, the Biblical record documented that *"...the Egyptians mistreated us, afflicted us, and laid hard bondage on us. Then we cried out to the Lord God of our fathers, and the Lord heard our voice and looked on our affliction and our labor and our* **oppression***"* (Deuteronomy 26:6-7). The Lord, moved with compassion, decided to bring the children of Israel out of the land of their **oppressors**. If you have never read the full story about the children of Israel, I encourage you to do so. One will see the power of the Lord through a story filled with love and encouragement.

After Moses was born, grew into a man, and led the children of Israel out of Egypt, the Lord gave him some commands to help Israel overcome the influence of the **oppressor** attribute. Now one would think that after *"four hundred and thirty years"* (Exodus 12:40) of bondage and **oppression**, the children of Israel would not need to be told not to **oppress** another person. But they did. This phenomenon illustrates the strength and corrosive nature of the **oppressor** attribute. The children of Israel, with their freedom and new wealth, allowed the influences of the negative attributes, including the **oppressor** attribute, in their lives. God had to put restraints in place to govern their behavior. Thus, Moses told the people from the Lord:

- *"You shall neither mistreat a stranger nor* **oppress** *him, for you were strangers in the land of Egypt"* (Exodus 22:21)

- *"Also you shall not* **oppress** *a stranger, for you know the heart of a stranger, because you were strangers in the land of Egypt"* (Exodus 23:9)

- *"In this Year of Jubilee, each of you shall return to his possession, and if you sell anything to your neighbor or buy from your neighbor's hand, you shall not* **oppress** *one another"* (Leviticus 25:14)

- *"Therefore you shall not* **oppress** *one another, but you shall fear your God; for I am the Lord your God"* (Leviticus 25:17)

- Concerning escaped slaves: *"He may dwell with you in your midst, in the place which he chooses within one of your gates, where it seems best to him; you shall not* **oppress** *him"* (Deuteronomy 23:16)

- *"You shall not* **oppress** *a hired servant who is poor and needy, whether one of your brethren or one of the aliens who is in your land within your gates"* (Deuteronomy 24:14)

Just as the Lord gave commands to Moses for the children of Israel to defeat the **oppressor** attribute, He also informed them of what would happen if they violated His commands. BTT helps one to see, since God knew their future, He gave them everything necessary to survive the onslaught of negative forces of the campaign poised to ensnare them. Thus, God had Moses tell the children of Israel, if they disobeyed His laws: *"...you shall grope* *at noonday, as a blind man gropes in darkness; you shall not prosper in your ways; you shall be only **oppressed** and plundered continually, and no one shall save you*" (Deuteronomy 28:29). Worse yet, Moses told them, "*A nation whom you have not known shall eat the fruit of your land and the produce of your labor, and you shall be only **oppressed** and crushed continually*" (Deuteronomy 28:33). With these warnings, the children of Israel could not plead ignorance to the knowledge of their future. But even with these warnings, they willfully sinned. After Moses died, Joshua led the children of Israel. When he died, the Lord placed a series of judges over the people to manage them. However, true to His Word, the Lord sent nations, heavily influenced by the **oppressor** attribute to **oppress** the children of Israel to modify their behavior.

The Book of Judges documented this well. In this Biblical reference, the Lord stated, "*Did I not deliver you from the Egyptians and from the Amorites and from the people of Ammon and from the Philistines? Also the Sidonians and Amalekites and Maonites **oppressed** you; and you cried out to Me, and I delivered you from their hand. Yet you have forsaken Me and served other gods. Therefore <u>I will deliver you no more</u>.* "*Go and cry out to the gods which you have chosen; let them deliver you in your time of distress.*" *And the children of Israel said to the Lord, "We have sinned! Do to us whatever seems best to You; only deliver us this day, we pray." So they put away the foreign gods from among them and served the Lord. And His soul could no longer endure the misery of Israel*" (Judges 10:11-16). Eventually, the children of Israel got tired of the judges that God had placed over them and they demanded a king instead. According to 1 Samuel 8:3-5, the new nation of Israel desired leadership like the other nations. Samuel, the last judge appointed by God, reluctantly crowned a king for them. Unfortunately, King Saul the first king allowed the influence of the wicked and **oppressor** attributes, and eventually went insane. The Lord replaced King Saul with King David whom Saul once tried to murder. The Biblical record documented that God made a covenant with David and told him, "*...I will appoint a place for My people Israel, and will plant them, that they may dwell in a place of their own and move no more; nor shall the sons of wickedness **oppress** them anymore...*" (2 Samuel 7:10). Although God did as He said, the nation of Israel failed to do their part and the negative forces of the war campaign overwhelmed their inner spirits.

The prophet Job provided great insights into the influence of the **oppressor** attribute. He became a victim of the greatest **oppressor** - Satan. But he kept his faith in God to see him through his affliction. He lost his entire family and wealth (Job 1:13-22) and his health to painful boils (Job 2:7) which caused him severe **depression**. His wife then allowed the influence of the **oppressor** attribute and told Job, "*...Curse God and die!*" (Job 2:9). She became an **oppressor** to Job instead of his helpmate. But this did not break Job's inner spirit. So, as Job suffered physically, mentally, and emotionally, Satan sent him misguided friends who allowed the influence of the **oppressor** attribute to corrupt them. They became Job's final **oppressors** in his spiritual battle. These were misguided but wise friends; Eliphaz, Bildad, Zophar and Elihu, and were used by Satan in an attempt to destroy a man influenced by the righteous attribute (Job 1:1; Ezekiel 14:14; 14:20). BTT allows one to see that this is the end-state for the negative forces of the war campaign, to eliminate all righteousness from the face of the earth. The Biblical record documented that Job confronted his **oppressors** after their continued verbal assaults on him and said "*This is the portion of a wicked man with God, and the heritage of **oppressors**, received from the Almighty: If his children are multiplied, it is for the sword; and his offspring shall not be satisfied with bread. Those who survive him shall be buried in death, and their widows shall not weep, though he heaps up silver like dust, and piles up clothing like clay— He may pile it up, but the just will wear it, and the innocent will divide the silver*" (Job 27:13-17). Job's comment was aimed at his friends. He wanted to help them understand the plight of people who allow the **oppressor** and the wicked attributes in their lives. BTT allows one to see that Job's statement applies to this very day.

The Psalmist also talked about the **oppressor** attribute. Using both prayers and songs, he asked the Lord to relieve him of his **oppressors**. Documented below are just a few of the insights he provided about the influence of the **oppressor** attribute for our learning. The Psalmist wrote:

- For people influenced by the wicked attribute, he wrote, "*His mouth is full of cursing and deceit and **oppression**; under his tongue is trouble and iniquity*" (Psalm 10:7) and that, "*They scoff and speak wickedly concerning **oppression**; they speak loftily*" (Psalm 73:8)

- "*Do not trust in **oppression**, nor vainly hope in robbery; if riches increase, do not set your heart on them*" (Psalm 62:10)

- Specifically to leaders with the **righteous** attribute, "*bring justice to the poor of the people; he will save the children of the needy, and will break in pieces the **oppressor***" (Psalm 72:4)

The Psalmist also documented a few pearls of wisdom to comfort people who become victims of one influenced by the **oppressor** attribute. He documented that the Lord:

- "*…will be a refuge for the **oppressed**, a refuge in times of trouble*" (Psalm 9:9)

- "*…will cause Your ear to hear, to do justice to the fatherless and the **oppressed**, that the man of the earth may **oppress** no more*" (Psalm 10:18)

- "*For the **oppression** of the poor, for the sighing of the needy, now I will arise,*" says the Lord; "*I will set him in the safety for which he yearns*" (Psalm 12:5)

- "*…executes righteousness and justice for all who are **oppressed***" (Psalm 103:6)

When Solomon penned the Book of Ecclesiastes during his epic search for truth, knowledge, and understanding of wisdom, he discovered some interesting facts about the influence of the **oppressor** attribute. He wrote, "*Then I returned and considered all the **oppression** that is done under the sun: And look! The tears of the **oppressed**, but they have no comforter— on the side of their **oppressors** there is power, but they have no comforter*" (Ecclesiastes 4:1). In other words, the influence of the **oppressor** attribute brought misery to both the **oppressed** and the **oppressor** alike. Neither person finds comfort when acts of

oppression occur. BTT allows one to see that this phenomenon is part of the grand strategy of the negative forces in the war campaign. This strategy keeps masses of people frustrated, upset, and unable to concentrate on the Truth of God's Word. For this phenomenon, Solomon concluded that the dead had it better than the living and people who never existed had it best according to Ecclesiastes 4:2-3. Further, Solomon documented, *"If you see the **oppression** of the poor, and the violent perversion of justice and righteousness in a province, do not marvel at the matter; for high official watches over high official, and higher officials are over them"* (Ecclesiastes 5:8). Once again, one can see the folly of allowing the influence of the ***oppressor*** attribute. God's justice is designed with accountability and responsibility built into it. Humanity causes justice to fail; not God. However, God is the Ultimate Judge and He will hold the highest officials accountable. However, Solomon still pointed out man's folly concerning the influence of the ***oppressor*** attribute when he said, *"Surely **oppression** destroys a wise man's reason..."* (Ecclesiastes 7:7). The point here is that wise people in the world see ***oppression*** and yet fail to see its true origin. They dismiss the fact that it stems from spiritual warfare to reason their own causes, effects, and solutions. Unfortunately, because of their ignorance to God's Truth, the overwhelming spiritual reality generated by the ***oppressor*** attribute simply blinds them and destroys their solutions. Truth lies in the understanding of spiritual warfare and the campaign itself. Solomon understood the war campaign.

The rest of the books of the Old Testament takes one back to the plight of God's people dealing with the ***oppressor*** attribute. The prophets of God continued their pleading with the nation of Israel to repent and remove the influence of the ***oppressor*** attribute from among them. Here are some of the many things from the prophets that documented the presence of the ***oppressor*** attribute's influence. The Biblical record documented:

The Prophet	What Was Said
Isaiah	*"Learn to do good; seek justice, rebuke the **oppressor**; defend the fatherless, plead for the widow"* (Isaiah 1:17)
	*"The people will be **oppressed**, everyone by another and every one by his neighbor; the child will be insolent toward the elder, and the base toward the honorable"* (Isaiah 3:5)
	*"As for My people, children are their **oppressors**, and women rule over them. O My people! Those who lead you cause you to err, and destroy the way of your paths"* (Isaiah 3:12)
	*"For the vineyard of the Lord of hosts is the house of Israel, and the men of Judah are His pleasant plant. He looked for justice, but behold, **oppression**; for righteousness, but behold, a cry for help"* (Isaiah 5:7)
	*"Therefore thus says the Holy One of Israel: "Because you despise this word, and trust in **oppression** and perversity, and rely on them, therefore this iniquity shall be to you like a breach ready to fall, a bulge in a high wall, whose breaking comes suddenly, in an instant"* (Isaiah 30:12-13)
	*"In transgressing and lying against the Lord, and departing from our God, speaking **oppression** and revolt, conceiving and uttering from the heart words of falsehood. Justice is turned back, and righteousness stands afar off; for truth is fallen in the street, and equity cannot enter"* (Isaiah 59:13-14)

Jeremiah	*"For thus has the Lord of hosts said: "Cut down trees, and build a mound against Jerusalem. This is the city to be punished. She is full of **oppression** in her midst"* (Jeremiah 6:6)
	*"O house of David! Thus says the Lord: "Execute judgment in the morning; and deliver him who is plundered out of the hand of the **oppressor**, lest My fury go forth like fire and burn so that no one can quench it, because of the evil of your doings"* (Jeremiah 21:12)
	*"Thus says the Lord: "Execute judgment and righteousness, and deliver the plundered out of the hand of the **oppressor**. Do no wrong and do no violence to the stranger, the fatherless, or the widow, nor shed innocent blood in this place"* (Jeremiah 22:3)
	Warns Shallum the son of Josiah, king of Judah: *"…your eyes and your heart are for nothing but your covetousness, for shedding innocent blood, and practicing **oppression** and violence"* (Jeremiah 22:17)
	*"Thus says the Lord of hosts: "The children of Israel were **oppressed**, along with the children of Judah; all who took them captive have held them fast; they have refused to let them go"* (Jeremiah 50:33)
Amos	*"Hear this word, you cows of Bashan, who are on the mountain of Samaria, who **oppress** the poor, who crush the needy, who say to your husbands, "Bring wine, let us drink!"* (Amos 4:1)
Hosea	*"A cunning Canaanite! Deceitful scales are in his hand; he loves to **oppress**"* (Hosea 12:7)
	*"Ephraim is **oppressed** and broken in judgment, because he willingly walked by human precept"* (Hosea 5:11)
Micah	*"They covet fields and take them by violence, also houses, and seize them. So they **oppress** a man and his house, a man and his inheritance"* (Micah 2:2)
Habakkuk	*"Will not your creditors rise up suddenly? Will they not awaken who **oppress** you? And you will become their booty"* (Habakkuk 2:7)
Zechariah	*"Do not **oppress** the widow or the fatherless, the alien or the poor. Let none of you plan evil in his heart against his brother"* (Zechariah 7:10)
Ezekiel	The prophet Ezekiel clarified that one has the *just* attribute and shall surely live, *"If he has not **oppressed** anyone…"* (Ezekiel 18:7)
	In contrast, Ezekiel clarified one does not have just attribute, *"If he has **oppressed** the poor and needy…"* (Ezekiel 18:12)
	Ezekiel pointed out all the sins of Jerusalem saying, *"In you they have made light of father and mother; in your midst they have **oppressed** the stranger; in you they have mistreated the fatherless and the widow"* (Ezekiel 22:7)
	*"The people of the land have used **oppressions**, committed robbery, and mistreated the poor and needy; and they wrongfully **oppress** the stranger"* (Ezekiel 22:29)

Table 26: Some of the Prophet's Warnings Concerning the Oppressor Attribute

The Old Testament of the Biblical record makes it clear that the influence of the **oppressor** attribute is bad One must not allow it to influence his or her inner spirit. Jesus Christ identifies Himself as the defender of the **oppressed** in the New Testament. The Biblical record documented that Jesus said, *"The Spirit of the Lord is upon Me, because He has anointed Me to preach the gospel to the poor; He has sent Me to heal the brokenhearted, to proclaim liberty to the captives and recovery of sight to the blind, to set at liberty those who* are ***oppressed**, to proclaim the acceptable year of the Lord"* (Luke 4:18-19). BTT allows one to see that God gave His Son, Jesus Christ, all authority to fix the issues of people's lives where their inner spirits are enslaved by the manifestations of the negative forces of the war campaign. This also includes the behaviors and acts of the ***oppressor*** attribute for those who believe in Him. However, one needs to understand that the negative forces of the campaign actively fight against Jesus and His Word with a vengeance. In fact, people heavily influenced by the ***oppressor*** attribute attacked Jesus. Sadly, what the prophet Isaiah prophesized in Isaiah 53 came to pass. The Biblical record documented in Isaiah 53:7-9:

> *"He was **oppressed** and He was afflicted, yet He opened not His mouth; He was led as a lamb to the slaughter, and as a sheep before its shearers is silent, so He opened not His mouth. He was taken from prison and from judgment, and who will declare His generation? For He was cut off from the land of the living; for the transgressions of My people He was stricken. And they made His grave with the wicked— but with the rich at His death, because He had done no violence, nor was any deceit in His mouth."*

Stephen reminded the nation of Israel of their past issues with the influence of the ***oppressor*** attribute before he was murdered. He told the Jewish high priest, *"But God spoke in this way: that his descendants would dwell in a foreign land, and that they would bring them into bondage and **oppress** them four hundred years"* (Acts 7:6). Stephen reminded them of the Pharaoh that did not know their patriarch Joseph, and how the Pharaoh, *"...dealt treacherously with our people, and **oppressed** our forefathers, making them expose their babies, so that they might not live"* (Acts 7:19). One may recall that this was the Pharaoh of Egypt who decreed the slaughter of countless Hebrew babies. The Lord saved Moses from this slaughter. Moses was able to grow up in the comfort of the Pharaoh's household. From his comfortable position, Moses saw the effects of the influence of the ***oppressor*** attribute firsthand on the Hebrew slaves. The Biblical record documented that on one occasion, Moses, *"...seeing one of them suffer wrong, he defended and avenged him who was **oppressed**, and struck down the Egyptian"* (Acts 7:24). Moses fled to Midian and the Lord revealed Himself there. He stated to Moses, *"I have surely seen the **oppression** of My people who are in Egypt; I have heard their groaning and have come down to deliver them. And now come, I will send you to Egypt"* (Acts 7:34). Thus, Stephen recounted to the Jews how the influence of the ***oppressor*** attribute caused many issues in their early history. According to Acts 8:58, the Jews rejected Stephen's words and stoned him to death.

Peter went to Cornelius's house to preach the gospel and commented on Jesus' role in dealing with the aftermath of people influenced by the source of the ***oppressor*** attribute. Peter told Cornelius, *"...how God anointed Jesus of Nazareth with the Holy Spirit and with power, who went about doing good and healing all who were **oppressed** by the <u>devil</u>, for God was with Him"* (Acts 10:38). Peter's comment deserves our close attention. For he shared a critical piece of information about the influence of the ***oppressor*** attribute. From Peter's statement, one learns that the devil is directly behind this attribute's ability to influence one's behavior. This is why this attribute has so much success in the campaign. Cornelius and his entire household were baptized into Christ after Peter talked with him. The Word of God and baptism placed Cornelius and his family firmly on the positive side of the war campaign from that day forward. As long as they stayed in God's Word, Cornelius and his family would have the tools to defeat the influence of the ***oppressor*** and any other negative attribute.

James documented some wisdom concerning this attribute and people blessed to be in the rich category. He highlighted an example of what some people in this category do towards people in the poor category when they allow the influence of the ***oppressor*** attribute in their inner spirit. Writing to Christians, James wrote, "*Listen, my beloved brethren: has God not chosen the poor of this world to be rich in faith and heirs of the kingdom which He promised to those who love Him? But you have dishonored the poor man. Do not the rich **oppress** you and drag you into the courts? Do they not blaspheme that noble name by which you are called?*" (James 2:5-7). BTT allows one to see that many people in the rich category end up on the side of the negative forces of the war campaign. This happens primarily because they do not know God's Word, are unaware of the spiritual war campaign, or feel they are above the Word of the Bible. BTT allows one to see that wealth can create a false sense of security. One will get the facts on this subject in Chapter VII on the people in the rich category. However, when a Christian defers to one in the rich category, because of partiality or favoritism over one in the poor category, that Christian has engaged in sin. Not only has he or she dishonored the person in the poor category, but he or she has also blasphemed the Christian name. Moreover, BTT allows one to see that the behavior is one of ***oppression*** for the one in the poor category. One must not show favoritism regardless of another person's status or financial state. God will judge one harshly for this self-righteous act. One should read James 5:1-8. It also documented the behavior of one influenced by the ***oppressor*** attribute, although the attribute was not named specifically. However, BTT allows one to see the behavior of the one in the rich category along with the influence of the ***oppressor*** and thief attributes that influenced that person's inner spirit.

The ***oppressor*** attribute's influence was active among the men and women of Sodom and Gomorrah. Peter documented their conduct when he wrote that God, "*...delivered righteous Lot, who was **oppressed** by the filthy conduct of the wicked, (for that righteous man, dwelling among them, tormented his righteous soul from day to day by seeing and hearing their lawless deeds)...*" (2 Peter 2:7-9). BTT allows one to see that filthy conduct is ***oppressive*** to anyone who obeys the will of God and lives for Christ. Anyone who lives his or her life around sustained filthy conduct is susceptible to the influences of the ***oppressor*** attribute. In addition, other negative attributes are sure to lurk in the filth too. But just like Lot, to be saved one must eventually leave the filth and depend on God. To do so, one must hear and believe the words written in the Biblical record to rise above the fog generated by the negative forces of the war campaign.

The **Seducer attribute**: The influence of this attribute causes a person to lead others astray by using enticing words and/or sexually provocative behavior. This attribute influences one to dress provocatively and attempts to keep all attention focused on himself or herself for the sole purpose of control. The ***seducer*** attribute's influence is more coercive, deceitful, and persuasive than the adulterer attribute. Like the adulterer attribute, Satan uses this ***unclean spirit*** to destroy husband and wife relationships. The ***seducer*** attribute seeks total control of a person, whereas the adulterer attribute initially simply seeks sport or temporary pleasure. Thus, one influenced by the ***seducer*** attribute uses persuasive words, looks, and behavior to influence others to:

- Commit inappropriate sexual relationship to include perverse and adulterous ones
- Commit disobedient and disloyal acts
- Stray from previous commitments by using false promises
- Engage in financial exploitation

Solomon used the image of a women influenced by the immoral attribute and involved in prostitution as a means to convey how strong the ***seducer*** attribute's influence was on an unsuspecting person. His example was not a derogatory statement towards women and nor was it about women at all. If he had meant it this way, the Spirit of wisdom would have corrected him immediately. She did not (Proverbs 8) and the example is document in the Biblical record. We must have faith. One cannot allow the negative forces of the war campaign to cloud his or her thoughts with deceptive worldly thinking. Thus, with this image, Solomon explained how the influence of the ***seducer*** attribute unites with the immoral attribute to ensnare an unsuspecting soul. The imagery provides form and substance for one's mind to visualize the interaction of these negative attributes in the physical world. Solomon documented how Wisdom herself, "*...delivers you from the immoral woman, from the **seductress** who flatters with her words, who forsakes the companion of her youth, and forgets the covenant of her God*" (Proverbs 2:16-17). Learning from the Spirit of wisdom, Solomon documented that one influenced by the ***seducer*** attribute uses the power of words to entice people's inner spirits. Proverbs 7:5-21 also documented more but specifically Solomon wrote, "*With her enticing speech she caused him to yield, with her flattering lips she **seduced** him*" (Proverbs 7:21). Here is the critical lessen not to be miss between these two important references on the ***seducer*** attribute. One influenced by this attribute has no power over another person until that person stops to listen to the ***seducer's*** words. Thus, when one has God's Word, he or she has no need to stop and hear words from someone else proclaiming it from another source. God's Word provides all one needs on. In fact, the Spirit of wisdom revealed how to escape the entrapment of one influenced by the ***seducer*** attribute. Solomon documented, "*... Reproofs of instruction are the way of life, to keep you from the evil woman, from the flattering tongue of a **seductress***" (Proverbs 6:23-24). What are reproofs of instruction? Solomon wrote, "*When wisdom enters your heart, and knowledge is pleasant to your soul, discretion will preserve you; understanding will keep you...*" (Proverbs 2:10-11). Reproofs are rebukes one gains from wisdom, knowledge, discretion, and understanding embedded in God's Word. These reproofs of instruction keeps one on the right path of life. However, reproofs are only useful when one is willing to listen to what is in God's written Word.

Solomon further documented that, "*...a **seductress** is a narrow well. She also lies in wait as for a victim, and increases the unfaithful among men*" (Proverbs 23:27-28). Using the same imagery of the prostitute, Solomon illustrated both the behavior and power of the influence of the **seducer** attribute. When this attribute influences one's inner spirit, it leads him or her to patiently wait for control of a person he or she desires. Solomon understood that the tools of this attribute are so good, many men fall prey to its intoxicating behavior. In the war campaign, men that fall to people influenced by this attribute are not only **seduced**, they also allow the influence of the unfaithful and adultery attributes in their inner spirit. Wow! God does not accept ignorance in this matter. One is only entrapped by a person influenced by the **seducer** attribute, when he or she is not content with what God has given them. There is a hidden desire for something else. This ancient attribute's influence knows how to draw secrets out.

Hence, Solomon stressed the marriage relationship with one's own wife and not allowing oneself to be **seduced** into an ungodly relationship. Solomon warned that this attribute's traps were for the wicked and he warned his son not to be counted among them. Thus Solomon documented, "*Drink water from your own cistern, and running water from your own well. Should your fountains be dispersed abroad, streams of water in the streets? Let them be only your own, and not for strangers with you. Let your fountain be blessed, and rejoice with the wife of your youth. As a loving deer and a graceful doe, let her breasts satisfy you at all times; and always be enraptured with her love. For why should you, my son, be enraptured by an immoral woman, and be embraced in the arms of a **seductress**? For the ways of man are before the eyes of the LORD, and He ponders all his paths. His own iniquities entrap the wicked man, and he is caught in the cords of his sin. He shall die for lack of instruction, and in the greatness of his folly he shall go astray*" (Proverbs 5:15-23). BTT allows one to see that the married person that falls prey to one with the **seducer** attribute is now guilty of the wicked, unfaithful, and adultery attributes too.

The Spirit of wisdom told Solomon of an important legal maneuver for dealing with one influenced by the **seducer** attribute. Twice Solomon documented, "*Take the garment of one who is surety for a stranger, and hold it as a pledge when it is for a **seductress***" (Proverbs 20:16) and "*Take the garment of him who is surety for a stranger, and hold it in pledge when he is surety for a **seductress***" (Proverbs 27:13). In both comments, BTT allows one to see the legal tactic of acquiring a piece of evidence to hold one influenced by the **seducer** attribute accountable. "Surety" is something tangible, written, or binding that can be used in a legal setting to show evidence of a transaction. One influenced by the **seducer** attribute will avoid formal evidence by keeping all agreements and statements verbal. However, "surety;" something binding or showing evidence of an agreement, will hold one influenced by the **seducer** attribute accountable in a court of law. The Bible provides an excellent example of this in Genesis 38:6-10 in the case of Tamar versus Judah. I encourage one to read God's Word on this matter.

Now consider what the rest of the Biblical record documents about the influence of the **seducer** attribute. In the Garden of Eden, the first example of the **seducer** attribute is found with a cunning serpent documented in Genesis 3:1. This serpent began a conversation with Eve to **seduce** her into taking its words over the Lord's Word. The Bible documented that Eve knew what God had said about eating from the tree of knowledge of good and evil (Genesis 2:9; 2:17), and she even repeated God's Word to the serpent (Genesis 3:2-3). However, she listened to the **seductive** words of the serpent anyway. The serpent told Eve that by eating from the tree,

"*...You will not surely die. For God knows that in the day you eat of it your eyes will be opened, and you will be like God, knowing good and evil*" (Genesis 3:4-5). The serpent **seduced** Eve with a thought that intoxicated her with desire. The Bible recorded, "*So when the woman saw that the tree was good for food, that it was pleasant to the eyes, and a tree desirable to make one wise, she took of its fruit and ate*" (Genesis 3:6). She disobeyed God's Word. Then she gave the fruit to her husband Adam and both fell into sin. But make no mistake, the **seducer** attribute initiated this event as it found an opportunity in the woman because of her desire to be wise. The point here is that the influence of the **seducer** attribute cannot **seduce** a person if there is no place to gain a foothold. This point hangs on two important variables to be effective. The first variable is one must know God's Word to be saved by it. The second variable is one must be obedient to God's Word to be saved by it. Only when one puts these variables in motion in his or her life, can one expect the protection necessary for defending oneself from the influence of the **seducer** attribute in the war campaign.

The women of Moab were identified with the influence of the **seducer** attribute. The Biblical record documented that they **seduced** many of the children of Israel in Acacia Grove after the Lord freed the children from bondage in Egypt. The Bible recorded that the women, "*...invited the people to the sacrifices of their gods, and the people ate and bowed down to their gods. So Israel was joined to Baal of Peor, and the anger of the Lord was aroused against Israel*" (Numbers 25:2-3). In this incident, the women of Moab practice **seductive** rituals surrounding the pagan god Baal. These practices were both satanic and sexually **seductive**. The Lord commanded Moses to "*Take all the leaders of the people and hang the offenders before the Lord, out in the sun, that the fierce anger of the Lord may turn away from Israel*" (Numbers 25:4). God commanded this punishment to rid the children of Israel of the people who allowed the influence of the **seducer** attribute in their camp. The action taken by the Lord illustrates the corrosive nature of this attribute. In a similar incident, the Lord used a plague, which took twenty-four thousand male Israelites lives to purge this attribute from among His people. The Biblical record documented that the Lord told Moses to, "*Harass the Midianites, and attack them; for they harassed you with their schemes by which they **seduced** you in the matter of Peor and in the matter of Cozbi, the daughter of a leader of Midian, their sister, who was killed in the day of the plague because of Peor*" (Numbers 25:17-18). Once again, one should read the entire account documented in the Book of Numbers Chapter 25 to understand the deceptive qualities of the influence of the **seducer** attribute.

The **seducer** attribute, when combined with other negative attributes, can bring down a kingdom. In fact, this happen with Solomon's son Rehoboam who listened to men influenced by the **seducer** attribute. After the elders had explained to Rehoboam how to handle a critical situation occurring in his kingdom (1 Kings 12:6-8), Rehoboam, "*...rejected the advice which the elders had given him, and consulted the young men who had grown up with him, who stood before him. And he said to them, "What advice do you give?"* (1 Kings 12: 8-9). These young men, influenced by the **seducer** attribute, **seduced** Rehoboam by their words. Look closely at the young men's response in 1 Kings 12: 10-11 which appealed to the negative attributes at work in Rehoboam's inner spirit. Their behavior, and Rehoboam's **seduction**, became the catalyst that split Solomon's kingdom.

King Manasseh allowed the influence of the **seducer** attribute in his life. In his case, the children of Israel let their guard down. The Biblical record documented that they, "*...paid no attention, and Manasseh **seduced** them to do more **evil** than the nations whom the Lord had destroyed before the children of Israel*" (2 Kings 21:9). 2 Chronicles 33:9 clarified "*...Manasseh **seduced** Judah and the inhabitants of Jerusalem....*" One can read earlier in the Biblical record that "*Manasseh was twelve years old when he became king, and he reigned fifty-five years in Jerusalem. His mother's name was Hephzibah. And he did evil in the sight of the Lord, according to the abominations of the nations whom the Lord had cast out before the children of Israel*" (2 Kings 21:1-2). Manasseh also set up a carved image of Asherah, a fertility goddess and the mother of Baal, in the Lord's temple. Specifically the Bible documented, "*He even set a carved image of Asherah that he had made, in the house of which the Lord had said to David and to Solomon his son, "In this house and in Jerusalem, which I have chosen out of all the tribes of Israel, I will put My name forever; and I will not make the feet of Israel wander anymore from the land which I gave their fathers—only if they are careful to do according to all that I have commanded them, and according to all the law that My servant Moses commanded them*" (2 Kings 21:7-8). The influence of the **seducer** attribute, along with other negative attributes, was strong in Manasseh's inner spirit and it cost him his kingdom.

The prophet Ezekiel documented that the **seducer** attribute influenced the false prophets of Israel. For their personal gain, this attribute led the false prophets to lie to the children of Israel about their security and **seduced** them into doing shoddy work repairing the wall of Jerusalem. The Lord told Ezekiel, "*Because, indeed, because they have **seduced** My people, saying, 'Peace!' when there is no peace—and one builds a wall, and they plaster it with untempered mortar— say to those who plaster it with untempered mortar, that it will fall. There will be flooding rain, and you, O great hailstones, shall fall; and a stormy wind shall tear it down*" (Ezekiel 13:10-11). BTT allows one to see how the false prophets **seduced** the children of Israel to believe that there was no danger facing them from outside forces. Their lackadaisical attitude led them to use inferior mortar on the walls. In other words, they took short cuts. Consequently, their negligence to obey the Lord to rebuild Jerusalem's wall by His standard, cost them their freedom.

The New Testament identifies Satan as the source of the **seducer** attribute. The Biblical record documented how Satan attempted to **seduce** Jesus in the wilderness using temptation. The Book of Matthew (Chapter 4:1-11), Mark (Chapter 1:12-13), and Luke (Chapter 4:1-13), documented this event for one's learning and mutual understanding of spiritual warfare. The documentation of this event is critical Jesus' provides the solution for defeating the influence of the **seducer** attribute specifically, and the other negative attributes in general. Please pay close attention to the underlined tactics of **seduction** used by the great **seducer** himself. Using Luke's account of the event in Luke 4:1-13, the Biblical record documented:

> "*Then Jesus, being filled with the Holy Spirit, returned from the Jordan and was led by the Spirit into the wilderness, being tempted for forty days by the devil. And in those days He ate nothing, and afterward, when they had ended, He was hungry. And the devil said to Him, "<u>If You are the Son of God, command</u>*

this stone to become bread." But Jesus answered him, saying, "It is written, 'Man shall not live by bread alone, but by every word of God.'" Then the devil, taking Him up on a high mountain, showed Him all the kingdoms of the world in a moment of time. And the devil said to Him, "All this authority I will give You, and their glory; for this has been delivered to me, and I give it to whomever I wish. Therefore, if You will worship before me, all will be Yours." And Jesus answered and said to him, "Get behind Me, Satan! For it is written, 'You shall worship the Lord your God, and Him only you shall serve.'" Then he brought Him to Jerusalem, set Him on the pinnacle of the temple, and said to Him, "If You are the Son of God, throw Yourself down from here. For it is written: 'He shall give His angels charge over you, to keep you,' and, 'In their hands they shall bear you up, lest you dash your foot against a stone.'" And Jesus answered and said to him, "It has been said, 'You shall not tempt the Lord your God.'" Now when the devil had ended every temptation, he departed from Him until an opportune time."*

One can easily see how Satan attempted to **seduce** Jesus while he was physically and emotionally exhausted after 40 days of fasting. However, Jesus was not spiritually exhausted. Through Jesus' example, BTT allows one to understand that even when one is physically and emotionally drained, God's Word used appropriately will give one the strength to still defeat the negative attributes. Even the **seducer** attributes, with its use of powerful and pervasive words, cannot defeat God's Word. One is susceptible to the words of one influenced by the **seducer** attribute when one's inner spirit is ill equipped. Make no mistake, while Jesus was on earth, He was susceptible to the same issues of life you or I face daily. The Bible even documented that, *"For we do not have a High Priest who cannot sympathize with our weaknesses, but was in all points tempted as we are, yet without sin"* (Hebrews 4:15). Jesus defeated the great **seducer**; Satan, with God's Word.

The Pharisees, chief priest, and the scribes of the Jewish people were influenced by the **seducer** attribute and they attempted to destroy Jesus. The Bible documented, *"...the chief priests and the scribes sought how they might take Him by trickery and put Him to death"* (Mark 14:1). Make no mistake, Satan was behind these men's pursuit to trap Jesus. Satan **seductively** convincing them that the nation of Israel had to be saved from Jesus (John 11:50; John 18:14). Eventually, the chief priest **seduced** Judas Iscariot, one of Jesus' eleven disciples, to betray Jesus. Judas was **seduced** by the chief priest's offer of money. This offer came sometimes after Judas began his walked with Jesus and the Bible confirms, *"...Judas Iscariot who also became a traitor"* in Luke 6:16. Judas susceptibility to those influenced by the **seducer** attribute occurred because he had other negative attributes already at work in his inner spirit. The Bible documented that Judas was a *"...a thief, and had the money box; and he used to take what was put in it"* (John 12:6). The thief and the other negative attributes already influencing Judas, made the **seduction** of the chief priest, scribes, and Pharisees' role easier. BTT allows one to see that the negative forces will always combine in the war campaign to take down anyone and everyone open to their influences to achieve their mission on the spiritual battlefield. In Judas' case, the negative forces combined to influence him to make a move against the Son of God. The behavior of the negative forces against Jesus indicates the serious nature of spiritual warfare. The Biblical record documented that, *"...Judas Iscariot, went to the* *chief priests and said, "What are you willing to give me if I deliver Him to you?" And they counted out to him thirty pieces of silver. So from that time he sought opportunity to betray Him"* (Matthew 26:14-16; Mark 14:10-11; Luke 22:3-6). When the opportunity arose for Judas to betray Jesus, the Biblical record documented, *"...Satan entered Judas, surnamed Iscariot, who was numbered among the twelve"* (Luke 22:3). BTT allows one to see how the **seducer** attribute brought the chief priest and Judas together at a decisive point in time. Judas; influenced by the thief attribute and <u>greed,</u> joined forces with the chief priest to take down Jesus. The **seducer** attribute's use of Judas and the chief priest gave a false impression of a decisive victory for the negative forces on the spiritual battlefield. However, BTT allows one to see that this was all in God's plan. Judas's **seduction** merely cost him his life. He committed suicide by hanging himself according to Matthew 23:5.

Caiaphas, one of the primary chief priests, allowed the influence of the **seducer** attribute. Caiaphas effectively illustrated the attribute while addressing the Sanhedrin after Jesus raised Lazarus from the dead. At a time when the Jewish council was confused over handling the demonstrated power of Jesus and His doctrine, the Biblical record documented that Caiaphas, *"...being high priest that year, said to them, "You know nothing at all, nor do you consider that it is expedient for us that one man should die for the people, and not that the whole nation should perish"* (John 11:49-50). Caiaphas's **seductive** words lulled the council into agreement and the Bible confirms, *"...from that day on, they plotted to put Him to death"* (John 11:53). The influence of the **seducer** attribute led Caiaphas and others to falsely charged Jesus with a crime and put Him to death.

Matthew 27:20-26 documented the influence of the **seducer** attribute among the crowd that stood before Pontius Pilate in the judgement of Jesus. The Bible documents that Pilate offered the Jews a choice between the death of Barabbas; a convicted criminal, and Jesus; the Son of God. But, the Bible also recorded that *"...the chief priests and elders **persuaded** the multitudes that they should ask for Barabbas and destroy Jesus"* (Matthew 27:20). This **persuasion** is a twisted form of **seduction** that leads people to do Satan's will. Because they had become hopelessly lost in the fog of the war, the **seducer** attribute influencing the chief priests and elders that day effectively advanced the war campaign for the negative forces.

Interestingly, the influence of the **seducer** attribute affected Saul before he was converted to Christianity and renamed Paul. He was among the Jewish leadership influenced by the **seducer** attribute. The attribute **seduced** Saul into believing the religious error perpetrated by the Jewish leadership that ignored the prophesies of the coming of Jesus. This religious error blinded Saul to the Truth concerning Jesus and God's Word. Saul's zeal for Judaism was genuine. But nonetheless, his **seduction,** influenced him to **seduce** others in his cause to destroy the Lord's church. In the Biblical record, once he was converted to the very doctrine he fought against, he documented some important effects the influence of the **seducer** attribute had on him. He wrote:

- *"...I am indeed a Jew, born in Tarsus of Cilicia, but brought up in this city at the feet of Gamaliel, taught according to the strictness of our fathers' law, and was zealous toward God as you all are today. I persecuted this Way to the death, binding and delivering into prisons both men and women, as also the high priest bears me witness, and all the council of the elders, from whom I also received letters to the brethren, and went to Damascus to bring in chains even those who were there to Jerusalem to be punished"* (Acts 22:3-5).

- *"Indeed, I myself thought I must do many things contrary to the name of Jesus of Nazareth. This I also did in Jerusalem, and many of the saints I shut up in prison, having received authority from the chief priests; and when they were put to death, I cast my vote against them. And I punished them often in every synagogue and compelled them to blaspheme; and being exceedingly enraged against them, I persecuted them even to foreign cities"* (Acts 26:9-11)

- *"For you have heard of my former conduct in Judaism, how I persecuted the church of God beyond measure and tried to destroy it. And I advanced in Judaism beyond many of my contemporaries in my own nation, being more exceedingly zealous for the traditions of my fathers"* (Galatians 1:13-14)

BTT allows one to see the horror of Paul's thinking as he got caught up in the business of Judaism and its prophesies over the written Word of God. Paul's words illustrate the strong delusive power of the **seducer** attribute. Then and now, the Biblical record reminds one that the world is under the *"...sway of the **wicked** one"* (John 5:19). This *"sway"* is from the great **seducer**; Satan, using the power of the **seducer** attribute to inflict spiritual warfare on earth. Satan's use of the **seducer** attribute in world affairs maintains the sway spoken of above.

Other people identified as being influence by the **seducer** attribute are Demetrius and Jews in the city of Galatia. In Demetrius' case, the influence of the attribute led him to **seduce** workers who shared similar occupations as his. Influenced by the **seducer** attribute, Demetrius led fellow workers in Ephesus to riot against Paul's preaching of Christ according to Acts 19:23-32. In the case of the Jews in Galatia, Paul documented that there were people who had begun **seducing** members of the Lord's church with another doctrine that was not from God. Galatians 1:6-9 documents this. In both cases, the power of the **seducer** attribute was strong and persuasive.

James documented the influence of the **seducer** attribute in a different way. He focused on how this attribute manifested itself through one's physical behavior and actions. James documented the correlation between the **seducer** attribute and the use of the tongue. He wrote, *"...the tongue is a little member and boasts great things. See how great a forest a little fire kindles! And the tongue is a fire, a world of iniquity. The tongue is so set among our members that it defiles the whole body, and sets on fire the course of nature; and it is set on fire by hell...It is an unruly evil, full of deadly poison"* (James 3:5-8). I encourage one to read the full discourse documented in James 3:1-12 for greater understanding and the analogies used to help one visualize the behavior. But from what is provided, one can see how the **seducer** attribute, once lodged in one's inner spirit, uses one's tongue to say things that **seduce** others to sin.

This is exactly why Jesus stated that it is, *"Not what goes into the mouth defiles a man; but what comes out of the mouth, this defiles a man"* (Matthew 15:11; Mark 7:20). The influence of the **seducer** attribute, as well as the other negative attributes, use the human mouth to say things that it should not. This is also why one must put God's Word into one's inner spirit so good things can come out of one's spiritual heart. The apostles Paul and Peter surely had the influence of the ***seducer*** attribute in mind when they wrote the following words by inspiration of the Holy Spirit. BTT allows one to see the ***seducer*** and the ***seduced*** as illustrated in the text of Paul and Peter as they wrote:

- *"If anyone teaches otherwise and <u>does not consent to wholesome words, even the words of our Lord Jesus Christ, and to the doctrine which accords with godliness</u>, he is proud, knowing nothing, but is obsessed with disputes and arguments over words, from which come envy, strife, reviling, evil suspicions, useless wranglings of men of corrupt minds and destitute of the truth, who suppose that godliness is a means of gain. From such withdraw yourself"* (1 Tim 6:3-5)

- *"But know this, that in the last days perilous times will come: For men will be lovers of themselves, lovers of money, boasters, proud, blasphemers, disobedient to parents, unthankful, unholy, unloving, unforgiving, slanderers, <u>without self-control</u>, brutal, <u>despisers of good</u>, traitors, headstrong, haughty, lovers of pleasure rather than lovers of God, having a form of godliness but denying its power. And from such people turn away! For of <u>this sort are those who creep into households and make captives</u> of gullible women loaded down with sins, <u>led away by various lusts</u>, always learning and never able to come to the knowledge of the truth"* (2 Timothy 3:1-7)

- *"But there were also false prophets among the people, even as there will be false teachers among you, who will <u>secretly bring in destructive heresies</u>, even denying the Lord who bought them, and bring on themselves swift destruction. And <u>many will follow their destructive ways</u>, because of whom the way of truth will be blasphemed. By covetousness they will exploit you with deceptive words; for a long time their judgment has not been idle, and their destruction does not slumber"* (Peter 2:1-3)

Finally, John captured the presence of the influence of the ***seducer*** attribute existing in an image of the Lord's church. John documented Jesus' Word concerning the church of Thyatira that, *"Nevertheless I have a few things against you, because you allow that woman Jezebel, who calls herself a prophetess, to teach and* ***seduce*** *My servants to commit* ***sexual immorality*** *and eat things sacrificed to idols"* (Revelation 2:20). From this Scripture, the Biblical record documents a warning. One must be very careful of the person one listens to that proclaiming God's Word. The image that Jesus' provided in this Scripture is clear. One must study the Bible and make sure his or her congregation is not the like the one Jesus' described. Even a preacher can fall under the influence of the ***seducer*** attribute. In the religious world, he or she will be cunning and well-spoken. They will use deception and ***persuasion*** tactics from this ancient attribute. Thus, one must know their Bible and the Truth contain within. This is key for defeating the influence of the ***seducer*** attribute in spiritual warfare and aiding the negative forces of the war campaign.

The **Backslider attribute**: This attribute influences one to walk away from God after learning and accepting His Word. Its influence reinvigorates past habits, behaviors, attitudes, and/or speech that one put away when he or she understood the Truth of the Biblical standard. This attribute causes one to "fall back" into a morally corrupt behavior after one learns and practices <u>*godly*</u> principles. Moreover, after one has come to know God and His Word, this is the attribute that influences one to revert to a worse condition beyond their learned knowledge of God. What sets this attribute apart from all of the other negative attributes is the fact that it specifically targets people who have been *"enlightened, and have tasted the heavenly gift, and have become partakers of the Holy Spirit, and have tasted the good word of God and the powers of the age to come..."* (Hebrews 6:4-5). This attribute specifically launches spiritual assaults against new Christians of Christ's teachings and the immature in God's Word to make them stumble. But the greater prize for the negative forces are people in Christ who have had the time to spiritually mature. Why? Because these are people with positive influences who can influence and lead positive changes in the direction of the war campaign. When the influence of the ***backslider*** attribute causes one in Christ to fall, the opportunities to ensnare others that followed this person's positive examples; adults and children, increases exponentially. For the one influenced by this attribute may "straddle the fence" for a period of time before falling completely away from Christ. In effect, this person may give the impression that they have the positive attributes and are among the positive forces of the campaign, while all along, living a lie. Hence, the Biblical record also interchangeably considers one with this attribute a ***transgressor*** of God's law.

    The Spirit of wisdom revealed to Solomon, that, *"The **backslider** in heart will be filled with his own ways, but a good man will be satisfied from above"* (Proverbs 14:14). This wisdom captures the essence of the things previously stated about this attribute. Wisdom explained that because of one's own desires; stored away instead of released from one's inner spirit upon conversion, one is influenced to ***backslide*** into past sin. When Christ dwells in one's spiritual heart, He set conditions for the maturing of His Word in one's heart through obedience to His Word. This obedience releases one's selfish desire formulated and stored up in one's spiritual heart from years of ignorance to God's Word. Continued obedience, patience, and spiritual maturing establishes self-control between one and his or her inner spirit. Self-control renders the influence of the ***backslider*** attribute powerless and God's way takes precedence over one's own desires.

    In the Old Testament of the Biblical record, the influence of the ***backslider*** attribute oscillated among the children of Israel in a deplorable fashion. First, understand that the Lord gave the children of Israel every opportunity to follow His Word. God even sent an angel to help the Israelite along their journey. The Lord said, *"Behold, I send an Angel before you to keep you in the way and to bring you into the place which I have prepared. Beware of Him and obey His voice; do not provoke Him, for He will not pardon your **transgressions**; for My name is in Him"* (Exodus 23:20-21). BTT helps one to see with clarity that the influence of the ***backslider*** attribute was not tolerated. However, from the beginning of the Israelite's journey to freedom, the influence of the ***backslider*** made itself known and thousands died along the way. The Lord said to Moses, *"...I have seen this people, and indeed it is a stiff-necked people!"*

(Exodus 32:9). Moses would later say to them, "*Now why do you **transgress** the command of the Lord? For this will not succeed*" (Numbers 14:41). Of course, they did not listen.

To control the influence of the **backslider** attribute, as well as the other negative attributes, the Lord gave Moses commands for the children of Israel to follow. Moses told them they would be stoned to death (Deuteronomy 17:5), "*If there is found among you, within any of your gates which the Lord your God gives you, a man or a woman who has been wicked in the sight of the Lord your God, in **transgressing** His covenant...*" (Deuteronomy 17:2). In fact, the Lord went on to state, "*Whoever is deserving of death shall be put to death on the testimony of two or three witnesses; he shall not be put to death on the testimony of one witness*" (Deuteronomy 17:6). This, seemingly harsh command from the Lord, highlighted the destructive, corrosive, and cancerous nature of the influence of the **backslider** attribute among God's people. Moses understood that to get the children of Israel to the Promised Land free of the negative attribute's influence, precise obedience to God's commandments was necessary. Some of the major **backsliding** events on the way to the Promised Land that occurred with Moses and the children of Israel included:

- The Israelites constant weeping over their travel to freedom, their complaining against Moses and Aaron, and their desire to die in the wilderness (Numbers 14:1-2)

- The request to make a god of a golden calf (Exodus 32)

- Their temptation of God ten times in the wilderness (Numbers 14:22)

All these events documented that, even though the Lord took great care of the children of Israel, they **backslid** into sin. God fed them with manna from heaven (Exodus 16:31; Numbers 11:7-9), quail (Exodus 16:13), fresh water (Numbers 20:8), and even provided them clothes and sandals that never wore out (Deuteronomy 29:5). After Moses's death, Joshua led the children of Israel into the Promised Land. As Joshua was about to die, he counseled the children of Israel on the influence of the **backslider** attribute as Moses did. First, documented in Joshua 23:11-13, Joshua told the children of Israel:

> "*Therefore take careful heed to yourselves, that you love the Lord your God. Or else, if indeed **you do go back**, and cling to the remnant of these nations— these that remain among you—and make marriages with them, and go in to them and they to you, know for certain that the Lord your God will no longer drive out these nations from before you. But they shall be snares and traps to you, and scourges on your sides and thorns in your eyes, until you perish from this good land which the Lord your God has given you.*"

Then he reminded them of the covenant with the Lord and said, "*When you have **transgressed** the covenant of the Lord your God, which He commanded you, and have gone and served other gods, and bowed down to them, then the anger of the Lord will burn against you, and you shall perish quickly from the good land which He has given you*" (Joshua 23:16). The people in turn replied to Joshua saying, "*Far be it from us that we should forsake the Lord* *to serve other gods; for the Lord our God is He who brought us and our fathers up out of the land of Egypt...*" (Joshua 24:16-17). But Joshua held his position and reiterated for clarity, "*You cannot serve the Lord, for He is a holy God. He is a jealous God; He will not forgive your **transgressions** nor your sins*" (Joshua 24:19) and told them to, "*...put away the foreign gods which are among you, and incline your heart to the Lord God of Israel*" (Joshua 24:23). The people agreed. Thus, Joshua made a covenant (a contract) and placed it in the Book of the Law of God. Soon after, Joshua died at the age of 110 (Joshua 24:29) and the period of the Judges begin.

The Biblical record documented, "*Then the anger of the Lord was hot against Israel; and He said, "Because this nation has **transgressed** My covenant which I commanded their fathers, and has not heeded My voice, I also will no longer drive out before them any of the nations which Joshua left when he died, so that through them I may test Israel, whether they will keep the ways of the Lord, to walk in them as their fathers kept them, or not*" (Judges 2:20-22). What happened? Well, the influence of the **backslider** attribute returned, and the children of Israel fell back to fulfilling their own evil desires. The Biblical record documented that "*...the children of Israel did evil in the sight of the Lord, and served the Baals; and they forsook the Lord God of their fathers, who had brought them out of the land of Egypt; and they followed other gods from among the gods of the people who were all around them, and they bowed down to them; and they provoked the Lord to anger. They forsook the Lord and served Baal and the Ashtoreths*" (Judges 2:11-13). The children of Israel allowed the influence of the **backslider** attribute in their inner spirits. They walked away from the commandments of the Lord; the only thing designed to protect and save them in spiritual warfare and the influence of the negative forces of the war campaign.

The Biblical record documented an incredible statement that had direct ties to the influence of the **backslider** attribute. This statement is critical for one to see because of its application to every generation. After Joshua died and the generation he had mentored died out too, the Bible documented, "*When all that generation had been gathered to their fathers, another generation arose after them who did not know the Lord nor the work which He had done for Israel*" (Judges 2:10). In other words, for all the influence the **backslider** attribute had on the children of Israel, eventually a generation was produced that had no knowledge of the Lord. This happens when sound teaching stops and parents no longer pass their knowledge to their children. Over time, each generation removed gets farther from the Truth. This precedent has continued to this very day in the same manner. The lesson here is that the influence of the **backslider** attribute will always be successful in the war campaign as masses of people fail to learn, respect, and teach God's Truth.

God sent His prophets to warn the nation of Israel to rid themselves of the influence of the **backslider** attribute, to repent, and to return to God. The Biblical record documents:

The Prophet	What Was Said
Isaiah	"For our <u>transgressions</u> are multiplied before You, and our sins testify against us; for our <u>transgressions</u> are with us, and as for our iniquities, we know them: in <u>transgressing</u> and lying against the Lord, and <u>departing from our God</u>,

	speaking oppression and revolt, conceiving and uttering from the heart words of falsehood" (Isaiah 59:12-13)
Jeremiah	*"Your own wickedness will correct you, and your **backslidings** will rebuke you. Know therefore and see that it is an evil and bitter thing that you have forsaken the Lord your God, and the fear of Me is not in you," Says the Lord God of hosts. For of old I have broken your yoke and burst your bonds; and you said, 'I will not **transgress**,' When on every high hill and under every green tree You lay down, playing the harlot"* (Jeremiah 2:19-20)
	The Lord asked the Jeremiah, *"...Have you seen what **backsliding** Israel has done? She has gone up on every high mountain and under every green tree, and there played the harlot. And I said, after she had done all these things, 'Return to Me.' But she did not return. And her treacherous sister Judah saw it"* (Jeremiah 3:6-7)
	*"Go and proclaim these words toward the north, and say: 'Return, **backsliding** Israel,' says the Lord; 'I will not cause My anger to fall on you"* (Jeremiah 3:12)
	*"Return, O **backsliding** children," says the Lord; "for I am married to you. I will take you, one from a city and two from a family, and I will bring you to Zion. And I will give you shepherds according to My heart, who will feed you with knowledge and understanding"* (Jeremiah 3:14-15)
	*"Return, you **backsliding** children, and I will heal your **backslidings**..."* (Jeremiah 3:22)
	*"Therefore a lion from the forest shall slay them, a wolf of the deserts shall destroy them; a leopard will watch over their cities. Everyone who goes out from there shall be torn in pieces, because their <u>transgressions</u> are many; their **backslidings** have increased"* (Jeremiah 5:6)
	*"Why has this people **slidden back**, Jerusalem, in a perpetual **backsliding**? They hold fast to deceit, they refuse to return. I listened and heard, but they do not speak aright. No man repented of his wickedness, saying, 'What have I done?' Everyone turned to his own course, as the horse rushes into the battle"* (Jeremiah 8:5-6)

Table 27: Some of the Prophet's Warnings about the Backslider Attribute

No one can deny that the influence of the **backslider** attribute had infiltrated the inner spirits of the people of Israel. However, one must understand that this attribute gained strength when the prophets and priest stopped teaching and enforcing God's Word. Had the religious leaders corrected Israel's leadership and parents when they initially started **backsliding** on God's Word, the behavior would not have replicated so fast among the people. Eventually, after a generation or two, God's Word became unknown by the later generations. False teachers, priest, and prophets exploited this condition for their own personal gain. One can learn this by continuing to be educated about each of the negative attributes and the war campaign.

In the New Testament of the Biblical record, Jesus addressed the influence of the **backslider** attribute and its strategy that causes one to stumble. His comments apply to a person who hears and accepts the His Word. Jesus said, *"When an **unclean spirit** goes out of a man, he goes through dry places, seeking rest, and finds none. Then he says, 'I will return to my house from which I came.' And when he comes, he finds it empty, swept, and put in order. Then he goes and takes with him seven other spirits more wicked than himself, and they enter* *and dwell there; and the last state of that man is worse than the first. So shall it also be with this wicked generation*" (Matthew 12:43-45). Jesus' insight provides the big picture as to why a person **backslides**. His Word is the only tool that can dislodge and remove **unclean spirits** from one's inner spirit. The Biblical record documents, "*For the word of God is living and powerful, and sharper than any two-edged sword, piercing even to the division of soul and spirit, and of joints and marrow, and is a <u>discerner</u> of the thoughts and intents of the heart*" (Hebrews 4:12). Thus, BTT allows one to see that when a person cleans up his or her life and begins to walk on the positive path, the negative attributes (**unclean spirits**) that left desires to return. However, to gain a strong enough influence to return, the negative attribute must combine with other negative attributes "*more wicked than himself.*" The reason for this combination is to enhance deception. These ancient attributes draw on knowledge from every aspect of one's former life to influence him or her to return to their old ways. These negative attributes are patient with their attack instead of using an outright assault. This constitutes spiritual warfare at the personal level in its finest form. Only study and maturity in God's Word, and obedience to it, can prevent the negative attributes from succeeding. Without a foundation in God's Word, the **backslider** attribute wins. The negative attributes will exploit one's weakness using temptation. Any momentary lowering of one's guard that causes one to steps away from God's Word, is an opening for the **backslider** attribute. Jesus said, if the negative attributes are successful, the state of that person's inner spirit will be "*worse than the first.*"

    BTT allows one to see that when one takes the steps necessary to rid himself or herself of the negative attributes, these spirits simply look for another place to go. Remember, spirits do not die; they just move somewhere else. They hang out until they find a susceptible person to influence or until a convenient opportunity presents itself to return to the original person's inner spirit. If one does not build a strong spiritual defense once one is cleansed, the negative attributes returns to trip one up. This is a continuous strategy of the negative forces of the campaign to attempt to cause one to **backslide**. BTT allows one to see the intelligence of these ancient spirits in that they bring other spirits with them to cause a cleansed inner spirit to stumble. BTT allows one to see that the force of the combined returning attributes can stir up past sinful behaviors, memories, or relationships that were long forgotten over time. One who puts on the whole armor of God (Ephesians 6:10-18), has the means to defeat the influence of this and the other negative attributes that it bring with it. Giving in to the temptations presented by influence of the **backslider** attribute is not the answer. Fighting the influence is the answer. For the Biblical record declares, "*...each one is tempted when he is drawn away by his own desires and enticed*" (James 1:14). When one **backslides** with even one of the negative attributes, his or her inner spirit becomes susceptible to multiple negative attributes through their temptation and influence. One must always keep in mind that the Bible declares, "*To him who overcomes I will grant to sit with Me on My throne, as I also overcame and sat down with My Father on His throne*" (Revelation 3:21). I want to be on God's side.

    Judas made his mark as one heavily influenced by the **backslider** attribute. Yes, the Biblical record revealed that Judas was a thief and he managed and stole from the disciple's moneybox according to John 12:6. However, one must always be mindful that Judas walked with Jesus and was taught the Word of God by the Son of God along with the other disciples. Judas had the words of life to change his life, but he allowed the influence of the **backslider** attribute to corrupt his inner spirit. The outward manifestation of the **backslider** attribute working in Judas' inner spirit lead to the betrayal of Jesus Christ for the sake of "...*thirty pieces of silver. So from that time he sought opportunity to betray Him*" (Matthew 26:14-16; Mark 14:10-11; Luke 22:3-6). When the opportunity arose for Judas to betray Jesus, the Biblical record documented, "...*Satan entered Judas, surnamed Iscariot, who was numbered among the twelve*" (Luke 22:3). BTT allows one to see that Judas **backslid** into his old ways of being a liar and a thief which took priority over God's Word and Jesus' life. Remember, it is what is behind one's behavior that is important to understand in spiritual warfare.

Paul commented on the influence of the **backslider** attribute when he wrote, "...*if I build again those things which I destroyed, I make myself a **transgressor***" (Galatians 2:18). The situation surrounding this text was Paul confronting Peter about his behavior in the presence of Christians and Jews. Peter, a Christian and apostle allowed the influence of the **backslider** attribute to put him in a sinful position. He **backslid** on the very Gospel he taught as he withdrew from the Gentiles when the Jews came around. Peter's behavior affected his companion, Barnabas, and other believing Jews according to Galatians 2:13. Paul saw this and corrected the situation immediately. Paul stopped the influence of the **backslider** attribute in its tracks. I encourage one to read this whole account of Paul and Peter's interaction to learn how the influence of the **backslider** attribute can covertly slip into one's inner spirit.

This wisdom from the Gospel is extremely important because it documents the influence of the **backslider** attribute affecting some Christians in the Lord's church today. James described this when he taught about partiality among God's people. James gave the example of a man who was blessed materially and entered an assembly (James 2:2). He wrote that if one paid attention to that man's financial wellbeing over others who were less fortunate, that behavior "...*dishonored the poor man...*" (James 2:6). In other words, the behavior is sin. This behavior indicates that one has **backslid** from the teaching of the Gospel. The influence of the **backslider** attribute operates by placing temptations in front of one whose been cleansed of his or her sins through baptism. After baptism, one should mature in the knowledge that as a Christian, "*There is neither Jew nor Greek, there is neither slave nor free, there is neither male nor female; for you are all one in Christ Jesus*" (Galatians 3:28). If this is learned, anything else that does not bring equal treatment and respect to all people is **backsliding** from what one has learned from the Gospel. The temptation to treat others differently must be overcome. James documented, "*Blessed is the man who endures temptation; for when he has been approved, he will receive the crown of life which the Lord has promised to those who love Him. Let no one say when he is tempted, "I am tempted by God"; for God cannot be tempted by evil, nor does He Himself tempt anyone. But each one is tempted when he is drawn away by his own desires and enticed. Then, when desire has conceived, it gives birth to sin; and sin, when it is full-grown, brings forth death*" (James 1:12-15). Temptation is the primary tool of the **backslider** attribute in the war campaign and this attribute knows how to effectively use this tool to regain and replenish forces on the negative side of the campaign.

The **Adulterer attribute**: The influence of this attribute leads one to establish a secondary physical relationship with another person or persons. This secondary relationship exists outside of one's primary contractual relationship that one originally committed. The secondary relationship can be purely based on emotional, sexual, or financial satisfaction. The influence of this attribute initially influences people to maintain their secondary relationship in secret. This is an indicator that something in the secondary relationship is Biblically wrong. In spiritual warfare, this relationship is morally illegal and "cheating." For the objective of the influence of the ***adulterer*** attribute is to destroy a sound relationship between two people, their family members and children, and their home. This strategy, perpetrated by the negative forces of the war campaign, is one of the most successful strategies today. This insidious attribute even destroys civility between people in a work environments and religious organizations. The influence of the ***adulterer*** attribute seeks to undermined God's design for a loving relationship between one man and one woman. Moreover, it desires to prove that God's design is false and open to interpretation by human enlightenment. In fact, when this attribute combines with the immoral attribute, they influence one to believe that open relationships are acceptable in the eyes of God. Open relationships can include men with multiple women, women with multiple men, men with men, women with women, and even adults with children in sexual relationships. The strength of this attribute is its persuasive ability to convince one that godly commitments are not important; but self-satisfaction of human desires are. The ***adulterer*** attribute influences the carnal side of man to prioritize human emotions and feelings over God's Word. This effective strategy blocks open communications in a godly relationships and eventually destroys one's home. The ***adulterer*** attribute influences either the husband or wife to believe that a contractual relationship is just a guideline. It conspires to teach that guidelines can always be broken if one is unhappy with the agreement. Therefore, divorce (breaking the contract) for any reason is an acceptable alternative to misery. If a divorce is not an immediate option, an extramarital affair will do. God never sanctioned any of these courses of actions in the Biblical record. In fact, BTT allows one to see that the options described above, break the contractual relationship between a husband and wife, and supports the same thinking used to sever one's relationship with God. People begin a relationship with the Lord only to forsake Him and align with the idols and false gods of the day. BTT will allow one to see that improper teaching about this attribute's influence, and refusal to accept Jesus' teaching on the subject, has rendered large numbers of men unqualified to serve in the established positions of the Lord's Church. These authorized positions are documented in Chapter XII of this book. Now before one stops reading this book over this statement, closely consider these three situations:

- The wives taken from foreign nations that intermarried with God's people in Ezra Chapters 9 and 10

- John the Baptist's rebuke of Herod for marring his brother's wife in Matthew 14:3-4; Mark 6:17-18; and Luke 3:19

- Paul's rebuke of the Corinthian church for allowing, and being proud of, a man that had his father's wife in 1 Corinthians Chapter 5

All these situations shared a common denominator disguised by the negative forces of the war campaign. In each situation, the common denominator is the influence of the ***adulterer*** attribute. Whether the behavior was ***adultery*** against God or ***adultery*** between consenting adults, it does not matter. The behavior, which is sin in the eyes of God, keeps one separated from God. The negative forces of the campaign suppress this knowledge as part of their strategy in spiritual warfare. Specifically, the ***adulterer*** attribute's influence convinces one that no matter what, his or her act of ***adultery*** is acceptable. For this attribute relies on man's self-righteous belief, identified by the Spirit of wisdom to Solomon, that *"All the ways of a man are pure in his own eyes…"* (Proverbs 16:2). However, this same Scripture ends with the Spirit of wisdom revealing that *"…the Lord weighs the spirits."* In this chapter, one will discover how the ***adulterer*** attribute has influenced many people with a lie in spiritual warfare.

BTT helps one to see that the Biblical record identified four states of sexual status. The four states are abstinence, fornication, ***adultery***, and married. Of course, abstinence is the practice of staying pure from sexual activity until marriage. Marriage is the union of a man and woman in a formal contractual relationship that joins the spirits of both people together as one flesh. Fornication is the opposite act of abstinence; one does not stay sexually pure. In fact, it is the indiscriminate behavior of having sexual intercourse with another person without the contractual commitment of marriage. Chapter X of this book will all of these states in more detail and address man's hybrid marriage constructs. Finally, there is the act of ***adultery*** in which one has sexual involvement with a person who made a commitment to another person through a marriage contract. Please keep these simple definitions in mind as one reads further.

The ***adulterer*** attribute is different from the seducer attribute. Although these attributes can combine for greater effectiveness in spiritual warfare, they must be viewed separately. The seducer attribute seeks total control of a person through words and materials for an intended purpose. Whereas the influence of the ***adulterer*** attribute, for the most part, seeks sport and temporary pleasure outside of an initial contractual agreement with another person. With this in mind, consider what the Spirit of wisdom revealed to Solomon about this attribute. Please understand that Solomon documented what the Spirit of wisdom revealed to him from the standpoint of a man's relationship with a woman. However, as one progresses in the reading, one will see that the influence of the ***adulterer*** attribute does not discriminate and is applicable to both men and women.

One of the first things Solomon documented about the influence of the ***adulterer*** attribute was that one who allows its influence lacks an understanding of its destructive nature. Solomon documented, *"Whoever commits **adultery** with a woman lacks understanding; he who does so destroys his own soul. Wounds and dishonor he will get, and his reproach will not be wiped away. For jealousy is a husband's fury; therefore, he will not spare in the day of vengeance. He will accept no recompense, nor will he be appeased though you give many gifts"* (Proverbs 6:32-35). From this thought, one can see the destructive nature of the influence of the ***adulterer*** attribute. First, the wound from this attribute is not just skin deep; it goes down to one's very soul. Secondly, the wound from this attribute brings dishonor and the reproach against God will not be wiped away. Thirdly, this attribute invites other negative forces from the war campaign to play in the sin it produces. BTT allows one to see that the jealous/envious, anger, furious, and violent attributes are ready to team up with the bloodthirsty attribute to set off a chain reaction over an **adulterous** affair. Since mankind's arrival on earth, this scenario has played out in every society on earth. Unfortunately, many people miss the cues before it is too late. This is what the **adulterer** attribute prefers, as it keeps strife and chaos alive in the campaign. The one who allows the influence of the **adulterer** attribute clearly lacks understanding and destroys everything around him or her. One must remember, destruction is not just limited to the initiator, both parties in the relationship are destroyed. But the negative forces of the war campaign want this information concealed.

Solomon taught his son that prostitutes in general had their inner spirits influenced by three **unclean spirits**. He documented , "*To keep you from the evil woman, from the flattering tongue of a seductress. Do not lust after her beauty in your heart, nor let her allure you with her eyelids. For by means of a* **harlot** *a man is reduced to a crust of bread; and an* **adulteress** *will prey upon his precious life*" (Proverbs 6: 24-26). BTT allows one to see the combined forces of the **adulterer**, seducer, and evil attributes working in this context. Further, one sees that Solomon described a woman so influenced by the negative forces of the war campaign, that she can destroy her victim's livelihood and life. Yes, both people are involved in sin together, but the influences of the **adulterer** attribute plays a major role in the entrapment.

King Agur, another contributor to Solomon's documentation wrote, "*This is the way of an* **adulterous** *woman: She eats and wipes her mouth, and says, "I have done no wickedness.*" (Proverbs 30:20). The Spirit of wisdom says otherwise. Not only was she and her actions *wicked*, but the man involved with her participated in a *wicked* act. Therefore, the participant is *wicked* too. Not only are they both guilty of the entrapment of the **adulterer** attribute, but they both have added numerical strength to the negative forces of the war campaign.

The influence of the **adulterer** attribute, much like the jealousy/envy attribute, shares a strong connection to the spiritual element of covetousness. To "covet" is to want, desire, or lust for a person or thing that one does not have in the most extreme way. Both the attribute and the element of covetousness play a significant role in the lives of the children of Israel. However, from the Lord's commands to the children of Israel, one can see that He did not want the Israelites to have anything to do with this element or the **adulterer** attribute. Moses told the children of Israel from the Lord, "*You shall not covet your neighbor's house; you shall not covet your neighbor's wife, nor his male servant, nor his female servant, nor his ox, nor his donkey, nor anything that is your neighbor's*" (Exodus 20:17). God knew that the element of covetousness would automatically open the door for the **adulterer** attribute. BTT helps one to see that the cravings for another person's spouse, caused by the element of covetousness, is like a powerful and addictive drug. When the influence of the **adulterer** attribute combines with the element of covetousness, this deadly combination produces an insatiable desire that can only be satisfied by the sinful behavior this attribute influences one to pursue. Without God's Word, one's soul is lost. BTT allows one to see that a person influenced by the **adulterer** attribute acts similar to one influenced by the lazy attribute. Both attributes cause one to prefer things worked for by others. Solomon documented for one influenced by the lazy attribute - "*He* *covets* greedily all day long..." (Proverbs 21:26) - as does one influenced by the **adulterer** attribute. This wisdom helps one to understand the ravenous desires invoked by the influence of the **adulterer** attribute. This attribute's hunger for pleasure will remain unsatisfied until it leads one to sin. For this attribute, the needs are mostly sexual in nature. Hence, Solomon documented for our learning, *"Can a man take fire to his bosom, and his clothes not be burned? Can one walk on hot coals, and his feet not be seared? So is he who goes in to his neighbor's wife; whoever touches her shall not be innocent"* (Proverbs 6:27-29). Now consider what the rest of the Biblical record documented about the **adulterer** attribute.

When *"...Jethro, the priest of Midian, Moses' father-in-law..."* (Exodus 18:1), met with Moses to help him organize the children of Israel, he gave him some instructions to help control the **adulterer** attribute. Jethro instructed Moses to select sound leaders who could stand before the people and serve as models of proper behavior. The Biblical record documented that Jethro told Moses, *"Listen now to my voice; I will give you counsel, and God will be with you: ...select from all the people able men, such as fear God, men of truth, hating covetousness; and place such over them to be rulers of thousands, rulers of hundreds, rulers of fifties, and rulers of tens"* (Exodus 18:19-21). BTT allows one to see that Jethro's recommendation was godly counsel. The presence of strong examples of godly behavior cripples the influence of the **adulterer** attribute for both sexual desires and material things.

Later, God gave the children of Israel a direct commandment concerning the influence of the **adulterer** attribute when He said in His Ten Commandments, *"You shall not commit adultery"* (Exodus 20:14; Deuteronomy 5:18). God's Word was simple and direct; no interpretation required. However, Moses still provided some clarification to other related areas tied to the influence of the **adulterer** attribute. For example, he told the children of Israel, *"You shall not covet your neighbor's house; you shall not covet your neighbor's wife, nor his male servant, nor his female servant, nor his ox, nor his donkey, nor anything that is your neighbor's"* (Exodus 20:17). One must connect the dots. When the element of covetousness is present, the influence of the **adulterer** attribute is near. As I stated earlier, this attribute will combine with the element of covetousness and develop an uncontrollable sin. There is no discrimination here; the attribute influences men and women equally and the element of covetousness can open the door to the influences of the perverse, immoral, and even the thief attributes. The point is, God hates the behavior caused by the influence of the **adulterer** attribute because it produces sins.

BTT allows one to see that the influence of the **adulterer** attribute took root among the children of Israel. Through Moses, the Lord clarified his position about this attribute more strongly and the consequence for falling prey to it. Moses documented, *"The man who commits **adultery** with another man's wife, he who commits **adultery** with his neighbor's wife, the **adulterer** and the **adulteress**, shall surely be put to death"* (Leviticus 20:10). This consequence of death illustrates how corrosive the influence of this attribute is and the damage it causes to one's home and society. God decreed death as the method for purging this corrosive attribute from among His people. The children of Israel "hated" this and refused to accept it. One will learn in the New Testament of the Biblical record that Moses chose a course of action that circumvented God's Word and it displeased Him. The course of action was the right to divorce one's spouse. Moses offered this to the people only because of the strong effects of the negative forces of the war campaign on the children of Israel. I will explain this in detail in the New Testament portion on this attribute.

The prophet Job documented a few insights about one who allows him or herself to be influenced by the **adulterer** attribute. Job wrote, *"The eye of the **adulterer** waits for the twilight, saying, 'No eye will see me'; and he disguises his face"* (Job 24:15). From Job's wisdom, one can see the level of detail invested by one influenced by the **adulterer** attribute as he or she considers committing an act of **adultery**. Their stealthy behavior clearly shows the behavior is wrong. In fact, Job compared the behavior of one influenced by the **adulterer** attribute to one influenced by both the bloodthirsty and thief attributes. He documented that, *"There are those who rebel against the light; they do not know its ways nor abide in its paths. The murderer rises with the light; he kills the poor and needy; and in the night he is like a thief. The eye of the **adulterer** waits for the twilight, saying, 'No eye will see me'; and he disguises his face. In the dark they break into houses which they marked for themselves in the daytime; they do not know the light. For the morning is the same to them as the shadow of death; if someone recognizes them, they are in the terrors of the shadow of death"* (Job 24:13-17). This remarkable piece of wisdom documents the insidious nature of the influence of the **adulterer** attribute. All these negative attributes operate in the shadows and those influenced by those attributes know their behavior is wrong.

All the prophets sent by the Lord warned the children of Israel about the rampant influence of the **adulterer** attribute among them. The Lord sent His prophets to warn the nation of Israel about the influence of the **adulterer** attribute. Moreover, He expressed how their behavior and interaction with foreign nations and their gods were **adulterous**. Here are a few of the many examples documented by the prophets to demonstrate the insidiousness of this attribute along with the element of <u>covetousness</u>. The Biblical record documented:

The Prophet	What Is Documented
Jeremiah	*"So it came to pass, through her casual **harlotry**, that she defiled the land and committed **adultery** with stones and trees"* (Jeremiah 3:9)
	"Because from the least of them even to the greatest of them, everyone is given to <u>covetousness</u>; and from the prophet even to the priest, everyone deals falsely" (Jeremiah 6:13)
	*"Will you steal, murder, commit **adultery**, swear falsely, burn incense to Baal, and walk after other gods whom you do not know, and then come and stand before Me in this house which is called by My name, and say, 'We are delivered to do all these abominations'?"* (Jeremiah 7:9-10)
	"Therefore I will give their wives to others, and their fields to those who will inherit them; because from the least even to the greatest everyone is given to <u>covetousness</u>; from the prophet even to the priest everyone deals falsely" (Jeremiah 8:10)
	*"Oh, that I had in the wilderness a lodging place for travelers; that I might leave my people, and go from them! For they are all **adulterers**, an assembly of treacherous men"* (Jeremiah 9:2)

		"Yet your eyes and your heart are for nothing but your <u>covetousness</u>, for shedding innocent blood, and practicing oppression and violence" (Jeremiah 22:17)
		"Also I have seen a horrible thing in the prophets of Jerusalem: They commit **adultery** and walk in lies; they also strengthen the hands of evildoers, so that no one turns back from his wickedness. All of them are like Sodom to Me, and her inhabitants like Gomorrah" (Jeremiah 23:14)
		"...because they have done disgraceful things in Israel, have committed **adultery** with their neighbors' wives, and have spoken lying words in My name, which I have not commanded them. Indeed I know, and am a witness, says the Lord" (Jeremiah 29:23)
	Hosea	"Hear the word of the Lord, you children of Israel, for the Lord brings a charge against the inhabitants of the land: "There is no truth or mercy or knowledge of God in the land. By swearing and lying, killing and stealing and committing **adultery**, they break all restraint, with bloodshed upon bloodshed" (Hosea 4:1-2)
	Malachi	"And I will come near you for judgment; I will be a swift witness against sorcerers, against **adulterers**, against perjurers, against those who exploit wage earners and widows and orphans, and against those who turn away an alien— Because they do not fear Me," Says the Lord of hosts" (Malachi 3:5)

Table 28: Some of the Prophets' Warnings about the Influence of the Adulterer Attribute and the Element of <u>Covetousness</u>

In the New Testament of the Biblical record, Jesus provided painful clarity of God's position on one influenced by the ***adulterer*** attribute. What Jesus said about this ***unclean spirit*** alone continues to split religious communities, and some in the Christian community, internally. What Jesus stated about this attribute identifies a key objective of the spiritual warfare. That objective is the destruction of the family unit; the godly relationship between a man and a woman. BTT allows one to see that Jesus took the teachings of the Old Testament concerning the ***adulterer*** attribute and provided clarity from God about its history. More importantly, Jesus restated God's specific commandments for controlling the power of this ***unclean spirit***. To set the stage for understanding, one must return to the Book of Genesis; the history of the beginning of all things. The Biblical record documented that God stated that in the beginning, "...*a man shall leave his father and mother and be joined to his wife, and they shall become one flesh*" (Genesis 2:24). I submit for one's consideration, this joining of a man and a woman is a marriage contract witnessed by God. The marriage establishes a spiritual contract between the man and woman's inner spirits unseen by the human eye. This union unites two human's inner spirits by a divine unseen element called "<u>love</u>." This unseen element is part of a divine construct designed for the lifetime of the people involved. BTT allows one to understand that the union of two physical flesh is not some form of a "she-male" aberration, but a spiritual construct designed by God for His purpose and will. I will cover this in detail in Chapter X of this book. For now, try to understand that the negative forces of the war campaign have distorted this fact among both the religious and secular communities since the beginning of mankind. Members of these communities, influenced by negative attributes, have made God's honorable union (Hebrews 13:4) a sideshow that simply anticipates failure. BTT allows one to see that the influence of the ***adulterer*** attribute leads one to hate the marriage agreement. The attribute, using the manipulation of time, perception, and events, does everything it can to influence a person in a marriage contract to believe he or she is living in a lie. Worse yet, this attribute deceives one to believe he or she is trapped in a relationship with the wrong person or is influenced to believe another person exists that he or she is spiritually meant to be with. When this level of deceit is reached, one allows the influence of other negative attributes and compromise occurs. Compromise can also include the influence of the bloodthirsty attribute. What a sad commentary.

Now, if one can accept everything stated above, then one will be able to accept the Word of Jesus that follows. After all, the Biblical record documented that Jesus stated Himself, "*...All authority has been given to Me in heaven and on earth*" (Matthew 28:18). It is His Word that one must listen to and not our own thoughts nor others influenced by the negative forces of the war campaign. Keeping the context of Genesis 2:24 in mind, read carefully Jesus' Word. I have adjusted the order only so one can see how Jesus' Word flowed between the harmonized Gospels. Additionally, I have added what the Holy Spirit inspired Paul to write to clarify confusing issues. The Bible documents from Jesus:

1. "*Have you not read that He who made them at the beginning 'made them male and female,' and said, 'For this reason a man shall leave his father and mother and be joined to his wife, and the two shall become one flesh'? So then, they are no longer two but one flesh. Therefore what God has joined together, let not man separate*" (Matthew 19:4-6)

2. "*You have heard that it was said to those of old, 'You shall not commit **adultery**.' But I say to you that whoever looks at a woman to <u>lust</u> for her has already committed **adultery** with her in his heart*" (Matthew 5:27-28)

3. "*Furthermore it has been said, 'Whoever divorces his wife, let him give her a certificate of divorce. But I say to you that whoever divorces his wife for any reason except **sexual immorality** causes her to commit **adultery**; and whoever marries a woman who is divorced commits **adultery**"* (Matthew 5:31-32)

4. "*Moses, because of the hardness of your hearts, permitted you to divorce your wives, <u>but from the beginning it was not so</u>. And I say to you, whoever divorces his wife, except for **sexual immorality**, and marries another, commits **adultery**; and whoever marries her who is divorced commits **adultery**"* (Matthew 19:8-9)

5. "*...Whoever divorces his wife and marries another commits **adultery** against her. And if a woman divorces her husband and marries another, she commits **adultery**"* (Mark 10:11-12)

6. "*Whoever divorces his wife and marries another commits **adultery**; and whoever marries her who is divorced from her husband commits **adultery**"* (Luke 16:18)

To a community entrenched in spiritual warfare, Paul led by the Holy Spirit added clarity to Jesus' divine teachings. He documented:

1. *"For the woman who has a husband is bound by the law to her husband as long as he lives. But if the husband dies, she is released from the law of her husband. So then if, while her husband lives, she marries another man, she will be called an **adulteress**; but if her husband dies, she is free from that law, so that she is no **adulteress**, though she has married another man"* (Romans 7:2, 3) [Paul reemphasized Jesus' teaching recorded in Matthew 5:31-32, Matthew 19:8-9]

2. *"...because of **sexual immorality**, let each man have his own wife, and let each woman have her own husband. Let the husband render to his wife the affection due her, and likewise also the wife to her husband. The wife does not have authority over her own body, but the husband does. And likewise the husband does not have authority over his own body, but the wife does. Do not deprive one another except with consent for a time, that you may give yourselves to fasting and prayer; and come together again so that Satan does not tempt you because of your lack of self-control"* (1 Corinthians 7:2-5)

3. *"But I say to the unmarried and to the widows: It is good for them if they remain even as I am; but if they cannot exercise self-control, let them marry. For it is better to marry than to burn with passion"* (1 Corinthians 7:8-9) [Paul's call for celibacy]

4. *"Now to the married I command, yet not I but the Lord: A wife is not to depart from her husband. But even if she does depart, let her remain unmarried or be reconciled to her husband. And a husband is not to divorce his wife"* (1 Corinthians 7:10-11). [For the husband, the same rules are implied; they did not require repeating]

5. *"But to the rest I, not the Lord, say: If any brother has a wife who does not believe, and she is willing to live with him, let him not divorce her. And a woman who has a husband who does not believe, if he is willing to live with her, let her not divorce him. For the unbelieving husband is sanctified by the wife, and the unbelieving wife is sanctified by the husband; otherwise your children would be unclean, but now they are holy. But if the unbeliever departs, let him depart; a brother or a sister is not under bondage in such cases. But God has called us to peace. For how do you know, O wife, whether you will save your husband? Or how do you know, O husband, whether you will save your wife?* (1 Corinthians 7:12-16)

6. *"Now concerning virgins: I have no commandment from the Lord; yet I give judgment as one whom the Lord in His mercy has made trustworthy. I suppose...because of the present distress—that it is good for a man to remain as he is: Are you bound to a wife? Do not seek to be loosed. Are you loosed from a wife? Do not seek a wife. But even if you do marry, you have not sinned; and if a virgin marries, she has not sinned. Nevertheless such will have trouble in the flesh, but I would spare you"* (1 Corinthians 7:25-28)

7. *"...if any man thinks he is behaving improperly toward his virgin* [JF: a relationship free of sex], *if she is past the flower of youth, and thus it must be, let him do what he wishes. He does not sin; let them marry. Nevertheless he who stands steadfast in his heart, having no necessity, but has power over his own will, and has so determined in his heart that he will keep his virgin, does well"* [JF: Remain in a celibate relationship] (1 Corinthians 7:36-37)

8. *"A wife is bound by law as long as her husband lives; but if her husband dies, she is at liberty to be married to whom she wishes, only in the Lord. But she is happier if she remains as she is, according to my judgment—and I think I also have the Spirit of God"* (1 Corinthians 7:39-40) [Two things: First, Paul's statement applied equally for men with the man implied. Second, Paul could not know if either person would be happier, but he used his personal judgement in this matter. He made it clear this portion of the statement was his judgement and not necessarily from the Holy Spirit]

Based on the Word of Jesus alone, one can see that allowing the influence of the **adulterer** attribute into one's inner spirit is bad. Further, Jesus clarifies that marriage is a contract for life. Because He has all authority for divine decisions, He authorized two exceptions for breaking the marriage contract. The first is when **sexual immorality** defiles the marriage relationship and the second is by the death of one's mate which Paul addressed in his follow-up statement. Outside of these two reasons, the Biblical record places every other activity into the **adulterer** attributes' area of spiritual warfare. Now, because of the influences of the negative forces of the campaign, the religious community and some in the Christian community will argue that both Jesus and Paul's word only applied to people who were living under the Mosaic Law. But consider this statement from Paul written by inspiration of the Holy Spirit and documented in Romans 2:12-24.

> *"For as many as have sinned without law will also perish without law, and as many as have sinned in the law will be judged by the law (for not the hearers of the law are just in the sight of God, but the doers of the law will be justified; for when Gentiles, who do not have the law, by nature do the things in the law, these, although not having the law, are a law to themselves, who show the work of the law written in their hearts, their conscience also bearing witness, and between themselves their thoughts accusing or else excusing them) in the day when God will judge the secrets of men by Jesus Christ, according to my gospel. Indeed you are called a Jew, and rest on the law, and make your boast in God, and know His will, and approve the things that are excellent, being instructed out of the law, and are confident that you yourself are a guide to the blind, a light to those who are in darkness, an instructor of the foolish, a teacher of babes, having the form of knowledge and truth in the law. You, therefore, who teach another, do you not teach yourself? You who preach that a man should not steal, do you steal? You who say, "Do not commit adultery," do you commit adultery? You who abhor idols, do you rob temples? You who make your boast in the law, do you dishonor God through breaking the law? For "the name of God is blasphemed among the Gentiles because of you," as it is written"*

Now, the act of cohabitation is as commonplace as it has been since the days of Noah. BTT allows one to see that this act is no more than a strategy conceived by the negative forces of the war campaign to simply circumvent God's plan of marriage. The act is a perceived way around the spiritual bond of marriage. It prevails because of a false premise that there are "no strings attached" and one can simply walk away at any time. During cohabitation, needs are fulfilled, and bonds of trust are established just as in a marriage contract. Often, children are produced. However, the relationship does not constitute a marriage. It remains a man and a woman in a state of cohabitation. Until a marriage contract is executed, both people live in a state of sin. Based on everything written prior to this point, this can be the only conclusion drawn. Meditate on this for a while and keep in mind there is spiritual wisdom and earthly wisdom. Do not be deceived.

For this reason, everyone who enters an illegitimate relationship of cohabitation places his or her soul in danger. The negative force's strategy of cohabitation is based on fornication. If one cannot exercise self-control, marriage is the only **honorable** option. Proper Biblical education will sustain a strong relationship. Without proper Biblical education on marriage, the negative forces of the war campaign simply gain forces in the war. This is a hard truth and many religious leaders avoid teaching on this subject. Their failure has allowed the influence of the **adulterer** attribute to flourish. Moreover, the false premise, "everybody is doing it" gets sanctioned as truth. Lawyers and judges also give legal sanction to the influence of the **adulterer** attribute as they authorize breaking the marriage bond for any and every cause. Their decisions undermine God's Word and His plan for the family unit. Make no mistake, they will be held accountable for their careless judgements and errors. Moreover, religious organizations across the world give approval to this deceitful strategy. Worldwide, their error gives legitimacy to unqualified people in positions of religious authority who continue to orchestrate other false doctrines. The Holy Spirit inspired Paul to document this when he wrote about people who, "*...knowing the righteous judgment of God, that those who practice such things are deserving of death, not only do the same but also approve of those who practice them*" (Romans 1:32). Please read Romans 1:26-32 for a full list of sinful behaviors referred to by Paul's statement.

The significance of the strategy enacted by the influence of the **adulterer** attribute cannot be overstated. People who allow this attribute's influence pray in vain to God. As long as one remains in an unclean state, God will not hear one's prayers. How can someone in an unclean state offer prayers to a Pure and Holy God on behalf of their home, community, or society when they themselves are in a state of sin? The answer is that one cannot! One's prayers are in vain. One must move from an unclean state to a repentant state for God to hear one's prayers. John even documented from the Holy Spirit, "*Now we know that God does not hear sinners; but if anyone is a worshiper of God and does His will, He hears him*" (John 9:31). Doing God's will is key. Within the war campaign, the negative attributes falsely convince people that they cannot know God's will. This false belief exasperates instability and strife in homes, communities, and societies without a spiritual means for resolution. But the Biblical record clearly documents, "*For this is the will of God, your sanctification: that you should abstain from **sexual immorality**; that each of you should know how to possess his own vessel in sanctification and honor, not in passion of lust, like the Gentiles who do not know God; that no one should take advantage of and defraud his brother in this matter, because the Lord is the avenger of all such, as we also forewarned you and testified. For God did not call us to uncleanness, but in holiness*" (1 Thessalonians 4:3-7). Please do not be deceived.

Jesus taught another crucial principle that needs review. He stated that, *"whoever looks at a woman to <u>lust</u> for her has already committed **adultery** with her in his heart"* (Matthew 5:27-28). This statement covers one's physical behavior of visually undressing or looking at a woman near or far off in a sexual way. This idea includes viewing pornography. These are sinful behaviors. The attitude behind the behavior corresponds to the influence of the immoral and **adulterer** attributes working together through the element of <u>lust</u>.

Thus, Paul wrote *"...in like manner also, that the women adorn themselves in modest apparel, with propriety and moderation, not with braided hair or gold or pearls or costly clothing, but, which is proper for women professing godliness, with good works"* (1 Timothy 9, 10). These words were not written to denigrate women in any way and nor were they to restrict women from braided hair, gold, pearls or costly clothing, as the negative forces of the war campaign want people to believe. Paul's words were for teaching respectability and moderation in spiritual warfare. BTT allows one to see that the element of <u>lust</u> is aroused by apparel and other cosmetics that accentuate the human body. The negative attributes use the fog of the campaign to stifle this knowledge. Paul's word provided knowledge from the Holy Spirit to help women engage in the fight of the campaign without drawing unwanted attention from people influenced by the negative attributes. When the element of <u>lust</u> is aroused, the influences of the **adulterer**, immoral, and perverse attributes find weak inner spirits to enter. God's Word and obedience provides the tools for defeating these attributes. This perspective allows one to spiritually mature with Paul's teaching.

The greater point from Paul is that women and men both have a responsibility to help each other combat the influences of the negative forces of the campaign. Positive dress apparel helps defeat the influences of the **adulterer** attribute. One must be careful of the message one's apparel sends to others. One must understand that the negative forces of the campaign will exploit dress apparel and cosmetics to cause people to stumble. Jesus stated, *"The lamp of the body is the eye. If therefore your eye is good, your whole body will be full of light. But if your eye is bad, your whole body will be full of darkness. If therefore the light that is in you is darkness, how great is that darkness!"* (Matthew 6:21-23). When a person looks upon attire that is inspired by people influenced by the negative forces and find he or she cannot look away, or the image festers in one's mind, then the element of <u>lust</u> is present. This element can make its way to one's inner spirit and cause one to be defiled. Defilement can come by way of the influences from the **adulterer** or a host of other negative attributes. Please do not listen to what the world says on this subject.

Jesus stated that the influence of the **adultery** attribute enters one's inner spirit. He stated, *"For out of the heart proceed evil thoughts, murders, **adulteries**, fornications, thefts, false witness, blasphemies. These are the things which defile a man..."* (Matthew 15:19-20). Mark also documented Jesus' statement and wrote, *"...Do you not perceive that whatever enters a man from outside cannot defile him, because it does not enter his heart but his stomach, and is eliminated, thus purifying all foods?"* And He said, *"What comes out of a man, that defiles a man. For from within, out of the heart of men, proceed evil thoughts, **adulteries**, fornications, murders, thefts, <u>covetousness</u>, wickedness, deceit, lewdness, an evil eye, blasphemy, pride, foolishness. All these evil things come from within and defile a man"* (Mark 7:18-21). BTT allows one to see that Jesus clearly states that the spiritual heart of the inner spirit can be defiled. Run from anyone who teaches otherwise. For this person is defiled and lost in the fog of spiritual warfare.

The Biblical record indicated that Jesus had strong feelings about the **adulterer** attribute. He called attention to it on many occasions. Jesus spoke of this attribute when He encountered a rich young ruler. When the rich young ruler asked Jesus what he should do to have eternal life (Matthew 19:16), Jesus responded, *"You shall not murder,' 'You shall not commit **adultery**,' 'You shall not steal,' 'You shall not bear false witness,'..."* (Matthew 19:18; Mark 10:19; Luke 18:20). The influence of the **adulterer** attribute was so important that Jesus addressed it with this young leader. The same was true in a second example of a Pharisee who compared himself to a tax collector. The Pharisee understood the gravity of allowing the influence of the **adulterer** attribute in his life. He said, *"...God, I thank You that I am not like other men—extortioners, unjust, **adulterers**, or even as this tax collector"* (Luke 18:11). Even though the Pharisee identified the negative attribute, he was wrong by putting himself on a pedestal above the tax collector. He still was in a sinful state. On the other hand, the tax collector, because he focused on his own issues and not on others, Jesus stated that he *"went down to his house justified rather than the other; for everyone who exalts himself will be humbled, and he who humbles himself will be exalted"* (Luke 18:14). The point here is that in both cases, Jesus pointed out that the **adulterer** attribute is a bad attribute to have.

Jesus taught the apostles and they continued spreading the Gospel to every corner of the earth according to Colossians 1:23. The apostles taught the same thing Jesus taught about this attribute and its deception. Here are some pearls of wisdom the apostles documented about the influence of the **adulterer** attribute and the element of <u>covetousness</u>. The Biblical record documented:

- *"Now the works of the flesh are evident, which are: **adultery**, fornication, uncleanness, lewdness, idolatry, sorcery, hatred, contentions, jealousies, outbursts of wrath, selfish ambitions, dissensions, heresies, envy, murders, drunkenness, revelries, and the like; of which I tell you beforehand, just as I also told you in time past, that those who practice such things will not inherit the kingdom of God"* (Galatians 5:19-21). Notice that the **adulterer** attribute leads the charge.

- *"Marriage is <u>**honorable**</u> among all, and the bed undefiled; but fornicators and **adulterers** God will judge. Let your conduct be without <u>covetousness</u>; be content with such things as you have. For He Himself has said, "I will never leave you nor forsake you"* (Hebrews 13:4-5)

- For the ungodly and unrighteous: *"And even as they did not like to retain God in their knowledge, God gave them over to a debased mind, to do those things which are not fitting; being filled with all unrighteousness, **sexual immorality**, wickedness, <u>covetousness</u>..."* (Romans 1:28-32)

- *"You, therefore, who teach another, do you not teach yourself? You who preach that a man should not steal, do you steal? You who say, "Do not commit **adultery**," do you commit **adultery**? You who abhor idols, do you rob temples?"* (Romans 2:21-22)

- *"Owe no one anything except to love one another, for he who loves another has fulfilled the law. For the commandments, "You shall not commit **adultery**," "You shall not murder," "You shall not steal," "You shall not bear false witness," "You shall not <u>covet</u>," and if there is any other commandment, are all summed up in this saying, namely, "You shall love your neighbor as yourself." Love does no harm to a neighbor; therefore love is the fulfillment of the law"* (Romans 13:8-10)

- *"I wrote to you in my epistle <u>not to keep company with</u> sexually immoral people. Yet I certainly did not mean with the sexually immoral people of this world, or with the <u>covetous</u>, or extortioners, or idolaters, since then you would need to go out of the world. But now I have written to you not to keep company with anyone named a brother, who is sexually immoral, or <u>covetous</u>, or an idolater, or a reviler, or a drunkard, or an extortioner—not even to eat with such a person. For what have I to do with judging those also who are outside? Do you not judge those who are inside? But those who are outside God judges. Therefore "put away from yourselves the evil person"* (1 Corinthians 5:9-12)

- *"…Do you not know that the unrighteous will not inherit the kingdom of God? Do not be deceived. Neither fornicators, nor idolaters, nor **adulterers**, nor homosexuals, nor sodomites, nor thieves, nor <u>covetous</u>, nor drunkards, nor revilers, nor extortioners will inherit the kingdom of God. And such were some of you. But you were washed, but you were sanctified, but you were justified in the name of the Lord Jesus and by the Spirit of our God"* (1 Corinthians 6:7-11)

- *"But fornication and all uncleanness or <u>covetousness</u>, let it not even be named among you, as is fitting for saints; neither filthiness, nor foolish talking, nor coarse jesting, which are not fitting, but rather giving of thanks. For this you know, that no fornicator, unclean person, nor <u>covetous</u> man, who is an idolater, has any inheritance in the kingdom of Christ and God. Let no one deceive you with empty words, for because of these things the wrath of God comes upon the sons of disobedience. Therefore do not be partakers with them"* (Ephesians 5:3-6)

- *"Therefore put to death your members which are on the earth: fornication, **uncleanness**, passion, evil desire, and <u>covetousness</u>, which is idolatry. Because of these things the wrath of God is coming upon the sons of disobedience, in which you yourselves once walked when you lived in them"* (Colossians 3:5)

- *"This is a faithful saying: If a man desires the position of a bishop, he desires a good work. A bishop then must be blameless, the husband of one wife, temperate, sober-minded, of good behavior, hospitable, able to teach; not given to wine, not violent, not greedy for money, but gentle, not quarrelsome, not <u>covetous</u>…"* (1 Timothy 3:1-7)

- *"If you really fulfill the royal law according to the Scripture, "You shall love your neighbor as yourself," you do well; but if you show partiality, you commit sin, and are convicted by the law as transgressors. For whoever shall keep the whole law, and yet stumble in one point, he is guilty of all. For He who said, "Do not commit **adultery**," also said, "Do not murder." Now if you do not commit **adultery**, but you do murder, you have become a transgressor of the law. So speak and so do as those who will be* *judged by the law of liberty. For judgment is without mercy to the one who has shown no mercy. Mercy triumphs over judgment" (James 2:8-13)*

- *"**Adulterers** and **adulteresses**! Do you not know that friendship with the world is enmity with God? Whoever therefore wants to be a friend of the world makes himself an enemy of God. Or do you think that the Scripture says in vain, "The Spirit who dwells in us yearns jealously"?" (James 4:1-5)*

- False prophets and false teachers *"...By <u>covetousness</u> they will exploit you with deceptive words; for a long time their judgment has not been idle, and their destruction does not slumber"* (2 Peter 2:1-3)

- False teachers: *"...They are spots and blemishes, carousing in their own deceptions while they feast with you, having eyes full of **adultery** and that cannot cease from sin, enticing unstable souls. They have a heart trained in <u>covetous</u> practices, and are accursed children. They have forsaken the right way and gone astray...they speak great swelling words of emptiness, they allure through the <u>lusts</u> of the flesh, through lewdness, the ones who have actually escaped from those who live in error"* (2 Peter 2:10-22)

The **Fool attribute**: The influence of this attribute is one of the most destructive negative attributes in the war campaign. It influences one to reject the Bible outright, including anything written or spoken about it, regardless of the evidence or facts that prove its reliability and Truth. The ***fool*** attribute influences one to act irrationally and to exhibit ridiculous behavior such as making faces or gestures when Biblical knowledge or instruction is made known. It leads one to sacrifice good sense or judgment, to behave in a manner that is unwise, and to speak in such a fashion as to demonstrate ignorance on any or all subjects while claiming superior knowledge. Most dangerous of all, people who allows the influenced by this attribute will be so busy trying to prove their point, they will miss important information that could save their life. Narcissistic behavior is a by-product of this attribute. The term "***silly***" is also associated with this attribute. It represents a smaller measure of the influence of the ***fool*** attribute in one's inner spirit.

The Spirit of wisdom revealed a lot of information to Solomon about the influence of the ***fool*** attribute. Documented in the early pages of the Book of Proverbs, the Spirit of wisdom revealed that, "...***fools*** *despise wisdom and instruction*" (Proverbs 1:7). To despise is a measure of behavior found in the hater attribute. This book documents the hater attribute later in this chapter. However, Wisdom stated that this is how strong the influence of this attribute makes one feel about wisdom and instruction. Further she revealed, "... ***fools*** *hate knowledge*" (Proverbs 1:22) and that, "...*the complacency of **fools** will destroy them*" (Proverbs 1:32). BTT allows one to see exactly what makes the influence of the ***fool*** attribute so dangerous. Influencing one to despise wisdom and instruction, to hate knowledge, and to be complacent makes a deadly recipe. Hence, the Spirit of wisdom pleaded for all people, influenced by the ***fool*** attribute, to seek understanding before it was too late. She said, "...*you **fools**, be of an understanding heart*" (Proverbs 8:5) and then went on to explain that her house was freely open to all. She said, *"Whoever is simple, let him turn in here!" As for him who lacks understanding, she says to him, "Come, eat of my bread and drink of the wine I have mixed. Forsake **foolishness** and live, and go in the way of understanding"* (Proverbs 9:4-6). Unfortunately, one learns from Wisdom that one influenced by the ***fool*** attribute does not listen to her or the Lord Himself. She said to Solomon, *"... **fools** die for lack of wisdom"* (Proverbs 10:21).

Solomon, after gaining an understating of the influence of the ***fool*** attribute asked, *"Why is there in the hand of a **fool** the purchase price of wisdom, since he has no heart for it?"* (Proverbs 17:16). BTT helps one to see that God blesses even one influenced by the ***fool*** attribute with the ability to gain wisdom. However, one with this attribute also has the freedom of choice. Often, one with this attribute will choose to ignore their ability to gain wisdom. They willfully dismiss God and His Word because their inner spiritual heart accepts the influence of the ***fool*** attribute. Instead of focusing on the important soul saving issues in front of them, *"...the eyes of a **fool** are on the ends of the earth"* (Proverbs 17:24). This means one influenced by the ***fool*** attribute has their priorities in the wrong order. Thus, Solomon documented, *"Wisdom is too lofty for a **fool**..."* (Proverbs 24:7). This simply meant that wisdom was out of reach. In fact, Solomon expressed that a person influenced by the ***fool*** attribute was not even capable of using a proverb - which is a wise saying - correctly. He stated, *"Like the legs of the lame that hang limp is a proverb in the mouth of **fools**"* (Proverbs 26:7) and *"Like a thorn that goes into the hand of a drunkard is a proverb in the mouth of **fools**"* (Proverbs 26:9). A proverb used by one influenced by the ***fool*** attribute, brings pain instead of wisdom to the hearer. Hence, these painful analogies demonstrate why it is important to protect one's self from the influences of the ***fool*** attribute.

Solomon learned much more about the destructive and deceptive ways of the influence of the ***fool*** attribute. Remember, Solomon sought out understanding of the influence of the ***fool*** attribute as much as he sought out wisdom. The Biblical record documented that he said, *"I applied my heart to know, to search and seek out wisdom and the reason of things, to know the wickedness of folly, even of **foolishness** and madness"* (Ecclesiastes 7:25). For time and space considerations, consider the many things the Spirit of wisdom revealed to Solomon listed in the Table below. Solomon documented:

"The way of a ***fool*** is right in his own eyes..." (Proverbs 12:15)	"... the heart of ***fools*** proclaims ***foolishness***" (Proverbs 12:23)	"A ***fool*** vents all his feelings..." (Proverbs 29:11)
"A ***fool*** has no delight in understanding, but in expressing his own heart" (Proverbs 18:2)	"The ***foolishness*** of a man twists his way, and his heart frets against the LORD" (Proverbs 19:3)	"...what is in the heart of ***fools*** is made known" (Proverbs 14:33)
"...the ***foolishness*** of ***fools*** is folly" (Proverbs 14:24)	"...a ***fool*** lays open his folly" (Proverbs 13:16)	"...the folly of ***fools*** is deceit" (Proverbs 14:8)
"Do not speak in the hearing of a ***fool***, for he will despise the wisdom of your words" (Proverbs 23:9)	"Understanding is a wellspring of life to him who has it. But the correction of	"Go from the presence of a ***foolish*** man, when you do not perceive in him the lips

	"***fools*** is folly" (Proverbs 16:22)	of knowledge" (Proverbs 14:7)
"...a prating ***fool*** will fall" (Proverbs 10:8 and 10:10)	"Luxury is not fitting for a ***fool***..." (Proverbs 19:10)	"...the companion of ***fools*** will be destroyed" (Proverbs 13:20)
"A wise man fears and departs from evil, but a ***fool*** rages and is self-confident" (Proverbs 14:16)	"It is honorable for a man to stop striving, since any ***fool*** can start a quarrel" (Proverbs 20:3)	"Let a man meet a bear robbed of her cubs, rather than a ***fool*** in his folly" (Proverbs 17:12)
"...the mouth of ***fools*** pours forth ***foolishness***" (Proverbs 15:2)	"... the mouth of the ***foolish*** is near destruction" (Proverbs 10:14)	"... it is an abomination to ***fools*** to depart from evil" (Proverbs 13:19)
"To do evil is like sport to a ***fool***..." (Proverbs 10:23)	"The devising of ***foolishness*** is sin..." (Proverbs 24:9)	"***Fools*** mock at sin..." (Proverbs 14:9)
"In the mouth of a ***fool*** is a rod of pride..." (Proverbs 14:3)	"... the mouth of ***fools*** feeds on ***foolishness***" (Proverbs 15:14)	"A ***fool's*** wrath is known at once..." (Proverbs 12:16)
"If a wise man contends with a ***foolish*** man, whether the ***fool*** rages or laughs, there is no peace" (Proverbs 29:9)	"A stone is heavy and sand is weighty, but a ***fool's*** wrath is heavier than both of them" (Proverbs 27:3)	"There is desirable treasure, and oil in the dwelling of the wise, but a ***foolish*** man squanders it" (Proverbs 21:20)
"Better is the poor who walks in his integrity than one who is perverse in his lips, and is a ***fool***" (Proverbs 19:1)	"Even a ***fool*** is counted wise when he holds his peace; when he shuts his lips, he is considered perceptive" (Proverbs 17:28)	"***Foolishness*** is bound up in the heart of a child; the rod of correction will drive it far from him" (Proverbs 22:15)
"A whip for the horse, a bridle for the donkey, and a rod for the ***fool's*** back" (Proverbs 26:3)	"Judgments are prepared for scoffers, and beatings for the backs of ***fools***" (Proverbs 19:29)	"As snow in summer and rain in harvest, so honor is not fitting for a ***fool***" (Proverbs 26:1)
"Rebuke is more effective for a wise man than a hundred blows on a ***fool***" (Proverbs 17:10)	"As a dog returns to his own vomit, so a ***fool*** repeats his folly" (Proverbs 26:11)	"A ***foolish*** son is a grief to his father, and bitterness to her who bore him" (Proverbs 17:25)
"The great God who formed everything gives the ***fool*** his hire and the transgressor his wages" (Proverbs 26:10)	"A ***fool's*** lips enter into contention, and his mouth calls for blows. A ***fool's*** mouth is his destruction, and his lips are the snare of his soul" (Proverbs 18:6-7)	"Though you grind a ***fool*** in a mortar with a pestle along with crushed grain, yet his ***foolishness*** will not depart from him" (Proverbs 27:22)
"A ***fool*** despises his father's instruction..." (Proverbs 15:5)	"... the father of a ***fool*** has no joy" (Proverbs 17:21)	A quick-tempered man acts ***foolishly***..." (Proverbs 14:17)
"...a ***foolish*** man despises his mother..." (Proverbs 15:20)	"...a ***foolish*** son is the grief of his mother" (Proverbs 10:1)	"A ***foolish*** son is the ruin of his father..." (Proverbs 19:13)

"Whoever hides hatred has lying lips, and whoever spreads slander is a **fool**" (Proverbs 10:18)	"Excellent speech is not becoming to a **fool**, much less lying lips to a prince" (Proverbs 17:7)	"He who sends a message by the hand of a **fool** cuts off his own feet and drinks violence" (Proverbs 26:6)
"Like one who binds a stone in a sling is he who gives honor to a **fool**" (Proverbs 26:8)	"A **foolish** woman is clamorous; She is simple, and knows nothing" (Proverbs 9:13)	"He who trusts in his own heart is a **fool**..." (Proverbs 28:26)
"Do you see a man hasty in his words? There is more hope for a **fool** than for him" (Proverbs 29:20)	"Do you see a man wise in his own eyes? There is more hope for a **fool** than for him" (Proverbs 26:12)	"He who troubles his own house will inherit the wind, and the **fool** will be servant to the wise of heart" (Proverbs 11:29)
"For three things the earth is perturbed, yes, for four it cannot bear up: For a servant when he reigns, a **fool** when he is filled with food, a hateful woman when she is married, and a maidservant who succeeds her mistress" (Proverbs 30:21-23)	"Do not answer a **fool** according to his folly, lest you also be like him. Answer a **fool** according to his folly, lest he be wise in his own eyes" (Proverbs 26:4-5)	"If you have been **foolish** in exalting yourself, or if you have devised evil, put your hand on your mouth. For as the churning of milk produces butter, and wringing the nose produces blood, so the forcing of wrath produces strife" (Proverbs 30:32-33)

Table 29: Pearls of Wisdom Concerning the Influence of the Fool Attribute

From this table, one can see that the Spirit of Wisdom revealed extensive knowledge to Solomon about the influence of the *fool* attribute in a variety of areas. One must remember that Wisdom revealed, "...*the complacency of **fools** will destroy them; but whoever listens to me will dwell safely, and will be secure, without fear of evil.*" (Proverbs 1:32-33). The Biblical record documents the truth about Wisdom. God's Word is Wisdom. Without it, one will never succeed in reaching heaven when this life is over. Hence, the Spirit of wisdom told Solomon, "*...shame shall be the legacy of **fools***" (Proverbs 3:35). Now consider what the rest of the Biblical record documents on this dangerous attribute and its role in spiritual warfare.

In the Old Testament, Aaron and Miriam allowed the influence of the *fool* attribute in their inner spirits. They challenged Moses' authority. When God began to punish them and Aaron saw that Miriam had been struck with leprosy (Numbers 12:10), Aaron cried to Moses saying, "*Oh, my lord! Please do not lay this sin on us, in which we have done **foolishly** and in which we have sinned*" (Numbers 12:11). Moses prayed, and the Lord responded on his behalf according to Numbers 12:14. The influence of the *fool* attribute led Aaron and Miriam to sin.

Before Moses died, he sang a song to the children of Israel and identified the presence of the influence of the *fool* attribute among them. The entire song is worth one's attention in the Book of Deuteronomy Chapter 32. In one part, Moses sang, "*Do you thus deal with the Lord, O **foolish** and unwise people? Is He not your Father, who bought you? Has He not made you and established you?*" (Deuteronomy 32:6). Moses reminded them of their troubled history. One can read from the Books of Exodus through Deuteronomy just how the *fool* attribute influenced the children of Israel to do things extremely unbecoming of a people that

God personally rescued from bondage. Their behavior at times could only be described as *foolish*, i.e. when they said "*...If only we had died in the land of Egypt! Or if only we had died in this wilderness!*" (Numbers 14:2). These two simple examples clearly identify the presence of the influence of the *fool* attribute among the children of Israel even after everything God had shown them.

The *fool* attribute can influence an entire nation, or it can simply influence the leader of a nation who then has major influence on the behavior of the entire nation. King Saul was such a leader. He allowed the influence of the *fool* attribute in his life and he lost his kingdom for it. The Lord sent the prophet Samuel to tell Saul, "*You have done foolishly. You have not kept the commandment of the Lord your God, which He commanded you. For now the Lord would have established your kingdom over Israel forever*" (1 Samuel 13:13). Later, Saul would confess to David, during a confrontation that "*I have sinned. Return, my son David. For I will harm you no more, because my life was precious in your eyes this day. Indeed I have played the fool and erred exceedingly*" (1 Samuel 26:21). God removed Saul from his office as king. However, before he left, the nation of Israel followed his *foolish* ways, acted *foolishly*, and were punished too.

When David became King, he allowed the influence of the *fool* attribute to lead him to decide to count the people of Israel and Judea. In reality, the Lord was angry at the nation of Israel, but David had a role in this too according to 2 Samuel 24:1. His army spent nine months and twenty days counting the people to provide David a number and the Biblical record documented, "*...in Israel eight hundred thousand valiant men who drew the sword, and the men of Judah were five hundred thousand men*" (2 Samuel 24:8-9). However, the Biblical record also documented that after the count was rendered, "*...David's heart condemned him after he had numbered the people. So David said to the Lord, "I have sinned greatly in what I have done; but now, I pray, O Lord, take away the iniquity of Your servant, for I have done very foolishly*" (2 Samuel 24:10). First Chronicles Chapter 21 provides more details about this account. A piece of information documented in this Book captured the fact that, "*...Satan stood up against Israel, and moved David to number Israel*" (1 Chronicles 21:1). This piece of information unmistakably lets one know who controls the influence of the *fool* attribute. BTT allows one to see that the nation of Israel was doing something wrong if the Lord allowed Satan to stand against them.

Next, Job's wife allowed the *fool* attribute to influence her after she lost her children and saw Job's affliction. After all the blessings she and Job had shared together, it was obviously the influence of the *fool* attribute led her to say to Job, "*Do you still hold fast to your integrity? Curse God and die!*" (Job 2:9). Job responded to her, "*You speak as one of the foolish women speaks. Shall we indeed accept good from God, and shall we not accept adversity?" In all this Job did not sin with his lips*" (Job 2:10). Moreover, Job's friends who came to sit and comfort him in his immense pain accused him of having the influence of the *fool* attribute. Eliphaz told him, "*Call out now; is there anyone who will answer you? And to which of the holy ones will you turn? For wrath kills a foolish man, and envy slays a simple one. I have seen the foolish taking root, but suddenly I cursed his dwelling place*" (Job 5:1-3). But Job stood strong in His love for God and told his wise friends, "*With Him are strength and prudence. The deceived and the deceiver are His. He leads counselors away plundered, and makes fools of the judges*"

(Job 12:17). Of course, Job was referring to his ***foolish*** wise friends who were now casting judgment on him. They had neither knowledge nor understanding of the events impacting Job.

In the Books of Psalms and Ecclesiastes, both writers documented a plethora of insights into the nature and behavior of one influence by the ***fool*** attribute. Once again, I will use the table format for space and convenience. David and Solomon documented:

*"Better a poor and wise youth than an old and **foolish** king who will be admonished no more"* (Ecclesiastes 4:13)	*"Arise, O God, plead Your own cause; remember how the **foolish** man reproaches You daily"* (Psalm 74:22)	*"Deliver me from all my transgressions; do not make me the reproach of the **foolish**"* (Psalm 39:8)
*"For he sees wise men die; likewise the **fool** and the senseless person perish, and leave their wealth to others. Their inner thought is that their houses will last forever, their dwelling places to all generations; they call their lands after their own names. Nevertheless man, though in honor, does not remain; he is like the beasts that perish. This is the way of those who are **foolish**, and of their posterity who approve their sayings"* (Psalm 49:10-13)	*"...I hated all my labor in which I had toiled under the sun, because I must leave it to the man who will come after me. And who knows whether he will be wise or a **fool**? Yet he will rule over all my labor in which I toiled and in which I have shown myself wise under the sun. This also is vanity"* (Ecclesiastes 2:18-19)	*"The wise man's eyes are in his head, but the **fool** walks in darkness. Yet I myself perceived that the same event happens to them all. So I said in my heart, "As it happens to the **fool**, it also happens to me, and why was I then more wise?" Then I said in my heart, "This also is vanity." For there is no more remembrance of the wise than of the **fool** forever, since all that now is will be forgotten in the days to come. And how does a wise man die? As the **fool**!"* (Ecclesiastes 2:14-16)
*"O Lord, how great are Your works! Your thoughts are very deep. A senseless man does not know, nor does a **fool** understand this"* (Psalm 92:5-6)	*"Remember this, that the enemy has reproached, O Lord, and that a **foolish** people has blasphemed Your name"* (Psalm 74:18)	*"When you make a vow to God, do not delay to pay it; for He has no pleasure in **fools**. Pay what you have vowed..."* (Ecclesiastes 5:4)

"I was so **foolish** and ignorant; I was like a beast before You" (Psalm 73:22)	"My wounds are foul and festering because of my **foolishness**" (Psalm 38:5)	"The **fool** folds his hands and consumes his own flesh" (Ecclesiastes 4:5)
"The **fool** has said in his heart, "There is no God." They are corrupt, they have done abominable works, there is none who does good" (Psalm 14:1; 53:1)	"Walk prudently when you go to the house of God; and draw near to hear rather than to give the sacrifice of **fools**, for they do not know that they do evil" (Ecclesiastes 5:1)	"For a dream comes through much activity, and a **fool's** voice is known by his many words" (Ecclesiastes 5:3)
"The heart of the wise is in the house of mourning, but the heart of **fools** is in the house of mirth. It is better to hear the rebuke of the wise than for a man to hear the song of **fools**. For like the crackling of thorns under a pot, so is the laughter of the **fool**. This also is vanity" (Ecclesiastes 7:4-6)	"A wise man's heart is at his right hand, but a **fool's** heart at his left. Even when a **fool** walks along the way, he lacks wisdom, and he shows everyone that he is a **fool**" (Ecclesiastes 10:2-3)	"The words of a wise man's mouth are gracious, but the lips of a **fool** shall swallow him up; the words of his mouth begin with **foolishness**, and the end of his talk is raving madness. (Ecclesiastes 10:12-13)
A **fool** also multiplies words. No man knows what is to be; who can tell him what will be after him? (Ecclesiastes 10:14)	The labor of **fools** wearies them, for they do not even know how to go to the city!" (Ecclesiastes 10:15)	"O God, You know my **foolishness**; and my sins are not hidden from You" (Psalm 69:5)
"Words of the wise, spoken quietly, should be heard rather than the shout of a ruler of **fools**" (Ecclesiastes 9:17)	"Do not hasten in your spirit to be angry, for anger rests in the bosom of **fools**" (Ecclesiastes 7:9)	"Do not be overly wicked, nor be **foolish**: Why should you die before your time?" (Ecclesiastes 7:17)

Table 30: Pearls of Wisdom from the Psalmist and Solomon Concerning the Fool Attribute

Wow! If one gained an understanding of the items revealed above, the influence of the *fool* attribute would be defeated in many homes and communities.

Next, the nation of Israel struggled with the influence of the *fool* attribute among its people before the Lord destroyed the nation. God sent His prophets to warn His people. Here are some of the many warnings given by the prophets from the Lord. The Bible recorded:

The Prophet	What Was Said
Isaiah	"For the **foolish** person will speak **foolishness**, and his heart will work iniquity: to practice ungodliness, to utter error against the Lord, to keep the hungry unsatisfied, and he will cause the drink of the thirsty to fail" (Isaiah 32:6)
	"Who frustrates the signs of the babblers, and drives diviners mad; Who turns wise men backward, and makes their knowledge **foolishness**..." (Isaiah 44:25)
Jeremiah	"For My people are **foolish**, they have not known Me. They are silly children, and they have no understanding. They are wise to do evil, but to do good they have no knowledge" (Jeremiah 4:22)
	"Therefore I said, "Surely these are poor. They are **foolish**; for they do not know the way of the Lord, the judgment of their God" (Jeremiah 5:4)
	"Hear this now, O **foolish** people, without understanding, who have eyes and see not, and who have ears and hear not..." (Jeremiah 5:21)
	"But they are altogether dull-hearted and **foolish**; a wooden idol is a worthless doctrine" (Jeremiah 10:8)
Ezekiel	"Thus says the Lord God: "Woe to the **foolish** prophets, who follow their own spirit and have seen nothing!" (Ezekiel 13:3)
Hosea	"Ephraim also is like a **silly** dove, without sense— they call to Egypt, they go to Assyria. Wherever they go, I will spread My net on them; I will bring them down like birds of the air; I will chastise them according to what their congregation has heard" (Hosea 7:11-12)

Table 31: The Prophet's Warnings about the Influence of the Fool Attribute

BTT allows one to see that the Old Testament clearly defined the behavior and attitude of one with the influence of the *fool* attribute; but more information is presented in the New Testament that is vital to our learning. Beginning with Jesus, He uses an analogy of a person building a house on sand to precisely illustrated the behavior of one influenced by this attribute. Most mature people understand the nature of sand and water; sand's loose granules easily wash away. To build a structure to live in on sand is clearly unwise. In fact, Jesus stated that only one influenced by the *fool* attribute would do so. When rains, flooding, and winds come along, this structure would eventually weaken and be destroyed. Jesus used this analogy to also illustrate the similarity of one influenced by the *fool* attribute and God's Word. Jesus said that everyone who does not build a strong foundation on good ground, in which the good ground represents His Word, has this attribute. Specifically, He said, *"But everyone who hears these sayings of Mine, and does not do them, will be like a **foolish** man who built his house on the sand"* (Matthew 7:26). These words of Jesus are free wisdom to all who will hear them. However, the negative forces of the war campaign, seeks to impede one's inner spirit from accepting even these simple words.

Other superb examples that Jesus used to illustrate the behavior of one influenced by the *fool* attribute included:

- The ten virgins: Jesus stated, *"Then the kingdom of heaven shall be likened to ten virgins who took their lamps and went out to meet the bridegroom. Now five of them were wise, and five were **foolish**. Those who were **foolish** took their lamps and took no oil with them..."* (Matthew 25:1-3). Jesus stated, *"...the **foolish** said to the wise, 'Give* *us some of your oil, for our lamps are going out."* (Matthew 25:8). The wise had none to spare, and the *foolish* were forced to go search for oil. Because of their lack of preparation, which is a sign of the *fool* attribute, they were lost.

- A rich man who became greedy: Jesus spoke a parable about a rich man whose ground yielded plentifully in Luke 12:16-21. But the man decided to tear down his barns and build newer and bigger barns to hoard more bounty and brag about his success. But Jesus said, *"...God said to him, 'Fool! This night your soul will be required of you; then whose will those things be which you have provided?"* (Luke 12:20). The *fool* attribute's influence on this wealthy man confused his priorities. His behavior cost him his soul.

Jesus also identified that the influence of the *fool* attribute lodges itself in one's inner spirit. He stated for one's learning, *"What comes out of a man, that defiles a man. For from within, out of the heart of men, proceed evil thoughts, adulteries, fornications, murders, thefts, covetousness, wickedness, deceit, lewdness, an evil eye, blasphemy, pride, foolishness. All these evil things come from within and defile a man"* (Mark 7:20-23). The big takeaway here is that the influence of the *fool* attribute, along with a host of other negative attributes that make it to one's inner spirit's heart, will defile a person. God's Word is the only protection that one's inner spirit has against the negative forces of the war campaign.

Jesus documented that the scribes and Pharisees allowed the *fool* attribute in their inner spirits. He called them out twice as "*Fools and blind!*" (Matthew 23:17; Matthew 23:19) because of their lack of understanding of spiritual matters. For the same reason, Jesus also told some of His disciples that they had allowed the influence of the *fool* attribute to temporarily blind them. The Biblical record documented that after Jesus' death, He met some of His disciples on the road to Emmaus and spoke to them. Jesus stated, *"...O foolish ones, and slow of heart to believe in all that the prophets have spoken!"* (Luke 24:25). In this instance, Jesus taught these disciples the words of life. The Bible documented that, *"...beginning at Moses and all the Prophets, He expounded to them in all the Scriptures the things concerning Himself"* (Luke 24:27). What is significant about this is that the Bible documented these men said, *"Did not our heart burn within us while He talked with us on the road, and while He opened the Scriptures to us?"* (Luke 24:32). Jesus' Word cleansed the influences of the *fool* attribute from the disciple's inner spirits.

Paul and the other disciples documented more pearls of wisdom about the *fool* attribute as the Holy Spirit led them to speak and write. Here are just a few of those pearls that are critical to our learning. The Biblical record documented:

- The *fool* attribute influences the ungodly and unrighteous: *"...because, although they knew God, they did not glorify Him as God, nor were thankful, but became futile in their thoughts, and their foolish hearts were darkened. Professing to be wise, they became fools..."* (Romans 1:21-22)

- One's conversations in life must not be *foolish*: *"But fornication and all uncleanness or covetousness, let it not even be named among you, as is fitting for saints; neither* *filthiness, nor **foolish** talking, nor coarse jesting, which are not fitting, but rather giving of thanks"* (Ephesians 5:3-4)

- One's behavior in life must not be ***foolish***: *"See then that you walk circumspectly, not as **fools** but as wise…"* (Ephesians 5:15)

- One must not chase after wealth: *"But those who desire to be rich fall into temptation and a snare, and into many **foolish** and harmful lusts which drown men in destruction and perdition"* (1 Timothy 6:9)

- One must avoid ***foolish*** dispute: *"But avoid **foolish** and ignorant disputes, knowing that they generate strife"* (2 Timothy 2:23) and *"…avoid **foolish** disputes, genealogies, contentions, and strivings about the law; for they are unprofitable and useless"* (Titus 3:9)

- One must do good works with faith that edifies the Lord: *"But do you want to know, O **foolish** man, that faith without works is dead?"* (James 2:20)

- One must submit to man's laws unless they are immoral or conflict with God: *"Therefore submit yourselves to every ordinance of man for the Lord's sake, whether to the king as supreme, or to governors, as to those who are sent by him for the punishment of evildoers and for the praise of those who do good. For this is the will of God, that by doing good you may put to silence the ignorance of **foolish** men—as free, yet not using liberty as a cloak for vice, but as bondservants of God"* (1 Peter 2:13-16)

BTT allows one to see that all the things documented above help one to withstand the influence of the ***fool*** attribute. The Gospel of Jesus Christ is the manual for defeating all the negative attributes and surviving spiritual warfare. I have placed a lot of emphasis on this because the influence of the ***fool*** attribute keeps an incredibly large number of the world's population, both religious and secular, in the dark about the living God. Paul, moved by the Holy Spirit, documented three critical truths to supports this fact. He wrote:

1. *"…the natural man does not receive the things of the Spirit of God, for they are **foolishness** to him; nor can he know them, because they are spiritually <u>discerned</u>"* (1 Corinthians 2:14)

2. *"Let no one deceive himself. If anyone among you seems to be wise in this age, let him become a **fool** that he may become wise. For the wisdom of this world is **foolishness** with God. For it is written, "He catches the wise in their own craftiness…"* (1 Corinthians 3:18-19)

3. *"For the message of the cross is **foolishness** to those who are perishing, but to us who are being saved it is the power of God. For it is written: "I will destroy the wisdom of the wise, and bring to nothing the understanding of the prudent." Where is the wise? Where is the scribe? Where is the disputer of this age? Has not God made **foolish** the wisdom of this world? For since, in the wisdom of God, the world through wisdom did not know God, it pleased God through the **foolishness** of the message preached to save those who believe. For Jews request a sign, and Greeks seek after wisdom; but we*

*preach Christ crucified, to the Jews a stumbling block and to the Greeks **foolishness**, but to those who are called, both Jews and Greeks, Christ the power of God and the wisdom of God. Because the **foolishness** of God is wiser than men, and the weakness of God is stronger than men. For you see your calling, brethren, that not many wise according to the flesh, not many mighty, not many noble, are called. But God has chosen the **foolish** things of the world to put to shame the wise, and God has chosen the weak things of the world to put to shame the things which are mighty; and the base things of the world and the things which are despised God has chosen, and the things which are not, to bring to nothing the things that are, that no flesh should glory in His presence*" (1 Corinthian 1:18-29)

Even as far back as the establishment of Christ's church in Galatia, the negative attributes slipped in and influenced people to backslide into error after they learned the Truth of the Gospel. The influence of the ***fool*** attribute was also present, for Paul documented "*O **foolish** Galatians! Who has bewitched you that you should not obey the truth, before whose eyes Jesus Christ was clearly portrayed among you as crucified?*" (Galatians 3:1). Further he said, "*Are you so **foolish**? Having begun in the Spirit, are you now being made perfect by the flesh?*" (Galatians 3:3). BTT helps one to see that some of the people in Christ's church in Galatia began turning to man's ways to save their souls and putting aside the Gospel of Christ; the only path to salvation.

For every Christian today, patience is critical for dealing with anyone influenced by the ***fool*** attribute. Patience is not only critical, but it is mandatory. Paul documented for all Christian's humility, "*...we ourselves were also once **foolish**, disobedient, deceived, serving various lusts and pleasures, living in malice and envy, hateful and hating one another*" (Titus 3:3). This sobering thought is for our benefit.

The **Simple attribute**: The influence of this attribute leads one to be naive when it comes to God's Word. Its influence keeps one from understanding the easy, straight forward, and basic principles that the Lord provided in the Biblical record. The ***simple*** attribute has nothing to do with people born with cognitive developmental disabilities or disabilities caused by brain damage from head trauma, drug use, or other physical conditions. This attribute deals with a negative spirit that can disrupt the connection between one's inner spirit and the physical brain. It causes one to respond to life's situations and scenarios with a child-like view that lacks spiritual maturity and knowledge. The ***simple*** attribute influences one to prefer not to hear hard teachings from the Lord. One influenced by this attribute will claim he or she prefers keeping his or her options open to all things. This includes any religious or pagan practice, tradition, or doctrine in any combination. The influence of the ***simple*** attribute strives to keep one in the dark on spiritual matters so that he or she can maintain their personal lifestyle choices and be unhindered by the perceived limitations of God's Word. In fact, this attribute strives to influence one to remain free of God in all sectors of one's life to the point of becoming atheistically defensive. Thus, this attribute's will rendering one completely ignorant of God's Word. Its influence is so debilitating that a person will lack the ability to see real dangers ahead of them. Moreover, one influenced by this attribute often believes people are free to live their lives anyway they wish as long as their lifestyles do not harm others. The ***simple*** lack the ability to see that this philosophy is part of the grand strategy of spiritual warfare designed to deliver large sums of people to the negative forces of the war campaign. For when the positive forces engage in tough teachings on topics such as abortion, assisted suicide, race relations, discrimination, or even homosexuality, people influenced by the ***simple*** attributes turn these topics into battle lines that their brains refuse to cross. The influence of the ***simple*** attribute will lead one to argue that ignorance is bliss on these and other tough subjects. Their life choice of ***simplicity*** will not entertain what the Lord has revealed on these and other Biblical subjects.

BTT also allows one to see that the full maturity of this attribute in one's inner spirit is the "***dumb***" spirit identified by the prophet Isaiah in Isaiah 56:10 and identified by Jesus in Mark 9:25. The Biblical record documented of Jesus that, "*...He rebuked the **unclean spirit**, saying to it: "Deaf and **dumb** spirit, I command you, come out of him and enter him no more!"* (Mark 9:25). Jesus was not being derogatory or condescending in the use of this term. He called out a behavior, identified by God, that one must not try to sugar coat or change to make it pleasing to one's ear. Jesus knew that this was a powerful ***unclean spirit*** that hindered the physical brain from making a spiritual connection. With this in mind, consider what the Spirit of wisdom taught Solomon.

In the first chapter of the Book of Proverbs, Solomon explained the reason for having proverbs and the enigma or paradox associated with them. Solomon wrote the proverbs for one, "*...to know wisdom and instruction, to perceive the words of understanding, to receive the instruction of wisdom, justice, judgment, and equity; to give prudence to the **simple**...*" (Proverbs 1:1-4). Given by the Spirit of wisdom and documented by Solomon, proverbs give prudence to people influenced by the ***simple*** attribute. Prudence means giving one the ability to govern and discipline oneself by use of reason, judgment, and knowledge that allows one to avoid danger or risks. In Chapter VII of this book, I will discuss the term "prudent" as a category of people among the harvest that Jesus spoke of in Matthew 9:37.

The Spirit of wisdom revealed to Solomon that she, "*...calls aloud outside; she raises her voice in the open squares. She cries out in the chief concourses, at the openings of the gates in the city she speaks her words: "How long, you **simple** ones, will you love **simplicity**?"*" (Proverbs 1:20-22). She revealed later that remaining in ***simplicity*** would seal one's fate. She told Solomon, "*For the turning away of the **simple** will slay them, and the complacency of fools will destroy them...*" (Proverbs 1:32). Remember, this attribute hinders a person from seeing danger coming their way because they choose to maintain a ***simple*** state of mind when it comes to God's Word.

In Chapter seven of the Book of Proverbs, Solomon documented a clear example of how one with the ***simple*** attribute easily falls to the <u>lust</u> of this world. The example used the illustration of a young man influenced by the ***simple*** attribute. He went to the house of one influenced by the immoral attribute engaged in prostitution. Please reread the chapter on the immoral attribute if one has forgotten the dangers of this negative attribute and its role in spiritual warfare. In this example, the ***simple*** attribute influenced this young man to go down the wrong path of life. Solomon documented, "*For at the window of my house I looked through my lattice, and saw among the **simple**, I perceived among the youths, a young man devoid of understanding, passing along the street near her corner; and he took the path to her house* *in the twilight, in the evening, in the black and dark night"* Proverbs 7:6-9). What happened next explained why knowledge of the influence of the *simple* attribute is so important. One will see that the influence of this attribute cost this young man his life. Solomon documented that, *"Immediately he went after her, as an ox goes to the slaughter, or as a fool to the correction of the stocks, till an arrow struck his liver. As a bird hastens to the snare, he did not know it would cost his life"* (Proverbs 7:22-23). In other words, the influence of the *simple* attribute blinded this young man and he willfully ignored the dangers that were around him. This is what the influence of the *simple* attribute does in homes and community every day because of the war campaign. This attribute influences young adults in great numbers. The attribute preys on youth's lack of knowledge and desire to be an adult too fast. For this reason, this attribute can do more damage to the world's youth than any other negative attribute traversing the campaign's battlefield.

    The Spirit of wisdom made several pleas for people influenced by the *simple* attribute to listen to her. She pleaded, *"O you **simple** ones, understand prudence, and you fools, be of an understanding heart"* (Proverbs 8:5). Further, she pleaded, *"Whoever is **simple**, let him turn in here!"* (Proverbs 9:4), hoping to redirect their path. Twice she revealed to Solomon that, *"A prudent man foresees evil and hides himself, but the **simple** pass on and are punished"* (Proverbs 22:3 and 27:12). BTT allows one to see that one who allows the influence of this attribute will ignore warning signs of trouble or danger to their own demise.

    Using imagery of a female prostitute influenced by the fool attribute, Wisdom revealed to Solomon that, *"A foolish woman is clamorous; she is **simple**, and knows nothing. For she sits at the door of her house, on a seat by the highest places of the city, to call to those who pass by, who go straight on their way: "Whoever is **simple**, let him turn in here"; And as for him who lacks understanding, she says to him, "Stolen water is sweet, and bread eaten in secret is pleasant." But he does not know that the dead are there, that her guests are in the depths of hell"* (Proverbs 9:13-18). I pray that one noticed that this woman used the same words as the Spirit of wisdom in Proverbs 9:4; *"Whoever is **simple**, let him turn in here!"* The influence of the fool attribute led this woman to deceptively use words that reached the inner spirits of one influenced by the *simple* attribute. This example of the foolish woman used a prostitute-like behavior to gain the attention of one influenced by the *simple* attribute. The result was destruction of the one who willfully entered her den of death. Conversely, in the war campaign, the result is eternal death for one's soul and the strengthening of the negative forces.

    Here are a few of the reasons why one with the *simple* attribute is so vulnerable. The Spirit of wisdom revealed to Solomon that, *"The **simple** believes every word..."* (Proverbs 14:15). Because of this, she further stated that *"The **simple** inherit folly..."* (Proverbs 14:18). That is to say, they inherit recklessness, irrationality, and even stupidity.

    There are always people who will scoff at what the Spirit of wisdom revealed. But one will learn that the scoffing comes from another ancient **unclean spirit** documented later in this book. However, for people like this, Wisdom told Solomon, *"Strike a scoffer, and the **simple** will become wary..."* (Proverbs 19:25) and *"When the scoffer is punished, the **simple** is made wise..."* (Proverbs 21:11). Rebuking and punishing people influenced by the scoffer attribute who ridicule the God's wisdom will help people influenced by the *simple* attribute. Corrective action against one influenced by the scoffer attribute allows one influenced by the *simple* attribute to wise up, and begin to understand the way of God. Yes! the *simple* can gain wisdom.

In the rest of the Biblical record, this attribute required very little documentation from the Lord. Eliphaz, one of the wise men who abused Job during his time of epic distress accused Job of having the *simple* attribute. Eliphaz said to Job, "*Call out now; is there anyone who will answer you? And to which of the holy ones will you turn? For wrath kills a foolish man, and envy slays a **simple** one*" (Job 5:2). Reading the Book of Job, one learns that Satan used Eliphaz to torment Job in his pain. Job never allowed the influence of the *simple* attribute in his inner spirit. His soundness of mind and the wisdom he espoused illuminates the pages of the Book of Job.

The Psalmist provided clues as to what can help those with the *simple* attribute gain wisdom. The Psalmist wrote, "*The law of the Lord is perfect, converting the soul; the testimony of the Lord is sure, making wise the **simple**...*" (Psalm 19:7). The Lord's testimony covers the pages of the Biblical record for everyone to see. But one influenced by the *simple* attribute must pick up the Book, read it, and believe its content. If anyone influenced by the *simple* attribute would just do this, the Psalmist said of the Lord, "*Your testimonies are wonderful; therefore my soul keeps them. The entrance of Your words gives light; it gives understanding to the **simple***" (Psalm 119:129-130). Further the Psalmist stated of himself, "*Gracious is the Lord, and righteous; Yes, our God is merciful. The Lord preserves the **simple**; I was brought low, and He saved me*" (Psalm 116:5-6). Yes! When the Psalmist found himself emotionally, physically, and spiritually drained by the pressures of life, he felt he had the influence of the *simple* attribute in his inner spirit. One can feel this way today when the struggles of this life overwhelms one's inner spirit. The deluge of misinformation, economic woes, crime, and the like, causes this feeling. The Psalmist recognized that God and His Word are the answers to overcome life's stresses.

The prophet Isaiah documented that the *simple* attribute influenced the leaders of the nation of Israel. He said of their leaders; their nation's "*...watchmen are blind, they are all ignorant; they are all **dumb** dogs, they cannot bark; sleeping, lying down, loving to slumber. Yes, they are greedy dogs which never have enough. And they are shepherds who cannot understand; they all look to their own way, every one for his own gain, from his own territory*" (Isaiah 56:10-11). Clearly, the *simple* attribute was doing its job of aiding the negative forces of the war campaign against the nation of Israel.

In the New Testament of the Biblical record, Paul provided a warning concerning divisive people within the Lord's church. Divisive people can easily deceive people influenced by the *simple* attribute. He documented, "*Now I urge you, brethren, note those who cause divisions and offenses, contrary to the doctrine which you learned, and avoid them. For those who are such do not serve our Lord Jesus Christ, but their own belly, and by smooth words and flattering speech deceive the hearts of the **simple***" (Romans 16:17-18). Yes! The body of Christ is composed of members of varying measures of spiritual maturity. Thus, Paul's stern warning is of grave importance. With people influenced by the *simple* attribute within the church, their faith requires greater protection while they spiritually mature. The negative forces will send divisive people to discourage and confuse those influenced by the *simple* attribute. The task of protecting them belongs to all that are more mature in God's Word. Christians must work to help people influenced by the ***simple*** attribute overcome this ***unclean spirit*** with the Truth from Jesus Christ. This is another reason that Christians are called to, "*Bear one another's burdens, and so fulfill the law of Christ*" (Galatians 6:2). Working with one influenced by the ***simple*** attribute is a chore, but a good work that God demands. Moreover, it keeps many people from becoming collateral damage along the path of the war campaign.

Paul recognized that there are some people who will argue for keeping some aspects of the influence of the ***simple*** attribute. Thus, to Christians in the Lord's church at Rome, he stated, "*...your obedience has become known to all. Therefore I am glad on your behalf; but I want you to be wise in what is good, and* ***simple*** *concerning evil*" (Romans 16:19). In other words, one must make sure one's focus is in the right place when it pertains to retaining an aspect of the ***simple*** attribute. If one does, one must make sure one maintains ***simplicity*** when it comes to the things that are evil and turn away from them. This is the focus of Paul statement. Other than this, the influence of the ***simple*** attribute remains on the negative forces side of the war campaign.

Finally, Paul warned Christians of the perilous times that would come and how the influence of the ***simple*** attribute would play a role in spiritual warfare. Paul wrote to Timothy and told him "*...know this, that in the last days perilous times will come: For men will be lovers of themselves, lovers of money, boasters, proud, blasphemers, disobedient to parents, unthankful, unholy, unloving, unforgiving, slanderers, without self-control, brutal, despisers of good, traitors, headstrong, haughty, lovers of pleasure rather than lovers of God, having a form of godliness but denying its power. And from such people turn away! For of this sort are those who creep into households and make captives of* ***gullible*** *women loaded down with sins, led away by various lusts, always learning and never able to come to the knowledge of the truth*" (2 Timothy 3:1-7). The women described in these Scriptures are women who will be influenced by the ***simple*** attribute. BTT allows one to see that the negative forces of the war campaign will impact women in various ways. These Scriptures indicated that there will be women influenced by the ***simple*** attribute, who will be exploited by men influenced by the wicked and evil attributes. The Gospel of Jesus Christ is the only hope in this situation. Until people with the positive attribute's help women influenced by the ***simple*** attribute spiritually mature, they will never understand what makes them stumble. Their ***gullibility*** will keep them lost in the fog generated by the negative forces of the war campaign. The inappropriate and ungodly behavior of men influenced by the wicked and evil attributes, and unsuspecting women with the ***simple*** attribute, can divide and destroy the Lord's church on the spiritual battlefield.

The **Unjust attribute**: The influence of this attribute causes an individual to turn a blind eye to justice and use the justice system to abuse and harm others. Acts of injustice, unfairness, discrimination, and partiality characterized this attribute. One influenced by the ***unjust*** attribute will create strife among his or her neighbors, communities, and society in  general, over such issues as race, gender, finance, and any other area. The influence of this attribute focuses on divisive tactics and perverting the legal system to support its actions. This attribute specifically loves the bounty of people in the legal profession whose sole role is to uphold the justice system. The influence of this attribute strives to compromise judges, lawyers, and the drafters and creators of earthly laws (also known as politicians). The people within these groups, who allow the influence of the ***unjust*** attribute, create barriers to God's Truth. The barriers are often greater than the harm created by other negative attributes because this attribute knows the laws well that protects their behavior. As one learns about the ***unjust*** attribute, one will be able to understand why Jesus specifically stated, "*Woe to you lawyers! For you have taken away the key of knowledge. You did not enter in yourselves, and those who were entering in you hindered*" (Luke 11:52), and "*Woe to you also, lawyers! For you load men with burdens hard to bear, and you yourselves do not touch the burdens with one of your fingers. Woe to you! For you build the tombs of the prophets, and your fathers killed them*" (Luke 11:46-47). I submit that Jesus referred to people in the legal profession of the religious and secular community alike.

Moreover, peace enforcement officials influenced by the ***unjust*** attribute cause immeasurable damage on the spiritual battlefield. The negative behaviors of rogue judges, lawyers, police, government officials and military leader's reinforce the negative attribute's offensive posture in spiritual warfare. These official's behaviors impact the physical, emotional, psychological, and spiritual level of the people they encounter which inadvertently increases the negative forces size as the encountered people respond. Only an infusion of God's Word can change this dynamic. An infusion of God's Word can begin the healing process at the spiritual level. Once healing begins here, the physical, emotional, and psychological levels can be healed. **Figure 21** attempts to illustrate this point. The fog generated by the negative forces hides this knowledge. Many healthcare professionals become part of the problem as they scoff at God's Word as a solution. Moreover, people influenced by the wicked attribute contribute to this problem by crafting and imposing government regulations that separate church and

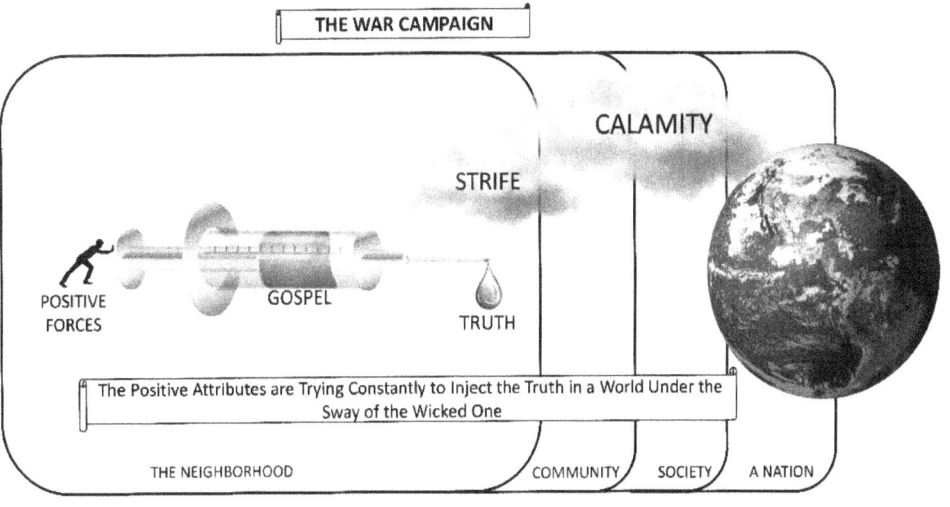

Figure 21: God's Word Provides Relief in the War Campaign

state to restrict knowledge from God's Word. Overall, the negative forces of the war campaign gain a steady influx of forces created officials influenced by the ***unjust*** attribute using a treacherous and corruptive strategy. The influence of the ***unjust*** attribute influences the creation and enforcement of immoral laws in spiritual warfare.

If it appears my condemnation of the legal community, including politicians, is harsh - it is; but God's condemnation is even worse. People working at any level of the justice system who allow the influence of the **unjust** attribute are the second greatest asset to the negative forces of the war campaign. The damage they do to the positive forces is second only to false teachers of the Gospel. The concept of segregation provides an example of the atrocity of the **unjust** attribute's influence on people in both the legal and political professions. BTT allows one to see that the practice of segregation by race was, and still remains, one of the greatest atrocities of spiritual warfare. People influenced by the **unjust** attribute perpetuated this practice and divided the secular, religious, and even the Christians communities, by skin color. Moreover, many lawyers and judges influenced by the **unjust** attribute fortified the practice with laws. These lawyers and judges abuse their authority and the justice system. For the spreading of the Gospel, segregation placed a wedge between God and believers who claim to read and teach the Gospel from His Word - the Bible. Hence, the influence of the **unjust** attribute divided entire congregations of people as they unknowingly walk on the negative path of life and prevented others from finding the path of light for generations. Refer to **Figures 10** and **11** in this book if necessary. God is not happy with this situation. Solomon documented, *"If you see the oppression of the poor, and the violent perversion of justice and righteousness in a province, do not marvel at the matter; for high official watches over high official, and higher officials are over them"* (Ecclesiastes 5:8). Please do not be deceived.

    The Spirit of wisdom revealed to Solomon two painful and indicting points about the influence of the **unjust** attribute. First, She revealed that *"An **unjust** man is an abomination to the righteous"* (Proverbs 29:27). This strong language revealed that the behavior of one influenced by the **unjust** attribute is so bad, that people with the righteous attribute will see them as an abomination. One influenced by the righteous attribute cannot tolerate this attribute's behaviors. Since the Spirit of wisdom revealed this, the opposite is also true. If one with the **unjust** attribute is not an abomination to one with the righteous attribute, then the one claiming the righteous attribute needs to examine himself or herself.

    The second painful and indicting point revealed to Solomon was that, *"When a wicked man dies, his expectation will perish, and the hope of the **unjust** perishes"* (Proverbs 11:7). From this wisdom, there is an obvious undeniable link between one with the wicked attribute and one with the **unjust** attribute. BTT allows one to see clearly that one exhibiting the behavior of the **unjust** attribute is emboldened by people influenced by the wicked attribute. Let this sink in a moment. It is this clarity that gives us the understanding of events occurring in spiritual warfare. The primary point here is that one must understand the way of one influenced by the wicked attribute and their impact on one influenced by the **unjust** attribute. Proportionally, the more the influence of the wicked attribute increases in the world, the more the influence of the **unjust** attribute also increases. However, when one influenced by the wicked attribute is removed by death, the hopes of one influenced by the **unjust** attribute will cease - proportionally.

    Further in the Old Testament, the Psalmist prayed to the Lord for help in dealing with people influenced by the **unjust** attribute. The Psalmist prayed, *"Vindicate me, O God, and plead my cause against an ungodly nation; oh, deliver me from the deceitful and **unjust** man! For You are the God of my strength..."* (Psalm 43:1). The Psalmist demonstrated the right way to deal with one influenced by the **unjust** attribute. One should never take up arms against people influenced by this **unclean spirit** because of the attribute's ancient and extensive knowledge of the legal system. Allowing God to handle people under the influence of this attribute is the best strategy. For it is the Lord who said, "*Vengeance is Mine*" (Deuteronomy 32:35; Romans 12:19; and Hebrews 10:30) and He will repay. If one influenced by the **unjust** attribute wrongs you, turn it over to the Lord and watch His power.

The Psalmist even documented that the Lord pays attention to the behavior of those influenced by the **unjust** attribute. He wrote, "*God stands in the congregation of the mighty; He judges among the gods. How long will you judge **unjustly**, and show partiality to the wicked? Selah. Defend the poor and fatherless; do justice to the afflicted and needy. Deliver the poor and needy; free them from the hand of the wicked. They do not know, nor do they understand; they walk about in darkness; all the foundations of the earth are unstable*" Psalm 82:1-5). BTT allows one to understand that where the Scripture states, "*He* [God] *judges among the gods,*" it means that God judges among the magistrates or judges of the legal profession. God knows their inner spirits when their rulings are just and **unjust**. They will be held accountable. The Scriptures explain that people influenced by the **unjust** attribute cause the foundations of the earth to be unstable. The foundations of the earth are the divine things God put in place to keep balance, order, and peace in the world. These foundations become unstable when people influenced by the **unjust** attribute pervert God's law. In spiritual warfare, as the legal system increase in perversions, as partiality increased toward the wicked, as the poor and fatherless lack defenses, and as the needy are afflicted, the foundation of the earth shake from instability. However, when the foundations become too unstable, God uses His <u>calamity</u> to get His people's attention. Rest assured, when the foundation unhinges from the weight of sin, Jesus Himself will return to fix the problem. However, one must understand the long-suffering God always provides an opportunity for repentance before His patience runs out. One must understand that the perversion of the law is part of the grand strategy crafted by people influenced by the **unjust** attribute of the war campaign. Leaders at all levels that claim the positive attributes cannot sit in silence when they become aware of abuses by people influenced by this attribute. If leaders remain silent, their silence is complicity and consent. One must get involved to correct the behaviors and actions of one influenced by the **unjust** attribute before the people impacted have their inner spirits broken.

All the prophets sent by God warned the nation of Israel about the influence of the **unjust** attribute. Here are just a few of the warnings. The prophets documented:

The Prophet	What Was Said
Isaiah	"*...Let grace be shown to the wicked, yet he will not learn righteousness; in the land of uprightness he will deal **unjustly**, and will not behold the majesty of the Lord*" (Isaiah 26:10)
Zephaniah	For Jerusalem: "*Woe to her who is rebellious and polluted, to the oppressing city! She has not obeyed His voice, she has not received correction; she has not trusted in the Lord, she has not drawn near to her God. Her princes in her midst are roaring lions; her judges are evening wolves that leave not a bone till morning. Her prophets are insolent, treacherous people; her priests have polluted the sanctuary, they have done violence to the law. The Lord is righteous in her midst, He will do no unrighteousness. Every morning He*

	*brings His justice to light; He never fails, but the **unjust** knows no shame"* (Zephaniah 3:1-5)

Table 32: Examples of the Prophets' Warnings about the Unjust Attribute

As you can see, the ***unjust*** attribute did great damage to the nation of Israel, as it does to any nation of people that it influences. Like the other negative attributes, when one can correct the manifestations of this attribute's behavior, correction must occur. With this said, consider what the New Testament of the Biblical record documents about this attribute.

As Jesus appeared in the Biblical record, while teaching people that they must love their enemies, He also taught them that God "...*makes His sun rise on the evil and on the good and sends rain on the just and on the **unjust***" (Matthew 5:45). This is a hard message today for many, but it simply signifies that God is still in control. The day one does not see the sunrise, one's life has ended. And yes, the blind can feel the sun; so, they are covered too. But until that time, one has time to make corrections in one's life. Jesus' comment is our example from God of His impartiality. Even one influenced by the ***unjust*** attribute can never say that God is ***unjust*** to him or her because God allows everyone the opportunity to see another day – another day to repent of sin. Irrespective of the choices one makes in life, God's reward and punishment is always just. BTT allows one to embrace this wonderful point of Jesus' message.

Next, Jesus commented on the shrewdness of people influenced by the ***unjust*** attribute. Compared to God's people, people influenced by the ***unjust*** attribute are quicker to respond to tough situations. In a parable documented in Luke 16:1-8, Jesus stated that a certain rich man found out that he had a steward influenced by the ***unjust*** attribute. After hearing accusations that this steward was wasting his goods, the rich man confronted the steward. In response, the ***unjust*** steward quickly devised a plan, collected money from the rich man's debtors, and made himself look good in the rich man's eyes. For the ***unjust*** steward's quick action, Jesus stated, "...*the master commended the **unjust** steward because he had dealt shrewdly. For the sons of this world are more shrewd in their generation than the sons of light*" (Luke 16:8). This comment documented how careful one must be of the craftiness of people influenced by the ***unjust*** attribute. For when people influenced by this attribute find themselves in a pinch, they will resolve their dilemmas using whatever means are at their disposal. This attribute's shrewdness demands that people influenced by positive attributes always be on their guard. For one influenced by the ***unjust*** attribute will use their shrewdness to gain an advantage over people influenced by the positive attributes in spiritual warfare.

Jesus stated several important facts concerning the influence of the ***unjust*** attribute in the lives of people. Some of the hardest hitting points included:

- "...*He who is faithful in what is least is faithful also in much; and he who is **unjust** in what is least is **unjust** also in much*" (Luke 16:10)

- To an "...***unjust*** *judge...*" (Luke 18:6) who did not fear God but responded to a widow's request for justice according to Luke 18:4, 5. Jesus said, "...*shall God not avenge His own elect who cry out day and night to Him, though He bears long with them? I tell you that He will avenge them speedily...*" (Luke 7-8)

- Using a parable about the Pharisee and the tax collector, Jesus said, "*The Pharisee stood and prayed thus with himself, 'God, I thank You that I am not like other men—extortioners, **unjust**, adulterers, or even as this tax collector*" (Luke 18:11) while the tax collector focused on what was really important in life. But it was the tax collector that went home, "*justified rather than the other; for everyone who exalts himself will be humbled, and he who humbles himself will be exalted*" (Luke 18:14)

Paul spoke about people influence by the **unjust** attribute when he gave his defense to Antonius Felix, the Governor of Judea. Paul told Felix, "*I have hope in God, which they themselves also accept, that there will be a resurrection of the dead, both of the just and the **unjust**. This being so, I myself always strive to have a conscience without offense toward God and men*" (Acts 24:15). You see, Paul understood the war campaign. He told Felix that God would judge people influenced by this attribute. Therefore, Paul wanted to keep his conscience clean before both God and men. People who allow the influence of the **unjust** attribute have a conscience problem. BTT allows one to see that Paul was stating that the conscience of one influenced by the **unjust** attribute offends God.

Peter later pointed out why the condemnation of one influenced by the **unjust** attribute was so great. He documented that Christ, "*...suffered once for sins, the **just** for the **unjust**, that He might bring us to God, being put to death in the flesh but made alive by the Spirit...*" (1 Peter 3:18). BTT allows one to see that because Christ sacrificed His life for people who allow the influence of the **unjust** attribute, there is no acceptable excuse for allowing this attribute's influence. Therefore, when He renders judgement, His judgement will be divinely <u>justified</u>! He has given instructions for defeating the **unjust** attribute, as well as examples to follow. For one who willfully allows the influence of the **unjust** attribute anyway, Peter documented, "*...the Lord knows how to deliver the godly out of temptations and to reserve the **unjust** under punishment for the day of judgment, and especially those who walk according to the flesh in the lust of uncleanness and despise authority...*" (2 Peter 2:9-10). This unprecedented clarity is hidden by the false teachings. False teachers hide this truth in the fog generated by the negative forces during spiritual warfare.

Jesus declared that there will be a time when it will be too late for one to change and accept the glorious Gospel. He said, "*Behold, I am coming quickly! Blessed is he who keeps the words of the prophecy of this book*" (Revelation 22:7). An angel of the Lord told John not to seal the words of this Book after this statement was made. He said the time is at hand in Revelation 22:10. Further, the angel said, "*He who is **unjust**, let him be **unjust** still; he who is filthy, let him be filthy still; he who is righteous, let him be righteous still; he who is holy, let him be holy still*" (Revelation 22:11). Then Jesus closed with this statement, "*...behold, I am coming quickly, and My reward is with Me, to give to every one according to his work. I am the Alpha and the Omega, the Beginning and the End, the First and the Last*" (Revelation 22:12-13). Based on these words, anyone influenced by the **unjust** attribute should strive to let it go now. Do not let Jesus return and catch one holding on to the influence of the **unjust** attribute or any other negative attribute. For when Jesus' justice is rendered, anyone influenced by this attribute will be lost in the deception perpetrated by the negative forces of the war campaign.

The **Scoffer attribute**: The influence of this attribute leads one to be insolent, contemptible, and disrespectful toward God and any form of Biblical Truth. The influence of the *scoffer* attribute causes one to sneer at anyone who comes to them with God's Word. A contemptuous facial expression marks their behavior. However, it is not just God's Word the *scoffer* ridicules. This attribute causes one to ridicule anything that they refuse to believe, along with any information that provides obvious warnings that indicate trouble is ahead. The influence of this attribute's manifested behavior is strongest when an audience is present. The attribute demonstrates physical outburst of contempt manifested as derision or *mockery*, which can lead others to abusive or nasty behaviors. Depending on the audience, spitting, tearing clothing, or other dramatic acts or gestures can be used to strengthen the *scoffer's* position. This behavior is especially true when the one influenced by the attribute strongly disagrees with another person's views or position. The influence of the *scoffer* attribute is extremely strong in religious and secular institutions of higher learning where professional credentials are at risk. Moreover, in these institutions, generations of people learn to actively *scoff* at and question the ancient boundaries God established to regulate godly behavior in mankind. Leaders influenced by the *scoffer* attribute in these institutions have become the chief obstructionist for learning both <u>discernment</u> of God's Word and His Truth. In the secular world, one influenced by the *scoffer* attribute pushes humanism, relativism, and creationism to argue there is no God. These institutions teach that man is the creator, author, and controller of his or her destiny. They believe evolution and critical thinking holds the key to true knowledge. Whereas in many religious communities, one influenced by the *scoffer* attribute becomes selective with God's Word. Religious academics pick and choose scriptures to make their professional arguments when they are convenient to their needs. Even people from these communities argue that spiritualism and enlightenment are the keys to knowledge, even though the Biblical record documents clearly that "...*God gives wisdom and knowledge*..." (Ecclesiastes 2:26). These are people who do not understand faith and they ignore the things they cannot physically justify. These same people establish their own wisdom over God's wisdom. Through religious and secular leadership, the *scoffer* attribute influences one to elevate himself or herself over the Word of God, while unknowingly aiding the negative forces of the war campaign. As one takes all this information into consideration, consider what the Spirit of wisdom revealed to Solomon about this divisive attribute.

One of the first things that Solomon learned from the Spirit of wisdom about this attribute was that, "...*scorners* delight in their *scorning*...." (Proverbs 1:22). Make no mistake, the Spirit of wisdom revealed that there was a fine line between *scoffing*, *scorning*, and *mocking*. All are part of the behavior of one influenced by the *scoffer* attribute. Where *scoffing* lends more toward simple ridicule; *scorning* and *mocking* are more intense behaviors of ridicule, belittling, and reviling. *Mocking's* intensity is followed up with physical hand gestures. It can include touching another person, i.e. slapping them on the head. This should tell one everything in a nutshell about this negative attribute. If one influenced by the *scoffer* attribute finds delight in his or her actions, they will keep doing it. Because the influence of this attribute brings one delight, he or she becomes a danger to themselves and others. Why? Because the Spirit of wisdom revealed inwardly, "*A **scoffer** seeks wisdom and does not find it...*" (Proverbs 14:6). In fact, Wisdom further revealed to Solomon, that "*A **scoffer** does not love one who corrects him, nor will he go to the wise*" (Proverbs 15:12). One should see the paradox for one influenced by the **scoffer** attribute. They want wisdom; but they do not want it from human sources. Thus, the Spirit of wisdom told Solomon "*Do not correct a **scoffer**, lest he hate you...*" (Proverbs 9:8) and "*He who corrects a **scoffer** gets shame for himself...*" (Proverbs 9:7). In other words, let the one influenced by the **scoffer** attribute deal with the consequences they create; leave them alone. For the Spirit of wisdom also revealed that "*... a **scoffer** does not listen to rebuke*" (Proverbs 13:1). Because of this, Solomon clearly understood Wisdom's statement that, "*...the **scoffer** is an abomination to men*" (Proverbs 24:9). One with the **scoffer** attribute may try to sell himself or herself as one in the wise category. But in the end, they are no more than an abomination.

A reason that one influenced by this attribute is an abomination to men is because "***Scoffers** set a city aflame...*" (Proverbs 29:8). In other words, BTT allows one to see that the power involved in this attribute's influence can lead one to cause so much strife that it can set an entire city in an uproar. In a fact filled meeting where truth and justice are taking place, a single person influenced by the **scoffer** attribute can become the catalyst for a citywide riot. One person influenced by the **scoffer** attribute can generate a mob mentality to distort and confuse the truth within minutes. An example of this is found in the Book of Acts. The Bible documents, "*...the Jews <u>who were not persuaded</u>, becoming envious, took some of the evil men from the marketplace, and gathering a mob, set all the city in an uproar and attacked the house of Jason, and sought to bring them out to the people*" (Acts 17:5). One can see how the catalytic power of this **unclean spirit** drives a strategy in spiritual warfare to grow forces against the positive attributes. The Spirit of wisdom told Solomon three critical rules for dealing with one influenced by the **scoffer** attribute. She said,

- "*Strike a **scoffer**, and the simple will become wary...*" (Proverbs 19:25)

- "*When the **scoffer** is punished, the simple is made wise...*" (Proverbs 21:11)

- "*Cast out the **scoffer**, and contention will leave; yes, strife and reproach will cease*" (Proverbs 22:10)

The most important thing that one should understand about this attribute is that God will handle the person who allows this influence of this attribute. The Spirit of wisdom shared with Solomon that "*Judgments are prepared for **scoffers**...*" (Proverbs 19:29). With this said, consider a few more pearls of wisdom that the Spirit of wisdom revealed to Solomon. Solomon documented:

"*He who begets a **scoffer** does so to his sorrow...*" (Proverbs 17:21)	"*Fools **mock** at sin...*" (Proverbs 14:9)	"*...if you **scoff**, you will bear it alone*" (Proverbs 9:12)
"*The eye that **mocks** his father, and **scorns** obedience to his mother, the ravens of the valley will pick*	"*A proud and haughty man—"**Scoffer**" is his name; He acts with*	"*He who **mocks** the poor reproaches his Maker; he who is glad at calamity will*

it out, and the young eagles will eat it" (Proverbs 30:17)	*arrogant pride"* (Proverbs 21:24)	*not go unpunished"* (Proverbs 17:5)

Table 33: Some Pearls of Wisdom Concerning the Scoffer Attribute

The Old Testament captured examples of the influence of the ***scoffer*** attribute. Some examples are:

Who	What They Did
Ishmael	The Biblical record documented: *"And Sarah saw the son of Hagar the Egyptian, whom she had borne to Abraham, **scoffing**. Therefore she said to Abraham, "Cast out this bondwoman and her son; for the son of this bondwoman shall not be heir with my son, namely with Isaac"* (Genesis 21:9)
Potiphar's wife falsely accused Joseph of this attributes influence	The Biblical record documented she told the guards that her husband had *"...brought in to us a Hebrew to **mock** us. He came in to me to lie with me, and I cried out with a loud voice"* (Genesis 39:13, 14), and told her husband *"...The Hebrew servant whom you brought to us came in to me to **mock** me..."* (Genesis 39:17)
The prophet Elijah used this attribute against false prophets	The Biblical record documented: *"...at noon, that Elijah **mocked** them and said, "Cry aloud, for he is a god; either he is meditating, or he is busy, or he is on a journey, or perhaps he is sleeping and must be awakened""* (1 Kings 18:27)
Some youths of a city that **scorned** the prophet Elijah	The Biblical record documented: *"Then he went up from there to Bethel; and as he was going up the road, some youths came from the city and **mocked** him, and said to him, "Go up, you baldhead! Go up, you baldhead!""* (2 Kings 2:23)
The nations of Israel and Judah	The Biblical record documented that when King Hezekiah sent out runners to them and *"...the runners passed from city to city through the country of Ephraim and Manasseh, as far as Zebulun; but they laughed at them and **mocked** them"* (2 Chronicles 30:10)
	Also, *"...they **mocked** the messengers of God, despised His words, and **scoffed** at His prophets, until the wrath of the Lord arose against His people, till there was no remedy"* (2 Chronicles 36:16)
Eliphaz, Bildad, and Zophar	Job told them *"I am one **mocked** by his friends, who called on God, and He answered him, the just and blameless who is ridiculed"* (Job 12:4)
	*"Will it be well when He [God] searches you out? Or can you **mock** Him as one **mocks** a man?"* (Job 13:9)
	*"My spirit is broken, my days are extinguished, the grave is ready for me. Are not **mockers** with me? And does not my eye dwell on their provocation?"* (Job 17:1-2)
	*"Listen carefully to my speech, and let this be your consolation. Bear with me that I may speak, and after I have spoken, keep **mocking**"* (Job 21:2-3)

Table 34: Examples of People Influenced by the Scoffer Attribute

The Psalmist commented on the influence of the ***scoffer*** attribute. He documented that this attribute can combine with the influence of the ungodly attribute. He wrote, *"But in my adversity they rejoiced and gathered together; attackers gathered against me, and I did not* *know it; they tore at me and did not cease; with ungodly **mockers** at feasts they gnashed at me with their teeth*" (Psalm 35:15-16). Further, he documented the combined influence of the ***scoffer***, proud, and wicked attributes. He wrote that people influenced by this combination will "*...**scoff** and speak wickedly concerning oppression; they speak loftily. They set their mouth against the heavens, and their tongue walks through the earth*" (Psalm 73:8-9). Later he would pray, "*Do not let me be ashamed, O Lord, for I have called upon You; let the wicked be ashamed; let them be silent in the grave. Let the lying lips be put to silence, which speak insolent things proudly and **contemptuously** against the righteous*" (Psalm 31:18). BTT allows one to see that the influence of the ***scoffer*** attribute can combine with many other negative attributes to create a deadly adversary against the positive forces of the campaign.

The Psalmist recognized how easy it was for anyone, including himself, to slip under the deceptive influence of the ***scoffer*** attribute. Consider this prayer from the Psalmist carefully. He prayed, "*Have mercy on us, O Lord, have mercy on us! For we are exceedingly filled with **contempt**. Our soul is exceedingly filled with the **scorn** of those who are at ease, with the **contempt** of the proud*" (Psalm 123:3-4). One should see that the influence of the ***scoffer*** attribute's deceptive qualities can easily cause one on the good path to stumble when looking at those on the bad path who appear to have an easy life. This is a strategy of deception in spiritual warfare.

God's prophets documented that the influence of the ***scoffer*** attribute was alive and well in the nation of Israel. The prophet's warnings from the Lord included:

- "*Now therefore, do not be **mockers**, lest your bonds be made strong; for I have heard from the Lord God of hosts, a destruction determined even upon the whole earth*" (Isaiah 28:22)

- "*In the day of our king, princes have made him sick, inflamed with wine; he stretched out his hand with **scoffers***" (Hosea 7:5)

- The Lord would say of the Chaldeans sent to destroy the nation of Israel: "*They **scoff** at kings, and princes are **scorned** by them. They deride every stronghold, for they heap up earthen mounds and seize it*" (Habakkuk 1:10)

There is little to expound on in the New Testament about the influence of the ***scoffer*** attribute. Jesus told His disciples that He would be delivered into the hands of people influenced by the ***scoffer*** attribute. He said, "*...the Son of Man will be betrayed to the chief priests and to the scribes; and they will condemn Him to death, and deliver Him to the Gentiles to **mock** and to scourge and to crucify. And the third day He will rise again*" (Matthew 20:18-19; Mark 10:33-34; Luke 18:32). BTT allows one to see that the fighting between the positive and negative attributes in the war campaign was severe as Jesus walked the earth. But it was God's plan that was in motion; not Satan's or man's plan. However, the manifestation of the negative attributes through man's behavior gave the appearance that the negative attributes were in control of the war campaign. On the day of Jesus' false arrest and condemnation by the Jews, the negative forces advanced on the spiritual battlefield. Jesus was sent to Pontius Pilate, but when he found out that Jesus was from Galilee (Luke 23:6), Pilate sent Him to Herod. Herod abused Jesus. The Bible documented, "*...Herod, with his men of war, treated Him with* *contempt* and **mocked** *Him, arrayed Him in a gorgeous robe, and sent Him back to Pilate. That very day Pilate and Herod became friends with each other, for previously they had been at enmity with each other"* (Luke 23:11-12). I highlighted this fact because BTT allows one to see that when the negative attributes influence people, friendships among people influenced by the negative forces will blossom over similar bad behaviors.

Here are more examples of the ***scoffer*** attribute's influence over man to consider from the New Testament:

Who	What They Did
The mob that Judas led to arrest Jesus	The Biblical record documented, *"Now the men who held Jesus **mocked** Him and beat Him. And having blindfolded Him, they struck Him on the face and asked Him, saying, "Prophesy! Who is the one who struck You?" And many other things they blasphemously spoke against Him"* (Luke 22:63-65)
Caiaphas, the scribes, and the elders	The Biblical record documented the manifestation of the ***scoffer*** attribute in their behavior in Matthew 26:57-68; Mark 14:53-65; Luke 22:66-71; and John 18:12-14, 19-24. The Biblical record documented that they *"...spat in His face and beat Him; and others struck Him with the palms of their hands, saying, "Prophesy to us, Christ! Who is the one who struck You?"* (Matthew 26:67-68)
Herod's solders	The Biblical record documented, *"Then, with his men of war, treated Him with **contempt** and **mocked** Him, arrayed Him in a gorgeous robe, and sent Him back to Pilate"* (Luke 23:11)
Pilate's solders	The Biblical record documented, the whole garrison around Jesus according to Matthew 27:27 and John 19:1. Afterwards, *"When they had twisted a crown of thorns, they put it on His head, and a reed in His right hand. And they bowed the knee before Him and **mocked** Him, saying, "Hail, King of the Jews!"* (Matthew 27:29)
	Afterwards, the Biblical record documented that these soldiers spit and hit Jesus and *"...when they had **mocked** Him, they took the robe off Him, put His own clothes on Him, and led Him away to be crucified"* (Matthew 27:31; Mark 15:20)
Jewish leaders, the chief priest, and the scribes, at the foot of Jesus cross.	The Biblical record documented, *"...the chief priests also, **mocking** with the scribes and elders, said, He saved others; Himself He cannot save. If He is the King of Israel, let Him now come down from the cross, and we will believe Him"* (Matthew 27:41-42; Mark 15:31)
	and *"...the rulers with them **sneered**, saying, "He saved others; let Him save Himself if He is the Christ, the chosen of God"* (Luke 23:35)
The solders at the foot of Jesus cross	The Biblical record documented, *"The soldiers also **mocked** Him, coming and offering Him sour wine, and saying, "If You are the King of the Jews, save Yourself"* (Luke 23:36)
Many Jews on the Day of Pentecost	On the Day of Pentecost when a sound from heaven came in the form of a mighty rushing wind; divided tongues like a fire appeared and sat on each disciple; they were filled with the Holy Spirit; they spoke with other languages; all according to Acts 2:2-4. Some Jews questioned what was occurring according to Acts 2:12, while *"Others **mocking** said, "They are full of new wine"* (Acts 2:13)

| The Epicurean and Stoic philosophers of Athens | The Biblical record documented that Paul told them of Jesus and, "...*when they heard of the resurrection of the dead, some **mocked**, while others said, "We will hear you again on this matter*" (Acts 17:32) |

Table 35: Examples of the Scoffer Attribute's Influence on Man's Behavior

Paul eloquently documented how many of the Old Testament patriarchs endured people influenced by the ***scoffer*** attribute. However, the patriarchs were well influenced by the faithful attribute. Hebrew Chapter 11: 17-40 documents their trials. Paul's discourse, while listing the many tribulations the patriarchs faced, also wrote, "*Still others had trial of **mockings** and scourgings, yes, and of chains and imprisonment*" (Hebrews 11:36). The influence of the faithful attribute, along with their belief, obedience, and reliance on God, got them through the pain and suffering they received from people influenced by the ***scoffer*** and other negative attributes.

Peter provided a strong warning to Christians about the influence of the ***scoffer*** attribute. He warned Christians that people influence by this attribute will come as the world gets closer for Christ return. He wrote, "*...that you may be mindful of the words which were spoken before by the holy prophets, and of the commandment of us, the apostles of the Lord and Savior, knowing this first: that **scoffers** will come in the last days, walking according to their own lusts...*" (2 Peter 3:3). Today, people influenced by the ***scoffer*** attribute from both the religious and secular communities, traverse the battlefield of the war campaign in countless numbers. Jude also commented on this. He said, "*...remember the words which were spoken before by the apostles of our Lord Jesus Christ: how they told you that there would be **mockers** in the last time who would walk according to their own ungodly lusts. These are sensual persons, who cause divisions, not having the Spirit*" (Jude 1:17-19). Jude provided a helpful description of one influenced by the ***scoffer*** attribute. One should also notice that the ungodly attribute is involved in their behavior. One must educate oneself about this attribute, its destructive nature, and protect the Lord's church from its influence. However, whatever troubles the influence of the ***scoffer*** attribute may bring, Christians must remember, "*Do not be deceived, God is not **mocked**; for whatever a man sows, that he will also reap*" (Galatians 6:7).

The **Proud attribute**: The influence of this attribute in the war campaign can cripple everyone - even Christians. This attribute influences people to believe that they are more important or simply just better, than another person, certain people, or even an entire race of people. This attribute is so corrosive that it causes personal character failures as one loses his or her  integrity, honor, fairness, and sound judgement. This deceptive attribute is so strong that it will cause one grounded in truth, to walk on the negative path just to keep from admitting he or she was wrong. When this attribute increases to its fullest measure in one's inner spirit, it opens a spiritual door to the influences of the evil, hater, and liar attributes. The influence of the ***proud*** attribute can even cripple relationships between Christians within the Lord's church. This attribute influences people through their conduct, their ability to greet others, and hinders the element of love from growing in their lives. The ***proud*** attribute uses a discrete strategy that can subversively divide whole congregations while increasing the negative force's strength in the war campaign. More importantly, BTT allows one to see that this attribute has some deadly by-products that creep into the inner spirits of the people who have become self-righteous. These by-products include boasting, arrogance, and stubbornness. Some important pearls of wisdom about these by-products are:

"Talk no more so very **proudly**; let no arrogance come from your mouth, for the Lord is the God of knowledge; and by Him actions are weighed" (1 Samuel 2:3)	"The fear of the Lord is to hate evil; **pride** and arrogance and the evil way and the perverse mouth I hate" (Proverbs 8:13)	"But if you have bitter envy and self-seeking in your hearts, do not boast and lie against the truth" (James 3:14)
"A proud and haughty man—"Scoffer" is his name; he acts with arrogant **pride**" (Proverbs 21:24)	"For rebellion is as the sin of witchcraft, and stubbornness is as iniquity and idolatry..." (1 Samuel 15:23)	"So I gave them over to their own stubborn heart, to walk in their own counsels" (Psalm 81:12)
"The boastful shall not stand in Your sight; You hate all workers of iniquity" (Psalm 5:5)	"...the wicked boasts of his heart's desire; He blesses the greedy and renounces the Lord" (Psalm 10:3)	"Let all be put to shame who serve carved images, who boast of idols. Worship Him, all you gods" (Psalm 97:7)
"Why do you boast in evil, O mighty man? The goodness of God endures continually" (Psalm 52:1)	"They utter speech, and speak insolent things; all the workers of iniquity boast in themselves" (Psalm 94:4)	"It is good for nothing," cries the buyer; but when he has gone his way, then he boasts" (Proverbs 20:14)
"Whoever falsely boasts of giving is like clouds and wind without rain" (Proverbs 25:14)	"Do not boast about tomorrow, for you do not know what a day may bring forth" (Proverbs 27:1)	"You who make your boast in the law, do you dishonor God through breaking the law?" (Romans 2:23)
The ungodly and unrighteous were "...backbiters, haters of God, violent, proud, boasters, inventors of evil things, disobedient to parents..." (Romans 1:30)	"Those who trust in their wealth and boast in the multitude of their riches, none of them can by any means redeem his brother, nor give to God a ransom for him..." (Psalm 49:6-7)	"For men will be lovers of themselves, lovers of money, boasters, **proud**, blasphemers, disobedient to parents, unthankful, unholy..." (2 Timothy 3:2)
"For not even those who are circumcised keep the law, but they desire to have you circumcised that they may boast in your flesh" (Galatians 6:13)	"For by grace you have been saved through faith, and that not of yourselves; it is the gift of God, not of works, lest anyone should boast" (Ephesians 2:8-9)	"Even so the tongue is a little member and boasts great things. See how great a forest a little fire kindles!" (James 3:5)
"For though I might desire to boast, I will not be a fool; for I will speak the truth. But I refrain, lest anyone should think of me above what he sees me to be or	"Let no one deceive himself. If anyone among you seems to be wise in this age, let him become a fool that he may become wise. For the wisdom of this world is	"Come now, you who say, "Today or tomorrow we will go to such and such a city, spend a year there, buy and sell, and make a profit"; whereas you do not know

hears from me" (2 Corinthians 12:6)	*foolishness with God. For it is written, "He catches the wise in their own craftiness"; and again, "The Lord knows the thoughts of the wise, that they are futile." Therefore let no one <u>boast</u> in men..."* (1 Corinthians 3:18-21)	*what will happen tomorrow. For what is your life? It is even a vapor that appears for a little time and then vanishes away. Instead you ought to say, "If the Lord wills, we shall live and do this or that." But now you <u>boast</u> in your <u>arrogance</u>. All such <u>boasting</u> is evil"* (James 4:13-16)

Table 36: By-products of the Proud Attribute

The Spirit of wisdom revealed to Solomon that the influence of the **proud** attribute is one the Lord specifically hates. Wisdom said, *"These six things the LORD hates, yes, seven are an abomination to Him: A **proud** look, a lying tongue, hands that shed innocent blood, a heart that devises wicked plans, feet that are swift in running to evil, a false witness who speaks lies, and one who sows discord among brethren"* (Proverbs 6:16-19). Further, Wisdom revealed to Solomon that, *"Everyone **proud** in heart is an abomination to the LORD; though they join forces, none will go unpunished"* (Proverbs 16:5). He also documented that *"The fear of the LORD is to hate evil; **pride** and <u>arrogance</u> and the evil way and the perverse mouth I hate"* (Proverbs 8:1-36). For anyone who loves God, Solomon documented how one should feel about the influence of the **proud** attribute since this is one of the chief attributes that creates strife and chaos in spiritual warfare. The Biblical record documented, *"He who is of a **proud** heart stirs up strife...."* (Proverbs 28:25) and *"By **pride** comes nothing but strife..."* (Proverbs 13:10). BTT allows one to see that the Spirit of wisdom's words are not complicated. Her words are clear and straightforward.

How does the influence of this attribute stir up strife? By the inappropriate things one influenced by this attribute says. Solomon documented, *"In the mouth of a fool is a rod of **pride**...."* (Proverbs 14:3). A rod of **pride** contains words that are hurtful, condemns, judges, and put others down. But also notice that the Spirit of wisdom identified a joining of the **proud** and fool attributes in Proverbs 14:3. This deadly combination serves up unrelenting strife. However, Wisdom also revealed to Solomon that the person with the **proud** attribute suffers for their actions. She revealed that *"A man's **pride** will bring him low..."* (Proverbs 29:23), and *"When **pride** comes, then comes shame..."* (Proverbs 11:2). Further, Solomon documented, *"**Pride** goes before destruction, and a haughty spirit before a fall"* (Proverbs 16:18). Moreover, Solomon documented for one's learning, *"The LORD will destroy the house of the **proud**, ..."* (Proverbs 15:25). **Figure 22** illustrates these Truths. In other words, the Lord is in control and He sets boundaries that even people influenced by the **proud** attribute can see but not pass. When they encroach too far, the Lord will stop the **proud** and destroy them. This should serve as warning to those who allow the influence of the **proud** attribute to have a place in their inner spirit. The Spirit of wisdom revealed to Solomon that it is, *"Better to be of a humble spirit with the lowly, than to divide the spoil with the **proud**"* (Proverbs 16:19). Remember, the Lord will destroy people influenced by the ***proud*** attribute. BTT allows one to see that when the Lord acts, everyone who partook in the actions led by people influenced with the ***proud*** attribute will also suffer punishment.

Later, the Spirit of wisdom revealed that the influence of the ***proud*** attribute can combine with the influence of the scoffer attribute. She told Solomon, "*A **proud** and haughty man—"Scoffer" is his name; he acts with arrogant **pride***" (Proverbs 21:24). BTT allows one to see that the union of these two attributes creates a formidable person on the spiritual battlefield. Having either of the attribute's influence alone is easier to contend with than the united attributes. United, a person's behavior is harder to contend with because they now display "*arrogant **pride**.*" This person's behavior makes them defiant. One will plant his or her foot firmly in the dirt and proclaim, "I know I'm right, and there is nothing that you or anyone else can say that will change my mind!" The influence of this union creates a person that is highly conceited, egotistical,

Figure 22: The Proud Attribute, Shame, and Destruction

stubborn, and superior. This union leads one to scoff and belittle everyone that he or she can mentally place beneath them. Thus, there is no reasoning with this person. But the Spirit of wisdom revealed to Solomon that all the behaviors and actions produced by the combining of these attributes and manifested in one's inner spirit is sin. Hence, Solomon documented, "*A haughty look, a **proud** heart, and the plowing of the wicked are sin*" (Proverbs 21:4).

Many examples of people influenced by the ***proud*** attribute exist in the Old Testament. A man named Lamech provides one of the first examples and its subtle documentation makes it easy to miss. The Bible documented that after God proclaimed, "*...whoever kills Cain, vengeance shall be taken on him sevenfold." And the Lord set a mark on Cain, lest anyone finding him should kill him*" (Genesis 4:15), a man named Lamech appeared. The influence of the ***proud*** attribute led Lamech to ***boast***, "*Adah and Zillah, hear my voice; wives of Lamech, listen to my speech! For I have killed a man for wounding me, even a young man for hurting me. If Cain shall be avenged sevenfold, then Lamech seventy-sevenfold*" (Genesis 4:23-24). What a ***prideful*** man. The influence of the **proud** attribute caused Lamech to express ***contempt*** toward the Almighty God. Some other examples of people in the Biblical record that had the ***proud*** attribute included:

Who	What Is Documented
Pharaoh and the Egyptians	Jethro, Moses father-in-law, stated to Moses, "*Blessed be the Lord, who has delivered you out of the hand of the Egyptians and out of the hand of Pharaoh, and who has delivered the people from under the hand of the Egyptians. Now I know that the Lord is greater than all the gods; for in the very thing in which they behaved **proudly**, He was above them*" (Exodus 18:10, 11). Also, the prophet Nehemiah documented "*You

	*showed signs and wonders against Pharaoh, against all his servants, and against all the people of his land. For You knew that they acted **proudly** against them. So You made a name for Yourself, as it is this day"* (Nehemiah 9:10)
	"And it came to pass, when Pharaoh was <u>stubborn</u> about letting us go, that the Lord killed all the firstborn in the land of Egypt, both the firstborn of man and the firstborn of beast..." (Exodus 13:15)
Peninnah, Elkanah second wife who tormented Hannah (1 Samuel 1:6)	After Samuel was born, Hannah prayed about Peninnah saying, *"Talk no more so very **proudly**; let no <u>arrogance</u> come from your mouth, for the Lord is the God of knowledge; and by Him actions are weighed"* (1 Samuel 2:3)
King Amaziah	*"Then Amaziah sent messengers to Jehoash...saying, "Come, let us face one another in battle"* (2 Kings 14:8). Jehoash responded, *"...You have indeed defeated Edom, and your **heart has lifted** you up. Glory in that, and stay at home; for why should you meddle with trouble so that you fall—you and Judah with you?" But Amaziah would not heed"* (2 Kings 14:9-14)
Uzziah, king of Judah	*"...as long as he sought the Lord, God made him prosper"* (2 Chronicles 26:5). However, it was also documented that *"...when he was strong **his heart was lifted up**, to his destruction, for he transgressed against the Lord his God by entering the temple of the Lord to burn incense on the altar of incense"* (2 Chronicles 26:16). The Lord struck him with leprosy for his **insolence** according to 2 Chronicles 26:21
King Hezekiah	*"In those days Hezekiah was sick and near death, and he prayed to the Lord; and He spoke to him and gave him a sign. But Hezekiah did not repay according to the favor shown him, for **his heart was lifted up**; therefore wrath was looming over him and over Judah and Jerusalem"* (2 Chronicles 32:24-25). Later it was documented that he, *"...humbled himself for the **pride** of his heart, he and the inhabitants of Jerusalem, so that the wrath of the Lord did not come upon them in the days of Hezekiah"* (2 Chronicles 32:26)
The Children of Israel	The prophet Nehemiah documented, *"...they and our fathers acted **proudly**, <u>hardened their necks</u>, and did not heed Your commandments"* (Nehemiah 9:16) and he said, *"...Yet they acted **proudly**, and did not heed Your commandments, but sinned against Your judgments, 'which if a man does, he shall live by them.' And they <u>shrugged their shoulders</u>, <u>stiffened their necks</u>, and would not hear"* (Nehemiah 9:29)
	"Listen to Me, you <u>stubborn-hearted</u>, who are far from righteousness..." (Isaiah 46:12)
	"They are all <u>stubborn</u> rebels, walking as slanderers. They are bronze and iron, they are all corrupters..." (Jeremiah 6:28)
	"For Israel is <u>stubborn</u> Like a stubborn calf; now the Lord will let them forage like a lamb in open country" (Hosea 4:16)
	"Thus with your mouth you have <u>boasted</u> against Me and multiplied your words against Me; I have heard them" (Ezekiel 35:13)

Ephraim	"*Woe to the crown of **pride**, to the drunkards of Ephraim, whose glorious beauty is a fading flower which is at the head of the verdant valleys, to those who are overcome with wine!*" (Isaiah 28:1; see also 28:3, 4)
Babylon	"*I will punish the world for its evil, and the wicked for their iniquity; I will halt the <u>arrogance</u> of the **proud**, and will lay low the haughtiness of the terrible*" (Isaiah 13:11) and, "*...Babylon, the glory of kingdoms, the beauty of the Chaldeans' **pride**, will be as when God overthrew Sodom and Gomorrah*" (Isaiah 13:19)
The king of Assyria	"*Therefore it shall come to pass, when the Lord has performed all His work on Mount Zion and on Jerusalem, that He will say, "I will punish the fruit of the <u>arrogant</u> heart of the king of Assyria, and the glory of his <u>haughty</u> looks*" (Isaiah 10:12)
Moab	"*We have heard of the **pride** of Moab— He is very **proud**— of his <u>haughtiness</u> and his **pride** and his wrath; but his lies shall not be so*" (Isaiah 16:6; see also 25:10-11), and "*We have heard the **pride** of Moab (He is exceedingly **proud**), of his loftiness and <u>arrogance</u> and **pride**, and of the <u>haughtiness of his heart</u>*" (Jeremiah 48:29)
Edom	"*Your fierceness has deceived you, the **pride** of your heart, O you who dwell in the clefts of the rock, who hold the height of the hill! Though you make your nest as high as the eagle, I will bring you down from there," says the Lord*" (Jeremiah 49:16; see also Obadiah 1:2-3), and "*But you should not have gazed on the day of your brother in the day of his captivity; nor should you have rejoiced over the children of Judah in the day of their destruction; nor should you have spoken **proudly** in the day of distress*" (Obadiah 1:12)
Babylon and the Chaldeans	"*Behold, I am against you, O most <u>haughty</u> one!" says the Lord God of hosts; "For your day has come, the time that I will punish you. The most **proud** shall stumble and fall, and no one will raise him up; I will kindle a fire in his cities, and it will devour all around him*" (Jeremiah 50:31-32)
King Nebuchadnezzar	He boasted, "*...Is not this great Babylon, that I have built for a royal dwelling by my mighty power and for the honor of my majesty?*" (Daniel 4:30) and the Bible documented that while the word was still in his mouth, "*a voice fell from heaven: "King Nebuchadnezzar, to you it is spoken: the kingdom has departed from you! And they shall drive you from men, and your dwelling shall be with the beasts of the field. They shall make you eat grass like oxen; and seven times shall pass over you, until you know that the Most High rules in the kingdom of men, and gives it to whomever He chooses*" (Daniel 4:31-32). Nebuchadnezzar would later admit "*Now I, Nebuchadnezzar, praise and extol and honor the King of heaven, all of whose works are truth, and His ways justice. And those who walk in **pride** He is able to put down*" (Daniel 4:37)
Belshazzar	He allowed the king, his lords, his wives, and his concubines to drink from the gold vessels used in the temple of the house of God in Jerusalem. In addition they drank wine, and praised the gods of gold and silver, bronze and iron, wood and stone. He also knew what had happened with King Nebuchadnezzar according to Daniel 5:20. But the

	Bible documented, "*But you his son, Belshazzar, have not humbled your heart, although you knew all this. And you have **lifted yourself up** against the Lord of heaven...*" (Daniel 5:22-23). The Bible documented that Belshazzar was slain that very night (Daniel 5:30-31)
Ashdod and the Philistines	"*A mixed race shall settle in Ashdod, and I will cut off the **pride** of the Philistines*" (Zechariah 9:6) and, "*He shall pass through the sea with affliction, and strike the waves of the sea: All the depths of the River shall dry up. Then the **pride** of Assyria shall be brought down, and the scepter of Egypt shall depart*" (Zechariah 10:11)
All the nations who mistreated the nation of Israel	"*This they shall have for their **pride**, because they have reproached and made <u>arrogant</u> threats against the people of the Lord of hosts. The Lord will be awesome to them, for He will reduce to nothing all the gods of the earth; people shall worship Him, each one from his place, indeed all the shores of the nations*" (Zephaniah 2:10-11)

Table 37: Examples of People Influenced by the Proud Attribute

For all the people list above, and for us today, we must keep in mind that the Biblical record documented that the Lord said, "*I will punish the world for its evil, and the wicked for their iniquity; I will halt the <u>arrogance</u> of the **proud**, and will lay low the <u>haughtiness</u> of the terrible*" (Isaiah 13:11). This warning from the Lord should be enough to understand that the **proud** attribute is a tool of Satan in spiritual warfare and God does not tolerate it on the spiritual battlefield.

Job, the Psalmist, and Solomon captured several more pearls of wisdom about the influence of the **proud** attribute. In the Psalmist case, he relied on the Lord to protect him from the attacks of people influenced by this attribute and he asked the Lord to deal with them. However, based on what the Psalmist addresses, one can learn a lot about the behavior of people influenced by this attribute from what they were physically doing to harm him. These men documented:

"*You rebuke the **proud**—the cursed, who stray from Your commandments*" (Psalm 119:21)	"*Rise up, O Judge of the earth; render punishment to the **proud**"* (Psalm 94:2)	"*The **proud** have me in great derision, yet I do not turn aside from Your law*" (Psalm 119:51)
"*Though the Lord is on high, yet He regards the lowly; but the **proud** He knows from afar*" (Psalm 138:6)	"*God will not withdraw His anger, the allies of the **proud** lie prostrate beneath Him*" (Job 9:13)	"*Blessed is that man who makes the Lord his trust, and does not respect the **proud**, nor such as turn aside to lies*" (Psalm 40:4)
"*...For the Lord preserves the faithful, and fully repays the **proud** person*" (Psalm 31:23)	"*Be surety for Your servant for good; do not let the **proud** oppress me*" (Psalm 119:122)	"*...the one who has a haughty look and a **proud** heart, him I will not endure*" (Psalm 101:5)
"*The **proud** have forged a lie against me...*" (Psalm 119:69)	"*The **proud** have dug pits for me...*" (Psalm 119:85)	"*The wicked in his **pride** persecutes the poor...*" (Psalm 10:2)
"*Let the **proud** be ashamed, for they treated me	"*Let not the foot of **pride** come against me, and let	"*The wicked in his **proud** countenance does not seek

wrongfully with falsehood; but I will meditate on Your precepts" (Psalm 119:78)	not the hand of the wicked drive me away" (Psalm 36:11)	God; God is in none of his thoughts" (Psalm 10:4)
"The end of a thing is better than its beginning; the patient in spirit is better than the **proud** in spirit" (Ecclesiastes 7:8)	"O God, the **proud** have risen against me, and a mob of violent men have sought my life, and have not set You before them" (Psalm 86:14)	"The **proud** have hidden a snare for me, and cords; they have spread a net by the wayside; they have set traps for me" (Psalm 140:5)
"Let the lying lips be put to silence, which speak insolent things **proudly** and **contemptuously** against the righteous" (Psalm 31:18) and "For the sin of their mouth and the words of their lips, let them even be taken in their **pride**, and for the cursing and lying which they speak" (Psalm 59:12)	Concerning those with the wicked attribute: "They have closed up their fat hearts; with their mouths they speak **proudly**" (Psalm 17:10) and "....**pride** serves as their necklace; violence covers them like a garment" (Psalm 73:6)	"May the Lord cut off all flattering lips, and the tongue that speaks **proud** things, who have said, "With our tongue we will prevail; our lips are our own; who is lord over us?" (Psalm 12:3-4)

Table 38: More Pearls of Wisdom from Job, the Psalmist, and Solomon Concerning the Influence of the Proud Attribute

As with the case of all the other negative attributes, the Lord sent His prophets to warn the nation of Israel about the influence of the **proud** attribute. These prophets pleaded with the nation of Israel to repent of the influence of this attribute, return to God, or face the consequence of their **_arrogance_**. The Biblical record documented:

The Prophet	What Was Said
Isaiah	"The **lofty looks** of man shall be humbled, the **haughtiness** of men shall be bowed down, and the Lord alone shall be exalted in that day. For the day of the Lord of hosts shall come upon everything **proud** and lofty, upon everything lifted up— and it shall be brought low" (Isaiah 2:11-12)
Jeremiah	"Thus says the Lord: 'In this manner I will ruin the **pride** of Judah and the great **pride** of Jerusalem. This evil people, who refuse to hear My words, who follow the dictates of their hearts, and walk after other gods to serve them and worship them, shall be just like this sash which is profitable for nothing..." (Jeremiah 13:9-11)
	"Hear and give ear: do not be **proud**, for the Lord has spoken" (Jeremiah 13:15)
	"But if you will not hear it, My soul will weep in secret for your **pride**; My eyes will weep bitterly and run down with tears, because the Lord's flock has been taken captive" (Jeremiah 13:17)
Ezekiel	"'Behold, the day! Behold, it has come! Doom has gone out; the rod has blossomed, **pride** has budded" (Ezekiel 7:10)
Hosea	"The **pride** of Israel testifies to his face; therefore Israel and Ephraim stumble in their iniquity; Judah also stumbles with them" (Hosea 5:5)

	"...the **pride** of Israel testifies to his face, but they do not return to the Lord their God, nor seek Him for all this" (Hosea 7:10)
Amos	"The Lord God has sworn by Himself, the Lord God of hosts says: "I abhor the **pride** of Jacob, and hate his palaces; therefore I will deliver up the city and all that is in it"" (Amos 6:8)
Habakkuk	"Behold the **proud**, his soul is not upright in him; but the just shall live by his faith. Indeed, because he transgresses by wine, he is a **proud** man, and he does not stay at home. Because he enlarges his desire as hell, and he is like death, and cannot be satisfied, he gathers to himself all nations and heaps up for himself all peoples" (Habakkuk 2:4-5)
Malachi	"Your words have been harsh against Me," says the Lord, "Yet you say, 'What have we spoken against You?' You have said, 'It is useless to serve God; what profit is it that we have kept His ordinance, and that we have walked as mourners before the Lord of hosts? So now we call the **proud** blessed, for those who do wickedness are raised up; they even tempt God and go free'" (Malachi 3:13-15)
	"For behold, the day is coming, burning like an oven, and all the **proud**, yes, all who do wickedly will be stubble. And the day which is coming shall burn them up," Says the Lord of hosts, "That will leave them neither root nor branch" (Malachi 4:1)

Table 39: Some of the Prophets' Warnings about the Influence of the Proud Attribute

In the New Testament of the Biblical record, Mary the mother of Jesus, was first to document the presence of the influence of the **proud** attribute. Mary visited Elizabeth, John the Baptist's mother and gave thanks to the Lord for her pregnancy saying, "*He has shown strength with His arm; He has scattered the **proud** in the imagination of their hearts*" (Luke 1:51). BTT allows one to see that Mary understood the Jews were expecting a messiah to come from royalty and not someone of her lowly status in life. God's use of Mary as a vessel for the Son of God completely shattered the ideas that the Jews had developed in their own minds.

After Jesus' birth, He grew and began His ministry. He documented that the influence of the **proud** attribute was among the many things that defiles people. Jesus told His disciples, "*What comes out of a man, that defiles a man. For from within, out of the heart of men, proceed evil thoughts, adulteries, fornications, murders, thefts, covetousness, wickedness, deceit, lewdness, an evil eye, blasphemy, **pride**, foolishness. All these evil things come from within and defile a man*" (Mark 7:20-23). One can see that when one allows the influence of the **proud** attribute in one's life, it penetrates down to the inner spirit and lodges in the spiritual heart. Until one purges this attribute from his or her inner spirit, defilement remains. Since defilement is within the inner spirit, the only cure for the influence of this attribute, as well as the other **unclean spirits**, is the Word of God. Without this cure, defilement becomes permanent and the negative forces of the war campaign will do everything possible to keep one from seeing, hearing, knowing and accepting this truth.

Paul documented the truth about the influence of the **proud** attribute when he wrote about the people who did not like to retain God in their knowledge. He documented that God would give them over to a debased mind to do the things which are not fitting; the things that are not pleasing to God, or inappropriate, or simply not decent. Paul documented that these are the people, "*...filled with all unrighteousness, sexual immorality, wickedness, covetousness, maliciousness; full of envy, murder, strife, deceit, evil-mindedness; they are whisperers, backbiters, haters of God, violent, **proud**, boasters, inventors of evil things, disobedient to parents, undiscerning, untrustworthy, unloving, unforgiving, unmerciful; who, knowing the righteous judgment of God, that those who practice such things are deserving of death, not only do the same but also approve of those who practice them*" (Romans 1:29-32). BTT helps one to understand that allowing the influence of the **proud** attribute into one's inner spirit leads one down a path that ends in a spiritual ambush.

Paul illustrated an example of a spiritual ambush when he spoke about elders' positions in the Lord's church. When he documented the qualifications for serving as an elder in the Lord's church, the Holy Spirit inspired him to write that the man cannot be, "*...a novice, lest being puffed up with **pride** he fall into the same condemnation as the devil*" (1 Timothy 3:6). BTT allows one to see that a novice; one lacking experience in spiritual, adult, family and business matters, can gets **puffed** up with the influence of the **proud** attribute. In the Lord's church, this behavior can lead to division and strife and split a congregation. An elder who is a novice in handling the Word of God can appear grounded, but in reality, harbor **unclean spirits**. Defilement is at the spiritual level and easily hidden. The manifestations of defilement show through one's behaviors, conduct, attitude, and words. However, to get what he desires, one can even hide his defilement for a time. With the influence of the **proud** attribute, it will be difficult for anyone to tell a novice of his error. The **proud** attribute will deceive him to think his way is based on knowledge and therefore, superior. In fact, the influence of the **proud** attribute on a novice can lead him to dismiss God's Word altogether. A situation like this will occur when the weight of responsibility of an eldership is placed on a novice's shoulders. Responsibilities such as watching out for other's souls and knowing they must give an account (Hebrews 13:17), and stopping people who "*subvert whole households, teaching things which they ought not, for the sake of dishonest gain*" (Titus 1:11), become major weights to bear. BTT allows one to see that the influence of the **proud** attribute will lead a novice down a negative path. For a congregation to place a novice in the eldership of the Lord's church, one can imply that a whole lot of people are lost in the fog of spiritual warfare. The negative forces will have successfully implemented a strategy to bring harm to the church in the long term.

Paul and some of the other disciples provided a few more pearls of wisdom about people influenced by the **proud** attribute. Here are just a few examples to help one identify and avoid people influenced by this attribute. These pearls will also help to identify if this attribute is residing in one's own inner spirit based on God's Word. The apostles wrote:

- "*If anyone teaches otherwise and does not consent to wholesome words, even the words of our Lord Jesus Christ, and to the doctrine which accords with godliness, he is **proud**, knowing nothing, but is obsessed with disputes and arguments over words, from which come envy, strife, reviling, evil suspicions, useless wranglings of men of corrupt minds and destitute of the truth, who suppose that godliness is a means of gain. From such withdraw yourself*" (1 Timothy 6:3-5)

- "*For men will be lovers of themselves, lovers of money, boasters, **proud**, blasphemers, disobedient to parents, unthankful, unholy, unloving, unforgiving, slanderers, without* *self-control, brutal, despisers of good, traitors, headstrong, haughty, lovers of pleasure rather than lovers of God, having a form of godliness but denying its power. And from such people turn away!"* (2 Timothy 3:2-5)

- *"...God resists the **proud**, but gives grace to the humble. Therefore submit to God. Resist the devil and he will flee from you. Draw near to God and He will draw near to you..."* (James 4:6-8)

- *"Likewise you younger people, submit yourselves to your elders. Yes, all of you be submissive to one another, and be clothed with humility, for "God resists the **proud**, but gives grace to the humble." Therefore humble yourselves under the mighty hand of God, that He may exalt you in due time, casting all your care upon Him, for He cares for you"* (1 Peter 5:5-7)

The **Hater attribute**: This attribute is among the most notorious and dangerous attributes of spiritual warfare. Its influence leads one to deny that he or she has the attribute. This attribute leads one to lose his humanity. The ***hater*** attribute is the root of prejudice, discrimination, and favoritism. It leads one to have the strongest negative emotional response against another person that one can have. The behavior  manifested by the influence of this attribute demonstrates an extreme ***dislike*** or antipathy for others, intense hostility, and a repugnance derived from fear, anger, or a sense of injury. With the influence of the ***hater*** attribute, strong negative behaviors are ignited without reason or cause. Skin color, language, wealth and poverty, education and a host of other physical characteristics become the scapegoat for justifying this attribute. However, these physical characteristics simply provide one influenced by the ***hater*** attribute a focal point to direct their behavior, attitude, and conduct toward. The Psalmist recognized this when he wrote, *"Let them not rejoice over me who are wrongfully my enemies; nor let them wink with the eye who **hate** me without a cause. For they do not speak peace, but they devise deceitful matters against the quiet ones in the land"* (Psalm 35:19-20). The mildest form, or smallest measure of influence from this attribute is "***dislike***." To ***dislike*** another person for any reason demonstrates spiritual immaturity. If left uncorrected, this smaller measure will blossom into the ***hater*** attribute. It has even crept into the Lord's church in some places. It is costing many good people their opportunity for heaven as they stumble in the fog generated by the negative forces of the war campaign. The attitude of ***dislike*** causes one to <u>complain</u>, <u>grumble</u>, and use other passive aggressive behaviors. In fact, the Biblical record documents that the ungodly attribute is involved in the behavior. Jude, speaking of the *"ungodly"* (Jude 1:15) documented, *"These are <u>grumblers</u>, <u>complainers</u>, walking according to their own <u>lusts</u>; and they mouth great swelling words, flattering people to gain advantage"* (Jude 1:16). The Biblical record even provided examples for one to understand this attitude in the Old Testament. The Bible documented, *"Now these things became our examples, to the intent that we should not lust after evil things as they also lusted... nor <u>complain</u>, as some of them also <u>complained</u>, and were destroyed by the destroyer. Now all these things happened to them as examples, and they were written for our admonition, upon whom the ends of the ages have come"* (1 Corinthians 10:6-11). Hence, the Biblical record documents:

- "*Do not <u>grumble</u> against one another, brethren, lest you be condemned. Behold, the Judge is standing at the door!*" (James 5:9)

- "*Be hospitable to one another without <u>grumbling</u>*" (1 Peter 4:9)

- "*Do all things without <u>complaining</u> and disputing, that you may become blameless and harmless, children of God without fault in the midst of a crooked and perverse generation, among whom you shine as lights in the world…*"(Philippians 2:14-15)

- "*…bearing with one another, and forgiving one another, if anyone has a <u>complaint</u> against another; even as Christ forgave you, so you also must do*" (Colossians 3:13).

BTT allows one to see that the influence of the **hater** attribute is unique in that it specifically targets race or gender to achieve division among God's creation. Regardless of one's credentials, experience, skills, or even education, the **hater** attribute will influence one to place race or gender as a discriminator to basic human rights. The influence of the attribute leads one to deny access to opportunities to others. One will establish a dividing line of superiority and inferiority with this attribute's influence. More importantly, this attribute can combine with the evil attribute. Radicalization comes from the union of these two attributes. When one becomes radicalized, the influence of the violent and bloodthirsty attributes boldly makes a play for one's inner spirit to strengthen the negative forces of the war campaign.

Before one says, "Wait a minute, the Bible commands Christians to hate certain things!" This is true. However, BTT allows one to understand that God commands God's people to <u>hate</u> the things that God Himself has specifically <u>said to hate</u>. This is different from allowing the influence of the **hater** attribute in one's inner spirit to dictate what Satan moves one to **hate**. This <u>discernment</u> is exactly why one must read the entire Biblical record to understand the full counsel of God's Word (Acts 20:27) and what it reveals. For one learning, Table 37 below documents from the Bible the things that God <u>hates</u>:

God Hates	**The Bible Documents**	**Where**
This attribute's influence against Him	"*…and He repays those who **hate** Him to their face, to destroy them. He will not be slack with him who **hates** Him; He will repay him to his face*"	Deuteronomy 7:10; see also Deuteronomy 32:41
Worship to false gods	"*You shall not worship the Lord your God in that way; for every abomination to the Lord which He <u>hates</u> they have done to their gods; for they burn even their sons and daughters in the fire to their gods*"	Deuteronomy 12:31
Worship to idols	"*You shall not set up a sacred pillar, which the Lord your God <u>hates</u>*"	Deuteronomy 16:22
Works of iniquity	"*The boastful shall not stand in Your sight; You <u>hate</u> all workers of iniquity*"	Psalm 5:5

Those influenced by the *wicked* and *violence* attributes	"*The Lord tests the righteous, but the wicked and the one who loves violence His soul hates*"	Psalm 11:5
A proud look, lying tongue, murders, devisers of wicked plans, people who run to evil, a lying witness, and one that sows discord	"*These six things the Lord hates, yes, seven are an abomination to Him: a proud look, a lying tongue, hands that shed innocent blood, a heart that devises wicked plans, feet that are swift in running to evil, a false witness who speaks lies, and one who sows discord among brethren*"	Proverbs 6:16-19
Human rituals done in His name	"*Your New Moons and your appointed feasts My soul hates; they are a trouble to Me, I am weary of bearing them*"	Isaiah 1:14; Also see Amos 5:21
Those who do injustice in His Holy name	"*For I, the Lord, love justice; I hate robbery for burnt offering; I will direct their work in truth, and will make with them an everlasting covenant*"	Isaiah 61:8
Evil thoughts against one's *neighbor* and the love of false oaths	"*Let none of you think evil in your heart against your neighbor; and do not love a false oath. For all these are things that I hate,' says the Lord*"	Zechariah 8:17
Divorce	"*For the Lord God of Israel says that He hates divorce, for it covers one's garment with violence," says the Lord of hosts. "Therefore take heed to your spirit, that you do not deal treacherously*"	Malachi 2:16

Table 40: Things God Specifically Hates

As one comes to grips with the wisdom documented above, the next step is to take what God *hates* and apply it to one's life. The Psalmist documented, "*Do I not hate them, O Lord, who **hate** You? And do I not loathe those who rise up against You? I hate them with perfect hatred; I count them my enemies*" (Psalm 139:21-22). BTT and *discernment* helps one to see that the Psalmist was not saying he *hated* the physical person. He *hated* the behaviors manifested in the inner spirit of the person. The Psalmist understood that he was to *hate* the negative behaviors manifested by the negative attributes (**unclean spirits**). He knew he was not to personally *hate* another person because he or she was made in the image of God. One must *hate* the behaviors driving people to negative actions and not the person themselves. As God has identified specific things He *hates*, one must do the same. From this, one can extrapolate the behaviors that everyone, specifically Christians, must *hate* with "perfect *hatred*" as commanded by God. The behaviors include:

- **Evil and wickedness:** "*The fear of the Lord is to hate evil...*" (Proverbs 8:13); "*I have hated the assembly of evildoers, and will not sit with the wicked*" (Psalm 26:5); "*You who love the Lord, hate evil! He preserves the souls of His saints; He delivers them out of the hand of the wicked*"(Psalm 97:10)

- **Debt:** "*...one who hates being surety is secure*" (Proverbs 11:15)

- **Lying:** "*A righteous man hates lying...*" (Proverbs 13:5); "*I hate and abhor lying, but I love Your law*" (Psalm 119:163)

- **Wicked intentions**: "*...and a man of wicked intentions is hated*" (Proverbs 14:17)

- **Bribes:** "*...he who hates bribes will live*" (Proverbs 15:27)

- **Covetousness:** "*...he who hates covetousness will prolong his days*" (Proverbs 28:16)

- **Idols**: "*I have hated those who regard useless idols; but I trust in the Lord*" (Psalm 31:6)

- **Backsliding:** "*I will set nothing wicked before my eyes; I hate the work of those who fall away; it shall not cling to me. A perverse heart shall depart from me; I will not know wickedness.*" (Psalm 101:3-4)

- **Every way not in accordance with God Holy word:** "*Through Your precepts I get understanding; therefore I hate every false way*" (Psalm 119:104); "*Therefore all Your precepts concerning all things I consider to be right; I hate every false way*" (Psalm 119:128). This includes the behaviors in 1 Corinthians 6:9-10 and Romans 1:18-32

- **Double-mindedness:** "*I hate the double-minded, but I love Your law*" (Psalm 119:113)

BTT allows one to clearly see that Christians have specific things identified by God to hate. Why? Because hating these things will keep one on the right path in life. Perfect hate occurs at the inner spirit level and teaches one at the cognitive (mental) level. If one does not learn to cognitively hate things at the level where rationalization, reason, and logic occurs, then the negative forces of the war campaign will find opportunities to take advantage of one's thoughts. Hating the things God hates at the cognitive level protects one from the negative attribute. However, it does not give one permission to allow the influence of the **hater** attribute as a means fight off other negative attributes. This would be a spiritual conundrum. One cannot use God's hate to justify similar behavior manifested by the influence of the **hater** attribute or any other negative attributes at any time. As one learns to hate the things that God hates, one grows in His word, gains the positive attributes, and gains the ability to fight off the negative attributes of spiritual warfare. Allowing the influence of the **hater** attribute takes one down the wrong path. For the influence of the **hater** attribute is an all-consuming **unclean spirit**. This means that the manifestation of this attribute leads a person through physical, emotional, and verbal displays of irrational behavior that leads to bitterness and strife. Often, the damage cause by this attribute is beyond repair for family, friends, coworkers, and the like. It strains relationships to the breaking point until someone is irrevocably hurt at the inner spirit level. It is at this level that the influence of the bloodthirsty attribute finds a foothold where positive relationships once existed.

I believe that the Spirit of wisdom revealed to Solomon the reason for all the things documented above. She revealed to Solomon that one who has allowed the influence of the **hater** attribute to cause them to **hate**, did so "*Because they **hated** knowledge and did not choose the fear of the Lord, they would have none of my counsel and despised my every rebuke. Therefore they shall eat the fruit of their own way, and be filled to the full with their own fancies*" (Proverbs 1:29-31). The reason given by the Spirit of wisdom answers the bulk of why one influenced by this attribute would randomly **hate** another of God's creation. In case you missed the answer, if one **hates** knowledge and chooses not to fear the Lord, he or she will eat the fruit of his or her own way and be filled with their own fancies. Wow! Proverbs 1:22 documents other reasons as described by the influences of the scoffer and fool attributes.

This leads to another critical piece of information that the Spirit of wisdom revealed to Solomon about the influence of this attribute and its correlation to things that are an <u>abomination</u> to the Lord. Wisdom not only revealed to Solomon that one influenced by the **hater** attribute had the liar attribute too, but She also revealed that there were several <u>abominations</u> in that person's spiritual heart. The Spirit of wisdom revealed, "*He who **hates**, disguises it with his lips, and lays up deceit within himself; when he speaks kindly, do not believe him, for there are seven <u>abominations</u> in his heart; though his **hatred** is covered by deceit, his wickedness will be revealed before the assembly*" (Proverbs 26:24-26). As one breaks this proverb apart, one must understand that one with the influence of the **hater** attribute will try to hide it. This person will lie. What this person lies about has the wicked attribute's involvement. So right here, three negative attributes are identified; the **hater**, liar, and wicked attributes influencing his or her inner spirit. Solomon also documented, "*Whoever hides **hatred** has lying lips, and whoever spreads slander is a fool*" (Proverbs 10:18) and, "*A lying tongue **hates** those who are crushed by it, and a flattering mouth works ruin*" (Proverbs 26:28). Strife and destruction result from the conditions created between the person influenced by the **hater** attribute and the person targeted by the **hater's hate**. It is this condition that Solomon documented, "***Hatred** stirs up strife…*" (Proverbs 10:12).

In addition, there is the other condition of the "seven <u>abominations</u>" that Proverbs 26:24-26 refers too in one's heart together with the combination of the **hater** and liar attributes. BTT allows one to see that the Lord identified these seven abominations. This opens a new area of discussion because it reveals that the influence of the **hater** attribute opens the door to a whole lot of wickedness that further defiles a person's behavior and mental state. Consider these seven things that God identified as <u>abominations</u> to Him. The Spirit of wisdom also provided additional information to help one acquire clarity and is critical for one's education, knowledge, and safety for gaining an understanding of spiritual warfare. The Spirit of Wisdom told Solomon the following:

1. "*For the perverse person is an <u>abomination</u> to the Lord…*" (Proverbs 3:32), and "*Those who are of a perverse heart are an <u>abomination</u> to the Lord…*" (Proverbs 11:20)

2. *"These six things the Lord <u>hates</u>, Yes, seven are an <u>abomination</u> to Him: A proud look, a lying tongue, hands that shed innocent blood, a heart that devises wicked plans, feet that are swift in running to evil, a false witness who speaks lies, and one who sows discord among brethren"* (Proverbs 6:16-19)

3. *"Dishonest scales are an <u>abomination</u> to the Lord, but a just weight is His delight"* (Proverbs 11:1)

    a. *"Diverse weights and diverse measures, they are both alike, an <u>abomination</u> to the Lord"* (Proverbs 20:10)

    b. *"Diverse weights are an <u>abomination</u> to the Lord, and dishonest scales are not good"* (Proverbs 20:23)

4. *"Lying lips are an <u>abomination</u> to the Lord, but those who deal truthfully are His delight"* (Proverbs 12:22)

5. *"The way of the wicked is an <u>abomination</u> to the Lord, but He loves him who follows righteousness"* (Proverbs 15:9)

    a. *"The sacrifice of the wicked is an <u>abomination</u> to the Lord, but the prayer of the upright is His delight"* (Proverbs 15:8)

    b. *"The sacrifice of the wicked is an <u>abomination</u>; how much more when he brings it with wicked intent!"* (Proverbs 21:27)

    c. *"The thoughts of the wicked are an <u>abomination</u> to the Lord, but the words of the pure are pleasant"* (Proverbs 15:26)

6. *"He who justifies the wicked, and he who condemns the just, both of them alike are an <u>abomination</u> to the Lord"* (Proverbs 17:15)

7. *"Everyone proud in heart is an <u>abomination</u> to the Lord; though they join forces, none will go unpunished"* (Proverbs 16:5)

From the things Solomon learned above, he further documented a few more pearls of wisdom concerning <u>abominations</u>. BTT allows one to see that the things Solomon documented above further links some of the behaviors of the negative attributes directly to the abominations. For instance, Solomon documented:

- *"…it is an <u>abomination</u> to fools to depart from evil"* (Proverbs 13:19)

- *"It is an <u>abomination</u> for kings to commit wickedness, for a throne is established by righteousness"* (Proverbs 16:12). (Note: This applies to all leadership positions)

- *"The devising of foolishness is sin, and the scoffer is an <u>abomination</u> to men"* (Proverbs 24:9)

- "*One who turns away his ear from hearing the law, even his prayer is an <u>abomination</u>*" (Proverbs 28:9)

- "*An unjust man is an <u>abomination</u> to the righteous, and he who is upright in the way is an <u>abomination</u> to the wicked.* (Proverbs 29:27)

Even in the New Testament of one's Bible, Jesus knew and taught what was an <u>abomination</u> to God. He said, "*You are those who justify yourselves before men, but God knows your hearts. For what is highly esteemed among men is an abomination in the sight of God*" (Luke 16:15). From Jesus statement, one can see the consistency of the entire Biblical record.

The influence of the **hater** attribute will typically combine with other negative attributes to enhance its influence over a person and lead them to commit greater destruction within the course of the war campaign. The Biblical record documented:

This Attribute teams with:	Solomon documented
The Fool attribute	"*How long, you simple ones, will you love simplicity? For scorners delight in their scorning, and fools **hate** knowledge*" (Proverbs 1:22)
The Scoffer attribute	"*Do not correct a scoffer, lest he **hate** you...*" (Proverbs 9:8)
The Adulterer attribute	Once the one with this attribute realizes their disgrace: "*And you mourn at last, when your flesh and your body are consumed, and say: "How I have **hated** instruction, and my heart despised correction! I have not obeyed the voice of my teachers, nor inclined my ear to those who instructed me!*" (Proverbs 5:11-13)
The Bloodthirsty attribute:	"*The bloodthirsty **hate** the blameless, but the upright seek his well-being*" (Proverbs 29:10)
The partners of one with the ***thief*** attribute	"*Whoever is a partner with a thief **hates** his own life; he swears to tell the truth, but reveals nothing*" (Proverbs 29:24)

Table 41: The Hater Attribute Can Combine With Other Negative Attributes

The Spirit of wisdom revealed a few more pearls of wisdom to Solomon about the influence of the **hater** attribute for our learning. These pearls included:

"*Whoever loves instruction loves knowledge, but he who **hates** correction is stupid*" (Proverbs 12:1)	"*He who spares his rod **hates** his son, but he who loves him disciplines him promptly*" (Proverbs 13:24)	"*The poor man is **hated** even by his own neighbor, but the rich has many friends*" (Proverbs 14:20)
"*Harsh discipline is for him who forsakes the way, and he who **hates** correction will die*" (Proverbs 15:10)	"*Seldom set foot in your neighbor's house, lest he become weary of you and **hate** you*" (Proverbs 25:17)	"*Better is a dinner of herbs where love is, than a fatted calf with **hatred***" (Proverbs 15:17)
The Spirit of wisdom said: "*Blessed is the man who listens to me, watching daily at my gates, waiting at the	"*All the brothers of the poor **hate** him; how much more do his friends go far from him! He may pursue them	"*For three things the earth is perturbed, yes, for four it cannot bear up: For a servant when he reigns, a

posts of my doors. For whoever finds me finds life, and obtains favor from the Lord; but he who sins against me wrongs his own soul; all those who **hate** me love death" (Proverbs 8:34-36)	with words, yet they abandon him" (Proverbs 19:7)	fool when he is filled with food, a **hateful** woman when she is married, and a maidservant who succeeds her mistress" (Proverbs 30:21-23)

Table 42: Some Pearls of Wisdom Concerning the Hater Attribute

Further in the Old Testament, one can reasonably state that the influence of the **hater** attribute was involved when Cain was influenced to **murder** his brother Abel in Genesis 4:3-8. This attribute combined with the bloodthirsty attribute to influence Cain to take Abel's life. Moreover, one can reasonably state that the **hater** attribute was among all the negative attributes that early on in Genesis, caused the Lord to grieve that he made mankind. The Biblical record documented that, "...*the Lord saw that the **wickedness** of man was great in the earth, and that every intent of the thoughts of his heart was only **evil** continually. And the Lord was sorry that He had made man on the earth, and He was grieved in His heart. So the Lord said, "I will destroy man whom I have created from the face of the earth, both man and beast, creeping thing and birds of the air, for I am sorry that I have made them." But Noah found grace in the eyes of the Lord*" (Genesis 6:5-8). God did as he said; He destroyed the wicked population from the earth. However, BTT allows one to see that although man's flesh was destroyed, the spirit of **hate** survived to find another opportune time to visit man. After the world was repopulated from the destruction of the great flood, this **unclean spirit** found willing hosts to influence. Some examples included:

Who	**What Is Documented**
Abimelech and the Philistinian	And Isaac said to them, "*Why have you come to me, since you **hate** me and have sent me away from you?*" (Genesis 26:27)
Esau	"*So Esau **hated** Jacob because of the blessing with which his father blessed him, and Esau said in his heart, "The days of mourning for my father are at hand; then I will kill my brother Jacob."*" (Genesis 27:41)
Joseph's brothers	"*But when his brothers saw that their father loved him more than all his brothers, they **hated** him and could not speak peaceably to him*" (Genesis 37:4)
	"*Now Joseph had a dream, and he told it to his brothers; and they **hated** him even more*" (Genesis 37:5)
	"*And his brothers said to him, "Shall you indeed reign over us? Or shall you indeed have dominion over us?" So they **hated** him even more for his dreams and for his words*" (Genesis 37:8)
The elders of Gilead	Jephthah said to them, "*Did you not **hate** me, and expel me from my father's house? Why have you come to me now when you are in distress?*" (Judges 11: 7)
Samson was accused of having the attribute	When he went to get his wife back that he sent back to her parents, Samson father-in-law "*...would not permit him to go in. Her father said, "I really thought that you thoroughly **hated** her; therefore I gave her to your companion...*" (Judges 15:1-2)

Amnon after he raped his sister Tamar	*"Then Amnon **hated** her exceedingly, so that the **hatred** with which he **hated** her was greater than the love with which he had loved her. And Amnon said to her, "Arise, be gone!"* (2 Samuel 13:15). Further, the record documents that Amnon had, *"…his servant put her out and bolted the door behind her"* (2 Samuel 13:18)
Absalom, Amnon brother	*"…Absalom spoke to his brother Amnon neither good nor bad. For Absalom **hated** Amnon, because he had forced his sister Tamar"* (2 Samuel 13:21, 22). The Biblical record documented that he had Amnon murdered according to 2 Samuel 13:28
The king of Israel at the time King Jehoshaphat ruled Judah	*"So the king of Israel said to Jehoshaphat, "There is still one man, Micaiah the son of Imlah, by whom we may inquire of the Lord; but I **hate** him, because he does not prophesy good concerning me, but evil." And Jehoshaphat said, "Let not the king say such things!""* (1 Kings 22:8; 2 Chronicles 18:7)
King Ahab	After King Jehoshaphat helped but lost in battle, the Biblical record documented, *"…Jehoshaphat the king of Judah returned safely to his house in Jerusalem. And Jehu the son of Hanani the seer went out to meet him, and said to King Jehoshaphat, "Should you help the wicked and love those who **hate** the Lord? Therefore the wrath of the Lord is upon you"* (2 Chronicles 19:1-2)
Haman and his followers	After Queen Esther exposed Haman's plans to annihilate the Jews, the Biblical record documented, *"…On the day that the enemies of the Jews had hoped to overpower them, the opposite occurred, in that the Jews themselves overpowered those who **hated** them"* (Esther 9:1) and *"Thus the Jews defeated all their enemies with the stroke of the sword, with slaughter and destruction, and did what they pleased with those who **hated** them"* (Esther 9:5)
The Philistines	*"Thus says the Lord God: "Because the Philistines dealt vengefully and took vengeance with a spiteful heart, to destroy because of the old **hatred**," therefore thus says the Lord God: "I will stretch out My hand against the Philistines…"* (Ezekiel 25:15-16)
Mount Seir	*"Because you have had an ancient **hatred**, and have shed the blood of the children of Israel by the power of the sword at the time of their calamity, when their iniquity came to an end, therefore, as I live," says the Lord God, "I will prepare you for blood, and blood shall pursue you; since you have not **hated** blood, therefore blood shall pursue you"* (Ezekiel 35:5-6)
	*"…I will do according to your anger and according to the envy which you showed in your **hatred** against them; and I will make Myself known among them when I judge you"* (Ezekiel 35:11)

Table 43: Examples of People Influenced by the Hater Attribute

The Lord gave Moses commands to protect the children of Israel from the influence of the **hater** attribute after they came out of bondage from Egypt. Moses documented:

- *"If you meet your enemy's ox or his donkey going astray, you shall surely bring it back to him again. If you see the donkey of one who **hates** you lying under its burden, and you would refrain from helping it, you shall surely help him with it"* (Exodus 23:4-5)

- *"You shall not **hate** your brother in your heart. You shall surely rebuke your neighbor, and not bear sin because of him. You shall not take vengeance, nor bear any grudge against the children of your people, but you shall love your neighbor as yourself: I am the Lord"* (Leviticus 19:17-18)

- *"If he pushes him out of **hatred** or, while lying in wait, hurls something at him so that he dies, or in enmity he strikes him with his hand so that he dies, the one who struck him shall surely be put to death. He is a murderer. The avenger of blood shall put the murderer to death when he meets him"* (Numbers 35:20-21)

- *"Then Moses set apart three cities on this side of the Jordan, toward the rising of the sun, that the manslayer might flee there, who kills his neighbor unintentionally, without having **hated** him in time past, and that by fleeing to one of these cities he might live..."* (Deuteronomy 4:42)

- *"And this is the case of the manslayer who flees there, that he may live: Whoever kills his neighbor unintentionally, not having **hated** him in time past...he shall flee to one of these cities and live..."'* (Deuteronomy 19:4-7)

- *"But if anyone **hates** his neighbor, lies in wait for him, rises against him and strikes him mortally, so that he dies, and he flees to one of these cities, then the elders of his city shall send and bring him from there, and deliver him over to the hand of the avenger of blood, that he may die. Your eye shall not pity him, but you shall put away the guilt of innocent blood from Israel, that it may go well with you"* (Deuteronomy 19:11-13)

Obedience to these few commands provided the children of Israel protection from the influence of the **hater** attribute. The commands were not hard or burdensome; they were fair. Because of this, God warned the children of Israel that if they were not obedient to His word, He would use two methods to correct their behavior. God used outsiders (other nations) and calamity. I will discuss God's use of calamity in Chapter IX of this book. For now, please understand that God allowed the **hater** attribute's influence with other nations. These nations punished the children of Israel for their inappropriate behavior. The Lord said, *"I also will do this to you: I will even appoint terror over you, wasting disease and fever which shall consume the eyes and cause sorrow of heart. And you shall sow your seed in vain, for your enemies shall eat it. I will set My face against you, and you shall be defeated by your enemies. Those who **hate** you shall reign over you, and you shall flee when no one pursues you. And after all this, if you do not obey Me, then I will punish you seven times more for your sins"* (Leviticus 26:16-18). I believe the unchanging God continues to use this method to get the attentions of those He loves even to this very day.

The Psalmist documented a few insights about the influence of the **hater** attribute. The insights included:

*"Your hand will find all Your enemies; Your right hand will find those who **hate** You. You shall make*	*"But to the wicked God says: "What right have you to declare My statutes, or take My covenant in your*	*"An oracle within my heart concerning the transgression of the wicked: There is no fear of God*

them as a fiery oven in the time of Your anger; the Lord shall swallow them up in His wrath, and the fire shall devour them" (Psalm 21:8-9)	mouth, seeing you **hate** instruction and cast My words behind you? When you saw a thief, you consented with him, and have been a partaker with adulterers. You give your mouth to evil, and your tongue frames deceit. You sit and speak against your brother; you slander your own mother's son" (Psalm 50:16-20)	before his eyes. For he flatters himself in his own eyes, when he finds out his iniquity and when he **hates**. The words of his mouth are wickedness and deceit; he has ceased to be wise and to do good. He devises wickedness on his bed; he sets himself in a way that is not good; he does not abhor evil." (Psalm 36:1-4)
"The **haters** of the Lord would pretend submission to Him, but their fate would endure forever" (Psalm 81:15)	"For behold, Your enemies make a tumult; and those who **hate** You have lifted up their head" (Psalm 83:2)	"Evil shall slay the wicked, and those who **hate** the righteous shall be condemned" (Psalm 34:21)

Table 44: Insights from the Psalmist on the Influence of the Hater Attribute

As with all the other negative attributes, the Lord sent His prophets to warn the nation of Israel to get rid of the influence of the ***hater*** attribute from among the people. Below are some of the many warnings the nation of Israel received from the Lord. They ignored them to their own peril. The prophet Jeremiah told the Jews about their people who went to Egypt and refused to <u>hate</u> what God said to <u>hate</u>. Jeremiah 44:2-6 informs us that the deceit of the negative forces of the war campaign cost this portion of the nation of Israel their lives for their misguided beliefs. Other warnings from the prophets included:

The Prophet	What Was Said
Ezekiel	"Behold, therefore, I stretched out My hand against you, diminished your allotment, and gave you up to the will of those who **hate** you, the daughters of the Philistines, who were ashamed of your lewd behavior" (Ezekiel 16:27)
Ezekiel	"For thus says the Lord God: 'Surely I will deliver you into the hand of those you **hate**, into the hand of those from whom you alienated yourself. They will deal **hatefully** with you, take away all you have worked for, and leave you naked and bare. The nakedness of your harlotry shall be uncovered, both your lewdness and your harlotry" (Ezekiel 23:28-29)
Amos	"They **hate** the one who rebukes in the gate, and they abhor the one who speaks uprightly" (Amos 5:10)
Amos	"Seek good and not evil, that you may live; so the Lord God of hosts will be with you, as you have spoken. **Hate** evil, love good; establish justice in the gate. It may be that the Lord God of hosts will be gracious to the remnant of Joseph" (Amos 5:14-15)
Micah	"And I said: "Hear now, O heads of Jacob, and you rulers of the house of Israel: Is it not for you to know justice? You who **hate** good and love evil; who strip the skin from My people...Then they will cry to the Lord, but He will

	not hear them; He will even hide His face from them at that time, because they have been evil in their deeds" (Micah 3:1-4)

Table 45: Warnings from the Prophets Concerning the Hater Attribute

As one studies the New Testament of the Biblical record, one learns that Zacharias, the father of John the Baptist, understood the influence of the **hater** attribute. He expressed his knowledge when he prophesized about Jesus' coming to the world. The Biblical record documented that he said, *"Blessed is the Lord God of Israel, for He has visited and redeemed His people, and has raised up a horn of salvation for us in the house of His servant David, as He spoke by the mouth of His holy prophets, who have been since the world began, that we should be saved from our enemies and from the hand of all who **hate** us, to perform the mercy promised to our fathers and to remember His holy covenant, the oath which He swore to our father Abraham: To grant us that we, being delivered from the hand of our enemies, might serve Him without fear, in holiness and righteousness before Him all the days of our life"* (Luke 1:68-75). BTT allows one to see that the influence of the **hater** attribute easily transitioned into the New Testament era.

When Jesus began His ministry, He made it crystal clear that anyone who follows Him cannot allow the influence of the **hater** attribute; even against one's own enemy. Jesus said, *"You have heard that it was said, 'You shall love your neighbor and **hate** your enemy.' But I say to you, love your enemies, bless those who curse you, do good to those who **hate** you, and pray for those who spitefully use you and persecute you, that you may be sons of your Father in heaven; for He makes His sun rise on the evil and on the good, and sends rain on the just and on the unjust"* (Matthew 5:43-45; Luke 6:27). In other words, one cannot allow the influence of the **hater** attribute to have any place in one's inner spirit at any time. BTT helps one to see that the arrest of the **hater** attribute's influence stops many other negative attributes from gaining a foothold on one's inner spirit. Controlling this one attribute preempts major attacks from other negative attributes in spiritual warfare .

To give the people of Jesus' time something tangible to understand, Jesus gave an example of one influenced by the **hater** attribute working for two different dominating priorities. Jesus stated, *"No one can serve two masters; for either he will **hate** the one and love the other, or else he will be loyal to the one and despise the other. You cannot serve God and mammon"* (Matthew 6:24; Luke 16:13). Clearly, when it comes to making the right choices in life, the influence of the **hater** attribute will skew one's vision and thoughts. Thus, one can see that Jesus ended the illustration with a direct comparison of serving God versus serving money (chasing, coveting, or worshiping it like a god). A choice must and will be made. Since Jesus taught, *"...seek first the kingdom of God and His righteousness, and all these things shall be added to you"* (Matthew 6:33), no other choice is acceptable to God. BTT allows one to see that God has established the priority. The influence of the **hater** attribute, on the other hand, obscures one's thinking into believing that he or she can have it both ways. Paul shared, *"Do you not know that to whom you present yourselves slaves to obey, you are that one's slaves whom you obey, whether of sin leading to death, or of obedience leading to righteousness?"* (Romans 6:16). Money has a deceitful way of influencing one's behavior when one ignores or does not know God's Word. The deceit is always in a negative direction. Many people become slaves to wealth and it becomes their priority. When this happens, one has made a choice to pursue it over God. When Jesus taught that one would either, "...***hate** the one and love the other, or else he will be loyal to the one and despise the other...*," who has the authority to dispute His Word? If the influence of the **hater** attribute is present in one's inner spirit, one will try to justify one's own actions and begin to **hate** God. The Old Testament confirmed this reaction from the influence of the **hater** attribute.

In another example designed to illustrate how deadly the influence of the **hater** attribute is to one's life, Jesus told a parable about a nobleman who went into a far country to receive a kingdom. This nobleman gave ten of his servants some money to invest until he returned home. But Jesus stated that, "...*his citizens **hated** him, and sent a delegation after him, saying, 'We will not have this man to reign over us'*" (Luke 19:14). Missing from the parable, BTT allows one to see that the citizens sending the delegation after the nobleman did not have good intentions. One can assume the intentions were influenced by negative forces from the war campaign. One can see that one of those negative attributes was the influence of the **hater** attribute. Be that as it may, the nobleman accomplished what he had set out to do. When he returned, he dealt harshly with those influenced by the **hater** attribute according to Luke 19: 27. BTT allows one to see that the nobleman did not allow the citizen's bad behavior to go unpunished. Jesus' parable illustrates that God will do the same to all who allow the influence of the **hater** attribute or any other negative attribute for that matter, to influence their inner spirit. The secondary point here is that leaders with positive attributes must act to keep the negative forces of the war campaign from advancing or gaining an advantage.

Jesus taught that the influence of the **hater** attribute would lead many people to target anyone who followed His teachings. His teaching covered the time for then and the future. A compilation of Jesus' teaching on the influence of the **hater** attribute is provided below. Please keep in mind that Jesus also taught that "*...he who endures to the end will be saved*" (Matthew 10:22; Mark 13:13). Jesus taught:

"And you will be **hated** by all for My name's sake. But he who endures to the end will be saved" (Matthew 10:22; Mark 13:13)	"If the world **hates** you, you know that it **hated** Me before it **hated** you. If you were of the world, the world would love its own. Yet because you are not of the world, but I chose you out of the world, therefore the world **hates** you" (John 15:18-19)	"...For everyone practicing evil **hates** the light and does not come to the light, lest his deeds should be exposed. But he who does the truth comes to the light, that his deeds may be clearly seen, that they have been done in God" (John 3:18-21)
"Blessed are you when men **hate** you, and when they exclude you, and revile you, and cast out your name as evil, for the Son of Man's sake. Rejoice in that day and leap for joy! For indeed your reward is great in	To His disciples: "Then they will deliver you up to tribulation and kill you, and you will be **hated** by all nations for My name's sake. And then many will be offended, will betray one another, and will **hate** one	"If I had not come and spoken to them, they would have no sin, but now they have no excuse for their sin. He who **hates** Me **hates** My Father also. If I had not done among them the works which no one else did, they

heaven, for in like manner their fathers did to the prophets" (Luke 6:22-23)	another. Then many false prophets will rise up and deceive many. And because lawlessness will abound, the love of many will grow cold. But he who endures to the end shall be saved" (Matthew 24:9-13; Luke 21:17)	would have no sin; but now they have seen and also **hated** both Me and My Father. But this happened that the word might be fulfilled which is written in their law, 'They **hated** Me without a cause'" (John 15:22-25)
"...The world cannot **hate** you, but it **hates** Me because I testify of it that its works are evil" (John 7:7)	Jesus pray to the Lord for His disciples, "I have given them Your word; and the world has **hated** them because they are not of the world, just as I am not of the world" (John 17:14)	

Table 46: Some of Jesus' Comments About the Influence of the Hater Attribute

The **hater** attribute continued its influence on the Jewish leadership and stirred up negative behaviors to stop the spread of Jesus' message. Unknowingly, the Jews were supporting the negative forces of the war campaign. Peter confirmed this when he told the Jews the reason that they murdered Jesus Christ. He said, *"Yet now, brethren, I know that you did it in ignorance, as did also your rulers"* (Acts 3:17). Satan influenced their actions. One can see the destructive nature of the **hater** attribute's influence demonstrated throughout the Book of Acts as the Gospel of Jesus Christ began to spread throughout the world. The persistent manifestation of the **hater** attribute's influence in people's attempt to stop the spread of the Gospel in its infancy, are captured below. Table 44 below documents some major offensive movements mounted by Satan's use of the **hater** attribute against the spread of the Gospel in the war campaign: The Biblical record documented that after the Day of Pentecost when the Holy Spirit came, and Christ's kingdom was established on earth, people influenced by the **hater** attribute attacked God's workers. The Bible documented:

Who	**What They Did**
The people, the priests, the captain of the temple, and the Sadducees	*"...came upon them, being greatly disturbed that they taught the people and preached in Jesus the resurrection from the dead. And they laid hands on them, and put them in custody until the next day, for it was already evening"* (Acts 4:1-3)
Their rulers, elders, and scribes, Annas the high priest, Caiaphas, John, and Alexander, and as many as were of the family of the high priest, that were gathered at Jerusalem (Acts 4:5, 6)	*"commanded them not to speak at all nor teach in the name of Jesus"* (Acts 4:18), and *"threatened them"* (Acts 4:21)
The high priest rose up, and all those who were	*"...they were filled with indignation, and laid their hands on the apostles and put them in the common prison"* (Acts 5:17-18)

with him (which is the sect of the Sadducees) (Acts 5:17)	
The high priest and those with him came and called the council together, with all the elders of the children of Israel, and sent to the prison to have them brought (Acts 5:21):	"...the high priest asked them, saying, 'Did we not strictly command you not to teach in this name? And look, you have filled Jerusalem with your doctrine, and intend to bring this Man's blood on us!'" (Acts 5:27, 28) and before they dismissed the apostles after they had, "beaten them, they commanded that they should not speak in the name of Jesus, and let them go" (Acts 5:40)
The Jews listening to Stephen's sermon (Acts 7)	"...they cried out with a loud voice, stopped their ears, and ran at him with one accord; and they cast him out of the city and stoned him..." (Acts 7:57-58)
The nation of Israel (Acts 8)	"...At that time a great persecution arose against the church which was at Jerusalem; and they were all scattered throughout the regions of Judea and Samaria, except the apostles" (Acts 8:1)
Saul (Acts 9)	"...breathing threats and murder against the disciples of the Lord, went to the high priest and asked letters from him to the synagogues of Damascus, so that if he found any who were of the Way, whether men or women, he might bring them bound to Jerusalem" (Acts 9:1-2)
The Jews	After Saul's conversion to Christianity (being renamed Paul), the Biblical record documented that "Immediately he preached the Christ in the synagogues, that He is the Son of God" (Acts 9:20) and he "confounded the Jews who dwelt in Damascus, proving that this Jesus is the Christ" (Acts 9:22). For this reason, "...the Jews plotted to kill him. But their plot became known to Saul. And they watched the gates day and night, to kill him" (Acts 9:23-24)
	Jews at Antioch: "...when the Jews saw the multitudes, they were filled with envy; and contradicting and blaspheming, they opposed the things spoken by Paul" (Acts 13:45) and "...the Jews stirred up the devout and prominent women and the chief men of the city, raised up persecution against Paul and Barnabas, and expelled them from their region" (Acts 13:50)
	Jews at Iconium: "...the multitude of the city was divided: part sided with the Jews, and part with the apostles. And when a violent attempt was made by both the Gentiles and Jews, with their rulers, to abuse and stone them..." (Acts 14:4-5)
	Jews at Derby: "Then Jews from Antioch and Iconium came there; and having persuaded the multitudes, they stoned Paul and dragged him out of the city, supposing him to be dead" (Acts 14:19)
	Jews at Philippi: "...the multitude rose up together against them; and the magistrates tore off their clothes and commanded them to be beaten with rods. And when they had laid many stripes on them, they threw them into prison, commanding the jailer to keep them securely. Having received such a charge, he put them

The Jews ~continued~	*into the inner prison and fastened their feet in the stocks"* (Acts 16:22-24)
	Jews at Thessalonica: *"...the Jews who were not persuaded, becoming envious, took some of the evil men from the marketplace, and gathering a mob, set all the city in an uproar and attacked the house of Jason, and sought to bring them out to the people"* (Acts 17:5), and *"...when the Jews from Thessalonica learned that the word of God was preached by Paul at Berea, they came there also and stirred up the crowds"* (Acts 17:13)
	Jews at Corinth: *"When Gallio was proconsul of Achaia, the Jews with one accord rose up against Paul and brought him to the judgment seat, 13 saying, "This fellow persuades men to worship God contrary to the law""* (Acts 18:12-13)
	Jews in Asia: *"...seeing him [Paul] in the temple, stirred up the whole crowd and laid hands on him, crying out, "Men of Israel, help! This is the man who teaches all men everywhere against the people, the law, and this place; and furthermore he also brought Greeks into the temple and has defiled this holy place"* (Acts 21:27, 28), and *"...all the city was disturbed; and the people ran together, seized Paul, and dragged him out of the temple; and immediately the doors were shut. Now as they were seeking to kill him..."* (Acts 21:30-31)
	Jews at Jerusalem: *"...some of the Jews banded together and bound themselves under an oath, saying that they would neither eat nor drink till they had killed Paul"* (Acts 23:12)
Herod (Acts 12)	*"...stretched out his hand to harass some from the church. Then he killed James the brother of John with the sword. And because he saw that it pleased the Jews, he proceeded further to seize Peter also. Now it was during the Days of Unleavened Bread. So when he had arrested him, he put him in prison, and delivered him to four squads of soldiers to keep him, intending to bring him before the people after Passover"* (Acts 12:1-4)
The Greeks following Demetrius (Acts 19)	After Demetrius convinced the people that Paul would hurt their trade in making idols and he was preaching that their goddess Diana was not a god at all (Acts 19:24-27), *"when they heard this, they were full of wrath and cried out, saying, "Great is Diana of the Ephesians!" So the whole city was filled with confusion, and rushed into the theater with one accord..."* (Acts 19: 28-29)
Ananias, the elders, and Tertullus, and orator	*"...gave evidence to the governor against Paul"* (Acts 24:1)

Table 47: Examples of the Hater Attribute's Influence on People who Attempted to Stop the Gospel

It is interesting that one of the greatest writers of the New Testament of the Biblical record was also one of the most notorious people influenced by the **hater** attribute. Paul, who converted to Christianity, had a full measure of the **hater** attribute at one time in his life according to Acts 8:3 and Acts 9:1-2. But God demonstrated that His Word would overcome any of the negative attributes including the influence of the **hater** attribute. After Paul heard the Gospel and was baptized (Acts 9:18), the Biblical record documented that "*Immediately he preached the Christ in the synagogues, that He is the Son of God*" (Acts 9:20) and he "*confounded the Jews who dwelt in Damascus, proving that this Jesus is the Christ*" (Acts 9:22). This is how powerful God's Word is and precisely why the Biblical record documents that, "*…the word of God is living and powerful, and sharper than any two-edged sword, piercing even to the division of soul and spirit, and of joints and marrow, and is a discerner of the thoughts and intents of the heart*" (Hebrews 4:12).

Now consider some of the many things that Paul shared about the influence of the **hater** attribute. Paul knew firsthand the effects of the influence of the **hater** attribute and what it could do in one's life. Thus, his insights should have even more meaning when one reads his words. Paul wrote a serious discourse about the consequences people suffer who are ungodly and unrighteous "*…who suppress the truth in unrighteousness, because what may be known of God is manifest in them, for God has shown it to them*" (Romans 1:18-19). He eloquently documented a full description of sin that people influenced by the ungodly and unrighteous attributes were involved in in Romans 1:24-31 to include stating that they were "*… **haters** of God…*" and "*…who, knowing the righteous judgment of God, that those who practice such things are deserving of death, not only do the same but also approve of those who practice them.*" One should notice how the **hater** attribute appeared in this list for the ungodly and unrighteous. Paul and the other apostles documented other pearls of wisdom about the influence of the **hater** attribute. Pearls for one's learning include:

- "*Now the works of the flesh are evident, which are: adultery, fornication, uncleanness, lewdness, idolatry, sorcery, **hatred**, contentions, jealousies, outbursts of wrath, selfish ambitions, dissensions, heresies, envy, murders, drunkenness, revelries, and the like; of which I tell you beforehand, just as I also told you in time past, that those who practice such things will not inherit the kingdom of God*" (Galatians 5:19-21)

- "*Remind them to be subject to rulers and authorities, to obey, to be ready for every good work, to speak evil of no one, to be peaceable, gentle, showing all humility to all men. For we ourselves were also once foolish, disobedient, deceived, serving various lusts and pleasures, living in malice and envy, **hateful** and **hating** one another*" (Titus 3:1-3)

- "*He who says he is in the light, and **hates** his brother, is in darkness until now. He who loves his brother abides in the light, and there is no cause for stumbling in him. But he who **hates** his brother is in darkness and walks in darkness, and does not know where he is going, because the darkness has blinded his eyes*" (1 John 2:9-11)

- "*Do not marvel, my brethren, if the world **hates** you. We know that we have passed from death to life, because we love the brethren. He who does not love his brother abides in death. Whoever **hates** his brother is a murderer, and you know that no murderer has eternal life abiding in him*" (1 John 3:13-15)

- "*If someone says, "I love God," and **hates** his brother, he is a liar; for he who does not love his brother whom he has seen, how can he love God whom he has not seen? And *this commandment we have from Him: that he who loves God must love his brother also"* (1 John 4:20-21)

Please do not be deceived by the influence of the ***hater*** attribute and aid the negative forces of the war campaign. Hate what God hates and nothing more; hate the behavior and not the person. The things that God hates have been laid out in this portion of my book which all relates to behavior and not man himself. Do not allow the ***hater*** attribute to influence you to ***hate*** another person who like you, is created in God's image.

Now before I closeout this portion on the ***hater*** attribute, BTT and <u>discernment</u> are necessary to see that this attribute has covertly crept into areas on the spiritual battlefield once held by the positive forces. This attribute's influence is expected in secular society, is rampant in religious communities, but now active among some of Christ's churches. In some of Christ's churches, the ***hater*** attribute's influence persists in the inner spirits of church elders, ministers, and immature Christians who refuse to accept that God "*...has made from one blood every nation of men to dwell on all the face of the earth...*" (Acts 17:26) and that He "*shows no partiality*" (Acts 10:34; Romans 2:11; Ephesians 6:9). Sadly, I write this from personal experience and continue to see the savage effects of this attribute in spiritual warfare on churches and members who actively practice segregation. This practice is ingrained in Christians who have not grasp the meaning of John's inspired words that, "*If someone says, "I love God," and ***hates*** his brother, he is a liar; for he who does not <u>love</u> his brother whom he has seen, how can he love God whom he has not seen?*" (1 John 4:20). These Christian's beliefs often slip out in their behaviors, attitudes, and conversations concerning other nationalities or races of people. Moreover, even if these Christians attempt to hide their true identity, their offspring's behaviors, words, and attitudes do not. Unfortunately, unless they examine themselves to make their "*...call and election sure...*" (2 Peter 1:10) and repent, they and their progeny will hear Jesus say "*I never knew you; depart from Me, you who practice lawlessness!*" (Matthew 7:23).

The **Liar attribute**: This is one of the most insidious attributes in the negative force's arsenal in the war campaign. One who allows the influence of this attribute has no honor. This attribute's influence leads one to distort both truth and reality in such small degrees and details that he or she begins believing their own fabrications. When this attribute matures, a person becomes skilled in manipulation and their oration and eye contact allows them to fabricate their own truths with remarkable speed, accuracy, confidence, and fidelity. In both spiritual and physical warfare, one who allows this attribute can become a master at deception and diversionary tactics. He or she will live in the ***lie*** they weave. When this attribute is extremely prevalent in one's life, he or she is labeled a "compulsive" ***liar*** by the world's standards. However, a ***liar*** is simply a ***liar*** in spiritual warfare, regardless of the degree to which one ***lies***. This attribute especially loves to influence children. BTT allows one to see that children are not born with the ability to decipher right from wrong. They must be taught. Without proper correction, negative behaviors develop innately as children grow and learn from their environments and living examples. Parents must correct negative behaviors or their children risks the ingraining of negative behaviors in their inner spirits. When negative attributes such as the ***liar*** attribute are left uncorrected, a host of other negative attributes will only reinforce it later. When parents ignore the influence of the ***liar*** attribute in their children, as this ***unclean spirit*** matures in their inner spirit, these children become menaces to their homes, communities, and society. The longer this attribute is allowed to influence one's inner spirit without correction, the harder it is to remove it over time. Why? Because this person's ability to develop <u>discernment</u> is lost; the lines between truth and lies blur. The line then becomes abstract values of perception and situational ethics begin to dominate each moment at hand. The Bible identified the ***liar*** attribute as the "***lying spirit***" in 1 Kings 22:22 and 2 Chronicles 18:21-22. However, this attribute appeared long before these Biblical references in the Garden of Eden with the serpent that ***deceived*** Eve as documented in Genesis 3:1-6.

BTT allows one to see that to ***deceive*** is to ***lie*** and all ***slanderous*** talk comes from the same ***unclean spirit*** – the ***liar*** attribute. There is no such thing as a "white ***lie***" or a ***lie*** of convenience that brings no harm. These are simply strategies perpetrated by the negative forces of the war campaign to makes one comfortable telling a ***lie***. When one becomes comfortable with "white ***lies***" or ***lies*** of convenience, greater ***lies*** will follow as <u>discernment</u> is lost. One will see this throughout the documentation of this attribute. But to express how powerful this attribute is on the spiritual battlefield, one need only to look at the so-called Holy Wars. There was nothing holy about these wars; nor did these wars have anything to do with the true teaching of Jesus Christ. The influence of the negative attributes and earthly wisdom inspired the Holy Wars. Nothing else. The Holy Wars simply aided the spread of the war campaign as it crossed the spiritual battlefield. The ***liar*** attribute was chief among the negative attributes ***deceptively*** claiming to spread Christianity. This claim was born from a ***lie***. In fact, Jesus told the Jewish High Priest, "*…I spoke openly to the world. I always taught in synagogues and in the temple, where the Jews always meet, and in secret I have said nothing*" (John 18:20). Had Jesus ever desired war to be used as a method to spread Christianity, He would have taught it to His apostles. They would have then led a revolt against the Jews and Saul of Tarsus when the persecution of Christians first began as documented in the Book of Acts. Saul took lead in the Jewish leadership for persecuting Christians because the ***liar*** attribute had ***deceived*** him. The Bible documented that when Stephen was murdered, "*Saul was consenting to his death…*" (Acts 8:1), and "*…he made havoc of the church, entering every house, and dragging off men and women, committing them to prison*" (Acts 8:3). Later, Ananias documented of Saul that he had, "*…authority from the chief priests to bind all who call on Your name*" (Acts 9:14). However, after Saul was converted to Christianity, he said of himself:

- "*I persecuted this Way to the death, binding and delivering into prisons both men and women, as also the high priest bears me witness, and all the council of the elders, from whom I also received letters to the brethren, and went to Damascus to bring in chains even those who were there to Jerusalem to be punished*" (Acts 22:4-5)

- "*Indeed, I myself thought I must do many things contrary to the name of Jesus of Nazareth. This I also did in Jerusalem, and many of the saints I shut up in prison, having received authority from the chief priests; and when they were put to death, I cast my vote against them. And I punished them often in every synagogue and compelled them to blaspheme; and being exceedingly enraged against them, I persecuted them even to foreign cities"* (Acts 26:9-11)

- *"For you have heard of my former conduct in Judaism, how I persecuted the church of God beyond measure and tried to destroy it"* (Galatians 1:13)

- *"If anyone else thinks he may have confidence in the flesh, I more so: circumcised the eighth day, of the stock of Israel, of the tribe of Benjamin, a Hebrew of the Hebrews; concerning the law, a Pharisee; concerning zeal, persecuting the church..."* (Philippians 3:4-6)

- *"...although I was formerly a blasphemer, a persecutor, and an insolent man; but I obtained mercy because I did it ignorantly in unbelief"* (1 Timothy 1:13)

Throughout the persecution of Christ's church by Saul, Christians followed the True teachings of Jesus Christ. They did not fight a physical war. Instead these Christians fought the spiritual war by continuing to teach and spread the Gospel of Jesus Christ <u>peacefully</u>. Christ's strategy prevailed. The Holy Wars, on the other hand, simply brought shame on the Gospel of Jesus Christ and strengthened other religious beliefs and practices on the spiritual battlefield. With this said, let us see what the Bible teaches about this attribute.

The Spirit of wisdom revealed to Solomon that, *"These six things the Lord hates, yes, seven are an abomination to Him: a proud look, a **lying** tongue, hands that shed innocent blood, a heart that devises wicked plans, feet that are swift in running to evil, a false witness who speaks **lies**, and one who sows discord among brethren"* (Proverbs 6:16-19). One should notice that the **liar** attribute is seen twice among the things that Lord hates. Although all of the things combined in one's inner spirit makes one an abomination to the Lord, the **liar** attribute stands prominently among them. Hence, Solomon would later document directly, *"**Lying** lips are an abomination to the Lord, but those who deal truthfully are His delight"* (Proverbs 12:22). BTT allows one to see that Solomon understood, in spiritual warfare, a person with **lying** lips, or a **lying** tongue, or one who speaks **lies,** sows discord among God's people. This wisdom is not hard to understand. Whether one's inner spirit is defiled with all seven things identified in Proverbs 6:16-19, or one willfully allows the influence of the **liar** attribute for personal gain, both are an abomination to the Lord. Why? Because in both cases the person has become a tool of Satan and a very dangerous **deceiver** operating on the spiritual battlefield in the war campaign.

Hence, Solomon continued to document that, *"A **lying** tongue hates those who are crushed by it..."* (Proverbs 26:28). BTT allows one to see that one influenced by the **liar** attribute does not care for the one harmed by his or her **lies**. Moreover, this verse reveals that this attribute can combine with the influence of the hater attribute an deliver a severe punch to the one crushed by the **lies**. In spiritual warfare, the combined strength of these two attributes form an alliance that is extremely detrimental to the positive forces. To make the situation even worse, Wisdom also revealed that *"An evildoer gives heed to **false lips**; a **liar** listens eagerly to a spiteful tongue"* (Proverbs 17:4). Thus, one influenced by the evil attribute joins in to bring harm to people on the good path. BTT allows one to put this proverb into perspective. People influenced by evil attribute listens to those influenced by the **liar** attribute. One influenced by the **liar** attribute gains information from people who want vengeance on other people. These are people with a "*spiteful tongues*" and eager to tear down the character, good works, and behavior of people influenced by positive attributes. These are the people whose words are laced with **lies**. Thus, in spiritual warfare, people with the evil and **liar** attributes traverse the battlefield eagerly waiting to hear **lies** from people with a spiteful tongue. In the war campaign, people influenced by the positive attributes will always be a target. This is why Solomon documented "*A righteous man hates **lying**...*" (Proverbs 13:5).

Solomon documented several hard lessons on how the **liar** attribute can influence people in the witness category. The witness category is documented later in Chapter VII of this book. Solomon learned that:

- "*A faithful witness does not **lie**, but a false witness will utter **lies***" (Proverbs 14:5)

- "*A true witness delivers souls, but a **deceitful** witness speaks **lies***" (Proverbs 14:25)

- "*A **false** witness will not go unpunished, and he who speaks **lies** will not escape*" (Proverbs 19:5) and "*...and he who speaks **lies** shall perish*" Proverbs 19:9

- "*Do not be a witness against your neighbor without cause, for would you **deceive** with your lips?*" (Proverbs 24:28) and "*Like a madman who throws firebrands, arrows, and death, is the man who **deceives** his neighbor, and says, "I was only joking!"*" (Proverbs 26:18-19)

Now to show one how complicated spiritual warfare is, the spirit of wisdom revealed that the **liar** attribute can combine with the hater attribute and their two manifested behaviors can mutate into a third attribute. Solomon documented that, "*Whoever hides **hatred** has **lying** lips, and whoever spreads **slander** is a fool*" (Proverbs 10:18). BTT allows one to see that a person who allows the hater attribute in their inner spirit and hides it from others has the **liar** attribute by their actions. If this same person now engages in **slandering** another person; the act of telling **lies** about that person, now they have allowed the fool attribute in their spirit. All three negative attributes are actively operating in this person's inner spirit at the same time. This is tough wisdom.

Solomon also learned that one can temporarily prosper physically when he or she allows the influence of the **liar** attribute. However, prosperity gained by **distorting** the truth also produces a fantasy state of mind within its host. Solomon documented this when he wrote, "*Getting treasures by a **lying** tongue is the fleeting fantasy of those who seek death*" (Proverbs 21:6). In other words, a **liar** may prosper temporarily, but his or her twisted state of mind proportionally increases with their prosperity which is leading them down a path of death. Hence, Solomon documented the words of Agur, the son of Jakeh, who stated, "*Two things I request of You (Deprive me not before I die): Remove **falsehood** and **lies** far from me; give me neither poverty nor riches— feed me with the food allotted to me; lest I be full and deny You, and say, "Who is the Lord?" Or lest I be poor and steal, and profane the name of my God*" (Proverbs 30:7-9). This has always been my personal prayer.

Solomon documented a final point for leaders when it comes to the **liar** attribute. He wrote, "*If a ruler pays attention to **lies**, all his servants become wicked*" (Proverbs 29:12). This proverbs documents a powerful Truth, yet a common problem, the world faces today. Leaders that lack *discernment* create many of the world's problems by allowing people influenced by the **liar** attribute to flourish in their organizations. Solomon documented for all leaders that, "*Excellent speech is not becoming to a fool, much less **lying** lips to a prince*" (Proverbs 17:7). Leaders cannot allow their subordinates or employees to maintain the influence of the **liar** attribute and go unpunished in their organizations. If so, the organization internal credibility, integrity, and morale will suffer. More importantly, people with the positive attributes will become the prime targets of people influence of the **liar** attribute because of spiritual warfare. The organization will eventually come to ruin. Unfortunately, when this happens, a lot of good people suffer and their integrity and reputations are often called into question simply because of their association with the organization. Because of spiritual warfare, good reputations and integrity can take years to repair.

Finally, Wisdom revealed God's Truth about the power of the **liar** attribute that should serve as an anchor for all who trust Him. Wisdom revealed to Solomon, "*The truthful lip shall be established forever, but a **lying** tongue is but for a moment*" (Proverbs 12:19). In other words, one who tells the truth has the real power; one who **lies** only has power for a moment. The pain that one endures from a **liar** may hurt for the moment; but God avenges those who are truthful and keeps their trust in Him. Hence, Solomon documented, "*What is desired in a man is kindness, and a poor man is better than a **liar**"* (Proverbs 19:22). God desires one to stand in truth in word, actions, and deeds. Even when it comes to God's Word, Solomon wrote, "*Do not add to His words, lest He rebuke you, and you be found a **liar***" (Proverbs 30:6). In all things God desires truthful lips. One must strive to keep the influence of the **liar** attribute far from one's inner spirit as possible. With this understanding, consider what the rest of the Old Testament documented about the **liar** attribute.

The Old Testament documented many examples of the influence of people who allowed the **liar** attribute. They used their tongues or deception as the tools of choice to achieve their goals for the negative forces of the war campaign. The Bible documented:

Who	What Was Done
The serpent	"*...the serpent said to the woman, "You will not surely die. For God knows that in the day you eat of it your eyes will be opened, and you will be like God, knowing good and evil*" (Genesis 3:4, 5). Eve would later tell God, "*The serpent **deceived** me, and I ate*" (Genesis 3:13)
Sarah, Abraham's wife	When the Lord asked her did she laugh about the message she heard, the Bible documented, "*...Sarah **denied** it, saying, "I did not laugh," for she was afraid. And He said, "No, but you did laugh!*" (Genesis 18:15)
Rebekah, the wife of Isaac	She crafted a deception plan to gain Jacob the birthright set aside for Esau documented in Genesis 27:5-18. Jacob carried out the plan.
Jacob	When Jacob went to Isaac his father, he **lied** and said, "*Jacob said to his father, "I am Esau your firstborn; I have done just as you told me..."* (Genesis 27:19); and when asked how he got the food so fast, "*... he said, "Because the Lord your God brought it to me*" (Genesis 27:20); and when asked was he really Esau, Jacob replied, "*I am*" (Genesis 27:24)
	When he switched Leah for Rachael for Jacob to marry, Jacob said, "*What is this you have done to me? Was it not for Rachel that I served you? Why

Laban	*then have you **deceived** me?"* (Genesis 29:25) and Jacob told Leah and Rachael, *"your father has **deceived** me and changed my wages ten times, but God did not allow him to hurt me"* (Genesis 31:7)
Achan of the children of Israel	*"Israel has sinned, and they have also transgressed My covenant which I commanded them. For they have even taken some of the accursed things, and have both stolen and **deceived**; and they have also put it among their own stuff"* (Joshua 7:11). Achan had stolen and **lied** about, *"a beautiful Babylonian garment, two hundred shekels of silver, and a wedge of gold weighing fifty shekels"* (Joshua 7:21) that he coveted buried in his tent.
The Gibeonites	*"...they worked craftily, and went and **pretended** to be ambassadors. And they took old sacks on their donkeys, old wineskins torn and mended, old and patched sandals on their feet, and old garments on themselves; and all the bread of their provision was dry and moldy"* (Joshua 9:4-5). Later, Joshua asked them, *"Why have you **deceived** us, saying, 'We are very far from you,' when you dwell near us?"* (Joshua 9:22)
Samson	Delilah claimed, *"Look, you have mocked me and told me **lies**. Now, please tell me what you may be bound with"* (Judges 16:10), and *"Until now you have mocked me and told me **lies**. Tell me what you may be bound with"* (Judges 16:13). He made the mistake of telling her the truth.
Michal, David's wife	She helped David escape from Saul and she *"...took an image and laid it in the bed, put a cover of goats' hair for his head, and covered it with clothes. So when Saul sent messengers to take David, she said, "He is sick."* (1 Samuel 19:13, 14). Saul would say, *"Why have you **deceived** me like this, and sent my enemy away, so that he has escaped?"* (1 Samuel 19:17)
David with the king of Gath	*"So he changed his behavior before them, **pretended** madness in their hands, scratched on the doors of the gate, and let his saliva fall down on his beard"* (1 Samuel 21:13)
Saul with a medium	*"When the woman saw Samuel, she cried out with a loud voice. And the woman spoke to Saul, saying, "Why have you **deceived** me? For you are Saul!"* (1 Samuel 28:12)
Amnon who raped his sister Tamar	He laid, *"...down and pretended to be ill; and when the king came to see him, Amnon said to the king, "Please let Tamar my sister come and make a couple of cakes for me in my sight, that I may eat from her hand"* (2 Samuel 13:5-6)
Absalom to King David	He convinced David to allow Amnon to come to a feast to celebrate (2 Samuel 13:23-27) but in reality, he had a plan to kill Amnon for raping Tamar according to (2 Samuel 13:28-29)
Joab, who sent a wise woman to lie to King David	*"And Joab sent to Tekoa and brought from there a wise woman, and said to her, "Please **pretend** to be a mourner, and put on mourning apparel; do not anoint yourself with oil, but act like a woman who has been mourning a long time for the dead. Go to the king and speak to him in this manner." So Joab put the words in her mouth"* (2 Samuel 14:2-3)
A false prophet to another prophet	*"He said to him, "I too am a prophet as you are, and an angel spoke to me by the word of the Lord, saying, 'Bring him back with you to your house, that he may eat bread and drink water.'" (He was **lying** to him.)"* (1 Kings 13:18)
The wife of Jeroboam	*"The Lord had said to Ahijah, "Here is the wife of Jeroboam, coming to ask you something about her son, for he is sick. Thus and thus you shall say to her; for it will be, when she comes in, that she will **pretend** to be*

	another woman." And so it was, when Ahijah heard the sound of her footsteps as she came through the door, he said, "Come in, wife of Jeroboam. Why do you **pretend** to be another person? For I have been sent to you with bad news" (1 Kings 14:5-6)
Moab	"We have heard of the pride of— He is very proud— of his haughtiness and his pride and his wrath; but his **lies** shall not be so" (Isaiah 16:6)
Pashhur	"And you, Pashhur, and all who dwell in your house, shall go into captivity. You shall go to Babylon, and there you shall die, and be buried there, you and all your friends, to whom you have prophesied **lies**" (Jeremiah 20:6)
Hananiah the prophet	The prophet Jeremiah said to him, "Hear now, Hananiah, the Lord has not sent you, but you make this people trust in a **lie**" (Jeremiah 28:15)
Ahab the son of Kolaiah, and Zedekiah the son of Maaseiah	The Lord called them out for **lying** to the nation of Israel in His name: "...who prophesy a **lie** to you in My name: Behold, I will deliver them into the hand of Nebuchadnezzar king of Babylon, and he shall slay them before your eyes. (Jeremiah 29:21)
Shemaiah the Nehelamite	"...Shemaiah has prophesied to you, and I have not sent him, and he has caused you to trust in a **lie**—" (Jeremiah 29:31)
Pharaoh king of Egypt	Called "...the great monster who **lies** in the midst of his rivers, who has said, 'My River is my own; I have made it for myself'" (Ezekiel 29:3)
The magicians, the astrologers, the sorcerers, and the Chaldeans	King Nebuchadnezzar knew they had the **liar** attribute and said to them "...if you do not make known the dream to me, there is only one decree for you! For you have agreed to speak **lying** and corrupt words before me till the time has changed. Therefore tell me the dream, and I shall know that you can give me its interpretation" (Daniel 2:9)
The kings of the North and South	"Both these kings' hearts shall be bent on evil, and they shall speak **lies** at the same table; but it shall not prosper, for the end will still be at the appointed time" (Daniel 11:27)
Ephraim	"...has encircled Me with **lies**, and the house of Israel with **deceit**..." (Hosea 11:12), and "...He daily increases **lies** and desolation. Also they make a covenant with the Assyrians, and oil is carried to Egypt" (Hosea 12:1)
The houses of Achzib	"Therefore you shall give presents to Moresheth Gath; the houses of Achzib shall be a **lie** to the kings of Israel" (Micah 1:14)
Nineveh	"Woe to the bloody city! It is all full of **lies** and robbery. Its victim never departs" (Nahum 3:1)
The diviners and idols	"For the idols speak delusion; The diviners envision **lies**, and tell false dreams; They comfort in vain. Therefore the people wend their way like sheep; they are in trouble because there is no shepherd" (Zechariah 10:2)
Idols	"What profit is the image, that its maker should carve it, the molded image, a teacher of **lies**, that the maker of its mold should trust in it, to make mute idols? (Habakkuk 2:18)

Table 48: Examples of the Influence of the Liar Attribute

When the children of Israel came out of bondage from the Egyptians, the Lord gave them simple but specific commands for dealing with the influence of the *liar* attribute. The Biblical record documented:

- *"If a person sins and commits a trespass against the Lord by **lying** to his neighbor about what was delivered to him for safekeeping, or about a pledge, or about a robbery, or if he has extorted from his neighbor, or if he has found what was lost and **lies** concerning it, and swears falsely—in any one of these things that a man may do in which he sins: then it shall be, because he has sinned and is guilty, that he shall restore what he has stolen, or the thing which he has extorted, or what was delivered to him for safekeeping, or the lost thing which he found, or all that about which he has **sworn falsely**. He shall restore its full value, add one-fifth more to it, and give it to whomever it belongs, on the day of his trespass offering"* (Leviticus 6:2-4)

- *"You shall not steal, nor deal falsely, nor **lie** to one another"* (Leviticus 19:11)

God's Word is straightforward and requires no educational degree to understand. Accepting the simplicity of God's Word is often the issue. The prophet Job understood this. The Biblical record documented that Job had to deal with friends who had allowed the **liar** attribute to influence them. They initially came to comfort him in his affliction. However, Satan used Job's friends to torment Job. They believed Job's condition came from his sins. After Eliphaz, Bildad, and Zophar verbally assaulted Job to get him to admit the sin that he had done, Job stated, *"Now therefore, be pleased to look at me; for I would never **lie** to your face"* (Job 6:28). Job did not allow the influence of the **liar** attribute in his inner spirit; nor did he believe that he had done anything wrong. Job speaking of God, acknowledged to his wise friends that, *"With Him are strength and prudence. The **deceived** and the **deceiver** are His"* (Job 12:16). In other words, Job knew the truth even though his friends did not. Moreover, Job chastised his friends saying, *"But you forgers of **lies**, you are all worthless physicians"* (Job 13:4) and *"How then can you comfort me with empty words, since **falsehood** remains in your answers?"* (Job 21:34). When one reads the Book of Job, BTT allows one to see that these friends were pawns of the negative forces and engaged in spiritual warfare. The influence of the **liar** attribute was strategically maneuvering these friends to take down a man with the righteous attribute (Ezekiel 14:14; 14:20). However, Job <u>discerned</u> their motive. He told them, *"If I have walked with **falsehood**, or if my foot has hastened to **deceit**, let me be weighed on honest scales, that God may know my integrity"* (Job 31:5). Job 42:10-18 informs one that Job was vindicated, his body healed, and his possessions were restored.

Other pearls of wisdom concerning the influence of the **liar** attribute found in the Old Testament include:

"Blessed is that man who makes the Lord his trust, and does not respect the proud, nor such as turn aside to **lies**" (Psalm 40:4)	God will: "...destroy those who speak **falsehood**; the Lord abhors the bloodthirsty and **deceitful** man" (Psalm 5:6)	"Behold, the wicked brings forth iniquity; yes, he conceives trouble and brings forth **falsehood**" (Psalm 7:14)
"Let the **lying** lips be put to silence, which speak insolent things proudly and contemptuously against the righteous" (Psalm 31:18)	"Take heed to yourselves, lest your heart be **deceived**, and you turn aside and serve other gods and	"The wicked are estranged from the womb; they go astray as soon as they are born, speaking **lies**" (Psalm 58:3)

	worship them" (Deuteronomy 11:16)	
The wicked: "*You give your mouth to evil, and your tongue frames **deceit**. You sit and speak against your brother; you **slander** your own mother's son*" (Psalm 50:19-20)	The Psalmist said, "*For the mouth of the wicked and the mouth of the **deceitful** have opened against me; they have spoken against me with a **lying** tongue*" (Psalm 109:2)	"*Whoever secretly **slanders** his neighbor, Him I will destroy; the one who has a haughty look and a proud heart, him I will not endure*" (Psalm 101:5)
The wicked: "*For the sin of their mouth and the words of their lips, let them even be taken in their pride, and for the cursing and **lying** which they speak*" (Psalm 59:12)	Enemies of God: "*They only consult to cast him down from his high position; they delight in **lies**; they bless with their mouth, but they curse inwardly*" (Psalm 62:4)	"*Surely men of low degree are a vapor, men of high degree are a **lie**; if they are weighed on the scales, they are altogether lighter than vapor*" (Psalm 62:9)
"*But the king shall rejoice in God; everyone who swears by Him shall glory; but the mouth of those who speak **lies** shall be stopped*" (Psalm 63:11)	"*Let the proud be ashamed, for they treated me wrongfully with **falsehood**; but I will meditate on Your precepts*" (Psalm 119:78)	"*The haters of the Lord would **pretend** submission to Him, but their fate would endure forever*" (Psalm 81:15)
"*My enemies speak evil of me: "When will he die, and his name perish? And if he comes to see me, he speaks **lies**; his heart gathers iniquity to itself; when he goes out, he tells it*" (Psalm 41:5-6)	"*I hate and abhor **lying**, but I love Your law*" (Psalm 119:163)	The Psalmist prayer: "*Remove from me the way of **lying**, and grant me Your law graciously*" (Psalm 119:29) and "*Deliver my soul, O Lord, from **lying** lips and from a deceitful tongue*" (Psalm 120:2)
"*I believed, therefore I spoke, I am greatly afflicted." I said in my haste, "All men are **liars**"*" (Psalm 116:10-11)	"*You reject all those who stray from Your statutes, for their deceit is **falsehood**"* (Psalm 119:118)	"*He who works **deceit** shall not dwell within my house; he who tells **lies** shall not continue in my presence*" (Psalm 101:7)
The children of Israel with God: "*Nevertheless they flattered Him with their mouth, and they **lied** to Him with their tongue; for their heart was not steadfast with Him, nor were they faithful in His covenant*" (Psalm 78:36-37)	The wicked: "*Why do you boast in evil, O mighty man? The goodness of God endures continually. Your tongue devises destruction, like a sharp razor, working **deceitfully**. You love evil more than good, **lying** rather than speaking righteousness*" (Psalm 52:1-3)	A prayer against all **liars**: "*Stretch out Your hand from above; rescue me and deliver me out of great waters, from the hand of foreigners, whose mouth speaks **lying** words, and whose right hand is a right hand of **falsehood***" (Psalm 144:7-8, 11)

Table 49: Pearls of Wisdom Concerning the Liar Attribute

As with all the other negative attributes, the influence of the **_liar_** attribute was extremely strong among the nation of Israel. Of course, God sent His prophets to plead with the people to reject this **_unclean spirit_** and return to Him; but they refused. Below are some of the many examples of the things that the Lord told the nation of Israel through the prophets. The Lord not only identified the attribute, but He specifically stated who had the attribute and the effects it had on the people. The warnings about this attribute could not be made any clearer. As one looks at the information below, please pay close attention to those things directed at the words, actions, and behaviors of this religious community. BTT allows one to see that the **_liar_** attribute's root was sourced from the **_lies_** and **_false_** teaching of false prophets and priest. The Bible documented:

The Prophet	**What Was Said**
Isaiah	"The elder and honorable, he is the head; the prophet who teaches **_lies_**, he is the tail" (Isaiah 9:15)
	"Because you have said, "We have made a covenant with death, and with Sheol we are in agreement. When the overflowing scourge passes through, it will not come to us, for we have made **_lies_** our refuge, and under **_falsehood_** we have hidden ourselves" (Isaiah 28:15)
	"That this is a rebellious people, **_lying_** children, children who will not hear the law of the Lord..." (Isaiah 30:9)
	"Also the schemes of the schemer are evil; he devises wicked plans to destroy the poor with **_lying_** words, even when the needy speaks justice" (Isaiah 32:7)
	"He feeds on ashes; a **_deceived_** heart has turned him aside; and he cannot deliver his soul, nor say, "Is there not a **_lie_** in my right hand?" (Isaiah 44:20)
	"Whom do you ridicule? Against whom do you make a wide mouth and stick out the tongue? Are you not children of transgression, offspring of **_falsehood_**..." (Isaiah 57:4)
	"And of whom have you been afraid, or feared, that you have **_lied_** and not remembered Me, nor taken it to your heart? Is it not because I have held My peace from of old that you do not fear Me?" (Isaiah 57:11)
	"For your hands are defiled with blood, and your fingers with iniquity; your lips have spoken **_lies_**, your tongue has muttered perversity. No one calls for justice, nor does any plead for truth. They trust in empty words and speak **_lies_**; they conceive evil and bring forth iniquity" (Isaiah 59:3-4)
	"In transgressing and **_lying_** against the Lord, and departing from our God, speaking oppression and revolt, conceiving and uttering from the heart words of **_falsehood_**" (Isaiah 59:13)
	"Then I said, "Ah, Lord God! Surely You have greatly **_deceived_** this people and Jerusalem, Saying, 'You shall have peace,' whereas the sword reaches to the heart" (Jeremiah 4:10)
	"They have **_lied_** about the Lord, and said, "It is not He. Neither will evil come upon us, nor shall we see sword or famine" (Jeremiah 5:12)
	"They are all stubborn rebels, walking as **_slanderers_**. They are bronze and iron, they are all corrupters..." (Jeremiah 6:28)
	"Do not trust in these **_lying_** words, saying, 'The temple of the Lord, the temple of the Lord, the temple of the Lord are these...'" (Jeremiah 7:4)

Jeremiah	"Behold, you trust in **lying** words that cannot profit" (Jeremiah 7:8)	
	"How can you say, 'We are wise, and the law of the Lord is with us'? Look, the false pen of the scribe certainly works **falsehood**" (Jeremiah 8:8)	
	"And like their bow they have bent their tongues for **lies**. They are not valiant for the truth on the earth. For they proceed from evil to evil, and they do not know Me," says the Lord. Everyone take heed to his neighbor, and do not trust any brother; for every brother will utterly supplant, and every neighbor will walk with **slanderers**" (Jeremiah 9:3-4)	
	"Everyone will **deceive** his neighbor, and will not speak the truth; they have taught their tongue to speak **lies**; they weary themselves to commit iniquity" (Jeremiah 9:5)	
	"Their tongue is an arrow shot out; it speaks **deceit**; one speaks peaceably to his neighbor with his mouth, but in his heart he **lies** in wait" (Jeremiah 9:8)	
	"Everyone is dull-hearted, without knowledge; every metalsmith is put to shame by an image; for his molded image is **falsehood**, and there is no breath in them" (Jeremiah 10:14)	
	"This is your lot, the portion of your measures from Me," says the Lord, "Because you have forgotten Me and trusted in **falsehood**" (Jeremiah 13:25)	
	"And the Lord said to me, "The prophets prophesy **lies** in My name. I have not sent them, commanded them, nor spoken to them; they prophesy to you a false vision, divination, a worthless thing, and the deceit of their heart" (Jeremiah 14:14)	
Jeremiah	"O Lord, my strength and my fortress, My refuge in the day of affliction, the Gentiles shall come to You from the ends of the earth and say, "Surely our fathers have inherited **lies**, worthlessness and unprofitable things"" (Jeremiah 16:19)	
	"Also I have seen a horrible thing in the prophets of Jerusalem: They commit adultery and walk in **lies**; They also strengthen the hands of evildoers, So that no one turns back from his wickedness. All of them are like Sodom to Me, And her inhabitants like Gomorrah" (Jeremiah 23:14)	
	"I have heard what the prophets have said who prophesy **lies** in My name, saying, 'I have dreamed, I have dreamed!' How long will this be in the heart of the prophets who prophesy **lies**? Indeed they are prophets of the deceit of their own heart..." (Jeremiah 23:25-26)	
	"Behold, I am against those who prophesy **false** dreams," says the Lord, "and tell them, and cause My people to err by their **lies** and by their recklessness. Yet I did not send them or command them; therefore they shall not profit this people at all," says the Lord" (Jeremiah 23:32)	
	"...do not listen to the words of the prophets who speak to you, saying, 'You shall not serve the king of Babylon,' for they prophesy a **lie** to you; for I have not sent them," says the Lord, "yet they prophesy a **lie** in My name, that I may drive you out, and that you may perish, you and the prophets who prophesy to you" (Jeremiah 27:14, 15)	
	"Also I spoke to the priests and to all this people, saying, "Thus says the Lord: 'Do not listen to the words of your prophets who prophesy to you, saying, "Behold, the vessels of the Lord's house will now shortly be brought back from Babylon"; for they prophesy a **lie** to you" (Jeremiah 27:16)	

	"*For thus says the Lord of hosts, the God of Israel: Do not let your prophets and your diviners who are in your midst **deceive** you, nor listen to your dreams which you cause to be dreamed*" (Jeremiah 29:8)	
	"*…because they have done disgraceful things in Israel, have committed adultery with their neighbors' wives, and have spoken **lying** words in My name, which I have not commanded them. Indeed I know, and am a witness, says the Lord*" (Jeremiah 29:23)	
	"*For they prophesy a **lie** to you, to remove you far from your land; and I will drive you out, and you will perish*" (Jeremiah 27:10)	
	"*Thus says the Lord: 'Do not **deceive** yourselves, saying, "The Chaldeans will surely depart from us," for they will not depart*" (Jeremiah 37:9)	
	"*I know his wrath,*" says the Lord, "*But it is not right; his **lies** have made nothing right*" (Jeremiah 48:30)	
	"*Everyone is dull-hearted, without knowledge; every metalsmith is put to shame by the carved image; for his molded image is **falsehood**, and there is no breath in them*" (Jeremiah 51:17)	
Ezekiel	"*…Because you have spoken nonsense and envisioned **lies**, therefore I am indeed against you,*" says the Lord God. "*My hand will be against the prophets who envision futility and who divine **lies**…*" (Ezekiel 13:8-9)	
	"*And will you profane Me among My people for handfuls of barley and for pieces of bread, killing people who should not die, and keeping people alive who should not live, by your **lying** to My people who listen to **lies**?*" (Ezekiel 13:19)	
	"*…with **lies** you have made the heart of the righteous sad, whom I have not made sad; and you have strengthened the hands of the wicked, so that he does not turn from his wicked way to save his life*" (Ezekiel 13:22)	
	"*While they see false visions for you, while they divine a **lie** to you, to bring you on the necks of the wicked, the slain whose day has come, whose iniquity shall end*" (Ezekiel 21:29)	
	"*In you are men who **slander** to cause bloodshed; in you are those who eat on the mountains; in your midst they commit lewdness*" (Ezekiel 22:9)	
	"*Her prophets plastered them with untempered mortar, seeing **false** visions, and divining **lies** for them, saying, 'Thus says the Lord God,' when the Lord had not spoken*" (Ezekiel 22:28)	
	"*She has grown weary with **lies**, and her great scum has not gone from her. Let her scum be in the fire!*" (Ezekiel 24:12)	
Hosea	"*By swearing and **lying**, killing and stealing and committing adultery, they break all restraint, with bloodshed upon bloodshed*" (Hosea 4:2)	
	"*They make a king glad with their wickedness, and princes with their **lies***" (Hosea 7:3)	
	"*Woe to them, for they have fled from Me! Destruction to them, because they have transgressed against Me! Though I redeemed them, yet they have spoken **lies** against Me*" (Hosea 7:13)	
	"*You have plowed wickedness; You have reaped iniquity. You have eaten the fruit of **lies**, because you trusted in your own way, in the multitude of your mighty men*" (Hosea 10:13)	
Micah	"*If a man should walk in a **false** spirit and speak a **lie**, saying, 'I will prophesy to you of wine and drink,' Even he would be the prattler of this people*" (Micah 2:11)	

	"For her rich men are full of violence, her inhabitants have spoken **lies**, and their tongue is deceitful in their mouth" (Micah 6:12)
Zechariah	"It shall come to pass that if anyone still prophesies, then his father and mother who begot him will say to him, 'You shall not live, because you have spoken **lies** in the name of the Lord.' And his father and mother who begot him shall thrust him through when he prophesies. "And it shall be in that day that every prophet will be ashamed of his vision when he prophesies; they will not wear a robe of coarse hair to **deceive**" (Zechariah 13:3-4)
Amos	"Thus says the Lord: "For three transgressions of Judah, and for four, I will not turn away its punishment, because they have despised the law of the Lord, and have not kept His commandments. Their **lies** lead them astray, **lies** which their fathers followed" (Amos 2:4)
Malachi	"But cursed be the **deceiver** who has in his flock a male, and takes a vow, but sacrifices to the Lord what is blemished— For I am a great King," Says the Lord of hosts, "and My name is to be feared among the nations"" (Malachi 1:14)

Table 50: The Prophets' Warning about the Influence of the Liar Attribute

As Jesus began his ministry and prepared His disciples for teaching God's Word, He warned them about the influence of the ***liar*** attribute. Jesus told them, "..."*Take heed that no one **deceives** you. For many will come in My name, saying, 'I am the Christ,' and will **deceive** many*" (Matthew 24:4-5). Jesus' statement was a major indicator that the influence of the ***liar*** attribute would play a large role during His ministry and the future. In fact, before the fall of Jerusalem, Jesus told the disciples, "*many false prophets will rise up and **deceive** many*" (Matthew 24:11; Mark 13:5-6; Luke 21:8), and "...***false*** *christs and false prophets will rise and show great signs and wonders to **deceive**, if possible, even the elect*" (Matthew 24:24; Mark 13:22). Interestingly, it was the influence of the ***liar*** attribute that was involved with the witnesses that ***falsely*** accused Jesus. The ***liar*** attribute's influence was so strong and pervasive among the Jewish leadership that it eventually led to the death of an innocent Jesus. BTT allows one to see that the negative forces of the war campaign used every strategy possible to strike a blow to the positive forces during the Jesus' ministry. Where it may appear that the negative forces succeeded by the crucifixion of Christ, the greater strategic plan of God was just unfolding for mankind.

Jesus' divine teaching shed light on the relationship between God and anyone influenced by the ***liar*** attribute. Jesus stated:

- "*He who says, "I know Him," and does not keep His commandments, is a **liar**, and the truth is not in him*" (1 John 2:4)

- "*...Who is a **liar** but he who denies that Jesus is the Christ? He is antichrist who denies the Father and the Son*" (1 John 2:21-22)

- "*If someone says, "I love God," and hates his brother, he is a **liar**; for he who does not love his brother whom he has seen, how can he love God whom he has not seen?*" (1 John 4:20)

- *"He who believes in the Son of God has the witness in himself; he who does not believe God has made Him a **liar**, because he has not believed the testimony that God has given of His Son"* (1 John 5:10)

The New Testament of the Biblical provided examples people influence by the ***liar*** attribute. Moreover, it provided future examples too. Some examples include:

Who	What Is Documented
Chief priest and Pharisees	They told Pilate, *"Sir, we remember, while He was still alive, how that **deceiver** said, 'After three days I will rise.'"* (Matthew 27:63)
Spies	Pharisees sent spies to watch Jesus who, *"...**pretended** to be righteous, that they might seize on His words, in order to deliver Him to the power and the authority of the governor"* (Luke 20:20)
The Jews at the feast (John 7:11)	*"And there was much complaining among the people concerning Him. Some said, "He is good"; others said, "No, on the contrary, He **deceives** the people"* (John 7:12)
Jews in general (John 8:48)	Jesus told them: *"Yet you have not known Him, but I know Him. And if I say, 'I do not know Him,' I shall be a **liar** like you; but I do know Him and keep His word"* (John 8:55)
	*"Why do you not understand My speech? Because you are not able to listen to My word. You are of your father the devil, and the desires of your father you want to do. He was a murderer from the beginning, and does not stand in the truth, because there is no truth in him. When he speaks a **lie**, he speaks from his own resources, for he is a **liar** and the father of it. But because I tell the truth, you do not believe Me"* (John 8:43-45)
Ananias and Sapphira	*"Ananias, why has Satan filled your heart to **lie** to the Holy Spirit and keep back part of the price of the land for yourself? While it remained, was it not your own? And after it was sold, was it not in your own control? Why have you conceived this thing in your heart? You have not **lied** to men but to God"* (Acts 5:3-4)
Tertullus, a Jewish orator accused Lysias, the commander who rescued Paul of this attribute	He falsely told Antonius Felix, governor of Judea that *"...the commander Lysias <u>came by and with great violence</u> took him out of our hands commanding his accusers to come to you..."* (Acts 24:7-8)
The ungodly and unrighteous	*"...exchanged the truth of God for the **lie**, and worshiped and served the creature rather than the Creator, who is blessed forever..."* (Romans 1:25)
Divisive people	*"...who are such do not serve our Lord Jesus Christ, but their own belly, and by smooth words and flattering speech **deceive** the hearts of the simple"* (Romans 16:18)
Evil men and impostors	*"But evil men and impostors will grow worse and worse, **deceiving** and being **deceived**"* (Timothy 3:13)
One's who think they are religious but cannot control their tongue	*"If anyone among you thinks he is religious, and does not bridle his tongue but **deceives** his own heart, this one's religion is useless"* (James 1:26)

Whoever loves and participated with this attribute	"*But outside are dogs and sorcerers and sexually immoral and murderers and idolaters, and whoever loves and practices a **lie**"* (Revelation 22:15)
It can overcome anyone	"*If we say that we have fellowship with Him, and walk in darkness, we **lie** and do not practice the truth*" (1 John 1:6)
Antichrists	"*For many **deceivers** have gone out into the world who do not confess Jesus Christ as coming in the flesh. This is a **deceiver** and an antichrist*" (2 John 1:7)

Table 51: Others Who Allowed the Influence of the Liar Attribute

Based on John 8:43-45, concerning the "Jews in general" in the Table above, BTT allows one to see clearly that the ***liar*** attribute is an ancient adversary. When Jesus spoke of the devil and said he was a murderer and a ***liar*** from the beginning, the word "beginning" is referring to the beginning of creation in the garden with Adam, Eve, and the serpent.

Further the Bible documents, "*Now the Spirit expressly says that in latter times some will depart from the faith, giving heed to deceiving spirits and doctrines of demons, speaking **lies** in hypocrisy, having their own conscience seared with a hot iron, forbidding to marry, and commanding to abstain from foods which God created to be received with thanksgiving by those who believe and know the truth*" (1 Timothy 4:1-2). Today, religious communities confirm this statement as they fall for the strategy of the ***liar*** attribute. Their actions, deeds, behaviors, and attitudes embolden the negative attributes as they engage in spiritual warfare. These ***unclean spirits*** twist the truth of the positive forces in the campaign by adding and subtracting from God's Word as they teach congregations of people around the world. BTT and <u>discernment</u> allows one to see that a person who allows the influence of the ***liar*** attribute sole purpose is to ***deceive***. Typically, the ***deception*** is for some measure of gain. But to ***deceive*** is to ***lie***; make no mistake, both come from the same ***unclean spirit***. A ***lie*** may be for monetary gain, control, or even to hide or justify one's sinful behavior. But regardless of the reason or rationale, one should never believe or trust a man or woman influenced by this attribute. Knowing God's Word helps to keep one from the ***deceit*** of the ***liar*** attribute. For these and many other reasons, the apostles documented several more pearls of wisdom about the ***liar*** attribute's strong influencing nature. By inspiration of the Holy Spirit, they documented:

"*Do not be **deceived**, my beloved brethren*" (James 1:16)	"*Do not be **deceived**: "Evil company corrupts good habits.*"" (1 Corinthians 15:33)	"*If we say that we have no sin, we **deceive** ourselves, and the truth is not in us*" (1 John 1:8)
"*Do not be **deceived**, God is not mocked; for whatever a man sows, that he will also reap*" (Galatians 6:7)	"*Now this I say lest anyone should **deceive** you with persuasive words*" (Colossians 2:4)	"*For if anyone thinks himself to be something, when he is nothing, he **deceives** himself*" (Galatians 6:3)
"*Let no one **deceive** himself. If anyone among you seems to be wise in this age, let him become a fool*	"*Therefore, putting away **lying**, "Let each one of you speak truth with his neighbor," for we are*	"*Let no one **deceive** you with empty words, for because of these things the wrath of God comes upon*

that he may become wise" (1 Corinthians 3:18)	members of one another" (Ephesians 4:25)	the sons of disobedience" (Ephesians 5:6)
Deacon's wives: *"Likewise, their wives must be reverent, not **slanderers**, temperate, faithful in all things"* (1 Timothy 3:11)	*"If we say that we have not sinned, we make Him a **liar**, and His word is not in us"* (1 John 1:10)	*"Little children, let no one **deceive** you. He who practices righteousness is righteous, just as He is righteous"* (1 John 3:7)
*"Do you not know that the unrighteous will not inherit the kingdom of God? Do not be **deceived**. Neither fornicators, nor idolaters, nor adulterers, nor homosexuals, nor sodomites, nor thieves, nor covetous, nor drunkards, nor revilers, nor extortioners will inherit the kingdom of God"* (1 Corinthians 6:9-10)	Older women: *"...the older women likewise, that they be reverent in behavior, not **slanderers**, not given to much wine, teachers of good things..."* (Titus 2:3)	*"But I fear, lest somehow, as the serpent **deceived** Eve by his craftiness, so your minds may be corrupted from the simplicity that is in Christ"* (2 Corinthians 11:3)

Table 52: Pearls of Wisdom Concerning the Influence of the Liar Attribute

The influence of the ***liar*** attribute, like all the negative attributes, comes from Satan. For one's benefit, the Biblical record documented, *"The coming of the lawless one is according to the working of Satan, with all power, signs, and **lying** wonders, and with all unrighteous deception among those who perish, because they did not receive the love of the truth, that they might be saved. And for this reason God will send them strong delusion, that they should believe the **lie**, that they all may be condemned who did not believe the truth but had pleasure in unrighteousness"* (2 Thessalonians 2:9-12). One must love the truth, which is the Gospel of Jesus Christ, to fight the influence of the ***liar*** attribute. The Mosaic Law was designed to lead the Jews to the Truth by teaching obedience. The Biblical record even documents, *"...the law was our tutor to bring us to Christ, that we might be justified by faith. But after faith has come, we are no longer under a tutor"* (Galatians 3:24-25). Today, the Gospel of Jesus Christ is God's Truth for all who believe in Him. In fact, Jesus bluntly told the Jewish leadership, *"You are of your father the devil, and the desires of your father you want to do. He was a murderer from the beginning, and does not stand in the truth, because there is no truth in him. When he speaks a **lie**, he speaks from his own resources, for he is a **liar** and the father of it"* (John 8:44). Jesus statement was universal in its application. Although He specifically said it to the Jews, its verbiage applies to all religious leaders who refuse to accept the authority of Jesus Christ today. Do not be ***deceived.***

Paul further documented, *"But we know that the law is good if one uses it lawfully, knowing this: that the law is not made for a righteous person, but for the lawless and insubordinate, for the ungodly and for sinners, for the unholy and profane, for murderers of fathers and murderers of mothers, for manslayers, for fornicators, for sodomites, for kidnappers, for **liars**, for perjurers, and if there is any other thing that is contrary to sound doctrine, according to the glorious gospel of the blessed God which was committed to my* *trust"* (1 Timothy 1:8-11). Unfortunately, the influence of the ***liar*** attribute masks this truth as one of the strategies of the war campaign. This attribute influences one's thoughts and behavior to use the Old Testament of the Biblical record unlawfully. Hence, ongoing spiritual warfare between the Christian community and religious communities.

In the Book of Revelation, the Bible documents the images of seven congregations in specific spiritual states engaged in the spiritual warfare. Two of the seven dealt with the presence of the ***liar*** attribute among their congregations. One congregation, the Church of Ephesus, correctly identified the influence of the ***liar*** attribute in ***false*** teachers that were among their congregation. Jesus stated, *"I know your works, your labor, your patience, and that you cannot bear those who are evil. And you have tested those <u>who say they are apostles and are not</u>, and have found them **liars**..."* (Revelation 2:2). However, the congregation was still failing as Jesus condemned them by stating, *"Nevertheless I have this against you, that you have left your first love. Remember therefore from where you have fallen; repent and do the first works, or else I will come to you quickly and remove your lampstand from its place—unless you repent"* (Revelations 2:4-5). On the other hand, the church of Philadelphia was doing what God wanted them to do; so much so, that Jesus stated, *"I know your works. See, I have set before you an open door, and no one can shut it; for you have a little strength, have kept My word, and have not denied My name. Indeed I will make those of the synagogue of Satan, <u>who say they are Jews and are not</u>, but **lie**—indeed I will make them come and worship before your feet, and to know that I have loved you"* (Revelation 3:8-9).

The influence of the ***liar*** attribute is documented well and in strong terms, in the Book of Revelation, regardless of one's maturity. In Revelations, confirmation of the attribute's existence extends into the future. All ***deception*** is from the ***unclean spirit*** of the ***liar*** attribute. BTT allows one to see that regardless of one's understanding of the Book of Revelation, the war campaign's end is already decided. God and the positive attributes will be triumphant! To see what happens to everyone who allows the influence of the ***liar*** attribute, as well as all the other negative attributes in their inner spirits, the Biblical record documents:

- *"So the great dragon was cast out, that serpent of old, called the Devil and Satan, who **deceives** the whole world; he was cast to the earth, and his angels were cast out with him"* (Revelation 12:9)

- *"The devil, who **deceived** them, was cast into the lake of fire and brimstone where the beast and the false prophet are. And they will be tormented day and night forever and ever"* (Revelation 20:10)

- John said the heavenly city established by God at the end of time and documented, *"...But there shall by no means enter it anything that defiles, or causes an abomination or a **lie**, but only those who are written in the Lamb's Book of Life"* (Revelation 21:27)

- *"Blessed are those who do His commandments, that they may have the right to the tree of life, and may enter through the gates into the city. But outside are dogs and sorcerers and sexually immoral and murderers and idolaters, and whoever loves and practices a **lie**. "I, Jesus, have sent My angel to testify to you these things in the*

churches. I am the Root and the Offspring of David, the Bright and Morning Star.'"
(Revelation 22:14-16)

The **Angry attribute**: This is a unique negative attribute in the war campaign that has three faces; *angry*, furious, and violent. I will address the furious and violent attributes next. For now, understand that each face causes an escalation in one's behavior by a different ***unclean spirit***. The escalation begins after one simply becomes "mad" or "upset" and does not control this natural emotional state. BTT allows one to see that this natural emotional state comes from the carnal side of man; it is part of God's design to allow the release of emotional tension that builds up from displeasure. The ***angry*** attribute is often confused with this unhappy disposition. For instance, a baby's displeasure or discomfort is different from being influenced by this negative attribute. A baby simply reacts to stimulus whether the stimulus is positive or negative. If the stimulus is warm, soothing, or pleasant, a baby's reaction will reflect the positive stimulus with a smile or cooing sound; however, if the stimulus is unpleasant, the baby will respond by crying or even screaming. But neither of these responses are due to an ***unclean spirit***. However, as a baby grows into a youth, develops cognitively and begin the process of reasoning, at some point the negative forces will be able to exploit the youth's inner spirit. There is no measure of time when this spiritual phenomenon begins to happen. However, in spiritual warfare, the negative attribute's influence in an immature inner spirit triggers negative outbursts of emotional responses and behavior. BTT allows one to see that the youth is still not accountable until he or she reaches an understanding of right and wrong. This is why good parenting and positive examples are so vital to a child's physical and spiritual development. Moreover, children's inner spirits exposed early to Christ's teachings can benefit from examples of other Christian adults and children. This exposure helps to develop children and aids parents in protecting them in the war campaign.

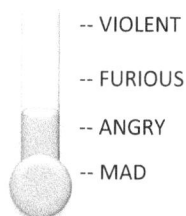
-- VIOLENT
-- FURIOUS
-- ANGRY
-- MAD

After a youth reaches an age of accountability, and automatically for adults of all ages, the influence of the ***angry*** attribute causes one to lose control of his or her emotions, thoughts, words, or behavior. One's temper; a person's state of mind seen in terms of their being angry or calm, makes a visual change. The attribute's influence is beyond the natural human emotion of frustration or disagreement. If one's temper is not controlled and goes beyond the point of being mad, then the door of the inner spirit opens to the influence of the ***angry*** attribute. If the attribute is allowed to enters one's inner spirit, one begins to lose control in a situation that does not warrant the distinctive and outward reaction created by this attribute. BTT allows one to understand that it is all right to get mad at a person, words, events, or even things; but, when one goes beyond this stage and one's visceral reaction escalates uncontrollably, then an ***unclean spirit*** is influencing one's inner spirit. Initially, the influence of the ***angry*** attribute is demonstrated by a strong emotional reaction. The reaction is similar to being upset or annoyed because of something perceived to be wrong. As this attribute matures, it leads one to excessive arguing, louder volumes of speech, shouting obscenities, and/or forcefully raising one's hands in irrational gestures. In most cases, a person can reason with another person influenced by the ***angry*** attribute and deescalate the attribute's influence. However, if the attribute lingers, it will escalate to one of its other spiritual faces; the furious or violent attributes. BTT helps one to see that alcohol, drugs, weapons, and fear, accelerates the influence of the ***angry*** attribute and often guarantees its escalation to the next state. Thus, if this attribute is not deescalated in one's inner spirit, it can begin a cycle of resentment and hate in the home that carries on for generations. Helpless children suffer from parents prone to frequent and spontaneous outburst of ***anger***. Here is what the Spirit of wisdom revealed to Solomon about this attribute.

Solomon learned that "*The <u>discretion</u> of a man makes him slow to **anger**, and his glory is to overlook a transgression*" (Proverbs 19:11). <u>Discretion</u> is the key for self-control. It allows one to be mad about something cognitively but keeps one's inner spirit in control. Without the element of <u>*discretion*</u>, the influence of the ***angry*** attributes creeps in and leads one to discard reason, good judgement, and control. Hence, Solomon wrote, "*...he who is slow to **anger** allays contention*" (Proverbs 15:18). This Scripture means, if one takes his or her time to weigh a situation when he or she gets mad, he or she can rationally alleviate the contention. For one who ignores this and loses control, Wisdom revealed that, "*An **angry** man stirs up <u>strife</u>...*" (Proverbs 29:22). Controlling ***anger*** keeps <u>strife</u> at bay. When <u>strife</u> is stirred up, everyone involved stays in contention. In chapter IX of this book, one will learn that the element of ***strife*** is an effective tool use by the negative forces of the war campaign. With this thought, Solomon documented that, "*He who is slow to **anger** is better than the mighty...*" (Proverbs 16:32). By controlling one's ***anger***, one is stronger (which is better) than one who allows the influence of this attribute to overthrow their inner spirit.

The Spirit of wisdom further taught Solomon, "*Make no friendship with an **angry** man...*" (Proverbs 22:24). Why? Because the influence of the ***angry*** attribute leads one down a path of trouble. For one's learning, Table 53 provides a few more pearls of wisdom that Solomon documented about the influence of the ***angry*** attribute:

"*A soft answer turns away wrath, but a harsh word stirs up **anger***" (Proverbs 15:1)	"*Wrath is cruel and **anger** a torrent...*" (Proverbs 27:4)	"*A gift in secret pacifies **anger**...*" (Proverbs 21:14)
"*Better to dwell in the wilderness, than with a contentious and **angry** woman*" (Proverbs 21:19)	"*He who sows iniquity will reap sorrow, and the rod of his **anger** will fail*" (Proverbs 22:8)	"*The north wind brings forth rain, and a backbiting tongue an **angry** countenance*" (Proverbs 25:23)
"*The wrath of a king is like the roaring of a lion; whoever provokes him to **anger** sins against his own life*" (Proverbs 20:2)		

Table 53: Some Pearls of Wisdom Concerning the Angry Attribute

In the Old Testament of the Biblical record, one of the earliest examples of the influence of the ***angry*** attribute appeared with Cain, the first born of Adam and Eve. The Biblical record documented that Cain was a tiller of the ground (Genesis 4:2), and his younger brother Abel, was a keeper of sheep. Both men made offerings to the Lord, but God was displeased with Cain's offering. The Bible documented that, "*Abel also brought of the firstborn of his flock and of their fat. And the Lord respected Abel and his offering, but He did not respect Cain and his offering. And Cain was very **angry**, and his countenance fell*" (Genesis 4:4, 5). Based on what is implied between the difference of Abel and Cain's offering, one should see that Cain's behavior opened an opportunity for the influence of the ***angry*** attribute. This influence became possible because of Cain's behavior; not because of what God did. The Biblical record confirmed that the Lord said to Cain, "*....Why are you **angry**? And why has your countenance fallen? If you do well, will you not be accepted? And if you do not do well, sin lies at the door. And its desire is for you, but you should rule over it*" (Genesis 4:6-7). Now clearly from the Text it is sin that desired Cain and wanted to rule him. Within this umbrella of sin was the influence of the ***angry*** attribute. The example documents that one provides the opportunity for this ***unclean spirit's*** entrance when one does not follow God's Word. Hence, a person is responsible for preparing and controlling one's own inner spirit. God told Cain- "*but you should rule over it.*" Other examples of people who allowed the influence of the ***angry*** attribute to influence their inner spirit and behavior include:

Who	**What Happened or What They Did**
Esau, Jacob's brother	After Jacob stole Esau's birthright, the Biblical record documented, "*...Esau hated Jacob because of the blessing with which his father blessed him, and Esau said in his heart, "The days of mourning for my father are at hand; then I will kill my brother Jacob*" (Genesis 27:45). So Rebekah told Jacob to flee, "*until your brother's **anger** turns away from you, and he forgets what you have done to him...*" (Genesis 27:45)
Jacob	"*Now when Rachel saw that she bore Jacob no children, Rachel envied her sister, and said to Jacob, "Give me children, or else I die!" And Jacob's **anger** was aroused against Rachel, and he said, "Am I in the place of God, who has withheld from you the fruit of the womb?*"" (Genesis 30:2)
	"*Then Jacob was **angry** and rebuked Laban, and Jacob answered and said to Laban: "What is my trespass? What is my sin, that you have so hotly pursued me?*" (Genesis 31:36). But Jacob controlled his anger and did not sin.
Dinah's brothers	After Shechem took Dinah and laid with her and her family found out, "*...the sons of Jacob came in from the field when they heard it; and the men were grieved and very **angry**, because he had done a disgraceful thing in Israel by lying with Jacob's daughter, a thing which ought not to be done*" (Genesis 34:7). They allowed this attribute to escalate.
	Jacob would prophesizes about Simeon and Levi: "*Let not my soul enter their council; let not my honor be united to their assembly; for in their **anger** they slew a man, and in their self-will they hamstrung an ox. Cursed be their **anger**, for it is fierce; and their wrath, for it is cruel! I will divide them in Jacob and scatter them in Israe*l" (Genesis 49:6-7)
Joseph's master	After the master's wife falsely accused Joseph: "*So it was, when his master heard the words which his wife spoke to him, saying, "Your servant did to me after this manner," that his **anger** was aroused*" (Genesis 39:19)

Pharaoh	*"And Pharaoh was **angry** with his two officers, the chief butler and the chief baker"* (Genesis 40:2) and put them in prison with Joseph.
Joseph's brothers	Joseph told them when he brought the entire family to Egypt *"...do not therefore be grieved or **angry** with yourselves because you sold me here; for God sent me before you to preserve life"* (Genesis 45:5)
Moses	He left Pharaoh's presence *"in great **anger**"* after the ninth plague had struck Egypt and he had pleaded with Pharaoh to let the children of Israel go before the final plague. (Exodus 11:8)
	He was ***angry*** with the Israelite after the Lord fed them in the Wilderness of Sin. Moses gave them clear instructions for handling the manna God gave them, *"Notwithstanding they did not heed Moses. But some of them left part of it until morning, and it bred worms and stank. And Moses was **angry** with them"* (Exodus 16:20)
	After receiving the Ten Commandments, *"So it was, as soon as he came near the camp, that he saw the calf and the dancing. So Moses' **anger** became hot, and he cast the tablets out of his hands and broke them at the foot of the mountain"* (Exodus 32:19) and Aaron, attempting to pacify Moses' ***anger*** said, *"...Do not let the **anger** of my lord become hot. You know the people, that they are set on evil"* (Exodus 32:22)
	When Aaron's sons did not follow the Lords instructions for the sin offering: *"Then Moses made careful inquiry about the goat of the sin offering, and there it was—burned up. And he was **angry** with Eleazar and Ithamar, the sons of Aaron..."* (Leviticus 10:16)
	When Korah, Dathan, Abiram, and On, lead, *"two hundred and fifty leaders of the congregation, representatives of the congregation, men of renown"* (Numbers 16:2) in rebellion: *"Then Moses was very **angry**, and said to the Lord, "Do not respect their offering. I have not taken one donkey from them, nor have I hurt one of them"* (Numbers 16:15). All the people in the rebellion died according to Numbers 16:32.
Balaam a false prophet	The Bible documented, *"And when the donkey saw the Angel of the Lord, she lay down under Balaam; so Balaam's **anger** was aroused, and he struck the donkey with his staff"* (Numbers 22:27)
The men of Israel under Gideon leadership	Gideon said to them, *"What have I done now in comparison with you? Is not the gleaning of the grapes of Ephraim better than the vintage of Abiezer? God has delivered into your hands the princes of Midian, Oreb and Zeeb. And what was I able to do in comparison with you?" Then their **anger** toward him subsided when he said that"* (Judges 8:2-3)
Samson	After his wife deceived him by giving the answers to his riddle to her relatives, *"Then the Spirit of the Lord came upon him mightily, and he went down to Ashkelon and killed thirty of their men, took their apparel, and gave the changes of clothing to those who had explained the riddle. So his **anger** was aroused, and he went back up to his father's house"* (Judges 14:19)
	Before he became king, Jabesh was considering a deal (essentially a surrender) with Nahash the Ammonite. To make the deal, the children of Israel would have to agree to have their right eyes put out. Well the Bible tells us, *"Then the Spirit of God came upon Saul when he heard this news, and his **anger** was greatly aroused"* (1 Samuel 11:6). Saul reunited the

Saul	armies of the children of Israel, defeated the Ammonites, and was crowned king in Gilgal (1 Samuel 11:11-15)
	When David fled from Saul after he tried to kill him and Jonathan, Saul's son, tried to intercede on David's behalf, the Bible documented, "*Then Saul's **anger** was aroused against Jonathan, and he said to him, "You son of a perverse, rebellious woman! Do I not know that you have chosen the son of Jesse to your own shame and to the shame of your mother's nakedness?"* (1 Samuel 20:30)
Jonathan	After the incident with Saul above. The Bible documented, "*...Jonathan arose from the table in fierce **anger**, and ate no food the second day of the month, for he was grieved for David, because his father had treated him shamefully*" (1 Samuel 20:34)
Abner	He was loyal to Saul until Ishbosheth, Saul son falsely accused him of sleeping with one of Saul's concubine named Rizpah. The Bible says, "*Then Abner became very **angry** at the words of Ishbosheth, and said, "Am I a dog's head that belongs to Judah? Today I show loyalty to the house of Saul your father, to his brothers, and to his friends, and have not delivered you into the hand of David; and you charge me today with a fault concerning this woman?"* (2 Samuel 3:8). Abner joined forces with David soon after.
King David	When Uzzah touched the ark of God and died the Bible documented, "*...David became **angry** because of the Lord's outbreak against Uzzah; and he called the name of the place Perez Uzzah to this day*" (2 Samuel 6:8)
King Asa	He foolishly tried to make a covenant with the king of Syria instead of relying on the Lord. The Lord sent Hanani the seer to warn him. The Bible documented, "*...Asa was **angry** with the seer, and put him in prison, for he was **enraged** at him because of this. And Asa oppressed some of the people at that time*" (2 Chronicles 16:10). His anger and foolishness cost him his life through a disease that started in his feet according to 2 Chronicles 16:11-14.
The prophet Jonah	After he preached the word of the Lord to the city of Nineveh. The people believed, repented of their sins, and the Lord relented from destroying the city. However, the Bible documented, "*But it displeased Jonah exceedingly, and he became **angry***" (Jonah 4:1). The Lord would ask Jonah, "*...Is it right for you to be **angry**?*" (Jonah 4:4)
	He also got angry over the death of a plant. The Biblical record documented, "*Then God said to Jonah, "Is it right for you to be **angry** about the plant?" And he said, "It is right for me to be **angry**, even to death!" But the Lord said, "You have had pity on the plant for which you have not labored, nor made it grow, which came up in a night and perished in a night. And should I not pity Nineveh, that great city, in which are more than one hundred and twenty thousand persons who cannot <u>discern</u> between their right hand and their left—and much livestock?"* (Jonah 4:9-11)

Table 54: Some Examples of People Who Allowed the Influence of the Angry Attribute

The Psalmist described how one can deescalate the influence of the ***angry*** attribute. He wrote, "*Be **angry**, and do not sin. Meditate within your heart on your bed, and be still*" (Psalm 4:4). This is the ultimate state of self-control of the inner spirit. The Lord knows that everyone is going to be influenced by the ***angry*** attribute from time to time; but the point is not to sin in that **anger**. To stop what one is doing and meditate on the issue at hand breaks the grip of the **angry** attribute. The influence of the **angry** attribute must not be allowed to mature. The Psalmist confirmed this thought when he documented, "*Cease from anger, and forsake wrath; do not fret—it only causes harm*" (Psalm 37:8). One must control one's inner spirit in which the influence of the **angry** attribute seeks entry. If not, escalation will occur that brings harm to another person. Escalation of this attribute is part of the strategy of the negative forces against other negative and positive forces in spiritual warfare. This strategy keeps instability and <u>strife</u> going in homes, communities, and societies worldwide.

In the Book of Ecclesiastes, Solomon documented a link between the pursuit of wealth and the influence of the **angry** attribute. Strongly stated as a warning to humanity, Solomon documented, "*And this also is a severe evil— just exactly as he came, so shall he go. And what profit has he who has labored for the wind? All his days he also eats in darkness, and he has much sorrow and sickness and **anger***" (Ecclesiastes 5:16-17). Many people in the rich category, discussed in Chapter VII of this book, say that there is a high degree of loneliness that comes with their financial status in life. Solomon acknowledged this too as he said sorrow, sickness, and **anger** becomes a part of life's equation. One becomes restricted in one's movements, loses the freedom to enjoy the company of friends, and many other things other people take for granted. Security, trust, and many other variables become a priority for people in the rich category. However, these items also open the door to the influence of the **angry** attribute. Moreover, without God's Word, spiritual warfare will ensure these other items bring pain. But at the end of the day, no wealth can leave with the person that owns them. Upon one's death, any wealth gained will remain on earth. Solomon documented "*exactly as he came, so shall he go.*" The context of Solomon writing suggest that this very thought may enhance the state of the **angry** attribute in one's life as he wrote, "*this also is a severe evil*". However, later he would contend, "*Do not hasten in your spirit to be **angry**, for **anger** rests in the bosom of fools*" (Ecclesiastes 7:9). Self-control of the inner spirit allows one to slow down in the heat of a tense situation. Mediating and feeding the inner spirit with God's Word provides one the tools for self-control. Without God's Word, the influence of the **angry** attribute will cause one to rest in the company of people influenced by the fool attribute.

The New Testament of the Biblical record brings life to the influence of the **angry** attribute's blinding capability. Jesus stated, "*You have heard that it was said to those of old, 'You shall not murder, and whoever murders will be in danger of the judgment'. But I say to you that whoever is **angry** with his brother without a cause shall be in danger of the judgment...*" (Matthew 5:21-22). BTT allows one to see that the influence of the **angry** attribute is a catalyst to more serious sins. Jesus is stating, for one to allow the influence of the **angry** attribute in one's inner spirit is just as bad as allowing the bloodthirsty (murderer) attribute in one's inner spirit. They are both ***unclean spirits***. Both will lead one to destruction and both are equally judged by God. When the influence of the **angry** attribute leads one to target their brother or sister for no reason, one has lost all self-control of one's inner spirit. BTT allows one to see that others are impacted by the manifested behavior of the **angry** attribute. The element of <u>strife</u> is spread among family members who then must take sides. This a spiritual warfare strategy and the negative forces use it to effectively destroy homes.

A few examples of individuals influenced by the ***angry*** attribute in the New Testament of the Biblical record include:

Who	What They Did
King Herod	*When he saw that he was deceived by the wise men, was exceedingly **angry**; and he sent forth and put to death all the male children who were in Bethlehem and in all its districts, from two years old and under, according to the time which he had determined from the wise men"* (Matthew 2:16). He allowed the attribute to escalate.
The brother of the prodigal son	Jesus said of the son that stayed home and worked, *"But he was **angry** and would not go in. Therefore his father came out and pleaded with him"* (Luke 15:28)
The Jews	After Jesus healed a man on the Sabbath (John 5:8-9), He point out their hypocrisy as He ask them, *"If a man receives circumcision on the Sabbath, so that the law of Moses should not be broken, are you **angry** with Me because I made a man completely well on the Sabbath?"* (John 7:23)

Table 55: More Examples of People Who Allowed the Influence of the Angry Attribute

Paul documented an important pearl of wisdom concerning the influence of the ***angry*** attribute. He wrote, "*Be **angry**, and do not sin": do not let the sun go down on your wrath, nor give place to the devil*" (Ephesians 4:26-27). From this Scripture, one can see the same situation facing Cain as the Lord told him to rule over the sin desiring him in Genesis 4:6-7. One must stop the influence of the ***angry*** attribute swiftly. Whatever it takes to extinguish the sting of this attribute in one inner spirit must be done; i.e. walking away, counting to ten, deep breaths, and/or quoting scriptures. If not, Satan will find an opportunity to enter one's spirit. Paul clearly documented that if one allows the influence of the ***angry*** attribute to fester into the night, Satan will gain a foothold in one's inner spirit and confuse one's thoughts with suspicions and false perceptions of the truth. Nightfall bring an escalation of this attribute's influence and invite the influence of the furious attribute to join it. This correlates well with Peter's comment that one must "*Be sober, be vigilant; because your adversary the devil walks about like a roaring lion, seeking whom he may devour*" (1 Peter 5:8). For anyone that claims Christ, Paul documented, "*Let all bitterness, wrath, **anger**, clamor, and evil speaking be put away from you, with all malice. And be kind to one another, tenderhearted, forgiving one another, even as God in Christ forgave you*" (Ephesians 4:31-32). He repeated this theme to the church in Colosse when he wrote, "*But now you yourselves are to put off all these: **anger**, wrath, malice, blasphemy, filthy language out of your mouth*" (Colossians 3:8). These comments serve to remind Christians that no one is immune to the influence of this attribute. It can cause one to stumble at any time. How one manages the influence of the ***angry*** attribute makes all the difference in the world. Paul's answer, which is the best answer until one masters the full control of one's inner spirit, is to not let the sun go down on your wrath. This is sound wisdom.

The **Furious attribute**: When the influence of the angry attribute reaches its full measure in one's inner spirit, if not arrested, it will spiritually mutate and become another **unclean spirit** called the *furious* attribute. This attribute is the second face of three powerful and related **unclean spirits**. This mutation of the *angry* attribute exhibits a behavior marked by an extremely stormy or turbulent temperament and appearance. The influence of this attribute causes one's verbal tone, perspiration, blood pressure, physical gestures, and other visual cues to increase exponentially. One becomes agitated, aggressive, and hostile but not to the tipping point of violence. Violence is the third face of this **unclean spirit**. BTT helps one to understand the influence of the *furious* attribute leads to crueler behavior toward others compared to the angry attribute. With the influence of this attribute, verbal abuse in the home is constant but not to the level of physical violence. However, this this attribute brings domestic violence to the home.

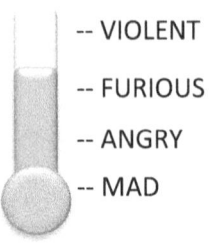

-- VIOLENT
-- FURIOUS
-- ANGRY
-- MAD

Solomon began to develop the distinction between the influence of the angry and *furious* attribute when he documented that, "*An **angry** man stirs up strife, and a **furious** man abounds in transgression*" (Proverbs 29:22). BTT allows one to see that where one influenced by the angry attribute causes <u>strife</u>, the influence of the *furious* attribute takes <u>strife</u> to a higher level. This attributes influence leads one into more destructive behaviors to get back at the person he or she initially became angry with. The influence of the *furious* attribute retards a person from hearing sound advice and counsel from others. They begin perceiving that any counsel or advice is an attack on them personally and isolate themselves from positive support or help. Hence, spiritual warfare is advanced as the negative forces of the war campaign begin unbalancing family, friends, and coworkers with knowledge of the situation and who believe they must take sides. For example, Solomon documented that "*… jealousy is a husband's **fury**; therefore he will not spare in the day of vengeance*" (Proverbs 6:34). BTT allows one to see that there are multiple people involved in this situation. There is the husband and wife; a third party involved with the wife; and the casual observers who serve as witness or friends of each person involved. However, as the *furious* attribute escalates and combine with other negative attributes, someone or ones may get hurt. In Proverb 6:34, the *furious* attribute combined with the jealousy/envy attribute. Whether a spouse, a lover, children, or in-laws, this insidious combination divides families and friends and supplies the negative forces of the war campaign. In this situation, the negative attributes can tip one over to the boiling point of the violent and bloodthirsty attributes. From Solomon's comment about the husband's behavior in Proverbs 6:34, one can see how the combined influences leads to a complete defilement of his inner spirit.

Further, Solomon learned that one should, "*Make no friendship with an **angry** man, and with a **furious** man do not go, lest you learn his ways and set a snare for your soul*" (Proverbs 22:24-25). From this statement, one can see the danger surrounding the influence of this attribute. Friendship with an angry person who never lets this **unclean spirit** go is a recipe for personal disaster. As the angry person allows their anger to mutate into *fury*, one that follows him or her places their soul in jeopardy. The longer one maintains a friendship with this person, the more likely one will learn their ways on their negative path of life. The fog of the war campaign hides this stark warning. All who ignore this wisdom fail to see that people who befriend a person with the *furious* attribute either ends up in prison or the grave. Consequently, the more hurtful aspect of this wisdom is that it reveals that one who learns the ways of the one influenced by the *furious* attribute places their soul in danger. This is especially true of innocent youth who find role models of people influenced by the *furious* attribute; from an early age, their soul is placed at risk. One with the positive attributes can rescue these youth by modeling good behavior, interaction, and positive relationships. Gangs began because of the influence of one with the *furious* attribute building relationships with younger people seeking positive but dominate role models.

As one studies the Old Testament of the Biblical record, one can see that the influence of the *furious* attribute was involved in the actions of Cain in Genesis 4:3-8. At some point in time, Cain made an offering to the Lord and murdering his brother in the field. Prior to Abel's murder, Cain allowed the angry attribute to give way to the *furious* attribute. Cain lost control of his inner spirit. Remember, the Lord said to Cain, *"If you do well, will you not be accepted? And if you do not do well, sin lies at the door. And its desire is for you, but you should rule over it"* (Genesis 4:7). God told Cain to get control over the sin (an umbrella of negative spirits) attempting to influence his inner spirit. Cain's answer was prayer, meditation, and obedience to God's Word. However, Cain rejected this path. Other examples of the *furious* attribute influencing the behavior and actions of people in the Old Testament included:

Who	**What Happened**
Esau	After Jacob stole his birthright: *"...Esau hated Jacob because of the blessing with which his father blessed him, and Esau said in his heart, "The days of mourning for my father are at hand; then I will kill my brother Jacob"* (Genesis 27:41), and Rebekah told Jacob to *"...flee to my brother Laban in Haran. And stay with him a few days, until your brother's **fury** turns away, until your brother's **anger** turns away from you, and he forgets what you have done ..."* (Genesis 27:43-45)
Simeon and Levi	Jacob, prophesying about his sons before he died stated, *"Cursed be their anger, for it is **fierce**; and their <u>wrath</u>, for it is cruel!"* (Genesis 49:7)
Naaman	After the prophet Elisha told Naaman what he needed to do to cure his leprosy, the Biblical record documented *"...Naaman became **furious**, and went away and said, "Indeed, I said to myself, 'He will surely come out to me, and stand and call on the name of the Lord his God, and wave his hand over the place, and heal the leprosy. Are not the Abanah and the Pharpar, the rivers of Damascus, better than all the waters of Israel? Could I not wash in them and be clean?" So he turned and went away in a <u>rage</u>"* (2 Kings 5:11-12)
King Uzziah,	As Azariah the priest and eighty other priests withstood Uzziah from entering the Lord's temple to burn incense to the Lord (2 Chronicles 26:19), the Bible documented, *"Then Uzziah became **furious**; and he had a censer in his hand to burn incense. And while he was angry with the priests, leprosy broke out on his forehead, before the priests in the house of the Lord, beside the incense altar"* (2 Chronicles 26:19)

Sanballat, governor of Samaria	When the Lord sent Nehemiah to Judah to begin rebuilding the Jerusalem wall, the Bible documented, "...*when Sanballat heard that we were rebuilding the wall, that he was **furious** and very indignant, and mocked the Jews*" (Nehemiah 4:1)
King Ahasuerus	The Bible documented that when, "*Queen Vashti refused to come at the king's command brought by his eunuchs; therefore the king was **furious**, and his anger burned within him*" (Esther 1:12)
Bigthan and Teresh, King Ahasuerus' eunuchs and doorkeepers	They "*became **furious** and sought to lay hands on King Ahasuerus*" on him. (Esther 2:21)
King Nebuchadnezzar	When the magicians, astrologers, sorcerers, and Chaldeans could not interpret his dream, the Bible says, "*For this reason the king was angry and very **furious**, and gave the command to destroy all the wise men of Babylon*" (Daniel 2:12)
	Also, when the Chaldeans accused Shadrach, Meshach, and Abed-Nego of disobeying his command to fall down and worship a golden image, the bible documented, "*...Nebuchadnezzar, in <u>rage</u> and **fury**, gave the command to bring Shadrach, Meshach, and Abed-Nego. So they brought these men before the king*" (Daniel 3:13)
	When these three men expressed their loyalty to God and presented their case to the king, the Bible documented, "*...Nebuchadnezzar was full of **fury**, and the expression on his face changed toward Shadrach, Meshach, and Abed-Nego. He spoke and commanded that they heat the furnace seven times more than it was usually heated*" (Daniel 3:19)

Table 56: Some Examples of People Who Allowed the Influence of the Furious Attribute

The prophet Isaiah revealed that the influence of the ***furious*** attribute can unite with the influence of the oppressor attribute in spiritual warfare. The nation of Israel experienced this phenomenon of spiritual warfare. The prophet Isaiah told the people from the Lord, "*I, even I, am He who comforts you. Who are you that you should be afraid of a man who will die, and of the son of a man who will be made like grass? And you forget the Lord your Maker, Who stretched out the heavens and laid the foundations of the earth; you have feared continually every day because of the **fury** of the oppressor, when he has prepared to destroy. And where is the **fury** of the oppressor?*" (Isaiah 51:12-13). Isaiah expressed to Israel that they had nothing to fear from this dreadful combination of attributes and the Lord was on their side.

In the New Testament, with the birth of Christ, the influence of the ***furious*** attribute appeared often in the Biblical record as the spiritual war increased in intensity. In fact, when King Herod saw that the wise men ignored his request to let him know where Jesus was born, he allowed the influence of the ***furious*** attribute in his inner spirit. Unfortunately, this **unclean spirit** rapidly mutated into the violent attribute and combined with the bloodthirsty attribute. The Biblical record documented that Herod became, "*...**exceedingly angry**; and he sent forth and put to death all the male children who were in Bethlehem and in all its districts, from two years old and under, according to the time which he had determined from the wise men*" (Matthew 2:16). With Herod, the influence of the ***furious*** attribute was expressed as "***exceedingly angry***." In other words, one could see the mutation of Herod's heightened stage of anger transitioning to the ***furious*** attribute. Moreover, BTT allows one to see that Herod experienced all the stages of escalation of anger; stemming from him first getting mad at the wise men's decision not to obey him. The negative forces of the war campaign found a rich and willing host in Herod.

As Jesus grew and began His ministry, the Bible documented a situation in which all three faces of the angry attribute are applied. During the situation, the influence of the ***furious*** and violent attributes are implied but clearly present. Here is what happened. Jesus went to a synagogue on the Sabbath day and read from the Book of the prophet Isaiah. When he finished reading, He told the Jews, "*Today this Scripture is fulfilled in your hearing*" (Luke 4:21). After a debate, the Biblical record documented, "*So all those in the synagogue, when they heard these things, were filled with <u>wrath</u>, and rose up and thrust Him out of the city; and they led Him to the brow of the hill on which their city was built, that they might throw Him down over the cliff*" (Luke 4:28). BTT allows one to see that the Jews allowed the influence of the angry attribute to escalate to the influence of the ***furious*** attribute. Then ***fury*** escalated to the violent attribute. The element of <u>wrath</u> became visible. I will cover the spiritual elements of <u>wrath</u> and <u>rage</u> with the next attribute. For now, understand that the crowd, confined to the space of the synagogue, provided fertile ground and opportunity for the influence of the ***furious*** attribute to quickly spread. The crowded environment fertilized a gang mentality when the negative forces of the campaign began working together in unison against the Son of God. Hence, the crowded conditions soon provided an opportunity for the influence of the violent and bloodthirsty attributes to lead many of the people down a dark path.

Within the war campaign, the influence of the ***furious*** attribute persistently sought anyone to influence to attack Jesus Christ. BTT allows one to see that during critical events in the life of Christ, the ***furious*** attribute was extremely active. One event occurred when Caiaphas the high priest, the scribes, and the elders assembled a Sanhedrin (the supreme council and tribunal of the Jews during postexilic times) to convict Jesus of a false crime. Caiaphas, influenced by the ***furious*** attribute, provided the opportunity for this **unclean spirit** to spread among the members of the Sanhedrin by his behavior. Look closely at the event documented in the Biblical record. The Bible documented that Caiaphas "*...tore his clothes, saying, "He has spoken blasphemy! What further need do we have of witnesses? Look, now you have heard His blasphemy! What do you think?" They answered and said, "He is deserving of death." Then they spat in His face and beat Him; and others struck Him with the palms of their hands, saying, "Prophesy to us, Christ! Who is the one who struck You?"*" (Matthew 26:65-68; Mark 14:63-65; Luke 22:71). BTT allows one to see how the ***furious*** attribute, influencing Caiaphas's behavior, opened the door for the attribute to spread among the members of the Sanhedrin as they witnessed his behavior, actions, and words. Based on the Biblical record's documentation of this event, the spread of this attribute led to the physical abuse of Jesus. This abuse came from the people who also allowed the influence of the ***furious*** attribute in their inner spirits.

Another event where the ***furious*** attribute was clearly present, but not identified, occurred when Jesus stood before the Jews facing judgement from Pontius Pilate. As Pilate made attempts to release Jesus because he knew that He was innocent, the Bible documented that, *"...the chief priests and elders persuaded the multitudes that they should ask for Barabbas and destroy Jesus"* (Matthew 27:20). What is unsaid here is the ***furious*** attribute was spread by the behavior of the chief priests and elders as they stirred up the crowd. One can see this in the crowd's response to Pilate as he attempted to release Jesus. The Bible documented that, *"Pilate said to them, "What then shall I do with Jesus who is called Christ?" They all said to him, "Let Him be crucified!" Then the governor said, "Why, what evil has He done?" But they cried out all the more, saying, "Let Him be crucified!" When Pilate saw that he could not prevail at all, but rather that <u>a tumult</u> was rising, he took water and washed his hands before the multitude, saying, "I am innocent of the blood of this just Person. You see to it." And all the people answered and said, "His blood be on us and on our children""* (Matthew 27:22-25). Overall, the reactions to Jesus and the Jew's response to Pilate, were indications of the presence of the influence of the ***furious*** attribute. Moreover, as this attribute's influence lingered in the inner spirits of the chief priests, elders, and the people, the violent attribute was gaining influence in the crowd. One can know this because the Bible documented that, *"that a tumult was rising"* according to Matthew 27:24. A tumult is an uproar, commotion, or chaos.

Now I would like one to consider the intelligence and strategy of the negative forces of the campaign. The ***furious*** attribute stopped short of mutating into the influence of the violent attribute. Why? Because of the possible response by Pilate and his Roman soldiers surrounding the Praetorium. If the ***furious*** attribute had escalated into the violent attribute and caused the Jews to escalate the tumult through violence, Pilate's soldiers would quickly bring an end to the whole situation. The Jewish leader and the crowd would suffer the wrath of the influences of the violent and bloodthirsty attributes from the Romans. The spiritual warfare perpetrated by the ***furious*** attribute and other negative forces present would not have succeeded in gaining Christ's conviction. Instead, there would have been a bloodbath of the Jewish crowd. But like a chess game, Satan maneuvered the influences of the negative forces where he could achieve his objectives in the war campaign. In this case, the negative attributes, working with the strength of the influence of the ***furious*** attribute, gained a win over the positive attributes. The evidence is Jesus' sentence to crucifixion.

The influence of the ***furious*** attribute continued after Jesus' crucifixion. As His apostles began spreading the Gospel throughout the world, BTT allows one to see the influence of this attribute in the following events:

The Perpetrators	What They Did
When the priests, the captain of the temple, and the Sadducees arrested Peter and John	"...being <u>greatly disturbed</u> that they taught the people and preached in Jesus the resurrection from the dead. And <u>they laid hands on them</u>, and put them in custody..." (Acts 4:2-3)
	"So when they had further <u>threatened them</u>, they let them go, finding no way of punishing them, because of the people, since they all glorified God for what had been done" (Acts 4:21)
When the high priest arrested the apostles by force	"Then the high priest rose up, and all those who were with him (which is the sect of the Sadducees), and they were <u>filled with indignation</u>, and <u>laid their hands on</u> the apostles and put them in the common prison" (Acts 5:17-18)

	After the apostles spoke to the Sanhedrin, the Bible documented "*When they heard this, they were **furious** and plotted to kill them*" (Acts 5:33)
	After debating how to handle the situation, the Sanhedrin had the apostles return "*…and <u>beaten them</u>, they <u>commanded</u> that they should <u>not speak in the name of Jesus</u>, and let them go*" (Acts 5:40)
The Jews that murdered Stephen	"*…they <u>cried out with a loud voice, stopped their ears, and ran at him</u> with one accord; and they cast him out of the city…*" (Acts 7:57-58)
Saul (before his conversion to Christianity)	"*…still <u>breathing threats</u> <u>and murder</u> against the disciples of the Lord, went to the high priest and asked letters from him to the synagogues of Damascus, so that if he found any who were of the Way, whether men or women, he might bring them bound to Jerusalem*" (Acts 9:1-2)

Table 57 Examples of Behavior Inspired by the Influence of the Furious Attribute:

The few examples above illustrated some of the many behaviors that corroborated the presence of the influence of the ***furious*** attribute. Once again, BTT and <u>discernment</u> allows one to see the behavior associated with this **unclean spirit** and its role in the war campaign.

The **Violent attribute**: The full measure of the influence from the furious attribute opens the door to the influence of the ***violent*** attribute. This is the third face of the angry attribute and it influences one on a path loaded with major consequences and pain. This attribute is the apex of anger where one is no longer able to control his or her inner spirit. This attribute influences one to go beyond making aggressive physical hand gestures, pushing, or verbally assaulting a person. It now influences one to the use

-- VIOLENT
-- FURIOUS
-- ANGRY
-- MAD

physical force; to physically attack or assault a person. It influences one to bring harm or damage to another person's flesh without taking the person's life. This is the attribute behind domestic ***violence*** at every level in the home. When the influence of the ***violent*** attribute combines with the influence of the oppressor attribute, the recipients of the anger behind these joint forces can have their inner spirits broken and stripped of all hope. One's behavior is often so intense that one appears to be in a blind <u>rage</u>. Because of the intense agitation created in their inner spirit, others must physically restrain a person who has allowed the influence of this attribute. The influence of the ***violent*** attribute leads to an expressive behavior that is more animated, hostile, and deviant than the furious attribute. Drugs, alcohol, and other negative influences such as the hater, evil, and jealousy/envy attributes, rapidly open the door for the influence of this attribute. If this attribute is not controlled, one's inner spirit becomes extremely susceptible to the influences of the bloodthirsty and perverse attributes. When this attribute combines with the perverse attribute, rape can occur with women, men, and even children. An extremely important point to understand about this attribute is that it, nor the behaviors that come from it, can be resolved by human laws or police actions. Resolution of the influence of this **unclean spirit** begins with knowledge of God's Word in the home with parents atoned to Biblical principles and a basic understanding of good and evil. This attribute germinates on the spiritual battlefield by ill-equipped or informed parents and the false teaching of God's Word.

Before I discuss the **violent** attribute, one must understand the elements of <u>wrath</u> and <u>rage</u>. The Biblical record identifies both elements, their differences are miniscule, and sometimes they overlap. Nonetheless, they play a role in spiritual warfare and having a working knowledge of them is important. <u>Rage</u> is violent uncontrollable anger seen through one's physical behavior such as hitting, cussing, slapping, etc. <u>Wrath</u> is considered extreme anger that is vengeful and full of indignation which deals with the mental state of one influenced by the **violent** attribute. One begins to cognitively think of ways to strongly get back at someone else, to harm them, to inflict pain on a person. The **violent** attribute spiritually makes use of both elements. The Spirit of Wisdom revealed to Solomon that, "<u>Wrath</u> *is cruel and anger a torrent...*" (Proverbs 27:4). Further she revealed that "*A <u>wrathful</u> man stirs up strife...*" (Proverbs 15:18) and "*A man who isolates himself seeks his own desire; he <u>rages</u> against all wise judgment*" (Proverbs 18:1). BTT allows one to see that both the elements of <u>wrath</u> and <u>rage</u> places one on a path where the outcome is not good for the person or persons whom he or she has come into contact. With these elements' spiritual link to the influence of the **violent** attribute, a person becomes a threat to his or her own family, community, and the society. This is why the Spirit of wisdom revealed to Solomon, "*He who is slow to <u>wrath</u> has great understanding, but he who is impulsive exalts folly*" (Proverbs 14:29). Further he documented, "*A wise man fears and departs from evil, but a fool <u>rages</u> and is self-confident*" (Proverbs 14:16). In other words, one must slow down and arrest these negative elements before the negative forces use the environment to grow the influence of the **violent** attribute to its fullest measure. Proverbs 14:16 means that one who does not learn to control his or her inner spirit will eventually be subject to the influences of the fool attribute because of self-confidence. God's Word provides the key required to ensure one does not place his or her soul at risk. A good example of one who arrested the element of <u>rage</u> is found with "*Naaman, commander of the army of the king of Syria, was a great and honorable man in the eyes of his master, because by him the Lord had given victory to Syria. He was also a mighty man of valor, but a leper*" (2 Kings 5:1). The Biblical record documents that Naaman was sent to Israel to be healed of his leprosy according to 2 Kings 5:2-6 which upset the King of Israel. Knowing he could not heal Naaman, the king tore his clothes. The Bible records that, "*Elisha the man of God heard that the king of Israel had torn his clothes*" (2 Kings 5:8) and he told the king essentially that he would take care of Naaman. Naaman went to see Elisha but Elisha did not come out to meet or speak with him. Instead, Elisha sent a massager to tell Naaman to "*Go and wash in the Jordan seven times, and your flesh shall be restored to you, and you shall be clean*" (2 Kings 5:10). However, this upset Naaman and the Biblical record documented, "*But Naaman became furious, and went away and said, "Indeed, I said to myself, 'He will surely come out to me, and stand and call on the name of the Lord his God, and wave his hand over the place, and heal the leprosy.' Are not the Abanah and the Pharpar, the rivers of Damascus, better than all the waters of Israel? Could I not wash in them and be clean?" So he turned and went away in a <u>rage</u>*" (2 Kings 5:11-12). BTT allows one to see that Naaman was about to lose a blessing from God because of the furious attribute. One can also visualize the element of <u>rage</u> developing in him. However, the Bible documented that one of Naaman servants calmed him down with God's

Truth according to 2 Kings 5:13. Thus the Bible recorded that Naaman, "...*went down and dipped seven times in the Jordan, according to the saying of the man of God; and his flesh was restored like the flesh of a little child, and he was clean*" (2 Kings 5:14).

Solomon documented some pearls of wisdom about the elements of <u>wrath</u> and <u>rage</u>. He documented:

"...the expectation of the wicked is <u>wrath</u>" (Proverbs 11:23)	"A fool's <u>wrath</u> is known at once..." (Proverbs 12:16)	"...wise men turn away <u>wrath</u>" (Proverbs 29:8)
"A soft answer turns away <u>wrath</u>, but a harsh word stirs up anger" (Proverbs 15:1)	"A man of great <u>wrath</u> will suffer punishment; for if you rescue him, you will have to do it again" (Proverbs 19:19)	"The king's <u>wrath</u> is like the roaring of a lion, but his favor is like dew on the grass" (Proverbs 19:12)
"A stone is heavy and sand is weighty, but a fool's <u>wrath</u> is heavier than both of them" (Proverbs 27:3)	"As messengers of death is the king's <u>wrath</u>, but a wise man will appease it" (Proverbs 16:14)	"The king's favor is toward a wise servant, but his <u>wrath</u> is against him who causes shame" (Proverbs 14:35)
"For as the churning of milk produces butter, and wringing the nose produces blood, so the forcing of <u>wrath</u> produces strife" (Proverbs 30:33)	"The <u>wrath</u> of a king is like the roaring of a lion; whoever provokes him to anger sins against his own life" (Proverbs 20:2	"If a wise man contends with a foolish man, whether the fool <u>rages</u> or laughs, there is no peace" (Proverbs 29:9)

Table 58: Some Pearls of Wisdom Concerning the Element of <u>Wrath</u> and <u>Rage</u>

This discussion on the elements of <u>wrath</u> and <u>rage</u> will now allow one to see how they and the influence of the **violent** attribute come together in the inner spirit of one who allows them. Thus, the Spirit of wisdom revealed to Solomon that, "*A **violent** man entices his neighbor, and leads him in a way that is not good. He winks his eye to devise perverse things; he purses his lips and brings about evil*" (Proverbs 16:29-30). This Scripture says a lot about the influence of the **violent** attribute. BTT allows one to see that the influence of this attribute opens the door to a host of negative attributes that are almost impossible to control. BTT also allows one to see that when this attribute enters people's inner spirit, it influences them to recruit others. In the proverb above, one can see that the **violent** attribute forms a triad with the perverse and evil attributes. This triad then uses methods of physical gestures (winking the eye) and lying (pursing the lips) to recruit a neighbor in deviant and illegal behaviors. Go back and read about the perverse and evil attribute's devastating influences when they are by themselves; then consider their impact when they come together as a triad with the aggression of the **violent** attribute. Nothing good comes from this triad. Remember, it is the combination of this and the perverse attributes that influences one into domestic violence and the rape of women, men, and children. Even if one allowed just the influence of the **violent** attribute into his or her inner spirit, neither their neighbors nor their neighborhoods are safe. Chapter VII of this book speaks about the people in the neighbor category. However, based on what one just read about the influence of the **violent** attribute, understand that it only gets worse.

The positive forces of the war campaign should worry when the influence of the ***violent*** attribute combines with the influence of the wicked and evil attributes. Solomon documented, *"Do not enter the path of the wicked, and do not walk in the way of evil. Avoid it, do not travel on it; turn away from it and pass on. For they do not sleep unless they have done evil; and their sleep is taken away unless they make someone fall. For they eat the bread of wickedness, and drink the wine of **violence**."* (Proverbs 4:14-17). This Scripture indicates that the influence of the ***violent*** attribute has an intoxicating affect and therefore, it may be additive. BTT allows one to see that this negative combination of influences will lead one to commit atrocities beyond comprehension. When this triad operates among the negative forces of the war campaign, no one influenced by the negative or positive attributes is safe. Further Solomon documented that, *"... **violence** covers the mouth of the wicked"* (Proverbs 10:6 and 10:11). Hence, one influenced by this attribute will publicly and privately speak about ***violent*** action to anyone who will listen. This accepted behavior makes many supporting souls culpable in spiritual warfare when they do nothing to stop this behavior.

The Spirit of wisdom revealed that the *"...**violence** of the wicked will destroy them, because they refuse to do justice"* (Proverbs 21:7). In other words, when the influence of the ***violent*** attribute unites with the influence of the wicked attribute, the combination is so intense that it eventually destroys the one influenced by this combination. However, prior to this person's destruction, their behavior will create massive spiritual and physical damage on the spiritual battlefield. But the influence of this combination blinds its host so badly that the one influenced by these attributes refuse to do justice even to save his or her own life. The cycle of ***violence*** they create has far reaching tentacles that last for generations. All of this illustrates the potency of the influence of the ***violent*** attribute in the both spiritual warfare and the war campaign itself.

Three more pearls of wisdom that Solomon documented from the Spirit of wisdom concerning the influence of the ***violent*** attribute included:

- *".... the soul of the unfaithful feeds on **violence**"* (Proverbs 13:2)

- *"Do not be envious of evil men, nor desire to be with them; for their heart devises **violence**, and their lips talk of troublemaking"* (Proverbs 24:1-2)

- *"He who sends a message by the hand of a fool cuts off his own feet and drinks **violence**"* (Proverbs 26:6)

As one reviews the rest of the Old Testament, one will first notice the ***violent*** attribute in Cain. Cain started with being mad and somewhere along the way, he allowed the influence of the angry attribute which escalate out of control in his inner spirit. God told Cain what he had to do when He said, *"Why are you angry? And why has your countenance fallen? If you do well, will you not be accepted? And if you do not do well, sin lies at the door. And its desire is for you, but you should rule over it.'"* (Genesis 4:6-7). Cain did not listen. This led to the influence of the furious attribute and then the ***violent*** attribute moved into his inner spirit. Suffice to say, the ***violent*** attribute opened the door for the bloodthirsty attribute's influence, and Cain murdered his brother Abel (Genesis 4:8). From this point on, the examples of the ***violent*** attribute grew. The Biblical record documented:

Who	What They Did
Lamech	He told his wives, "*Adah and Zillah, hear my voice; wives of Lamech, listen to my speech! For I have killed a man for wounding me, even a young man for hurting me*" (Genesis 4:23)
Mankind (before the great flood)	"*...saw that the wickedness of man was great in the earth, and that every intent of the thoughts of his heart was only evil continually. And the Lord was sorry that He had made man on the earth, and He was grieved in His heart*" (Genesis 6:5, 6), and "*The earth also was corrupt before God, and the earth was filled with **violence***" (Genesis 6:11)
	"*And God said to Noah, "The end of all flesh has come before Me, for the earth is filled with **violence** through them; and behold, I will destroy them with the earth*" (Genesis 6:13)
Simeon and Levi	After Shechem and his family were circumcised so that Shechem could marry Dinah, the sister of Simeon and Levi, whom he violated earlier (Genesis 34:1-24), the Bible documented, "*Now it came to pass on the third day, when they were in pain, that two of the sons of Jacob, Simeon and Levi, Dinah's brothers, each **took his sword and came boldly** upon the city and killed all the males. And they killed Hamor and Shechem his son with the edge of the sword, and took Dinah from Shechem's house, and went out*" (Genesis 34:25-26)
	Jacob, prophesying about his sons before he died stated, "*Cursed be their anger, for it is **fierce**; and their <u>wrath</u>, for it is cruel!*" (Genesis 49:7)
The children of Israel after they reached the Promised Land	"*They did not destroy the peoples, concerning whom the Lord had commanded them, but they mingled with the Gentiles and learned their works; they served their idols, which became a snare to them. They even sacrificed their sons and their daughters to demons, and **shed innocent blood**, the blood of their sons and daughters, whom they **sacrificed** to the idols of Canaan; and the land was polluted with blood*" (Psalms 106:34-38)
King Saul	"*...there was a famine in the days of David for three years, year after year; and David inquired of the Lord. And the Lord answered, "It is because of Saul and his bloodthirsty house, because he killed the Gibeonites""* (2 Samuel 21:1)
Joab the son of Zeruiah	"*he shed the blood of war in peacetime, and put the blood of war on his belt that was around his waist, and on his sandals that were on his feet*" (1 Kings 2:5)
King Ahab and his wife Jezebel	Jezebel crafted a letter in Ahab's name to proclaim a feast for Naboth according to 1 Kings 21:8-10. She coordinated a scheme to murder Naboth. The Biblical record documented, "*And two men, scoundrels, came in and sat before him; and the scoundrels witnessed against him, against Naboth, in the presence of the people, saying, "Naboth has blasphemed God and the king!" Then they took him outside the city and **stoned him with stones**, so that he died*" (1 Kings 21:13-15). Then "*So it was, when Ahab heard that Naboth was dead, that Ahab got up and went down to take possession of the vineyard of Naboth the Jezreelite*" (1 Kings 21:16)

Sennacherib king of Assyria	The prophet Amos told King Hezekiah that the Lord heard his prayer concerning Sennacherib and the Lord said, "…'*But I know your dwelling place, your going out and your coming in, and your <u>rage</u> against Me. Because your <u>rage</u> against Me and your tumult have come up to My ears, therefore I will put My hook in your nose and My bridle in your lips, and I will turn you back by the way which you came*" (2 Kings 19:27-28; Isaiah 37:28-29)
Manasseh	"*Manasseh **shed very much innocent blood**, till he had filled Jerusalem from one end to another, besides his sin by which he made Judah sin, in doing evil in the sight of the Lord*" (2 Kings 21:16). His punishment was so severe that Lord said, "*Behold, I am bringing such calamity upon Jerusalem and Judah, that whoever hears of it, both his ears will tingle*" (2 Kings 21:12). You see, the Lord revealed that Manasseh's sins and **bloodthirstiness** was great, "*…because of the **innocent blood** that he had shed; for he had filled Jerusalem with **innocent blood**, which the Lord would not pardon*" (2 Kings 21:16)
The children of Israel	"*But a prophet of the Lord was there, whose name was Oded; and he went out before the army that came to Samaria, and said to them: "Look, because the Lord God of your fathers was angry with Judah, He has delivered them into your hand; but you have killed them in a <u>rage</u> that reaches up to heaven*" (2 Chronicles 28:9)
King Ahasuerus	After Queen Esther told the king of Haman plot to exterminate the Jews, The Bible documented, that the king "*arose in his <u>wrath</u> from the banquet of wine and went into the palace garden; but Haman stood before Queen Esther, pleading for his life…*" (Esther 7:7)
	The Bible also documented that after, "*…they hanged Haman on the gallows that he had prepared for Mordecai. Then the king's <u>wrath</u> subsided*" (Esther 7:10)
Bigthan and Teresh, King Ahasuerus' eunuchs and doorkeepers	The Biblical record documented that they, "*became furious and **sought to lay hands on** King Ahasuerus*" on him. (Esther 2:21)
Haman	When he "*…saw that Mordecai did not bow or pay him homage, Haman was filled with <u>wrath</u>*" (Esther 3:5)
Elihu	The Biblical record documented, *the <u>wrath</u> of Elihu, the son of Barachel the Buzite, of the family of Ram, was aroused against Job; his <u>wrath</u> was aroused because he justified himself rather than God. Also against his three friends his <u>wrath</u> was aroused, because they had found no answer, and yet had condemned Job. Now because they were years older than he, Elihu had waited to speak to Job. When Elihu saw that there was no answer in the mouth of these three men, his <u>wrath</u> was aroused*" (Job 32:2-5)
	When the magicians, astrologers, sorcerers, and Chaldeans could not interpret his dream, the Bible says, "*For this reason the king was angry and **very furious**, and gave the command to destroy all the wise men of Babylon*" (Daniel 2:12)

King Nebuchadnezzar	"Then Nebuchadnezzar, in <u>rage</u> and fury, gave the command to bring Shadrach, Meshach, and Abed-Nego. So they brought these men before the king" (Daniel 3:13)
	When these three men expressed their loyalty to God and presented their case to the king, the Bible documented, "...*Nebuchadnezzar was full of fury, and* **the expression on his face changed** *toward Shadrach, Meshach, and Abed-Nego. He spoke and commanded that they heat the furnace seven times more than it was usually heated*" (Daniel 3:19)
	"..."*And the king of the South shall be moved with <u>rage</u>, and go out and fight with him, with the king of the North, who shall muster a great multitude; but the multitude shall be given into the hand of his enemy*" (Daniel 11:11)
	"For ships from Cyprus shall come against him; therefore he shall be grieved, and return in <u>rage</u> against the holy covenant, and do damage. "So he shall return and show regard for those who forsake the holy covenant" (Daniel 11:30)
Moab	The prophet Isaiah documented, "*We have heard of the pride of Moab— He is very proud— of his haughtiness and his pride and his <u>wrath</u>; but his lies shall not be so*" (Isaiah 16:6)
	And the Lord said, "*I know his <u>wrath</u>,*" says the Lord, "*But it is not right; his lies have made nothing right*" (Jeremiah 48:30)
Shallum the son of Josiah	"*Yet your eyes and your heart are for nothing but your covetousness, for shedding innocent blood, and practicing oppression and* **violence**" (Jeremiah 22:17)
The rich city of Tyre	The Lord said, "*By the abundance of your trading you became filled with* **violence** *within, and you sinned; therefore I cast you as a profane thing out of the mountain of God; and I destroyed you, O covering cherub, from the midst of the fiery stones*" (Ezekiel 28:16)
Egypt and Edom	"*Egypt shall be a desolation, and Edom a desolate wilderness, because of* **violence** *against the people of Judah, for they have shed innocent blood in their land*" (Joel 3:19)
	To Edom: "*For* **violence** *against your brother Jacob, shame shall cover you, and you shall be cut off forever*" (Obadiah 1:10)
The children of Israel	"*For they do not know to do right,' Says the Lord, 'who store up* **violence** *and robbery in their palaces*" (Amos 3:10)
	To Jerusalem and Samaria: "*Woe to you who put far off the day of doom, who cause the seat of* **violence** *to come near*" (Amos 6:3)
	"*Woe to those who devise iniquity, and work out evil on their beds! At morning light they practice it, because it is in the power of their hand. They covet fields and take them by* **violence**, *also houses, and seize them. So they oppress a man and his house, a man and his inheritance*" (Micah 2:1-2)
	"*For her rich men are full of* **violence**, *her inhabitants have spoken lies, and their tongue is deceitful in their mouth*" (Micah 6:12)
Nineveh	"*But let man and beast be covered with sackcloth, and cry mightily to God; yes, let everyone turn from his evil way and from the* **violence** *that is in his hands*" (Jonah 3:8)
	For Judah: "*O Lord, how long shall I cry, and You will not hear? Even cry out to You,* "**Violence**!" *And You will not save. Why do You show me*

	*iniquity, and cause me to see trouble? For plundering and **violence** are before me; there is strife, and contention arises*" (Habakkuk 1:2-3)
	To Jerusalem: "*Her prophets are insolent, treacherous people; her priests have polluted the sanctuary, they have done **violence** to the law*" (Zephaniah 3:4)

Table 59: Examples of People Who Allowed the Influence of the Violent Attribute

The Lord gave Moses instructions concerning the influence of the ***violent*** attribute. However, BTT and <u>discernment</u> is required to see and understand what the Lord said to the children of Israel. Moses documented, "*He who strikes a man so that he dies shall surely be put to death*" (Exodus 21:12). Embedded in this law is the consequence for one who allows the influence of the ***violent*** attribute to control their inner spirit. The law covers two attributes; the bloodthirsty and the ***violent*** attributes. In this case, one can see that the influence of the ***violent*** attribute leads to physical harm. Likewise, if that same man dies, the influence of the bloodthirsty attribute is involved. To allow the influence of the ***violent*** attribute to get out of control, automatically establishes guilt. Satan has confused this message through the perversion of the legal system as part of spiritual warfare. Man is responsible for controlling his inner spirit, which includes the influence of the ***violent*** attribute. Where the influence of the ***violent*** attribute is involved, there is no such thing as an accident. This is consistent with the application of God's Word.

David wrote a song to the Lord to express his appreciation for deliverance from the hand of Saul and all his enemies. In the song, twice David commented on the ***violent*** attribute that influenced his adversaries. He wrote, "*The God of my strength, in whom I will trust; My shield and the horn of my salvation, My stronghold and my refuge; My Savior, You save me from **violence**"* (2 Samuel 22:3). Next he wrote, "*It is God who avenges me, and subdues the peoples under me; He delivers me from my enemies. You also lift me up above those who rise against me; You have delivered me from the **violent** man. Therefore I will give thanks to You, O Lord, among the Gentiles, and sing praises to Your name*" (2 Samuel 22:48-50). David's prayer teaches several important principles. Most importantly, one should gave thanks to God Who is the True deliverer from people influenced by the ***violent*** attribute. David's words should serve as an example for one to follow today. One must learn God's Word and pray.

Within the context of the Book of Job, Job's three wise friends accused him of allowing the influence of the ***violent*** attribute in his activities as a reason for the calamity he was going through. They had no idea of the cause of Job's suffering, but they made accusations freely. Job knew this was not the case. Job told them, "*My face is flushed from weeping, and on my eyelids is the shadow of death; although no **violence** is in my hands, and my prayer is pure*" (Job 16:16-17). At one point during Job's suffering, he questioned why people who knew God, would allow the influence of the ***violent*** attribute in their lives. Job stated, "*Since times are not hidden from the Almighty, why do those who know Him see not His days? Some remove landmarks; they seize flocks **violently** and feed on them; they drive away the donkey of the fatherless; they take the widow's ox as a pledge. They push the needy off the road; all the poor of the land are forced to hide*" (Job 24:1-4). Although this question troubled Job, and he could clearly identify the behaviors associated with the attribute, he accepted that God was still in control. He rightfully told his wise friends that the Lord would judge people influenced by the **violent** attribute and all other sinners for their actions, in due time.

Toward the end of the Book of Job, it is clear that he understood how the influence of the **violent** attribute worked. During his time of affliction, Job told his three wise but tormenting friends, that *"If you should say, 'How shall we persecute him?'—since the root of the matter is found in me, be afraid of the sword for yourselves; for <u>wrath</u> brings the punishment of the sword, that you may know there is a judgment"* (Job 19:28-29). Job's friends were trying to convince him that he was the cause of his own affliction by the sin that he had secretly committed. They were attempting to get him to confess to their perceived lie. From the context, it appeared that these wise friends had allowed the element of <u>wrath</u> in their behavior and speech. Job perceived that this element and the influence of the angry attribute was leading them down a path to persecute him. Job told them to be afraid for their own lives. He used the image of a sword to illustrate they would be judged for their error. Job was right.

The Psalmist simply documented that one must, *"Cease from **anger**, and forsake <u>wrath</u>; do not fret—it only causes harm"* (Psalm 37:8). Just as Solomon had documented, the Psalmist also documented that the influence of the **violent** attribute only causes harm and does no one any good. One must arrest the influence of the **violent** attribute at the early stage of the angry attribute. The Psalmist prayed to the Lord to help him deal with people who had allowed the influence of the **violent** attribute. The Biblical record documented that he prayed, *"Attend to me, and hear me; I am restless in my complaint, and moan noisily, because of the voice of the enemy, because of the oppression of the wicked; for they bring down trouble upon me, and in <u>wrath</u> they hate me"* (Psalm 55:2-3). BTT also allows one to see from the Psalmist's prayers that the influence of the **violent** attribute can combine with the influence of the hater attribute. This combination creates major trouble for whomever it targets. In spiritual warfare, prayer is the only weapon that fights the union of these combined **unclean spirits**.

David and Solomon documented a few more pearls of wisdoms that one needs to see concerning the influence of the **violent** attribute. The following pearls of wisdom are from the prayers of David and a thought from Solomon.

*"Why do the nations **rage**, and the people plot a vain thing?"* (Psalm 2:1)	Concerning the wicked: *"...pride serves as their necklace; **violence** covers them like a garment"* (Psalm 73:6)	*"The nations **raged**, the kingdoms were moved; He uttered His voice, the earth melted"* (Psalm 46:6)
"Arise, O Lord, in Your anger; lift Yourself up because of the <u>rage</u> of my enemies; rise up for me to the judgment You have commanded!" (Psalm 7:6)	The wicked: *"His trouble shall return upon his own head, and his **violent** dealing shall come down on his own crown"* (Psalm 7:16)	*"The Lord tests the righteous, but the wicked and the one who loves **violence** His soul hates"* (Psalm 11:5)
"For He will deliver the needy when he cries, the poor also, and him who has no helper. He will spare the poor and needy, and will	*"He [the Lord] delivers me from my enemies. You also lift me up above those who rise against me; You have delivered me from the*	*"If you see the oppression of the poor, and the **violent** perversion of justice and righteousness in a province, do not marvel at the matter;*

save the souls of the needy. He will redeem their life from oppression and *violence*; and precious shall be their blood in His sight" (Psalm 72:12-14)	*violent* man" (Psalm 18:48)	for high official watches over high official, and higher officials are over them" (Ecclesiastes 5:8)
"Deliver me, O Lord, from evil men; Preserve me from *violent* men, who plan evil things in their hearts; they continually gather together for war" (Psalm 140:1-2)	"Keep me, O Lord, from the hands of the wicked; preserve me from *violent* men, who have purposed to make my steps stumble" (Psalm 140:4)	"Do not deliver me to the will of my adversaries; for false witnesses have risen against me, and such as breathe out *violence*" (Psalm 27:12)

Table 60: Some Pearls of Wisdom Concerning the Influence of the Violent Attribute

The influence of the ***violent*** attribute was extremely active among the nation of Israel. As with all the other negative attributes, the Lord sent His prophets to warn them to repent. Remember, when this attribute combines with the oppressor attribute, it can break the spirits of its recipients and strip them of hope. Thus, the Lord used strong language to get the nation's attention. Here are a few of the warnings from the prophets:

The Prophet	What Was Said
Isaiah	"...your iniquities have separated you from your God; and your sins have hidden His face from you, so that He will not hear. For your hands are defiled with blood, and your fingers with iniquity; your lips have spoken lies, your tongue has muttered perversity...their works are works of iniquity, and the act of **violence** is in their hands" (Isaiah 59:2-6)
Jeremiah	"...Cut down trees, and build a mound against Jerusalem. This is the city to be punished. She is full of oppression in her midst. As a fountain wells up with water, so she wells up with her wickedness. **Violence** and plundering are heard in her. Before Me continually are grief and wounds" (Jeremiah 6:6-7)
	"...Execute judgment and righteousness, and deliver the plundered out of the hand of the oppressor. Do no wrong and do no **violence** to the stranger, the fatherless, or the widow, nor shed innocent blood in this place" (Jeremiah 22:3)
Ezekiel	"**Violence** has risen up into a rod of wickedness; none of them shall remain, none of their multitude, none of them; nor shall there be wailing for them. The time has come, the day draws near..." (Ezekiel 7:11-12)
	"Make a chain, for the land is filled with crimes of blood, and the city is full of **violence**" (Ezekiel 7:23)
	"Have you seen this, O son of man? Is it a trivial thing to the house of Judah to commit the abominations which they commit here? For they have filled the land with **violence**; then they have returned to provoke Me to anger. Indeed they put the branch to their nose" (Ezekiel 8:17)
	"...say to the people of the land, 'Thus says the Lord God to the inhabitants of Jerusalem and to the land of Israel: "They shall eat their bread with anxiety,

| | *and drink their water with dread, so that her land may be emptied of all who are in it, because of the **violence** of all those who dwell in it*" (Ezekiel 12:19) |

Table 61: Some of the Prophets' Warnings About the Influence of the Violent Attribute

Before I leave the Old Testament, one can learn something about the influence of the ***violent*** attribute though a false teaching that had permeated the nation of Israel and their legal system. The people had perverted God's "accountability for sin" by punishing entire households. Children and young adults received punishment for the sins of their parents and parents for the sins of their adult children. If the influence of the ***violent*** attribute got involved, the inflicted punishments became even more perverted, brutal, and heinous. Thus, the Lord had the prophet Ezekiel explain the accountability of sin to the nation of Israel through some easy to understand examples. Ezekiel used an example of a person influenced by the just attribute. The just attribute is one of the seven positive attributes and is discussed in Chapter VI of this book. Using the criteria for the just attribute given by God, Ezekiel taught the nation of Israel:

- If a man is just and does what is lawful and right, "*...has not oppressed anyone, but has restored to the debtor his pledge; has robbed no one by **violence**, but has given his bread to the hungry and covered the naked with clothing...*" (Ezekiel 18:7; see Ezekiel 18:5-9 for the whole criteria). This man has the influence of the just attribute according to Ezekiel 18:9.

- If a man had a son who "*...oppressed the poor and needy, robbed by **violence**, not restored the pledge, lifted his eyes to the idols, or committed abomination...*" (Ezekiel 18:12; see Ezekiel 18:10-13 for the whole criteria), this son did not have the influence of the just attribute. The son is accountable for his own sins according to Ezekiel 18:3.

- If however, a man's son sees his father sin, but does not do them. If the son has not "*...oppressed anyone, nor withheld a pledge, nor robbed by **violence**, but has given his bread to the hungry and covered the naked with clothing...*" (Ezekiel 18:16), this son has the influence of the just attribute, but his father does not. The father is accountable for his own sins alone and must not be imposed on the son according to Ezekiel 18:17.

Thus, Ezekiel explained during these examples that, "*As for his father, because he cruelly oppressed, robbed his brother by **violence**, and did what is not good among his people, behold, he shall die for his iniquity*" (Ezekiel 18:18). You see, God is thorough and just. He laid down the standard in His Holy Hord for all mankind to follow. No one, especially ones who allow the influence of the ***violent*** attribute, will have an excuse for his or her behavior when the Day of Judgement comes.

In the New Testament of the Biblical record, Jesus stated, "*And from the days of John the Baptist until now the kingdom of heaven suffers **violence**, and the **violent** take it by force. For all the prophets and the law prophesied until John. And if you are willing to receive it, he is Elijah who is to come. He who has ears to hear, let him hear!*" (Matthew 11:12-14). From Jesus' statement, it is evident that Satan increased his use of the influence of the ***violent*** attribute in spiritual warfare to change the dynamic of war campaign in both the earthly and the spiritual realms. BTT helps one to understand that:

- John the Baptist had been placed in prison prior to Jesus statement (Matthew 11:2)

- Jesus knew John's time one earth was about to come to a ***violent*** end

- Herod the tetrarch (Matthew 14:1) beheaded John in prison and, "*his head was brought on a platter...*" (Matthew 14:11) to the daughter of Herodias, Herod's unlawful wife (Matthew 14:4)

- All the prophets and the law prophesied prior to John's death mark the beginning of a new era under Jesus Christ.

- From the time of John's birth up the time that Jesus began His ministry, the influence of the ***violent*** attribute in spiritual warfare was so powerful that "*the kingdom of heaven suffers **violence***". This metaphorically illustrated the ***violent*** conflict occurring across the spiritual battlefield on God's people.

- People influenced by the ***violent*** attribute take God's people, who metaphorically are the community of "*the kingdom of heaven*", by force - "*...the **violent** take it by force*". This is the spiritual war campaign manifested on earth. God's prophets and His people (then and today), John the Baptist, the apostles, an even Jesus Christ Himself, suffer in God's kingdom from the "***violence*** by force" inflicted by people who allow this attribute. This statement documents the increasing effects of the ***violent*** attribute from spiritual warfare spilling into the earthy realm. This attribute's influence will increase in intensity until Jesus returns. However, His Gospel is the balm that keeps life tolerable for all who obey His Word and one has His confirmation that, "*Heaven and earth will pass away, but My words will by no means pass away*" (Matthew 24:35)

Why was John the Baptist so important to Satan in the context of the war campaign? Because John's life mission was to pave the way for the coming of Jesus Christ and His Gospel into the world according to Matthew 3:1-17; Mark 1:2-11; Luke 3:1-22; and John 1:19-34. Satan's plan was to stop John. This gave the negative forces of the war campaign a perceived victory over the positive forces. The influence of the ***violent*** attribute led Herod to take John's life. However, the negative forces failed because the era of Jesus and His ministry had already begun. The strategies playing out at that moment in time were some of the greatest strategies ever conceived.

Other examples of the ***violent*** attribute influencing people to the point of harming others or even combining with the bloodthirsty attribute to cause murder, included:

Who	What Is Documented
The Jews in the synagogue on the Sabbath in Luke 4:16	The Biblical record documented, "*all those in the synagogue, when they heard these things, were filled with <u>wrath</u>, and rose up and **thrust Him out of the city**; and they led Him to the brow of the hill on which their city was built, that they might **throw Him down over the cliff**"* (Luke 4:28-29)

The scribes and Pharisees	"...they were filled with <u>rage</u>, and discussed with one another what they might do to Jesus" (Luke 6:11)
The captain and the officers of Herod's temple (The first time they put the apostles in prison in Acts 5:18)	The second time they arrested them, the Bible documented, "...the captain went with the officers and brought them without **violence**, for they feared the people, lest they should be stoned" (Acts 5:26)
The Jews that murdered Stephen	"Then they cried out with a loud voice, stopped their ears, and ran at him with one accord; and they **cast him out of the city and stoned him**..." (Acts 7:57-58)
Saul (before his conversion to Christianity)	"...still **breathing threats and murder** against the disciples of the Lord, went to the high priest and asked letters from him to the synagogues of Damascus, so that if he found any who were of the Way, whether men or women, he might **bring them bound** to Jerusalem" (Acts 9:1-2)
Herod	The Bible documented, "...Herod the **king stretched out his hand to harass** some from the church. Then he killed James the brother of John with the sword. And because he saw that it pleased the Jews, he **proceeded further to seize** Peter also..." (Acts 12:1-3)
	The Lord sent an angel and freed Peter. When he escaped, Herod, "searched for him and not found him, he examined the guards **and commanded that they should be put to death**" (Acts 12:19)
Unbelieving Jews in Iconium	When Paul and Barnabas were preaching the Gospel and a great multitude of Jews and Greeks in Iconium believed, the Bible documented, "...the unbelieving Jews stirred up the Gentiles and poisoned their minds against the brethren" (Acts 14:2) and the city became divided. Thus, the Bible documented, "...a **violent** attempt was made by both the Gentiles and Jews, with their rulers, to abuse and stone them..." (Acts 14:5), and Paul and Barnabas were forced to flee the city.
Jews from Asia against Paul	The Bible documented"...seeing him in the temple, **stirred up the whole crowd and laid hands on him**" (Acts 21:27), and...
	"...all the city was disturbed; and the people ran together, **seized** Paul, and **dragged** him out of the temple; and immediately the doors were shut. Now as they were **seeking to kill** him, news came to the commander of the garrison that all Jerusalem was in an uproar" (Acts 21:30-31)
Demetrius	He had the attribute and it used him to stir up workers of his similar occupation against Paul. He told them Paul would stop their profession of making idols of the goddess Diana. The Biblical record documented, "...when they heard this, they were full of <u>wrath and cried out</u>, saying, "Great is Diana of the Ephesians!" (Acts 19:28)
	"When he reached the stairs, he had to be carried by the soldiers because of the **violence** of the mob" (Acts 21:35)
	"...raised their voices and said, "Away with such a fellow from the earth, for he is not fit to live!" Then, as they **cried out and tore off their clothes and threw dust into the air**" (Acts 22:22-23)

The Jews dedicated to killing Paul after his conversion to Christianity	"...some of the Jews banded together and bound themselves under an oath, saying that they would **neither eat nor drink till they had killed** Paul. Now there were more than forty who had formed this conspiracy. They came to the chief priests and elders, and said, "We have bound ourselves under **a great oath that we will eat nothing until we have killed** Paul" (Acts 23:12-14)
The ungodly and unrighteous	The Bible documented, among a long list of unclean things in Romans 1:24-31, that "*...they are whisperers, backbiters, haters of God, **violent**, proud, boasters, inventors of evil things, disobedient to parents, un<u>discerning</u>, untrustworthy, unloving, unforgiving, unmerciful; who, knowing the righteous judgment of God, that those who practice such things are deserving of death, not only do the same but also approve of those who practice them*" (Romans 1:18-19)

Table 62: Other Examples of People Who Allowed the Influence of the Violent Attribute

BTT allows one to see that after Paul's conversion to Christianity, he and the other apostles taught about the influence of the **violent** attribute. They also emphasized the element of <u>wrath</u>. They understood the destructive power of the influence of the **violent** attribute combined with the element of <u>wrath</u> in spiritual warfare. Thus, when Paul quoted the Lord saying "*Beloved, do not avenge yourselves, but rather give place to <u>wrath</u>; for it is written, "Vengeance is Mine, I will repay," says the Lord*" (Romans 12:19), he argued to stop the influence of the **violent** attribute in its tracks and not allow it to mature. Paul understood that **violence** results in vengeance and vengeance belongs to the Lord. To give place to the element of <u>wrath</u> is to enlist whatever positive behaviors that are necessary to deescalate the element and allow it to pass. This is difficult wisdom; many people find it impossible to do. However, the Holy Spirit told Paul it can be done and it is the reason Paul documented this wisdom. More pearls of wisdom from the apostles included:

"And you, fathers, do not provoke your children to <u>wrath</u>, but bring them up in the training and admonition of the Lord" (Ephesians 6:4)	"But now you yourselves are to put off all these: anger, <u>wrath</u>, malice, blasphemy, filthy language out of your mouth" (Colossians 3:8)	"So then, my beloved brethren, let every man be swift to hear, slow to speak, slow to <u>wrath</u>; for the <u>wrath</u> of man does not produce the righteousness of God" (James 1:19-20)
"Now the works of the flesh are evident, which are: adultery, fornication, uncleanness, lewdness, idolatry, sorcery, hatred, contentions, jealousies, outbursts of <u>wrath</u>...those who practice such things will not inherit the kingdom of God" (Galatians 5:19-21)	"Let all bitterness, <u>wrath</u>, anger, clamor, and evil speaking be put away from you, with all malice. And be kind to one another, tenderhearted, forgiving one another, even as God in Christ forgave you." (Ephesians 4:31-32)	"For God did not appoint us to <u>wrath</u>, but to obtain salvation through our Lord Jesus Christ, who died for us, that whether we wake or sleep, we should live together with Him" (1 Thessalonians 5:9-10)
"Be angry, and do not sin": do not let the sun go down	"I desire therefore that the men pray everywhere,	

on your <u>wrath</u>, nor give place to the devil" (Ephesians 4:26-27)	lifting up holy hands, without <u>wrath</u> and doubting…" (1 Timothy 2:8)	

Table 63: More Pearls of Wisdom Concerning the Violent Attribute and the Element of <u>Wrath</u>

BTT allows one to see that the influence of the ***violent*** attribute, not only destroys its host, but also brings harm to anyone associated with the attribute. Hence, Paul documented that one influenced by the ***violent*** attribute must not hold a leadership position in the Lord's church. Based on the qualifications given by inspiration of the Holy Spirit, Paul documented that a bishop, which is an elder in the Lord's church, cannot have the influence of this attribute. He wrote that one serving in an elder's position must be, "*…temperate, sober-minded, of good behavior, hospitable, able to teach, not given to wine, not **violent**…not a novice, lest being puffed up with pride he fall into the same condemnation as the devil…*" (1 Timothy 3:2-7). Paul reiterated this position when he wrote Titus, stating, "*…a <u>bishop</u> must be blameless, as a steward of God, not self-willed, not quick-tempered, not given to wine, not **violent**, not greedy for money…*" (Titus 1:5-7). No congregation that claims Jesus Christ as its Head should ever consider a man to serve as an elder or minister with a history of ***violence*** to serve in a leadership position. The influence of the ***violent*** attribute would lead that man to chaos, split a congregation, and lead many of the members away from the Lord. Moreover, no business or organization should ever entrust their leadership to a person influenced by the ***violent*** attribute. Not only would this be foolish, but it also is a recipe for disaster for the whole organization. The negative forces of the war campaign strive to blind people to these simple but important facts to orchestrate a win on the spiritual battlefield.

The **Bloodthirsty attribute**: The influence of this attribute is the most dangerous of all the attributes. This attribute's influence leads one to ***murder*** another human being or animal, to eagerly hurt others, and to enjoy the sight of violence or ***bloodshed***. This attribute's influence of the inner spirit causes mental instability in one's thoughts, words, and actions. The full measure of the ***bloodthirsty*** attribute influences one to have no shame or remorse for himself or herself over their negative behavior. In fact, one with this attribute will show no empathy or sympathy for the person he or she seeks to harm. Its influence destroys one's discretion and one will ***murder*** with or without cause, for financial gain, or just for sport. When the ***bloodthirsty*** attribute combines with either the ***violent*** or ***hater*** attribute, the one influenced will completely lose control of their inner spirit; they become mentally, emotionally, and physically unbridled. The situation one is physically engaged in blurs as the influence of the ***bloodthirsty*** attribute leaves its host mentally and emotionally undetached. This state leads one to brazenly ***kill*** indiscriminately. The full measure of this attribute's influence will lead one to ***murder*** adults or children, regardless of familiarity; i.e. parents, babies, children, friends, or even acquaintances. Because of this attribute, the farther the bloodline is from a victim, the less concern this person will have for the victim's life. Hence, when one asks a person with the full measure of this attribute why they behaved the way they did? The response is often a blank stare produced from a cognitive gap.

They do not know why they **killed**; they just did, as if the act was a reaction to an unknown stimulus. However, BTT allows one to see the reason behind the behavior. The full measure of the **bloodthirsty** attribute overpowered their inner spirit rendering the carnal side temporary ignorant to their outer behavior and actions. One may appear to be insane or one may claim he or she "blacked out" from all rational thought and reason. However, this lapse caused by one's bad judgement in no way releases him or her from the accountability and consequence of the behavior manifested by the influenced of the **bloodthirsty** attribute. Why? Because the person allowed this attribute's influence in the first place. The means to control this **unclean spirit** is freely identified by God's written Word. Thus, this behavior constitutes sin and God commands punishment for such behavior.

Moreover, there is another point one needs to understand about this heinous attribute. BTT allows one to see that the **murder** of the innocent extends to the unborn child. God, speaking through the prophet Jeremiah, stated "*Before I formed you in the womb I knew you; Before you were born I sanctified you; I ordained you a prophet to the nations*" (Jeremiah 1:5). This statement, supported by many other writers in the Biblical records, indicates that life begins at conception and therefore that life is a living innocent being. Therefore, to destroy or terminate the life of this being constitutes **murder**. Do not be **deceived**. The practice of abortion is simply man's clinical name for **murdering** an innocent being created by God. The **bloodthirsty** attribute's influence is behind everyone who practices this heinous and ungodly act. When this attribute combines with the influence of the **perverse** attributes, even unborn children are not safe.

BTT allows one to see that one's own personal bad choices in life provides the opportunity for the **bloodthirsty** attribute to enter one's inner spirit. Bad choices begin with the choice to ignore God's Word. For this reason, God put the death penalty in place for people who allow the influence of this heinous attribute. The divine penalty for **murdering** one of God's creations is the forfeiture of one's own life. Yes, God sanctioned the death penalty. First, the Biblical record documents the death penalty as a punishment. This punishment is a consequence to extremely bad behavior. Secondly, penalty serves as a safeguard for homes, communities, and even societies. However, God put in place safeguards to govern accidental **killings**. He authorized places of sanctuary until trials were held, penalties for false witnesses, and punishments for irresponsible lawyers and judges. Peace results from following God's Word. Sin develops and spreads by ignoring God's Word. Irresponsible judges, lawyers, and politicians who pervert the legal system as pawns of spiritual warfare, have created opportunities for sin to prevail on the spiritual battlefield. Regardless, the death penalty for this attribute is mandatory and crucial for maintaining peace, order, and civility in a society. Moreover, it keeps the negative forces of the war campaign in check. BTT and <u>discernment</u> helps one to come to this understanding that is contrary to today's political, social, psychological, philosophical, and theological (religious) wisdom. However, one will learn from this book that people in society who intentionally **shed innocent blood** have a spiritual problem.

The Spirit of wisdom revealed to Solomon that there were, "*...six things the Lord hates, yes, seven are an abomination to Him: a proud look, a lying tongue, hands that **shed innocent blood**, a heart that devises wicked plans, feet that are swift in running to evil, a false witness who speaks lies, and one who sows discord among brethren*" (Proverbs 6:16-19).

Shedding innocent blood is an act caused by one influenced by the ***bloodthirsty*** attribute. God hates this behavior. If God ***hates*** this behavior, then the person that allows the ***bloodthirsty*** attribute to influence them to perform this type of behavior is condemned. For this reason, Solomon would document that, "*A man burdened with **bloodshed** will flee into a pit; let no one help him*" (Proverbs 28:17). In other words, when a person allows the influences of the ***bloodthirsty*** attribute to lead their actions, they have determined their own path to walk. No one can or should defend this personal's personal choice. Based on God's law, they must face the consequences of their actions on their own. Legal defense tactics to aid one influenced by this attribute subverts the balance between the positive and negative forces of the war campaign. BTT lets one see that these helpers, whether a judge, lawyer, friend, or family member, will also face God's judgement for their part in spiritual warfare. The one that ***shed innocent blood*** must face a fair and impartial review of their crime. If warranted, execution by the death penalty is mandated.

The Spirit of wisdom also revealed to Solomon that, "*The **bloodthirsty** hate the blameless...*" (Proverbs 29:10). This Scripture illustrates that the influence of the ***bloodthirsty*** attribute can unite with the influence of the hater attribute. This deadly combination places one influenced by the blameless attribute, a positive attribute discussed in Chapter VI of this book, in mortal danger. There is no earthly rationale that explains the actions behind this combined attribute's behavior. But based on the Spirit of wisdom's insight into the combined behavior, one influenced by the blameless attribute can expect no more from one with this combination other than hatred and ***murder***.

The ***bloodthirsty*** attribute will find a way to ***shed innocent blood***. Consider this scenario documented by Solomon in Proverbs 1:10-19 says,

> "*My son, if sinners entice you, do not consent. If they say, "Come with us, let us lie in **wait to shed blood**; let us lurk secretly for the innocent without cause; let us swallow them alive like Sheol, and whole, like those who go down to the Pit; we shall find all kinds of precious possessions, we shall fill our houses with spoil; cast in your lot among us, let us all have one purse"— My son, do not walk in the way with them, keep your foot from their path; for their feet run to evil, and they make haste to **shed blood**. Surely, in vain the net is spread in the sight of any bird; but they lie in wait for their own blood, they lurk secretly for their own lives. So are the ways of everyone who is greedy for gain; it takes away the life of its owners*"

From the above scenario, the behavior of one influenced by the ***bloodthirsty*** attribute is on full display. Regardless of all the other things occurring in this scenario, the mindset of the one influenced by ***bloodthirsty*** attribute is to take the life of someone who is innocent. Personal gain is simply a distractor to the real underlying issue. ***Murder*** is the issue. No matter what the reason, the one influenced by the ***bloodthirsty*** attribute and anyone that participates in the activity, are all guilty of the ***bloodthirsty*** attribute's influence. Moreover, in this scenario, all participants are guilty of ***murder*** and the penalty of death for their actions must take precedent. BTT allows one to see this through Solomon's statement that, "*...they lie in wait* *for their own blood, they lurk secretly for their own lives."* This is God's divine penalty of death revealed against their behavior and bad choices. Judges are to review and exhaust all of God's established divine guidance in their exercise of justice. But when judges do not know God, the negative forces of the campaign advance on the spiritual battlefield.

The first recorded appearance of the **bloodthirsty** attribute in the Old Testament is documented in the behavior of Cain, Adam and Eve's first born (Genesis 4:1-2). The Biblical record documented that Cain allowed the negative attributes to influence him over an offering he prepared for God according to Genesis 4:3-7. The **bloodthirsty** attribute influenced his inner spirit after he allowed all three faces of the angry attribute to mature. The **bloodthirsty** attribute influenced Cain to **murder** Abel. The Biblical record documented, *"Now Cain talked with Abel his brother; and it came to pass, when they were in the field, that Cain rose up against Abel his brother and **killed** him"* (Genesis 4:8). BTT helps one to understand that through Cain, the **bloodthirsty** attribute accomplished its mission within the realm of spiritual warfare to **murder** Abel - an innocent man. BTT and <u>discernment</u> allows one to see that Abel allowed the blameless attribute in his inner spirits and honored God through his offering. Cain did not. One can also know that the **bloodthirsty** attribute continued to seek others it could influence because the Biblical record documented that God intervened to spare Cain's life from other people. The Bible documented that the Lord Himself stated, *"...whoever **kills** Cain, vengeance shall be taken on him sevenfold." And the Lord set a mark on Cain, lest anyone finding him should **kill** him"* (Genesis 4:15). God spared Cain's life. The reason God spared Cain is His alone to know. But clearly, the influence of the **bloodthirsty** attribute was alive and well in the world and its dangerous influence roamed the earth seeking others willing to allow its influence.

The influence of the **bloodthirsty** attribute was documented in the life of Lamech. Lamech proudly boasted to his two wives, *"Adah and Zillah, hear my voice; wives of Lamech, listen to my speech! For I have **killed** a man for wounding me, even a young man for hurting me. If Cain shall be avenged sevenfold, then Lamech seventy-sevenfold"* (Genesis 4:23-24). BTT allows one to see that Lamech allowed the influence of the **bloodthirsty** attribute, combined with the *proud* attribute, in his inner spirit. His words demonstrated contempt for the Almighty God. But God cleared the world of the growing number of people influenced by this attribute when He made the decision to destroy all flesh on earth according to Genesis Chapter 6. The Biblical record documented that, *"...the Lord saw that the **wickedness** of man was great in the earth, and that every intent of the thoughts of his heart was only **evil** continually. And the Lord was sorry that He had made man on the earth, and He was grieved in His heart. So the Lord said, "I will destroy man whom I have created from the face of the earth, both man and beast, creeping thing and birds of the air, for I am sorry that I have made them"* (Genesis 6:5-7). The great flood came and only Noah, his family, and the animals that the Lord brought aboard the ark were saved according to Genesis 6:8-22; through Chapters 7, 8, and 9. The Biblical record documented, *"And all flesh died that moved on the earth: birds and cattle and beasts and every creeping thing that creeps on the earth, and every man. All in whose nostrils was the breath of the spirit of life, all that was on the dry land, died. So He destroyed all living things which were on the face of the ground: both man and cattle, creeping thing and bird of the air. They were destroyed from the earth. Only Noah and those who were* *with him in the ark remained alive. And the waters prevailed on the earth one hundred and fifty days"* (Genesis 7:21-24). BTT allows one to see that God cleansed the earth for a new beginning. However, the positive and negative attributes lived on since they were spirits. The spirits were only available to mankind by his or her personal choice.

After the flood, the Lord gave Noah and his family a critical command concerning the influence of the **bloodthirsty** attribute. The Lord said, *"Every moving thing that lives shall be food for you. I have given you all things, even as the green herbs. But you shall not eat flesh with its life, that is, its blood. Surely for your lifeblood I will demand a reckoning; from the hand of every beast I will require it, and from the hand of man. From the hand of every man's brother I will require the life of man. "Whoever **sheds** man's **blood**, by man his blood shall be shed; for in the image of God He made man"* (Genesis 9:3-6). From God's statement, one sees the death penalty mandated by the word of the Almighty God. God's Word condemns the behavior of anyone allowing the influence of the **bloodthirsty** attribute. This attribute destroys the very image of God on earth manifested through His fleshly creation. Let that soak in a little. This important fact is vital to the balance of the positive and negative forces engaged in spiritual warfare. What God said after the flood is hard for the carnal man's mind to grasp, but the spiritual mind can understand it perfectly. This is why spiritual things must be compared with things that are spiritual. If not, understanding this war campaign is impossible. Paul confirmed this when he documented, *"These things we also speak, not in words which man's wisdom teaches but which the Holy Spirit teaches, comparing spiritual things with spiritual"* (1 Corinthians 2:13).

Carnal man, blessed with the gift of free will, allowed the influence of the **bloodthirsty** attribute back into his life. Consider some of the many examples in the Biblical record that documented people who allowed the influenced of the **bloodthirsty** attribute and what they did under the attribute's influence. I will also point out people temporarily influenced by this attribute too. One will understand these few examples when one sees them. The Biblical record documented:

Who	What Is Documented
The Egyptians	Abram told his wife, *"...when the Egyptians see you, that they will say, 'This is his wife'; and they will **kill** me, but they will let you live"* (Genesis 12:12)
Esau	*"...Esau hated Jacob because of the blessing with which his father blessed him, and Esau said in his heart, "The days of mourning for my father are at hand; then I will **kill** my brother Jacob"* (Genesis 27:41)
Simeon and Levi	After Shechem and his family were circumcised so that Shechem could marry Dinah, the sister of Simeon and Levi, whom he violated earlier (Genesis 34:1-24), the Bible documented, *"Now it came to pass on the third day, when they were in pain, that two of the sons of Jacob, Simeon and Levi, Dinah's brothers, each took his sword and came boldly upon the city and **killed** all the males. And they **killed** Hamor and Shechem his son with the edge of the sword, and took Dinah from Shechem's house, and went out"* (Genesis 34:25-26)
	They agree to, *"Come therefore, let us now **kill** him and cast him into some pit; and we shall say, 'Some wild beast has devoured him'. We shall see*

The brothers of Joseph	*what will become of his dreams!"* (Genesis 37:20). Reuben, the oldest, eventually came to his senses and said, *"Shed no blood, but cast him into this pit which is in the wilderness, and do not lay a hand on him"—that he might deliver him out of their hands, and bring him back to his father"* (Genesis 37:22)
Pharaoh, king of Egypt	He commanded the midwives, *"...When you do the duties of a midwife for the Hebrew women, and see them on the birthstools, if it is a son, then you shall **kill** him; but if it is a daughter, then she shall live"* (Exodus 1:16; 2:15)
Moses (Temporarily)	*"...he saw an Egyptian beating a Hebrew, one of his brethren. So he looked this way and that way, and when he saw no one, he **killed** the Egyptian and hid him in the sand"* (Exodus 2:11-12)
The children of Israel after they reached the Promised Land	*"They did not destroy the peoples, concerning whom the Lord had commanded them, but they mingled with the Gentiles and learned their works; they served their idols, which became a snare to them. They even sacrificed their sons and their daughters to demons, and **shed innocent blood**, the blood of their sons and daughters, whom they **sacrificed** to the idols of Canaan; and the land was polluted with blood"* (Psalms 106:34-38)
King Saul	*"...there was a famine in the days of David for three years, year after year; and David inquired of the Lord. And the Lord answered, "It is because of Saul and his **bloodthirsty** house, because he **killed** the Gibeonites""* (2 Samuel 21:1)
Doeg the Edomite	*"Doeg the Edomite turned and struck the priests, and killed on that day eighty-five men who wore a linen ephod. Also Nob, the city of the priests, he struck with the edge of the sword, both men and women, children and nursing infants, oxen and donkeys and sheep—with the edge of the sword"* (1 Samuel 22:18-19)
Shimei falsely accused David of this attribute	He publicly yelled, *"...Come out! Come out! You **bloodthirsty** man, you rogue! The Lord has brought upon you all the blood of the house of Saul, in whose place you have reigned; and the Lord has delivered the kingdom into the hand of Absalom your son. So now you are caught in your own evil, because you are a **bloodthirsty** man!""* (2 Samuel 16:7-8)
David (Temporarily)	After he had an affair with Bathsheba, Uriah's wife, the prophet Nathan told David from the Lord, *"Why have you despised the commandment of the Lord, to do evil in His sight? You have **killed** Uriah the Hittite with the sword; you have taken his wife to be your wife, and have **killed** him with the sword of the people of Ammon"* (2 Samuel 12:9; See also 2 Samuel 11:15-17)
Absalom, Amnon brother	*"Now Absalom had commanded his servants, saying, "Watch now, when Amnon's heart is merry with wine, and when I say to you, 'Strike Amnon!' then **kill** him. Do not be afraid. Have I not commanded you? Be courageous and valiant"* (2 Samuel 13:28)
Joab the son of Zeruiah	*"he **shed the blood** of war **in peacetime,** and put the blood of war on his belt that was around his waist, and on his sandals that were on his feet"* (1 Kings 2:5)
The woman choosing to **spit** her child	*"Then the woman whose son was living spoke to the king, for she yearned with compassion for her son; and she said, "O my lord, give her the living child, and by no means **kill** him!" But the other said, "Let him be neither mine nor yours, but **divide him."*** (1 Kings 3:26)

King Ahab and his wife Jezebel	Jezebel crafted a letter in Ahab's name to proclaim a feast for Naboth according to 1 Kings 21:8-10. She coordinated a scheme to **murder** Naboth. The Biblical record documented, *"And two men, scoundrels, came in and sat before him; and the scoundrels witnessed against him, against Naboth, in the presence of the people, saying, "Naboth has blasphemed God and the king!" Then they took him outside the city and **stoned him** with stones, **so that he died**"* (1 Kings 21:13-15). Then *"So it was, when Ahab heard that Naboth was dead, that Ahab got up and went down to take possession of the vineyard of Naboth the Jezreelite"* (1 Kings 21:16)
Jozachar and Shimeath, King Joash's servants	*"And his servants arose and formed a conspiracy, and **killed** Joash in the house of the Millo, which goes down to Silla. For Jozachar the son of Shimeath and Jehozabad the son of Shomer, his servants, **struck him**. So he died..."* (2 Kings 12:20-21). King Amaziah *"executed his servants who had **murdered** his father the king"* (2 Kings 14:5)
Manasseh	*"Manasseh shed very much **innocent blood**, till he had filled Jerusalem from one end to another, besides his sin by which he made Judah sin, in doing evil in the sight of the Lord"* (2 Kings 21:16). His punishment was so severe that Lord said, *"Behold, I am bringing such calamity upon Jerusalem and Judah, that whoever hears of it, both his ears will tingle"* (2 Kings 21:12). You see, the Lord revealed that Manasseh's sins and **bloodthirstiness** was great, *"...because of the **innocent blood** that he had shed; for he had filled Jerusalem with **innocent blood**, which the Lord would not pardon"* (2 Kings 21:16)
Haman	He planned to, *"...to **destroy**, to **kill**, and to **annihilate** all the Jews, both young and old, little children and women, in one day, on the thirteenth day of the twelfth month, which is the month of Adar, and to plunder their possessions"* (Esther 3:13)
Shallum the son of Josiah	*"Yet your eyes and your heart are for nothing but your covetousness, **for shedding innocent blood**, and practicing oppression and violence"* (Jeremiah 22:17)
Edom, called Mount Sheir (see Ezekiel verse 35:15; 25:8 for reference)	*"Because you have had an ancient hatred, and have **shed the blood** of the children of Israel by the power of the sword at the time of their calamity, when their iniquity came to an end, therefore, as I live," says the Lord God, "I will prepare you for blood, and blood shall pursue you; since you have not hated blood, therefore blood shall pursue you"* (Ezekiel 35:5-6)
Egypt	*"Egypt shall be a desolation, and Edom a desolate wilderness, because of violence against the people of Judah, for they have **shed innocent blood** in their land"* (Joel 3:19)

Table 64: Some Examples of People Who Allowed the Influence of the Bloodthirsty Attribute

Before one leaves this Table, one should understand that Doeg the Edomite provides the ultimate example of one's behavior when influenced by the full measure of the **bloodthirsty** attribute. For this sadistic attribute influences one to **kill** indiscriminately and without conscience. When the wicked attribute influenced King Saul to order his guards to senselessly **murder** the Lord's priests, the Biblical record documented *"...the servants of the king would not lift their hands to strike the priests of the Lord"* (1 Samuel 22:17). However, when the King turned to Doeg, he did not hesitate to **murder** the priest. In fact, the Biblical record informs one that Doeg not only **murdered** eighty-five men serving as priest (1 Samuel 22:18), he went to their city and **murdered**, "*both men and women, children and nursing infants, oxen and donkeys and sheep—with the edge of the sword*" (1 Samuel 22:19). Even today and throughout history, the **bloodthirsty** attribute has influenced many people to commit atrocities of even greater magnitudes. This includes acts of genocide. As one considers the many examples of people who were influenced by the **bloodthirsty** attribute after the great flood, one must always keep in mind that their behavior was always driven by their own choices. Hence, God gave specific instructions concerning this attribute, the means for defeating it, the means for protecting oneself from it, and even the means for judging its influence in case of an accident. To be direct about the influence of the **bloodthirsty** attribute, God commands, "*You shall not* ***murder***" (Exodus 20:13; Deuteronomy 5:17). Plain and simple.

The Table below documents some of the laws God gave to Moses for governing His people where it pertains to the influence of the **bloodthirsty** attribute. Try to keep in mind that these laws punished the guilty and protected the innocent. This fact has been distorted by leaders in both the religious and secular communities by the influences of the negative attributes of the war campaign. The Biblical record documented:

"*Keep yourself far from a false matter; do not **kill** the innocent and righteous. For I will not justify the wicked*" (Exodus 23:7)	"*Moreover you shall take no ransom for the life of a **murderer** who is guilty of death, but he shall surely be put to death*" (Numbers 35:31)	"*And whoever **kills** an animal shall restore it; but whoever **kills** a man shall be put to death*" (Leviticus 24:21)
"*He who **strikes** a man so that he **dies** shall surely be put to death. However, if he did not lie in wait, but God delivered him into his hand, then I will appoint for you a place where he may flee*" (Exodus 20:12-13)	"*He who **strikes a man so that he dies** shall surely be put to death*" (Exodus 21:12), and "*Whoever **kills** any man shall surely be put to death*" (Leviticus 24:17)	"*…if a man acts with premeditation against his neighbor, to **kill** him by treachery, you shall take him from My altar, that he may die*" (Exodus 21:14)
"*But if he strikes him with an iron implement, so that he dies, he is a **murderer**; the **murderer** shall surely be put to death*" (Numbers 35:16)	"*And if he strikes him with a stone in the hand, by which one could die, and he does die, he is a **murderer**; the **murderer** shall surely be put to death*" (Numbers 35:17)	"*Or if he strikes him with a wooden hand weapon, by which one could die, and he does die, he is a **murderer**; the **murderer** shall surely be put to death*" (Numbers 35:18)
"*The avenger of blood himself shall put the **murderer** to death; when he meets him, he shall put him to death*" (Numbers 35:19)	"*If he pushes him out of hatred or, while lying in wait, hurls something at him so that he dies, or in enmity he strikes him with his hand so that he dies, the one who struck him shall surely be put to death. He is	"*Whoever **kills** a person, the **murderer** shall be put to death on the testimony of witnesses; but one witness is not sufficient testimony against a person for the **death penalty**" (Numbers 35:30)

	a ***murderer***. *The avenger of blood shall put the **murderer** to death when he meets him*" (Numbers 35:20-21)

Table 65: God's Commands Concerning the Influence of the Bloodthirsty Attribute

In the thoroughness of the Lord, He provided for accidental deaths. The Lord commanded the establishment of "Sanctuary cities" and their conditions for use were clear, reasonable, and perfect when executed correctly. These were safe cities for one to stay until a court <u>*discerned*</u> justice for the legal status of the person in question. Consider closely what the Lord provided for governing accidental deaths for someone accused of having the ***bloodthirsty*** attribute. The Bible documented:

A person could flee there that ***killed*** someone unintentionally:	"*...that the **manslayer** might flee there, who **kills** his neighbor unintentionally, without having hated him in time past, and that by fleeing to one of these cities he might live...*" (Deuteronomy 4:42)
A person was safe in the cities of refuge even from the avenger of blood:	"*They shall be cities of refuge for you from the avenger, that the **manslayer** may not die until he stands before the congregation in judgment*" (Numbers 35:12)
	"*...he shall flee to one of these cities and live; lest the avenger of blood, while his anger is hot, pursue the **manslayer** and overtake him, because the way is long, and **kill** him, though he was not deserving of death, since he had not hated the victim in time past*" (Deuteronomy 19:5-6)
The cities of refuges were for everyone:	"*These six cities shall be for refuge for the children of Israel, for the stranger, and for the sojourner among them, that anyone who **kills** a person accidentally may flee there*" (Numbers 35:15)
The congregation could place a person in a refuge city if they belief a death was caused accidentally:	"*...the congregation shall judge between the **manslayer** and the avenger of blood according to these judgments. So the congregation shall deliver the **manslayer** from the hand of the avenger of blood, and the congregation shall return him to the city of refuge where he had fled, and he shall remain there until the death of the high priest who was anointed with the holy oil*" (Numbers 35:24-25)
If a person accused of ***killing*** enters a city of refuge but leaves before the case is settled:	"*But if the **manslayer** at any time goes outside the limits of the city of refuge where he fled, and the avenger of blood finds him outside the limits of his city of refuge, and the avenger of blood **kills** the **manslayer**, he shall not be guilty of blood, because he should have remained in his city of refuge until the death of the high priest. But after the death of the high priest the **manslayer** may return to the land of his possession*" (Numbers 35:26-28)
No ransom is allowed to be taken for a person fleeing to a city of refuge:	"*And you shall take no ransom for him who has fled to his city of refuge, that he may return to dwell in the land before the death of the priest. So you shall not pollute the land where you are; for blood defiles the land, and no atonement can be made for the land,*

	*for the **blood that is shed** on it, except by the **blood** of him who **shed** it"* (Numbers 35:32-33)
A person influenced by the ***bloodthirsty*** attribute that is guilty of killing a person cannot use the city of refuge as a hiding place:	*"But if anyone hates his neighbor, lies in wait for him, rises against him and **strikes him mortally**, so that he dies, and he flees to one of these cities, then the elders of his city shall send and bring him from there, and deliver him over to the hand of the avenger of blood, that he may die. Your eye shall not pity him, but you shall put away the **guilt of innocent blood** from Israel, that it may go well with you"* (Deuteronomy 19:11-13)

Table 66: God's Commands and the use of Sanctuary Cities

God provided even more instructions to deal with situations surrounding one influenced by the ***bloodthirsty*** attribute. God provided a method for justice even when a ***murder*** occurred, and accountability seemed questionable. God, in His wisdom, placed the responsibility on the leaders of His people to give an account. In other words, the elders had to know their people, had to have taught the people the way of God and consequences of false testimony, asked the appropriate questions, and exercise <u>discernment</u>. Here is the account of God's amazing perfection of wisdom and judgement He gave to Moses to teach the people. The Bible documented in Deuteronomy 21:1-9"

> *"If anyone is found **slain**, lying in the field in the land which the Lord your God is giving you to possess, and it is not known who **killed** him, then your elders and your judges shall go out and measure the distance from the **slain** man to the surrounding cities. And it shall be that the elders of the city nearest to the **slain** man will take a heifer which has not been worked and which has not pulled with a yoke. The elders of that city shall bring the heifer down to a valley with flowing water, which is neither plowed nor sown, and they shall break the heifer's neck there in the valley. Then the priests, the sons of Levi, shall come near, for the Lord your God has chosen them to minister to Him and to bless in the name of the Lord; by their word every controversy and every assault shall be settled. And all the elders of that city nearest to the **slain** man shall wash their hands over the heifer whose neck was broken in the valley. Then they shall answer and say, 'Our hands have not shed this blood, nor have our eyes seen it. Provide atonement, O Lord, for Your people Israel, whom You have redeemed, and do not **lay innocent blood** to the charge of Your people Israel.' And atonement shall be provided on their behalf for the blood. So you shall put away the guilt of **innocent blood** from among you when you do what is right in the sight of the Lord."*

Further in the Lord's thoroughness, where the influence of the ***bloodthirsty*** attribute was concerned, animals that ***killed*** humans fell under God's divine law of the death penalty. This may be a little harder for one to make the connection, but BTT allows one to see that punishment for the influence of the ***bloodthirsty*** attribute also applies to animals ***murdering*** humans. Regardless of earthy wisdom, when an animal indiscriminately terminates an innocent life made in the image of God, the death penalty is required. The Biblical record documented:

- *"If an ox **gores** a man or a woman **to death**, then the ox shall surely be stoned, and its flesh shall not be eaten; but the owner of the ox shall be acquitted"* (Exodus 12:28)

- *"But if the ox tended to thrust with its horn in times past, and it has been made known to his owner, and he has not kept it confined, so that it has **killed** a man or a woman, the ox shall be stoned and its owner also shall be put to death"* (Exodus 12:29)

- *"If the ox **gores** a male or female servant, he shall give to their master thirty shekels of silver, and the ox shall be stoned"* (Exodus 12:32)

The key point is the act of **murder** is not to be tolerated from man or animal. The great God of the universe requires an accounting for the senseless death of His creation and punishment is required.

Here is another important point to understand about the influence of this attribute. Leaders influenced by the **bloodthirsty** attribute will lead people into unnecessary conflicts, battles, and wars. This happens because the influence of this attribute unites with the proud attribute and shuts down any positive counsel that may be given. A great example of this occurred with King Amaziah documented in 2 Kings 14:9-14. The influence of this and the proud attribute's involvement in the king's behavior stood out prominently. King Amaziah and his people paid a high price because of the influence of the **bloodthirsty** attribute. Please take the time to read this amazing account of King Amaziah's folly. Now consider what Solomon learned from the Spirit of wisdom.

Job and the Psalmist captured a few more pearls of wisdom about the influence of the **bloodthirsty** attribute in the Biblical record. In these pearls of wisdom, one should make a mental note of the relationship between the **bloodthirsty** and the poor, needy, innocent, and helpless people. For spiritual warfare is seen in each pearl of wisdom. These two wise men wrote:

- *"The **murderer** rises with the light; he **kills** the poor and needy; and in the night he is like a thief"* (Job 24:14)

- *"... The Lord abhors the **bloodthirsty** and deceitful man"* (Psalms 5:6)

- For one with the wicked and **bloodthirsty** attributes: *"The wicked in his proud countenance does not seek God; God is in none of his thoughts. His ways are always prospering; Your judgments are far above, out of his sight; as for all his enemies, he sneers at them. He has said in his heart, "I shall not be moved; I shall never be in adversity." His mouth is full of cursing and deceit and oppression; under his tongue is trouble and iniquity. He sits in the lurking places of the villages; in the secret places he **murders** the innocent; his eyes are secretly fixed on the helpless. He lies in wait secretly, as a lion in his den; He lies in wait to catch the poor; he catches the poor when he draws him into his net. So he crouches, he lies low, that the helpless may fall by his strength. He has said in his heart, "God has forgotten; He hides His face; He will never see"* (Psalms 10:4-11). And *"They slay the widow and the stranger, and **murder** the fatherless"* (Psalms 94:6)

As with all the negative attributes, the Lord sent his prophets to warn the nation of Israel about the impact, devastation and corruption caused by the influence of **bloodthirsty** attribute. Consider the next Table and the warnings from the prophets. The Biblical record documented:

The Prophet	What Was Said
Isaiah	For *people with the wicked and bloodthirsty attributes*: *"Their feet run to evil, and they make haste to* **shed innocent blood**; *their thoughts are thoughts of iniquity; wasting and destruction are in their paths"* (Isaiah 59:7)
Jeremiah	*"if you thoroughly amend your ways and your doings, if you thoroughly execute judgment between a man and his neighbor, if you do not oppress the stranger, the fatherless, and the widow, and do not* **shed innocent blood** *in this place, or walk after other gods to your hurt, then I will cause you to dwell in this place, in the land that I gave to your fathers forever and ever"* (Jeremiah 7:5-7)
	"Will you steal, **murder**, *commit adultery, swear falsely, burn incense to Baal, and walk after other gods whom you do not know..."* (Jeremiah 7:9)
	"Execute judgment and righteousness, and deliver the plundered out of the hand of the oppressor. Do no wrong and do no violence to the stranger, the fatherless, or the widow, nor **shed innocent blood** *in this place"* (Jeremiah 22:3)
	"Because of the sins of her prophets and the iniquities of her priests, who **shed** *in her midst the* **blood** *of the just"* (Lamentations 4:13)
Ezekiel	*"I will judge you as women who break wedlock or* **shed blood** *are judged; I will bring blood upon you in fury and jealousy"* (Ezekiel 16:38)
	"You have become guilty by the **blood** *which you have* **shed**, *and have defiled yourself with the idols which you have made. You have caused your days to draw near, and have come to the end of your years; therefore I have made you a reproach to the nations, and a mockery to all countries"* (Ezekiel 22:4)
	"Look, the princes of Israel: each one has used his power to **shed blood** *in you"* (Ezekiel 22:6)
	"In you they take bribes to **shed blood**; *you take usury and increase; you have made profit from your neighbors by extortion, and have forgotten Me," says the Lord God"* (Ezekiel 22:12)
	"Her princes in her midst are like wolves tearing the prey, to **shed blood**, *to destroy people, and to get dishonest gain"* (Ezekiel 22:27)
	"Therefore say to them, 'Thus says the Lord God: "You eat meat with blood, you lift up your eyes toward your idols, and **shed blood**. *Should you then possess the land? You rely on your sword, you commit abominations, and you defile one another's wives. Should you then possess the land?"* (Ezekiel 33:25-27)

Table 67: Some of the Prophet's Warnings about the Influence of the Bloodthirsty Attribute

In the New Testament of the Biblical record, Jesus immediately began teaching about the influence of the ***bloodthirsty*** attribute. The Jewish leadership failed to correctly teach on this attribute, so Jesus clarified the Lord's Word about it. Jesus stated, *"You have heard that it was said to those of old, 'You shall not **murder**, and whoever **murders** will be in danger of the judgment.' But I say to you that whoever is angry with his brother without a cause shall be in danger of the judgment..."* (Matthew 5:21-22). You see, the Jewish leadership taught that murder and being angry with one's brother without a cause, were different crimes with different punishments. However, Jesus said "no!" Why? Because both sins have an **unclean spirit** behind the behavior that is driving the sin. Sin is sin in the eyes of God. Only man gives weights for one sin over another. This allows him to justify his actions. But with God, this will not stand. BTT allows one to see that one who allows the ***bloodthirsty*** attribute and one who allows the angry attribute with his brother without a cause are both equally in danger of the judgment. Jesus knew that if the angry attribute influenced one to be angry against his brother without a cause, the influence of the ***bloodthirsty*** attribute would be nearby. In spiritual warfare, these two attributes would lead one to ***murder***. Consider Cain and Abel's situation for proof. In spiritual warfare, there is no difference in the sin that is created by the behaviors of these attributes. Therefore, both are serious because they both bring harm to others in the war campaign. Therefore, one cannot allow the influence of the ***bloodthirsty*** attribute to go unpunished.

In the case above; being angry with one's brother without a cause, involves evil thoughts. Why else would one be angry with his or her sibling without a cause? This condition can only exist when there are evil thoughts on one side that were never vetted or discussed. Hence, Jesus taught, *"...out of the heart proceed evil thoughts, **murders**, adulteries, fornications, thefts, false witness, blasphemies"* (Matthew 15:19; Mark 7:21). In Matthew 5:21-22, what starts out as anger in the inner spirit, if not purged by God's Word, is followed up by the furious, violent, and eventually the ***bloodthirsty*** attributes. But there is another negative attribute identified too. When Jesus said, *"...out of the heart proceed evil thoughts..."*, He clarified that the influence of the evil attribute was already involved prior to the other items in the text. Thus, Jesus provided clear insight into spiritual warfare and its effects on the inner spirit when God's Word is not present. The end result is destruction, pain and suffering. Some more examples Jesus used to teach His followers about the influence of the ***bloodthirsty*** attribute included:

- A rich young ruler seeking advice on eternal life, *"...You shall not **murder**,' 'You shall not commit adultery,' 'You shall not steal,' 'You shall not bear false witness..."* (Matthew 19:18; Mark 10:19). Notice that the physical manifestation of the ***bloodthirsty*** attribute was first on Jesus' list.

- A parable about *some wicked vinedressers* with the attribute. He stated, *"But when the vinedressers saw the son, they said among themselves, 'This is the heir. Come, let us **kill** him and seize his inheritance.' So they took him and cast him out of the vineyard and **killed** him"* (Matthew 21:38-39; Mark 12:5-8; Luke 20:14-15). The behavior of the vinedressers was a direct manifestation of the influence of the ***bloodthirsty*** attribute and greed in the lives of these people. This spirit's influence convinced them to plot the death of the heir of the vineyard.

- A parable about invited guest to a wedding feast who had the attribute. He stated that when the guests were invited, "...*they made light of it and went their ways, one to his own farm, another to his business. And the rest seized his servants, treated them spitefully, and **killed** them. But when the king heard about it, he was furious. And he sent out his armies, destroyed those **murderers**, and burned up their city. Then he said to his servants, 'The wedding is ready, but those who were invited were not worthy* (Matthew 22:5-8)

The Biblical record indicated that people influenced by the **bloodthirsty** attribute were seeking to harm Jesus and prevent anyone from carrying His message to the world. BTT helps one to see that this was part of Satan's grand strategy. He used, and is still using, the negative forces through spiritual warfare to stop the Gospel of Christ from reaching people who desire God's Truth. Within the war campaign, the negative forces covet people influenced by the **bloodthirsty** attribute. Beginning with the Jews who were initially given the oracles of God, the Biblical record documented others who had and have the influence of this attribute:

Who	**What Is Documented**
The Chief priests, scribes, elders of the people and Caiaphas	They "...*plotted to take Jesus by trickery and **kill** Him*" (Matthew 26:3-4; Mark 14:1)
	"...*the chief priests **plotted** to put Lazarus to **death** also, because on account of him many of the Jews went away and believed in Jesus*" (John 12:10-11)
	Peter and the other apostles stated, "*We ought to obey God rather than men. The God of our fathers raised up Jesus whom you **murdered** by hanging on a tree*" (Acts 5:29-30)
	Stephen said to them, "*Which of the prophets did your fathers not persecute? And they **killed** those who foretold the coming of the Just One, of whom you now have become the betrayers and **murderers**...*" (Acts 7:52)
Pharisees and scribes	Jesus said, "...*you are witnesses against yourselves that you are sons of those who **murdered** the prophets*" (Matthew 23:31)
	"*Therefore, indeed, I send you prophets, wise men, and scribes: some of them you will **kill and crucify**, and some of them you will scourge in your synagogues and persecute from city to city, that on you may come all the **righteous blood shed** on the earth, from the blood of righteous Abel to the blood of Zechariah, son of Berechiah, whom you **murdered** between the temple and the altar*" (Matthew 23:34-35; Luke 11:46-51)
	"*You are of your father the devil, and the desires of your father you want to do. He was a **murderer** from the beginning, and does not stand in the truth, because there is no truth in him. When he speaks a lie, he speaks from his own resources, for he is a liar and the father of it*" (John 8:44)
	"...*the Jews sought all the more to **kill** Him, because He not only broke the Sabbath, but also said that God was His Father, making Himself equal with God*" (John 5:18)
	"*Did not Moses give you the law, yet none of you keeps the law? Why do you seek to **kill** Me?*" (John 7:19)

The Jews against Jesus:	"*Men of Israel, hear these words: Jesus of Nazareth, a Man attested by God to you by miracles, wonders, and signs which God did through Him in your midst, as you yourselves also know— Him, being delivered by the determined purpose and foreknowledge of God, you have taken by lawless hands, have **crucified**, and **put to death**; whom God raised up, having loosed the pains of death, because it was not possible that He should be held by it*" (Acts 2:22-24)
	"*Therefore let all the house of Israel know assuredly that God has made this Jesus, whom you **crucified**, both Lord and Christ*" (Acts 2:26)
	"*The God of Abraham, Isaac, and Jacob, the God of our fathers, glorified His Servant Jesus, whom you delivered up and denied in the presence of Pilate, when he was determined to let Him go. But you denied the Holy One and the Just, and asked for a **murderer** to be granted to you, and **killed** the Prince of life, whom God raised from the dead, of which we are witnesses*" (Acts 3:14)
Barabbas	Jewish leadership and they persuaded the Roman government to release, "*to them the one they requested, who for rebellion and **murder** had been thrown into prison; but he delivered Jesus to their will*" (Luke 23:25; Mark 15:7; Luke 23:19)
Pontius Pilate	He made the final decision to **shed the innocent blood** of Jesus. After Pilate examined Jesus he said, "*You have brought this Man to me, as one who misleads the people. And indeed, having examined Him in your presence, I have found no fault in this Man concerning those things of which you accuse Him…*" (Luke 23:14; John 18:38)
	"*So Pilate, wanting to gratify the crowd, released Barabbas to them; and he **delivered** Jesus, after he had scourged Him, **to be crucified**" (Mark 15:15)
Herod the king	"*…stretched out his hand to harass some from the church. Then he **killed** James the brother of John with the sword. And because he saw that it pleased the Jews, he proceeded further to seize Peter also…*" (Acts 12:1-3)
The Jews that murdered Stephen	"*Then they cried out with a loud voice, stopped their ears, and ran at him with one accord; and they cast him out of the city and **stoned** him…*" (Acts 7:57-58)
Saul (before his conversion to Christianity)	"*…still breathing threats and **murder** against the disciples of the Lord, went to the high priest and asked letters from him to the synagogues of Damascus, so that if he found any who were of the Way, whether men or women, he might bring them bound to Jerusalem*" (Acts 9:1-2)
	"*…when the **blood** of Your martyr Stephen was **shed**, I also was standing by **consenting to his death**, and guarding the clothes of those who were **killing** him*" (Acts 22:20)
	"*Indeed, I myself thought I must do many things contrary to the name of Jesus of Nazareth. This I also did in Jerusalem, and many of the saints I shut up in prison, having received authority from the chief priests; and **when they were put to death, I cast my vote against them**. And I punished them often in every synagogue and compelled them to blaspheme; and being exceedingly enraged against them, I persecuted them even to foreign cities*" (Acts 26:9-11)
	"*…Saul increased all the more in strength, and confounded the Jews who dwelt in Damascus, proving that this Jesus is the Christ. Now after many*

The Jews dedicated to killing Paul	*days were past, the Jews **plotted to kill** him. But their plot became known to Saul. And they watched the gates day and night, **to kill** him"* (Acts 9:22-24)
	*"And he spoke boldly in the name of the Lord Jesus and disputed against the Hellenists, but they attempted **to kill** him"* (Acts 9:29)
	*"...some of the Jews banded together and bound themselves under an oath, saying that they would neither eat nor drink till they had killed Paul. Now there were more than forty who had formed this conspiracy. They came to the chief priests and elders, and said, "We have bound ourselves under a great oath that we will eat nothing until we have **killed** Paul"* (Acts 23:12-14)
	Paul would later quote from Proverbs 1:16 about them: *"Their feet are swift to **shed blood**..."* (Romans 3:15)
The ungodly and unrighteous	*"...God gave them over to a debased mind, to do those things which are not fitting; being filled with all unrighteousness... **murder**, ...who, knowing the righteous judgment of God, that those who practice such things are deserving of death, not only do the same but also approve of those who practice them"* (Romans 1:28-32)

Table 68: More Examples of the Bloodthirsty Attribute's Influence on People's Behavior

Despite Jesus hardships, He still successfully taught the Gospel to His disciples against the backdrop of abuse from the Jews. The Jewish leadership allowed the influence of the **bloodthirsty** attribute to affect their behavior and thoughts. However, Jesus' apostles successfully took His Truth (the Gospel) out to the world. Paul documented this when he wrote about the Gospel, *"...which was preached to every creature under heaven"* (Colossians 1:23). Some final pearls of wisdom that the apostles documented about the **bloodthirsty** attribute included:

- *"For the commandments, "You shall not commit adultery," "You shall not **murder**," "You shall not steal," "You shall not bear false witness," "You shall not covet," and if there is any other commandment, are all summed up in this saying, namely, "You shall love your neighbor as yourself"* (Romans 13:9)

- *"Now the works of the flesh are evident, which are: adultery, fornication, uncleanness, lewdness, idolatry, sorcery, hatred, contentions, jealousies, outbursts of wrath, selfish ambitions, dissensions, heresies, envy, **murders**, drunkenness, revelries, and the like; of which I tell you beforehand, just as I also told you in time past, that those who practice such things will not inherit the kingdom of God"* (Galatians 5:19-21)

- *"...the law is not made for a righteous person, but for the lawless and insubordinate, for the ungodly and for sinners, for the unholy and profane, for **murderers** of fathers and **murderers** of mothers, for **manslayers**, for fornicators, for sodomites, for kidnappers, for liars, for perjurers, and if there is any other thing that is contrary to sound doctrine, according to the glorious gospel of the blessed God..."* (1 Timothy 1:9-11)

- Speaking of God: *"For He who said, "Do not commit adultery," also said, "Do not **murder**." Now if you do not commit adultery, but you do **murder**, you have become a transgressor of the law"* (James 2:11)

- *"You lust and do not have. You **murder** and **covet** and cannot obtain. You fight and war. Yet you do not have because you do not ask"* (James 4:2)

- To people in the rich category with **bloodthirsty** attribute – *"You have condemned, you have **murdered** the just; he does not resist you"* (James 5:6)

- *"But let none of you suffer as a **murderer**, a thief, an evildoer, or as a busybody in other people's matters"* (1 Peter 4:15)

- *"Cain who was of the wicked one and **murdered** his brother. And why did he **murder** him? Because his works were evil and his brother's righteous"* (1 John 3:12)

- *"Whoever hates his brother is a **murderer**, and you know that no **murderer** has eternal life abiding in him"* (1 John 3:15)

- *"But let none of you suffer as a **murderer**, a thief, an evildoer, or as a busybody in other people's matters. Yet if anyone suffers as a Christian, let him not be ashamed, but let him glorify God in this matter"* (1 Peter 4:15-16)

- *"But the cowardly, unbelieving, abominable, **murderers**, sexually immoral, sorcerers, idolaters, and all liars shall have their part in the lake which burns with fire and brimstone, which is the second death"* (Revelation 21:8)

- *"...outside are dogs and sorcerers and sexually immoral and **murderers** and idolaters, and whoever loves and practices a lie"* (Revelation 22:15)

Based on all the evidence above, BTT allows one to see that the influence of the **bloodthirsty** attribute is the most physically dangerous attribute that one can allow to influence his or her inner spirit. The long-term psychological and emotional damage that this attribute inflicts on the home, community, and society is immeasurable. Moreover, the physical manifestations of **murder** can lead to retaliatory responses that exponentially increase the size of the negative forces in the war campaign. This attribute's deception can lead whole communities into strife and chaos because of revenge. However, the ones that suffer the most are children and the innocent.

BTT also allows one to see that the Lord provided the method for dealing with one who allows the influence of this heinous attribute. The method begins with parents taking the responsibility for teaching their children based on the Lord's standard, the way of God, obedience to His Word, and knowledge of right from wrong. As they grow up, this education provides children the foundation they need to understand spiritual warfare as described in the Bible. Parents are the first line of defense for teaching children <u>discernment</u>. When children are not taught to <u>discern</u> right and wrong, they have no fighting chance to defend themselves against the negative forces of the war campaign. BTT allows one to see that as children grow and reach an age of accountability, the multitude of choices presented by the negative forces can gain the upper hand influencing them toward the negative path of life. God's Word, tough love, and discipline are then required to correct their poor choices. The alternative, ignoring the behavior created by poor choices, only invites spiritual chaos and conflict. It is this spiritual chaos and conflict that eventually invites the influence of the ***bloodthirsty*** attribute. This is where God's Word and Satan's use of spiritual warfare conflict for most of humanity.

If a child refused the teachings of his parent, reaches an age of accountability, and <u>willfully</u> takes the life of another of God's creation, then he or she has allowed the influence of the ***bloodthirsty*** attribute to dominate their inner spirit. The penalty for this person's behavior is the forfeiture of his or her own life. Plain and simple - this person must face the death penalty. This wisdom defies worldly wisdom, but this is because of spiritual warfare and the fog generated by the negative forces in the war campaign. The death penalty is God's divine method for purging the sin caused by the ***bloodthirsty*** attribute out of a family, community, and a society. God's way ensures peace and civility in the world. When a perverted justice system through favoritism, prejudice, and money allows people influenced by this attribute to go free, people influenced by the positive attributes should be concerned. In the war campaign as humanity moves further from God's wisdom for dealing with this attribute, it will live with the increasing pain and suffering created by the senseless, indiscriminate, and abusive behavior of the attribute's influence. BTT allows one to see that this attribute's influence ensures the negative forces maintain numerically superior forces in the campaign by eliminating the positive forces at every opportunity. Only by learning God's Word, and understanding the war campaign, can one have hope to survive this war as it manifests itself on earth through the influence of human behavior.

Finally, consider this sobering thought. The influence of the ***bloodthirsty*** attribute is always seeking new hosts worldwide. Moreover, no matter how many prisons are built, one influenced by the ***bloodthirsty*** attribute can return to society. Please do not be deceived. The ancient wisdom of the negative attributes will create ways to gather their forces together through actions like time served, pardons, bribes, escapes, and legal technicalities. In other words, permanent incarceration is never guaranteed. Even Barabbas, a ***murder*** (Mark 15:7), was released from prison in exchange for the life of an innocent man – Jesus Christ – according to Matthew 27:26 and Mark 15:15. Once one influenced by the ***bloodthirsty*** attribute returns to society, strife will resumes unless God's Word is used to defeat this ***unclean spirit***.

CHAPTER VI: The Positive Attributes

"All the nations will be gathered before Him, and He will separate them one from another, as a shepherd divides his sheep from the goats. And He will set the sheep on His right hand, but the goats on the left."

~ Matthew 25:32-34

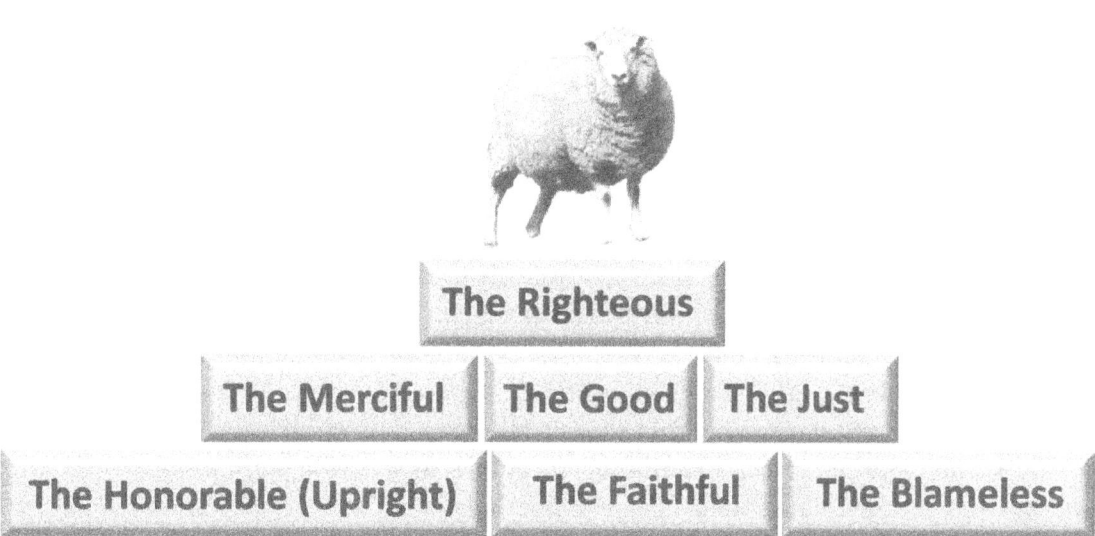

INTRODUCTION

The positive attributes are the strongest divine creation ever to exist in the universe and specifically on earth. These attributes, when applied properly have the ability to defeat all of the negative attributes in spiritual warfare and alter the course of the war campaign in a positive direction. Do not get hung up on their small numbers. Remember that God is in control. Each positive attribute can stand on its own. However, only the influence of the *righteous* attribute can get one to heaven. Why? Because the *righteous* attribute comprises all the other positive attributes knitted together by the element of <u>love</u>. **Figure 23** illustrates this thought and this book's documentation will clarify the full ramification of the *righteous* attribute. For now, one simply needs to understand that when these attributes influence one's inner spirit, he or she can become a formidable warrior on the spiritual battlefield. Within these people rest the fruit of the Spirit which is, "*...love, joy, peace, longsuffering, kindness, goodness, faithfulness, gentleness, self-control. <u>Against such there is no law</u>. And those who are Christ's have crucified the flesh with its passions and desires*" (Galatians 5: 23-24). These are the people who live in the Spirit and also walk in the Spirit of God.

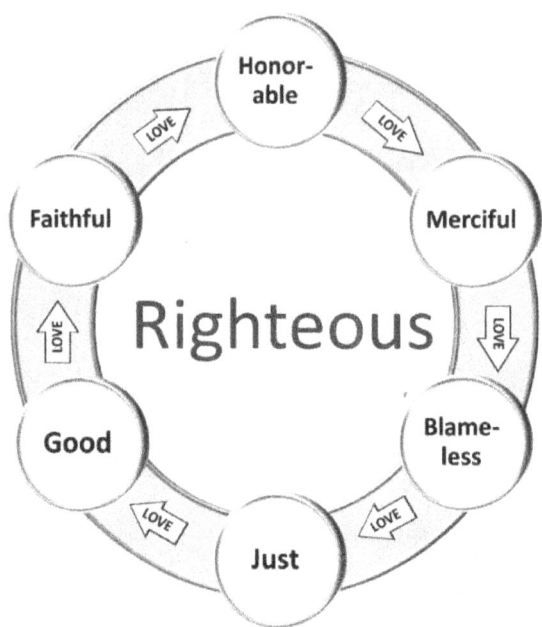

Figure 23: The Positive Forces

One will learn how the supernatural element of <u>love</u> binds all the positive attributes together to produce an amazing child of God. This is the <u>love</u> documented by Paul when he wrote concerning all the Old Testament commandments, "*... and if there is any other commandment, are all summed up in this saying, namely, "You shall <u>love</u> your neighbor as yourself." <u>Love</u> does no harm to a neighbor; therefore <u>love</u> is the fulfillment of the law*" (Romans 13:9-10). Further, Paul stated, "<u>Love</u> *suffers long and is kind;* <u>love</u> *does not envy;* <u>love</u> *does not parade itself, is not puffed up; does not behave rudely, does not seek its own, is not provoked, thinks no evil; does not rejoice in iniquity, but rejoices in the truth; bears all things, believes all things, hopes all things, endures all things.* <u>Love</u> *never fails...*" (1 Corinthians 13:4-8). BTT allows one to see that one must cleanse oneself of the negative attributes to stand firmly among the positive forces of the war campaign. Paul told this to the church in Corinth when he wrote, "*...let us cleanse ourselves from all filthiness of the flesh and spirit, perfecting holiness in the fear of God*" (2 Corinthians 7:1). One cannot perfect holiness without the element of <u>love</u>. In fact, one's unclean state (one in which a person refuses to submit to God and repent of sin) will not allow God's love to penetrate his or her inner spirit because the two oppose each other. But for one who is willing to give up his or her unclean state (repent and submit to God) and accept the love of Christ, John documented, "*And we have known and believed the <u>love</u> that*

God has for us. God is <u>love</u>, and he who abides in <u>love</u> abides in God, and God in him" (1 John 4:16).

For Christians maturing in the knowledge of God, the Holy Spirit inspired Peter to document, "*...giving all diligence, add to your faith virtue, to virtue knowledge, to knowledge self-control, to self-control perseverance, to perseverance godliness, to godliness brotherly kindness, and to brotherly kindness love. For if these things are yours and abound, you will be neither barren nor unfruitful in the knowledge of our Lord Jesus Christ. For he who lacks these things is shortsighted, even to blindness, and has forgotten that he was cleansed from his old sins. Therefore, brethren, be even more diligent to make your call and election sure, for if you do these things you will never stumble; for so an entrance will be supplied to you abundantly into the everlasting kingdom of our Lord and Savior Jesus Christ*" (2 Peter 1:5-11). Peter's words confirmed the existence of good in the world and one cannot allow the negative attributes to rob one of this fact. Unfortunately, many people struggle with <u>discernment</u> today which makes the knowledge of the positive attributes harder to see in a world of wickedness and perversion. Be that as it may, the individual positive attributes originated from the divine nature of God Himself. God is the author of the positive forces and it stands to reason that these forces are part of His Spirit. He will make the positive attributes available to anyone who submits to Him and is obedient to His Holy Word so that one can stand strong against the negative forces in spiritual warfare. Meditate on this while considering God and the identification of the positive attributes in the Scriptures below. The Biblical record documented:

"*Trust in the Lord, and do **good**; dwell in the land, and feed on His **faithfulness**"* (Psalm 37:3)	"*Your **mercy**, O Lord, is in the heavens; Your **faithfulness** reaches to the clouds*" (Psalm 36:5)	"*Your **faithfulness** endures to all generations; You established the earth, and it abides*" (Psalm 119:90)
"*Hear my prayer, O Lord, Give ear to my supplications! In Your **faithfulness** answer me, and in Your **righteousness**"* (Psalm 143:1)	"*I have not hidden Your **righteousness** within my heart; I have declared Your **faithfulness** and Your salvation...*" (Psalm 40:10)	"*I know, O Lord, that Your judgments are right, and that in **faithfulness** You have afflicted me*" (Psalm 119:75)
"*With the **merciful** You will show Yourself **merciful**; with a **blameless** man You will show Yourself **blameless**...*" (2 Samuel 22:26-28; Psalm 18:23-27)	"*He has remembered His **mercy** and His **faithfulness** to the house of Israel; all the ends of the earth have seen the salvation of our God*" (Psalm 98:3)	"*...I will praise You— And Your **faithfulness**, O my God! To You I will sing with the harp, O Holy One of Israel*" (Psalm 71:22)
"*All Your commandments are **faithful**; they persecute me wrongfully; Help me!*" (Psalm 119:86)	"*O Lord God of hosts, Who is mighty like You, O Lord? Your **faithfulness** also surrounds You*" (Psalm 89:8)	"*Your testimonies, which You have commanded, are **righteous** and very **faithful**"* (Psalm 119:138)

"It is good to give thanks to the Lord, and to sing praises to Your name, O Most High; to declare Your lovingkindness in the morning, and Your **faithfulness** every night..." (Psalm 92:1-2)	Further he said, since we now have Christ serving as the High Priest over the house of God, "*Let us hold fast the confession of our hope without wavering, for He who promised is **faithful***" (Hebrews 10:23)	Jesus Christ as, "*...the **faithful** witness, the firstborn from the dead, and the ruler over the kings of the earth. To Him who loved us and washed us from our sins in His own blood...*" (Revelation 1:5)
"Therefore know that the Lord your God, He is God, the **faithful** God who keeps covenant and **mercy** for a thousand generations with those who love Him and keep His commandments..." (Deuteronomy 7:9-10)	John wrote, "*...If we confess our sins, He is **faithful** and just to forgive us our sins and to cleanse us from all unrighteousness. If we say that we have not sinned, we make Him a liar, and His word is not in us*" (1 John 1:5-10)	Paul, speaking of Jesus wrote, "*Therefore, in all things He had to be made like His brethren, that He might be a **merciful** and **faithful** High Priest in things pertaining to God, to make propitiation for the sins of the people*" (Hebrews 2:17)
"Have mercy upon me, O God, according to Your lovingkindness; according to the multitude of Your tender **mercies**...I acknowledge my transgressions, and my sin is always before me. Against You, You only, have I sinned, and done this evil in Your sight— that You may be found **just** when You speak, and **blameless** when You judge" (Psalm 51:1-4)	"*Therefore let him who thinks he stands take heed lest he fall. No temptation has overtaken you except such as is common to man; but God is **faithful**, who will not allow you to be tempted beyond what you are able, but with the temptation will also make the way of escape, that you may be able to bear it*" (1 Corinthians 10:13)	"But as God is **faithful**, our word to you was not Yes and No. For the Son of God, Jesus Christ, who was preached among you by us—by me, Silvanus, and Timothy—was not Yes and No, but in Him was Yes. For all the promises of God in Him are Yes, and in Him Amen, to the glory of God through us" (2 Corinthians 1:18-20)
"...These things says the Amen, the **Faithful** and True Witness, the Beginning of the creation of God..." (Revelation 3:14-15)	"*...the Lord is **faithful**, who will establish you and guard you from the **evil** one*" (2 Thessalonians 3:3)	"God is **faithful**, by whom you were called into the fellowship of His Son, Jesus Christ our Lord" (1 Corinthians 1:9)
"Through the Lord's **mercies** we are not consumed, because His compassions fail not. They are new every morning; Great is Your **faithfulness**" (Lamentations 3:22-23)	"Ephraim has encircled Me with lies, and the house of Israel with deceit; but Judah still walks with God, even with the Holy One who is **faithful**" (Hosea 11:12)	"O Lord, You are my God. I will exalt You, I will praise Your name, for You have done wonderful things; Your counsels of old are **faithfulness** and truth" (Isaiah 25:1)
"And the heavens will praise Your wonders, O Lord; Your **faithfulness** also in the assembly of the saints" (Psalm 89:5)	"... let those who suffer according to the will of God commit their souls to Him in doing good, as to a **faithful** Creator" (1 Peter 4:19)	"He shall judge the world in **righteousness**, and He shall administer judgment for the peoples in **uprightness**" (Psalm 9:8)

And further he wrote of Christ, "Therefore, holy brethren, partakers of the heavenly calling, consider the Apostle and High Priest of our confession, Christ Jesus, who was **faithful** to Him who appointed Him, as Moses also was **faithful** in all His house" (Hebrews 3:1-2)	"We give thanks to You, O God, we give thanks! For Your wondrous works declare that Your name is near. "When I choose the proper time, I will judge **uprightly**. The earth and all its inhabitants are dissolved; I set up its pillars firmly" (Psalm 75:1-3)	"I will sing of the **mercies** of the Lord forever; with my mouth will I make known Your **faithfulness** to all generations. For I have said, "**Mercy** shall be built up forever; Your **faithfulness** You shall establish in the very heavens" (Psalm 89:1-2)
"**Righteous** are You, O Lord, and **upright** are Your judgments" (Psalm 119:137)	"**Good** and **upright** is the Lord; therefore He teaches sinners in the way" (Psalm 25:8)	"His work is **honorable** and glorious, and His **righteousness** endures forever" (Psalm 111:3)
"He will judge your people with **righteousness**, and your poor with **justice**" (Psalm 72:2)	"The works of His hands are verity and **justice**; all His precepts are sure" (Psalm 111:7)	"God is a **just** judge, and God is angry with the wicked every day" (Psalm 7:11)
"The works of His hands are verity and **justice**; all His precepts are sure. They stand fast forever and ever, and are done in truth and **uprightness**" (Psalm 111:7-8)	"He loves **righteousness** and **justice**; the earth is full of the **goodness** of the Lord" (Psalm 33:5)	"He is the Rock, His work is perfect; for all His ways are **justice**, a God of truth and without injustice; **righteous** and **upright** is He" (Deuteronomy 32:4)
"Your **righteousness** is like the great mountains; Your judgments are a great deep; O Lord, You preserve man and beast" (Psalm 36:6)	"...You are God, ready to pardon, gracious and **merciful**, slow to anger, abundant in <u>kindness</u>, and did not forsake them" (Nehemiah 9:17)	"Now I saw heaven opened, and behold, a white horse. And He who sat on him was called **Faithful** and True, and in **righteousness** He judges and makes war" (Revelation 19:11)
"For the Lord loves **justice**, and does not forsake His saints; they are preserved forever, but the descendants of the wicked shall be cut off" (Psalm 37:28)	"...To declare that the Lord is **upright**; He is my rock, and there is no unrighteousness in Him" (Psalm 92:15)	"He will bring **justice** to the poor of the people; He will save the children of the needy, and will break in pieces the oppressor" (Psalm 72:4)
"**Righteousness** and **justice** are the foundation of Your throne; **mercy** and truth go before Your face" (Psalm 89:14)	"Clouds and darkness surround Him; **Righteousness** and **justice** are the foundation of His throne" (Psalm 97:2)	"Blessed be the Lord, For He has shown me His marvelous <u>kindness</u> in a strong city!" (Psalm 31:21)
"The Lord executes **righteousness** and **justice** for all who are oppressed" (Psalm 103:6)	"For His **merciful** <u>kindness</u> is great toward us, and the truth of the Lord endures forever. Praise the Lord!" (Psalm 117:2)	"He shall bring forth your **righteousness** as the light, and your **justice** as the noonday" (Psalm 37:6)

"Let, I pray, Your **merciful** _kindness_ be for my comfort, According to Your word to Your servant" (Psalm 119:76)	"Through the Lord's **mercies** we are not consumed, because His _compassions_ fail not" (Lamentations 3:22)	"For You, Lord, are **good**, and ready to _forgive_, and abundant in **mercy** to all those who call upon You" (Psalm 86:5)
"You answered them, O Lord our God; You were to them God-Who-_forgives_, Though You took vengeance on their deeds" (Psalm 99:8)	"Unto the upright there arises light in the darkness; He is gracious, and full of _compassion_, and **righteous**" (Psalm 112:4)	"The Lord has made known His salvation; His **righteousness** He has revealed in the sight of the nations" (Psalm 98:2)
"But there is _forgiveness_ with You, That You may be feared" (Psalm 130:4)	"But You, O Lord, are a God full of _compassion_, and gracious, longsuffering and abundant in **mercy** and truth" (Psalm 86:15)	"For the Lord is **good**; His **mercy** is everlasting, and His truth endures to all generations" (Psalm 100:5)
"Oh, taste and see that the Lord is **good**; blessed is the man who trusts in Him!" (Psalm 34:8)	"The Lord is gracious and full of _compassion_, Slow to anger and great in **mercy**" (Psalm 145:8)	"The Lord is **good** to all, and His tender **mercies** are over all His works" (Psalm 145:9)
"Bless the Lord, O my soul, and forget not all His benefits: Who _forgives_ all your iniquities, who heals all your diseases, who redeems your life from the pit and crowns you with love and _compassion_, who satisfies your desires with **good** things so that your youth is renewed like the eagle's" (Psalm 103:2-5)	"_His **mercy** endures forever_" documented seven times in the Books of Chronicles (1 Chronicles 16:34; 41; 17:13; 2 Chronicles 5:13; 7:3; 7:6; and 20:21); once in Ezra (Ezra 3:11); thirty-two times in the Psalms (Psalm 106:1; 107:1; 118:1-4; 29; 136:1-26; and 138:8) and once in the Book of Jeremiah (Jeremiah 33:11)	"For the Lord your God is God of gods and Lord of lords, the great God, mighty and awesome, who shows no partiality nor takes a bribe. He administers **justice** for the fatherless and the widow, and loves the stranger, giving him food and clothing" (Deuteronomy 10:17-18))
"Listen to Me, My people; and give ear to Me, O My nation: For law will proceed from Me, and I will make My **justice** rest as a light of the peoples" (Isaiah 51:4)	"So rend your heart, and not your garments; return to the Lord your God, for He is gracious and **merciful**, slow to anger, and of great _kindness_; and He relents from doing harm" (Joel 2:13)	"Oh, how great is Your **goodness**, which You have laid up for those who fear You, which You have prepared for those who trust in You in the presence of the sons of men!" (Psalm 31:19)
"He has made His wonderful works to be remembered; the Lord is gracious and full of _compassion_" (Psalm 111:4)	"Praise the Lord! Oh, give thanks to the Lord, for He is **good**! For His **mercy** endures forever" (Psalm 106:1; Psalm 136:1)	"Teach me to do Your will, for You are my God; Your Spirit is **good**. Lead me in the land of **uprightness**" (Psalm 143:10)
"Praise the Lord, for the Lord is **good**; sing praises to His name, for it is pleasant" (Psalm 135:3)	"Gracious is the Lord, and **righteous**; Yes, our God is **merciful**" (Psalm 116:5)	"The Lord is **righteous**; He has cut in pieces the cords of the wicked" (Psalm 129:4)

"Let the heavens declare His **righteousness**, for God Himself is Judge" (Psalm 50:6)	"His work is honorable and glorious, and His **righteousness** endures forever" (Psalm 111:3)	"The Lord is **righteous** in all His ways, gracious in all His works" (Psalm 145:17)
"The heavens declare His **righteousness**, and all the peoples see His glory" (Psalm 97:6)	"...for all Your commandments are **righteousness**" (Psalm 119:172)	"...Your **righteousness**, O God, is very high, You who have done great things; O God, who is like You?" (Psalm 71:19)
"Then He said, "I will make all My **goodness** pass before you, and I will proclaim the name of the Lord before you. I will be gracious to whom I will be gracious, and I will have <u>compassion</u> on whom I will have <u>compassion</u>" (Exodus 33:19)	"Therefore the Lord will wait, that He may be gracious to you; and therefore He will be exalted, that He may have mercy on you. For the Lord is a God of **justice**; blessed are all those who wait for Him" (Isaiah 30:18)	"But the **mercy** of the Lord is from everlasting to everlasting on those who fear Him, and His **righteousness** to children's children, to such as keep His covenant, and to those who remember His commandments to do them" (Psalm 103:17-18)
"The entirety of Your word is truth, and every one of Your **righteous** judgments endures forever" (Psalm 119:160)	"The fear of the Lord is clean, enduring forever; the judgments of the Lord are true and **righteous** altogether" (Psalm 19:9)	"The Lord, the Lord God, **merciful** and gracious, longsuffering, and abounding in **goodness** and truth..." (Exodus 34:6)
"The **righteousness** of Your testimonies is everlasting..." (Psalm 119:144)	"Your **righteousness** is an everlasting **righteousness**, and Your law is truth" (Psalm 119:142)	

Table 69: God Contains All the Positive Attributes Himself

With the above Scriptures in mind, let us consider the positive attributes documented in the Biblical record.

The **Merciful attribute**: The influence of this attribute allows one to acquire the spiritual elements of _kindness_, _compassion_, and _forgiveness_. In fact, these elements form the initial measure of the influence of the **merciful** attribute. 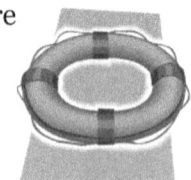 BTT allows one to see that if one cannot extend these three elements to others, even if the person has caused him or her harm, the full measure of the influence of the **merciful** attribute is never attained. However, achieving this attribute is imperative because it provides one the ability to spiritually mature to righteousness. The influence of the **merciful** attribute leads one to share their resources with people less fortunate. One will provide relief to people in the poor and needy categories who may be experiencing hard times, oppressed, or suffering. Moreover, this is the attribute that influences one to have the feelings for sympathy and empathy for someone else's misfortune. BTT allows one to see that by seeking God's wisdom, one can begin to learn and understand the depth of this ancient attribute. But one must understand this important point about the **merciful** attribute. Having this attribute is great on the spiritual battlefield. However, to get one's soul into heaven from this side of life requires more than just this attribute alone. One must have the righteous attribute; the sum of all the positive attributes combined and God's grace, to gain an entrance into heaven. This point will become clear by the end of this Chapter.

Solomon documented the importance of this attribute early on in his writings. He wrote, _"Let not **mercy** and truth forsake you; bind them around your neck, write them on the tablet of your heart, and so find favor and high esteem in the sight of God and man"_ (Proverbs 3:3-4). From this verse alone, one can see the benefits of the influence of the **merciful** attribute. Both God and man highly esteem people influenced by this attribute. Further, the person influenced by this attribute will _"find favor"_ which is to be liked, approved of, and supported.

The Spirit of wisdom revealed to Solomon that when the influence of the **merciful** attribute and Truth are together, they form a formidable team in the war campaign. Here are three major points that Solomon documented about this combination. Together they:

- ...grow in the inner spirits of people who plan good things for others. Solomon documented, _"Do they not go astray who devise evil? But **mercy** and truth belong to those who devise good"_ (Proverbs 14:22)

- ...can help one find _forgiveness_ from sinful behavior and activity. Solomon documented, _"In **mercy** and truth atonement is provided for iniquity; and by the fear of the Lord one departs from evil"_ (Proverbs 16:6)

- ...preserve sound leadership. Solomon documented, _"**Mercy** and truth preserve the king, and by loving _kindness_ he upholds his throne"_ (Proverbs 20:28)

Solomon was not the only one to gain this wisdom about the **merciful** attribute and truth working together. David also understood. David documented of this team that, _"**Mercy** and truth have met together; righteousness and peace have kissed. Truth shall spring out of the earth, and righteousness shall look down from heaven. Yes, the Lord will give what is good; and our land will yield its increase. Righteousness will go before Him, and shall make His footsteps our pathway."_ (Psalm 85:10-13). BTT allows one to see that when the influence of the ***merciful*** attribute is present and demonstrated in one's inner spirit, truth germinates. The powerful combination of ***mercy*** and truth opens the door for the influence of the righteous attribute to flourish and peace to enter one's life. All these things illustrate the creation of a healthy environment for one to spiritually grow. This is why David wrote, "*Righteousness and justice are the foundation of Your throne;* ***mercy*** *and truth go before Your face*" (Psalm 89:14). Further, David documented, "*All the paths of the Lord are* ***mercy*** *and truth, to such as keep His covenant and His testimonies*" (Psalm 25:10).

    The influence of the ***merciful*** attribute is powerful. This attribute influences one to do good things for one's self, as well as for others. One with the influence of this attribute will not beat himself or herself up each time a mistake is made. When one learns to allow for mistakes in one's own spiritual life, personal growth and maturity takes place. Spiritual growth and maturity from mistakes free one up to help others, even to the point of showing ***mercy*** to another person experiencing hard times. Here are a few more pearls of wisdom that the Spirit of wisdom revealed to Solomon concerning the influence of the ***merciful*** attribute. Solomon documented:

- "*The* ***merciful*** *man does good for his own soul, but he who is cruel troubles his own flesh*" (Proverbs 11:17)

- "*He who despises his neighbor sins; but he who has* ***mercy*** *on the poor, happy is he*" (Proverbs 14:21)

- "*He who covers his sins will not prosper, but whoever confesses and forsakes them will have* ***mercy***" (Proverbs 28:13)

- "*He who oppresses the poor reproaches his Maker, but he who honors Him has* ***mercy*** *on the needy*" (Proverbs 14:31)

- "*A righteous man regards the life of his animal, but the tender* ***mercies*** *of the wicked are cruel*" (Proverbs 12:10)

- "*What is desired in a man is* <u>*kindness*</u>, *and a poor man is better than a liar*" (Proverbs 19:22)

- "*He who follows righteousness and* ***mercy*** *finds life, righteousness, and honor*" (Proverbs 21:21)

Solomon provided some bonus information for one's learning near the end of the Book of Proverbs. He documented the value of finding the right person to marry. In Proverbs 31:10-31, he documented that a virtuous wife, "*...opens her mouth with wisdom, and on her tongue is the law of* <u>*kindness*</u>" (Proverbs 31:26). This vital piece of information allows one to see that the right mate can make all the difference in the world when the negative forces of the war campaign come against one's inner spirit. Two people working together as a team can survive in the war campaign better than one by himself. Hence, Solomon documented, "*Two are better than one, because they have a good reward for their labor. For if they fall, one will lift up his* *companion. But woe to him who is alone when he falls, for he has no one to help him up"* (Ecclesiastes 4:9-10). A good husband and wife team provides positive light and guidance on the spiritual battlefield. With this said, the Old Testament of the Biblical record, provided numerous examples of individuals to whom the Lord showed **mercy** and who in turn, provided examples for the things to come. Some examples included:

Examples	What Is Documented
Lot and his family	For reasons far beyond hospitality, Lot demonstrated this attribute to the visitors of Sodom and Gomorrah because he knew the inhabitant's vile behavior. The Biblical record documented, *"Now the two angels came to Sodom in the evening, and Lot was sitting in the gate of Sodom. When Lot saw them, he rose to meet them, and he bowed himself with his face toward the ground. And he said, "Here now, my lords, please turn in to your servant's house and spend the night, and wash your feet; then you may rise early and go on your way." And they said, "No, but we will spend the night in the open square." But he insisted strongly; so they turned in to him and entered his house. Then he made them a feast, and baked unleavened bread, and they ate."* (Genesis 19:1-3)
Isaac	Rebekah met Abraham's servant, heard and believed his story, and became Isaac's wife. The Biblical record documented that the servant said, *"Blessed be the Lord God of my master Abraham, who has not forsaken His **mercy** and His truth toward my master..."* (Genesis 24:27)
Joseph	The Biblical record says, *"Then Joseph's master took him and put him into the prison, a place where the king's prisoners were confined. And he was there in the prison. But the Lord was with Joseph and showed him **mercy**, and He gave him favor in the sight of the keeper of the prison"* (Genesis 39:20-21)
The children of Israel	As they were led out of Egyptian bondage. The Biblical record says of the Lord, *"You in Your **mercy** have led forth the people whom You have redeemed; You have guided them in Your strength to Your holy habitation"* (Exodus 15:13)
To thousands	The Biblical record documented the Lord said of Himself, *"...For I, the Lord your God, am a jealous God, visiting the iniquity of the fathers upon the children to the third and fourth generations of those who hate Me, but showing **mercy** to thousands, to those who love Me and keep My commandments"* (Exodus 20:5-6; Deuteronomy 5:9-10)
Aaron	God had Moses warn Aaron, after the death of his two sons for offering a profane fire before the Lord, *"Tell Aaron your brother not to come at just any time into the Holy Place inside the veil, before the **mercy** seat which is on the ark, lest he die; for I will appear in the cloud above the **mercy** seat"* (Leviticus 16:1-2)
David and his son Solomon	David, in a song to the Lord in 2 Samuel 22 1-51, concluded about the Lord, *"He is the tower of salvation to His king, and shows **mercy** to His anointed, to David and his descendants forevermore"* (2 Samuel 22:51)
The prophet Ezra through	The Biblical record says, *"Blessed be the Lord God of our fathers, who has put such a thing as this in the king's heart, to beautify the house of the Lord which is in Jerusalem, and has extended **mercy** to me before the king and his counselors, and before all the king's mighty princes. So I was*

King Artaxerxes	*encouraged, as the hand of the Lord my God was upon me; and I gathered leading men of Israel to go up with me"* (Ezra 7:27-28)
The reassembled children of Israel after captivity	The Biblical record documented that Ezra, speaking to the people, said, *"For we were slaves. Yet our God did not forsake us in our bondage; but He extended **mercy** to us in the sight of the kings of Persia, to revive us, to repair the house of our God, to rebuild its ruins, and to give us a wall in Judah and Jerusalem"* (Ezra 9:9)
	King Hezekiah sent runners throughout all Israel and Judah stating, *"...if you return to the Lord, your brethren and your children will be treated with **compassion** by those who lead them captive, so that they may come back to this land; for the Lord your God is gracious and **merciful**, and will not turn His face from you if you return to Him"* (2 Chronicles 30:9). The Bible documented, that some *"runners passed from city to city through the country of Ephraim and Manasseh, as far as Zebulun; but they laughed at them and mocked them. Nevertheless some from Asher, Manasseh, and Zebulun humbled themselves and came to Jerusalem. Also the hand of God was on Judah to give them singleness of heart to obey the command of the king and the leaders, at the word of the Lord"* (2 Chronicles 30:10-12).

Table 70: Examples of People Influenced by the Merciful Attribute

Before going further into the influence of the **merciful** attribute itself, I need to address a point about the application of this attribute. The Lord specifically told Moses and Joshua that there were times to allow the influence of this attribute as well as times to withhold this attribute when carrying out God's commands. This may sound strange however, BTT allows one to see that during the time of the Old Testament, God had a mission for the children of Israel that included taking control of the land occupied by wicked nations. God's directives did not include extending **mercy** to these nations. God's directives took priority over allowing the influence of the **merciful** attribute. In these situations, showing **mercy** was sinful and had severe consequences. Moses told the children of Israel, *"When the Lord your God brings you into the land which you go to possess, and has cast out many nations before you, the Hittites and the Girgashites and the Amorites and the Canaanites and the Perizzites and the Hivites and the Jebusites, seven nations greater and mightier than you, and when the Lord your God delivers them over to you, you shall conquer them and utterly destroy them. You shall make no covenant with them nor show **mercy** to them"* (Deuteronomy 7:2). Many in the religious world want to dismiss these words because they failed to understand the extent of the influence of wicked and evil's contamination. This is a strategy used in spiritual warfare to blind God's people to the war campaign. Because of this, Moses told the children of Israel what God would do for them IF they were obedient. Moses said, *"...it shall come to pass, because you listen to these judgments, and keep and do them, that the Lord your God will keep with you the covenant and the **mercy** which He swore to your fathers"* (Deuteronomy 7:12). Wow! BTT allows one to see that the Lord knew how devastating and corrosive the influences of the wicked and evil attributes were going to be on the children of Israel. Today, we need to learn from this example. In Deuteronomy 13:12-17, the Lord instructed Moses to tell the children of Israel not to show any **mercy** to people enticing them to serve other gods. God called these people corrupt (Deuteronomy 13:13) and their behavior an abomination (Deuteronomy 13:14). Further He told

Moses that, *"...you shall surely strike the inhabitants of that city with the edge of the sword, utterly destroying it, all that is in it and its livestock—with the edge of the sword. And you shall gather all its plunder into the middle of the street, and completely burn with fire the city and all its plunder, for the Lord your God. It shall be a heap forever; it shall not be built again. So none of the accursed things shall remain in your hand, that the Lord may turn from the fierceness of His anger and show you* **mercy**, *have* compassion *on you and multiply you, just as He swore to your fathers..."* (Deuteronomy 13:15-17).

In other words, one must restrain the influence of the **merciful** attribute if a behavior compromises God's Word. Even Joshua understood this and was obedient. When he led the children of Israel into the Promised Land, the Biblical record documented in Joshua 11:16-23,

> *"Thus Joshua took all this land: the mountain country, all the South, all the land of Goshen, the lowland, and the Jordan plain—the mountains of Israel and its lowlands, from Mount Halak and the ascent to Seir, even as far as Baal Gad in the Valley of Lebanon below Mount Hermon. He captured all their kings, and struck them down and killed them. Joshua made war a long time with all those kings. There was not a city that made peace with the children of Israel, except the Hivites, the inhabitants of Gibeon. All the others they took in battle. For it was of the Lord to harden their hearts, that they should come against Israel in battle, that He might utterly destroy them, and that they might receive no* **mercy**, *but that He might destroy them, as the Lord had commanded Moses. And at that time Joshua came and cut off the Anakim from the mountains: from Hebron, from Debir, from Anab, from all the mountains of Judah, and from all the mountains of Israel; Joshua utterly destroyed them with their cities. None of the Anakim were left in the land of the children of Israel; they remained only in Gaza, in Gath, and in Ashdod. So Joshua took the whole land, according to all that the Lord had said to Moses; and Joshua gave it as an inheritance to Israel according to their divisions by their tribes. Then the land rested from war."*

BTT allows one to plainly see that there is a time to withhold the application of the **merciful** attribute. This attribute is withheld when its application conflicts with God's Word. Please try to understand, the negative forces of the war campaign will promote deceivers who will attempt to confuse the use of the **merciful** attribute along with the elements of forgiveness, kindness, and compassion. A few examples for one's learning include:

Examples	What Is Documented
Pharaoh	He lied to Moses and Aaron, after the eighth plague on Egypt and asked them, *"Now therefore, please forgive my sin only this once, and entreat the Lord your God, that He may take away from me this death only"* (Exodus 10:17). Pharaoh, influenced by the liar attribute, caused God to bring another plague on Egypt.
	When Gideon died, the Biblical record documented *"the children of Israel again played the harlot with the Baals, and made Baal-Berith their god. Thus*

The children of Israel	*the children of Israel did not remember the Lord their God, who had delivered them from the hands of all their enemies on every side; nor did they show <u>kindness</u> to the house of Jerubbaal (Gideon) in accordance with the good he had done for Israel"* (Judges 8:33-35)
Joash the king	When Jehoiada the priest died, the Bible documented, *"...the leaders of Judah came and bowed down to the king. And the king listened to them. Therefore they left the house of the Lord God of their fathers, and served wooden images and idols..."* (2 Chronicles 24:17-18). Joash was the king. God sent prophets to bring them back to the Lord, but they would not listen" (2 Chronicles 24:19). God sent the prophet Zechariah, the son of Jehoiada the priest, and the Bible documented, *"Thus Joash the king did not remember the <u>kindness</u> which Jehoiada his father had done to him, but killed his son; and as he died, he said, "The Lord look on it, and repay!"* (2 Chronicles 24:22)

Table 71: The Elements of <u>*Forgiveness*</u>, <u>*Kindness*</u>, and <u>*Compassion*</u>

God was with the children of Israel when they kept His commandments. He did not forsake them; however, they turned their backs on Him constantly. The Biblical record makes it clear that God's "...***mercy*** *endures forever.*" This is stated seven times in the Books of the Chronicles (1 Chronicles 16:34-41; 17:13; 2 Chronicles 5:13; 7:3; 7:6; and 20:21), once in the Book of Ezra (Ezra 3:11), and thirty-two times in the Book of Psalms (Psalm 106:1; 107:1; 118:1-4; 29; 136:1-26; and 138:8) and once in the Book of Jeremiah (Jeremiah 33:11). Even so, the children of Israel still turned their backs on the Lord. However, they received constant education about this attribute and the elementary principles about the elements of <u>*kindness*</u>, <u>*compassion*</u>, and <u>*forgiveness*</u> from Moses and God's prophets.

Moses pleaded with God to <u>*forgive*</u> the children of Israel after they made a golden calf and bowed down to worship it in the wilderness according to Exodus Chapter 32. Their sin was so grave and wicked that Moses pleaded, *"Oh, these people have committed a great sin, and have made for themselves a god of gold! Yet now, if You will <u>forgive</u> their sin—but if not, I pray, blot me out of Your book which You have written"* (Exodus 32: 31-32). God did not accept Moses' plea and the Biblical record documented *"...the Lord plagued the people because of what they did with the calf which Aaron made"* (Exodus 32:35). Their behavior was an abomination to the Lord. To gain <u>*forgiveness*</u> of their sins from the Lord, the following are some of the many commands that Moses had to give the children of Israel. These commands also helped to reinforce the weakened influence of the ***merciful*** attribute that had not matured in their inner spirits. Moses commanded from the Lord:

Sin Committed	**The Offering**	**The Priest Role**
If the whole congregation of Israel sins unintentionally and the sin becomes known... (Leviticus 4:13-14; Numbers 15:25-26)	A young bull without blemish	The priest will conduct a ceremony (Leviticus 4:15-19) and,"...*make atonement for them, and it shall be <u>forgiven</u> them*" (Leviticus 4:20)
If a ruler sins and does something unintentionally against any of the	A male kid of the goats, without blemish	The priest will conduct a ceremony (Leviticus 4:24-25) and, "...*make atonement*

commandments of the Lord... (Leviticus 4:22-23)		*for him concerning his sin, and it shall be forgiven him"* (Leviticus 4:26)
If anyone of the common people sins unintentionally by doing something against any of the commandments of the Lord ...(Leviticus 4:27-28; Numbers 15:28)	A female kid of the goats without blemish	The priest will conduct a ceremony (Leviticus 4:24-25) and *"...make atonement for him, and it shall be forgiven him"* (Leviticus 4:31)
If he brings a lamb as his sin offering...(Leviticus 4:32)	A female lamb without blemish	The priest will conduct a ceremony (Leviticus 4:33-34) and *"...shall make atonement for his sin that he has committed, and it shall be forgiven him"* (Leviticus 4:35)
If a person sins in a matter of an oath, touches any unclean thing, touches human uncleanness, or swears, speaking thoughtlessly with his lips to do evil or to do good...(Leviticus 5:1-4). When guilt is established in any of these matters, and offering will be made.	A female lamb, kid of the goats (Leviticus 5:6), or two turtledoves or two young pigeons (Leviticus 5:7)	When guilty is established, the priest will conduct a ceremony (Leviticus 5:8-9) and *"...shall make atonement on his behalf for his sin which he has committed, and it shall be forgiven him"* (Leviticus 5:10)
If the person cannot bring two turtledoves or two young pigeons (Leviticus 5:11)	Then one-tenth of an ephah of fine flour	The priest will conduct a ceremony (Leviticus 5:12) and *"...shall make atonement for him, for his sin that he has committed in any of these matters; and it shall be forgiven him..."* (Leviticus 5:13)
"If a person commits a trespass, and sins unintentionally in regard to the holy things of the Lord..." (Leviticus 5:15)	... a ram without blemish, a valuation in shekels of silver according to the shekel of the sanctuary as a trespass offering, and restitution for the harm that he has done (Leviticus 5:15-16)	The priest shall make atonement for him with the ram of the trespass offering, and it shall be forgiven him. (Leviticus 5:16)
"If a person sins, and commits any of these things which are forbidden to be done by the commandments of the Lord, though he does not know it, yet he is guilty and shall bear his iniquity" (Leviticus 5:17)	A ram without blemish from the flock, with a valuation, as a trespass offering (Leviticus 5:18)	*"...So the priest shall make atonement for him regarding his ignorance in which he erred and did not know it, and it shall be forgiven him"* (Leviticus 5:18)

If a person sins by lying to his neighbor, (Leviticus 6:1-4)	A ram, a valuation, restore what he lied about at full value plus one-fifth more (Leviticus 6:4-6)	"So the priest shall make atonement for him before the Lord, and he shall be <u>forgiven</u> for any one of these things that he may have done in which he trespasses" (Leviticus 6:7)
Whoever lies carnally with a woman who is betrothed to a man as a concubine, and who has not at all been redeemed nor given her freedom (Leviticus 19:20)	"…for this there shall be scourging; but they shall not be put to death…" (Leviticus 19:20) and he will offer a ram (Leviticus 19:21)	The priest shall make atonement for him…and the sin which he has committed shall be <u>forgiven</u> him. Leviticus 19:22

Table 72: God's Commands to the Children of Israel to Receive <u>*Forgiveness*</u>

Moses was not the only Old Testament leader to plead with the children of Israel to repent of their sins. Many other people told them about the influence of the **merciful** attribute and the elements of <u>*forgiveness*</u>, <u>*kindness*</u>, and <u>*compassion*</u>. Examples included:

- Joshua who said to the people, *"You cannot serve the Lord, for He is a holy God. He is a jealous God; He will not <u>forgive</u> your transgressions nor your sins. If you forsake the Lord and serve foreign gods, then He will turn and do you harm and consume you, after He has done you good"* (Joshua 24:19-20)

- The Lord told Solomon: *"if My people who are called by My name will humble themselves, and pray and seek My face, and turn from their wicked ways, then I will hear from heaven, and will <u>forgive</u> their sin and heal their land"* (2 Chronicles 7:14)

In addition, there are numerous examples of people in the Old Testament who demonstrated the influence of the **merciful** attribute and the elements of <u>*kindness*</u>, <u>*compassion*</u>, <u>*forgiveness*</u> to others. A few examples for one's learning include:

Examples	What Is Documented
Sarah	She demonstrated <u>*kindness*</u> to her husband Abram by letting their enemies know she was Abram's sister and wife. The Biblical record documented from Abram, *"…when God caused me to wander from my father's house, that I said to her, 'This is your <u>kindness</u> that you should do for me: in every place, wherever we go, say of me, "He is my brother."'"* (Genesis 20:13)
Abraham	Demonstrated <u>*kindness*</u> to Abimelech. The Bible documented that when Abimelech realized God was with Abraham, he asked Abraham, *"Now therefore, swear to me by God that you will not deal falsely with me, with my offspring, or with my posterity; but that according to the <u>kindness</u> that I have done to you, you will do to me and to the land in which you have dwelt"* (Genesis 21:23).
Rebekah	Abraham sent a servant to find a wife for his son Isaac. The Bible documented that he saw Rebekah during his journey. The Bible records the servant said, *"Now let it be that the young woman to whom I say, 'Please let down your pitcher that I may drink,' and she says, 'Drink, and I will also give your*

	camels a drink'—let her be the one You have appointed for Your servant Isaac. And by this I will know that You have shown <u>kindness</u> to my master" (Genesis 24:14). Rebekah became Isaac's wife (Genesis 24:67)
Chief Butler	After interpreting his dream for him while they were both in prison, he asked the chief butler to *"...remember me when it is well with you, and please show <u>kindness</u> to me; make mention of me to Pharaoh, and get me out of this house"* (Genesis 40:14) Two years later (Genesis 41:1) the chief butler remember and showed <u>kindness</u> to Joseph (Genesis 41:9)
Pharaoh daughter	She demonstrated <u>compassion</u> for Moses. The Biblical record documented, *"And when she opened it, she saw the child, and behold, the baby wept. So she had <u>compassion</u> on him, and said, "This is one of the Hebrews' children."* (Exodus 2:6)
Rahab	She showed <u>kindness</u> to the men that spied out the city of Jericho. The Bible documented that she said to the spies, *"Now therefore, I beg you, swear to me by the Lord, since I have shown you <u>kindness</u>, that you also will show <u>kindness</u> to my father's house, and give me a true token..."* (Joshua 2:12). The spies kept their agreement and Rahab and her family were spared when Jericho was captured by the children of Israel (Joshua 6:22-25)
Certain spies	These men of Joseph went up against Bethel, and the Biblical record documented, *"...when the spies saw a man coming out of the city, they said to him, "Please show us the entrance to the city, and we will show you **mercy**. So he showed them the entrance to the city, and they struck the city with the edge of the sword; but they let the man and all his family go"* (Judges 1:24-25)
Ruth	She worked in the fields to make enough to take care of Naomi, her mother-in-law. Boaz told her, *"Blessed are you of the Lord, my daughter! For you have shown more <u>kindness</u> at the end than at the beginning, in that you did not go after young men, whether poor or rich"* (Ruth 3:10)
The Kenites	The Biblical record documented, *"...Saul said to the Kenites, "Go, depart, get down from among the Amalekites, lest I destroy you with them. For you showed <u>kindness</u> to all the children of Israel when they came up out of Egypt." So the Kenites departed from among the Amalekites"* (1 Samuel 15:6)
Jonathan	He showed <u>kindness</u> to David, risking his own life, as Saul sought to kill him. The Bible documented, *"And you shall not only show me the <u>kindness</u> of the Lord while I still live, that I may not die; but you shall not cut off your <u>kindness</u> from my house forever, no, not when the Lord has cut off every one of the enemies of David from the face of the earth." So Jonathan made a covenant with the house of David, saying, "Let the Lord require it at the hand of David's enemies""* (1 Samuel 20:14-16)
Abigail's	David showed **kindness** to her when She demonstrated <u>forgiveness</u>, <u>kindness</u>, and <u>compassion</u> as she asked David to spare the life of her wicked husband *"Please <u>forgive</u> the trespass of your maidservant. For the Lord will certainly make for my lord an enduring house, because my lord fights the battles of the Lord, and evil is not found in you throughout your days"* (1 Samuel 25:28)
The men of Jabesh Gilead	The Bible documented that David said, *"So David sent messengers to the men of Jabesh Gilead, and said to them, "You are blessed of the Lord, for you have shown this <u>kindness</u> to your lord, to Saul, and have buried him. And now may*

	the Lord show kindness and truth to you. I also will repay you this kindness, because you have done this thing"" (2 Samuel 2:5-6)
David	He showed *kindness* to Mephibosheth. The Bible documented, *"Now David said, "Is there still anyone who is left of the house of Saul, that I may show him kindness for Jonathan's sake?"* (2 Samuel 9:1). Mephibosheth, who had lame feet (2 Samuel 9:3) was identified, and *"...David said to him, "Do not fear, for I will surely show you kindness for Jonathan your father's sake, and will restore to you all the land of Saul your grandfather; and you shall eat bread at my table continually.""* (2 Samuel 9:7)
	The Biblical record documented, *"Then David said, "I will show kindness to Hanun the son of Nahash, as his father showed kindness to me."* (2 Samuel 10:2; 1 Chronicles 19:2)
David forgave Absalom	Absalom burned David's servant Joab's field because he had not seen David in two years according to 2 Samuel 14:28-30. He got an audience with David because of this incident and the Biblical record documented that Absalom, *"...came to the king and bowed himself on his face to the ground before the king. Then the king kissed Absalom"* (2 Samuel 14:33) as a sign of *forgiveness*.
David to Ittai the Gittite	Ittai was a foreigner. The Biblical record documented that David said to Ittai, *"...Why are you also going with us? Return and remain with the king. For you are a foreigner and also an exile from your own place. In fact, you came only yesterday. Should I make you wander up and down with us today, since I go I know not where? Return, and take your brethren back.* **Mercy** *and truth be with you"* (2 Samuel 15:19-20). But after Ittai spoke to David, David allowed Ittai, his family and all his men to travel with him according to 2 Samuel 15:22.
David to Shimei	Shimei was a man from the family of the house of Saul who cursed and threw stones at David as he passed by (2 Samuel 16:5-7). The Biblical record tells us that when David took the throne, *"...Now Shimei the son of Gera fell down before the king when he had crossed the Jordan"* (2 Samuel 19:18). Shimei pleaded for his life and admitted that he had sinned according to 2 Samuel 19:20. David, because of the ***merciful*** attribute allowed Shimei to live that day.
	The Biblical record documented that David showed *kindness* to Barzilla, *"a very aged man, eighty years old. And he had provided the king with supplies while he stayed at Mahanaim, for he was a very rich man"* (2 Samuel 19:32). David took Barzilla son, Chimham, under his wing (2 Samuel 19:37) and he *"kissed Barzillai and blessed him, and he returned to his own place"* (2 Samuel 19:39)
Solomon	He continued showing *kindness* to the sons of Barzillai because of David. The Bible documented that David told Solomon as he took over the throne, *"But show kindness to the sons of Barzillai the Gileadite, and let them be among those who eat at your table, for so they came to me when I fled from Absalom your brother"* (1 Kings 2:7)
A woman fighting for the life of her child	Two women gave birth at the same time (1 Kings 3:16-21). After one of the mother's child died, she took the other mother's child as her own by switching her son's dead body for the living. For the true mother, standing before Solomon to judge the case, the Bible documented *"Then the woman whose son was living spoke to the king, for she yearned with compassion for her son;*

	and she said, "O my lord, give her the living child, and by no means kill him!" But the other said, "Let him be neither mine nor yours, but divide him" (1 Kings 3:26)

Table 73: Examples of the Influence of the Merciful Attribute and the Elements of <u>*Forgiveness*</u>, <u>*Kindness*</u>, and <u>*Compassion*</u>

David documented an interesting truth concerning the relationship between God and one influenced by the **merciful** attribute. He documented, *"With the **merciful** You will show Yourself **merciful**; with a blameless man You will show Yourself blameless; with the pure You will show Yourself pure; and with the devious You will show Yourself shrewd. You will save the humble people; but Your eyes are on the haughty, that You may bring them down"* (2 Samuel 22:26-28; Psalm 18:25-27). The key point here is: If one wants **mercy** from God, one must show **mercy** to others. One must strive to acquire this attribute, allow its influence, and demonstrate this attribute to remain on the positive side of the war campaign. When David penned the Book of Psalms, through his writings, he taught that God provides unlimited **mercy** to His creation. However, one must still ask for God's **mercy** because asking shows submission to God. For one's example, the Psalmist documented that he:

- Asked the Lord to "*have **mercy** on him*" ten times in Psalm 4:1; 6:2; 9:13; 25:16; 27:7; 30:10; 31:9; 51:1; 86:15, 16; 123:3

- Asked the Lord "*to be **merciful** to him*" seven times according to Psalm 41:4; 41:10; 56:1; 57:1; 86:3; 119:58; 119:132

- Asked the Lord to remember him according to His **mercy** in Psalm 25:7 and to "*show us Your **mercy***" in Psalm 85:7

Just as David demonstrated the requirement to ask God for **mercy**, he also prayed that the Lord withhold **mercy** from people who were influenced by the wicked attribute and those whose mouths were simply deceitful (Psalm 109:1-29), especially if they harm the poor and needy. The whole text is worth reading but to summarize it, David prayed that people with the wicked and liar attributes be shown no **mercy**, *"Because he did not remember to show **mercy**, but persecuted the poor and needy man, that he might even slay the broken in heart"* (Psalm 109:16). The point here is prayer is a powerful tool. Prayer changes negative behavior in people used by the negative forces of the war campaign.

As the children of Israel grew into a powerful nation, their struggles to mature the **merciful** attribute, as well as the elements of <u>*kindness*</u>, <u>*compassion*</u>, and <u>*forgiveness*</u>, expanded. As Solomon became king and reestablished and consecrated the Lord's temple, he had to once again sanctify the people before they could stand before the Lord. Some of the things Solomon prayed to God to allow the nation of Israel to stand in His presence included:

- "*...hear the supplication of Your servant and of Your people Israel, when they pray toward this place. Hear in heaven Your dwelling place; and when You hear, <u>forgive</u>*" (1 Kings 8:30; 2 Chronicles 6:21)

- "*...hear in heaven, and <u>forgive</u> the sin of Your people Israel, and bring them back to the land which You gave to their fathers*" (1 Kings 8:34; 2 Chronicles 6:25)

- "*...hear in heaven, and <u>forgive</u> the sin of Your servants, Your people Israel, that You may teach them the good way in which they should walk; and send rain on Your land which You have given to Your people as an inheritance*" (1 Kings 8:36; 2 Chronicles 6:27)

- "*...hear in heaven Your dwelling place, and <u>forgive</u>, and act, and give to everyone according to all his ways, whose heart You know (for You alone know the hearts of all the sons of men)*" (1 Kings 8:39; 2 Chronicles 6:30)

- "*...and <u>forgive</u> Your people who have sinned against You, and all their transgressions which they have transgressed against You; and grant them <u>compassion</u> before those who took them captive, that they may have <u>compassion</u> on them*" (1 Kings 8:50; 2 Chronicles 6:39)

The items above made a powerful prayer. These prayers emphasized that Solomon understood what his father, David who was also the Psalmist, wrote when he penned, "*For the Lord is good; His **mercy** is everlasting, and His truth endures to all generations*" (Psalm 100:5). Below are more pearls of wisdom that concern the influence of the **merciful** attribute and the elements of <u>forgiveness</u>, <u>kindness</u>, and <u>compassion</u>. These pearls help one to understand the Old Testament writers knew their values. The Bible documented:

For Leaders: "*For the king trusts in the Lord, and through the **mercy** of the Most High he shall not be moved*" (Psalm 21:7)	"*Blessed is he whose transgression is <u>forgiven</u>, whose sin is covered*" (Psalm 32:1)	"*Many sorrows shall be to the wicked; but he who trusts in the Lord, **mercy** shall surround him*" (Psalm 32:10)
"*Righteousness and justice are the foundation of Your throne; **mercy** and truth go before Your face*" (Psalm 89:14)	"*The wicked borrows and does not repay, but the righteous shows **mercy** and gives*" (Psalm 37:21)	"*But as for me, I will walk in my integrity; redeem me and be **merciful** to me*" (Psalm 26:11)
"*I have been young, and now am old; yet I have not seen the righteous forsaken, nor his descendants begging bread. He is ever **merciful**, and lends; and his descendants are blessed*" (Psalm 37:25-26)	"*Let the righteous strike me; It shall be a <u>kindness</u>. And let him rebuke me; it shall be as excellent oil; let my head not refuse it. For still my prayer is against the deeds of the wicked*" (Psalm 141:5)	"*To him who is afflicted, <u>kindness</u> should be shown by his friend, even though he forsakes the fear of the Almighty.*" (Job 6:14)
"*For though I were righteous, I could not answer Him; I would beg **mercy** of my Judge*" (Job 9:15)	"*Surely goodness and **mercy** shall follow me all the days of my life; and I will dwell in the house of the Lord forever*" (Psalm 23:6)	"*All the paths of the Lord are **mercy** and truth, to such as keep His covenant and His testimonies*" (Psalm 25:10)

"For the Lord will judge His people, and He will have <u>compassion</u> on His servants" (Psalm 135:14)	"Though He causes grief, yet He will show <u>compassion</u> according to the multitude of His **mercies**" (Lamentations 3:32)	
"**Mercy** and truth have met together; righteousness and peace have kissed. Truth shall spring out of the earth, and righteousness shall look down from heaven. Yes, the Lord will give what is good; and our land will yield its increase. Righteousness will go before Him, and shall make His footsteps our pathway" (Psalm 85:10-13)	For Leaders: "For You, O God, have heard my vows; You have given me the heritage of those who fear Your name. You will prolong the king's life, his years as many generations. He shall abide before God forever. Oh, prepare **mercy** and truth, which may preserve him!" (Psalm 61:5-7)	

Table 74: Some Pearls of Wisdom Concerning the Influence of the Merciful Attribute

As the nation of Israel grew, the people's rejection of God also grew proportionately. Just as with the other attributes, the Lord sent His prophets to warn the nation of Israel and their leaders to repent and return to Him. The prophets warned the nation of Israel about the lack of the **merciful** attribute's influence and the elements of <u>kindness</u>, <u>compassion</u>, and <u>forgiveness</u> among the leaders and the people. Some of the many warnings included:

The Prophet	What Was Said
Isaiah	"Their land is also full of idols; they worship the work of their own hands, that which their own fingers have made. People bow down, and each man humbles himself; therefore do not <u>forgive</u> them" (Isaiah 2:8-9)
Isaiah	He told the nation of Israel, "The righteous perishes, and no man takes it to heart; **merciful** men are taken away, while no one considers that the righteous is taken away from evil" (Isaiah 57:1)
Jeremiah	"Go and cry in the hearing of Jerusalem, saying, 'Thus says the Lord: "I remember you, the <u>kindness</u> of your youth, the love of your betrothal, when you went after Me in the wilderness, in a land not sown" (Jeremiah 2:2)
Jeremiah	"It may be that the house of Judah will hear all the adversities which I purpose to bring upon them, that everyone may turn from his evil way, that I may <u>forgive</u> their iniquity and their sin." (Jeremiah 36:3)
Jeremiah	Because the nation of Israel lacked the **merciful** attribute, the Lord sent a people to destroy them that also lacked the merciful attribute. The Biblical record documented, "Thus says the Lord: "Behold, a people comes from the north country, and a great nation will be raised from the farthest parts of the earth. They will lay hold on bow and spear; they are cruel and have no **mercy**; their voice roars like the sea; and they ride on horses, as men of war set in array against you, O daughter of Zion" (Jeremiah 6:22, 23; Jeremiah 50:41-42)

	"*With a little wrath I hid My face from you for a moment; but with everlasting <u>kindness</u> I will have **mercy** on you," Says the Lord, your Redeemer*" (Isaiah 54:8)
	Prior to destruction of Jerusalem, some of the nation of Israel decided to go to Egypt for protection. The Lord sent Jeremiah to warn them to repent and return to Him and He would protect them from the king of Babylon they feared (Jeremiah 42:7-12). Jeremiah told them from the Lord, "*...I will show you **mercy**, that he may have **mercy** on you and cause you to return to your own land*" (Jeremiah 42:12). Unfortunately, the people made the wrong choice and went on to Egypt according to Jeremiah 43:7 and were punished because King Nebuchadnezzar of Babylon, whom they feared, came and defeated the army of Pharaoh Necho, king of Egypt, destroying the nation and placing the nation in bondage according the Jeremiah 46.
Daniel	"*To the Lord our God belong **mercy** and <u>forgiveness</u>, though we have rebelled against Him*" (Daniel 9:9)
	He warned King Nebuchadnezzar, after interpreting a second dream for him saying, "*Therefore, O king, let my advice be acceptable to you; break off your sins by being righteous, and your iniquities by showing **mercy** to the poor. Perhaps there may be a lengthening of your prosperity*" (Daniel 4:27). But the Biblical record tells us that King Nebuchadnezzar did not listen to the Lord or Daniel. The King went on to say, "*Is not this great Babylon, that I have built for a royal dwelling by my mighty power and for the honor of my majesty?*" (Daniel 4:30). And the Biblical record also tells us that the very hour he spoke he was removed from his throne by a condition that drove him to eat grass in the fields like a wild animal (Daniel 4:31-33). During this time, he humbled himself and came to recognize and glorify God. Because of his true repentance, the Biblical record documented that King Nebuchadnezzar and his kingdom were restored. God showed him **mercy** according to Daniel 4:34-37.
From the Book of Lamentations	"*The hands of the <u>compassionate</u> women Have cooked their own children; they became food for them in the destruction of the daughter of my people*" (Lamentations 4:10)
Hosea	"*Hear the word of the Lord, You children of Israel, for the Lord brings a charge against the inhabitants of the land: "There is no truth or **mercy** or knowledge of God in the land*" (Hosea 4:1)
	He called them to repentance. He said, "*Sow for yourselves righteousness; reap in **mercy**; break up your fallow ground, for it is time to seek the Lord, till He comes and rains righteousness on you*" (Hosea 10:12)
	He also told them, "*So you, by the help of your God, return; observe **mercy** and justice, and wait on your God continually*" (Hosea 12:6)
Micah	He documented some facts to the nation of Israel, told them what the Lord expected of them, and at the same time, asked them a pointed question from the Lord. He stated that God, "*...has shown you, O man, what is good; and what does the Lord require of you but to do justly, to love **mercy**, and to walk humbly with your God?*" (Micah 6:8)
	He warned the people from the Lord saying, "*Thus says the Lord of hosts: 'Execute true justice, show **mercy** and <u>compassion</u> everyone to his brother. Do not oppress the widow or the fatherless, the alien or the poor. Let none of you plan evil in his heart against his brother*" (Zechariah 7:9-10)

Zechariah	Sadly, the Biblical record documented, *"But they refused to heed, shrugged their shoulders, and stopped their ears so that they could not hear. Yes, they made their hearts like flint, refusing to hear the law and the words which the Lord of hosts had sent by His Spirit through the former prophets. Thus great wrath came from the Lord of hosts. Therefore it happened, that just as He proclaimed and they would not hear, so they called out and I would not listen,"* says the Lord of hosts. *"But I scattered them with a whirlwind among all the nations which they had not known. Thus the land became desolate after them, so that no one passed through or returned; for they made the pleasant land desolate"* (Zechariah 7:11-14)

Table 75: The Prophets' Warnings about the Influence of the Merciful Attributes

When Jesus came to the world, one can immediately see that He placed a premium on acquiring the influence of the **merciful** attribute. The people of His day were seriously hurting under both Jewish and Roman authority. So, Jesus taught everyone that heard Him about the influence of the **merciful** attribute and demonstrated the attribute through His example. Documented below are some of the numerous things He taught.

- In a famous sermon He gave on a mount, He taught, *"Blessed are the **merciful**, for they shall obtain **mercy**"* (Matthew 5:7)

- To Pharisees who questioned Jesus' disciples after He sat and ate with Matthew, a tax collector, and other tax collectors and sinners that came to eat with Him (Matthew 9:9, 10), He taught, *"Those who are well have no need of a physician, but those who are sick. But go and learn what this means: 'I desire **mercy** and not sacrifice.' For I did not come to call the righteous, but sinners, to repentance"* (Matthew 9:12-13)

- When the Pharisees complained because Jesus' disciples plucked and ate grain on the Sabbath (Matthew 12:1, 2), Jesus taught them, *"Have you not read what David did when he was hungry, he and those who were with him: how he entered the house of God and ate the showbread which was not lawful for him to eat, nor for those who were with him, but only for the priests? Or have you not read in the law that on the Sabbath the priests in the temple profane the Sabbath, and are blameless? Yet I say to you that in this place there is One greater than the temple. But if you had known what this means, 'I desire **mercy** and not sacrifice,' you would not have condemned the guiltless. For the Son of Man is Lord even of the Sabbath"* (Matthew 12:3-8)

- He warned the Pharisees and scribes, *"Woe to you, scribes and Pharisees, hypocrites! For you pay tithe of mint and anise and cummin, and have neglected the weightier matters of the law: justice and **mercy** and faith. These you ought to have done, without leaving the others undone"* (Matthew 23:23)

- He taught the people to, *"...love your enemies, do good, and lend, hoping for nothing in return; and your reward will be great, and you will be sons of the Most High. For He is kind to the unthankful and evil. Therefore be **merciful**, just as your Father also is **merciful**"* (Luke 6:35-36)

- He taught a lawyer about the influence of the **merciful** attribute (Luke 10:25) after the lawyer tried to test Him. Jesus taught him a parable about a good Samaritan, a priest, and Levite who saw a man left for dead by robbers. At the end of the parable, Jesus asked the lawyer, "*So which of these three do you think was neighbor to him who fell among the thieves?" And he said, "He who showed **mercy** on him." Then Jesus said to him, "Go and do likewise"*" (Luke 10:35-37)

- He taught a parable to some people, "*...who trusted in themselves that they were righteous, and despised others...*" (Luke 18:9). He taught, "*Two men went up to the temple to pray, one a Pharisee and the other a tax collector. The Pharisee stood and prayed thus with himself, 'God, I thank You that I am not like other men—extortioners, unjust, adulterers, or even as this tax collector. I fast twice a week; I give tithes of all that I possess.' And the tax collector, standing afar off, would not so much as raise his eyes to heaven, but beat his breast, saying, 'God, be **merciful** to me a sinner!' I tell you, this man went down to his house justified rather than the other; for everyone who exalts himself will be humbled, and he who humbles himself will be exalted*" (Luke 18:10-14)

- He taught, "*Therefore be **merciful**, just as your Father also is **merciful**"* (Luke 6:36)

All the items above that Jesus taught defied the wisdom of the world. Jesus also taught a great deal on the elements of _kindness_, _compassion_, and _forgiveness_. In fact, He emphasized the need for _forgiving_ others when He gave the people an example of how to pray in Matthew 6: 8-13. Jesus told them when they prayed to ask God to, "*..._forgive_ us our debts, as we _forgive_ our debtors*" (Matthew 6:12) or said another way, "*..._forgive_ us our sins, for we also _forgive_ everyone who is indebted to us...*" (Luke 11:4). One can see the same thoughts captured in the teachings of Jesus as He compared "*...the kingdom of heaven to a certain king who wanted to settle accounts with his servants*" in Matthew 18:23. To answer a question Peter asked about, "*...how often shall my brother sin against me, and I _forgive_ him? Up to seven times?*" (Matthew 18:21), Jesus told Peter a story about a servant who could not pay the king what he owed him. The servant pleaded with the king to have patience and he was so, "*moved with _compassion_, released him, and forgave him the debt*" (Matthew 18:27). Then the same servant, freed of his debt, found one of his fellow servants. He caught him by the throat and demanded money owed to him according to Matthew 18:28. When the servant begged and asked for patience, the demanding servant, "*...threw him into prison till he should pay the debt*" (Matthew 18:30). The king found out, called the servant he _forgave_, and said, "*Should you not also have had _compassion_ on your fellow servant, just as I had _pity_ on you?*" (Matthew 18:33). The king punished that wicked servant for his insolent behavior. Thus, Jesus said to Peter, "*So My heavenly Father also will do to you if each of you, from his heart, does not _forgive_ his brother his trespasses*" (Matthew 18:35). Only the negative attributes using spiritual warfare can confuse Jesus' straightforward answer. Do not be deceived.

Jesus further explained blasphemy against the Holy Spirit is an _unforgivable_ sin. The Biblical record documented that He said, "*...I say to you, every sin and blasphemy will be _forgiven_ men, but the blasphemy against the Spirit _will not_ be _forgiven_ men. Anyone who speaks a word against the Son of Man, it will be _forgiven_ him; but whoever speaks against* *the Holy Spirit, it will not be forgiven him, either in this age or in the age to come*" (Matthew 12:31-32). Mark also captured Jesus' important point more clearly. His account of Jesus' Word stated, "*Assuredly, I say to you, all sins will be forgiven the sons of men, and whatever blasphemies they may utter; but he who blasphemes against the Holy Spirit never has forgiveness, but is subject to eternal condemnation...*" (Mark 3:28-29). Even Luke documented Jesus' Word on this subject, "*And anyone who speaks a word against the Son of Man, it will be forgiven him; but to him who blasphemes against the Holy Spirit, it will not be forgiven*" (Luke 12:10). No matter how one wants to read these Scriptures, Jesus' Word remains clear and true. Unfortunately, the influence of the negative forces on the war campaign is leading people to spiritual death in this area. There are people influenced by the ancient negative attributes in religious communities worldwide that are blinding others with words of blasphemy against the Holy Spirit through their deception and behavior.

Jesus told the Pharisees and scribes (Luke 15:2) a parable about a son who took his inheritance and left his father only to squander it as documented in Luke 15:11-32. In this parable, Jesus illustrated the influence of the **merciful** attribute in the life of a father, while at the same time, illustrating the power of the element of compassion. After the son squandered his inheritance, it did not take him long to join the ranks of those in the poor category. The Bible documented, "*...he would gladly have filled his stomach with the pods that the swine ate, and no one gave him anything*" (Luke 15:16). When he came to his senses, the Bible documented "*...he arose and came to his father. But when he was still a great way off, his father saw him and had compassion, and ran and fell on his neck and kissed him*" (Luke 15:20). Like this father and son, God rejoices when and errant person repents and returns to His Truth. This same teaching applies to one who leaves the positive side of the war campaign; leaving puts them on the side of the vast number of the negative forces. There is no middle ground. If this person comes to his or her senses and returns to the positive forces, great rejoicing occurs with the Lord and all His people. One reduction in the negative force's numbers is a cause for rejoicing.

As Jesus taught about the influence of the **merciful** attribute and the elements of forgiveness, kindness, and compassion, He demonstrated **merciful** behavior to His disciples and all the people who believed and listened to Him. Some examples include:

Examples	**What Is Documented**
A Paralytic Man	On a paralytic man: The Biblical record documented He saw the faith of the men who brought the paralytic to Him, "*...He said to the paralytic, "Son, be of good cheer; your sins are forgiven you*" (Matthew 9:1-2; Mark 2:5; Luke 5:20)
	Jesus told the scribes who said within themselves, "*This Man blasphemes!*" (Matthew 9:3; Mark 2:7; Luke 5:21), "*For which is easier, to say, 'Your sins are forgiven you,' or to say, 'Arise and walk'? But that you may know that the Son of Man has power on earth to forgive sins*"—then He said to the paralytic, "*Arise, take up your bed, and go to your house*" (Matthew 9:5-6; Mark 2:9-10; Luke 5:23-24)
Two blind men	The Biblical records documents, "*When Jesus departed from there, two blind men followed Him, crying out and saying, "Son of David, have **mercy** on us!*" (Matthew 9:27). Because of the **merciful** attribute, He does.
	The Biblical record documented that He, "*...went about all the cities and villages, teaching in their synagogues, preaching the gospel of the kingdom,*

To the multitudes	*and healing every sickness and every disease among the people. But when He saw the multitudes, He was moved with <u>compassion</u> for them, because they were weary and scattered, like sheep having no shepherd"* (Matthew 9:35-36)
	"And when Jesus went out He saw a great multitude; and He was moved with <u>compassion</u> for them, and healed their sick" (Matthew 14:14)
A mother with a possessed child	The Biblical records documents, *"And behold, a woman of Canaan came from that region and cried out to Him, saying, "Have **mercy** on me, O Lord, Son of David! My daughter is severely demon-possessed"* (Matthew 15:22). Because of the **merciful** attribute, He demonstrates His mercy to the woman and her daughter.
4000 people feed	*"Now Jesus called His disciples to Himself and said, "I have <u>compassion</u> on the multitude, because they have now continued with Me three days and have nothing to eat. And I do not want to send them away hungry, lest they faint on the way.""* (Matthew 15:32; Mark 8:2; 9)
A man with an epileptic son	The Biblical records documents the man pleading, *"Lord, have **mercy** on my son, for he is an epileptic and suffers severely; for he often falls into the fire and often into the water"* (Matthew 17:15). Because of the **merciful** attribute, He demonstrates His **mercy** to the man and his son.
Two blind men siting by the road	The Biblical records documents, *"And behold, two blind men sitting by the road, when they heard that Jesus was passing by, cried out, saying, "Have **mercy** on us, O Lord, Son of David!" Then the multitude warned them that they should be quiet; but they cried out all the more, saying, "Have **mercy** on us, O Lord, Son of David!"* (Matthew 20:30-31; Mark 10:47-48; Luke 18:38-39). The Gospel of Mark tells us that one of the men was named Bartimaeus (Mark 10:46). Thus, *"…Jesus had <u>compassion</u> and touched their eyes. And immediately their eyes received sight, and they followed Him"* (Matthew 20:34)
A leper kneeling to Him	*"…Jesus, moved with <u>compassion</u>, stretched out His hand and touched him, and said to him, "I am willing; be cleansed"* (Mark 1:41)
A demon-possessed man	He was healed and wanted to travel with Jesus, but the Biblical record documented, *"…Jesus did not permit him, but said to him, "Go home to your friends, and tell them what great things the Lord has done for you, and how He has had <u>compassion</u> on you."* (Mark 5:19)
A woman with a blood disease	The Bible documented that Jesus said to her, *"Daughter, your faith has made you well. Go in peace, and be healed of your affliction"* (Mark 5:34)
5000 people	The Biblical record documented that Jesus *"…when He came out, saw a great multitude and was moved with <u>compassion</u> for them, because they were like sheep not having a shepherd. So He began to teach them many things"* (Mark 6:34; 44)
A demon-possessed boy	A father brought his son to Jesus for healing. He told Jesus, *"…often he has thrown him both into the fire and into the water to destroy him. But if You can do anything, have <u>compassion</u> on us and help us"* (Mark 9:22). Jesus healed the son.
A widow's son	A widow brought her dead son to Jesus and the Bible documented, *"When the Lord saw her, He had <u>compassion</u> on her and said to her, "Do not weep.""*

	(Luke 7:13). Jesus healed her son and the Bible recorded, "*So he who was dead sat up and began to speak. And He presented him to his mother*" (Luke 7:15)
A Sinful Woman	Jesus was invited to a Pharisees home to eat (Luke 7:36). A woman there looked after Jesus. Jesus told the Pharisee, "*Therefore I say to you, her sins, which are many, are forgiven, for she loved much. But to whom little is forgiven, the same loves little. Then He said to her, "Your sins are forgiven." And those who sat at the table with Him began to say to themselves, "Who is this who even forgives sins?*" (Luke 7:47-49)
A certain Samaritan	After a priest and a Levite passed by a wounded man on the side of the road who was a victim of thieves according to Luke 10:30-32, Jesus said, "*…a certain Samaritan, as he journeyed, came where he was. And when he saw him, he had compassion*" (Luke 10:33)
Ten lepers	As Jesus passed through Samaria and Galilee, in a small village ten men stood far off. The Biblical records documents, "*And they lifted up their voices and said, "Jesus, Master, have **mercy** on us!*" (Luke 17:13). Because of the **merciful** attribute, Jesus heals all ten but only one comes back to thank Him
Those who murdered Jesus	"Then Jesus said, "*Father, forgive them, for they do not know what they do." And they divided His garments and cast lots*" (Luke 23:34)

Table 76: Jesus' Examples of the Influence of the Merciful Attribute and the Elements of _Forgiveness_, _Kindness_, and _Compassion_

Before Jesus left the earth, He had taught His disciples the primary wisdom they needed to know until the Holy Spirit came and empowered them. Their empowerment came on the Day of Pentecost as documented in Acts 2:1-4. From that day forward, the disciples, now called apostles, began teaching the Truth from the Gospel of Jesus Christ to the world. This included the things that they understood about the influence of the **merciful** attribute and the elements of _kindness_, _compassion_, and _forgiveness_. Jesus empowered Paul with the same knowledge as His other apostles when Paul converted from Judaism to Christianity through his baptism into Christ. Once baptized, Paul preached and taught the exact same doctrine Christ taught the other apostles. Do not let anyone deceive you on this fact. Paul's preaching was consistent with the other apostles. They all shared the same Spirit and positive attributes.

All the apostles taught that the Lord gave Jesus the authority to _forgive_ sin, which was necessary to reach heaven in a pure state. _Forgiveness_ of sin demonstrated God's **mercy** toward man. The concept is far above man's comprehension. But Biblically, the act of _forgiveness_ refreshes man's inner spirit and soul. The following are some key Scriptures surrounding this truth.

- Peter and the other apostles declared, "*The God of our fathers raised up Jesus whom you murdered by hanging on a tree. Him God has exalted to His right hand to be Prince and Savior, to give repentance to Israel and forgiveness of sins*" (Acts 5:30-31)

- Paul stated, "*Therefore let it be known to you, brethren, that through this Man is preached to you the forgiveness of sins; and by Him everyone who believes is justified from all things from which you could not be justified by the law of Moses*" (Acts 13:38-39)

- Jesus appeared to Paul for him to believe, be baptized, and preach Jesus to the people to, "*to open their eyes, in order to turn them from darkness to light, and from the power of Satan to God, that they may receive <u>forgiveness</u> of sins and an inheritance among those who are sanctified by faith in Me*" (Acts 26:18)

- Paul wrote, "*In Him we have redemption through His blood, the <u>forgiveness</u> of sins, according to the riches of His grace…*" (Ephesians 1:7)

- Paul documented, "*He has delivered us from the power of darkness and conveyed us into the kingdom of the Son of His love, in whom we have redemption through His blood, the <u>forgiveness</u> of sins*" (Colossians 1:13-14)

- Paul also documented, "*And you, being dead in your trespasses and the uncircumcision of your flesh, He has made alive together with Him, having <u>forgiven</u> you all trespasses…*" (Colossians 2:13)

Paul also documented for one's learning that not every person would have the same measure of influence from the **merciful** attribute. Regardless of the measure one receives, one must display that measure with cheerfulness. Paul wrote to the members of the early church in Rome documented in Romans 12:1-8,

> "*For I say, through the grace given to me, to everyone who is among you, not to think of himself more highly than he ought to think, but to think soberly, as God has dealt to each one a measure of faith. For as we have many members in one body, but all the members do not have the same function, so we, being many, are one body in Christ, and individually members of one another. Having then gifts differing according to the grace that is given to us, let us use them: if prophecy, let us prophesy in proportion to our faith; or ministry, let us use it in our ministering; he who teaches, in teaching; he who exhorts, in exhortation; he who gives, with liberality; he who leads, with diligence; he who shows* **mercy**, *with cheerfulness*"

During the time of the apostles, the teaching of the Gospel rapidly spread throughout the world. People far and wide heard the teachings about the influence of the **merciful** attribute along with teaching on the elements of <u>forgiveness</u>, <u>kindness</u>, and <u>compassion</u>. Two quick examples include:

Lydia	The Biblical record documented she demonstrated <u>kindness</u> to Paul and others travelling with him. The Bible recorded, "*And when she and her household were baptized, she begged us, saying, "If you have judged me to be faithful to the Lord, come to my house and stay." So she persuaded us*" (Acts 16:15)
The natives of Malta	Paul documented when they were shipwrecked in Malta, "*…the natives showed us unusual <u>kindness</u>; for they kindled a fire and made us all welcome, because of the rain that was falling and because of the cold*" (Acts 28:2)

Table 77: Some Examples of People who Demonstrated the Element of <u>Kindness</u>

In closing, here are some final pearls of wisdom from the apostles concerning the influence of the **merciful** attribute, and the elements of _forgiveness_, _kindness_, and _compassion_ for one's application. The Bible documented:

"*If we confess our sins, He is faithful and just to forgive us our sins and to cleanse us from all unrighteousness*" (1 John 1:9)	"*And the prayer of faith will save the sick, and the Lord will raise him up. And if he has committed sins, he will be forgiven*" (James 5:15)	"*Judge not, and you shall not be judged. Condemn not, and you shall not be condemned. Forgive, and you will be forgiven*" (Luke 6:37)
Jesus said, "*For if you forgive men their trespasses, your heavenly Father will also forgive you. But if you do not forgive men their trespasses, neither will your Father forgive your trespasses*" (Matthew 6:14-15)	"*Indeed we count them blessed who endure. You have heard of the perseverance of Job and seen the end intended by the Lord—that the Lord is very compassionate and merciful*" (James 5:11)	"*Blessed are those whose lawless deeds are forgiven, and whose sins are covered...*" (Romans 4:7)
"*And on some have compassion, making a distinction; but others save with fear, pulling them out of the fire, hating even the garment defiled by the flesh*" (Jude 1:22-23)	"*So speak and so do as those who will be judged by the law of liberty. For judgment is without **mercy** to the one who has shown no **mercy**. **Mercy** triumphs over judgment*" (James 2:13)	"*Therefore, in all things He had to be made like His brethren, that He might be a **merciful** and faithful High Priest in things pertaining to God, to make propitiation for the sins of the people*" (Hebrews 2:17)
Paul wrote of himself, "*And I thank Christ Jesus our Lord who has enabled me, because He counted me faithful, putting me into the ministry, although I was formerly a blasphemer, a persecutor, and an insolent man; but I obtained **mercy** because I did it ignorantly in unbelief*" (1 Timothy 1:12-13)	"*Therefore, as the elect of God, holy and beloved, put on tender **mercies**, kindness, humility, meekness, longsuffering; bearing with one another, and forgiving one another, if anyone has a complaint against another; even as Christ forgave you, so you also must do*" (Colossians 3:12-13)	"*...all of you be of one mind, having compassion for one another; love as brothers, be tenderhearted, be courteous; not returning evil for evil or reviling for reviling, but on the contrary blessing, knowing that you were called to this, that you may inherit a blessing*" (1 Peter 3:8-9)
"*But when the kindness and the love of God our Savior toward man appeared, not by works of righteousness which we have done, but according to His mercy He saved us, through the washing of regeneration and renewing of the Holy Spirit...*" (Titus 3:4-5)	"*And whenever you stand praying, if you have anything against anyone, forgive him, that your Father in heaven may also forgive you your trespasses. But if you do not forgive, neither will your Father in heaven forgive your trespasses*" (Mark 11:25-26)	"*But the fruit of the Spirit is love, joy, peace, longsuffering, kindness, goodness, faithfulness, gentleness, self-control. Against such there is no law. And those who are Christ's have crucified the flesh with its passions and desires*" (Galatians 5:22-24)

"But the wisdom that is from above is first pure, then peaceable, gentle, willing to yield, full of **mercy** and good fruits, without partiality and without hypocrisy" (James 3:17). You see, God is thorough. Even His wisdom contains the **merciful** attribute and He will give this wisdom to everyone who asks Him according to James 1:5 (*If any of you lacks wisdom, let him ask of God, who gives to all liberally and without reproach, and it will be given to him*).	"...*giving all diligence, add to your faith virtue, to virtue knowledge, to knowledge self-control, to self-control perseverance, to perseverance godliness, to godliness brotherly <u>kindness</u>, and to brotherly <u>kindness</u> love. For if these things are yours and abound, you will be neither barren nor unfruitful in the knowledge of our Lord Jesus Christ. For he who lacks these things is shortsighted, even to blindness, and has forgotten that he was cleansed from his old sins*" (2 Peter 1:5-9)	"*Therefore if there is any consolation in Christ, if any comfort of love, if any fellowship of the Spirit, if any affection and **mercy**, fulfill my joy by being like-minded, having the same love, being of one accord, of one mind. Let nothing be done through selfish ambition or conceit, but in lowliness of mind let each esteem others better than himself. Let each of you look out not only for his own interests, but also for the interests of others*" (Philippians 2:1)
Take heed to yourselves. If your brother sins against you, rebuke him; and if he repents, <u>forgive</u> him. And if he sins against you seven times in a day, and seven times in a day returns to you, saying, 'I repent,' you shall <u>forgive</u> him"" (Luke 17:3)	Paul also wrote of himself stating, "*This is a faithful saying and worthy of all acceptance, that Christ Jesus came into the world to save sinners, of whom I am chief. However, for this reason I obtained **mercy**, that in me first Jesus Christ might show all longsuffering, as a pattern to those who are going to believe on Him for everlasting life*" (1 Timothy 1:15-16)	

Table 78: More Pearls of Wisdom Concerning the Influence of the Merciful Attribute and the Elements of <u>**Forgiveness**</u>, <u>**Kindness**</u>, and <u>**Compassion**</u>

I specifically saved a point for the end of this section. The Biblical record documents of God, "*You have a mighty arm; strong is Your hand, and high is Your right hand. Righteousness and justice are the foundation of Your throne; **mercy** and truth go before Your face. Blessed are the people who know the joyful sound! They walk, O Lord, in the light of Your countenance*" (Psalms 89:13-15). To survive spiritual warfare, one must acquire <u>*discernment*</u> and know the joyful sound of the influence of the **mercy** attribute and Truth.

The **Just attribute**: The influence of this attribute leads one to look upon God's creations and treat everyone and everything with fairness, equity, impartiality, and respect. The influence of the *just* attribute causes one to be morally strong in all of one's behavior, actions, and words, and to stand against all forms of bigotry, prejudice, and hatred. In fact, one influenced by this attribute abhors these three things. This  attribute's influence is consistent and does not change because of circumstances, situations, or the status of people involved. Based on obedience to God's Word, people influenced by this attribute do what is right. Equity and *justice*, without regard for race, gender, or personal belief, are the foundation of this attribute's existence. This attribute and the element of *justice* are inexplicably connected. BTT allows one to see that anyone with a measure of the positive attributes can acquire this attribute. For without the influence of this attribute, abuse of authority occurs. The abuse of *justice* is a clear indication that the influence of the ***just*** attribute is not present. However, God, the ultimate Judge, will have the last word. Hence, just because one displays an earthly title of "judge" does not mean that person is influenced by the ***just*** attribute. No! Just like the ratio of positive to negative attributes, so are there proportionate numbers of earthly judges in the positive and negative forces of the war campaign. Moreover, like the merciful attribute, one must understand this important point about the ***just*** attribute. Having this attribute is great on the spiritual battlefield. However, to get one's soul into heaven from this side of life requires more than just this attribute alone. One must have the righteous attribute; the sum of all the positive attributes combined and God's grace, to gain an entrance into heaven. This point will become clear by the end of this Chapter.

The Spirit of wisdom revealed to Solomon, "*that the path of the **just** is like the shining sun, that shines ever brighter unto the perfect day*" (Proverbs 4:18). Thus, people influenced by the ***just*** attribute walk on a path that sheds light to a world living in darkness. Solomon wrote, "*It is a joy for the **just** to do justice...*" (Proverbs 21:15). The influence of the ***just*** attribute allows one to see that it is a blessing to extend the element of *justice* to others and to execute fully their role in being ***just.*** True leaders understand this. They know the ramifications of their actions and decisions on others – both the good and the evil. You see, the Spirit of wisdom explained to Solomon that, "*To do righteousness and justice is more acceptable to the Lord than sacrifice*" (Proverbs 21:3).

The influence of the ***just*** attribute causes one to expand one's knowledge. Solomon documented, "*Give instruction to a wise man, and he will be still wiser; teach a **just** man, and he will increase in learning*" (Proverbs 9:9). There is no limit to what one influenced by the ***just*** attribute can learn, do, or provide to others when one continues on the right path. However, throughout history, there have been many people influenced by the negative attributes, who seek to stop the education of those influenced by the ***just*** attribute. The ancient negative forces know that knowledge is powerful. They understand that one influenced by the ***just*** attribute who increases in the knowledge of God's Word, can become a disruptive force to their capabilities in spiritual warfare. Therefore, anyone influenced by the negative attributes who throw their weight against people with the ***just*** attribute are an *abomination* to the Lord. In fact, the Spirit of wisdom informed Solomon that, "*He who **justifies** the wicked, and he who condemns the **just**, both of them alike are an abomination to the LORD*" (Proverbs 17:15). To be in a state of abomination with the creator of the universe is no small matter. Further, Solomon documented, *"Evil men do not understand justice, but those who seek the Lord understand all"* (Proverbs 28:5). I pray for all who allow the influences of the negative attributes to place them in this position. For one must understand that, *"The curse of the Lord is on the house of the wicked, but He blesses the home of the **just**"* (Proverbs 3:33).

BTT allows one to see that the element of *justice* will always be incorporated in the outcome of one's decisions, actions, and efforts when one has the influence of the ***just*** attribute. The relationship between the ***just*** attribute and *justice* are inseparable. In fact, one of the very reasons Solomon documented the proverbs was for one to understand *justice* and by default, gain the influence of the ***just*** attribute. The Biblical record documented, *"The proverbs of Solomon the son of David, king of Israel: To know wisdom and instruction, to perceive the words of understanding, to receive the instruction of wisdom, justice, judgment, and equity; to give prudence to the simple, to the young man knowledge and discretion—A wise man will hear and increase learning, and a man of understanding will attain wise counsel, to understand a proverb and an enigma, the words of the wise and their riddles"* (Proverbs 1:1-6). Thus, the Spirit of wisdom revealed several pearls of wisdom to Solomon that correlate this relationship:

"The violence of the wicked will destroy them, because they refuse to do justice" (Proverbs 21:7)	*"A wicked man accepts a bribe behind the back to pervert the ways of justice"* (Proverbs 17:23)	*"Better is a little with righteousness, than vast revenues without justice"* (Proverbs 16:8)
Wisdom's said, *"By me kings reign, and rulers decree justice"* (Proverbs 8:15)	*"The king establishes the land by justice, but he who receives bribes overthrows it"* (Proverbs 29:4)	*"Many seek the ruler's favor, but justice for man comes from the Lord"* (Proverbs 29:26)
"It is not for kings, O Lemuel, it is not for kings to drink wine, nor for princes intoxicating drink; lest they drink and forget the law, and pervert the justice of all the afflicted" (Proverbs 31:4-5)	The Spirit of wisdom *"...traverse the way of righteousness, in the midst of the paths of justice, that I may cause those who love me to inherit wealth, that I may fill their treasuries"* (Proverbs 8:20-21)	*"He [God] guards the paths of justice, and preserves the way of His saints. Then you will understand righteousness and justice, equity and every good path"* (Proverbs 2:8-9)
"Much food is in the fallow ground of the poor, and for lack of justice there is waste" (Proverbs 13:23)	*"A disreputable witness scorns justice, and the mouth of the wicked devours iniquity"* (Proverbs 19:28)	*"Dishonest scales are an abomination to the Lord, but a **just** weight is His delight"* (Proverbs 11:1)

Table 79: Some Pearls of Wisdom Concerning the Influence of the Just Attribute

The Old Testament of the Biblical record documented many examples of people influenced by the ***just*** attribute. Some of the more familiar people include:

Examples	What Is Documented
Noah	*"This is the genealogy of Noah. Noah was a **just** man, perfect in his generations. Noah walked with God"* (Genesis 6:9)

Abraham	*"And the Lord said, "Shall I hide from Abraham what I am doing, since Abraham shall surely become a great and mighty nation, and all the nations of the earth shall be blessed in him? For I have known him, in order that he may command his children and his household after him, that they keep the way of the Lord, to do righteousness and <u>justice</u>, that the Lord may bring to Abraham what He has spoken to him"* (Genesis 18:17-19)
David	*"So David reigned over all Israel; and David administered judgment and <u>justice</u> to all his people"* (2 Samuel 8:15; 1 Chronicles 18:14)
Solomon	*"...all Israel heard of the judgment which the king had rendered; and they feared the king, for they saw that the wisdom of God was in him to administer <u>justice</u>"* (1 Kings 3:28)
Solomon	The Queen of Sheba recognized the influence of the **just** attribute in Solomon. She said, *"Blessed be the Lord your God, who delighted in you, setting you on the throne of Israel! Because the Lord has loved Israel forever, therefore He made you king, to do <u>justice</u> and righteousness."* (1 Kings 10:9; 2 Chronicles 9:8)
Job	The Biblical record documented, *"There was a man in the land of Uz, whose name was Job; and that man was blameless and upright, and one who feared God and shunned evil"* (Job 1:1)

Table 80: A Few Examples of People Who Allowed the Influence of the Just Attribute

Further, in the Biblical record, the Lord told the children of Israel through Moses that, *"You shall follow what is altogether **just**, that you may live and inherit the land which the Lord your God is giving you"* (Deuteronomy 16:20). The importance of this command cannot be overstated. The Lord desired for His people to attain and maintain the influence of the ***just*** attribute. The reason was simple; the children of Israel were going to a land filled with wickedness and their role was to cleanse and inherit it. BTT allows one to see that because God gave the children of Israel the command in Deuteronomy 16:20 to pursue the influence of the ***just*** attribute, it also meant that it was achievable. The children of Israel were to acquire and mature the influence of the ***just*** attribute to protect them from becoming like the people in the land they would inherit. Just as important, the Lord gave Moses clear commands for the children of Israel concerning the behavior necessary for retaining this **clean spirit**. Only by maintaining the behavior God specified, could one maintain the influence of the ***just*** attribute in his or her inner spirit. I personally like these commands because they established simple measures to identify inappropriate behaviors, which are still applicable today. Consider Table 81 below. Some of them clearly specify the ***just*** attribute while others simply state the behavior that marks the influence of the ***just*** attribute without using its name. Moses documented:

"You shall not circulate a false report. Do not put your hand with the wicked to be an unrighteous witness" (Exodus 23:1)	*"You shall not follow a crowd to do evil; nor shall you testify in a dispute so as to turn aside after many to pervert <u>justice</u>"* (Exodus 23:2)	*"You shall not show partiality to a poor man in his dispute"* (Exodus 23:3)
*"If you meet your enemy's ox or his donkey going	*"If you see the donkey of one who hates you lying under	*"You shall not pervert <u>justice</u> due the stranger or

astray, you shall surely bring it back to him again" (Exodus 23:4)	*its burden, and you would refrain from helping it, you shall surely help him with it"* (Exodus 23:5)	*the fatherless, nor take a widow's garment as a pledge"* (Deuteronomy 24:17)
"And you shall take no bribe, for a bribe blinds the <u>discerning</u> and perverts the words of the righteous" (Exodus 23:8)	*"…you shall not oppress a stranger, for you know the heart of a stranger, because you were strangers in the land of Egypt"* (Exodus 23:9)	*"Cursed is the one who perverts the <u>justice</u> due the stranger, the fatherless, and widow.' "And all the people shall say, 'Amen!'"* (Deuteronomy 27:19)
*"You shall have a perfect and **just** weight, a perfect and **just** measure, that your days may be lengthened in the land which the Lord your God is giving you"* (Deuteronomy 25:15)	*"You shall appoint judges and officers in all your gates, which the Lord your God gives you, according to your tribes, and they shall judge the people with **just** judgment"* (Deuteronomy 16:18)	*"You shall not pervert the judgment of your poor in his dispute. Keep yourself far from a false matter; do not kill the innocent and righteous. For I will not **justify** the wicked"* (Exodus 23:6-7)
"You shall not pervert <u>justice</u>; you shall not show partiality, nor take a bribe, for a bribe blinds the eyes of the wise and twists the words of the righteous" (Deuteronomy 16:19)	*"…if a man finds a betrothed young woman in the countryside, and the man forces her and lies with her, then only the man who lay with her shall die. But you shall do nothing to the young woman; there is in the young woman no sin deserving of death, for just as when a man rises against his neighbor and kills him, even so is this matter"* (Deuteronomy 22:25-26)	*"If there is a dispute between men, and they come to court, that the judges may judge them, and they **justify** the righteous and condemn the wicked, then it shall be, if the wicked man deserves to be beaten, that the judge will cause him to lie down and be beaten in his presence, according to his guilt, with a certain number of blows. Forty blows he may give him and no more, lest he should exceed this and beat him with many blows above these, and your brother be humiliated in your sight"* (Deuteronomy 25:1-3)

Table 81: God's Commands Concerning the Influence of the Just Attribute

The most important point of these pearls of wisdom is that Moses told the children of Israel, *"You shall follow what is altogether **just**…"* (Deuteronomy 16:20). This statement validates the simplicity of God's wisdom and His desire for His people to survive spiritual warfare.

The Biblical record documented examples of people in authority who lacked the influence of the ***just*** attribute and the issues that they caused. A prime example was Samuel's sons Joel and Abijah. These men were judges over Israel according to 1 Samuel 18:1. Samuel placed his sons in their positions and the Biblical record documented that they *"…did not walk* *in his* [Samuel] *ways; they turned aside after dishonest gain, took bribes, and perverted justice*" (1 Samuel 8:3). In fact, the inappropriate behavior of these two men as religious leaders and judges played a significant role in the children of Israel's demand for a king according to 1 Samuel 8:4. BTT allows one to see that Israel's demand – "*make us a king to judge us like all the nations*" (1 Samuel 8:5) – came from the negative force's use of spiritual warfare on the people. Why would I say this? Because the influences of the wicked attribute led the other nation's kings. This is why God had the nation of Israel subdue the people and take their lands. Go back and reread about the wicked attribute if one has forgotten this fact. To gain a king was a downgrade for Israel. Israel's best leadership came from judges appointed by God who allowed the influence of the **just** attribute.

A man named Absalom is another example of a person who lacked the influence of the **just** attribute. He desired to be in authority and masqueraded as if he had the influence of the **just** attribute. In reality, Absalom allowed the influence of the wicked and liar attributes. Absalom plotted to take the throne from David and lost his life for treason. BTT allows one to see the effect of the negative forces of the war campaign fighting the positive forces in this example. The Biblical record documented about Absalom, "*Now in all Israel there was no one who was praised as much as Absalom for his good looks. From the sole of his foot to the crown of his head there was no blemish in him. And when he cut the hair of his head—at the end of every year he cut it because it was heavy on him—when he cut it, he weighed the hair of his head at two hundred shekels according to the king's standard*" (2 Samuel 14:25-26). If the proud attribute does not immediately come to mind, then I have not done a good job writing this book. But let me continue. Verses 28-33 of 2 Samuel chapter 14 informs us how Absalom became upset because he had not seen the king in two years of living in Jerusalem. So, he had his servants burn his neighbor Joab's, field to get the king's attention. Then, the Biblical record tells us:

> "*After this it happened that Absalom provided himself with chariots and horses, and fifty men to run before him. Now Absalom would rise early and stand beside the way to the gate. So it was, whenever anyone who had a lawsuit came to the king for a decision, that Absalom would call to him and say, "What city are you from?" And he would say, "Your servant is from such and such a tribe of Israel." Then Absalom would say to him, "Look, your case is good and right; but there is no deputy of the king to hear you." Moreover Absalom would say, "Oh, that I were made judge in the land, and everyone who has any suit or cause would come to me; then I would give him justice." And so it was, whenever anyone came near to bow down to him, that he would put out his hand and take him and kiss him. In this manner Absalom acted toward all Israel who came to the king for judgment. So Absalom stole the hearts of the men of Israel*"

Now one should see a lot of things wrong here. Even the practice of bowing down and kissing Absalom's hand is reflected in our society today. However, to make a long story short, Absalom attempted a coup and failed. His death was just as interesting as his life. At the end of the coup, Absalom attempted to escape on a donkey. According to the Biblical record, "*...The mule went under the thick boughs of a great terebinth tree, and his head caught in the* *terebinth; so he was left hanging between heaven and earth. And the mule which was under him went on*" (2 Samuel 18:9). Joab, one of David's servants, found Absalom and the Biblical record documented that, "*...he took three spears in his hand and thrust them through Absalom's heart, while he was still alive in the midst of the terebinth tree. And ten young men who bore Joab's armor surrounded Absalom, and struck and killed him*" (2 Samuel 18:14-15). As difficult as it is to comprehend, through the lens of spiritual warfare, Absalom received justice for his wicked behavior against a righteous man. God had placed King David in his leadership position. The negative forces, using spiritual warfare, influenced Absalom's actions against David because of his selfish desire for power. One should read the entire account as recorded in the scriptures to have a full appreciation of the fact that David allowed the influence of the ***just*** attribute and God protected his walk for his obedience to His word. When David was firmly established as king, he would go on to say, "*The God of Israel said, the Rock of Israel spoke to me: 'He who rules over men must be **just**, ruling in the fear of God*" (2 Samuel 23:3). This is a faithful saying that applies to this very day. David also prayed for people with the ***just*** attribute. He prayed, "*Oh, let the wickedness of the wicked come to an end, but establish the **just**; for the righteous God tests the hearts and minds*" (Psalm 7:9). Prayer is the weapon of choice for one influenced by the ***just*** attribute. This is why David prayed, "*Hear a **just** cause, O Lord, attend to my cry; give ear to my prayer which is not from deceitful lips*" (Psalm 17:1). One must understand that God protects one influenced by the ***just*** attribute, but one must seek the protection through prayer and obedience to God.

Another insight into the influence of the ***just*** attribute is documented in the Book of Job. This Biblical record documented spiritual warfare and the ***just*** attribute unlike any other Book in the Bible. In this portion of the Biblical record, Job allowed the influence of the ***just*** attribute but was attacked by three of his wise friends, plus one young understudy. All these attackers lacked the influence of the ***just*** attribute. Job 1: 9-10 documented that Satan desired Job and he used Job's wise friends as tormenters. These men became Satan's assailants and tried to convince Job that he did not have the ***just*** attribute nor any other positive attribute, for that matter.

One cannot gain an appreciation for the Book of Job, nor the depth of information it provides on the war campaign, in a single soundbite. The discourse between Job and his friends is complicated. However, for Job's part of the discourse, the influence of the ***just*** attribute in his life is easily recognized. To begin with, Eliphaz, Bildad, and Zophar primarily focused on trying to convince Job that he was unrighteous and wicked. From this position, they argued that he could not have the influence of the ***just*** attribute. Eliphaz argued that God was chastening him for wrongdoing to which Job responded, "*Yield now, let there be no injustice! Yes, concede, my righteousness still stands! Is there injustice on my tongue? Cannot my taste discern the unsavory?*" (Job 6:29-30). Bildad, at the same time argued "*Does God subvert judgment? Or does the Almighty pervert justice?*" (Job 8:3). He tried to get Job to see that all the things that had happened to him were because God was taking a ***just*** stand against him, and if this were the case, Job's position was **unjust.** This wrangling of words demonstrated one of the classic strategies of spiritual warfare used by the negative forces of the war campaign. Eliphaz, Bildad, and Zophar made no headway in convincing Job that he was in sin. This angered Elihu, the understudy, which gave Satan a foothold to launch a more ferocious verbal assault on Job to break Job's inner spirit. The Biblical record documented that, "...*the <u>wrath</u> of Elihu, the son of Barachel the Buzite, of the family of Ram, was aroused against Job; his <u>wrath</u> was aroused because he **justified** himself rather than God*" (Job 32:2). One can see that Elihu's assault was completely godless; he was full of the negative attributes in his inner spirit and it showed in his comments to Job. Elihu launched a vicious verbal attack on Job while also chastising his elders - Eliphaz, Bildad, and Zophar – according to Job 32:3. Below are some of Elihu's comments. Keep in mind that Elihu's comments were designed to assault Job at the cognitive and spiritual level while disproving the ***just*** attribute influenced Job. Elihu argued:

- "*Great men are not always wise, nor do the aged always understand <u>justice</u>*" (Job 32:9)

- "*If you have anything to say, answer me; speak, for I desire to **justify** you*" (Job 33:32)

- "*Hear my words, you wise men; give ear to me, you who have knowledge. For the ear tests words as the palate tastes food. Let us choose <u>justice</u> for ourselves; let us know among ourselves what is good. "For Job has said, 'I am righteous, but God has taken away my <u>justice</u>...*" (Job 34:1-5)

- "*Surely God will never do wickedly, nor will the Almighty pervert <u>justice</u>*" (Job 34:12)

- "*If you have understanding, hear this; listen to the sound of my words: Should one who hates <u>justice</u> govern? Will you condemn Him who is most **just**?*" (Job 34:16-17)

- "*Surely God will not listen to empty talk, nor will the Almighty regard it. Although you say you do not see Him, yet <u>justice</u> is before Him, and you must wait for Him. And now, because He has not punished in His anger, nor taken much notice of folly, therefore Job opens his mouth in vain; he multiplies words without knowledge*" (Job 35:13-16)

- "*Behold, God is mighty, but despises no one; He is mighty in strength of understanding. He does not preserve the life of the wicked, but gives <u>justice</u> to the oppressed*" (Job 36:5-6)

- "*But you are filled with the judgment due the wicked; judgment and <u>justice</u> take hold of you*" (Job 36:17)

- "*As for the Almighty, we cannot find Him; He is excellent in power, in judgment and abundant <u>justice</u>; He does not oppress. Therefore men fear Him; He shows no partiality to any who are wise of heart*" (Job 37:23-24)

Elihu's comments were disrespectful to both Job and his wise friends alike. Elihu used the spiritual warfare strategy of confusion by mixing some truths about God and <u>justice</u> to call Job unjust. This same strategy is employed today by the wicked to fight the ***just***. To achieve their objective, no one on the positive forces side is safe. However, when one stays true to God, He will fight the battles and vindicate His people in the end. Thus, after all that Job endured, the Lord spoke directly to him. In Chapters 38 through 42 of the Book of Job, the Bible documents the amazing and inspiring Word of God. The Lord then addressed Eliphaz in Job 42:7, who passed God's message to Bildad and Zophar. God ignored Elihu. However, all their fates rested on Job shoulders. For the Lord instructed Job's tormentors to "...*take for yourselves seven bulls and seven rams, go to My servant Job, and offer up for yourselves a burnt offering; and My servant Job shall pray for you. For I will accept him, lest I deal with you according to your folly; because you have not spoken of Me what is right, as My servant Job has*" (Job 42:8). BTT allows one to see that the influence of the ***just*** attribute will help one to stand strong in God's Word through the battles of the war campaign.

The Psalmist and Solomon documented a few more pearls of wisdom about the influence of the ***just*** attribute. For our learning, they wrote:

David declared, "*I know that the Lord will maintain the cause of the afflicted, and justice for the poor*" (Psalm 140:12)	"*The King's strength also loves justice; You have established equity; You have executed justice and righteousness in Jacob*" (Psalm 99:4)	"*Blessed are those who keep justice, and he who does righteousness at all times!*" (Psalm 106:3)
"*The humble He guides in justice, and the humble He teaches His way*" (Psalm 25:9)	"*The wicked plots against the **just**, and gnashes at him with his teeth*" (Psalm 37:12)	"*The mouth of the righteous speaks wisdom, and his tongue talks of justice*" (Psalm 37:30)
"*If you see the oppression of the poor, and the violent perversion of justice and righteousness in a province, do not marvel at the matter; for high official watches over high official, and higher officials are over them*" (Ecclesiastes 5:8)	"*Wisdom strengthens the wise more than ten rulers of the city. For there is not a **just** man on earth who does good and does not sin*" (Ecclesiastes 7:19-20)	"*Lord, You have heard the desire of the humble; You will prepare their heart; You will cause Your ear to hear, to do justice to the fatherless and the oppressed, that the man of the earth may oppress no more*" (Psalm 10:17-18)
"*There is a vanity which occurs on earth, that there are **just** men to whom it happens according to the work of the wicked; again, there are wicked men to whom it happens according to the work of the righteous. I said that this also is vanity*" (Ecclesiastes 8:14)	David prayed, "*Oh, let the wickedness of the wicked come to an end, but establish the **just**; for the righteous God tests the hearts and minds*" (Psalm 7:9)	
"*I have seen everything in my days of vanity: There is a **just** man who perishes in his righteousness, and there is a wicked man who prolongs life in his wickedness. Do not be overly righteous, nor be*	"*Happy is he who has the God of Jacob for his help, whose hope is in the Lord his God, Who made heaven and earth, the sea, and all that is in them; Who keeps truth forever, Who executes justice for the oppressed,*	"*God stands in the congregation of the mighty; He judges among the gods. How long will you judge **unjustly**, and show partiality to the wicked? Defend the poor and fatherless; do justice to the*

overly wise: Why should you destroy yourself? Do not be overly wicked, nor be foolish: Why should you die before your time? It is good that you grasp this, and also not remove your hand from the other; for he who fears God will escape them all" (Ecclesiastes 7:15-18)	Who gives food to the hungry. The Lord gives freedom to the prisoners" (Psalm 146:5-7)	afflicted and needy. Deliver the poor and needy; free them from the hand of the wicked" (Psalm 82:1-4)

Table 82: Some of the Pearls of Wisdom Concerning the Influence of the Just Attribute

As the children of Israel became their own nation, the influence of the *just* attribute was lost in spiritual warfare. Although the influence of the *just* attribute was critical for maintaining a fair, legal, and impartial judicial system, Israel's religious leaders stopped teaching about it and the people pursued their own legal means. Israel discarded this attribute's influence. The collapse of the judicial system opened the door to the vilest behaviors manifested by the negative attributes. The negative forces of the war campaign gained a foothold in the inner spirits of Israel's religious and nonreligious leaders and the people in general. Thus, God sent His prophets to call for repentance. The biblical record documented:

The Prophet	What Was Said
Isaiah	"Wash yourselves, make yourselves clean; Put away the evil of your doings from before My eyes. Cease to do evil. Learn to do good; seek <u>justice</u>, rebuke the oppressor; defend the fatherless, plead for the widow" (Isaiah 1:16-17)
	"How the faithful city has become a harlot! It was full of <u>justice</u>; righteousness lodged in it, but now murderers" (Isaiah 1:21)
	If the nation of Israel were to repent, Isaiah said from the Lord, "*I will restore your judges as at the first, and your counselors as at the beginning. Afterward you shall be called the city of righteousness, the faithful city. Zion shall be redeemed with <u>justice</u>, and her penitents with righteousness. The destruction of transgressors and of sinners shall be together, and those who forsake the Lord shall be consumed*" (Isaiah 1:26-28)
	"For the vineyard of the Lord of hosts is the house of Israel, and the men of Judah are His pleasant plant. He looked for <u>justice</u>, but behold, oppression; for righteousness, but behold, a cry for help" (Isaiah 5:7)
	"…In fact, in the day of your fast you find pleasure, and exploit all your laborers. No one calls for <u>justice</u>, nor does any plead for truth. They trust in empty words and speak lies; they conceive evil and bring forth iniquity" (Isaiah 58:3-4)
Jeremiah	"Run to and fro through the streets of Jerusalem; see now and know; and seek in her open places if you can find a man, if there is anyone who executes <u>judgment</u>, who seeks the truth, and I will pardon her" (Jeremiah 5:1)
Ezekiel	"Thus says the Lord God: "Enough, O princes of Israel! Remove violence and plundering, execute <u>justice</u> and righteousness, and stop dispossessing My people," says the Lord God" (Ezekiel 45:9). The Lord identified the corruption,

		cheating, and scandals that had so badly marred Israel's business practices in Ezekiel 45:10-17
Amos		"Seek the Lord and live, lest He break out like fire in the house of Joseph, and devour it, with no one to quench it in Bethel— you who turn <u>justice</u> to wormwood, and lay righteousness to rest in the earth!" (Amos 5:6-7)
		"Do horses run on rocks? Does one plow there with oxen? Yet you have turned <u>justice</u> into gall, and the fruit of righteousness into wormwood..." (Amos 6:12)
		"For I know your manifold transgressions and your mighty sins: afflicting the **just** and taking bribes; diverting the poor from <u>justice</u> at the gate" (Amos 5:12)
		"Hate evil, love good; establish <u>justice</u> in the gate. It may be that the Lord God of hosts will be gracious to the remnant of Joseph" (Amos 5:15)
		"Take away from Me the noise of your songs, for I will not hear the melody of your stringed instruments. But let <u>justice</u> run down like water, and righteousness like a mighty stream" (Amos 5:23-24)
Micah		"And I said: "Hear now, O heads of Jacob, and you rulers of the house of Israel: Is it not for you to know <u>justice</u>?" (Micah 3:1)
		"But truly I am full of power by the Spirit of the Lord, and of <u>justice</u> and might, to declare to Jacob his transgression and to Israel his sin. Now hear this, you heads of the house of Jacob and rulers of the house of Israel, who abhor <u>justice</u> and pervert all equity, who build up Zion with bloodshed and Jerusalem with iniquity: her heads judge for a bribe, her priests teach for pay, and her prophets divine for money. Yet they lean on the Lord, and say, "Is not the Lord among us? No harm can come upon us"" (Micah 3:8-11)
		"He has shown you, O man, what is good; and what does the Lord require of you but to do **justly**, to love mercy, and to walk humbly with your God?" (Micah 6:8)
Habakkuk		"O Lord, how long shall I cry, and You will not hear? Even cry out to You, "Violence!" And You will not save. Why do You show me iniquity, and cause me to see trouble? For plundering and violence are before me; there is strife, and contention arises. Therefore the law is powerless, and <u>justice</u> never goes forth. For the wicked surround the righteous; therefore perverse judgment proceeds" (Habakkuk 1:2-4)
		Well, the Lord answered Habakkuk's question. I encourage you to read His answer. One should pay close attention to the end of God's answer. Allow me to be a spoiler. God answered Habakkuk in Habakkuk 1:5-11. God made it clear that the problem was in the people themselves. He said because of the proud attribute, "*Then his mind changes, and he transgresses; he commits offense, ascribing this power to his god*" (Habakkuk 1:11)
		"Then the Lord answered me and said: "Write the vision and make it plain on tablets, that he may run who reads it. For the vision is yet for an appointed time; but at the end it will speak, and it will not lie. Though it tarries, wait for it; because it will surely come, it will not tarry. Behold the proud, his soul is not upright in him; but the **just** shall live by his faith" (Habakkuk 2:2-4)
		"Her prophets are insolent, treacherous people; her priests have polluted the sanctuary, they have done violence to the law. The Lord is righteous in her midst, He will do no unrighteousness. Every morning He brings His <u>justice</u> to light; He never fails, but the unjust knows no shame" (Zephaniah 3:4-5)
		"Thus says the Lord of hosts: 'Execute true <u>justice</u>, show mercy and compassion everyone to his brother. Do not oppress the widow or the fatherless, the alien

Zephaniah	or the poor. Let none of you plan evil in his heart against his brother. But they refused to heed, shrugged their shoulders, and stopped their ears so that they could not hear. Yes, they made their hearts like flint, refusing to hear the law and the words which the Lord of hosts had sent by His Spirit through the former prophets. Thus great wrath came from the Lord of hosts" (Zechariah 7:9-12)
	"These are the things you shall do: Speak each man the truth to his neighbor; give judgment in your gates for truth, *justice*, and peace; Let none of you think evil in your heart against your neighbor; and do not love a false oath. For all these are things that I hate,' says the Lord" (Zechariah 8:16-17)

Table 83: The Prophets' Warnings Concerning the Influence of the Just Attribute

One cannot read all the warnings concerning the influence of the ***just*** attribute and say that God did not give the nation of Israel a chance to repent. The negative forces of the war campaign found fertile ground in the inner spirits of Israel's leadership, its prophets, priest, and people. In fact, conditions were so bad that Isaiah documented these sad words in Isaiah 59:8-15:

"The way of peace they have not known, and there is no justice in their ways; they have made themselves crooked paths; whoever takes that way shall not know peace. Therefore justice is far from us, nor does righteousness overtake us; we look for light, but there is darkness! For brightness, but we walk in blackness! We grope for the wall like the blind, and we grope as if we had no eyes; we stumble at noonday as at twilight; we are as dead men in desolate places. We all growl like bears, and moan sadly like doves; we look for justice, but there is none; for salvation, but it is far from us. For our transgressions are multiplied before You, and our sins testify against us; for our transgressions are with us, and as for our iniquities, we know them: In transgressing and lying against the Lord, and departing from our God, speaking oppression and revolt, conceiving and uttering from the heart words of falsehood. Justice is turned back, and righteousness stands afar off; for truth is fallen in the street, and equity cannot enter. So truth fails, and he who departs from evil makes himself a prey. Then the Lord saw it, and it displeased Him that there was no justice."

In addition, explicit warnings had to be given to specific people like King Shallum for his role in hindering the influence of the ***just*** attribute by his wicked behavior. Jeremiah documented a specific "woe" to Shallum in Jeremiah 22:17 when he wrote from the Lord:

"Woe to him who builds his house by unrighteousness and his chambers by injustice, who uses his neighbor's service without wages and gives him nothing for his work, who says, 'I will build myself a wide house with spacious chambers, and cut out windows for it, paneling it with cedar and painting it with vermilion.' Shall you reign because you enclose yourself in cedar? Did not your father eat and drink, and do justice and righteousness?

> *Then it was well with him. He **judged** the cause of the poor and needy; then it was well. Was not this knowing Me?" says the Lord"* (Jeremiah 22:13-16)

King Shallum lacked the influence of the ***just*** attribute. We know this because Jeremiah points out that his ways were corrupt. The Lord, speaking through Jeremiah confronted Shallum by saying, *"Yet your eyes and your heart are for nothing but your covetousness, for shedding innocent blood, and practicing oppression and violence."* (Jeremiah 22:17). This was a practice of total injustice; a display of bad behavior from one who lacks the influence of the ***just*** attribute.

God gave the prophet Ezekiel the standard for one to claim the influence of the ***just*** attribute. Ezekiel documented that one is considered to have the ***just*** attribute's influence if they meet the standards found in Ezekiel 18:5-8:

- Does what is lawful and right
- Has not eaten on the mountains (temple worship on mountain tops)
- Has not lifted his eyes to the idols
- Has not defiled his neighbor's wife
- Has not approached a woman during her impurity
- Has not oppressed anyone, but has restored to the debtor his pledge
- Has not robbed anyone by violence
- Has given his bread to the hungry
- Has covered the naked with clothing
- Has not exacted usury (in the sense of *overcharging* and *extortion*)
- Has not taken any increase (in the sense of *illegal gain*)
- Has withdrawn his hand from iniquity
- Has executed true ***judgment*** between man and man

The opposite of anything on this list makes one unjust. Israel was engaged in unjust behavior. At the end of this list, Ezekiel concluded from the Lord that the maturing of the influence of the ***just*** attribute was contingent on one also acquiring the faithful attribute. Ezekiel documented, *"If he has walked in My statutes and kept My judgments faithfully— He is **just**; He shall surely live!" Says the Lord God"* (Ezekiel 18:9). Of course, the "My" in this passage is God. The prophet Habakkuk, on the other hand, simply documented from the Lord that, *"...the **just** shall live by his faith"* (Habakkuk 2:2-4). Habakkuk also documented some very strong "woes" that correlated to the requirements for the influence of the ***just*** attribute that Ezekiel documented from the Lord. Consider the behaviors below against the standards Ezekiel documented and see if the influence of the ***just*** attribute is not forthcoming in his writing. Habakkuk documented:

- *Woe to him who increases what is not his* (Habakkuk 2:6-8)

- *Woe to him who covets evil gain for his house that he may set his nest on high that he may be delivered from the power of disaster*! (Habakkuk 2:9-11)

- *Woe to him who builds a town with bloodshed, who establishes a city by iniquity*! (Habakkuk 2:12-14)

- *Woe to him who gives drink to his neighbor, pressing him to your bottle, even to make him drunk, that you may look on his nakedness!* (Habakkuk 2:15-17)

- *Woe to him who says to wood, 'Awake!' To silent stone, 'Arise! It shall teach!'* (Habakkuk 2:18-20)

Habakkuk told the nation of Israel that any of the behaviors practiced above indicates that one does not have the influence of the **just** attribute dwelling in his or her inner spirit. The items he documented only increase the negative force's boundaries in the war campaign. Thus, Habakkuk documented one of the simplest pearls of wisdom surrounding the influence of the **just** attribute. The Lord told him directly, "*Behold the proud, his soul is not upright in him; but the **just** shall live by his faith*" (Habakkuk 2:4).

Here are some final pearls of wisdoms from the Old Testament prophets that then and now, pertain to the influence of the **just** attribute.

"...*Woe to men valiant for mixing intoxicating drink, who **justify** the wicked for a bribe, and take away justice from the righteous man!* (Isaiah 5:22-23)	"...*the schemes of the schemer are evil; he devises wicked plans to destroy the poor with lying words, even when the needy speaks justice*" (Isaiah 32:7)	"*The way of the **just** is uprightness; O Most Upright, You weigh the path of the **just***" (Isaiah 26:7)
"*Woe to those who decree unrighteous decrees, who write misfortune, which they have prescribed to rob the needy of justice, and to take what is right from the poor of My people, that widows may be their prey, and that they may rob the fatherless*" (Isaiah 10:1-2)	"*Oh Lord, I know the way of man is not in himself; it is not in man who walks to direct his own steps. O Lord, correct me, but with justice; not in Your anger, lest You bring me to nothing*" (Jeremiah 10:23-24)	"*Seek the Lord, all you meek of the earth, who have upheld His justice. Seek righteousness, seek humility. It may be that you will be hidden in the day of the Lord's anger*" (Zephaniah 2:3)
"*You have wearied the Lord with your words; Yet you say, "In what way have we wearied Him?" In that you say, "Everyone who does evil is good in the sight of the Lord, and He delights in them," Or, "Where is the God of justice?*" (Malachi 2:17)		

Table 84: A Few More Pearls of Wisdom from the Prophets Concerning the Just Attribute

As one reviews the New Testament, one learns that the spirit of the **just** attribute plays a significant role in the operation of spiritual warfare. God sending His Son, Jesus Christ, was vital to the role of the **just** attribute at a time when most of the people in the world had lost their way. Now before one examines the New Testament for this wisdom pertaining to this attribute, one should know that the Old Testament documented important information concerning the correlation between Jesus and the ***just*** attribute. Here are some examples:

- The warning: *"Thus says the Lord: "Keep justice, and do righteousness, for My salvation is about to come, and My righteousness to be revealed"* (Isaiah 56:1)

- The birth of the Savior: *"For unto us a Child is born, unto us a Son is given; and the government will be upon His shoulder. And His name will be called Wonderful, Counselor, Mighty God, Everlasting Father, Prince of Peace. Of the increase of His government and peace there will be no end, upon the throne of David and over His kingdom, to order it and establish it with judgment and justice from that time forward, even forever. The zeal of the Lord of hosts will perform this"* (Isaiah 9:6-7)

- His entrance: *"Rejoice greatly, O daughter of Zion! Shout, O daughter of Jerusalem! Behold, your King is coming to you; He is **just** and having salvation, lowly and riding on a donkey, a colt, the foal of a donkey. I will cut off the chariot from Ephraim and the horse from Jerusalem; the battle bow shall be cut off. He shall speak peace to the nations; His dominion shall be 'from sea to sea, and from the River to the ends of the earth"* (Zechariah 9:9-10). [**Sadly, the Jewish leadership rejected Him**]

- His purpose: *"Therefore thus says the Lord God: "Behold, I lay in Zion a stone for a foundation, a tried stone, a precious cornerstone, a sure foundation; whoever believes will not act hastily. Also I will make justice the measuring line, and righteousness the plummet; the hail will sweep away the refuge of lies, and the waters will overflow the hiding place"* (Isaiah 28:16-17)

- His life on earth: *"Yet it pleased the Lord to bruise Him; He has put Him to grief. When You make His soul an offering for sin, He shall see His seed, He shall prolong His days, and the pleasure of the Lord shall prosper in His hand. He shall see the labor of His soul, and be satisfied. By His knowledge My righteous Servant shall **justify** many, for He shall bear their iniquities"* (Isaiah 53:10-11)

- His resurrection: *"In mercy the throne will be established; and One will sit on it in truth, in the tabernacle of David, judging and seeking justice and hastening righteousness"* (Isaiah 16:5)

- The day of Pentecost: *"Until the Spirit is poured upon us from on high, and the wilderness becomes a fruitful field, and the fruitful field is counted as a forest. Then justice will dwell in the wilderness, and righteousness remain in the fruitful field"* (Isaiah 32:15-16)

- His full purpose revealed: *"Behold! My Servant whom I uphold, My Elect One in whom My soul delights! I have put My Spirit upon Him; He will bring forth justice to the Gentiles. He will not cry out, nor raise His voice, nor cause His voice to be heard in the street. A bruised reed He will not break, and smoking flax He will not quench; He will bring forth justice for truth. He will not fail nor be discouraged, till He has established justice in the earth; and the coastlands shall wait for His law"* (Isaiah 42:1-4)

BTT allows one to understand that one of Jesus' personal missions when He came into the world was to reestablish the spirit of *justice* on earth with the Word of God. I do not want one to have the impression that the influence of the **just** attribute had fled the world. In fact, there were remnants of people among the Jewish nation and Gentiles who retained this attribute's influence and remained **just** in their behavior. Table 82 below identifies a few examples of people with the active influence of this attribute. The Bible documented:

Who	What Is Documented
Joseph, Mary's husband	*"Then Joseph her husband, being a **just** man, and not wanting to make her a public example, was minded to put her away secretly"* (Matthew 1:19)
John the Baptist	John preached against Herod's unlawful married to his brother's wife Herodias. The Biblical record says, *"Therefore Herodias held it against him and wanted to kill him, but she could not; for Herod feared John, knowing that he was a **just** and holy man, and he protected him. And when he heard him, he did many things, and heard him gladly"* (Mark 6:19-20)
Jesus	Pontius Pilate's wife came to understand that Jesus had this attribute. The Biblical record documented, *"While he was sitting on the judgment seat, his wife sent to him, saying, "Have nothing to do with that **just** Man, for I have suffered many things today in a dream because of Him"* (Matthew 27:19)
Jesus	*"When Pilate saw that he could not prevail at all, but rather that a tumult was rising, he took water and washed his hands before the multitude, saying, "I am innocent of the blood of this **just** Person. You see to it"* (Matthew 27:24)
Simeon	*"And behold, there was a man in Jerusalem whose name was Simeon, and this man was **just** and devout, waiting for the Consolation of Israel, and the Holy Spirit was upon him"* (Luke 2:25). Simeon documented, : *"Lord, now You are letting Your servant depart in peace, according to Your word; for my eyes have seen Your salvation which You have prepared before the face of all peoples, a light to bring revelation to the Gentiles, and the glory of Your people Israel"* (Luke 2:28-32)
Joseph of Arimathea	*"Now behold, there was a man named Joseph, a council member, a good and **just** man. He had not consented to their decision and deed. He was from Arimathea, a city of the Jews, who himself was also waiting for the kingdom of God. This man went to Pilate and asked for the body of Jesus"* (Luke 23:50-52)
Peter	He demonstrated this attribute with Cornelius. The Biblical record documented that Peter stated, *"... In truth I perceive that God shows no partiality. But in every nation whoever fears Him and works righteousness is accepted by Him"* (Act 10:34-35)
Cornelius	*"...Cornelius the centurion, a **just** man, one who fears God and has a good reputation among all the nation of the Jews, was divinely instructed by a holy angel to summon you to his house, and to hear words from you"* (Acts 10:22)
	*"You are witnesses, and God also, how devoutly and **justly** and blamelessly we behaved ourselves among you who believe; as you know*

| The apostles | *how we exhorted, and comforted, and charged every one of you, as a father does his own children, that you would walk worthy of God who calls you into His own kingdom and glory"* (1 Thessalonians 2:10-12) |

Table 85: Examples of People Who Allowed the Influence of the Just Attribute

Now the reason there are Gentile examples is because the Bible specifically stated, "*...(for not the hearers of the law are **just** in the sight of God, but the doers of the law will be justified; for when Gentiles, who do not have the law, by nature do the things in the law, these, although not having the law, are a law to themselves, who show the work of the law written in their hearts, their conscience also bearing witness, and between themselves their thoughts accusing or else excusing them) in the day when God will judge the secrets of men by Jesus Christ, according to my gospel*" (Romans 2:13-16).

As the New Testament era began to unfold, an angel of the Lord told John the Baptist's father, Zacharias, that he would have a son whose mission was to prepare the world for the coming of Jesus according to Luke 1:13-17. Within this context, the angel stated that John would, "*...go before Him* [Jesus] *in the spirit and power of Elijah, 'to turn the hearts of the fathers to the children,' and the disobedient to the wisdom of the **just**, to make ready a people prepared for the Lord*" (Luke 1:17). As one can see from the angel's statement, people with the ***just*** attribute would play an important role in the balance of the war campaign.

Thus, as Jesus began His ministry, He shared some poignant information about the relationship between God and the ***just*** attribute. First, He made it clear that God is in control of life itself. Because God Himself is ***Just;*** He "*...makes His sun rise on the evil and on the good, and sends rain on the **just** and on the unjust.*" (Matthew 5:45). God treats all humanity with justice. God also expects everyone, whether religious or secular, believer or nonbeliever, to do the same. Because God is ***just***, He gives everyone an opportunity to hear Him and make the choice to listen to His Word or ignore Him. However, with every choice comes responsibility, accountability, and consequences. When one cannot be ***just***, fair, or equal in one's treatment of another person, the Lord's expectation does not change. Thus, the one who engages in the negative behavior of being unjust can only expect harsh justice based on God's standard.

The wisdom in Jesus' Word is profound. He taught that one who receives blessings from God must help others who lack resources or have needs. In Jesus' eyes, this is ***just*** and expected of people who are influenced by the ***just*** attribute. This concept ensures opportunities for the fortunate to reach out to the less fortunate; even "sinners." Just think what would happen if one was led to follow Christ over a simple act of humility or gesture of kindness. This amplifies the idea behind Jesus' discussion over the lost sheep in Luke 15:4-6. Hence Jesus said, "*I say to you that likewise there will be more joy in heaven over one sinner who repents than over ninety-nine **just** persons who need no repentance*" (Luke 15:7). Yes, a person influenced by the ***just*** attribute is important, but so is the person in a state of sin that repents. A person who is influenced by the ***just*** attribute and striving to meet the standards of the attribute itself, already has a better chance of salvation than one who never knew God's Truth. BTT allows one to see that when one repents from sin, is baptized, and begins a journey on the right path, the angels rejoice. Why? Because a soul is saved, and the negative forces are decreased by one person in the war campaign. This is praiseworthy and worth every Christian's rejoicing.

Jesus provided more insight into the influence of the ***just*** attribute and its importance over the course of His ministry. Here are some more examples:

- When He called the Pharisees a "*Brood of vipers*". He told them "*...by your words you will be <u>justified</u>, and by your words you will be condemned*" (Matthew 12:34-37)

- When He compared heaven to a dragnet. He said "*...the kingdom of heaven is like a dragnet that was cast into the sea and gathered some of every kind, which, when it was full, they drew to shore; and they sat down and gathered the good into vessels, but threw the bad away. So it will be at the end of the age. The angels will come forth, separate the wicked from among the **just**, and cast them into the furnace of fire. There will be wailing and gnashing of teeth*" (Matthew 13:47-50)

- When He called the Pharisees and scribes hypocrites and blind guides. He told them that they, "*...pay tithe of mint and anise and cummin, and have neglected the weightier matters of the law: <u>justice</u> and mercy and faith. These you ought to have done, without leaving the others undone...*" (Matthew 23:23-24; Luke 11:42)

- When He corrected a lawyer in Luke 10:25-37 who "*...wanting to <u>justify</u> himself...*" (Luke 10:27-29)

- When He corrected the Pharisees after teaching that "*No servant can serve two master...*" in (Luke 16:13). The Biblical record documented, "*Now the Pharisees, who were lovers of money, also heard all these things, and they derided Him. And He said to them, "You are those who <u>justify</u> yourselves before men, but God knows your hearts. For what is highly esteemed among men is an abomination in the sight of God*" (Luke 16:14-15)

- When He gave some thoughts to consider for helping the poor, maimed, lame and blind people of the world. He told the people, instead of inviting friends, brothers, relatives or rich neighbors who can pay you back, consider inviting "*...the poor, the maimed, the lame, the blind. And you will be blessed, because they cannot repay you; for you shall be repaid at the resurrection of the **just***" (Luke 14:12-14)

For one to acquire the full measure of the ***just*** attribute, one must also have the faithful attribute. Pulling from the knowledge of the Old Testament, Paul reiterated that, "*...The **just** shall live by faith*" (Romans 1:17). As the Holy Spirit inspired him, Paul built on this statement by documenting that the Lord was involved in the union between the ***just*** and faithful attributes. He documented, "*Now the **just** shall live by faith; but if anyone draws back, My soul has no pleasure in him*" (Hebrews 10:38). Of course, the "*My*" of this passage is the Almighty God. Why would God's soul have no pleasure in one who draws back? It is simple. God gave His Son's life for the unjust. Peter documented this when he wrote, "*For Christ also suffered once for sins, the **just** for the unjust, that He might bring us to God, being put to death in the flesh but made alive by the Spirit...*" (1 Peter 3:18). However, also of importance is the fact that this scripture documents that both the ***just*** and faith attributes must work in unison if one desires to grow spiritually, defend one's self during spiritual warfare and to survive the war campaign. Some final pearls of wisdom concerning the influence of this attribute include:

Speaking of the Mosaic Law, Paul documented, *"But that no one is **justified** by the law in the sight of God is evident, for "the **just** shall live by faith"* (Galatians 3:11). In addition, Paul told them, *"...the law was our tutor to bring us to Christ, that we might be **justified** by faith"* (Galatians 3:24)	Paul said, *"For I am not ashamed of the gospel of Christ, for it is the power of God to salvation for everyone who believes, for the Jew first and also for the Greek. For in it the righteousness of God is revealed from faith to faith; as it is written, "The **just** shall live by faith"* (Romans 1:16-17)	*"For there is no partiality with God. For as many as have sinned without law will also perish without law, and as many as have sinned in the law will be judged by the law (for not the hearers of the law are **just** in the sight of God, but the doers of the law will be **justified**..."* (Romans 2:11-13)
Speaking of the Jews, Paul told Felix, *"...there will be a resurrection of the dead, both of the **just** and the unjust. This being so, I myself always strive to have a conscience without offense toward God and men"* (Acts 24:13-16)	God said, *"Now the **just** shall live by faith; but if anyone draws back, My soul has no pleasure in him"* (Hebrews 10:38)	Consider this Scripture from the standpoint of the employer to employee relationship. *Masters, give your bondservants what is **just** and fair, knowing that you also have a Master in heaven"* (Colossians 4:1)
Another name elders were called are bishops: *"...a bishop must be blameless, as a steward of God, not self-willed, not quick-tempered, not given to wine, not violent, not greedy for money, but hospitable, a lover of what is good, sober-minded, **just**, holy, self-controlled, holding fast the faithful word as he has been taught, that he may be able, by sound doctrine, both to exhort and convict those who contradict"* (Titus 1:7-9)	To keep one's mind focused on <u>godliness</u>, Paul wrote, *"Finally, brethren, whatever things are true, whatever things are noble, whatever things are **just**, whatever things are pure, whatever things are lovely, whatever things are of good report, if there is any virtue and if there is anything praiseworthy—meditate on these things. The things which you learned and received and heard and saw in me, these do, and the God of peace will be with you"* (Philippians 4:8-9)	For people in the rich category on the negative forces side, James documented: *"Indeed the wages of the laborers who mowed your fields, which you kept back by fraud, cry out; and the cries of the reapers have reached the ears of the Lord of Sabaoth [literally, in Hebrew, means Hosts]. You have lived on the earth in pleasure and luxury; you have fattened your hearts as in a day of slaughter. You have condemned, you have murdered the **just**; he does not resist you"* (James 5:5-6)

Table 86: Some Pearls of Wisdom Concerning the Just Attribute

These pearls of wisdom highlight the fact that God, who created the standard for the influence of the ***just*** attribute, will judge the world with <u>justice</u> and righteousness. On the Day of Judgement, one's spiritual condition will be either ***just*** or unjust. Only people who are influenced by the ***just*** attribute and the other positive attributes, will have a hope of salvation. The Psalmist documented of the Lord, *"Righteousness and <u>justice</u> are the foundation of Your* *throne; mercy and truth go before Your face. Blessed are the people who know the joyful sound! They walk, O Lord, in the light of Your countenance. In Your name they rejoice all day long, and in Your righteousness they are exalted"* (Psalm 89:14-16).

The **Upright/Honorable attribute**: This attribute influences one to live a life marked by the highest personal standards of honesty, integrity, and moral character. It influences one to respect God, His Son, and His Holy Word and to strive to live and walk in a *godly* manner. A *godly* manner is a wholesome life with high standards gleaned from examples found in the Biblical record, those identified by Jesus' Word, and positive examples set by parents, family members, and friend.  The element of *godliness* will be discussed later in this chapter. Further, the **upright/honorable** attribute gives one the moral courage to do what is right while facing adversity. Its influence leads one to reject mankind's philosophies of situational ethics, relativism, and socially engineered tolerance that strives to redefine God's Word or makes it obsolete. Learning about this attribute begins in the home from parents who teach respect for all authority. Hence, the Bible documents *"Children, obey your parents in the Lord, for this is right. "***Honor** *your father and mother," which is the first commandment with promise: "that it may be well with you and you may live long on the earth""* (Ephesians 6:1-3). As children learn to **honor** their own parents, they develop the morale courage necessary to stand up and combat the negative force's actions and destructive behaviors originating from spiritual warfare. Especially when these behaviors bring harm to another human being. Additionally, the ***upright/honorable*** attribute influences one to promote behaviors of fairness and impartiality without prejudice, malice, or deceit. BTT allows one to see that the Old Testament writers referred to this attribute mostly by the name "***upright***," while the New Testament writers primarily used the name "***honorable***." The two names synonymously identify the same positive spirit of the war campaign. BTT also allows one to see that just because people have the term "**honorable**" attached to their human title or wears a robe, does not mean that this positive attribute influences them. The negative forces of the war campaign and spiritual warfare have used this false tactic to cover up injustices worldwide. Do not be deceived. Moreover, like the last two attributes, one must understand this important point about the ***upright/honorable*** attribute. Having this attribute is great on the spiritual battlefield. However, to get one's soul into heaven from this side of life requires more than just this attribute alone. One must have the righteous attribute; the sum of all the positive attributes combined and God's grace, to gain an entrance into heaven. This point will become clear by the end of this Chapter.

The Spirit of wisdom revealed to Solomon that God loves this attribute. Solomon documented of God that, *"He stores up sound wisdom for the **upright**; He is a shield to those who walk **uprightly**"* (Proverbs 2:7). For one influenced by this attribute, God has wisdom ready and available for his or her use. However, one must still ask God for that wisdom, walk in a *godly* manner, and study His Word to acquire it. This is consistent with Solomon's request of God and the reference found in the New Testament that states specifically *"If any of you lacks wisdom, let him ask of God, who gives to all liberally and without reproach, and it will be given to him"* (James 1:5). Moreover, as one influenced by this attribute accesses the sound wisdom God stores up for him or her, God also provides a "*shield*" or protection according to Proverbs 2:7. This knowledge is significantly important in spiritual warfare. For the negative forces will always move against one influenced by the **upright/honorable** attribute. BTT allows one to see that God's shield is essential for one who has this attribute and has acquired wisdom from God. For the negative forces of the war campaign will rally to prevent one from espousing God's wisdom to the world. This statement is true because Solomon documented, "*...he who is **upright** in the way is an <u>abomination</u> to the wicked*" (Proverbs 29:27). The use of the word "abomination" in the text is strong and deliberate. This documented fact means that people who are influenced by the *wicked attribute* will use everything in their power to destroy those influenced by the **upright/honorable** attribute. Thus, the Spirit of wisdom warned leaders, "*...to punish the righteous is not good, nor to strike princes for their **uprightness*** (Proverbs 17:26). People who are influenced with this attribute serve a special purpose in the fight between good and evil. Earthly leaders must do their part to protect and preserve individuals influenced by the **upright/honorable** attribute. If not, those influenced by the wicked attribute will increase and spread their venom to everyone who hears them or cowers to their oppressive tactics. When people influenced by this positive attribute are suppressed, wickedness spreads to consume organizations, communities, and nations.

Why do people influenced by the wicked attribute want the destruction of those with the **upright/honorable** attribute? Because the Spirit of wisdom revealed to Solomon that, "*Folly is joy to him who is destitute of <u>discernment</u>, but a man of understanding walks **uprightly***" (Proverbs 15:21). BTT allows one to see that people destitute of <u>discernment</u> are enamored with, caught up in, and lost in foolishness (folly). Folly keeps chaos goings. Folly hides the agendas of those influenced by the wicked attribute's thirst for personal gain. However, people influenced by the **upright/honorable** attribute can see through the folly and become a stumbling block to the wicked. People influenced by the **upright/honorable** calls out folly with Truth. Thus, the wicked love to keep people lost in folly. Please go back and look closely at the influence of the fool and wicked attributes in this book. Their separate or combined strengths makes formidable adversaries in spiritual warfare. But for one influenced by the **upright/honorable** attribute, Solomon documented that, "*...the way of the **upright** is a highway*" (Proverbs 15:19) and "*The highway of the **upright** is to depart from evil; he who keeps his way preserves his soul*" (Proverbs 16:17). In other words, people who attain this attribute walk in a way that is completely different from people who are caught up in the affairs of the world. They behave in a manner that demonstrates the good path of life. They model the Biblical requirements of being set apart (1 Peter 2:9) and not conforming to the standards of the world (Romans 12:2). Solomon further documented in Proverbs 2:10-15 that:

> "*When wisdom enters your heart, and knowledge is pleasant to your soul, discretion will preserve you; understanding will keep you, to deliver you from the way of evil, from the man who speaks perverse things, from those who leave the paths of **uprightness** to walk in the ways of darkness; who rejoice in doing evil, and delight in the perversity of the wicked; whose ways are crooked, and who are devious in their paths; ...*"

BTT allows one to see that the negative attributes, especially the wicked, evil, and perverse attributes, strive to pull people with the influence of the **upright/honorable** attribute to the negative path. Solomon even documented, "*Whoever causes the **upright** to go astray in an evil way, he himself will fall into his own pit* (Proverbs 28:10). The negative forces of the campaign deceive many in the fog of the war on this point. This is why the word "whoever" is used in the text. For good people, deceived by the negative forces, often fail to see that their actions are degrading the good that exists in the world. Even good people with good intentions, can cause people influenced by the **upright/honorable** attribute to stumble from time to time; thus, staying focused on God's Word is paramount. The good attribute will be fully discussed later in this chapter.

The Spirit of wisdom further revealed to Solomon that, "*A wicked man hardens his face, but as for the **upright**, he establishes his way*" (Proverbs 21:29). Clearly, the Biblical record is indicating that God gives everything necessary to succeed in the war campaign to one influenced by the **upright/honorable** attribute. People with this attribute will take their time to establish their steps in God's Word to ensure they are going in the right direction. People influenced by the wicked attribute reject this knowledge and will harden their face against it. For the wicked know God's provisions includes the wisdom to turn away from evil and keep one's feet planted in a direction toward godliness. In fact, the Biblical record even documented that, "*...secret counsel is with the **upright***" (Proverbs 3:32). This secret counsel is not by a direct personal discussion between oneself and God through the speaking in tongues as false teachers profess. This false belief and practice contradicts God's Word since the Bible states specifically, "*God, who at various times and in various ways spoke in time past to the fathers by the prophets, has in these last days spoken to us by His Son, whom He has appointed heir of all things, through whom also He made the worlds...*" (Hebrews 1:1-2). In these last days, we all equally have Jesus' Word as it is recorded in the Bible. No man or woman gets another word from Jesus or it would make God's Word a lie. Proverbs 3:32 simply documents the strong connection to God through consistent prayer and study of His Word which allows access to His wisdom He stores up according to Proverbs 2:7. Prayer remains one's only way to communicate with God. Solomon documented that, "*...the prayer of the **upright** is the Lord's delight*" (Proverbs 15:8) and "*The way of the LORD is strength for the **upright**...*" (Proverbs 10:29). Solomon captures the takeaway from these two great passages when he documented, "*The righteousness of the **upright** will deliver them...*" (Proverbs 11:6). In other words, BTT allows one to see that the seed of righteousness is embedded in the influence of this attribute and will influence one toward salvation. A few more pearls of wisdom the Spirit of wisdom revealed to Solomon concerning the **upright/honorable** attribute included:

"By the blessing of the **upright** the city is exalted" (Proverbs 11:11)	"The mouth of the **upright** will deliver others from sin" (Proverbs 12:6)	"Among the **upright** there is favor" (Proverbs 14:9)
"The **upright** seek the well-being of the blameless" (Proverbs 29:10)	"...the unfaithful shall be a ransom for the **upright** (Proverbs 21:18)	"The integrity of the **upright** will guide them..." (Proverbs 11:3)

"For the **upright** will dwell in the land, and the blameless will remain in it; but the wicked will be cut off from the earth, and the unfaithful will be uprooted from it" (Proverbs 2:21-22)	"He who walks in his **uprightness** fears the Lord, but he who is perverse in his ways despises Him" (Proverbs 14:2)	"...the tent of the **upright** will flourish" (Proverbs 14:11)

Table 87: Some Pearls of Wisdom Concerning the Upright/Honorable Attribute

Finally, Solomon documented a simple but worthy statement that helps one identify a man or woman who allows the influence of the **upright/honorable** attribute to lead in their spirits. He wrote, "*It is **honorable** for a man to stop striving, since any **fool** can start a quarrel*" (Proverbs 20:3). One who knows when to walk away from useless debates or arguments demonstrates the **upright/honorable** attribute. Solomon rightfully stated that any **fool** can start a quarrel.

The rest of the Old Testament documented the **upright/honorable** attribute well by the actions and behavior of the people who allowed this **clean spirit's** influence. Here are a few examples:

Who	What Is Documented
Deborah	"*Now Deborah, a prophetess, the wife of Lapidoth, was judging Israel at that time*" (Judges 4:4)
Ruth	Demonstrated the attribute with her mother-in-law when she said, "*Entreat me not to leave you, or to turn back from following after you; for wherever you go, I will go; and wherever you lodge, I will lodge; your people shall be my people, and your God, my God. Where you die, I will die, and there will I be buried. The Lord do so to me, and more also, if anything but death parts you and me*" (Ruth 1:16-17)
Boaz	Demonstrated the attribute through all his dealing with Ruth. The Biblical record documented, "*And Boaz said to the elders and all the people, "You are witnesses this day that I have bought all that was Elimelech's, and all that was Chilion's and Mahlon's, from the hand of Naomi. Moreover, Ruth the Moabitess, the widow of Mahlon, I have acquired as my wife, to perpetuate the name of the dead through his inheritance, that the name of the dead may not be cut off from among his brethren and from his position at the gate. You are witnesses this day*" (Ruth 4:9-10)
Jabez	The record documented that, "*...Jabez was more **honorable** than his brothers, and his mother called his name Jabez, saying, "Because I bore him in pain"* (1 Chronicles 4:9)
Samuel	A servant told Saul, "*Look now, there is in this city a man of God, and he is an **honorable** man; all that he says surely comes to pass. So let us go there; perhaps he can show us the way that we should go*" (1 Samuel 9:6)
David	The prophet Ahimelech told King Saul that David had this attribute. The Biblical record documented, "*So Ahimelech answered the king and said, "And who among all your servants is as faithful as David, who is the king's son-in-law, who goes at your bidding, and is **honorable** in your house...*" (1 Samuel 22:14-15)

		Achish, the king of Gath (1 Samuel 21:10) identified the attribute in David. The Biblical record documented, "*Then Achish called David and said to him, "Surely, as the Lord lives, you have been **upright**, and your going out and your coming in with me in the army is good in my sight. For to this day I have not found evil in you since the day of your coming to me. Nevertheless the lords do not favor you*" (1 Samuel 29:6)
		King Solomon confirmed that David had the attribute. Solomon said to the Lord, "*You have shown great mercy to Your servant David my father, because he walked before You in truth, in righteousness, and in **uprightness** of heart with You; You have continued this great kindness for him, and You have given him a son to sit on his throne, as it is this day*" (1 Kings 3:6)
		The Lord also acknowledged that David had this attribute. The Lord told Solomon, "*Now if you walk before Me as your father David walked, in integrity of heart and in **uprightness**, to do according to all that I have commanded you, and if you keep My statutes and My judgments, then I will establish the throne of your kingdom over Israel forever, as I promised David your father, saying, 'You shall not fail to have a man on the throne of Israel.'*" (1 Kings 9:4-5)
	Naaman	The Biblical record documented, "*Now Naaman, commander of the army of the king of Syria, was a great and **honorable** man in the eyes of his master, because by him the Lord had given victory to Syria. He was also a mighty man of valor, but a leper*" (2 Kings 5:1). The Lord healed Naaman of his leprosy according to 2 Kings 5:13-14
	Ester	She demonstrated this attribute. After Mordecai, her father in law, told Ester of a plot to annihilate the Jews by a man named Haman, he also told her, "*...who knows whether you have come to the kingdom for such a time as this?*" (Ester 4:14). She, as Queen Ester made the decision to expose Haman's plot to the King, her husband. The Bible documented that she said, "*Go, gather all the Jews who are present in Shushan, and fast for me; neither eat nor drink for three days, night or day. My maids and I will fast likewise. And so I will go to the king, which is against the law; and if I perish, I perish!*" (Ester 4:16)
	Job	The Biblical record documented, "*There was a man in the land of Uz, whose name was Job; and that man was blameless and **upright**, and one who feared God and shunned evil*" (Job 1:1)
		Twice it is recorded, "*Then the Lord said to Satan, "Have you considered My servant Job, that there is none like him on the earth, a blameless and **upright** man, one who fears God and shuns evil?*" (Job 1:8 and 2:3). The Lord told Satan, "*...And still he holds fast to his <u>integrity</u>, although you incited Me against him, to destroy him without cause*" (Job 2-3)

Table 88: Some Examples of People Who Allowed the Influence of the Upright/Honorable Attribute

Moses told the children of Israel that they lacked the **upright** attribute. He said to them, "*It is not because of your righteousness or the **uprightness** of your heart that you go in to possess their land, but because of the wickedness of these nations that the Lord your God drives them out from before you, and that He may fulfill the word which the Lord swore to your fathers, to Abraham, Isaac, and Jacob*" (Deuteronomy 9:5). Moses documented that the influence of the ***upright/honorable*** attribute was not germinating properly among the Israelites. However, because God made a promise to their forefathers, God in His ***uprightness*** and **honor**, kept His promise. Moses told the people, "*He is the Rock, His work is perfect; for all His ways are justice, a God of truth and without injustice; righteous and **upright** is He*" (Deuteronomy 32:4).

The Book of Job provided a rare glimpse of the fight between the positive and negative forces of the war campaign as it unfolded among some very wise men. The ratio of the battle was one man influenced by the positive attributes against four men influenced by the negative attributes. Looking at this battle from the standpoint of the **upright/honorable** attribute's influence, BTT allows one to see that the brutal strategy of the negative forces was to convince Job that he did not have this attribute influencing his inner spirit. In this case, the negative forces that influenced Job's tormentors attempted to destroy him emotionally, psychologically, and spiritually while he was in extreme physical pain. The Biblical record documented that Job had lost all His children and livelihood (Job 1:13-19), was struck with painful boils from his feet to his head (Job 2:7), his wife questioned his *integrity* and told him to die (Job 2:9), and three of his friends (Eliphaz, Bildad, and Zophar) tormented him. These friends brought along a fourth man named Elihu who is believed to be an understudy. But Satan used them all against Job. Consider a few of the many things that Job's tormentors accused him of to destroy his confidence and convince him that the influence of the **upright/honorable** attribute did not dwell in his spirit:

- Eliphaz accused Job of sin. He told Job, "*But now it comes upon you, and you are weary; it touches you, and you are troubled. Is not your reverence your confidence? And the integrity of your ways your hope? Remember now, whoever perished being innocent? Or where were the **upright** ever cut off? Even as I have seen, those who plow iniquity and sow trouble reap the same*" (Job 4:5-8)

- Eliphaz accuses Job of wickedness. He said, "*Is not your wickedness great, and your iniquity without end?*" (Job 22:5) and said, "*You have not given the weary water to drink, and you have withheld bread from the hungry. But the mighty man possessed the land, and the **honorable** man dwelt in it*" (Job 22:7-8)

- Bildad accused him of not having the influence of the **upright/honorable** attribute. He told Job, "*If you were pure and **upright**, surely now He [God] would awake for you, and prosper your **rightful** dwelling place*" (Job 8:6)

- Elihu spoke from his anger to prove himself. He falsely told Job, "*My words come from my **upright** heart; my lips utter pure knowledge*" (Job 33:3) and then he proceeded to launch a verbal assault against Job that contradicted the older three men, the wisdom of Job, and most importantly - God's Word. His vicious verbal assault covered Chapters 32 through 37 of the Book of Job with vain philosophies and ramblings that demonstrated Satan's use of him during Job's suffering. I encourage one to read this interesting assault to fully appreciate the influence of the negative attribute on Elihu in the war campaign.

Job responded to all the accusations by keeping focused on the Lord. He countered their arguments after every verbal assault, but they did not listen. Here are just a few of the points Job made concerning the influence of the **upright/honorable** attribute.

- First, after telling the men that they were miserable comforters (Job 16:2) he said if the situation were reversed, "*...I would strengthen you with my mouth, and the comfort of my lips would relieve your grief*" (Job 16:5)

- He defended the righteousness of God but asked for relief from his suffering. He said, "***Upright*** *men are astonished at this, and the innocent stirs himself up against the hypocrite. Yet the righteous will hold to his way, and he who has clean hands will be stronger and stronger*" (Job 17:8-9)

- He told the men, if he could find God and go to His court, he could plead his case. He said, "*There the* ***upright*** *could reason with Him, and I would be delivered forever from my Judge*" (Job 23:7)

The beautiful thing about all the discourse between Job and his accusers is the fact that it is documented for our learning. The Lord kept His eye on the situation and vindicated Job according to Job Chapter 42. In fact, the Biblical record documented that because Job allowed the influence of the **upright/honorable** attribute, as well as the other positive attributes, "*...the Lord restored Job's losses when he prayed for his friends. Indeed the Lord gave Job twice as much as he had before*" (Job 42:10).

In addition to Job's situation, one can learn many other pearls of wisdom about the influence of the **upright/honorable** attribute documented by David and Solomon. These men provided some of the best pearls of wisdom that one can have to appreciate this attribute. Here are some of the things they documented.

"*My defense is of God, Who saves the* ***upright*** *in heart*" (Psalm 7:10)	"*For the Lord is righteous, He loves righteousness; His countenance beholds the* ***upright***" (Psalm 11:7)	"*Rejoice in the Lord, O you righteous! For praise from the* ***upright*** *is beautiful*" (Psalm 33:1)
"*Oh, continue Your lovingkindness to those who know You, and Your righteousness to the* ***upright*** *in heart*" (Psalm 36:10)	"*Let my vindication come from Your presence; let Your eyes look on the things that are* ***upright***" (Psalm 17:2)	"*For the Lord God is a sun and shield; the Lord will give grace and glory; no good thing will He withhold from those who walk* ***uprightly***" (Psalm 84:11)
"*Light is sown for the righteous, and gladness for the* ***upright*** *in heart*" (Psalm 97:11)	"*Let integrity and* ***uprightness*** *preserve me, for I wait for You*" (Psalm 25:21)	"*The Lord knows the days of the* ***upright***, *and their inheritance shall be forever*" (Psalm 37:18)
"*Be glad in the Lord and rejoice, you righteous; and shout for joy, all you* ***upright*** *in heart!*" (Psalm 32:11)	"*The righteous shall be glad in the Lord, and trust in Him. And all the* ***upright*** *in heart shall glory*" (Psalm 64:10)	"*Praise the Lord! I will praise the Lord with my whole heart, in the assembly of the* ***upright*** *and in the congregation*" (Psalm 111:1)
"*I will praise You with* ***uprightness*** *of heart,*	"*Do good, O Lord, to those who are good, and to those*	"*Surely the righteous shall give thanks to Your name;*

when I learn Your righteous judgments" (Psalm 119:7)	who are **upright** in their hearts" (Psalm 125:4)	the **upright** shall dwell in Your presence" (Psalm 140:13)
"Teach me to do Your will, for You are my God; Your Spirit is good. Lead me in the land of **uprightness**" (Psalm 143:10)	"Mark the blameless man, and observe the **upright**; for the future of that man is peace" (Psalm 37:37)	Truly, this only I have found: That God made man **upright**, but they have sought out many schemes" (Ecclesiastes 7:29)
David documented, "*I know also, my God, that You test the heart and have pleasure in* **uprightness**. *As for me, in the* **uprightness** *of my heart I have willingly offered all these things; and now with joy I have seen Your people, who are present here to offer willingly to You*" (1 Chronicles 29:17)	"And moreover, because the Preacher was wise, he still taught the people knowledge; yes, he pondered and sought out and set in order many proverbs. The Preacher sought to find acceptable words; and what was written was **upright**—words of truth" (Ecclesiastes 12:9-10)	"This is the way of those who are foolish, and of their posterity who approve their sayings. Like sheep they are laid in the grave; death shall feed on them; the **upright** shall have dominion over them in the morning; and their beauty shall be consumed in the grave, far from their dwelling" (Psalm 49:13-14)
"Lord, who may abide in Your tabernacle? Who may dwell in Your holy hill? He who walks **uprightly**, and works righteousness, and speaks the truth in his heart; he who does not backbite with his tongue, nor does evil to his neighbor, nor does he take up a reproach against his friend; in whose eyes a vile person is despised, but he honors those who fear the Lord; he who swears to his own hurt and does not change; he who does not put out his money at usury, nor does he take a bribe against the innocent. He who does these things shall never be moved" (Psalm 15:1-5)	"Praise the Lord! Blessed is the man who fears the Lord, who delights greatly in His commandments. His descendants will be mighty on earth; the generation of the **upright** will be blessed. Wealth and riches will be in his house, and his righteousness endures forever. Unto the **upright** there arises light in the darkness; he is gracious, and full of compassion, and righteous" (Psalm 112:1-4)	"The Lord knows the thoughts of man, that they are futile. Blessed is the man whom You instruct, O Lord, and teach out of Your law, that You may give him rest from the days of adversity, until the pit is dug for the wicked. For the Lord will not cast off His people, nor will He forsake His inheritance. But judgment will return to righteousness, and all the **upright** in heart will follow it" (Psalm 94:11-15)

Table 89: Pearls of Wisdom Concerning the Upright/Honorable Attribute

As stated earlier, within the war campaign, people influenced by the wicked attribute always try to stop people influenced by the ***upright/honorable*** attribute even by murder. Look closely at what the Psalmist documented:

- *"For look! The wicked bend their bow, they make ready their arrow on the string, that they may shoot secretly at the **upright** in heart"* (Psalm 11:2)

- *"The wicked have drawn the sword and have bent their bow, to cast down the poor and needy, to slay those who are of **upright** conduct"* (Psalm 37:14)

- *"Do you indeed speak righteousness, you silent ones? Do you judge **uprightly**, you sons of men? No, in heart you work wickedness; you weigh out the violence of your hands in the earth"* (Psalm 58:1)

The prophets of the Old Testament warned the nation of Israel about their lack of the ***upright/honorable*** attribute. Remember, the negative forces of the war campaign overran the nation of Israel because their prophets failed to teach God's Word. Even though the nation of Israel was stubborn, God still required His people to allow the influence of the ***upright/honorable*** attribute. Thus, the prophets repeatedly warned them that the Lord would destroy them if they did not repent of their wickedness. The Biblical record captured the warnings pertaining to their failure to allow the influence of the ***upright/honorable*** attribute. I encourage one to read one's own Bible to fully appreciate and understand these warnings. Some of the warnings were:

The Prophet	What Was Said
Isaiah	*"For behold, the Lord, the Lord of hosts, takes away from Jerusalem and from Judah the stock and the store, the whole supply of bread and the whole supply of water; the mighty man and the man of war, the judge and the prophet, and the diviner and the elder; the captain of fifty and the **honorable** man, the counselor and the skillful artisan, and the expert enchanter. I will give children to be their princes, and babes shall rule over them. The people will be oppressed, everyone by another and every one by his neighbor; the child will be insolent toward the elder, and the base toward the **honorable**"* (Isaiah 3:1-5)
	*"Therefore my people have gone into captivity, because they have no knowledge; their **honorable** men are famished, and their multitude dried up with thirst. Therefore Sheol has enlarged itself and opened its mouth beyond measure; their glory and their multitude and their pomp, and he who is jubilant, shall descend into it. People shall be brought down, each man shall be humbled, and the eyes of the lofty shall be humbled. But the Lord of hosts shall be exalted in judgment, and God who is holy shall be hallowed in righteousness"* (Isaiah 5:13-16)
	*"For the people do not turn to Him who strikes them, nor do they seek the Lord of hosts. Therefore the Lord will cut off head and tail from Israel, palm branch and bulrush in one day. The elder and **honorable**, he is the head; the prophet who teaches lies, he is the tail. For the leaders of this people cause them to err, and those who are led by them are destroyed. Therefore the Lord will have no joy in their young men, nor have mercy on their fatherless and widows; for everyone is a hypocrite and an evildoer, and every mouth speaks folly..."* (Isaiah 9:13-17)

		For the city of Tyre: "*Who has taken this counsel against Tyre, the crowning city, whose merchants are princes, whose traders are the **honorable** of the earth? The Lord of hosts has purposed it, to bring to **dishonor** the pride of all glory, to bring into contempt all the **honorable** of the earth*" (Isaiah 23:8-9)
		"*The way of the just is **uprightness**; O Most **Upright**, You weigh the path of the just*" (Isaiah 26:7)
		"*With my soul I have desired You in the night, yes, by my spirit within me I will seek You early; for when Your judgments are in the earth, the inhabitants of the world will learn righteousness. Let grace be shown to the wicked, yet he will not learn righteousness; in the land of **uprightness** he will deal unjustly, and will not behold the majesty of the Lord. Lord, when Your hand is lifted up, they will not see. But they will see and be ashamed for their envy of people; yes, the fire of Your enemies shall devour them*" (Isaiah 26:9-11)
		"*The sinners in Zion are afraid; fearfulness has seized the hypocrites: "Who among us shall dwell with the devouring fire? Who among us shall dwell with everlasting burnings?" He who walks righteously and speaks **uprightly**, he who despises the gain of oppressions, who gestures with his hands, refusing bribes, who stops his ears from hearing of bloodshed, and shuts his eyes from seeing evil: He will dwell on high; his place of defense will be the fortress of rocks; bread will be given him, his water will be sure*" (Isaiah 33:14-16)
		"*The righteous perishes, and no man takes it to heart; merciful men are taken away, while no one considers that the righteous is taken away from evil. He shall enter into peace; they shall rest in their beds, each one walking in his **uprightness**. "But come here, you sons of the sorceress, you offspring of the adulterer and the harlot! Whom do you ridicule? Against whom do you make a wide mouth and stick out the tongue? Are you not children of transgression, offspring of falsehood, inflaming yourselves with gods under every green tree, slaying the children in the valleys, under the clefts of the rocks?*" (Isaiah 57:1-5)
	Amos	"*They hate the one who rebukes in the gate, and they abhor the one who speaks **uprightly**"* (Amos 5:10)
	Micah	"*You who are named the house of Jacob: "Is the Spirit of the Lord restricted? Are these His doings? Do not My words do good to him who walks **uprightly**?*" (Micah 2:7)
		"*The faithful man has perished from the earth, and there is no one **upright** among men. They all lie in wait for blood; every man hunts his brother with a net. That they may successfully do evil with both hands—the prince asks for gifts, the judge seeks a bribe, and the great man utters his evil desire; so they scheme together. The best of them is like a brier; the most **upright** is sharper than a thorn hedge; the day of your watchman and your punishment comes; now shall be their perplexity*" (Micah 7:2-4)
	Habakkuk	"*Then the Lord answered me and said: "Write the vision and make it plain on tablets, that he may run who reads it. For the vision is yet for an appointed time; but at the end it will speak, and it will not lie. Though it tarries, wait for it; because it will surely come, it will not tarry. Behold the proud, his soul is not **upright** in him; but the just shall live by his faith*" (Habakkuk 2:2-4)

Table 90: Some of the Prophets' Warnings Concerning the Influence of the Upright/Honorable Attribute

In the New Testament, Jesus addressed the influence of the **upright/honorable** attribute through a parable to the people. He said, "*When you are invited by anyone to a wedding feast, do not sit down in the best place, lest one more **honorable** than you be invited by him; and he who invited you and him come and say to you, 'Give place to this man,' and then you begin with shame to take the lowest place. But when you are invited, go and sit down in the lowest place, so that when he who invited you comes he may say to you, 'Friend, go up higher.' Then you will have glory in the presence of those who sit at the table with you. For whoever exalts himself will be <u>humbled</u>, and he who <u>humbles</u> himself will be exalted*" (Luke 14:8-11). BTT helps one to understand that those influenced by the **upright/honorable** attribute must never exploit this blessing. To "show off" this attribute by seeking the best seat for attention simply identifies one's own self-righteousness. To be seen or to elevate one's own status is not from God. The driving force behind this negative behavior is not the way of the positive influence of the **upright/honorable** attribute at all. A host, or others influenced by this attribute, will recognize people with the true attribute and respond appropriately. Consequently, one who abuses his or her measure of this attribute makes him or herself a target for the negative forces of spiritual warfare. The negative forces love to find ways to embarrass people with the **upright/honorable** attribute as a means of chipping away at their <u>integrity</u> and destroying their <u>credibility</u>. Moreover, the greater impact is the loss of credible examples of people with this positive spirit for the world to see.

Moreover, in Luke 14:8-11 above, Jesus identified a correlation between this attribute and the spiritual element of <u>humility</u>. In fact, as One with the **upright/honorable** attribute, He demonstrated the element of <u>humility</u> by his very act of coming to this earth. Paul documented that Christ's example should be exemplified by Christians when he wrote, "*Let this mind be in you which was also in Christ Jesus, who, being in the form of God, did not consider it robbery to be equal with God, but made Himself of no reputation, taking the form of a bondservant, and coming in the likeness of men. And being found in appearance as a man, He <u>humbled</u> Himself and became obedient to the point of death, even the death of the cross*" (Philippians 2:5-8). Interestingly, the prophets of the Old Testament confirm <u>humility</u> when they documented, "*He has shown you, O man, what is good; and what does the LORD require of you but to do justly, to love mercy, and to walk <u>humbly</u> with your God?*" (Micah 6:8), and "*For the Lord takes pleasure in His people; He will beautify the <u>humble</u> with salvation*" (Psalm 149:4).

Jesus taught more on the influence of the **upright/honorable** attribute when He taught the proper behavior to demonstrate while hosting an event or activity. When Jesus was invited to the home of one of the Pharisees (Luke 14:1), He explained to His host, "*When you give a dinner or a supper, do not ask your friends, your brothers, your relatives, nor rich neighbors, lest they also invite you back, and you be repaid. But when you give a feast, invite the poor, the maimed, the lame, the blind. And you will be blessed, because they cannot repay you; for you shall be repaid at the resurrection of the just*" (Luke 14:12-14). In other words, providing for people who truly need the support is the real demonstration of the influence of the **upright/honorable.** BTT allows one to see that supporting people who cannot afford to help themselves is selfless service. Selfless service is truly **upright**, **honorable**, and just. Please do not miss the fact that when one is influenced by the **upright/honorable** attribute and does as Jesus stated above, one gains another positive attribute in the process. For one's selfless service to people in the poor category or people with the needy attribute, one gains a measure of the just attribute.

One can see the strong influence of Jesus' Gospel on Paul as he taught about the influence of the **upright/honorable** attribute. Comparing the worth and function of members of the Lord's church to the parts of the human body, Paul brilliantly illustrated the influence of the **upright/honorable** attribute. I strongly encourage reading the entire example captured in 1 Corinthians 12:12-27. From the example, Paul concluded that "...*the body is not one member but many...those members of the body which seem to be weaker are necessary. And those members of the body which we think to be less* **honorable**, *on these we bestow greater* **honor**; *and our unpresentable parts have greater modesty, but our presentable parts have no need. But God composed the body, having given greater* **honor** *to that part which lacks it, that there should be no schism in the body, but that the members should have the same care for one another. And if one member suffers, all the members suffer with it; or if one member is* **honored**, *all the members rejoice with it. Now you are the body of Christ, and members individually*" (1 Corinthians 12:14-27). BTT allows one to see that when this strategy is applied, even the smallest problems go away. Everyone involved gains the powerful element of <u>respect</u> and everyone has a purpose. When one influenced by the **upright/honorable** attribute shows <u>respect</u> to others, this positive behavior then promotes dignity and self-worth. There are many reasons for the disparity of blessings and skills in the Lord's church. However, what is important is that God requires everyone to be treated the same. One with the influence of the **upright/honorable** attribute instinctively knows this and carries out God's command without hesitation or question.

A Christian's relationship to another Christian must always be one of **uprightness** and **honor**. Accordingly, a Christian must display this same behavior to his or her enemy to remain among the positive forces of the war campaign. A Christian sets the example of <u>respect</u>, <u>love</u>, **uprightness**, and **honor**. BTT allows one to see that God expects one's behavior to be consistent with this attribute as well as the other positive attributes, if one desires to stay on the positive path of life.

However, like Jesus, Paul also documented how the influence of the **upright/honorable** attribute played a role in marriage. He documented, "*Marriage is* **honorable** *among all, and the bed undefiled; but fornicators and adulterers God will judge. Let your conduct be without covetousness; be content with such things as you have. For He Himself has said, "I will never leave you nor forsake you." So we may boldly say: The Lord is my helper; I will not fear. What can man do to me?*" (Hebrews 13:4-6). BTT helps one to recognize the influences of the adultery and immoral attributes cause many people to stumble. Even people in sound marriages who are influenced by the **upright/honorable** attribute are prone to stumble when they let their guard down. As painful as it may be, when it comes to the commitment of marriage, the influence of the **upright/honorable** attribute in one's inner spirit, is not possible when one commits and willfully remains in sin. Remember, to defile the marriage bed is sin. When the marriage's contractual relationship is broken because of sin, the negative forces of the war campaign gain another, if not two more soldiers. Marriage is voluntary, applies only to a man and woman, and is always done in God's presence (whether one wants to accept this fact or not). This authorized union is **honorable** in the eyes of God and should never be taken lightly; those who do so, lack *discernment*. The Biblical record documents, *"For the Lord God of Israel says that He hates divorce, for it covers one's garment with violence," Says the Lord of hosts. "Therefore take heed to your spirit, that you do not deal treacherously"* (Malachi 2:16). To this end, Peter also documented, *"Beloved, I beg you as sojourners and pilgrims, abstain from fleshly lusts which war against the soul, having your conduct* **honorable** *among the Gentiles, that when they speak against you as evildoers, they may, by your good works which they observe, glorify God in the day of visitation"* (1 Peter 2:11-12).

One must protect the influence of the **upright/honorable** attribute. BTT allows one to see that the Bible; God's Word, is the source of that protection. For marriage as discussed above, one can see that the negative forces have not just led an attack on the **honorable** institution of marriage, they have also launched a strategic initiative to redefine marriage. The initiative is to redefine marriage to include men with men, women with women, adults with children, and even a person with an animal or material objects. This subject is covered in more detail in Chapter X of this book. For now, try to understand that the negative forces are using this strategy to destroy the Biblical foundation of the home. This covert maneuver has gathered support by many in the secular community and far worse, many in religious communities. Religious people support this insidious spiritual tactic because they lack *discernment* and have no respect for God. God forbid when these ideas enter Christ's church. This strategy is forged in sin and is not from God. The negative forces have deceived many people in the fog of spiritual warfare and false teachers are leading millions of people into darkness. Many churches around the world have fallen silent on this subject, but God has not. He is not pleased and is showing His displeasure through His *calamity*. God's *calamity* is discussed in Chapter IX of this book. Paul placed emphasis on the fact that sins of this nature will cause people to face spiritual death. He documented, *"...knowing the righteous judgment of God, that those who practice such things are deserving of death, not only do the same but also approve of those who practice them"* (Romans 1:32).

Finally, BTT allows one to see that the influence of the **upright/honorable** attribute leads one to gain the spiritual elements of *humility* and *godliness*. First, consider the correlation between the **upright/honorable** attribute and the element of *humility*. BTT allows one to see that an **upright/honorable** person is one who is *humble*, and a *humble* person displays *humility*. James documented, *"Humble yourselves in the sight of the Lord, and He will lift you up"* (James 4:10). Likewise, Peter documented, *"...you younger people, submit yourselves to your elders. Yes, all of you be submissive to one another, and be clothed with humility, for "God resists the proud, but gives grace to the humble." Therefore humble yourselves under the mighty hand of God, that He may exalt you in due time, casting all your care upon Him, for He cares for you"* (1 Peter 5:5-6). One who is obedient to God's Word, will *humble* himself or herself to the people that God has put in place to enforce and teach it His Word. Hence, the element of *humility* is an **upright/honorable** behavior in God's eyes. In fact, Jesus stated, *"...whoever humbles himself as this little child is the greatest in the kingdom of heaven"* (Matthew 18:4). Many reject this idea because of the fog generated by the negative forces in spiritual warfare. People deceived by the fog are the very ones, Peter warns to be, *"...sober, be* *vigilant; because your adversary the devil walks about like a roaring lion, seeking whom he may devour"* (1 Peter 5:8). Satan deceives and devours many souls each day because of the lack of spiritual knowledge and <u>discernment</u>. Consider a few pearls of wisdom documented in the Biblical record concerning the correlation between the **upright/honorable** attribute and the element of <u>humility</u>.

"Arise, O Lord! O God, lift up Your hand! Do not forget the <u>humble</u>" (Psalm 10:12)	"Surely He scorns the scornful, but gives grace to the <u>humble</u>" (Proverbs 3:34)	"By <u>humility</u> and the fear of the Lord are riches and **honor** and life" (Proverbs 22:4)
"The fear of the Lord is the instruction of wisdom, and before **honor** is <u>humility</u>" (Proverbs 15:33)	"Before destruction the heart of a man is haughty, and before **honor** is <u>humility</u>" (Proverbs 18:12)	"When pride comes, then comes shame; but with the <u>humble</u> is wisdom" (Proverbs 11:2)
"Better to be of a <u>humble</u> spirit with the lowly, than to divide the spoil with the proud" (Proverbs 16:19)	"When they cast you down, and you say, 'Exaltation will come!' Then He will save the <u>humble</u> person" (Job 22:29)	"When He avenges blood, He remembers them; He does not forget the cry of the <u>humble</u>" (Psalm 9:12)
"But as for me, when they were sick, my clothing was sackcloth; I <u>humbled</u> myself with fasting; and my prayer would return to my own heart" (Psalm 35:13)	"Lord, You have heard the desire of the <u>humble</u>; You will prepare their heart; You will cause Your ear to hear..." (Psalm 10:17)	"So do this, my son, and deliver yourself; for you have come into the hand of your friend: Go and <u>humble</u> yourself; plead with your friend" (Proverbs 6:3)
"For You will save the <u>humble</u> people, but will bring down haughty looks" (Psalm 18:27)	"The <u>humble</u> He guides in justice, and the <u>humble</u> He teaches His way" (Psalm 25:9)	"The Lord lifts up the <u>humble</u>; He casts the wicked down to the ground" (Psalm 147:6)
"A man's pride will bring him low, but the <u>humble</u> in spirit will retain **honor**" (Proverbs 29:23)	"The <u>humble</u> shall see this and be glad; and you who seek God, your hearts shall live" (Psalm 69:32)	"My soul shall make its boast in the Lord; the <u>humble</u> shall hear of it and be glad" (Psalm 34:2)
"Seek the Lord, all you meek of the earth, who have upheld His justice. Seek righteousness, seek <u>humility</u>. It may be that you will be hidden in the day of the Lord's anger" (Zephaniah 2:3)	"Let no one cheat you of your reward, taking delight in <u>false humility</u> and worship of angels, intruding into those things which he has not seen, vainly puffed up by his fleshly mind..." (Colossians 2:18)	"These things indeed have an appearance of wisdom in self-imposed religion, <u>false humility</u>, and neglect of the body, but are of no value against the indulgence of the flesh" (Colossians 2:23)
"And whoever exalts himself will be <u>humbled</u>, and he who <u>humbles</u> himself will be exalted" (Matthew 23:12; Luke 14:11; Luke 18:14)	"But He gives more grace. Therefore, He says: "God resists the proud, but gives grace to the <u>humble</u>" (James 4:6)	"...to speak evil of no one, to be peaceable, gentle, showing all <u>humility</u> to all men..." (Titus 3:2)
"Let no one cheat you of your reward, taking delight in false <u>humility</u> and	"These things indeed have an appearance of wisdom in self-imposed religion, false	"Be of the same mind toward one another. Do not set your mind on high

worship of angels, intruding into those things which he has not seen, vainly puffed up by his fleshly mind..." (Colossians 2:18)	*humility, and neglect of the body, but are of no value against the indulgence of the flesh"* (Colossians 2:23)	*things, but associate with the humble. Do not be wise in your own opinion"* (Romans 12:16)
"...in humility correcting those who are in opposition, if God perhaps will grant them repentance, so that they may know the truth..." (2 Timothy 2:25)	*"Therefore, as the elect of God, holy and beloved, put on tender mercies, kindness, humility, meekness, longsuffering..."* (Colossians 3:12)	*"For thus says the High and Lofty One Who inhabits eternity, whose name is Holy: "I dwell in the high and holy place, with him who has a contrite and humble spirit, to revive the spirit of the humble, and to revive the heart of the contrite ones"* (Isaiah 57:15)

Table 91: The Correlation between the Upright/Honorable Attribute and Humility

Second, BTT allows one to see that an **upright/honorable** person is one who displays a _godly_ behavior. The spiritual element of _godliness_ sets one apart from the world's behaviors, words, and attitudes. In fact, it is this spiritual element that is seen as, *"...**honorable** among the Gentiles, that when they speak against you as evildoers, they may, by your good works which they observe, glorify God in the day of visitation"* (1 Peter 2:12). _Godliness_ is **upright/honorable** behavior in God's eyes. This is the element that divides Christians from the religious world and prevents Christ's church from mimicking secular society to attract others to His Kingdom. Here are a few pearls of wisdom to consider from the Biblical record concerning the correlation between the **upright/honorable** attribute and element of _godliness_.

"...having a form of godliness but denying its power. And from such people turn away!" (2 Timothy 3:5)	*"...but, which is proper for women professing godliness, with good works"* (1 Timothy 2:10)	*"But reject profane and old wives' fables, and exercise yourself toward godliness"* (1 Timothy 4:7)
"...as His divine power has given to us all things that pertain to life and godliness, through the knowledge of Him who called us by glory and virtue..." (2 Peter 1:3)	*"For bodily exercise profits a little, but godliness is profitable for all things, having promise of the life that now is and of that which is to come"* (1 Timothy 4:8)	*"But you, O man of God, flee these things and pursue righteousness, godliness, faith, love, patience, gentleness"* (1 Timothy 6:11)
"If anyone teaches otherwise and does not consent to wholesome words, even the words of our Lord Jesus Christ, and to the doctrine which	*"...useless wranglings of men of corrupt minds and destitute of the truth, who suppose that godliness is a means of gain. From such withdraw yourself. Now*	*"But also for this very reason, giving all diligence, add to your faith virtue, to virtue knowledge, to knowledge self-control, to self-control perseverance, to*

accords with <u>godliness</u>, he is proud, knowing nothing, but is obsessed with disputes and arguments over words, from which come envy, strife, reviling, evil suspicions…" (1 Timothy 6:3-4)	*<u>godliness</u> with contentment is great gain"* (1 Timothy 6:5-6)	*perseverance <u>godliness</u>, to <u>godliness</u> brotherly kindness, and to brotherly kindness love"* (2 Peter 1:5-7)
"Therefore I exhort first of all that supplications, prayers, intercessions, and giving of thanks be made for all men, *for kings and all who are in authority, that we may lead a quiet and peaceable life in all <u>godliness</u> and reverence"* (1 Timothy 2:1-2)	*"And without controversy great is the mystery of <u>godliness</u>: God was manifested in the flesh, justified in the Spirit, seen by angels, preached among the Gentiles, believed on in the world, received up in glory"* (1 Timothy 3:16)	*"Therefore, since all these things will be dissolved, what manner of persons ought you to be in holy conduct and <u>godliness</u>…"* (2 Peter 3:11)

Table 92: The correlation between the Upright/Honorable Attribute and Godliness

     One must pursue and allow the influence of the ***upright/honorable*** attribute in one's life. Moreover, one must do everything humanly possible to protect people who have acquired this attribute. For as people with this attribute are lost in the confusion, distortion, and chaos of spiritual warfare, generations of people will suffer from the loss of their positive examples. Men and women with the elements of <u>humility</u> and <u>godliness</u> are the foundation of a good society. Please do not be ***deceived.***

The **Blameless attribute**: This attribute influences one to always be aware of his or her behavior, words, and actions around others. It influences one to strive to be on his or her best behavior regardless of the circumstance, location, or audience; it never shows partiality and represents fairness in all aspects of behavior. One who possesses the influence of the ***blameless*** attribute strives to leave people who observe his or her behavior, unable to  say or think negatively of them. Its influence allows one to walk in truth and establish relationships that exemplify trust and confidence. Often, "good character" is mistakenly identified as the outward manifestation of the ***blameless*** attribute. However, this attribute influences much more than just good character. This attribute helps one to be above reproach. To be above reproach is to reach a state where one is beyond criticism, above suspicion, or without fault. No, it does not mean that one is perfect. But it implies that one behaves with standards of high morality and integrity. Further, one influenced by this attribute can and will make mistakes. Again this person is not perfect or immune to the effects of spiritual warfare. However, when he or she makes a mistake, he or she corrects it and repents. Just like the last three attributes, BTT allows one to see the ***blameless*** attribute alone cannot save one's soul. One must attain the righteous attribute; the sum of all the positive attributes combined and God's grace. This point will become clear by the end of this Chapter.

It may seem hard to find a person influenced by the ***blameless*** attribute, but the Spirit of wisdom shared with Solomon that, "...*the upright will dwell in the land, and the* ***blameless*** *will remain in it*" (Proverbs 2:21). This sacred wisdom documents that there will always be people around with this attribute. People influenced by this attribute will be around as long as the earth exists. For people who are striving to acquire the full measure of this attribute, the Spirit of wisdom revealed to Solomon that they would have help. She revealed that, "...*the righteousness of the* ***blameless*** *will direct his way aright...*" (Proverbs 11:5) and "...*righteousness guards those who's way is* ***blameless***..." (Proverbs 13:6). This wisdom is significant. For one who strives to live ***blamelessly,*** the influence of the righteous attribute supports his or her inner spirit. These combined attributes feed one's inner spirit for greater service to the Lord. To this end, the Spirit of wisdom revealed to Solomon that, "...*the* ***blameless*** *in their ways are the Lord's delight*" (Proverbs 11:20). What a wonderful thought to know that if one allows the influence of this attribute into one's life, he or she can have a special relationship with the Lord.

When one absorbs all the information above and strives to live a ***blameless*** life by allowing the influence of this attribute, the Lord provides even more support. Solomon documented, "...*the* ***blameless*** *will inherit good*" (Proverbs 28:10). BTT allows one to see that there is no qualification or quantification as to what the good is that is inherited. Why? Because whatever God provides will be beyond one's imagination. Thus, if one continues to grow, mature, and walk in the positive direction that the influence of this attributes leads, then as Solomon documented, "...*whoever walks* ***blamelessly*** *will be saved...*" (Proverbs 28:18). This is the end state one should desire in spiritual warfare. For walking ***blamelessly*** means following the path that Jesus and the apostles laid out in God's Word. This walk excludes man-made religious edicts, traditions, and doctrines. God's Word contains the only path to righteousness and His salvation. Walking ***blamelessly*** in this Proverb documents the movement, direction, and action on the good path that applies in both the physical and spiritual realms. The strategies employed by the negative forces of the war campaign focus on decoupling ***blamelessness*** from eternal salvation. However, BTT allows one to see the inextricable connection between the two. One learns that by maturing in God's Word and allowing the ***blameless*** attribute to influence one's inner spirit, the other positive attributes will come. All the positive attributes are required in spiritual warfare to survive the war campaign; Proverbs 28:18 simply calls out a ***blameless*** walk before God. God's grace fills in the gap when one sincerely strives to live a godly life.

The significance of the things written above gain greater importance as one begins to fully understand how the influence by the ***blameless*** attribute works in one's life. For instance, to be ***blameless,*** this attribute influences one to show fairness and impartiality to everyone; not just select people. One with this attribute will strive to do what is right in the eyes of men, and more importantly, in the eyes of God. Because of this, the negative forces through spiritual warfare will always seek to retaliate against this ***clean spirit***. Specifically, Solomon documented that, "*the bloodthirsty hate the* ***blameless***, *but the upright seek his well-being.*" (Proverbs 29:10). In this scripture, the Spirit of wisdom revealed to Solomon that there are people influenced by the bloodthirsty and hater attributes combined influence who specifically target people with the ***blameless*** attribute. There is no earthly logic for this person's negative behavior. However, through the lens of spiritual warfare, this person's behavior against one influenced by the ***blameless*** attribute can be known. Conversely, Proverbs 29:10 also informs one that among the positive forces, people influenced by the upright/honorable attribute seek the wellbeing of people influenced by the ***blameless*** attribute. This positive spirit provides the ***blameless*** a source of support and protection.

Now, as one considers the meaning of Proverbs 29:10 a little more, BTT allows one to see through the fog deployed by the negative forces of the war campaign. The negative forces have deceived both the religious and secular communities alike to think that actions perpetrated against all innocent people are simply wayward crimes. This deception prevails due to both community's lack of <u>discernment</u>. Both communities fail to see the reality of the negative force's crimes. For among the innocent are people influenced by the ***blameless*** attribute who are casualties of the war campaign. The bloodthirsty and hater attributes in spiritual warfare are united and influencing people who unknowingly harm some people influenced by the ***blameless*** attribute on the spiritual battlefield. This is one of the many unseen strategies employed by the negative forces used to shake the faith of people influenced by the positive attributes.

In the Old Testament of the Biblical record, Moses told the people that, *"You shall be **blameless** before the L*ORD *your God"* (Deuteronomy 18:13). This statement indicates the full measure of this positive attribute is achievable. For clarity, Moses provided some specifics to the children of Israel when he said, *"When you come into the land which the Lord your God is giving you, you shall not learn to follow the abominations of those nations. There shall not be found among you anyone who makes his son or his daughter pass through the fire, or one who practices witchcraft, or a soothsayer, or one who interprets omens, or a sorcerer, or one who conjures spells, or a medium, or a spiritist, or one who calls up the dead. For all who do these things are an abomination to the Lord, and because of these abominations the Lord your God drives them out from before you. You shall be **blameless** before the Lord your God. For these nations which you will dispossess listened to soothsayers and diviners; but as for you, the Lord your God has not appointed such for you"* (Deuteronomy 18:9-14). In spiritual warfare, the influence of the ***blameless*** attribute helps one to <u>discern</u> and avoid such things mentioned above.

Moses, and many others, served as examples of people who allowed the influence of the ***blameless*** attribute in the Old Testament. A few examples of these people and what they specifically did when the attribute influenced their inner spirits include:

Who	**What Is Documented**
Abraham	The Biblical record tells us, *"When Abram was ninety-nine years old, the Lord appeared to Abram and said to him, "I am Almighty God; walk before Me and be **blameless**. And I will make My covenant between Me and you, and will multiply you exceedingly." Then Abram fell on his face, and God talked with him, saying: "As for Me, behold, My covenant is with you, and you shall be a father of many nations. No longer shall your name be called Abram, but your name shall be Abraham; for I have made you a father of many nations"* (Genesis 17:1-5)

Joseph	He refused the advance of Potiphar's deceitful wife. After Potiphar "...*left all that he had in Joseph's hand, and he did not know what he had except for the bread which he ate*" (Genesis 39:6), the Biblical record documented, "...*it came to pass after these things that his master's wife cast longing eyes on Joseph, and she said, "Lie with me"* (Genesis 39:7)
	"...*she spoke to Joseph day by day, that he did not heed her, to lie with her or to be with her*" (Genesis 39:10)
	"...*it happened about this time, when Joseph went into the house to do his work, and none of the men of the house was inside, 12 that she caught him by his garment, saying, "Lie with me." But he left his garment in her hand, and fled and ran outside*" (Genesis 39:11-12)
The tribes of Reuben and Gad	They made an agreement with Moses to fight with the children of Israel until every one of them, "...*received his inheritance*" (Numbers 32:18), on the other side of Jordan and beyond. The Biblical record documented that Moses told them, "...*If you do this thing, if you arm yourselves before the Lord for the war, and all your armed men cross over the Jordan before the Lord until He has driven out His enemies from before Him, and the land is subdued before the Lord, then afterward you may return and be **blameless** before the Lord and before Israel; and this land shall be your possession before the Lord. But if you do not do so, then take note, you have sinned against the Lord; and be sure your sin will find you out. Build cities for your little ones and folds for your sheep, and do what has proceeded out of your mouth*" (Numbers 32:20-24).
Rahab, a harlot in Jericho and two men from the children of Israel	Rahab helped these two men who came to spy on Jericho, her country (Numbers 2:2). To help her, the men made an agreement with her, and contingent upon her keeping it, all parties of the agreement would not bear any sin in their activities. The Biblical record documented that the men said to Rahab, "*We will be **blameless** of this oath of yours which you have made us swear, unless, when we come into the land, you bind this line of scarlet cord in the window through which you let us down, and unless you bring your father, your mother, your brothers, and all your father's household to your own home. So it shall be that whoever goes outside the doors of your house into the street, his blood shall be on his own head, and we will be **guiltless**. And whoever is with you in the house, his blood shall be on our head if a hand is laid on him. And if you tell this business of ours, then we will be free from your oath which you made us swear." Then she said, "According to your words, so be it." And she sent them away, and they departed. And she bound the scarlet cord in the window*" (Joshua 2:17-21; also see Joshua 6:25)
Samson	Samson married a Philistine woman against his parent's wishes, but the Biblical record documented, "...*his father and mother did not know that it was of the Lord—that He was seeking an occasion to move against the Philistines. For at that time the Philistines had dominion over Israel*" (Judges 14:3). Over time, Samson left his wife and his father-in-law gave her to "...*his companion, who had been his best man*" (Judges 14:20). Samson wanted her back, but the father-in-law refused him according to Judges 15:2. Thus Samson said to his father-in-law, "...*This time I shall be **blameless** regarding the Philistines if I harm them!*" (Judges 15:3). And Judges 15:3-17 documented that Samson burns up the Philistine's stocks, standing grain, vineyards, and olive groves. Samson retained the **blameless** attribute in the eyes of the Lord and the Biblical record

	documents that he, "...*judged Israel twenty years in the days of the Philistines*" (Judges 15:30)
David	He documented, "*The Lord rewarded me according to my righteousness; according to the cleanness of my hands He has recompensed me. For I have kept the ways of the Lord, and have not wickedly departed from my God. For all His judgments were before me; and as for His statutes, I did not depart from them. I was also **blameless** before Him, and I kept myself from my iniquity. Therefore the Lord has recompensed me according to my righteousness, according to my cleanness in His eyes*" (2 Samuel 22:21-25)
	"*I was also **blameless** before Him, and I kept myself from my iniquity. Therefore the Lord has recompensed me according to my righteousness, according to the cleanness of my hands in His sight. With the merciful You will show Yourself merciful; with a **blameless** man You will show Yourself **blameless**; with the pure You will show Yourself pure; and with the devious You will show Yourself shrewd. For You will save the humble people, but will bring down haughty looks*" (Psalm 18:23-27; Also documented in 2 Samuel 22:26-28)
Job	The Biblical record documented, "*There was a man in the land of Uz, whose name was Job; and that man was **blameless** and upright, and one who feared God and shunned evil*" (Job 1:1)
	Also, the Lord identified Job as one with the influence of the **blameless** attribute twice. The Bible records, "*Then the Lord said to Satan, "Have you considered My servant Job, that there is none like him on the earth, a **blameless** and upright man, one who fears God and shuns evil?*" (Job 1:8; 2:3)

Table 93: Some Examples of People Who Allowed the Influence of the Blameless Attribute

Some additional pearls of wisdom documented in the Old Testament of the Biblical record include:

- Bildad's comment to Job. Bildad stated, "*Behold, God will not cast away the **blameless**, nor will He uphold the evildoers*" (Job 8:20). Bildad's statement is true. However, he misapplied it to accuse Job falsely of a hidden guilt.

- Job, corrected Bildad's misapplied statement when he said, "*Though I were righteous, my own mouth would condemn me; though I were **blameless**, it would prove me perverse. I am **blameless**, yet I do not know myself; I despise my life. It is all one thing; therefore I say, 'He destroys the **blameless** and the wicked'*" (Job 9:20-22)

- David documented: "*The law of the Lord is perfect, converting the soul; the testimony of the Lord is sure, making wise the simple; the statutes of the Lord are right, rejoicing the heart; the commandment of the Lord is pure, enlightening the eyes; the fear of the Lord is clean, enduring forever; the judgments of the Lord are true and righteous altogether. More to be desired are they than gold, yea, than much fine gold; sweeter also than honey and the honeycomb. Moreover by them Your servant is warned, and in keeping them there is great reward. Who can understand his errors? Cleanse me from secret faults. Keep back Your servant also from presumptuous sins; let them not have dominion over me. Then I shall be **blameless**, and I shall be innocent of great* *transgression. Let the words of my mouth and the meditation of my heart be acceptable in Your sight, O Lord, my strength and my Redeemer"* (Psalms 19:7-14)

- o *"Let my heart be **blameless** regarding Your statutes, that I may not be ashamed"* (Psalm 119:80)

- o *"Mark the **blameless** man, and observe the upright; for the future of that man is peace. But the transgressors shall be destroyed together; the future of the wicked shall be cut off"* (Psalm 37:37-38)

- o And he called on the Lord to protect him and the **blameless** from people with the wicked attribute. David prayed to God to hide him from their secret plots, *"...who sharpen their tongue like a sword, and bend their bows to shoot their arrows—bitter words, that they may shoot in secret at the **blameless**; suddenly they shoot at him and do not fear"* (Psalm 64:3-4)

Finally, from the Old Testament, one learns that the influence of the **blameless** attribute does not allow discriminatory, prejudice, or bigoted behavior. The Book of First Samuel provides an example when the Lord sent Samuel to meet with Jesse the Bethlehemite. According to 1 Samuel 16:1, the Lord told Samuel that a king would come from Jesse's household. The Biblical record documented, *"Thus Jesse made seven of his sons pass before Samuel. And Samuel said to Jesse, "The Lord has not chosen these." And Samuel said to Jesse, "Are all the young men here?" Then he said, "There remains yet the youngest, and there he is, keeping the sheep"* (1 Samuel 16:10-11). Why were none of the first seven chosen? Because by man's standards, the influences of the negative attributes would inject discriminatory, prejudice, or bigoted ideas into the decision process. But with God, one learns as Samuel and Jesse did, *"Do not look at his appearance or at his physical stature, because I have refused him. For the Lord does not see as man sees; for man looks at the outward appearance, but the Lord looks at the heart"* (1 Samuel 16:7). Samuel's obedience to God allowed him to demonstrate the **blameless** attribute influencing his inner spirit. We must do the same.

In the New Testament, Jesus' life was an example for those influenced by the **blameless** attribute. He explained the influence of this attribute to the Pharisees when they complained to him about his hungry disciples plucking and eating heads of grain on the Sabbath. The Pharisees complained, *"...Look, Your disciples are doing what is not lawful to do on the Sabbath!"* (Matthew 12:2). To which Jesus replied, *"Have you not read what David did when he was hungry, he and those who were with him: how he entered the house of God and ate the showbread which was not lawful for him to eat, nor for those who were with him, but only for the priests? Or have you not read in the law that on the Sabbath the priests in the temple profane the Sabbath, and are **blameless**? Yet I say to you that in this place there is One greater than the temple. But if you had known what this means, 'I desire mercy and not sacrifice,' you would not have condemned the **guiltless**. For the Son of Man is Lord even of the Sabbath"* (Matthew 12:3-8). BTT allows one to see that <u>discernment</u> works hand in hand with the influence of the **blameless** attribute. Rules and traditions do not determine **blamelessness,** God does. Within the Scripture above, Jesus documented an association between the **blameless** and the merciful attributes. In spiritual matters with God, this combination allows one to be *guiltless* before God in spiritual matters. Man's lack of understanding of spiritual things, may hold another man's actions in contempt, but God will not. Consider the world's condemnation of people in the poor category. One influenced by the ***blameless*** and merciful attributes cannot condemn this category of people nor hold them in contempt. For one with the ***blameless*** and merciful attributes know that people in the poor category are also children of God, they serve a purpose, and they deserve respect.

Jesus set the ultimate example of one influenced by the ***blameless*** attribute. The New Testament also documents other people influenced by this attribute for our examples. A few of the examples include:

Examples	What Is Documented
Zacharias and Elizabeth	The Biblical record documented, "*There was in the days of Herod, the king of Judea, a certain priest named Zacharias, of the division of Abijah. His wife was of the daughters of Aaron, and her name was Elizabeth. And they were both righteous before God, walking in all the commandments and ordinances of the Lord **blameless***" (Luke 1:5-6)
Mary	She had the ***blameless*** attribute in the eyes of the Lord because the Biblical record documented, "*...the angel said to her, "Do not be afraid, Mary, for you have found favor with God*" (Luke 1:30)
John the Baptist	When the Holy Spirit fell on Zacharias, he prophesized: "*And you, child, will be called the prophet of the Highest; For you will go before the face of the Lord to prepare His ways, to give knowledge of salvation to His people by the remission of their sins, through the tender mercy of our God...*" (Luke 1:56-58). John maintained the ***blameless*** attribute to carry out his mission.
Paul	In his dedication to following the law of Moses before he became a Christian, Paul said of himself, "*...If anyone else thinks he may have confidence in the flesh, I more so: circumcised the eighth day, of the stock of Israel, of the tribe of Benjamin, a Hebrew of the Hebrews; concerning the law, a Pharisee; concerning zeal, persecuting the church; concerning the righteousness which is in the law, **blameless***" (Philippians 3:4-6)
Paul and the other apostles	After his baptism and conversion to Christianity, Paul documented of himself and the other apostles, "*You are witnesses, and God also, how devoutly and justly and **blamelessly** we behaved ourselves among you who believe; as you know how we exhorted, and comforted, and charged every one of you, as a father does his own children, that you would walk worthy of God who calls you into His own kingdom and glory*" (1 Thessalonians 2:10-12)

Table 94: More Examples of People Who Allowed the Influence of the Blameless Attribute

Paul's conversion to Christianity occurred after the crucifixion of Jesus and after the apostles began taking the Gospel to the world. Paul taught the same exact Gospel message as the other apostles. Through his writings, the Holy Spirit inspired him to document some important pearls of wisdom concerning the influence of the ***blameless*** attribute. From Paul's writings, BTT allows one to see that to acquire and achieve the full measure of the ***blameless*** attribute in one's inner spirit, one must work daily on certain positive behaviors until these behaviors becomes routine. He wrote one must:

The Behavior	What Is Documented
Study and learn God's Word	To the church in Corinth, he wrote. *"I thank my God always concerning you for the grace of God which was given to you by Christ Jesus, that you were enriched in everything by Him in all utterance and all knowledge, even as the testimony of Christ was confirmed in you, so that you come short in no gift, eagerly waiting for the revelation of our Lord Jesus Christ, who will also confirm you to the end, that you may be **blameless** in the day of our Lord Jesus Christ"* (1 Corinthians 1:4-8)
Not engage in divisive practices	*"Now I say this, that each of you says, "I am of Paul," or "I am of Apollos," or "I am of Cephas," or "I am of Christ." Is Christ divided? Was Paul crucified for you? Or were you baptized in the name of Paul? I thank God that I baptized none of you except Crispus and Gaius, lest anyone should say that I had baptized in my own name"* (1 Corinthians 1:12-15)
Learn to do all things without complaining and disputing	*"Do all things without complaining and disputing, that you may become **blameless** and harmless, children of God without fault in the midst of a crooked and perverse generation, among whom you shine as lights in the world, holding fast the word of life..."* (Philippians 2:14-16)
After baptism continue to walk **blamelessly**	*"...you, who once were alienated and enemies in your mind by wicked works, yet now He has reconciled in the body of His flesh through death, to present you holy, and **blameless**, and above reproach in His sight— if indeed you continue in the faith, grounded and steadfast, and are not moved away from the hope of the gospel which you heard, which was preached to every creature under heaven, of which I, Paul, became a minister"* (Colossians 1:21-23)
Increase and abound in love to one another and to all	*"...may the Lord make you increase and abound in love to one another and to all, just as we do to you, so that He may establish your hearts **blameless** in holiness before our God and Father at the coming of our Lord Jesus Christ with all His saints"* (1 Thessalonians 3:12-13)
Treat members of the Lord's church and outsiders with respect	*"Do not rebuke an older man, but exhort him as a father, younger men as brothers, older women as mothers, younger women as sisters, with all purity"* (1 Timothy 5:1-2)
Honor true widows	*"Honor widows who are really widows. But if any widow has children or grandchildren, let them first learn to show piety at home and to repay their parents; for this is good and acceptable before God. Now she who is really a widow, and left alone, trusts in God and continues in supplications and prayers night and day. But she who lives in pleasure is dead while she lives. And these things command, that they may be **blameless**. But if anyone does not provide for his own, and especially for those of his household, he has denied the faith and is worse than an unbeliever"* (1 Timothy 5:3-8)
Speak and teach the words of the	*"If anyone teaches otherwise and does not consent to wholesome words, even the words of our Lord Jesus Christ, and to the doctrine which accords with godliness, he is proud, knowing nothing, but is obsessed with disputes*

Gospel as they are and not add to them	*and arguments over words, from which come envy, strife, reviling, evil suspicions, useless wranglings of men of corrupt minds and destitute of the truth, who suppose that godliness is a means of gain. From such withdraw yourself"* (1 Timothy 6:3-5)
Flee the love of money and foolish and harmful lusts (1 Timothy 6:9-10)	*"But you, O man of God, flee these things and pursue righteousness, godliness, faith, love, patience, gentleness. Fight the good fight of faith, lay hold on eternal life, to which you were also called and have confessed the good confession in the presence of many witnesses. I urge you in the sight of God who gives life to all things, and before Christ Jesus who witnessed the good confession before Pontius Pilate, that you keep this commandment without spot,* **blameless** *until our Lord Jesus Christ's appearing..."* (1 Timothy 6:11-14)

Table 95: Positive Behaviors to Mature the Blameless Attribute in One's Inner Spirit

The influence of the **blameless** attribute on Paul was profound. The Holy Spirit's influence on him led him to express a seriousness about the Gospel of Jesus Christ unseen anywhere in history. Next to Jesus' example, Paul's example is one worthy of following. When Paul wrote his second letter to the church in Corinth, commenting about the apostles handling of God's Word, he stated, *"We then, as workers together with Him also plead with you not to receive the grace of God in vain. For He says: "In an acceptable time I have heard you, and in the day of salvation I have helped you." Behold, now is the accepted time; behold, now is the day of salvation. We give no offense in anything, that our ministry may not be* **blamed**" (2 Corinthians 6:1-3). Paul wanted everyone who was baptized into Christ to take his or her Christian responsibilities as seriously as he did. He did not want to bring **blame** or shame on his or the apostle's work in the ministry of the Gospel. Paul expressed this same seriousness in other areas, because of the influence of the **blameless** attribute. Two examples included:

- Transparency in handing contributions to the Lord's church and its distribution. As Titus prepared to transport a lavish gift from the churches in Corinth to other needy congregations, Paul wrote, *"And we have sent with him the brother whose praise is in the gospel throughout all the churches, and not only that, but who was also chosen by the churches to travel with us with this gift, which is administered by us to the glory of the Lord Himself and to show your ready mind, avoiding this: that anyone should* **blame** *us in this lavish gift which is administered by us—providing honorable things, not only in the sight of the Lord, but also in the sight of men"* (2 Corinthians 8:18-21).

- Showing favoritism, discrimination, or prejudice. Paul corrected an apostle caught in this sin. When Peter temporarily lost the influence of the **blameless** attribute, Paul documented, *"Now when Peter had come to Antioch, I withstood him to his face, because he was to be* **blamed**; *for before certain men came from James, he would eat with the Gentiles; but when they came, he withdrew and separated himself, fearing those who were of the circumcision. And the rest of the Jews also played the hypocrite with him, so that even Barnabas was carried away with their hypocrisy"* (Galatians 2:11-13).

In the first example above, BTT allows one to see that if one does not take precautions to do things transparently and correctly, especially the handling of money, people will find fault where none exists. Perception and suspicion, mixed with the influence of the liar attribute, allows the negative forces to cast a shadow of unjustified **blame** over one's character. Perception, suspicion, and the liar attribute override reality in spiritual warfare to bring harm to people influenced by the positive attributes. Wherever possible, the negative forces use this strategy to plant seeds of **blame**. For in spiritual warfare, positive forces are *guilty* until proven innocent. Paul corrected the situation in this example to ensure Titus's *integrity* and the **blameless** attribute stayed intact from misperceptions and false accusations. Paul nor Titus gave the negative forces of the campaign an opportunity to exploit the good work done by the positive forces and the churches in Corinth.

In the second example, BTT allows one to see how negative behavior and bad judgement can cripple the influence of the **blameless** attribute in one's inner spirit. In the example with Peter in Galatians 2:11-13, he demonstrated favoritism, discrimination, and possibly a prejudicial behavior toward new Christians when some Jews came around. The Bible documented that he "*withdrew and separated himself*" from Christians in the presence of unconverted Jews. Because of spiritual warfare, his hypocrisy was so powerful that even the converted Jews and Barnabas began to follow his lead. BTT allows one to see that Peter initially had the influence of the **blameless** attribute. However, the attribute left his inner spirit during his hypocrisy. When Paul saw Peter's behavior, he immediately confronted and corrected him. Paul, influenced by the **blameless** attribute, held Peter accountable for his actions. Had Paul overlooked the situation, the **blameless** attribute would have forsaken his inner spirit too and the negative forces of the war campaign would have scored a decisive victory. Through this example, one can see that one must take a stand for what is right in the eyes of God to retain the **blameless** attribute's influence. Moreover, BTT allows one to see that holding Christian's accountable stops sin from spreading in the body of Christ.

Unfortunately, because of the fog of the war campaign, many in the religious community are caught-up in this very sin each day. Despite the fact that Paul, a converted Jew himself, documented from the Holy Spirit, that "*There is neither Jew nor Greek, there is neither slave nor free, there is neither male nor female; for you are all one in Christ Jesus*" (Galatians 3:28), many in the religious community continue to claim that God has authorized the practice of Judaism alongside of Christianity today. This **false** teaching seeks to place God in a state of hypocrisy. For God sent His Son Jesus Christ to convert Jews through Christ's teachings. The negative attribute's influence through spiritual warfare has successfully confused the religious community. Many people in these communities uphold the practice of Judaism or mix Mosaic doctrines with Christ's Word in their assemblies, teachings, and worship to God. This divisive tactic continues to cost countless souls their opportunity to reach heaven. Peter was **guilty** of hypocrisy and so is everyone who perpetuates this belief today. The Truth is this. The nation of Israel separated itself from God long before Christianity appeared. Please read carefully what the prophet Isaiah documented long ago in the Book of Isaiah in Isaiah 59:1-8:

> "*Behold, the Lord's hand is not shortened, that it cannot save; nor His ear heavy, that it cannot hear. But your iniquities have separated you from your*

God; and your sins have hidden His face from you, so that He will not hear. For your hands are defiled with blood, and your fingers with iniquity; your lips have spoken lies, your tongue has muttered perversity. No one calls for justice, nor does any plead for truth. They trust in empty words and speak lies; they conceive evil and bring forth iniquity. They hatch vipers' eggs and weave the spider's web; he who eats of their eggs dies, and from that which is crushed a viper breaks out. Their webs will not become garments, nor will they cover themselves with their works; their works are works of iniquity, and the act of violence is in their hands. Their feet run to evil, and they make haste to shed innocent blood; their thoughts are thoughts of iniquity; wasting and destruction are in their paths. The way of peace they have not known, and there is no justice in their ways; they have made themselves crooked paths; whoever takes that way shall not know peace"

People who are claiming that God has authorized the practice of Judaism alongside of Christianity today are guilty of a grave sin. **False** teachers, and all who follow in their error will be **blamed** and condemned for this religious error when Christ returns. Please do not be deceived.

Paul reemphasized the fact that one can be **blameless** before God, and it is His desire that one strives to acquire this state. He wrote, *"Blessed be the God and Father of our Lord Jesus Christ, who has blessed us with every spiritual blessing in the heavenly places in Christ, just as He chose us in Him before the foundation of the world, that we should be holy and without **blame** before Him in love…"* (Ephesians 1:3-4). Here, Paul was not just speaking about the apostles. He wrote this letter to the saints (those in Christ's church) in Ephesus. This same message applies to everyone who accepts Christ through <u>baptism</u> and become part of His kingdom by striving to live a godly life. Hence, when Paul told the Thessalonian congregation, *"Now may the God of peace Himself sanctify you completely; and may your whole spirit, soul, and body be preserved **blameless** at the coming of our Lord Jesus Christ"* (1 Thessalonians 5:23), it also applied to the Christians of today. The words are spiritual encouragement for all the people on the side of the positive forces of the campaign striving to live and remain **blameless** among this wicked and perverse generation.

Peter also captured this same thought concerning the influence of the **blameless** attribute. Peter understood the strategies generated by the negative forces and the power of the **blameless** attribute first hand; for at one time, he was not **blameless** nor did he have the attribute. He denied knowing Jesus after walking with Him and the disciples according to Matthew 26:69-74; Mark 14:66-71; Luke 22:54-60; and John 18:15-26. Jesus restored Peter in the faith. More importantly, Peter recognized that Jesus was going to return to earth one day, so he wrote, *"Therefore, beloved, looking forward to these things, be diligent to be found by Him in peace, without spot and **blameless**…"* (2 Peter 3:14). When Jesus returns, everybody will wish he or she had acquired the influence of the **blameless** attribute on the Day of Accountability.

God, in His infinite wisdom, established a way for Christians and people of the world to see living examples of people who are influenced by the **blameless** attribute. Beginning in the

1st Century, with the assembly of Christians on the first day of each week after the Day of Pentecost, the Lord established physical positions of responsibility for men to lead His church. These positions are part of the operational and organizational structure for an assembly of God's people. Unfortunately, the negative forces use spiritual warfare to distort God's structure with immeasurable inaccuracies. However, God's Word stands. The Biblical record only identifies four positions in the Lord's church and all are required to have the influence of the ***blameless*** attribute. The Biblically authorized positions are elders, a minister(s), teachers, and deacons. BTT automatically allows one to see that the negative forces of the war campaign have distorted this structure throughout the world. However, for one to retain the influence of the ***blameless*** attribute, one must follow the Lord's command and the pattern He authorized. The Biblical record documented that Christ's church must strive to have:

- Elders: synonymous with bishops (1 Timothy 3:1), overseers (Acts 20:28), pastors and shepherds (Ephesians 4:11), and presbytery (1 Timothy 4:14). The Biblical record documents, "*A bishop then must be **blameless**...*" (1 Timothy 3:2) and, "*...if a man is **blameless**, the husband of one wife, having faithful children not accused of dissipation or insubordination. For a bishop must be **blameless**, as a steward of God...*" (Titus 1:6-7). These men by default are to serve as ministers and teachers if no others are available to help in these two roles.

- A minister(s): By default, this man must have the influence of the ***blameless*** attribute as he preaches the Gospel of Jesus Christ to the assembly. Paul documented, "*How then shall they call on Him in whom they have not believed? And how shall they believe in Him of whom they have not heard? And how shall they hear without a preacher? And how shall they preach unless they are sent? As it is written: "How beautiful are the feet of those who preach the gospel of peace, who bring glad tidings of good things!*" (Romans 10:14-15)

- Teachers: James documented, "*My brethren, let not many of you become teachers, knowing that we shall receive a stricter judgment. For we all stumble in many things. If anyone does not stumble in word, he is a perfect man, able also to bridle the whole body*" (James 3:1-2)

- Deacons: They support the eldership in the conduct of Lord's work for the church for specific tasks. Nothing else. The Biblical record documents that they must be tested, "*... then let them serve as deacons, being found **blameless**...*" (1 Timothy 3:10). The ***blameless*** attribute is important here because of the example they must set for the rest of the congregation.

Once again as defined above, to serve in leadership positions in Christ's church, one is required to have a measure of the ***blameless*** attribute. If this attribute is not present in the people selected for these positions, the negative forces of the war campaign gains opportunities to corrupt the assembly. Unfortunately, many religious organizations have dismissed the role of an eldership and replaced it with boards, committees, and a preacher running the organization. These are organizations by man's designs and not from God's divine pattern that He established beginning with the 1st Century church. Boards, committees, and preacher-led church structures create ripe environments for the negative forces to flourish. Chapter XII of this book covers this fact in detail. For now, understand that these organizations trample the ***blameless*** attribute's influence. One must leave these organizations and seek God's Truth through His Word to be saved in the war campaign. Even righteous Lot, having the influence of the ***blameless*** attribute, left his home (2 Peter 2:8) to remain in the Lord. Please do not be deceived.

It takes BTT to fully digest the implication of having the influence of the ***blameless*** attribute in one's inner spirit. However, the reward for acquiring and maturing this attribute is substantial. Paul documented for Christians, "*...you, who once were alienated and enemies in your mind by wicked works, yet now He has reconciled in the body of His flesh through death, to present you holy, and **blameless**, and above reproach in His sight— if indeed you continue in the faith, grounded and steadfast, and are not moved away from the hope of the gospel which you heard, which was preached to every creature under heaven, of which I, Paul, became a minister*" (Colossians 1:21-23). Paul's statement acknowledged that one can achieve a state of ***blamelessness***. BTT allows one to see that this state comes by allowing one's inner spirit to be influenced by the ***blameless*** attribute and one's obedience to God's Word. From Paul's statement, by continuing with faith and obedience, staying grounded and steadfast, and maintaining the hope that is developed through the study of the Gospel, one will live with God one day. However, Paul pointed out that "*wicked works*" cause people to be alienated from God and become His enemy. Wicked works can be works people create to edify God outwardly, but inwardly are simply works to glorify the person. These works are born from selfish ambitions that appear good but have no significance to God. Paul warned the churches in Corinth and Philippi about selfish ambition and other negative behaviors when he wrote, "*For I fear lest, when I come, I shall not find you such as I wish, and that I shall be found by you such as you do not wish; lest there be contentions, jealousies, outbursts of wrath, selfish ambitions, backbitings, whisperings, conceits, tumults...*" (2 Corinthians 12:20), and "*Let nothing be done through selfish ambition or conceit, but in lowliness of mind let each esteem others better than himself*" (Philippians 2:3). All these things stop the influence of the **blameless** attribute from feeding one's inner spirit. For people who will say to Jesus on the Day of Judgement, "*Lord, Lord, have we not prophesied in Your name, cast out demons in Your name, and done many wonders in Your name?*" (Matthew 7:22). He will respond, "*I never knew you; depart from Me, you who practice lawlessness!*" (Matthew 7:23). <u>Discernment</u> is critical for avoiding this situation and for one to remain **blameless**. To acquire and mature the **blameless** attribute, one must study God's Word and seek its understanding. This is the only way to ensure one avoids the negative path of life and remains ***blameless*** in the war campaign.

The **Good attribute**: People influenced by the ***good*** attribute make up the largest portion of the positive forces in the war campaign. Why? Because this attribute's influence can extend to, and be seen in, large populations of people in religious and secular communities. However, this attribute by itself does not make one a Christian and nor will it save one's soul. It simply means the spirit of the ***good*** attribute does not discriminate and is available to everyone. In fact, one will learn that even people influenced by

the negative forces can behave in a ***good*** manner sometimes. Jesus Himself said, "*...if you love those who love you, what credit is that to you? For even sinners love those who love them. And if you do **good** to those who do **good** to you, what credit is that to you? For even sinners do the same*" (Luke 6:32-33). In other words, a specific situation or event may cause one to allow the influence of a very small measure of this attribute at the carnal level. But if that person does not allow the attribute to influence their inner spirit, it will soon depart. The prophet Micah documented that God "*...has shown you, O man, what is **good**; and what does the Lord require of you but to do justly, to love mercy, and to walk humbly with your God?*" (Micah 6:8). BTT allows one to see for this attribute to grow, it must combine with other positive attributes; specifically, the just, upright/honorable, merciful, and faithful attributes. With this combination influencing one's inner spirit, the ***good*** attribute is nourished and can lead one to do what is considered morally right and decent in the world. It causes one to be benevolent and to have empathy for others regardless of race, gender, or nationality. Because it is the right thing to do, this attribute influences one to extend his or her hands to help another person in times of conflict, regardless of the situation or condition. Based on all the above, one can see that this attribute is extremely complex, and one must carefully study God's Word to fully appreciate this ***clean spirit's*** influence and impact on the inner spirit. As one begins to read this chapter keep this very important fact in mind: One who considers himself to be ***good***, but ignores, allows, or fails to speak out on the actions of the wicked are complicit in those actions and will be held accountable by God. BTT allows one to see that a ***good*** person without God's Truth is just a lost soul in the war campaign. Hence, to get one's soul into heaven from this side of life requires more than just this attribute alone. One must attain the righteous attribute; the sum of all the positive attributes combined and God's grace.

The influence of the ***good*** attribute in one's inner spirit works directly with the cognitive and emotional side of one's physical brain. This attribute often manifests itself as a positive reaction and is accompanied by an emotion, a gesture, or some other form of positive behavior. Its influences can remove walls of discrimination, partiality, favoritism, and hate. Moreover, the attribute can be seen in small measures in non-believers. Often, because of the nature of this attribute, it is mistaken as the merciful attribute. However, as much as they work together, these spirits are very different. A more tragic mistake made by many people is believing that being ***good*** alone will give them favor with God when they die. They foolishly believe the ***good*** things they do in life will make up for any sins they have committed. Unfortunately, these are people unaware that they have been deceived by a strategy perpetrated by the negative forces in spiritual warfare. The Spirit of wisdom addressed this error with Solomon as he documented "*Most men will proclaim each his own **goodness**, but who can find a faithful man?*" (Proverbs 20:6). In other words, to have an opportunity for heaven, the ***good*** and faithful attributes must be present in one's inner spirit. This combination influences one seek what God defines as ***good*** and be obedient to the whole counsel of God (Acts 20:27). This is consistent with God's statement that, "*...My thoughts are not your thoughts, nor are your ways My ways,*" says the Lord" (Isaiah 55:8).

Now the positive forces of the war campaign benefit from religious organizations and parents that teach positive behavior from the Bible. For embedded in their teachings are truths about the ***good*** attribute from God. However, God's desires one to mature so that small measures of the attribute can influence one to pursue greater understandings of His True will. BTT allows one to see that one can acquire a small amount of the influence of the **good** attribute and, because of one's lifestyle and behavior, remain estranged from God. Examples of people in this category are those who give, feed the hungry, and even protect others from the negative forces, but refuse to hear and obey what the Biblical record documents from the Lord. They are not on the negative side of the war campaign, but they easily succumb with each strike from the negative forces or fall as collateral causalities on the spiritual battlefield. Unfortunately, in Revelations 3:15-21, Jesus described these people as "Lukewarm." Or worse yet, the people of Matthew 7:21-23.

<u>Discernment</u> and BTT are necessary to identify people influenced by this attribute. The Bible documents, "*...Satan himself transforms himself into an angel of light*" (2 Corinthians 11:14). Satan can masquerade as someone or something **good**. In other words, there are people influenced by the negative forces of the campaign who pose as people influenced by the **good** attribute. There are also works, charities, governmental policies, and ideas that seem **good** at the time but in the end lead to death. In physical warfare, spies are an example of people who pose as *good* people but whose real intentions are to bring harm. There are many charities and governmental programs that fall in this category. One must apply God's Word and <u>discernment</u> to establish the intent of these *good* works to avoid sanctioning an effort that violates God's Word. Satan, posing as an angel of light, has crafted many charities that keep many people lost in spiritual warfare. These charities' time, money, and energy support the negative forces of the war campaign. A simple example can be charities that engage in activities on Sundays that lure people away from God's worship services. Although the charity may be for a **good** cause, its demands force **good** people to choose between it and the Lord. BTT and <u>discernment</u> must be applied; do not be deceived.

The Spirit of wisdom revealed to Solomon that gaining the full measure of the **good** attribute requires commitment. It requires walking a different path and following a different doctrine than the rest of the world. Solomon learned that one must:

- Accept God's wisdom. He documented, "*For the Lord gives wisdom; from His mouth come knowledge and understanding; He stores up sound wisdom for the upright; He is a shield to those who walk uprightly; He guards the paths of justice, and preserves the way of His saints. Then you will understand righteousness and justice, equity and every **good** path*" (Proverbs 2:6-9)

- Accept God's doctrine. He taught his children stating, "*Hear, my children, the instruction of a father, and give attention to know understanding; for I give you **good** doctrine: Do not forsake my law*" (Proverbs 4:2)

- Walk in the way of God. He documented for those that give in to the influences of the immoral and adultery attributes (Proverbs 2:16-17), "*...nor do they regain the path of life - so you may walk in the way of **goodness**, and keep to the paths of righteousness*" (Proverbs 2:19-20).

Solomon learned that wisdom and understanding are the keys to finding the influence of the **good** attribute. He documented that, "*He who gets wisdom loves his own soul; he who* *keeps understanding will find **good**"* (Proverbs 19:8). Interestingly, the Spirit of wisdom revealed that understanding was part of the equation tied to the Lord. She told him, *"For the Lord gives wisdom; from His mouth come knowledge and understanding..."* (Proverbs 2:6). BTT allows one to see that if one desires the full measure of the **good** attribute's influence, one must seek the Lord first. Without the Lord, the **good** attribute may only influence one's behavior with minimal short-term cognitive results.

The **good** attribute's influence is always with people influenced by the other positive attributes. For example, Solomon documented that, *"The desire of the righteous is only **good**..."* (Proverbs 11:23) and, *"as evil pursues sinners, but to the righteous, **good** shall be repaid"* (Proverbs 13:21). He documented that, *"the merciful man does **good** for his own soul, but he who is cruel troubles his own flesh"* (Proverbs 11:17). He also documented that, *"...the blameless will inherit **good**"* (Proverbs 28:10) and for, *"those who rebuke the **wicked**, they will have delight and a **good** blessing will come upon them"* (Proverbs 24:25). In fact, since marriage is **honorable** (Hebrews 13:4), the Spirit of wisdom even revealed to Solomon that, *"He who finds a wife finds a **good** thing, and obtains favor from the LORD"* (Proverbs 18:22). Why? Because Proverbs 31:10-29 reveals the characteristics of a virtuous wife. In these writings, one learns that *"her worth is far above rubies. The heart of her husband safely trusts her; so he will have no lack of gain. She does him **good** and not evil all the days of her life"* (Proverbs 31:10-12). Further, her work supporting the relationship is **good**, as the Proverbs reveals, *"from her profits she plants a vineyard. She girds herself with strength, and strengthens her arms. She perceives that her merchandise is **good**, and her lamp does not go out by night"* (Proverbs 31:16-18).

The Spirit of wisdom revealed some trusted behavioral signs of one influenced by the **good** attribute to Solomon. Solomon documented:

The Behavior	What Is Documented
Always shares and quick to help others	*"Do not withhold **good** from those to whom it is due, when it is in the power of your hand to do so. Do not say to your neighbor, "Go, and come back, and tomorrow I will give it," when you have it with you"* (Proverbs 3:27-28)
Does not show favoritism or partiality	*"To show partiality is not **good**, because for a piece of bread a man will transgress"* (Proverbs 28:21). He also documented, *"These things also belong to the wise: It is not **good** to show partiality in judgment"* (Proverbs 24:23) and *"It is not **good** to show partiality to the wicked..."* (Proverbs 18:5)
Does not cheat or deceive	*"Diverse weights are an abomination to the LORD, and dishonest scales are not **good**"* (Proverbs 20:23). In addition, he documented, *"It is **good** for nothing," cries the buyer; but when he has gone his way, then he boasts"* (Proverbs 20:14)
Does not harm people	*"Whoever rewards evil for **good**, evil will not depart from his house"* (Proverbs 17:13), and *"Also, to punish the righteous is not **good**..."* (Proverbs 17:26)

Does not reject hearing God's Word	"*...it is not **good** for a soul to be without knowledge, and he sins who hastens with his feet*" (Proverbs 19:2), and "*He who heeds the word wisely will find **good**, and whoever trusts in the LORD, happy is he*" (Proverbs 16:20)
Guards their ***good*** reputation closely	"*A **good** name is to be chosen rather than great riches, loving favor rather than silver and gold*" (Proverbs 22:1)
Strives to support future generations	"*A **good** man leaves an inheritance to his children's children*" (Proverbs 13:22)

Table 96: Trusted Signs of One Who Allows the Influence of the Good Attribute

The Spirit of wisdom summed up all of the above by revealing to Solomon, "*He who has a deceitful heart finds no **good**...*" (Proverbs 17:20). Solomon understood this and allowed the influences of the ***good*** attribute, as well as the other ***clean spirits***, to guide him through most of his reign as king. He understood the influence of the ***good*** attribute comes when one honestly seeks the attribute on God's terms. He wrote, "*He who earnestly seeks **good** finds favor, but trouble will come to him who seeks evil*" (Proverbs 11:27). He elaborated that, "*A **good** man obtains favor from the LORD...*" (Proverbs 12:2), that "***Good** understanding gains favor...*" (Proverbs 13:15) and that "*...a **good** man will be satisfied from above*" (Proverbs 14:14). To have favor from God brings satisfaction. When one has the influence of the ***good*** attribute, the favor and satisfaction one receives evokes prayer and thanksgiving. For these things, Solomon wrote, "*A man will be satisfied with **good** by the fruit of his mouth...*" (Proverbs 12:14). In other words, there is a reciprocal correlation to prayer, thanksgiving, supplication, and the fruit that comes from one's mouth because of God's magnificent favor. The importance of this cannot be overstated. One influenced by the ***good*** attribute speaks ***good*** things to others, which changes lives for the positive. The Spirit of wisdom revealed to Solomon that, "*Anxiety in the heart of man causes depression, but a **good** word makes it glad*" (Proverbs 12:25), and "*A man has joy by the answer of his mouth, and a word spoken in due season, how **good** it is!*" (Proverbs 15:23). Solomon also documented that "*A merry heart does **good**, like medicine, but a broken spirit dries the bones*" (Proverbs 17:22). When one influenced by the ***good*** attribute speaks ***good*** things, the Spirit of wisdom revealed to Solomon that, "*... a **good** report makes the bones healthy*" (Proverbs 15:30), and "*As cold water to a weary soul, so is **good** news from a far country*" (Proverbs 25:25).

In contrast to all the positive things cited above, one must understand that the negative attributes seek to hinder the ***good*** attribute's effectiveness. Solomon documented, "*A violent man entices his neighbor, and leads him in a way that is not **good**...*" (Proverbs 16:29). In another example, Solomon documented, "*Do they not go astray who devise evil? But mercy and truth belong to those who devise **good***" (Proverbs 14:22). However, God confirms that He is in control. Solomon documented, "*The eyes of the LORD are in every place, keeping watch on the evil and the **good***" (Proverbs 15:3). Moreover, one can find comfort and hope in knowing that "*The evil will bow before the **good**, and the wicked at the gates of the righteous*" (Proverbs 14:19). Thus, one can see that having the ***good*** attribute is extremely important.

Solomon compared the knowledge of wisdom to the **goodness** of honey to illustrate the **goodness** of God's wisdom. He told his son, "*My son, eat honey because it is **good**, and the honeycomb which is sweet to your taste; so shall the knowledge of wisdom be to your soul; if you have found it, there is a prospect, and your hope will not be cut off*" (Proverbs 24:13-14). In contrast, Solomon said, "*It is not **good** to eat much honey; so to seek one's own glory is not glory*" (Proverbs 25:27). From these two proverbs, one can see that balance is key when it comes to the influence of the **good** attribute in one's life. The importance of balance will become even clearer as one continues to read.

Before journeying through the rest of the Biblical record to see all the wonderful information provided by the Lord on the influence of the **good** attribute, one must understand that the Lord Himself knows what is **good**. As the Creator of **good**, His handiwork demonstrated this attribute when He formed the universe. Because God created all things, He had the unquestionable right to define what is **good** through His handiwork because of His divine wisdom and knowledge. To this end, God defined what is **good** by the following examples of His majestic handiwork:

- He created the heavens, the earth, and light and "*...And God saw the light, that it was **good**; and God divided the light from the darkness*" (Genesis 1:1-4)

- He separated the waters and the land: "*And God called the dry land Earth, and the gathering together of the waters He called Seas. And God saw that it was **good***" (Genesis 1:10)

- He put vegetation on the earth**:** "*And the earth brought forth grass, the herb that yields seed according to its kind, and the tree that yields fruit, whose seed is in itself according to its kind. And God saw that it was **good***" (Genesis 1:12)

- He made the sun, moon, and stars: "*God set them in the firmament of the heavens to give light on the earth, and to rule over the day and over the night, and to divide the light from the darkness. And God saw that it was **good***" (Genesis 1:17-18)

- He made the animals of the seas and oceans and flying animals: "*So God created great sea creatures and every living thing that moves, with which the waters abounded, according to their kind, and every winged bird according to its kind. And God saw that it was **good***" (Genesis 1:21)

- He made every kind of beast and everything that crawled: "*And God made the beast of the earth according to its kind, cattle according to its kind, and everything that creeps on the earth according to its kind. And God saw that it was **good***" (Genesis 1:25)

- He observed all of His work: "*Then God saw everything that He had made, and indeed it was very **good**. So the evening and the morning were the sixth day*" (Genesis 1:31)

- He made "*...every tree grow that is pleasant to the sight and **good** for food. The tree of life was also in the midst of the garden, and the tree of the knowledge of **good** and evil*" (Genesis 2:9)

- He placed the gold in Havilah: *"Now a river went out of Eden to water the garden, and from there it parted and became four riverheads. The name of the first is Pishon; it is the one which skirts the whole land of Havilah, where there is gold. And the gold of that land is **good**. Bdellium and the onyx stone are there"* (Genesis 2:12)

Universally, one sees that the Lord knows what is **good**. Therefore, it only stands to reason that He universally knows what is not **good**. So, as God created mankind in His own image to inhabit the earth which was **good**, He also said, *"...It is not good that man should be alone; I will make him a helper comparable to him"* (Genesis 2:18). Thus, God created the woman from one of the man's ribs according to Genesis 2:21-22. Here is where the war campaign becomes visible on earth.

The Biblical record documented that, *"...the Lord God took the man and put him in the Garden of Eden to tend and keep it. And the Lord God commanded the man, saying, "Of every tree of the garden you may freely eat; but of the tree of the knowledge of **good** and **evil** you shall not eat, for in the day that you eat of it you shall surely die"* (Genesis 2:15-17). BTT allows one to see that everything up to the point of the creation of man and woman was **good** and had the influence of the **good** attribute. However, a spirit of something not good then entered God's creation. A negative spirit influenced a serpent that God had made of which the Bible documented as, *"...more cunning than any beast of the field which the Lord God had made..."* (Genesis 3:1). The serpent, influenced by a negative spirit, deceived man's helper into eating from the tree of the knowledge of **good** and evil. The serpent told her that, *"...God knows that in the day you eat of it your eyes will be opened, and you will be like God, knowing **good** and evil." So when the woman saw that the tree was **good** for food, that it was pleasant to the eyes, and a tree desirable to make one wise, she took of its fruit and ate. She also gave to her husband with her, and he ate"* (Genesis 3:5-6). Both the woman and man ate of the fruit. The knowledge that came from this tree opened the door for the full measure of the influences of both the positive and negative attributes and destroyed their innocence. The Bible documents that *"Then the Lord God said, "Behold, the man has become like one of Us, to know **good** and evil. And now, lest he put out his hand and take also of the tree of life, and eat, and live forever"*— (Genesis 3:22). Because God's creations acquired the influences of the **good** and evil attribute at the same time, they became unclean. This unclean state separated the man, woman, and serpent from the rest of God's pure creation. Therefore, the Biblical record documented that God removed them from their earthly paradise, called the "Garden of Eden," forever. From that day forward, the war campaign between the positive attributes, which leads humanity back to God, and the negative attributes that lead humanity away from God, would fight on the earth for souls in spiritual combat.

Not all was lost. The man and woman, known as Adam and Eve, had a lot of work to do because of their sin. They bore the responsibility of teaching **good** and evil to their children. One should know that sometimes they were successful and sometimes they were not successful. This fact is clear because the Biblical record documented that Cain, Adam and Eve's first born, murdered Abel, their youngest son. Cain lacked the influence of the **good** attribute. In addition, after many generations a time came when the negative forces of the war campaign overpowered the positive forces. This period grieved God so much that He said, *"I will destroy man whom I have created from the face of the earth, both man and beast, creeping thing and birds of the* *air, for I am sorry that I have made them." But Noah found grace in the eyes of the Lord"* (Genesis 6:6-8). The Lord saved Noah and his family to repopulate the earth. Noah had the responsibility to teach his descendants about the influences of **good** and evil in the new world. BTT allows one to see, over generations and spiritual warfare, the positive and negative attributes continued their fight. Consequently, there are many examples of people in the Old Testament who demonstrated the influence of the **good** attribute. Some examples include:

Who	**What Example Was Provided**
King Abimelech	He displayed the influence of the **good** attribute to Isaac after Isaac camped in the king's kingdom in the land of Gerar according to Genesis 26:1-27. As Isaac departed, Abimelech, his friend Ahuzzath, and Phichol the commander of Abimelech's army said, "*... We have certainly seen that the Lord is with you. So we said, 'Let there now be an oath between us, between you and us; and let us make a covenant with you, that you will do us no harm, since we have not touched you, and since we have done nothing to you but **good** and have sent you away in peace. You are now the blessed of the Lord'*" (Genesis 26:28-29)
Joseph	After he interpreted a butler's dream, the Bible recorded, "*When the chief baker saw that the interpretation was **good**, he said to Joseph, "I also was in my dream, and there were three white baskets on my head...."*" (Genesis 40:16)
	He interpreted the dreams of a Pharaoh and provided him with advice. To this, the biblical record documents, "*So the advice was **good** in the eyes of Pharaoh and in the eyes of all his servants*" (Genesis 41:37)
Jethro	Jethro, Moses' father-in-law, told Moses that he was not allowing the influence of the **good** attribute by taking on so much of the burden of the children of Israel. Jethro told Moses, "*The thing that you do is not **good**"* (Exodus 18:17). He helped Moses organize the people for better managed, command, and control (Exodus 18:19-26)
Moses	Demonstrated the attribute to Hobab, the son of Reuel the Midianite. Moses said to him, "*...Please do not leave, inasmuch as you know how we are to camp in the wilderness, and you can be our eyes. And it shall be, if you go with us—indeed it shall be—that whatever **good** the Lord will do to us, the same we will do to you*" (Numbers 10:31-32)
Joshua	He allowed the Gibeonites to live among the children of Israel after the elders had been deceived, formed a covenant with them, and then wanted to kill them according to Joshua Chapter 9. When the Gibeonites rouge was exposed, they said to Joshua, "*And now, here we are, in your hands; do with us as it seems **good** and right to do to us*" (Joshua 9:25). Joshua honored the oath before God to let them live, and removed them from the children of Israel so they would not kill them according to Joshua 9:26. However, as punishment for their rouge, he condemned them to be, "*...woodcutters and water carriers for the congregation and for the altar of the Lord, in the place which He would choose, even to this day*" (Joshua 9:27)
	He was judge of Israel. He destroyed the altar of Baal and cut down the wooden images beside it (Judges 6:30); took three hundred select men and destroyed, Zebah and Zalmunna and their armies (Judges 8:10); and destroyed the cities of Succoth and Penuel that refused to provide food for his

Gideon	men prior to the fight (Judges 8:5-9). However, the Bible documented, "*...as soon as Gideon was dead, that the children of Israel again played the harlot with the Baals, and made Baal-Berith their god. Thus the children of Israel did not remember the Lord their God, who had delivered them from the hands of all their enemies on every side; nor did they show kindness to the house of Jerubbaal (Gideon) in accordance with the **good** he had done for Israel*" (Judges 8:33-35)
Ruth	Naomi identified the attribute in Ruth as she went out and gleaned the fields of Boaz to gather food for her and Naomi to eat. Naomi said to Ruth, "*...It is **good**, my daughter, that you go out with his young women, and that people do not meet you in any other field*" (Ruth 2:22) and she did as Naomi instructed.
Hannah	Clearly, she had the **good** attribute that demonstrated by her behavior to Elkahah (her husband) and Peninnah (Elkahah's second wife) who verbally abused her. The Biblical record documented that because Hannah could not have children, Peninnah, "*her rival also provoked her severely, to make her miserable, because the Lord had closed her womb*" (1 Samuel 1:6). But Hannah endured and petitioning God for a child. Eli heard and blessed her saying, "*...Go in peace, and the God of Israel grant your petition which you have asked of Him*" (1 Samuel 1:17) and the Biblical record documents, "*So it came to pass in the process of time that Hannah conceived and bore a son, and called his name Samuel, saying, "Because I have asked for him from the Lord*" (1 Samuel 1:20)
Children of Israel	For a brief time under their first king, Samuel provided them everything they needed to acquire, maintain, and grow the influence of the **good** attribute among them. However, as one may already know, their maintenance of the *good* attribute was short lived. The Biblical record documented, "*For the Lord will not forsake His people, for His great name's sake, because it has pleased the Lord to make you His people. Moreover, as for me, far be it from me that I should sin against the Lord in ceasing to pray for you; but I will teach you the **good** and the right way. Only fear the Lord, and serve Him in truth with all your heart; for consider what great things He has done for you. But if you still do wickedly, you shall be swept away, both you and your king*" (1 Samuel 12:22-25). For a brief time, after this warning, the people and Saul agreed to pursue the **good** attribute and obey God's Word.
	Jonathan, Saul's son protected David and tried to tell Saul of the influence of the *good* attribute that resided in David. However, Saul envied David and tried to kill him. The Bible documented, "*Thus Jonathan spoke well of David to Saul his father, and said to him, "Let not the king sin against his servant, against David, because he has not sinned against you, and because his works have been very **good** toward you*" (1 Samuel 19:4)
David ~continued~	Saul would eventually acknowledge to David, "*You are more righteous than I; for you have rewarded me with **good**, whereas I have rewarded you with evil. And you have shown this day how you have dealt well with me; for when the Lord delivered me into your hand, you did not kill me. For if a man finds his enemy, will he let him get away safely? Therefore may the Lord reward you with **good** for what you have done to me this day*" (1 Samuel 24:17-19)

	Achish recognized the influence of the **good** attribute in David. The Biblical record documented that, "...*Achish answered and said to David, "I know that you are as **good** in my sight as an angel of God..."* (1 Samuel 29:9), but Achish asked David to leave because the princes of the Philistines were afraid of him.
	He exercised the influence of the **good** attribute with Mephibosheth, the grandson of Saul. After hearing Mephibosheth's story over a land dispute with Ziba, one of Saul's servants, Mephibosheth said of Ziba to David, "*And he has slandered your servant to my lord the king, but my lord the king is like the angel of God. Therefore do what is **good** in your eyes*" (2 Samuel 19:27). David simply decided they would split the land
	He exercised the influence of the **good** attribute with Shemei who cursed and threw rocks at him. David retrained his men from killing Shemei and said, "*...It may be that the Lord will look on my affliction, and that the Lord will repay me with **good** for his cursing this day*" (2 Samuel 16:12)
	Araunah the Jebusite recognized the **good** attribute in David. He said to David, "*...Let my lord the king take and offer up whatever seems **good** to him. Look, here are oxen for burnt sacrifice, and threshing implements and the yokes of the oxen for wood*" (2 Samuel 24:22). David would not take anything without paying and he paid him fifty shekels of silver for his property according to 2 Samuel 24:24
	Ornan the Jebusite recognized the **good** attribute in David. David would not accept his property to make a sacrifice to the Lord without paying a fair price for it. Like Araunah, Ornan also said, "*Take it to yourself, and let my lord the king do what is **good** in his eyes. Look, I also give you the oxen for burnt offerings, the threshing implements for wood, and the wheat for the grain offering; I give it all*" (1 Chronicles 21:23). David would not take anything with paying and he paid him six hundred shekels of gold for his property according to 1 Chronicles 21:25
Abigail	She was the wife of Nabal and the Biblical record documented, "*Now there was a man in Maon whose business was in Carmel, and the man was very rich. He had three thousand sheep and a thousand goats. And he was shearing his sheep in Carmel. The name of the man was Nabal, and the name of his wife Abigail. And she was a woman of **good** understanding and beautiful appearance; but the man was harsh and evil in his doings. He was of the house of Caleb*" (1 Samuel 25:2-3)
David's men of war	Although David's military treated Nabal's worker well, Nabal did not return the favor to David. The Biblical record documented, "*Now one of the young men told Abigail, Nabal's wife, saying, "Look, David sent messengers from the wilderness to greet our master; and he reviled them. But the men were very **good** to us, and we were not hurt, nor did we miss anything as long as we accompanied them, when we were in the fields*" (1 Samuel 25:14-15)
Solomon	Shimei recognized the influence of the *good* attribute in Solomon. Solomon, to honor David's request not to harm Shimei, told him to build a house in Jerusalem and stay in it and the day he leaves it, he would die according to 1 Kings 2:36-37. Shimei acknowledged, "*The saying is **good**. As my lord the king has said, so your servant will do." So Shimei dwelt in Jerusalem many days*" (1 Kings 2:38). Shimei broke the agreement and the Bible documented Solomon had Shimei executed according to 1 Kings 2:46.

	Solomon asked God for a full measure of the influence of the **good** attribute when he asked the Lord, "*Therefore give to Your servant an understanding heart to judge Your people, that I may <u>discern</u> between **good** and evil. For who is able to judge this great people of Yours?*" (1 Kings 3:9). The Lord granted Solomon's request according to 1 Kings 3:10-14.
Jeroboam's child	Ahijah, a prophet of God, told Jeroboam's wife who had come to him in disguise to inquire about Jeroboam's kingdom. The Lord told him, "*Arise therefore, go to your own house. When your feet enter the city, the child shall die. And all Israel shall mourn for him and bury him, for he is the only one of Jeroboam who shall come to the grave, because in him there is found something **good** toward the Lord God of Israel in the house of Jeroboam*" (1 Kings 14:12-13). The child was the only one found to have the influence of the **good** attribute in Jeroboam's kingdom.
King Asa	As king of Judah, the Bible documented, "*Asa did what was **good** and right in the eyes of the Lord his God, for he removed the altars of the foreign gods and the high places, and broke down the sacred pillars and cut down the wooden images*" (2 Chronicles 14:2-3).
King Jehoshaphat	He had a measure of the *good* attribute. Jehu the son of Hanani the seer told King Jehoshaphat, "*Should you help the wicked and love those who hate the Lord? Therefore the wrath of the Lord is upon you. Nevertheless **good** things are found in you, in that you have removed the wooden images from the land, and have prepared your heart to seek God*" (2 Chronicles 19:2-3).
King Hezekiah	The Biblical record documented that he "*...gave encouragement to all the Levites who taught the **good** knowledge of the Lord; and they ate throughout the feast seven days, offering peace offerings and making confession to the Lord God of their fathers*" (2 Chronicles 30:22)
	He "*...did throughout all Judah, and he did what was **good** and right and true before the Lord his God*" (2 Chronicles 31:20)
	He prayed, "*Remember now, O Lord, I pray, how I have walked before You in truth and with a loyal heart, and have done what was **good** in Your sight." And Hezekiah wept bitterly*" (2 Kings 20:3; Isaiah 38:2-3)
	The Biblical record documented of him, "*Now the rest of the acts of Hezekiah, and his **goodness**, indeed they are written in the vision of Isaiah the prophet, the son of Amoz, and in the book of the kings of Judah and Israel*" (2 Chronicles 32:32)
The prophet Jehoiada	The Bible documents that he, "*...grew old and was full of days, and he died; he was one hundred and thirty years old when he died. And they buried him in the City of David among the kings, because he had done **good** in Israel, both toward God and His house*" (2 Chronicles 24:15-16)
Josiah	The Bible documented, "*Now the rest of the acts of Josiah and his **goodness**, according to what was written in the Law of the Lord, and his deeds from first to last, indeed they are written in the book of the kings of Israel and Judah*" (2 Chronicles 35:26-27)
Ezra	The Biblical record says specifically of Ezra, "*For Ezra had prepared his heart to seek the Law of the Lord, and to do it, and to teach statutes and ordinances in Israel*" (Ezra 7:10)

	Further, the king told Ezra, *"And whatever seems **good** to you and your brethren to do with the rest of the silver and the gold, do it according to the will of your God"* (Ezra 7:18)
Nehemiah	The Bible documented of Him, *"But the former governors who were before me laid burdens on the people, and took from them bread and wine, besides forty shekels of silver. Yes, even their servants bore rule over the people, but I did not do so, because of the fear of God...Yet in spite of this I did not demand the governor's provisions, because the bondage was heavy on this people"* (Nehemiah 5:15-18)
	And he simply prayed, *"Remember me, my God, for **good**, according to all that I have done for this people"* (Nehemiah 5:19)
Mordecai	The Biblical record documented, *"...Mordecai the Jew was second to King Ahasuerus, and was great among the Jews and well received by the multitude of his brethren, seeking the **good** of his people and speaking peace to all his countrymen"* (Esther 10:3)
Daniel	*"But Daniel purposed in his heart that he would not defile himself with the portion of the king's delicacies, nor with the wine which he drank; therefore he requested of the chief of the eunuchs that he might not defile himself"* (Daniel 1:8). Because of this, the Biblical record tells us, *"Now God had brought Daniel into the favor and **goodwill** of the chief of the eunuchs"* (Daniel 1:9)

Table 97: Examples of People Who Allowed the Influence of the Good Attribute

In addition to the examples of people with the influence of the ***good*** attribute, there were people who <u>did not have</u> the ***good*** attribute. Remember, every person identified in the Chapter V: The Negative Attributes, was an example of one without the influence of the ***good*** attribute. A few more specific examples include:

Who	What Is Documented
Hophni and Phinehas	These men were Eli the prophet's sons. They had the immoral and evil attributes and the Bible documented that they even, *"...lay with the women who assembled at the door of the tabernacle of meeting"* (1 Samuel 2:22). Eli said to them, *"..."Why do you do such things? For I hear of your evil dealings from all the people. No, my sons! For it is not a **good** report that I hear. You make the Lord's people transgress"* (1 Samuel 2:23-24). But Eli did not punish them. However, God punished the three of them. Hophni and Phinehas died at the hands of the Philistines (1 Samuel 4:11) and Eli fell off his seat backwards, broke his neck, and died (1 Samuel 4:18), then Samuel took over as the prophet for Israel.
Joel and Abijah	Samuel's sons lack the influence of the ***good*** attribute. The Biblical record documented, *"Now it came to pass when Samuel was old that he made his sons judges over Israel. The name of his firstborn was Joel, and the name of his second, Abijah; they were judges in Beersheba. But his sons did not walk in his ways; they turned aside after dishonest gain, took bribes, and perverted justice"* (1 Samuel 8:1-3)
Rehoboam	After hearing a plea from Jeroboam to *"...lighten the burdensome service of your father, and his heavy yoke which he put on us, and we will serve you"* (1 Kings 12:4), the elders counseled Rehoboam *"...If you will be a servant to these people today, and serve them, and answer them, and speak **good***

	words to them, then they will be your servants forever" (1 Kings 12:7; 2 Chronicles 10:7). But Rehoboam rejected the elder's council in favor of the counsel of younger men who grew up with him. This bad counsel and Rehoboam decision split Solomon's kingdom. The Biblical record documents, *"So Israel has been in rebellion against the house of David to this day"* (1 Kings 12:19)
Some Jewish nobles and rulers	Nehemiah 5:1-11 documented that Nehemiah became very angry and rebuked the nobles and rulers because *"Each of you is exacting usury from his brother." So I called a great assembly against them. And I said to them, "According to our ability we have redeemed our Jewish brethren who were sold to the nations. Now indeed, will you even sell your brethren? Or should they be sold to us?" Then they were silenced and found nothing to say. Then I said, "What you are doing is not **good**..."* The nobles and rulers agreed to stop and return wheat they took from their own people according to Nehemiah 5:12

Table 98: Examples of People Who Lacked the Influence of the Good Attribute

BTT allows one to see that the influence of the ***good*** attribute, like the other attributes, expresses itself through one's behavior. One can also see the expression of this attribute in how one handles situations between one's self and others. How one responds to situations demonstrate the influence of the ***good*** attribute. Based on the Lord's commands, Moses told the children of Israel what the Lord required concerning the ***good*** attribute. Based on specific scenarios, Moses documented the following:

Scenarios	**The Required Response**
Mishaps due to dangerous situation	*"...if a man opens a pit, or if a man digs a pit and does not cover it, and an ox or a donkey falls in it, the owner of the pit shall make it **good**; he shall give money to their owner, but the dead animal shall be his"* (Exodus 21:33-34)
Mishaps due to chance during honest agreements	*"If a man delivers to his neighbor a donkey, an ox, a sheep, or any animal to keep, and it dies, is hurt, or driven away, no one seeing it, then an oath of the Lord shall be between them both, that he has not put his hand into his neighbor's goods; and the owner of it shall accept that, and he shall not make it **good**"* (Exodus 22:10-11)
	*"But if, in fact, it is stolen from him, he shall make restitution to the owner of it. If it is torn to pieces by a beast, then he shall bring it as evidence, and he shall not make **good** what was torn"* (Exodus 22:12-13)
Possessions borrowed	*"And if a man borrows anything from his neighbor, and it becomes injured or dies, the owner of it not being with it, he shall surely make it **good**. If its owner was with it, he shall not make it **good**; if it was hired, it came for its hire"* (Exodus 22:14-15)
Oaths	*"...if a person swears, speaking thoughtlessly with his lips to do evil or to do **good**, whatever it is that a man may pronounce by an oath, and he is unaware of it—when he realizes it, then he shall be guilty in any of these matters"* (Leviticus 5:4)
Killing another person's livestock	*"Whoever kills an animal shall make it **good**, animal for animal"* (Leviticus 24:18)

Recognizing authority and honoring commitments	"*If it is an animal that men may bring as an offering to the Lord, all that anyone gives to the Lord shall be holy. He shall not substitute it or exchange it,* **good** *for bad or bad for* **good**; *and if he at all exchanges animal for animal, then both it and the one exchanged for it shall be holy*" (Leviticus 27:9-10)
	"*And when a man dedicates his house to be holy to the Lord, then the priest shall set a value for it, whether it is* **good** *or bad; as the priest values it, so it shall stand*" (Leviticus 27:14)
The Ten Commandments	"*And you shall do what is right and* **good** *in the sight of the Lord, that it may be well with you, and that you may go in and possess the* **good** *land of which the Lord swore to your fathers...*" (Deuteronomy 6:18)
	"*And the Lord commanded us to observe all these statutes, to fear the Lord our God, for our* **good** *always, that He might preserve us alive, as it is this day*" (Deuteronomy 6:24)
	"*And now, Israel, what does the Lord your God require of you, but to fear the Lord your God, to walk in all His ways and to love Him, to serve the Lord your God with all your heart and with all your soul, and to keep the commandments of the Lord and His statutes which I command you today for your* **good**?" (Deuteronomy 10:13)
	"*Observe and obey all these words which I command you, that it may go well with you and your children after you forever, when you do what is* **good** *and right in the sight of the Lord your God*" (Deuteronomy 12:28)
	"*See, I have set before you today life and* **good**, *death and evil, in that I command you today to love the Lord your God, to walk in His ways, and to keep His commandments, His statutes, and His judgments, that you may live and multiply; and the Lord your God will bless you in the land which you go to possess*" (Deuteronomy 30:15-16)
Giving Thanks	"*When you have eaten and are full, then you shall bless the Lord your God for the* **good** *land which He has given you*" (Deuteronomy 8:10)

Table 99: Scenarios that Offer Opportunities to Demonstrate the Influence of the Good Attribute

The Biblical record documented a unique method not seen with any of the other attributes, for spreading the influence of the **good** attribute to others. BTT allows one to see several <u>specific</u> situations in the Old Testament where this unique method was applied. The method used was possibly due to the intensity of spiritual warfare in the war campaign and the negative force's use of the element of <u>fear</u>. The method was the use of the phrase, "*Be of* **good** *courage.*" Sometimes the phrase changed slightly, but it always conveyed the same meaning of spiritual strength, power, and encouragement. One will see a similar method in the New Testament. Here are some of the many times one can see this phrase used:

Who Said It	Who It Was Said To And The Reference
	Twelve men were selected, one from each tribe of the children of Israel, to leave the Wilderness of Paran to spy out the land of Canaan (Numbers 13:1-16). He told them, "*...see what the land is like: whether the people who dwell in it are strong or weak, few or many; whether the land they dwell in is good or bad; whether the cities they inhabit are like camps or strongholds; whether the*

Moses	land is rich or poor; and whether there are forests there or not. <u>Be of **good** courage</u>. And bring some of the fruit of the land." Now the time was the season of the first ripe grapes" (Numbers 13:18-20)
	The transfer of leadership and spiritual authority to Joshua. The Bible documented, "Then He inaugurated Joshua the son of Nun, and said, "<u>Be strong and of **good** courage</u>; for you shall bring the children of Israel into the land of which I swore to them, and I will be with you" (Deuteronomy 31:23)
	Moses said to Joshua in the sight of all Israel, "Be strong and of **good** courage, do not fear nor be afraid of them; for the Lord your God, He is the One who goes with you. He will not leave you nor forsake you." Then Moses called Joshua and said to him in the sight of all Israel, "<u>Be strong and of **good** courage</u>, for you must go with this people to the land which the Lord has sworn to their fathers to give them, and you shall cause them to inherit it" (Deuteronomy 31:6-7)
The Lord	After Moses died, the Lord told Joshua to, "<u>Be strong and of **good** courage</u>, for to this people you shall divide as an inheritance the land which I swore to their fathers to give them" (Joshua 1:6)
	The Lord also said to Joshua, "This Book of the Law shall not depart from your mouth, but you shall meditate in it day and night, that you may observe to do according to all that is written in it. For then you will make your way prosperous, and then you will have **good** success. Have I not commanded you? <u>Be strong and of **good** courage</u>; do not be afraid, nor be dismayed, for the Lord your God is with you wherever you go" (Joshua 1:8-9)
The leaders of the Reubenites, the Gadites, and half the tribe of Manasseh	Before Moses died, he promised the Reubenites, the Gadites, and half the tribe of Manasseh, land on the side of Jordan that they were currently on. They understood and accepted Joshua's authority and said to him, "...All that you command us we will do, and wherever you send us we will go. Just as we heeded Moses in all things, so we will heed you. Only the Lord your God be with you, as He was with Moses. Whoever rebels against your command and does not heed your words, in all that you command him, shall be put to death. Only <u>be strong and of **good** courage</u>" (Joshua 1:16-18). Joshua honored Moses's promise and let them return to their lands once they helped capture the land the Lord had given the rest of the children of Israel (Joshua 22:1-4)
Joshua	After the children of Israel defeated the armies (Joshua 10:20) of five kings (Joshua 10:23), he told his captains, "Come near, put your feet on the necks of these kings." And they drew near and put their feet on their necks. Then Joshua said to them, "Do not be afraid, nor be dismayed; <u>be strong and of **good** courage</u>, for thus the Lord will do to all your enemies against whom you fight. And afterward Joshua struck them and killed them, and hanged them on five trees; and they were hanging on the trees until evening" (Joshua 10:24-26)
Joab	Serving as David's military commander, he told his brother Abishai to, "<u>Be of **good** courage</u>, and let us be strong for our people and for the cities of our God. And may the Lord do what is **good** in His sight" (2 Samuel 10:12; 1 Chronicles 19:13). The Biblical record documented, "...David killed seven hundred charioteers and forty thousand horsemen of the Syrians, and struck Shobach the commander of their army, who died there" (2 Samuel 10:18)

David	He told His son Solomon, "*Be strong and of **good** courage; do not fear nor be dismayed*" (1 Chronicles 22:13)
	He told Solomon again, "*Be strong and of **good** courage, and do it; do not fear nor be dismayed, for the Lord God—my God—will be with you. He will not leave you nor forsake you, until you have finished all the work for the service of the house of the Lord*" (1 Chronicles 28:20)
Shechaniah, the son of Jehiel	Ezra had the task to tell the children of Israel to put away their pagan wives and children. Shechaniah told Ezra, "*Arise, for this matter is your responsibility. We also are with you. Be of **good** courage, and do it*" (Ezra 10:4). Ezra carried out the task according to Ezra 10:5-44.
The Psalmist	He wrote for us, "*I would have lost heart, unless I had believed that I would see the **goodness** of the Lord in the land of the living. Wait on the Lord; be of **good** courage, and He shall strengthen your heart; wait, I say, on the Lord!*" (Psalm 27:13-14)
	"*Be of **good** courage, and He shall strengthen your heart, all you who hope in the Lord*" (Psalm 31:24)

Table 100: Examples of the Use of the Phrase "Be of Good Courage"

One would think that the influence of the **good** attribute would have a heavy presence among the children of Israel after they gained their freedom from bondage in Egypt. However, this was not the case. The influences of the negative attributes flourished as Moses tried to lead the people to the Promised Land. The people sinned, complained, and rebelled so much that Moses documented, "*...the Lord heard the sound of your words, and was angry, and took an oath, saying, 'Surely not one of these men of this evil generation shall see that **good** land of which I swore to give to your fathers...*" (Deuteronomy 1:34-35). BTT allows one to see that the Lord directed His statement at the adults; not the innocent children. In fact, the Biblical record documented, "*Moreover your little ones and your children, who you say will be victims, who today have no knowledge of **good** and evil, they shall go in there; to them I will give it, and they shall possess it*" (Deuteronomy 1:39). The little ones and children were the babies, infants, and toddlers; a new generation, which had not been corrupted from spiritual warfare. God selected Joshua from this population to lead His people into the Promised Land.

The Biblical record documented that as Joshua approached one hundred and ten years of age (Joshua 24:29), he prepared the people for his departure to be with the Lord. He reminded the generation of people under his leadership of all the **good** things the Lord had done for them (Joshua 23:11-16). Further, he warned, "*If you forsake the Lord and serve foreign gods, then He will turn and do you harm and consume you, after He has done you **good***" (Joshua 24:20). Joshua's warning was short lived; for after he died, the negative forces of the war campaign influenced the children of Israel with a vengeance.

It is difficult for one to comprehend all the things the Lord does for one that strives for a full measure of the influence from the **good** attribute. But the Lord provides the wisdom for one to comprehend his **goodness**. The Psalmist wrote, "*The fear of the Lord is the beginning of wisdom; a **good** understanding have all those who do His commandments. His praise endures forever*" (Psalm 111:10). Further, Solomon documented that, "*...God gives wisdom and knowledge and joy to a man who is **good** in His sight; but to the sinner He gives the work of gathering and collecting, that he may give to him who is **good** before God. This also is vanity* *and grasping for the wind*" (Ecclesiastes 2:26). BTT allows one to see that the influence of the **good** attribute is rewarding to one's life. Moreover, Solomon provided some insight as to where some of God's favor comes from - sinners who gather and collect God's resources. Further, David documented that, "*The steps of a **good** man are ordered by the Lord, and He delights in his way*" (Psalm 37:23) and, "*...the Lord God is a sun and shield; the Lord will give* grace *and glory; no **good** thing will He withhold from those who walk uprightly*" (Psalm 84:11). Consequently, as a sign of warning, David documented, "*Those also who render evil for **good**, they are my adversaries, because I follow what is **good***" (Psalm 38:20).

    The prophet Nehemiah identified the **good** attribute as a positive spirit that comes from the Lord. Nehemiah documented, "*You also gave Your **good** Spirit to instruct them, and did not withhold Your manna from their mouth, and gave them water for their thirst*" (Nehemiah 9:20). Nehemiah reiterated that the influence of the **good** attribute comes from God and He provides this **clean spirit** freely to anyone who will hear His voice. Today, hearing comes through His written Holy Word. The influence of the **good** attribute matures by obedience and studying God's Word.

    Job highlighted an important pearl of wisdom about the influence of the **good** attribute. People who do not understand God often overlooked this pearl. Although one may have the influence of the **good** attribute in his or her inner spirit, it does not mean that one will never see trials or tribulation. One who thinks this does not understand the nature of spiritual warfare. Job understood this perfectly. When his wife was ready to give up on him after he had lost everything that had value, he said to her, "*...You speak as one of the foolish women speaks. Shall we indeed accept **good** from God, and shall we not accept adversity?" In all this Job did not sin with his lips*" (Job 2:10). Even during a time when he sat through a verbal assault by his friends, Eliphaz, Bildad, and Zophar, Job reflected on his life and told his tormentors, "*Have I not wept for him who was in trouble? Has not my soul grieved for the poor? But when I looked for **good**, evil came to me; and when I waited for light, then came darkness*" (Job 30:25-26). Job's made this statement to chastise his three wise friends who oppressed him rather than comforted him. To make matters worse, his friends brought with them an understudy named Elihu, who felt compelled to verbally assault Job. Elihu made a comment that deserves one's attention. By the words he spoke to Job, his statements proved that he did not have the influence of the **good** attribute in his inner spirit. Elihu, like the others, espoused misguided wisdom to Job. But in this case, after putting down Eliphaz, Bildad, and Zophar, he elevated himself over Job and said to them all, "*Hear my words, you wise men; give ear to me, you who have knowledge. For the ear tests words as the palate tastes food. Let us choose justice for ourselves; let us know among ourselves what is **good***" (Job 34:2-4). BTT allows one to see that Elihu desired to use worldly wisdom to define what was **good** over God's wisdom. Elihu's words demonstrated spiritual warfare at its best state. Do not be deceived.

    Elihu promoted a worldly practice that in progress today. The practice is defining what is **good** by the world's standards apart from God's definition. The proud and wicked attributes were influencing Elihu. He did not allow the influence of the **good** attribute to enter in the discussion between him and the others. This is a common strategy used by the negative forces in spiritual warfare. The influence of the **good** attribute guides one to the **good** things of the Lord through the study of His Word. BTT allows one to see that one, on his or her own accord, does not have the authority to define what is **good** for God's creation. God has already defined what is **good** by His Holy Word. The influence of the **good** attribute provides understanding to one's inner spirit through the application of God's Word.

The negative attributes through spiritual warfare influence people to fight against everyone influenced by the **good** attribute. Solomon documented for one's learning that, *"Wisdom is better than weapons of war; but one sinner destroys much **good**"* (Ecclesiastes 9:18). The heavy hitters of the negative attributes that influence people against the **good** attribute include:

- The fool attribute: The Biblical record documents, *"The fool has said in his heart, "There is no God." They are corrupt, they have done abominable works, there is none who does **good**"* (Psalm 14:1; Psalm 53:1)

- The wicked and liar attributes: The Biblical record documents, *"...The words of his mouth are wickedness and deceit; he has ceased to be wise and to do **good**. He devises wickedness on his bed; he sets himself in a way that is not **good**; he does not abhor evil"* (Psalm 36:3-4)

- The evil, hater, and liar attributes: The Biblical record documents, *"Why do you boast in evil, O mighty man? The **goodness** of God endures continually. Your tongue devises destruction, like a sharp razor, working deceitfully. You love evil more than **good**, lying rather than speaking righteousness. Selah. You love all devouring words, you deceitful tongue"* (Psalm 52:1-4)

The Psalmist also referenced the dilemma that man creates by attempting to redefine what is **good**, independent of the influence of the **good** attribute that comes from God. The Psalmist documented that, *"There are many who say, "Who will show us any **good**?" Lord, lift up the light of Your countenance upon us"* (Psalm 4:6). BTT allows one to see that the Psalmist, addressing the dilemma, also answers it by calling on the Lord. The Psalmist and Solomon documented additional pearls of wisdom that pertained to the **good** attribute. They wrote:

*"Yes, the Lord will give what is **good**; and our land will yield its increase"* (Psalm 85:12)	*"It is **good** for me that I have been afflicted, that I may learn Your statutes"* (Psalm 119:71)	*"Depart from evil, and do **good**; and dwell forevermore"* (Psalm 37:27)
*"The Lord looks down from heaven upon the children of men, to see if there are any who understand, who seek God. They have all turned aside, they have together become corrupt; there is none who does **good**, no, not one"* (Psalm 14:2, 3; Psalm 53:2-3)	*"Oh, taste and see that the Lord is **good**; blessed is the man who trusts in Him! Oh, fear the Lord, you His saints! There is no want to those who fear Him. The young lions lack and suffer hunger; but those who seek the Lord shall not lack any **good** thing"* (Psalm 34:8-10)	*"You prepare a table before me in the presence of my enemies; You anoint my head with oil; my cup runs over. Surely **goodness** and mercy shall follow me all the days of my life; and I will dwell in the house of the Lord forever"* (Psalm 23:6)

"My heart is overflowing with a **good** theme; I recite my composition concerning the King; my tongue is the pen of a ready writer" (Psalm 45:1)	"O Lord, You are the portion of my inheritance and my cup; You maintain my lot. The lines have fallen to me in pleasant places; Yes, I have a **good** inheritance" (Psalm 16:5-6)	"I have proclaimed the **good** news of righteousness in the great assembly; indeed, I do not restrain my lips, O Lord, You Yourself know" (Psalm 40:9)
"O my soul, you have said to the Lord, "You are my Lord, my **goodness** is nothing apart from You" (Psalm 16:2)	"Those also who render evil for **good**, they are my adversaries, because I follow what is **good**" (Psalm 38:20)	"Fierce witnesses rise up; they ask me things that I do not know. They reward me evil for **good**, to the sorrow of my soul" (Psalm 35:12)
"Do **good**, O Lord, to those who are **good**, and to those who are upright in their hearts" (Psalm 125:4)	"It is **good** to give thanks to the Lord, and to sing praises to Your name, O Most High..." (Psalm 92:1)	"Trust in the Lord, and do **good**; dwell in the land, and feed on His faithfulness" (Psalm 37:3)
"Behold, how **good** and how pleasant it is for brethren to dwell together in unity!" (Psalm 133:1)	"A **good** man deals graciously and lends; he will guide his affairs with discretion" (Psalm 112:5)	"The steps of a **good** man are ordered by the Lord, and He delights in his way" (Psalm 37:23)
"Oh, give thanks to the Lord, for He is **good**! For His mercy endures forever" (Psalm 107:1; Psalm 118:1; Psalm 118:29)	"Praise the Lord! For it is **good** to sing praises to our God; for it is pleasant, and praise is beautiful" (Psalm 147:1)	"Sing to the Lord, bless His name; proclaim the **good** news of His salvation from day to day" (Psalm 96:2)
"Why do you boast in evil, O mighty man? The **goodness** of God endures continually. Your tongue devises destruction, like a sharp razor, working deceitfully. You love evil more than **good**, lying rather than speaking righteousness. Selah. You love all devouring words, you deceitful tongue" (Psalm 52:1-4)	"... will guard my ways, lest I sin with my tongue; I will restrain my mouth with a muzzle, while the wicked are before me." I was mute with silence, I held my peace even from **good**; and my sorrow was stirred up. My heart was hot within me; while I was musing, the fire burned. Then I spoke with my tongue..." (Psalm 39:1-3)	"Come, you children, listen to me; I will teach you the fear of the Lord. Who is the man who desires life, and loves many days, that he may see **good**? Keep your tongue from **evil**, and your lips from speaking deceit. Depart from **evil** and do **good**; seek peace and pursue it" (Psalm 34:11-14)
"For the Lord God is a sun and shield; the Lord will give grace and glory; no **good** thing will He withhold from those who walk uprightly" (Psalm 84:11)	"Teach me **good** judgment and knowledge, for I believe Your commandments" (Psalm 119:66) "You are **good**, and do **good**; teach me Your statutes" (Psalm 119:68)	"Blessed is the man You choose, and cause to approach You, that he may dwell in Your courts. We shall be satisfied with the **goodness** of Your house, Of Your holy temple" (Psalm 65:4)
"The fool has said in his heart, "There is no God." They are corrupt, they have	"Nothing is better for a man than that he should eat and drink, and that his soul	"The fear of the Lord is the beginning of wisdom; a **good** understanding have

done abominable works, there is none who does **good**" (Psalm 14:1; Psalm 53:1)	should enjoy **good** in his labor. This also, I saw, was from the hand of God" (Ecclesiastes 2:24)	all those who do His commandments. His praise endures forever" (Psalm 111:10)
"Because of the house of the Lord our God I will seek your **good**" (Psalm 122:9)	"A **good** name is better than precious ointment..." (Ecclesiastes 7:1)	"For there is not a just man on earth who does **good** and does not sin" (Ecclesiastes 7:20)
"Oh, that men would give thanks to the Lord for His **goodness**, and for His wonderful works to the children of men! For He satisfies the longing soul, and fills the hungry soul with **goodness**" (Psalm 107:8-9)	"I know that nothing is better for them than to rejoice, and to do **good** in their lives, and also that every man should eat and drink and enjoy the **good** of all his labor—it is the gift of God" (Ecclesiastes 3:12-13)	"Let us hear the conclusion of the whole matter: Fear God and keep His commandments, for this is man's all. For God will bring every work into judgment, including every secret thing, whether **good** or evil" (Ecclesiastes 12:14)
"An oracle within my heart concerning the transgression of the wicked: there is no fear of God before his eyes. For he flatters himself in his own eyes, when he finds out his iniquity and when he hates. The words of his mouth are wickedness and deceit; he has ceased to be wise and to do **good**. He devises wickedness on his bed; he sets himself in a way that is not **good**; he does not abhor evil" (Psalm 36:1-4)	"For the mouth of the wicked and the mouth of the deceitful have opened against me; they have spoken against me with a lying tongue. They have also surrounded me with words of hatred, and fought against me without a cause. In return for my love they are my accusers, but I give myself to prayer. Thus they have rewarded me **evil** for **good**, and hatred for my love" (Psalm 109:2-5)	"Bless the Lord, O my soul; and all that is within me, bless His holy name! Bless the Lord, O my soul, and forget not all His benefits: Who forgives all your iniquities, Who heals all your diseases, Who redeems your life from destruction, Who crowns you with lovingkindness and tender mercies, Who satisfies your mouth with **good** things, so that your youth is renewed like the eagle's" (Psalm 103:1-5)
"Whom have I in heaven but You? And there is none upon earth that I desire besides You. My flesh and my heart fail; but God is the strength of my heart and my portion forever. For indeed, those who are far from You shall perish; You have destroyed all those who desert You for harlotry. But it is **good** for me to draw near to God; I have put my trust in the Lord GOD, that I may	"For God gives wisdom and knowledge and joy to a man who is **good** in His sight; but to the sinner He gives the work of gathering and collecting, that he may give to him who is **good** before God. This also is vanity and grasping for the wind" (Ecclesiastes 2:26)	"All things come alike to all: one event happens to the righteous and the wicked; to the **good**, the clean, and the unclean; to him who sacrifices and him who does not sacrifice. As is the **good**, so is the sinner; he who takes an oath as he who fears an oath" (Ecclesiastes 9:2)

declare all Your works" (Psalm 73:25-28)		

Table 101: Some Pearls of Wisdom Concerning the Good Attribute

As with the other attributes, God sent His prophets to warn the nation of Israel to repent and seek the influence of the ***good*** attribute. Here are a few of the many examples one can find in the Old Testament:

The Prophet	What Was Said
Isaiah	*"Wash yourselves, make yourselves clean; put away the evil of your doings from before My eyes. Cease to do evil, learn to do **good**; seek justice, rebuke the oppressor; defend the fatherless, plead for the widow"* (Isaiah 1:16-17)
	*"Woe to those who call evil **good**, and **good** evil; who put darkness for light, and light for darkness; who put bitter for sweet, and sweet for bitter!"* (Isaiah 5:20)
	*"I have stretched out My hands all day long to a rebellious people, who walk in a way that is not **good**, according to their own thoughts; a people who provoke Me to anger continually to My face; who sacrifice in gardens, and burn incense on altars of brick; who sit among the graves, and spend the night in the tombs; who eat swine's flesh, and the broth of abominable things is in their vessels; who say, 'Keep to yourself, do not come near me, for I am holier than you!' These are smoke in My nostrils, a fire that burns all the day"* (Isaiah 65:2-5)
Jeremiah	*"I brought you into a bountiful country, to eat its fruit and its **goodness**. But when you entered, you defiled My land and made My heritage an abomination"* (Jeremiah 2:7)
	*"For My people are foolish, they have not known Me. They are silly children, and they have no understanding. They are wise to do evil, but to do **good** they have no knowledge"* (Jeremiah 4:22)
	*"But this people has a defiant and rebellious heart; they have revolted and departed. They do not say in their heart, "Let us now fear the Lord our God, who gives rain, both the former and the latter, in its season. He reserves for us the appointed weeks of the harvest." Your iniquities have turned these things away, and your sins have withheld **good** from you"* (Jeremiah 5:23-25)
	*"Thus says the Lord: "Stand in the ways and see, and ask for the old paths, where the **good** way is, and walk in it; then you will find rest for your souls. But they said, 'We will not walk in it.'"* (Jeremiah 6:16)
	*"Now therefore, speak to the men of Judah and to the inhabitants of Jerusalem, saying, 'Thus says the Lord: "Behold, I am fashioning a disaster and devising a plan against you. Return now everyone from his evil way, and make your ways and your doings **good**"'"* (Jeremiah 18:11)
Jeremiah ~continued~	For being so disobedient, he prayed, *"Give heed to me, O Lord, and listen to the voice of those who contend with me! Shall evil be repaid for **good**? For they have dug a pit for my life. Remember that I stood before You to speak **good** for them, to turn away Your wrath from them. Therefore deliver up their children to the famine, and pour out their blood by the force of the sword; let their wives become widows and bereaved of their children. Let*

	their men be put to death, their young men be slain by the sword in battle" (Jeremiah 18:19-20)
	*"For I have set My face against this city for adversity and not for **good**,"* says the Lord. *"It shall be given into the hand of the king of Babylon, and he shall burn it with fire'"* (Jeremiah 21:10)
Book of Lamentations	*"The Lord is **good** to those who wait for Him, to the soul who seeks Him"* (Lamentations 3:25)
	*"It is **good** that one should hope and wait quietly for the salvation of the Lord"* (Lamentations 3:26)
	*"It is **good** for a man to bear the yoke in his youth"* (Lamentations 3:27)
Ezekiel	While explaining to the people that one is accountable for his or her own sins only, and not for the sins of others, he told them from the Lord in a comparison of a sinful father and a son who had not sinned, *"As for his father, because he cruelly oppressed, robbed his brother by violence, and did what is not **good** among his people, behold, he shall die for his iniquity"* (Ezekiel 18:18). The son was not to be punished for the father's sin which was a false teaching of that day.
Hosea	*"Harlotry, wine, and new wine enslave the heart. My people ask counsel from their wooden idols, and their staff informs them. For the spirit of harlotry has caused them to stray, and they have played the harlot against their God. They offer sacrifices on the mountaintops, and burn incense on the hills, under oaks, poplars, and terebinths, because their shade is **good**. Therefore your daughters commit harlotry, and your brides commit adultery"* (Hosea 4:11-13)
	*"Israel has rejected the **good**; the enemy will pursue him"* (Hosea 8:3).
Amos	*"Seek **good** and not evil, that you may live; so the Lord God of hosts will be with you, as you have spoken. Hate evil, love **good**; establish justice in the gate. It may be that the Lord God of hosts will be gracious to the remnant of Joseph."* (Amos 5:14-15)
Micah	*"Hear now, O heads of Jacob, and you rulers of the house of Israel: Is it not for you to know justice? You who hate **good** and love evil; who strip the skin from My people, and the flesh from their bones; who also eat the flesh of My people, flay their skin from them, break their bones, and chop them in pieces like meat for the pot, like flesh in the caldron"* (Micah 3:1-3)
	*"He has shown you, O man, what is **good**; and what does the Lord require of you but to do justly, to love mercy, and to walk humbly with your God?"* (Micah 6:8)
Nahum	*"The Lord is **good**, a stronghold in the day of trouble; and He knows those who trust in Him"* (Nahum 1:7)
Malachi	*"You have wearied the Lord with your words; yet you say, "In what way have we wearied Him?" In that you say, "Everyone who does evil is **good** in the sight of the Lord, and He delights in them," Or, "Where is the God of justice?"* (Malachi 2:17)

Table 102: The Prophets' Warnings Concerning the Influence of the Good Attribute

Unfortunately, the Biblical record documented that the nation of Israel failed to heed the Lord's warnings from the prophets and He destroyed their original nation. But the spirit of the **good** attribute continued in a remnant of those who were obedient to His Word.

The amount of information on the influence of the ***good*** attribute contained in the New Testament of the Biblical record is staggering. At the end of this chapter, I hope that one will agree that the importance of the influence of the ***good*** attribute cannot be overstated.

God provided illustrations of the ***good*** attribute using common things in nature. This allowed people to immediately grasp His concept. Nature's examples allow one to visually see the differences between ***good*** and bad. Beginning with John the Baptist, he documented the by-product of the efforts of one influenced by the ***good*** attribute using an illustration of a fruit bearing tree. After referring to the Pharisees and Sadducees as a brood of vipers, since they only came to see what he was doing, John sternly warned them, "*...bear fruits worthy of repentance...even now the ax is laid to the root of the trees. Therefore every tree which does not bear **good** fruit is cut down and thrown into the fire*" (Matthew 3:7-10; Luke 3:9). BTT allows one to see that John used the fruit tree illustration and the actions of an ax to illustrate what would happen to the Pharisees and Sadducees not producing for God. Although these religious teachers had God's Word and all the prophecies of the Messiah to come, they failed to use the knowledge properly. They lacked the influence of the ***good*** attribute and their work only led to the cultivation of like-minded teachers and students; more fruit that also lacked the influence of the ***good*** attribute. Jesus' Word came to spiritually cut down and burn the efforts of everyone who allowed the influence of the negative forces of the war campaign.

Thus, when Jesus arrived and began His ministry, He also illustrated the influence of the ***good*** attribute using an example of a fruit tree. Fruit trees were plentiful and provided a quick reference for illustrating the influence of ***good*** and bad to the people of Jesus' day. The production of ***good*** or bad fruit, from appearance to taste, easily conveyed spiritual concepts. Jesus expanded the images He used from the fruit tree to other things such as salt, light, the eye, soil, seed, and fish. The Biblical record documented:

The Item Used	What Is Documented
Fruit tree	"*Beware of false prophets, who come to you in sheep's clothing, but inwardly they are ravenous wolves. You will know them by their fruits. Do men gather grapes from thornbushes or figs from thistles? Even so, every **good** tree bears **good** fruit, but a bad tree bears bad fruit. A **good** tree cannot bear bad fruit, nor can a bad tree bear **good** fruit. Every tree that does not bear **good** fruit is cut down and thrown into the fire. Therefore by their fruits you will know them*" (Matthew 7:15-20; Luke 6:43-44)
	"*Either make the tree **good** and its fruit **good**, or else make the tree bad and its fruit bad; for a tree is known by its fruit. Brood of vipers! How can you, being evil, speak **good** things? For out of the abundance of the heart the mouth speaks. A **good** man out of the **good** treasure of his heart brings forth **good** things, and an evil man out of the evil treasure brings forth evil things. But I say to you that for every idle word men may speak, they will give account of it in the day of judgment. For by your words you will be justified, and by your words you will be condemned*" (Matthew 12:33-37; Luke 6:45)
Salt	"*You are the salt of the earth; but if the salt loses its flavor, how shall it be seasoned? It is then **good** for nothing but to be thrown out and trampled underfoot by men*" (Matthew 5:13; Mark 9:50). In the Book of Luke, Jesus

	says, "*Salt is **good**; but if the salt has lost its flavor, how shall it be seasoned?*" (Luke 14:34)
Light	"*Let your light so shine before men, that they may see your **good** works and glorify your Father in heaven*" (Matthew 5:16)
One's eye	"*The lamp of the body is the eye. If therefore your eye is **good**, your whole body will be full of light. But if your eye is bad, your whole body will be full of darkness. If therefore the light that is in you is darkness, how great is that darkness!*" (Matthew 6:22-23; Luke 11:33-36)
Soil (for farming)	Based on Jesus' parable of the Seed and the Sower, He said, "*But others fell on **good** ground and yielded a crop: some a hundredfold, some sixty, some thirty*" (Matthew 13:8; Mark 4:8; Luke 8:8)
	Explaining the parable to His disciples, Jesus said, "*...he who received seed on the **good** ground is he who hears the word and understands it, who indeed bears fruit and produces: some a hundredfold, some sixty, some thirty.*" Another parable He put forth to them, saying: "*The kingdom of heaven is like a man who sowed **good** seed in his field...*" (Matthew 13:23-24; Mark 4:20)
	Luke recorded, ""*But the ones that fell on the **good** ground are those who, having heard the word with a <u>noble</u> and **good** heart, keep it and bear fruit with patience*" (Luke 8:15)
Seed	Jesus spoke a parable in Matthew 13:24 of a man who sowed seed in his field. In the parable, the Biblical record documented, "*So the servants of the owner came and said to him, 'Sir, did you not sow **good** seed in your field? How then does it have tares?* (Matthew 13:27)
	As the field produced *good* (wheat) and bad (tares) together, the servants wanted to separate them but, the owner stopped them. Jesus explained to the disciples, "*...He who sows the **good** seed is the Son of Man. The field is the world, the **good** seeds are the sons of the kingdom, but the tares are the sons of the wicked one. The enemy who sowed them is the devil, the harvest is the end of the age, and the reapers are the angels. Therefore as the tares are gathered and burned in the fire, so it will be at the end of this age....*" (Matthew 13:37-43)
Fish in a net	Jesus said, "*Again, the kingdom of heaven is like a dragnet that was cast into the sea and gathered some of every kind, which, when it was full, they drew to shore; and they sat down and gathered the **good** into vessels, but threw the bad away. So it will be at the end of the age. The angels will come forth, separate the wicked from among the just, and cast them into the furnace of fire. There will be wailing and gnashing of teeth*" (Matthew 13:47-50)

Table 103: Imagery Jesus used as Examples to Teach on the Influence of the Good Attribute

Jesus' parable of the Sower and the Seed provides perfect clarity of the influence of the **good** attribute. He brilliantly explained that the Word of God came in the form of a singular "*seed*" to the world in Luke 8:12. The *seed* is identified as "*God's Word*" in Mark 4:14 and is also documented as the "*word of the kingdom*" in Matthew 13:19. In the parable, God's Word came to people that had a measure of the **good** attribute (Matthew 13:8; Mark 4:8; and Luke 8:8) who were on **good** ground or soil. They were influenced by the attribute but had not allowed it to mature in their inner spirit. As God's Word came to them, some received it (implied), understood it, accepted it (Mark 4:20) and then kept it (Luke 8:15). Jesus stated that these people, "...*having heard the word with a **noble** and **good** heart, keep it and bear fruit with patience*" (Luke 8:15). In other words, the **good** attribute matures when combined with God's Word. This combination in a person with a **noble** and **good** heart takes God's Word to produce more followers or soldiers on the positive side of the war campaign. Incidentally, to be **noble** is synonymous to being **honorable**. This means a measure of the honorable/upright attribute is involved. Specifically, the Bible documents that this person "*...yielded a crop: some a hundredfold, some sixty, some thirty*" (Matthew 13:8; Mark 4:8; Luke 8:8). Thus, this attribute's efforts lead to the conversion of souls on the **good** ground and others. Chapter VIII explains Jesus' parable of the sower and Seed in detail. One will see that this parable explains spiritual warfare and lays out the entire war campaign. Jesus summed up the importance of the **good** attribute combined with God's Word when he stated, "*...the hour is coming in which all who are in the graves will hear His voice and come forth—those who have done **good**, to the resurrection of life, and those who have done evil, to the resurrection of condemnation*" (John 5:28-29). Jesus' Word leaves no room for confusion. God expects mankind to pursue the **good** attribute or give an account on the Day of Judgement.

Jesus thoroughly described the expected behavior of one with the **good** attribute's influence. Like all the other positive attributes, He made His points using parables. Today, no one can read Jesus' Word and misunderstand what having the influence of the **good** attribute is all about. A few of the numerous pearls of wisdom Jesus offered to the world include:

- "*You have heard that it was said, 'You shall love your neighbor and hate your enemy.' But I say to you, love your enemies, bless those who curse you, do **good** to those who hate you, and pray for those who spitefully use you and persecute you, that you may be sons of your Father in heaven; for He makes His sun rise on the evil and on the **good**, and sends rain on the just and on the unjust*" (Matthew 5:43-45)

- "*But I say to you who hear: Love your enemies, do **good** to those who hate you, bless those who curse you, and pray for those who spitefully use you. To him who strikes you on the one cheek, offer the other also. And from him who takes away your cloak, do not withhold your tunic either. Give to everyone who asks of you. And from him who takes away your goods do not ask them back. And just as you want men to do to you, you also do to them likewise. But if you love those who love you, what credit is that to you? For even sinners love those who love them. And if you do **good** to those who do good to you, what credit is that to you? For even sinners do the same. And if you lend to those from whom you hope to receive back, what credit is that to you? For even sinners lend to sinners to receive as much back. But love your enemies, do **good**, and lend, hoping for nothing in return; and your reward will be great, and you will be sons of the Most High. For He is kind to the unthankful and evil. Therefore be merciful, just as your Father also is merciful*" (Luke 6:27-36)

- "*Take heed that you do not do your charitable deeds before men, to be seen by them. Otherwise you have no reward from your Father in heaven*" (Matthew 6:1)

- "*Ask, and it will be given to you; seek, and you will find; knock, and it will be opened to you. For everyone who asks receives, and he who seeks finds, and to him who *knocks it will be opened. Or what man is there among you who, if his son asks for bread, will give him a stone? Or if he asks for a fish, will he give him a serpent? If you then, being evil, know how to give **good** gifts to your children, how much more will your Father who is in heaven give **good** things to those who ask Him! Therefore, whatever you want men to do to you, do also to them, for this is the Law and the Prophets."* (Matthew 7:7-12; Luke 11:9-13)

Jesus illustrated the ***good*** attribute's influence through His conduct and behavior. The Biblical record documented the ***good*** attribute when Jesus healed:

Who	Where Documented
A man with leprosy	Matthew 8:1-4; Mark 1:40-45; Luke 5:12-16
A centurion's servant	Matthew 8:5-13; Luke 7:1-10
Peter's mother-in-law	Matthew 8:14-15; Mark 1:29-31; Luke 4:38-39
Many demon-possessed	Matthew 8:16
Two demon-possessed men	Matthew 8:28-32; Mark 5:1-20; Luke 8:26-39
A paralytic man	Matthew 9:1-7; Mark 2:1-12; Luke 5:17-26
A girl who died	Matthew 9:18-19; 23-26; Mark 5:21-43; Luke 8:40-42;49-56
A woman with hemophilia	Matthew 9:20-22; Mark 5:25-34; Luke 8:43-48
Two blind men	Matthew 9:27-31
A mute, demon-possessed man	Matthew 9:32-34
A man with a withered hand	Matthew 12:10-14; Mark 3:4; Luke 6:9
A demon- possessed, blind, mute man	Matthew 12:22-30; Mark 3:22-27; Luke 11:14-23
A woman's daughter	Matthew 15:21-28; Mark 7:24-30
Many lame, blind, mute, maimed, etc...	Matthew 15:29-31
An epileptic boy	Matthew 17:14-21; Mark 9:14-29; Luke 9:37-42
Two blind men	Matthew 20:29-34; Mark 10:46-52; Luke 1:35-43
Jesus also:	
Ate with tax collectors	Matthew 9:9-13; Mark 2:13-17; Luke 5:27-32
Feed five thousand people	Matthew 14:13-21; Mark 6:30-44; Luke 9:10-17; John 6:1-14
Feed four thousand	Matthew 15:32-38; Mark 8:1-10

Table 104: Jesus' Demonstration of the Influence of the Good Attribute

From the examples above, one can see how the influence of the ***good*** attribute manifested itself through Jesus' work on earth. However, there were still people influenced by the hater attribute who wanted to take His life. These were people who refused to accept that Jesus was the Son of God and that He was providing them living examples to follow. When the Jews took stones to kill Jesus, the Biblical record documented that He said to them, *"Many **good** works I have shown you from My Father. For which of those works do you stone Me?" The Jews answered Him, saying, "For a **good** work we do not stone You, but for blasphemy, and because You, being a Man, make Yourself God"* (John 10:32-33). Consider for a moment, only God could do the things that Jesus did. Yet, they rejected Him. They could neither see that Jesus was God in the flesh, nor understand the influence of the ***good*** attribute working in Him on God's behalf. Because of the intensity of spiritual warfare, the Jewish leadership eventually condemned Jesus to die.

Jesus had the ability to share the spirit of the ***good*** attribute to others by His Word. He used a method similar to an Old Testament method. He used the phrase "*be of **good** cheer*," instead of the phrase "*be of **good** courage*." Here are some examples:

What Jesus Did	What Is Documented
Healed the paralytic man	"*Then behold, they brought to Him a paralytic lying on a bed. When Jesus saw their faith, He said to the paralytic, "Son, <u>be of **good** cheer</u>; your sins are forgiven you*" (Matthew 9:2)
Healed the woman of hemophilia	"*…Jesus turned around, and when He saw her He said, "<u>Be of **good** cheer</u>, daughter; your faith has made you well." And the woman was made well from that hour*" (Matthew 9:22; Luke 8:48)
Walked on the sea and scared his disciples	"*But immediately Jesus spoke to them, saying, "<u>Be of **good** cheer</u>! It is I; do not be afraid*" (Matthew 14:27; Mark 6:50)
Healed a blind man	"*So Jesus stood still and commanded him to be called. Then they called the blind man, saying to him, "<u>Be of **good** cheer</u>. Rise, He is calling you*" (Matthew 20:29-34; Mark 10:49; Luke 18:35-43)
Comforted His disciples	"*These things I have spoken to you, that in Me you may have peace. In the world you will have tribulation; <u>but be of **good** cheer</u>, I have overcome the world*" (John 16:33)
Comforted Paul for the task ahead of him	"*But the following night the Lord stood by him and said, "<u>Be of **good** cheer</u>, Paul; for as you have testified for Me in Jerusalem, so you must also bear witness at Rome*" (Acts 23:11)

Table 105: Jesus Spreading the Seed for the Influence of the Good Attribute

Both of these phrases still have the same impact today when spoken by leaders in the face of adversity and <u>fear</u> on the spiritual battlefield. Some final examples and teachings from Jesus on the influence of the ***good*** attribute included:

- …the landowner who agreed to pay laborers a fixed wage for their work. Some laborers worked more than others worked. They expected higher wages but that was not the agreement. The landowner said, "*Is it not lawful for me to do what I wish with my own things? Or is your eye evil because I am **good**?*" (Matthew 20:15)

- …the king who arranged a marriage for his son. After hearing excuses from those invited by invitation, he allowed both ***good*** and bad to come to the feast. The Bible says, "*So those servants went out into the highways and gathered together all whom they found, both bad and **good**. And the wedding hall was filled with guests*" (Matthew 22:10). But the king put out one who came unprepared.

- …the wealthy man and his servants. He gave them talents to invest based on their abilities according to Matthew 25:15; Luke 19:12-27. When he returned, to one he said, "*…Well done, **good** and faithful servant; you were faithful over a few things, I will *make you ruler over many things. Enter into the joy of your lord"* (Matthew 25:21) and to another he said, *"...Well done, **good** and faithful servant; you have been faithful over a few things, I will make you ruler over many things. Enter into the joy of your lord"* (Matthew 25:23). But he cast one out for being wicked and unprofitable according to Matthew 25:26-30.

- ...the **good** Samaritan. Although the attribute is never identified in this parable, the man's actions demonstrated the attribute compared to two other people who did not have the attribute. In the parable, the Samaritan comes across a man that had fallen among thieves of who, *"...stripped him of his clothing, wounded him, and departed, leaving him half dead"* (Luke 10:30). Even though the Samaritan did not know the man, he took him to an inn and left money for the innkeeper to take care of the man. On top of this, he told the innkeeper that he would pay any additional fees for the man on his return to the in. Sadly, a priest and a Levite saw the same man and ignored his condition and situation as they passed by.

- The woman who put expensive oil on Jesus' hair before His betrayal. The disciples complained but the Biblical record says, *"But when Jesus was aware of it, He said to them, "Why do you trouble the woman? For she has done a **good** work for Me"* (Matthew 26:10; Mark 14:6-7)

An enduring piece of information that Jesus shared about the influence of the **good** attribute is the fact that the **good** attribute is necessary to make it to heaven. One should consider Jesus' Word closely. He stated in John 5:25-29:

> *"Most assuredly, I say to you, the hour is coming, and now is, when the dead will hear the voice of the Son of God; and those who hear will live. For as the Father has life in Himself, so He has granted the Son to have life in Himself, and has given Him authority to execute judgment also, because He is the Son of Man. Do not marvel at this; for the hour is coming in which all who are in the graves will hear His voice and come forth—those who have done **good**, to the resurrection of life, and those who have done **evil**, to the resurrection of condemnation"*

You see, when Jesus called out, *"those who have done **good**, to the resurrection of life,"* He was speaking about the people who allowed the influence of the **good** attribute to impact their behavior, conduct, work, speech, etc.... These are the people who follow God's Word all the way to gain a crown of life according to James 1:12. The negative forces of the campaign create fog to keep people confused from seeing this Truth in the war. Be that as it may, Jesus says, *"I am the door. If anyone enters by Me, he will be saved, and will go in and out and find pasture. The thief does not come except to steal, and to kill, and to destroy. I have come that they may have life, and that they may have it more abundantly. "I am the **good** shepherd. The **good** shepherd gives His life for the sheep"* (John 10:11). Further He said, *"I am the **good** shepherd; and I know My sheep, and am known by My own"* (John 10:14). Jesus Christ Himself, the ultimate expression of the **good** attribute, is the gate keeper to heaven. The Bible documents, *"...God anointed Jesus of Nazareth with the Holy Spirit and with power, who went about doing **good** and healing all who were oppressed by the devil, for God was with Him"*

(Acts 10:38). Thus, it is by His rules and definition of what is **good** that one gains access to heaven. Since Jesus' example is based on obedience to God's Word, His example leads people who hear Him to "...*an antitype which now saves us—<u>baptism</u> (not the removal of the filth of the flesh, but the answer of a **good** conscience toward God), through the resurrection of Jesus Christ...*" (1 Peter 3:21-22). One must strive to acquire the influence of the **good** attribute, be <u>baptized</u>, and live faithfully until death to gain the crown of life according to Revelations 2:10.

To close out the four gospels, here are more examples of people influenced by the **good** attribute.

Who	What Is Documented
Luke	"*Inasmuch as many have taken in hand to set in order a narrative of those things which have been fulfilled among us, just as those who from the beginning were eyewitnesses and ministers of the word delivered them to us, it seemed **good** to me also, having had perfect understanding of all things from the very first, to write to you an orderly account, most excellent Theophilus, that you may know the certainty of those things in which you were instructed*" (Luke 1:1-4)
Mary	Instead of focusing on housework like Martha when Jesus was present, she opted to hear what He had to say. Because of this, Jesus said, "*Martha, Martha, you are worried and troubled about many things. But one thing is needed, and Mary has chosen that **good** part, which will not be taken away from her*" (Luke 10:41-42)
Joseph of Arimathea	"*Now behold, there was a man named Joseph, a council member, a **good** and just man*" (Luke 23:50)
Philip	Based on his actions. The Biblical record documented, "*Philip found Nathanael and said to him, "We have found Him of whom Moses in the law, and also the prophets, wrote—Jesus of Nazareth, the son of Joseph." And Nathanael said to him, "Can anything **good** come out of Nazareth?" Philip said to him, "Come and see"* (John 1:45-46)
The first Christians	When the first group of people was baptized into Christ (Acts 2:41) after the Day of Pentecost, the Biblical record documented, about three thousand souls, "*...had all things in common, and sold their possessions and goods, and divided them among all, as anyone had need. So continuing daily with one accord in the temple, and breaking bread from house to house, they ate their food with gladness and simplicity of heart, praising God and having favor with all the people. And the Lord added to the church daily those who were being saved*" (Acts 2:41-47)
	And great grace was upon them all. Nor was there anyone among them who lacked; for all who were possessors of lands or houses sold them, and brought the proceeds of the things that were sold, and laid them at the apostles' feet; and they distributed to each as anyone had need. (Acts 4:32-35)
Joses	"*...who was also named Barnabas by the apostles (which is translated Son of Encouragement), a Levite of the country of Cyprus, having land, sold it, and brought the money and laid it at the apostles' feet*" (Acts 4:36-37)
Peter and John	The Bible documented that Peter told the Sanhedrin after bringing him in for healing a man, "*If we this day are judged for a **good** deed done to a helpless man, by what means he has been made well, let it be known to you all, and to all the people of Israel, that by the name of Jesus Christ of Nazareth, whom*

403

	you crucified, whom God raised from the dead, by Him this man stands here before you whole...." (Acts 4:9-11)
Seven men to help widows	The apostles directed, "*Therefore, brethren, seek out from among you seven men of **good** reputation, full of the Holy Spirit and wisdom, whom we may appoint over this business...*" (Acts 6:3). The church identified and selected seven men to serve the Hellenist widows.
Tabitha	The Biblical record documents, "*At Joppa there was a certain disciple named Tabitha, which is translated Dorcas. This woman was full of **good** works and charitable deeds which she did...*" (Acts 9:36, 37). She died. Peter went to her, prayed, and she returned to life by the power of Jesus Christ according to the Biblical record of Acts 9:39-42.
Cornelius	He sent men to get Peter and the Bible documents, "*And they said, "Cornelius the centurion, a just man, one who fears God and has a **good** reputation among all the nation of the Jews, was divinely instructed by a holy angel to summon you to his house, and to hear words from you*" (Acts 10:22)
Barnabas	The Biblical record says, "*For he was a **good** man, full of the Holy Spirit and of faith. And a great many people were added to the Lord*" (Acts 11:24)
Ananias	Paul said of him, "*Then a certain Ananias, a devout man according to the law, having a **good** testimony with all the Jews who dwelt there came to me; and he stood and said to me, 'Brother Saul, receive your sight.' And at that same hour I looked up at him*" (Acts 22:12-13)
Paul	The Biblical record documented, "Then Paul, looking earnestly at the council, said, "*Men and brethren, I have lived in all **good** conscience before God until this day*" (Acts 23:1) Also not, Jesus told him, "*...Be of **good** cheer, Paul; for as you have testified for Me in Jerusalem, so you must also bear witness at Rome*" (Acts 23:11)
Demetrius	The Bible documented that he "*has a **good** testimony from all, and from the truth itself. And we also bear witness, and you know that our testimony is true*" (3 John 1:12)
Many others	Paul presented a list of people in Hebrews 11:4-38. He documented that Abel, Enoch, Noah, Abraham, Sarah, Isaac, Jacob, Joseph, Moses, Rahab, Gideon, Barak, Samson, Jephthah, David, Samuel, and the prophets. Paul documented that "*...all these, having obtained a **good** testimony through faith, did not receive the promise, God having provided something better for us, that they should not be made perfect apart from us*" (Hebrews 11:39-40)

Table 106: More Examples of People Who Allowed the Influence of the Good Attribute

After Paul's conversion to Christianity, he began spreading the Gospel of Jesus Christ to the Jews. He documented the role of the ***good*** attribute's influence between God and man based on God's standard. I implore one to consider Paul's discourse closely. By inspiration of the Holy Spirit, Paul documented in Romans 2:1-11:

> "*Therefore you are inexcusable, O man, whoever you are who judge, for in whatever you judge another you condemn yourself; for you who judge practice the same things. But we know that the judgment of God is according to truth against those who practice such things. And do you think this, O man, you who judge those practicing such things, and doing the same, that you will escape the judgment of God? Or do you despise the riches of His*

> ***goodness**, forbearance, and longsuffering, not knowing that the **goodness** of God leads you to repentance? But in accordance with your hardness and your impenitent heart you are treasuring up for yourself wrath in the day of wrath and revelation of the righteous judgment of God, who "will render to each one according to his deeds": eternal life to those who by patient continuance in doing **good** seek for glory, honor, and immortality; but to those who are self-seeking and do not obey the truth, but obey unrighteousness—indignation and wrath, tribulation and anguish, on every soul of man who does evil, of the Jew first and also of the Greek; but glory, honor, and peace to everyone who works what is **good**, to the Jew first and also to the Greek. For there is no partiality with God."*

BTT allows one to see that in the relationship between God and humanity, the influence of the **good** attribute makes a big difference. This attribute helps one to understand the need to prioritize the works of God over the works of self or others. The **good** works that come out of the influence of the **good** attributes leads one to *"glory, honor, and immortality."* One should also notice that when it comes to the **good** works influenced by this attribute, there is no separation between the Jew and anyone else. Paul documented, *"…there is no partiality with God."* In fact, for people who teach that the Jews have priority with God above Christians, Paul documented a stern warning. He said, *"…Because of unbelief they were broken off, and you stand by faith. Do not be haughty, but fear. For if God did not spare the natural branches, He may not spare you either. Therefore consider the **goodness** and severity of God: on those who fell, severity; but toward you, **goodness**, if you continue in His **goodness**. Otherwise you also will be cut off. And they also, if they do not continue in unbelief, will be grafted in, for God is able to graft them in again"* (Romans 11:20-23). BTT allows one to understand that the influence of the **good** attribute is necessary for one to remain on the **good** path of life and receive God's **goodness.** It is God's **goodness** that saves one from everlasting destruction. God's **goodness** is synonymous with His grace. However, God's grace is on an unfathomably higher level of **goodness**.

Paul went on to document that, *"…when we were still without strength, in due time Christ died for the ungodly. For scarcely for a righteous man will one die; yet perhaps for a **good** man someone would even dare to die. But God demonstrates His own love toward us, in that while we were still sinners, Christ died for us"* (Romans 5:6-8). This statement from Paul highlights the blinding and corrosive nature of spiritual warfare. It emphasizes spiritual priorities from the standpoint of engaging in the spiritual fight. Paul statement suggests people might sacrifice their lives for a **good** man, but rarely for one that is righteous; the attribute that embodies all the positive attributes in spiritual warfare. Most people cannot <u>discern</u> what is **good** from what is best. To do so, one must *"…be transformed by the renewing of your mind, that you may prove what is that **good** and acceptable and perfect will of God"* (Romans 12:2). Conforming to the wisdom of the world leads to spiritual blindness. Allowing the influence of the **good** attribute and striving to develop the attribute in one's inner spirit is one's only hope to *"prove what is that **good** and acceptable and perfect will of God."* The **good** attribute sets one on the path towards BTT, or as Paul documented, the *"renewing of your mind"* to accept a direction opposite of the world's view.

The Biblical record identifies bad conduct and behavior. For the maturing of the ***good*** attribute steers one away from bad conduct and behavior. This undisputed information comes from the Holy Spirit who inspired men to document God's Word. Essential indicators that one **does not have** the influence of the ***good*** attribute include:

The Indicator	What Is Documented
General areas	*"But know this, that in the last days perilous times will come: For men will be lovers of themselves, lovers of money, boasters, proud, blasphemers, disobedient to parents, unthankful, unholy, unloving, unforgiving, slanderers, without self-control, brutal, despisers of **good**, traitors, headstrong, haughty, lovers of pleasure rather than lovers of God, having a form of godliness but denying its power. And from such people turn away! For of this sort are those who creep into households and make captives of gullible women loaded down with sins, led away by various lusts, always learning and never able to come to the knowledge of the truth"* (2 Timothy 3:1-7)
Practicing behavior that is unfit for Christians	*"…do those things which are not fitting; being filled with all unrighteousness, sexual immorality, wickedness, covetousness, maliciousness; full of envy, murder, strife, deceit, evil-mindedness; they are whisperers, backbiters, haters of God, violent, proud, boasters, inventors of evil things, disobedient to parents, un<u>discerning</u>, untrustworthy, unloving, unforgiving, unmerciful; who, knowing the righteous judgment of God, that those who practice such things are deserving of death, not only do the same but also approve of those who practice them"* (Romans 1:28-32)
Listening to deceiving spirits and doctrines of demons	*"Now the Spirit expressly says that in latter times some will depart from the faith, giving heed to deceiving spirits and doctrines of demons, speaking lies in hypocrisy, having their own conscience seared with a hot iron, forbidding to marry, and commanding to abstain from foods which God created to be received with thanksgiving by those who believe and know the truth"* (1 Timothy 4:1-3)
Worshippers of creatures and those who dishonoring their bodies (Perverse and immoral attributes involved)	*"Professing to be wise, they became fools, and changed the glory of the incorruptible God into an image made like corruptible man—and birds and four-footed animals and creeping things. Therefore God also gave them up to uncleanness, in the lusts of their hearts, to dishonor their bodies among themselves, who exchanged the truth of God for the lie, and worshiped and served the creature rather than the Creator, who is blessed forever"* (Romans 1:23-25)
Practice Homosexuality and the like	*"For this reason God gave them up to vile passions. For even their women exchanged the natural use for what is against nature. Likewise also the men, leaving the natural use of the woman, burned in their lust for one another, men with men committing what is shameful, and receiving in themselves the penalty of their error which was due"* (Romans 1:26-27)
Congregations that praise God with open acts of	Within the church of Corinthian, a son had his father's wife and the congregation accepted and applauded the behavior. Paul documented, *"Your glorying is not **good**. Do you not know that a little leaven leavens*

sexual immorality present	*the whole lump?"* (1 Corinthians 5:6). He directed them, *"In the name of our Lord Jesus Christ, when you are gathered together, along with my spirit, with the power of our Lord Jesus Christ, deliver such a one to Satan for the destruction of the flesh, that his spirit may be saved in the day of the Lord Jesus"* (1 Corinthians 5:4-5)
Bad behavior	*"...the works of the flesh are evident, which are: adultery, fornication, uncleanness, lewdness, idolatry, sorcery, hatred, contentions, jealousies, outbursts of wrath, selfish ambitions, dissensions, heresies, envy, murders, drunkenness, revelries, and the like; of which I tell you beforehand, just as I also told you in time past, that those who practice such things will not inherit the kingdom of God"* (Galatians 5:19-21)
Inability to teach about Christ	*"For though by this time you ought to be teachers, you need someone to teach you again the first principles of the oracles of God; and you have come to need milk and not solid food. For everyone who partakes only of milk is unskilled in the word of righteousness, for he is a babe. But solid food belongs to those who are of full age, that is, those who by reason of use have their senses exercised to <u>discern</u> both **good** and evil"* (Hebrews 5:12-14)
Turning one's back on God, the Gospel, or His church	*"For it is impossible for those who were once enlightened, and have tasted the heavenly gift, and have become partakers of the Holy Spirit, and have tasted the **good** word of God and the powers of the age to come, if they fall away, to renew them again to repentance, since they crucify again for themselves the Son of God, and put Him to an open shame"* (Hebrews 6:4-6)
Listeners and accepters of worldly wisdom over God's wisdom	*"Who is wise and understanding among you? Let him show by **good** conduct that his works are done in the meekness of wisdom. But if you have bitter envy and self-seeking in your hearts, do not boast and lie against the truth. This wisdom does not descend from above, but is earthly, sensual, demonic. For where envy and self-seeking exist, confusion and every **evil** thing are there. But the wisdom that is from above is first pure, then peaceable, gentle, willing to yield, full of mercy and **good** fruits, without partiality and without hypocrisy"* (James 3:13-17)
	"For there are many insubordinate, both idle talkers and deceivers, especially those of the circumcision, whose mouths must be stopped, who subvert whole households, teaching things which they ought not, for the sake of dishonest gain" (Titus 1:10-11)
	*"...Therefore rebuke them sharply, that they may be sound in the faith, not giving heed to Jewish fables and commandments of men who turn from the truth. To the pure all things are pure, but to those who are defiled and unbelieving nothing is pure; but even their mind and conscience are defiled. They profess to know God, but in works they deny Him, being abominable, disobedient, and disqualified for every **good** work"* (Titus 1:13-16)
The lack of self-control	*"Where do wars and fights come from among you? Do they not come from your desires for pleasure that war in your members? You lust and do not have. You murder and covet and cannot obtain. You fight and war. Yet you do not have because you do not ask. You ask and do not*

	receive, because you ask amiss, that you may spend it on your pleasures" (James 4:1-3)
Trying to please God and the secular friends	*"Adulterers and adulteresses! Do you not know that friendship with the world is enmity with God? Whoever therefore wants to be a friend of the world makes himself an enemy of God. Or do you think that the Scripture says in vain, "The Spirit who dwells in us yearns jealously"? But He gives more grace. Therefore He says: "God resists the proud, but gives grace to the humble.""* (James 4:4-6)
Resisting God's Word	*"Therefore submit to God. Resist the devil and he will flee from you. Draw near to God and He will draw near to you. Cleanse your hands, you sinners; and purify your hearts, you double-minded"* (James 4:7-8)
Speaking evil of fellow Christians	*"Do not speak evil of one another, brethren. He who speaks evil of a brother and judges his brother, speaks evil of the law and judges the law. But if you judge the law, you are not a doer of the law but a judge. There is one Lawgiver, who is able to save and to destroy. Who are you to judge another?"* (James 4:11-12)
Boasting of the future	*"Come now, you who say, "Today or tomorrow we will go to such and such a city, spend a year there, buy and sell, and make a profit"; whereas you do not know what will happen tomorrow. For what is your life? It is even a vapor that appears for a little time and then vanishes away. Instead you ought to say, "If the Lord wills, we shall live and do this or that." But now you boast in your arrogance. All such boasting is evil"* (James 4:13-16)
Pursuit of wealth over God	*"But those who desire to be rich fall into temptation and a snare, and into many foolish and harmful lusts which drown men in destruction and perdition. For the love of money is a root of all kinds of evil, for which some have strayed from the faith in their greediness, and pierced themselves through with many sorrows"* (1 Timothy 6:9-10)
The misuse of wealth	*"Come now, you rich, weep and howl for your miseries that are coming upon you! Your riches are corrupted, and your garments are moth-eaten. Your gold and silver are corroded, and their corrosion will be a witness against you and will eat your flesh like fire. You have heaped up treasure in the last days. Indeed the wages of the laborers who mowed your fields, which you kept back by fraud, cry out; and the cries of the reapers have reached the ears of the Lord of Sabaoth. You have lived on the earth in pleasure and luxury; you have fattened your hearts as in a day of slaughter. You have condemned, you have murdered the just; he does not resist you"* (James 5:1-6)
The lack of patience	*"Therefore be patient, brethren, until the coming of the Lord. See how the farmer waits for the precious fruit of the earth, waiting patiently for it until it receives the early and latter rain. You also be patient. Establish your hearts, for the coming of the Lord is at hand"* (James 5:7-8)
Grumbling	*"Do not grumble against one another, brethren, lest you be condemned. Behold, the Judge is standing at the door! My brethren, take the prophets, who spoke in the name of the Lord, as an example of suffering and patience"* (James 5:9-10)
Swearing by oath	*"But above all, my brethren, do not swear, either by heaven or by earth or with any other oath. But let your "Yes" be "Yes," and your "No," "No," lest you fall into judgment"* (James 5:12)

Foolish things	"But avoid foolish disputes, genealogies, contentions, and strivings about the law; for they are unprofitable and useless. Reject a divisive man after the first and second admonition, knowing that such a person is warped and sinning, being self-condemned" (Titus 3:9-11)
Fornication, uncleanness, covetousness	"But fornication and all uncleanness or covetousness, let it not even be named among you, as is fitting for saints; neither filthiness, nor foolish talking, nor coarse jesting, which are not fitting, but rather giving of thanks. For this you know, that no fornicator, unclean person, nor covetous man, who is an idolater, has any inheritance in the kingdom of Christ and God" (Ephesians 5:3-5)
All uncleanness	"Therefore put to death your members which are on the earth: fornication, uncleanness, passion, evil desire, and covetousness, which is idolatry. Because of these things the wrath of God is coming upon the sons of disobedience, in which you yourselves once walked when you lived in them" (Colossians 3:5-7)

Table 107: Examples That Indicate the Absence of the Influence of the Good Attribute

The things written above are easy to understand and require no interpretation. BTT allows one to see that one truly influenced by the ***good*** attribute would not engage in these types of behaviors. Conversely, just as the Biblical record documents what constitutes conducts and behaviors that **<u>are not good</u>**, the Holy Spirit led these same men to document what is ***good*** or positive conduct and behavior. This information is unparalleled in its amount, quality, and clarity. The inspired writers documented the following undisputed information from the Word of God by inspiration of the Holy Spirit:

The Indicator	What Is Documented
Concerning marriage	"But I say to the unmarried and to the widows: It is **good** for them if they remain even as I am; but if they cannot exercise self-control, let them marry. For it is better to marry than to burn with passion" (1 Corinthians 7:8-9)
	Further: "Now concerning virgins: I have no commandment from the Lord; yet I give judgment as one whom the Lord in His mercy has made trustworthy. I suppose therefore that this is **good** because of the present distress—that it is **good** for a man to remain as he is: Are you bound to a wife? Do not seek to be loosed. Are you loosed from a wife? Do not seek a wife. But even if you do marry, you have not sinned; and if a virgin marries, she has not sinned. Nevertheless such will have trouble in the flesh, but I would spare you" (1 Corinthians 7:25-28)
	"...It is **good** for a man not to touch a woman. Nevertheless, because of **sexual immorality**, let each man have his own wife, and let each woman have her own husband. Let the husband render to his wife the affection due her, and likewise also the wife to her husband" (1 Corinthians 7:1-3)
	"Marriage is honorable among all, and the bed undefiled; but fornicators and adulterers God will judge" (Hebrews 13:4)
	"Husbands, love your wives, just as Christ also loved the church and gave Himself for her..." (Ephesians 5:25)

The family relationship	"*Husbands, love your wives and do not be bitter toward them*" (Colossians 3:19)
	"*Husbands, likewise, dwell with them with understanding, giving honor to the wife, as to the weaker vessel, and as being heirs together of the grace of life, that your prayers may not be hindered*" (1 Peter 3:7)
	"*Wives, submit to your own husbands, as to the Lord*" (Ephesians 5:22)
	"*Wives, submit to your own husbands, as is fitting in the Lord*" (Colossians 3:18)
	"*Wives, likewise, be submissive to your own husbands, that even if some do not obey the word, they, without a word, may be won by the conduct of their wives, when they observe your chaste conduct accompanied by fear. Do not let your adornment be merely outward—arranging the hair, wearing gold, or putting on fine apparel— rather let it be the hidden person of the heart, with the incorruptible beauty of a gentle and quiet spirit, which is very precious in the sight of God. For in this manner, in former times, the holy women who trusted in God also adorned themselves, being submissive to their own husbands, as Sarah obeyed Abraham, calling him lord, whose daughters you are if you do **good** and are not afraid with any terror*" (1 Peter 3:1-6)
	"*Children, obey your parents in the Lord, for this is right*" (Ephesians 6:1)
	"*Children, obey your parents in all things, for this is well pleasing to the Lord*" (Colossians 3:20)
	"*Honor your father and mother,*" which is the first commandment with promise: "*that it may be well with you and you may live long on the earth*" (Ephesians 6:2-3)
	"*And you fathers, do not provoke your children to wrath, but bring them up in the training and admonition of the Lord*" (Ephesians 6:4)
	"*Fathers, do not provoke your children, lest they become discouraged*" (Colossians 3:21)
One's spiritual walk	"*I say then: Walk in the Spirit, and you shall not fulfill the lust of the flesh. For the flesh lusts against the Spirit, and the Spirit against the flesh; and these are contrary to one another, so that you do not do the things that you wish. But if you are led by the Spirit, you are not under the law*" (Galatians 5:16-18)
	"*And walk in love, as Christ also has loved us and given Himself for us, an offering and a sacrifice to God for a sweet-smelling aroma*" (Ephesians 5:2)
	"*Walk as children of light (for the fruit of the Spirit is in all **goodness**, righteousness, and truth), finding out what is acceptable to the Lord*" (Ephesians 5:9-10)
	"*See then that you walk circumspectly, not as fools but as wise, redeeming the time, because the days are evil*" (Ephesians 5:15-16)
	"*And whatever you do in word or deed, do all in the name of the Lord Jesus, giving thanks to God the Father through Him*" (Colossians 3:17)
	"*Walk in wisdom toward those who are outside, redeeming the time*" (Colossians 4:5)
	"*Now by this we know that we know Him, if we keep His commandments. He who says, "I know Him," and does not keep His commandments, is a liar, and the truth is not in him. But whoever keeps His word, truly the love of*

One's spiritual walk	*God is perfected in him. By this we know that we are in Him. He who says he abides in Him ought himself also to walk just as He walked"* (1 John 2:3-6)
	"...be strong in the Lord and in the power of His might" (Ephesians 6:10)
	"Put on the whole armor of God, that you may be able to stand against the wiles of the devil" (Ephesians 6:11)
One's conversation	*"Let your speech always be with grace, seasoned with salt, that you may know how you ought to answer each one"* (Colossians 4:6)
	"Therefore, putting away lying, "Let each one of you speak truth with his neighbor," for we are members of one another" (Ephesians 4:25)
	"Do not lie to one another, since you have put off the old man with his deeds, and have put on the new man who is renewed in knowledge according to the image of Him who created him, where there is neither Greek nor Jew, circumcised nor uncircumcised, barbarian, Scythian, slave nor free, but Christ is all and in all" (Colossians 3:9-11)
	*"Let no corrupt word proceed out of your mouth, but what is **good** for necessary edification, that it may impart grace to the hearers"* (Ephesians 4:29)
	"Let all bitterness, wrath, anger, clamor, and evil speaking be put away from you, with all malice" (Ephesians 4:31)
	"But now you yourselves are to put off all these: anger, wrath, malice, blasphemy, filthy language out of your mouth" (Colossians 3:8)
	"And do not be drunk with wine, in which is dissipation; but be filled with the Spirit, speaking to one another in psalms and hymns and spiritual songs, singing and making melody in your heart to the Lord, giving thanks always for all things to God the Father in the name of our Lord Jesus Christ, submitting to one another in the fear of God" (Ephesians 5:18-21)
	"Let the word of Christ dwell in you richly in all wisdom, teaching and admonishing one another in psalms and hymns and spiritual songs, singing with grace in your hearts to the Lord" (Colossians 3:16)
	"Do all things without complaining and disputing, that you may become blameless and harmless, children of God without fault in the midst of a crooked and perverse generation, among whom you shine as lights in the world, holding fast the word of life ..." (Philippians 2:14-16)
One's thoughts	*"Let no one deceive you with empty words, for because of these things the wrath of God comes upon the sons of disobedience. Therefore do not be partakers with them"* (Ephesians 5:6-7)
	"Therefore do not be unwise, but understand what the will of the Lord is" (Ephesians 5:17)
	"If then you were raised with Christ, seek those things which are above, where Christ is, sitting at the right hand of God" (Colossians 3:1)
	"Set your mind on things above, not on things on the earth" (Colossians 3:2)
Concerning Truth	One must make, *"...supplications, prayers, intercessions, and giving of thanks be made for all men, for kings and all who are in authority, that we may lead a quiet and peaceable life in all godliness and reverence. For this is **good** and acceptable in the sight of God our Savior, who desires all men to be saved and to come to the knowledge of the truth"* (1 Timothy 2:1-4)

	"...that the men pray everywhere, lifting up holy hands, without wrath and doubting..." (1 Timothy 2:8)	
	"*Continue earnestly in prayer, being vigilant in it with thanksgiving...*" (Colossians 4:2)	
Concerning Truth	"*Brethren, if anyone among you wanders from the truth, and someone turns him back, let him know that he who turns a sinner from the error of his way will save a soul from death and cover a multitude of sins*" (James 5:19-20)	
Concerning food	"*For every creature of God is **good**, and nothing is to be refused if it is received with thanksgiving; for it is sanctified by the word of God and prayer*" (1 Timothy 4:4-5)	
Behavior **in** the Lord's Church	"*And let us consider one another in order to stir up love and **good** works, not forsaking the assembling of ourselves together, as is the manner of some, but exhorting one another, and so much the more as you see the Day approaching*" (Hebrews 10:24-25)	
	"*...all of you be of one mind, having compassion for one another; love as brothers, be tenderhearted, be courteous; not returning evil for evil or reviling for reviling, but on the contrary blessing, knowing that you were called to this, that you may inherit a blessing. For "He who would love life and see **good** days, let him refrain his tongue from evil, and his lips from speaking deceit. Let him turn away from evil and do **good**; let him seek peace and pursue it. For the eyes of the Lord are on the righteous, and His ears are open to their prayers; but the face of the Lord is against those who do evil*" (1 Peter 3:8-12)	
	"*And above all things have fervent love for one another, for "love will cover a multitude of sins." Be hospitable to one another without grumbling. As each one has received a gift, minister it to one another, as **good** stewards of the manifold grace of God*" (1 Peter 4:8-10)	
	"*Beloved, do not imitate what is evil, but what is **good**. He who does **good** is of God, but he who does evil has not seen God*" (3 John 1:11)	
	"*Bear one another's burdens, and so fulfill the law of Christ*" (Galatians 6:2)	
	"*Honor all people. Love the brotherhood. Fear God. Honor the king*" (1 Peter 2:17)	
	"*But reject profane and old wives' fables, and exercise yourself toward godliness*" (1 Timothy 4:7)	
	"*And we urge you, brethren, to recognize those who labor among you, and are over you in the Lord and admonish you, and to esteem them very highly in love for their work's sake. Be at peace among yourselves. Now we exhort you, brethren, warn those who are unruly, comfort the fainthearted, uphold the weak, be patient with all. See that no one renders evil for evil to anyone, but always pursue what is **good** both for yourselves and for all*" (1 Thessalonians 5:12-15)	
Elders	"*This is a faithful saying: If a man desires the position of a bishop, he desires a **good** work. A bishop then must be blameless, the husband of one wife, temperate, sober-minded, of **good** behavior...Moreover he must have a **good** testimony among those who are outside, lest he fall into reproach and the snare of the devil*" (1 Timothy 3:1-7)	
	"*Now faith is the substance of things hoped for, the evidence of things not seen. For by it the elders obtained a **good** testimony*" (Hebrews 11:1-2)	

Elders	*Shepherd the flock of God which is among you, serving as overseers, not by compulsion but willingly, not for dishonest gain but eagerly; nor as being lords over those entrusted to you, but being examples to the flock; and when the Chief Shepherd appears, you will receive the crown of glory that does not fade away"* (1 Peter 5:2-4)
	*"...if a man is blameless, the husband of one wife, having faithful children not accused of dissipation or insubordination. For a bishop must be blameless, as a steward of God, not self-willed, not quick-tempered, not given to wine, not violent, not greedy for money, but hospitable, a lover of what is **good**, sober-minded, just, holy, self-controlled, holding fast the faithful word as he has been taught, that he may be able, by sound doctrine, both to exhort and convict those who contradict"* (Titus 1:5-9)
(Preaching and Teaching)	*"If anyone speaks, let him speak as the oracles of God. If anyone ministers, let him do it as with the ability which God supplies, that in all things God may be glorified through Jesus Christ, to whom belong the glory and the dominion forever and ever. Amen"* (1 Peter 4:11)
	"...teaching us that, denying ungodliness and worldly lusts, we should live soberly, righteously, and godly in the present age..." (Titus 2:12)
	*"Remind them to be subject to rulers and authorities, to obey, to be ready for every **good** work, to speak evil of no one, to be peaceable, gentle, showing all humility to all men"* (Titus 3:1-2)
	Paul told Timothy, *"If you instruct the brethren in these things, you will be a **good** minister of Jesus Christ, nourished in the words of faith and of the **good** doctrine which you have carefully followed"* (1 Timothy 4:6)
(Members of the Body)	*"Do not rebuke an older man, but exhort him as a father, younger men as brothers, older women as mothers, younger women as sisters, with all purity"* (1 Timothy 5:1-2)
--- Older Men	*"...that the older men be sober, reverent, temperate, sound in faith, in love, in patience..."* (Titus 2:2)
--- Older and Younger Women	*"...the older women likewise, that they be reverent in behavior, not slanderers, not given to much wine, teachers of **good** things— that they admonish the young women to love their husbands, to love their children, to be discreet, chaste, homemakers, **good**, obedient to their own husbands, that the word of God may not be blasphemed"* (Titus 2:3-5)
	*"...women adorn themselves in modest apparel, with propriety and moderation, not with braided hair or gold or pearls or costly clothing, but, which is proper for women professing godliness, with **good** works"* (1 Timothy 2:9, 10).
--- Younger Men	*"Likewise, exhort the young men to be sober-minded, in all things showing yourself to be a pattern of **good** works; in doctrine showing integrity, reverence, incorruptibility, sound speech that cannot be condemned, that one who is an opponent may be ashamed, having nothing evil to say of you"* (Titus 2:6-8)
--- Younger people in general	*Likewise you younger people, submit yourselves to your elders. Yes, all of you be submissive to one another, and be clothed with humility, for "God resists the proud, but gives grace to the humble." Therefore humble yourselves under the mighty hand of God, that He may exalt you in due time, casting all your care upon Him, for He cares for you. Be sober, be vigilant; because your adversary the devil walks about like a roaring lion, seeking*

	whom he may devour. Resist him, steadfast in the faith, knowing that the same sufferings are experienced by your brotherhood in the world. But may the God of all grace, who called us to His eternal glory by Christ Jesus, after you have suffered a while, perfect, establish, strengthen, and settle you" (1 Peter 5-10)
Deacons	*"For those who have served well as deacons obtain for themselves a **good** standing and great boldness in the faith which is in Christ Jesus"* (1 Timothy 3:13)
Widows	*"Honor widows who are really widows"* (1 Timothy 5:3)
-- with children or grand-children	*"But if any widow has children or grandchildren, let them first learn to show piety at home and to repay their parents; for this is **good** and acceptable before God"* (1 Timothy 5:4)
-- under sixty years of age	*"Do not let a widow under sixty years old be taken into the number, and not unless she has been the wife of one man, well reported for **good** works: if she has brought up children, if she has lodged strangers, if she has washed the saints' feet, if she has relieved the afflicted, if she has diligently followed every **good** work"* (1 Timothy 5:9-10)
Irresponsible people	*"But if anyone does not provide for his own, and especially for those of his household, he has denied the faith and is worse than an unbeliever"* (1 Timothy 5:8)
One's Behavior **outside** the Lord's church	*"Therefore submit yourselves to every ordinance of man for the Lord's sake, whether to the king as supreme, or to governors, as to those who are sent by him for the punishment of evildoers and for the praise of those who do **good**. For this is the will of God, that by doing **good** you may put to silence the ignorance of foolish men—as free, yet not using liberty as a cloak for vice, but as bondservants of God"* (1 Peter 2:13-16)
One's Behavior **outside** the Lord's church	*"And who is he who will harm you if you become followers of what is **good**? But even if you should suffer for righteousness' sake, you are blessed. "And do not be afraid of their threats, nor be troubled." But sanctify the Lord God in your hearts, and always be ready to give a defense to everyone who asks you a reason for the hope that is in you, with meekness and fear; having a **good** conscience, that when they defame you as evildoers, those who revile your **good** conduct in Christ may be ashamed. For it is better, if it is the will of God, to suffer for doing **good** than for doing evil"* (1 Peter 3:13-17)
	*"But the fruit of the Spirit is love, joy, peace, longsuffering, kindness, **goodness**, faithfulness, gentleness, self-control. Against such there is no law". And those who are Christ's have crucified the flesh with its passions and desires"* (Galatians 5:22-24)
	"Be angry, and do not sin": do not let the sun go down on your wrath, nor give place to the devil" (Ephesians 4:26-27)
	*"Let him who stole steal no longer, but rather let him labor, working with his hands what is **good**, that he may have something to give him who has need"* (Ephesians 4:28)
	"And do not grieve the Holy Spirit of God, by whom you were sealed for the day of redemption" (Ephesians 4:30)
	"And be kind to one another, tenderhearted, forgiving one another, even as God in Christ forgave you" (Ephesians 4:32)

		"Therefore, as the elect of God, holy and beloved, put on tender mercies, kindness, humility, meekness, longsuffering; bearing with one another, and forgiving one another, if anyone has a complaint against another; even as Christ forgave you, so you also must do" (Colossians 3:12-13)
		"But above all these things put on love, which is the bond of perfection" (Colossians 3:14)
		"...be imitators of God as dear children" (Ephesians 5:1)
		"...let the peace of God rule in your hearts, to which also you were called in one body; and be thankful" (Colossians 3:15)
	One's companion-ship	*"And have no fellowship with the unfruitful works of darkness, but rather expose them. For it is shameful even to speak of those things which are done by them in secret. But all things that are exposed are made manifest by the light, for whatever makes manifest is light. Therefore He says: "Awake, you who sleep, arise from the dead, and Christ will give you light.""* (Ephesians 5:11-14)
	Work Relation-ships (The Employee)	*"Bondservants, be obedient to those who are your masters according to the flesh, with fear and trembling, in sincerity of heart, as to Christ; not with eyeservice, as men-pleasers, but as bondservants of Christ, doing the will of God from the heart, with **goodwill** doing service, as to the Lord, and not to men, knowing that whatever **good** anyone does, he will receive the same from the Lord, whether he is a slave or free"* (Ephesians 6:5-8)
		"Bondservants, obey in all things your masters according to the flesh, not with eyeservice, as men-pleasers, but in sincerity of heart, fearing God. And whatever you do, do it heartily, as to the Lord and not to men, knowing that from the Lord you will receive the reward of the inheritance; for you serve the Lord Christ. But he who does wrong will be repaid for what he has done, and there is no partiality" (Colossians 3:22-25)
		"Let as many bondservants as are under the yoke count their own masters worthy of all honor, so that the name of God and His doctrine may not be blasphemed. And those who have believing masters, let them not despise them because they are brethren, but rather serve them because those who are benefited are believers and beloved. Teach and exhort these things" (1 Timothy 6:1-2)
		*"Exhort bondservants to be obedient to their own masters, to be well pleasing in all things, not answering back, not pilfering, but showing all **good** fidelity, that they may adorn the doctrine of God our Savior in all things"* (Titus 2:9-10)
		*"Servants, be submissive to your masters with all fear, not only to the **good** and gentle, but also to the harsh. For this is commendable, if because of conscience toward God one endures grief, suffering wrongfully. For what credit is it if, when you are beaten for your faults, you take it patiently? But when you do **good** and suffer, if you take it patiently, this is commendable before God"* (1 Peter 2:18-20)
	(The Employer)	*"And you, masters, do the same things to them, giving up threatening, knowing that your own Master also is in heaven, and there is no partiality with Him"* (Ephesians 6:9)
		"Masters, give your bondservants what is just and fair, knowing that you also have a Master in heaven" (Colossians 4:1)

Concerning people with wealth	*"Command those who are rich in this present age not to be haughty, nor to trust in uncertain riches but in the living God, who gives us richly all things to enjoy. Let them do **good**, that they be rich in **good** works, ready to give, willing to share, storing up for themselves a **good** foundation for the time to come, that they may lay hold on eternal life"* (1 Timothy 6:17-19)

Table 108: Examples of Behaviors That Indicate the Presence of the Influence of the Good Attribute

Along with all the information presented, the apostles also documented the correlation between the influence of the **good** attribute and works, a **good** conscience, a **good** confession and fighting the **good** fight with the positive forces of the war campaign. To begin with, one influenced by the **good** attribute will automatically be involved in **good** works. In fact, it is safe to say that one does not have the influence of the **good** attribute if one refuses to engage in **good** works, because God commands these works; He does not request them. **Good** works go hand in hand with the progression and maturity of a Christian. *Good **works*** causes growth in a Christian. Studying the Word of God is a **good** work and a measure of the influence of the **good** attribute is always involved. The correlation is clear because God's Word is clear. Concerning the **good** attribute and **good** works, the Holy Spirit led the inspired writers to document the following pearls of wisdom:

- *"Now may our Lord Jesus Christ Himself, and our God and Father, who has loved us and given us everlasting consolation and **good** hope by grace, comfort your hearts and establish you in every **good** word and work"* (2 Thessalonians 2:16-17)

- *"Nevertheless the solid foundation of God stands, having this seal: "The Lord knows those who are His," and, "Let everyone who names the name of Christ depart from iniquity." But in a great house there are not only vessels of gold and silver, but also of wood and clay, some for honor and some for dishonor. Therefore if anyone cleanses himself from the latter, he will be a vessel for honor, sanctified and useful for the Master, prepared for every **good** work"* (2 Timothy 2:19-21)

- *"All Scripture is given by inspiration of God, and is profitable for doctrine, for reproof, for correction, for instruction in righteousness, that the man of God may be complete, thoroughly equipped for every **good** work"* (2 Timothy 3:17)

- Paul told Titus, *"This is a faithful saying, and these things I want you to affirm constantly, that those who have believed in God should be careful to maintain **good** works. These things are **good** and profitable to men"* (Titus 3:8)

- *"Beloved, I beg you as sojourners and pilgrims, abstain from fleshly lusts which war against the soul, having your conduct honorable among the Gentiles, that when they speak against you as evildoers, they may, by your **good** works which they observe, glorify God in the day of visitation"* (1 Peter 2:11-12)

- For all Christians: *"And let our people also learn to maintain **good** works, to meet urgent needs, that they may not be unfruitful"* (Titus 3:14)

- *"Now may the God of peace who brought up our Lord Jesus from the dead, that great Shepherd of the sheep, through the blood of the everlasting covenant, make you complete in every **good** work to do His will, working in you what is well pleasing in His sight, through Jesus Christ, to whom be glory forever and ever. Amen "*(Hebrews 13:20-21)

BTT allows one to see that **good** works fortify one's inner spirit. This is why Paul wrote, *"...whatever you do in word or deed, do all in the name of the Lord Jesus, giving thanks to God the Father through Him"* Colossians 3:17). This fortification helps one to maintain a **good** conscience and a **good** confession, which is necessary to remain among the positive forces of the war campaign and for fighting the **good** fight. Paul recognized this, and with the help of the Holy Spirit, he documented the words that best explains this aspect of the positive forces of the campaign. Paul documented:

- *"Pray for us; for we are confident that we have a **good** conscience, in all things desiring to live honorably"* (Hebrews 13:18)

- He charges Timothy, *"...wage the **good** warfare, having faith and a **good** conscience, which some having rejected, concerning the **faith** have suffered shipwreck..."* (1 Timothy 1:18-19)

- *"...pursue righteousness, godliness, faith, love, patience, gentleness. Fight the **good** fight of faith, lay hold on eternal life, to which you were also called and have confessed the **good** confession in the presence of many witnesses. I urge you in the sight of God who gives life to all things, and before Christ Jesus who witnessed the **good** confession before Pontius Pilate, that you keep this commandment without spot, blameless until our Lord Jesus Christ's appearing, which He will manifest in His own time..."* (1 Timothy 6:11-15)

- During his physical fatigue, he said, *"For I am already being poured out as a drink offering, and the time of my departure is at hand. I have fought the **good** fight, I have finished the race, I have kept the faith"* (2 Timothy 4:6-7)

- *"You therefore must endure hardship as a **good** soldier of Jesus Christ"* (2 Timothy 2:3)

There are countless pearls of wisdom to be learned about the influence of the **good** attribute and the behavior it inspires in the rest of the New Testament. Here are a few more to close out this chapter on the **good** attribute. The Biblical record documented:

"Let love be without hypocrisy. Abhor what is evil. Cling to what is **good**" (Romans 12:9)	"Do not be deceived: "evil company corrupts **good** habits" (1 Corinthians 15:33)	"Do not be overcome by evil, but overcome evil with **good**" (Romans 12:21)
"Repay no one evil for evil. Have regard for **good** things in the sight of all men" (Romans 12:17)	"... be wise in what is **good**, and simple concerning evil" (Romans 16:19)	"Therefore, to him who knows to do **good** and does not do it, to him it is sin" (James 4:17)

"...work out your own salvation with fear and trembling; for it is God who works in you both to will and to do for His **good** pleasure" (Philippians 2:13)	"Every **good** gift and every perfect gift is from above, and comes down from the Father of lights, with whom there is no variation or shadow of turning" (James 1:17)	"Let him who is taught the word share in all **good** things with him who teaches" (Galatians 6:6)
"It is **good** neither to eat meat nor drink wine nor do anything by which your brother stumbles or is offended or is made weak" (Romans 14:21)	"Therefore let those who suffer according to the will of God commit their souls to Him in doing **good**, as to a faithful Creator" (1 Peter 4:19)	"For we are His workmanship, created in Christ Jesus for **good** works, which God prepared beforehand that we should walk in them" (Ephesians 2:10)
"...whoever has this world's goods, and sees his brother in need, and shuts up his heart from him, how does the love of God abide in him?" (1 John 3:17)	"And God is able to make all grace abound toward you, that you, always having all sufficiency in all things, may have an abundance for every **good** work" (2 Corinthians 9:8)	"...Christ came as High Priest of the **good** things to come, with the greater and more perfect tabernacle not made with hands, that is, not of this creation" (Hebrews 9:11)
"We then who are strong ought to bear with the scruples of the weak, and not to please ourselves. Let each of us please his neighbor for his **good**, leading to edification" (Romans 15:1-2)	"For we must all appear before the judgment seat of Christ, that each one may receive the things done in the body, according to what he has done, whether **good** or bad" (2 Corinthians 5:10)	"And do not be conformed to this world, but be transformed by the renewing of your mind, that you may prove what is that **good** and acceptable and perfect will of God" (Romans 12:2)
"Rejoice always, pray without ceasing, in everything give thanks; for this is the will of God in Christ Jesus for you. Do not quench the Spirit. Do not despise prophecies. Test all things; hold fast what is **good**. Abstain from every form of evil" (1 Thessalonians 5:16-22)	"... brethren, do not grow weary in doing **good**. And if anyone does not obey our word in this epistle, note that person and do not keep company with him, that he may be ashamed. Yet do not count him as an enemy, but admonish him as a brother" (2 Thessalonians 3:13-15)	"Therefore do not let your **good** be spoken of as evil; for the kingdom of God is not eating and drinking, but righteousness and peace and joy in the Holy Spirit. For he who serves Christ in these things is acceptable to God and approved by men" (Romans 14:16-18)
"Some men's sins are clearly evident, preceding them to judgment, but those of some men follow later. Likewise, the **good** works of some are clearly evident, and those that are otherwise cannot be hidden" (1 Timothy 5:24-25)	"Hold fast the pattern of sound words which you have heard from me, in faith and love which are in Christ Jesus. That **good** thing which was committed to you, keep by the Holy Spirit who dwells in us" (2 Timothy 1:13-14)	"Therefore by Him let us continually offer the sacrifice of praise to God, that is, the fruit of our lips, giving thanks to His name. But do not forget to do **good** and to share, for with such sacrifices God is well pleased" (Hebrews 13:15-16)

"...let us not grow weary while doing **good**, for in due season we shall reap if we do not lose heart. Therefore, as we have opportunity, let us do **good** to all, especially to those who are of the household of faith" (Galatians 6:7-10)	"...brethren, whatever things are true, whatever things are noble, whatever things are just, whatever things are pure, whatever things are lovely, whatever things are of **good** report, if there is any virtue and if there is anything praiseworthy—meditate on these things" (Philippians 4:8)	"Jesus Christ is the same yesterday, today, and forever. Do not be carried about with various and strange doctrines. For it is **good** that the heart be established by grace, not with foods which have not profited those who have been occupied with them" (Hebrews 13:8-9)
"And let us not grow weary while doing **good**, for in due season we shall reap if we do not lose heart. Therefore, as we have opportunity, let us do **good** to all, especially to those who are of the household of faith" (Galatians 6:9-10)	"Therefore, to him who knows to do **good** and does not do it, to him it is sin" (James 4:17) AND "...do not forget to do **good** and to share, for with such sacrifices God is well pleased" (Hebrews 13:16)	"Therefore let those who suffer according to the will of God commit their souls to Him in doing **good**, as to a faithful Creator" (1 Peter 4:19)

Table 109: Some Pearls of Wisdom Concerning the Influence of the Good Attribute

Before I leave the ***good*** attribute, I must address a false and widespread practice that has overwhelmed the religious community. This is the practice of giving material gifts, either by mass distribution or lottery, to people inside and outside the "church" to show the ***goodness*** of God. The practice involves holding some event in the name of Jesus, mixed with preaching, motivational sale's pitches, emotional and shaming tactics, and then the distribution of gifts for all who came to participate. This practice has nothing to do with God's ***goodness*** but everything to do with ***deception*** by spiritual warfare. Jesus said, "*Ask, and it will be given to you; seek, and you will find; knock, and it will be opened to you. For everyone who asks receives, and he who seeks finds, and to him who knocks it will be opened...*" (Matthew 7:7-10). BTT allows one to see that Jesus was referring to spiritual needs and not carnal satisfaction. False teachers have twisted this Scripture to mean physical gifts that satisfy the flesh. This tactic works on emotions and leads people to believe they are involved in a ***good*** work for the Lord. Jesus said, "*...seek first the kingdom of God and His righteousness, and all these things shall be added to you.*" (Matthew 6:33). In other words, God will supply the things one needs if they seek Him first. The practice of giving gifts to lure people to "church" to win some to Christ is no more than a strategy conceived by the negative forces of the war campaign. In fact, this strategy places God second to the material gifts one came to claim. Please do not be deceived.

The **Faithful attribute**: The influence of this attribute leads one to believe, trust, and hold on to God at the inner spirit level; not just at the cognitive level. Next to the pure Word of God itself, this attribute is one of the greatest defenses against the negative forces of the war campaign. This attributes influences one to grow in his or her commitment and conviction to Christ and His church (not a man-made organization). In addition, it leads one to honor spiritual and personal commitments, especially commitments to the church, one's spouse, and family. The *faithful* attribute influences one to read and seek the meaning of the words documented in the Biblical record. It leads one to question and dismiss things from others that simply do not correlate with God's written Word. It empowers one to have trust and loyalty in the rest of the positive attributes that are unseen by the naked eye, yet visible through the matured transformed mind. This attribute is unique in that it and the element of belief are spiritually wedded to each other. One must believe in the one God, His Holy Spirit, and His Son Jesus Christ to acquire this attribute. The **faith** attribute's influence can never mature without belief in this trio. Belief without the trio is vain *faith*; which is not from this attribute, but from Satan. This understanding will become clear in the New Testament portion of this chapter. Moreover, as with the previous attributes, to get one's soul into heaven from this side of life requires more than just this attribute alone. One must have the righteous attribute; the sum of all the positive attributes combined and God's _grace_, to gain an entrance into heaven. This point will also become clear by the end of this Chapter.

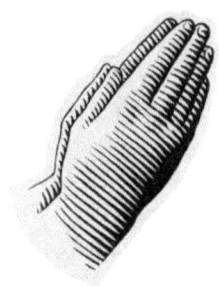

A very important point to understand is this attribute alone does not save anyone. Paul made this clear when he documented, "*For by _grace_ you have been saved through **faith**, and that not of yourselves; it is the gift of God, not of works, lest anyone should boast*" (Ephesians 2:8-9). When one allows the *faithful* attribute, believes God's Word and is obedient to it, then God's _grace_ saves one spiritually. It is important to know this upfront before one reads the rest of this chapter. God's _grace_, which is synonymous with God's goodness, but on an unfathomably higher level, is explained later in this book. The point here is that acquiring the influence of the *faithful* attribute alone will not get one to heaven, but it will protect one in the war campaign. To get God's _grace_, one needs to understand what one believes and has *faith* in - that is to say, the things that guides one's inner spirit in Truth. This knowledge is derived from universal Truths that God established. The Biblical record documented:

- "*The entirety of Your word is truth, and every one of Your **righteous** judgments endures forever*" (Psalms 119:160)

- "*You are near, O Lord, and all Your commandments are truth*" (Psalms 119:151)

- "*Your righteousness is an everlasting **righteousness**, and Your law is truth*" (Psalms 119:142)

- "*Your testimonies, which You have commanded, are **righteous** and very **faithful***" (Psalm 119:138)

- *"For the Lord is **good**; His **mercy** is everlasting, and His truth endures to all generations"* (Psalms 100:5)

- *"For the word of the Lord is right, and all His work is done in truth"* (Psalms 33:4)

- *"The fear of the Lord is clean, enduring forever; the judgments of the Lord are true and **righteous** altogether"* (Psalms 19:9)

The Scriptures above summarize God's universal Truths. As one learns about the Almighty God and accepts His Truth, one begins to acquire the influence of the ***faithful*** attribute with time and patience invested in studying His Word. Studying God's Word feeds the ***faithful*** attribute and causes it to mature. When one refuses to believe God's Word, the ***faithful*** attribute has no foundation to rest on for growth in one's inner spirit. Consequently, the negative forces using spiritual warfare, sends every distraction possible to ensure that the ***faithful*** attribute never gains an opportunity to establish a foundation. These distractions include influencing one to question the very existence of God.

With this information in mind, one can understand why Solomon documented that, "*A **faithful** witness does not lie...*" (Proverbs 14:5). This statement applies to the universal Truth he learned from His father, David, and sited previously from the Psalms. One that allows the influence of the ***faithful*** attribute witnesses God's Truths through the application of His Word. One who lies about God's Word is <u>faithless</u> and has the influence of the liar attribute; a negative attribute discussed earlier. Living a life with God in one's life makes lying a foreign concept. The Spirit of wisdom revealed to Solomon that, "*The eyes of the Lord preserve knowledge, but He overthrows the words of the <u>faithless</u>*" (Proverbs 22:12). This verse refers to one who has no ***faith*** in God. Until this person repents and seeks God, their inner spirit will remain <u>faithless,</u> and the influence from the ***faithful*** attribute will remain elusive.

With the influence of this attribute and growth in God's Word, one becomes an ambassador of God to others whose ***faith*** may be weak. In fact, Solomon documented that, "*...a **faithful** ambassador brings health*" (Proverbs 13:17) and, "*A **faithful** man will abound with blessings...*" (Proverbs 28:20). People influenced by the ***faithful*** attribute have a positive behavioral countenance that demonstrates the <u>love</u> of God. That <u>love</u> radiates in such a way that the spiritual elements of <u>joy</u>, <u>comfort</u>, and <u>peace</u> spreads to others near them. I will cover these spiritual elements later in this chapter. However, Solomon gave an indication that finding people influenced by the ***faithful*** attribute can sometimes be difficult. He wrote, "*Most men will proclaim each his own goodness, but who can find a **faithful** man?*" (Proverbs 20:6). Please understand that Solomon is not saying people influenced by the ***faithful*** attribute are not abundant on earth. BTT helps one see that with so many religious groups competing for one's attention and claiming to be ***faithful*** to God's Word, those who have the influence of this attribute are hard to identify. People with the ***faithful*** attribute do not alter God's Word for any reason. Hence, confusion is a primary strategy used in spiritual warfare. The negative forces generate fog daily to twist God's Word and keep people lost in it. Although there are many people around with the ***faithful*** attribute's influence leading people out of the fog to the truth of the True Gospel, the negative force's grip remains strong.

Solomon shared an important pearl of wisdom for helping people who came out of the fog of spiritual warfare. He wrote that, "...*he who is of a **faithful** spirit conceals a matter*" (Proverbs 11:13). BTT allows one to see that this is not for hiding matters that are either criminal or illegal. This verse refers to indiscretions and mistakes made by people who stumbled but are now committed to _godliness_ and striving to live by God's Word. These are people who desire to do right, who genuinely seek guidance, support, and are open to correction. People influenced by the ***faithful*** attribute will provide confidential help and support while keeping the indiscretions or mistakes out of public view. The idea is "loving one's fellow man or woman with godly _love_" through their stumble. This _love_ ensures that the negative forces of the war are not given a vulnerability to exploit in the person's weakness. If exploitation occurs, one now gained to the positive side of the campaign may be lost to the opposing side of the war again.

One influenced by a full measure of the ***faithful*** attribute fully understands and appreciates his or her role among the positive forces of the campaign. Solomon documented the relationship as follows: *"Like the cold of snow in time of harvest is a **faithful** messenger to those who send him, for he refreshes the soul of his masters."* (Proverbs 25:13). Through this proverb, BTT allows one to see that one influenced by the ***faithful*** attribute refreshes the inner spirit of others. You see, during Solomon's time, leaders depended on "runners" to get their orders to the front lines of the battle. The job of these runners, also known as messengers, were often fatal. Moreover, messengers' reliability were poor due to poor benefits, defection, loss of the message, or bribery. Thus, for the ***faithful*** messenger, who was successful in their mission, their success refreshed the soul of their leadership. This is the same on the spiritual battlefield. Consider this proverb from the standpoint of a congregation that sends missionaries out to the spiritual battlefield with God's message. Congregations and their leadership are refreshed when they receive word that their missionaries are turning souls to Christ. The one influenced by the ***faithful*** attribute who carried the message, refreshes the inner spirits of everyone involved. The influence of the ***faithful*** attribute on the messenger ensures the accurate delivery of the message; for the negative forces are constantly trying to compromise the message. Meditate on Proverbs 25:13 for a while to appreciate its powerful message. For it also applies to a congregation's elders that bring in a minister who handles God's Word well and grounds the congregation in God's Truth.

Moving forward in the Biblical record, from the murder of Abel to the great flood, the influence of the ***faithful*** attribute took a backseat to the growth of the war campaign. After the flood of Noah's day, the influence of wickedness began retaking the world with a vengeance. One must remember from Noah's days forward, thousands of years passed and generations of people stopped passing on the knowledge of God to their progeny. However, a small remnant of believers did. The Psalmist documented the results of the greater failure as he wrote about the people influenced by the proud, liar, and bloodthirsty attributes in Psalms 5:5-6. He wrote, "...*there is no **faithfulness** in their mouth; their inward part is destruction; their throat is an open tomb; they flatter with their tongue*" (Psalm 5:9). Further, he revealed the attitude of people influenced by these attributes towards God. He wrote that, "...*they have rebelled against You*" (Psalm 5:10). During the Psalmist's life, chaos ruled the world as the negative force's generated fog through spiritual warfare. He wrote in a song, *"Help, Lord, for the godly man ceases! For the **faithful** disappear from among the sons of men"* (Psalm 12:1). One can imagine the Psalmist's pain as he penned these words. But later he would write, "*Oh, <u>love</u> the Lord, all you His saints! For the Lord preserves the **faithful**...*" (Psalm 31:23). Throughout the Old Testament, there were numerous examples of people who allowed the influence of the **faithful** attribute to lead in their inner spirits and God preserved them during their allotted time on earth to accomplish His will. This does not imply that these people lost their freedom of choice. No! These are people who spiritually matured and follow God of their own free will. One must view this proverb from the spiritual aspect of the war campaign and not an earthly perspective. Consider the next few examples:

Examples	What Is Documented
Abel	"*By **faith** Abel offered to God a more excellent sacrifice than Cain, through which he obtained witness that he was righteous, God testifying of his gifts; and through it he being dead still speaks*" (Hebrews 11:4)
Enoch	"*By **faith** Enoch was taken away so that he did not see death, "and was not found, because God had taken him"; for before he was taken he had this testimony, that he pleased God. But without **faith** it is impossible to please Him, for he who comes to God must believe that He is, and that He is a rewarder of those who diligently seek Him*" (Hebrews 11:5-6)
Noah	"*By **faith** Noah, being divinely warned of things not yet seen, moved with godly fear, prepared an ark for the saving of his household, by which he condemned the world and became heir of the righteousness which is according to **faith**"* (Hebrews 11:7)
Abraham	"*By **faith** Abraham obeyed when he was called to go out to the place which he would receive as an inheritance. And he went out, not knowing where he was going. By **faith** he dwelt in the land of promise as in a foreign country, dwelling in tents with Isaac and Jacob, the heirs with him of the same promise, for he waited for the city which has foundations, whose builder and maker is God*" (Hebrews 11:8-10)
	"*By **faith** Abraham, when he was tested, offered up Isaac, and he who had received the promises offered up his only begotten son, of whom it was said, "In Isaac your seed shall be called," concluding that God was able to raise him up, even from the dead, from which he also received him in a figurative sense...*" (Hebrews 11:17-19)
Sarah	"*By **faith** Sarah herself also received strength to conceive seed, and she bore a child when she was past the age, because she judged Him **faithful** who had promised*" (Hebrews 11:11)
Isaac	"*By **faith** Isaac blessed Jacob and Esau concerning things to come*" (Hebrews 11:20)
Jacob	"*By **faith** Jacob, when he was dying, blessed each of the sons of Joseph, and worshiped, leaning on the top of his staff*" (Hebrews 11:21)
Joseph	"*By **faith** Joseph, when he was dying, made mention of the departure of the children of Israel, and gave instructions concerning his bones*" (Hebrews 11:22)
Moses' Parents	"*By **faith** Moses, when he was born, was hidden three months by his parents, because they saw he was a beautiful child; and they were not afraid of the king's command*" (Hebrews 11:23)

Moses	"*By **faith** Moses, when he became of age, refused to be called the son of Pharaoh's daughter, choosing rather to suffer affliction with the people of God than to enjoy the passing pleasures of sin, esteeming the reproach of Christ greater riches than the treasures in Egypt; for he looked to the reward.* (Hebrews 11:24-26)
	"*By **faith** he forsook Egypt, not fearing the wrath of the king; for he endured as seeing Him who is invisible. By **faith** he kept the Passover and the sprinkling of blood, lest he who destroyed the firstborn should touch them*" (Hebrews 11:27-28)
	Moses and the Israelites "*By **faith** they passed through the Red Sea as by dry land, whereas the Egyptians, attempting to do so, were drowned*" (Hebrews 11:29)
	After Aaron and Miriam challenged his authority, the Lord said, "*...Hear now My words: If there is a prophet among you, I, the Lord, make Myself known to him in a vision; I speak to him in a dream. Not so with My servant Moses; He is **faithful** in all My house. I speak with him face to face, even plainly, and not in dark sayings; and he sees the form of the Lord. Why then were you not afraid to speak against My servant Moses?*" (Numbers 12:6-8)
Joshua	Joshua took the fortified city of Jericho without weapons, The Bible documented, "*By **faith** the walls of Jericho fell down after they were encircled for seven days*" (Hebrews 11:30)
Rahab	"*By **faith** the harlot Rahab did not perish with those who did not believe, when she had received the spies with peace*" (Hebrews 11:31)
Gideon, Barak, Samson, Jephthah, David, Samuel, and the prophets	"*...who through **faith** subdued kingdoms, worked righteousness, obtained promises, stopped the mouths of lions, quenched the violence of fire, escaped the edge of the sword, out of weakness were made strong, became valiant in battle, turned to flight the armies of the aliens. Women received their dead raised to life again. Others were tortured, not accepting deliverance, that they might obtain a better resurrection. Still others had trial of mockings and scourgings, yes, and of chains and imprisonment. They were stoned, they were sawn in two, were tempted, were slain with the sword. They wandered about in sheepskins and goatskins, being destitute, afflicted, tormented— of whom the world was not worthy. They wandered in deserts and mountains, in dens and caves of the earth. And all these, having obtained a good testimony through faith, did not receive the promise...*" (Hebrews 11:32-39)
Hannah	Although not stated, her action and behavior clearly indicated that she had the ***faithful*** attribute. From her behavior at the tabernacle of the Lord (1 Samuel 1:13-17), to her actions with Samuel (1 Samuel 1:20-28), to her life after she honored her promise to the Lord; "*...the Lord visited Hannah, so that she conceived and bore three sons and two daughters. Meanwhile the child Samuel grew before the Lord*" (1 Samuel 2:21)
Samuel, Hannah's son	A man of God, speaking of Samuel, told the prophet Eli that the Lord said, "*...I will raise up for Myself a **faithful** priest who shall do according to what is in My heart and in My mind. I will build him a sure house, and he shall walk before My anointed forever*" (1 Samuel 2:35)
David	Saul asked Ahimelech about David. Ahimelech said to the king, "*...who among all your servants is as **faithful** as David, who is the king's son-in-

	law, who goes at your bidding, and is honorable in your house? ..." (1 Samuel 22:14)
The wise woman in the city of Abel of Beth Maachiah	She helped Joab capture Sheba who took refuge in her city. When Joab was about to destroy the city to get to Sheba, she got Joab's attention and said, "*I am among the peaceable and **faithful** in Israel. You seek to destroy a city and a mother in Israel. Why would you swallow up the inheritance of the Lord?*" (2 Samuel 20:19). Her behavior saved the entire city from destruction.
Jehoiaha, the priest, and the workmen repairing the house of the Lord	"*So it was, whenever they saw that there was much money in the chest, that the king's scribe and the high priest came up and put it in bags, and counted the money that was found in the house of the Lord. Then they gave the money, which had been apportioned, into the hands of those who did the work, who had the oversight of the house of the Lord... they repaired the house of the Lord with it. Moreover they did not require an account from the men into whose hand they delivered the money to be paid to workmen, for they dealt **faithfully**"* (2 Kings 12:10-15)
Hilkiah, high priest and workmen who rebuilt the temple	The Biblical record documented, that King Josiah told Hilkiah to deliver money into the hands of those doing the work and said, "*However there need be no accounting made with them of the money delivered into their hand, because they deal **faithfully**"* (2 Kings 22:7). Their behavior was confirmed in 2 Chronicles as the Biblical record documented, "*And the men did the work **faithfully**..."* (2 Chronicles 34:12)
Daniel	The Biblical record documented that, "*...the governors and satraps sought to find some charge against Daniel concerning the kingdom; but they could find no charge or fault, because he was **faithful**; nor was there any error or fault found in him*" (Daniel 6:4)
King Jehoshaphat	The attribute's influence led him to surround himself with others with the attribute. The Biblical record documented, "*Moreover in Jerusalem, for the judgment of the Lord and for controversies, Jehoshaphat appointed some of the Levites and priests, and some of the chief fathers of Israel, when they returned to Jerusalem. And he commanded them, saying, "Thus you shall act in the fear of the Lord, **faithfully** and with a loyal heart..."* (2 Chronicles 19:8-9). One should note that there was a time when this king faith became weak and he aligned himself with King Ahab, a wicked king of Israel, for at the time which is documented in 2 Chronicles 18.
King Hezekiah	The Biblical record documented that, "*...he opened the doors of the house of the Lord and repaired them. Then he brought in the priests and the Levites, and gathered them in the East Square, and said to them: "Hear me, Levites! Now sanctify yourselves, sanctify the house of the Lord God of your fathers, and carry out the rubbish from the holy place*" (2 Chronicles 29:3-5)
	Moreover, King Hezekiah trust and encouragement of the priest and Levites lead them to **faithful** actions. The Bible documented ""*Then they **faithfully** brought in the offerings, the tithes, and the dedicated things..."* (2 Chronicles 31:12)
	"*Thus Hezekiah did throughout all Judah, and he did what was good and right and true before the Lord his God. And in every work that he began in the service of the house of God, in the law and in the commandment, to seek his God, he did it with all his heart. So he prospered*" (2 Chronicles 31:20-21)
	The Bible documents "*Kore the son of Imnah the Levite, the keeper of the East Gate, was over the freewill offerings to God, to distribute the offerings*

Kore and his assistants	*of the Lord and the most holy things. And under him were Eden, Miniamin, Jeshua, Shemaiah, Amariah, and Shecaniah, his **faithful** assistants in the cities of the priests, to distribute allotments to their brethren by divisions, to the great as well as the small...for in their **faithfulness** they sanctified themselves in holiness"* (2 Chronicles 31:13-18)
Hananiah	The Biblical record documented, *"Then it was, when the wall was built and I had hung the doors, when the gatekeepers, the singers, and the Levites had been appointed, that I gave the charge of Jerusalem to my brother Hanani, and Hananiah the leader of the citadel, for he was a **faithful** man and feared God more than many"* (Nehemiah 7:1-2)
The men selected to maintain the wall and serve in the temple:	Nehemiah selected men to maintain the wall and serve in the temple *"And I appointed as treasurers over the storehouse Shelemiah the priest and Zadok the scribe, and of the Levites, Pedaiah; and next to them was Hanan the son of Zaccur, the son of Mattaniah; for they were considered **faithful**, and their task was to distribute to their brethren"* (Nehemiah 13:13)

Table 110: Examples of People Who Allowed the Influence of the Faithful Attribute

One can understand the value of the influence of the ***faithful*** attribute as one reads about Moses and his struggles with the children of Israel. God was ***faithful*** to the children of Israel to bring them out of bondage and into a land He promised to their forefather Abraham (Genesis 17:8-10). Moses was ***faithful*** (Exodus 33:12-13) to God as he carried out the will of God. However, the children of Israel did not allow the ***faithful*** attribute's influence as they left the Egyptian's bondage. Moses documented in a song that the influence of the ***faithful*** attribute never took root among the children of Israel. He sang that God said, *"...'I will hide My face from them, I will see what their end will be, for they are a perverse generation, children in whom is no **faith**"* (Deuteronomy 32:20). The influence of the ***faithful*** attribute never took root in generations of the children of Israel. From their time in bondage, through ten supernatural plagues on Egypt, through their release from bondage, and even through their travels in the wilderness. Even the Psalmist documented that the Lord, *"...established a testimony in Jacob, and appointed a law in Israel, which He commanded our fathers, that they should make them known to their children; that the generation to come might know them, the children who would be born, that they may arise and declare them to their children, that they may set their <u>hope</u> in God, and not forget the works of God, but keep His commandments; and may not be like their fathers, a stubborn and rebellious generation, a generation that did not set its heart aright, and whose <u>spirit</u> was not **faithful** to God"* (Psalm 78:8). Additionally, he wrote that *"...their heart was not steadfast with Him, nor were they **faithful** in His covenant"* (Psalm 78:37). Yet, the Psalmist stated firmly of the Lord, *"Your testimonies, which You have commanded, are righteous and very **faithful**"* (Psalm 119:138). If Israel had just listened and <u>believed</u> the testimonies of God, the influence of the ***faithful*** attribute may have found fertile ground to root.

Sadly, the children of Israel grew into a nation that proportionally grew in their ***unfaithfulness*** toward the Lord. Over time and after numerous warning from God's prophets, God destroyed the nation of Israel. The prophet Isaiah documented from the Lord, *"How the*

faithful city has become a harlot! It was full of justice; Righteousness lodged in it, but now murderers. Your silver has become dross, your wine mixed with water. Your princes are rebellious, and companions of thieves; everyone <u>loves</u> bribes, and follows after rewards. They do not defend the fatherless, nor does the cause of the widow come before them" (Isaiah 1:21-23). The prophet Hosea documented from the Lord, "*O Ephraim, what shall I do to you? O Judah, what shall I do to you? For your **faithfulness** is like a morning cloud, and like the early dew it goes away*" (Hosea 6:4). The prophet Micah recorded from the Lord, "*The **faithful** man has perished from the earth, and there is no one upright among men. They all lie in wait for blood; every man hunts his brother with a net*" (Micah 7:2). What a sad commentary. The negative forces of the war campaign and spiritual warfare consumed the nation of Israel.

The prophet Ezekiel provided some insights into the areas that prevented the influence of the ***faithful*** attribute from germinating among the nation of Israel. He documented the intimate relationship between the influence of the ***faithful*** attribute and that of the just attribute. Ezekiel documented from God that one is considered a just person if he or she met the requirements of Ezekiel 18:5-8. The requirements were:

- Does what is lawful and right
- Has not eaten on the mountains (temple worship on mountain tops)
- Has not lifted his eyes to the idols (carved images of gods, animals, symbols)
- Has not defiled his neighbor's wife
- Has not approached a woman during her impurity
- Has not oppressed anyone, but has restored to the debtor his pledge
- Has not robbed anyone by violence
- Has given his bread to the hungry
- Has covered the naked with clothing
- Has not exacted usury (in the sense of *overcharging* and *extortion*)
- Has not taken any increase (in the sense of *illegal gain*)
- Has withdrawn his hand from iniquity
- Has executed true judgment between man and man

During the time of the prophets, the nation of Israel was involved in activities opposite of the list above, i.e. they were lifting their eyes to idols. Ezekiel documented that maturing the influence of the just attribute was contingent on acquiring the ***faithful*** attribute. In other words, the children of Israel had to <u>believe</u> every one of the items that Ezekiel documented above from the Lord and do them. Further, the Lord said, "*If he has walked in My statutes and kept My judgments **faithfully**— he is just; he shall surely live!" Says the Lord God*" (Ezekiel 18:9). The prophet Habakkuk also documented from the Lord that, "*...the just shall live by his **faith***" (Habakkuk 2:2-4). The nation of Israel clearly needed the influence of the ***faithful*** attribute. Habakkuk went on to document some very strong "woes" from the Lord that coincided with Ezekiel's list above. Habakkuk warned:

- *Woe to him who increases what is not his.* (Habakkuk 2:6-8)

- *Woe to him who covets evil gain for his house that he may set his nest on high that he may be delivered from the power of disaster!* (Habakkuk 2:9-11)

- *Woe to him who builds a town with bloodshed, who establishes a city by iniquity!* (Habakkuk 2:12-14)

- *Woe to him who gives drink to his neighbor, pressing him to your bottle, even to make him drunk, that you may look on his nakedness!* (Habakkuk 2:15-17)

- *Woe to him who says to wood, 'Awake!' To silent stone, 'Arise! It shall teach!'* (Habakkuk 2:18-20)

BTT allows one to see that the negative attribute's growth did not stop with the Old Testament. All the behaviors manifested by the negative attributes transitioned to the New Testament of the Biblical record without interference because man's disbelief and lack of respect for God continued to increase. However, God's unchanged Word remained. Now before I transition to the New Testament, I need to bring one's attention to an important point about the people who died under the Mosaic Law of the Old Testament influence by the ***faithful*** attribute. Paul mentioned many of the people in Table 107 who allowed the influence of the ***faithful*** attribute in their lives in Hebrews 11:4-39. An important point Paul highlighted was that, "*These all died in **faith**, not having received the promises, but having seen them afar off were assured of them, embraced them and confessed that they were strangers and pilgrims on the earth*" (Hebrews 11:13). They all believed in God's Word and allowed the influence of the ***faithful*** attribute to lead in their inner spirits. Paul further wrote, "*And all these, having obtained a good testimony through **faith**, did not receive the promise, God having provided something better for us, that they should not be made perfect apart from us*" (Hebrews 11:39-40). Just like the people of the Old Testament, we can pursue the influence of the ***faithful*** attribute and find perfection just like them. What is great today is the fact that one has God's Word in written form. Not only did God provide His Son as a sacrifice for our sins, but He also provided written instructions through the prophets and apostles to navigate the war campaign and find the righteous path to eternal life. The Bible provides this knowledge and the means to acquire the influence of the ***faithful*** attribute while on this earth.

As Jesus came on the scene in the New Testament, He pointed out how little the influence of the ***faithful*** attribute had germinated among those who supposedly followed the teachings of Judaism. Jesus' comments included:

To Whom	What Jesus Said
The people of Israel	While teaching on the subject of "worrying", Jesus taught the people, "*Now if God so clothes the grass of the field, which today is, and tomorrow is thrown into the oven, will He not much more clothe you, O you of little **faith**?*" (Matthew 6:30; Luke 12:28)
	During a storm when Jesus and His disciples were out in a boat and Jesus went to sleep. The disciples woke Him up out of frustration and fear. They pleaded with Jesus to save them, but He simply responded, "*...Why are you*

His disciples	*fearful, O you of little **faith**?" Then He arose and rebuked the winds and the sea, and there was a great calm"* (Matthew 8:26; Mark 4:40)
	While Jesus was teaching the disciples about the leaven of the Pharisees and Sadducees, they misunderstood Him. They forgot to bring bread on their journey and thought He spoke about them. The Bible documented, *"But Jesus, being aware of it, said to them, "O you of little **faith**, why do you reason among yourselves because you have brought no bread?"* (Matthew 16:8)
	When the disciples could not heal a boy who severely suffered from epilepsy, the Bible documented, *"...Jesus answered and said, "O <u>faithless</u> and perverse generation, how long shall I be with you? How long shall I bear with you? Bring him here to Me"* (Matthew 17:17; Mark 9:19; Luke 9:41). And when they asked Jesus privately why they could not heal the boy, He stated, *"...Because of your <u>unbelief</u>; for assuredly, I say to you, if you have **faith** as a mustard seed, you will say to this mountain, 'Move from here to there,' and it will move; and nothing will be impossible for you. However, this kind does not go out except by prayer and fasting"* (Matthew 17:20-21; Mark 9:29)
Peter specifically	He stepped out of a boat, started to walk on the water, and then became afraid and began to sink. The Bible says, *"And immediately Jesus stretched out His hand and caught him, and said to him, "O you of little **faith**, why did you <u>doubt</u>?"* (Matthew 14:31)

Table 111: Examples of People Who Lacked the Faithful Attribute

Jesus' statements above did not mean the influence of the ***faithful*** attribute was non-existent. It simply meant that the measure of the attribute's influence was very minimal among the people. The New Testament thoroughly documents examples of the ***faithful*** attribute's strong presence during and after Jesus' time on earth. Here are some of the many examples:

Example	What Is Documented
Men who brought a paralytic to Jesus	The Bible says, *"Then behold, they brought to Him a paralytic lying on a bed. When Jesus saw their **faith**, He said to the paralytic, "Son, be of good cheer; your sins are forgiven you"* (Matthew 9:2; Mark 2:5; Luke 5:20)
A woman	She touched Jesus' garment while a crowd of people surrounded him. The Bible documented, when the woman touched the hem of His garment, *"...Jesus turned around, and when He saw her He said, "Be of good cheer, daughter; your **faith** has made you well." And the woman was made well from that hour"* (Matthew 9:22; Mark 5:34; Luke 8:48)
Two blind men	They called out for Jesus' mercy. The Bible documented, *"Then He touched their eyes, saying, "According to your **faith** let it be to you"* (Matthew 9:29)
A woman of Canaan	She sought out Jesus to heal her severely demon-possessed daughter The Bible tells us, *"Then Jesus answered and said to her, "O woman, great is your **faith**! Let it be to you as you desire." And her daughter was healed from that very hour"* (Matthew 15:28)
Blind Bartimaeus	He ignored others who told him to be quiet and when Jesus called him, he threw aside his garments, rose, and came to Jesus. Telling Jesus his desire, the Bible says, *"Then Jesus said to him, "Go your way; your **faith** has made*

	you well." And immediately he received his sight and followed Jesus on the road (Mark 10:52; Luke 18:42)
A woman at the house of Simon	She began washing Jesus' feet with her tears, wiping them with her hair, kissed His feet, and anointed them with a fragrant oil. Simon thought Jesus was unaware of who the woman was. But Jesus was aware, and he corrected Simon for his thoughts. The Bible documents, *"Then He said to the woman, "Your **faith** has saved you. Go in peace"* (Luke 7:50)
Ten lepers	Jesus cleansed all ten of them but only one returned to glorify God and fell at Jesus' feet and thanked Him. The one that return was considered a foreigner according to Luke 17:18. Jesus said to him, *"…Arise, go your way. Your **faith** has made you well"* (Luke 17:19)
A centurion	He came to Jesus and pleaded for the healing of his paralyzed and tormented servant. He stopped Jesus from going with him because He knew the power of Jesus' Word according to Matthew 8:8-10; Luke 7:2-8. The Bible documented that, *"When Jesus heard it, He marveled, and said to those who followed, "Assuredly, I say to you, I have not found such great **faith**, not even in Israel!"* (Matthew 8:10; Luke 7:9)
Stephen	The Biblical record documented that the apostle sought men *"…of good reputation, full of the Holy Spirit and wisdom, whom we may appoint…"* (Acts 6:3), over the business of caring for widows from the Hellenist's community. The Bible documents that, *"…they chose Stephen, a man full of **faith** and the Holy Spirit…"* (Acts 6:5)
	Also, *"Then the word of God spread, and the number of the disciples multiplied greatly in Jerusalem, and a great many of the priests were obedient to the **faith**. And Stephen, full of **faith** and power, did great wonders and signs among the people"* (Acts 6:7-8)
Barnabas	The Bible says that when Barnabas came to the church in Jerusalem and saw the grace of God, *"…he was glad, and encouraged them all that with purpose of heart they should continue with the Lord. For he was a good man, full of the Holy Spirit and of **faith**. And a great many people were added to the Lord"* (Acts 11:23-24)
A man in the city of Lystra	The Biblical record documented, *"…a certain man without strength in his feet was sitting, a cripple from his mother's womb, who had never walked. This man heard Paul speaking. Paul, observing him intently and seeing that he had **faith** to be healed, said with a loud voice, "Stand up straight on your feet!" And he leaped and walked"* (Acts 14:8-10)
Lydia	The Bible documented, *"Now a certain woman named Lydia heard us. She was a seller of purple from the city of Thyatira, who worshiped God. The Lord opened her heart to heed the things spoken by Paul. And when she and her household were baptized, she begged us, saying, "If you have judged me to be **faithful** to the Lord, come to my house and stay." So she persuaded us"* (Acts 16:14-15)
Timothy	Paul sent him to Corinth and stated, *"For this reason I have sent Timothy to you, who is my beloved and **faithful** son in the Lord, who will remind you of my ways in Christ, as I teach everywhere in every church"* (1 Corinthians 4:17)
	And Paul wrote, *"I thank God, whom I serve with a pure conscience, as my forefathers did, as without ceasing I remember you in my prayers night and day, greatly desiring to see you, being mindful of your tears, that I may be*

	*filled with joy, when I call to remembrance the genuine **faith** that is in you, which dwelt first in your grandmother Lois and your mother Eunice, and I am persuaded is in you also"* (2 Timothy 1:3-5)
Tychicus	Paul wrote, *"But that you also may know my affairs and how I am doing, Tychicus, a beloved brother and **faithful** minister in the Lord, will make all things known to you; whom I have sent to you for this very purpose, that you may know our affairs, and that he may comfort your hearts"* (Ephesians 6:21-22)
	Paul wrote, *"Tychicus, a beloved brother, **faithful** minister, and fellow servant in the Lord, will tell you all the news about me"* (Colossians 4:7)
Epaphras	Paul documented, *"as you also learned from Epaphras, our dear fellow servant, who is a **faithful** minister of Christ on your behalf..."* (Colossians 1:7)
Onesimus	Paul wrote, "with Onesimus, a ***faithful*** and beloved brother, who is one of you...." (Colossians 4:9)
Titus	Paul wrote, *"To Titus, a true son in our common **faith**: Grace, mercy, and peace from God the Father and the Lord Jesus Christ our Savior"* (Titus 1:4)
Philemon	Paul identified him as a "...*beloved friend and fellow laborer...*" (Philemon 1:1-2), and said, *"I thank my God, making mention of you always in my prayers, hearing of your love and faith which you have toward the Lord Jesus and toward all the saints, that the sharing of your **faith** may become effective by the acknowledgment of every good thing which is in you in Christ Jesus. For we have great joy and consolation in your love, because the hearts of the saints have been refreshed by you, brother"* (Philemon 1:4-7)
Silvanus	Peter said, *"By Silvanus, our **faithful** brother as I consider him, I have written to you briefly, exhorting and testifying that this is the true grace of God in which you stand"* (1 Peter 5:12)
Gaius	John wrote, *"Beloved, you do **faithfully** whatever you do for the brethren and for strangers, who have borne witness of your love before the church. If you send them forward on their journey in a manner worthy of God, you will do well, because they went forth for His name's sake, taking nothing from the Gentiles. We therefore ought to receive such, that we may become fellow workers for the truth"* (3 John 1:5-7)
The church in Rome	Paul commended the congregation for the ***faithful*** attribute that flourished amongst their brethren. He wrote, *"First, I thank my God through Jesus Christ for you all, that your **faith** is spoken of throughout the whole world"* (Romans 1:8; Romans 1:11-12)
The church of Ephesus	Paul documented, *"Paul, an apostle of Jesus Christ by the will of God, to the saints who are in Ephesus, and **faithful** in Christ Jesus: Grace to you and peace from God our Father and the Lord Jesus Christ"* (Ephesians 1:1-2)
	And he wrote, *"Therefore I also, after I heard of your **faith** in the Lord Jesus and your love for all the saints, do not cease to give thanks for you, making mention of you in my prayers..."* (Ephesians 1:15-16)
The church in Philippi	One can see a measure of Paul's profound joy as he wrote, *"Yes, and if I am being poured out as a drink offering on the sacrifice and service of your **faith**, I am glad and rejoice with you all"* (Philippians 2:17)
The church at Colosse	Paul documented, *"To the saints and **faithful** brethren in Christ who are in Colosse: Grace to you and peace from God our Father and the Lord Jesus Christ. We give thanks to the God and Father of our Lord Jesus Christ,*

	*praying always for you, since we heard of your **faith** in Christ Jesus and of your <u>love</u> for all the saints..."* (Colossians 1:2-4)
The church in Thessalonica	Paul wrote, *"We give thanks to God always for you all, making mention of you in our prayers, remembering without ceasing your work of **faith**, labor of <u>love</u>, and patience of <u>hope</u> in our Lord Jesus Christ in the sight of our God and Father, knowing, beloved brethren, your election by God"* (1 Thessalonians 1:2-4)
	And, *"...Your **faith** toward God has gone out, so that we do not need to say anything"* (1 Thessalonians 1:8)
	And, *"...because your **faith** grows exceedingly, and the <u>love</u> of every one of you all abounds toward each other, so that we ourselves boast of you among the churches of God for your patience and **faith** in all your persecutions and tribulations that you endure..."* (2 Thessalonians 1:3-4)
	This church was under attack by people with the negative attributes. Paul fled their location because of fierce opposition he and the apostles received from the Jews. Because of all this, Paul wrote, *"...Timothy has come to us from you, and brought us good news of your **faith** and <u>love</u>, and that you always have good remembrance of us, greatly desiring to see us, as we also to see you— therefore, brethren, in all our affliction and distress we were <u>comforted</u> concerning you by your **faith**."* (1 Thessalonians 3:1-7)
	Also, Paul told them, *"For what thanks can we render to God for you, for all the <u>joy</u> with which we rejoice for your sake before our God, night and day praying exceedingly that we may see your face and perfect what is lacking in your **faith**?"* (1 Thessalonians 3:9-10)

Table 112: Examples of People Who Allowed the Influence of the Faithful Attribute

Now with all these examples, one should see the importance of acquiring the ***faithful*** attribute and striving to gain its full measure. Moreover, BTT allows one to see that this is the attribute that helps one:

- <u>Overcome disbelief.</u> Jesus said, *"Have **faith** in God. For assuredly, I say to you, whoever says to this mountain, 'Be removed and be cast into the sea,' and does not <u>doubt</u> in his heart, but believes that those things he says will be done, he will have whatever he says. Therefore I say to you, whatever things you ask when you pray, believe that you receive them, and you will have them"* (Mark 11:22-24)

- <u>Overcome doubt</u>. Jesus said, *"... "Assuredly, I say to you, if you have **faith** and do not <u>doubt</u>, you will not only do what was done to the fig tree, but also if you say to this mountain, 'Be removed and be cast into the sea,' it will be done"* (Matthew 21:21)

- <u>Prioritize spiritual matters</u> over worldly matters. Jesus said, *"Woe to you, scribes and Pharisees, hypocrites! For you pay tithe of mint and anise and cummin, and have neglected the weightier matters of the law: justice and mercy and **faith**. These you ought to have done, without leaving the others undone"* (Matthew 23:23)

- <u>Appreciate the blessings</u> God has already provided. Jesus said, *"...He who is **faithful** in what is least is **faithful** also in much; and he who is unjust in what is least is unjust* *also in much. Therefore if you have not been **faithful** in the unrighteous mammon, who will commit to your trust the true riches? And if you have not been **faithful** in what is another man's, who will give you what is your own? ...*" (Luke 16:9-13)

All the reasons presented above express the importance of the influence of the ***faithful*** attribute. However, there is an even greater reason exposed by Jesus after He told His disciples of His impending betrayal and death. All four of the Gospel writers - Matthew, Mark, Luke, and John - captured a discussion Jesus had with His disciples and their reaction. The Biblical record documented, "*...All of you will be made to stumble because of Me this night, for it is written: 'I will strike the Shepherd, and the sheep of the flock will be scattered*'" (Matthew 26:31; Mark 14:27). Peter followed up by stating that, "*Even if all are made to stumble because of You, I will never be made to stumble*" (Matthew 26:33; Mark 14:29), and he said with the other disciples in agreement, "*Even if I have to die with You, I will not deny You!*" (Matthew 26:35; Mark 14:31; John 13:37). Luke documented a little more detail. Luke documented that Satan was directly involved in trying to stop the influence of the ***faithful*** attribute and Simon Peter became a prime target. Luke documented, "*And the Lord said, "Simon, Simon! Indeed, Satan has asked for you, that he may sift you as wheat. But I have prayed for you, that your **faith** should not fail; and when you have returned to Me, strengthen your brethren." But he said to Him, "Lord, I am ready to go with You, both to prison and to death"*" (Luke 22:31-33). The Bible documents that to advance the war campaign, Satan, can and will manipulate one's situation to inflict damage in the earthly realm of the physical battlefield to hinder the works of the positive attributes. No one is immune. However, in this case, Jesus interceded on Peter's behalf. Jesus prayed for Peter to strengthen his inner spirit. BTT allows one to see that Jesus provided both an example and the key to strengthen the positive attributes that influences one's inner spirit. Prayer is the key. BTT allows one to see that the influence of the pride attribute prevented Peter from hearing Jesus' Word. BTT also allows one to see the influence of the ***faithful*** attribute was weakened in Peter after the betrayal of Jesus. Remember, the twelve disciples grew close to each other as they walked with Jesus, the Son of God. For one of their own team members to betray Jesus and turn Him over to the Jews in the manner Judas did, was traumatic. Peter and the other disciples witnessed Judas, one of their close team members, betray their Teacher with a kiss and then turn Him over to a mob (Matthew 26:48-50; Mark 14:44-46; Luke 22:47-54). Satan orchestrated the event by influencing people and this action successfully weakened the influence of the ***faithful*** attributes among Jesus' core <u>believers</u>. BTT allows one to see on that night, both physical warfare and spiritual warfare collided. In fact, these events were so overwhelming for Peter that, just as Jesus had told him, he stumbled that very night. Peter denied that he knew Jesus, the Son of God, according to Matthew 26:69-75; Mark 14:66-72; Luke 22:55-62; and John 18:15-18, 25-27. However, the influence of the ***faithful*** attribute remained in his inner spirit in a small weakened measure. BTT allows one to see this because Peter remained with the other disciples after Jesus' arrest and death. Had the influence of the ***faithful*** attribute completely left Peter, he would have parted company from the other disciples and returned to the world. Had this occurred, Peter like Judas, could have been lost to the negative forces of the war campaign. Clearly, Jesus' prayer for Peter, documented in Luke 22:31-33, worked. He was eventually restored, gained a full measure of the influence of the *faithful* attribute, and wrote the books of First and Second Peter in the Bible.

Jesus gave the world three superior parables to explain how the influence of the *faithful* attribute can protect one's soul during the war campaign. To fully appreciate the role the influence of the *faithful* attribute plays in one's life, I encourage one to read these parables. His parables were about:

- A "... *faithful* and wise servant, whom his master made ruler over his household" documented in Matthew 24:45-51 and Luke 12:41-48.

- A comparison of the kingdom of heaven to "...a man traveling to a far country, who called his own servants and delivered his goods to them" documented in Matthew 25:14-30 and Luke 19:11-27. Of the three servants he called, two allowed the influenced of the *faithful* attribute and one did not.

- An unjust judge and a *faithful* widow who sought justice documented in Luke 18:2-8

In each of these parables, BTT allows one to see that Jesus recognized the influence of the *faithful* attribute as one of the most important positive attributes to have. Even Jesus' disciples recognized this importance. They asked Jesus to increase the measure of the *faithful* attribute growing within them. They asked, "...*Increase our faith.*" So the Lord said, "*If you have faith as a mustard seed, you can say to this mulberry tree, 'Be pulled up by the roots and be planted in the sea,' and it would obey you*" (Luke 17:5-6). Why is the influence of this attribute so important? First, when one acquires it, it indicates that the good, honorable, merciful, blameless, and just attributes are also influencing one's inner spirit. More importantly, to achieve the righteous attribute, one must have the matured *faithful* attribute's influence. This fact helps one to understand a disconcerting point Jesus made in the parable of the unjust judge. At the end of the parable, Jesus said, "...*Hear what the unjust judge said. And shall God not avenge His own elect who cry out day and night to Him, though He bears long with them? I tell you that He will avenge them speedily. Nevertheless, when the Son of Man comes, will He really find faith on the earth?*" (Luke 18:6-8). Even though one can see from the parable that the judge was *unjust*, the real emphasis is not the judge's behavior. The real gem is found in the behavior of the widow who allowed the influence of the *faithful* attribute. People with the *faithful* attribute demonstrate it by doing what God requires them to do. This widow's behavior and actions demonstrated persistence. Her persistence demonstrated the *faithful* attribute's influence in her life and her belief that God would provide for her; not the judge. Jesus' question is, when He returns will He find the same persistence in people who claim the influence of the *faithful* attribute on the Day of Judgement? BTT allows one to see that the measure of *faith* that the widow demonstrated is the example of what one must strive for and acquire now.

Paul documented a considerable amount of information on the influence of the *faithful* attribute. He began by documenting how one acquires the influence of this attribute as he wrote, "...*faith comes by hearing, and hearing by the word of God*" (Romans 10:17). In other words, one acquires this attribute by hearing what God's Word says. Later he wrote, "...*faith is the substance of things hoped for, the evidence of things not seen"* (Hebrews 11:1). In other words, having the influence of the ***faithful*** attribute opens one's spiritual understanding to the element of *hope* and its full spiritual power. With the ***faithful*** attribute's influence, God's promises can help one's inner spirit develop a yearning for the things of God. This yearning cannot be measured by any physical instrument or science of man. Based on Paul's statements above, BTT allows one to see why Christians are to, "...*walk by **faith**, not by sight*" (2 Corinthians 5:7). One's ***faithful*** walk brings opportunity, growth, and reward along the journey. But here is the catch: There is no empirical evidence or measure for God's blessings; just spiritual measures. Paul and the other apostles documented the benefits of the influence of the ***faithful*** attribute:

Benefits	What Is Documented
Brings justification and access to God's *grace*	Paul documented, *"Therefore, having been justified by **faith**, we have peace with God through our Lord Jesus Christ, through whom also we have access by **faith** into this grace in which we stand, and rejoice in hope of the glory of God"* (Romans 5:1-2)
Provides *discernment* on wisdom	*"...your **faith** should not be in the wisdom of men but in the power of God...."* (1 Corinthians 2:4-8), and *"If any of you lacks wisdom, let him ask of God, who gives to all liberally and without reproach, and it will be given to him. But let him ask in **faith**, with no doubting, for he who doubts is like a wave of the sea driven and tossed by the wind"* (James 1:5-6)
Clarifies that the supernatural element of *grace* is involved with this maturing attribute	*"But as you abound in everything—in **faith**, in speech, in knowledge, in all diligence, and in your love for us—see that you abound in this grace also"* (2 Corinthians 8:7), and *"For by grace you have been saved through **faith**, and that not of yourselves; it is the gift of God, not of works, lest anyone should boast"* (Ephesians 2:8-9)
Provides clarity as to how it is matured	*"But also for this very reason, giving all diligence, add to your **faith** virtue, to virtue knowledge, to knowledge self-control, to self-control perseverance, to perseverance godliness, to godliness brotherly kindness, and to brotherly kindness love. For if these things are yours and abound, you will be neither barren nor unfruitful in the knowledge of our Lord Jesus Christ. For he who lacks these things is shortsighted, even to blindness, and has forgotten that he was cleansed from his old sins. Therefore, brethren, be even more diligent to make your call and election sure, for if you do these things you will never stumble; for so an entrance will be supplied to you abundantly into the everlasting kingdom of our Lord and Savior Jesus Christ"* (2 Peter 1:5-11)
Provides the clarity to escape the corruption of the world	Peter wrote, *"...Grace and peace be multiplied to you in the knowledge of God and of Jesus our Lord, as His divine power has given to us all things that pertain to life and godliness, through the knowledge of Him who called us by glory and virtue, by which have been given to us exceedingly great and precious promises, that through these you may be partakers of the divine nature, having escaped the corruption that is in the world through lust"* (2 Peter 1:1-4)

Helps one to recognize that God has provided everything needed "*...that pertain to life and godliness*" through Jesus.	Peter wrote, "*Grace and peace be multiplied to you in the knowledge of God and of Jesus our Lord, as His divine power has given to us all things that pertain to life and godliness, through the knowledge of Him who called us by glory and virtue, by which have been given to us exceedingly great and precious promises, that through these you may be partakers of the divine nature, having escaped the corruption that is in the world through lust*" (2 Peter 1:2-4)
Helps one overcome the negative attribute	John wrote, "*This is the message which we have heard from Him and declare to you, that God is light and in Him is no darkness at all. If we say that we have fellowship with Him, and walk in darkness, we lie and do not practice the truth. But if we walk in the light as He is in the light, we have fellowship with one another, and the blood of Jesus Christ His Son cleanses us from all sin. If we say that we have no sin, we deceive ourselves, and the truth is not in us. If we confess our sins, He is* **faithful** *and just to forgive us our sins and to cleanse us from all unrighteousness. If we say that we have not sinned, we make Him a liar, and His word is not in us*" (1 John 1:5-10)
	John wrote, "*If someone says, "I love God," and hates his brother, he is a liar; for he who does not love his brother whom he has seen, how can he love God whom he has not seen? And this commandment we have from Him: that he who loves God must love his brother also*" (1 John 4:20-21)
	Paul wrote take, "*...the shield of* **faith** *with which you will be able to quench all the fiery darts of the wicked one*" (Ephesians 6:16), and "*You are all sons of light and sons of the day. We are not of the night nor of darkness. Therefore let us not sleep, as others do, but let us watch and be sober. For those who sleep, sleep at night, and those who get drunk are drunk at night. But let us who are of the day be sober, putting on the breastplate of* **faith** *and love, and as a helmet the hope of salvation*" (1 Thessalonians 5:5-8)
Helps one to keep God's commandments as documented in the Gospel	John wrote, "*For this is the love of God, that we keep His commandments. And His commandments are not burdensome. For whatever is born of God overcomes the world. And this is the victory that has overcome the world—our* **faith**. *Who is he who overcomes the world, but he who believes that Jesus is the Son of God?*" (1 John 5:3-5)
Helps one to fully understand the true purpose of baptism	Paul documented: "*In Him you were also circumcised with the circumcision made without hands, by putting off the body of the sins of the flesh, by the circumcision of Christ, buried with Him in baptism, in which you also were raised with Him through* **faith** *in the working of God, who raised Him from the dead*" (Colossians 2:11-12)
Helps one to strengthen one's inner spirit until the end	Peter documented, "*Blessed be the God and Father of our Lord Jesus Christ, who according to His abundant mercy has begotten us again to a living hope through the resurrection of Jesus Christ from the dead, to an inheritance incorruptible and undefiled and that does not fade away, reserved in heaven for you, who are kept by the power of God through* **faith** *for salvation ready to be revealed in the last time. In this you greatly rejoice, though now for a little while, if need be, you have been grieved by various trials, that the genuineness of your* **faith**, *being much*

	*more precious than gold that perishes, though it is tested by fire, may be found to praise, honor, and glory at the revelation of Jesus Christ, whom having not seen you <u>love</u>. Though now you do not see Him, yet believing, you rejoice with <u>joy</u> inexpressible and full of glory, receiving the end of your **faith**—the salvation of your souls."* (1 Peter 1:3-9)

Table 113: The Benefits of the Faithful Attribute's Influence

When one reads about all the benefits of acquiring the influence of the ***faithful*** attribute, it is natural to wonder what else is necessary to acquire it. Surely there is more than just, "*...**faith** comes by hearing, and hearing by the word of God*" (Romans 10:17). Well, the Biblical record provides that answer too. This positive attribute, like the others, starts with accepting the universal Truths documented at the beginning of this chapter. The New Testament of the Biblical record offers more clarity to include:

- Paul told Timothy, "*Hold fast the pattern of sound words which you have heard from me, in **faith** and <u>love</u> which are in Christ Jesus*" (2 Timothy 1:13)

- After Peter healed the lame man in the Book of Acts, He told the Jews that were astonished at the healing, "*...And His name, through **faith** in His name, has made this man strong, whom you see and know. Yes, the **faith** which comes through Him has given him this perfect soundness in the presence of you all*" (Acts 3:16)

- One must have the influence of the ***faithful*** attribute that steers one towards Jesus and not in any other religious or spiritual direction. Paul documented, "*...I kept back nothing that was helpful, but proclaimed it to you, and taught you publicly and from house to house, testifying to Jews, and also to Greeks, repentance toward God and **faith** toward our Lord Jesus Christ*" (Acts 20:20-21)

- One must seek God's righteousness and His Law of ***faith***. "*But now the righteousness of God apart from the law is revealed, being witnessed by the Law and the Prophets, even the righteousness of God, through **faith** in Jesus Christ, to all and on all who believe. For there is no difference; for all have sinned and fall short of the glory of God, being justified freely by His grace through the redemption that is in Christ Jesus, whom God set forth as a propitiation by His blood, through **faith**, to demonstrate His righteousness, because in His forbearance God had passed over the sins that were previously committed, to demonstrate at the present time His righteousness, that He might be just and the justifier of the one who has **faith** in Jesus. Where is boasting then? It is excluded. By what law? Of works? No, but by the law of **faith**. Therefore we conclude that a man is justified by **faith** apart from the deeds of the law*" (Romans 3:21-28)

The other question is, if the influence of the ***faithful*** attribute is so important, why did the Jews not accept its influence to lead them to Christ? The Biblical record answers this valid question. However, I must warn that the answer upsets the religious community today, including some who call themselves Christians who are not teaching this Truth. BTT allows one to see clearly that God shows no favoritism, nor holds any special place in heaven for the Jews, the doctrine of Judaism, or any other religious belief outside of the Gospel of Jesus Christ. God, the Creator of the universe, the King of kings, and Lord of lords, confirmed this Himself when He said of Jesus, *"This is My beloved Son. Hear Him!"* (Matthew 17:5; Mark 9:7; Luke 9:35). From then on, what Jesus said and revealed to the apostles ruled. This truth was expressed several times to the Jews in the Biblical record. The Bible recorded:

- Paul, speaking of God, documented, *"Or is He the God of the Jews only? Is He not also the God of the Gentiles? Yes, of the Gentiles also, since there is one God who will justify the circumcised [the Jews] by **faith** and the uncircumcised [the Gentiles] through **faith**. Do we then make void the law through **faith**? Certainly not! On the contrary, we establish the law"* (Romans 3:29-31)

- The practice of Judaism under the Law of Moses: *"Therefore the law was our tutor to bring us to Christ, that we might be justified by faith. But after faith has come, we are no longer under a tutor. For you are all sons of God through **faith** in Christ Jesus. For as many of you as were baptized into Christ have put on Christ"* (Galatians 3:24-27)

    - And Jesus said: *"Do not think that I came to destroy the Law or the Prophets. I did not come to destroy but to fulfill"* (Matthew 5:17)

    - Thus, Paul documented that the Law of Moses was finished upon Jesus' crucifixion and resurrection: *"And you, being dead in your trespasses and the uncircumcision of your flesh, He has made alive together with Him, having forgiven you all trespasses, having wiped out the handwriting of requirements that was against us, which was contrary to us. And He has taken it out of the way, having nailed it to the cross. Having disarmed principalities and powers, He made a public spectacle of them, triumphing over them in it"* (Colossians 2:13-15)

- But the Jews rejected the message that Jesus Christ delivered. Because of this, Paul wrote, *"...Because of unbelief they were broken off, and you stand by **faith**. Do not be haughty, but fear"* (Romans 11:20)

- The Jews' rejection of Christ goes way back in their lineage and history. Paul explained that their ancestors rebelled and hardened their hearts against the word of God in Hebrew 3:7-19. Why? They lacked the **faithful** attribute. Paul documented, *"For indeed the gospel was preached to us as well as to them; but the word which they heard did not profit them, not being mixed with **faith** in those who heard it"* (Hebrews 4:2)

- Speaking of the Gentiles, Paul documented, *"...God, who knows the heart, acknowledged them by giving them the Holy Spirit, just as He did to us, and made no distinction between us and them, purifying their hearts by **faith**. Now therefore, why do you test God by putting a yoke on the neck of the disciples which neither our fathers nor we were able to bear? But we believe that through the grace of the Lord Jesus Christ we shall be saved in the same manner as they"* (Acts 15:8-11)

- From this same idea, Paul connects the element of <u>justification</u> and the **faithful** attribute. He wrote, *"Therefore, having been <u>justified</u> by **faith**, we have <u>peace</u> with God* *through our Lord Jesus Christ, through whom also we have access by **faith** into this <u>grace</u> in which we stand, and rejoice in <u>hope</u> of the glory of God*" (Romans 5:1-2)

- To emphasize this very point even more, Paul compares the current condition of the Gentiles (all of us) to the Jews (those originally set aside by God) by saying, "*What shall we say then? That Gentiles, who did not pursue righteousness, have attained to righteousness, even the righteousness of **faith**; but Israel, pursuing the law of righteousness, has not attained to the law of righteousness. Why? Because they did not seek it by **faith**, but as it were, by the works of the law. For they stumbled at that stumbling stone*" (Romans 9:30-31)

Once again, my writing is not to denigrate the Jews, their beliefs or practices. This is only to document God's Truth and show how spiritual warfare has deceived so many good people in the world. Paul also shared that just like the other positive attributes, the influence of the ***faithful*** attribute, initially comes to people in varying amounts. He wrote, "*For I say, through the <u>grace</u> given to me, to everyone who is among you, not to think of himself more highly than he ought to think, but to think soberly, as God has dealt to each one a measure of **faith***" (Romans 12:3). One must nurture and grow this attribute through obedience to God's Word and practice. Discipline is key for growing this attribute. When Paul wrote, "*Receive one who is weak in the **faith**, but not to disputes over <u>doubtful</u> things*" (Romans 14:1), the statement had a double meaning. A Christian should receive another person that is weak in the Gospel as well as one that has a weaker measure of the ***faithful*** attribute. <u>Discernment</u> allows one to distinguish between the two. However, in both cases, the stronger person is required to help the weaker person grow.

When the influence of the ***faithful*** attribute combines with <u>*discernment*</u>, one can begin to grasp some of the harder concepts documented in the Biblical record that specifically pertain to this attribute. There are four major areas where maturing Christians need this combination for understanding the difficult concepts concerning this attribute.

The first area concerns the fact that there is only one Gospel, which is the only ***faith*** or religious belief that can save one's soul. BTT allows one to see that the influence of the ***faithful*** attribute is necessary for understanding this Faith. Paul documented the Holy Spirit revealed that "*There is one body and one Spirit, just as you were called in one <u>hope</u> of your calling; one Lord, one **faith**, one <u>baptism</u>; one God and Father of all, who is above all, and through all, and in you all*" (Ephesians 4:4-6). BTT allows one to see that this is a critical point to understand because of escalating spiritual warfare and the war campaign. Jesus established the "One **Faith**" for all mankind to believe and pursue to get to God the Father of the universe. However, in doing so, He did not remove the freedom of choice given to all. Thus Paul further documented, "*Now the Spirit expressly says that in latter times some will depart from the **faith**, giving heed to deceiving spirits and doctrines of demons, speaking lies in hypocrisy, having their own conscience seared with a hot iron, forbidding to marry, and commanding to abstain from foods which God created to be received with thanksgiving by those who believe and know the truth*" (1 Timothy 4:1-3). In other words, attacks against the belief of the "One **Faith**" by the negative forces of the war campaign were divinely predicted. However, the influence of the ***faithful*** attribute helps one to stay true to only the teachings of the Gospel of

Jesus Christ which is the "One **Faith**." BTT also allows one to see that the rise of men and women who falsely claim to follow the teachings of Christ are tools of Satan. Their false teachings have and will continue to derail many who believe the true Gospel. This is why the war campaign continues. In fact, the Biblical record even documented that, *"For such are false apostles, deceitful workers, transforming themselves into apostles of Christ. And no wonder! For Satan himself transforms himself into an angel of light. Therefore it is no great thing if his ministers also transform themselves into ministers of righteousness, whose end will be according to their works"* (2 Corinthians 11:13-15). This is why Paul instructed Timothy, *"If you instruct the brethren in these things, you will be a good minister of Jesus Christ, nourished in the words of faith and of the **good** doctrine which you have carefully followed"* (1 Timothy 4:6). When one allows the influence of the ***faithful*** attribute and is obedient to God's Word, the Gospel will nourish one's inner spirit and feed the ***faithful*** attribute for one's maturity. The ***faithful*** attribute will help one to follow the true teachings of Jesus Christ and lead one to compare what the world teaches against the written Word of God.

The second area concerns the fact the Lord's church has a defined structure and purpose. The structure and purpose were designed by God, not man; and Jesus specifically said *"...and the gates of Hades shall not prevail against it"* (Matthew 16:18). The structure contains a membership of people added to the Christ's church through <u>baptism</u> (Acts 2:47), and elders, ministers, and teachers. Deacons come from the membership to serve in an administrative role to support the elders only when there is a need. The elders, a primary minister, and teachers share in the strict responsibility of teaching and enforcing the Biblical teachings of Christ without alteration. This includes:

- Stopping false teachers and doctrines from entering the Lord's church: *"For there are many insubordinate, both idle talkers and deceivers, especially those of the circumcision, whose mouths must be stopped, who subvert whole households, teaching things which they ought not, for the sake of dishonest gain"* (Titus 1:10-11)

- Taking the Gospel as it is. Paul stated, *"...the things that you have heard from me among many witnesses, commit these to **faithful** men who will be able to teach others also. You therefore must endure hardship as a good soldier of Jesus Christ. No one engaged in warfare entangles himself with the affairs of this life, that he may please him who enlisted him as a soldier"* (2 Timothy 2:2-5)

- Leading everyone into the unity of the Gospel. This church structure is necessary until: *"...we all come to the unity of the **faith** and of the knowledge of the Son of God, to a perfect man, to the measure of the stature of the fullness of Christ; that we should no longer be children, tossed to and fro and carried about with every wind of doctrine, by the trickery of men, in the cunning craftiness of deceitful plotting..."* (Ephesians 4:13-14)

- Correcting false teachings as Paul charged Timothy to *"...charge some that they teach no other doctrine, nor give heed to fables and endless genealogies, which cause disputes rather than godly edification which is in **faith**. Now the purpose of the commandment is <u>love</u> from a pure heart, from a good conscience, and from sincere* *faith*, *from which some, having strayed, have turned aside to idle talk, desiring to be teachers of the law, understanding neither what they say nor the things which they affirm"* (1 Timothy 1:4-7)

- o Therefore, James documented, *"My brethren, let not many of you become teachers, knowing that we shall receive a stricter judgment"* (James 3:1)

- Identifying false teachers and their doctrine: *"But shun profane and idle babblings, for they will increase to more ungodliness. And their message will spread like cancer. Hymenaeus and Philetus are of this sort, who have strayed concerning the truth, saying that the resurrection is already past; and they overthrow the **faith** of some"* (2 Timothy 2:16-18)

- Understanding the full Truth in the fact that, *"...in the last days perilous times will come: For men will be lovers of themselves, lovers of money, boasters, proud, blasphemers, disobedient to parents, unthankful, unholy, unloving, unforgiving, slanderers, without self-control, brutal, despisers of good, traitors, headstrong, haughty, lovers of pleasure rather than lovers of God, having a form of godliness but denying its power. And from such people turn away! For of this sort are those who creep into households and make captives of gullible women loaded down with sins, led away by various lusts, always learning and never able to come to the knowledge of the truth."* (2 Timothy 3:1-7)

- Clearly understanding that *"...evil men and impostors will grow worse and worse, deceiving and being deceived"* (2 Timothy 3:13)

Just to be clear, leadership in the Lord's church contains elders. This is not to say that newly formed churches of the Lord must have elders immediately. Remember, the church is established within one's inner spirits (1 Corinthians 3:16) when one is baptized into Christ. Hence Paul asked, *"...do you not know that your body is the temple of the Holy Spirit who is in you, whom you have from God, and you are not your own?"* (1 Corinthians 6:19). Thus, when people who are influenced by the ***faithful*** attribute come together to worship the Lord in Spirit and truth (John 4:23-24), that location where they meet forms a physical structure called a church. In reality, the structure is Christians coming together as one body in Christ, in decency and order (1 Corinthians 14:40), to worship God collectively (Ephesians 2:19-22). If following the Bible and studying it like the Bereans (Acts 17:11), this group of ***faithful*** people will seek out someone to minister to them. They will grow this body of believers and strive to install elders. This is part of a natural progression of a healthy church where all things are done *"...decently and in order"* (1 Corinthians 14:40). Moreover, it is the pattern set forth from God. Elders in established churches of Christ must demonstrate the influence of the ***faithful*** attribute and discernment because they have the awesome responsibility of keeping sound ministers and teachers in positions. In fact, Paul told Titus to, *"...set in order the things that are lacking, and appoint elders in every city as I commanded you— if a man is blameless, the husband of one wife, having **faithful** children not accused of dissipation or insubordination"* (Titus 1:5-6). Paul stressed that prior to becoming an elder, the man must be, *"holding fast the*

faithful word as he has been taught, that he may be able, by sound doctrine, both to exhort and convict those who contradict" (Titus 1:9).

The third area concerns a unique connection between the influence of the ***faithful*** attribute and physical work. BTT allows one to see God requires this attribute and work. The ***faithful*** attribute's influence is demonstrated by "good *works.*" James does a beautiful job explaining the correlation between good works and the influence of the ***faithful*** attribute in James 2:14-26. The Holy Spirit inspired James to write:

> "What does it profit, my brethren, if someone says he has **faith** but does not have works? Can **faith** save him? If a brother or sister is naked and destitute of daily food, and one of you says to them, "Depart in <u>peace</u>, be warmed and filled," but you do not give them the things which are needed for the body, what does it profit? Thus also **faith** by itself, if it does not have works, is dead. But someone will say, "You have **faith**, and I have works." Show me your **faith** without your works, and I will show you my **faith** by my works. You believe that there is one God. You do well. Even the demons believe— and tremble! But do you want to know, O foolish man, that **faith** without works is dead? Was not Abraham our father justified by works when he offered Isaac his son on the altar? Do you see that **faith** was working together with his works, and by works **faith** was made perfect? And the Scripture was fulfilled which says, "Abraham believed God, and it was accounted to him for righteousness." And he was called the friend of God. You see then that a man is justified by works, and not by **faith** only. Likewise, was not Rahab the harlot also justified by works when she received the messengers and sent them out another way? For as the body without the spirit is dead, so **faith** without works is dead also."

From James' words , one can see the strong connection between the influence of the ***faithful*** attribute and what it leads one to do – that is – good works that edify God; not works that bring glory to one's self or men. Thus, for those who teach or identify the act of <u>baptism</u> as a work or refuse to do it because it is a work and has nothing to do with salvation, are false teachers. No Biblical writer, taught by Jesus or inspired by the Holy Spirit, ever called <u>baptism</u> or the "act of <u>baptism</u>" a work as some profess it to be. More importantly, the Biblical writers documented the necessity of the act. Chapter X of this book will cover this fact.

The fourth area concerns the fact that the Holy Spirit inspired Paul to document a standard for widows under sixty years of age who are part of the Lord's church. This standard, like the subject of divorce and remarriage, is difficult to accept by many Christians. However, the influence of the ***faithful*** attribute and the <u>comfort</u> of the Scriptures, help one to understand that the standard serves a purpose in the overall war campaign. Paul documented that widows under sixty years must meet a stiff standard to move into the household of a Christian couple. If not, Paul said to refuse them. Here is the standard and Paul's rationale documented in 1 Timothy 5:9-16 as inspired by the Holy Spirit:

> "Do not let a widow under sixty years old be taken into the number, and not unless she has been the wife of one man, well reported for good works: if she

has brought up children, if she has lodged strangers, if she has washed the saints' feet, if she has relieved the afflicted, if she has diligently followed every good work. But refuse the younger widows; for when they have begun to grow wanton against Christ, they desire to marry, having condemnation because they have cast off their first faith. And besides they learn to be idle, wandering about from house to house, and not only idle but also gossips and busybodies, saying things which they ought not. Therefore I desire that the younger widows marry, bear children, manage the house, give no opportunity to the adversary to speak reproachfully. For some have already turned aside after Satan. If any believing man or woman has widows, let them relieve them, and do not let the church be burdened, that it may relieve those who are really widows."

BTT allows one to see that this action keeps the influences of the negative forces outside the doors of one's home and the Lord's church. It was a hard teaching then and it remains a hard teaching today. This standard applies to the church that Christ established. Any other religious organization can do as they please, but God will not be mocked. In Christ's church enforcement of this standard is necessary. It takes a strong measure of the ***faithful*** attribute to enforce this standard.

To follow up on these four areas, within the Biblical record are some ***faithful*** sayings that coexist with the influence of the ***faithful*** attribute. All these sayings are worth one's meditation to strengthen and mature the ***faithful*** attribute's influence within one's inner spirit. The ***faithful*** sayings are:

- *"And the <u>grace</u> of our Lord was exceedingly abundant, with **faith** and <u>love</u> which are in Christ Jesus. This is a **faithful** saying and worthy of all acceptance, that Christ Jesus came into the world to save sinners, of whom I am chief. However, for this reason I obtained mercy, that in me first Jesus Christ might show all longsuffering, as a pattern to those who are going to believe on Him for everlasting life"* (1 Timothy 1:14-16)

- *"This is a **faithful** saying: If a man desires the position of a bishop, he desires a good work"* (1 Timothy 3:1). The full qualifications are in 1 Timothy 3:1-7. The Lord's church must strive to have elders.

- *"But reject profane and old wives' fables, and exercise yourself toward godliness. For bodily exercise profits a little, but <u>godliness</u> is profitable for all things, having promise of the life that now is and of that which is to come. This is a **faithful** saying and worthy of all acceptance. For to this end we both labor and suffer reproach, because we trust in the living God, who is the Savior of all men, especially of those who believe. These things command and teach"* (1 Timothy 4:7-11)

- *"This is a **faithful** saying: For if we died with Him, we shall also live with Him. If we endure, we shall also reign with Him. If we deny Him, He also will deny us. If we are faithless, He remains **faithful**; He cannot deny Himself"* (2 Timothy 2:11-13)

- *"This is a **faithful** saying, and these things I want you to affirm constantly, that those who have believed in God should be careful to maintain good works. These things are good and profitable to men"* (Titus 3:8)

There are two more very important connections the influence of the ***faithful*** attribute has for resisting the negative forces of the war campaign. The first is a connection to wisdom and the second is a connection to a spiritual element called <u>steadfastness</u>. First, James documented *"If any of you lacks wisdom, let him ask of God, who gives to all liberally and without reproach, and it will be given to him. But let him ask in **faith**, with no <u>doubting</u>, for he who <u>doubts</u> is like a wave of the sea driven and tossed by the wind. For let not that man suppose that he will receive anything from the Lord; he is a double-minded man, unstable in all his ways"* (James 1:5-8). BTT allows one to see that God will supply one with wisdom if one allows the influence of the ***faithful*** attribute. However, if one allows the attribute but also allows the spiritual element of <u>doubt</u> to enter one's mind, a spiritual conundrum occurs. This conundrum produces internal fighting between the inner spiritual heart and the physical mind which leads to instability. An unstable person in spiritual warfare is a liability for the positive forces of the campaign. Hence, one should not expect anything from God. Here are a few more situations and pearls of wisdom concerning the element of <u>doubt</u> for one's consideration:

*"And immediately Jesus stretched out His hand and caught him, and said to him, "O you of little **faith**, why did you <u>doubt</u>?"* (Matthew 14:31)	*"Then the Jews surrounded Him and said to Him, "How long do You keep us in <u>doubt</u>? If You are the Christ, tell us plainly."* (John 10:24)	*"I desire therefore that the men pray everywhere, lifting up holy hands, without wrath and <u>doubting</u>…"* (1 Timothy 2:8)
*"So Jesus answered and said to them, "Assuredly, I say to you, if you have **faith** and do not <u>doubt</u>, you will not only do what was done to the fig tree, but also if you say to this mountain, 'Be removed and be cast into the sea,' it will be done"* (Matthew 21:21)	*"For assuredly, I say to you, whoever says to this mountain, 'Be removed and be cast into the sea,' and does not <u>doubt</u> in his heart, but believes that those things he says will be done, he will have whatever he says"* (Mark 11:23)	*"But he who <u>doubts</u> is condemned if he eats, because he does not eat from **faith**; for whatever is not from **faith** is sin"* (Romans 14:23)
"And He said to them, "Why are you troubled? And why do <u>doubts</u> arise in your hearts?" (Luke 24:38)	*"Receive one who is weak in the **faith**, but not to disputes over <u>doubtful</u> things"* (Romans 14:1)	*"But let him ask in **faith**, with no <u>doubting</u>, for he who <u>doubts</u> is like a wave of the sea driven and tossed by the wind"* (James 1:6)

Table 114: Situations and Pearls of Wisdom Concerning the Element of <u>Doubt</u>

Secondly, James documented a direct connection to the **faithful** attribute and the spiritual element of <u>steadfastness</u>. James wrote, *"My brethren, count it all <u>joy</u> when you fall into various trials, knowing that the testing of your **faith** produces patience. But let patience have its perfect work, that you may be perfect and complete, lacking nothing"* (James 1:2-4). The term patience in this context means <u>steadfastness</u>. Peter explained the element of *steadfastness* by documenting that all Christians should be waiting *steadfastly* for - "*new heavens and a new earth in which righteousness dwells*" (2 Peter 3:13) – and then stating, "*Therefore, beloved, looking forward to these things, be diligent to be found by Him in peace, without spot and blameless; and consider that the longsuffering of our Lord is salvation...*" (2 Peter 3:14-15). One must understand that acquiring the influence of the ***faithful*** attribute takes work, study, patience, and obedience to God's Word. To shake one's ***faith*** before it becomes permanent and grows, the negative forces of the war campaign use an arsenal of tricks to test the influence of the ***faithful*** attribute in one's inner spirit. To have a better understanding of the *steadfast* element, here are some other places in the Biblical record where one can see its importance. The Biblical record documented:

Who	What Is documented
Solomon	Concerning David's son, God said, "*Moreover I will establish his kingdom forever, if he is steadfast to observe My commandments and My judgments, as it is this day*" (1 Chronicles 28:7)
David	He prayed, "*Create in me a clean heart, O God, and renew a steadfast spirit within me*" (Psalm 51:10; See also Psalm 57:7; Psalm 78:37; Psalm 108:1; and Psalm 112:7)
King Darius	After God saved David and his companions in the lion's den, King Darius proclaimed, "*I make a decree that in every dominion of my kingdom men must tremble and fear before the God of Daniel. For He is the living God, and steadfast forever; His kingdom is the one which shall not be destroyed, and His dominion shall endure to the end*" (Daniel 6:26)
3,000 people	After Peter's first sermon, and about three thousand souls were *baptized* into Christ, the Biblical record documented, "*And they continued steadfastly in the apostles' doctrine and fellowship, in the breaking of bread, and in prayers*" (Acts 2:42)
The Holy Spirit inspired	For Christian's behavior: "*Let love be without hypocrisy. Abhor what is evil. Cling to what is good. Be kindly affectionate to one another with brotherly love, in honor giving preference to one another; not lagging in diligence, fervent in spirit, serving the Lord; rejoicing in hope, patient in tribulation, continuing steadfastly in prayer...*" (Romans 12:9-12)
	Concerning celibacy: "*Nevertheless he who stands steadfast in his heart, having no necessity, but has power over his own will, and has so determined in his heart that he will keep his virgin, does well*" (1 Corinthians 7:37)
	Good works for the Lord: "*Therefore, my beloved brethren, be steadfast, immovable, always abounding in the work of the Lord, knowing that your labor is not in vain in the Lord*" (1 Corinthians 15:58)
	Paul and the apostles prayed for the Corinthian brethren: "*And our hope for you is steadfast, because we know that as you are partakers of the sufferings, so also you will partake of the consolation*" (2 Corinthians 1:7)
	For the church in Colosse: "*And you, who once were alienated and enemies in your mind by wicked works, yet now He has reconciled in the body of His flesh through death, to present you holy, and blameless, and above reproach in His sight— if indeed you continue in the **faith**, grounded and steadfast, and are not moved away from the hope of the gospel which you heard, which was*

Paul to write	*preached to every creature under heaven, of which I, Paul, became a minister"* (Colossians 1:21-23)	
	And Paul wrote the church in Colosse: *"For though I am absent in the flesh, yet I am with you in spirit, rejoicing to see your good order and the steadfastness of your faith in Christ"* (Colossians 2:5)	
	"For if the word spoken through angels proved steadfast, and every transgression and disobedience received a just reward, how shall we escape if we neglect so great a salvation, which at the first began to be spoken by the Lord, and was confirmed to us by those who heard Him…" (Hebrews 2:2-3)	
	"For we have become partakers of Christ if we hold the beginning of our confidence steadfast to the end…" (Hebrews 3:14)	
	"This hope we have as an anchor of the soul, both sure and steadfast, and which enters the Presence behind the veil…" (Hebrews 6:19)	
The Holy Spirit inspired Peter to write	Speaking of the Satan, Peter wrote, *"Resist him, steadfast in the **faith**, knowing that the same sufferings are experienced by your brotherhood in the world"* (1 Peter 5:9)	
	"You therefore, beloved, since you know this beforehand, beware lest you also fall from your own steadfastness, being led away with the error of the wicked; but grow in the grace and knowledge of our Lord and Savior Jesus Christ" (2 Peter 3:17-18)	

Table 115: The Faithful Attribute and the Element of <u>Steadfastness</u>

Finally, to fully appreciate the ***faithful*** attribute, the apostles documented a few more pearls of wisdom about this ***clean spirit***. These pearls included:

"…it is required in stewards that one be found **faithful**" (1 Corinthians 4:2)	"And now abide **faith**, hope, love, these three; but the greatest of these is love" (1 Corinthians 13:13)	Jesus Christ provides "…boldness and access with confidence through **faith** in Him" (Ephesians 3:12)
"For I say, through the grace given to me, to everyone who is among you, not to think of himself more highly than he ought to think, but to think soberly, as God has dealt to each one a measure of **faith**" (Romans 12:3)	"I have been crucified with Christ; it is no longer I who live, but Christ lives in me; and the life which I now live in the flesh I live by **faith** in the Son of God, who loved me and gave Himself for me" (Galatians 2:20)	Paul documented, "…if Christ is not risen, then our preaching is empty and your **faith** is also empty" (1 Corinthians 15:14). Further, "…if Christ is not risen, your **faith** is futile; you are still in your sins!" (1 Corinthians 15:17)
"Do not destroy the work of God for the sake of food. All things indeed are pure, but it is evil for the man who eats with offense. It is good neither to eat meat nor drink wine nor do anything by which your brother stumbles or is offended or is made weak. Do you have **faith**? Have it to yourself	"Do not be deceived, God is not mocked; for whatever a man sows, that he will also reap. For he who sows to his flesh will of the flesh reap corruption, but he who sows to the Spirit will of the Spirit reap everlasting life. And let us not grow weary while doing good, for in due season we shall reap if we	"For the love of money is a root of all kinds of evil, for which some have strayed from the faith [this is the Gospel] in their greediness, and pierced themselves through with many sorrows. But you, O man of God, flee these things and pursue righteousness, godliness, **faith**, love,

*before God. Happy is he who does not condemn himself in what he approves. But he who <u>doubts</u> is condemned if he eats, because he does not eat from **faith**; for whatever is not from **faith** is sin"* (Romans 14:20-23)	*do not lose heart. Therefore, as we have opportunity, let us do good to all, especially to those who are of the household of **faith**"* (Galatians 6:7-10)	*patience, gentleness. Fight the good fight of **faith**, lay hold on eternal life, to which you were also called and have confessed the good confession in the presence of many witnesses"* (1 Timothy 6:10-12)
*"Now the just shall live by **faith**; but if anyone draws back, My soul has no pleasure in him"* (Hebrews 10:38). The "My" documented here is God.	*"Remember those who rule over you, who have spoken the word of God to you, whose **faith** follow, considering the outcome of their conduct"* (Hebrews 13:7)	*"For in Christ Jesus neither circumcision nor uncircumcision avails anything, but **faith** working through <u>love</u>"* (Galatians 5:6)
*"...a man is not justified by the works of the law but by **faith** in Jesus Christ, even we have believed in Christ Jesus, that we might be justified by **faith** in Christ and not by the works of the law; for by the works of the law no flesh shall be justified"* (Galatians 2:16)	The Negative forces: *"These will make war with the Lamb, and the Lamb will overcome them, for He is Lord of lords and King of kings; and those who are with Him are called, chosen, and **faithful**"* (Revelation 17:14)	Paul told the church of Ephesus: *"<u>Peace</u> to the brethren, and <u>love</u> with **faith**, from God the Father and the Lord Jesus Christ. Grace be with all those who <u>love</u> our Lord Jesus Christ in sincerity. Amen"* (Ephesians 6:23-24)
*"But the fruit of the Spirit is <u>love</u>, <u>joy</u>, <u>peace</u>, longsuffering, kindness, goodness, **faithfulness**, gentleness, self-control. Against such there is no law. And those who are Christ's have crucified the flesh with its passions and desires. If we live in the Spirit, let us also walk in the Spirit. Let us not become conceited, provoking one another, envying one another"* (Galatians 5:22)	*"Listen, my be<u>love</u>d brethren: Has God not chosen the poor of this world to be rich in **faith** and heirs of the kingdom which He promised to those who <u>love</u> Him? But you have dishonored the poor man. Do not the rich oppress you and drag you into the courts? Do they not blaspheme that noble name by which you are called?"* (James 2:5-7)	*"Therefore we also, since we are surrounded by so great a cloud of witnesses, let us lay aside every weight, and the sin which so easily ensnares us, and let us run with endurance the race that is set before us, looking unto Jesus, the author and finisher of our **faith**, who for the <u>joy</u> that was set before Him endured the cross, despising the shame, and has sat down at the right hand of the throne of God"* (Hebrews 12:1-2)
That God can *"grant you, according to the riches of His glory, to be strengthened with might through His Spirit in the inner man, that Christ may dwell in your hearts*	*"Examine yourselves as to whether you are in the **faith**. Test yourselves. Do you not know yourselves, that Jesus Christ is in you?—unless indeed you are disqualified"*	*"But as you abound in everything—in **faith**, in speech, in knowledge, in all diligence, and in your <u>love</u> for us—see that you abound in this grace also"* (2 Corinthians 8:7)

through *faith*; ...." (Ephesians 3:16-17)	(2 Corinthians 13:5)	
Deacon's wives must meet a standard. "*Likewise, their wives must be reverent, not slanderers, temperate, **faithful** in all things*" (1 Timothy 3:11)	"*Here is the patience of the saints; here are those who keep the commandments of God and the **faith** of Jesus*" (Revelation 14:12)	"*Flee also youthful lusts; but pursue righteousness, **faith**, love, peace with those who call on the Lord out of a pure heart*" (2 Timothy 2:22)
"*My brethren, count it all joy when you fall into various trials, knowing that the testing of your **faith** produces patience. But let patience have its perfect work, that you may be perfect and complete, lacking nothing*" (James 1:2-4)	"*If anyone has an ear, let him hear. He who leads into captivity shall go into captivity; he who kills with the sword must be killed with the sword. Here is the patience and the **faith** of the saints*" (Revelation 13:9-10)	"*...we desire that each one of you show the same diligence to the full assurance of hope until the end, that you do not become sluggish, but imitate those who through **faith** and patience inherit the promises*" (Hebrews 6:11-12)
"*Therefore let him who thinks he stands take heed lest he fall. No temptation has overtaken you except such as is common to man; but God is **faithful**, who will not allow you to be tempted beyond what you are able, but with the temptation will also make the way of escape, that you may be able to bear it*" (1 Corinthians 10:13)	Paul stated, "*For I am not ashamed of the gospel of Christ, for it is the power of God to salvation for everyone who believes, for the Jew first and also for the Greek. For in it the righteousness of God is revealed from **faith** to **faith**; as it is written, "The just shall live by **faith**"* (Romans 1:16-17)	"*...let us draw near with a true heart in full assurance of **faith**, having our hearts sprinkled from an evil conscience and our bodies washed with pure water. Let us hold fast the confession of our hope without wavering, for He who promised is **faithful***" (Hebrews 10:22-23)

Table 116: Some Pearls of Wisdom Concerning the Faithful Attribute

The **Righteous attribute**: The full measure of this attribute allows one to be a formidable spiritual warrior on the battlefield of the war campaign. One with this attribute stands up for God's Word, Jesus Christ, and all that is *right* in the face of adversity. The influence of this attribute leads an individual to exercise morally high standards based on God's Word, to act and demonstrate behavior in accordance with divine and moral laws, and to make decisions based on the ethics and Truths found in the Bible. Emotional, situational, or relative dictates,  precedence, or philosophies of the world never come from this attribute. God is always at the forefront of every decision made by one with this attribute. For one to have the *righteous* attribute, one must be in a state of maturing all the other positive attributes (merciful, just, blameless, good, honorable/upright, and faithful). BTT allows one to see that all the other positive attributes are spiritually embodied in this attribute with the element of <u>love</u>. **Figure 24** illustrates this truth. When one has this attribute, it radiates throughout one's behavior. You see, when one acquires this attribute, one becomes a formidable warrior among the positive forces of the war campaign and a leader on the spiritual battlefield. Because of the former statements, the *righteous* attribute is harder to obtain than the other positive attributes. But acquiring this attribute is achievable. God desires everyone to strive for and achieve a state of *righteousness*. However, BTT allows one to see and understand that one cannot decided for himself or herself when this attribute is achieved. Nor can any human alive ordain another person as "*righteous*." God is the only One who can decide when one achieves a state of *righteousness* and acquires this attribute. Only God knows the measure for its full achievement. Someone may observe another person's *righteousness* but the person observed can never declare or decide for themselves that they are *righteous*. Please do not be *deceived* on this matter.

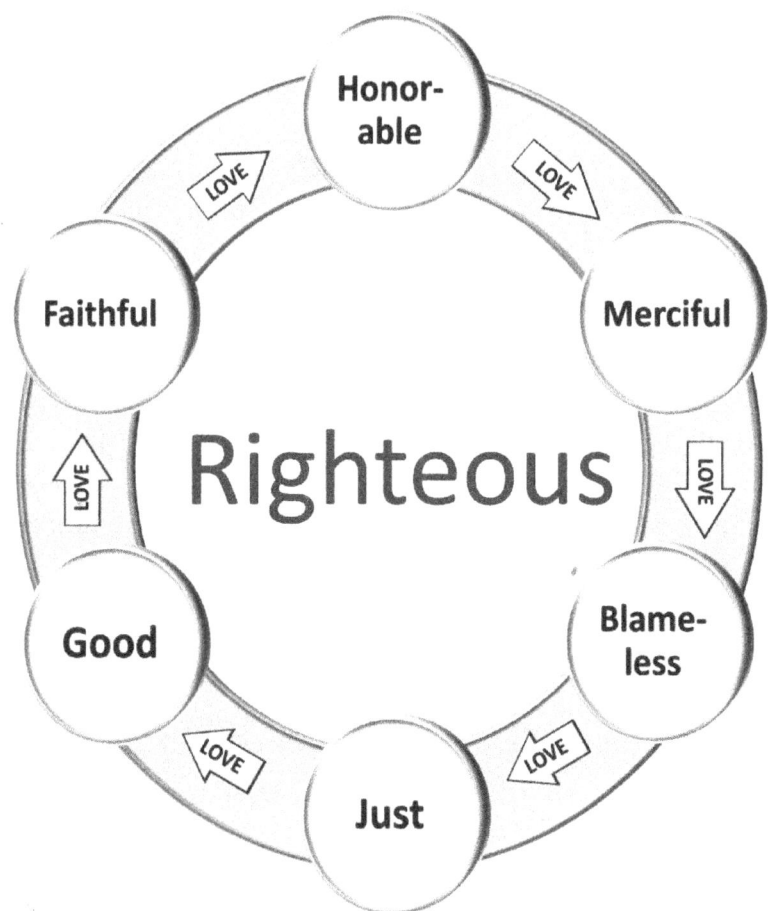

Figure 24: The Righteous Attribute and the Element of Love

One's requirement is simply to strive for it by mastering the other positive attributes. Even Solomon understood that "*He who follows **righteousness** and mercy finds life, **righteousness**, and honor*" (Proverbs 21:21). In this context, to "follow" is to pursue. One must pursue God's **righteousness** to access heaven; not man's brand of **righteousness**. For the religious community that believes otherwise, Paul documented, "*For they being ignorant of God's **righteousness**, and seeking to establish their own **righteousness**, have not submitted to the **righteousness** of God*" (Romans 10:3) and the Bible aptly documents "*As it is written: "There is none **righteous**, no, not one..."* (Romans 3:10).

Just so one understands the full ramification of striving to fully acquire the **righteous** attribute, try to embrace Paul's inspired words from the Holy Spirit documented in Romans 8:31-39. He wrote,

> "*What then shall we say to these things? If God is for us, who can be against us? He who did not spare His own Son, but delivered Him up for us all, how shall He not with Him also freely give us all things? Who shall bring a charge against God's elect? It is God who justifies. Who is he who condemns? It is Christ who died, and furthermore is also risen, who is even at the right hand of God, who also makes intercession for us. Who shall separate us from the love of Christ? Shall tribulation, or distress, or persecution, or famine, or nakedness, or peril, or sword? As it is written:*
>
> > "*For Your sake we are killed all day long; we are accounted as sheep for the slaughter.*"
>
> *Yet in all these things we are more than conquerors through Him who loved us. For I am persuaded that neither death nor life, nor angels nor principalities nor powers, nor things present nor things to come, nor height nor depth, nor any other created thing, shall be able to separate us from the love of God which is in Christ Jesus our Lord.*"

Paul's statement above reflects the knowledge and life of one truly influenced by the **righteous** attribute. With these words in mind, one should understand why Satan desires to take down those who have attained the **righteous** attribute. BTT allows one to see that for the **righteous**, or those striving for **righteousness**, Satan and his negative forces constantly place traps on their path. When Satan or his negative force's efforts cannot get a **righteous** person directly, their family members and friends become the target for an indirect attack. This tactic is true even in physical warfare. The prophet Job provided a superior example of this strategy. Satan went after his children, his wife, and then his friends (Job 1:13—19; 2:9). Like Job, regardless of the fiery darts (Ephesians 6:16) hurdled one's way, one must stand against the wiles of Satan (Ephesians 6:11). Like Job, an indicator that one is on the path of **righteousness** is when he or she can <u>*forgive*</u> another person's adversarial behavior especially when the behavior is taken to the extreme. One can consider the examples of Jesus (Luke 23:34) and Stephen (Acts 7:60) if one desires to jump ahead of the knowledge contained in this chapter. In fact, true knowledge of this attribute is so important that one should know upfront that the Biblical record documents, "*Little children, let no one **deceive** you. He who practices*

righteousness* is *righteous, *just as He is **righteous***" (1 John 3:7). Thus, consider the many things that Solomon learned from the Spirit of wisdom about this attribute.

One of the earliest lessons Solomon learned about the influence of the ***righteous*** attribute was: for one to understand it, one must first seek wisdom, <u>discernment</u>, and understanding. In other words, acquiring this attribute requires spiritual and mental work. He documented if, "*...you incline your ear to wisdom, and apply your heart to understanding; Yes, if you cry out for <u>discernment</u>, and lift up your voice for understanding, if you seek her as silver, and search for her as for hidden treasures; then you will understand the fear of the Lord, and find the knowledge of God. For the LORD gives* wisdom; *from His mouth come knowledge and understanding; He stores up sound wisdom for the upright; He is a shield to those who walk* uprightly; *He guards the paths of justice, and preserves the way of His saints. Then you will understand **righteousness** and justice, equity and every good path*" (Proverbs 2:2-9). From Solomon's statement, one can see the labor required to achieve the influence of the ***righteous*** attribute includes the discipline to walk on a path that is different from the world. It is only through God's wisdom that one can understand the nature of all the other positive attributes. The Spirit of wisdom shared with Solomon that she is the key for one to "*walk in the way of goodness, and keep to the paths of **righteousness***" (Proverbs 2:20).

As Wisdom revealed herself to Solomon, the influence of the ***righteous*** attribute was present. She told Solomon, documented in Proverbs 8:1-36, the following things:

- "*Listen, for I will speak of excellent things, and from the opening of my lips will come **right** things; for my mouth will speak truth; wickedness is an abomination to my lips*" (Proverbs 8:6-7)

- "*All the words of my mouth are with **righteousness**; nothing crooked or perverse is in them*" (Proverbs 8:8)

- "*They are all plain to him who understands, and **right** to those who find knowledge*" (Proverbs 8:9)

- "*Riches and honor are with me, enduring riches and **righteousness***" (Proverbs 8:18)

- "*My fruit is better than gold, yes, than fine gold, and my revenue than choice silver. I traverse the way of **righteousness**, in the midst of the paths of justice, that I may cause those who love me to inherit wealth, that I may fill their treasuries*" (Proverbs 8:19-21)

The Spirit of wisdom ended her discourse by telling Solomon, "*Blessed is the man who listens to me, watching daily at my gates, waiting at the posts of my doors. For whoever finds me finds life, and obtains favor from the LORD; but he who sins against me wrongs his own soul; all those who hate me love death*" (Proverbs 8:34-36). From this point on, one will see how the influence of the ***righteous*** attribute and God's wisdom are tethered.

The Lord takes care of one that allows the influence of the ***righteous*** attribute. The Spirit of wisdom revealed to Solomon that, "*The LORD will not allow the **righteous** soul to famish...*" (Proverbs 10:3). One can see that the Lord Himself feeds the soul of one with this attribute. God's Word provides the spiritual nourishment for spiritual and physical strength for one to resist and fight the negative forces of the war campaign. In fact, Solomon learned that, "*The **righteous** eats to the satisfying of his soul....*" (Proverbs 13:25). And since the Lord feeds the soul of those who allow the influence of the ***righteous*** attribute, Wisdom also revealed that, "*Blessings are on the head of the **righteous**...*" (Proverbs 10:6). Solomon learned further that:

- "*The memory of the **righteous** is blessed...*" (Proverbs 10:7)
    - "*The thoughts of the **righteous** are **right**...*" (Proverbs 12:5)

- "*The mouth of the **righteous** is a well of life...*" (Proverbs 10:11)
    - "*The mouth of the **righteous** brings forth wisdom...*" (Proverbs 10:31)
    - "*The lips of the **righteous** feed many...*" (Proverbs 10:21)
    - "*The lips of the **righteous** know what is acceptable...*" (Proverbs 10:32)
    - "***Righteous** lips are the delight of kings, and they love him who speaks what is*
      right" (Proverbs 16:13)
    - "*The tongue of the **righteous** is choice silver...*" (Proverbs 10:20)

- "*The fruit of the **righteous** is a tree of life...*" (Proverbs 11:30)

- "*The silver-haired head is a crown of glory, if it is found in the way of **righteousness***" (Proverbs 16:31)

- "*The labor of the **righteous** leads to life...*" (Proverbs 10:16)

From the Scriptures above, one can plainly see that the influence of the ***righteous*** attribute is both special and powerful. Moreover, the Spirit of wisdom shared with Solomon that, "*The **righteous** will never be removed...*" (Proverbs 10:30). This fact is consistent with an earlier statement by the Spirit of wisdom when she revealed to Solomon that, "*...**righteousness** delivers from death*" (Proverbs 10:2). Make no mistake, God empowers this attribute in ways that one can never fully understand in this lifetime. Yes, one with this attribute will experience physical death as all humanity does. But until that time, God's indwelling spirit ensures a good life (spiritual) with eternal benefits after death.

The benefits of the influence of the ***righteous*** attribute are much more significant than those of the good attribute. Since this attribute embodies all the positive attributes, BTT allows one to see that this attribute's influence makes a holistic difference in the life of its owner. In fact, people who encounter one influenced by this attribute reap the blessings of their presence. Biblical examples are found in the studies of Noah and his family, Abraham and his household, Joseph and his brothers, Moses and the children of Israel, and Jesus and His followers just to name a few. Consider the many pearls of wisdom that Solomon learned about the influence of the ***righteous*** attribute and its nature from the Spirit of wisdom in Table 117. He learned:

"The desire of the **righteous** is only good..." (Proverbs 11:23)	"A **righteous** man hates lying..." (Proverbs 13:5)	"The hope of the **righteous** will be gladness..." (Proverbs 10:28)
"...the **righteous** are bold as a lion" (Proverbs 28:1)	"...the **righteous** will flourish like foliage" (Proverbs 11:28)	"....the **righteous** has a refuge in his death" (Proverbs 14:32)
"He who speaks truth declares **righteousness**..." (Proverbs 12:17)	"**Righteousness** guards him whose way is blameless..." (Proverbs 13:6)	"...the desire of the **righteous** will be granted" (Proverbs 10:24)
"The **righteousness** of the blameless will direct his way aright..." (Proverbs 11:5)	"The wicked shall be a ransom for the **righteous**..." (Proverbs 21:18)	"....the wealth of the sinner is stored up for the **righteous**" (Proverbs 13:22)
"... the **righteous** gives and does not spare" (Proverbs 21:26)	"...the Lord hears the prayer of the **righteous**" (Proverbs 15:29)	"**Righteousness** exalts a nation..." (Proverbs 14:34)
"The **righteousness** of the upright will deliver them..." (Proverbs 11:6)	"No grave trouble will overtake the **righteous**..." (Proverbs 12:21)	"A **righteous** man regards the life of his animal..." (Proverbs 12:10)
"The **righteous** man walks in his integrity; his children are blessed after him" (Proverbs 20:7)	"The evil will bow before the good, and the wicked at the gates of the **righteous**" (Proverbs 14:19)	"He who follows **righteousness** and mercy finds life, **righteousness**, and honor" (Proverbs 21:21)
"The heart of the **righteous** studies how to answer..." (Proverbs 15:28)	"... the posterity of the **righteous** will be delivered" (Proverbs 11:21)	"When the **righteous** rejoice, there is great glory...." (Proverbs 28:12)
"In the way of **righteousness** is life, and in its pathway there is no death" (Proverbs 12:28)	"... through knowledge the **righteous** will be delivered" (Proverbs 11:9)	"... he who sows **righteousness** will have a sure reward" (Proverbs 11:18)
"As **righteousness** leads to life, so he who pursues evil pursues it to his own death" (Proverbs 11:19)	"The **righteous** should choose his friends carefully, for the way of the wicked leads them astray" (Proverbs 12:26)	"...to do **righteousness** and <u>justice</u> is more acceptable to the LORD than sacrifice" (Proverbs 21:3)
"The **righteous** considers the cause of the poor, but the wicked does not understand such knowledge" (Proverbs 29:7)	"The way of the wicked is an abomination to the LORD, but He loves him who follows **righteousness**" (Proverbs 15:9)	"The father of the **righteous** will greatly rejoice, and he who begets a wise child will delight in him. Let your father and your mother be glad, and let her who bore you rejoice" (Proverbs 23:24-25)

Table 117: Some Pearls of Wisdom Concerning the Righteous Attribute

Table 117 easily helps one to see the richness of the **righteous** attribute in the inner spirit of one who allows its influence. To seek the Lord by following His Word, searching out His wisdom, and acquiring all the other positive attributes, one can achieve the **righteous** attribute. To do anything less places one at odds with the Lord's desires. One can easily find him or herself in an unjust state because of their attitude and behavior. Thus, Solomon documented that *"An unjust man is an abomination to the **righteous**..."* (Proverbs 29:27). People who have acquired a measure of the ***righteous*** attribute will never tolerate the behavior of one influenced by the unjust attribute.

Later in Chapter IX of this book, one will learn how God's use of "<u>calamity</u>" in the war campaign affects the actions of the negative forces. I do not want to spoil this portion of one's reading about this topic here but one should know that Solomon documented some important truths concerning people influenced by the ***righteous*** attribute and this divine phenomenon. The Spirit of wisdom informed Solomon that, *"When the whirlwind passes by, the wicked is no more, but the **righteous** has an everlasting foundation"* (Proverbs 10:25). Said more plainly, Solomon understood and documented, *"The **righteous** is delivered from trouble..."* (Proverbs 11:8), and *"...the house of the **righteous** will stand"* (Proverbs 12:7). In other words, people influenced by the ***righteous*** attribute will survive through God's <u>calamity</u>. Why? Because God's <u>calamity</u> is not for the people influenced by the ***righteous*** attribute. One will learn in Chapter IV of this book that there are times when spiritual warfare becomes too overwhelming for the positive forces. God can, will, and does use <u>calamity</u> to maintain balance on the battlefield of the war campaign. Thus, the Spirit of wisdom assured Solomon that, *"...the root of the **righteous** cannot be moved"* (Proverbs 12:3). People who are influenced by the ***righteous*** attribute are necessary for the aftermath of the <u>calamity</u>. With God's Word and support, they bring understanding and hope to those impacted by the <u>calamity</u> – on both sides of the war! Hence, Solomon documented that *"...the root of the **righteous** yields fruit"* (Proverbs 12:12). This means there will be conversion during spiritual warfare to include some from the negative side. But for sure, the Spirit of wisdom told Solomon, *"The wicked is ensnared by the transgression of his lips, but the **righteous** will come through trouble"* (Proverbs 12:13). People influenced by the ***righteous*** attribute stand up and edify God while leading others through the darkness of sin, chaos, and confusion (which is the fog of the war campaign) while even facing the threats of death.

With this understanding, BTT allows one to see the importance of having people who allow the influence of the ***righteous*** attribute and leadership. Solomon, as both a godly man and leader, personally learned a lot about the ***righteous*** attribute in his position. The Spirit of wisdom told him directly, *"It is an abomination for kings to commit wickedness, for a throne is established by **righteousness**"* (Proverbs 16:12) and *"Take away the wicked from before the king, and his throne will be established in **righteousness**"* (Proverbs 25:5). These principles applied to Solomon and moreover, they spiritually apply to all leadership positions. Leaders that allow wicked counsel or surround themselves with people influenced by the wicked attribute, are wicked leaders themselves. The corrosive nature of wickedness corrupts everything it touches. Eventually, if it is not controlled, one's entire organization is consumed in the wickedness allowed by its wicked leader. BTT allows one to see such things as, when people influenced by the wicked attribute multiply, their transgressions increase (Proverbs 29:16); when they arise, men hide themselves (Proverbs 28:28); when they rule, the people groan (Proverbs 29:2); others join forces with them (Proverbs 11:21); they do deceptive work (Proverbs 11:18); people in their ignorance will call them *"**righteous**"* (Proverbs 24:24); they punish those with the **righteous** attribute (Proverbs 17:26); and they exercise partiality and overthrow the **righteous** in judgment (Proverbs 18:5). Solomon learned all these truths from the Spirit of wisdom.

The Spirit of wisdom informed Solomon that, *"He who says to the wicked, "You are* ***righteous****," him the people will curse; nations will abhor him. But those who rebuke the wicked will have delight, and a good blessing will come upon them"* (Proverbs 24:24-25). Moreover, the Spirit of wisdom informed Solomon that people with the influence of the **righteous** attribute will see the wicked fall from power. Wisdom told him, *"...the* ***righteous*** *will see their fall"* (Proverbs 29:16) and *"...when they perish, the* ***righteous*** *increase"* (Proverbs 28:28). Yes, God's Word is Truth, but one must have <u>discernment</u> to see and understand it; for the fall of the wicked occurs each day as God demonstrates His Truth and shows that He is in control. Hence, Paul documented *"Oh, the depth of the riches both of the wisdom and knowledge of God! How unsearchable are His judgments and His ways past finding out!"* (Romans 11:33) for one's knowledge.

Happiness and <u>peace</u> abound when one, especially one in a leadership position, allows the **righteous** attribute to influence his or her behavior and actions. The Spirit of wisdom told Solomon, *"When the* ***righteous*** *are in authority, the people rejoice..."* (Proverbs 29:2) and *"When it goes well with the* ***righteous****, the city rejoices; and when the wicked perish, there is jubilation"* (Proverbs 11:10). Further, Solomon documented, *"By transgression an evil man is snared, but the* ***righteous*** *sings and rejoices"* (Proverbs 29:6). These statements complement Solomon's documentation of the fact that, *"The light of the* ***righteous*** *rejoices, but the lamp of the wicked will be put out"* (Proverbs 13:9). Therefore, leaders need the influence of the **righteous** attribute to combat the spread of the negative attributes and spiritual warfare in their sphere of influence. King Lemuel added this closing point to the writings of the Book of Proverbs. He documented: *"Open your mouth for the speechless, in the cause of all who are appointed to die. Open your mouth, judge* ***righteously****, and plead the cause of the poor and needy"* (Proverbs 31:8-9).

The Spirit of wisdom also revealed to Solomon a correlation between the influence of the **righteous** attribute and wealth. Unfortunately, wealth like wickedness, has a corrosive side. Wealth offers people a false sense of security and blind them of their need for God. Solomon came to understand that, *"The name of the LORD is a strong tower; the* ***righteous*** *run to it and are safe. The rich man's wealth is his strong city, and like a high wall in his own esteem"* (Proverbs 18:10-11). Wealth deceives one's inner spirit into thinking that one has protection from all adversaries. When one's inner spirit gets comfortable in the deception, one's spiritual heart also hardens to hearing God's Word. One loses control of his or her inner spirit as worldly comforts and luxuries take precedence. With time and circumstance, one slowly becomes a hostage to the negative forces of the war campaign as wickedness consumes one's inner spirit. God's Word provides the only understanding and resolution to this paradox. Solomon documented that, *"The* ***righteous*** *God wisely considers the house of the wicked, overthrowing the wicked for their wickedness"* (Proverbs 21:12). If a person influenced by the **righteous** attribute can reach one blinded by the deceitfulness of wealth, that person can have a chance for salvation before their day of judgement. For the Spirit of wisdom further revealed to Solomon that, *"Riches do not profit in the day of wrath, but* ***righteousness*** *delivers from* *death"* (Proverbs 11:4). This Truth from Wisdom revealed that the influence of the ***righteous*** attribute can save in both the earthly and spiritual realms.

Spiritually, one also needs to know that one influenced by the ***righteous*** attribute also has wealth. Solomon document that, "*In the house of the **righteous** there is much treasure, but in the revenue of the wicked is trouble*" (Proverbs 15:6). People who allow the influence of the ***righteous*** attribute recognize that everything they have comes from the Lord. The ***righteous*** attribute's influence allows one to see that he or she is simply a caretaker of God's assets; from the smallest items to the largest. Everything is a blessing from the Lord - this is wealth. Furthermore, the wealth of one influenced by the ***righteous*** attribute is beyond earthy riches. Therefore, one influenced by this attribute appreciates the wealth found in all things. In fact, Wisdom revealed to Solomon that, "*Riches and honor are with me, enduring riches and **righteousness**. My fruit is better than gold, yes, than fine gold, and my revenue than choice silver. I traverse the way of **righteousness**, in the midst of the paths of justice, that I may cause those who love me to inherit wealth, that I may fill their treasuries*" (Proverbs 8:18-21). Those who allow the influence of the ***righteous*** attribute have Wisdom's wealth and know Wisdom's value. Hence, Solomon documented, "*Better is a little with **righteousness**, than vast revenues without justice*" (Proverbs 16:8). In other words, even the smallest measure of the ***righteous*** attribute is better than having vast wealth without Wisdom's knowledge to use it. BTT allows one to see that Wisdom revealed a spiritual principle here. The principle indicates that one will use wealth unjustly when no measure of the influence of the ***righteous*** attribute is present in one's inner spirit. The divine comparison here is that having a small measure of ***righteousness*** is far greater than having vast amounts of wealth without the influence of the just attribute. If one does not have the influence of the just attribute, then one is influenced by the unjust attribute; its opposite **unclean spirit**. It is one or the other in spiritual warfare. Either way, one blessed with wealth will either bring much good or great harm to the forces of the campaign. Chapter VII discusses people in the rich category and provides a greater understanding of this topic.

The Spirit of Wisdom revealed to Solomon that "*Evil pursues sinners, but to the **righteous**, **good** shall be repaid*" (Proverbs 13:21). From the previous chapter on the good attribute, one already knows this attribute's influence makes up the ***righteous*** attribute. So, it stands to reason, God blesses one influenced by the ***righteous*** attribute with good. This also supports another point that Solomon documented and recorded, "*If the **righteous** will be recompensed on the earth, how much more the ungodly and the sinner*" (Proverbs 11:31). Please do not miss this important point. Wisdom clearly revealed to Solomon that God will "<u>make amends for loss or harm suffered</u>" or "<u>compensate</u>" one influenced by the ***righteous*** attribute. However, from the same context, one can see a warning to people who are influenced by the ungodly attribute and sinners. God will render compensation to them too. However, the compensation will not be good. Please take heed to Wisdom's warning.

Finally, so as not to leave one with the impression that one with the ***righteous*** attribute is some super human, Solomon learned that one with the ***righteous*** attribute can be hurt or stumble under the intensity of spiritual warfare. I stated at the beginning of this chapter that one who acquires this attribute is a formidable warrior in the campaign. This is true. But just as true is the fact that one that acquires the full measure of the wicked attribute is also a formidable warrior. However, God is with the ***righteous***. Solomon documented, *"Do not lie in wait, O wicked man, against the dwelling of the **righteous**; do not plunder his resting place; for a **righteous** man may fall seven times and rise again, but the wicked shall fall by calamity"* (Proverbs 24:15-16). Yes, one influenced by the ***righteous*** attribute can fall in spiritual combat. Wisdom further revealed to Solomon that, *"A **righteous** man who falters before the wicked is like a murky spring and a polluted well"* (Proverbs 25:26). The fall of a ***righteous*** person, like a murky spring and a polluted well, is nasty and a major setback to all the positive forces of the war campaign. One must consider all the souls that looked up to this person's example and become discouraged when the ***righteous*** person falls. If one looks closely at what the Spirit of wisdom revealed to Solomon, one sees that he or she who attains the ***righteous*** attribute, *"may fall seven times and rise again"* according to Proverbs 24:16. The key however is that this person must get up and get back into the fight. This Proverb provides an everlasting hope for all who strive to achieve the ***righteous*** attribute. No other positive attribute can boast this great pearl of wisdom documented in Proverbs 24:16. Thus, the importance of pursuing the ***righteous*** attribute becomes even more significant as one begins to understand the war campaign. One may stumble, but one that pursues this attribute can get back up and continue the fight. Now let us see what more one can learn about the ***righteous*** attribute in the Biblical record.

The Biblical record provided many examples of people in the Old Testament that obtained the influence of the ***righteous*** attribute. Here are some of the examples that either the Lord spoke directly about or whom someone else identified based on the person's ***righteous*** behavior.

Who	**What Is Documented**
Abel	Jesus told the Pharisees they had blood on their hand. From *"... the blood of **righteous** Abel to the blood of Zechariah, son of Berechiah, whom you murdered between the temple and the altar"* (Matthew 23:31-35)
	*"By faith Abel offered to God a more excellent sacrifice than Cain, through which he obtained witness that he was **righteous**, God testifying of his gifts; and through it he being dead still speaks"* (Hebrews 11:4)
	*"For this is the message that you heard from the beginning, that we should love one another, not as Cain who was of the wicked one and murdered his brother. And why did he murder him? Because his works were evil and his brother's **righteous**"* (1 John 3:12)
Noah, Daniel, and Job	Then the Lord said to Noah, *"Come into the ark, you and all your household, because I have seen that you are **righteous** before Me in this generation"* (Genesis 7:1)
	The Lord told the prophet Ezekiel concerning the state of the nation of Israel's sin, that *"Even if these three men, Noah, Daniel, and Job, were in it, they would deliver only themselves by their **righteousness**,"* says the Lord God" (Ezekiel 14:14)
	Further, in Ezekiel 14:15-20, the Lord explains to Ezekiel the persistent unfaithfulness was at such a level that even sending wild beast, sword, and pestilence would not save it. And the Lord said, *"...even though Noah, Daniel, and Job were in it, as I live,"* says the Lord God, *"they would deliver neither*

	son nor daughter; they would deliver only themselves by their **righteousness**" (Ezekiel 14:20)
	"By faith Noah, being divinely warned of things not yet seen, moved with godly fear, prepared an ark for the saving of his household, by which he condemned the world and became heir of the **righteousness** which is according to faith" (Hebrews 11:7)
	"For if God did not spare the angels who sinned, but cast them down to hell and delivered them into chains of darkness, to be reserved for judgment; and did not spare the ancient world, but saved Noah, one of eight people, a preacher of **righteousness**..." (2 Peter 2:4-5)
Melchi-zedek	"For this Melchizedek, king of Salem, priest of the Most High God, who met Abraham returning from the slaughter of the kings and blessed him, to whom also Abraham gave a tenth part of all, first being translated "king of **righteousness**," and then also king of Salem, meaning "king of peace,"..." (Hebrews 7:2)
Abraham	"And he believed in the Lord, and He accounted it to him for **righteousness**" (Genesis 15:6)
	Paul said, "For what does the Scripture say? Abraham believed God, and it was accounted to him for **righteousness**" (Romans 4:3)
	"For the promise that he would be the heir of the world was not to Abraham or to his seed through the law, but through the **righteousness** of faith" (Romans 4:13) and "And therefore "it was accounted to him for **righteousness**" (Romans 4:22)
	"And the Scripture was fulfilled which says, "Abraham believed God, and it was accounted to him for **righteousness**." And he was called the friend of God" (James 2:23)
Lot	"...and delivered **righteous** Lot, who was oppressed by the filthy conduct of the wicked (for that **righteous** man, dwelling among them, tormented his **righteous** soul from day to day by seeing and hearing their lawless deeds)" (2 Peter 2:7-8)
Jacob	When he bargained with Laban, he said, "Let me pass through all your flock today, removing from there all the speckled and spotted sheep, and all the brown ones among the lambs, and the spotted and speckled among the goats; and these shall be my wages. So my **righteousness** will answer for me in time to come, when the subject of my wages comes before you: every one that is not speckled and spotted among the goats, and brown among the lambs, will be considered stolen, if it is with me" (Genesis 30:32-33)
Tamar	Judah identified Tamar's actions to be synonymous to the **righteous** attribute. After she patiently waited for a husband, according to the traditions of the time from Judah, she was forced to trick him as he reneged on his obligations and promise. The Biblical record documented that Judah acknowledge the issue and said, "...She has been more **righteous** than I, because I did not give her to Shelah my son." And he never knew her again" (Genesis 38:26)
Phinehas	"Then they despised the pleasant land; they did not believe His word, but complained in their tents, and did not heed the voice of the Lord. Therefore He raised His hand in an oath against them, to overthrow them in the wilderness, to overthrow their descendants among the nations, and to scatter them in the lands. They joined themselves also to Baal of Peor, and ate sacrifices made to

	the dead. Thus they provoked Him to anger with their deeds, and the plague broke out among them. Then Phinehas stood up and intervened, and the plague was stopped. And that was accounted to him for **righteousness** to all generations forevermore" (Psalm 106:24-31)
Ishbosheth	He was Saul's forty years old son, who reigned over Israel for two years according to 2 Samuel 2:10. The Biblical record documented that Baanah and Rechab, "...*two men who were captains of troops*" (2 Samuel 4:2-3), went to Ishbosheth's home and murdered him according to 2 Samuel 4:5-8. David caught Baanah and Rechab and the Biblical record documented that he said to them, "...*How much more, when wicked men have killed a **righteous** person in his own house on his bed? Therefore, shall I not now require his blood at your hand and remove you from the earth?" So David commanded his young men, and they executed them...*" (2 Samuel 4:9-12)
Zechariah	Jesus told the Pharisees they had blood on their hand. From "... *the blood of **righteous** Abel to the blood of Zechariah, son of Berechiah, whom you murdered between the temple and the altar*" (Matthew 23:31-35)
David	He said of himself, "*The Lord rewarded me according to my **righteousness**; according to the cleanness of my hands He has recompensed me. For I have kept the ways of the Lord, and have not wickedly departed from my God. For all His judgments were before me; and as for His statutes, I did not depart from them. I was also blameless before Him, and I kept myself from my iniquity. Therefore the Lord has recompensed me according to my **righteousness**, according to my cleanness in His eyes*" (2 Samuel 22:21-25)
	After David made it known to Saul that he could have killed him, Saul said to David, "..."*You are more **righteous** than I; for you have rewarded me with good, whereas I have rewarded you with evil*" (1 Samuel 24:17)
	Solomon, speaking about father David, prayed to the Lord, "...*You have shown great mercy to Your servant David my father, because he walked before You in truth, in **righteousness**, and in uprightness of heart with You; You have continued this great kindness for him, and You have given him a son to sit on his throne, as it is this day*" (1 Kings 3:6)
Solomon	The Queen of Sheba recognized this attribute in Solomon. She stated, "*Blessed be the Lord your God, who delighted in you, setting you on the throne of Israel! Because the Lord has loved Israel forever, therefore He made you king, to do justice and **righteousness**"* (1 Kings 10:9; 2 Chronicles 9:8)
Gideon, Barak, Samson, Jephthah, David, Samuel and the prophets	Of whom the Biblical record said, "...*who through faith subdued kingdoms, worked **righteousness**, obtained promises, stopped the mouths of lions, quenched the violence of fire, escaped the edge of the sword, out of weakness were made strong, became valiant in battle, turned to flight the armies of the aliens*" (Hebrews 11:33-34)

Table 118: Examples of People Who Allowed the Influence of the Righteous Attribute

What is so fascinating about Abraham is how the influence of the ***righteous*** attribute led in his spirit and the relationship he had with God. This attribute's influence was so profound in Abraham's inner spirit that the Lord heard his pleas for the lives of the people living in the cities of Sodom, Gomorrah, and the other cities on the plains. This example documents the power one can achieve through prayer, with obedience to the Lord and achievement of the full measure of the **righteous** attribute. Abraham petitioned the Lord and the Bible documented:

- *"Would You also destroy the **righteous** with the wicked? Suppose there were fifty **righteous** within the city; would You also destroy the place and not spare it for the fifty **righteous** that were in it? Far be it from You to do such a thing as this, to slay the **righteous** with the wicked, so that the **righteous** should be as the wicked; far be it from You! Shall not the Judge of all the earth do **right**?" So the Lord said, "If I find in Sodom fifty **righteous** within the city, then I will spare all the place for their sakes"* (Genesis 18:23-26)

- *Suppose there were five less than the fifty **righteous**; would You destroy all of the city for lack of five?" So He said, "If I find there forty-five, I will not destroy it"* (Genesis 18:28)

- *"Suppose there should be forty found there?" So He said, "I will not do it for the sake of forty"* (Genesis 18:29)

- *"Then he said, "Let not the Lord be angry, and I will speak: Suppose thirty should be found there?" So He said, "I will not do it if I find thirty there"* (Genesis 18:30)

- *"...Suppose twenty should be found there?" So He said, "I will not destroy it for the sake of twenty"* (Genesis 18:31)

- *Then he said, "Let not the Lord be angry, and I will speak but once more: Suppose ten should be found there?" And He said, "I will not destroy it for the sake of ten"* (Genesis 18:32)

Sadly, Genesis 19 documented that after Abraham petitioned the Lord, only four people initially survived the destruction of the cities on the plains. The Biblical record documented that Lot stated, *"Indeed now, your servant has found favor in your sight, and you have increased your mercy which you have shown me by saving my life..."* (Genesis 19:19). Lot, his wife, and two daughters escaped the destruction. However, the negative forces of the war campaign pursued Lot and his family as they left the city. The Bible documented that Lot's wife died leaving the city (Genesis 19:26) because she did not follow God's precise instructions. She looked back and died. Lot's two daughters sinned too. Upon reaching safety in the mountains according to Genesis 19:31-35, they allowed the influence of the immoral and perverted attributes in their inner spirits. From their immoral behavior, the Bible documented *"...both the daughters of Lot were with child by their father. The firstborn bore a son and called his name Moab; he is the father of the Moabites to this day. And the younger, she also bore a son and called his name Ben-Ammi; he is the father of the people of Ammon to this day."* (Genesis 19:36-38). As for the cities on the plain, the Bible documented, *"...the Lord rained brimstone and fire on Sodom and Gomorrah, from the Lord out of the heavens. So He overthrew those cities, all the plain, all the inhabitants of the cities, and what grew on the ground"* (Genesis 19:23-25) and *"The whole land is brimstone, salt, and burning; it is not sown, nor does it bear,* nor does any grass grow there, like the overthrow of Sodom and Gomorrah, Admah, and Zeboiim, which the Lord overthrew in His anger and His wrath" (Deuteronomy 29:23). And still further "...as Sodom and Gomorrah, and the cities around them in a similar manner to these, having given themselves over to sexual immorality and gone after strange flesh, are set forth as an example, suffering the vengeance of eternal fire" (Jude 1:7). The Lord destroys whole cities and nations when the presence of the **righteous** attribute is absent. Unfortunately, when BTT and <u>discernment</u> are lost, God's destruction is often hard to see because of the fog from the war campaign.

As one moves forward in the Biblical record, Moses documented that all the commandments given to the children of Israel from the Lord were **righteous**. Their obedience to the commandments would have helped them acquire the influence of the **righteous** attribute. Moses documented, *"...what great nation is there that has such statutes and* **righteous** *judgments as are in all this law which I set before you this day?"* (Deuteronomy 4:8) and, *"...the Lord commanded us to observe all these statutes, to fear the Lord our God, for our good always, that He might preserve us alive, as it is this day. Then it will be* **righteousness** *for us, if we are careful to observe all these commandments before the Lord our God, as He has commanded us"* (Deuteronomy 6:24-25). Some of the statutes, judgments, and commandments that Moses referred to are:

- *"Keep yourself far from a false matter; do not kill the innocent and* **righteous**. *For I will not justify the wicked"* (Exodus 23:7)

- *"...you shall take no bribe, for a bribe blinds the <u>discerning</u> and perverts the words of the* **righteous**" (Exodus 23:8)

- *"You shall do no injustice in judgment. You shall not be partial to the poor, nor honor the person of the mighty. In* **righteousness** *you shall judge your neighbor"* (Leviticus 19:15)

- *"Then I commanded your judges at that time, saying, 'Hear the cases between your brethren, and judge* **righteously** *between a man and his brother or the stranger who is with him"* (Deuteronomy 1:16)

- *"You shall not pervert justice; you shall not show partiality, nor take a bribe, for a bribe blinds the eyes of the wise and twists the words of the* **righteous**" (Deuteronomy 16:19)

- *"And if the man is poor, you shall not keep his pledge overnight. You shall in any case return the pledge to him again when the sun goes down, that he may sleep in his own garment and bless you; and it shall be* **righteousness** *to you before the Lord your God"* (Deuteronomy 24:12-13)

- *"If there is a dispute between men, and they come to court, that the judges may judge them, and they justify the* **righteous** *and condemn the wicked, then it shall be, if the wicked man deserves to be beaten, that the judge will cause him to lie* *down and be beaten in his presence, according to his guilt, with a certain number of blows"* (Deuteronomy 25:1-2)

- Moses commanded the judges *"...judges at that time, saying, 'Hear the cases between your brethren, and judge **righteously** between a man and his brother or the stranger who is with him"* (Deuteronomy 1:16). For he said to all the nation of Israel under his leadership, *"For what great nation is there that has God so near to it, as the Lord our God is to us, for whatever reason we may call upon Him? And what great nation is there that has such statutes and **righteous** judgments as are in all this law which I set before you this day?"* (Deuteronomy 4:7-8)

- *"...the Lord commanded us to observe all these statutes, to fear the Lord our God, for our good always, that He might preserve us alive, as it is this day. Then it will be **righteousness** for us, if we are careful to observe all these commandments before the Lord our God, as He has commanded us"* (Deuteronomy 6:24-25)

All the things from the Lord that Moses commanded the children of Israel gave them the opportunity to acquire and nourish the influence of the ***righteous*** attribute among themselves. BTT allows one to see that the children of Israel's obedience to God's commands were paramount if they wanted the influence of this attribute. And just to be clear on this matter, Moses told them that this attribute was not automatic. In fact, as God cleared the wicked nations out of the way of the Israelites, Moses told them in Deuteronomy 9:4-6,

*"Do not think in your heart, after the Lord your God has cast them out before you, saying, 'Because of my **righteousness** the Lord has brought me in to possess this land'; but it is because of the wickedness of these nations that the Lord is driving them out from before you. It is not because of your **righteousness** or the uprightness of your heart that you go in to possess their land, but because of the wickedness of these nations that the Lord your God drives them out from before you, and that He may fulfill the word which the Lord swore to your fathers, to Abraham, Isaac, and Jacob. Therefore understand that the Lord your God is not giving you this good land to possess because of your **righteousness**, for you are a stiff-necked people"*

One can see that the Lord knew the children of Israel's hearts and the strength of the negative forces of the war campaign. One must remember, although the children of Israel were God's chosen people, they still had the ability to choose their own path. This Truth applies to us today.

After generations passed and Israel grew into a nation, the ***righteous*** attribute's influence weakened among most of the people. When Solomon became king, he built and dedicated the temple to the Lord, and he prayed, *"When anyone sins against his neighbor, and is forced to take an oath, and comes and takes an oath before Your altar in this temple, then hear in heaven, and act, and judge Your servants, condemning the wicked, bringing his way on his head, and justifying the **righteous** by giving him according to his **righteousness**"* (1 Kings 8:31-32; 2 Chronicles 6:23). Based on Solomon's petition to God, one can surmise that spiritual warfare was running rampant among the people of Israel. Solomon did everything he could to bring the battlefield back in balance by strengthening the positive forces with leaders who were influenced by the positive attributes.

In the Book of Job, one learns that Eliphaz, Bildad, Elihu argued with Job about his **righteousness** and the attribute's influence in his inner spirit.

Eliphaz argued:

- *"Can a mortal be more **righteous** than God? Can a man be more pure than his Maker? If He puts no trust in His servants, if He charges His angels with error, how much more those who dwell in houses of clay, whose foundation is in the dust, who are crushed before a moth? They are broken in pieces from morning till evening; they perish forever, with no one regarding. Does not their own excellence go away? They die, even without wisdom"* (Job 4:17-21)

- *"What is man, that he could be pure? And he who is born of a woman, that he could be **righteous**?"* (Job 15:14)

- *"Is it any pleasure to the Almighty that you are **righteous**? Or is it gain to Him that you make your ways blameless?"* (Job 22:3)

- Eventually, Eliphaz accused Job of the influence of the wicked attribute. According to Job 22:15-20, Eliphaz told Job that God cut him down and Eliphaz concluded, *"The **righteous** see it and are glad, and the innocent laugh at them..."* (Job 22:19).

Bildad argued:

- *"Dominion and fear belong to Him; He makes peace in His high places. Is there any number to His armies? Upon whom does His light not rise? How then can man be **righteous** before God? Or how can he be pure who is born of a woman? If even the moon does not shine, and the stars are not pure in His sight, how much less man, who is a maggot, and a son of man, who is a worm?"* (Job 25:1-6)

The Biblical record documented that Eliphaz, Bildad, and Zophar, *"...ceased answering Job, because he was **righteous** in his own eyes"* (Job 32:1). They ceased answering out of sarcasm and scorn toward Job, not from a belief that Job was **right**. Because of this, Elihu, a younger man accompanying Eliphaz, Bildad, and Zophar (Job 32:4), spoke out under the influence of the angry attribute (Job 32:2-3). His verbal assault on Job brought to bear all the inappropriate and violent expressions of the negative forces from the war campaign. He argued:

- *"Look, in this you are not **righteous**. I will answer you, for God is greater than man"* (Job 33:12)

- *"Hear my words, you wise men; give ear to me, you who have knowledge. For the ear tests words as the palate tastes food. Let us choose justice for ourselves; let us know among ourselves what is good. For Job has said, 'I am **righteous**, but God has taken away my justice...'"* (Job 34:2-5)

- "Moreover Elihu answered and said: "Do you think this is **right**? Do you say, 'My **righteousness** is more than God's'?" (Job 35:1-2)

- "If you are **righteous**, what do you give Him? Or what does He receive from your hand? Your wickedness affects a man such as you, and your **righteousness** a son of man" (Job 35:7-8)

- "Elihu also proceeded and said: "Bear with me a little, and I will show you that there are yet words to speak on God's behalf. I will fetch my knowledge from afar; I will ascribe **righteousness** to my Maker. For truly my words are not false; one who is perfect in knowledge is with you" (Job 36:1-4)

- "Behold, God is mighty, but despises no one; He is mighty in strength of understanding. He does not preserve the life of the wicked, but gives justice to the oppressed. He does not withdraw His eyes from the **righteous**; but they are on the throne with kings, for He has seated them forever, and they are exalted" (Job 36:5-7)

Job responded to each of the men's accusation in a way that demonstrated both his wisdom and the influence of the **righteous** attribute. Here are just a few of the essential things Job said about this attribute:

- "My eye has also grown dim because of sorrow, and all my members are like shadows. Upright men are astonished at this, and the innocent stirs himself up against the hypocrite. Yet the **righteous** will hold to his way, and he who has clean hands will be stronger and stronger" (Job 17:7-9)

- "My lips will not speak wickedness, nor my tongue utter deceit. Far be it from me that I should say you are right; till I die I will not put away my integrity from me. My **righteousness** I hold fast, and will not let it go; my heart shall not reproach me as long as I live" (Job 27:4-6)

- "Because I delivered the poor who cried out, the fatherless and the one who had no helper. The blessing of a perishing man came upon me, and I caused the widow's heart to sing for joy. I put on **righteousness**, and it clothed me; my justice was like a robe and a turban. I was eyes to the blind, and I was feet to the lame. I was a father to the poor, and I searched out the case that I did not know. I broke the fangs of the wicked, and plucked the victim from his teeth." (Job 29:12-17)

All evidence points to the fact that Job allowed the influence of the **righteous** attribute to lead his inner spirit. He stood firm against his adversaries disguised as his friends. Thus, God restored everything he had plus more according to the Biblical record in Job 42:12-17.

The Psalmist documented a treasure trove of wisdom about the **righteous** attribute. He defined the scope, breath, and depths of this attribute from God's perspective as the owner of this positive spirit. The Psalmist documented:

"He loves **righteousness** and justice; the earth is full	"He shall judge the world in **righteousness**, and He shall administer judgment	"Oh, let the nations be glad and sing for joy! For You shall judge the people

of the goodness of the Lord" (Psalm 33:5)	for the peoples in uprightness" (Psalm 9:8)	*righteously*, and govern the nations on earth" (Psalm 67:4)
"Deliver me in Your *righteousness*, and cause me to escape; incline Your ear to me, and save me" (Psalm 71:2)	"The Lord executes *righteousness* and justice for all who are oppressed" (Psalm 103:6)	"In You, O Lord, I put my trust; let me never be ashamed; deliver me in Your *righteousness*" (Psalm 31:1)
"For He is coming to judge the earth. With *righteousness* He shall judge the world, and the peoples with equity" (Psalm 98:9)	"Lead me, O Lord, in Your *righteousness* because of my enemies; make Your way straight before my face" (Psalm 5:8)	"Vindicate me, O Lord my God, according to Your *righteousness*; and let them not rejoice over me" (Psalm 35:24)
"Revive me, O Lord, for Your name's sake! For Your *righteousness*' sake bring my soul out of trouble" (Psalm 143:11)	"Oh, continue Your lovingkindness to those who know You, and Your *righteousness* to the upright in heart" (Psalm 36:10)	"I will praise the Lord according to His *righteousness*, and will sing praise to the name of the Lord Most High" (Psalm 7:17)
"For You have maintained my *right* and my cause; You sat on the throne judging in *righteousness*" (Psalm 9:4)	"For He is coming, for He is coming to judge the earth. He shall judge the world with *righteousness*, and the peoples with His truth" (Psalm 96:13)	"Say among the nations, "The Lord reigns; the world also is firmly established, it shall not be moved; He shall judge the peoples *righteously*" (Psalm 96:10)
"My eyes fail from seeking Your salvation and Your *righteous* word" (Psalm 119:123)	"Behold, I long for Your precepts; revive me in Your *righteousness*" (Psalm 119:40)	"I have sworn and confirmed that I will keep Your *righteous* judgments" (Psalm 119:106)
"My tongue also shall talk of Your *righteousness* all the day long; for they are confounded, for they are brought to shame who seek my hurt" (Psalm 71:24)	"My mouth shall tell of Your *righteousness* and Your salvation all the day, for I do not know their limits. I will go in the strength of the Lord GOD; I will make mention of Your *righteousness*, of Yours only" (Psalm 71:15-16)	"Add iniquity to their iniquity, and let them not come into Your *righteousness*. Let them be blotted out of the book of the living, and not be written with the *righteous*" (Psalm 69:27-28)

Table 119: Pearls of Wisdom from the Psalmist Concerning the Righteous Attribute

Solomon and David identified some of the ongoing battles that occur in spiritual warfare between people who are influenced by the ***righteous*** attribute and people influenced by some of the negative attributes. Here are a few of the struggles these men captured that exposed parts of the campaign. Consider these examples closely. BTT allows one to see how the positive and negative forces engage in battles in the spiritual realm, while the manifestation of their struggle appears through behaviors in the earthly realm. These men documented the struggle between the influence of the ***righteous*** attribute and...

- The ungodly attribute: *"Blessed is the man who walks not in the counsel of the ungodly, nor stands in the path of sinners, nor sits in the seat of the scornful; but his delight is in the law of the Lord, and in His law he meditates day and night. He shall be like a tree planted by the rivers of water, that brings forth its fruit in its season, whose leaf also shall not wither; and whatever he does shall prosper. The ungodly are not so, but are like the chaff which the wind drives away. Therefore the ungodly shall not stand in the judgment, nor sinners in the congregation of the **righteous**. For the Lord knows the way of the **righteous**, but the way of the ungodly shall perish"* (Psalm 1:1-6)

- The evil and hater attributes: *"The eyes of the Lord are on the **righteous**, and His ears are open to their cry. The face of the Lord is against those who do evil, to cut off the remembrance of them from the earth. The **righteous** cry out, and the Lord hears, and delivers them out of all their troubles. The Lord is near to those who have a broken heart, and saves such as have a contrite spirit. Many are the afflictions of the **righteous**, but the Lord delivers him out of them all. He guards all his bones; not one of them is broken. Evil shall slay the wicked, and those who hate the **righteous** shall be condemned"* (Psalm 34:15-21)

- The evil, liar, and wicked attributes: *"Why do you boast in evil, O mighty man? The goodness of God endures continually. Your tongue devises destruction, like a sharp razor, working deceitfully. You love evil more than good, lying rather than speaking **righteousness**. You love all devouring words, you deceitful tongue. God shall likewise destroy you forever; He shall take you away, and pluck you out of your dwelling place, and uproot you from the land of the living. The **righteous** also shall see and fear, and shall laugh at him, saying, "Here is the man who did not make God his strength, but trusted in the abundance of his riches, and strengthened himself in his wickedness"* (Psalm 52:1-7)

- The wicked attribute: *"There is a vanity which occurs on earth, that there are just men to whom it happens according to the work of the wicked; again, there are wicked men to whom it happens according to the work of the **righteous**. I said that this also is vanity"* (Ecclesiastes 8:14)

    - *"I have seen everything in my days of vanity: There is a just man who perishes in his **righteousness**, and there is a wicked man who prolongs life in his wickedness. Do not be overly **righteous**, nor be overly wise: Why should you destroy yourself?"* (Ecclesiastes 7:15-16)

- The fool attribute: *"The fool says in his heart, "There is no God." They are corrupt, their deeds are vile; there is no one who does good. The Lord looks down from heaven on all mankind to see if there are any who understand, any who seek God. All have turned away, all have become corrupt; there is no one who does good, not even one. Do all these evildoers know nothing? They devour my people as though eating bread; they never call on the Lord. There they are in great fear, for God is with the generation of the **righteous**"* (Psalm 14:1-5)

- The unjust, wicked, violent, and perverse attributes: *"Shall the throne of iniquity, which devises evil by law, have fellowship with You? They gather together against the life of the **righteous**, and condemn innocent blood. But the Lord has been my defense, and my God the rock of my refuge. He has brought on them their own iniquity, and shall cut them off in their own wickedness; the Lord our God shall cut them off"* (Psalm 94:20-23)

    o *Moreover I saw under the sun: In the place of judgment, wickedness was there; and in the place of **righteousness**, iniquity was there. I said in my heart, "God shall judge the **righteous** and the wicked, for there is a time there for every purpose and for every work"* (Ecclesiastes 3:16-17)

    o *"If you see the oppression of the poor, and the violent perversion of justice and **righteousness** in a province, do not marvel at the matter; for high official watches over high official, and higher officials are over them"* (Ecclesiastes 5:8)

David, Solomon, and several prophets sent by God documented some enduring pearls of wisdom about the influence of the **righteous** attribute. These pearls highlighted the importance God placed on this attribute's influence on the inner spirit. Please study these pearls closely and meditate on their importance. The Biblical record documented:

*"The wicked borrows and does not repay, but the **righteous** shows mercy and gives"* (Psalm 37:21)	*"Let Your priests be clothed with **righteousness**, and let Your saints shout for joy"* (Psalm 132:9)	*"For You, O Lord, will bless the **righteous**; with favor You will surround him as with a shield"* (Psalm 5:12)
*"Cast your burden on the Lord, and He shall sustain you; He shall never permit the **righteous** to be moved"* (Psalm 55:22)	*"Let the lying lips be put to silence, which speak insolent things proudly and contemptuously against the **righteous**"* (Psalm 31:18)	*"Blessed are those who keep justice, and he who does **righteousness** at all times!"* (Psalm 106:3)
*"The Lord tests the **righteous**, but the wicked and the one who loves violence His soul hates"* (Psalm 11:5)	God *"...restores my soul; He leads me in the paths of **righteousness** for His name's sake"* (Psalm 23:3)	*"Light is sown for the **righteous**, and gladness for the upright in heart"* (Psalm 97:11)
*"The **righteous** shall be glad in the Lord, and trust in Him. And all the upright in heart shall glory"* (Psalm 64:10)	*"...let the **righteous** be glad; let them rejoice before God; yes, let them rejoice exceedingly"* (Psalm 68:3)	*"Surely the **righteous** shall give thanks to Your name; the upright shall dwell in Your presence"* (Psalm 140:13)
*"Be glad in the Lord and rejoice, you **righteous**; and shout for joy, all you upright in heart!"* (Psalm 32:11)	*"Rejoice in the Lord, O you **righteous**! For praise from the upright is beautiful"* (Psalm 33:1)	*"Rejoice in the Lord, you **righteous**, and give thanks at the remembrance of His holy name"* (Psalm 97:12)
*"The **righteous** shall flourish like a palm tree, He shall grow like a cedar in Lebanon. Those who are*	*"Blessed is the man whom You instruct, O Lord, and teach out of Your law, that You may give him rest from*	*"Those who trust in the Lord are like Mount Zion, which cannot be moved, but abides forever. As the mountains*

planted in the house of the Lord shall flourish in the courts of our God. They shall still bear fruit in old age; they shall be fresh and flourishing, to declare that the Lord is upright; He is my rock, and there is no unrighteousness in Him" (Psalm 92:12-15)	the days of adversity, until the pit is dug for the wicked. For the Lord will not cast off His people, nor will He forsake His inheritance. But judgment will return to **righteousness**, and all the upright in heart will follow it" (Psalm 94:12-15)	surround Jerusalem, so the Lord surrounds His people from this time forth and forever. For the scepter of wickedness shall not rest on the land allotted to the **righteous**, lest the **righteous** reach out their hands to iniquity" (Psalm 125:1-3)
"Let the **righteous** strike me; it shall be a kindness. And let him rebuke me; it shall be as excellent oil; let my head not refuse it. For still my prayer is against the deeds of the wicked" (Psalm 141:5)	"The mouth of the **righteous** speaks wisdom, and his tongue talks of justice. The law of his God is in his heart; none of his steps shall slide. The wicked watches the **righteous**, and seeks to slay him" (Psalm 37:30-32)	"A little that a **righteous** man has is better than the riches of many wicked. For the arms of the wicked shall be broken, but the Lord upholds the **righteous**" (Psalm 37:16-17)
"The voice of rejoicing and salvation is in the tents of the **righteous**; the right hand of the Lord does valiantly" (Psalm 118:15)	"The Lord opens the eyes of the blind; the Lord raises those who are bowed down; the Lord loves the **righteous**" (Psalm 146:8)	"I have been young, and now am old; yet I have not seen the **righteous** forsaken, nor his descendants begging bread" (Psalm 37:25)
"...Everyone who is found written in the book. And many of those who sleep in the dust of the earth shall awake, some to everlasting life, some to shame and everlasting contempt. Those who are wise shall shine like the brightness of the firmament, and those who turn many to **righteousness** like the stars forever and ever" (Daniel 12:1-3)	"Praise the Lord! Blessed is the man who fears the Lord, who delights greatly in His commandments. His descendants will be mighty on earth; the generation of the upright will be blessed. Wealth and riches will be in his house, and his **righteousness** endures forever. Unto the upright there arises light in the darkness; he is gracious, and full of compassion, and **righteous**" (Psalm 112:1-4)	"The **righteous** cry out, and the Lord hears, and delivers them out of all their troubles. The Lord is near to those who have a broken heart, and saves such as have a contrite spirit. Many are the afflictions of the **righteous**, but the Lord delivers him out of them all. He guards all his bones; not one of them is broken. Evil shall slay the wicked, and those who hate the **righteous** shall be condemned" (Psalm 34:17-21)
"The **righteous** shall inherit the land, and dwell in it forever" (Psalm 37:29)	"The eyes of the Lord are on the **righteous**, and His ears are open to their cry" (Psalm 34:15)	"... God is with the generation of the **righteous**" (Psalm 14:5)
"...the ungodly shall not stand in the judgment, nor sinners in the congregation	"When a **righteous** man turns away from his **righteousness**, commits	"Listen to Me, you who follow after **righteousness**, you who

of the **righteous**. For the Lord knows the way of the **righteous**, but the way of the ungodly shall perish" (Psalm 1:5-6)	iniquity, and dies in it, it is because of the iniquity which he has done that he dies" (Ezekiel 18:26)	seek the Lord: Look to the rock from which you were hewn, and to the hole of the pit from which you were dug" (Isaiah 51:1)
"For I considered all this in my heart, so that I could declare it all: that the **righteous** and the wise and their works are in the hand of God" (Ecclesiastes 9:1)	"Say to the **righteous** that it shall be well with them, for they shall eat the fruit of their doings" (Isaiah 3:10)	"The work of **righteousness** will be peace, and the effect of **righteousness**, quietness and assurance forever" (Isaiah 32:17)
"The **righteous** shall rejoice when he sees the vengeance; he shall wash his feet in the blood of the wicked, so that men will say, "Surely there is a reward for the **righteous**; surely He is God who judges in the earth" (Psalm 58:10-11)	"The Lord shall judge the peoples; judge me, O Lord, according to my **righteous**-ness, and according to my integrity within me. Oh, let the wickedness of the wicked come to an end, but establish the just; for the **righteous** God tests the hearts and minds" (Psalm 7:8-9)	"No weapon formed against you shall prosper, and every tongue which rises against you in judgment You shall condemn. This is the heritage of the servants of the Lord, and their **righteousness** is from Me," Says the Lord" (Isaiah 54:17)
"Listen to Me, you who know **righteousness**, you people in whose heart is My law: Do not fear the reproach of men, nor be afraid of their insults. For the moth will eat them up like a garment, and the worm will eat them like wool; but My **righteousness** will be forever, and My salvation from generation to generation" (Isaiah 51:7-8)	"...With my soul I have desired You in the night, yes, by my spirit within me I will seek You early; for when Your judgments are in the earth, the inhabitants of the world will learn **righteousness**. Let grace be shown to the wicked, yet he will not learn **righteousness**; in the land of uprightness he will deal unjustly, and will not behold the majesty of the Lord" (Isaiah 26:9-10)	"He who walks **righteously** and speaks uprightly, he who despises the gain of oppressions, who gestures with his hands, refusing bribes, who stops his ears from hearing of bloodshed, and shuts his eyes from seeing evil: He will dwell on high; his place of defense will be the fortress of rocks; bread will be given him, his water will be sure" (Isaiah 33:15-16)
"For since the beginning of the world men have not heard nor perceived by the ear, nor has the eye seen any God besides You, Who acts for the one who waits for Him. You meet him who rejoices and does **righteousness**, who remembers You in Your ways. You are indeed angry,	"...when a **righteous** man turns from his **righteousness** and commits iniquity, and I lay a stumbling block before him, he shall die; because you did not give him warning, he shall die in his sin, and his **righteousness** which he has done shall not be remembered; but his	"But if a wicked man turns from all his sins which he has committed, keeps all My statutes, and does what is lawful and right, he shall surely live; he shall not die. None of the transgressions which he has committed shall be remembered against him; because of the **righteousness** which he

*for we have sinned— in these ways we continue; and we need to be saved. But we are all like an unclean thing, and all our **righteousnesses** are like filthy rags; we all fade as a leaf, and our iniquities, like the wind, have taken us away"* (Isaiah 64:4-5)	*blood I will require at your hand. Nevertheless if you warn the **righteous** man that the **righteous** should not sin, and he does not sin, he shall surely live because he took warning; also you will have delivered your soul"* (Ezekiel 3:20-21)	*has done, he shall live. Do I have any pleasure at all that the wicked should die?"* says the Lord God, *"and not that he should turn from his ways and live?"* (Ezekiel 18:21-23)
*"...The **righteousness** of the **righteous** shall be upon himself, and the wickedness of the wicked shall be upon himself"* (Ezekiel 18:20)	*"When the **righteous** turns from his **righteousness** and commits iniquity, he shall die because of it"* (Ezekiel 33:18)	
*"But when a **righteous** man turns away from his **righteousness** and commits iniquity, and does according to all the abominations that the wicked man does, shall he live? All the **righteousness** which he has done shall not be remembered; because of the unfaithfulness of which he is guilty and the sin which he has committed, because of them he shall die. Yet you say, 'The way of the Lord is not fair.' Hear now, O house of Israel, is it not My way which is fair, and your ways which are not fair?"* (Ezekiel 18:24-25)	*"He who walks uprightly, and works **righteousness**, and speaks the truth in his heart; He who does not backbite with his tongue, nor does evil to his neighbor, nor does he take up a reproach against his friend; in whose eyes a vile person is despised, but he honors those who fear the Lord; he who swears to his own hurt and does not change; he who does not put out his money at usury, nor does he take a bribe against the innocent. He who does these things shall never be moved"* (Psalm 15:2-5)	*"...the **righteous** will be in everlasting remembrance. He will not be afraid of evil tidings; his heart is steadfast, trusting in the Lord. His heart is established; he will not be afraid, until he sees his desire upon his enemies. He has dispersed abroad, he has given to the poor; his **righteousness** endures forever; his horn will be exalted with honor. The wicked will see it and be grieved; he will gnash his teeth and melt away; the desire of the wicked shall perish"* (Psalm 112:5-10)
*"...the salvation of the **righteous** is from the Lord; He is their strength in the time of trouble. And the Lord shall help them and deliver them; He shall deliver them from the wicked, and save them, because they trust in Him"* (Psalm 37:39-40)		*"Who is wise? Let him understand these things. Who is prudent? Let him know them. For the ways of the Lord are **right**; the **righteous** walk in them, but transgressors stumble in them"* (Hosea 14:9)

Table 120: More Pearls of Wisdoms Concerning the Righteous Attribute

As with all the other attributes, the Lord sent His prophets to warn the nation of Israel to repent, return to Him, and to seek out the influence of the ***righteous*** attribute. The next Table offers many examples in which the Lord expressed frustration with the nation of Israel concerning the absence of this attribute. But as one looks at this Table, here is one of the most important takeaways to understand in spiritual warfare. The prophet Habakkuk cried to the Lord, *"Why do You show me iniquity, and cause me to see trouble? For plundering and violence are before me; there is <u>strife</u>, and <u>contention</u> arises. Therefore the law is powerless, and justice never goes forth. For the wicked surround the **righteous**; therefore perverse judgment proceeds"* (Habakkuk 1:1-4). The Biblical record documented:

The Prophet	What Was Said
Isaiah	*"Come now, and let us reason together," says the Lord, "Though your sins are like scarlet, they shall be as white as snow; though they are red like crimson, they shall be as wool. If you are willing and obedient, you shall eat the good of the land; but if you refuse and rebel, you shall be devoured by the sword"; for the mouth of the Lord has spoken. How the faithful city has become a harlot! It was full of justice; **righteousness** lodged in it, but now murderers"* (Isaiah 1:18-21)
	*"...restore your judges as at the first, and your counselors as at the beginning. Afterward you shall be called the city of **righteousness**, the faithful city"* (Isaiah 1:26)
	*"For the vineyard of the Lord of hosts is the house of Israel, and the men of Judah are His pleasant plant. He looked for justice, but behold, oppression; for **righteousness**, but behold, a cry for help"* (Isaiah 5:7)
	*"Woe to men mighty at drinking wine, woe to men valiant for mixing intoxicating drink, who justify the wicked for a bribe, and take away justice from the **righteous** man!"* (Isaiah 5:22-23)
	*"Listen to Me, you stubborn-hearted, who are far from **righteousness**: I bring My **righteousness** near, it shall not be far off; My salvation shall not linger. And I will place salvation in Zion, for Israel My glory"* (Isaiah 46:12-13)
	*"Hear this, O house of Jacob, who are called by the name of Israel, and have come forth from the wellsprings of Judah; who swear by the name of the Lord, and make mention of the God of Israel, but not in truth or in **righteousness**..."* (Isaiah 48:1)
	*"Oh, that you had heeded My commandments! Then your peace would have been like a river, and your **righteousness** like the waves of the sea"* (Isaiah 48:18)
	*"The **righteous** perishes, and no man takes it to heart; merciful men are taken away, while no one considers that the **righteous** is taken away from evil"* (Isaiah 57:1)
	*"Therefore justice is far from us, nor does **righteousness** overtake us; we look for light, but there is darkness! For brightness, but we walk in blackness!" We grope for the wall like the blind, and we grope as if we had no eyes; we stumble at noonday as at twilight; we are as dead men in desolate places. We all growl like bears, and moan sadly like doves; we look for justice, but there is none; for salvation, but it is far from us. For our transgressions are multiplied before You, and our sins testify against us; for our transgressions are with us, and as for our iniquities, we know them: In transgressing and lying against the Lord, and departing from our God, speaking oppression and revolt, conceiving and uttering from the heart words of falsehood. Justice is turned back, and*

	righteousness *stands afar off; for truth is fallen in the street, and equity cannot enter. So truth fails, and he who departs from evil makes himself a prey"* (Isaiah 59:9-15)
Jeremiah	*"...Backsliding Israel has shown herself more **righteous** than treacherous Judah"* (Jeremiah 3:11)
	*"But, O Lord of hosts, You who test the **righteous**, and see the mind and heart, let me see Your vengeance on them; for I have pleaded my cause before You"* (Jeremiah 20:12)
	*"...'hear the word of the Lord, O king of Judah, you who sit on the throne of David, you and your servants and your people who enter these gates! Thus says the Lord: "Execute judgment and **righteousness**, and deliver the plundered out of the hand of the oppressor. Do no wrong and do no violence to the stranger, the fatherless, or the widow, nor shed innocent blood in this place. For if you indeed do this thing, then shall enter the gates of this house, riding on horses and in chariots, accompanied by servants and people, kings who sit on the throne of David. But if you will not hear these words, I swear by Myself," says the Lord, "that this house shall become a desolation""* (Jeremiah 22:2-5)
Ezekiel	To the *foolish prophets, "...who follow their own spirit and have seen nothing!"* (Ezekiel 13:3) and *"...envisioned futility and false divination, saying, 'Thus says the Lord!' But the Lord has not sent them; yet they hope that the word may be confirmed"* (Ezekiel 13:6), the Lord warned, *"Because with lies you have made the heart of the **righteous** sad, whom I have not made sad; and you have strengthened the hands of the wicked, so that he does not turn from his wicked way to save his life"* (Ezekiel 13:22)
	*"As I live," says the Lord God, "neither your sister Sodom nor her daughters have done as you and your daughters have done. Look, this was the iniquity of your sister Sodom: She and her daughter had pride, fullness of food, and abundance of idleness; neither did she strengthen the hand of the poor and needy. And they were haughty and committed abomination before Me; therefore I took them away as I saw fit. Samaria did not commit half of your sins; but you have multiplied your abominations more than they, and have justified your sisters by all the abominations which you have done. You who judged your sisters, bear your own shame also, because the sins which you committed were more abominable than theirs; they are more **righteous** than you. Yes, be disgraced also, and bear your own shame, because you justified your sisters"* (Ezekiel 16:48-52)
	*"Son of man, set your face toward Jerusalem, preach against the holy places, and prophesy against the land of Israel; and say to the land of Israel, 'Thus says the Lord: "Behold, I am against you, and I will draw My sword out of its sheath and cut off both **righteous** and wicked from you. Because I will cut off both **righteous** and wicked from you, therefore My sword shall go out of its sheath against all flesh from south to north, that all flesh may know that I, the Lord, have drawn My sword out of its sheath; it shall not return anymore"* (Ezekiel 21:2-5)
	But ***righteous*** *men will judge them after the manner of adulteresses, and after the manner of women who shed blood, because they are adulteresses, and blood is on their hands"* (Ezekiel 23:45)

	"Thus says the Lord God: "Enough, O princes of Israel! Remove violence and plundering, execute justice and **righteousness**, and stop dispossessing My people," says the Lord God" (Ezekiel 45:9)
	"Therefore you, O son of man, say to the children of your people: 'The **righteousness** of the **righteous** man shall not deliver him in the day of his transgression; as for the wickedness of the wicked, he shall not fall because of it in the day that he turns from his wickedness; nor shall the **righteous** be able to live because of his **righteousness** in the day that he sins. When I say to the **righteous** that he shall surely live, but he trusts in his own **righteousness** and commits iniquity, none of his **righteous** works shall be remembered; but because of the iniquity that he has committed, he shall die" (Ezekiel 33:12-13)
Daniel	To King Nebuchadnezzar, David warned, "Therefore, O king, let my advice be acceptable to you; break off your sins by being **righteous**, and your iniquities by showing mercy to the poor. Perhaps there may be a lengthening of your prosperity" (Daniel 4:27)
Hosea	The Lord directed Hosea to, "..."Go, take yourself a wife of harlotry and children of harlotry, for the land has committed great harlotry by departing from the Lord." (Hosea 1:2). By reading the Biblical record, one learns that Gomer, Hosea's wife, committed *adultery* (Hosea 3:1) but Hosea forgive and redeemed her according to the Biblical record of Hosea 3:2, 3. The example was used to let the nation of Israel know that God was willing to take Israel back as His bride if the people repented. Hosea warned Israel from the Lord, "*I will betroth you to Me forever; yes, I will betroth you to Me in **righteousness** and justice, in lovingkindness and mercy; I will betroth you to Me in faithfulness, and you shall know the Lord*" (Hosea 2:19)
	"Sow for yourselves **righteousness**; reap in mercy; break up your fallow ground, for it is time to seek the Lord, till He comes and rains **righteousness** on you. You have plowed wickedness; you have reaped iniquity. You have eaten the fruit of lies, because you trusted in your own way, in the multitude of your mighty men." (Hosea 10:12-13)
Amos	"Thus says the Lord: "For three transgressions of Israel, and for four, I will not turn away its punishment, because they sell the **righteous** for silver, and the poor for a pair of sandals" (Amos 2:6)
	"You who turn justice to wormwood, and lay **righteousness** to rest in the earth!" (Amos 5:7)
	"I hate, I despise your feast days, and I do not savor your sacred assemblies. Though you offer Me burnt offerings and your grain offerings, I will not accept them, nor will I regard your fattened peace offerings. Take away from Me the noise of your songs, for I will not hear the melody of your stringed instruments. But let justice run down like water, and **righteousness** like a mighty stream" (Amos 5:21-24)
	"Do horses run on rocks? Does one plow there with oxen? Yet you have turned justice into gall, and the fruit of **righteousness** into wormwood..." (Amos 6:12)
	He asked the Lord, when shown the sins of the nation of Israel, "*Why do You show me iniquity, and cause me to see trouble? For plundering and violence are before me; there is strife, and contention arises. Therefore the law is powerless, and justice never goes forth. For the wicked surround the **righteous**; therefore perverse judgment proceeds*" (Habakkuk 1:4). The Lord

Habakkuk	told Habakkuk the He was in control and, *"Look among the nations and watch—be utterly astounded! For I will work a work in your days which you would not believe, though it were told you"* (Habakkuk 1:5)
	He asked the Lord a second question in which he said, *"You are of purer eyes than to behold evil, and cannot look on wickedness. Why do You look on those who deal treacherously, and hold Your tongue when the wicked devours a person more **righteous** than he?"* (Habakkuk 1:13). God responded with a consistent truth. The Bible recorded the Lord's comments in Habakkuk 2:2-20 for which I can summarize once again by saying – God is in control!
Zephaniah	*"Seek the Lord, all you meek of the earth, who have upheld His justice. Seek **righteousness**, seek humility. It may be that you will be hidden in the day of the Lord's anger"* (Zephaniah 2:3)
Malachi	The Bible documented, *"Then those who feared the Lord spoke to one another, and the Lord listened and heard them; so a book of remembrance was written before Him for those who fear the Lord and who meditate on His name. "They shall be Mine," says the Lord of hosts, "On the day that I make them My jewels. And I will spare them as a man spares his own son who serves him." Then you shall again <u>discern</u> between the **righteous** and the wicked, between one who serves God and one who does not serve Him"* (Malachi 3:16-18)

Table 121: The Prophet's Warnings about the Influence of the Righteous Attribute

The Lord was serious about the nation of Israel repenting and turning away from sin. BTT allows one to see that God's warnings were clear. However, Israel rejected God's warnings and the influence of the ***righteous*** attribute. Yet, this attribute remained in a remnant of the Jewish nation. For this remnant, the Lord told them, *"The Gentiles shall see your **righteousness**, and all kings your glory. You shall be called by a new name, which the mouth of the Lord will name"* (Isaiah 62:2). That new name today is "Christian" which is documented in Acts 11:26. As for the rest of the nation, the Biblical record documented from the prophet Ezekiel, *"Yet the house of Israel says, 'The way of the Lord is not fair.' O house of Israel, is it not My ways which are fair, and your ways which are not fair? Therefore I will judge you, O house of Israel, every one according to his ways," says the Lord God. "Repent, and turn from all your transgressions, so that iniquity will not be your ruin. Cast away from you all the transgressions which you have committed, and get yourselves a new heart and a new spirit. For why should you die, O house of Israel? For I have no pleasure in the death of one who dies," says the Lord God. "Therefore turn and live!"'* (Ezekiel 18:29-32). Most Jews refused then; and their practices, traditions, and doctrines persist today. Thus, Jesus ushered in a new covenant with a remnant of Jews and the Gentiles.

The Lord always wants His people to strive for the ***righteous*** attribute. BTT allows one to see that since He desired people who would worship Him in spirit and truth (John 4:24), He established the criteria long ago as to how His worship must be done. Worship to and for the Almighty God is to be done His way; not man's way. David documented this criterion which included all the positive attributes, when he wrote, *"Lord, who may abide in Your tabernacle? Who may dwell in Your holy hill? He who walks uprightly, and works **righteousness**, and speaks the truth in his heart; he who does not backbite with his tongue, nor does evil to his neighbor, nor does he take up a reproach against his friend; in whose eyes a vile person is* *despised, but he honors those who fear the Lord; he who swears to his own hurt and does not change; he who does not put out his money at usury, nor does he take a bribe against the innocent. He who does these things shall never be moved"* (Psalms 15:1-5).

Now some of the New Testament characters found as examples of people who were influenced by the **righteous** attribute include:

Who	What Is Documented
John the Baptist	I told you earlier that he had the **righteous** attribute. Now consider what Jesus told the chief priest and the elders of the people, *"...Assuredly, I say to you that tax collectors and harlots enter the kingdom of God before you. For John came to you in the way of **righteousness**, and you did not believe him; but tax collectors and harlots believed him; and when you saw it, you did not afterward relent and believe him"* (Matthew 21:31-32)
Zacharias and Elizabeth	The Biblical record documented, *"There was in the days of Herod, the king of Judea, a certain priest named Zacharias, of the division of Abijah. His wife was of the daughters of Aaron, and her name was Elizabeth. And they were both **righteous** before God, walking in all the commandments and ordinances of the Lord blameless"* (Luke 1:5-6)
Mary	Implied by Elizabeth and the actions surrounding Mary. The Bible documented: *"Now Mary arose in those days and went into the hill country with haste, to a city of Judah, and entered the house of Zacharias and greeted Elizabeth. And it happened, when Elizabeth heard the greeting of Mary, that the babe leaped in her womb; and Elizabeth was filled with the Holy Spirit. Then she spoke out with a loud voice and said, "Blessed are you among women, and blessed is the fruit of your womb! But why is this granted to me, that the mother of my Lord should come to me? For indeed, as soon as the voice of your greeting sounded in my ears, the babe leaped in my womb for joy. Blessed is she who believed, for there will be a fulfillment of those things which were told her from the Lord"* (Luke 1:39-45)
Jesus	The Biblical record documented that a Centurion declared His **righteousness**. The Bible recorded, *"So when the centurion saw what had happened, he glorified God, saying, "Certainly this was a **righteous** Man!"* (Luke 23:47)

Table 122: Some Examples of People Who Allowed the Influence of the Righteous Attribute

Additional information is provided about the influence of the **righteous** attribute in the four Gospels of the New Testament. This information explicitly expresses that this attribute is gravely important for mankind and the maintenance of world peace and order. Jesus Christ provides a clue of this when He approached John the Baptist and desired to be <u>baptized</u> by him. According to the Biblical record, John tried to prevent Jesus from being <u>baptized</u>. The Bible documented, *"And John tried to prevent Him, saying, "I need to be <u>baptized</u> by You, and are You coming to me?" But Jesus answered and said to him, "Permit it to be so now, for thus it is fitting for us to fulfill all **righteousness**." Then he allowed Him"* (Matthew 3:14-15). Thus, Jesus' behavior, from His early education as a youth (Luke 2:40), through His <u>baptism</u>, fulfilled the **righteousness** of God. Moreover, Jesus' behavior established the pattern for everyone who desired to become His followers under His name (Christians). Following His teachings exclusively gives one the ability to acquire the influence of the *righteous* attribute. Pearls of wisdom about the *righteous* attribute from the Master Teacher Himself included:

"Blessed are those who hunger and thirst for **righteousness**, for they shall be filled" (Matthew 5:6)	"Blessed are those who are persecuted for **righteousness**' sake, for theirs is the kingdom of heaven" (Matthew 5:10)	"But seek first the kingdom of God and His **righteousness**, and all these things shall be added to you" (Matthew 6:33)
"Then the **righteous** will shine forth as the sun in the kingdom of their Father. He who has ears to hear, let him hear!" (Matthew 13:43)	"….go and learn what this means: 'I desire mercy and not sacrifice.' For I did not come to call the **righteous**, but sinners, to repentance" (Matthew 9:13; Mark 2:13-17; Luke 5:27-32)	For I say to you, that unless your **righteousness** exceeds the **righteousness** of the scribes and Pharisees, you will by no means enter the kingdom of heaven" (Matthew 5:17-20)
Jesus said to His disciples, "But blessed are your eyes for they see, and your ears for they hear; for assuredly, I say to you that many prophets and **righteous** men desired to see what you see, and did not see it, and to hear what you hear, and did not hear it" (Matthew 13:16-17)	"…unless your **righteousness** exceeds the **righteousness** of the scribes and Pharisees, you will by no means enter the kingdom of heaven" (Matthew 5:20)	"He who receives you receives Me, and he who receives Me receives Him who sent Me. He who receives a prophet in the name of a prophet shall receive a prophet's reward. And he who receives a **righteous** man in the name of a **righteous** man shall receive a **righteous** man's reward. And whoever gives one of these little ones only a cup of cold water in the name of a disciple, assuredly, I say to you, he shall by no means lose his reward" (Matthew 10:41)

Table 123: Pearls of Wisdom From Jesus Concerning the Influence of the Righteous Attribute

Jesus spiritually taught the people who would hear Him. He explained to them that the wisdom of God produced all the positive attributes, including the *righteous* attribute. Conversely, He told them that discipline and obedience to God's Word was necessary. However, the negative forces of the war campaign vigorously tried to prevent people from hearing Jesus' message through spiritual warfare. These negative forces influenced the Jews, to whom the Gospel message came first, to revolt and close their ears. As the Jew's behavior aided the negative forces of the war campaign, Jesus call out the behavior of the scribes and Pharisees who were unable to perceive the role that the influence of the *righteous* attribute played in their inner spirits. Jesus said to them:

- *"Woe to you, scribes and Pharisees, hypocrites! For you are like whitewashed tombs which indeed appear beautiful outwardly, but inside are full of dead men's bones and*

> *all uncleanness. Even so you also outwardly appear **righteous** to men, but inside you are full of hypocrisy and lawlessness"* (Matthew 23:27-28)

- *"Woe to you, scribes and Pharisees, hypocrites! Because you build the tombs of the prophets and adorn the monuments of the **righteous**, and say, 'If we had lived in the days of our fathers, we would not have been partakers with them in the blood of the prophets'"* (Matthew 23:29-30)

- *"Therefore you are witnesses against yourselves that you are sons of those who murdered the prophets. Fill up, then, the measure of your fathers' guilt. Serpents, brood of vipers! How can you escape the condemnation of hell? Therefore, indeed, I send you prophets, wise men, and scribes: some of them you will kill and crucify, and some of them you will scourge in your synagogues and persecute from city to city, that on you may come all the **righteous** blood shed on the earth, from the blood of **righteous** Abel to the blood of Zechariah, son of Berechiah, whom you murdered between the temple and the altar"* (Matthew 23:31-35)

The scribes' and Pharisees' behavioral responses to Jesus was as expected. They responded with irritation and indignation. The Biblical record documented the Pharisees, *"...watched Him, and sent spies who pretended to be **righteous**, that they might seize on His words, in order to deliver Him to the power and the authority of the governor"* (Luke 20:20). However, the Biblical record also indicated that Jesus understood what was behind their behavior and motives. Satan influenced the people who were attempting to stop Him from carrying out His mission on earth. Yes, Jesus knew the specifics of the war campaign. He understood that because of the Jews' selfish desires and refusal to acknowledge God, the influences of the negative attributes would lead them to do negative things. Thus, Jesus spoke in parables to those who could hear His voice through the fog of spiritual warfare.

Jesus shared a correlation between the influence of the ***righteous*** attribute and His final return to earth in Matthew 25:31-46. **Figure 25** illustrates this correlation by documenting the influence of the ***righteous*** attribute's role in the war campaign to one's end-state at the war's conclusion. BTT also allows one to see that Jesus' Word is clear even in the fog of the war campaign; there is no confusion. David said, *"Your word is a lamp to my feet and a light to my path"* (Psalm 119:105). To have the influence of the ***righteous*** attribute matters. One must seek this attribute and acquire it by striving to master the other six attributes and the element of <u>love</u> in one's life. Then God, with His <u>grace</u>, will decide one's outcome with the achievement of the ***righteous*** attribute. Thus, in another parable, Jesus spoke of a Pharisee and the tax collector who were both praying to God in the same temple. The Pharisee, claiming **righteousness** for himself, prayed to God by pointing out how clean he was and simultaneously pointing out the unclean state of the tax collector. Jesus said of this situation that there are some people who *"...trusted in themselves that they were **righteous**, and despised others..."* (Luke 18:9). Clearly, the Pharisee lacked the ***righteous*** attribute's influence. He publicly wore a masquerade. Inwardly, the influences of the negative forces of the war campaign led him.

Before Jesus left the earth to return to His father in heaven, He left the world with three critical Truths that pertain to the influence of the ***righteous*** attribute. All three of these Truths centered on the facts that He had this attribute; He had the power to give and use it; and one could acquire it and its power through the Gospel He left behind.

> "When the Son of Man comes in His glory, and all the holy angels with Him, then He will sit on the throne of His glory. All the nations will be gathered before Him, and He will separate them one from another, as a shepherd divides his sheep from the goats. And He will set the <u>sheep on His right hand</u>, but the <u>goats on the left</u>"

"Then He will also say to those on the left hand, 'Depart from Me, you cursed, into the everlasting fire prepared for the devil and his angels: for I was hungry and you gave Me no food; I was thirsty and you gave Me no drink; I was a stranger and you did not take Me in, naked and you did not clothe Me, sick and in prison and you did not visit Me.' "Then they also will answer Him, saying, 'Lord, when did we see You hungry or thirsty or a stranger or naked or sick or in prison, and did not minister to You?' Then He will answer them, saying, 'Assuredly, I say to you, inasmuch as you did not do it to one of the least of these, you did not do it to Me.'"	"Then the King will say to those on His right hand, 'Come, you blessed of My Father, inherit the kingdom prepared for you from the foundation of the world: for I was hungry and you gave Me food; I was thirsty and you gave Me drink; I was a stranger and you took Me in; I was naked and you clothed Me; I was sick and you visited Me; I was in prison and you came to Me.' "Then the **righteous** will answer Him, saying, 'Lord, when did we see You hungry and feed You, or thirsty and give You drink? When did we see You a stranger and take You in, or naked and clothe You? Or when did we see You sick, or in prison, and come to You?' And the King will answer and say to them, 'Assuredly, I say to you, inasmuch as you did it to one of the least of these My brethren, you did it to Me.'"
"And these will go away into everlasting punishment..."	"...but the **righteous** into eternal life."

Figure 25: The Separation of the Righteous and the Wicked

Look closely at these three truths from Jesus Himself:

- First, He told His disciples, "*I can of Myself do nothing. As I hear, I judge; and My judgment is **righteous**, because I do not seek My own will but the will of the Father who sent Me*" (John 5:30)

- Second, based on the above statement and what He taught His disciples about "**righteous** judgment," He taught them how to use the same **righteous** judgment when dealing with the world. Jesus taught, "*Do not judge according to appearance, but judge with **righteous** judgment*" (John 7:24)

- Thirdly, after Jesus taught His disciples about **righteous** judgment, He departed and sent the Holy Spirit back to them to give them the strength, conviction, and understanding to both teach and set in writing everything necessary for life, to understand the influence of the **righteous** attribute, and to know the necessity of **righteous** judgment. Jesus told His disciples, "*...I will send Him to you. And when He has come, He will convict the world of sin, and of **righteousness**, and of judgment: of sin, because they do not believe in Me; of **righteousness**, because I go to My Father and you see Me no more; of judgment, because the ruler of this world is judged*" (John 16:5-11)

On the Day of Pentecost, the Holy Spirit came into the world and rested on the disciples just as Jesus had said according to Acts 2:1-4. An important thought for one to consider is as the Holy Spirit entered the earth, the negative attributes of the war campaign intensified their efforts to influence mankind. The negative forces not only influenced people not to listen, but also to violently reject and block others from hearing the Gospel message of Jesus Christ. Even as the Holy Spirit arrived, and people were able to witness its power based on the events occurring in Acts 2:5-12, the Biblical record documented, "*Others mocking said, "They are full of new wine."*" (Acts 2:13). I submit this mocking was part of the fog created by the negative forces of the campaign to stir up ridicule, confusion, and keep as many people as possible in darkness. One evidence to support this point involved Paul, who had the influence of the **righteous** attribute and who confronted a man who was influenced by the wicked attribute. Their encounter reflected the day-to-day struggle between the positive and negative forces in spiritual warfare. The Biblical record documented that Sergius Paulus, the proconsul on the island of Paphos an intelligent man, called for Barnabas and Paul so that he could hear the Word of God according to Acts 13:6-8. However, Sergius Paulus had a sorcerer and false prophet who worked for him. This man was a Jew named Bar-Jesus, also translated as Elymas according to Acts 13:6. The Biblical record documented that Elymas tried to stop Barnabas and Paul from seeing Sergius Paulus. In fact, the Biblical record documented that Elymas, "*withstood them, seeking to turn the proconsul away from the faith*" (Acts 13:8). Thus, this is where one learns that the influence of the **righteous** attribute is far more powerful than the influence of the wicked attribute. The Bible says, "*Then Saul, who also is called Paul, filled with the Holy Spirit, looked intently at him and said, "O full of all deceit and all fraud, you son of the devil, you enemy of all **righteousness**, will you not cease perverting the straight ways of the Lord? And now, indeed, the hand of the Lord is upon you, and you shall be blind, not seeing the sun for a time." And immediately a dark mist fell on him, and he went around seeking someone to lead him by the hand. Then the proconsul believed, when he saw what had been done, being astonished at the teaching of the Lord*" (Acts 13:9-12). The gem in this incident is one learns that there are people in the world that are "*enemies of all **righteousness**.*" But more important is the knowledge that prayer of one influenced by the **righteous** attribute today has power to stop sinful activity. To keep the perspective, Paul did not blind Elymas. God did as He responded to Paul's prayer. God responded because of Paul's **righteousness**.

Paul also reasoned with others about the influence of the **righteous** attribute and the Gospel of Jesus Christ. The Bible documented that he, "*reasoned about **righteousness**, self-control, and the judgment to come*" with Felix, the governor of Caesarea (Acts 23:23-24), in Acts 24:10-21. However, the Biblical record also documented that, "*...Felix was afraid and answered, "Go away for now; when I have a convenient time I will call for you. Meanwhile he also hoped that money would be given him by Paul, that he might release him. Therefore* *he sent for him more often and conversed with him.* " (Acts 24:25-26). Paul also reasoned with the Jewish leadership over the influence of the ***righteous*** attribute because they placed the act of circumcision above what Jesus taught. Romans 2:25-29 documents Paul's debate. One should look closely at how the ***righteous*** attribute's influence and the inner spirit are connected. Paul told them,

> *"...circumcision is indeed profitable if you keep the law; but if you are a breaker of the law, your circumcision has become uncircumcision. Therefore, if an uncircumcised man keeps the **righteous** requirements of the law, will not his uncircumcision be counted as circumcision? And will not the physically uncircumcised, if he fulfills the law, judge you who, even with your written code and circumcision, are a transgressor of the law? For he is not a Jew who is one outwardly, nor is circumcision that which is outward in the flesh; but he is a Jew who is one inwardly; and circumcision is that of the heart, in the Spirit, not in the letter; whose praise is not from men but from God"*

Still further in the Biblical record, the Holy Spirit led Paul to document, *"Circumcision is nothing and uncircumcision is nothing, but keeping the commandments of God is what matters"* (1 Corinthians 7:19). He explained to the Jews, and for one's knowledge today, that a person by their own doing cannot achieve ***righteousness.*** Paul documented, *"As it is written: "There is none **righteous**, no, not one..."* (Romans 3:10). Paul provided the reason in Romans 3:19-26. One really needs to grasp this and strive to allow BTT for understanding God's plan and how the ***righteous*** attribute fits. The Holy Spirit inspired Paul to document the following words:

> *"Now we know that whatever the law says, it says to those who are under the law, that every mouth may be stopped, and all the world may become guilty before God. Therefore by the deeds of the law no flesh will be <u>justified</u> in His sight, for by the law is the knowledge of sin. But now the **righteousness** of God apart from the law is revealed, being witnessed by the Law and the Prophets, even the **righteousness** of God, through faith in Jesus Christ, to all and on all who believe. For there is no difference; for all have sinned and fall short of the glory of God, being <u>justified</u> freely by His <u>grace</u> through the redemption that is in Christ Jesus, whom God set forth as a propitiation by His blood, through faith, to demonstrate His **righteousness**, because in His forbearance God had passed over the sins that were previously committed, to demonstrate at the present time His **righteousness**, that He might be just and the justifier of the one who has faith in Jesus."*

Paul concluded his entire Biblical argument by saying that not all the things we can now read about Abraham of the Old Testament were just for Abraham's sake. Paul wrote, *"Now it was not written for his sake alone that it was imputed to him, but also for us. It shall be imputed to us who believe in Him who raised up Jesus our Lord from the dead, who was delivered up because of our offenses, and was raised because of our justification*" (Romans 4:23-25). BTT allows one to see that this important knowledge reinforces the need to strive to acquire the influence of the ***righteous*** attribute. God recognizes this attribute and one must have it on the day of salvation.

Paul documented that the influence of the ***righteous*** attribute comes from God and is available as a free gift for those who are obedient to His Word. Paul illustrated the power of this attribute by comparing Jesus' obedience and Adam's disobedience in the Garden of Eden. While speaking of these two men, he said of Adam, "*...if by the one man's offense death reigned through the one, much more those who receive abundance of <u>grace</u> and of the gift of **righteousness** will reign in life through the One, Jesus Christ.) Therefore, as through one man's offense judgment came to all men, resulting in condemnation, even so through one Man's **righteous** act the free gift came to all men, resulting in justification of life. For as by one man's disobedience many were made sinners, so also by one Man's obedience many will be made **righteous**.* (Romans 5:17-19). BTT allows one to see that the influence of the ***righteous*** attribute is a free gift from God that comes through Jesus Christ. But to gain it, one must be obedient. To what, one might ask? To the Gospel of Jesus Christ. Jesus came to earth and left examples of obedience and left His Holy Word to the apostles to record for humanity. His example included demonstrations of the influence of all the positive attributes combined with <u>love</u>. This obedience places one on the right path for achieving the gift of ***righteousness***. God's <u>grace</u> then covers everything in between while one is striving to achieve ***righteousness***. Going back to Romans 5:17-19, Paul wanted everyone to understand that when one truly allows Jesus to dominate in one's life, "*...those who receive abundance of <u>grace</u> and of the gift of **righteousness** will reign in life through the One, Jesus Christ...*" (Romans 5:17). Hence, the Bible records by Christ's sacrifice and "*...obedience many will be made **righteous***" (Romans 5:19). Paul concludes by stating, "*...where sin abounded, <u>grace</u> abounded much more, so that as sin reigned in death, even so <u>grace</u> might reign through **righteousness** to eternal life through Jesus Christ our Lord*" (Romans 5:20-21). In other words, God's <u>grace</u> and the pursuit of the ***righteous*** attribute are spiritually joined. Please do not listen to false teachers who want to convince the world that God's <u>grace</u> covers sinners as they continue to live a life of sinful activity. This false teaching has deceived many in the religious community who are dying on the spiritual battlefield of the war campaign. God desires everyone to leave his or her life of sin and hear the Word of His Son Jesus Christ. God desires one to live, "*...as obedient children, not conforming yourselves to the former <u>lusts</u>, as in your ignorance; but as He who called you is holy, you also be holy in all your conduct, because it is written, "Be holy, for I am holy."* (1 Peter 1:14-16). This means hearing the Truth and accepting it, which leads one to <u>baptism</u> and putting on Christ in one's life. With Christ, the ***right*** tools, and striving for the ***righteous*** attribute, then and only then does God's <u>grace</u> protect one in the spiritual war. The negative forces have distorted this wisdom through the fog of the war campaign. One does not get God's <u>grace</u> just for living; one must live obediently to His Word.

Further, Paul documented how God's <u>grace</u> and the influence of the ***righteous*** attribute work within one's inner spirit to guide one through the battles of spiritual warfare. He documented in Romans 8:2-11:

> *"For the law of the Spirit of life in Christ Jesus has made me free from the law of sin and death. For what the law could not do in that it was weak through the flesh, God did by sending His own Son in the likeness of sinful flesh, on account of sin: He condemned sin in the flesh, that the **righteous** requirement of the law might be fulfilled in us who do not walk according to the flesh but according to the Spirit. For those who live according to the flesh set their minds on the things of the flesh, but those who live according to the Spirit, the things of the Spirit. For to be carnally minded is death, but to be spiritually minded is life and peace. Because the carnal mind is enmity against God; for it is not subject to the law of God, nor indeed can be. So then, those who are in the flesh cannot please God. But you are not in the flesh but in the Spirit, if indeed the Spirit of God dwells in you. Now if anyone does not have the Spirit of Christ, he is not His. And if Christ is in you, the body is dead because of sin, but the Spirit is life because of **righteousness**. But if the Spirit of Him who raised Jesus from the dead dwells in you, He who raised Christ from the dead will also give life to your mortal bodies through His Spirit who dwells in you"*

BTT allows one to see that the influence of the **righteous** attribute is only available when one allows the Spirit of Jesus to dwell in one's inner spirit. Once again, from the above, Paul documented, *"...if Christ is in you, the body is dead because of sin, but the Spirit is life because of **righteousness**. But if the Spirit of Him who raised Jesus from the dead dwells in you, He who raised Christ from the dead will also give life to your mortal bodies through His Spirit who dwells in you"* (Romans 8:10-11). The Holy Spirit confirmed this fact by providing John with three **righteous** statements for one's learning today. John documented:

- *"If you know that He is **righteous**, you know that everyone who practices **righteousness** is born of Him"* (1 John 2:29)

- *"...let no one deceive you. He who practices **righteousness** is **righteous**, just as He is **righteous**"* (1 John 3:7)

- *"In this the children of God and the children of the devil are manifest: Whoever does not practice **righteousness** is not of God, nor is he who does not love his brother"* (1 John 3:10)

Based on these statements, Paul did everything he could to persuade the Jews about Jesus, His message, and the truth about the influence of the **righteous** attribute. Applicable to the religious condition of the Jews, both then and today, the Holy Spirit led Paul to document these pointed words in Romans 9:30-33 and 10:1-4:

> *"What shall we say then? That Gentiles, who did not pursue **righteousness**, have attained to **righteousness**, even the **righteousness** of faith; but Israel, pursuing the law of **righteousness**,*

*has not attained to the law of **righteousness**. Why? Because they did not seek it by faith, but as it were, by the works of the law. For they stumbled at that stumbling stone. As it is written: "Behold, I lay in Zion a stumbling stone and rock of offense, and whoever believes on Him will not be put to shame." Brethren, my heart's desire and prayer to God for Israel is that they may be saved. For I bear them witness that they have a zeal for God, but not according to knowledge. For they being ignorant of God's **righteousness**, and seeking to establish their own **righteousness**, have not submitted to the **righteousness** of God. For Christ is the end of the law for **righteousness** to everyone who believes"*

Peter used this reasoning to say that the Jews, "*...stumble, being disobedient to the word, to which they also were appointed*" (1 Peter 2:8), whereas to the Christian, "*But you are a chosen generation, a royal priesthood, a holy nation, His own special people, that you may proclaim the praises of Him who called you out of darkness into His marvelous light...*" (1 Peter 2:9). Paul further explained that the apostles were given the honor to teach the Gospel of Jesus Christ. The apostles' efforts provided the wisdom for everyone to acquire the influence of the **righteous** attribute through reconciliation to God, by accepting His Son Jesus Christ. Paul wrote, "*Now then, we are ambassadors for Christ, as though God were pleading through us: we implore you on Christ's behalf, be reconciled to God. For He made Him who knew no sin to be sin for us, that we might become the **righteousness** of God in Him*" (2 Corinthians 5:21). Embedded in Paul's statement is the importance for pursuing the **righteous** attribute. Jesus' death gave everyone the ability to achieve **righteousness** through Him. BTT allows one to see that the ability to achieve **righteousness** through Christ begins with one's reconciliation to God, by accepting His Son Jesus Christ. Reconciliation occurs with <u>baptism</u> which places one in Christ and opens the spiritual door for **righteousness**. Yes, there is an order to things in life and God has established it.

BTT allows one to see that the negative forces of the war campaign are actively keeping humanity from a reconciliation with God. Throughout history, the negative forces have employed false apostles, and deceitful religious workers who "*...transforming themselves into apostles of Christ. And no wonder! For Satan himself transforms himself into an angel of light. Therefore it is no great thing if his ministers also transform themselves into ministers of **righteousness**, whose end will be according to their works*" (2 Corinthians 11:12-15). These false ministers, often ignorant of the fact that they are being used by **deceiving spirits**, espouse doctrines of demons (1 Timothy 4:1). These ancient doctrines are powerful enough to cause even people who have found Christ to stumble. Hence, Paul warned, "*We then, as workers together with Him also plead with you not to receive the <u>grace</u> of God in vain*" (2 Corinthians 6:1). For this reason, <u>discernment</u> and BTT are key to surviving the war campaign.

In fact, Peter wrote about the false teachers and the relationship between them and the influence of the **righteous** attribute. He documented that false teachers, under the influence of the negative forces of the campaign would, "*...secretly bring in destructive heresies, even denying the Lord who bought them, and bring on themselves swift destruction. And many will follow their destructive ways, because of whom the way of truth will be blasphemed. By* *covetousness they will exploit you with deceptive words; for a long time their judgment has not been idle, and their destruction does not slumber"* (2 Peter 2:1-3). In other words, **false** teacher's words, actions, and behaviors are directly opposite of a person influenced by the **righteous** attribute. He further documented that they:

- [are] *"...like natural brute beasts made to be caught and destroyed, speak evil of the things they do not understand, and will utterly perish in their own corruption, and will receive the wages of unrighteousness, as those who count it pleasure to carouse in the daytime. They are spots and blemishes, carousing in their own deceptions while they feast with you, having eyes full of adultery and that cannot cease from sin, enticing unstable souls. They have a heart trained in covetous practices, and are accursed children"* (2 Peter 2:12-14)

- *"...have forsaken the **right** way and gone astray, following the way of Balaam the son of Beor, who loved the wages of unrighteousness; but he was rebuked for his iniquity..."* (2 Peter 2:15-16)

- *"...are wells without water, clouds carried by a tempest, for whom is reserved the blackness of darkness forever. For when they speak great swelling words of emptiness, they allure through the lusts of the flesh, through lewdness, the ones who have actually escaped from those who live in error. While they promise them liberty, they themselves are slaves of corruption; for by whom a person is overcome, by him also he is brought into bondage. For if, after they have escaped the pollutions of the world through the knowledge of the Lord and Savior Jesus Christ, they are again entangled in them and overcome, the latter end is worse for them than the beginning. For it would have been better for them not to have known the way of **righteousness**, than having known it, to turn from the holy commandment delivered to them"* (2 Peter 2:17-21)

BTT allows one to see that Paul was conscious of the sacrifice it took to acquire the influence of the **righteous** attribute. He understood its worth and put things in perspective when he documented, *"Yet indeed I also count all things loss for the excellence of the knowledge of Christ Jesus my Lord, for whom I have suffered the loss of all things, and count them as rubbish, that I may gain Christ and be found in Him, not having my own **righteousness**, which is from the law, but that which is through faith in Christ, the **righteousness** which is from God by faith..."* (Philippians 3:8-9). In other words, the influence of the **righteous** attribute, starting with the influence of the faith attribute and the indwelling Spirit of Jesus Christ, is worth the sacrifice of everything worldly. Nothing else is important because everything will be lost if one does not survive spiritual warfare. As one strives to live a life of obedience to God's Word and acquire the **righteous** attribute, one will be able to say like Paul, *"...there is laid up for me the crown of **righteousness**, which the Lord, the **righteous** Judge, will give to me on that Day, and not to me only but also to all who have loved His appearing"* (2 Timothy 4:8).

To encourage and support one through the tough times of spiritual warfare, the apostles documented these final pearls of wisdom about the influence of the **righteous** attribute. By the inspiration and power of the Holy Spirit, they wrote for our learning:

The Gospel of Christ is the power of God to salvation for everyone who believes. The Biblical record declares "...the **righteousness** of God is revealed from faith to faith; as it is written, "The just shall live by faith" (Romans 1:16-17)	"...do not present your members as instruments of unrighteousness to sin, but present yourselves to God as being alive from the dead, and your members as instruments of **righteousness** to God" (Romans 6:13)	"...the kingdom of God is not eating and drinking, but **righteousness** and peace and joy in the Holy Spirit. For he who serves Christ in these things is acceptable to God and approved by men" (Romans 14:17-18)
"For with the heart one believes unto **righteousness**, and with the mouth confession is made unto salvation" (Romans 10:10)	"For scarcely for a **righteous** man will one die; yet perhaps for a good man someone would even dare to die" (Romans 5:7)	"...we, according to His promise, look for new heavens and a new earth in which **righteousness** dwells" (2 Peter 3:13)
"...God shows no partiality. But in every nation whoever fears Him and works **righteous-ness** is accepted by Him" (Acts 10:35)	"Awake to **righteousness**, and do not sin; for some do not have the knowledge of God... (1 Corinthians 15:34)	Be "...filled with the fruits of **righteousness** which are by Jesus Christ, to the glory and praise of God" (Philippians 1:11)
"Truly, these times of ignorance God overlooked, but now commands all men everywhere to repent, because He has appointed a day on which He will judge the world in **righteousness** by the Man whom He has ordained. He has given assurance of this to all by raising Him from the dead." (Acts 17:30-31)	"...Walk as children of light (for the fruit of the Spirit is in all goodness, **righteousness**, and truth), finding out what is acceptable to the Lord. And have no fellowship with the unfruitful works of darkness, but rather expose them. For it is shameful even to speak of those things which are done by them in secret" (Ephesians 5:8-12)	"For the grace of God that brings salvation has appeared to all men, teaching us that, denying ungodliness and worldly lusts, we should live soberly, **righteously**, and godly in the present age, looking for the blessed hope and glorious appearing of our great God and Savior Jesus Christ..." (Titus 2:11-14)
"...put on the breastplate of **righteousness**..." (Ephesians 6:14)	"Now the fruit of **righteousness** is sown in peace by those who make peace" (James 3:18)	
"...be renewed in the spirit of your mind, and that you put on the new man which was created according to God, in true **righteousness** and holiness." (Ephesians 4:17-24)	"My little children, these things I write to you, so that you may not sin. And if anyone sins, we have an Advocate with the Father, Jesus Christ the **righteous**" (1 John 2:1)	"...let every man be swift to hear, slow to speak, slow to wrath; for the wrath of man does not produce the **righteousness** of God" (James 1:20)
Paul warned Timothy about "But you, O man of God, flee these things and pursue **righteousness**, godliness,	"Do not seal the words of the prophecy of this book, for the time is at hand. He who is unjust, let him be	"For everyone who partakes only of milk is unskilled in the word of **righteousness**, for he is a

faith, _love, patience, gentleness_" (1 Timothy 6:9-11).Flee, those who desire to be rich fall, _foolish and harmful lusts, straying from the faith in their_ greediness.	unjust still; he who is filthy, let him be filthy still; he who is **righteous**, let him be **righteous** still; he who is holy, let him be holy still" (Revelation 22:10-11)	babe. But solid food belongs to those who are of full age, that is, those who by reason of use have their senses exercised to _discern_ both good and evil" (Hebrews 5:13-14)
"Do you not know that to whom you present yourselves slaves to obey, you are that one's slaves whom you obey, whether of sin leading to death, or of obedience leading to **righteousness**?" (Romans 6:16)	"Now no chastening seems to be joyful for the present, but painful; nevertheless, afterward it yields the _peaceable_ fruit of **righteousness** to those who have been trained by it" (Hebrews 12:11)	"But even if you should suffer for **righteousness**' sake, you are blessed...For it is better, if it is the will of God, to suffer for doing good than for doing evil" (1 Peter 3:14-17)
"...the eyes of the Lord are on the **righteous**, and His ears are open to their prayers; but the face of the Lord is against those who do evil" (1 Peter 3:12)	"Flee also youthful _lusts_; but pursue **righteousness**, faith, _love, peace_ with those who call on the Lord out of a pure heart" (2 Timothy 2:22)	"Now "If the **righteous** one is scarcely saved, where will the ungodly and the sinner appear?" (1 Peter 4:18)
"...the law is good if one uses it lawfully, knowing this: the law is not made for a **righteous** person, but for "...the lawless, insubordinate, ungodly, sinners, unholy, profane, murderers, manslayers, fornicators, sodomites, kidnappers, liars, perjurers, and any other thing that is contrary to sound doctrine, according to the glorious gospel of the blessed God" (1 Timothy 1:8-11)	"Do not be unequally yoked together with unbelievers. For what fellowship has **righteousness** with lawlessness? And what communion has light with darkness?" (2 Corinthians 6:14). Remember, the Bible documented, "...Come out from among them and be separate, says the Lord. Do not touch what is unclean, and I will receive you" (Roman 6:17; Isaiah 52:11)	"...having been set free from sin, you became slaves of **righteousness**. I speak in human terms because of the weakness of your flesh. For just as you presented your members as slaves of uncleanness, and of lawlessness leading to more lawlessness, so now present your members as slaves of **righteousness** for holiness. For when you were slaves of sin, you were free in regard to **righteousness**" (Romans 6:18-20)
"Confess your trespasses to one another, and pray for one another, that you may be healed. The effective, fervent prayer of a **righteous** man avails much" (James 5:16)	"All Scripture is given by inspiration of God, and is profitable for doctrine, for reproof, for correction, for instruction in **righteousness**, that the man of God may be complete, thoroughly equipped for every good work" (2 Timothy 3:16-17)	When Jesus was reviled, He "...did not revile in return; when He suffered, He did not threaten, but committed Himself to Him who judges **righteously**; who Himself bore our sins in His own body on the tree, that we, having died to sins, might live for **righteousness**—by

		whose stripes you were healed" (1 Peter 2:24)

Table 124: More Pearls of Wisdom Concerning the Righteous Attribute

    To close out this chapter on the ***righteous*** attribute, the Psalmist provided two facts that one can always hold on to concerning this attribute. He documented, "*...For God is with the generation of the **righteous***" (Psalm 14:5), and "*...the salvation of the **righteous** is from the Lord; He is their strength in the time of trouble. And the Lord shall help them and deliver them; He shall deliver them from the wicked, and save them, because they trust in Him*" (Psalm 37:39-40). Moreover, the Psalmist documented that God, "*...preserves the souls of His saints; He delivers them out of the hand of the wicked*" (Psalm 97:10). The ***righteous*** are God's saints. For all who seek the influence of this attribute, this is a reminder and hope that throughout the course of the war campaign, all who strive to acquire the full measure of the ***righteous*** attribute have the Lord on their side. For this reason, people striving to live ***righteously*** never give up the good fight. Even under direct attack by the adversary, they stand even stronger to encourage others more. They never give up! They cannot. For in their inner spirits, they know what is at stake in the war campaign - souls.

CHAPTER VII: The Harvest

"The harvest truly is plentiful, but the laborers are few."

~ Matthew 9:37

INTRODUCTION

This chapter is dedicated to eight prominent categories identified by Solomon and the apostles. These eight categories, found among the **harvest**, play a significant role in the balance of the campaign. From these categories, one will learn two important lessons: First, how the people in the categories impact spiritual warfare and the war campaign and second; why their conversions to either the positive or the negative side of the campaign are so important. One may recall from chapter IV of this book, it is the **harvest** on the battlefield that provides the physical resources and support to the campaign. Those resources include manpower, finances, logistics, maintenance, guidance and instruction, and consistent leadership. One will learn in this chapter that the behavior and actions of every single person makes a difference in the campaign. As one reads each section dedicated to these categories, their roles will become very clear when influenced by either the positive or negative attributes.

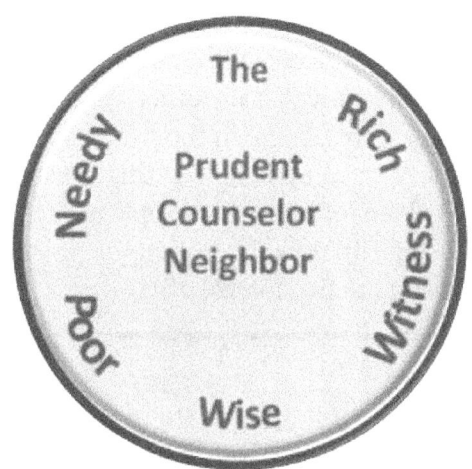

Figure 26: Categories of the Harvest

Jesus made a fascinating statement that I believe was a reference to the war campaign. The Biblical record documented, "*...Jesus went about all the cities and villages, teaching in their synagogues, preaching the gospel of the kingdom, and healing every sickness and every disease among the people. But when He saw the multitudes, He was moved with compassion for them, because they were weary and scattered, like sheep having no shepherd. Then He said to His disciples, "The* **harvest** *truly is plentiful, but the laborers are few. Therefore pray the Lord of the* **harvest** *to send out laborers into His* **harvest**" (Matthew 9:35-38). Luke also documented that, "*...the Lord appointed seventy others also, and sent them two by two before His face into every city and place where He Himself was about to go. Then He said to them, "The* **harvest** *truly is great, but the laborers are few; therefore pray the Lord of the* **harvest** *to send out laborers into His* **harvest**. *Go your way; behold, I send you out as lambs among wolves*" (Luke 10:1-3). From Jesus' statement, and His reference of the "**harvest**," one can unmistakably see that He was referring to people worldwide in need of His Gospel message. **Figure 26** captures some of the categories that people in the **harvest** can find themselves in.

Thanks to the writers of the Biblical record, the definition of the **harvest** is even more refined through the lens of the war campaign. BTT allows one to see that the **harvest** not only represents people, but through the lens of BTT, one can see the **harvest** contains different categories of people. It is analogous to a farmer's land that contains different crops growing on different parts of the farm prior to a **harvest**. Or it is like an army made up of different categories of soldiers, i.e. cavalry, infantry, artillery, etc.... In both analogies, an observer would see a field to **harvest** or an army to fight independent of what makes up either one. Hence, Jesus simply identified the **harvest** to His disciples without discriminating who was in it.

Please remember from the introduction of this book, the **harvest** has many more categories than I have placed in this chapter. However, the few selected will provide one a basic understanding of the complexity of the **harvest**. These categories were never meant to be a source for division but simple descriptors of characteristics. Unfortunately, spiritual warfare and fog has deceived humanity. Satan, using spiritual warfare, turned the categories of the **harvest** against each other. Thus, as the positive or the negative attributes influence the categories of people in the **harvest**, they in turn support either the positive or negative forces of the war campaign. For this reason, both sides of the campaign are locked in a spiritual struggle to influence the people in each of the categories. **Figure 27** depicts the delicate balance of the spiritual fight between the positive and negative forces with the people of the **harvest** in between the two forces.

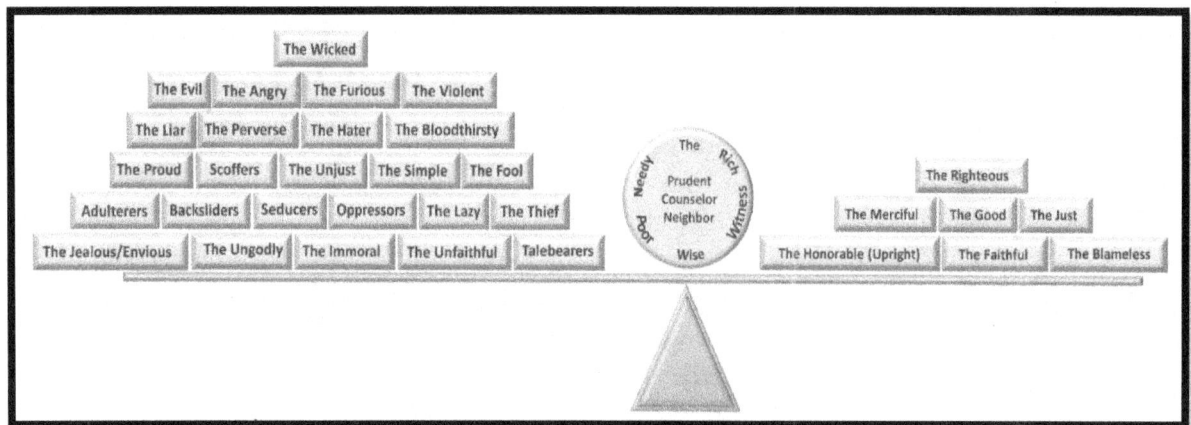

Figure 27: The Balancing Scale of Spiritual Warfare

BTT allows one to see that there are many categories of people in the **harvest**. For example, on the physical side of life, there are leaders and followers, men and a women, masters and slaves, fathers and mothers, parents and children, married and single and widows, etc.... On the spiritual side of life, there are saints and sinners, the saved and the lost, believers and nonbelievers, and many more. Thus, BTT allows one to see that each category has its place in the Biblical record. I will leave this research for another time. However as stated earlier, God's categories were not meant as tools of division. Mankind influenced by the negative attributes created worldly division. Even religious categories such as Evangelicals, Protestants, Catholics, Mormons, Buddhist, Hindus, Muslims, and on and on are not Biblical but manmade divisions born out of spiritual warfare. The Holy Spirit inspired Paul to document for one's knowledge, *"There is one body and one Spirit, just as you were called in one hope of your calling; one Lord, one faith, one baptism; one God and Father of all, who is above all, and through all, and in you all"* (Ephesians 4:4-6). BTT allows one to see that God's categories define the nature of a person and does not divide from the oneness He established. Worldly division is from sin. In fact, when it comes to the oneness of Jesus' kingdom, He Himself stated, *"...Every kingdom divided against itself is brought to desolation, and every city or house divided against itself will not stand"* (Matthew 12:25). In the context of the war campaign, every impersonator of Christ's church and any belief not of Christ, will fail. But until the failure occurs, man's traditions, false practices, and misunderstandings of God's Word will continue to cause people to be lost in the fog of the war campaign until Jesus intervenes with His return. Jesus simply said, "*The* **harvest** *is plentiful, but the labors are few.*" The numbers of the positive forces, especially those striving to acquire the full measure of the righteous attribute, are few.

    For this chapter of the book, each category will be in **bold** font. The positive or negative attribute influencing the category will remain in a ***bold italic*** font. All spiritual elements will retain their double <u>underlined</u>. This method will help one easily concentrate on the point being made about the person in the category.

The **Neighbor category:** Every living person on earth falls into this category. It is one of the most important categories to understand in the **harvest** because it impacts every boundary of the spiritual battlefield. In fact, improper understanding of this category cost people their souls. Even some Christians are compromised because of their lack of understanding of people who make up the **neighbor** category.

Jesus defined who existed in the **neighbor** category and the rest of the Biblical record documented the details necessary for understanding the category. In the Book of Luke, a lawyer confronted Jesus in an attempt to test Him on the subject of the **neighbor.** The conversation started when the lawyer asked "*Teacher, what shall I do to inherit eternal life?*" (Luke 10:25), to which Jesus asked him, "*What is written in the law? What is your reading of it?*" (Luke 10:26). The lawyer responded with "*You shall love the Lord your God with all your heart, with all your soul, with all your strength, and with all your mind,' and 'your **neighbor** as yourself*" according to Luke 10:27. Jesus told the lawyer he was correct. However, the lawyer wanted to justify himself in the eyes of Jesus. Thus, the lawyer went on to ask, "*And who is my **neighbor**?*" (Luke 10:29). BTT allows one to see that with Jesus's response, one can gain the full definition of the people in the **neighbor** category. Jesus, responded to the lawyer with an illustration of a man who was beaten, robbed, and left for dead on the side of the road by thieves. He explained that a priest and Levite, of whom people considered ***righteous***, saw this beaten man. Separately they both passed by and ignored the man. However, a Samaritan of whom the Jews considered unclean, saw the man and "*...had compassion...*" (Luke 10:33). This Samaritan "*...bandaged the man wounds, set him on his own animal, brought him to an inn, and took care of him, gave them to the innkeeper two denarii when he departed, and told the innkeeper to, 'Take care of him; and whatever more you spend, when I come again, I will repay you'*" (Luke 10:34-35). At the end of this response, Jesus then asked the scribe "*who was the **neighbor**?*" The lawyer replied, "*...He who showed **mercy** on him.*" Then Jesus said to him, "*Go and do likewise.*" (Luke 10:34-35).

From this whole discourse, if one steps back to observe the whole incident from the macro level, one can see that everyone involved had the responsibility for being each other's **neighbor**. But when one comes down to the micro level, where spiritual warfare is taking place and the positive or negative attributes have had an opportunity to influence everyone involved, the details of the people in the **neighbor** category are exposed. The secular community has no clue of who is in the **neighbor** category until they are taught. In the religious community, improper teaching of the people in the **neighbor** category has given way to cognitive boundaries, which then become physical boundaries of race, color, and gender across the spiritual battlefield. However, within the Christian community, one understands every member of God's creation is a potential brother or sister in Christ and therefore one's **neighbor**. Hence, no discrimination, separation, or prejudice can be tolerated because God views this behavior as sin. God said so in His written Word. The Christian community understands that Christ's kingdom consists of all races and nationality; thus, everyone is part of the **neighbor** category itself. If not, the negative forces of the war campaign will prevail through the element of <u>strife</u> and division. For ***just*** as John documented, "*If someone says, "I <u>love</u> God," and **hates** his brother, he is a <u>liar</u>; for he who does not <u>love</u> his brother whom he has seen, how can he <u>love</u>*

God whom he has not seen?" (1 John 4:20), the same principle applies to everyone in the **neighbor** category. Once again, every **neighbor** is a potential brother or sister in Christ and Christians cannot allow the ***hater*** attribute, or any other negative attribute, to rob him or her of this relationship. First John 4:20 broadly states that one cannot sincerely <u>love</u> God while harboring **hate** for one's **neighbor** who one can physically see. The Scripture is not about proximity; it is about truth and genuine <u>love</u>; the relationship the ***hater*** attribute desires to destroy. When the influence of the positive or negative attributes affect a person, one will either look at one of God's human creations with <u>love</u> or disdain. It does not matter if that person is next door, on the other side of a land-border, or overseas in another country; in this world, we are all **neighbors**. With this understanding of who the **neighbor** is, now consider what the **neighbor** does.

One must understand the role of people in the **neighbor** category. The Spirit of wisdom told Solomon, "*Do not devise **evil** against your **neighbor**, for he dwells by you for safety's sake*" (Proverbs 3:29). One cannot emphasize the importance of this statement enough. People in the **neighbor** category play a vital role in both physical protection, as well as spiritual protection, against the forces unleashed in the war campaign. A healthy relationship among **neighbors** allows families to keep watch from others attempting to bring harm. If one takes the time to meditate on the application of this statement, one would find it true in every scenario of one's life, with the understanding that there are both ***good*** and bad **neighbors**. However, one must keep in mind that it is not the person, it is the influence of the positive or negative attributes in this or her life that leads them in a ***good*** or bad direction. ***False*** teachers dilute this Truth when they are void of God's Word. They become self-centered to which the Spirit of wisdom told Solomon, "*He who is <u>devoid of wisdom</u> **despises** his **neighbor**, but a man of understanding holds his peace*" (Proverbs 11:12). Still further Wisdom shared, "*He who **despises** his **neighbor** sins...*" (Proverbs 14:21). To this end, here are some of the many pearls of wisdom that Solomon learned about the **neighbor** category when the negative attribute's influences are involved. Solomon documented:

"*The hypocrite with his mouth destroys his **neighbor**...*" (Proverbs 11:9)	"*A man who **flatters** his **neighbor** spreads a net for his feet*" (Proverbs 29:5)
"*The poor man is **hated** even by his own **neighbor**, but the rich has many friends*" (Proverbs 14:20)	"*A **violent** man entices his **neighbor**, and leads him in a way that is not **good***" (Proverbs 16:29)
"*Can a man take fire to his bosom, and his clothes not be burned? Can one walk on hot coals, and his feet not be seared? So is he who goes in to his **neighbor's** wife; whoever touches her <u>shall not be innocent</u>*" (Proverbs 6:27-29)	"*Like a madman who throws firebrands, arrows, and death, is the man who **deceives** his **neighbor**, and says, "I was only joking!"*" (Proverbs 26:18-19)
"*The soul of the **wicked** desires **evil**; his **neighbor** finds no favor in his eyes*" (Proverbs 21:10)	"*A man who bears **false witness** against his **neighbor** is like a club, a sword, and a sharp arrow*" (Proverbs 25:18)

Table 125: The Negative Attribute's Influence on People in the Neighbor Category

In contrast, Solomon documented several pearls of wisdom that one must beware of to maintain a healthy relationship with one's **neighbor**. These pearls are only understandable when the influences of the positive attributes are present in one's inner spirit. Solomon documented:

*"Do not withhold **good** from those to whom it is due, when it is in the power of your hand to do so. Do not say to your **neighbor**, "Go, and come back, and tomorrow I will give it," when you have it with you"* (Proverbs 3:27-28)	*"Do not be a **witness** against your **neighbor** without cause, for would you **deceive** with your lips? Do not say, "I will do to him **just** as he has done to me; I will render to the man according to his work.""* (Proverbs 24:28-29)
*"Do not forsake your own friend or your father's friend, nor go to your brother's house in the day of your calamity; better is a **neighbor** nearby than a brother far away"* (Proverbs 27:10)	*"Do not go hastily to court; for what will you do in the end, when your **neighbor** has put you to shame? Debate your case with your **neighbor**, and do not disclose the secret to another; lest he who hears it expose your shame, and your reputation be ruined"* (Proverbs 25:8-10)
*"Seldom set foot in your **neighbor's** house, lest he become weary of you and **hate** you"* (Proverbs 25:17)	*"The first one to plead his cause seems right, until his **neighbor** comes and examines him"* (Proverbs 18:17)

Table 126: The Positive Attribute's Influence on People in the Neighbor Category

All the items above will help one maintain healthy relationships with the **neighbor** category. To dispute the wisdom espoused by the Spirit of wisdom to Solomon is to endanger one's own life through the application of worldly knowledge. Now consider what the rest of the Biblical record has to say about the **neighbor** category.

The Lord viewed all the children of Israel as each other's **neighbors**. Because of this view, He gave Moses specific commands for growing the positive attributes among them. The commands promoted peace and harmony among the children of Israel. BTT allows one to see that the children of Israel were one big community of millions of **neighbors**. Thus, God's commands promoted the positive attributes while protecting the children of Israel from the influences of the negative attributes. As one looks at the commands documented in Table 124, pay close attention to how the positive and negative forces of the war campaign are woven throughout the application of God's commands. The Biblical record documented that the Lord commanded:

Commands	What Is Documented
For the Passover meal	*"And if the household is too small for the lamb, let him and his **neighbor** next to his house take it according to the number of the persons; according to each man's need you shall make your count for the lamb"* (Exodus 12:4)
For general living	*"You shall not bear **false witness** against your **neighbor**. You shall not <u>covet</u> your **neighbor's** house; you shall not <u>covet</u> your **neighbor's** wife, nor his male servant, nor his female servant, nor his ox, nor his donkey, nor anything that is your **neighbor's**"* (Exodus 20:16, 17; Deuteronomy 5:20-21)

	"*Cursed is the one who <u>attacks</u> his **neighbor** secretly.' "And all the people shall say, 'Amen!'"* (Deuteronomy 27:24). "Attacks" is associated with the elements of <u>rage</u> and <u>wrath</u>.
For cases of **murder**	"*But if a man acts with **premeditation** against his **neighbor**, to **kill** him by **treachery**, you shall take him from My altar, that he may die*" (Exodus 21:14)
In cases where unintentional **murder** occurs	"*Then Moses set apart three cities on this side of the Jordan, toward the rising of the sun, that the manslayer might flee there, who kills his **neighbor** unintentionally, without having **hated** him in time past, and that by fleeing to one of these cities he might live...*" (Deuteronomy 4:41-42)
	"*And this is the case of the manslayer who flees there, that he may live: Whoever kills his **neighbor** unintentionally, not having **hated** him in time past— as when a man goes to the woods with his **neighbor** to cut timber, and his hand swings a stroke with the ax to cut down the tree, and the head slips from the handle and strikes his **neighbor** so that he dies— he shall flee to one of these cities and live...*" (Deuteronomy 19:4-5)
	"*But if anyone **hates** his **neighbor**, lies in wait for him, <u>**rises against**</u> him and **strikes him mortally**, so that he **dies**, and he flees to one of these cities, then the elders of his city shall send and bring him from there, and deliver him over to the hand of the avenger of blood, that he may die. Your eye shall not pity him, but you shall put away the **guilt of innocent blood** from Israel, that it may go well with you*" (Deuteronomy 19:11-13)
For cases of **thief**	"*If a man delivers to his **neighbor** money or articles to keep, and it is **stolen** out of the man's house, if the **thief** is found, he shall pay double. If the **thief** is not found, then the master of the house shall be brought to the judges to see whether he has put his hand into his **neighbor's** goods. For any kind of **trespass**, whether it concerns an ox, a donkey, a sheep, or clothing, or for any kind of lost thing which another claims to be his, the cause of both parties shall come before the judges; and whomever the judges condemn shall pay double to his **neighbor**"* (Exodus 22:7-9)
For no-fault cases and then **theft** is discovered	"*If a man delivers to his **neighbor** a donkey, an ox, a sheep, or any animal to keep, and it dies, is hurt, or driven away, no one seeing it, then an oath of the Lord shall be between them both, that he has not put his hand into his **neighbor's** goods; and the owner of it shall accept that, and he shall not make it **good**. But if the animal was **stolen** from the **neighbor**, restitution must be made to the owner. If it was torn to pieces by a wild animal, the **neighbor** shall bring in the remains as evidence and shall not be required to pay for the torn animal*" (Exodus 22:10-13)
For cases of borrowing	"*And if a man borrows anything from his **neighbor**, and it becomes injured or dies, the owner of it not being with it, he shall surely make it **good**. But if the owner is with the animal, the borrower will not have to pay. If the animal was hired, the money paid for the hire covers the loss*" (Exodus 22:14-15)
For cases of lending on credit	"*At the end of every seven years you shall grant a release of debts. And this is the form of the release: Every creditor who has lent anything to his **neighbor** shall release it; he shall not require it of his **neighbor** or his brother, because it is called the Lord's release*" (Deuteronomy 15:1-2)

For cases where a pledge is made	*"If you ever take your **neighbor's** garment as a pledge, you shall return it to him before the sun goes down"* (Exodus 22:26)
For cases when ***lying*** is involved	*"If a person sins and commits a trespass against the Lord by **lying** to his **neighbor** about what was delivered to him for safekeeping, or about a pledge, or about a **robbery**, or if he has **extorted** from his **neighbor**, or if they find lost property and **lie** about it, or if they swear **falsely** about any such sin that people may commit— when they sin in any of these ways and realize their guilt, they must return what they have **stolen or taken by extortion**, or what was entrusted to them, or the lost property they found, or w**hate**ver it was they swore **falsely** about. They must make restitution in full, add a fifth of the value to it and give it all to the owner on the day they present their guilt offering"* (Leviticus 6:2-5). Plus, the individual must make a trespass offering to the Lord.
For cases when ***immorality*** is involved	*"Moreover you **shall not lie carnally** with your **neighbor**'s wife, to defile yourself with her"* (Leviticus 18:20)
	*"If a young woman who is a virgin is betrothed to a husband, and a man finds her in the city and lies with her, then you shall bring them both out to the gate of that city, and you shall stone them to death with stones, the young woman because she did not cry out in the city, and the man because he humbled his **neighbor's** wife; so you shall put away the **evil** from among you"* (Deuteronomy 22:23-24)
	*"But if a man finds a betrothed young woman in the countryside, and the man forces her and lies with her, then only the man who lay with her shall die. But you shall do nothing to the young woman; there is in the young woman no sin deserving of death, for **just** as when a man <u>rises against</u> his **neighbor** and **kills** him, even so is this matter"* (Deuteronomy 22:25-26)
For cases when ***adultery*** is involved	*"The man who commits **adultery** with another man's wife, he who commits **adultery** with his **neighbor**'s wife, the **adulterer** and the **adulteress**, shall surely be put to death"* (Leviticus 20:10)
For cases where cheating is involved	*"You shall not cheat your **neighbor**, nor **rob** him. The wages of him who is hired shall not remain with you all night until morning"* (Leviticus 19:13)
	*"When you come into your **neighbor's** vineyard, you may eat your fill of grapes at your pleasure, but you shall not put any in your container. When you come into your **neighbor's** standing grain, you may pluck the heads with your hand, but you shall not use a sickle on your **neighbor's** standing grain"* (Deuteronomy 23:24-25)
For cases where judgment is involved	*"You shall do no <u>injustice</u> in judgment. You shall not be partial to the poor, nor **honor** the person of the mighty. In **righteousness** you shall judge your **neighbor**"* (Leviticus 19:15)
For cases where gossip and rumors are involved	*"You shall not go about as a **talebearer** among your people; nor shall you take a stand against the life of your **neighbor**: I am the Lord. 'You shall not **hate** your brother in your heart. You shall surely rebuke your **neighbor**, and not bear sin because of him. You shall not take vengeance, nor bear any **grudge** against the children of your people, but you shall <u>love</u> your **neighbor** as yourself: I am the Lord"* (Leviticus 19:16-18)

For cases where disfigurement is caused	*"If a man causes disfigurement of his **neighbor**, as he has done, so shall it be done to him— fracture for fracture, eye for eye, tooth for tooth. The one who has inflicted the injury must suffer the same injury"* (Leviticus 24:19)
For cases where selling and buying are involved	*"And if you sell anything to your **neighbor** or buy from your **neighbor**'s hand, you shall not **oppress** one another"* (Leviticus 25:14)
For cases involving property boundaries	*"You shall not remove your **neighbor's** landmark, which the men of old have set, in your inheritance which you will inherit in the land that the Lord your God is giving you to possess"* (Deuteronomy 19:14)
	*"Cursed is the one who moves his **neighbor**'s landmark.' "And all the people shall say, 'Amen!'"* (Deuteronomy 27:17)

Table 127: God's Commands for the Neighbor Category

If the world applied these simple commands today, imagine all the positive changes that could occur. Once again, the influence of the positive attributes on the **neighbor** category cannot be overstated. Naomi had **neighbors** influenced by the positive attributes who helped her name Boaz and Ruth's first child. The Biblical record documented, *"...the **neighbor** women gave him a name, saying, "There is a son born to Naomi." And they called his name Obed. He is the father of Jesse, the father of David"* (Ruth 4:17). Likewise, Saul lost his kingdom to a **neighbor** influenced by the positive attributes. The prophet Samuel told Saul, *"...The Lord has torn the kingdom of Israel from you today, and has given it to a **neighbor** of yours, who is better than you"* (1 Samuel 15:28). In 1 Samuel 28:16-17, one learns that the **neighbor** was David. When David took over the throne, he documented an important point about the **neighbor** category and worshipping God when the question was asked, *"Who had the right to abide in the Lord's tabernacle or dwell in His holy hill?"* David's reply contained the person who had not done *"...**evil** to his **neighbor**..."* (Psalm 15:3) had the right to abide in the Lord's tabernacle or dwell in His holy hill. This perspective makes a huge difference in the way one looks at the **neighbor** category because it identifies a division between people serving on the positive or negative side of the war campaign. BTT allows one to see that the negative attribute's influence on people in the **neighbor** category led to the destruction of the nation of Israel. The following negative behaviors were rampant because of the negative attribute's influences:

- ***Oppression*** and <u>disrespect</u>**:** *"The people will be **oppressed**, everyone by another and every one by his **neighbor**; the child will be insolent toward the elder, and the base toward the **honorable**"* (Isaiah 3:5)

- ***Lying*****:** *"And like their bow they have bent their tongues for **lies**. They are not valiant for the truth on the earth. For they proceed from **evil** to **evil**, and they do not know Me," says the Lord. Everyone take heed to his **neighbor**, and do not trust any brother; for every brother will utterly **supplant**, and every **neighbor** will walk with **slanderers**. Everyone will **deceive** his **neighbor**, and will **not speak the truth**; they have taught their tongue to speak <u>lies</u>; they weary themselves to commit **iniquity**"* (Jeremiah 9:3-5)

- ***Deception***: *"Their tongue is an arrow shot out; it speaks **deceit**; one speaks peaceably to his **neighbor** with his mouth, but in his heart he lies in wait"* (Jeremiah 9:8)

- ***Cheating:*** *Woe to him who builds his house by **unrighteousness** and his chambers by <u>injustice</u>, who uses his **neighbor's** service without wages and gives him nothing for his work…"* (Jeremiah 22:13)

- ***False*** prophesizing and teaching<u>:</u> *"I have heard what the prophets have said who prophesy **lies** in My name, saying, 'I have dreamed, I have dreamed!' How long will this be in the heart of the prophets who prophesy **lies**? Indeed they are prophets of the **deceit** of their own heart, who try to make My people forget My name by their dreams which everyone tells his **neighbor**, as their fathers forgot My name for Baal"* (Jeremiah 23:25-27) and *"Therefore behold, I am against the prophets," says the Lord, "who **steal** My words every one from his **neighbor**"* (Jeremiah 23:30)

- ***Adultery***: *"…because they have done disgraceful things in Israel, have committed **adultery** with their **neighbors'** wives, and have spoken **lying** words in My name, which I have not commanded them. Indeed I know, and am a **witness**, says the Lord"* (Jeremiah 29:23)

- ***Perversion and extortion***: *"One commits abomination with his **neighbor's** wife; another **lewdly defiles** his daughter-in-law; and another in you **violates** his sister, his father's daughter. In you they take bribes to **shed blood**; you take **usury** and **increase**; you have made profit from your **neighbors** by **extortion**, and have forgotten Me," says the Lord God."* (Ezekiel 22:11-12)

- <u>Alcohol abuse</u>: *"Woe to him who gives drink to his **neighbor**, pressing him to your bottle, even to make him **drunk**, that you may **look on his nakedness**! You are filled with shame instead of glory. You also—drink! And be exposed as uncircumcised! The cup of the Lord's right hand will be turned against you, and utter shame will be on your glory."* (Habakkuk 2:15-16)

Because of the negative attribute's influence on the **neighbor** category, the nation of Israel lost respect internally for each other. The Lord eventually destroyed their nation.

When Jesus came on the scene in the New Testament, He brought even more knowledge and clarity about the **neighbor** category. Specifically, He provided clarification on who the people in the **neighbor** category were. Jesus stated, *"You have heard that it was said, 'You shall <u>love</u> your **neighbor** and **hate** your enemy.' But I say to you, <u>love</u> your enemies, bless those who curse you, do **good** to those who **hate** you, and pray for those who spitefully use you and persecute you, that you may be sons of your Father in heaven; for He makes His sun rise on the **evil** and on the **good**, and sends rain on the **just** and on the **unjust**"* (Matthew

5:43-45). From this clarification, Jesus placed everyone in the **neighbor** category; the *good* and the *evil* and the *just* and *unjust*. Even one's enemy falls into the **neighbor** category. Jesus followed up His teaching with an even greater principle when He stated, "*You shall love the Lord your God with all your heart, with all your soul, and with all your mind.' This is the first and great commandment. And the second is like it: 'You shall love your* **neighbor** *as yourself.' On these two commandments hang all the Law and the Prophets*" (Matthew 22:37-40; Mark 12:31; Luke 10:27). In other words, Jesus verified that the Mosaic Law and the things God's prophets taught and said, all pointed to the *love* one must have for God and your **neighbor**. Therefore, to *love* God, one must *love* one's **neighbor**. The *love* expressed here applies to all people in one's **neighbor***hood* and the world. Everyone in the **neighbor** category deserves the same *love* that one would have for oneself, God and His Son Jesus Christ.

The apostles handled Christ's teaching about the **neighbor** category with the same level of consistency as Jesus and all the prophets before Him. Some additional pearls of wisdom they documented about the people in the **neighbor** category included:

- "*…Owe no one anything except to love one another, for he who loves another has fulfilled the law. For the commandments, "You shall not commit* **adultery**,*" "You shall not* **murder**,*" "You shall not* **steal**,*" "You shall not bear* **false witness**,*" "You shall not covet," and if there is any other commandment, are all summed up in this saying, namely, "You shall love your* **neighbor** *as yourself." Love does no harm to a* **neighbor**; *therefore love is the fulfillment of the law*" (Romans 13:8-10)

- "*Let each of us please his* **neighbor** *for his* **good**, *leading to edification*" (Romans 15:2)

- "*…all the law is fulfilled in one word, even in this: "You shall love your* **neighbor** *as yourself*" (Galatians 5:14)

- "*Therefore, putting away lying,* "*Let each one of you speak truth with his* **neighbor**,*" for we are members of one another…*" (Ephesians 4:25)

- "*If you really fulfill the royal law according to the Scripture, "You shall love your* **neighbor** *as yourself," you do well; but if you* **show partiality**, *you commit sin, and are convicted by the law as* **transgressors**" (James 2:8-9)

Based on the above, BTT allows one to see how understanding the **neighbor** category is essential to understanding Jesus' meaning behind the **harvest** and the need for laborers. Unfortunately, many church going people today have unknowingly forfeited their opportunity for heaven because of the influence of the ***hater*** attribute. This attribute disqualifies one from heavenly access because of the harbored resentment against one's **neighbor**. In Christianity, there are no immigrants, foreigners, or "them" and "us"; all are **neighbors** in the **harvest**. People who understand God's Word and its application to this category, realize sharing the Gospel's Truth with **neighbors** increases the positive forces of the war campaign. One cannot share the Gospel when one has inadvertently created a mental barrier with his or her **neighbor**. Therefore, one cannot perform God's will. Properly teaching the Gospel arms everyone with the correct knowledge for defeating the negative forces of the war campaign. True, not everyone will hear the message; but for those who do, safety nets are established in one's community that can provide both physical and spiritual protection. The most important perspective one should have of the **neighbor** category is the fact that the positive protection afforded by God's Word will provide security for the world's children; the innocent and beneficiaries of the next generation.

The **Counselor category:** People found in this category are those who have taken on the responsibility to give **counsel**, **advice** or their opinion on matters that pertain to God or *godly* matters. People in this category may be paid professionals or anyone in general that happens to be someone's friend, a  coworker, or a lecturer in a general forum. The worst offender in this category is one who randomly provides **counsel** or **advice** on spiritual matters and whose idle words end up influencing someone to take a path that supports their ***evil*** desires. BTT allows one to see that, depending on the positive or negative attributes influencing the person in the **counselor** category, their spoken words can have a major impact on listeners. The consequences of the **counseling** or **advising**, whether on worldly or spiritual matters, can lead one to support either the positive or the negative forces of the war campaign. Moreover, social media, automation, and other virtual medians are making it possible for people in this category to share words of spiritual **counsel** and **advice** indiscriminately. Based on the **counselor's** motivation, this indiscriminate form of **council** or **advice** can have unpredictable affects in spiritual warfare. Hence, in the Christian community, face to face and individual/family **counseling** is always recommended; not with an audience or for show.

To see the impact of the positive and negative attributes on one in the **counselor** category, the Spirit of wisdom revealed to Solomon "**Counsel** *is mine, and sound wisdom; I am understanding, I have strength. By me kings reign, and rulers decree justice. By me princes rule, and nobles, all the judges of the earth*" (Proverbs 8:14-16). Based on Wisdom's statement, BTT allows one to see, that if the words of **counsel** are not from God, one had better be careful. Wisdom herself is the source of positive **counsel** for people in the **counselor** category. When people in this category refuse to use information from the Source, Wisdom documents their demise. She stated, "*...because you disdained all my* **counsel**, *and would have none of my rebuke, I also will laugh at your calamity; I will* **mock** *when your terror comes, when your terror comes like a storm, and your destruction comes like a whirlwind, when distress and anguish come upon you*" (Proverbs 1: 25-27). Further, Wisdom stated for people in general, "*Because they* **hated** *knowledge and did not choose the fear of the LORD, they would have none of my* **counsel** *and despised my every rebuke. Therefore they shall eat the fruit of their own way, and be filled to the full with their own fancies* (Proverbs 1: 29-31). One must keep in mind, that the people in the **counsel** category are just like you and me. They are subject to the same influences of the positive or negative attributes. However, when they chose to give **counsel** or **advice**, Wisdom makes it clear that God has a say too. Thus, when one speaks, he or she will be rewarded or punished based on their input on the spiritual battlefield. Knowing and accepting the true Source of positive **counsel,** makes all the difference in spiritual warfare. The prophet Isaiah understood this and documented, "*O Lord, You are my God. I will exalt You, I will praise Your name, for You have done wonderful things; Your* **counsels** *of old are faithfulness and truth*" (Isaiah 25:1).

Solomon further documented "*…a man of understanding will attain wise* **counsel**, *to understand a proverb and an enigma, the words of the wise and their riddles*" (Proverbs 1: 5-6). People who understand how things work seek wise **counsel** to know and understand more. They know that people wiser than themselves can give **counsel** to move them further in their pursuits. Once again, depending on the type of **counsel** the person of understanding receives, he or she could turn to the positive or negative path of life. The acceptance of positive or negative **counsel** also coincides with the person of understanding's desires. Hence, Solomon wrote, "*The way of a **fool** is **right** in his own eyes, but he who heeds* **counsel** *is **wise***" (Proverbs 12:15). God's Word is positive **counsel**. But to the ***foolish***, God's positive **counsel** means nothing. **Fools** reject God's positive **counsel**. Thus, Solomon wrote, "*Listen to* **counsel** *and receive instruction, that you may be wise in your latter days. There are many plans in a man's heart, nevertheless the LORD's* **counsel**—*that will stand*" (Proverbs 19:20-21). Even the prophet Jeremiah wrote "*You are great in* **counsel** *and mighty in work, for Your eyes are open to all the ways of the sons of men, to give everyone according to his ways and according to the fruit of his doings*" (Jeremiah 32:19). Jeremiah's warning pertained to everyone, but especially to people in the **counselor** category choosing to **counsel** or **advise** others in matters pertaining to God. Based on this warning, God will "*give everyone according to his ways and according to the fruit of his doings*". This includes a **counselor**.

The Spirit of wisdom explained to Solomon that people in the **counselor** category serve a critical role in the war campaign - whether for good or bad. Some of the things that Solomon documented from the Spirit of wisdom included:

- "*Where there is no* **counsel**, *the people fall; but in the multitude of* **counselors** *there is safety*" (Proverbs 11:14)

- "*Without* **counsel**, *plans go awry, but in the multitude of* **counselors** *they are established*" (Proverbs 15:22)

- "*Plans are established by* **counsel**; *by wise* **counsel** *wage war*" (Proverbs 20:18)

- "*A wise man is strong, yes, a man of knowledge increases strength; for by wise* **counsel** *you will wage your own war, and in a multitude of* **counselors** *there is safety*" (Proverbs 24:5-6)

- "*The thoughts of the* **righteous** *are* **right**, *but the* **counsels** *of the* **wicked** *are* **deceitful**" (Proverbs 12:5)

- "***Deceit*** *is in the heart of those who devise **evil**, but* **counselors** *of peace have joy*" (Proverbs 12:20)

- "**Counsel** *in the heart of man is like deep water, but a man of understanding will draw it out*" (Proverbs 20:5)

- "*Do not **envy** the **oppressor**, and choose none of his ways; for the **perverse** person is an abomination to the LORD, but His secret **counsel** is with the **upright***" (Proverbs 3:31-32)

- "*There is no wisdom or understanding or **counsel** against the LORD*" (Proverbs 21:30)

One must understand that when the positive or negative attributes influence one giving **counsel** to another, their **counsel** can persuade one to join either the positive or negative side of the war campaign. For this reason one can see why <u>discernment</u> is critical. When one's inner spirit is capable of <u>discern</u>ing what one hears, he or she will walk toward the ***right*** path of life. BTT allows one to see that <u>discernment</u> comes from wisdom that comes from the Lord according to Proverbs 2:2-9. Solomon documented that one should, "*Listen to **counsel** and receive instruction, that you may be wise in your latter days*" (Proverbs 19:20). Further, he wrote, "*Have I not written to you excellent things of **counsels** and knowledge that I may make you know the certainty of the words of truth, that you may answer words of truth to those who send to you?*" (Proverbs 22:20-21). What Solomon documented from the Spirit of wisdom was all positive **counsel**. But the <u>discernment</u> that comes from knowing God's Word and being obedient to it, is the only way of protecting oneself from negative **counselors** operating on behalf of the negative forces. This is another reason why parents must be very cautious of who is providing their children **counsel** or **advice**. A true Christian **counselor** always consults the Bible prior to giving **counsel** or **advice**. For one who is a **counselor** of the positive forces of the campaign understand, "*For unto us a Child is born, unto us a Son is given; and the government will be upon His shoulder. And His name will be called Wonderful, **Counselor**, Mighty God, Everlasting Father, Prince of Peace*" (Isaiah 9:6). Jesus and His Word is the source of True **counsel** and **advice**.

The Biblical record is full of examples of people who received either good or bad **counsel** from a person and even animals in the **counselor** category. The Book of Numbers in chapter 22, provides an example of an animal providing positive **counsel**. In this example, a donkey stopped on a road three times because it saw an angel blocking the road. Balaam, the donkey's master, beat the donkey each time because he could not see the angel. Eventually, the Lord opened the donkey's mouth to **counsel** Balaam stating, "*Am I not your donkey on which you have ridden, ever since I became yours, to this day? Was I ever disposed to do this to you?*" (Numbers 22:30). To this **counsel**, Balaam replied "No!" and the Lord opened Balaam's spiritual eyes (Numbers 22:31). Then the angel said to him, "*Why have you struck your donkey these three times? Behold, I have come out to stand against you, because your way is **perverse** before Me. The donkey saw Me and turned aside from Me these three times. If she had not turned aside from Me, surely I would also have killed you by now, and let her live*" (Numbers 22:32-33). The donkey's positive **counsel** saved Balaam's life. A few more examples of positive **counsel** from one in the **counselor** category documented in the Biblical record include:

Who	What Is Documented
Jethro	Moses father-in-law provided positive **counsel** to Moses that helped him relieve the stress of leadership according to Exodus 18:17-23
Children of Israel	After some **perverted** men from the tribe of Benjamin attempted to **sodomize** a priest and **raped** a woman in Judges Chapter 19, the Bible documented that the Levite who survived the assault said to the Israel, "*Look! All of you are children of Israel; give your **advice** and **counsel** here and now!*" (Judges 20:7). Their positive **counsel** removed sin from the nation of Israel. The Biblical record documented that the carnage was great according to Judges 20:35-48.
Daniel	He provided positive **counsel** to King Nebuchadnezzar who was having troubling dreams that deprived him of his sleep. The negative **counsel** of his "*...magicians, the astrologers, the sorcerers, and the Chaldeans...*" (Daniel 2:2) did no good. In fact, King Nebuchadnezzar decided to **kill** them, and the Bible documented, "*Then with **counsel** and wisdom Daniel answered Arioch, the captain of the king's guard, who had gone out to **kill** the wise men of Babylon...*" (Daniel 2:14) which spared them from the king's <u>wrath</u>. Daniel's positive **counsel** brought the king comfort and sleep.
John the Baptist	He **counseled** the Pharisees to repent. He said, "*Brood of vipers! Who warned you to flee from the <u>wrath</u> to come? Therefore bear fruits worthy of repentance...*" (Matthew 3:7-8)
	He **counseled** Herod about his **immoral** marriage. He told Herod, "*It is <u>not lawful</u> for you to have your brother's wife*" (Mark 6:18)
Jesus	He **counseled** the moneychangers who had set up shop in the temple of God. He said to them, "*It is written, 'My house shall be called a house of prayer,' but you have made it a 'den of **thieves**'*" (Matthew 21:13; Mark 11:17; John 2:16)
	He **counseled** the rich young ruler on eternal life in of Matthew 19:16-26; Mark 10:17-22; and Luke 18:18-23. However, the young man had a hard time receiving Jesus' **counsel** and he walked away sorrowful according to Matthew 19:22; Mark 10:22; and Luke 18:23
	He **counseled** the Sadducees on their **false** doctrine concerning the resurrection. He said to them, "*Are you not therefore mistaken, because you do not know the Scriptures nor the power of God?*" (Mark 12:24)
	He **counseled** to people to beware of the scribes. He said to them, "*Beware of the scribes, who desire to go around in long robes, love greetings in the marketplaces, the best seats in the synagogues, and the best places at feasts, who devour widows' houses, and for a pretense make long prayers. These will receive greater condemnation*" (Luke 20:46-47)
	He **counseled** Nicodemus on <u>baptism</u>. He said, "*Most assuredly, I say to you, unless one is born again, he cannot see the kingdom of God*" (John 3:3)
Elizabeth	She **counseled** Mary about baby Jesus inside her womb. She said, "*Blessed are you among women, and blessed is the fruit of your womb!*" (Luke 1:42)
Philip	He **counseled** Nathanael about Jesus before they became disciples. Philip said, "*We have found Him of whom Moses in the law, and also the prophets, wrote— Jesus of Nazareth, the son of Joseph.*" And Nathanael said to him, "*Can anything good come out of Nazareth?*" Philip said to him, "*Come and see*" (John 1:46-47)

Paul	He **counseled** the Epicureans and Stoic philosophers of Athens in Acts 17:18-34 about the "unknown God" statue in the Areopagus

Table 128: Examples of the Positive Attribute's Influence on People in the Counselor Category

Conversely, there are examples of people in the **counselor** category who were influenced by the negative attributes and provided negative **counsel** to others. Genesis 3 provides an example of an animal providing negative **counsel**. A serpent in the Garden of Eden, influenced by the negative attributes, **counseled** Eve to eat from a tree that God had told her not to eat from according to Genesis 3:1-5. The woman told the serpent, "*We may eat the fruit of the trees of the garden; but of the fruit of the tree which is in the midst of the garden, God has said, 'You shall not eat it, nor shall you touch it, lest you die.'*" (Genesis 3:2-3). But the serpent ***advised*** her that, "*You will not surely die. For God knows that in the day you eat of it your eyes will be opened, and you will be like God, knowing good and **evil**.*" (Genesis 3: 4-5). This negative **counsel** *seduced* Eve, now tainted by the element of doubt, to eat from the tree. One might infer that Eve **advised** Adam to eat the fruit after he observed that nothing seemingly happened to Eve. One can infer this because the Bible documented that the Lord said to Adam, "*Because you have heeded the voice of your wife...*" (Genesis 3:17), he was punished. With God's command violated, they both lost their place in God's paradise because of their negative behavior. A few other examples of negative **counsel** given by one in the **counselor** category include:

Who	What Is Documented
Balaam	Moses directed the son of Eleazar the priest (Numbers 31:6) to lead an army against the Midianites (Numbers 31:7-8). However, Phinehas, Eleazar's son, ignored Moses' command to completely destroy the people. He saved the Midianite women for the Israelites. After the war, Moses was ***angry*** with the leaders of the Army (Numbers 31:14) and he said to them, "*Look, these women caused the children of Israel, through the **counsel** of Balaam, to **trespass** against the Lord in the incident of Peor, and there was a plague among the congregation of the Lord*" (Numbers 31:16)
Ahithophel	"*David's **counselor**, from his city—from Giloh*" (2 Samuel 15:12) gave negative **counsel** three times. The Biblical record documented that the "*...**advice** of Ahithophel, which he gave in those days, **was as if one had inquired at the oracle of God**. So was all the **advice** of Ahithophel both with David and with Absalom*" (2 Samuel 16:23). The first example of his negative **counsel** is found in 2 Samuel 15:12-34; the second in 2 Samuel 16:21-22; and a third in 2 Samuel Chapters 17 and 18. Ahithophel hung himself when he was exposed according to 2 Samuel 17:23
The people of the land	In the Book of Ezra, people in the negative **counsel** category attempted to discourage work on the restoration of the Lord's temple in Jerusalem. The Biblical documented that, "*Then the people of the land tried to discourage the people of Judah. They troubled them in building, and hired **counselors** against them to frustrate their purpose all the days of Cyrus king of Persia, even until the reign of Darius king of Persia*" (Ezra 4:4-5). Their efforts failed.

Bildad, Zophar, and Elihu	In the Book of Job, three wise and one younger man, lead verbal assaults on the prophet Job using negative **counsel** while he was stricken and bed ridden. However, Job shut all of them down when he said to Bildad, one of the adversaries, "*How have you helped him who is without power? How have you saved the arm that has no strength? How have you **counseled** one who has no wisdom? And how have you declared sound **advice** to many?*" (Job 26:2-3). You see, Job recognized that these men were full of the negative **counsel** and was of no value to him or anyone else.
Governors of the kingdom, administrators, satraps, **counselor**s, and advisors	In the book of Daniel, negative **counselors** and **advisors** tried to have Daniel ***killed*** under King Darius leadership. They **conspired**, along with the governors of the kingdom, the administrators and satraps to, "*...establish a royal statute and to make a firm decree, that whoever petitions any god or man for thirty days, except you, O king, shall be cast into the den of lions. Now, O king, establish the decree and sign the writing, so that it cannot be changed, according to the law of the Medes and Persians, which does not alter." Therefore King Darius signed the written decree*" (Daniel 6:6-9). Of course, this was to trap Daniel. It backfired. For the Lord sent an angel to, "*...shut the lions' mouths...*" (Daniel 6:22). Because Daniel was innocent, the king was, "*...exceedingly glad...*" (Daniel 6:23) and, "*...the king gave the command, and they brought those men who had **accused** Daniel, and they cast them into the den of lions—them, their children, and their wives; and the lions overpowered them, and broke all their bones in pieces before they ever came to the bottom of the den*" (Daniel 6:24)
King Herod	He secretly called the wise men and **counseled** them to discover where young Jesus was, so he could ***kill*** him. He said, "*Go and search carefully for the young Child, and when you have found Him, bring back word to me, that I may come and worship Him also*" (Matthew 2:8). Herod had no intention of worshipping Jesus.
Satan	He **counseled** Jesus on three occasions: Satan told Jesus to "*...command that these stones become bread*" (Matthew 4:3; Luke 4:3); to "*...throw Yourself down...*" (Matthew 4:6; Luke 4:9-12); and to "*...fall down and worship me*" (Matthew 4:9; Luke 4:7)
Caiaphas	He **counseled** the Jews to ***kill*** Jesus when he said, "*You know nothing at all, nor do you consider that it is expedient for us that one man should **die** for the people, and not that the whole nation should perish*" (John 11:49-50)
	He **counseled** the Sanhedrin on Jesus' ***false*** guilt. He said to them, "*He has spoken blasphemy! What further need do we have of witnesses? Look, now you have heard His blasphemy! What do you think?" They answered and said, "He is deserving of death*" (Matthew 26:65-66)
The chief priests	They **counseled** the people to ask for Barabbas' release from his death sentence instead of freeing Jesus; an innocent man. (Mark 15:6-13)
	They **consulted** with the elders and **counseled** the soldiers who guarded Jesus tomb. The Biblical record documented, "*When they had assembled with the elders and **consulted** together, they gave a large sum of money to the soldiers, saying, "Tell them, 'His disciples came at night and **stole** Him away while we slept.' So they took the money and did as they were*

	instructed; and this saying is commonly reported among the Jews until this day" (Matthew 28:12-15)
The Pharisees	They **counseled** a healed man that had been born blind from birth to deny the power of Jesus. When the man would not comply, *"They answered and said to him, "You were completely born in sins, and are you teaching us?" And <u>they cast him out</u>"* (John 9:34)
The Sanhedrin	This group of religious leaders **counseled** Peter and John and told them, *"...not to speak at all nor teach in the name of Jesus"* (Acts 4:18)
Demetrius	A silversmith who **counseled** the people to <u>revolt against</u> the Gospel and Paul's teaching in Acts 19:23-41

Table 129: Examples of the Negative Attribute's Influence on People in the Counselor Category

These examples are enough for one to understand the nature of the people in the **counselor** category. One can see how the positive or negative attributes can influence their behavior in the war campaign. **Counselors** who fail to understand God's Word will face punishment from the Lord as documented in the Biblical record. The prophet Job said that when it comes to God, *"With Him are strength and prudence. The **deceived** and the **deceiver** are His. He leads **counselors** away plundered, and makes **fools** of the judges"* (Job 12:16-17). Why does the Lord care about people in the **counselor** category? Because their **counsel** and **advice** can either, lead one toward the path of ***righteousness*** or deep into a path of darkness. One cannot overstate the power of the influence that people in the **counselor** category possess. The Psalmist said, *"Blessed is the man who walks not in the **counsel** of the **ungodly**, nor stands in the path of sinners, nor sits in the seat of the **scornful**..."* (Psalm 1:1). One needs <u>discernment</u> to stay away from the **counsel** of people influenced by the ***ungodly*** attribute. As for the people who allow themselves to be influenced by the ***wicked***, ***evil***, ***proud***, ***liar***, and ***bloodthirsty*** attributes (Psalms 5:4-6), and who accepts negative **counsel**, David prayed *"...Let them fall by their own **counsels**; cast them out in the multitude of their **transgressions**, for they have <u>rebelled</u> against You"* (Psalm 5:9-10). This prayer applies even today. But as one prays, one must remember to ***hate*** the behavior of the person and not the physical person. One must let God take care of all people who espouse negative **counsel** and leads others astray.

All of God's prophets documented that the nation of Israel's demise occurred due in part to its leadership listening to people in the **counselor** category who were influenced by the negative attributes. This serves as a great source of learning for us today. Starting back before Israel was a nation and moving to the present time, the Biblical record documented from the Lord:

- *"But My people would not heed My voice, and Israel would have none of Me. So I gave them over to their own <u>stubborn</u> heart, to walk in their own **counsels**"* (Psalm 81:11-12)

- *"They soon forgot His works; they did not wait for His **counsel**, but <u>lusted</u> exceedingly in the wilderness, and tested God in the desert"* (Psalm 106:13-14)

- *"Many times He delivered them; but they <u>rebelled</u> in their **counsel**, and were brought low for their **iniquity**"* (Psalm 106:43)

- *"Because they rebelled against the words of God, and **despised** the **counsel** of the Most High, therefore He brought down their heart with labor; they fell down, and there was none to help"* (Psalm 107:11-12)

- *"Woe to those who seek deep to hide their **counsel** far from the Lord, and their works <u>are in the dark</u>; they say, "Who sees us?" and, "Who knows us?"* (Isaiah 29:15)

- *"Woe to the <u>rebellious</u> children," says the Lord, "Who take **counsel**, but not of Me, and who devise plans, but not of My Spirit, that they may add sin to sin..."* (Isaiah 30:1-2)

- *"Yet they did not obey or incline their ear, but followed the **counsels** and the dictates of their **evil** hearts, and **went backward** and not forward"* (Jeremiah 7:24)

- *"...there at the door of the gate were twenty-five men, among whom I saw Jaazaniah the son of Azzur, and Pelatiah the son of Benaiah, princes of the people. And He said to me: "Son of man, these are the men who **devise iniquity** and give **wicked** counsel in this city..."* (Ezekiel 11:1-4)

Throughout the New Testament of the Biblical record, the importance of people in the **counselor** category supporting the positive forces of the war campaign were worth their weight in gold. From the birth of Christ, His ministry, and the life He led up to His death, the number of people **counseling** and **advising** others exploded on the spiritual battlefield. Contentions between Jesus teachings and other religious beliefs, practices, and traditions brought out people ripened with the influences of the positive or negative attributes. However, Jesus' followers never placed feel good **counsel** and **advice** over the truth of God's Word. Even after Jesus's death, His apostles continued to take God's Word out to the world through preaching and positive **counsel** from Christ's Word. Paul documented the importance of positive **counsel** when he stated, *"For I have not shunned to declare to you the whole **counsel** of God"* (Acts 20:27). BTT allows one to see that in spiritual warfare, the *"whole **counsel** of God"* is always positive. Christians that are part of the **counselor** category always consult the Bible first to give sound **counsel** and **advice** to others. These are the people that know where positive **counsel** comes from. Isaiah stated long ago, *"For unto us a Child is born, unto us a Son is given; and the government will be upon His shoulder. And His name will be called Wonderful, **Counselor**, Mighty God, Everlasting Father, Prince of Peace"* (Isaiah 9:6). When one turns to a person in the **counselor** category that recognizes Jesus Christ as the Chief **Counselor**, his or her **counsel** and **advice** will always put one on a positive path in the war campaign.

In the Book of Revelations from Chapter 1:9 through Chapter 3:22, Jesus provided sound **counsel** to seven churches that serve as spiritual images of churches on the spiritual battlefield. These seven churches are worthy of one's study and contemplation. These spiritual images will help one <u>know</u> if he or she is currently worshipping in a place where Christ truly exists. Please do not accept negative **counsel** from people in the **counselor** category who reject these images from Christ. The negative forces of the war campaign are maintaining a fog in the war to keep unsuspecting souls confused and lost over Christ's **counsel**. The negative forces strategy, strengthened by people in the **counselor** category who reject or misunderstand God's Word, supports *false* organizations and worships designed to *deceived* masses of people. Further, their ability to *deceive* is enhanced by social, broadcast, and written media, distributed at astonishing speeds across the spiritual battlefield twenty-four hours a day. Please do not be deceived. One's failure to understand what Jesus has presented will condemn one to support the negative forces of the war campaign. To make this very point clear, one should meditate on the words captured in the Book of Jeremiah Chapter 14. Here the Biblical record speaks of prophets who provided negative **counsel** and the people who accepted that **counsel**. Jeremiah wrote in Jeremiah 14:13-16:

> *"Then I said, "Ah, Lord God! Behold, the prophets say to them, 'You shall not see the sword, nor shall you have famine, but I will give you assured peace in this place.' " And the Lord said to me, "The prophets prophesy lies in My name. I have not sent them, commanded them, nor spoken to them; they prophesy to you a false vision, divination, a worthless thing, and the deceit of their heart. Therefore thus says the Lord concerning the prophets who prophesy in My name, whom I did not send, and who say, 'Sword and famine shall not be in this land'—'By sword and famine those prophets shall be consumed! And the people to whom they prophesy shall be cast out in the streets of Jerusalem because of the famine and the sword; they will have no one to bury them—them nor their wives, their sons nor their daughters—for I will pour their wickedness on them.'"*

The **Witness category:** This category is an important category of the **harvest** because it represents people who either will defend or deny what they read in God's Word. People in this category will also defend or deny what they have seen of other's behavior due to the influence of the positive or negative attributes in their lives. When the *liar*, *hater*, *wicked*, or *evil* attributes influence people of this category, they will inflict untold harm on people with positive attributes and Christians. From an earthly standpoint, a **witness** is one who observes something and can make a statement about what he or she knows or has observed. This **witness's** statement, called a <u>testimony</u>, can be given to a friend or to someone in the professional establishment, i.e. police, a lawyer, or a judge in a courtroom setting. But here is where the influence of the positive and negative attributes comes in to play. A person in the **witness** category, influenced by the *liar* attribute or other negative attributes, will provide a written or verbal statement of *lies*. This **witness's** behavior can bring harm to an innocent person. This is spiritual warfare and the desired outcome of the negative forces of the war campaign. Conversely, one in the **witness** category influenced by the positive attributes can only provide a statement of truth. To do anything less places the person on the bad path of life. Refer back to **Figure 10** if necessary. Hence, a Christian is slow to speak (James 1:19) as he or she considers their words. Moreover, in both cases, everyone who hears or reads the *testimony* faces the same positive or negative influences when rendering a decision to believe or not believe the **witness**' statement. Without the application of *discernment* in both cases, an innocent person's life is uncertain. This is the reality of spiritual warfare and the war campaign itself. What is disconcerting about this process is the fact that one in the **witness** category can provide ***false*** *testimony* and walk away unharmed. This happens when the judicial system gives responsible people the authority to correct an *injustice* and they choose not to do what is ***right***. In addition, when a ***false*** **witness** is not held accountable for their ***false*** *testimony*, the negative forces exploit the ensuing situation. BTT allows one to see that the negative forces use the spiritual element of *fear* to immobilize many people influenced by the **good** and **just** attributes. This spiritual element causes some people within the positive forces to remain silent. But these are the same type of people Jesus described when He said to His disciples, "*Why are you so fearful? How is it that you have no* ***faith****?*" BTT allows one to see that Jesus made a direct correlation between the element of *fear* and having no ***faith***. *Fear* causes disruption among the positive forces. In fact, when the negative attributes influence people in the **witness** category, they become susceptible to **deception**, ***false*** *testimony*, and bribery. These **witnesses** can destroy a person's reputations by ***falsely*** claiming to see or know something that is not true. Their **accusations** show partiality and contempt. Based on what is at stake, people influenced by either the positive or the negative attributes, are targets of these **witnesses**. When influenced by the negative attributes, everyone in this category depends on their own personal desires or the profit they can gain from their *testimony*, actions, and behavior.

    BTT allows one to see that in spiritual warfare, truth lies somewhere between one's inner spirit and God. Man can only *discern* the truth of one in the **witness** category by the answers from his or her mouth, his or her physical behavior, or his or her emotional state. People in the **witness** category, influenced by the positive attributes, will see through **deception**, ***false*** *testimony*, and *bribery*. Hence, getting the Gospel message to people living in this category is essential. For in the war campaign, spiritual warfare can place anyone in the **witness** category at any given time. This is especially true as the Gospel of Jesus Christ sheds light on sin and the negative forces retaliate to keep people in darkness. Thus, anyone can be placed in a situation in which one will be called to **testify** for or against another person's behavior, actions, or words. This prospect has major consequences attached to it in the war campaign.

    The Spirit of wisdom made Solomon keenly aware that God *hates* anyone in the **witness** category who allows the influence of the negative attributes. Wisdom told Solomon, "*These six things the LORD* *hates*, *yes, seven are an abomination to Him: A* **proud** *look, a* **lying** *tongue,* **hands that shed innocent blood***, a heart that devises* **wicked** *plans, feet that are swift in running to* **evil***, a* ***false*** **witness** *who speaks* **lies***, and one who* *sows discord* *among brethren*" (Proverbs 6:16-19). Why would the Lord take such a strong position on a person like this in the **witness** category influenced by the negative attributes? Well, possibly because of the damage they do to the reputations of His people. Solomon learned, "*He who speaks truth declares* **righteousness***, but a* ***false*** **witness***,* **deceit**" (Proverbs 12:17) and, "*A* **faithful** **witness** *does not* **lie***, but a* ***false*** **witness** *will utter* **lies**" (Proverbs 14:5). This latter statement was repeated with even more clarity as Solomon documented in Proverbs 14:25 that, "*A true* **witness** *delivers souls, but a* **deceitful** **witness** *speaks* **lies**." BTT allows one to see that one in the **witness** category, influenced by the negative attributes, can steer others away from the Truth of the Gospel by ***deceit***. His or her **witness** about ***false*** religious matters, traditions, or worldly beliefs, can be so convincing that the message of the True Gospel is lost in the fog of spiritual warfare. Conversely, one in the **witness** category influenced by the positive attributes can lead others to Christ and the Truth.

The challenges for one in the **witness** category influenced by the negative attributes is even more pronounced when one considers that Solomon documented, "*A <u>disreputable</u>* **witness *scorns*** <u>*justice*</u>*, and the mouth of the **wicked** devours iniquity*" (Proverbs 19:28). Simply put, a person in the **witness** category influenced by the negative attributes will ***mock*** and bring shame to the <u>*justice*</u> system, while people who allow the influence of the **wicked** attribute <u>*love*</u> the ***immorality*** displayed by a <u>*disreputable*</u> **witness's** behavior. One influenced by the **wicked** attribute will take in every word of a <u>*disreputable*</u> **witness** and use it in ***deceitful*** ways across the spiritual battlefield against the positive forces. BTT allows one to see that the <u>*disreputable*</u> **witness** provides an arsenal of ***evil*** possibilities to support the negative forces of the war campaign during spiritual warfare.

The Spirit of wisdom further shared with Solomon that a person in the **witness** category influenced by the negative attributes, can expect punishment. Thus, Solomon documented a principle found in three proverbs for everyone influenced by the negative attributes. He documented:

- "*A **false** witness will not go unpunished, and he who speaks **lies** will not escape*" (Proverbs 19:5)

- "*A **false** witness will not go unpunished, and he who speaks **lies** shall perish*" (Proverbs 19:9)

- "*A **false** witness shall perish, but the man who hears him will speak endlessly*" (Proverbs 21:28)

BTT allows one to see from these Scriptures, a ***false witness*** will not escape and will be punished for his or her actions. However, the Spirit of wisdom identifies a reality in the third Scripture above. The reality is this. Although a ***false* witness** will eventually die, his or her ***false*** <u>*testimony*</u> will continue to live on through the people who heard it. BTT allows one to see that ***false statements*** continue to live by people influenced by the negative forces of the campaign. The life of a ***lie*** can continue well beyond the life of the person who told the ***lie***. Reasons vary but ***lies*** persist because of gossip, rumors, and people who ignore facts nor desire to hear truth. This principle demonstrates the power of words as well as the capability of a person in the **witness** category in spiritual warfare. Hence, the truth of the Gospel must be spoken and passed on to counter ***lies*** perpetrated by the negative forces of the war campaign. Moreover, God has a way to always bring out the truth. Hence, Solomon documented, "*The first one to plead his cause seems **right**, until his neighbor comes and examines him*" (Proverbs 18:17). A Christian understands the value of not being hasty with both words and actions. Even the Spirit of wisdom expressed to Solomon, "*Do you see a man hasty in his words? There is more hope for a **fool** than for him*" (Proverbs 29:20).

Finally, to keep the influence of the negative attributes away, Solomon documented two very important concepts for people in the **witness** category to ponder. He wrote, "*Do not be a* **witness** *against your neighbor without cause, for would you* ***deceive*** *with your lips? Do not say, "I will do to him* ***just*** *as he has done to me; I will render to the man according to his work*" (Proverbs 24:28, 29). When one perceives that one's neighbor has done wrong, it is necessary for one to step back and consider the reason behind the neighbor's actions. Hasty conclusions open the door for the negative attributes to enter one's inner spirit. In Solomon's second important concept, he documented, "*A man who bears* ***false*** **witness** *against his neighbor is like a club, a sword, and a sharp arrow*" (Proverbs 25:18). In other words, if the neighbor's decision was ***just***, but one jumped to a hasty conclusion, the damage inflicted will be like a deep painful wound that is difficult to close. Consider other items identified in the Biblical record about the **witness** category.

The Lord gave Moses commands for the children of Israel to live by which included requirements for people who found themselves in the **witness** category. Some example included:

- "*You shall not bear* ***false*** **witness** *against your neighbor*" (Exodus 20:16; Deuteronomy 5:20)

- "*You shall not circulate a* ***false report***. *Do not put your hand with the* ***wicked*** *to be an* ***unrighteous*** **witness**" (Exodus 23:1)

- "*If a person sins in hearing the utterance of an oath, and is a* **witness**, *whether he has seen or known of the matter—if he does not tell it, he bears guilt*" (Leviticus 5:1)

- "*If any man's wife goes astray and behaves* ***unfaithfully*** *toward him, and a man* ***lies*** *with her carnally, and it is hidden from the eyes of her husband, and it is concealed that* ***she has defiled herself***, *and there was no* **witness** *against her, nor was she caught— if the* ***spirit of jealousy*** *comes upon him and he becomes* ***jealous*** *of his wife...*" (Numbers 5:12-14), there is a procedure the priest and both parties must follow laid out in Numbers 5:15-31 to determine her innocence or guilt.

- "*Whoever* ***kills*** *a person, the* ***murderer*** *shall be put to death on the* <u>testimony</u> *of* **witnesses**; *but one* **witness** *is not sufficient* <u>testimony</u> *against a person for the death penalty*" (Numbers 35:30)

    - "*Whoever is deserving of death shall be put to death on the* <u>testimony</u> *of two or three* **witnesses**; *he shall not be put to death on the* <u>testimony</u> *of one* **witness**. *The hands of the* **witnesses** *shall be the first against him to put him to death, and afterward the hands of all the people. So you shall put away the* ***evil*** *from among you*" (Deuteronomy 17:6-7)

- "*One* **witness** *shall not rise against a man concerning any iniquity or any sin that he commits; by the mouth of two or three* **witnesses** *the matter shall be established. If a* ***false*** **witness** *rises against any man to* <u>testify</u> *against him of wrongdoing, then both men in the controversy shall stand before the Lord, before the priests and the judges* *who serve in those days. And the judges shall make careful inquiry, and indeed, if the* **witness** *is a **false** **witness**, who has <u>testified</u> **falsely** against his brother, then you shall do to him as he thought to have done to his brother; so you shall put away the* **evil** *from among you"* (Deuteronomy 19:15-19)

The Biblical record documented in 1 Kings Chapter 21, a classic example of people in the **witness** category abusing their responsibility as **witnesses**. The example involved a man named Naboth, influenced by the positive attributes, and King Ahab and Queen Jezebel, who were overwhelmed with negative attributes. Ahab was the king of Samaria and he wanted Naboth's land to grow a vineyard so badly that it made him physically sick. He laid in his bed, turned away from people, and refused to eat according to 1 Kings 21:4. When Jezebel saw her husband in this condition, the Bible documented that she said, *"...Why is your spirit so sullen that you eat no food?"* (1 Kings 21:5). BTT allows one to see that the influences of the **wicked** attribute were so strong in Jezebel that she could see that it was Ahab's inner spirit that was extremely **depressed**. So, she **wickedly** plotted to take the land from Naboth using people in the **witness** category who were influenced by the negative attributes. The Biblical record documented that Jezebel wrote a letter to the elders of Israel sealed with the king's seal to *"Proclaim a fast, and seat Naboth with high **honor** among the people; and seat two men,* **scoundrels**, *before him to bear* **witness** *against him, saying, "You have blasphemed God and the king." Then take him out, and* **stone him, that he may die**.*"* (1 Kings 21:9-10). The elders carried out this **wicked** scheme. The Biblical record documented that on the day of the fast, *"...two men,* **scoundrels**, *came in and sat before him; and the* **scoundrels** *witnessed against him, against Naboth, in the presence of the people, saying, "Naboth has blasphemed God and the king!" Then they took him outside the city and* **stoned him with stones, so that he died**" (1 Kings 21:13). When Jezebel heard that Naboth was **murdered**, she told her husband to take possession of Naboth vineyard. At that moment in time, people in the **witness** category influenced by the negative forces prevailed over one man among the positive forces. An innocent life was **murdered**.

The Psalmist spoke of people, influenced by the **wicked**, **evil**, **liar**, **hater**, and other negative attributes, in the **witness** category that became his **accusers**. In Psalms 109:1-29, he provided a series of things they did toward him as their leader and king. The Psalmist wrote in general, *"For the mouth of the* **wicked** *and the mouth of the* **deceitful** *have opened against me; they have spoken against me with a* **lying** *tongue. They have also surrounded me with words of* **hatred**, *and fought against me without a cause. In return for my <u>love</u> they are my* **accusers**, *but I give myself to prayer. Thus they have rewarded me* **evil** *for* **good**, *and* **hatred** *for my <u>love</u>"* (Psalms 109:2-5). BTT allows one to see that the Psalmist's "**accusers**" were people in the **witness** category influenced by the negative attributes.

In the Book of Hosea, the Lord shared that each one of His prophets served in the **witness** category and had the positive attributes. To the nation of Israel, the Lord said, *"I have also spoken by the prophets, and have multiplied visions; I have given symbols through the* **witness** *of the prophets"* (Hosea 12:10). The point here is that the things that the Lord gave the prophets for the nation of Israel were **righteous** and positive. The prophets were **witnesses** from God who brought positive <u>testimony</u> to the people for their welfare. However, the nation of Israel lacked the <u>discernment</u> needed to distinguish the truth, because there were many people in the **witness** category influenced by the negative attributes, who provided ***false testimony*** against the prophets and the Word of the Lord. Without God's Word, discernment of the truth is impossible. This message is consistent with the prophet Malachi's message from the Lord. The Lord told the people that He would serve as the ultimate **witness** against those who refused His Word. Malachi documented from the Lord, "*...I will come near you for judgment; I will be a swift* **witness** *against sorcerers, against* **adulterers**, *against* **perjurers**, *against those who* exploit *wage earners and widows and orphans, and against those who turn away an alien— because they do not fear Me," says the Lord of hosts*" (Malachi 3:5). From here, consider the New Testament's insights into the **witness** category.

Jesus documents that people in the **witness** category influenced by the negative attributes, have an inner spirit problem. He stated, "*For out of the heart proceed* **evil** *thoughts,* **murders**, **adulteries**, **fornications**, **thefts**, **false** **witness**, *blasphemies. These are the things which defile a man...*" (Matthew 15:19-20). BTT allows one to see that the negative attributes lodge themselves in one's spiritual heart when one allows their influences. Only God's Word can purge these attributes from one's inner spirit and provide future protection. God's Word prepares the spiritual heart for acceptance of the positive attributes. Hence, when one finds him or herself in the **witness *category*** and needs to protect oneself during a time of spiritual warfare, Jesus gave the following instructions. He said, "*...if your brother sins against you, go and tell him his fault between you and him alone. If he hears you, you have gained your brother. But if he will not hear, take with you one or two more, that 'by the mouth of two or three* **witnesses** *every word may be established.' And if he refuses to hear them, tell it to the church. But if he refuses even to hear the church, let him be to you like a heathen and a tax collector*" (Matthew 18:15-17). One should notice that Jesus used the same principles set forth by God in Deuteronomy 17:6-7; 19:15-19. The reality about the Scriptures documented in Matthew 18:15-17 is the fact that it applies to everyone. However, when God's way is unknown or incorrectly taught, abuse on the spiritual battlefield occurs in unquantifiable amounts.

Jesus pointed out to the scribes and Pharisees that they were among the people in the **witness** category influenced by the negative attributes. He said to them, "*Woe to you, scribes and Pharisees, hypocrites! Because you build the tombs of the prophets and adorn the monuments of the* **righteous**, *and say, 'If we had lived in the days of our fathers, we would not have been partakers with them* **in the blood of** *the prophets.' Therefore you are* **witnesses** *against yourselves that you are sons of those who* **murdered** *the prophets*" (Matthew 23:31). Similarly, Jesus told them, "*Woe to you! For you build the tombs of the prophets, and your fathers* **killed** *them. In fact, you bear* **witness** *that you approve the deeds of your fathers; for they indeed* **killed** *them, and you build their tombs*" (Luke 11:47-48). Clearly, the behavior and actions of the scribes and Pharisees demonstrated they were in the **witness** category and influenced by negative attributes.

Jesus' illegitimate trial and the accusations brought against Him demonstrated another classic example of people in the **witness** category influenced by the negative attributes. The Biblical record documented, "*...the chief priests, the elders, and all the council sought* ***false testimony*** *against Jesus to put Him to death, but found none. Even though many* ***false*** **witnesses** *came forward, they found none. But at last two* ***false*** **witnesses** *came forward...*" (Matthew 26:59-60). Mark documented, "*For many bore* ***false*** **witness** *against Him, but* *their <u>testimonies</u> did not agree...*" (Mark 14:56-58). In fact, the Biblical record documented the high priest became his own ***false* witness** against Jesus. The high priest, "*...tore his clothes, saying, "He has spoken blasphemy! What further need do we have of* **witnesses***? Look, now you have heard His blasphemy!*" (Matthew 26:65; Mark 14:63). As the crowd and the high priest participated in the **witness** category against the Son of God, their words, actions, and behaviors showed a substantial manifestation of the negative attributes working in their inner spirits.

Finally, the apostles provided some pearls of wisdom about the people in the **witness** category. These pearls documented the influence of either the positive or the negative attributes on this category. These pearls of wisdom included:

- "*Owe no one anything except to <u>love</u> one another, for he who <u>loves</u> another has fulfilled the law. For the commandments, "You shall not commit* **adultery***," "You shall not* **murder***," "You shall not* **steal***," "You shall not bear* ***false* witness***," "You shall not <u>covet</u>," and if there is any other commandment, are all summed up in this saying, namely, "You shall <u>love</u> your neighbor as yourself." <u>Love</u> does no harm to a neighbor; therefore <u>love</u> is the fulfillment of the law*" (Romans 13:8-10)

- "*...By the mouth of two or three* **witnesses** *every word shall be established*" (2 Corinthians 13:1)

- "*Do not receive an* **accusation** *against an elder except from two or three* **witnesses**" (1 Timothy 5:19)

- "*And the things that you have heard from me among many* **witnesses***, commit these to* ***faithful*** *men who will be able to teach others also*" (2 Timothy 2:2)

- "*Therefore we also, since we are surrounded by so great a cloud of* **witnesses***, let us lay aside every weight, and the sin which so easily ensnares us, and let us run with endurance the race that is set before us, looking unto Jesus, the author and finisher of our* **faith***, who for the joy that was set before Him endured the cross, despising the shame, and has sat down at the* **right** *hand of the throne of God*" (Hebrews 12:1-2)

- "*This is He who came by water and blood—Jesus Christ; not only by water, but by water and blood. And it is the Spirit who bears* **witness***, because the Spirit is truth. For there are three that bear* **witness** *in heaven: the Father, the Word, and the Holy Spirit; and these three are one. And there are three that bear* **witness** *on earth: the Spirit, the water, and the blood; and these three agree as one. If we receive the* **witness** *of men, the* **witness** *of God is greater; for this is the* **witness** *of God which He has <u>testified</u> of His Son. He who believes in the Son of God has the* **witness** *in himself; he who does not believe God has made Him a* **liar***, because he has not believed the <u>testimony</u> that God has given of His Son*" (1 John 5:6-10)

BTT allows one to see that the **harvest** has untold numbers of people in the **witness** category. Some operate in public while others work in secret. These people can either validate one's character, reputation, or activity or operate in secrecy to destroy one behind closed doors. Spiritually, one in the **witness** category always supports either the positive or the negative forces of the war campaign. One has no choice in this matter because indecision is a choice in and of itself. A *false* **witness** corrupts as many people as possible with *false* testimony; especially in cases against the positive forces, their *good* works, and God's Word overall. Hence, this category requires exposure to the Gospel of Jesus Christ to strengthen the balance between the positive and negative forces of the war campaign. Remember, a person in the **witness** category who has tasted the *goodness* of God (Hebrews 6:4-6), cannot keep silent when *evil* is present. **Witnesses** in the positive forces of the war campaign, who have experienced the divine nature of God and seen His providential power, are like Jesus' disciples of whom He said, "*I tell you that if these should keep silent, the stones would immediately cry out*" (Luke 19:40). If one does keep silent, either he or she lacks spiritual maturity, or the positive attributes are not present in their lives. Do not be deceived, for one can easily find one's inner spirit compromised.

The **Prudent category:** BTT allows one to see that one must use the Hebrew term transliterated as "*châkâm*[1]" to understand this category of people from those in the wise category. The people of the wise category will be discussed next. From the Hebrew language, the **prudent** are skillful (in technical work), wise (in administration), and learned or educated people. Where wisdom is best understood as the accumulation of knowledge, experience, and discernment, which allows one to appropriately apply the information he or she acquired, **prudence** is more specific, focused, and task oriented. People in this category offer great skills and capabilities to forces involved in either physical or spiritual warfare. For people in the *prudent* category are self-motivated, and can govern and discipline themselves using "reason". They exercise skills in judgment primarily based on the knowledge they acquire. They exercise practical sense and shrewdness in managing their affairs and they exercise caution and suspicion when it comes to danger or risk. They are a people blessed with the innate capability to turn knowledge into professional skills, talents, and capabilities. Hence, BTT allows one to see that the negative attributes prefer to keep people confused about people in the **prudent** category because of the capabilities they can bring to the positive forces. In spiritual warfare today, people identified as prodigies, eccentric, high IQs, and in some cases autistic, are placed in the **prudent** category. But this is man's idea and not supported by Scripture. Anyone can be **prudent** for everyone has a skill, talent, or capability that is a gift from God. Sometimes the gift takes a while to discover but every level or degree is important to God. It is how one uses his or her skills, talents, or capabilities in spiritual warfare that make the difference. With this idea in mind, let us consider the Proverbs.

Twice, the Spirit of wisdom revealed to Solomon that, "*A* **prudent** *man foresees* **evil** *and hides himself, but the* **simple** *pass on and are punished*" (Proverbs 22:3 and 27:12). Clearly, based on this proverb alone, a person that is **prudent** can exercise positive or negative behaviors that will protect him or her in spiritual warfare. Why is this possible? The Biblical

---

[1] Strong's # 2450 - חָכָם - Old Testament Hebrew Lexical Dictionary. (n.d.). Retrieved from https://www.studylight.org/lexicons/hebrew/2450.html. Accessed 18 February 2019

record documented several things that explain one's actions in the **prudent** category. First, the Spirit of wisdom revealed to Solomon, "...*the* **prudent** *are crowned with knowledge*" (Proverbs 14:18). It simply means there are some people in the world who are blessed with the gift of knowledge. These people can take in information from multiple sources, and quicker than the average person, convert that information to useable knowledge. However, this person is no better than you or I. They may have the innate ability to process information faster, but it is how he or she uses that knowledge that makes the difference. In fact, the Spirit of wisdom revealed a fact to Solomon that makes one in the **prudent** category even more interesting. She revealed that the "*the heart of the* **prudent** *acquires knowledge...*" (Proverbs 18:15). Since the fleshly heart only pumps blood through the human body, it stands to reason that the author is referring to the spiritual heart. This understanding is critical for understanding spiritual warfare. For people blessed to be in the **prudent** category have a gift for rapidly gaining and processing information into knowledge at the inner spirit level. Therefore, if the information acquired by the spiritual heart is tainted by the negative attributes, the owner of that inner spirit is also tainted. Conversely, if the information acquired by the spiritual heart comes from the positive attributes, the owner of that inner spirit is filled with ***goodness***.

This is why the Spirit of wisdom further revealed, "*Every* **prudent** *man acts with knowledge...*" (Proverbs 13:16). This scripture reveals the nexus where all things come together. BTT helps one understand that a person in the **prudent** category can foresee ***evil*** and hide according to Proverbs 22:3 and 27:12. He or she is acting with the knowledge (Proverbs 13:16) that he or she is crowned with according to Proverbs 14:18. This person's behavior will either be from the influences of a positive or negative spiritual stimulus. The behavior is positive if the person acts with their knowledge to engage in spiritual warfare at a future time and let others know of the ***evil*** that is ahead. The behavior is negative if the same person saw ***evil*** with the knowledge he or she obtained and hid without helping or warning others. This person's behavior is sinful. Clearly, the negative attributes were influencing this person's decision to protect only himself or herself instead of helping others. Let us dig deeper on this point.

The Spirit of wisdom revealed that, "*A* **prudent** *man conceals knowledge...*" (Proverbs 12:23). BTT allows one to see that this is not knowledge of something illegal or ***immoral***. This is general knowledge or knowledge of another person's personal mistakes that if used improperly will bring harm. Hence, this Scripture indicates that the influences of either the positive or the negative attributes is inferred. If a **prudent** man conceals knowledge (not of something illegal) so another person can start his or her life anew, this is a positive act for all involved. This positive behavior demonstrates confidentiality and respect. In this scenario, the **prudent** person demonstrates the acquired wisdom from above that is, "...*first pure, then peaceable, gentle, willing to yield, full of* **mercy** *and* **good** *fruits, without partiality and without hypocrisy*" (James 3:17). This **prudent** person's positive influence strives to help another person overcome negative attributes and any shame associated with it. Hence, Solomon documented that, "...*a* **prudent** *man covers shame*" (Proverbs 12:16). When one knows that another person has stumbled and treats the knowledge confidentially, the erring person has an opportunity to recover from his or her stumble. For leaders, this positive behavior allows subordinates to make mistakes and recover from those mistakes personally and professionally without *fear*. An erring person is encouraged, supported, and properly mentored by a **prudent** person influenced by positive attributes. From this scenario, one can understand Solomon's proverb that states, "*He who covers a transgression seeks love, but he who repeats a matter separates friends*" (Proverbs 17:9). Thus, a **prudent** leader influenced by the negative attributes who learns of his or her subordinate's error, may use the erring persons shame for control and advantage. This leader will more likely seek special favors or publicly shame the erring person. This behavior mentally and spiritually destroys the one who stumbled. This person's personal and professional growth ceases as the shame crushes his or her inner spirit. BTT allows one to see that the ***oppressor*** attribute is involved in this leader's behavior too.

In another scenario that still focuses on Proverbs 12:23, if a **prudent** person conceals knowledge and allows harm to come to others, this is a negative act. The **prudent** person applied earthly wisdom in the scenario. That is, the wisdom applied "*...does not descend from above, but is earthly, sensual, demonic*" (James 3:15). ***Evil*** and other negative attributes will influence a **prudent** person to refuse to share knowledge that can help another person's situation. This **prudent** person's action causes many people to move into the camp of the negative forces. In addition to this scenario, if one in the **prudent** category conceals knowledge of something that is illegal or a crime, he or she is involved in sin. Clearly the influence of the negative attributes is involved and the person's decision is swayed by the negative force's use of spiritual warfare.

BTT allows one to see that a **prudent** person who conceals knowledge (Proverbs 12:23) stands at the demarcation of choice. One who struggles with a decision to help or not help others when they have the knowledge to do so is an indication of the influence of the negative attributes in their inner spirit. When trouble is approaching, one in the **prudent** category blessed with knowledge and the positive attributes, would never hesitate to help others avoid trouble. Now this does not eliminate one's time to contemplate whether an action is ***right*** or wrong. For contemplation is part of the human dynamic between the cognitive mind and inner spirit. In fact, the Spirit of wisdom revealed to Solomon that "*...the* **prudent** *considers well his steps*" (Proverbs 14:15). This statement informs one that the people of the **prudent** category weigh their options well and do not make decisions hastily. They mentally and spiritually wrestle with their choices before reaching a decision and direction to journey. Hence, a **prudent** person influenced by the positive attributes use God's written Word to guide their actions.

Solomon documented, "*...he who receives correction is* **prudent**" (Proverbs 15:5). In the context of Solomon's writing, God's correction is implied. BTT allows one to see that anyone who receives God's correction, through His Holy Word, falls in the **prudent** category. Correction comes to all who strive to walk on the ***right*** path of life. This is why Solomon wrote, "*The wisdom of the* **prudent** *is to understand his way...*" (Proverbs 14:8). In other words, the wisdom a **prudent** person acquires is the key for understanding the path he or she walks. In spiritual warfare, the positive and negative attributes desire to influence one in the **prudent** category's understanding. Doing so influences him or her to choose sides in the war campaign. BTT allows one to see that the spiritual tug of war occurring between the positive and negative forces reemphasizes the importance of <u>discernment</u>. If one lacks the discipline to <u>discern</u> **right** from ***wrong***, earthly wisdom (James 3:15) will overtake <u>godly</u> wisdom (James 3:17). Without <u>discernment</u>, the negative forces of the war campaign will influence one in the **prudent** category to reason their own path. When left to one's own reasoning, one in the **prudent** category will walk toward *evil* without realizing it. The Biblical record scripturally establishes this idea where it documents:

- *"The way of a **fool** is **right** in his own eyes..."* (Proverbs 12:15)

- *"All the ways of a man are pure in his own eyes..."* (Proverbs 16:2)

- *"Every way of a man is **right** in his own eyes..."* (Proverbs 21:2)

- *"O Lord, I know the way of man is not in himself; it is not in man who walks to direct his own steps"* (Jeremiah 10:23)

God's wisdom gives people in this **prudent** category true understanding. Some other areas that one can study about people in the **prudent** category include:

- *"The wise in heart will be called* **prudent**...*"* (Proverbs 16:21). This illustrates the complexity of the people in the **harvest**. This scriptures document one can be in two or more categories of the **harvest** at the same time.

- *"...a* **prudent** *wife is from the Lord"* (Proverbs 19:14). This illustrates that a **prudent** person does not have to face choices in life alone. God knows what every adult man needs in life if one simply trusts in Him.

- *"Walk* **prudently** *when you go to the house of God; and draw near to hear rather than to give the sacrifice of **fools**, for they do not know that they do **evil**"* (Ecclesiastes 5:1). This Scripture documents the effects of either the positive or the negative attribute on a **prudent** person and the care they must exercise in the presence of the Almighty God. Showing respect for God requires focus and understanding.

Now consider what the rest of the Biblical record documents about people in the **prudent** category. First, keep in mind that God crowns the **prudent** with knowledge (Proverbs 14:18) and this knowledge translates into professional skills, talents, and capabilities. With this understanding, here are some of the numerous examples found in the Biblical record of people in this category who supported the positive forces of the war campaign. The Bible documented:

Who	What Is Documented
Abel	*"...Now Abel was a keeper of sheep..."* (Genesis 4:2)
Jabal and Jubal	*"...Jabal. He was the father of those who dwell in tents and have livestock. His brother's name was Jubal. He was the father of all those who play the harp and flute"* (Genesis 4:20-21)
Noah	*"Make yourself an ark of gopherwood; make rooms in the ark, and cover it inside and outside with pitch. And this is how you shall make it..."* (Genesis 6:14-15)
Nimrod	*"...he began to be a mighty one on the earth. He was a mighty hunter before the Lord; therefore it is said, "Like Nimrod the mighty hunter before the Lord"* (Genesis 10:8-9)
Esau	*"...Esau was a skillful hunter, a man of the field..."* (Genesis 25:27)

Artisans who made Aaron and Aaron's sons holy garments	The Lord told Moses to "*...speak to all who are gifted artisans, whom I have filled with the spirit of wisdom, that they may make Aaron's garments, to consecrate him, that he may minister to Me as priest. And these are the garments which they shall make: a breastplate, an ephod, a robe, a skillfully woven tunic, a turban, and a sash...*" (Exodus 28:3-4)
Bezalel and Aholiab	"*Bezalel the son of Uri, the son of Hur, of the tribe of Judah; and He has filled him with the Spirit of God, in wisdom and understanding, in knowledge and all manner of workmanship, to design artistic works, to work in gold and silver and bronze, in cutting jewels for setting, in carving wood, and to work in all manner of artistic workmanship. And He has put in his heart the ability to teach, in him and Aholiab the son of Ahisamach, of the tribe of Dan. He has filled them with skill to do all manner of work of the engraver and the designer and the tapestry maker, in blue, purple, and scarlet thread, and fine linen, and of the weaver—those who do every work and those who design artistic works*" (Exodus 35:30-35)
David	He was "*a man who is a skillful player on the harp*" (1 Samuel 16:16). "*Then one of the servants answered and said, "Look, I have seen a son of Jesse the Bethlehemite, who is skillful in playing, a mighty man of valor, a man of war,* **prudent** *in speech, and a handsome person; and the Lord is with him.*" (1 Samuel 16:18)
Sidonians	"*...For you know there is none among us who has skill to cut timber like the Sidonians*" (1 Kings 5:6)
Huram	"*...Huram from Tyre. He was the son of a widow from the tribe of Naphtali, and his father was a man of Tyre, a bronze worker; he was filled with wisdom and understanding and skill in working with all kinds of bronze work...*" (1 Kings 7: 13-14)
	"*...a skillful man, endowed with understanding...*" and "*...master craftsman*" who is "*...skilled to work in gold and silver, bronze and iron, stone and wood, purple and blue, fine linen and crimson, and to make any engraving and to accomplish any plan which may be given to him...*" (2 Chronicles 2: 13-14)
44,760 valiant men	"*The sons of Reuben, the Gadites, and half the tribe of Manasseh had forty-four thousand seven hundred and sixty valiant men, men able to bear shield and sword, to shoot with the bow, and skillful in war, who went to war*" (1 Chronicles 5:18)
Chenaniah	"*Chenaniah, leader of the Levites, was instructor in charge of the music, because he was skillful...*" (1 Chronicles 15:22)
Workmen of every skill	"*Moreover there are workmen with you in abundance: woodsmen and stonecutters, and all types of skillful men for every kind of work*" (1 Chronicles 22:15)
288 musicians	"*Moreover David and the captains of the army separated for the service some of the sons of Asaph, of Heman, and of Jeduthun, who should prophesy with harps, stringed instruments, and cymbals. And the number of the skilled men performing their service was... So the number of them, with their brethren who were instructed in the songs of the Lord, all who were skillful, was two hundred and eighty-eight*" (1 Chronicles 25:1-7)
Uzziah and other men	"*Then Uzziah prepared for them, for the entire army, shields, spears, helmets, body armor, bows, and slings to cast stones. And he made devices*

	in Jerusalem, invented by skillful men, to be on the towers and the corners, to shoot arrows and large stones..." (2 Chronicles 26:14-15)
Others of the Levites	"...Others of the Levites, all of whom were skillful with instruments of music, were over the burden bearers and were overseers of all who did work in any kind of service. And some of the Levites were scribes, officers, and gatekeepers" (2 Chronicles 34:12-13)
Ezra	"...this Ezra came up from Babylon; and he was a skilled scribe in the Law of Moses, which the Lord God of Israel had given" (Ezra 7:6)
Daniel, Hananiah, Mishael, and Azariah	"As for these four young men, God gave them knowledge and skill in all literature and wisdom; and Daniel had understanding in all visions and dreams" (Daniel 1:17)
Joseph and his Son Jesus	"Is this not the carpenter's son? Is not His mother called Mary? And His brothers James, Joses, Simon, and Judas?" (Matthew 3:55). And for Jesus, "Is this not the carpenter, the Son of Mary, and brother of James, Joses, Judas, and Simon? And are not His sisters here with us?" So they were offended at Him" (Mark 6:3)
Paul, Aquila, and Pricilla	"...he found a certain Jew named Aquila, born in Pontus, who had recently come from Italy with his wife Priscilla (because Claudius had commanded all the Jews to depart from Rome); and he came to them. So, because he was of the same trade, he stayed with them and worked; for by occupation they were tentmakers" (Acts 18:2-3)
The apostles, prophets, evangelists, pastors, and teachers	"And He Himself gave some to be apostles, some prophets, some evangelists, and some pastors and teachers, for the equipping of the saints for the work of ministry, for the edifying of the body of Christ..." (Ephesians 4:11-12)

Table 130: Examples of People in the Prudent Category Influenced by Positive Attributes

BTT allows one to see that each of the people listed in Table 130 were in the **prudent** category and crowned with knowledge. One can see how the knowledge translated to professional skills, talents, and capabilities as they were influenced by the positive attributes in their inner spirits. These **prudent** people supported the positive forces. But the Biblical record also provides examples of people in the **prudent** category influence by the negative attributes. One can consider for oneself, the damage that these people did on the spiritual battlefield. Examples include:

Who	What Is Documented
Cain	"...Cain was a tiller of the ground" (Genesis 4:2)
Tubal-Cain	"...Tubal-Cain, an instructor of every craftsman in bronze and iron..." (Genesis 4:22)
The magicians of Egypt	"Now it came to pass in the morning that his spirit was troubled, and he sent and called for all the magicians of Egypt and all its wise men. And Pharaoh told them his dreams, but there was no one who could interpret them for Pharaoh" (Genesis 41:8)

	"But Pharaoh also called the wise men and the sorcerers; so the magicians of Egypt, they also did in like manner with their enchantments" (Exodus 7:11)
	"Then the magicians of Egypt did so with their enchantments; and Pharaoh's heart grew hard, and he did not heed them, as the Lord had said" (Exodus 7:22; Exodus 8:7; Exodus 8:18-19; Exodus 9:11)
People who practice witchcraft, soothsaying, interprets omens, sorcery, spell conjurers, medium, spiritist, or who call up the dead	*"When you come into the land which the Lord your God is giving you, you shall not learn to follow the abominations of those nations. There shall not be found among you anyone who makes his son or his daughter pass through the fire, or one who practices witchcraft, or a soothsayer, or one who interprets omens, or a sorcerer, or one who conjures spells, or a medium, or a spiritist, or one who calls up the dead"* (Deuteronomy 18:9-11)
The nation of Israel	*"...they left all the commandments of the Lord their God, made for themselves a molded image and two calves, made a wooden image and worshiped all the host of heaven, and served Baal. And they caused their sons and daughters to pass through the fire, practiced witchcraft and soothsaying, and sold themselves to do evil in the sight of the Lord, to provoke Him to anger. Therefore the Lord was very angry with Israel, and removed them from His sight; there was none left but the tribe of Judah alone"* (2 Kings 17:16-18)
King Manasseh	*"...he rebuilt the high places which Hezekiah his father had destroyed; he raised up altars for Baal, and made a wooden image, as Ahab king of Israel had done; and he worshiped all the host of heaven and served them. He also built altars in the house of the Lord, of which the Lord had said, "In Jerusalem I will put My name." And he built altars for all the host of heaven in the two courts of the house of the Lord. Also he made his son pass through the fire, practiced soothsaying, used witchcraft, and consulted spiritists and mediums. He did much evil in the sight of the Lord, to provoke Him to anger. He even set a carved image of Asherah that he had made, in the house of which the Lord"* (2 Kings 21:3-7) *and sorcery* (2 Chronicles 33:6)
The diviners of Babylon	*"Who frustrates the signs of the babblers, and drives diviners mad; who turns wise men backward, and makes their knowledge foolishness..."* (Isaiah 44:25)
Magicians, astrologers, sorcerers, and soothsayers	*"Then the king gave the command to call the magicians, the astrologers, the sorcerers, and the Chaldeans to tell the king his dreams. So they came and stood before the king"* (Daniel 2:2), *and soothsayers* (Daniel 2:27; Daniel 4:7)
Governors, satraps, advisors, counselors, and administrators, in King Darius's kingdom	*"All the governors of the kingdom, the administrators and satraps, the counselors and advisors, have consulted together to establish a royal statute and to make a firm decree, that whoever petitions any god or man for thirty days, except you, O king, shall be cast into the den of lions"* (Daniel 6:7)
Idol craftsmen	*"Now they sin more and more, and have made for themselves molded images, idols of their silver, according to their skill; all of it is the work of craftsmen. They say of them, "Let the men who sacrifice kiss the calves!""* (Hosea 13:2)

Simon the sorcerer	"...there was a certain man called Simon, who previously practiced sorcery in the city and astonished the people of Samaria, claiming that he was someone great, to whom they all gave heed, from the least to the greatest, saying, "This man is the great power of God.""" (Acts 8:9-10)
Elymas the sorcerer	"...Elymas the sorcerer (for so his name is translated) withstood them, seeking to turn the proconsul away from the **faith**" (Acts 13:8)
Demetrius	"For a certain man named Demetrius, a silversmith, who made silver shrines of Diana, brought no small profit to the craftsmen" (Acts 19:24)
Alexander the coppersmith	Paul told Timothy that he, "...did me much harm. May the Lord repay him according to his works" (2 Timothy 4:14)

Table 131: Examples of People in the Prudent Category Influenced by Negative Attributes

Moving forward in the Biblical record, the nation of Israel had people in the **prudent** category among them. The negative forces influenced their behavior and they used their knowledge for *evil*. Thus, God sent Isaiah to deliver a strong "woe" to Israel and pointed out the *folly*. Isaiah told them, "*Woe to those who are wise in their own eyes, and* **prudent** *in their own sight!*" (Isaiah 5:21). Remember, a "woe" from the Almighty God is not a mild warning. Later Isaiah gave another stern warning from the Lord. The Biblical record documented that the Lord said, "*Therefore, behold, I will again do a marvelous work among this people, a marvelous work and a wonder; for the wisdom of their wise men shall perish, and the understanding of their* **prudent** *men shall be hidden*" (Isaiah 29:14). However, there is more to the story than just the destruction of Israel and punishment of the people in the **prudent** category. BTT allows one to see that people in the **prudent** category can be both believers and nonbelievers. One can see this point clearly in the fact that God used a nonbeliever, the King of Assyria, to punish the nation of Israel. Nevertheless, even for this king, he was not immune to the influence of the negative attributes. The king failed to realize that it is how one uses the blessing of knowledge that makes the difference. Here is what happened. Isaiah documented, after the fall of Israel and Jerusalem, the Lord said in Isaiah 10:12-14:

> "*...I will punish the fruit of the <u>arrogant</u> heart of the king of Assyria, and the glory of his <u>haughty</u> looks." For he says: "By the strength of my hand I have done it, and by my wisdom, for I am* **prudent***; also I have removed the boundaries of the people, and have <u>robbed</u> their treasuries; so I have put down the inhabitants like a valiant man. My hand has found like a nest the riches of the people, and as one gathers eggs that are left, I have gathered all the earth; and there was no one who moved his wing, nor opened his mouth with even a peep*"

You see, the King of Assyria failed to recognize that the Lord allowed him to destroy the nation of Israel and Jerusalem; it was not by his own hand. Even though he was a man in the **prudent** category, he allowed himself to be influenced by the negative attributes. The Lord punished him because the ***proud*** attribute influenced him to sin by <u>boasting</u>.

But Isaiah was not the only prophet to warn the people in the **prudent** category among the nation of Israel. The prophet Hosea documented, "*Who is wise? Let him understand these things. Who is **prudent**? Let him know them. For the ways of the Lord are **right**; the **righteous** walk in them, but transgressors stumble in them*" (Hosea 14:9). The prophet Amos also documented, "*Therefore the **prudent** keep silent at that time, for it is an **evil** time*" (Amos 5:13). Yes, the nation of Israel fell into apostasy partly because people in the **prudent** category saw *evil* approaching and failed to warn the nation of the truth. The **prudent** played a significant role in the nation of Israel's demise. God will apply His same wrath today to people in the **prudent** category who see His truth coming to fruition from His Holy Word and remain silent.

The New Testament of the Biblical record documented that Jesus also identified the fact that there were people in the **prudent** category. Jesus stated in a prayer, "*... thank You, Father, Lord of heaven and earth, that You have hidden these things from the wise and **prudent** and have revealed them to babes*" (Matthew 11:25; Luke 10:21-22). BTT allows one to see that God chose to hide His Truth from people in the **prudent** category while revealing it to people He chose according to Luke 10:1-12. Besides the twelve disciples, Jesus selected and taught seventy people His Gospel message and gave them the mission of preparing the Jewish world for its delivery. The Truth they had, and the power they were given to deliver it, was exceedingly great. Jesus did not reveal His Truth and power to the people in the wise and **prudent** categories because the influences of the negative attributes working in their inner spirits would have corrupted God's Word during its delivery. In fact, Jesus chastised some of the cities that rejected His Word according to Luke 10:13-16 and Matthew 11:20-24. When the seventy returned "*...with joy, saying, "Lord, even the demons are subject to us in Your name"*" (Luke 10:17), Jesus had to remind them Who gave them their authority. He told them "*Nevertheless do not rejoice in this, that the spirits are subject to you, but rather rejoice because your names are written in heaven*" (Luke 10: 20). Jesus gave these disciples spiritual powers for a short time to advance His ministry. Jesus did not want the disciples to rejoice over their abilities because He understood men. Jesus knew the disciple's new abilities could give way to exploitation by the negative attributes in the war campaign. Jesus reminded the disciples of this fact so that the influence of the ***proud*** attribute could not gain a foothold in their inner spirits. Nevertheless, even these seventy would eventually leave Jesus as He taught them greater knowledge from God's Word according to John 6:66. The seventy disciples left Jesus side saying, "*This is a hard saying; who can understand it?*" (John 6:60).

When Paul spoke of the people who were "*inventors of evil things*" in Romans 1:30, more than likely he was referring to people in the **prudent** category influenced by the negative attributes. Moreover, when he wrote 1 Corinthians 1:18-25, he was speaking of people with all the negative attributes and people in the **prudent** category as well. He wrote:

> "*For the message of the cross is **foolishness** to those who are perishing, but to us who are being saved it is the power of God. For it is written:*
>
>> "*I will destroy the wisdom of the wise, and bring to nothing the understanding of the **prudent**.*"

BTT allows one to see that when people in the **prudent** category allow the negative forces of spiritual warfare to influence their reasoning, God brings their understanding to nothing. They cannot understand the majesty of God, His Son, or the Holy Spirit because they reject the whole Gospel of Jesus Christ. Moreover, the idea that an Almighty God would sacrifice His Son for humanity to live, defies reason for most **prudent** people. Why? Because the negative forces of the war campaign generate fog that prevents them from seeing this Truth. The fact that the Biblical record documents, *"For as the heavens are higher than the earth, so are My ways higher than your ways, and My thoughts than your thoughts"* (Isaiah 55:9), has no meaning to **prudent** people influenced by the negative attributes. These are a people who insists on using their skills, talents, or capabilities, inappropriately to vainly worship the Almighty God. **Prudent** people influenced by the positive attributes are obedient to God's Word, submit to authority, and follow Christ's direction exclusively. Until Jesus and His Truth are accepted, their knowledge is in vain because it leads them down a path of darkness and the soul lost in torment.

The **Wise Category:** Next to the people of the poor category, this is probably the second largest category of people in the **harvest**. This community ranges from the formally educated in institutions of higher learning, to those who have become **wise** from years of experience, to those who are street **wise** from living through life's hardships and pain. However, in the war campaign, none of these matters. What matters is how one's inner spirit allows the influence of the positive and negative attributes to use the wisdom he or she has acquired. Make no mistake, hearing God's Word makes a major difference in the lives of people in the **wise** category. One in this category has the innate ability to think critically, to analyze, to create, and to find practical solutions for solving problems. The difference between one in this category and one in the prudent category is often hard to see. However, BTT allows one to see that where a person in the prudent category has a spiritual gift for processing knowledge into one or more skills, talents, or capabilities; a person in the **wise** category think at a higher level to connect broader concepts together using the spiritual gifts of people in the prudent category. For example, where a prudent person may have the spiritual gift to read music and play one or more instruments, a **wise** person can bring multiple prudent people together to create an orchestra and play a symphony. In addition, because of the beauty and complexity of God's workmanship, a person can exist in both the **wise** and prudent categories.

People in the **wise** category are often described as geniuses, intellectuals, or brilliant. For this reason, the negative attributes especially desire people in this category for their ability to advance the war campaign in their favor. The positive attributes rely on God. BTT allows one to see that when the positive attributes influence people in this category, God's gifts to humanity edify Him. These gifts can include all the sciences, mathematics, art, architecture, geology, medicine, and the like. Conversely, when the negative attributes influence people in this category, God's gifts to humanity are used to deny Him. Worldly <u>*wisdom*</u> takes precedence over God *"...because, although they knew God, they did not glorify Him as God, nor were thankful, but became futile in their thoughts, and their **foolish** hearts were darkened"* (Romans 1:27).

Hence, enlightenment, philosophy, evolution, scientology, humanism, relativism, and a host of other ideologies based on earthly _wisdom_, leads people away from the one True God. The negative attributes prevent many people in the **wise** category from hearing the Gospel because of the fog of the war campaign. They are ***self*-wise** in their cognitive minds while their spiritual hearts are captive to the influence of the negative attributes. Their spiritual hearts get seared shut (1 Timothy 4:2) and their souls are lost. Only God's Word, their submission to it, and repentance will free their spiritual hearts to give them the opportunity for salvation.

Now one needs to be clear on the difference between _wisdom_ and being in the **wise category.** The two are not the same. _Wisdom_ is a spiritual element that comes from God and Satan alike. God's _wisdom_ makes a person **wise** with _godly wisdom_ and saves one's soul. Conversely, Satan's _wisdom_ makes a person "smart" with earthly _wisdom_ that is demonic by nature. This _wisdom_ simply condemns one's life and soul to eternal damnation. No amount of Satan's _wisdom_ can save one's soul. The fog generated by the negative forces in spiritual warfare has blinded the religious community to this fact. The teachings on "hell" and other hard spiritual topics have taken a back seat to "positive-only" messages and motivational talks. Thus, the Bible documents the following information on the spiritual element of _godly wisdom_:

- "*For the Lord gives _wisdom_; from His mouth come knowledge and understanding...*" (Proverbs 2:6)

- "*The Lord by _wisdom_ founded the earth; by understanding He established the heavens; by His knowledge the depths were broken up, and clouds drop down the dew*" (Proverbs 3:19-20)

- "*The _fear_ of the Lord is the instruction of _wisdom_, and before **honor** is _humility_*" (Proverbs 15:33)

- "*There is no _wisdom_ or understanding or counsel against the Lord*" (Proverbs 21:30)

- "*...if you have bitter **envy** and _self-seeking_ in your hearts, do not _boast_ and **lie** against the truth. This _wisdom_ does not descend from above, but is earthly, sensual, demonic. For where **envy** and _self-seeking_ exist, confusion and every **evil** thing are there. But the _wisdom_ that is from above is first pure, then _peaceable_, gentle, willing to yield, full of **mercy** and **good** fruits, without partiality and without hypocrisy*" (James 3:14-17)

The point here is that there is a _wisdom_ accessible to the positive forces that come from God. This _wisdom_ came through the Spirit of _wisdom_ of the Old Testament and today comes through the work of the Holy Spirit in the New Testament. BTT allows one to see that God moved men to document the Holy Spirit's Word in the Bible. The inspired words of the apostles provide all _godly wisdom_ one requires for salvation today. In contrast, there is a _wisdom_ accessible to the negative forces that comes from Satan which is also documented throughout the Biblical record. Satan's _wisdom_ is passed down by word of mouth through academic forums, secret organizations, and religious practices and traditions. These things scar generations over lifetimes. Depending on the condition of a person's inner spirit, a person will either accept or reject the _wisdom_ they hear and the source espousing it. Knowing this Truth allows one to understand the impact that the positive or negative attributes have on anyone that falls in the **wise** category.

The Spirit of <u>wisdom</u> revealed to Solomon several benefits that God's <u>wisdom</u> provides for people in the **wise** category. She taught him:

- *"When <u>wisdom</u> enters your heart, and knowledge is pleasant to your soul, discretion will preserve you; understanding will keep you, to deliver you from the way of **evil**..."* (Proverbs 2:10-12)

- *"Hear instruction and be **wise**, and do not disdain it. Blessed is the man who listens to me, watching daily at my gates, waiting at the posts of my doors. For whoever finds me finds life, and obtains favor from the LORD; but he who sins against me wrongs his own soul; all those who **hate** me <u>love</u> death."* (Proverbs 8:35-36)

- *"Through <u>wisdom</u> a house is built, and by understanding it is established; by knowledge the rooms are filled with all precious and pleasant riches"* (Proverbs 24:3-4)

- *"He who gets <u>wisdom</u> <u>loves</u> his own soul; he who keeps understanding will find **good**"* (Proverbs 19:8) and *"So shall the knowledge of <u>wisdom</u> be to your soul; if you have found it, there is a prospect, and your hope will not be cut off"* (Proverbs 24:14)

- *"<u>Wisdom</u> rests in the heart of him who has understanding..."* (Proverbs 14:33) and *"<u>Wisdom</u> is in the sight of him who has understanding, but the eyes of a **fool** are on the ends of the earth"* (Proverbs 17:24)

- *"Happy is the man who finds <u>wisdom</u>, and the man who gains understanding; for her proceeds are better than the profits of silver, and her gain than fine gold. She is more precious than rubies, and all the things you may desire cannot compare with her"* (Proverbs 3:13-15) and, *"How much better to get <u>wisdom</u> than gold! And to get understanding is to be chosen rather than silver"* (Proverbs 16:16) and, *"Buy the truth, and do not sell it, also <u>wisdom</u> and instruction and understanding"* (Proverbs 23:23)

Now consider some of the many pearls of <u>wisdom</u> the Spirit of <u>wisdom</u> revealed to Solomon about people in the **wise** category influenced by the positive attributes.

"The lips of the **wise** disperse knowledge..." (Proverbs 15:7)	"...he who heeds counsel is **wise**" (Proverbs 12:15)	"A **wise** man <u>fears</u> and departs from **evil**..." (Proverbs 14:16)
"**Wise** people store up knowledge..." (Proverbs 10:14)	"...**wise** men turn away <u>wrath</u> (Proverbs 29:8)	"...he who wins souls is **wise**" (Proverb 11:30)
"Give instruction to a **wise** man, and he will be still **wiser**..." (Proverbs 9:9)	"A **wise** son makes a father glad, but a **foolish** man despises his mother" (Proverb 15:20)	"The ear that hears the rebukes of life will abide among the **wise**" (Proverbs 15:31)

"... Rebuke a **wise** man, and he will <u>love</u> you" (Proverbs 9:8)	"The **wise** in heart will receive commands..." (Proverbs 10:8)	"...the ear of the **wise** seeks knowledge" (Proverbs 18:150
"A **wise** man is strong, yes, a man of knowledge increases strength..." (Proverbs 24:5)	"The heart of the **wise** teaches his mouth, and adds learning to his lips" (Proverbs 16:23)	"Plans are established by counsel; by **wise** counsel <u>wage</u> war" (Proverbs 20:18)
"A **fool** vents all his feelings, but a **wise** man holds them back" (Proverbs 29:11)	"The tongue of the **wise** uses knowledge **rightly**..." (Proverbs 15:2)	"...the tongue of the **wise** promotes health" (Proverbs 12:18)
"The crown of the **wise** is their riches..." (Proverbs 14:24)	"...the lips of the **wise** will preserve them" (Proverbs 14:3)	"The **wise** shall inherit glory..." (Proverbs 3:35)
"He who walks with **wise** men will be **wise**, but the companion of **fools** will be destroyed" (Proverbs 13:20)	The **wise** in heart will be called prudent, and sweetness of the lips increases learning" (Proverbs 16:21)	"...for by **wise** counsel you will wage your own war, and in a multitude of counselors there is safety" (Proverbs 24:6)
"The king's favor is toward a **wise** servant, but his <u>wrath</u> is against him who causes shame" (Proverbs 14:35)	"A **wise** man scales the city of the mighty, and brings down the trusted stronghold" (Proverbs 21:22)	"The law of the **wise** is a fountain of life, to turn one away from the snares of death (Proverbs 13:14)
"Like an earring of gold and an ornament of fine gold is a **wise** rebuker to an obedient ear" (Proverbs 25:12)	"He who trusts in his own heart is a **fool**, but whoever walks **wisely** will be delivered" (Proverbs 28:26)	"...A **wise** son makes a glad father, but a **foolish** son is the grief of his mother" (Proverbs 10:1)
"...the **fool** will be servant to the **wise** of heart" (Proverbs 11:29)	"A **wise** son heeds his father's instruction..." (Proverbs 13:1)	"He who gathers in summer is a **wise** son..." (Proverbs 10:5)
"The **wise** woman builds her house, but the **foolish** pulls it down with her hands" (Proverbs 14:1)	"A **wise** servant will rule over a son who causes shame, and will share an inheritance among the brothers" (Proverbs 17:2)	"A **wise** king sifts out the **wicked**, and brings the threshing wheel over them" (Proverbs 20:26)
"<u>Wisdom</u> is found on the lips of him who has understanding, but a rod is for the back of him who is devoid of understanding" (Proverbs 10:13)	"...he who begets a **wise** child will delight in him. Let your father and your mother be glad, and let her who bore you <u>rejoice</u>" (Proverbs 23:24-25)	Concerning a virtuous wife: "She opens her mouth with <u>wisdom</u>, and on her tongue is the law of <u>kindness</u>" (Proverbs 31:26)
"...when the **wise** is instructed, he receives knowledge" (Proverbs 21:11)	"...there is desirable treasure, and oil in the dwelling of the **wise**..." (Proverbs 21:20)	"Whoever <u>loves</u> <u>wisdom</u> makes his father rejoice..." (Proverbs 29:3)
"A man will be commended according to his <u>wisdom</u>, but he who is of a **perverse**	"Listen to counsel and receive instruction, that you may be **wise** in your latter days" (Proverbs 19:20)	"The way of life winds upward for the **wise**, that he may turn away from hell below" (Proverbs 15:24)

heart will be despised" (Proverbs 12:8)		
"The mouth of the **righteous** brings forth <u>wisdom</u>..." (Proverbs 10:31)	"Answer a **fool** according to his **folly**, lest he be **wise** in his own eyes" (Proverbs 26:5)	The <u>wisdom</u> of the prudent is to understand his way..." (Proverbs 14:8)
"A **wise** man will hear and increase learning, and a man of understanding will attain **wise** counsel, to understand a proverb and an enigma, the words of the **wise** and their riddles" (Proverb 1:5-6)	"The rod and rebuke give <u>wisdom</u>, but a child left to himself brings shame to his mother" (Proverbs 29:15)	"Rebuke is more effective for a **wise** man than a hundred blows on a **fool**" (Proverbs 17:10)

Table 132: Pearls of <u>Wisdom</u> Concerning People in the Wise Category Who Allow the Influences of the Positive Attributes

In contrast, the Spirit of <u>wisdom</u> revealed pearls of wisdom that apply to people in the **wise** category who allowed the influences of the negative attributes. Solomon documented:

"...**fools** despise <u>wisdom</u> and instruction" (Proverbs 1:7)	"If you are **wise**, you are **wise** for yourself..." (Proverbs 9:12)	"...**fools** die for lack of <u>wisdom</u>" (Proverbs 10:21)
"These things also belong to the **wise**: It is not **good** to show partiality in judgment" (Proverbs 24:23)	"In the multitude of words sin is not lacking, but he who restrains his lips is **wise**" (Proverbs 10:19)	"Wine is a **mocker**, strong drink is a brawler, and whoever is led astray by it is not **wise**" (Proverbs 20:1)
"If a **wise** man contends with a **foolish** man, whether the **fool** <u>rages</u> or laughs, there is no peace" (Proverbs 29:9)	Do not speak in the hearing of a **fool**, for he will despise the <u>wisdom</u> of your words" (Proverbs 23:9)	"Why is there in the hand of a **fool** the purchase price of <u>wisdom</u>, since he has no heart for it?" (Proverbs 17:16)
"Even a **fool** is counted **wise** when he holds his <u>peace</u>; when he shuts his lips, he is considered perceptive" (Proverbs 17:28)	"Do not be **wise** in your own eyes; fear the LORD and depart from **evil**. It will be health to your flesh, and strength to your bones (Proverbs 3:7-8)	"Do you see a man **wise** in his own eyes? There is more hope for a **fool** than for him" (Proverbs 26:12)
"The **lazy** man is **wiser** in his own eyes than seven men who can answer sensibly" (Proverbs 26:16)	"A man who isolates himself seeks his own desire; he <u>rages</u> against all **wise** judgment" (Proverbs 18:1)	"A **scoffer** seeks <u>wisdom</u> and does not find it, but knowledge is easy to him who understands" (Proverbs 14:6)
"A **scoffer** does not <u>love</u> one who corrects him, nor will he go to the **wise**" (Proverbs 15:12)	"<u>Wisdom</u> is too lofty for a **fool**; he does not open his mouth in the gate" (Proverbs 24:7)	"When **pride** comes, then comes shame; but with the <u>humble</u> is <u>wisdom</u>" (Proverbs 11:2)

"By **pride** comes nothing but strife, but with the well-advised is <u>wisdom</u>" (Proverbs 13:10)	"Do not answer a **fool** according to his **folly**, lest you also be like him" (Proverbs 26:4)	"The rich man is **wise** in his own eyes…" (Proverbs 28:11)
"He who is devoid of <u>wisdom</u> despises his neighbor, but a man of understanding holds his <u>peace</u>" (Proverbs 11:12)	"To do **evil** is like sport to a **fool**, but a man of understanding has <u>wisdom</u>" (Proverbs 10:23)	

Table 133: Pearls of <u>Wisdom</u> Concerning People in the Wise Category Who Allow the Influences of the Negative Attributes

Finally, Solomon documented some examples one can find in nature to understand the behaviors of people in the **wise** category who allow the influence of the negative attributes. He wrote, "*Go to the ant, you **sluggard**! Consider her ways and be **wise**, which, having no captain, overseer or ruler, provides her supplies in the summer, and gathers her food in the harvest. How long will you **slumber**, O **sluggard**? When will you rise from your **sleep**?*" (Proverbs 6:6-9). Further, Solomon documented a standard of behavior for people in the **wise** category influenced by the positive attributes. Using the words of Agur, Solomon documented, "*There are four things which are little on the earth, but they are exceedingly **wise**: The ants are a people not strong, yet they prepare their food in the summer; the rock badgers are a feeble folk, yet they make their homes in the crags; the locusts have no king, yet they all advance in ranks; the spider skillfully grasps with its hands, and it is in kings' palaces*" (Proverbs 30:24-28). These living examples are God's provisions for identifying behaviors of people in the **wise** category who are influenced by either the positive attributes or the negative attributes during spiritual warfare.

Eve learned from the serpent in the Garden of Eden that she could be in the **wise** category by violating God's command in Chapter Three of the Book of Genesis. She ate from the tree of knowledge of **good** and **evil** (Genesis 2:16, 17) and the Biblical record documented, "*So when the woman saw that the tree was **good** for food, that it was pleasant to the eyes, and a tree desirable to make one **wise**, she took of its fruit and ate. She also gave to her husband with her, and he ate*" (Genesis 3:6). Through Eve's initial bite, the negative attributes were set free on God's creation and future generations of people falling into the **wise** category.

Another example of people in the **wise** category influenced by the negative attributes worked for an Egyptian Pharaoh in Genesis 41:8. The Biblical record referred to these people in the **wise** category as the "*magicians of Egypt and all its **wise** men.*" Pharaoh called them to interpret his dream, but they were incapable. However, God provided one in the **wise** category influenced by the positive attributes. The Biblical record documented that Joseph, who had been sitting in the Pharaoh's prison (Genesis 41:14), was in the **wise** category, and was capable of interpreting Pharaoh's dream. Joseph told the Pharaoh, "*It is not in me; God will give Pharaoh an answer of <u>peace</u>*" (Genesis 41:16) and Joseph explained Pharaoh's dream documented in Genesis 41:33-41. BTT allows one to see from this example that one in the **wise** category influenced by the positive attributes, will automatically give glory to the Source of his or her <u>wisdom</u>; that is God. Likewise, one can read about another person in the **wise** category influenced by the negative attributes who initiated an act of genocide against the Hebrew people. The Biblical record documented how a new king in Egypt (Exodus 1:8), who did not know Joseph or his people, said, *"Look, the people of the children of Israel are more and mightier than we; come, let us deal shrewdly with them, lest they multiply, and it happen, in the event of war, that they also join our enemies and fight against us, and so go up out of the land"* (Exodus 1:8-10). This king listened to **unwise** counselors and made some **unwise** decisions that included:

- *"Therefore they set taskmasters over them to afflict them with their burdens. And they built for Pharaoh supply cities, Pithom and Raamses"* (Exodus 1:11)

- *"So the Egyptians made the children of Israel serve with rigor. And they made their lives bitter with hard bondage—in mortar, in brick, and in all manner of service in the field. All their service in which they made them serve was with rigor"* (Exodus 1:13-14)

- *"The King of Egypt told the Hebrew midwifes: "When you do the duties of a midwife for the Hebrew women, and see them on the birthstools, if it is a son, then you shall **kill** him; but if it is a daughter, then she shall live"* (Exodus 1:16)

- *"So Pharaoh commanded all his people, saying, "Every son who is born you shall **cast into the river**, and every daughter you shall save alive""* (Exodus 1:22)

All the examples above illustrate the power of people in the **wise** category when influenced by the negative attributes. Even when Moses came on the scene, one can read about how he confronted Pharaoh and his **wise** men influenced by the negative attributes. In one example, the Biblical record documented *"...Pharaoh also called the **wise** men and the sorcerers; so the magicians of Egypt, they also did in like manner with their **enchantments**"* (Exodus 7:11). But God eventually silenced these **wise** men as His plagues on Egypt increased in intensity. By the fourth plague, the Biblical record documents of the **wise** men influenced by the negative attributes, *"...the magicians so worked with their **enchantments** to bring forth lice, but they could not. So there were lice on man and beast. Then the magicians said to Pharaoh, "This is the finger of God."* (Exodus 8:18-19). Of course, Pharaoh eventually allowed the children of Israel to leave Egypt.

Once the children of Israel were out of Egyptian captivity, people in the **wise** category with the positive attributes were necessary to help Moses manage the great multitude of people. The Biblical record identified some of the people in the **wise** category with the positive attributes such as the gifted artisans whom the Lord, *"...filled with the spirit of <u>wisdom</u>, that they may make Aaron's garments, to consecrate him, that he may minister to Me as priest"* (Exodus 28:3). There was also Bezalel. The Lord *"...filled him with the Spirit of God, in <u>wisdom</u>, in understanding, in knowledge, and in all manner of workmanship, to design artistic works, to work in gold, in silver, in bronze, in cutting jewels for setting, in carving wood, and to work in all manner of workmanship"* (Exodus 31:3-5; Exodus 35:31). There were also women identified in the **wise** category influenced by the positive attribute. The Biblical record documented, *"And all the women whose hearts stirred with <u>wisdom</u> spun yarn of goats' hair"* (Exodus 35:26). Later, Moses' father-in-law, Jethro met Moses and provided **wise** counsel for organizing the children of Israel as documented in Exodus 18:17-23. Moses had become overwhelmed leading the children of Israel and he said, "*...I alone am not able to bear you. The Lord your God has multiplied you, and here you are today, as the stars of heaven in multitude*" (Deuteronomy 1:9-10). But Jethro was in the **wise** category and the influence of the positive attributes allowed him to support Moses. Based on Jethro's **wise** counsel, Moses turned to the children of Israel and said, "*Choose **wise**, understanding, and knowledgeable men from among your tribes, and I will make them heads over you*" (Deuteronomy 1:13). The Biblical record documented from Moses, "*So I took the heads of your tribes, **wise** and knowledgeable men, and made them heads over you, leaders of thousands, leaders of hundreds, leaders of fifties, leaders of tens, and officers for your tribes*" (Deuteronomy 1:15). As Moses himself was in the **wise** category, he followed the Lord's guidance and gave strict guidance to the judges that he appointed. The Bible records documented that Moses said, "*Then I commanded your judges at that time, saying, 'Hear the cases between your brethren, and judge **righteously** between a man and his brother or the stranger who is with him. You shall not show partiality in judgment; you shall hear the small as well as the great; you shall not be afraid in any man's presence, for the judgment is God's. The case that is too hard for you, bring to me, and I will hear it.' And I commanded you at that time all the things which you should do*" (Deuteronomy 1:16-18). Later, Moses commanded the children of Israel that, "*You shall not **pervert** justice; you shall not show partiality, nor take a bribe, for a bribe blinds the eyes of the **wise** and twists the words of the **righteous***" (Deuteronomy 16:19).

Countless other examples of people in the **wise** category either influenced by the positive or negative attributes exist throughout the Old Testament. I pray one will open one's own Bible to review this rich study of people in this category, including people like David, the **wise** women in the city of Abel of Beth, Maachah (2 Samuel 20:16-22), Solomon, Huram from Tyre (1 Kings 7:14), Zechariah (1 Chronicles 26:14), Jehonathan (1 Chronicles 27:32), Ezra (Ezra 7:25), the **wise** men who understood the times (Esther 1:13-15), Job, Daniel, Hananiah, Mishael, and Azariah (Daniel 1:19-20), the **wise** men of Babylon (Daniel 2:2-48; Daniel 5:7-8), the **wise** men from Edom (Obadiah 1:8), and many others. In fact, the entire Book of Job dedicates itself to the positive and negative discourse from five men in the **wise** category. Job influenced by the positive attributes takes on Eliphaz, Bildad, Zophar, and Elihu; four **wise** men heavily influenced by the negative attributes. The Lord found Job ***righteous*** when He interceded and Job 42:8 informs us that God placed the fates of the other four men in Job's hands.

To be in the **wise** category with the influence of the positive attributes, David documented that one must fear the Lord. He wrote, "*The fear of the Lord is the beginning of wisdom; a **good** understanding have all those who do His commandments. His praise endures forever*" (Psalm 111:10). However, those who do not fear the Lord, are unwise and influenced by the negative attributes. David documented, "*...concerning the transgression of the **wicked**: There is no fear of God before his eyes. For he **flatters** himself in his own eyes, when he finds out his iniquity and when he **hates**. The words of his mouth are **wickedness** and **deceit**; he has ceased to be **wise** and to do **good**. He devises **wickedness** on his bed; he sets himself in a way that is not **good**; he does not abhor **evil***" (Psalm 36:1-4). Further David wrote of them, "*...God shall shoot at them with an arrow; suddenly they shall be wounded. So

He will make them stumble over their own tongue; all who see them shall flee away. All men shall fear, and shall declare the work of God; for they shall **wisely** *consider His doing"* (Psalm 64:7-9). In other words, the _fear_ of the Lord will move people into the **wise** category when _calamity_ strikes. Although many will allow the negative forces of the war campaign to harden their hearts, they will stumble over their own _wisdom_ when the Lord's acts.

Consider some more of the rich pearls of _wisdom_ provided by the Psalmist and Solomon about the people in the **wise** category. Table 129 identifies the influences of either the positive or the negative attributes on this category of people. The Bible documented:

*"Whoever is **wise** will observe these things, and they will understand the lovingkindness of the Lord"* (Psalm 107:43)	*"Surely **oppression** destroys a **wise** man's reason, and a bribe debases the heart"* (Ecclesiastes 7:7)	*"Do not be overly **righteous**, nor be overly **wise**: Why should you destroy yourself?"* (Ecclesiastes 7:16)
From David's prayer to the Lord: *"Who knows the power of Your **anger**? For as the fear of You, so is Your _wrath_. So teach us to number our days, that we may gain a heart of _wisdom_"* (Psalm 90:11-12)	*"It is better to hear the rebuke of the **wise** than for a man to hear the song of **fools**. For like the crackling of thorns under a pot, so is the laughter of the **fool**. This also is vanity"* (Ecclesiastes 7:5-6)	*"The words of a **wise** man's mouth are gracious, but the lips of a **fool** shall swallow him up; the words of his mouth begin with **foolishness**, and the end of his talk is raving madness"* (Ecclesiastes 10:12-13)
*"You, through Your commandments, make me **wiser** than my enemies; for they are ever with me"* (Psalm 119:98)	*"Do not say, "Why were the former days better than these?" For you do not inquire **wisely** concerning this"* (Ecclesiastes 7:10)	*"If the ax is dull, and one does not sharpen the edge, then he must use more strength; but _wisdom_ brings success"* (Ecclesiastes 10:10)
*"The mouth of the **righteous** speaks _wisdom_, and his tongue talks of _justice_"* (Psalm 37:30)	*"_Wisdom_ strengthens the **wise** more than ten rulers of the city"* (Ecclesiastes 7:19)	*"The words of the **wise** are like goads, and the words of scholars are like well-driven nails, given by one Shepherd"* (Ecclesiastes 12:11)
*"Who is like a **wise** man? And who knows the interpretation of a thing? A man's _wisdom_ makes his face shine, and the sternness of his face is changed"* (Ecclesiastes 8:1)	*"Whatever your hand finds to do, do it with your might; for there is no work or device or knowledge or _wisdom_ in the grave where you are going"* (Ecclesiastes 9:10)	*"_Wisdom_ is **good** with an inheritance, and profitable to those who see the sun. For _wisdom_ is a defense as money is a defense, but the excellence of knowledge is that _wisdom_ gives life to those who have it"* (Ecclesiastes 7:11-12)
*"Understand, you senseless among the people; and you **fools**, when will you be **wise**? He who planted the*	*"Better to go to the house of mourning than to go to the house of feasting, for that is the end of all men; and the*	*"For there is not a **just** man on earth who does **good** and does not sin. Also do not take to heart everything*

ear, shall He not hear? He who formed the eye, shall He not see? He who instructs the nations, shall He not correct, he who teaches man knowledge? The Lord knows the thoughts of man, that they are futile." (Psalm 94:8-11)	living will take it to heart. Sorrow is better than laughter, for by a sad countenance the heart is made better. The heart of the **wise** is in the house of mourning, but the heart of **fools** is in the house of mirth" (Ecclesiastes 6:8)	people say, lest you hear your servant cursing you. For many times, also, your own heart has known that even you have cursed others. All this I have proved by <u>wisdom</u>. I said, "I will be **wise**"; but it was far from me" (Ecclesiastes 7:20-24)
"...and a **wise** man's heart <u>discerns</u> both time and judgment, because for every matter there is a time and judgment, though the misery of man increases greatly. For he does not know what will happen; so who can tell him when it will occur? No one has power over the spirit to retain the spirit, and no one has power in the day of death. There is no release from that war, and **wickedness** will not deliver those who are given to it" (Ecclesiastes 8:5-8)	"I returned and saw under the sun that— The race is not to the swift, nor the battle to the strong, nor bread to the **wise**, nor riches to men of understanding, nor favor to men of skill; but time and chance happen to them all. For man also does not know his time: Like fish taken in a cruel net, like birds caught in a snare, so the sons of men are snared in an **evil** time, when it falls suddenly upon them" (Ecclesiastes 9:11, 12)	"Dead flies putrefy the perfumer's ointment, and cause it to give off a foul odor; so does a little **folly** to one respected for <u>wisdom</u> and **honor**. A **wise** man's heart is at his right hand, but a **fool's** heart at his left. Even when a **fool** walks along the way, he lacks <u>wisdom</u>, and he shows everyone that he is a **fool**" (Ecclesiastes 10:1-3)
"When I applied my heart to know <u>wisdom</u> and to see the business that is done on earth, even though one sees no sleep day or night, then I saw all the work of God, that a man cannot find out the work that is done under the sun. For though a man labors to discover it, yet he will not find it; moreover, though a **wise** man attempts to know it, he will not be able to find it" (Ecclesiastes 8:16-17)		

Table 134: More Pearls of <u>Wisdom</u> Concerning the People of the Wise Category

Solomon documented an important correlation between people in the **wise** category and the war campaign. Solomon conceded, "*For I considered all this in my heart, so that I could declare it all: that the **righteous** and the **wise** and their works are in the hand of God. People know neither <u>love</u> nor **hatred** by anything they see before them*" (Ecclesiastes 9:1). It is when Solomon stated that, "*...People know neither <u>love</u> nor **hatred** by anything they see before* *them,*" that one gains an insight into the war campaign. Solomon understood it is not what one physically sees that cause a person to *love* or **hate**. No! It is what drives the influences behind one's behavior that cause one to *love* or **hate**. Solomon understood the war campaign. His education from the Spirit of *wisdom* gave him an understanding of the inner spirit of a man and the influences of the positive and negative attributes influencing behaviors. If a person allows the influence of the positive attributes in his or her inner spirit, his or her outward behavior will reflect *love*. Conversely, if a person allows the influence of the negative attributes in his or her inner spirit, his or her outward behavior will reflect **hate**. BTT provides the lens to see this perspective beyond the flesh. When the positive or negative attributes influence one's inner spirit, one's inward spirit becomes spiritually connected to either side of the campaign. The spiritual manifestation of the positive or negative attributes appears as physical behaviors. Solomon conveyed this *wisdom*.

With the above thoughts in mind, consider how the children of Israel lost their way as they became a great nation. The negative forces used spiritual warfare to corrupt their leaders, prophets, and priest in the **wise** category. The Lord sent numerous prophets to warn the children of Israel to return to Him or have their nation destroyed. Here are a few examples where one can see how people in the **wise** category influenced by negative attributes, led the nation of Israel toward destruction. The Biblical record documented from the Lord through the prophets:

- "*Woe to those who are* **wise** *in their own eyes, and prudent in their own sight!*" (Isaiah 5:21). Just before this verse, the Lord had said, "*Woe to those who call* **evil good**, *and* **good evil**; *who put darkness for light, and light for darkness; who put bitter for sweet, and sweet for bitter!* (Isaiah 5:20)

- "*Therefore, behold, I will again do a marvelous work among this people, a marvelous work and a wonder; for the wisdom of their* **wise** *men shall perish, and the understanding of their prudent men shall be hidden*" (Isaiah 29:14)

- "*Thus says the Lord, your Redeemer, and He who formed you from the womb: "I am the Lord, who makes all things, Who stretches out the heavens all alone, Who spreads abroad the earth by Myself; Who frustrates the signs of the babblers, and drives diviners mad; who turns* **wise** *men backward, and makes their knowledge* **foolishness***…*" (Isaiah 44:24-25)

- "*For My people are* **foolish,** *they have not known Me. They are* **silly** *children, and they have no understanding. They are* **wise** *to do* **evil**, *but to do* **good** *they have no knowledge*" (Jeremiah 4:22)

- "*How can you say, 'We are* **wise**, *and the law of the Lord is with us'? Look, the* **false** *pen of the scribe certainly works* **falsehood**. *The* **wise** *men are ashamed, they are dismayed and taken. Behold, they have rejected the word of the Lord; so what wisdom do they have?*" (Jeremiah 8:8-9)

From the items documented above by the prophets, one should see both the importance and role the people in the **wise** category played in the nation of Israel's destruction. The influences of the negative attributes cost the nation its place with the Lord. Israel rejected God's Word given by the **wise** counsel of His prophets. For Israel's disobedience, God destroyed the nation along with the people who were in the **wise** category and influenced by the negative attributes.

The New Testament documented people in the **wise** category influenced by the positive attributes. Beginning with the birth of Jesus, the Bible also identified Zacharias, Elizabeth, John the Baptist, Mary, and Joseph as people in the **wise** category and influenced by the positive attributes. In addition, there were the **wise** men who came seeking Jesus but disobeyed King Herod who wanted to ***kill*** Jesus according to Matthew 2:16. The Bible documented, "*...Herod, when he saw that he was **deceived** by the wise men, was exceedingly **angry**; and he sent forth and **put to death** all the male children who were in Bethlehem and in all its districts, from two years old and under, according to the time which he had determined from the wise men*" (Matthew 2:16). Herod was **wise** but influenced by the negative attributes. From Herod's example, once again one can see that people influenced by the negative attributes in the **wise** category are capable of heinous activities.

BTT allows one to see that Jesus was in the **wise** category and had a full measure of this ***clean spirit***. The Bible documents, "*...the Child grew and became strong in spirit, filled with wisdom; and the grace of God was upon Him*" (Luke 2:40). Later the Bible records that, "*...Jesus increased in wisdom and stature, and in favor with God and men*" (Luke 2:46-52) and when He went to teach in the Jew's synagogue, "*...they were astonished and said, "Where did this Man get this wisdom and these mighty works?*" (Matthew 13:54). Jesus provided examples of how people influenced with the positive attributes in the **wise** category, should behave. He documented that people should:

- Use God's Word to defeat Satan's use of the negative attributes. Jesus defeated Satan's temptations this way as documented in Matthew 4:1-11; Mark 1:12, 13; and Luke 4:1-13

- Establish and build on a strong spiritual foundation as documented in Matthew 7:24-27

- Do ***good*** works even when no one is watching. Matthew 24:45-51 and Luke 12:42-48 documents this principle taught in Jesus parable of the ***faithful*** servant

- Prepare and always be prepared. Jesus taught this principle in a parable about **wise** and ***foolish*** virgins documented in Matthew 25:1-13

Jesus also acknowledged that there were people influenced by the negative attributes in the **wise** category who make it their mission to stop the Word of God from reaching people. Jesus heavily condemned one such group of people when He said "*...Woe to you also, lawyers! For you load men with burdens hard to bear, and you yourselves do not touch the burdens with one of your fingers*" (Luke 11:46) and "*Woe to you lawyers! For you have taken away the key of knowledge. You did not enter in yourselves, and those who were entering in you hindered*" (Luke 11:52). When He prepared His disciples and sent them out to teach the Gospel to the world, the Biblical record documented, "*Therefore settle it in your hearts not to meditate beforehand on what you will answer; for I will give you a mouth and wisdom which all your* *adversaries will not be able to contradict or resist*" (Luke 21:14-15). If one were to read the Book of Acts, one would see that Jesus' statement was true. In fact, Stephen, a disciple of Christ (Acts 6:5) was in the **wise** category and offers a great example for one to study. The Biblical record documented people influenced by the negative attributes in the **wise** category, tried to dispute Stephen's teaching of the Gospel of Jesus Christ. Specifically, the Bible documents, "*...there arose some from what is called the Synagogue of the Freedmen (Cyrenians, Alexandrians, and those from Cilicia and Asia), disputing with Stephen. And they were not able to resist the wisdom and the Spirit by which he spoke*" (Acts 6:9-10). Since they could not resist his words, they ***falsely*** accused him according to Acts 6:11-13 and brought him before the Jewish council (Acts 7:1-53). Even the council could not resist God's Words. The Bible documented "*When they heard these things they were cut to the heart, and they gnashed at him with their teeth*" (Acts 7:54), and "*...they cried out with a loud voice, stopped their ears, and ran at him with one accord; and they cast him out of the city and **stoned him**...*" (Acts 7:57-58). That day, the negative forces influencing people in the **wise** category advanced on the spiritual battlefield in the war campaign. Interestingly, the Biblical record documented that before Paul became a Christian, he was in the **wise** category and influenced by negative attributes according to Acts 22:5. He was present on the day of Stephen's ***murder*** according to Acts 7:58-59.

Thankfully, Paul converted to Christ. The Biblical record documented his conversion in Chapter 9 in the Book of Acts. Ironically, through the providential hand of God, Paul found himself among the people influenced by the positive attributes in the **wise** category with a mission to correct other people in the **wise** category influenced by the negative attributes. Paul, steeped in the knowledge of the Old Testament, Judaism, and Jewish traditions took on the negative forces influencing the Jews that opposed the Gospel of Jesus Christ. Also, Paul would teach the true Gospel even to people in the **wise** category that were lost because of ancient *wisdoms* and philosophies that permeated the entire world. For example, the Biblical record documented that while Paul was in Athens, "*...his spirit was provoked within him when he saw that the city was given over to **idols**. Therefore he reasoned in the synagogue with the Jews and with the Gentile worshipers, and in the marketplace daily with those who happened to be there. Then certain Epicurean and Stoic philosophers encountered him. And some said, "What does this babbler want to say?*" (Acts 17:16-18). It was Paul's inner spirit that led him to act when he saw all the idols. Some of the Epicurean and Stoic philosophers knew that Paul preached Jesus because they stated, "*He seems to be a proclaimer of foreign gods," because he preached to them Jesus and the resurrection*" (Acts 17:18). Thus, they led Paul to the Areopagus and the Biblical record documented that, "*...all the Athenians and the foreigners who were there spent their time in nothing else but either to tell or to hear some new thing*" (Acts 17:21). In other words, these Epicurean and Stoic philosophers heard and spread earthly *wisdom* through these forums by anyone who came and stood on their platform to speak in their hearing. Many religious and secular institutions today replicate this same practice. However, the most important part about this practice is the negative forces of the war campaign have always used forums like these in their strategy to keep ancient *wisdom* strong in the inner spirits of people confused or unaware of the actual message of the Bible. For this reason, Paul took an opportunity to address the forum and introduce everyone in his hearing to Jesus Christ. BTT allows one to see that Paul's inner spirit revealed to him that the people were "religious" (Acts 17:22). With this knowledge, he then selected an altar with the inscription "TO THE UNKNOWN GOD" on it and said to them, *"Therefore, the One whom you worship without knowing, Him I proclaim to you..."* (Acts 17:23). Unfortunately, after Paul introduced Jesus to the people in the **wise** category, the negative forces tightened their grip on the people and most of them rejected the message. The Biblical record documented, *"...when they heard of the resurrection of the dead, some **mocked**, while others said, "We will hear you again on this matter." So Paul departed from among them. However, some men joined him and believed, among them Dionysius the Areopagite, a woman named Damaris, and others with them"* (Acts 13:32-34).

From Paul's conversion to the Gospel forward, he worked tirelessly alongside the other apostles to provide more pearls of _wisdom_ about the people in the **wise** category. For one's learning, here are some of the pearls of _wisdom_ documented in the Biblical record.

- There are people in the **wise** category influenced by the negative attributes: *"Professing to be **wise**, they became **fools**, and changed the glory of the incorruptible God into an image made like corruptible man—and birds and four-footed animals and creeping thing"* (Romans 1:22-23)

- Concerning the Gospel of Jesus Christ: *"For I do not desire, brethren, that you should be ignorant of this mystery, lest you should be **wise** in your own opinion, that blindness in part has happened to Israel until the fullness of the Gentiles has come in"* (Romans 11:25)

- *"Be of the same mind toward one another. Do not set your mind on high things, but associate with the _humble_. Do not be **wise** in your own opinion"* (Romans 12:16)

- *"For your obedience has become known to all. Therefore I am glad on your behalf; but I want you to be **wise** in what is **good**, and **simple** concerning **evil**"* (Romans 16:19)

- *"For the message of the cross is **foolishness** to those who are perishing, but to us who are being saved it is the power of God. For it is written: "I will destroy the _wisdom_ of the **wise**, and bring to nothing the understanding of the prudent." Where is the **wise**? Where is the scribe? Where is the disputer of this age? Has not God made **foolish** the _wisdom_ of this world? For since, in the _wisdom_ of God, the world through _wisdom_ did not know God, it pleased God through the **foolishness** of the message preached to save those who believe"* (1 Corinthians 1:18-21)

- *"For Jews request a sign, and Greeks seek after _wisdom_; but we preach Christ crucified, to the Jews a stumbling block and to the Greeks **foolishness**, but to those who are called, both Jews and Greeks, Christ the power of God and the _wisdom_ of God. Because the **foolishness** of God is **wiser** than men, and the weakness of God is stronger than men. For you see your calling, brethren, that not many **wise** according to the flesh, not many mighty, not many noble, are called. But God has chosen the **foolish** things of the world to put to shame the **wise**, and God has chosen the weak things of the world to put to shame the things which are mighty; and the base things of the world and the things which are despised God has chosen, and the things which *are not, to bring to nothing the things that are, that no flesh should glory in His presence. But of Him you are in Christ Jesus, who became for us <u>wisdom</u> from God—and **righteousness** and sanctification and redemption—that, as it is written, "He who glories, let him glory in the Lord."* (1 Corinthians 1:22-31)

- *"Let no one deceive himself. If anyone among you seems to be* **wise** *in this age, let him become a* **fool** *that he may become* **wise**. *For the <u>wisdom</u> of this world is* **foolishness** *with God. For it is written, "He catches the* **wise** *in their own craftiness"; and again, "The Lord knows the thoughts of the* **wise**, *that they are futile"* (1 Corinthians 3:18-20)

- *"Therefore, my beloved, flee from <u>idolatry</u>. I speak as to* **wise** *men; judge for yourselves what I say"* (1 Corinthians 10:14-15)

- *"See then that you walk circumspectly, not as* **fools** *but as* **wise**, *redeeming the time, because the days are* **evil**" (Ephesians 5:15, 16)

- *"Therefore, if you died with Christ from the basic principles of the world, why, as though living in the world, do you subject yourselves to regulations — "Do not touch, do not taste, do not handle," which all concern things which perish with the using — according to the commandments and doctrines of men? These things indeed have an appearance of <u>wisdom</u> in self-imposed religion,* **false** <u>humility</u>, *and neglect of the body, but are of no value against the indulgence of the flesh."* (Colossians 2:20-23)

- *"Let the word of Christ dwell in you richly in all <u>wisdom</u>, teaching and admonishing one another in psalms and hymns and spiritual songs, singing with <u>grace</u> in your hearts to the Lord"* (Colossians 3:16)

- *"Walk in <u>wisdom</u> toward those who are outside, redeeming the time. Let your speech always be with <u>grace</u>, seasoned with salt, that you may know how you ought to answer each one"* (Colossians 4:5-6)

- *"But* **evil** *men and impostors will grow worse and worse,* **deceiving** *and being* **deceived**. *But you must continue in the things which you have learned and been assured of, knowing from whom you have learned them, and that from childhood you have known the Holy Scriptures, which are able to make you* **wise** *for salvation through* **faith** *which is in Christ Jesus"* (2 Timothy 3:13-15)

- *"If any of you lacks <u>wisdom</u>, let him ask of God, who gives to all liberally and without reproach, and it will be given to him. But let him ask in* **faith**, *with no <u>doubting</u>, for he who <u>doubts</u> is like a wave of the sea driven and tossed by the wind. For let not that man suppose that he will receive anything from the Lord; he is a double-minded man, unstable in all his ways."* (James 1:5-8)

- *"Who is* **wise** *and understanding among you? Let him show by* **good** *conduct that his works are done in the meekness of <u>wisdom</u>. But if you have bitter* **envy** *and self-seeking in your hearts, do not <u>boast</u> and* **lie** *against the truth. This <u>wisdom</u> does not descend from above, but is earthly, sensual, demonic. For where* **envy** *and self-seeking exist, confusion and every* **evil** *thing are there. But the <u>wisdom</u> that is from above is* *first pure, then <u>peaceable</u>, gentle, willing to yield, full of* **mercy** *and* **good** *fruits, without <u>partiality</u> and without hypocrisy"* (James 3:13-17)

From everything documented about the people in the **wise** category of the **harvest**, one should understand why this category of people is important to the positive and negative forces of the war campaign. Laborers of the Gospel are essential for reaching and converting the people of the *wise* category to the True Gospel of Jesus Christ. Moreover, their abilities to use God's *wisdom* among the positive forces, is essential on the spiritual battlefield to aid in the formulation of strategies to spread the Gospel during spiritual warfare. Likewise, the negative forces gather people in the *wise* category every day to stop the positive forces and more importantly - the Word of God - from advancing on the spiritual battlefield.

The Needy Category: This category of people often finds themselves mixed in with the people of the poor category. But this category represents a distinct and separate category of people who are part of the **harvest**. The people of this category may or may not be poor. However, they are a people who never seem to have enough of the things they desire such as money, food, attention, affection, or even emotional support. People in the **needy** category are ones who because of  circumstance always **need** someone else's help. Their **need** is not because they lack intelligence or suffer from some form of handicap. No! Their **need** often has more to do with their inability to make smart choices in life or to be satisfied with what they have. When they choose their own ways over God's way, they find themselves overextended by their own decisions. In most cases, they fail to think through their decisions before they act, weigh, or count the cost (Luke 14:28). When one in the **needy** category allows the influence of the negative attributes, his or her personal desires stress the inner spirits of others. People with the positive attributes have their patience and understanding pushed to their carnal limits as the **needy** become burdens to their friends, family, and even members of the church. However, patience and understanding are a two-way street. Depending on the influences of the positive or negative forces, people in the **needy** category will express either appreciation or their ***anger*** toward others trying to support their **needs**. BTT allows one to see that patience may not be in great supply for the one in this category. However, without patience and <u>discernment</u>, the one responding to the people in this category can easily find himself in danger of the influence of the negative forces.

The Spirit of wisdom informed Solomon that, *"He who* **oppresses** *the poor reproaches his Maker, but he who* **honors** *Him has* **mercy** *on the* **needy***"* (Proverbs 14:31). In other words, people who honor God, have ***mercy*** on the **needy**. This implies that one must have patience with the people in the **needy** category and try to respond to their **needs** in a manner that glorifies God. For people who do not understand this wisdom, Agur, another wise contributor to the Book of Proverbs documented, *"There is a generation whose teeth are like swords, and whose fangs are like knives, to devour the poor from off the earth, and the* **needy** *from among men"* (Proverbs 30:14). This <u>wisdom</u> remains true to this very day.

King Lemuel was another contributor to the Book of Proverbs who spoke about people in the **needy** category. He addressed leader's responsibility to this category when he documented, *"Open your mouth, judge* **righteously***, and plead the cause of the poor and*

needy" (Proverbs 31:9). In other words, one cannot simply ignore people in the **needy** category. Like everyone else, the **needy** deserve the same fair and impartial <u>justice</u>. Hence, the Biblical record documents the value and importance of a virtuous wife because, "*She extends her hand to the poor, yes, she reaches out her hands to the* **needy**" (Proverbs 31:20). A virtuous wife can help a man distinguish ***right*** from wrong when dealing with the **needy**. A ***good*** husband and wife team will <u>discern</u> a true **need** over a person's well-developed scheme. In His infinite wisdom, God knew exactly what He was doing when He created marriage.

As Moses led the children of Israel out of captivity and into the wilderness, the Biblical record documented two examples of people in the **needy** category influenced by the negative attributes. Both examples deal with the children of Israel complaining against Moses and Aaron saying, "*Oh, that we had died by the hand of the Lord in the land of Egypt, when we sat by the pots of meat and when we ate bread to the full! For you have brought us out into this wilderness to* **kill** *this whole assembly with hunger*" (Exodus 16:3). Please understand that this serious accusation implied Moses and Aaron had the influence of the ***bloodthirsty*** attribute. Moses cautioned the people stating, "*...Your complaints are not against us but against the Lord*" (Exodus 16:8). Now consider these two examples:

In the first example, the Lord provided manna from heaven for the children of Israel to eat to satisfy their **need**. The Bible documented that the manna, "*...was like white coriander seed, and the taste of it was like wafers made with honey*" (Exodus 16:31). Moses told the Israelite, "*This is the thing which the Lord has commanded: 'Let every man gather it according to each one's* **need**, *one omer for each person, according to the number of persons; let every man take for those who are in his tent.'*" (Exodus 16:16). Further, the Bible documented "*So when they measured it by omers, he who gathered much had nothing left over, and he who gathered little had no lack. Every man had gathered according to each one's* **need**" (Exodus 16:18). However, the Biblical record also documented, "*Notwithstanding they did not heed Moses. But some of them left part of it until morning, and it bred worms and stank. And Moses was* ***angry*** *with them. So they gathered it every morning, every man according to his* **need**. *And when the sun became hot, it melted*" (Exodus 16:20-21). Thus, one can see that when the negative attributes began to influence the people in the **needy** category, sin occurred.

Similarly, in the second example, the Bible documented, "*Now the mixed multitude who were among them yielded to intense craving; so the children of Israel also wept again and said: "Who will give us meat to eat? We remember the fish which we ate freely in Egypt, the cucumbers, the melons, the leeks, the onions, and the garlic; but now our whole being is dried up; there is nothing at all except this manna before our eyes!*" (Numbers 11:4-6). The people complained about meat even though they had flocks of animals with them. However, the Lord heard their complaints and provided, "*...quail from the sea and left them fluttering near the camp, about a day's journey on this side and about a day's journey on the other side, all around the camp, and about two cubits above the surface of the ground*" (Numbers 11:31). But this time the influence of the negative attributes on the people in the **needy** category drew the <u>wrath</u> of God. The Biblical record documented, "*But while the meat was still between their teeth, before it was chewed, the <u>wrath</u> of the Lord was aroused against the people, and the Lord struck the people with a very great plague. So he called the name of that place Kibroth Hattaavah, because there they buried the people who had <u>yielded to craving</u>*" (Numbers 11:33-

34). Allowing the influence of the negative attributes is not ***good*** for people in the **needy** category.

For dealing with the people in the **needy** category, the Lord gave Moses a few commands for the nation of Israel to observe. These commands included:

- "*If there is among you a* poor *man of your brethren, within any of the gates in your land which the Lord your God is giving you, you shall not harden your heart nor shut your hand from your* poor *brother, but you shall open your hand wide to him and willingly lend him sufficient for his* **need***, whatever he* **needs**" (Deuteronomy 15:7-9)

- "*For the* poor *will never cease from the land; therefore I command you, saying, 'You shall open your hand wide to your brother, to your* poor *and your* **needy***, in your land.*" (Deuteronomy 15:11)

- "*You shall not* **oppress** *a hired servant who is* poor *and* **needy***, whether one of your brethren or one of the aliens who is in your land within your gates*" (Deuteronomy 24:14)

There are many other pearls of wisdom documented in the Old Testament about people in the **needy** category, their treatment, and the influences of the positive or negative attributes on them. Here are a few to consider:

To judges and leaders at every level: "*Defend the* poor *and fatherless; do <u>justice</u> to the afflicted and* **needy***. Deliver the* poor *and* **needy***; free them from the hand of the* **wicked**" (Psalm 82:3-4)	"*There are those who rebel against the light; they do not know its ways nor abide in its paths. The* **murderer** *rises with the light; he* **kills** *the* poor *and* **needy***; and in the night he is like a <u>thief</u>*" (Job 24:13-14)	"*The* **wicked** *shall be turned into hell, and all the nations that forget God. For the* **needy** *shall not always be forgotten; the expectation of the* poor *shall not perish forever*" (Psalm 9:17-18)
"*For the* **oppression** *of the* poor*, for the sighing of the* **needy***, now I will arise,*" *says the Lord;* "*I will set him in the safety for which he yearns*" (Psalm 12:5)	"*He raises the* poor *out of the dust, and lifts the* **needy** *out of the ash heap, that He may seat him with princes—with the princes of His people*" (Psalm 113:7-8)	"*He will bring <u>justice</u> to the* poor *of the people; He will save the children of the* **needy***, and will break in pieces the* **oppressor**" *(Psalm 72:4)*
"*...He will deliver the* **needy** *when he cries, the* poor *also, and him who has no helper*" (Psalm 72:12)	"*He will spare the* poor *and* **needy***, and will save the souls of the* **needy**" (Psalm 72:13)	A person is **unjust**: "*...If he has* **oppressed** *the* poor *and* **needy**..." (Ezekiel 18:12)
"*All my bones shall say,* "*Lord, who is like You, delivering the* poor *from him who is too strong for him, yes, the* poor *and the* **needy** *from him who plunders him?*" (Psalm 35:10)	"*The* poor *and* **needy** *seek water, but there is none, their tongues fail for thirst. I, the Lord, will hear them; I, the God of Israel, will not forsake them*" (Isaiah 41:17)	"*Also the schemes of the schemer are* **evil***; he devises* **wicked** *plans to destroy the* poor *with* **lying** *words, even when the* **needy** *speaks <u>justice</u>*" (Isaiah 32:7)

"The **wicked** have drawn the sword and have bent their bow, to cast down the poor and **needy**, to slay those who are of **upright** conduct. Their sword shall enter their own heart, and their bows shall be broken" (Psalm 37:14-15)	"Since times are not hidden from the Almighty, why do those who know Him see not His days? "Some remove landmarks; they seize flocks **violently** and feed on them; they drive away the donkey of the fatherless; they take the widow's ox as a pledge. They push the **needy** off the road; all the poor of the land are forced to hide" (Job 24:4)	"Woe to those who decree **unrighteous** decrees, who write misfortune, which they have prescribed to **rob** the **needy** of justice, and to take what is **right** from the poor of My people, that widows may be their prey, and that they may **rob** the fatherless" (Isaiah 10:1-2)

Table 135: Pearls of Wisdom Concerning the People of the Needy Category

The prophet Jeremiah documented the treatment of people in the **needy** category living among the nation of Israel. The **needy** were ***oppressed*** by people in the rich category with the **wicked** attribute's influence. Jeremiah wrote that the Lord stated, *"For among My people are found **wicked** men; they lie in wait as one who sets snares; they set a trap; they catch men. As a cage is full of birds, so their houses are full of **deceit**. Therefore they have become great and grown rich. They have grown fat, they are sleek; yes, they surpass the deeds of the **wicked**; they do not plead the cause, the cause of the fatherless; yet they prosper, and the **right** of the **needy** they do not defend. Shall I not punish them for these things?' says the Lord. 'Shall I not avenge Myself on such a nation as this?'"* (Jeremiah 5:26-29). The Lord did punish the nation of Israel. In the same vein, the prophet Amos documented the behavior and treatment of the people in the **needy** category living in the nation of Israel. He said, *"Hear this word, you cows of Bashan, who are on the mountain of Samaria, who **oppress** the poor, who crush the **needy**, who say to your husbands, "Bring wine, let us drink!"* (Amos 4:1). Amos did not mince words. He told the people directly that God was fed up with their sinful behavior. Thus, he went on to tell them that their destruction was imminent. He told them, *"Hear this, you who swallow up the **needy**, and make the poor of the land fail, saying: "When will the New Moon be past, that we may sell grain? And the Sabbath, that we may trade wheat? Making the ephah small and the shekel large, **falsifying** the scales by **deceit**, that we may buy the poor for silver, and the **needy** for a pair of sandals— even sell the bad wheat?"* (Amos 8:4-6). The nation of Israel, especially those who treated the people in the **needy** category poorly, paid with their lives during the destruction of their nation.

In the New Testament, Jesus addressed the people in the **needy** category and everyone who prayed for their **needs**. Jesus stated, *"...do not use vain repetitions as the heathen do. For they think that they will be heard for their many words. Therefore do not be like them. For your Father knows the things you have **need** of before you ask Him"* (Matthew 6:7-8). In other words, Jesus taught people how to pray and He provided them the awareness that God already knew their **needs**. However, BTT allows one to see that the requirement to ask God to satisfy one's **needs** still remains. Why? Because the discipline demonstrates obedience and submission to Him. This discipline keeps one focused on God and the influence of the negative attributes away. One must think spiritually on this and not carnally. Thus, through the providence and power of God, people in the **needy** category have their **needs** met. Moreover, Jesus said, "*...do not worry, saying, 'What shall we eat?' or 'What shall we drink?' or 'What shall we wear?' For after all these things the Gentiles seek. For your heavenly Father knows that you* **need** *all these things. But seek first the kingdom of God and His* **righteousness**, *and all these things shall be added to you. Therefore do not worry about tomorrow, for tomorrow will worry about its own things. Sufficient for the day is its own trouble*" (Matthew 6:31-34; Luke 22:22-31). BTT allows one to see that when people in the **needy** category hear and accept the Gospel of Jesus Christ, they find satisfaction within their inner spirit for all their spiritual **needs**. This satisfaction can also bring relief to their physical **needs** as well through God's providential hand. Satisfaction of both areas of need helps one to become a useful and *faithful* member of the positive forces fighting in the war campaign. Furthermore, their knowledge and personal experiences provide a wealth of understanding to better help others in **need** as they once were.

The Biblical record documents that Jesus is the answer for everyone who finds himself or herself in the **needy** category. When it came to the sickness of the nation of Israel, the Biblical record documented that people gathered around Jesus and the disciples in the city of Bethsaida and they, "*...received them and spoke to them about the kingdom of God, and healed those who had* **need** *of healing*" (Luke 9:11). Later, after the death of Jesus, the apostles carried on these benevolent acts. The Bible documented, "*Then those who gladly received his word were baptized; and that day about three thousand souls were added to them. And they continued steadfastly in the apostles' doctrine and fellowship, in the breaking of bread, and in prayers. Then fear came upon every soul, and many wonders and signs were done through the apostles. Now all who believed were together, and had all things in common, and sold their possessions and goods, and divided them among all, as anyone had* **need**" (Acts 2:41-45). Notice how the people in the **needy** category had their **needs** meet. Also, notice from the text that the people in this category who found satisfaction and relief, were of the people who heard the Gospel of Christ, were baptized, and were committed. These people stayed in God's Word and became part of the positive forces of the war campaign. Therefore, God met their **needs**.

Later, Acts 4:32-37 documented this same process. The Bible recorded, "*Now the multitude of those who believed were of one heart and one soul; neither did anyone say that any of the things he possessed was his own, but they had all things in common. And with great power the apostles gave witness to the resurrection of the Lord Jesus. And great grace was upon them all. Nor was there anyone among them who lacked; for all who were possessors of lands or houses sold them, and brought the proceeds of the things that were sold, and laid them at the apostles' feet; and they distributed to each as anyone had* **need**. *And Joses, who was also named Barnabas by the apostles (which is translated Son of Encouragement), a Levite of the country of Cyprus, having land, sold it, and brought the money and laid it at the apostles' feet*". Once again, the Biblical record provides the example of how people in the **needy** category found satisfaction for their **needs**. The Lord expects people He blesses to take care of others that are less fortunate. This includes people in the **needy** category. One should always keep in mind that the **needy** are different from the people in the poor category. I will discuss the people in the poor category at the end of this chapter.

The Hellenist widows, documented in Acts Chapter 6, provides another example of people in the **needy** category. The Bible documented, "*...there arose a complaint against the Hebrews by the Hellenists, because their widows were neglected in the daily distribution*" (Acts 6:1). To satisfy this **need**, the apostles wisely stated, "*...seek out from among you seven men of **good** reputation, full of the Holy Spirit and <u>wisdom</u>, whom we may appoint over this business...*" (Acts 6:3). By selecting men from among the people of their own nationality, they appropriately responded to and satisfied the widows' cultural **needs**.

The Holy Spirit led the apostles to document some pearls of wisdom for our learning about the people in the **needy** category. BTT allows one to make the appropriate application for one in this category using a spiritual lens. The apostles documented:

- "*Let <u>love</u> be without hypocrisy. Abhor what is **evil**. Cling to what is **good**. Be kindly affectionate to one another with brotherly <u>love</u>, in **honor** giving preference to one another; not lagging in diligence, fervent in spirit, serving the Lord; rejoicing in <u>hope</u>, <u>patient</u> in tribulation, continuing steadfastly in prayer; distributing to the **needs** of the saints, given to hospitality*" (Romans 12:9-13)

- "*And my God shall supply all your **need** according to His riches in glory by Christ Jesus*" (Philippians 4:19)

- "*And let our people also learn to maintain **good** works, to meet urgent **needs**, that they may not be unfruitful*" (Titus 3:14)

- "*Let us therefore come boldly to the throne of <u>grace</u>, that we may obtain **mercy** and find <u>grace</u> to help in time of **need***" (Hebrews 4:16)

- "*For though by this time you ought to be teachers, you **need** someone to teach you again the first principles of the oracles of God; and you have come to **need** milk and not solid food*" (Hebrews 5:12)

- "*Therefore do not cast away your confidence, which has great reward. For you have **need** of endurance, so that after you have done the will of God, you may receive the promise...*" (Hebrews 10:35-36)

- "*What does it profit, my brethren, if someone says he has **faith** but does not have works? Can **faith** save him? If a brother or sister is naked and destitute of daily food, and one of you says to them, "Depart in peace, be warmed and filled," but you do not give them the things which are **needed** for the body, what does it profit? Thus also **faith** by itself, if it does not have works, is dead*" (James 2:14-17)

- "*But whoever has this world's goods, and sees his brother in **need**, and shuts up his heart from him, how does the <u>love</u> of God abide in him?*" (1 John 3:17)

As a final thought, the Biblical record documented that it is possible for an entire church of people to be in the **needy** category and not know it. How? Wealth can cloud one's vision.

This fog is exactly what Jesus described in the Book of Revelations. John documented Jesus' Word about the church of the Laodiceans. This church is described as the "*...the lukewarm church...*" (Revelations 3:16). Jesus said, "*Because you say, 'I am rich, have become wealthy, and have **need** of nothing'—and do not know that you are wretched, miserable, poor, blind, and naked...*" (Revelation 3:17). He told this church to be zealous and repent and further told them, "*Behold, I stand at the door and knock. If anyone hears My voice and opens the door, I will come in to him and dine with him, and he with Me. To him who overcomes I will grant to sit with Me on My throne, as I also overcame and sat down with My Father on His throne*" (Revelation 3:20-21). Clearly, this congregation's people were in the **needy** category. The congregation **needed** spiritual <u>discernment</u> and healing. What is troubling is the fact that the people were in a church thinking they were serving God and did not see their own condition. The reality is, they were lost in the fog generated by the negative forces through spiritual warfare. This example expresses why Jesus desired true laborers for the **harvest**. Laborers, even for people worshipping in the Laodicean-like congregations today, can help people in the **needy** category see the true light of Christ.

The Poor Category: This is the largest of all the categories of the **harvest** and the people cover the entire earth. For this category of people, the term **poor** includes people who are spiritually, physically, emotionally, mentally, and economically **poor**. However, the majority of this chapter will focus on being economically **poor** because spiritual warfare uses economics to convince the carnal side of man to think he or she is spiritually, physically, emotionally, and mentally poor. The influence  of the negative attributes uses wealth as a means to attack people on the spiritual battlefield of the war campaign. For this reason, people in the **poor** category can find themselves in either physical or spiritual <u>poverty</u>. Physical <u>poverty</u> is the state in which one is extremely deficient in the material things, i.e. money, collateral, and bartering items. Physical <u>poverty</u> forces one to survive below the lowest level of human subsistence. Similarly, spiritual <u>poverty</u> is the state in which one's inner spirit is deprived of the spiritual subsistence, i.e. ***faith*** (Hebrews 11:1), <u>*belief*</u> (Matthew 6:33), or other things that provides <u>*hope*</u> beyond the physical sustainment of this life. It also provides the bulk of the human capital for the war campaign; the people who bolster the positive and negative forces of the war. The positive or negative attributes make an incredible impact on the inner spirit of people in this category because of their status in life. The reality is, people in this category who are physically **poor** do not have the financial resources for all the worldly clutter and traps that wealth brings. Conversely, their desires for financial resources opens the door for the negative forces influence in the campaign. BTT allows one to see that around the world, the bulk of the people in this category are in a survival mode. It is the survival mode that the negative forces exploit in Spiritual warfare which makes the Gospel message harder to hear. However, the positive forces know that when people of this category hear the Truth, their outlook on life and even their very status, can improve. Some of the strongest laborers of the Gospel are produced from this category of people.

First, BTT allows one to see that there is a spiritual phenomenon that keeps people in the **poor** category by shaping one's state of mind through environmental surroundings and circumstance. But one can overcome this phenomenon. As long as one has a mindset of **poorness**, one will remain in the **poor** category. However, with God there are always opportunities to overcome this category if one's inner spirit will accept His Word. The Spirit of wisdom revealed pearls of wisdom that support this statement. Solomon documented the following behaviors that come from a mindset of **poorness**:

- Being <u>lazy</u>: "*He who has a <u>slack</u> hand becomes* **poor**..." (Proverbs 10:4)

- Inability to grasp opportunity: "*Much food is in the fallow ground of the* **poor**..." (Proverbs 13:23). "*Fallow*" means "*unplanted,*" "*unseeded,*" or "*uncultivated,*" or "*unused.*"

- A dislike for correction: "<u>*Poverty*</u> *and shame will come to him who disdains correction...*" (Proverbs 13:18)

- Talking instead of working: "*In all labor there is profit, but <u>idle</u> chatter leads only to <u>poverty</u>*" (Proverbs 14:23)

- The lack of planning: "*The plans of the diligent lead surely to plenty, but those of everyone who is hasty, surely to <u>poverty</u>*" (Proverbs 21:5)

- Drinking and eating excessively: "*...the drunkard and the glutton will come to <u>poverty</u>, and drowsiness will clothe a man with rags*" (Proverbs 23:21)

- The inappropriate pursuit and use of wealth: "*A man with an **evil** eye hastens after riches, and does not consider that <u>poverty</u> will come upon him*" (Proverbs 28:22) and that, "*He who <u>loves</u> pleasure will be a* **poor** *man...*" (Proverbs 21:17)

- Being ***foolish*** instead of working: Solomon learned that, "*He who tills his land will have plenty of bread, but he who follows **frivolity** will have <u>poverty</u> enough!*" (Proverbs 28:19)

All the behaviors above will keep one in the **poor** category. And yes, there are people in the **poor** category who chose to be in the category. The Spirit of wisdom revealed to Solomon, "*There is one who makes himself rich, yet has nothing; and one who makes himself* **poor**, *yet has great riches*" (Proverbs 13:7). In other words, there are people that give up everything and find happiness living on the simple pleasures of life. These are people in the **poor** category who may or may not be pursuing God; their reasons are personal and their choice. Solomon learned these things from the Spirit of wisdom which makes the knowledge a reliable insight into the nature of people of the **poor** category. Thus, as one considers all the items above, one can understand Solomon's comment that, "*...The destruction of the* **poor** *is their <u>poverty</u>*" (Proverbs 10:15). In other words, what is killing people in the **poor** category is the <u>*poverty*</u> itself whether environmental, circumstantial, self-inflicted, or spiritual; these variables of <u>*poverty*</u> are literally destroying them. However, their situation can change if they listen to God's Word and become obedient to it.

The Spirit of wisdom revealed to Solomon that many people in the **poor** category deal with overwhelming depression and loneliness. This happens because the negative forces of the war campaign influence many people who could render assistance, mentorship, and guidance, to stay away from people in this category. Some people turn their backs completely and treat the **poor** as if they have a disease. Solomon learned:

- *"All the brothers of the **poor hate** him; how much more do his friends go far from him! He may pursue them with words, yet they abandon him"* (Proverbs 19:7)

- *"...the **poor** is separated from his friend"* (Proverbs 19:4)

- *"The **poor** man is **hated** even by his own neighbor..."* (Proverbs 14:20)

One should pay close attention to the above Scriptures. BTT allows one to see that the **hater** attribute is involved and clearly influencing people to cause division. Further, this division extends even to those in the **poor** category who make honest pleas, requests, and petitions for basic subsistence. Wisdom revealed to Solomon that *"The **poor** man uses entreaties, but the rich answers roughly"* (Proverbs 18:23). In short, people in the *rich* category and often people in general who have more than people in the **poor** category, speak inappropriately to the people of this category. Still, there are even more challenges for the people in the **poor** category that keep them down and susceptible to the negative forces of the campaign. The Spirit of wisdom revealed some additional painful facts about people influenced by the negative attributes attitudes towards those who happen to be in the **poor** category. She revealed to Solomon:

- *"Like a roaring lion and a charging bear is a **wicked** ruler over **poor** people"* (Proverbs 28:15)

- *"The rich rules over the **poor**, and the borrower is servant to the lender"* (Proverbs 22:7)

- *"A **poor** man who **oppresses** the **poor** is like a driving rain which leaves no food"* (Proverbs 28:3)

With all the above said, consider these pearls of wisdom from the Spirit of wisdom to provide further insight about the people in the **poor** category. Within these pearls, BTT allows one to see God's expectation for the treatment of the people in this category by those who profess to have the influence of the positive attributes. Please read these carefully. Solomon documented:

*"What is desired in a man is <u>kindness</u>, and a **poor** man is better than a **liar**"* (Proverbs 19:22)	*"He who **oppresses** the **poor** reproaches his Maker..."* (Proverbs 14:31)	*"The rich and the **poor** have this in common, the LORD is the maker of them all"* (Proverbs 22:2)

The **righteous** are concerned for the **poor**. "*The **righteous** considers the cause of the **poor**, but the **wicked** does not understand such knowledge*" (Proverbs 29:7)	"*Do not **rob** the **poor** because he is **poor**, nor **oppress** the afflicted at the gate; for the LORD will plead their cause, and plunder the soul of those who plunder them*" (Proverbs 22:22-23)	"*One who increases his possessions by usury and extortion gathers it for him who will pity the **poor***" (Proverbs 28:8)
A virtuous wife cares for the **poor**. "*She extends her hand to the **poor**, yes, she reaches out her hands to the needy*" (Proverbs 31:20)	"*He who **oppresses** the **poor** to increase his riches, and he who gives to the rich, will surely come to poverty*" (Proverbs 22:16)	The **merciful** are concern for the **poor**. "*He who has pity on the **poor** lends to the LORD, and He will pay back what he has given*" (Proverbs 19:17)
The **merciful** are happy to support the **poor**. "*...he who has **mercy** on the **poor**, happy is he*" (Proverbs 14:21)	"*He who has a generous eye will be blessed, for he gives of his bread to the **poor***" (Proverbs 22:9)	"*He who gives to the **poor** will not lack, but he who hides his eyes will have many curses*" (Proverbs 28:27)
"*Whoever shuts his ears to the cry of the **poor** will also cry himself and not be heard*" (Proverbs 21:13)	"*He who **mocks** the **poor** reproaches his Maker; he who is glad at calamity will not go unpunished*" (Proverbs 17:5)	"*Better is the **poor** who walks in his integrity than one who is **perverse** in his lips, and is a **fool**"* (Proverbs 19:1)
"*Better is the **poor** who walks in his integrity than one **perverse** in his ways, though he be rich*" (Proverbs 28:6)	"*The ransom of a man's life is his riches, but the **poor** does not hear rebuke*" (Proverbs 13:8)	"*The rich man is **wise** in his own eyes, but the **poor** who has understanding searches him out*" (Proverbs 28:11)

Table 136: Pearls of Wisdom Concerning the People in the Poor Category

From the pearls of wisdom above, one should understand that anyone can become an ***oppressor*** of people in this category. However, one should also keep in mind that Wisdom revealed to Solomon, "*The **poor** man and the **oppressor** have this in common: The LORD gives light to the eyes of both*" (Proverbs 29:13). Thus, God is in control and He will judge appropriately. Solomon also learned that leaders at every level have a responsibility for people in the **poor** category. The Spirit of wisdom revealed to him that, "*The king who judges the **poor** with truth, his throne will be established forever*" (Proverbs 29:14). King Lemuel documented that one must, "*Open your mouth, judge **righteously**, and plead the cause of the **poor** and needy*" (Proverbs 31:9). While King Agur explained that, "*There is a generation that curses its father, and does not bless its mother. There is a generation that is pure in its own eyes, yet is not washed from its filthiness. There is a generation—oh, how lofty are their eyes! And their eyelids are lifted up. There is a generation whose teeth are like swords, and whose fangs are like knives, to devour the **poor** from off the earth, and the needy from among men*" (Proverbs 30:11-14). To understand their responsibilities to the people in the **poor** category, leaders must acquire the influences of the positive attributes. If not, leaders with the negative attributes will destroy both the people in the **poor** category and themselves in the process. This is part of the strategy of the negative forces hidden in the fog of spiritual warfare.

To sum up the Proverbs, King Agur provided some great words that Solomon recorded concerning the influence of the positive or negative attributes. He prayed to God saying, "*Two things I request of You (deprive me not before I die): remove **falsehood** and **lies** far from me; give me neither poverty nor riches— feed me with the food allotted to me; lest I be full and deny You, and say, "Who is the LORD?" or lest I be **poor** and **steal**, and **profane** the name of my God*" (Proverbs 30:7-9). This should be part of the prayer for everyone who wishes to support the positive forces of the war campaign. With this said, consider what the rest of the Biblical record documents about the people in the **poor** category.

First, God made it clear to the children of Israel that partiality, discrimination, and **unjust** behavior toward people in the **poor** category was unacceptable. He gave Moses several regulatory commands for Israel to follow. The Biblical record documented:

"*If you lend money to any of My people who are **poor** among you, you shall not be like a moneylender to him; you shall not charge him interest*" (Exodus 22:25)	"*You shall not show partiality to a **poor** man in his dispute*" (Exodus 23:3)	"*You shall not **pervert** the judgment of your **poor** in his dispute*" (Exodus 23:6)
The Ransom offering: "*Everyone included among those who are numbered, from twenty years old and above, shall give an offering to the Lord. The rich shall not give more and the **poor** shall not give less than half a shekel...*" (Exodus 30:14-15)	"*You shall not **oppress** a hired servant who is **poor** and needy.... Each day you shall give him his wages, and not let the sun go down on it, for he is **poor** and has set his heart on it; lest he cry out against you to the Lord, and it be sin to you*" (Deuteronomy 24:14-15)	"*And if one of your brethren who dwells by you becomes **poor**, and sells himself to you, you shall not compel him to serve as a slave. As a hired servant and a sojourner he shall be with you, and shall serve you until the Year of Jubilee*" (Leviticus 25:39-40)
"*Six years you shall sow your land and gather in its produce, but the seventh year you shall let it rest and lie fallow, that the **poor** of your people may eat...*" (Exodus 23:10-11)	*And you shall not glean your vineyard, nor shall you gather every grape of your vineyard; you shall leave them for the **poor** and the stranger: I am the Lord your God*" (Leviticus 19:10; 23:22)	"*You shall do no injustice in judgment. You shall not be partial to the **poor**, nor **honor** the person of the mighty. In **righteousness** you shall judge your neighbor*" (Leviticus 19:15)
"*If one of your brethren becomes **poor**, and has sold some of his possession, and if his redeeming relative comes to redeem it, then he may redeem what his brother sold.... But if he is not able to have it restored to himself, then what was	"*If one of your brethren becomes **poor**, and falls into poverty among you, then you shall help him, like a stranger or a sojourner, that he may live with you. Take no usury or interest from him; but fear your God, that your brother may	The Trespass offering: "*...if he is **poor** and cannot afford it, then he shall take one male lamb as a trespass offering to be waved, to make atonement for him, one-tenth of an ephah of fine flour mixed with oil as a grain offering, a log of oil,

sold shall remain in the hand of him who bought it until the Year of Jubilee; and in the Jubilee it shall be released, and he shall return to his possession..." (Leviticus 25:25-28)	live with you. You shall not lend him your money for usury, nor lend him your food at a profit." (Leviticus 25:35-37)	and two turtledoves or two young pigeons, such as he is able to afford: one shall be a sin offering and the other a burnt offering" (Leviticus 14:21-22)
"Now if a sojourner or stranger close to you becomes rich, and one of your brethren who dwells by him becomes **poor**, and sells himself to the stranger or sojourner close to you, or to a member of the stranger's family, after he is sold he may be redeemed again..." (Leviticus 25:47-49)	A person concentrated to the Lord for service: "But if he is too **poor** to pay your valuation, then he shall present himself before the priest, and the priest shall set a value for him; according to the ability of him who vowed, the priest shall value him" (Leviticus 27:8)	"If there is among you a **poor** man of your brethren, within any of the gates in your land which the Lord your God is giving you, you shall not harden your heart nor shut your hand from your **poor** brother but you shall open your hand wide to him and willingly lend him sufficient for his need, whatever he needs" (Deuteronomy 15:7-8)
Beware lest there be a **wicked** thought in your heart, saying, 'The seventh year, the year of release, is at hand,' and your eye be **evil** against your **poor** brother and you give him nothing, and he cry out to the Lord against you, and it become sin among you" (Deuteronomy 15:9)	"...the **poor** will never cease from the land; therefore I command you, saying, 'You shall open your hand wide to your brother, to your **poor** and your needy, in your land'" (Deuteronomy 15:11)	"...if the man is **poor**, you shall not keep his pledge overnight. You shall in any case return the pledge to him again when the sun goes down, that he may sleep in his own garment and bless you; and it shall be **righteousness** to you before the Lord your God." (Deuteronomy 24:12-13)

Table 137: God's Commands Concerning the Treatment of People in the Poor Category

Given by the Lord for the children of Israel, the items listed in Table 136 regulated Israel's behavior regarding the treatment of the people in the **poor** category. Moreover, God identified sin by His commands. When one violated His commands, one found himself or herself in a state of sin. In addition, BTT allows one to see how the positive or negative attributes affected both the people who dealt with the people of the **poor** category and the people in the category itself.

Other people in the Biblical record who shared pearls of wisdom about people in the **poor** category included Hannah, who gave birth to Samuel, and Job while defending himself against four *false* accusers. The Biblical record documented:

- Hannah stated, "*The Lord makes **poor** and makes rich; He brings low and lifts up. He raises the **poor** from the dust and lifts the **beggar** from the ash heap, to set them among princes and make them inherit the throne of glory. For the pillars of the earth are the Lord's, and He has set the world upon them*" (1 Samuel 2:7-8)

- Job, talking about people influenced by the **wicked** attribute and their war against the people in the **poor** category, stated:

    - *"Some remove landmarks; they seize flocks **violently** and feed on them; they drive away the donkey of the fatherless; they take the widow's ox as a pledge. They push the needy off the road; all the **poor** of the land are forced to hide"* (Job 24:2-4)

    - *Some snatch the fatherless from the breast, and take a pledge from the **poor**. They cause the **poor** to go naked, without clothing; and they take away the sheaves from the hungry"* (Job 24:9-10)

    - And still others: *"There are those who rebel against the light; they do not know its ways nor abide in its paths. The **murderer** rises with the light; he **kills** the **poor** and needy; and in the night he is like a **thief**"* (Job 24:13-14)

One can learn so much more from Job. As a man blessed to be in the rich category, he documented the proper relationship that one should have with people in the **poor** category. To his accusers, and for our example, Job documented:

- *"The voice of nobles was hushed, and their tongue stuck to the roof of their mouth. When the ear heard, then it blessed me, and when the eye saw, then it approved me; because I delivered the **poor** who cried out, the fatherless and the one who had no helper"* (Job 29:10-12)

- *"I put on **righteousness**, and it clothed me; my justice was like a robe and a turban. I was eyes to the blind, and I was feet to the lame. I was a father to the **poor**, and I searched out the case that I did not know. I broke the fangs of the **wicked**, and plucked the victim from his teeth"* (Job 29:14-17)

- *"Have I not wept for him who was in trouble? Has not my soul grieved for the **poor**?"* (Job 30:25)

- *"If I have kept the **poor** from their desire, or caused the eyes of the widow to fail, or eaten my morsel by myself, so that the fatherless could not eat of it (But from my youth I reared him as a father, and from my mother's womb I guided the widow); if I have seen anyone perish for lack of clothing, or any **poor** man without covering; if his heart has not blessed me, and if he was not warmed with the fleece of my sheep; if I have raised my hand against the fatherless, when I saw I had help in the gate; then let my arm fall from my shoulder, let my arm be torn from the socket. For destruction from God is a terror to me, and because of His magnificence I cannot endure"* (Job 31:16-23)

Clearly, Job understood spiritual warfare and the war campaign. Job was among the positive forces doing what he could to help the people in the **poor** category and shield them from the clutches of the negative forces of the war campaign. Moreover, as one in the rich category, Job put his resources toward their wellbeing for he understood that he was merely a caretaker of God's riches. God blessed Job with his possessions and he served the Lord with them.

Consider some final pearls of wisdom from King David and Solomon. They both documented the special relationship between the people of the **poor** category and the Lord. Do not lose sight of the fact that the relationship between the Lord and the people of the **poor** category is contingent on their hearing and being obedient to the Lord's Word. This is consistent throughout the Biblical record. King David and Solomon documented:

"For the needy shall not always be forgotten; the expectation of the **poor** *shall not perish forever"* (Psalm 9:18)	*"I know that the Lord will maintain the cause of the afflicted, and justice for the* **poor***"* (Psalm 140:12)	*"...He shall stand at the* **right** *hand of the* **poor***, to save him from those who condemn him"* (Psalm 109:30-31)
"He will bring justice to the **poor** *of the people; he will save the children of the needy, and will break in pieces the* **oppressor***"* (Psalm 72:4)	*"Better a* **poor** *and wise youth than an old and* **foolish** *king who will be admonished no more"* (Ecclesiastes 4:13)	*"He has dispersed abroad, He has given to the* **poor***; His* **righteousness** *endures forever; His horn will be exalted with* **honor***"* (Psalm 112:9)
"Blessed is he who considers the **poor***; the Lord will deliver him in time of trouble"* (Psalm 41:1)	*"For the Lord hears the* **poor***, and does not despise His prisoners"* (Psalm 69:33)	*"The* **wicked** *in his* **pride** *persecutes the* **poor***; let them be caught in the plots which they have devised"* (Psalm 10:2)
"For the **oppression** *of the* **poor***, for the sighing of the needy, now I will arise,"* says the Lord; *"I will set him in the safety for which he yearns"* (Psalm 12:5)	*"All my bones shall say, "Lord, who is like You, delivering the* **poor** *from him who is too strong for him, yes, the* **poor** *and the needy from him who plunders him?"* (Psalm 35:10)	*"He raises the* **poor** *out of the dust, and lifts the needy out of the ash heap, that He may seat him with princes—with the princes of His people"* (Psalm 113:7)
"If you see the **oppression** *of the* **poor***, and the* **violent perversion** *of justice and* **righteousness** *in a province, do not marvel at the matter; for high official watches over high official, and higher officials are over them"* (Ecclesiastes 5:8)	*"The* **wicked** *have drawn the sword and have bent their bow, to cast down the* **poor** *and needy, to slay those who are of* **upright** *conduct. Their sword shall enter their own heart, and their bows shall be broken."* (Psalm 37:14-15)	People with the **wicked** attribute: *"He lies in wait secretly, as a lion in his den; he lies in wait to catch the* **poor***; he catches the* **poor** *when he draws him into his net"* (Psalm 10:9)
"...He will deliver the needy when he cries, the **poor** *also, and him who has no helper. He will spare the* **poor** *and needy, and will save the souls of the needy.*	*"Have all the workers of iniquity no knowledge, who eat up my people as they eat bread, and do not call on the Lord? There they are in great fear, for God is*	

He will redeem their life from **oppression** and **violence**; and precious shall be their blood in His sight" (Psalm 72:12-14)	with the generation of the **righteous**. You shame the counsel of the **poor**, but the Lord is his refuge" (Psalm 14:4-6)

Table 138: Pearls of Wisdom from the Psalmist and Solomon Concerning People in the Poor Category

Finally, as the nation of Israel grew ***wicked*** and corrupted by the influence of the negative attributes, the people in the **poor** category suffered even more. The Biblical record documented how the Lord sent His prophets to the nation of Israel warning them to repent and return to Him. The treatment of the people in the **poor** category showed up numerous times in those warnings. The Bible documented:

The Prophet	What Is Documented
Isaiah	"*The Lord will enter into judgment with the elders of His people and His princes: "For you have eaten up the vineyard; the plunder of the **poor** is in your houses. What do you mean by crushing My people and grinding the faces of the **poor**?" Says the Lord God of hosts*" (Isaiah 3:14-15)
	"*Woe to those who decree **unrighteous** decrees, who write misfortune, which they have prescribed to **rob** the needy of justice, and to take what is **right** from the **poor** of My people, that widows may be their prey, and that they may **rob** the fatherless*" (Isaiah 10:1-2)
	"*Also the schemes of the schemer are **evil**; he devises **wicked** plans to destroy the **poor** with **lying** words, even when the needy speaks justice*" (Isaiah 32:7)
	Concerning fasting: "*Is this not the fast that I have chosen: to loose the bonds of **wickedness**, to undo the heavy burdens, to let the **oppressed** go free, and that you break every yoke? Is it not to share your bread with the hungry, and that you bring to your house the **poor** who are cast out...?*" (Isaiah 58:6-7)
Jeremiah	"*Also on your skirts is found the **blood** of the lives of the **poor** innocents. I have not found it by secret search, but plainly on all these things*" (Jeremiah 2:34)
Ezekiel	The prophet Ezekiel explained that one can identify one who claims they have the ***just***_attribute by how they treat people in the **poor** category. He documented that if one "*...has **oppressed** the **poor** and needy...*" (Ezekiel 18:4-18), the ***unjust*** attribute influences this person's behavior.
	However, if the person has "*has given his bread to the hungry and covered the naked with clothing; who has withdrawn his hand from the **poor** and not received usury or increase, but has executed My judgments and walked in My statutes*" (Ezekiel 18:16-17), the ***just*** attribute influences this person's behavior.
	"*Thus says the Lord: "For three transgressions of Israel, and for four, I will not turn away its punishment, because they sell the **righteous** for silver, and the **poor** for a pair of sandals. They pant after the dust of the earth which is on the head of the **poor**, and **pervert** the way of the **humble**. A man and his father go in to the same girl, to defile My holy name. They lie down by every*

Amos	*altar on clothes taken in pledge, and drink the wine of the condemned in the house of their god"* (Amos 2:6-8)
	*"Hear this word, you cows of Bashan, who are on the mountain of Samaria, who **oppress** the **poor**, who crush the needy, who say to your husbands, "Bring wine, let us drink!"* (Amos 4:1)
	*"Therefore, because you tread down the **poor** and take grain taxes from him, though you have built houses of hewn stone, yet you shall not dwell in them; you have planted pleasant vineyards, but you shall not drink wine from them. For I know your manifold transgressions and your mighty sins: Afflicting the **just** and <u>taking bribes</u>; diverting the **poor** from <u>justice</u> at the gate"* (Amos 5:11-12)
	*"Hear this, you who swallow up the needy, and make the **poor** of the land fail, saying: "When will the New Moon be past, that we may sell grain? And the Sabbath, that we may trade wheat? Making the ephah small and the shekel large, **falsifying** the scales by **deceit**, that we may buy the **poor** for silver, and the needy for a pair of sandals— even sell the **bad** wheat?"* (Amos 8:4-6)

Table 139: The Prophet's Warnings about the People in the Poor Category

The prophet Ezekiel laid the blame of the fall of the nation of Israel on the religious community and their leaders. He explained his position based on what he received from the Lord. These religious leader's actions had a major impact on the people in the **poor** category; the largest population in the nation of Israel at that time. As a testament even for us today, Ezekiel documented that, *"The conspiracy of her prophets in her midst is like a roaring lion tearing the prey; they have devoured people; they have taken treasure and precious things; they have made many widows in her midst. Her priests have violated My law and profaned My holy things; they have not distinguished between the holy and unholy, nor have they made known the difference between the unclean and the clean; and they have hidden their eyes from My Sabbaths, so that I am profaned among them. Her princes in her midst are like wolves tearing the prey, **to shed blood**, to destroy people, and to get **dishonest** <u>gain</u>. Her prophets plastered them with untempered mortar, seeing **false** <u>visions</u>, and <u>divining</u> **lies** for them, saying, 'Thus says the Lord God,' when the Lord had not spoken. The people of the land have used **oppressions**, committed **robbery**, and mistreated the **poor** and needy; and they wrongfully **oppress** the stranger"* (Ezekiel 22:25-29). Israel was in a state of chaos and its corrupt *and* **wicked** prophets, priest, and leaders were the blame. The Lord, true to His Word, destroyed the nation and scattered the people abroad. This is the same state today that religious leaders worldwide are in. Only a remnant of Christians are still teaching God's Word unchanged.

As the New Testament begins, Jesus acknowledges the people in the **poor** category early in the Gospel. He stated, *"Blessed are the **poor** in spirit, for theirs is the kingdom of heaven.* (Matthew 5:3). In this statement, Jesus addressed the condition of the inner spirit of the people. Those in the **poor** category would have especially found this statement comforting since their economic situation left much to be desired. It is also important to see that Jesus comments on the **poor** aspect first in the whole discourse known as the "Beatitudes" in Matthew 5:3-11. Further, Jesus identified the people of the **poor** category when two of John the Baptist's disciples came to Him to inquire if He was the Christ. He said, "*...Go and tell John the things which you hear and see: The blind see and the lame walk; the lepers are cleansed and the deaf hear; the dead are raised up and the* **poor** *have the gospel preached to them. And blessed is he who is not offended because of Me*" (Matthew 11:4-6; Luke 7:22). BTT allows one to see that Jesus identified Himself by the work He was doing among the people in the **poor** category. People in the **poor** category's inner spirits were refreshed when they heard the preaching of the Gospel. They began to understand the importance of God's Word in their lives and the transformative difference it makes.

Spread throughout the rest of the New Testament, there are many confirmations of the people in the **poor** category. Teachings from Jesus and the apostles clearly illustrated one's ***faith*** is on display by one's response to people who are in this category. As part of the **harvest**, Jesus commands one's appropriate attention to their plight. The Biblical record documents:

- To the rich young ruler, Jesus said: "*If you want to be perfect, go, sell what you have and give to the* **poor**, *and you will have treasure in heaven; and come, follow Me*" (Matthew 19:21)

- Jesus chastised Judas and the disciples who complained about oil used for Him. Judas exclaimed, "*...Why this waste? For this fragrant oil might have been sold for much and given to the* **poor**." *But when Jesus was aware of it, He said to them, "Why do you trouble the woman? For she has done a* **good** work *for Me. For you have the* **poor** *with you always, but Me you do not have always*" (Matthew 26:8-11; Mark 14:3-9; and John 12:1-8)

- Judas behavior was not from the positive attributes. The Biblical record documented of Judas, "*...not that he cared for the* **poor**, *but because he was a* **thief**, *and had the money box; and he used to* **take** *what was put in it*" (John 12:6)

- For the **poor** widow contributing to the treasury, Jesus stated, "*this* **poor** *widow has put in more than all those who have given to the treasury; for they all put in out of their abundance, but she out of her* poverty *put in all that she had, her whole livelihood*" (Mark 12:41-44 and Luke 21:1-4)

- Jesus speaking of His responsibility said, "*The Spirit of the Lord is upon Me, because He has anointed Me To preach the gospel to the* **poor**..." (Luke 4:18)

- Concerning one's responsibility, Jesus stated "*But when you give a feast, invite the* **poor**, *the maimed, the lame, the blind. And you will be blessed, because they cannot repay you; for you shall be repaid at the resurrection of the* **just**" (Luke 14:13-14; 21)

- Zacchaeus recognized the **poor**. He stated to Jesus, "*...Look, Lord, I give half of my* **good***s to the* **poor**; *and if I have taken anything from anyone by* **false** accusation, *I restore fourfold*" (Luke 19:8)

- The Macedonian and Achaian churches recognized the **poor**. Paul documented "*For it pleased those from Macedonia and Achaia to make a certain contribution for the* **poor** *among the saints who are in Jerusalem*" (Romans 15:26)

- Paul recognized the **poor**. He stated, *"But this I say: He who sows sparingly will also reap sparingly, and he who sows bountifully will also reap bountifully. So let each one give as he purposes in his heart, not grudgingly or of necessity; for God <u>loves</u> a cheerful giver. And God is able to make all grace abound toward you, that you, always having all sufficiency in all things, may have an abundance for every **good** work: As it is written: "He has dispersed abroad, He has given to the **poor**; His **righteousness** endures forever"* (2 Corinthians 9:6-9)

- The Galatian church recognized the **poor**. Paul documented, *"They desired only that we should remember the **poor**, the very thing which I also was eager to do"* (Galatians 2:10)

- James recognized the **poor**. He wrote, *"Let the **lowly** brother glory in his exaltation, but the rich in his humiliation, because as a flower of the field he will pass away. For no sooner has the sun risen with a burning heat than it withers the grass; its flower falls, and its beautiful appearance perishes. So the rich man also will fade away in his pursuits"* (James 1:9-11)

God <u>loves</u> the **poor** of this world and the Biblical record provides the evidence as documented above. For this reason, people in this category are sought by the attributes on both sides of the war campaign. Thus, it is extremely important for people influenced by the positive forces to reach out and help people in the **poor** category. If not, the negative forces will grow their strength exponentially in spiritual warfare. If the people in the **poor** category, the largest population of people in the world, respond to the negative stimuli, chaos will ensue and the influence of the **hater** and **violent** attributes will gain a greater foothold in the world. Christians must share God's Word with the people in the **poor** category at every opportunity.

Luke 16:19-31 and James 2:1-13 documents two superior examples of spiritual warfare. These examples illustrate the pressures people in the **poor** category experience and God's great <u>love</u> for them. Both examples deal with people in the **poor** and rich categories. In the Book of Luke, Jesus spoke of a person in the **poor** category named Lazarus. The Bible documented that *"...a certain **beggar** named Lazarus, full of sores, who was laid at his gate, desiring to be fed with the crumbs which fell from the rich man's table"* (Luke 16:20-21). The man in the rich category *"...was clothed in purple and fine linen and fared sumptuously every day"* (Luke 16:19). What is so important about Jesus' comparison is that He laid out what occurs in the war campaign when the positive or negative attributes influences one's behavior in either of these categories. The comparison also exposed what happens to one's soul when one dies. For Lazarus, one can infer from the text that he knew God's Word and was obedient to it because he was *"...carried by the angels to Abraham's bosom"* (Luke 16:22). However, the rich man's case was completely different. Jesus said of him, *"...being in torments in Hades, he lifted up his eyes and saw Abraham afar off, and Lazarus in his bosom"* (Luke 16:23). BTT allows one to see that the rich man had the opportunity and resources to help Lazarus in life. However, based on his documented behavior, he rejected this opportunity. The Bible documented that from his tormented state, the rich man cried out to Abraham for help. However, Abraham replied, *"Son, remember that in your lifetime you received your **good** things, and likewise Lazarus **evil*** *things; but now he is comforted and you are tormented"* (Luke 16:25). Moreover, when the rich man recognized the truth of the war campaign, he asked Abraham to send Lazarus back from the dead to warn his five brothers according to Luke 16:27-28. Nevertheless, Abraham told him truthfully why this could not be done (Luke 16:26). His response is well worth reading. Consider the discourse between Abraham and the rich man very closely. Abraham said, *"They have Moses and the prophets; let them hear them.' And he said, 'No, father Abraham; but if one goes to them from the dead, they will repent.' But he said to him, 'If they do not hear Moses and the prophets, neither will they be persuaded though one rise from the dead"* (Luke 16 29-31). This Truth applies today. All the categories of people in the **harvest** have the Bible at their disposal or have the opportunity to hear God's Word today. In some countries, this opportunity may be more difficult; however, man cannot limit God's hand. If there is a desire, the providence of God will make a way. For the prophet Isaiah documented from the Lord, *"For as the rain comes down, and the snow from heaven, and do not return there, but water the earth, and make it bring forth and bud, that it may give seed to the sower and bread to the eater, so shall My word be that goes forth from My mouth; It shall not return to Me void, but it shall accomplish what I please, and it shall prosper in the thing for which I sent it"* (Isaiah 55:10-11). In fact, the resources of people in the rich category are one of the vehicles used to aid in this effort. However, one cannot allow the fog generated by the negative forces through spiritual warfare blind one to this Truth. If one does, based on Jesus' example and the conclusion above, the consequences are forever.

The second example deals with the element of *favoritism* used against people in the **poor** category. In this example, a person in the **poor** category and a person in the rich category are in the same physical location. The **poor** person was "***dishonored***" (James 2:6) in the presence of the rich person by the behavior of the people present. The people present, influenced by negative attributes, "***honored***" the rich person based on his appearance. In other words, because of spiritual warfare, the Biblical record documented, *"...have you not shown partiality among yourselves, and become judges with **evil** thoughts?"* (James 2:4). What makes this example so important is the fact that the setting is in the Lord's church. BTT allows one to see this fact by the use of the term "assembly" in James 2:2, and the knowledge that James' letter was for the people in Christ's church. Further, James documented God's Law that everyone among the positive forces are to observe. James documented, *"If you really fulfill the royal law according to the Scripture, "You shall love your neighbor as yourself," you do well; but if you show partiality, you commit sin, and are convicted by the law as **transgressors**. For whoever shall keep the whole law, and yet stumble in one point, he is guilty of all"* (James 2:8-10). Moreover, James documented that for one to remain on the positive forces side of the campaign, one must, *"...speak and so do as those who will be judged by the law of liberty. For judgment is without **mercy** to the one who has shown no **mercy**. **Mercy** triumphs over judgment"* (James 12-13). The fog generated by the negative forces during spiritual warfare involves the use of *partiality* and *favoritism* to divide the positive forces, and more importantly; God's people. One will see these examples again in the chapter on the rich category from the perspective of people in that category.

The negative forces of the war campaign have successfully perpetuated a ***false*** teaching about Jesus' status. This must be addressed. Using the Gospel of Jesus Christ, promoters of the prosperity movement ***falsely*** teach that Jesus was in the rich category while on earth. This is taught despite all the Biblical documentation to the contrary. This teaching is a classic example of how the negative forces use spiritual warfare to twist Scripture. Many in the religious community then spreads this ***false*** and misleading doctrine. This ***false*** doctrine continues to lead many **good** people down the bad path of life. The Biblical record documented, "*For you know the <u>grace</u> of our Lord Jesus Christ, that <u>though He was rich, yet for your sakes He became</u> **poor**, that you through His <u>poverty</u> might become rich*" (2 Corinthians 8:9). BTT allows one to see that in this Scriptural reference, Jesus' wealth stems from the fact that He, as the Son of God, owns everything that exists. The Biblical record confirms this fact as it documents, "*He was in the beginning with God. All things were made through Him, and without Him nothing was made that was made*" (John 1:2-3). Jesus is wealthy beyond imagination as the Son of God and we are the caretakers of His physical wealth regardless of the amount. Nevertheless, when Jesus put on human flesh, He put away His wealth for our sakes. For our sake, He became a person in the **poor** category so that He could experience life unencumbered by His Spiritual embodiment. The Bible even documents that Jesus, "*...being in the form of God, did not consider it robbery to be equal with God, but made Himself of no reputation, taking the form of a bondservant, and coming in the likeness of men*" (Philippians 2:6-7). Jesus gave up everything to live among us in the form of a bondservant; a person bound in service without wages, i. e. a slave. He was not rich or pursuing wealth. This Truth confirms the Biblical record's documentation that, "*...we do not have a High Priest who cannot sympathize with our weaknesses, but was in all points tempted as we are, yet without sin*" (Hebrews 4:15). Still further, the Bible documented that Jesus Himself said, "*Foxes have holes and birds of the air have nests, but the Son of Man has nowhere to lay His head*" (Matthew 8:20; Luke 9:58). Why? Jesus lived primarily among the people of the **poor** category. Jesus sacrificed all he had according 2 Corinthians 8:9, so that "*you through His <u>poverty</u> might become rich*". BTT allows one to see that this is spiritual wealth; not carnal wealth.

Consider the contradiction His life would represent to the Bible if He lived in luxury while on earth. The Holy Spirit provides one principle that states, "*For the <u>love</u> of money is a root of all kinds of **evil**, for which some have strayed from the **faith** in their <u>greediness</u>, and pierced themselves through with many sorrows*" (1 Timothy 6:10). This principle signifies that the prosperity movement is not from God but is simply another strategy used by the negative forces of the war campaign to cause many people to stumble in the fog of the war. People promoting this ***false*** teaching were identified by Paul when he wrote to Timothy stating, "*But know this, that in the last days perilous times will come: For men will be lovers of themselves, <u>lovers of money</u>, <u>boasters</u>, **proud**, blasphemers, disobedient to parents, unthankful, unholy, unloving, unforgiving, **slanderers**, **without self-control**, **brutal**, **despisers of good**, traitors, headstrong, **haughty**, lovers of pleasure rather than <u>lovers of God</u>, having a form of **godliness** but denying its power. <u>And from such people turn away</u>!*" (2 Timothy 3:1-5). Anyone following religious teachers who espouse this ***false*** doctrine will be lost when Jesus returns.

One can also consider that Satan even offered Jesus wealth. As Jesus was being tempted in the wilderness, He turned Satan's offer down because Jesus was well aware of the war campaign. For one's knowledge, the Bible documents, "*...the devil took Him up on an* *exceedingly high mountain, and showed Him all the kingdoms of the world and their glory. And he said to Him, "All these things I will give You if You will fall down and worship me"* (Matthew 4:8-9). Using Scripture, Jesus rejected Satan stating, *"Away with you, Satan! For it is written, 'You shall worship the Lord your God, and Him only you shall serve"* (Matthew 4:10). If Jesus had accepted Satan's offer, the prosperity movement would have a Scriptural foundation. But Satan lost. The prosperity movement is only kept alive in the war campaign by **false** teachers. In fact, Paul likely had to deal with a situation concerning the roots of an early prosperity movement in the regions of Achaia. The Bible indicates that there appeared to be **false** teachers preaching the Gospel by taking people's money for person gain. Paul went there and attempted to set the correct example in 2 Corinthians 11:7-15. He said, *"Did I commit sin in <u>humbling</u> myself that you might be exalted, because I preached the gospel of God to you free of charge?* (2 Corinthians 11:7). After his discussion, he warned *"But what I do, I will also continue to do, that I may cut off the opportunity from those who desire an opportunity to be regarded just as we are in the things of which they boast. For such are **false** apostles, **deceitful** workers, transforming themselves into apostles of Christ. And no wonder! For Satan himself transforms himself into an angel of light. Therefore it is no great thing if his ministers also transform themselves into ministers of **righteousness**, whose end will be according to their works"* (2 Corinthians 11:12-15).

Because of Jesus' great awareness of spiritual warfare, the war campaign, the future ramification of His decisions, and His commitment to God, He rejected Satan's offer documented in Matthew 4:8-9. Thus, one should not be involved in this **false** movement. Jesus stated Himself, *"For where your treasure is, there your heart will be also"* (Matthew 6:21; Luke 12:34). Jesus' Word is written to show that anyone preaching a Biblical theology that He was in the **rich** category while on earth and He wants you to be too, is influenced by the **liar** attribute. Where the Scripture documents that, *"...yet for your sakes He became **poor**, that you through His <u>poverty</u> might become rich"* in 2 Corinthians 8:9, the author is talking about becoming spiritually rich is Christ's Word and the knowledge of God. But **false** teachers twist this Truth to simply justify their own pursuit of <u>wealth</u>. They operate in the fog generated by the negative forces of the war campaign and their teachings **dishonor** God, Jesus, and the people in the **poor** category. In fact, their contradiction blasphemes the Holy Spirit's teaching by Paul documented in 2 Timothy 3:1-5. People who pursue <u>wealth</u> in the name of God are in error. This **false** teaching is increasing the negative forces in the campaign, while tilting the balance of the war toward the negative force's favor and inviting God's <u>calamity</u>. Jesus understood the role of money in human affairs. But He warned that it must be respected. In fact, Jesus said, *"...make friends for yourselves by **unrighteous** mammon, that when you fail, they may receive you into an everlasting home. He who is **faithful** in what is least is **faithful** also in much; and he who is **unjust** in what is least is **unjust** also in much. Therefore if you have not been **faithful** in the **unrighteous** mammon, who will commit to your trust the true riches? And if you have not been **faithful** in what is another man's, who will give you what is your own? No servant can serve two masters; for either he will **hate** the one and <u>love</u> the other, or else he will be loyal to the one and despise the other. You cannot serve God and mammon"* (Luke 16:9-13). "Mammon" and "money" are synonymous terms in this Biblical context. Thus, Jesus taught, *"...seek the kingdom of God, and all these things shall be added to you"* (Luke

12:31). One must trust God in this matter. If one chooses to ignore this message, the consequences are his or hers alone.

Lastly, consider the case of the church of the Laodiceans in the Book of Revelation. Jesus documented that this church was spiritually bankrupt. This congregation had lost their way in the war campaign and although they had physical wealth, the people's inner spirits belonged in the spiritually **poor** category. The people spiritually had nothing based on Jesus' standard. He called the congregation "lukewarm" and said, "...*I will vomit you out of My mouth. Because you say, 'I am rich, have become wealthy, and have need of nothing'—and do not know that you are wretched, miserable,* **poor***, blind, and naked— I counsel you to buy from Me gold refined in the fire, that you may be rich; and white garments, that you may be clothed, that the shame of your nakedness may not be revealed; and anoint your eyes with eye salve, that you may see. As many as I love, I rebuke and chasten. Therefore be zealous and repent...*" (Revelation 3:14-22). The image of this church represents many congregations today that believe they are doing the work of God. Please do not be **deceived**. For the Bible documents, "*For the time has come for judgment to begin at the house of God; and if it begins with us first, what will be the end of those who do not obey the gospel of God?*" (1 Peter 4:17).

The **Rich Category:** The people in this category provide the bulk of the resources that bolsters the advancement of either the positive or the negative forces of the war campaign. The influence of wealth and its intentional and unintentional uses can never be underestimated. People influenced by the positive attributes in the **rich** category, share their wealth among the positive forces of the campaign to accomplish the works of God. These works include such things as supporting the efforts to spread the Gospel within the context of the Scriptures, helping the poor, the needy, widows, and orphans. These works can also include supporting a safe place for teaching the Gospel and having the essential materials available for worship. Even if one's home is the only available place for Christians to meet in an area consumed in ***wickedness***, the assets of one in the **rich** category can go a long way to help support this ***good*** work.

When people in the **rich** category are influenced by the negative attributes, the influences of the ***wickedness***, ***evil***, ***proud***, and ***perverse*** attributes can accomplish staggering amounts of damage through spiritual warfare. Simply based on the sheer numbers of negative forces, the availability of wealth opens countless opportunities against the positive forces to include the invention of ***evil*** things (Romans 1:30). The combination of sins produced against the positive forces can be staggering but is part of the grand strategy of the negative forces. When unrestrained resources support the negative forces, God's Word becomes the target of alternative and ***false*** doctrines. Unrestrained resources, especially with bribes, can make discernment difficult in the fog of the campaign. Bribes and special favors sway the minds of people who either do not know the Almighty God, are not committed to him, or simply do not care. Moreover, breaches in the religious community due to bribes and the love of money lead to the convergence of boundaries on the spiritual battlefield which fuels apostasy. BTT allows one to see that breaches begin with the hiring of a ***false*** teacher for "itching ear" (2 Timothy 4:3) who seeks wealth under the false premise that money is the secret for accomplishing ***good*** works. Under this ***false*** premise, sound doctrine takes a backseat to worldly practices, traditions of men, and ***idolatrous*** philosophies generated by the negative attributes. These ***false*** teachers promote and grow <u>wealth</u> through strategies based on congregational numbers and contributions. They sway religious communities using ***deception*** in spiritual warfare. Overtime, the religious leader's apparel changes, facilities become elaborate and ornate to attract the masses, and the church building itself is glamorized over ***godly*** worship. Hence, the Holy Spirit inspired Paul to write about ***false*** teachers who teach people to "*...exchanged the truth of God for the **lie**, and worshiped and served the creature rather than the Creator, who is blessed forever. Amen*" (Romans 1:25).

As <u>wealth</u> spread among the negative forces, <u>resources</u> for printing, distributing, and circulating ***false*** Biblical doctrine and teachings spread. In fact, BTT allows one to see the spread of apostasy by these <u>resources</u> and Paul documented, "*Now the Spirit expressly says that in latter times some will depart from the **faith**, giving heed to deceiving spirits and doctrines of demons, speaking **lies** in hypocrisy, having their own conscience seared with a hot iron, forbidding to marry, and commanding to abstain from foods which God created to be received with thanksgiving by those who* believe *and know the truth*" (1 Timothy 4:1-3). The <u>resources</u> of people in the **rich** category even fund the travel and expenses of ***false*** teachers throughout the campaign's battlefield. Jesus condemned the religious leaders of His time when he stated, "*Woe to you, scribes and Pharisees, hypocrites! For you travel land and sea to win one proselyte, and when he is won, you make him twice as much a son of hell as yourselves*" (Matthew 23:15). When the negative forces of the campaign are involved in the inner spirits of people in the **rich** category, nothing is off limits to their desires. As one continues reading this chapter, BTT will allow one to see that the misuse of <u>wealth</u> even causes Christians to fall away from the Truth.

In this chapter of the book, one will also learn about another dark side of the misuse of <u>wealth</u>. It deals with people in the **rich** category's influence over weaker people, <u>wealth</u> pursuers, and dreamers who desire <u>wealth</u> over everything else. These people influenced by the negative attributes blindly support the schemes of people in the **rich** category. In the prosperity movement, this constitutes a large population of people hoping to gain <u>wealth</u>, status, and/or positions of favor that give them an advantage over others. BTT allows one to see that these are people who have accepted worldly wisdom (James 3:15) in hopes of gaining ***godly*** favor. But in reality, the influences of the negative forces have trapped these people hopelessly in sin. The hidden influence that people in the **rich** category have over people who desire <u>wealth</u> is difficult to document, explain, or measure. However, the influence can be seen in the behavior of people willing to risk their souls for unseen favors. Their behavior from time to time alters the balance of spiritual warfare simply because of their <u>greed</u>. The strategy behind the behavior, conceived by the negative forces, entangles and traps many ***good*** people. God's Word and the teaching of His Truth exposes and breaks this negative strategy. Hence, sharing the true Gospel of Jesus Christ to this category of people among the **harvest** is critical to the overall efforts of the positive forces of the war campaign.

The Biblical record documented that Solomon was in the **rich** category. However, he never asked nor sought to be <u>wealthy</u>. God gave him <u>wealth</u>. God told Solomon, because he only asked for wisdom, "*...and have not asked long life for yourself, nor have asked* **riches** *for* *yourself, nor have asked the life of your enemies, but have asked for yourself understanding to <u>discern justice</u>, behold, I have done according to your words; see, I have given you a wise and understanding heart, so that there has not been anyone like you before you, nor shall any like you arise after you. And I have also given you what you have not asked: both* **riches** *and* **honor***, so that there shall not be anyone like you among the kings all your days"* (1 Kings 3:11-13). Solomon's inner spirit had access to the Spirit of wisdom and she revealed many things to him that allowed him to acquire significant <u>wealth</u>. In fact, the Spirit of wisdom told him, *"Receive my instruction, and not <u>silver</u>, and knowledge rather than choice <u>gold</u>; for wisdom is better than <u>rubies</u>, and all the things one may desire cannot be compared with her"* (Proverbs 8:10-11). Within this statement from Wisdom, a pearl of wisdom is given. Instruction and knowledge yields spiritual <u>wealth</u>. I will revisit this important pearl later. For now, accept that Solomon understood what true <u>wealth</u> was. Wisdom further revealed, *"***Riches** *and* **honor** *are with me, enduring* **riches** *and* **righteousness***. My fruit is better than <u>gold</u>, yes, than fine <u>gold</u>, and my <u>revenue</u> than choice <u>silver</u>. I traverse the way of* **righteousness***, in the midst of the paths of <u>justice</u>, that I may cause those who <u>love</u> me to inherit <u>wealth</u>, that I may fill their <u>treasuries</u>"* (Proverbs 8: 18-21). BTT allows one to see through Wisdom's words that God provided Solomon's <u>wealth</u> both spiritually and physically. I believe this principle still applies to those who <u>love</u> and obey the Lord.

Further, the Spirit of wisdom also revealed that, *"The blessing of the LORD makes one* **rich***, and He adds no sorrow with it"* (Proverbs 10:22). This is a spiritual Truth worthy of one's meditation. First it documents that the Lord's blessings will place one in the **rich** category. The blessing may be spiritual, physical, or both. Regardless, it is the second part of the proverb that is even more important. When blessings are from the Lord, there are no sorrows with them. This is a clear indication that the blessing is from the Lord. Ill-gotten <u>wealth</u> from any other source will have pain and sorrow associated with it. Moreover, Wisdom revealed to Solomon that, *"<u>Wealth</u> gained by <u>dishonesty</u> will be diminished..."* (Proverbs 13:11). With this understanding, now consider some pearls of wisdom about people in the **rich** category influenced by either the positive or the negative attributes. Remember, one who accepts God's Word manifests the positive attributes through their behavior. Conversely, one who rejects God's Word manifests negative attributes through their behavior. For people influenced by the positive attributes in the **rich** category, the Spirit of wisdom revealed to Solomon:

Concerning wisdom and understanding: *"…Yes, if you cry out for <u>discernment</u>, and lift up your voice for understanding, if you seek her as* **silver***, and search for her as for hidden* **treasures***; then you will understand the <u>fear</u> of the Lord, and find the knowledge of God"* (Proverbs 2:1-5)	*"Happy is the man who finds wisdom, and the man who gains understanding; for her* **proceeds** *are better than the* **profits** *of* **silver***, and her gain than* **fine gold***. She is more precious than* **rubies***, and all the things you may desire cannot compare with her. Length of days is in her* **right** *hand, in her left hand*	*"Through wisdom a house is built, and by understanding it is established; by knowledge the rooms are filled with all <u>precious and pleasant</u>* **riches***"* (Proverbs 24:3-4)

	riches and **honor**. Her ways are <u>ways of pleasantness</u>, and all her paths are <u>peace</u>" (Proverbs 3:13-17)	
"By <u>humility</u> and the fear of the LORD are **riches** and **honor** and life" (Proverbs 22:4)	"In all labor there is **profit**, but **idle** chatter leads only to <u>poverty</u>" (Proverbs 14:23)	"…he who trusts in the LORD will be **prospered**" (Proverbs 28:25)
"The crown of the wise is their **riches**…" (Proverbs 14:24)	"… the hand of the diligent makes **rich**" (Proverbs 10:4)	"…the soul of the diligent shall be made **rich**" (Proverbs 13:4)
"The generous soul will be made **rich**, and he who waters will also be watered himself" (Proverbs 11:25)	"One who **increases his possessions** by usury and **extortion** gathers it for him who will pity the poor" (Proverbs 28:8)	"Be diligent to know the state of your flocks, and attend to your herds; for **riches** are not forever, nor does a crown endure to all generations" (Proverbs 27:23-24)

Table 140: Pearls of Wisdom Concerning the Positive Attribute's Influence on People in the Rich Category

For people influenced by the negative attributes in the **rich** category, the Spirit of wisdom revealed to Solomon:

"An **inheritance gained** hastily at the beginning will not be blessed at the end" (Proverbs 20:21)	"Getting **treasures** by a **lying** tongue is the fleeting fantasy of those who seek death" (Proverbs 21:6)	"Better is the poor who walks in his <u>integrity</u> than one **perverse** in his ways, though he be **rich**" (Proverbs 28:6)
Concerning those who are just <u>greedy</u>: "He who is <u>greedy</u> for **gain** troubles his own house…" (Proverbs 15:27)	"Bread **gained** by **deceit** is sweet to a man, but afterward his mouth will be filled with gravel" (Proverbs 20:17)	"He who **oppresses** the poor to increase his **riches**, and he who gives to the **rich**, will surely come to <u>poverty</u>" (Proverbs 22:16)
"The **rich** man is wise in his own eyes…" (Proverbs 28:11)	"… ruthless men retain **riches**" (Proverbs 11:16)	"…the **rich** answers roughly" (Proverbs 18:23)
"Better is a little with the fear of the LORD, than great **treasure** with trouble" (Proverbs 15:16)	"The **rich** man's <u>wealth</u> is his strong city…" (Proverbs 10:15 and 18:11)	"The **rich** rules over the poor, and the borrower is servant to the lender" (Proverbs 22:7)
"The ransom of a man's life is his **riches**, but the poor does not hear rebuke" (Proverbs 13:8)	"The **rich** man's <u>wealth</u> is his strong city, and like a high wall in his own esteem" (Proverbs 18:11)	"…the **rich** has many friends" (Proverbs 14:20) because, "<u>Wealth</u> makes many friends…" (Proverbs 19:4)

"He who trusts in his **riches** will fall..." (Proverbs 11:28)	"**Treasures** of **wickedness** profit nothing..." (Proverbs 10:2)	"**Riches** do not **profit** in the day of <u>wrath</u>..." (Proverbs 11:4)
"...a companion of harlots wastes his <u>wealth</u>" (Proverbs 29:3)	"...He who <u>loves</u> wine and oil will not be **rich**" (Proverbs 21:17)	"...in the **revenue** of the **wicked** is trouble" (Proverbs 15:6)
"...the <u>wealth</u> of the sinner is stored up for the **righteous**" (Proverbs 13:22)	"...he who hastens to be **rich** will not go unpunished" (Proverbs 28:20)	"Better is a little with the fear of the LORD, than great **treasure** with trouble" (Proverbs 15:16)
"A **good** name is to be chosen rather than great **riches**, loving favor rather than **silver** and **gold**" (Proverbs 22:1)	Concerning those who's **just evil**: "A man with an **evil** eye hastens after **riches**, and does not consider that <u>poverty</u> will come upon him" (28:22)	"There is one who makes himself **rich**, yet has nothing; and one who makes himself poor, yet has great **riches**" (Proverb 13:7)
"Do not overwork to be **rich**; because of your own understanding, cease! Will you set your eyes on that which is not? For **riches** certainly make themselves wings; they fly away like an eagle toward heaven" (Proverbs 23:4, 5)	Concerning those who plan **murder** for **gain**: "...in vain the net is spread in the sight of any bird; but they lie in wait for their own blood, they lurk secretly for their own lives. So are the ways of everyone who is <u>greedy</u> for **gain**; it takes away the life of its owners" (Proverbs 1:11-19)	

Table 141: Pearls of Wisdom Concerning the Negative Attribute's Influence on People in the Rich Category

Fittingly, Solomon documented a piece of wisdom from another wise man who had a **good** philosophy about being in the **rich** category. A man named Agur prayed to God and stated, "*Two things I request of You (deprive me not before I die): remove **falsehood** and **lies** far from me; give me neither <u>poverty</u> nor **riches**— feed me with the food allotted to me; lest I be full and deny You, and say, "Who is the LORD?" or lest I be poor and **steal**, and **profane** the name of my God*" (Proverbs 30:7-9). This should be everyone's approach toward **riches**, especially if one claims the influence of the positive attributes; for in the end, there is one thing that one can be sure of according to the Spirit of wisdom. That is, "*The **rich** and the poor have this in common, the LORD is the maker of them all*" (Proverbs 22:2). By this statement, one can rest assured that God is in control. What God gives, He can just as easily take away. Thus, one can find him or herself in either category at any time.

The Biblical record documented scores of people in the **rich** category along with the examples of their behavior when the positive or negative attributes influenced them. Every example documented in the Biblical record is worth one's full attention and study. Here are a few examples of individuals influenced by the positive attributes in the **rich** category:

Abraham (Genesis 13:2)	Jacob (Genesis 30:43)	Boaz (Ruth 2:1)
Joseph, Isaac's son (Genesis 41:37-45)	Esau, Jacob's brother (Genesis 32:14-15)	King David (1 Chronicles 29:10-15)
The children of Israel (Exodus 12:35-26; 32:1-6)	Solomon (1 Kings 10:23; 2 Chronicles 9:22);	King Jehoshaphat (2 Chronicles 17:5)
King Jehoash (2 Kings 12:4-16)	King Cyrus of Persia (Ezra 1:1)	King Artaxerxes (Ezra 7:15-17)
Mithredath the treasurer and Sheshbazzar the prince of Judah (Ezra 2:64-67)	Some heads of the father's houses of the children of Israel (Ezra 2:68-69)	King Josiah and Hilkiah (2 Kings 22:2; 2 Kings 22:4-7; 2 Chronicles 34:9-17)
Ezra (Ezra 8:25-27)	Job (Job 1:2-3)	Zacchaeus (Luke 19:2)
Joseph from Arimathea (Matthew 27:57-59)	People in the early church (Acts 2:44-47; Acts 4:1-23; Acts 4:32-35)	Joses, who was also named Barnabas (Acts 4:36-37)

Table 142: Examples of People in the Rich Category Influenced by the Positive Attributes

Conversely, here are examples of individuals in the **rich** category influenced by the negative attributes:

Lot (Genesis 13:5-7)	King Jehoiakim (2 Kings 23:35)	Barzillai (2 Samuel 19:32)
The lords of the Philistines (Judges 16:5)	Joel and Abijah, the sons of Samuel (1 Samuel 8:1-3)	King Hezekiah (2 Kings 20:13; Isaiah 39:1-2)
King Ahab (1 Kings 16:29-33; 1 Kings 21:2-16)	Laban, the brother of Rebekah, (Genesis 29:18-20; Genesis 31:38-42)	The king of the Chaldeans (2 Chronicles 36:17-19)
King Menahem (2 Kings 15:20)	King Ahaz (2 Chronicles 28:21)	Nabal (1 Samuel 25:2-3)
King Nebuchadnezzar (2 Kings 24:13)	King Ahasuerus (Esther 1:1-9)	Haman (Esther 5:11)
King Belshazzar (Daniel 5:1-28)	Ephraim (Hosea 12:7-8)	Simon (Acts 8:9-20)
Ananias and his wife Sapphira (Acts 5:1-2)	Chief priest and Pharisees (Matthew 28:11-15; Mark 14:10-11; Luke 16:14; Luke 22:5)	Men who used a possessed girl for *profit* (Acts 16:16)
Demetrius, a silversmith (Acts 19:24)		

Table 143: Examples of People in the Rich Category Influenced by the Negative Attributes

BTT allows one to see that the children of Israel went from the *poor* category as slaves in Egypt, to people in the **rich** category after they gained their freedom. This transformation literally occurred overnight. The Biblical record documented that God told Moses about the children of Israel's transformation before the plagues on Egypt. God said, *"And I will give this people favor in the sight of the Egyptians; and it shall be, when you go, that you shall not go empty-handed. But every woman shall ask of her neighbor, namely, of her who dwells near* *her house, articles of <u>silver</u>, articles of <u>gold</u>, and <u>clothing</u>; and you shall put them on your sons and on your daughters. So you shall plunder the Egyptians*" (Exodus 3:21-22). After the last plagues and Pharaoh's release of the people, the Biblical record documented, "*Now the children of Israel had done according to the word of Moses, and they had asked from the Egyptians articles of <u>silver</u>, articles of <u>gold</u>, and <u>clothing</u>. And the Lord had given the people favor in the sight of the Egyptians, so that they granted them what they requested. Thus they plundered the Egyptians*" (Exodus 12:35-36). The transformation of the children of Israel to the **rich** category was complete. However, their new status invited the influence of the negative attributes for multiple reasons. The reason included the fact that they were a people:

- Enriched overnight going from literally nothing to extreme <u>wealth</u>
- Enslaved for generations and could only watch their <u>wealthy</u> capturers live sumptuously
- Lacked education on <u>wealth</u> management but now free to <u>buy</u> as they please
- Enslaved and now free

Taking these factors into consideration, God gave the children of Israel strict rules to follow. These rules would help them regulate their new <u>wealth</u> and provide a defense against the influence of the negative attributes. One might ask if all the children of Israel were in the **rich** category, why was there an issue? The Biblical record provides an answer. The Biblical record documented that when, "*...the children of Israel journeyed from Rameses to Succoth, about six hundred thousand men on foot, besides children. A mixed multitude went up with them also, and flocks and herds—a great deal of livestock*" (Exodus 12:37, 38). The "mixed multitude" documented that there was an unknown number of people who were not necessarily in the **rich** category among the children of Israel. These people were possibly foreigners and slaves. Therefore, God gave the children of Israel, now a people in the **rich** category, commands to control abuse. I implore one to take the time and read the specifics in one's own Bible. Here are some of those commands:

For eating the Passover meal: "*...No foreigner shall eat it. But every man's servant who is bought for **money**, when you have circumcised him, then he may eat it*" (Exodus 12:43-44)	Concerning servants: *If you **buy** a Hebrew servant, he shall serve six years; and in the seventh he shall go out free and <u>pay</u> nothing...*" (Exodus 21: 1-6)	"*At the end of every third year you shall bring out the **tithe** of your produce of that year and store it up within your gates*" (Deuteronomy 14:28)
Concerning the death of someone else livestock: "*...if a man opens a pit, or if a man digs a pit and does not cover it, and an ox or a donkey falls in it, the owner of the pit shall make it **good**; he shall give **money** to their owner,	Concerning daughters for marriage: "*And if a man **sells** his daughter to be a female slave, she shall not go out as the male slaves do... If he takes another wife, he shall not diminish her food, her clothing, and her marriage rights. And if	Concerning animals and attacks: "*...if the ox tended to thrust with its horn in times past, and it has been made known to his owner, and he has not kept it confined, so that it has **killed** a man or a woman, the ox shall be stoned and

but the dead animal shall be his" (Exodus 21:33-34)	*he does not do these three for her, then she shall go out free, without* **paying money***"* (Exodus 21:7-11)	*its owner also shall be put to death. If there is imposed on him a sum of* **money***, then he shall* **pay** *to* **redeem** *his life…"* (Exodus 21:28-32)
"if he is too poor to <u>pay</u> *your* **valuation***, then he shall present himself before the priest, and the priest shall set a* **value** *for him; according to the ability of him who vowed, the priest shall* **value** *him"* (Leviticus 27:8)	*"If one man's ox hurts another's, so that it dies, then they shall* **sell** *the live ox and divide the* **money** *from it; and the dead ox they shall also divide"*(Exodus 21:35)	*"…if it was known that the ox tended to thrust in time past, and its owner has not kept it confined, he shall surely* **pay** *ox for ox, and the dead animal shall be his own"* (Exodus 21:36)
"If a man **steals** *an ox or a sheep, and slaughters it or* **sells** *it, he shall* **restore** *five oxen for an ox and four sheep for a sheep"* (Exodus 22:1)	*"If the sun has risen on him, there shall be guilt for his* **bloodshed***. He should make* **full restitution***; if he has nothing, then* **he shall be sold** *for his* **theft***"* (Exodus 22:3)	*"If the* **theft** *is certainly found alive in his hand, whether it is an ox or donkey or sheep, he shall* **restore double***"* (Exodus 22:4)
"And if a man **borrows** *anything from his neighbor, and it becomes injured or dies, the owner of it not being with it, he shall surely make it* **good***…"* (Exodus 22:15)	*"If fire breaks out and catches in thorns, so that stacked grain, standing grain, or the field is consumed, he who kindled the fire shall surely* **make restitution***"* (Exodus 22:6)	*"If a man delivers to his neighbor* **money** *or articles to keep, and it is* **stolen** *out of the man's house, if the* **thief** *is found, he shall* **pay double***"* (Exodus 22:7)
"For any kind of trespass, …ox, donkey, sheep, clothing, or any kind of lost thing which another claims to be his, the cause of both parties shall come before the judges; and whomever the judges condemn shall **pay double** *to his neighbor"* (Exodus 22:9)	*"If a man causes a field or vineyard to be grazed, and lets loose his animal, and it feeds in another man's field, he shall* **make restitution** *from the best of his own field and the* **best of his own vineyard***"* (Exodus 22:5)	*"If a man entices a virgin who is not betrothed, and lies with her, he shall surely* **pay** *the bride-price for her to be his wife. If her father utterly refuses to give her to him, he shall* **pay money** *according to the bride-price of virgins"* (Exodus 22:16-17)
"If you **lend money** *to any of My people who are poor among you, you shall not be like a* **moneylender** *to him; you shall not charge him* **interest***"* (Exodus 22:25)	*"You shall not* **lend** *him your* **money** *for usury, nor* **lend** *him your food at a* **profit***"* (Leviticus 25:37)	The **valuation** or **price** for a person or property consecrated to service to the Lord by a vow are found in Leviticus 27:3-7
"The Lord will open to you His **good** *treasure, the heavens, to give the rain to your land in its season, and to bless all the work of your*	*"…if he who dedicates the field ever wishes to* **redeem** *it, then he must add one-fifth of the* **money** *of your* **valuation** *to it, and*	*"You shall not charge* <u>interest</u> *to your brother…To a foreigner you may charge* **interest***, but to your brother you shall not*

hand. *You shall* **lend** *to many nations, but you shall not* **borrow**" (Deuteronomy 28:12)	*it shall belong to him"* (Leviticus 27:19)	*charge* **interest**..." (Deuteronomy 23:19-20)
Concerning the holy offering: "*No outsider shall eat the holy offering; one who dwells with the priest, or a hired servant, shall not eat the holy thing. But if the priest* **buys** *a person with his* **money**, *he may eat it; and one who is born in his house may eat his food*" (Leviticus 22:10-11)	"*Now if a sojourner or stranger close to you becomes* **rich**, *and one of your brethren who dwells by him becomes poor, and* **sells** *himself to the stranger or sojourner close to you, or to a member of the stranger's family, after he is* **sold** *he may be* **redeemed** *again...*" (Leviticus 25:47-54)	"*You shall truly* **tithe** *all the* **increase** *of your grain that the field produces year by year...the* **tithe** *of your grain, new wine, oil, firstborn of your herds and your flocks, that you may learn to fear the Lord your God always*" (Deuteronomy 14:22-23)
For an animal: "*...the priest shall set a* **value** *for it, whether it is* **good** *or bad; as you, the priest,* **value** *it, so it shall be. But if he wants at all to* **redeem** *it, then he must add one-fifth to your* **valuation**" (Leviticus 27:12-13)	For one's house: "*If he who dedicated it wants to* **redeem** *his house, then he must add one-fifth of the* **money** *of your* **valuation** *to it, and it shall be his*" (Leviticus 27:15)	"*If a man dedicates to the Lord part of a field of his* **possession**, *then your* **valuation** *shall be according to the seed for it...*" (Leviticus 27:16-17)
"*...if he dedicates his field after the Jubilee, then the priest shall reckon to him the* **money** *due according to the years that remain till the Year of Jubilee, and it shall be* **deducted** *from your* **valuation**" (Leviticus 27:18)	Concerning offering of atonement: "*The* **rich** *shall not* **give more** *and the poor shall not* **give less** *than half a* **shekel**, *when you give an offering to the Lord, to make atonement for yourselves*" (Exodus 30:15)	To the descendants of Esau living in the territory of Mount Seir. The Lord told Moses: "*You shall* **buy** *food from them with* **money**, *that you may eat; and you shall also* **buy** *water from them with* **money**, *that you may drink*" (Deuteronomy 2:6)
"*And if a man dedicates to the Lord a field which he has* **bought**, *which is not the field of his* **possession**, *then the priest shall reckon to him the worth of your* **valuation**... *In the Year of Jubilee the field shall return to him from whom it was* **bought**, *to the one who owned the land as a* **possession**...*twenty* **gerahs** *to the* **shekel**" (Leviticus 27:22-25)	For the dedication of Levites instead of the firstborns: "*...Moses took the redemption* **money** *from those who were over and above those who were* **redeemed** *by the Levites. From the firstborn of the children of Israel he took the* **money**, *one thousand three hundred and sixty-five* **shekels**, *according to the* **shekel** *of the*	Concerning female captives: Deuteronomy 21:10-13 laid out a procedure for marriage. In addition, the Bible documents, "*And it shall be, if you have no delight in her, then you shall set her free, but you certainly shall not sell her for* **money**; *you shall not treat her* **brutally**, *because you have humbled her*" (Deuteronomy 21:14)

	sanctuary" (Numbers 3:49-50)	
As the Israelites entered the territory of King Sihon, they were to **buy** food and water from him. Moses said, *"You shall **sell** me food for **money**, that I may eat, and give me water for **money**, that I may drink; only let me pass through on foot..."* (Deuteronomy 2:28)	Concerning **money** gained from ***immoral*** activity: *"There shall be no **ritual harlot** of the daughters of Israel, or a **perverted** one of the sons of Israel. You shall not bring the **wages** of a **harlot** or the **price** of a dog to the house of the Lord your God for any vowed offering, for both of these are an abomination to the Lord your God"* (Deuteronomy 23:17-18)	

Table 144: Commands from God to Guide the Children of Israel Now Living in the Rich Category

All the items documented in Table 144 helped manage the behaviors of the children of Israel, taught them respect for their <u>wealth</u>, and gave them wisdom for avoiding the influence of the negative attributes. To show that Moses recognized the spirits of the positive and negative attributes, from the Lord's commands, Moses stated in Deuteronomy 8:11-20,

> *"Beware that you do not forget the Lord your God by not keeping His commandments, His judgments, and His statutes which I command you today, lest—when you have **eaten and are full**, and have **built beautiful houses** and dwell in them; and when your **herds and your flocks multiply**, and your **silver** and **gold are multiplied**, and **all that you have is multiplied**; when your **heart is lifted up**...then you say in your heart, 'My power and the might of my hand have **gained** me this <u>wealth</u>.' "And you shall remember the Lord your God, for it is He who gives you power to get <u>wealth</u>, that He may establish His covenant which He swore to your fathers, as it is this day. Then it shall be, if you by any means forget the Lord your God, and <u>follow other gods</u>, and <u>serve them</u> and <u>worship them</u>, I testify against you this day that you shall surely perish. As the nations which the Lord destroys before you, so you shall perish, because you would not be obedient to the voice of the Lord your God."*

Moses' words summed up the manifestation of the spiritual warfare that would grow among the children of Israel. He warned them of the behaviors and consequences from the spiritual struggle between the positive and negative attributes. As the children of Israel grew into a nation, the influence of the positive and negative attributes on people in the **rich** category became evident. Before the fall of the nation of Israel, the Lord sent numerous prophets to warn the people to repent. The warning was also for those influenced by the negative attributes in the **rich** category. Below are some of the many warnings the Lord gave through His prophets. In terms of the war campaign, these warnings are applicable to those in the **rich** category today. The Bible documented:

The Prophet	What Is Documented
Isaiah	"...they are filled with eastern ways; they are soothsayers like the Philistines, and they are pleased with the children of foreigners. Their land is also full of **silver** and **gold**, and there is **no end to their treasures**; their land is also **full of horses**, and there is **no end to their chariots**" (Isaiah 2:6-7) and "And so it shall be: instead of a sweet smell there will be a stench; instead of a <u>sash</u>, a rope; instead of **well-set hair**, baldness; instead of a **rich robe**, a girding of sackcloth; and branding instead of beauty" (Isaiah 3:24)
	"His watchmen are blind, they are all ignorant; they are all dumb dogs, they cannot bark; sleeping, **lying** down, loving to slumber. Yes, they are <u>greedy</u> dogs which **never have enough**. And they are shepherds who cannot understand; they all look to their own way, every one for his own <u>gain</u>, from his own territory. Come," one says, "I will bring wine, and we will fill ourselves with intoxicating drink; tomorrow will be as today, and **much more abundant**" (Isaiah 56:11)
Jeremiah	"... they have become great and grown **rich**. They have **grown fat**, they are **sleek**; yes, they surpass the deeds of the **wicked**; they do not plead the cause, the cause of the fatherless; yet they **prosper**, and the **right** of the needy they do not defend" (Jeremiah 5:26-31)
	"...let the **rich** man glory in his **riches**; but let him who glories glory in this, that he understands and knows Me, that I am the Lord, exercising lovingkindness, judgment, and **righteousness** in the earth. For in these I delight," says the Lord" (Jeremiah 9:23-24)
	"As a partridge that broods but does not hatch, so is he who gets **riches**, but not by **right**; It will leave him in the midst of his days, and at his end he will be a **fool**" (Jeremiah 17:11)
	"The <u>conspiracy</u> of her prophets in her midst is like a roaring lion tearing the prey; they have devoured people; they have taken **treasure** and **precious things**; they have made many widows in her midst" (Ezekiel 22:25) and "Her princes in her midst are like wolves tearing the prey, to **shed blood**, to destroy people, and to get **dishonest** gain. Her prophets plastered them with untempered mortar, seeing **false** visions, and divining **lies** for them, saying, 'Thus says the Lord God,' when the Lord had not spoken" (Ezekiel 22:27-29)
Ezekiel	"...In you they take **bribes** to **shed blood**; you take **usury** and **increase**; you have made **profit** from your neighbors by **extortion**, and have forgotten Me," says the Lord God. "Behold, therefore, I beat My fists at the **dishonest profit** which you have made, and at the **bloodshed** which has been in your midst" (Ezekiel 22:6-13)
	"...Thus says the Lord God: "...With your wisdom and your understanding you have **gained riches** for yourself, and gathered **gold** and **silver** into your **treasuries**; by your great wisdom in trade you have **increased** your **riches**, and your **heart is lifted up** because of your **riches**..." (Ezekiel 28:1-10)
Micah	"Now hear this, you heads of the house of Jacob and rulers of the house of Israel, who abhor <u>justice</u> and **pervert** all equity, who build up Zion with **bloodshed** and Jerusalem with iniquity: her heads judge for a **bribe**, her priests teach for **pay**, and her prophets divine for **money**..." (Micah 3:9-12)

	*"The Lord's voice cries to the city—Wisdom shall see Your name: ... Shall I count pure those with the **wicked** scales, and with the bag of **deceitful** weights? For her **rich** men are full of **violence**, her inhabitants have spoken **lies**, and their tongue is **deceitful** in their mouth.* (Micah 6:9-12)
Habakkuk	*"Woe to him who covets **evil** gain for his house, that he may set his nest on high, that he may be delivered from the power of disaster! ..."* (Habakkuk 2:9-11)

Table 145: The Prophets' Warnings to the People in the Rich Category

Now before one leaves the Old Testament, consider some pearls of wisdom that people blessed with <u>wisdom</u> made about people in the **rich** category. These pearls cover both the Jews and people in general. The Biblical record documented:

The **rich** and **wicked**: "... *They spend their days in <u>wealth</u>, and in a moment go down to the grave. Yet they say to God, 'Depart from us, for we do not desire the knowledge of Your ways. Who is the Almighty, that we should serve Him? And what **profit** do we have if we pray to Him?' Indeed their **prosperity** is not in their hand; the counsel of the **wicked** is far from me"* (Job 21:13-16)	*"Though he heaps up **silver** like dust, and **piles up clothing** like clay—he may pile it up, but the **just** will wear it, and the innocent will divide the **silver**. He builds his house like a moth, like a booth which a watchman makes. The **rich** man will lie down, but not be gathered up; he opens his eyes, and he is no more. Terrors overtake him like a flood..."* (Job 27:16-23)	*"...For he sees wise men die; likewise the **fool** and the **senseless** person perish, and leave their <u>wealth</u> to others. Their inner thought is that their houses will last forever, their dwelling places to all generations; they call their lands after their own names. Nevertheless man, though in **honor**, does not remain; he is like the beasts that perish"* (Psalm 49:10-12)
*"There is one alone, without companion: he has neither son nor brother. Yet there is no end to all his labors, nor is his eye satisfied with **riches**. But he never asks, "For whom do I toil and deprive myself of **good**?" This also is vanity and a <u>grave misfortune</u>"* (Ecclesiastes 4:8)	*"...Those who trust in their <u>wealth</u> and <u>boast</u> in the multitude of their **riches**, none of them can by any means **redeem** his brother, nor give to God a ransom for him—for the redemption of their souls is **costly**, and it shall cease forever...* (Psalm 49:5-8)	The man who: *"...<u>boast</u> in **evil**...The **righteous** also shall see and fear, and shall laugh at him, saying, "Here is the man who did not make God his strength, but trusted in the **abundance** of his **riches**, and strengthened himself in his **wickedness**"* (Psalm 52:1-7)
*"Do not be afraid when one becomes **rich**, when the glory of his **house is increased**; for when he dies he shall <u>carry nothing away</u>; his glory shall not descend after him. Though while he lives he blesses himself (For men will praise*	*"Do not curse the king, even in your thought; do not curse the **rich**, even in your bedroom; for a bird of the air may carry your voice, and a bird in flight may tell the matter"* (Ecclesiastes 10:20)	*"If I have made **gold** my hope, or said to **fine gold**, 'You are my confidence'; if I have rejoiced because my <u>wealth</u> was great, and because my hand had **gained much**...this also would be an iniquity deserving of judgment, for I*

you when you do well for yourself)..." (Psalm 49:16-18)		*would have denied God who is above"* (Job 31:24-28)
*"As for every man to whom God has given **riches** and <u>wealth</u>, and given him power to eat of it, to receive his heritage and rejoice in his labor—this is the gift of God"* (Ecclesiastes 5:19)	*"A little that a **righteous** man has is better than the **riches** of many **wicked**. For the arms of the **wicked** shall be broken, but the Lord upholds the **righteous**"* (Psalm 37:16-17)	*"Do not trust in **oppression**, nor vainly hope in **robbery**; if **riches increase**, do not set your heart on them"* (Psalm 62:9-10)
*"The sleep of a laboring man is sweet, whether he eats little or much; but the **abundance** of the **rich** will not permit him to sleep. There is a severe **evil** which I have seen under the sun: **riches** kept for their owner to his hurt. But those **riches** perish through misfortune..."* (Ecclesiastes 5:12-13)	*"Praise the Lord! Blessed is the man who fears the Lord, who delights greatly in His commandments. His descendants will be mighty on earth; the generation of the **upright** will be blessed. <u>Wealth</u> and **riches** will be in his house, and his **righteousness** endures forever..."* (Psalm 112:1-10)	*"There is an **evil** which I have seen under the sun, and it is common among men: a man to whom God has given **riches** and <u>wealth</u> and **honor**, **so that he lacks nothing** for himself of all he desires; yet God does not give him power to eat of it, but a foreigner consumes it. This is vanity, and it is an **evil** affliction"* (Ecclesiastes 6:1-2)
*"Wisdom is **good** with an inheritance, and **profitable** to those who see the sun. For wisdom is a defense as **money** is a defense, but the excellence of knowledge is that wisdom gives life to those who have it"* (Ecclesiastes 7:11-12)	*"Because of **laziness** the building decays, and through **idleness** of hands the house leaks. A feast is made for laughter, and wine makes merry; but **money** answers everything"* (Ecclesiastes 10:16-19)	*"Moreover the **profit** of the land is for all; even the king is served from the field. He who loves **silver** will not be satisfied with **silver**; nor he who loves **abundance**, with **increase**"* (Ecclesiastes 5:9-10)

Table 146: Pearls of Wisdom Concerning People in the Rich Category

The Psalmist documented an observation he made about people in the **rich** category influenced by the ***wicked***, ***ungodly***, and other negative attributes. He documented in Psalm 73:2-12:

> *"I saw the **prosperity** of the **wicked**. For there are no pangs in their death, but their strength is firm. They are not in trouble as other men, nor are they plagued like other men. Therefore **pride** serves as their necklace; **violence** covers them like a garment. Their eyes bulge with **abundance**; they **have more** than heart could wish. They **scoff** and speak **wickedly** concerning **oppression**; they **speak loftily**. They set their mouth against the heavens, and their tongue walks through the earth. Therefore his people return here, and waters of a full cup are drained by them. And they say, "How does God know? And is there knowledge in the Most High?" Behold, these are the **ungodly**, who are always at ease; they **increase** in **riches**"*

From this observation, no one should be surprised at the behavior of people in the **rich** category who allowed themselves to be influenced by the negative attributes. The positive forces of the campaign have many reasons for concern when people in the **rich** category allow the influence of the negative forces. There are even greater pains when people in the **rich** category commit their <u>wealth</u> towards supporting the negative forces of the war. Their <u>wealth</u> creates weapons of war for <u>profit</u> instead of <u>investments</u> in peace by spreading the Gospel. This is why Jesus documented that the laborers are few. Laborers are needed to reach out to people in the **rich** category to lead them to the positive side of the campaign. This is not only **good** for the positive forces, but also **good** for the souls of the people in the **rich** category. The Lord desires everyone to be saved (1 Timothy 2:4). However, one can only be saved by hearing and accepting His Truth. Although the work of the laborer is difficult, it is the desire of the Lord and worth every soul.

As Jesus came on the scene, one of the first things He told everyone striving to be in the **rich** category was "*Do not lay up for yourselves* **treasures** *on earth, where moth and rust destroy and where* **thieves** *break in and* **steal**; *but lay up for yourselves* **treasures** *in heaven, where neither moth nor rust destroys and where* **thieves** *do not break in and* **steal**. *For where your* **treasure** *is, there your heart will be also*" (Matthew 6:19-21). This statement set the tone for His ministry concerning earthly **riches** and the command for everyone in the **rich** category to follow. Below are some of the many pearls of wisdom from Jesus that have a direct correlation to the people in the **rich** category. Jesus makes the identification of the positive and negative force's influences from spiritual warfare very clear. Jesus said:

"*No one can serve two masters; for either he will* **hate** *the one and* <u>love</u> *the other, or else he will be loyal to the one and* **despise** *the other. You cannot serve God and* **mammon**" (Matthew 6:24)	"*Now he who received seed among the thorns is he who hears the word, and the cares of this world and the* **deceitful-ness** *of* **riches** *choke the word, and he becomes unfruitful*" (Matthew 13:22; Mark 4:19; Luke 8:14)	Stated to a **rich** young ruler: "*If you want to be perfect, go,* **sell** *what you have and* **give** *to the poor, and you will have* **treasure** *in heaven; and come, follow Me*" (Matthew 19:21; Mark 10:21)
"*...it is hard for a* **rich** *man to enter the kingdom of heaven. And again I say to you, it is easier for a camel to go through the eye of a needle than for a* **rich** *man to enter the kingdom of God*" (Matthew 19:23-24; Luke 18:22-25)	"*...How hard it is for those who have* **riches** *to enter the kingdom of God! ...how hard it is for those who trust in* **riches** *to enter the kingdom of God! It is easier for a camel to go through the eye of a needle than for a* **rich** *man to enter the kingdom of God*" (Mark 10:23-25)	"*If anyone desires to come after Me, let him deny himself, and take up his cross, and follow Me ...For what* **profit** *is it to a man if he* **gains** *the whole world, and loses his own soul? Or what will a man give in exchange for his soul? ...*" (Matthew 16:26; Mark 8:36)
"*For what* **profit** *is it to a man if he* **gains** *the whole world, and is himself destroyed or lost?*" (Luke 9:25)	"*But woe to you who are* **rich**, *for you have received your* **consolation**...*Woe to you when all men speak well of you, for so did their*	"*No servant can serve two masters; for either he will* **hate** *the one and* <u>love</u> *the other, or else he will be loyal to the one and despise*

	*fathers to the **false** prophets*" (Luke 6:24-26)	*the other. You cannot serve God and **mammon***" (Luke 16:13)
Concerning a *poor* widow who put **money** into the treasury: "*...many who were **rich** <u>put in</u> much. ...this poor widow has <u>put in</u> more than all those who have given to the **treasury**; for they all put in out of their **abundance**, but she out of her <u>poverty</u> put in all that she had, her whole livelihood.*" (Mark 12:41-44 and Luke 21:1-4)	"*Why do you test Me, you hypocrites? Show Me the <u>tax</u> **money**.*" So they brought Him a denarius. And He said to them, "*Whose image and inscription is this?*" They said to Him, "*Caesar's.*" And He said to them, "*Render therefore to Caesar the things that are Caesar's, and to God the things that are God's*" (Matthew 22:16-22)	In the parable of the **unprofitable** servant: "*...to everyone who has, more will be given, and he will have **abundance**; but from him who does not have, even what he has will be taken away. And cast the **unprofitable** servant into the outer darkness. There will be weeping and gnashing of teeth'*" (Matthew 25:14-30)

Table 147: Jesus' Teaching About the Rich Category and the effects of Spiritual Warfare

Jesus told a parable about a <u>wealthy</u> man and his inappropriate thinking. This parable provided an excellent example of the behavior emanating from one influenced by the negative attributes in the **rich** category. Jesus said, "*The ground of a certain **rich** man **yielded plentifully**. And he thought within himself, saying, 'What shall I do, since I have no room to store my crops?' So he said, 'I will do this: I will pull down my barns and **build greater**, and there I will store all my crops and my goods. And I will say to my soul, "Soul, you have many goods laid up for many years; take your ease; eat, drink, and be merry."' But God said to him, '**Fool**! This night your soul will be required of you; then whose will those things be which you have provided?' So is he who lays up **treasure** for himself, and is not **rich** toward God*" (Luke 12:16-21). One can see this **rich** man's <u>wealth</u> became his stronghold. Instead of him using his assets for God through **good** works, i.e. supporting the *poor*, the *needy*, orphans, widows, or even the advancement of God's Word, he hoarded his <u>wealth</u>. This man did exactly what Jesus said <u>not to do</u> in Matthew 6:19-21 as stated earlier. BTT allows one to see that the negative attribute's influences had corrupted the **rich** man's spiritual heart. He became a pawn of the negative forces in the campaign and these forces influenced him to believe that he was in control of his life. Clearly, he was not. This is the important message hidden in the fog of the negative forces through spiritual warfare. Do not be **deceived**.

Another prime example of how the negative attribute influences the thinking of people in the **rich** category is seen in the behavior of a **rich** young ruler who approached Jesus about eternal life. Matthew, Mark, and Luke documented this encounter. The **rich** ruler approached Jesus and asked, "***Good** Teacher, what shall I do to inherit eternal life?*" (Matthew 19:16, Mark 10:17, and Luke 18:18). According to Matthew, Mark, and Luke's harmonized accounts of the discussion, Jesus told the **rich** ruler, "*You know the commandments: 'Do not commit **adultery**,' 'Do not **murder**,' 'Do not **steal**,' 'Do not bear **false witness**,' '**Honor** your father and your mother*'" (Luke 18:20). Mark also documented, "*Do not **defraud***" (Mark 10:19) and Matthew documented "*You shall <u>love</u> your neighbor as yourself*" (Matthew 19:19) as part of the list. Interestingly, the Bible documented that the **rich** ruler said to Jesus, "*All these things I have kept from my youth. What do I still lack?*" (Matthew 19:20; Mark 10:20; and Luke 18:21). Think on this for a moment. BTT allows one to see from this **rich** ruler's statement that he was doing ***good***. However, by now one should understand that doing ***good*** is not enough. Hence, Jesus looked at this **rich** ruler, "*...<u>loved</u> him, and said to him, "One thing you lack: Go your way,* **sell** *whatever you have and give to the poor, and you will have* **treasure** *in heaven; and come, take up the cross, and follow Me*" (Mark 10:21). Matthew documented from the conversation, "*If you want to be perfect, go,* **sell** *what you have and give to the poor, and you will have* **treasure** *in heaven; and come, follow Me*" (Matthew 19:21). Whereas Luke captured from the conversation, "*You still lack one thing.* **Sell** *all that you have and distribute to the poor, and you will have* **treasure** *in heaven; and come, follow Me*" (Luke 18:22). All these accounts are true with the understanding that Jesus was not telling or implying that the **rich** young ruler sacrifice everything and join the people of the poor category. This is what the negative forces wanted the **rich** young ruler to believe. The ***unclean spirits*** influenced him to that end. His ears were closed to Jesus' full message because his <u>wealth</u> blinded him from seeing the purpose of Jesus' Word. This is still happening today. Jesus simply told this man to share some of God's blessings that he had become a caretaker of with people less fortunate. BTT allows one to see that Jesus' knowledge of the spiritual warfare and the war campaign would have saved this ruler from the traps of the negative forces pulling at his inner spirit. Jesus knew that this ruler had a hidden problem; his <u>wealth</u> was his security, life, and strength. Remember, Jesus' had said earlier, "*No one can serve two masters; for either he will* **hate** *the one and <u>love</u> the other, or else he will be loyal to the one and* **despise** *the other. You cannot serve God and* **mammon**" (Matthew 6:24). Unfortunately, the **rich** ruler did not stay to inquire more from Jesus. He allowed the fog of the war to stop him from hearing Jesus' Truth and the Bible documented that this **rich** young ruler was, "*...sad at this word, and went away sorrowful, for he had* **great possessions**" (Mark 10:22; Matthew 19:22). Both Matthew and Luke documented the **rich** young ruler left Jesus, "<u>*very*</u> *sorrowful*" while Luke also emphasized the fact he was "<u>*very*</u> **rich**" (Luke 18:23). This was a tragedy for the soul of one who was in the **rich** category and a caretaker of **vast amounts** of God's **resources**. Nevertheless, Jesus' message for the people in the **rich** category did not end here.

    Directly after this conversation, Jesus made a startling statement that is important for everyone in the **rich** category to know because of the war campaign. Using Mark's account, the Bible documented that, "*Jesus looked around and said to His disciples, "How hard it is for those who have* **riches** *to enter the kingdom of God!" And the disciples were astonished at His words. But Jesus answered again and said to them, "Children, how hard it is for those who trust in* **riches** *to enter the kingdom of God! It is easier for a camel to go through the eye of a needle than for a* **rich** *man to enter the kingdom of God*"" (Mark 10:23-25). At this point, possibly after thinking about all the commandments that the **rich** young ruler claimed he had kept, the disciples began questioning their own status. They asked Jesus, "*Who then can be saved?*" (Matthew 19:25; Mark 10:26; and Luke 18:26). This is the most important question of the war campaign. Jesus responded, "*With men it is impossible, but not with God; for with God all things are possible*" (Matthew 19:26; Mark 10:27; and Luke 18:27). BTT allows one to see that in the war campaign, there is nothing one can do to save oneself. But with God, one will survive. **Riches** cannot save, but God can. Moreover, <u>wealth</u> makes it harder, not impossible, but harder to be saved and get to heaven because of the negative attributes ***deception*** and spiritual warfare. For all who sacrifice for Christ and the spreading of the Gospel, Jesus declared, "*Assuredly, I say to you, there is no one who has left house or brothers or sisters or father or mother or wife or children or lands, for My sake and the gospel's, who shall not* **receive a hundredfold** *now in this time—houses and brothers and sisters and mothers and children and lands, with* <u>persecutions</u>—*and in the age to come, eternal life. But many who are first will be last, and the last first*" (Mark 10:29-31; Matthew 19:28-30; and Luke 18:29-30). Based on Jesus' Word, the bottom line is this: God will compensate everyone that sacrifices for Christ and His Gospel. However, for the people in the **rich** category, the negative attributes make Christ's message harder to see in the fog of spiritual warfare.

Jesus also told a story about a man in the **rich** category and his response to Lazarus, a man in the poor category. By far, this is one of the most insightful looks into the life and death of a person in the **rich** category who allowed the negative attributes to influence his or her life. In the Book of Luke, Jesus spoke of a person in the **rich** category, who "...*was* **clothed in purple and fine linen and fared sumptuously every day**" (Luke 16:19). Conversely, Lazarus a beggar, was "...*full of sores, who was laid at his gate, desiring to be fed with the crumbs which fell from the* **rich** *man's table*" (Luke 16:20-21). Here is what is so important about Jesus' comparison. Jesus described what occurs in the war campaign when the positive or negative attributes influences one's behavior in the **rich** category. Both men died, and Jesus documented what happened to their souls. Jesus documented that the **rich** man's soul would not make it to heaven. He said when the **rich** man died, "...*being in torments in Hades, he lifted up his eyes and saw Abraham afar off, and Lazarus in his bosom*" (Luke 16:23). Yet Lazarus, tormented on earth, died and was "...*carried by the angels to Abraham's bosom*" (Luke 16:22). What happened here? BTT allows one to see that the **rich** man allowed the negative forces of the campaign to cloud his judgement with the <u>wealth</u> he had acquired. This **rich** man had had the chance to support the positive forces but made the choice not to. The Biblical record documented that the **rich** man cried out to Abraham from his tormented state for help. But Abraham replied, "*Son, remember that in your lifetime you received your* **good things**, *and likewise Lazarus* **evil** *things; but now he is comforted and you are tormented*" (Luke 16:25). This is when the **rich** man realized the Truth of spiritual warfare. He asked Abraham to send Lazarus back from the dead to warn his five brothers according to Luke 16:27 and 28. But Abraham told him the Truth of why this could not be done (Luke 16:26) (This is worth reading for oneself). Consider the discourse between Abraham and the man in the **rich** category very closely. Abraham said, "*They have Moses and the prophets; let them hear them.' And he said, 'No, father Abraham; but if one goes to them from the dead, they will repent.' But he said to him, 'If they do not hear Moses and the prophets, neither will they be persuaded though one rise from the dead*" (Luke 16 29-31). This stinging Truth applies today. All the categories of people in the **harvest** have the Biblical record at their disposal and the opportunity to hear God's Word today. Yes, in some countries, this may be more difficult, but man cannot limit God's hand. If there is a desire, the providence of God will make a way and the **resources** of the people in the **rich** category will be used to facilitate this effort. One cannot allow the fog generated by the negative forces blind one to the truth of the Gospel of Jesus Christ. For if one does, based on Jesus' example and conclusion above, the consequences are forever. This chilling story documents a reality for people in the **rich** category who allow the negative attributes to take them down the wrong path in life.

Another thought regarding people in the **rich** category concerns charities and philanthropies. These are activities of man and should never be confused with works from God. BTT allows one to see that if one wants God's recognition for using one's <u>wealth</u>, one must give to the things identified in God's Word. Jesus told the Pharisees who attempted to trap him over an issue about paying taxes to "*Render therefore to Caesar the things that are Caesar's, and to God the things that are God's*" (Matthew 22:21; Mark 12:17; Luke 20:25). At the micro level, the context of this Scripture deals with taxation. However, at the macro level of spiritual warfare, this Scripture deals with the use of **money** for the appropriate things. Today, as it was long ago, people in the **rich** category use their **resources** for bandages instead of repairing the wounds created by the negative behavior of people influenced by the negative attributes. This strategy used in spiritual warfare only serves to provide people in the **rich** category satisfaction from ***false honors***. Do not be ***deceived*** by this ancient strategy. BTT allows one to see the macro-level application of giving to charities for the works of God correctly. His blessings are to be used for His works. In fact, one should consider Jesus' statement concerning charitable deeds closely. He stated in Matthew 6:1-4:

> "*Take heed that you do not do your charitable deeds before men, to be seen by them. Otherwise you have no* **reward** *from your Father in heaven. Therefore, when you do a charitable deed, do not sound a trumpet before you as the hypocrites do in the synagogues and in the streets, that they may have glory from men. Assuredly, I say to you, they have their* **reward**. *But when you do a charitable deed, do not let your left hand know what your right hand is doing, that your charitable deed may be in secret; and your Father who sees in secret will Himself* **reward** *you openly*"

The negative forces of the campaign lay traps for everyone, but especially for people in the **rich** category through charitable gifts and philanthropies. Do not allow the negative attributes to ***deceive*** one's inner spirit on this matter. Hearing God's Word is the first step to breaking the grip of the negative forces on one's inner spirit. <u>Wealth</u> **invested** in the true works of God are the only **investments** with an eternal **return**.

After Jesus' departure and the apostles began to spread His Gospel, examples of people in the **rich** category became very evident. As Christ's church began to take shape, the Biblical record documented, "*Now all who believed were together, and had all things in common, and <u>sold</u> their* **possessions** *and* **goods**, *and divided them among all, as anyone had need. So continuing daily with one accord in the temple, and breaking bread from house to house, they ate their food with gladness and simplicity of heart, praising God and having favor with all the people. And the Lord added to the church daily those who were being saved*" (Acts 2:44-47). The Scriptures above are packed with wisdom and one should not miss all the aspects of what occurred. First, BTT allows one to see there were people from the **rich** and poor categories <u>baptized</u> into Christ who created the first congregation of believers in Christ's church. Next, because of the teachings of Christ, the people in the **rich** category "**sold** *their* **possessions** *and* **goods**, *and divided them among all, as anyone had need.*" The people in the **rich** category "shared what they had; they did not **sell** "everything" they had! The context is that the people in the **rich** category **sold** enough to take care of the needs of the people in the poor and needy categories. God, nor His teachings, ever told a person to become poor for the sake of being in the poor category. Once again, this idea comes from a strategy in spiritual warfare and through *false* teachers. God desires everyone to use His **resources** wisely as caretakers of His vast earthly **treasure**. Third, the people in the **rich** category became a family with everyone else in the Lord's church. There was no <u>partiality</u> or bias; just "*gladness and simplicity of heart*" displayed among multiple races and ethnics of people within the body of Christ. Remember, the Biblical record documented that this first congregation was made up of "*...Galileans, Parthians, Medes, Elamites, those dwelling in Mesopotamia, Judea and Cappadocia, Pontus and Asia, Phrygia and Pamphylia, Egypt and the parts of Libya adjoining Cyrene, visitors from Rome, both Jews and proselytes, Cretans and Arabs...*" according to Acts 2:7-11. No <u>prejudice</u> or <u>discrimination</u> existed in this body because they accepted the Truth that God had, "*...made from one blood every nation of men to dwell on all the face of the earth...*" (Acts 17:26). Nor was there any separation between people in the **rich**, poor, or other categories of the **harvest**. This was Jesus's church that provided the pattern for a unique creation made up of people obedient to His Word. The Biblical record documented that "*...the Lord added to the church daily those who were being saved*" (Acts 2:47) through the process of <u>baptism</u> according to Acts 2:38. BTT allows one to see that God had established a true pattern for His church for all the people of the **harvest** to come together and worship.

Later in the Book of Acts, Christ's church grew. People in the **rich** category influenced by the positive attributes, were actively engaged. The Biblical record documented, "*Now the multitude of those who* believed *were of one heart and one soul; neither did anyone say that any of the* **things he possessed** *was his own, but they had all things in common. And with great power the apostles gave* **witness** *to the resurrection of the Lord Jesus. And great grace was upon them all. Nor was there anyone among them who lacked; for all who were* **possessors of lands or houses sold** *them, and* **brought the proceeds** *of the things that were* **sold**, *and laid them at the apostles' feet; and they distributed to each as anyone had need*" (Acts 4:32-35). BTT allows one to see this pattern for Christ's church is still the same. People <u>baptized</u> into Christ gained one spiritual heart and share with each other. The influences of the positive attributes inspire this type of positive behavior. The idea of people in the **rich** category giving from their <u>wealth</u> to aid others is a <u>godly</u> principle going back to the Book of Genesis. Regardless of the measure of <u>wealth</u>, people influenced by the positive attributes understand that they are simply stewards of God's vast **resources**. The negative forces *falsely* claim that helping others with <u>wealth</u> is "redistribution or socialism." However, people influenced by the positive attributes in the **rich** category know this process is called "support" through the bond of <u>love</u>. Consider a comparison of Joses, Ananias, and Sapphira. These were all people in the **rich** category.

The Biblical record documented that Joses, "*...having* **land**, **sold it**, *and brought the* **money** *and laid it at the apostles' feet*" (Acts 4:37). Joses' behavior exemplified the influences of the positive attributes. He wanted to support Christ's church in a way that reflected the teachings of Christ. He gave of his <u>wealth</u> to support Christ's church, the people in both the *needy* and *poor* categories of the **harvest** and furthered the spread of the Gospel. Conversely, Ananias and his wife Sapphira, allowed the influences of the negative attributes. As members of Christ's church, they made bad decisions with their <u>wealth</u>. The Bible documented that Ananias "...**sold** *a* **possession**. *And he kept back part of the* **proceeds**, *his wife also being aware of it, and* **brought a certain part** *and laid it at the apostles' feet*" (Acts 5:1-2). BTT allows one to see from the **transaction** that takes place, both Ananias and Sapphira had at some point committed the whole **possession** they **sold** to Christ's church. However, at the time of giving, they only brought a part of what was **sold** to the church. Here is where the negative attributes influenced their inner spirits. Peter, by inspiration of the Holy Spirit, knew what this **rich** couple had committed. When Ananias brought the **proceeds** of his **sale** and laid it, "*at the apostles' feet*", Peter asked, "*Ananias, why has Satan filled your heart to* **lie** *to the Holy Spirit and keep back part of the* **price of the land** *for yourself? While it remained, was it not your own? And after it was* **sold***, was it not in your own control? Why have you conceived this thing in your heart? You have not* **lied** *to men but to God*" (Acts 5:3-4). One can see that the ***wicked*** attribute led Ananias to conceive a scheme and the ***liar*** attribute influenced him to state ***falsely*** his **sale** amount of the **possession** in the presence of the Holy Spirit operating in the Lord's church. Because of this, and to instill the importance of the Holy Spirit and Christ's church, Ananias dropped dead (Acts 5:5). But Satan did not stop there with the negative forces. Sapphira was unaware of what happened to her husband. The Bible documented that, "*...three hours later when his wife came in, not knowing what had happened. And Peter answered her, "Tell me whether you* **sold the land** *for so much?" She said, "Yes,* ***for so much***.*""* (Acts 5:7-8). BTT allows one to see that Peter asked Sapphira if the **land sold** for the amount that Ananias had previously stated and laid at the apostle's feet. Her response indicated that the negative forces of the war campaign had influenced her. Peter asked her, "*How is it that you have agreed together to test the Spirit of the Lord?*" (Acts 5:9). Sapphira forfeited her life too, because the influences of the negative attributes had corrupted this family who had become part of Christ's initial church. Satan, uses attributes of the negative forces to influence the inner spirits of people in the church to try to gain a foothold in the assembly. One might ask if Ananias and Sapphira had to die for this infraction. The answer lies in understanding spiritual warfare. In its infancy, Christ's church which was made up of people like you and me, could not start off with people already influenced by Satan. These people had to be purged from the body of Christ. The Holy Spirit was present and protected this precious work. Any attempt by ***unclean spirits*** to corrupt the purity of Christ's initial church was purged. Make no mistake, BTT allows one to see that both Ananias and Sapphira were Christians but they allowed themselves to fall because of <u>greed</u>. They were <u>baptized</u> into the same Truth with all the other people working in the initial vineyard of Christ. Therefore, their behavior was not tolerated, and they were purged from the body of Christ. The Biblical record documented that the consequence of their egregious act brought, "*...great <u>fear</u> came upon all the church and upon all who heard these things*" (Acts 5:11). After Christ's church was established, men trained in the Gospel of Jesus Christ, became responsible and accountable for protecting Christ's church. Hence, Paul would teach that elders would bear this responsibility. Elders must understand spiritual warfare and hold closely the wisdom that, "*A little leaven leavens the whole lump*" (Galatians 5:9). Elders, then and today, are responsible for the offensive posture of the Lord's church. They are required to purge the negative forces from Christ's church and stop spiritual warfare in its tracks. Chapter XII of this book outlines the Biblical foundation, qualifications, role, and responsibilities for elders in the body of Christ.

There were many people in the **rich** category, influenced by the positive attributes, that had a relationship with the Gospel of Jesus Christ and His church. Here are just a few:

- Cornelius: "*a devout man and one who feared God with all his household, who* **gave alms generously** *to the people, and prayed to God always*" (Acts 10:2)

- Lydia: "a **seller of purple** from the city of Thyatira, who worshiped God" (Acts 16:14) who **owned her own home** according to Acts 16:15

- Joseph of Arimathea: "*Now when evening had come, there came a* **rich** *man from Arimathea, named Joseph, who himself had also become a disciple of Jesus*" (Matthew 27:57)

Conversely, there were people influenced by the negative attributes in the **rich** category who abused their _wealth_. Examples include:

- Those who owned a girl that followed Paul: "*a certain slave girl possessed with a spirit of divination met us, who brought her masters* **much profit** *by fortune-telling*" (Acts 16:16)

- Demetrius and the silversmiths of Ephesus: "*a silversmith, who made* **silver** *shrines of Diana,* **brought no small profit** *to the craftsmen*" (Acts 19:24)

BTT allows one to see that people in the **rich** category are no different from anyone else when it comes to the influences of the positive and negative attributes. However, because the **rich** are blessed with greater **resources**, God places a greater expectation on the use of those **resources**. However, without the knowledge of spiritual warfare and the war campaign, the negative forces bury people in the **rich** category in the fog of spiritual darkness. **Resources** are important to both sides of the campaign and both forces strive to convert people in this category to their respective side. BTT allows one to see that God simply desires everyone blessed with His wealth to be like the Psalmist who said, "*I have rejoiced in the way of Your testimonies, as much as in all* **riches**" (Psalm 119:14). Even in the Book of the First Chronicles, it was known that, "*Yours, O Lord, is the greatness, the power and the glory, the victory and the majesty; for all that is in heaven and in earth is Yours; Yours is the kingdom, O Lord, and You are exalted as head over all*" (1 Chronicles 29:11).

The apostles provided several important pearls of wisdom on the behavior of people in the **rich** category influenced by either the positive or the negative attributes. Here are some of those pearls:

An elder of Jesus' church must meet qualifications. He cannot be "...*greedy for* **money**, *but gentle, not quarrelsome, not covetous*..." (1 Timothy 3:1-7; Titus 1:5-7)	Elders are to protect Christ's church: "*For there are many insubordinate, both* **idle** *talkers and* **deceivers**, *especially those of the circumcision, whose mouths must be stopped, who subvert whole households, teaching things which they ought not, for the sake of* **dishonest gain**" (Titus 1:10-11)	"*Likewise deacons must be reverent, not double-tongued, not given to much wine, not greedy for* **money**, *holding the mystery of the* **faith** *with a pure conscience*..." (1 Timothy 3:8-13)
"*But those who desire to be* **rich** *fall into temptation and a snare, and into many* **foolish** *and harmful* lusts *which drown men in destruction and perdition. For the* **love of money** *is a root of all kinds of* **evil**, *for which some have strayed from the* **faith** *in their* greediness, *and pierced themselves through with many sorrows*" (1 Timothy 6:9-10)	"*Command those who are* **rich** *in this present age not to be* **haughty**, *nor to trust in uncertain* **riches** *but in the living God, who gives us* **richly** *all things to enjoy. Let them do* **good**, *that they be* **rich** *in* **good** *works, ready to* **give**, willing to share, storing *up for themselves a* **good** *foundation for the time to come, that they may lay hold on eternal life*" (1 Timothy 6:17-19)	"*But know this, that in the last days perilous times will come: For men will be lovers of themselves,* **lovers of money**...*lovers of pleasure rather than* lovers *of God, having a form of* **godliness** *but denying its power. And from such people turn away! For of this sort are those who creep into households and make captives of gullible women loaded down with sins*..." (2 Timothy 3:1-7)
"*Let the lowly brother glory in his exaltation, but the* **rich** *in his humiliation, because as a flower of the field he will pass away. For no sooner has the sun risen with a burning heat than it withers the grass; its flower falls, and its beautiful appearance perishes. So the* **rich** *man also will fade away in his pursuits*" (James 1:9-11)	"*Come now, you* **rich**, *weep and howl for your miseries that are coming upon you! Your* **riches** *are corrupted, and your garments are moth-eaten. Your* **gold** *and* **silver** *are corroded, and their corrosion will be a* **witness** *against you and will eat your flesh like fire. You have heaped up* **treasure** *in the last days. Indeed the* **wages** *of the laborers who mowed your fields, which you kept back by* **fraud**, *cry out; and the cries of the reapers have reached the ears of the Lord of Sabaoth. You have lived on the earth in* **pleasure** *and* **luxury**; *you have* **fattened your hearts** *as in*	"*By this we know* love, *because He laid down His life for us. And we also ought to lay down our lives for the brethren. But whoever has this* **world's goods**, *and sees his brother in need, and shuts up his heart from him, how does the* love *of God abide in him? My little children, let us not* love *in word or in tongue, but in deed and in truth*" (1 John 3:16-18)

| | *a day of slaughter. You have condemned, you have **murdered** the **just**; he does not resist you"* (James 5:1-6) | |

Table 148: Pearls of Wisdom from the Apostles Concerning People in the Rich Category

    James documented the influence of the negative attributes on Christians that react differently around people in the **rich** category. In James 2:1-13, he provided an example of the elements of <u>favoritism</u> and <u>partiality</u>. The example involved a person in the **rich** category <u>favored</u> over a person in the poor category. In his example, the person in the poor category was "***dishonored***" (James 2:6) because people influenced by spiritual warfare "***honored***" the person in the **rich** category purely because of that person's appearance or perceived <u>wealth</u>. In this case, James asked, "*...have you not shown <u>partiality</u> among yourselves, and become judges with **evil** thoughts?*" (James 2:4). What makes this example so bad is the fact that this incident occurred in the Lord's church as identified by the term "assembly" in the context of James 2:2. God's laws were violated by the bad behavior displayed. James documented, "*If you really fulfill the royal law according to the Scripture, "You shall <u>love</u> your neighbor as yourself," you do well; but if you show <u>partiality</u>, you commit sin, and are convicted by the law as **transgressors**. For whoever shall keep the whole law, and yet stumble in one point, he is guilty of all*" (James 2:8-10). Moreover, James documented that for one to remain on the positive forces' side of the campaign, one must, "*...speak and so do as those who will be judged by the law of liberty. For judgment is without **mercy** to the one who has shown no **mercy**. **Mercy** triumphs over judgment*" (James 12-13). The negative forces of the war campaign use fog to advance a strategy of <u>partiality</u> and <u>favoritism</u> to divide the positive forces, and more importantly, God's people. Please do not get lost in the fog. James's comments require no explanation. For all who claim to be a Christian, this is a standing directive from the Lord for one to live by.

    Finally, in the Book of Revelation, Jesus warned how an entire congregation of people, in the **rich** category, stumbled because of the negative attributes. For the church of the Laodiceans, Jesus stated, "*I know your works, that you are neither cold nor hot. I could wish you were cold or hot. So then, because you are lukewarm, and neither cold nor hot, I will vomit you out of My mouth. Because you say, 'I am **rich**, have become <u>wealthy</u>, and have need of nothing'—and do not know that you are wretched, miserable, poor, blind, and naked— I counsel you to **buy** from Me **gold** refined in the fire, that you may be **rich**; and white garments, that you may **be clothed**, that the shame of your nakedness may not be revealed; and anoint your eyes with eye salve, that you may see*" (Revelation 3:15-18). In many places in the world, this image of the church continues to thrive today. If one finds himself or herself within a congregation with this image, one should leave it as fast as one can. If not, based on the truth of the war campaign, one will forfeit his or her opportunity to reach heaven.

    In conclusion, one of the most important things that one in the **rich** category can do is share their <u>wealth</u> as prescribed by the Gospel of Jesus Christ. **Riches** are a blessing from God. One must know Christ to know that God desires one to use their <u>wealth</u> appropriately. Paul documented, "...*He who* **sows sparingly** *will also* **reap sparingly**, *and he who* **sows bountifully** *will also* **reap bountifully**. *So let each one* **give** *as he purposes in his heart, not grudgingly or of necessity; for God* <u>loves</u> *a cheerful giver. And God is able to make all* <u>grace</u> *abound toward you, that you, always having* **all sufficiency in all things**, *may have an* **abundance** *for every* **good** *work. As it is written: "He has* <u>dispersed abroad</u>, *He has given to the poor; His* **righteousness** *endures forever"*" (2 Corinthians 9:6-9). The fog generated by the negative forces during spiritual warfare, twists this message's meaning to line the pockets of the ***ungodly***. Thus, Jesus requires laborers in the **harvest** to reach out to everyone across the spiritual battlefield. This includes the people in the **rich** category. They and their **resources** from God's blessings play a vital role in extending the Gospel to the lost throughout the world.

CHAPTER VIII: What Happens in the Harvest When the Influences of the Attributes are Allowed?

"The harvest truly is plentiful, but the laborers are few"

~ Matthew 9:37

Within the Biblical record, Jesus documented the harsh reality of the war campaign, spiritual warfare, and the toil it takes on mankind. In a parable documented by Matthew, Mark, and Luke, Jesus provided context and clarity about the works of the laborers of the **harvest** on the spiritual battlefield. When Jesus told His disciples *"The **harvest** truly is plentiful, but the laborers are few"* (Matthew 9:37), He shed light on the magnitude of the war campaign compared to the small numbers of people engaged on the side of the positive forces.

Jesus used a parable about a sower sowing a single seed to describe the actions of the laborers among the positive forces. BTT allows one to see that from the sower's work, negative forces rallied to counter his efforts. This counteraction perfectly illustrates the war campaign and why it is unfolding. In addition, the parable reveals the importance of BTT and <u>discernment</u>. The parable is documented in **Table 149** below and provides a harmonized view of Matthew, Mark, and Luke's accounts for clarity. Please use your Bible to follow Jesus' Word. The Scriptures read as follows:

Matthew 13:3-9	**Mark 4:2-9**	**Luke 8:4-8**
"Then He spoke many things to them in parables, saying: "Behold, a sower went out to sow. And as he sowed, some seed fell by the wayside; and the birds came and devoured them. Some fell on stony places, where they did not have much earth; and they immediately sprang up because they had no depth of earth. But when the sun was up they were scorched, and because they had no root they withered away. And some fell among thorns, and the thorns sprang up and choked them. But others fell on good ground and yielded a crop: some a hundredfold, some sixty, some thirty. He who has ears to hear, let him hear!"	"Then He taught them many things by parables, and said to them in His teaching: "Listen! Behold, a sower went out to sow. And it happened, as he sowed, that some seed fell by the wayside; and the birds of the air came and devoured it. Some fell on stony ground, where it did not have much earth; and immediately it sprang up because it had no depth of earth. But when the sun was up it was scorched, and because it had no root it withered away. And some seed fell among thorns; and the thorns grew up and choked it, and it yielded no crop. But other seed fell on good ground and yielded a crop that sprang up,	And when a great multitude had gathered, and they had come to Him from every city, He spoke by a parable: "A sower went out to sow his seed. And as he sowed, some fell by the wayside; and it was trampled down, and the birds of the air devoured it. Some fell on rock; and as soon as it sprang up, it withered away because it lacked moisture. And some fell among thorns, and the thorns sprang up with it and choked it. But others fell on good ground, sprang up, and yielded a crop a hundredfold." When He had said these things He cried, "He who has ears to hear, let him hear!"

| | | increased and produced: some thirtyfold, some sixty, and some a hundred." And He said to them, "He who has ears to hear, let him hear!" | |

Table 149: A Text Side-by-Side Comparison of the Sower and the Seed Parable

Now consider these same Scriptures from a graphic view. **Figure 28** illustrates the seed that fell in various places, the Biblical record documented:

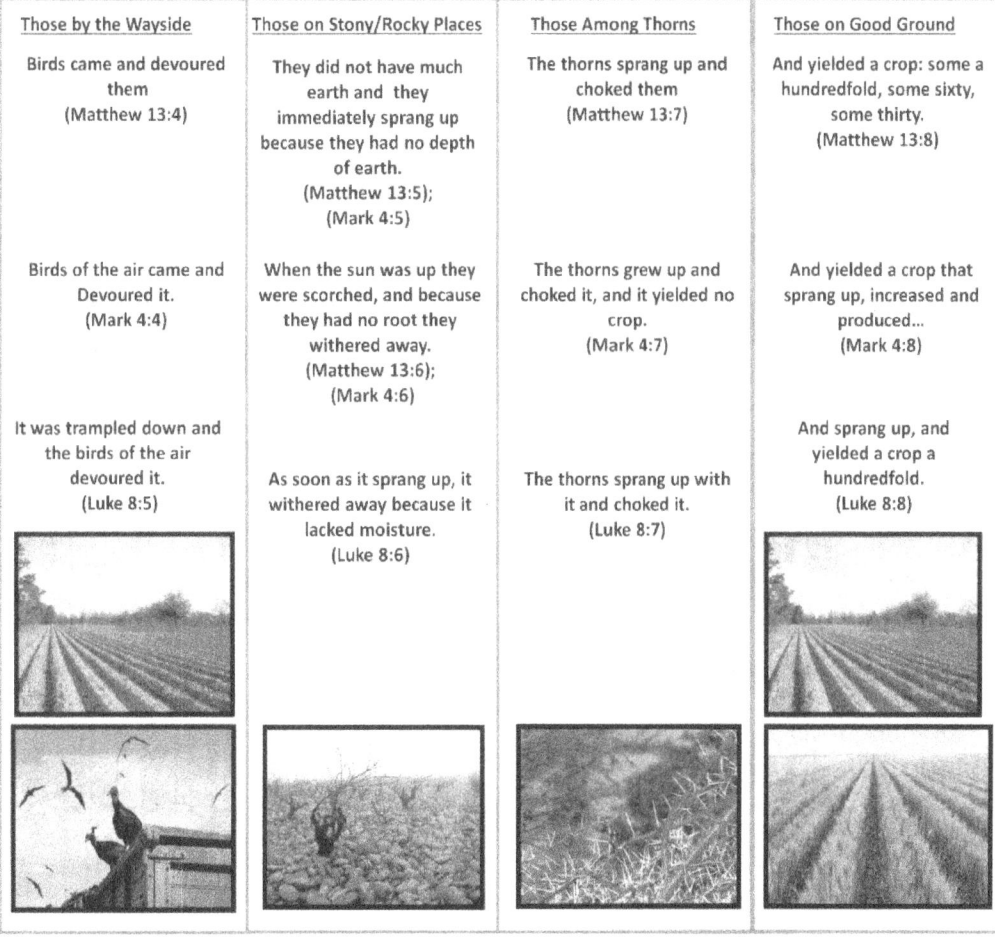

Figure 28: A Graphic Side-by-Side view of the Sower and the Seed Parable

Additionally, if one reads the account of the parables, one will realize that each account begins with the fact that a sower went out to sow seed, and some of the seed fell on different areas of the ground. BTT allows one to see that where the seed fell provided the parameters of the entire spiritual battlefield. However, Jesus' disciples did not understand this. They came to Jesus and asked Him to explain the meaning of the parable and He responded, "...*Do you not understand this parable? How then will you understand all the parables?*" (Mark 4:13). Then He explained the parable to the disciples. Table 150 provides the harmonized account of what

Jesus told His disciples across the accounts <u>heard</u> by Matthew, Mark, and Luke. The Gospel writers documented:

Matthew 13:18-23	Mark 4:14-20	Luke 8:11-15
"Then He spoke many things to "Therefore hear the parable of the sower: When anyone hears the word of the kingdom, and does not understand it, then the wicked one comes and snatches away what was sown in his heart. This is he who received seed by the wayside. But he who received the seed on stony places, this is he who hears the word and immediately receives it with joy; yet he has no root in himself, but endures only for a while. For when tribulation or persecution arises because of the word, immediately he stumbles. Now he who received seed among the thorns is he who hears the word, and the cares of this world and the deceitfulness of riches choke the word, and he becomes unfruitful. But he who received seed on the good ground is he who hears the word and understands it, who indeed bears fruit and produces: some a hundredfold, some sixty, some thirty."	*"The sower sows the word. And these are the ones by the wayside where the word is sown. When they hear, Satan comes immediately and takes away the word that was sown in their hearts. These likewise are the ones sown on stony ground who, when they hear the word, immediately receive it with gladness; and they have no root in themselves, and so endure only for a time. Afterward, when tribulation or persecution arises for the word's sake, immediately they stumble. Now these are the ones sown among thorns; they are the ones who hear the word, and the cares of this world, the deceitfulness of riches, and the desires for other things entering in choke the word, and it becomes unfruitful. But these are the ones sown on good ground, those who hear the word, accept it, and bear fruit: some thirtyfold, some sixty, and some a hundred."*	*"Now the parable is this: The seed is the word of God. Those by the wayside are the ones who hear; then the devil comes and takes away the word out of their hearts, lest they should believe and be saved. But the ones on the rock are those who, when they hear, receive the word with joy; and these have no root, who believe for a while and in time of temptation fall away. Now the ones that fell among thorns are those who, when they have heard, go out and are choked with cares, riches, and pleasures of life, and bring no fruit to maturity. But the ones that fell on the good ground are those who, having heard the word with a noble and good heart, keep it and bear fruit with patience.*

Table 150: The Side-by-Side Comparison of Jesus' Explanation of the Sower and the Seed Parable

Jesus' explanation allows one to see the interaction between the physical and spiritual realms of the war campaign. He defined what the seed was. The laborers carried the seed to the people of the **harvest**. Then He explained what happened with the people of the **harvest** who received the seed. **Figure 29** provides a harmonized graphic for clarity of Jesus' parable.

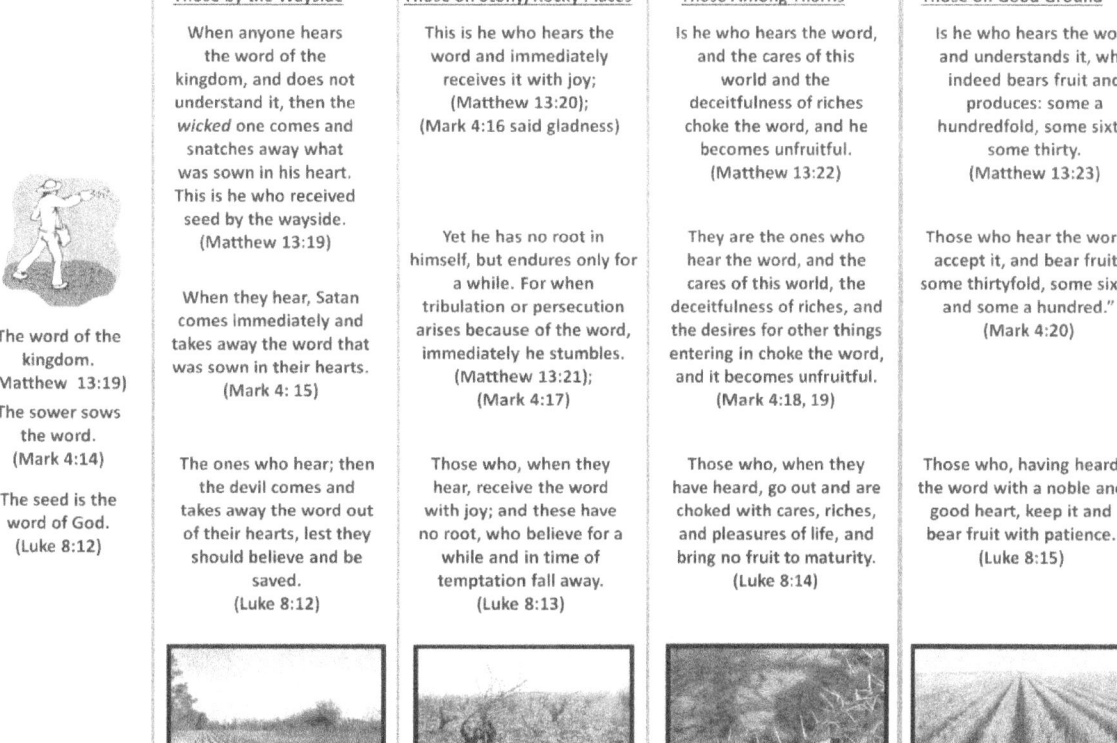

Figure 29: The Graphic Explanation of Jesus' Sower and Seed Parable

Using this graphic, one can see that the sower was spreading a seed. I will identify the sower last to prevent the active negative attributes from clouding one's understanding. BTT allows one to see that the sower's actions is the catalyst for everything that takes place in the parable. It is important for one to understand that the sower was spreading a unique seed. The Seed is singular; not "seeds." This is the first important lesson in BTT and *discernment*. One must pay attention to the details recorded in the Bible to understand the spiritual war. Next, the Biblical record documented that the sower's seed being spread was the Word (Mark 4:14), the Word of the kingdom (Matthew 13:19), and the Word of God (Luke 8:12). These three proclamations all referred to the Gospel of Jesus Christ. The seed is singular because it was created as a singular Gospel message that came from God that decreed, *"There is one body and one Spirit, just as you were called in one hope of your calling; one Lord, one **faith**, one baptism; one God and Father of all, who is above all, and through all, and in you all"* (Ephesians 4:6-6). In other words, this seed is unique and contains the "one" doctrine authorized by its designer - God. BTT allows one to see that the germination of this unique seed yields a unique crop. Because of this, there are hosts of negative forces that want this seed destroyed. If one simply pays attention to the details of this parable, one will learn the truth about the war campaign and spiritual warfare.

All the earth's populations are the fields in which this seed spreads without discrimination. It represents the trillions of people of every race, ethnicity, and gender that populates every location of every country on earth. One can see this from Jesus' statement, *"when anyone hears."* The term *"anyone"* represents a broad open-ended statement for all humanity. Thus, the field is also the battlefield of the positive and negative attributes in the spiritual realm.

First, the seed fell among the people on the wayside. Consider the term "wayside" as people who live on the edge of life. These are people that are just living. They are people who may have never considered, thought about, or made a commitment to God. In general, these are people who do not feel they have a need for God in their lives and believe their lives are fine the way they are. In most cases, these are people who do not want religious accountability. They neither support nor deny a belief in God, nor will they defend Christ to the exclusion of any other belief, god, or deity. They believe in "live and let live" and that one should keep their faith to themselves. But consider what happened when the seed fell among them. Some <u>heard</u> it, but they did not understand it (Matthew 13:19). To be clear, the Biblical record documented that they <u>heard</u> the word of the kingdom, they <u>received</u> it, but they <u>did not understand it</u>. Because of these three important points, the ***wicked*** one came and snatched away everything sown in their spiritual hearts. Mark clarified that the ***wicked*** one was Satan (Mark 4:15), while Luke documented that the ***wicked*** one was the "devil." BTT allows one to see that Satan, the devil, and the ***wicked*** one are the same person. Together, the three Gospel writers' documentation defeats any confusion on who is leading the negative forces of the war campaign. Satan, the devil, and the ***wicked*** one are all one and the same negative spiritual entity and the three harmonized Scriptures clarify this fact. However, the negative forces of the campaign use fog to ***deceive*** people to point out these authors simply contradict each other. Please do not be ***deceived***. These details captured by the three Gospel writers tells one who is leading the charge to immediately take the seed away (Mark 4:15) from one's inner spirit.

Satan controls the negative attributes which influences people to create confusion, deception, perversion, and manipulation of the sowed seed. The influences of the negative attributes cause some people to wrestle with sin in their past and current lives. Mark documented that Jesus said, "*For from within, out of the heart of men, proceed **evil thoughts, adulteries, fornications, murders, thefts, covetousness, wickedness, deceit, lewdness, an evil eye, blasphemy, pride, foolishness***" (Mark 7:23-23). Negativism, with the help of other people hanging out on the wayside, can keep one from accepting God's Word. Negativism and bad behavior will cease from one's life by pursuing the Gospel. When one accepts God's Word, an immature spirit and poor choices reopens the door for Satan. Jesus told the Jewish leadership, "*Why do you not understand My speech? Because you are not able to listen to My word. You are of your father the **devil**, and the desires of your father you want to do. He was a **murderer** from the beginning, and does not stand in the truth, because there is no truth in him. When he speaks a **lie**, he speaks from his own resources, for he is a **liar** and the father of it. But because I tell the truth, you do not <u>believe</u> Me*" (John 8:43-45). For this reason, Satan, the great deceiver, converts large populations of people to the negative forces of the war campaign. He snatches or takes the word away immediately, "*lest they should <u>believe</u> and be saved*" (Luke 8:12). BTT allows one to see that Satan acts decisively when one hears and receives the seed which is the word (Mark 4:14), the word of the kingdom (Matthew 13:19), and the Word of God (Luke 8:12). Why? Because one's very belief in the word can lead one to take the steps toward True salvation.

Luke 17:11-19 provides an example of people on the wayside of life. The example documents ten lepers who came to Jesus for healing. Jesus healed all the lepers, but only one returned to thank Jesus. All ten of them could have returned to Jesus to learn and gain more from Him; but the other nine took from Jesus and returned to the world without seeking more. The nine allowed the influence of the negative forces to lead them away from the source of salvation. However, their decision was their own personal choice to take the path they chose. Perhaps, these are the people who Paul said, "*Do not be **deceived**: "**Evil** company corrupts good habits." Awake to **righteousness**, and do not sin; for some do not have the knowledge of God. I speak this to your shame*" (1 Corinthians 15:33-34). Paul wrote his letter to the people in Christ's church, yet some did not have the knowledge of God. This lack of knowledge was shameful and documents that there are people sitting in the Lord's church who are on the wayside. These people show up at church out of a sense of obligation; they do not come to learn, grow, fellowship, or partake in activities with the congregation. Their own poor behavior identifies them. One can observe that their lives inside and outside of the church are completely different. The **wicked** also see this contradiction and exploit every opportunity with this person until he or she slides out of the body of Christ. In this case, because of complacency, one who may have been hanging on to small measures of the positive attributes begins to aid the negative forces through their behavior.

Next, the seed fell on people in stony and rocky places. The first thing one should notice is, just like those by the wayside, these people heard and received the word. The difference between these people and the people of the wayside is how they accepted the word. They received the seed with *joy* and *gladness* according to all three Gospel writers. Matthew even stated that they received it immediately. However, these people did not develop a root or foundation in the Gospel to build on. BTT helps one to understand that the development of a root in the Gospel is important for stability. A root in the Gospel, just like the root of a plant, allows one to stand strong when *tribulations* or *storms* occur. I will discuss these two variables shortly. For now, just understand that people never develop a root because of their inconsistency in studying God's Word, poor attendance at church, or their lack of commitment to opportunities to learn the Gospel through Bible studies. This is why the Bible specifically calls for everyone who receives God's Word to, "*Be diligent to present yourself approved to God, a worker who does not need to be ashamed, **rightly** dividing the word of truth*" (2 Timothy 2:15). The context of this "be diligent" means to study. Consider the consequences these people faced in the war.

Matthew and Mark documented that because of the seed, the people in the stony and rocky places only endured for a while when spiritual variables like *tribulation* and *persecution* were introduced. These two variables caused stumbling and Luke introduced a third variable of *temptation*. Of the three variables, it was the variable of *temptation* which caused people to fall away. However, BTT helps one to understand that these three variables play a pivotal role in the war campaign. This trio forces people to make choices in life. Depending on the measure of the seed that has made its way to one's inner spirit, the influence of the positive and negative attributes will determine how one might respond to these variables. The Bible record documents some pearls of wisdom about these three variables. The Bible documents:

For the *tribulation* (synonymous with *trials*):

- Paul and Barnabas, after returning to Lystra, Iconium, and Antioch, "...*strengthening the souls of the disciples, exhorting them to continue in the **faith**, and saying, "We must through many tribulations enter the kingdom of God*" (Acts 14:21-22)

- "*...but to those who are self-seeking and do not obey the truth, but obey* **unrighteousness**—*indignation and wrath, tribulation and anguish, on every soul of man who does **evil**...*" (Romans 2:8-9)

- "*...we also glory in tribulations, knowing that tribulation produces perseverance; and perseverance, character; and character, hope. Now hope does not disappoint, because the love of God has been poured out in our hearts by the Holy Spirit who was given to us*" (Romans 5:3-5)

- "*Blessed be the God and Father of our Lord Jesus Christ, the Father of **mercies** and God of all comfort, who comforts us in all our tribulation, that we may be able to comfort those who are in any trouble, with the comfort with which we ourselves are comforted by God*" (2 Corinthians 1:3-4)

- "*My brethren, count it all joy when you fall into various trials, knowing that the testing of your **faith** produces patience. But let patience have its perfect work, that you may be perfect and complete, lacking nothing*" (James 1:2-4)

For *persecution*:

- Jesus taught there would be gains from the Gospel but with *persecution*. Jesus said, "*...Assuredly, I say to you, there is no one who has left house or brothers or sisters or father or mother or wife or children or lands, for My sake and the gospel's, who shall not receive a hundredfold now in this time—houses and brothers and sisters and mothers and children and lands, with persecutions—and in the age to come, eternal life. But many who are first will be last, and the last first*" (Mark 10:29-31)

- "*...so that we ourselves boast of you among the churches of God for your patience and* ***faith*** *in all your persecutions and tribulations that you endure, which is manifest evidence of the righteous judgment of God, that you may be counted worthy of the kingdom of God, for which you also suffer; since it is a **righteous** thing with God to repay with tribulation those who trouble you, and to give you who are troubled rest with us...*" (2 Thessalonians 1:4-7)

- "*Yes, and all who desire to live **godly** in Christ Jesus will suffer persecution*" (2 Timothy 3:12)

For _temptation_:

- Jesus said, "*Watch and pray, lest you enter into temptation. The spirit indeed is willing, but the flesh is weak*" (Matthew 26:41; Mark 14:38)

- "*No temptation has overtaken you except such as is common to man; but God is **faithful**, who will not allow you to be tempted beyond what you are able, but with the temptation will also make the way of escape, that you may be able to bear it*" (1 Corinthians 10:13)

- "*But those who desire to be rich fall into temptation and a snare, and into many **foolish** and harmful lusts which drown men in destruction and perdition*" (1 Timothy 6:9)

- "*Brethren, if a man is overtaken in any trespass, you who are spiritual restore such a one in a spirit of gentleness, considering yourself lest you also be tempted*" (Galatians 6:1)

- "*Blessed is the man who endures temptation; for when he has been approved, he will receive the crown of life which the Lord has promised to those who love Him. Let no one say when he is tempted, "I am tempted by God"; for God cannot be tempted by **evil**, nor does He Himself tempt anyone. But each one is tempted when he is drawn away by his own desires and enticed. Then, when desire has conceived, it gives birth to sin; and sin, when it is full-grown, brings forth death.*" (James 1:12-16)

- "*…the Lord knows how to deliver the **godly** out of temptations and to reserve the **unjust** under punishment for the Day of Judgment…*" (2 Peter 2:9)

Based on the information above, BTT helps one see that these three variables; _tribulation_ (and _trials_), _persecution_, and _temptation_, are part of spiritual warfare. Every person must overcome them in the war campaign. Moreover, BTT allows one to see that the variable _temptation_, enables some of the greatest strategies used by the negative forces to cause the positive forces to stumble. The negative forces use _temptation_ in short-term and long-term strategies to lure people into traps. These traps keep the simple and unbelievers entangled in sin while effectively trapping people influenced by the positive attributes who become complacent and comfortable. The negative force's goal is to cause one with positive attributes to stumble and then use the result against others of the positive forces. Even Jesus faced _temptation_ which exposed parts of the war campaign according to Matthew 4:1-11. His example and approach for dealing with this variable demonstrated how to defeat the negative forces using God's Word. Thus, Paul documented that "*No temptation has overtaken you except such as is common to man; but God is faithful, who will not allow you to be tempted beyond what you are able, but with the temptation will also make the way of escape, that you may be able to bear it*" (1 Corinthians 10:13). Moreover, the Bible documents that for everyone who allows the influence of the positive attributes, "*…the Lord knows how to deliver the **godly** out of temptations and to reserve the unjust under punishment for the Day of Judgment…*" (2 Peter 2:9). The Bible documents, "*Blessed is the man who endures temptation; for when he has been* *approved, he will receive the crown of life which the Lord has promised to those who love Him"* (James 1:12). Once again, seeking and acquiring the positive attributes are important for surviving spiritual warfare. Thus, Paul reminds the mature Christian, *"Who shall separate us from the love of Christ? Shall tribulation, or distress, or persecution, or famine, or nakedness, or peril, or sword? Yet in all these things we are more than conquerors through Him who loved us"* (Romans 8:35-37).

A person who never hears God's Word, or one who hears but never matures, will buckle under the weight of these variables. A person who receives God's Words has a greater chance of overcoming these variables because they can anticipate them and be prepared for the campaign's challenges. But know this *"...that if the master of the house had known what hour the **thief** would come, he would have watched and not allowed his house to be broken into"* (Matthew 24:43; Luke 12:39). BTT helps one to understand that the Gospel provides spiritual information that prepares one's inner spirit with safety protocols. These protocols strengthen the root that allows a foundation for God's Word to open one's spiritual heart to the influences of the positive attributes. Without the Gospel, the influences of the negative attributes will automatically overtake one who has heard and received the word. One will stumble and eventually fall away if the word does not mature.

It is very important to understand that one can "fall away" from the Gospel of Jesus Christ. This Biblical fact contradicts today's ***false*** teachers. The negative forces use spiritual warfare to embolden ***false*** teachers to claim that once one is saved, they will always be saved. The Bible actually teaches that if one is baptized into Christ, *"...it is impossible for those who were once enlightened, and have tasted the heavenly gift, and have become partakers of the Holy Spirit, and have tasted the good word of God and the powers of the age to come, if they fall away, to renew them again to repentance, since they crucify again for themselves the Son of God, and put Him to an open shame"* (Hebrews 6:4-6). Only people who achieve BTT and discernment, will accept this information as God's Truth. God will not extend His grace to anyone who willfully sins and remains disobedient to His Word while refusing to repent from that sin. Understand that the "once saved, always saved" doctrine is born out of a strategy of the negative forces to keep people lost in the fog of the war campaign. Do not be ***deceived***.

BTT allows one to see that the people in the stony and rocky places can be people in one's home or work place. They can be people who reject the Gospel, friends who place barriers in the way of one's learning, or even religious leaders who teach things contrary to God's Word. The Biblical record provides evidence of all these scenarios. BTT allows one to see a few examples of the people among the stony and rocky places in the Biblical record. For examples, the Biblical record documented:

- *"How could one chase a thousand, and two put ten thousand to flight, unless their rock had sold them, and the Lord had surrendered them? For their rock is not like our Rock, even our enemies themselves being judges. For their vine is of the vine of Sodom and of the fields of Gomorrah; their grapes are grapes of gall, their clusters are bitter"* (Deuteronomy 32:30-32)

- What the Lord would do for Israel if they repent: "*Then I will give them one heart, and I will put a new spirit within them, and take the stony heart out of their flesh, and give them a heart of flesh...*" (Ezekiel 11:19)

- "*O Lord, are not Your eyes on the truth? You have stricken them, but they have not grieved; You have consumed them, but they have refused to receive correction. They have made their faces harder than rock; they have refused to return*" (Jeremiah 5:3)

From these few Scriptures, BTT allows one to see that the people represented by the stones and rocks are those that have hardened their hearts against the Almighty God and their countenance is cold. They are a people who, "*...because lawlessness will abound, the love of many will grow cold*" (Matthew 24:12). They represent the people that Paul described as **ungodly** and **unrighteous**, "*...who suppress the truth in **unrighteousness**, because what may be known of God is manifest in them, for God has shown it to them*" (Romans 1:18-19). The people of the stones and rocks can hear the Gospel, but few will heed its words.

Beyond the wayside and rocks, the seed fell to people among thorns. Once again, the Biblical record documented that these people also heard the Word. Luke, in harmony with Matthew and Mark, documented that they heard the Word and "went out," which implies that they did not try to keep the Word to themselves. They shared the **good** news of the Gospel with others. BTT helps one to see that as they attempted to "*Go therefore and make disciples of all the nations, baptizing them in the name of the Father and of the Son and of the Holy Spirit, teaching them to observe all things that I have commanded you; and lo, I am with you always, even to the end of the age...*" (Matthew 28:19-20; Mark 16:15), something happened. The harmonized Biblical record documents that four variables affected them. The variables were:

Variable	Where
The cares of this world	Matthew 123:22; Mark 4:19; Luke 8:14
The **deceitfulness** of riches	Matthew 123:22; Mark 4:19; Luke 8:14
The desires for other things	Mark 4:19
The pleasures of life	Luke 8:14

Table 151: Spiritual Variables in Spiritual Warfare

These four variables are simply distractors of God's Word. These distractors are strategies used by the negative forces of the war campaign in the physical realm. These distractors are some of the most effective strategies ever devised by Satan for the war campaign. They grab one's attention until the Word of God is "*choked*" out of one's life. The diversion of one's attention to physical distractors creates a tourniquet-like process on one's inner spirit that slowly cuts off the feeding of God's Word to one's spirit. Instead of maturing spiritually, one immerses himself or herself in ***folly***. One never reaches maturity in the Gospel, learns discernment, or achieves BTT. In other words, these distractors simply aid the progression of the negative attribute in one's inner spirit. Had the person among the thorns matured the seed, they would have understood God's priorities over their own. They would have learned that by seeking, "*...first the kingdom of God and His **righteousness**...*" (Matt 6:33), everything **good** and necessary for life would follow. With God as the priority, the four distractors have no power over one's inner spirit or mind. Without God, the four distractors combine with the negative attributes and choke the Word of God from an immature Christian. BTT helps one to see that Judas fell in this category and he eventually committed suicide. In Matthew 27:5, Judas betrayed the Son of God for thirty pieces of silver (Matthew 26:15). Judas got distracted. When Jesus became a prisoner, Judas **killed** himself. Simon the Sorcerer of Acts 8:9-24 also fell in this category. He offered the apostles money for the power to lay his hands-on others, so they could receive the Holy Spirit. Satan choked the Seed out of Simon by distracting him with the ***deceitfulness*** of riches.

The Biblical record shared some other clues about the people among the thorns. Consider these Biblical references:

- People whom God told the Israelites to move off the land: "*But if you do not drive out the inhabitants of the land from before you, then it shall be that those whom you let remain shall be irritants in your eyes and <u>thorns</u> in your sides, and they shall harass you in the land where you dwell*" (Numbers 33:55; see also Joshua 23:13 and Judges 2:3)

- The way of people influenced by the ***lazy*** attribute: "*The way of the **lazy** man is like a hedge of <u>thorns</u> ...*" (Proverbs 15:19)

- The way of people influenced by the ***perverse*** attribute: "<u>*Thorns*</u> *and snares are in the way of the **perverse**; he who guards his soul will be far from them*" (Proverbs 22:5)

BTT helps one to see that the thorns represent people who reject and ***mock*** God. They are the people who keep chaos going in the world by creating distractors to counteract opportunities for God's Word to root in one's inner spirit. People, specifically people in the **rich** category influenced by the ***wicked***, ***fool***, ***scoffer***, ***perverse***, ***unfaithful***, ***ungodly***, and the ***immoral*** attributes, relish in the creation of distractors which fits in the category of the ***thorns*** in the war campaign. BTT also allows one to see that many charitable and philanthropic activities, along with their creators who disguise their causes under religious pretense, are among the ***thorns***. These activities and their causes ensnare many who claim the name of Christ. This includes believers who conveniently skip serving the Lord on the day He designated to assemble on by attending charitable activities disguised as ***good*** and acceptable works for the Lord. This deceptive strategy is just another part of the fog generated by the negative forces of the war campaign to ensnare people influenced by the ***simple*** attribute. Only Biblical transformational thinkers can see the destruction occurring in local churches as the influence of the negative attributes use distractors on both the spiritual and physical battlefields.

Finally, the seed fell on ***good*** ground. All three of the Gospel accounts of Jesus' parable documented that these people <u>heard</u> it, <u>received</u> it (implied), <u>understood</u> it, <u>accepted</u> it (Mark 4:20) and then <u>kept</u> it (Luke 8:15). The parable documented that something was different about these people. Luke documented that they had a ***noble*** and ***good*** heart. This means that two positive attributes, the ***upright/honorable*** and ***good*** attributes, were actively influencing their inner spirits. BTT let one see that these people <u>received</u> the same Seed as the people of the thorns, stones, and wayside. But the Seed was not snatched away or choked out of them, and nor were the people distracted.

Before going further, consider this about the people on ***good*** ground. First, they were not Christians prior to the time the Seed fell on them. BTT allows one to see that this confirms the fact that there are people in the world who have small measures of the positive attributes, excluding the ***righteous*** attribute, who have not obeyed the Gospel of Jesus Christ. They innately allow small measures of the ***good, merciful, just, upright/honorable, blameless, and faithful*** attributes because of positive influences, examples, and experiences they are exposed to in their lives. Nonetheless, they have not fully come to know and commit to God and His Son Jesus Christ. This also means that without the Seed, although these people are on ***good*** ground; they are still spiritually lost. This truth documents the nexus of the physical and spiritual realms of the campaign. Where they meet documents where baptism brings one's inner spirit in contact with the spiritual blood of Jesus and obedience to the Word of God. A laborer must introduce God's Word to one who lacks this Truth. God does not communicate His Word directly to anyone outside of the Bible itself. For the people who mature the Seed (Christians), they are generally safe among the people on ***good*** ground. However, because of the fog in spiritual warfare, one must keep in mind that bribes and other strategies of the negative forces can also corrupt people on the ***good*** ground. Hence, just as Jesus warned His disciples, "*Behold, I send you out as sheep in the midst of wolves. Therefore be **wise** as serpents and harmless as doves*" (Matthew 10:16), so must the Christian be. However, Biblical insight informs one that most people on the ***good*** ground are receptive to listening to God's Word from those who possess it because of the condition of their inner spiritual heart. Hence, this **harvest** is plentiful. Perhaps the woman at the well in John 4:5-26, or the ***good*** Samaritan in Luke 10:25-37, can serve as examples of people on ***good*** ground who had not necessarily accepted Christ. They both already had a measure of the ***good*** attribute but still needed Jesus to be saved.

A broader perspective of the people on ***good*** ground includes many of the people who make up the religious community. There are many people in this community with a large measure of the ***good*** attribute but have not fully come to understand the Bible to be become a Christian. They are not saved even though ***false*** teaching from the Bible and traditions of men state otherwise. Nicodemus in John 3:1-9 is an excellent example of one who fell in this category of religious people. Saul, who eventually was renamed Paul, provided another strong example of one who was religious but made a change to become a Christian. In fact, in Saul case, he attempted to destroy Christianity until he learned the Truth and became a Christian.

Another very important aspect about the people on ***good*** ground, who accepted the Seed, is they used it to gain others. They used another spiritual element called "*patience*." BTT helps one to understand that *patience* is critical for a Christian's survival in spiritual warfare. Christians learn to appreciate the element of *patience* early in their spiritual walk. Most Christians remember that this element also worked with them. Consider the following passages of Scriptures to help reach this important understanding.

- "*For whatever things were written before were written for our learning, that we through the patience and comfort of the Scriptures might have hope*" (Romans 15:4)

- "*Now may the God of <u>patience</u> and <u>comfort</u> grant you to be like-minded toward one another, according to Christ Jesus...*" (Romans 15:5)

- "*Now may the Lord direct your hearts into the <u>love</u> of God and into the <u>patience</u> of Christ*" (2 Thessalonians 3:5)

- To overcome the negative attributes: "*But you, O man of God, flee these things and pursue **righteousness**, **godliness**, **faith**, <u>love</u>, <u>patience</u>, gentleness. Fight the **good** fight of **faith**, lay hold on eternal life, to which you were also called and have confessed the **good** confession in the presence of many witnesses*" (1 Timothy 6:11-12)

- "*...that you do not become sluggish, but imitate those who through **faith** and <u>patience</u> inherit the promises*" (Hebrews 6:12)

- "*...knowing that the testing of your **faith** produces <u>patience</u>*" (James 1:3)

- "*But let <u>patience</u> have its perfect work, that you may be perfect and complete, lacking nothing*" (James 1:4)

- "*My brethren, take the prophets, who spoke in the name of the Lord, as an example of suffering and <u>patience</u>*" (James 5:10)

The people on **good** ground who have fully accepted Christ and are obedient to the Seed, use the element of <u>patience</u> to successfully spread the Word of God to others. Some of these people can easily identify with the people they bring the Seed to as Paul reminded us all, "*...Do you not know that the **unrighteous** will not inherit the kingdom of God? Do not be **deceived**. Neither **fornicators**, **nor idolaters**, **nor adulterers**, **nor homosexuals**, **nor sodomites**, **nor thieves**, **nor covetous**, **nor drunkards**, **nor revilers**, **nor extortioners** will inherit the kingdom of God. <u>And such were some of you</u>. But you were washed, but you were sanctified, but you were justified in the name of the Lord Jesus and by the Spirit of our God*" (1 Corinthians 6:9-11). Emphasis is on the underlined portion of this text.

These are people who produced other Christians, of which the Biblical record compares to the reproduction of fruit. Jesus documented that their efforts yielded large numbers of converts to the kingdom of God; some thirtyfold, some sixtyfold, some hundredfold. Within this portion of the parable, BTT brings one full circle to the correlation of the war campaign and Jesus' Word when He said, "*...The **harvest** truly is plentiful, but the laborers are few.*'" (Matthew 9:37; Luke 10:2). The laborers are few because spiritual warfare incapacitates large numbers of humanity through deception. To this point, one can understand what Jesus meant when He told His disciples, "*When a strong man, fully armed, guards his own palace, his goods are in peace. But when a stronger than he comes upon him and overcomes him, he takes from him all his armor in which he trusted, and divides his spoils. He who is not with Me is against Me, and he who does not gather with Me scatters*" (Luke 11:21-23). In other words, one who relies on materialism, prosperity, or **false** teachings will not withstand the wilds of the **wicked** one on the battlefield of the war campaign. Satan will physically and spiritually overcome and take everything one has and divide it among the negative forces of the campaign.

This is happening today. <u>Wealth</u> is simply being redistributed among people influenced by the negative attributes who are emboldened by the negative forces who **covet** and lust for more. The second part of this Scripture is that people who are not spreading this Truth from Jesus Christ are automatically aiding the negative forces and helping to scatter the people of the **harvest**. If one is not with Jesus and His one doctrine, one is with Satan on the spiritual battlefield. There is no middle ground. This wisdom is both deep and troubling at the same time.

The Bible provides some clues about the spreading of the Seed and the yield it produces. The yield is identified as "<u>fruit</u>." More importantly, because of spiritual warfare, one learns there is **good** and **bad** <u>fruit</u> depending on the source of its producer. The Bible documents:

- *"Beware of **false** prophets, who come to you in sheep's clothing, but inwardly they are ravenous wolves. You will know them by their <u>fruits</u>. Do men gather grapes from thornbushes or figs from thistles? Even so, every **good** tree bears **good** <u>fruit</u>, but a **bad** tree bears **bad** <u>fruit</u>. A **good** tree cannot bear **bad** <u>fruit</u>, nor can a **bad** tree bear **good** <u>fruit</u>. Every tree that does not bear **good** <u>fruit</u> is cut down and thrown into the fire. Therefore by their <u>fruits</u> you will know them"* (Matthew 7:15-20)

- *"Every branch in Me that does not bear <u>fruit</u> He takes away; and every branch that bears <u>fruit</u> He prunes, that it may bear more <u>fruit</u>"* (John 15:2)

- *"What <u>fruit</u> did you have then in the things of which you are now ashamed? For the end of those things is death. But now having been set free from sin, and having become slaves of God, you have your <u>fruit</u> to holiness, and the end, everlasting life"* (Romans 6:21-22)

- *"Therefore, my brethren, you also have become dead to the law through the body of Christ, that you may be married to another—to Him who was raised from the dead, that we should bear <u>fruit</u> to God. For when we were in the flesh, the sinful passions which were aroused by the law were at work in our members to bear <u>fruit</u> to death"* (Romans 7:4-5)

One can now identify the sower of the Seed that produces the good fruit. Jesus clearly stated, *"Abide in Me, and I in you. As the branch cannot bear **fruit** of itself, unless it abides in the vine, neither can you, unless you abide in Me. "I am the vine, you are the branches. He who abides in Me, and I in him, bears much **fruit**; for without Me you can do nothing"* (John 15:4). People who accept the Seed; the Word (Mark 4:14), the Word of the kingdom (Matthew 13:19), and the Word of God (Luke 8:12), the way Jesus says in His Gospel, becomes the sower of the Seed. There is no substitute method. Substitutes invite the elements of **strife** and **calamity** of which I cover in the next chapter of this book. Only Jesus' disciples today, who use His Word correctly and are obedient to it, can produce the fruit from the **harvest** that God seeks.

One can now see that Jesus' parable of the sower clearly documents a deep look into spiritual warfare, the war campaign, and the battlefield on which the war takes place. One must look at the Scriptures through a strategic lens of warfighting to see the full meaning of God's Word and its application to spiritual warfare. BTT provides the strategic lens that allows one to view the physical challenges facing the world from a moral, ethical, just, and **righteous** point of view. In addition, BTT allows one to see fair and ***just*** solutions for today's problems. The Gospel of Jesus Christ provides solutions. For God's Word:

- Is True - "*All Scripture is given by inspiration of God, and is profitable for doctrine, for reproof, for correction, for instruction in* **righteousness**, *that the man of God may be complete, thoroughly equipped for every* **good** *work*" (2 Tim 3:16-17)

- Will help one grow - "*Therefore, laying aside all malice, all* **deceit**, *hypocrisy,* **envy**, *and all* **evil** *speaking, as newborn babes, desire the pure milk of the word, that you may grow thereby, if indeed you have tasted that the Lord is gracious*" (1 Pet 2:1-3)

- Will give one _hope_ - "*For whatever things were written before were written for our learning, that we through the_ patience _and_ comfort _of the Scriptures might have_ hope*" (Rom 15:4)

- Will save one's soul "*But Simon Peter answered Him, "Lord, to whom shall we go? You have the words of eternal life"*" (John 6:68)

CHAPTER IX: Why Identification of the Attributes is Critical for Winning the War Campaign

*"... For plundering and **violence** are before me; there is <u>strife</u>, and <u>contention</u> arises. Therefore the law is powerless, and justice never goes forth. For the **wicked** surround the **righteous**; therefore **perverse** judgment proceeds"*

~ Habakkuk 1:1-4 ~

One can never expect to solve the growing number of complex issues the world is experiencing if one never identifies the root cause of the issues. This rule applies in the physical and the spiritual realms because the two coexist and impact each other. However, in the spiritual realm, the complex issues have greater consequences because one's soul is at stake. For this reason, identifying the attributes correctly and understanding them is crucial for the Christian's survival in the war campaign. When one ignores the attributes or rejects their existence, then one can never understand spiritual warfare or even begin to fathom the root cause of all the chaos and mayhem the world is experiencing today. But make no mistake, chaos and mayhem are increasing worldwide as they did before the time of Noah and God destroyed all life during the great flood. Solomon reminded us, *"That which has been is what will be, that which is done is what will be done, and there is nothing new under the sun"* (Ecclesiastes 1:9). Hence, chaos and mayhem will continue to increase until Jesus eventually returns. The question is – what side of the war campaign will you be on when Christ returns?

BTT allows one to see that the positive attributes are hard to grasp due to years of ***false*** teachings about them. The negative attributes have invested time through generations of people redefining these ***clean spirits***. Through spiritual warfare, Satan has hidden the original meaning, purpose, and role of the positive attribute by redefining them. The prophet Isaiah tried to warn the world of this in a statement he made to the nation of Israel; the people who had the true oracles of God (Romans 3:2). Isaiah stated, *"Woe to those who call **evil good**, and **good evil**; who put darkness for light, and light for darkness; who put bitter for sweet, and sweet for bitter!"* (Isaiah 5:20). This statement did not only apply to the **good** attribute, it applied to the redefining of all the attributes. Had God's people remained true to the oracles of God, understanding the positive attributes may have been much simpler.

Moreover, the fact that the root of the positive attributes are part of the divine nature of God makes understand them antithetical to the thinking of mankind. When Paul wrote, *"These things we also speak, not in words which man's wisdom teaches but which the Holy Spirit teaches, comparing spiritual things with spiritual. But the natural man does not receive the things of the Spirit of God, for they are foolishness to him; nor can he know them, because they are spiritually <u>discerned</u>"* (1 Corinthians 2:13-14), he was writing about the Gospel. However, BTT allows one to see that spiritual warfare, all the attributes, and the war campaign itself are all part of the Gospel message. The fact is, centuries of spiritual warfare have conditioned mankind to emphasize the negative over the positive attributes. The goals of the negative attributes are first to hinder anything positive from God and then to destroy whatever message comes from God. Their tactic begins with confusing anything from the positive attributes with fog. To confirm this very point, I often ask people to consider the words of Philippians 4:8 which says, "...*whatever things are true, whatever things are noble, whatever things are just, whatever things are pure, whatever things are lovely, whatever things are of good report, if there is any virtue and if there is anything praiseworthy—meditate on these things.*" Next, I ask them to pick one item from this Scripture and tell me one recent positive thing that has happened in their lives that meets the positive nature of the item they selected. The results are always the same. After long pauses, ninety-plus percent of the people surveyed cannot offer a single positive thing. This is a sad commentary.

However, this reality is the result of daily assaults from covert influences of the negative attributes. These influences come through unfiltered social media, television, radio and music, and companionship with people influenced by the negative attributes. But to live as God desires one to live, a man and woman must learn how to defeat the negativism by allowing the influences of the positive attributes. Everything starts in the home in spiritual warfare. **Figure 30** shows the influences of the positive forces in the home when God's Word is present. Understanding and accepting this truth is essential if one want to survive the war campaign. Whether a home has two parents or a single parent; whether children in

Figure 30: The Positive Attributes and the Home

the home are by birth or adopted, exposure to the Truth of God's Word is the only protection a home has in spiritual warfare. Knowledge of the positive attribute's role, along with an understanding of the war campaign, can set everyone on the right path of life and salvation.

For the traditional family based on the Biblical model, the basic Family Cycle looks like what is illustrated in **Figure 31**. Essentially, this figure illustrates how everything starts when men and women come together and create children. Whether a man and woman come together in marriage or not, if children are produced, both parents have the inherent responsibility for teaching their children the way they should go in life according to Proverbs 22:6 and Ephesians

Figure 31: A Basic Look at the Family Cycle

6:4. This responsibility is not abrogated just because the man or woman wants no part of it. When children are produced, the man and woman that produced them inherit a spiritually fixed responsibly that they are eternally held accountable for completing. Satan, spiritual warfare, and all the negative forces of the war campaign wants this truth stricken from God's creation. As children grow and leave the home, they begin the cycle depicted in **Figure 31** for themselves. Just as the negative attributes surround their parents, so will these forces surround these new young adults as they leave the home. But the goal of spiritual warfare is to split the home anywhere it can along the cycle. Hence, when single parent, or fatherless children, or two parents homes overrun by the negative force's influences become the norm, each of their successive generation will get further away from God's original family design. If successive generations fail to be exposed to the True teachings of God's Word along the way, the end-state will result in a breakdown of the moral fabric that underpins strong homes, communities, and societies around the world. As societies succumb to the influences of negative forces, eventually nations fail. Sadly, the negative force's influences are so gradual and well-orchestrated that generations of people never see the results in their lifetime. However, for godly parents blessed to see the lives of their grand or great grand-children who turn to the world, God's Word and prayer provides their only comfort. Therefore, understanding the positive attributes early in life is critical. Not only for the current generation, but for future generations as well.

As I stated in my introduction, religious leadership and ***false*** teachers in academia are accountable for the lack of knowledge about the positive attributes in society. In addition to this group, people who claim to be spiritual, but neither religious or Christian, have emerged to further add confusion in the war campaign. Please do not be ***deceived***. Their actions are just another part of the strategy in spiritual warfare to entrap uneducated souls. Do not confuse any of these groups with the Christian community. In fact, from the Biblical record, as one meditates on the idea of what is Christian and what is religious, here are four important points to remember:

- *"…if you died with Christ from the basic principles of the world, why, as though living in the world, do you subject yourselves to regulations— "Do not touch, do not taste, do not handle," which all concern things which perish with the using—according to the commandments and doctrines of men? These things indeed have an appearance of wisdom in self-imposed religion, false humility, and neglect of the body, but are of no value against the indulgence of the flesh"* (Colossians 2:20-23)

- *"If anyone among you thinks he is religious, and does not bridle his tongue but deceives his own heart, this one's religion is useless"* (James 1:26)

- *"Pure and undefiled religion before God and the Father is this: to visit orphans and widows in their trouble, and to keep oneself unspotted from the world"* (James 1:27)

- And if a follower of Christ, Jesus said, *"But why do you call Me 'Lord, Lord,' and not do the things which I say? Whoever comes to Me, and hears My sayings and does them, I will show you whom he is like: He is like a man building a house, who dug deep and laid the foundation on the rock. And when the flood arose, the stream beat vehemently against that house, and could not shake it, for it was founded on the rock. But he who heard and did nothing is like a man who built a house on the earth without a foundation, against which the stream beat vehemently; and immediately it fell. And the ruin of that house was great"* (Luke 6:6-49)

These distinctions are important to understand in spiritual warfare and the war campaign. For most religious leaders, ***false*** teachers in academia, and spiritualist cannot <u>discern</u> God's Word. These are the same people who have placed themselves and self-knowledge over the Word of God. The negative attributes profoundly influence their inner spirits and they are unaware of their captivity. Paul captured this idea when he told the Jews of his time, *"Do you not know that to whom you present yourselves slaves to obey, you are that one's slaves whom you obey, whether of sin leading to death, or of obedience leading to **righteousness**?"* (Romans 6:16). Further Paul documented, *"Now the Spirit expressly says that in latter times some will depart from the **faith**, giving heed to deceiving spirits and doctrines of demons, speaking lies in hypocrisy, having their own conscience seared with a hot iron, forbidding to marry, and commanding to abstain from foods which God created to be received with thanksgiving by those who believe and know the truth"* (1 Timothy 4:1-3). But here is the most important point of all. These religious leaders, ***false*** teachers in academia, spiritualist, <u>and their followers</u> will all answer to God for their ***deception***. Ignorance on the Day of Judgement will not be excused for the Biblical record documents for all, *"Truly, these times of ignorance God overlooked, but now commands all men everywhere to repent, because He has appointed a day on which He will judge the world in **righteousness** by the Man whom He has ordained. He has given assurance of this to all by raising Him from the dead."* (Acts 17:30-31).

To make spiritual warfare even more complicated, one must understand that there are additional elements that exist on the spiritual battlefield beyond the attributes and the fog. Religious leaders and scholars have failed to see the strategic significance of these elements although they have impacted spiritual warfare and the balance of the campaign since the beginning of time. These elements are "<u>*strife*</u>" and "<u>*calamity*</u>." The element of <u>*strife*</u> comes from man influenced by the negative attributes. However, the element of <u>*calamity*</u> comes from God and occurs in an epic supernatural manner. The operation of these two elements can occur separately or combine to destroy entire households, churches, communities, societies and even nations. It takes BTT and <u>*discernment*</u> to grasp the operation of these elements. However, the full operation of the element of <u>*calamity*</u> may never be fully understood in one's lifetime as it can impact masses of people over generations to complete God's will.

I will begin with the element of <u>*strife*</u> and then discuss <u>*calamity*</u>. I want to keep these terms separated for one to see their roles in the war campaign. Both elements will appear in an <u>*italic underlined*</u> font. The attributes will maintain their ***bold italic text*** while the eight categories will simply be in **bold text**; not italic.

STRIFE

"The beginning of strife is like releasing water; therefore stop contention before a quarrel starts"

~ Proverbs 17:14

The online Merriam-Webster dictionary's defines *strife* in the following way:

- bitter sometimes **violent** conflict or dissension <political *strife*>
- an act of contention: fight, struggle
- exertion or contention for superiority

This worldly definition is enough if one desires only to know that *strife* exists. However, if one desires to fully understand spiritual warfare and the war campaign, one must open God's Word. The Biblical record is the only document humanity has for understanding the full ramifications of this element. The Spirit of wisdom revealed some interesting things to Solomon about this element and its origin. First, Wisdom revealed that *strife* is the by-product of several of the negative attributes. Here are some examples Solomon documented:

- "**Hatred** *stirs up strife, but love covers all sins*" (Proverbs 10:12). The influence of the **hater** attribute brings *strife*.

- "*By **pride** comes nothing but strife, but with the well-advised is wisdom*" (Proverbs 13:10), and, "*He who is of a **proud** heart stirs up strife, but he who trusts in the Lord will be prospered*" (Proverbs 28:25). The influence of the **proud** attribute brings *strife*.

- "*An **angry** man stirs up strife, and a **furious** man abounds in transgression*" (Proverbs 29:22), and "*He who loves transgression loves strife, and he who exalts his gate seeks destruction*" (Proverbs 17:19), and "*A **wrathful** man stirs up strife, but he who is slow to **anger** allays contention*" (Proverbs 15:18), and "*For as the churning of milk produces butter, and wringing the nose produces blood, so the forcing of **wrath** produces strife*" (Proverbs 30:33). The influence of the **angry**, **furious**, and **violent** attributes brings *strife*.

- "*A **perverse** man sows' strife, and a whisperer separates the best of friends*" (Proverbs 16:28). The influence of the **perverse** attribute brings *strife*.

- "*Where there is no wood, the fire goes out; and where there is no **talebearer**, strife ceases*" (Proverbs 26:20). The influence of the **talebearer** attribute brings *strife*.

- "*Cast out the **scoffer**, and contention will leave; yes, strife and reproach will cease*" (Proverbs 22:10). The influence of the **scoffer** attribute brings *strife*.

From these verses, BTT allows one to see the magnitude of the social problems that homes, communities, nations and the world experiences when the negative attributes cause *strife*. The element of *strife* destroys good relationships and brings vital communications to a standstill. But one should also consider, the negative attributes working together magnify the negative attributes influences on unmeasurable levels and cause _strife_ to flow in countless directions. The results lead to skirmishes and physical conflict. Even people who do not even know what started the original issue get caught up in the turmoil. These are the people who simply become collateral damage to the _strife_ generated by spiritual warfare. Moreover, BTT allows one to see that when the ***furious*** and ***violent*** attributes begin to influence people's inner spirits, ***bloodshed*** and death are somewhere near. But here is the greater condemnation. The church is the place to learn about these attributes and their ability to create the element of _strife_. When churches fail in this responsibility, parents have no means to protect themselves; and children grow up without the Truth. If parents do not learn these things, they cannot teach their children properly. If children never learn these things, generations move further away from the Truth of the Gospel and the negative forces of the war campaign rule using the element of _strife_. I submit to you that this is a significant part of the problem the world faces today.

The Spirit of wisdom summed this idea up by using three metaphors to explain the harmful effects of the element of _strife_ to Solomon. BTT allows one to see the truth and potency behind Wisdom's comments. She revealed to Solomon:

- *"Better is a dry morsel with quietness, than a house full of feasting with _strife_"* (Proverbs 17:1)

- *"The beginning of _strife_ is like releasing water; therefore stop **contention** before a quarrel starts"* (Proverbs 17:14)

- *"As charcoal is to burning coals, and wood to fire, so is a **contentious** man to kindle _strife_"* (Proverbs 26:21)

Through these proverbial metaphors, one can see the destructive nature of the element of _strife_. The bottom line from the Spirit of Wisdom to Solomon was, "*stop **contention** before a quarrel starts.*" If Wisdom said it, it must be true.

Consider what the rest of the Biblical record documented about the element of _strife_. Starting in the Book of Genesis, one can see that Cain experienced the element of _strife_ when he rose up and ***murdered*** his brother Abel. The Lord asked Cain, "..."*Why are you **angry**? And why has your countenance fallen? If you do well, will you not be accepted? And if you do not do well, sin lies at the door. And its desire is for you, but you should rule over it*"" (Genesis 4:6-7). One should see that the Lord saw the element of _strife_ growing in Cain because of the ***angry*** and ***furious*** attributes (Proverbs 15:18; 17:19) and God gave Cain the remedy for it. Moreover, the Lord told Cain in advance what the results would be if he did not rule over the negative forces desiring to influence his inner spirit and stop the element of _strife_. The choice was with Cain. The _strife_ in Cain was internal. Abel did nothing to provoke Cain other than by doing God's will. The Biblical record documented that Cain failed to listen to God. It documented, "...*Cain rose up against Abel his brother and **killed** him*" (Genesis 4:8). From the beginning of mankind, this first example documented the power of the element of _strife_.

Later in the Book of Genesis, the element of _strife_ appeared between the households of Abram and Lot. The Biblical record documented that these two men were both in the **rich** category. BTT allows one to see that the positive attributes influenced them. They had so much **wealth** that "*...the land was not able to support them, that they might dwell together, for their **possessions were so great** that they could not dwell together. And there was* <u>strife</u> *between the herdsmen of Abram's livestock and the herdsmen of Lot's livestock...*" (Genesis 13:6-7). BTT allows one to see that the crowded conditions became fertile ground for the negative attributes. In fact, BTT allows one to see that the positive attributes influencing the inner spirits of Abram and Lot were mature enough to protect them. Therefore, the negative attributes went after their herdsmen. Please do not miss this small point. Abram, trusting in the Lord, took the high ground to stop the element of <u>strife</u> from spreading by suggesting he and Lot separate their two camps. Consider the words of Abram and how he stopped the element of <u>strife</u> in its tracks. The Biblical record documented in Genesis 13:8-11:

> "*So Abram said to Lot, "Please let there be no* <u>strife</u> *between you and me, and between my herdsmen and your herdsmen; for we are brethren. Is not the whole land before you? Please separate from me. If you take the left, then I will go to the right; or, if you go to the right, then I will go to the left." And Lot lifted his eyes and saw all the plain of Jordan, that it was well watered everywhere (before the Lord destroyed Sodom and Gomorrah) like the garden of the Lord, like the land of Egypt as you go toward Zoar. Then Lot chose for himself all the plain of Jordan, and Lot journeyed east. And they separated from each other."*

There are many more examples that capture illustrations of the element of <u>strife</u> found in the Book of Genesis. For this reason, I encourage you to continue to read your Bible with a <u>discern</u>ing eye now that you know what to look for. Moving on, Moses dealt with the element of <u>strife</u> as it attempted to destroy God's people once they left the Egyptian captivity. BTT allows one to see how the element of <u>strife</u> soured the Israelite's behavior in the Books of Exodus and Numbers. The Biblical record documented from the Lord, "*For in the Wilderness of Zin, during the* <u>strife</u> *of the congregation, you rebelled against My command to hallow Me at the waters before their eyes." (These are the waters of Meribah, at Kadesh in the Wilderness of Zin)*" (Numbers 27:14). The element of <u>strife</u> was so corrosive among the Israelites that the Lord had to slay many of the people before they even reached the Promised Land.

The element of <u>strife</u> plagued the children of Israel from the time they left Egypt forward. I encourage you to read the Bible from the perspective of the war campaign to appreciate how the negative attributes and the element of <u>strife</u> influenced the Israelites to sin repeatedly. However, keep in mind, the element of <u>strife</u> remained among the children of Israel because they continued to allow the negative attribute's influence in their inner spirits. They refused to truly repent or stay obedient to God's Word. Even when they did repent, because they were a "stiff-necked" people (see Exodus 32:9; Exodus 33:3; Exodus 33:5; Exodus 34:9; Deuteronomy 9:6; Deuteronomy 9:13; Deuteronomy 10:16; 2 Chronicles 30:8; Acts 7:51), they reverted back to sin.

David the Psalmist commented on how the **goodness** of God is unaffected by the element of <u>strife</u>. However, for people to taste God's **goodness**, conditions do apply. David documented, "*Oh, how great is Your **goodness**, which You have laid up for those who* <u>fear</u> *You, which You have prepared for those who trust in You in the presence of the sons of men!*

You shall hide them in the secret place of Your presence from the plots of man; You shall keep them secretly in a pavilion from the <u>strife</u> of tongues" (Psalm 31:19-20). BTT allows one to see that God's **goodness** is available to those who <u>*fear*</u> and trust Him. <u>*Fear*</u> and trust are His conditions. God keeps His **goodness** in places unseen by humanity and away from the element of <u>strife</u>; the by-product of numerous negative attributes.

The Psalmist clearly understood where the element of <u>strife</u> originated. He knew that the negative attributes were present when he saw the manifestation of bad behaviors among his people. Because he understood that the issues were spiritual in nature, I believe, it prodded him to call on the Lord for help instead of relying on physical means or self-knowledge to resolve the issues. BTT allows one to see the Psalmist's view when he documented these words in Psalm 55:9-15. Look closely at the last sentence. He wrote:

> *"Destroy, O Lord, and divide their tongues, for I have seen **violence** and <u>strife</u> in the city. Day and night they go around it on its walls; iniquity and trouble are also in the midst of it. Destruction is in its midst; **oppression** and **deceit** do not depart from its streets. For it is not an enemy who reproaches me; then I could bear it. Nor is it one who **hates** me who has exalted himself against me; then I could hide from him. But it was you, a man my equal, my companion and my acquaintance. We took sweet **counsel** together, and walked to the house of God in the throng. Let death seize them; let them go down alive into hell, for **wickedness** is in their dwellings and among them."*

One should see that behind the carnal thoughts of men were negative attributes influencing their behavior. These negative influences created the element of <u>strife</u>. The Psalmist called on the Lord to intervene. God could immediately destroy the spiritual influences and stop the spiritual warfare surrounding the Psalmist. However, BTT allows one to see that the first line of defense for stopping <u>strife</u> belongs to people who claim the **good** attributes. The Lord intervenes when His people become too few to make a difference. But this is seldom the case.

In the Book of Isaiah, the author documented how some of the negative attributes had deceived the nation of Israel's leadership. The negative attributes had influenced the religious leadership to incorporate the element of <u>strife</u> into one of God's activities. This activity was "fasting." Through the prophet Isaiah, God pointed out their corruption and the correct use of this activity. The Biblical record documented in Isaiah 58:3-9:

> *"Why have we fasted,' they say, 'and You have not seen? Why have we afflicted our souls, and You take no notice? In fact, in the day of your fast you find pleasure, and exploit all your laborers. Indeed you fast for <u>strife</u> and debate, and to strike with the fist of **wickedness**. You will not fast as you do this day, to make your voice heard on high. Is it a fast that I have chosen, a day for a man to afflict his soul? Is it to bow down his head like a bulrush, and to spread out sackcloth and ashes? Would you call this a fast, and an acceptable day to the Lord? "Is this not the fast that I have chosen: To loose the bonds of **wickedness**, to undo the heavy burdens, to let the **oppressed** go free, and that you break every yoke? Is it not to share your bread with the hungry, and that you bring to your house the **poor** who are*

*cast out; when you see the naked, that you cover him, and not hide yourself from your own flesh? Then your light shall break forth like the morning, your healing shall spring forth speedily, and your **righteousness** shall go before you; the glory of the Lord shall be your rear guard. Then you shall call, and the Lord will answer; You shall cry, and He will say, 'Here I am.'"*

BTT allows one to see that God sets specific rules for the activities that He requires from man. But when the negative forces through spiritual warfare get involved, the generated fog distorts and confuses God's commands. This is what happened to Israel's religious leadership. They introduced the element of <u>strife</u> into an activity that God had defined. Changing His standard amounted to nothing but sin. The negative forces used a **deceptive** strategy that influenced the people to think they had the authority to change God's established standard. This **lie** cost them dearly. They fasted and God ignored their pleas.

The prophet Habakkuk commented on the element of <u>strife</u> as he saw the problems infesting the nation of Israel. He said to the Lord, *"Why do You show me iniquity, and cause me to see trouble? For plundering and **violence** are before me; there is <u>strife</u>, and **contention** arises. Therefore the law is powerless, and justice never goes forth. For the **wicked** surround the **righteous**; therefore **perverse** judgment proceeds"* (Habakkuk 1:3-4). What a powerful statement. BTT allows one to see that while the element of <u>strife</u> is present, **perversion** and **wickedness** are also in play. Remember, **perversion** and **wickedness** come from the **perverse** and **wicked** attributes; two **unclean spirits** that caused major damage in the conduct of spiritual warfare. These attributes produce and then feed on the element of <u>strife</u>. This is a spiritual process occurring in the war campaign. Therefore, rationalization by worldly science or academia is futile. As <u>strife</u> keeps confusion and contention going in the world, the negative attributes influence leaders to place barriers between God and His Word.

As the Old Testament closes and the New Testament begins, one can see the element of <u>strife</u> as it traverses the pages of the Biblical record. Paul made this point when he documented a fact about people who attempt to block the knowledge of the one True God from their minds. Paul documented this painful statement in Romans 1:28-31:

> *"And even as they did not like to retain God in their knowledge, God gave them over to a debased mind, to do those things which are not fitting; being filled with all **unrighteousness, sexual immorality, wickedness, covetousness, maliciousness; full of envy, murder, <u>strife</u>, deceit, evil-mindedness**; they are **whisperers, backbiters, haters of God, violent, proud, boasters, inventors of evil things, disobedient to parents, un<u>discerning</u>, untrustworthy, unloving, unforgiving, unmerciful**; who, knowing the righteous judgment of God, that those who practice such things are deserving of death, not only do the same but also approve of those who practice them."*

One should understand from Paul's statement that all the negative attributes are documented somewhere in this lineup along with the element of <u>strife</u>. For those who know God and are content to follow Him and Jesus Christ, Paul wrote, *"Let us walk properly, as in the day, not in revelry and drunkenness, not in lewdness and <u>lust</u>, not in <u>strife</u> and **envy**. But* *put on the Lord Jesus Christ, and make no provision for the flesh, to fulfill its lusts*" (Romans 13:13-14). The Biblical record reveals the truth about the element of *strife* and Christ's Gospel is the key for one's protection against it.

When Paul wrote his letter to the church in Corinth, he warned them about the element of *strife*. Before this warning, he pointed out their lack of spiritual maturity for understanding God's Word. He wrote, "*And I, brethren, could not speak to you as to spiritual people but as to carnal, as to babes in Christ. I fed you with milk and not with solid food; for until now you were not able to receive it, and even now you are still not able; for you are still carnal. For where there are **envy**, strife, and divisions among you, are you not carnal and behaving like mere men?*" (1 Corinthians 3:1-3). BTT allows one to see that the negative attributes were influencing the behaviors of the congregation in the Corinthian church. The attributes were causing divisions among the people. In fact, the element of *strife* was causing the congregation to argue and divide themselves over who taught them the Gospel according to 1 Corinthians 3:4. Paul explained to them, "*Who then is Paul, and who is Apollos, but ministers through whom you believed, as the Lord gave to each one? I planted, Apollos watered, but God gave the increase. So then neither he who plants is anything, nor he who waters, but God who gives the increase. Now he who plants and he who waters are one, and each one will receive his own reward according to his own labor*" (1 Corinthian 3:5-8). Division is simply a mindset brought on by the element of *strife*. Division is prevalent in the religious community. Unfortunately, it has taken root and some of Christ's churches too.

Paul provided an excellent lesson on what a Christian's attitude should be even amid attacks by those influenced by the negative attributes. He first documented to the church in Philippi that, "*...I want you to know, brethren, that the things which happened to me have actually turned out for the furtherance of the gospel, so that it has become evident to the whole palace guard, and to all the rest, that my chains are in Christ...*" (Philippians 1:12-13). Then he went on to say, "*Some indeed preach Christ even from **envy** and strife, and some also from **goodwill**: The former preach Christ from **selfish ambition**, not sincerely, supposing to add affliction to my chains; but the latter out of love, knowing that I am appointed for the defense of the gospel. What then? Only that in every way, whether in pretense or in truth, Christ is preached; and in this I rejoice, yes, and will rejoice*" (Philippians 1:15-18). BTT allows one to see that Paul's comments require the context occurring with his circumstance at the time to understand his statement. He was not rationalizing the use of the element of *strife* as a means to further the Gospel of Jesus Christ in the world. No! He was simply saying during the times of his imprisonment, if people influenced by the ***jealous/envious*** attribute preached Christ for their own selfish ambition, or if they used the element of *strife* to add affliction to his chains, he did not care as long as the preaching of Jesus occurred. Paul was stating that it is Jesus Christ and His message that is important; it is not about him and nor is it about us today. Like Paul, I am nothing compared to the Word of Jesus Christ.

When Paul wrote to Timothy, he shared some pearls of wisdom about the element of *strife*. First, where it concerned the Gospel, he told Timothy, "*If anyone teaches otherwise and does not consent to wholesome words, even the words of our Lord Jesus Christ, and to the doctrine which accords with godliness, he is **proud**, knowing nothing, but is obsessed with disputes and arguments over words, from which come **envy**, strife, reviling, **evil***

suspicions, *useless wranglings of men of corrupt minds and destitute of the truth, who suppose that **godliness** is a means of gain. From such withdraw yourself"* (1 Timothy 6:3-5). Paul's letter to Timothy was directed to Christians who wanted to argue over God's clear Word. This is very important to understand. Paul told Timothy that negative attributes were present and were influencing the behavior behind the people's actions and the element of <u>strife</u> would follow. Paul rightly told Timothy to withdraw from those individuals. He did not want Timothy or anyone else to get lost in the fog of their ***folly***. This comment leads to another pearl of wisdom about the element of <u>strife</u> for Timothy.

Paul stated, *"Flee also youthful lusts; but pursue **righteousness**, **faith**, love, peace with those who call on the Lord out of a pure heart. But avoid **foolish** and ignorant disputes, knowing that they generate <u>strife</u>. And a servant of the Lord must not quarrel but be gentle to all, able to teach, patient, in humility correcting those who are in opposition, if God perhaps will grant them repentance, so that they may know the truth, and that they may come to their senses and escape the snare of the devil, having been taken captive by him to do his will"* (2 Timothy 2:22-26). Paul's words expressed many of the things that happen when the negative attributes influence one's inner spirit. One becomes a captive of the devil; the negative force's leader. BTT allows one to see that Paul clearly drew a correlation between the influence of the ***fool*** attribute and the element of <u>strife</u>. The influence of the ***fool*** attribute on humanity has generated incredible amounts of the element of <u>strife</u> between believers of the Biblical record and non-believers. But as Paul told Timothy, one must not quarrel; for quarrels, arguments, or disputes produce the element of <u>strife</u>. This means the negative attributes are empowered as spiritual warfare blossoms. BTT allows one to see, not only are the people involved in the <u>strife</u> impacted, <u>strife</u> also shipwrecks the ***faith*** and conscience of others listening or observing the dispute according to 1 Timothy 1:19. The Holy Spirit led Paul to document that it is better to avoid ***foolish*** and ignorant disputes rather than entangle oneself in them. One must simply learn to walk away from the traps baited by people influenced by the negative attributes.

Finally, to place more emphasis on the results of the element of <u>strife</u>, if it not controlled, James expressed what occurs. He wrote, *"Where do wars and fights come from among you? Do they not come from your desires for pleasure that war in your members? You **lust** and do not have. You **murder** and **covet** and cannot obtain. You fight and war. Yet you do not have because you do not ask. You ask and do not receive, because you ask amiss, that you may spend it on your pleasures"* (James 4:1-3). BTT allows one to see that if the element of <u>strife</u> working in one's inner spirit is not controlled, it will lead one to physical confrontation and even war. The element of <u>strife</u> leads one to acquire the influences of the ***anger***, ***furious***, and ***violent*** attributes which eventually leads to ***bloodshed***. Remember, the ***angry***, ***furious***, and ***violent*** attributes are all progressively dangerous negative attributes.

With this said, consider the impact of the element of <u>strife</u> on people in leadership positions ranging from teachers, church leaders, businesses, the military, the government, or a leader of a country. When the element of <u>strife</u> influences a leader, chaos reins at every echelon below them. Therefore, understanding the element of <u>strife</u> from the Biblical perspective is crucial for understanding what occurs holistically in every one's life. The element of <u>strife</u> on an uninformed leader has great impact on his or her inner spirits and the people who are completely unaware of spiritual warfare and its danger.

CALAMITY

"That they may know from the rising of the sun to its setting that there is none besides Me. I am the Lord, and there is no other; I form the light and create darkness, I make peace and create <u>calamity</u>; I, the Lord, do all these things."

~ Isaiah 45:6-7

The element of <u>calamity</u>, fully documented in the Biblical record, is far different from the element of <u>strife</u>. The Merriam-Webster dictionary defines <u>calamity</u> as a state of deep distress or misery caused by major misfortune or loss from a natural or an economic catastrophe. However, spiritual warfare suggests much more than this definition. BTT suggests that when the negative attributes and the element of <u>strife</u> rises to epic levels, God may use a supernatural phenomenon known as <u>calamity</u>. *Calamities* come in the form of earthly phenomena. These phenomena supernaturally restore the balance of the war campaign. This may be to refocus people on God's omnipotent power, or to get the attention of His people, or to purge Christ's church of some hidden sin within its midst. Stop reading for a moment and meditate on this thought. <u>Calamity</u> in the war campaign comes about because of epic sin on the spiritual battlefield for mankind cannot fathom the power, reach, or all the forms of spiritual **wickedness** in the world. The influence of **wickedness** is so corrosive that the people influenced by it "… *do not know, nor do they understand; they walk about in darkness;* **<u>all the foundations of the earth are unstable</u>**" (Psalms 82:5). This knowledge is deep and a lot to digest.

Now for clarity, I am not talking about the random weather conditions that come in the form of hurricanes, tornadoes, floods, famine, plagues, drought, pestilence, earthquakes, fire, hail, or snow that are governed by the natural laws of nature that God put in place. God controls the natural weather activity. The Biblical record documents that God said, "*While the earth remains, seedtime and harvest, cold and heat, winter and summer, and day and night shall not cease*" (Genesis 8:22). Further, the Biblical writers wrote:

- "…*He changes the times and the seasons…*" (Daniel 2:21)

- "*He appointed the moon for seasons; the sun knows its going down*" (Psalm 104:19)

- "*He caused an east wind to blow in the heavens; and by His power He brought in the south wind*" (Psalm 78:26)

- "*For He commands and raises the stormy wind, which lifts up the waves of the sea*" (Psalm 107:25)

And nor am I referring to the natural sicknesses or diseases that befalls the body due to age, weather, wounds, or plagues. I am referring to God's <u>calamity</u> that occurs in such an epic way and on such a large scale to groups of people that the human mind cannot comprehend it or the outcome. The Biblical record documents supernatural events of this nature in numerous places. Moreover, BTT allows one to see that short of taking one's life, like the **rich** man in Luke 12: 16-21, God in his infinite wisdom has multiple ways to get one's attention when the things of this life take precedence over Him. Even economic destruction has a way of removing the blinders that hinder one from seeing the Almighty God. Through these measures, God demonstrates His great _love_ and _longsuffering_ for people's souls; sometimes on a massive scale. When God's _calamity_ comes, He brings it to fulfill His Word. The Psalmist documented, "_Fire and hail, snow and clouds; stormy wind, fulfilling His word…_" (Psalm 148:8). Moreover, he documented "_Upon the **wicked** He will rain coals; fire and brimstone and a burning wind shall be the portion of their cup_" (Psalm 11:6). But of all the Biblical writers, the prophet Amos illustrated the difference between the natural weather and God's use of _calamity_ in his writings about the nation of Israel's disobedience. Amos wrote from the Lord as documented in Amos 4:7-13

> "_I also withheld rain from you, when there were still three months to the harvest. I made it rain on one city, I withheld rain from another city. One part was rained upon, and where it did not rain the part withered. So two or three cities wandered to another city to drink water, but they were not satisfied; yet you have not returned to Me," says the Lord. "I blasted you with blight and mildew. When your gardens increased, your vineyards, your fig trees, and your olive trees, the locust devoured them; yet you have not returned to Me," says the Lord. "I sent among you a plague after the manner of Egypt; your young men I killed with a sword, along with your captive horses; I made the stench of your camps come up into your nostrils; yet you have not returned to Me," says the Lord. "I overthrew some of you, as God overthrew Sodom and Gomorrah, and you were like a firebrand plucked from the burning; yet you have not returned to Me," says the Lord. "Therefore thus will I do to you, O Israel; because I will do this to you, prepare to meet your God, O Israel!" For behold, He who forms mountains, and creates the wind, Who declares to man what his thought is, and makes the morning darkness, Who treads the high places of the earth—The Lord God of hosts is His name_"

When God's _calamity_ strikes, God's people must recognize it for what it is, repent, pray, and refocus on His will. BTT allows one to see that others will be afraid for a time, but will revert to their normal way of life and remain spiritually lost. They are lost because of the fog generated by the negative forces of the war campaign. The fog retards them from seeing or hearing the Truth. The Biblical record reveals facts about this, but before I go any further, I must make one thing clear. The human mind fathoming the scope of God's use of _calamity_ is not possible. His timing, ways, and results are wide-reaching. More importantly, God's timing for His use of _calamity_ is unknowable by man's measures from science, theology, or mathematical calculations. God's actions are unfathomable for three distinct truths that God shared in the Biblical record by His inspired writers. They are:

- "_But You, O Lord, are a God full of compassion, and gracious, longsuffering and abundant in mercy and truth_" (Psalm 86:15; also Exodus 34:6)

- "But, beloved, do not forget this one thing, that with the Lord <u>one day is as a thousand years, and a thousand years as one day</u>" (2 Peter 3:8; also Psalm 90:4)

- "For as the heavens are higher than the earth, so are <u>My ways higher than your ways, and My thoughts than your thoughts</u>" (Isaiah 55:9)

In other words, the very attributes of God Himself allow Him to have an abundance of <u>patience</u> with His creation which gives mankind the opportunity to repent, or through generations, the opportunity to refocus on Him. The Bible even documented that, "*The Lord is not slack concerning His promise, as some count slackness, but is longsuffering toward us, not willing that any should perish but that all should come to repentance*" (2 Peter 3:9). However, if one rejects his or her opportunity for repentance, his or her choice will gain them the same status and consequences as the people of the nation of Israel. The Lord told them, "*My eye will not spare, nor will I have pity; I will repay you according to your ways, and your abominations will be in your midst. Then you shall know that I am the Lord who strikes*" (Ezekiel 7:9). This warning still applies to everyone who refuses to repent of sin.

God's creation tends to forget the past. Solomon documented, "*There is no remembrance of former things, nor will there be any remembrance of things that are to come by those who will come after*" (Ecclesiastes 1:11). Be that as it may, God allows His creation maximum time to make corrections. Sadly, few people take the opportunity to correct themselves. This has been true throughout time. And yet, God's longsuffering remains firm. Thus, BTT allows one to understand that when God decides to use *calamity*, its use is necessary. I believe God uses *calamity* to make corrections in the balance of spiritual warfare. This happens when the negative forces of the war campaign reach epic levels and God decides He will no longer tolerate the negative force's actions. In fact, Jesus Himself had the ability to command God's *calamity*. For example, when the mob came to arrest Him on the night He was betrayed, He told Peter (John 18:10) to "*Put your sword in its place, for all who take the sword will perish by the sword. Or do you think that I cannot now pray to My Father, and He will provide Me with more than twelve legions of angels? ...*" (Matthew 26:52-54). Twelve legions of angels would have decimated the nation of Israel. God's *calamity* would have been swift. But Jesus understood the war campaign before Him and controlled the moment. Moreover, Jesus could extend the use of God's calamity to others. The Book of Luke provides an example of this. The Bible documented Jesus, "*...sent messengers before His face. And as they went, they entered a village of the Samaritans, to prepare for Him. But they did not receive Him, because His face was set for the journey to Jerusalem. And when His disciples James and John saw this, they said, "Lord, do You want us to <u>command fire to come down from heaven and consume them</u>, just as Elijah did?" But He turned and rebuked them, and said, "You do not know what manner of spirit you are of. For the Son of Man did not come to destroy men's lives but to save them." And they went to another village*" (Luke 9:52-56). In this example, Jesus demonstrated His deity and His ability to extend His authority to others. James and John demonstrated the influence of the negative attributes as the fog of spiritual warfare momentarily blinded their inner spirits. They were ready to misuse the power that Jesus had empowered them with.

To give one an even greater understanding of God's calamity, consider how the spiritual battlefield's conditions were shaped to invite His calamity on the nation of Israel in the Old Testament. While reading this discourse, think about the world's conditions today to visualize the spiritual battlefield. The prophet Isaiah documented the following words in Isaiah 59:1-15:

> "Behold, the Lord's hand is not shortened, that it cannot save; nor His ear heavy, that it cannot hear. But your iniquities have separated you from your God; and your sins have hidden His face from you, so that He will not hear. For your hands are **defiled with blood**, and your fingers with iniquity; your lips have spoken **lies**, your tongue has muttered **perversity**. No one calls for justice, nor does any plead for truth. They trust in empty words and speak **lies**; they conceive **evil** and bring forth iniquity. They hatch vipers' eggs and weave the spider's web; he who eats of their eggs dies, and from that which is crushed a viper breaks out. Their webs will not become garments, nor will they cover themselves with their works; their works are works of iniquity, and the act of **violence** is in their hands. Their feet run to **evil**, and they make haste to **shed innocent blood**; their thoughts are thoughts of iniquity; wasting and destruction are in their paths. The way of peace they have not known, and there is **no justice** in their ways; They have made themselves crooked paths; whoever takes that way shall not know peace. Therefore justice is far from us, nor does **righteousness** overtake us; we look for light, but there is darkness! For brightness, but we walk in blackness! We grope for the wall like the blind, and we grope as if we had no eyes; and stumble at noonday as at twilight; we are as dead men in desolate places. We all growl like bears, and moan sadly like doves; we look for justice, but there is none; for salvation, but it is far from us. For our transgressions are multiplied before You, and our sins testify against us; for our transgressions are with us, and as for our iniquities, we know them: In **transgressing** and **lying** against the Lord, and departing from our God, speaking **oppression** and **revolt**, conceiving and uttering from the heart words of **falsehood**. Justice is turned back, and **righteousness** stands afar off; for truth is fallen in the street, and equity cannot enter. So truth fails, and he who departs from **evil** makes himself a prey."

With this image now in mind, consider what the Spirit of wisdom revealed about God's calamity. First, Wisdom revealed to Solomon how she looked upon those with the **simple** attribute; a negative attribute identified earlier in this book. Please consider closely what Wisdom said. Solomon documented, "*How long, you **simple** ones, will you love **simplicity**? For **scorners** delight in their scorning, and **fools hate** knowledge. Turn at my rebuke; surely I will pour out my spirit on you; I will make my words known to you. Because I have called and you refused, I have stretched out my hand and no one regarded, because you disdained all my **counsel**, and would have none of my rebuke, I also will laugh at your calamity; I will **mock** when your terror comes, when your terror comes like a storm, and your destruction comes like a whirlwind, when distress and anguish come upon you*" (Proverbs 1:22-27). Wisdom placed her emphasis on people influenced by the **simple** attribute in this proverb. However, she also identified the **scoffer** and **fool** attributes in the text. She did not tell

Solomon that people influenced by the **simple** attribute would receive *calamity* by a physical *storm* or *whirlwind*. No! BTT allows one to see their *calamity* would come "like" those two natural disasters. In other words, the person influenced by the **simple** attribute would experience something as severe as these natural disasters. Wisdom's words described the severity of God's *calamity* that would befall a person with the **simple** attribute if they continued their **simple** path. One must understand, when God's Word says to do something, and the influence of the **simple** attribute leads one to ignore God's Word and remain in a **simple** state of mind enjoying sin and the pleasures of life, God's *calamity* will be severe. BTT allows one to see that God's *calamity* is severe because personal choices and behavior do not allow one to see God's *calamity* coming. Unfortunately, often when friends, neighbors, relatives, or others offer warnings to people influenced by the **simple** attribute, their personal desires for **simplicity** retards their hearing and they continue down the dark path of life. This is why the influence of the **simple** attribute falls among the negative attributes. One's state of mind is a choice and one's desire to remain in this state is detrimental to one's soul.

Later the Spirit of wisdom declared to Solomon that *calamity* struck people who allowed the combined influences of the **wicked** and **perverse** attributes and involved themselves in **evil** activities. She revealed to him, "A worthless person, a **wicked** man, walks with a **perverse** mouth; he winks with his eyes, he shuffles his feet, he points with his fingers; **perversity** is in his heart, he **devises evil** continually, he sows discord. Therefore his *calamity* shall come suddenly; suddenly he shall be *broken without remedy*" (Proverbs 6:12-15). Before one dwell on the results of God's *calamity* for this person, consider the fact that this person also "*sowed discord.*" This discord is another way of saying that the person, with all the negative attributes identified influencing his or her inner spirit, also generated the element of *strife*. BTT allows one to see that a person with this combination of negative attributes influencing their behavior and generating *strife*, is a major force to contend with in spiritual warfare. Whether they are aware or unaware of their behavior, this person can exponentially advance the negative forces of the war campaign. Wisdom revealed to Solomon that *calamity* for this person would come suddenly, and "*... he shall be broken without remedy.*" King Jehoram (2 Chronicles 21:18) and King Herod (Acts 12:23) are examples of this occurrence documented in the Biblical record.

Consider some more pearls of wisdom that specifically pertain to people with the **wicked** attribute and their demise through *calamity*. The Spirit of wisdom revealed to Solomon:

- "*Do not lie in wait, O **wicked** man, against the dwelling of the **righteous**; do not plunder his resting place; for a **righteous** man may fall seven times and rise again, but the **wicked** shall fall by calamity*" (Proverbs 24:15-16)

- "*When the whirlwind passes by, the **wicked** is no more, but the **righteous** has an everlasting foundation*" (Proverbs 10:25)

But one should not think that God's *calamity* comes only to people influenced by the **wicked** attribute. No! The Spirit of wisdom also revealed to Solomon that *calamity* comes to:

- People who rejoice over another person's _calamity_. Wisdom shared, "*He who **mocks** the **poor** reproaches his Maker; he who is glad at _calamity_ will not go unpunished*" (Proverbs 17:5)

- People who associate with people given to change. Solomon stated, "*My son, _fear_ the Lord and the king; do not associate with those given to change; for their _calamity_ will rise suddenly, and who knows the ruin those two can bring?*" (Proverbs 24:21-22)

- People who harden their hearts against God. Solomon documented, "*Happy is the man who is always reverent, but he who hardens his heart will fall into _calamity_*" (Proverbs 28:14)

These powerful Biblical references should create grave concern for anyone who allows the influence of the negative attributes in their life. In Proverbs 24:21-22, Wisdom is specifically speaking about associating with people who alter God's unchanging Word. Religious leaders that change God's Word, and everyone who associates with these leaders, will face God's _calamity_. The Lord says in the Biblical record that, "*…I am the Lord, I do not change…*" (Malachi 3:6). When He sent His Son to die for the sins of man, the Bible also recorded "*Jesus Christ is the same yesterday, today, and forever. Do not be carried about with various and strange doctrines. For it is **good** that the heart be established by _grace_, not with foods which have not profited those who have been occupied with them*" (Hebrews 13:8-9). The spiritual element of _grace_ comes from God and He alone extends it to people who are trying their best to be obedient to His Word as He has given it - unchanged. God's Word leads one to **righteousness** and nothing else; and certainly, no manmade law can. This is why Paul stated, "*I do not set aside the _grace_ of God; for if **righteousness** comes through the law, then Christ died in vain*" (Galatians 2:21). This knowledge is significant, and one must try to understand that God will bring _calamity_ to change agents of His Word. When _calamity_ comes, it will happen suddenly. BTT allows one to see when God's _calamity_ comes, everyone found in association with the guilty risk consumption in His _wrath_. The negative forces of the war campaign relish **false** teachings about God's _grace_ and change agents who distort His Word.

One of the final things that the Spirit of wisdom revealed to Solomon about God's _calamity_ was, "*Do not forsake your own friend or your father's friend, nor go to your brother's house in the day of your _calamity_; better is a **neighbor** nearby than a brother far away*" (Proverbs 27:10). BTT suggests that when one experiences _calamity_ in one's life, one should not drag family members into it who live far away. They have no ability to analyze the truth behind the issues from a distance. Distance only invites the element of _strife_ to the table. BTT allows one to see the truth behind this proverb. A person in the **neighbor** category, someone close by, will more than likely know what is really behind the _calamity_, i.e. sinful activity. Therefore, a **neighbor**, especially one not related by blood, can provide an untainted, fair, and truthful assessment for the reason behind the _calamity_. At the same time, a **neighbor** can offer comfort and recommendation for dealing with the aftermath. Solomon learned that if one becomes a victim of God's _calamity_, approaching someone nearby in the **neighbor** category is the best option for understanding the _calamity_ and gaining a solution.

So, what can the Old Testament tell one about <u>*calamity*</u>? Well, one of the first **calamities** that one learns from God comes from the early pages in the Book of Genesis. BTT allows one to see that God used a <u>*calamity*</u> when He drove Adam and Eve from the garden. The Biblical record documented, *"So He drove out the man; and He placed cherubim at the east of the garden of Eden, and a flaming sword which turned every way, to guard the way to the tree of life"* (Genesis 3:24). For one to be forcibly removed from paradise and all they had ever known; to see a cherubim and a flaming sword blocking the entrance back to paradise, and to enter a world that they had to tame to make their home, was a <u>*calamity*</u> by every stretch of the imagination. Simply for most people, to see a cherubim would be a <u>*calamity*</u>. The prophet Ezekiel documented, *"This is the living creature I saw under the God of Israel by the River Chebar, and I knew they were cherubim. Each one had four faces and each one four wings, and the likeness of the hands of a man was under their wings"* (Ezekiel 10:19-21). Seeing this creature will bring <u>*calamity*</u> to the average person. Thus, this whole event was supernatural. Unfortunately, the generations that proceeded from their union gave way to the next great <u>*calamity*</u> to come.

Generations after Adam and Eve's eviction from the Garden of Eden, the Biblical record documented that, *"...the Lord saw that the **wickedness** of man was great in the earth, and that every intent of the thoughts of his heart was only **evil** continually. And the Lord was sorry that He had made man on the earth, and He was grieved in His heart. So the Lord said, "I will destroy man whom I have created from the face of the earth, both man and beast, creeping thing and birds of the air, for I am sorry that I have made them." But Noah found grace in the eyes of the Lord"* (Genesis 6:5-8). This destruction from the Lord was the second major <u>*calamity*</u> of mankind. One can know that God did what He said because the Biblical record documented His statement of, *"...behold, I Myself am bringing <u>floodwaters</u> on the earth, to destroy from under heaven all flesh in which is the breath of life; everything that is on the earth shall die"* (Genesis 6:17). The Lord gave Noah specific instructions and time to construct an ark to save his family along with select animals according to Genesis 6:13-22. When Noah completed his work, the Biblical record documented that, *"And it came to pass after seven days that the waters of the <u>flood</u> were on the earth. In the six hundredth year of Noah's life, in the second month, the seventeenth day of the month, on that day all the fountains of the great deep were broken up, and the windows of heaven were opened. And the rain was on the earth forty days and forty nights"* (Genesis 7:10-12), and *"...The waters increased and lifted up the ark, and it <u>rose high above the earth</u>"* (Genesis 7:17). The Biblical record documented God's preciseness in His use of <u>*calamity*</u> on the world.

At the end of this <u>*calamity*</u>, God cleared the great waters from the earth placing them in the areas now known as oceans, lakes, rivers, polar regions, etc.... The Biblical record documented that the Lord then said to Noah, *"Thus I establish My covenant with you: Never again shall all flesh be cut off by the waters of the <u>flood</u>; never again shall there be a <u>flood</u> to destroy the earth"* (Genesis 9:11) and, *"...I will remember My covenant which is between Me and you and every living creature of all flesh; the waters shall never again become a <u>flood</u> to destroy all flesh"* (Genesis 9:15). The Lord sealed this covenant for all generations to see by placing a rainbow in the sky to this very day. The Lord said, *"The rainbow shall be in the cloud, and I will look on it to remember the everlasting covenant between God and every living* *creature of all flesh that is on the earth." And God said to Noah, "This is the sign of the covenant which I have established between Me and all flesh that is on the earth"* (Genesis 9:16-17). BTT allows one to see the great <u>flood</u> was a <u>calamity</u> to purge the negative attribute's influences from God's creation. Mankind received an opportunity to move forward with a fresh start. The rainbow in the sky confirms this epic <u>calamity</u> and it signifies today that God is still in control.

The Biblical record documented that Noah's family had many children after God's <u>calamity</u>. Genesis 10:1-33 documents a list of the nations that were born from Noah's children and their generations. This Biblical reference ends with the statement, *"These were the families of the sons of Noah, according to their generations, in their nations; and from these the nations were divided on the earth after the <u>flood</u>"* (Genesis 10:32). In other words, nations of people were born as time moved forward. In fact, these nations occupied one massive area and God used another <u>calamity</u> to make them move and populate the world as He told them to do previously in Genesis 8:15-19. Genesis chapter 11 documented the <u>calamity</u>. In this part of the Biblical record, the purpose of the <u>calamity</u> was simple to understand. The Bible recorded in Genesis 11:1-4:

> *"Now the whole earth had one language and one speech. And it came to pass, as they journeyed from the east, that they found a plain in the land of Shinar, and they dwelt there. Then they said to one another, "Come, let us make bricks and bake them thoroughly." They had brick for stone, and they had asphalt for mortar. And they said, "Come, let us build ourselves a city, and a tower whose top is in the heavens; let us make a name for ourselves, lest we be scattered abroad over the face of the whole earth."*

From this point, BTT allows one to see that God was tolerant of man's actions up to a point. But one should also understand, generations of people staying in one spot who all thought and spoke alike, was not a good long-term plan. The scenario created a ripe battleground for the negative forces of the war campaign. So the Biblical record documented the Lord's thinking, the <u>calamity</u> He brought on them, and why He did what was necessary. The Biblical record documented in Genesis 11:5-9:

> *"But the Lord came down to see the city and the tower which the sons of men had built. And the Lord said, "Indeed the people are one and they all have one language, and this is what they begin to do; now nothing that they propose to do will be withheld from them. Come, let Us go down and there confuse their language, that they may not understand one another's speech." So the Lord <u>scattered them abroad from there over the face of all the earth</u>, and they ceased building the city. Therefore its name is called Babel, because there the Lord <u>confused the language</u> of all the earth; and from there the Lord <u>scattered them abroad over the face of all the earth</u>."*

Critics argue that in this instance, there was no reason for the Lord to use a <u>calamity</u>. The people would have eventually dispersed because of a lack of food and other resources. However, these same critics miss the point. The fact was, when Noah and his family came off the ark in the first place, the Lord told them to, *"Be fruitful and multiply, <u>and fill the earth</u>"* (Genesis 9:1). Given whatever time God allowed, they failed to do as God had commanded. BTT allows one to understand that over time, **false** leaders stepped up to deny and defy God's Word. Whoever said, "*Come, let us build ourselves a city, and a tower whose top is in the heavens; let us make a name for ourselves, <u>lest we be scattered abroad over the face of the whole earth</u>*" (Genesis 11:4), was defying God. The negative attributes once again began influencing leader's inner spirits and the negative forces were emboldened again.

The next <u>calamity</u> God used for His purpose was a <u>famine</u>. The Biblical record documented that God used <u>famines</u> in the land to move people from their comfort zones to new locations that He designated. Here are three instances.

- "*Now there was a <u>famine</u> in the land, and Abram went down to Egypt to dwell there, for the <u>famine</u> was severe in the land*" (Genesis 12:10). Abram, who was renamed Abraham by God, moved his entire household from the country he was born in to Egypt. This move made history.

- "*There was a <u>famine</u> in the land, besides the first <u>famine</u> that was in the days of Abraham. And Isaac went to Abimelech king of the Philistines, in Gerar*" (Genesis 26:1). In this instance, God told Isaac to remain where he was and not go to Egypt (Genesis 26:2) and He would bless him. Isaac choose to obey God and made history.

- "*...but after them seven years of <u>famine</u> will arise, and all the plenty will be forgotten in the land of Egypt; and the <u>famine</u> will deplete the land. So the plenty will not be known in the land because of the <u>famine</u> following, for it will be <u>very severe</u>*" (Genesis 41:30-31). In this instance, the providence of God elevated Joseph to a status second only to Pharaoh in Egypt since he **rightly** interpreted Pharaoh's dream of a severe <u>famine</u>. The <u>famine</u> came, and the Biblical record documented it was "*in all lands*" (Genesis 41:54) and "*over all the face of the earth*" (Genesis 41:56-57). This <u>famine</u> made history with impacts to the entire children of Israel as Joseph's whole family reunited in Egypt.

Two **witnesses** of God's use of <u>calamity</u> were Abram and Lot. Beginning with Abram, after Pharaoh's men took Sarai from Abram, the Lord brought <u>calamity</u> to Pharaoh and his household. The Biblical record documented that, "*...the Lord <u>plagued</u> Pharaoh and his house with great <u>plagues</u> because of Sarai, Abram's wife*" (Genesis 12:17). The <u>plague</u> was a <u>calamity</u> on Pharaoh and his household of epic proportions.

In the case of Lot, although he could not look directly at God's <u>calamity</u>, he was a **witness** to the destruction of Sodom and Gomorrah by God's <u>calamity</u>. The Lord told Abram that, "*Because the outcry against Sodom and Gomorrah is great, and because their sin is very grave, I will go down now and see whether they have done altogether according to the outcry against it that has come to Me; and if not, I will know*" (Genesis 18:20-21) and if confirmed, He would destroy the cities with His <u>calamity</u>. What is fascinating about this event is the fact that Jesus and two angels, according to Genesis 18:2-3, came to confirm the conditions of the cities. During the discourse between Abram and Jesus, one learns that God would not destroy the cities if ten **righteous** souls could be found between them according to Genesis 18:32. The Biblical record documented that the angels confirmed the depraved condition of the cities and said to Lot, "*...we will destroy this place, because the outcry against them has grown great* *before the face of the Lord, and the Lord has sent us to destroy it"* (Genesis 19:13). Well, Lot and his family were allowed to move to a place of safety; a city named Zoar (Genesis 19:22). Then God's <u>calamity</u> rained down from the heavens on the cities in the form of <u>fire</u> and <u>brimstone</u> (Genesis 19:23). Please do not fall for the negative forces **lie** that this event never happened or the cities, if they were destroyed, occurred because of a volcano. One can know that this was God's <u>calamity</u> because it was so epic that when Lot's wife turned to look at it, something incredible happened. She violated God's command not to look back at the destruction (Genesis 19:17). The Bible documented that as she and Lot were escaping, she *"...looked back behind him, and she became a pillar of salt"* (Genesis 19:26). Clearly, this <u>calamity</u> was not from the effects of a volcano. Moreover, because it is recorded in the Biblical record, it did happen.

Next Jacob moved his entire household to Egypt to protected them from a <u>*famine*</u>. BTT allows one to see that God's <u>calamity</u> caused Jacob's entire household to move for His future purpose. In fact, Joseph would explain to his brothers in Genesis 45:5-8:

> *"But now, do not therefore be grieved or* **angry** *with yourselves because you sold me here; for God sent me before you to preserve life. For these two years the <u>famine</u> has been in the land, and there are still five years in which there will be neither plowing nor harvesting. And God sent me before you to preserve a posterity for you in the earth, and to save your lives by a <u>great deliverance</u>. So now it was not you who sent me here, but God; and He has made me a father to Pharaoh, and lord of all his house, and a ruler throughout all the land of Egypt."*

The Lord used <u>calamity</u> to free the children of Israel from Pharaoh's bondage in the land of Egypt. God also used this <u>calamity</u> to show the nation of Egypt that their gods and idols were **false** and the Almighty God was real. One can know this because the Biblical record documented that by the seventh <u>plague</u> on Egypt, the Lord told Pharaoh through Moses, *"for at this time I will send all My <u>plagues</u> to your very heart, and on your servants and on your people, that you may know that there is none like Me in all the earth"* (Exodus 9:14). From Exodus chapter 4 through chapter 12, the Biblical record documented all the <u>calamities</u> that God brought on Egypt to humble Pharaoh. Consider the following events:

#	The <u>Calamity</u>	Where Documented	The Epic Event
1st	All the waters became blood	Exodus 7:14-25	Plague
2nd	Epic proportion of frogs	Exodus 8:1-15	Plague
3rd	Epic proportion of lice	Exodus 8:16-19	Plague
4th	Epic proportion of flies	Exodus 8:20-32	Plague
5th	Livestock dies	Exodus 9:1-7	Disease/<u>pestilence</u>
6th	Boils develop on the people	Exodus 9:8-12	Disease
7th	Severe hail, fire and thunder	Exodus 9:13-35	<u>Calamity</u> using weather
8th	Epic proportion of locusts	Exodus 10:1-15	Plague

| 9th | Perpetual darkness | Exodus 10:21-27 | The hand of God |
| 10th | Death | Exodus 11; 12 :29, 30 | Plague |

Table 152: God's *Calamity* on Pharaoh and Egypt

After all the *calamities* Pharaoh experienced by the hand of God, the Biblical record documented that he released the children of Israel from bondage and they were able to leave Egypt. In fact, the Bible recorded, "*...the Egyptians urged the people, that they might send them out of the land in haste. For they said, "We shall all be dead"*" (Exodus 12: 33). Clearly, when God decides to use *calamity*, His purpose succeeds despite the thoughts or behaviors of unbelievers.

When the children of Israel came out of Egypt, BTT allows one to see that they knew the power of God and His use of *calamity.* They had seen what God unleashed on the Egyptians first hand. However, their freedom opened the door to the full onslaught of negative influences of spiritual warfare. The negative forces attacked as forceful as possible using the strategy of **deception** and the elements of *greed* and *lust*. However, Moses saw the effects and warned the children of Israel that, "*If you diligently heed the voice of the Lord your God and do what is* ***right*** *in His sight, give ear to His commandments and keep all His statutes, I will put none of the diseases on you which I have brought on the Egyptians. For I am the Lord who heals you*" (Exodus 15:26). God's desire was for the children of Israel to succeed. However, He does not discriminate in punishing disobedience. He used *calamity* to correct His people ***justly***. God's punishment became necessary. The Biblical record documented that the children of Israel began to turn to **idolatry**. Specifically, the Bible documented "*...the Lord plagued the people because of what they did with the calf which Aaron made*" (Exodus 32:35). God's *calamity* came to the people even before they reached the Promised Land.

Moses explained precisely the rules of engagement existing between the Lord and the children of Israel. Within the Book of Leviticus of the Biblical record, one can see that Moses clearly told the people that they would experience God's *calamity* if they were not true to the Lord. Chapter 26 of the Book of Leviticus highlighted the promised blessings and retribution the children of Israel would encounter based on their obedience. Here are three examples from the Lord that pertain to *calamity*:

- "*I also will do this to you: I will even appoint terror over you, wasting disease and fever which shall consume the eyes and cause sorrow of heart. And you shall sow your seed in vain, for your enemies shall eat it*" (Leviticus 26:16)

- "*...'Then, if you walk contrary to Me, and are not willing to obey Me, I will bring on you seven times more plagues, according to your sins*" (Leviticus 26:21)

- "*And I will bring a sword against you that will execute the vengeance of the covenant; when you are gathered together within your cities I will send pestilence among you; and you shall be delivered into the hand of the enemy*" (Leviticus 26:25)

After Moses taught the children about the way of the Lord and provided them the laws to keep them safe, one would think they would be obedient knowing the consequences. However, the Book of Numbers exposed the truth. God used *calamity* to purge the spiritual

wickedness that was influencing them to sin from among the children of Israel. Just because the children of Israel where identified as God's people did not mean they were immune to the influences of spiritual warfare. If anything, after everything they had **witnessed** from the Lord, the children of Israel should have been more aware of the war campaign. However, choice remained with the people as it does with us today. So, consider some of the events that occurred as documented in the Book of Numbers.

First, the Lord designated a group of people to help His priest Aaron when he performed his functions in God's sanctuary. The Levites had this role. The Levites were to remain "spiritually and physically clean" to perform the work inside God's designated place of worship. The massive number of Israelites themselves would have invited God's <u>calamity</u> if they entered God's Holy Tabernacle. Therefore, God designated a smaller group of people to meet His strict requirements. The Biblical record documented, "*And I have given the Levites as a gift to Aaron and his sons from among the children of Israel, to do the work for the children of Israel in the tabernacle of meeting, and to make atonement for the children of Israel, that there be no <u>plague</u> among the children of Israel when the children of Israel come near the sanctuary*" (Numbers 8:19).

Next, the Lord provided the children of Israel food in abundance (Numbers 11:31-32) and after they complained (Numbers 11:1) and "*yielded to intense cravings*" (Numbers 11:4), their sinful behavior invited God's <u>calamity</u>. The Biblical record documented, "*But while the meat was still between their teeth, before it was chewed, the wrath of the Lord was aroused against the people, and the Lord struck the people with a very great <u>plague</u>*" (Numbers 11:33). This was God's <u>calamity</u>, not an act of nature.

Next, the Lord directed Moses and Aaron to have the children of Israel take the land of Canaan. Instead, the people refused, complained, and wanted to **kill** Moses and Aaron. Once again, their sinful behavior invited God's <u>calamity</u>. The Biblical record documented that, "*...all the congregation said to stone them with stones. Now the glory of the Lord appeared in the tabernacle of meeting before all the children of Israel*" (Numbers 14:10). This was serious. The Lord told Moses, "*<u>I will strike them</u> with the <u>pestilence</u> and disinherit them, and I will make of you a nation greater and mightier than they*" (Numbers 14:12). However, Numbers 14:13-23 documented that Moses interceded on behalf of the people. For a time, Moses's actions caused God to relent from His <u>calamity</u>. The Lord directed them to continue with the mission to go to Canaan. Moses sent several men to spy out the land so that he could plan his strategy. These men were now in the **witness** category. Unfortunately, when the men returned, all but two of them allowed the influences of the negative attributes. The **liar** attribute influenced most of the men to provide bad reports about the land. Only Joshua and Caleb told the truth about what they saw. They understood God's strategy for them to acquire the land. As for the other men, God's <u>calamity</u> struck them. The Biblical record documented, "*...those very men who brought the **evil** report about the land, died by the <u>plague</u> before the Lord*" (Numbers 14:37).

God used <u>calamity</u> on the children of Israel when four men named Korah, Dathan, Abiram, and On, "*...took men; and they rose up before Moses with some of the children of Israel, two hundred and fifty leaders of the congregation, representatives of the congregation, men of renown. They gathered together against Moses and Aaron, and said to them, "You take too much upon yourselves, for all the congregation is holy, every one of them, and the Lord is* *among them. Why then do you exalt yourselves above the assembly of the Lord?"* (Numbers 16:1-3). Moses attempted to talk with them. However, his attempt was to no avail according to Number 16:4-15. God's <u>calamity</u> came in the form of an <u>earthquake</u> that opened the earth and then closed. This <u>calamity</u> was something the people had never seen before (Numbers 16:30). The Biblical record documented that, "...*the <u>ground split</u> apart under them, and the <u>earth opened its mouth and swallowed them up</u>, with their households and all the men with Korah, with all their goods. So they and all those with them went down alive into the pit; the <u>earth closed over them</u>, and they perished from among the assembly. Then all Israel who were around them fled at their cry, for they said, "Lest the earth swallow us up also!" And <u>a fire came out from the Lord</u> <u>and consumed</u> the two hundred and fifty men who were offering incense*" (Numbers 16:31-35). God's use of <u>calamity</u> is real. One would think that this <u>calamity</u> would have ended further discussion about God's appointment of Moses and Aaron to their leadership positions, but it did not. God brought another <u>calamity</u> to the people to make His point and the Biblical record documented that on the very next day, "...*all the congregation of the children of Israel* **complained** *against Moses and Aaron, saying, "You have* **killed** *the people of the Lord"* (Numbers 16:41). The Lord came back to His sanctuary and He was not happy. He told Moses and Aaron to get out of the way for He was going to destroy the people according to Numbers 16:44. Moses and Aaron fell to the ground. BTT allows one to see that Moses and Aaron's prostrate position was an act of respect; not cowering out of <u>fear</u>. Their prayers saved the Israelites from destruction. Consequently, the Biblical record documented the following <u>calamity</u> that took place in Numbers 16:46-50:

> *"So Moses said to Aaron, "Take a censer and put fire in it from the altar, put incense on it, and take it quickly to the congregation and make atonement for them; for wrath has gone out from the Lord. The <u>plague</u> has begun." Then Aaron took it as Moses commanded, and ran into the midst of the assembly; and already the <u>plague</u> had begun among the people. So he put in the incense and made atonement for the people. And he stood between the dead and the living; so the <u>plague</u> was stopped. Now those who died in the <u>plague</u> were fourteen thousand seven hundred, besides those who died in the Korah incident. So Aaron returned to Moses at the door of the tabernacle of meeting, for the <u>plague</u> had stopped."*

BTT allows one to see God used <u>calamity</u> to purge His people of sin. But even after these events, some of the children of Israel allowed the influences of the negative attributes to return and they chose to turn back towards sin. This is a testament of the strong influences of the negative attributes. Hence, the Biblical record captured another <u>calamity</u> as the children of Israel made their way to the Promised Land. In Numbers 21:4-9, the Biblical record documented a method the Lord used to discipline the children of Israel because of their constant grumbling and complaining. The <u>calamity</u> identified involved poisonous snakes. As the children of Israel journeyed from Mount Hor by the Way of the Red Sea to go around the land of Edom, the Biblical record documented that, "...*the soul of the people became very discouraged on the way. And the people spoke against God and against Moses: "Why have you brought us up out of Egypt to die in the wilderness? For there is no food and no water, and our soul loathes this worthless bread." So the Lord sent <u>fiery serpents</u> among the people,* *and they bit the people; and many of the people of Israel died. Therefore the people came to Moses, and said, "We have sinned, for we have spoken against the Lord and against you; pray to the Lord that He take away the <u>serpents</u> from us." So Moses prayed for the people. Then the Lord said to Moses, "Make a <u>fiery serpent</u>, and set it on a pole; and it shall be that everyone who is bitten, when he looks at it, shall live." So Moses made a bronze serpent, and put it on a pole; and so it was, if a <u>serpent had bitten anyone</u>, when he looked at the <u>bronze serpent</u>, he lived."* You see, the <u>bronze serpent</u> gave the people something physical to look at and gave them <u>hope</u> while at the same time teaching them discipline. BTT also allows one to see that the serpents were a form of <u>calamity</u> from God. Many of the people died during this purge of the Israelite's camp from sins.

Interestingly, today the symbol of the serpent on a pole is used in the medical community and alchemy community by the Greeks to represent life and healing as pictured in **Figure 32.** In reality, humanity has rejected or chosen not to remember where this symbol originated. This is the way of the negative attribute's use of fog on the spiritual battlefield to eat away at the glory of the Almighty God. Sadly, the Biblical record informs us that King Hezekiah had to destroy the *"...wooden image and broke in pieces the bronze serpent that Moses had made; for until those days the children of Israel burned incense to it, and called it Nehushtan"* (2 Kings 18:4). Israel had turned the very item that saved them into an item of sin.

Figure 32: Today's use of the Serpent and Pole

The children of Israel experienced the next <u>calamity</u> as they, *"...remained in Acacia Grove, and the people began to commit **harlotry** with the women of Moab. They invited the people to the **sacrifices of their gods**, and the people ate and **bowed down** to their gods. So Israel was joined to Baal of Peor, and the anger of the Lord was aroused against Israel"* (Number 25:1-3). BTT allows one to see that **harlotry** and **idol** worship committed by the children of Israel was sin. Because of the sin, the Lord sent <u>calamity</u> in the form of a <u>plague</u> among the people. Initially the Lord told Moses how to resolve the problem in Numbers 25:4 by separating the offenders. However, the problem was inflamed according to Numbers 25:5 when, *"...one of the children of Israel came and presented to his brethren a Midianite woman in the sight of Moses and in the sight of all the congregation of the children of Israel, who were weeping at the door of the tabernacle of meeting"* (Numbers 25:6). Then the Lord immediately sent a <u>plague</u> on the Israelites. The Biblical record documented in Numbers 25:7-11:

> *"Now when Phinehas the son of Eleazar, the son of Aaron the priest, saw it, he rose from among the congregation and took a javelin in his hand; and he went after the man of Israel into the tent and thrust both of them through, the man of Israel, and the woman through her body. So the <u>plague</u> was stopped among the children of Israel. And those who died in the <u>plague</u> were*

twenty-four thousand. Then the Lord spoke to Moses, saying: "Phinehas the son of Eleazar, the son of Aaron the priest, has turned back My wrath from the children of Israel, because he was zealous with My zeal among them, so that I did not consume the children of Israel in My zeal"

In the Book of Deuteronomy, there are critical verses that explain how the Lord used <u>calamity</u> as an agent of change. Depending on their obedience or sin, the Lord told the children of Israel through Moses, what to expect. First, based on their obedience to God's Word, Moses told them that the Lord would "...*take away from you all <u>sickness</u>, and will afflict you with none of the <u>terrible</u> <u>diseases</u> of Egypt which you have known, but will lay them on all those who **hate** you*" (Deuteronomy 7:15). Considering all the <u>calamities</u> the children of Israel saw in Egypt, obedience should have been a reasonable choice. BTT allows one to see this option was a blessing from the Lord. However, because of man's freewill to choose and spiritual warfare, the second options were curses. The Biblical record documented that, for lack of obedience to the Lord's commands, the following <u>calamity</u> was available at His discretion.

- *"The Lord will send on you cursing, confusion, and rebuke in all that you set your hand to do, until you are destroyed and until you perish quickly, because of the **wickedness** of your doings in which you have forsaken Me. The Lord will make the <u>plague</u> cling to you until He has consumed you from the land which you are going to possess. The Lord will strike you with <u>consumption</u>, with <u>fever, with inflammation, with severe burning fever, with the sword, with scorching, and with mildew</u>; they shall pursue you until you perish. And your heavens which are over your head shall be bronze, and the earth which is under you shall be iron. The Lord will <u>change the rain of your land to powder and dust</u>; from the heaven it shall come down on you until you are destroyed"* (Deuteronomy 28:20-24)

- *"If you do not carefully observe all the words of this law that are written in this book, that you may <u>fear</u> this glorious and awesome name, THE LORD YOUR GOD, then the Lord will bring upon you and your descendants <u>extraordinary</u> <u>plagues</u>—<u>great and prolonged plagues</u>—and <u>serious and prolonged sicknesses</u>. Moreover He will bring back on you all the <u>diseases</u> of Egypt, of which you were <u>afraid</u>, and <u>they shall cling to you</u>. Also every <u>sickness</u> and every <u>plague</u>, which is not written in this Book of the Law, will the Lord bring upon you until you are destroyed"* (Deuteronomy 28:58-61)

From this point on, many <u>calamities</u> came upon the children of Israel. These <u>calamities</u> occurred until God purged the original adult generation out from the group that left Egypt. Their children crossed over into the Promised Land as millions of people died by <u>calamity</u> for refusing to be obedient to the Lord. BTT allows one to see that Joshua took a pure generation of God's people into the Promised Land. However, even they were susceptible to the influences of spiritual warfare. The campaign intensified as the negative forces maneuvered to destroy God's work. After Joshua's death, the Lord placed a series of judges over the children of Israel to <u>discern</u> right and wrong and to guide them with God's commandments, statues, and laws. But the children of Israel became increasingly disobedient and **unfaithful**. In fact, the Biblical record documented that, "*Wherever they went out, the hand of the Lord was against them for <u>calamity</u>, as the Lord had said, and as the Lord had sworn to them. And they were <u>greatly distressed</u>*" (Judges 2:15). The children of Israel and the nations around them from this point forward, experienced _calamities_ from God. BTT allows one to see that the _calamities_ had a two-fold purpose; first to get Israel's attention and change their behavior, and second to punish the nation's that harmed or persuaded Israel to sin.

In the Book of Ruth, God's _calamity_ moved Naomi and her two daughters-in-laws back to the land of Judah. The Biblical record documented, "..._in the days when the judges ruled, that there was a famine in the land. And a certain man of Bethlehem, Judah, went to dwell in the country of Moab, he and his wife and his two sons_" (Ruth 1:1). This family was Elimelech and Naomi and their two sons Mahlon and Chilion. Mahlon and Chilion had wives named Ruth and Orpah. During the _famine_, all the men died according to the Biblical record documented in Ruth 1:3-5. This was a family _calamity_ in and of itself. According to Ruth 1:6, Naomi had heard that there was food in Judah, so she packed up her belongings and headed there. Both Ruth and Orpah followed, but Naomi released them to return to their own people. However, Ruth would not leave Naomi. If one were to read the Book of Ruth, one would understand the divine hand of God through this _calamity_. Ruth's positive behavior played a significant role in God's plan; clearly, the influence of the positive attributes resided in her inner spirit. This was even though she was a, "_women of Moab_" (Ruth 1:4) and not a descendent of the children of Israel. Ruth married Boaz, a relative of Elimelech and descendant of the children of Israel. Their union produced a son named, "_Obed. He is the father of Jesse, the father of David_" (Ruth 14:17). God's _calamity_ in the form of a _famine_, moved Ruth in a direction for God's use.

In the Book of First Samuel, it was God's _calamity_ that forced the return of the ark of God to the nation of Israel that they had lost to the Philistines during a battle. One should read the entire event to gain a full appreciation of what occurred before the nation of Israel lost the ark of God. It is a fascinating read that gives one a feel for the fact that the nation of Israel had sinned against God. Israel initially went into battle without the ark of God against the Philistines and lost, "_about four thousand men of the army in the field_" (1 Samuel 4:2). They prepared for a second battle and this time brought the ark of God. Before this battle, the Biblical record made it clear that the Philistines knew about God's use of _calamity_, but this did not stop their leadership's determination to defeat God's people. BTT allows one to see an important lesson taught here about the influences of the negative forces. That is, until God intervenes, the negative forces prevail when sin weakens the positive forces. Please consider these next events closely. In 1 Samuel 4:5-11:

> "_And when the ark of the covenant of the Lord came into the camp, all Israel shouted so loudly that the earth shook. Now when the Philistines heard the noise of the shout, they said, "What does the sound of this great shout in the camp of the Hebrews mean?" Then they understood that the ark of the Lord had come into the camp. So the Philistines were afraid, for they said, "God has come into the camp!" And they said, "Woe to us! For such a thing has never happened before. Woe to us! Who will deliver us from the hand of these mighty gods? These are the gods who struck the Egyptians with all the plagues in the wilderness. Be strong and conduct yourselves like men, you Philistines, that you do not become servants of the Hebrews, as they have been to you. Conduct yourselves like men, and fight!" So the Philistines fought, and Israel was defeated, and every man fled to his tent. There was a_

very great slaughter, and there fell of Israel thirty thousand foot soldiers. Also the ark of God was captured; and the two sons of Eli, Hophni and Phinehas, died."

BTT allows one to see that God is a ***just*** God. The nation of Israel had the ark of God, but they had not repented from their sin and the ark became useless to them as they fought the Philistines. They received punishment and defeat for their disobedience. Their loss during the war was their <u>calamity</u> from God. But there is more to this story. The Philistines took the ark of God and set it before their god. The Biblical record documented, "*...they brought it into the house of Dagon and set it by Dagon*" (1 Samuel 5:2). The next morning, the Bible documented that Dagon had, "*fallen on its face to the earth before the ark of the Lord. So they took Dagon and set it in its place again. And when they arose early the next morning, there was Dagon, fallen on its face to the ground before the ark of the Lord. The head of Dagon and both the palms of its hands were broken off on the threshold; only Dagon's torso was left of it*" (1 Samuel 5:3-4). After these events, the Dagon priests and Philistine leadership realized the ark of God had to go. They then sent it to the city of Gath instead of returning it to the nation of Israel. However, the Philistines quickly learned that God was in control. In fact, the Biblical record documented that God's <u>calamity</u> struck them. The Bible documented, "*But the hand of the Lord was heavy on the people of Ashdod, and He ravaged them and struck them with <u>tumors</u>, both Ashdod and its territory*" (1 Samuel 5:6). Also, the Bible recorded, "*So it was, after they had carried it away, that the hand of the Lord was against the city with a very great destruction; and He <u>struck the men of the city</u>, both small and great, and <u>tumors</u> broke out on them*" (1 Samuel 5:9). The Philistines then sent the ark of God to the city of Ekron, and the Biblical record documented, "*So it was, as the ark of God came to Ekron, that the Ekronites cried out, saying, "They have brought the ark of the God of Israel to us, to **kill** us and our people!" So they sent and gathered together all the lords of the Philistines, and said, "Send away the ark of the God of Israel, and let it go back to its own place, so that it does not **kill** us and our people." For there was a deadly destruction throughout all the city; the hand of God was very heavy there. And the men who did not die <u>were stricken with the tumors</u>, and the cry of the city went up to heaven*" (1 Samuel 5:10-12). After all this, the Philistines returned the ark of God to its rightful –owners, the nation of Israel, as documented in 1 Samuel chapter 6. One can see from the example that God's <u>calamity</u> achieved His intended purpose.

In the Book of Second Samuel, God used <u>calamity</u> on an entire nation. The Biblical record documented; "*Now there was a <u>famine</u> in the days of David for three years, year after year; and David inquired of the Lord. And the Lord answered, "It is because of Saul and his **bloodthirsty** house, because he **killed** the Gibeonites*" (2 Samuel 21:1). I encourage you to read the Biblical record of the Gibeonites to appreciate the full account of Saul's behavior. However, know that the negative attributes played a major role in influencing him. For the Gibeonites knew and the Biblical record documented, that "*Saul had sought to **kill** them in his zeal for the children of Israel and Judah*" (2 Samuel 21:2). Therefore, God used <u>calamity</u> to get Saul's attention because he was still a king and unrepentant leader in a position of significant authority and responsibility.

Both before and after he became king of Israel, David faced a series of personal <u>calamities</u> in his life. David would say of his enemies, "*They confronted me in the day of my calamity, but the Lord was my support*" (2 Samuel 22:19). David understood the nature of God's use of *calamity*, and rather than turning away, he allowed it to strengthen his relationship with God. For example, in 2 Samuel 24, the Bible documented that, "*...the anger of the Lord was aroused against Israel, and He moved David against them to say, "Go, number Israel and Judah"* (2 Samuel 24:1). First, understand that the Lord was not angry with David. The Bible clearly states that He was angry at the nation of Israel. Therefore, David commanded Joab, the commander of his army according to 2 Samuel 24:2, to execute God's command. Now BTT allows one to understand that the Lord already knew how many people were among the nation of Israel. God's commandment was an opportunity for David to demonstrate his obedience to the Lord. In addition, during the counting, the people had time to repent of their sin prior to the Lord disciplining them by His *calamity*.

One needs to apply BTT to see and understand the next sequence of events. The Biblical record documented that, "*David's heart condemned him after he had numbered the people. So David said to the Lord, "I have sinned greatly in what I have done; but now, I pray, O Lord, take away the iniquity of Your servant, for I have done very **foolishly***" (2 Samuel 24:10). David felt guilty for counting the people in his kingdom, but in reality, he could not see God's hand behind his actions. He was simply being obedient as he allowed the influences of the positive attributes to lead his inner spirit. In the spiritual realm, the positive attributes influencing David were moving against the negative forces in the war campaign that had influenced the nation of Israel to sin. One can be sure of this because once the count was complete, the Lord sent word to the prophet Gad with a message for David. The Biblical record documented, "*So Gad came to David and told him; and he said to him, "Shall seven years of famine come to you in your land? Or shall you flee three months before your enemies, while they pursue you? Or shall there be three days' plague in your land? Now consider and see what answer I should take back to Him who sent me*" (2 Samuel 24:13; 1 Chronicles 21:12). BTT allows one to understand that the three options were against the nation of Israel and not David; even the option for David to flee was against Israel. A nation without a king would have started an internal *calamity* within the **wicked** leaders of Israel. Externally, a nation without leadership would be a prime target for their enemies. The Biblical record documented that David decided to let the Lord choose. Thus, the Bible recorded, "*So the Lord sent a plague upon Israel from the morning till the appointed time. From Dan to Beersheba seventy thousand men of the people died*" (2 Samuel 24:15; 1 Chronicles 21:14). In other words, seventy thousand men who chose to allow the influences of the negative attributes, died by God's *calamity*. God purged the people caught up in sin from among His people. Even as the war campaign progresses today, God still purges the sinful and unrepentant from among His people.

Here is how this *calamity* stopped. The Bible documented that David went to Araunah, the Jebusite, to buy land to build an altar to the Lord. The Bible recorded, "*Then Araunah said, "Why has my lord the king come to his servant?" And David said, "To buy the threshing floor from you, to build an altar to the Lord, that the plague may be withdrawn from the people*" (2 Samuel 24:21). David could have just taken the land. Araunah even offered it to him freely. However, David refused. David wanted to ensure that he did what was **right** in the sight of the Lord. This demonstrated that David had acquired all the positive attributes and God counted him among the **righteous**. The Bible documented that, "*...David bought the threshing floor* *and the oxen for fifty shekels of silver. And David built there an altar to the Lord, and offered burnt offerings and peace offerings. So the Lord heeded the prayers for the land, and the <u>plague</u> was withdrawn from Israel"* (2 Samuel 24:24-25; 1 Chronicles 21:22). Thus, God's <u>calamity</u> ceased when a man, influenced by the **righteous** attributes, called on the name of Lord. Just having the other positive attributes (**upright/honorable**, **merciful**, **blameless**, **faithful**, **just**, and **good**) by themselves were not enough. It was the **righteous** attribute that made the difference in this example.

In the Book of first Kings, the Lord made it clear that even the nations that surrounded the nation of Israel would come to know His <u>calamity</u>. When King Solomon finished building the temple of the Lord, the Lord came and visited it according to 1 Kings Chapter 9. Within this reading, one learns that the Lord gave Solomon a stern warning that included the use of <u>calamity</u>. In 1 Kings 9:6-9, the Lord said:

> *"But if you or your sons at all turn from following Me, and do not keep My commandments and My statutes which I have set before you, but go and **serve other gods and worship them**, then I will cut off Israel from the land which I have given them; and this house which I have consecrated for My name I will cast out of My sight. Israel will be a proverb and a byword among all peoples. And as for this house, which is exalted, everyone who passes by it will be astonished and will hiss, and say, 'Why has the Lord done thus to this land and to this house?' Then they will answer, 'Because they forsook the Lord their God, who brought their fathers out of the land of Egypt, and have **embraced other gods**, and **worshiped them and served them**; therefore the Lord has brought all this <u>calamity</u> on them.'"*

BTT allows one to see that God remained consistent in His Word and His use of <u>calamity</u>. Below are more examples of this fact for one to consider.

God used <u>calamity</u> to get the attention of both the nation of Israel and King Ahab. The Bible documented, *"In the thirty-eighth year of Asa king of Judah, Ahab the son of Omri became king over Israel; and Ahab the son of Omri reigned over Israel in Samaria twenty-two years. Now Ahab the son of Omri did **evil** in the sight of the Lord, more than all who were before him. And it came to pass, as though it had been a trivial thing for him to walk in the sins of Jeroboam the son of Nebat, that he took as wife Jezebel the daughter of Ethbaal, king of the Sidonians; and he went and **served Baal and worshiped him**. Then he set up an altar for Baal in the temple of Baal, which he had built in Samaria. And Ahab made a **wooden image**. Ahab did more to provoke the Lord God of Israel to anger than all the kings of Israel who were before him"* (1 Kings 16:29-33). The Lord sent the prophet Elijah to proclaim a <u>calamity</u> in the form of a <u>drought</u>. The Biblical record documented that, *"...Elijah the Tishbite, of the inhabitants of Gilead, said to Ahab, "As the Lord God of Israel lives, before whom I stand, there shall not be <u>dew nor rain</u> these years, except at my word"* (1 Kings 17:1). BTT allows one to see that because Ahab was so **evil**, the Lord told Elijah where to hide after he delivered God's message according to 1 Kings 17:2. Elijah did as the Lord said. Later, the Lord had Elijah to return and speak to Ahab. The Biblical record documented, *"So Elijah went to present himself to Ahab; and there was a severe <u>famine</u> in Samaria"* (1 Kings 18:2). Ahab accused Elijah for causing the nation of Israel's problems. To this, Elijah said, *"I have not* *troubled Israel, but you and your father's house have, in that you have forsaken the commandments of the Lord and have* **followed the Baals**. *Now therefore, send and gather all Israel to me on Mount Carmel, the four hundred and fifty prophets of Baal, and the four hundred prophets of Asherah, who eat at Jezebel's table."* (1 Kings 18:18-19). Elijah had set up a competition between the Lord and the four hundred and fifty prophets and their gods - Baal and Asherah. Elijah had the nation of Israel there as **witnesses**. The Biblical record documented the entire event in 1 Kings 18:20-39. Please read this on your own to fully appreciate God's magnificence. Of course, the Lord won, and the Bible documented, *"Now when all the people saw it, they fell on their faces; and they said, "The Lord, He is God! The Lord, He is God!" And Elijah said to them, "Seize the prophets of Baal! Do not let one of them escape!" So they seized them; and Elijah brought them down to the Brook Kishon and executed them there. Then Elijah said to Ahab, "Go up, eat and drink; for there is the sound of abundance of rain"* (1 Kings 18:39-41). When God's <u>calamity</u> ended, the Biblical record documented, *"...that the sky became <u>black with clouds and wind</u>, and there was <u>a heavy rain</u>...."* (1 Kings 18:45).

BTT is necessary to comprehend the awesome and unseen nature of the Almighty Living God. The Lord's presence on earth alone brings <u>calamity</u>. Elijah found this out first hand as he went up into the mountains and spent the night in a cave according to 1 Kings 19:9. Elijah had fled to the mountains because Jezebel had placed a bounty on his head and wanted him dead according to 1 Kings 19:14. However, the Lord called him out of the cave and said, *"..."Go out, and stand on the mountain before the Lord." And behold, the Lord passed by, and a <u>great and strong wind tore into the mountains and broke the rocks in pieces</u> before the Lord, but the Lord was not in the <u>wind</u>; and after the <u>wind</u> an <u>earthquake</u>, but the Lord was not in the <u>earthquake</u>; and after the <u>earthquake</u> a <u>fire</u>, but the Lord was not in the <u>fire</u>; and after the <u>fire</u> a still small voice. So it was, when Elijah heard it, that he wrapped his face in his mantle and went out and stood in the entrance of the cave. Suddenly a voice came to him, and said, "What are you doing here, Elijah?" And he said, "I have been very zealous for the Lord God of hosts; because the children of Israel have forsaken Your covenant, torn down Your altars, and* **killed** *Your prophets with the sword. I alone am left; and they seek to take my life"* (1 Kings 19:11-14). Consider all of God's <u>calamities</u> that Elijah **witnessed** for himself. The Lord sent him off the mountain with instructions and His protection. The Lord also told Elijah that he was not alone. In fact, the Lord revealed to him, *"Yet I have reserved seven thousand in Israel, all whose knees* **have not bowed to Baal**, *and* **every mouth that has not kissed him**" (1 Kings 19:18). A remnant of God's people remained in the land with Jezebel. BTT allows one to see that a remnant will always remain with God while the masses follow a different voice. This Truth is also seen in the ratio of positive to negative attributes in the war campaign.

As evil as Ahab was, he understood what it meant to have <u>calamity</u> come from the Lord. To illustrate this point, the Biblical record documented that Elijah went to Ahab with a direct message from the Lord. When they first met, Ahab said to Elijah, *"Have you found me, O my enemy?"* (1 Kings 21:20). BTT allows one to understand that this was not a greeting of mutual respect, but one influenced by the **hater** attribute. Nonetheless, Elijah responded, *"I have found you, because you have sold yourself to do* **evil** *in the sight of the Lord: 'Behold, I will bring <u>calamity</u> on you. I will take away your posterity, and will cut off from Ahab every male* *in Israel, both bond and free"* (1 Kings 21:21). There is a whole lot more to God's message in 1 Kings 22-26 and I encourage you to read it. Elijah's response scared Ahab so badly that the Biblical record documented that he, *"tore his clothes and put sackcloth on his body, and fasted and lay in sackcloth, and went about mourning"* (1 Kings 21:27). BTT allows one to see that Ahab repented. Because of this, the Lord said to Elijah, *"See how Ahab has <u>humbled</u> himself before Me? Because he has <u>humbled</u> himself before Me, I will not bring the <u>calamity</u> in his days. In the days of his son I will bring the <u>calamity</u> on his house"* (1 Kings 21:29). God spared Ahab a <u>calamity</u>; however, Ahab had already corrupted his son. Thus, God's foretold <u>calamity</u> was **just**. Keep in mind, Ahab's son had his own choices to make; he had the right to follow God.

In the Book of Second Kings, God used <u>calamity</u> to get the attention of the nation of Israel and their king. In fact, the Biblical record documented that Ben-Hadad, king of Syria, took advantage of God's <u>calamity</u> to inflict harm on God's people in Samaria. The Biblical record documented, *"And it happened after this that Ben-Hadad king of Syria gathered all his army, and went up and besieged Samaria. And there was a great <u>famine</u> in Samaria; and indeed they besieged it until a donkey's head was sold for eighty shekels of silver, and one-fourth of a kab of dove droppings for five shekels of silver"* (2 Kings 6:24-25). The siege and <u>famine</u> combined forced the people into a situation where they turned to cannibalism to remain alive according to 2 Kings 6:26-31. I will spare you the details recorded in the Biblical record, but I encourage you to read this gruesome portion of the Biblical record for yourself. The prophet Elisha and the elders of Samaria met with Israel's king and he recognized that the <u>calamity</u> facing Samaria was from the Lord. The Biblical record documented, *"And while he was still talking with them, there was the messenger, coming down to him; and then the king said, "Surely this <u>calamity</u> is from the Lord; why should I wait for the Lord any longer?"* (2 Kings 6:33). BTT allows one to see that the nation of Israel and the king had to make a choice. God's <u>longsuffering</u> and <u>patience</u> would allow Him to take them back if they made the **right** choice. I encourage you to read the rest of the Biblical record to see what they did.

God used <u>calamity</u> to get the attention of the nation of Israel and King Manasseh. The Biblical record documented, *"Because Manasseh king of Judah has done these abominations (he has acted more **wickedly** than all the Amorites who were before him, and has also made Judah sin with his **idols**), therefore thus says the Lord God of Israel: 'Behold, I am bringing such <u>calamity</u> upon Jerusalem and Judah, that whoever hears of it, both his ears will tingle"* (2 Kings 21:11-12). BTT allows one to see that when a nation refuses to do what the Lord commands, conditions are set up for leaders with negative attributes to lead. When He sees fit, the Lord can and will exercise His option to use <u>calamity</u> to refocus people back to the truth.

In the Book of Second Chronicles, after Solomon had completed the Temple of the Lord, the Lord made an important point to Solomon. The Biblical record documented, *"Then the Lord appeared to Solomon by night, and said to him: "I have heard your prayer, and have chosen this place for Myself as a house of sacrifice. When I shut up heaven and there is <u>no rain</u>, or command <u>the locusts to devour the land</u>, or send <u>pestilence</u> among My people, if My people who are called by My name will <u>humble</u> themselves, and pray and seek My face, and turn from their **wicked** ways, then I will hear from heaven, and will forgive their sin and heal their land"* (2 Chronicles 7:12-14). BTT allows one to see the correlation between the Lord's use of _calamity_ and repentance. People who follow God's Word must _humble_ themselves before Him or face His _calamity_. BTT also allows one to see that God's _calamity_ comes automatically for those who do not know the Lord. Therefore, the Biblical record goes on to document for Solomon and for our learning today, these words in 2 Chronicles 7:19-22:

> *"But if you turn away and forsake My statutes and My commandments which I have set before you, and go and serve other gods, and worship them, then I will <u>uproot</u> them from My land which I have given them; and this house which I have sanctified for My name I will <u>cast out</u> of My sight, and will make it a proverb and a byword among all peoples. "And as for this house, which is exalted, everyone who passes by it will be astonished and say, 'Why has the Lord done thus to this land and this house?' Then they will answer, 'Because they forsook the Lord God of their fathers, who brought them out of the land of Egypt, and **embraced other gods**, and **worshiped them** and **served them**; therefore He has brought all this <u>calamity</u> on them.'"*

In addition, the prophet Elijah wrote a letter to King Jehoram and told him that the Lord would use _calamity_ to get his and the nation of Israel's attention. Here is the letter documented in 2 Chronicles 21:12-15:

> *"Thus says the Lord God of your father David: Because you have not walked in the ways of Jehoshaphat your father, or in the ways of Asa king of Judah, but have walked in the way of the kings of Israel, and have made Judah and the inhabitants of Jerusalem to play the **harlot** like the **harlotry** of the house of Ahab, and also have **killed** your brothers, those of your father's household, who were better than yourself, behold, the Lord will <u>strike</u> your people with a <u>serious affliction</u>—your children, your wives, and all your possessions; and you will become <u>very sick</u> with a <u>disease</u> of your intestines, until your intestines come out by reason of the <u>sickness</u>, day by day."*

King Jehoram did not heed the words of the Lord and the Biblical record documented that _calamity_ came. The Bible recorded, *"After all this the Lord struck him in his intestines with an incurable <u>disease</u>. Then it happened in the course of time, after the end of two years, that his intestines came out because of his <u>sickness</u>; so <u>he died in severe pain</u>. And his people made no burning for him, like the burning for his fathers"* (2 Chronicles 21:18-19). One can see that the Lord did as He said. King Jehoram had the option to repent but did not.

Most people, even people partially familiar with the Biblical record, tend to know of the epic _calamity_ that Job experienced. What is important about this _calamity_ is that Ezekiel 14:14 and Ezekiel 14:20 identified Job as a **righteous** man. Moreover, the Biblical record documented that he was, *"...**blameless** and **upright**, and one who feared God and shunned **evil**"* (Job 1:1). So, there must be a prolific point for one to learn if someone like Job could experience the _calamity_ that he experienced. However, before revealing the point, understand Job did experience God's _calamity_. God allowed Satan to attempt to influence Job's behavior and attitude. The Biblical record documented that Satan said to God, *"...You have blessed the work of his hands, and his **possessions have increased** in the land. But now, stretch out*

Your hand and touch all that he has, and he will surely curse You to Your face!" And the Lord said to Satan, "Behold, all that he has is in your power; only do not lay a hand on his person." So Satan went out from the presence of the Lord" (Job 1:10-12). Satan had authority to try to influence Job, but he could not take Job's life. BTT allows one to see that Satan used the spiritual warfare against Job. The Biblical record documented the following:

Calamity	**What Is Documented**	**Job's Response**
First	*"A messenger came to Job and said, "The oxen were plowing and the donkeys feeding beside them, when the Sabeans **raided** them and took them away—indeed they have **killed** the servants with the edge of the sword; and I alone have escaped to tell you!"* (Job 1:14-15)	None
Second	*"While he was still speaking, another also came and said, "The **fire of God fell from heaven and burned up** the sheep and the servants, and consumed them; and I alone have escaped to tell you!"* (Job 1:16)	None
Third	*"While he was still speaking, another also came and said, "The Chaldeans formed three bands, **raided** the camels and took them away, yes, and **killed** the servants with the edge of the sword; and I alone have escaped to tell you!"* (Job 1:17)	None
Fourth	*"While he was still speaking, another also came and said, "Your sons and daughters were eating and drinking wine in their oldest brother's house, and suddenly **a great wind** came from across the wilderness and **struck** the four corners of the house, and it fell on the young people, and they are dead; and I alone have escaped to tell you!"* (Job 1:18-19)	*"Then Job arose, tore his robe, and shaved his head; and he fell to the ground and worshiped. And he said: "Naked I came from my mother's womb, and naked shall I return there. The Lord gave, and the Lord has taken away; blessed be the name of the Lord."* **In all this Job did not sin nor charge God with wrong**" (Job 1:20-22)
Fifth	*"So Satan went out from the presence of the Lord, and **struck** Job with **painful boils** from the sole of his foot to the crown of his head"* (Job 2:7)	*"And he took for himself a potsherd with which to scrape himself while he sat in the midst of the ashes"* (Job 2:8)
Sixth	*"Then his wife said to him, "Do you still hold fast to your integrity? Curse God and die!"* (Job 2:9)	*"But he said to her, "You speak as one of the foolish women speaks. Shall we indeed accept good from God, and shall we not accept adversity?"* **In all this Job did not sin with his lips**" (Job 2:10)

Seventh	*"Now when Job's three friends heard of all this adversity that had come upon him, each one came from his own place—Eliphaz the Temanite, Bildad the Shuhite, and Zophar the Naamathite. For they had made an appointment together to come and mourn with him, and to comfort him"* (Job 2:11) Elihu, an understudy of the wise men, commented when he felt the other men are not making progress with their accusations against Job. His comments are found in Job chapters 32-36)	Job 2:7 thru Job 37 captures the discourse between Job and the four men. God told them they will be punished and what they must do," *...My wrath is aroused against you and your two friends, for you have not spoken of Me what is right, as My servant Job has"* (Job 42: 7). AND **Job did not sin and is restored**, *"And the Lord restored Job's losses when he prayed for his friends. Indeed the Lord gave Job twice as much as he had before"* (Job 42:10)

Table 153: God's <u>*Calamity*</u> and Job

As one reviews the <u>*calamity*</u> Job experienced, one should also observe his behavior and response to each event. Within the context of Job's behavioral and verbal responses, one finds answers to the prolific point God reveals. It is one thing to say that God is in control, but when adversity strikes, it is a whole different thing to show by one's behavior and speech that one believes God is in control. This is the lesson from Job. BTT allows one to see that Job stood firm against the negative forces of the war campaign through this <u>*calamity*</u>. Moreover, many people miss another aspect of God's <u>*calamity*</u> surrounding Job. That is, Job was not the only one experiencing the <u>*calamity*</u>. Everyone else in his family also experienced God's <u>*calamity*</u>. The Book of Job did not elaborate on what was happening in the lives of Job's children. However, it is revealed, *"...when the days of feasting had run their course, that Job would send and sanctify them, and he would rise early in the morning and offer burnt offerings according to the number of them all. For Job said, "It may be that my sons have sinned and cursed God in their hearts." Thus Job did regularly"* (Job 1:5). Based on this information, BTT allows one to see that the negative forces of the war campaign were knocking on the door of Job's children. The negative forces went after Job's family to get to Job. BTT allows one to see that Job's children had to fight and defend against spiritual warfare on their own. If Job's children got lost in the fog of the negative forces, they faced their own consumption in the war campaign. Job, as a parent grieved this reality, as all parents should. Unfortunately, the record did not record a favorable outcome for them according to Job 1:18-19. As God's <u>*calamity*</u> came, Job's children had to give an account for themselves. Thus, Job understood spiritual warfare and the war campaign and made his wisdom clear when he documented about God, *"He shall deliver you in six troubles, Yes, in seven no **evil** shall touch you"* (Job 5:19). Job provided a major pearl of wisdom here. He stood strong through seven major crises (see Table 148) and the Lord delivered him and restored all that he lost. In fact, the Biblical record documented that, *"...the Lord blessed the latter days of Job more than his beginning..."* (Job 42:12). One should take away the fact that God is in control. Even through <u>*calamity,*</u> if one is ***faithful*** and obedient to God, He will be ***faithful*** in return.

In the Book of Psalms, the author documented God's use of <u>*calamity*</u>. The Psalmist emphasized the fact that God was in control of humanity and that He used <u>*calamity*</u> as a physical illustration of His authority. The Psalmist drew a distinction between the normal earthly processes that occur as part of nature and the epic events that consume the life of God's creation when the negative attributes gain too great of a foothold. The Psalmist wrote of God:

- *"You broke open the fountain and the flood; You dried up mighty rivers. The day is Yours, the night also is Yours; You have prepared the light and the sun. You have set all the borders of the earth; You have made summer and winter"* (Psalm 74:15-17)

- *"The voice of Your thunder was in the whirlwind; the lightnings lit up the world; the earth trembled and shook"* (Psalm 77:18)

- Dealing with the Egyptians who held the children of Israel in bondage: *"He made a path for His anger; He did not spare their soul from death, but gave their life over to the plague..."* (Psalm 78:50)

- *"Moreover He called for a famine in the land; He destroyed all the provision of bread"* (Psalm 105:16)

- *"For He commands and raises the stormy wind, which lifts up the waves of the sea"* (Psalm 107:25) and *"He calms the storm, so that its waves are still"* (Psalm 107:29)

- *"Fire and hail, snow and clouds; stormy wind, fulfilling His word..."* (Psalm 148:8)

From these Biblical references, one can see that God uses *calamity* to fulfill His Word (Psalms 148:8). From this point, I will pick a few examples of God's use of *calamity* to get the nation of Israel and their leadership's attention as the Lord spoke through His prophets. Afterwards, I will show how the Lord used *calamity* to punish other nations for their interference and the harm they inflicted on the nation of Israel. Pleases consider Table 154:

The Prophet	**What Was Said**
Isaiah	*"You will be punished by the Lord of hosts with thunder and earthquake and great noise, with storm and tempest and the flame of devouring fire"* (Isaiah 29:6)
	"I am the Lord, and there is no other; there is no God besides Me. I will gird you, though you have not known Me, that they may know from the rising of the sun to its setting that there is none besides Me. I am the Lord, and there is no other; I form the light and create darkness, I make peace and create calamity; I, the Lord, do all these things'" (Isaiah 45:5-7)
	"Then the Lord said to me: "Out of the north calamity shall break forth on all the inhabitants of the land" (Jeremiah 1:14)
	*"For the house of Israel and the house of Judah have dealt very treacherously with Me," says the Lord. They have **lied** about the Lord, and said, "It is not He. Neither will **evil** come upon us, nor shall we see sword or famine. And the prophets become wind, for the word is not in them. Thus shall it be done to them"* (Jeremiah 5:11-13)

Jeremiah	"Hear, O earth! Behold, I will certainly bring <u>calamity</u> on this people— The fruit of their thoughts, because they have not heeded My words nor My law, but rejected it" (Jeremiah 6:19)
	"Therefore thus says the Lord: "Behold, I will surely bring <u>calamity</u> on them which they will not be able to escape; and though they cry out to Me, I will not listen to them" (Jeremiah 11:11)
	"...therefore thus says the Lord of hosts: 'Behold, I will punish them. The young men shall <u>die by the sword</u>, their sons and their daughters shall die by <u>famine</u>..." (Jeremiah 11:22)
	"They shall die <u>gruesome deaths</u>; they shall not be lamented nor shall they be buried, but they shall be like refuse on the face of the earth. They shall be <u>consumed by the sword</u> and by <u>famine</u>, and their corpses shall be meat for the birds of heaven and for the beasts of the earth" (Jeremiah 16:4)
	"I will <u>strike</u> the inhabitants of this city, both man and beast; they shall die of <u>a great pestilence</u>" (Jeremiah 21:6)
	When Israel said, "That is hopeless! So we will walk according to our own plans, and we will every one obey the dictates of his **evil** heart" (Jeremiah 18:12). God responded, "I will <u>scatter them</u> as with an <u>east wind</u> before the enemy; I will show them the back and not the face in the day of their <u>calamity</u>" (Jeremiah 18:17)
	King Nebuchadnezzar of Babylon invaded the nation of Israel and his armies were the tool of God's <u>calamity</u> on the nation according to Jeremiah 21:7. The Biblical record documented, that Jeremiah told the people, "...'Thus says the Lord: "Behold, I set before you the way of life and the way of death. He who remains in this city shall <u>die by the sword</u>, by <u>famine</u>, and by <u>pestilence</u>; but he who goes out and defects to the Chaldeans who besiege you, he shall live, and his life shall be as a prize to him. For I have set My face against this city for adversity and not for **good**," says the Lord. "It shall be given into the hand of the king of Babylon, and he shall <u>burn it with fire</u>"' (Jeremiah 21:8-10)
	"Behold, a <u>whirlwind</u> of the Lord has gone forth in fury— A <u>violent whirlwind</u>! It will fall <u>violently</u> on the head of the **wicked**" (Jeremiah 23:19)
	As people fled to Egypt for protection, Jeremiah went there and told them, "...then it shall be that the sword which you feared shall overtake you there in the land of Egypt; the <u>famine</u> of which you were afraid shall follow close after you there in Egypt; and there you shall die. So shall it be with all the men who set their faces to go to Egypt to dwell there. They shall <u>die by the sword</u>, by <u>famine</u>, and by <u>pestilence</u>. And none of them shall remain or escape from the disaster that I will bring upon them'" (Jeremiah 42:16, 17; 44:12-13)
Ezekiel	"One-third of you shall die of the <u>pestilence</u>, and be consumed with <u>famine</u> in your midst; and one-third shall <u>fall by the sword</u> all around you; and I will <u>scatter</u> another third to all the winds, and I will draw out a sword after them" (Ezekiel 5:12)
	"And they shall know that I am the Lord; I have not said in vain that I would bring this <u>calamity</u> upon them." Thus says the Lord God: "Pound your fists and stamp your feet, and say, 'Alas, for all the **evil** abominations of the house of Israel! For they shall <u>fall by the sword</u>, by <u>famine</u>, and by <u>pestilence</u>. He who is far off shall die by the <u>pestilence</u>, he who is near shall <u>fall by the sword</u>, and he who remains and is besieged shall die by the <u>famine</u>. Thus will I spend My fury upon them" (Ezekiel 6:10-12)

	"The <u>sword is outside</u>, and the <u>pestilence</u> and <u>famine</u> within. Whoever is in the field will <u>die by the sword</u>; and whoever is in the city, <u>famine</u> and <u>pestilence</u> will devour him" (Ezekiel 7:15)
	"But I will spare a few of their men from the sword, from <u>famine</u>, and from <u>pestilence</u>, that they may declare all their abominations among the Gentiles wherever they go. Then they shall know that I am the Lord" (Ezekiel 12:16)
Amos	"If a trumpet is blown in a city, will not the people be afraid? If there is <u>calamity</u> in a city, will not the Lord have done it?" (Amos 3:6)
	"For surely I will command, and will sift the house of Israel among all nations, as grain is sifted in a sieve; yet not the smallest grain shall fall to the ground. All the sinners of My people shall die by the sword, who say, 'The <u>calamity</u> shall not overtake nor confront us'" (Amos 9:9-10)

Table 154: The Prophets' Identification of God's _Calamity_ on the Nation of Israel

After the destruction of the nation of Israel, God punished the nations documented below that inflicted harm on the nation of Israel. God's _calamity_ came to those nations for allowing the negative forces of the war campaign to dominate in their inner spirit and their role in corrupting the nation of Israel:

- Moab: "_The <u>calamity</u> of Moab is near at hand, and his affliction comes quickly_" (Jeremiah 48:16)

- Dedan: "_Flee, turn back, dwell in the depths, O inhabitants of Dedan! For I will bring the <u>calamity</u> of Esau upon him, the time that I will punish him_" (Jeremiah 49:8)

- Edom: "_Edom also shall be an astonishment; everyone who goes by it will be astonished and will hiss at all its <u>plagues</u>_" (Jeremiah 49:17)

- Kedar and Hazor: "_Their camels shall be for booty, and the multitude of their cattle for plunder. I will scatter to all winds those in the farthest corners, and I will bring their <u>calamity</u> from all its sides," says the Lord_" (Jeremiah 49:32)

- Babylon and Babylonia: "_Because of the wrath of the Lord she shall not be inhabited, but she shall be wholly desolate. Everyone who goes by Babylon shall be horrified and hiss at all her <u>plagues</u>_" (Jeremiah 50:13), and "_A <u>drought</u> is against her waters, and they will be dried up. For it is the land of **carved images**, and they are insane with their **idols**_" (Jeremiah 50:38)

- Mount Seir: "_Because you have had an **ancient hatred**, and have **shed the blood** of the children of Israel by the power of the sword at the time of their <u>calamity</u>, when their iniquity came to an end..._" (Ezekiel 35:5)

- Gog: _For in My jealousy and in the fire of My wrath I have spoken: 'Surely in that day there shall be <u>a great earthquake</u> in the land of Israel,_ (Ezekiel 38:19), and "_And I will bring him to judgment with <u>pestilence</u> and bloodshed; I will rain down on him, on his troops, and on the many peoples who are with him, <u>flooding rain</u>, <u>great hailstones</u>, <u>fire</u>, and <u>brimstone</u>_" (Ezekiel 38:22)

- Nineveh: *"The Lord is slow to anger and great in power, and will not at all acquit the **wicked**. The Lord has His way in the <u>whirlwind</u> and in the <u>storm</u>, and the clouds are the dust of His feet"* (Nahum 1:3), and *"But with an <u>overflowing flood</u> He will make an utter end of its place, and darkness will pursue His enemies"* (Nahum 1:8)

In addition, the prophet Ezekiel revealed a major point about <u>calamity</u> from the Lord that is often overlooked. In the Book of Ezekiel, Ezekiel gave a strict warning to the prophets who ***falsely*** prophesized things from God in Ezekiel 13:2. Because of their **lies**, the Lord had Ezekiel give them a direct message. I want to share this message because I believe what is documented foreshadows God's <u>calamity</u> on society today because of **false** ministers and teachers of world religions. This applies even more to the **false** teachers in the Lord's church who are simply advancing the negative forces of the war campaign. Ezekiel documented in Ezekiel 13:8-16 the following:

> *"Therefore thus says the Lord God: "Because you have spoken nonsense and **envisioned lies**, therefore I am indeed against you," says the Lord God. "My hand will be against the prophets who **envision futility** and who **divine lies**; they shall not be in the assembly of My people, nor be written in the record of the house of Israel, nor shall they enter into the land of Israel. Then you shall know that I am the Lord God. Because, indeed, because they have **seduced** My people, saying, 'Peace!' when there is no peace—and one builds a wall, and they plaster it with untempered mortar— say to those who plaster it with untempered mortar, that it will fall. There will be <u>flooding rain</u>, and you, O <u>great hailstones</u>, shall fall; and a <u>stormy wind</u> shall tear it down. Surely, when the wall has fallen, will it not be said to you, 'Where is the mortar with which you plastered it?'" Therefore thus says the Lord God: "I will cause a <u>stormy wind</u> to break forth in My fury; and there shall be a <u>flooding rain</u> in My anger, and <u>great hailstones</u> in fury to consume it. So I will break down the wall you have plastered with untempered mortar, and bring it down to the ground, so that its foundation will be uncovered; it will fall, and you shall be consumed in the midst of it. Then you shall know that I am the Lord. "Thus will I accomplish My wrath on the wall and on those who have plastered it with untempered mortar; and I will say to you, 'The wall is no more, nor those who plastered it, that is, the prophets of Israel who prophesy concerning Jerusalem, and who see visions of peace for her when there is no peace,'" says the Lord God."*

BTT allows one to see that the Lord established sanctuaries and places of learning about Him and His way on the battlefield of the war campaign. In the ancient days, it was His Tabernacle; and for the Jews, the synagogue. However, today the sanctuary and place of learning is Jesus' church that He established. However, when God's people become complacent, ***false*** teachers rise. God's Word is the mortar that strengthened the foundation of humanity with His wisdom. This mortar protects humanity from the influences of the negative attributes that are so prevalent in the spiritual war. For the nation of Israel, the prophets and priests became corrupt and taught **lies** and *"untempered"* mortar filled the foundation of the people. This untempered mortar was the improper teaching of the Word of God and therefore it made the people weak. They were unable to stand when God's <u>calamity</u> came for the people influenced by the **wicked** attribute. When the nation of Israel fell, God's _calamity_ consumed the people spiritually immature in His Word, the priest, and the *false* prophets. One will see this again in the New Testament.

BTT allows one to plainly see that the Lord used _calamity_ to correct and purge sin from among His people in the Old Testament. But is there clear evidence that God used _calamity_ in the New Testament and now? Yes! BTT allows one to see that God used _calamity_ in the New Testament and is using it today. Generations today remain in the fog generated by the negative forces. Let us see what the New Testament documented on this subject.

The four Gospels of Matthew, Mark, Luke, and John thoroughly documents God's _calamity_. Please keep in mind this one Scripture as I begin. Paul documented, *"For whatever things were written before were written for our learning, that we through the patience and comfort of the Scriptures might have hope"* (Romans 15:4). This statement captures the essential knowledge that informs one that the entire Old Testament of the Biblical record does not need repeating in the New Testament for one to believe it. The past knowledge was for one's learning; one must now grow from what one has learned. With that said, one must understand that God's people of the New Testament were still dealing with God's _calamity_ from the Old Testament. God's _calamity_ from the judgement He pronounced on the nation of Israel and the surrounding nations had not ceased. Do not forget this important point. Generations of the nation of Israel had not repented of the sins identified from the past. Moreover, the prophets, chief priest, Pharisees, Sadducees, and scribes kept the people in the fog of the negative forces of the war campaign. Hence, Jesus called the Jewish leadership *"blind guides"* according to Matthew 23:16; and verse 24. However, a minority of people influenced by the positive forces were among the Jews too. BTT allows one to see that there was a remnant of Jews influenced by the ***faithful*** attribute living among the Jews of that time. These ***faithful*** Jew's condition was much like Lot of whom the Biblical record documented, *"...was **oppressed** by the **filthy conduct** of the **wicked** (for that **righteous** man, dwelling among them, tormented his **righteous** soul from day to day by seeing and hearing their lawless deeds)"* (2 Peter 2:7-8). According to the first part of the four Gospel writers, Jesus Christ and John the Baptist were born from two families of the remnant. In fact, a prophecy about this remnant is found in the Old Testament where it is stated, *"The remnant of Israel shall do no **unrighteousness** and speak no **lies**, nor shall a **deceitful** tongue be found in their mouth; for they shall feed their flocks and lie down, and no one shall make them _afraid_"* (Zephaniah 3:13).

When Jesus Christ arrived, He served as a major disrupting force to the war campaign. Because the Jews and surrounding nations were still dealing with God's _calamity_, the Biblical record documented, *"...Jesus went about all Galilee, teaching in their synagogues, preaching the gospel of the kingdom, and healing all kinds of _sickness_ and all kinds of _disease_ among the people. Then His fame went throughout all Syria; and they brought to Him all _sick_ people who were afflicted with various _diseases_ and torments, and those who were demon-possessed, epileptics, and paralytics; and He healed them"* (Matthew 4:23-24). Jesus was teaching the Jews in their synagogues and BTT allows one to see that as He taught them God's Word, He was healing people from the sting of God's _calamity_, which started long ago. In other words, within His teachings and preaching, Jesus was providing relief from God's _calamity_. He was the source of relief sent by God for those who believed in Him. His teachings provided the Jews the wisdom for defending themselves against spiritual warfare. Please pay close attention to the next thought, as it is extremely important for preparing for spiritual warfare and the war campaign.

Early in His ministry, Jesus gave a message to the people that was similar to the Lord's message to the nation of Israel. Consider Jesus's statement and the Lord's statement in **Table 155**.

Matthew 7:24-29	*"Therefore whoever hears these sayings of Mine, and does them, I will liken him to a **wise** man who built his house on the rock: and the rain descended, the floods came, and the winds blew and beat on that house; and it did not fall, for it was founded on the rock. "But everyone who hears these sayings of Mine, and does not do them, will be like a **foolish** man who built his house on the sand: and the rain descended, the floods came, and the winds blew and beat on that house; and it fell. And great was its fall." And so it was, when Jesus had ended these sayings, that the people were astonished at His teaching, for He taught them as one having authority, and not as the scribes"*
Luke 6:46-49	*"But why do you call Me 'Lord, Lord,' and not do the things which I say? Whoever comes to Me, and hears My sayings and does them, I will show you whom he is like: He is like a man building a house, who dug deep and laid the foundation on the rock. And when the flood arose, the stream beat vehemently against that house, and could not shake it, for it was founded on the rock. But he who heard and did nothing is like a man who built a house on the earth without a foundation, against which the stream beat vehemently; and immediately it fell. And the ruin of that house was great."*
Ezekiel 13:10-16	*"...and one builds a wall, and they plaster it with untempered mortar— say to those who plaster it with untempered mortar, that it will fall. There will be flooding rain, and you, O great hailstones, shall fall; and a stormy wind shall tear it down. Surely, when the wall has fallen, will it not be said to you, 'Where is the mortar with which you plastered it?'" Therefore thus says the Lord God: "I will cause a stormy wind to break forth in My fury; and there shall be a flooding rain in My anger, and great hailstones in fury to consume it. So I will break down the wall you have plastered with untempered mortar, and bring it down to the ground, so that its foundation will be uncovered; it will fall, and you shall be consumed in the midst of it. Then you shall know that I am the Lord. "Thus will I accomplish My wrath on the wall and on those who have plastered it with untempered mortar; and I will say to you, 'The wall is no more, nor those who plastered it, that is, the prophets of Israel..."*

Table 155: The Wisdom of the House and Foundation

BTT allows one to see the correlation between the foundation of the house that Jesus spoke about and the foundation of the wall that Ezekiel spoke about. God's Word strengthens the house and the wall's foundation. God's Word is spiritual mortar that strengthens one spiritually during times of calamity. Moreover, God's Word strengthens one's inner spirit against the negative attributes during spiritual warfare. For Christians, Paul stated *"...do you not know that your body is the temple of the Holy Spirit who is in you, whom you have from God, and you are not your own?"* (1 Corinthians 6:19). BTT allows one to see that without the Word of God, one's house or bodily temple, foundation, and inner spirit, will fail when God's <u>calamity</u>, or even spiritual warfare occurs. Without a strong spiritual foundation, one simply becomes collateral damage in the war campaign. Paul provided more wisdom to this point when he documented, *"...if Christ is in you, the body is dead because of sin, but the Spirit is life because of **righteousness**"* (Romans 8:10). BTT allows one to see that this is what Jesus told the people, just like the Lord told Ezekiel. Untempered mortar is the same as ***false*** doctrine to the inner spirit. Hence, <u>discernment</u> and BTT are paramount.

Now just to be crystal clear about this foundation, BTT allows one to see that the foundation that Christians build their spiritual house with and on is God's Word. It is the spiritual mortar of the foundation that makes Christians, *"...no longer strangers and foreigners, but fellow citizens with the saints and members of the household of God, having been built on the foundation of the apostles and prophets, Jesus Christ Himself being the chief cornerstone, in whom the whole building, being fitted together, grows into a holy temple in the Lord, in whom you also are being built together for a dwelling place of God in the Spirit"* (Ephesians 2:19-22). Christians know that *"...no other foundation can anyone lay than that which is laid, which is Jesus Christ"* (1 Corinthians 3:11). Further they wholeheartedly believe the Holy Spirit's Word to Paul when he wrote Timothy stating, *"the solid foundation of God stands, having this seal: "The Lord knows those who are His," and, "Let everyone who names the name of Christ depart from iniquity"* (2 Timothy 2:19). Hence, for the ***righteous***, the Spirit of wisdom revealed to Solomon, *"When the <u>whirlwind</u> passes by, the **wicked** is no more, but the **righteous** has an everlasting foundation"* (Proverbs 10:25).

Later in the Gospel accounts, the Biblical record specifically documented what Jesus was doing as the disrupting force to the Jew's <u>calamity</u>. The Bible documented, *"Then Jesus went about all the cities and villages, teaching in their synagogues, preaching the gospel of the kingdom, and healing every <u>sickness</u> and every <u>disease</u> among the people"* (Matthew 9:35). In other words, as Jesus taught the Gospel to the Jewish's nation, the <u>calamity</u> they experienced began to cease for those accepting His Word. The Gospel that Jesus taught was the balm that healed the Jews of God's <u>calamity</u>. This may be a different way to look at the events taking place, but as one begins to understand spiritual warfare and the war campaign, God's strategy among the Jews becomes clearer. The Bible even documents, *"...Jesus said to those Jews who believed Him, "If you abide in My word, you are My disciples indeed. And you shall know the truth, and the truth shall make you free""* (John 8:31-32). The Book of Amos also shed light on this fact where it documented, *"Seek **good** and not **evil**, that you may live; so the Lord God of hosts will be with you, as you have spoken. **Hate evil**, love **good**; establish justice in the gate. It may be that the Lord God of hosts will be <u>gracious</u> to the remnant of Joseph"* (Amos 5:14-15). Jesus would bring that <u>grace</u> to the remnant of Joseph.

BTT allows one to see that Jesus affected both the physical and spiritual realms of the campaign. Jesus' physical acts among the people did more than just heal them of natural <u>sicknesses</u>. His power cleansed the influences of the negative attributes from the inner spirits of the people. Jesus' balm, God's Word, allowed the Jews that believed in Him to come out of the fog generated by the negative forces. In fact, the Biblical record documented, *"And the*

***unclean spirits**, whenever they saw Him, fell down before Him and cried out, saying, "You are the Son of God""* (Mark 3:11). Other references include:

- The man with **unclean spirits**. The Bible documented that after Jesus spoke to the **unclean spirits** that wanted to leave him, *"...at once Jesus gave them permission. Then the **unclean spirits** went out and entered the swine (there were about two thousand); and the herd ran violently down the steep place into the sea, and drowned in the sea"* (Mark 5:13)

- *"Then they were all amazed and spoke among themselves, saying, "What a word this is! For with authority and power He commands the **unclean spirits**, and they come out"* (Luke 4:36)

- *"When the sun was setting, all those who had any that were <u>sick</u> with <u>various diseases</u> brought them to Him; and He laid His hands on every one of them and healed them"* (Luke 4:40)

In other words, the negative attributes (**unclean spirits**) were so prevalent that God's <u>calamity</u> hung over the Jewish nation in the form of a <u>sickness</u> at a pandemic level. Remember what the Lord had Moses tell the children of Israel in the Old Testament? The Biblical record documented that the Lord said, *"... if you walk contrary to Me, and are not willing to obey Me, I will bring on you seven times more <u>plagues</u>, according to your sins"* (Leviticus 26:21). Connect the dots from the Old to the New Testament. These <u>plagues</u> were epic, unquestionably came from God, and persist to this very day. But, the negative forces of the war campaign will downplay God's <u>calamity</u> by teaching that the <u>sicknesses</u> that Jesus dealt with were simply due to the unsanitary conditions of that day. Do not be deceived. Jesus, as evidenced by Legion and others, talked to the **unclean spirits** (the negative attributes) that influenced the people.

There were so many <u>sick</u> people that Jesus received help because He was in His human body on earth. The Biblical record documented, *"And when He had called His twelve disciples to Him, He gave them power over **unclean spirits**, to cast them out, and to heal all kinds of <u>sickness</u> and all kinds of <u>disease</u>"* (Matthew 10:1; Mark 3:15; Luke 9:1). BTT allows one to see that the **unclean spirits** mentioned here were still negative attributes and the reason for God's <u>calamity</u> in the first place. Some might say that it is wrong to say that Jesus had help in this area from the twelve disciples. However, BTT allows one to see that when Jesus became flesh and blood, He limited His own powers on earth according to Philippians 2:8. In His human form, He trained twelve other men to help Him carry out God's mission. The training of the twelve men was for their benefit. The training prepared them for fighting spiritual warfare, the war campaign, and the future delivery of the Gospel message to the world. Moreover, this was part of God's strategy as documented by Jesus himself when He said, *"I have manifested Your name to the men whom You have given Me out of the world. They were Yours, You gave them to Me, and they have kept Your word. Now they have known that all things which You have given Me are from You. For I have given to them the words which You have given Me; and they have received them, and have known surely that I came forth from You; and they have believed that You sent Me"* (John 17:6-8).

To understand the magnitude of the _calamity_ affecting the Jewish nation, the Bible documents that Jesus, "..._came down with them and stood on a level place with a crowd of His disciples and a great multitude of people from all Judea and Jerusalem, and from the seacoast of Tyre and Sidon, who came to hear Him and be healed of their diseases, as well as those who were tormented with_ **unclean spirits**. _And they were healed. And the whole multitude sought to touch Him, for power went out from Him and healed them all_" (Luke 6:17-19). Jesus had the power to stop the _calamity plaguing_ the Jewish nation without the disciple's help. However, He chose not to. Just as He spoke to the _storm_ in Matthew 14:32, Mark 4:39, Mark 6:51, and Luke 8:24, and the _storm_ obeyed His voice; He also had the authority to stop God's _calamity_ on the Jews. The Biblical record also acknowledged that people were following Jesus because of what He could do. These people would later serve in the **witness** category. It was recorded, "_Then a great multitude followed Him, because they saw His signs which He performed on those who were diseased_" (John 6:2).

BTT allows one to see that the negative attribute's influences on humanity had a purpose and strategy within the war campaign. Remember, attributes are ancient **_spirits_**. They understood what the birth of Christ meant, and they understood the predictions from the Old Testament. This knowledge led Satan to ramp up his negative forces to entrench people in the fog of the war. Entrenchment was necessary to overpower Jesus, the One who would usher in a new covenant between God and man. Thus, the negative attributes concentrated their attacks on the nation of Israel; the people given the original oracle of God according to Romans 3:2. Israel then became a stronghold against Jesus and this led Jesus to pronounce from God an epic _calamity_ against the nation of the Jews. Jesus said, "_For nation will rise against nation, and kingdom against kingdom. And there will be famines, pestilences, and earthquakes in various places_" (Matthew 24:7-8; Mark 13:8; Luke 21:11). In fact, concerning the destruction of the temple in Jerusalem, Jesus even told His disciples, "_Do you see these great buildings? Not one stone shall be left upon another, that shall not be thrown down_" (Mark 13:2). BTT allows one to see that this was not a prediction of the end of the world. Jesus was announcing the destruction of the Jewish nation by Rome as documented in many historical records. Historians document that the Romans destroyed the Jewish temple around 70 A.D.

Please do not confuse this _calamity_ with the final great _calamity_ that will occur when the world ends, and Jesus returns. Peter documents the final great _calamity_ in the Book of Second Peter. The order of magnitude clarifies the difference between what Jesus stated in Mark 13:2 and what Peter documented. Peter documented that when this great _calamity_ comes from the Lord, "..._the Lord will come as a thief in the night, in which the heavens will pass away with a great noise, and the elements will melt with fervent heat; both the earth and the works that are in it will be burned up. Therefore, since all these things will be dissolved, what manner of persons ought you to be in holy conduct and_ **godliness**, _looking for and hastening the coming of the day of God, because of which the heavens will be dissolved, being on fire, and the elements will melt with fervent heat?_" (2 Peter 3:10-12). Remember, Jesus told the people to flee to the mountains in Matthew 24:16, Mark 13:14, and Luke 21:21 to escape God's _calamity_. In the _calamity_ Peter describes, there will be no mountains or any other place to flee to.

Prior to the fall of the Jewish nation, the people witnessed other _calamities_ from the Lord to get their attention. The Lord in His _longsuffering_, _compassion_, and **mercy**, gave the Jews every opportunity to repent, even with the sacrifice of His Son Jesus Christ. The Biblical record documented that during Jesus death:

- _"...the centurion and those with him, who were guarding Jesus, saw the earthquake and the things that had happened, they feared greatly, saying, "Truly this was the Son of God!"_ (Matthew 27:54)

- _"...the veil of the temple was torn in two from top to bottom; and the earth quaked, and the rocks were split, and the graves were opened; and many bodies of the saints who had fallen asleep were raised; and coming out of the graves after His resurrection, they went into the holy city and appeared to many"_ (Matthew 27:51-53; Mark 15:38)

- _"...there was a great earthquake; for an angel of the Lord descended from heaven, and came and rolled back the stone from the door, and sat on it"_ (Matthew 28:2)

After Jesus' death, but still before the fall of Jerusalem, the Bible continues to document God's _calamities_ to get the Jews' attention. BTT allows one to see that although many were being _baptized_ and turning to Christ, according to Acts 2:41-42 and Acts: 5:14; resistance to the Gospel from the Jews was also growing exponentially according to Acts 7:51-60; 8:1-3. Resistance came from men influenced by the negative attributes as the war campaign increased in intensity to stop the spread of the Gospel. However, here is where the application of BTT and _discernment_ is required. After the Holy Spirit arrived, the concentration of Christianity was in and around Jerusalem in Acts 2:1-4. One is never told how many of the people in Acts 2:9-11, remained in Jerusalem as the church grew exponentially. What one does know from the Biblical record is that after the first sermon by Peter, about _"three thousand souls"_ were _baptized_ into Christ according to Acts 2:41. However, BTT allows one to see that God did not desire these Christians to stay in Jerusalem. In fact, Jesus told His disciples, _"...that repentance and remission of sins should be preached in His name to all nations, beginning at Jerusalem"_ (Luke 2:47); to _"Go into all the world and preach the gospel to every creature. He who believes and is baptized will be saved; but he who does not believe will be condemned"_ (Mark 16:15-16); and to, _"Go therefore and make disciples of all the nations, baptizing them in the name of the Father and of the Son and of the Holy Spirit, teaching them to observe all things that I have commanded you..."_ (Matthew 28: 19-20). Just as the Old Testament (Genesis 11) indicates that as they grew in number, the people desired to remain around the Tower of Babel, so did these new Christians desire to remain in Jerusalem where they were comfortable with the Word of God. But God used a _calamity_ in both instances to move the people out of their comfort zones. In the case of the Christians in and around Jerusalem, the Biblical record documented that the Lord used a man name Saul to scatter the Christians abroad. Later, Saul's conversion to Christianity placed him in a position to serve as a major leader among the positive forces in the war campaign. For one's knowledge, the Bible documented, _"At that time a great persecution arose against the church which was at Jerusalem; and they were all scattered throughout the regions of Judea and Samaria, except the apostles...As for Saul, he made havoc_ of the church, entering every house, and dragging off men and women, committing them to prison. Therefore <u>those who were scattered went everywhere</u> preaching the word" (Acts 8:1-4). BTT allows one to see that God used <u>calamity</u> to enforce His will. People of all the nations listed in Acts 2:9-11 were scattered (Acts 8:1) to fulfill what Jesus commanded in Luke 24:46-48, Mark 16: 15-16, and Matthew 28: 19-20 as stated earlier. BTT is required for this idea but this is why this book has been written to provide an understanding of the war campaign.

After this <u>calamity</u> and as the Gospel spread throughout the world, the Biblical record documented other <u>calamities</u>. Here are a few of those <u>calamities</u>:

- <u>Famine</u>: "Then one of them, named Agabus, stood up and showed by the Spirit that there was going to be a great <u>famine</u> throughout all the world, which also happened in the days of Claudius Caesar" (Acts 11:28)

- <u>Earthquake</u>: "Suddenly there was a great <u>earthquake</u>, so that the foundations of the prison were shaken; and immediately all the doors were opened and everyone's chains were loosed" (Acts 16:26). Interestingly, this <u>quake</u> occurred after the Jews beat both Paul and Silas and then locked them in prison to stop them from teaching the Gospel.

- <u>Disease</u>: "...so that even handkerchiefs or aprons were brought from his body to the sick, and the <u>diseases</u> left them and the **evil spirits** went out of them" (Acts 19:12) and later after Paul healed Publius' father of <u>fever</u> and <u>dysentery</u>, "...the rest of those on the island who had <u>diseases</u> also came and were healed" (Acts 28:9)

The death of King Herod is another event documented in the Book of Acts of an exceptional example of God's <u>calamity</u>. The Biblical record documented that the **immoral** and **ungodly** attributes influenced Herod. People showering him with **flattery** and **blasphemy seduced** his thinking as the influence of the **pride** attribute seared his spiritual heart. He failed to correct the people and acknowledge God in their presence. Because of his behavior, God sent an immediate <u>calamity</u> to him. Herod died horribly. The Biblical record documented in Acts 12:20-24:

> "Now Herod had been **very angry** with the people of Tyre and Sidon; but they came to him with one accord, and having made Blastus the king's personal aide their friend, they asked for peace, because their country was supplied with food by the king's country. So on a set day Herod, arrayed in royal apparel, sat on his throne and gave an oration to them. And the people kept shouting, "The voice of a god and not of a man!" Then immediately an angel of the Lord <u>struck him</u>, because he did not give glory to God. And he was <u>eaten by worms</u> and died. But the word of God grew and multiplied."

One should pay close attention to the outcome of this <u>calamity</u>. The Biblical record documented that after King Herod died, the Word of God grew and multiplied because of God's <u>calamity</u>. In other words, the negative forces suffered a major defeat that day during the war campaign.

A very important point that Christians today must understand is that the nation of Israel rejected the Gospel of Jesus Christ; the key for their salvation and the balm for the Lord's *calamity*. BTT allows one to see that when Peter took the Gospel of Christ to Cornelius and his household in Chapter Ten of the Book of Acts, and these non-Jews accepted Christ, the positive forces of the war campaign expanded exponentially. This expansion became even more real when Paul and Barnabas stopped trying to help the Jews understand the Gospel of Jesus Christ. The Bible documented in Acts 13:44-47, *"On the next Sabbath almost the whole city came together to hear the word of God. But when the Jews saw the multitudes, they were filled with **envy**; and contradicting and blaspheming, they opposed the things spoken by Paul. Then Paul and Barnabas grew bold and said, "It was necessary that the word of God should be spoken to you first; but since you reject it, and judge yourselves unworthy of everlasting life, behold, we turn to the Gentiles. For so the Lord has commanded us: 'I have set you as a light to the Gentiles, that you should be for salvation to the ends of the earth.'"*

Later, Paul, a Jew himself, exclaimed to the Jewish leadership in Corinth, *"..."Your blood be upon your own heads; I am clean. From now on I will go to the Gentiles"* (Acts 18:6). In these instances, the negative forces lost a decisive spiritual battle. They did not stop the Gospel of Jesus Christ by silencing Paul or the other apostles. In fact, the positive forces multiplied, and the Jews forfeited their only protection from God's *calamity*. Moreover, their decision condemned them to God's *calamity* and *strife* to this very day.

Peter, like all the other New Testament writers, often reflected on the Old Testament to show the continuity of God Word between both Testaments. Peter did this with examples of *calamities* from the Old Testament to illustrate the continuity of God's method for dealing with sinful activity on a Biblical scale. Peter, inspired by the Holy Spirit, documented in 2 Peter 2:4-11 the following:

> *"For if God did not spare the angels who sinned, but cast them down to hell and delivered them into chains of darkness, to be reserved for judgment; and did not spare the ancient world, but saved Noah, one of eight people, a preacher of righteousness, bringing in the flood on the world of the **ungodly**; and turning the cities of Sodom and Gomorrah into ashes, condemned them to destruction, making them an example to those who afterward would live **ungodly**; and delivered **righteous** Lot, who was **oppressed** by the **filthy conduct** of the **wicked** (for that **righteous** man, dwelling among them, tormented his **righteous** soul from day to day by seeing and hearing their lawless deeds)— then the Lord knows how to deliver the **godly** out of temptations and to reserve the **unjust** under punishment for the day of judgment, and especially those who walk according to the flesh in the lust of uncleanness and despise authority. They are presumptuous, self-willed. They are not afraid to speak **evil** of dignitaries, whereas angels, who are greater in power and might, do not bring a reviling accusation against them before the Lord."*

In the example above, Peter illustrated God's use of three epic *calamities* to demonstrate His authority and power. At the same time, God purged the world of sinful behavior. In each case, God's actions dealt a major blow to the negative forces fighting in the war campaign. BTT allows one to see that God uses *calamity* when the negative attribute's influences extend beyond a boundary He has set. When the balance of the campaign becomes too unbalanced in favor of the negative forces, _calamity_ provides the opportunity for the positive forces to regain spiritual ground.

James shared that Christians always have an avenue to strengthen each other when God's _calamity_ is present. When there are spiritual and natural _sicknesses_ dominating one's life, James documented, "*Is anyone among you suffering? Let him pray. Is anyone cheerful? Let him sing psalms. Is anyone among you _sick_? Let him call for the elders of the church, and let them pray over him, anointing him with oil in the name of the Lord. And the prayer of **faith** will save the _sick_, and the Lord will raise him up. And if he has committed sins, he will be forgiven. Confess your trespasses to one another, and pray for one another, that you may _be healed_. The effective, fervent prayer of a **righteous** man avails much*" (James 5:13-16). In other words, the prayers of the **righteous** are effective in relieving both natural and spiritual _sickness_ today if it is God's will. The importance of this Scripture must not be taken lightly. This is why Paul talked about the importance of examining one's self when he gave instructions for participating in God's communion in 1 Corinthians 11:23-26. Paul stated that if one takes the communion of the Lord, "*in an _unworthy manner_ will be guilty of the body and blood of the Lord*" (1 Corinthians 11:27). Doing so invites God's _calamity_ to people in His church who take His communion in a sinful state. Therefore, Paul said, "*...let a man examine himself, and so let him eat of the bread and drink of the cup. For he who eats and drinks in an _unworthy manner_ eats and drinks judgment to himself, not _discerning_ the Lord's body. For this reason, many are _weak_ and _sick_ among you, and many sleep. For if we would judge ourselves, we would not be judged. But when we are judged, we are chastened by the Lord, that we may not be condemned with the world*" (1 Corinthian 11: 28-32). Paul's references to _weak_, _sick_ and spiritually dead were not necessarily by natural illnesses. God's _calamity_ on the person perpetrating a fraud in His church plays a role. However, the prayers of the **righteous** help people in this state. Prayers can alleviate God's _calamity_ by helping people to realize their need for repentance as they perform a self-examination of themselves. Until the person comes to grips with their own personal state of sin and repents, prayers can only buy one time in the war campaign. One living in sin cannot use prayer to defend against God's _calamity_. One must be clean, not perfect, but clean for God to hear one's prayers. Please meditate on this wisdom and let it sink in. Remember, the Holy Spirit inspired Peter to write, "*...as He who called you is holy, you also be holy in all your conduct...*" (1 Peter 1:15).

God's use of _calamity_ is thoroughly documented in the Book of Revelations, both figuratively and literally. Whether one views the reading from the perspective of the destruction of Israel or the end of the world, God's _calamity_ stands supreme. The references are too numerous to go over in detail but some of the references are as follows:

- _Earthquakes_: Revelation 6:12; 8:5; 11:13; 11:19; and 16:18

- _Fire_: Revelation 8:5; 9:18

- _Plagues_: Revelation 9:18; 9:20; 11:6; 15:6; 15:8; 15:11; 16:9; 16:21; 18:4; 18:8

- *Famine*: Revelation 18:8

- *Hail*: Revelation 11:19; and 16:21

Of all the comments on God's *calamity* in the Book of Revelation, a significant one warns each of us about changing God's Words. John, inspired by the Holy Spirit, concluded Revelation by stating, "*For I testify to everyone who hears the words of the prophecy of this book: If anyone adds to these things, God will add to him the plagues that are written in this book; and if anyone takes away from the words of the book of this prophecy, God shall take away his part from the Book of Life, from the holy city, and from the things which are written in this book*" (Revelation 22:18-19). God's Word is final. People who take the Biblical record out of context to enrich themselves or lead others through the wide gate (Matthew 7:13) will face God's *calamity*, on earth and in death. Paul declared, "*It is a fearful thing to fall into the hands of the living God*" (Hebrews 10:31).

Without the proper identification of the attributes, one can never understand the correlation between spiritual warfare, the war campaign, and the elements of *strife* and *calamity*. BTT allows one to see that the negative forces bring the element of *strife*. By its nature, *strife's* role is to keep confusion and disagreement in motion. *Strife* keeps people in the fog of the campaign. Confusion and disagreements prevent the influence of the positive attributes from entering one's inner spirit. *Strife* also prevents unity at all levels. On the other hand, God's *calamity* gets His people's attention today and purges sin from among His congregations on the spiritual battlefield. God may use *calamity* during periods of *strife* when large numbers of His people are seriously impacted, or He may use *calamity* when the negative forces cross His spiritual boundaries and unbalance the war campaign too much in Satan's favor. When this happens, even Christians can experience God's *calamity* when they refuse to speak up and stand for God and His Word. Their example weakens Christ's church on the spiritual battlefield. It is the Christian's duty to understand God's way and make sure they have not slipped off the **good** path by unknowingly spreading error. The Biblical record and the evidence presented in this chapter supports this supposition.

CHAPTER X: Is God's *Calamity* Occurring in the World Today?

*"Thus says the Lord: "Stand in the ways and see, and ask for the old paths, where the **good** way is, and walk in it; then you will find rest for your souls. But they said, 'We will not walk in it.' Also, I set watchmen over you, saying, 'listen to the sound of the trumpet!' But they said, 'We will not listen.' Therefore hear, you nations, and know, O congregation, what is among them. Hear, O earth! Behold, I will certainly bring calamity on this people—the fruit of their thoughts, because they have not heeded My words nor My law, but rejected it"*

~ Jeremiah 6:16-19

It is easy to see that the world today, is experiencing the element of *strife* at all levels in society. However, it is harder to see that God's *calamity* is also occurring outside of the natural processes of storms, whirlwinds (which includes tornadoes and hurricanes), floods, famine, plagues, drought, pestilence and disease, earthquakes, tsunamis, fire, hail, and snow that come from the decay of our ecological systems or the sickness of our decaying physical bodies. But I firmly believe the world is experiencing God's *calamity* in epic proportions. I believe the prophet Zephaniah confirmed this when he wrote, *"Seek the Lord, all you meek of the earth, who have upheld His justice. Seek **righteousness**, seek humility. It may be that you will be hidden in the day of the Lord's anger"* (Zephaniah 2:3). The Lord's anger is His *calamity* in the world that purges His church and maintains the balance in the war campaign for His remnant. Now before one gets upset with this statement, please consider that the Lord Himself told Moses, *"I will have **mercy** on whomever I will have **mercy**, and I will have compassion on whomever I will have compassion." So then it is not of him who wills, nor of him who runs, but of God who shows **mercy**. For the Scripture says to the Pharaoh, "For this very purpose I have raised you up, that I may show My power in you, and that My name may be declared in all the earth." Therefore He has **mercy** on whom He wills, and whom He wills He hardens"* (Romans 9:15-18). The point of this scripture is Pharaoh and all of Egypt had the opportunity to personally **witness** the power of the Almighty God by His *calamity* while the children of Israel, remained untouched. Pharaoh and the Egyptians still rejected God and His name was declared in all the earth by their destruction. Moreover, after the children of Israel **witnessed** God's magnificent power, they **backslid** into sin and were punished too. Today, with the loss of *discernment* in the world, recognizing God's movements by His *calamity* are more difficult. The negative force's fog and ***false*** teaching from the religious communities have blinded most of the world. For the religious community has been **deceived** for so long, including some in Christ's church, that the downward spiral of man is now in a state of freefall. Paul documented that the Gospel, the only thing available to open their eyes, is hidden from them. Why? Because *"...it is veiled to those who are perishing, whose minds the god of this age has blinded, who do not believe, lest the light of the gospel of the glory of Christ, who is the image of God, should shine on them"* (2 Corinthians 4:3-4). Man's choice to follow man's doctrines, traditions, and creeds has invited God's *calamity* worldwide although the Biblical record documents:

- God said, *"This is My beloved Son, in whom I am well pleased. Hear Him!"* (Matthew 17:5)

- Jesus said, *"All authority has been given to Me in heaven and on earth"* (Matthew 28:18). And He said,

    o *"Go into all the world and preach the gospel to every creature. He who believes and is <u>baptized</u> will be saved; but he who does not believe will be condemned"* (Mark: 16:15-16)

    o *"But why do you call Me* **[Jesus]** *'Lord, Lord,' and not do the things which I say?"* (Luke 6:46)

- Paul documented that *"God, who at various times and in various ways spoke in time past to the fathers by the prophets, has in these last days spoken to us by His Son* **[Jesus]**, *whom He* **[God]** *has appointed heir of all things, through whom also He made the worlds; who being the brightness of His glory and the express image of His person, and upholding all things by the word of His power, when He had by Himself purged our sins, sat down at the right hand of the Majesty on high..."* (Hebrews 1:1-3)

- Peter declared, *"For Moses truly said to the fathers, 'The Lord your God will raise up for you a Prophet like me from your brethren. Him you shall hear in all things, whatever He says to you. And it shall be that every soul who will not hear that Prophet shall be utterly destroyed from among the people"* (Acts 3:22-23)

God left no room for substitutes, alternative philosophies, or additional religious beliefs outside of His Son's Word. In fact, the Holy Spirit led Paul to document, *"But even if we, or an angel from heaven, preach any other gospel to you than what we have preached to you, let him be accursed. As we have said before, so now I say again, if anyone preaches any other gospel to you than what you have received, let him be accursed"* (Galatians 1:8). Jesus' Word takes preeminence in Christ's church; not inspirational, emotional, motivational, or political discourses from the pulpit. These tactics only serve to elevate man while God's Word becomes filler material. One must understand that in spiritual warfare, every spoken word or activity taken out of context from God's Word is contraband to God. The negative attributes know this well and they hide this fact. They influence people to provide alternative Biblical beliefs and practices in the name of religion. The negative attributes influence ***false*** teachers to claim they received messages directly from God or that they have a private interpretation of His Word given by the Holy Spirit. In addition, they claim the ability to speak in secret tongues only understandable between them and God. The Lord dealt with this during the time of Ezekiel. As ***false*** teachers and prophets claimed these things, God said Israel's prophets plastered their people, *"...with untempered mortar, seeing false visions, and divining lies for them, saying, 'Thus says the Lord God,' when the Lord had not spoken"* (Ezekiel 22:28). Today, God speaks through His inspired Word, delivered by His Son Jesus Christ to His apostles of whom the Holy Spirit guided their thoughts and documentation. Simplified, God stated, *"This is My beloved Son, in whom I am well pleased. Hear Him!"* (Matthew 17:5; Mark 9:7; Luke 9:35). To counter God's actions, Satan deployed ***false*** teachers in spiritual warfare to deceive and compromise.

Christians who embrace the Holy Spirit's Word through Paul that, *"A little leaven leavens the whole lump"* (Galatians 5:9) understand spiritual warfare. When too much leavening occurs, by God's standard, His <u>calamity</u> is necessary to purge camouflaged negative forces from among His people. Just to ensure my point is clear, Christians are the people of Christ's church - the enduring church that strives to maintain the pattern of the church born after the Day of Pentecost. This is the one church that exists in many locations on the spiritual battlefield. The Biblical record confirms this statement and the pattern. I will cover the pattern God provided for His church in Chapter XII because its identification is critical on a battlefield filled with counterfeits erected to **deceive** and destroy souls. For now, consider the significance of the Scripture that says, *"For the time has come for judgment to begin at the house of God; and if it begins with us first, what will be the end of those who do not obey the gospel of God?"* (1 Peter 4:17). BTT allows one to see that congregations of imposters at some point after the Day of Pentecost, left Christ's church and the Lord's defined pattern of worship. Generationally, these imposters continued to populate the spiritual battlefield. Regardless, the Lord's church and His established pattern remains as an ark of safety on the battlefield where proper teaching, preaching, and worship to God occurs. Think about Noah's Ark. With Noah's Ark and God's epic _calamity_ in mind, let us explore His _calamity_ today and why it is occurring.

Although there are many reasons that one can point to as a flashpoint for God's _calamity_, I would like to offer seven critical reasons that I have observed over time. As one reads my seven reasons for God's _calamity_ today, please keep in mind that God said, *"When I shut up heaven and there is no rain, or command the locusts to devour the land, or send pestilence among My people, if My people who are called by My name will _humble_ themselves, and pray and seek My face, and turn from their **wicked** ways, then I will hear from heaven, and will forgive their sin and heal their land"* (1 Chronicles 7:13-14). God's _calamity_ and words directed at the nation of Israel then, still applies today. However, since Jesus visited the world to provide the balm of salvation, God's _calamity_ has increased with man's rejection of His Son and His remedy. Thus, my seven reasons for God's _calamity_ are:

1. **False** teaching of God's Word has reach epic levels

2. The religious community's *false* representation of the numbers of Christians in the world

3. The senseless division within the Lord's church over race, politics, and personal opinions

4. The negative forces significant advances to alter God's divine plan for of His male and female creation

5. The incredible and increasing numbers of the religious community's **deceived** in denying God's requirement for water _baptism_

6. The increasing number of people abiding in Christ's church who refuse to partake in evangelism

7. The escalating number of men who have abdicated their role as men, as spiritual leaders in His church, and in their homes

To begin with, I believe the first critical reason for God's *calamity* today is because ***false*** teaching of God's Word has reached epic levels. The Holy Spirit inspired Paul to comment on this when he wrote, *"For we are not, as so many, peddling the word of God; but as of sincerity, but as from God, we speak in the sight of God in Christ"* (2 Corinthians 2:17). There are many ***false*** teachers, whose numbers have grown exponentially since Christ's original church was established, *"peddling the Word of God"*. Why? The Holy Spirits, through Paul's writings, allows one to see that God's Word is *"peddled"* (meaning *sold, marketed, hawked,* or *touted)* for earthy gain; not because of sincerity towards God. This is a major strategy used by the negative forces in spiritual warfare to create and maintain division and *strife* between people in Christ and everyone else. The result of this ***false*** teaching is the knowledge of the True God, His power, and His Truth are being diluted at a staggering pace. God's Word is rapidly being replaced by the gods of men ruled by man's wisdom and money. The real Truth that is hidden in the fog of the war campaign is *"...the world is passing away, and the lust of it; but he who does the will of God abides forever"* (1 John 2:17). Jesus stated for everyone to hear, *"Heaven and earth will pass away, but My words will by no means pass away"* (Matthew 24:35; Matthew 5:18; Mark 13:31; Luke 21:33). Moreover, in the Old Testament God said, *"For My thoughts are not your thoughts, nor are your ways My ways," says the Lord. "For as the heavens are higher than the earth, so are My ways higher than your ways, and My thoughts than your thoughts. For as the rain comes down, and the snow from heaven, and do not return there, but water the earth, and make it bring forth and bud, that it may give seed to the sower and bread to the eater, so shall My word be that goes forth from My mouth; It shall not return to Me void, but it shall accomplish what I please, and it shall prosper in the thing for which I sent it"* (Isaiah 55:8-11). Regardless of ***false*** teachers' twisting of God's Word, His Word still accomplishes what He pleases. God's Word still stands as each generation rejects the God of Truth and allows Satan to use the negative forces to fill the void at a staggering pace. However, just as the prophets of old warned the nation of Israel, God's *calamity* is occurring today in the war campaign. Ezekiel recorded God's eternal Word stating, *"Therefore thus says the Lord God: "I will cause a stormy wind to break forth in My fury; and there shall be a flooding rain in My anger, and great hailstones in fury to consume it. So I will break down the wall you have plastered with untempered mortar, and bring it down to the ground, so that its foundation will be uncovered; it will fall, and you shall be consumed in the midst of it. Then you shall know that I am the Lord"* (Ezekiel 13:13-14).

The negative attributes fill any void where God's Word is not present. **Perverting** His Word is not new. A prophet foretold of the ***perversion*** as far back as a few generations after Adam and Eve. Jude documented that, *"...Enoch, the seventh from Adam, prophesied about these men also, saying, "Behold, the Lord comes with ten thousands of His saints, to execute judgment on all, to convict all who are **ungodly** among them of all their **ungodly** deeds which they have committed in an **ungodly** way, and of all the harsh things which **ungodly** sinners have spoken against Him"* (Jude 14-15). Moreover, one must understand the extent of the negative influences that were on the men identified by Enoch. Jude documented that they spoke *"...**evil** of whatever they do not know; and whatever they know naturally, like brute beasts, in these things they corrupt themselves. Woe to them! For they have gone in the way* *of Cain, have run <u>greedily</u> in the error of Balaam for profit, and perished in the rebellion of Korah. These are spots in your <u>love</u> feasts, while they feast with you without fear, serving only themselves. They are clouds without water, carried about by the winds; late autumn trees without fruit, twice dead, pulled up by the roots; <u>raging</u> waves of the sea, foaming up their own shame; wandering stars for whom is reserved the blackness of darkness forever"* (Jude 10-13). The men that Enoch spoke of transferred demonic wisdom, doctrines, and traditions (1 Timothy 4:1-2) to generations after them. Their works continue to pass on through ***false*** teaching in homes, places of worship, and many religious educational programs to this very day. ***False*** teachers breathe in the fog generated by the negative attributes and corrupt the people listening to their ***deceit*** and ***folly***.

As one moves forward, Moses documented the influences of the negative forces of the war campaign on priests and prophets who spoke things that did not come from God. Moses documented, "*...when a prophet speaks in the name of the Lord, if the thing does not happen or come to pass, that is the thing which the Lord has not spoken; the prophet has spoken it presumptuously; you shall not be afraid of him*" (Deuteronomy 18:22). BTT allows one to see that the same ***false*** practices continue today. The prophet Jeremiah, as well as the other prophets, documented this phenomenon. An example from Jeremiah stated, "*The prophets prophesy **falsely**, and the priests rule by their own power; and My people <u>love</u> to have it so...*" (Jeremiah 5:31). Even after Jesus came and taught His apostles the Gospel and they taught others and established Christ's church with the true Gospel, ***false*** teachers increased. Even within Christ's church, something happened. Jude documented, "*For certain men have crept in unnoticed, who long ago were marked out for this condemnation, **ungodly** men, who turn the <u>grace</u> of our God into **lewdness** and deny the only Lord God and our Lord Jesus Christ*" (Jude 1:4). These were men who crept into the Lord's church and distorted the teaching of the true Gospel. However, God's pure Word continues to stay with His remnant. God, in His all-powerful way, made a way for His people to get out the true Gospel message. By His Almighty power, the world has God's Word in written form.

Unfortunately, because the negative forces strategically exploits gaps, today a gap is being exploited among God's remnant using Bible translations. BTT allows one to see the Holy Spirit's involvement during the translation of the Bible from its original Hebrew and Greek. Then, by the providence of God and the development of the printing press, mass production of the Bible became possible with the printing of the King James version of the Bible. The printing of this Bible gave many people the opportunity to hear and see God's Word in their spoken language. However, God never intended His Word to stop in the 17th Century language and colloquialism. The event that happened on the Day of Pentecost proved this fact. When the Holy Spirit came as documented in Acts 2:6-11, His coming did more than just fulfill Old Testament prophesy. His coming also fulfilled Jesus' promise to His disciples before He died to send back a Helper and Comforter, who are synonymous with the Holy Spirit. Jesus made this promise in the Book of John where it is documented numerous times. Specifically, he documented, "*But the Helper, the Holy Spirit, whom the Father will send in My name, He will teach you all things, and bring to your remembrance all things that I said to you*" (John 14:26). Moreover, the Holy Spirit provided evidence that God intended the teaching of His Word to reach people in a way that they would understand it in their own language. The Bible documented that when the Holy Spirit came with the <u>*sound of a rushing wind*</u> in Acts 2:6-11:

> "...*when this <u>sound</u> occurred, the multitude came together, and were confused, because everyone heard <u>them speak in his own language</u>. Then they were all amazed and marveled, saying to one another, "Look, are not all these who speak Galileans? And <u>how is it that we hear</u>, each <u>in our own language</u> in which we were born? Parthians and Medes and Elamites, those dwelling in Mesopotamia, Judea and Cappadocia, Pontus and Asia, Phrygia and Pamphylia, Egypt and the parts of Libya adjoining Cyrene, visitors from Rome, both Jews and proselytes, Cretans and Arabs—<u>we hear them speaking in our own tongues</u> the wonderful works of God."*

My point is, people of the Lord's church who insist on teaching today's people with 17th Century language are carelessly losing many people to the fog generated by the negative forces of the war campaign. Very few teachers today can handle 17th Century language in a manner that provides a "clear" understanding of God's Word without constantly defining it for clarity to their audience. One needs to ask, why use an archaic 17th Century language to teach people today? One should be very careful when using the King James Bible in today' public assembly since many of its words, when used in the correct colloquialism and syntax, becomes irrelevant to people today. It is a great study tool, but I question its value as a teaching tool to a lost and dying world. The negative forces of the campaign are spiritually exploiting this point. Using spiritual warfare, the negative attributes are convincing good people seeking to know God's Word, to close their ears to teachers who refuse to adjust in this area. There is nothing holy about the King James Bible translation as some people would have the world believe. What is Holy is God's Word and His spiritual food contained within the Bible. One must strive to treat God's Word in a way that all can understand. In physical and spiritual warfare, clear communication is vital to transfer clear and consistent orders from leadership to troops to ensure a successful mission. Words matter and their meanings must provide a common understanding to the hearers. If not, confusion will rule. The idea can be seen in Paul's message to the Corinthian church over the issue of speaking in tongues. BTT allows one to see the same principle applies to clear communication in warfare – spiritual or physical. Paul stated: "*Even things without life, whether flute or harp, when they make a sound, unless they make a distinction in the sounds, how will it be known what is piped or played? For if the trumpet makes an uncertain sound, who will prepare for battle? So likewise you, unless you utter by the tongue words easy to understand, how will it be known what is spoken? For you will be speaking into the air. There are, it may be, so many kinds of languages in the world, and none of them is without significance. Therefore, if I do not know the meaning of the language, I shall be a foreigner to him who speaks, and he who speaks will be a foreigner to me*" (1 Corinthians 14:7-11). Hence, clear communication in the modern language of the people receiving God's Word is vital for educating, preparing, carrying out Christ's directives, and fighting spiritual war. The element of <u>discernment</u> dictates clear communication, but many Christians fail to understand this often because of the influence of the **pride** attribute. The negative forces of the war campaign are exploiting the confusion with the fog of the battle among many members of the bodies of Christ. This confusion continues to hinder both conversions and growth on the spiritual battlefield and explains why God's *calamity* is impacting His church today.

A few more earthly variables further complicate ***false*** teaching and the exploited gap mentioned above. The negative forces influence is increasing worldwide due to,

a) The use of social media and its ability to spread ***false doctrines*** at a rapid pace, and

b) Most academic institutions offering divinity, theology, and philosophical hybrid degrees to satisfy the appetite of the growing community of people desiring to understand God's Word through a professor's eyes

Both of these variables are exponentially increasing ***false*** teachers' effectiveness. For item "a", a ***false*** message spreads like cancer at speeds and locations unimagined in the past. The Holy Spirit led James to document, "*If anyone among you thinks he is religious, and does not bridle his tongue but **deceives** his own heart, this one's religion is useless*" (James 1:26). Social media creates an electronic tongue that cannot be bridled. When ***false*** teachers use this medium of communications, in spiritual warfare James documented, "*Even so the tongue is a little member and boasts great things. See how great a forest a little fire kindles! And the tongue is a fire, a world of iniquity. The tongue is so set among our members that it defiles the whole body, and sets on fire the course of nature; and it is set on fire by hell*" (James 3:5-6). BTT allows one to see that James spoke of the physical tongue. But in spiritual warfare, that same tongue is extended into the spiritual realm by the misuse of modern tools used for ***evil***.

Unfortunately, many of the students attending academic institutions sited in variable "b", fail to realize the dangers of their ***false*** teachers. BTT allows one to see that if a teacher is influenced by negative attributes, the words they espouse will also be tainted. BTT allows one to see that many academic institutions of higher education employ professors who do not accept that the Biblical record has "*some things hard to understand, which untaught and unstable people twist to their own destruction, as they do also the rest of the Scriptures*" (2 Peter 3:16). Because of the ***proud*** attribute, these professors feel compelled to provide an answer from their own cognitive resources. In other words, some of them feel free to make an answer up. Balaam of the Old Testament said it right when he stated to Balak, "*…If Balak were to give me his house full of silver and gold, I could not go beyond the word of the Lord, to do **good** or **bad** of my own will. What the Lord says, that I must speak'?*" (Numbers 24:13). Balaam did not heed his own words as do many religious academics. Thus, the institution's students graduate and spread ***false*** teachings and error.

But it does not stop here. Due to the use of social media today, an unprecedented phenomenon has occurred that has never before been accomplished in the history of mankind. Because of unconstrained resources, technology, and social media, the image and sound of a person proclaiming Jesus can be transmitted from a pulpit and simultaneously broadcasted to millions of people in different countries across the globe. One who proclaims Christ while influenced by negative attributes can inflict major damage on people simply listening to each ***false*** broadcast. This is occurring today. Their pseudo-educations, laced with secular theologies, philosophies, and science permeates the physical landscape, airways, and spiritual battlefield. Their words, spread through social media and enhanced by high definition presentations, multimedia graphics, and entertainment, and are so convincing that even many of God's people are **deceived**. Moreover, thousands of charismatic religious and spiritual men and women are serving as radio and television host in record numbers. They offer their religious and secular audiences, "thoughts or words from God, Jesus, or the Gospel" on their programs. However, they fail to understand the influence they have over their listeners or the level of damage they are causing in spiritual warfare by their soundbites of misguided **counsel** and **advice**. Jesus' warning, "...*whoever causes one of these little ones who believe in Me to sin, it would be better for him if a millstone were hung around his neck, and he were drowned in the depth of the sea*" (Matthew 18:6; Mark 9:42; Luke 17:2), applies to them. For the negative forces of the war campaign have mass produced a Jesus-concept that has successfully created apostasy on the spiritual battlefield. This includes places that were once arks of safety on the spiritual battlefield. These *false* teachers divide God's creation by mass producing a fog of confusion to hide their **deceptive** practices. Paul documented, "*For such are **false** apostles, **deceitful** workers, transforming themselves into apostles of Christ. And no wonder! For Satan himself transforms himself into an angel of light. Therefore it is no great thing if his ministers also transform themselves into ministers of **righteousness**, whose end will be according to their works*" (2 Corinthians 11:13-15). To this end, Jesus said, "*Take heed what you hear...*" (Mark 4:23). The fact that Jesus said, "*He who has ears to hear, let him hear*" (Matthew 11:15; 13:9; 13:43; Mark 4:9; 4:23; 7:16; Luke 8:8; 10:16; 14:35; and 8 times in the Book of Revelations), seventeen times tells one that hearing His Truth is important. God does not want one to listen to every John and Jane Doe that quotes the Bible. Jesus' statements concerned hearing spiritual Truth from Him. Hence, Jesus bluntly said, "*He who is of God hears God's Words; therefore you do not hear, because you are not of God*"(John 8:47). Please do not be **deceived**.

    False teachers have created religious division and invited God's <u>calamity</u>. BTT allows one to see that throughout His Biblical record, God only divided people on the side of either ***good*** or ***evil***. These two categories contained sheep or goats, believers or unbelievers, the saved or the lost, Christians or sinners, etc..., but they are all synonyms for ***good*** or ***evil***. However, the negative forces strategically divide God's creation into religious groups. **False** teachers subdivide the religious community into denominations and non-denominations. Further subdivisions of Christians, Catholics, Baptists, Methodists, Protestants, and Mormons, and on and on, continue. These groups even subdivide into conservative, liberal, evangelical, fundamental, born-again, and on and on. Beyond all of these, there are other religious groups that have nothing to do with Christianity. Moreover, politics and race add another division and more reasons for God's <u>calamity</u>. This book will address politics and race later in this chapter. None of this division is from God. These divisions based on ***false*** teachers' interpretation of God's Word, amounts to gospels different from what Paul and the other apostles delivered. Paul, foreseeing such division through the Holy Spirit's inspiration said to the church of Galatia, "*I marvel that you are turning away so soon from Him who called you in the <u>grace</u> of Christ, to a different gospel, which is not another; but there are some who trouble you and want to **pervert** the gospel of Christ. But even if we, or an angel from heaven, preach any other gospel to you than what we have preached to you, let him be accursed. As we have said before, so now I say again, if anyone preaches any other gospel to you than what you have received, let* *him be accursed*" (Galatians 1:6-9). Given by the Holy Spirit, Paul's pronouncement stands today as if Jesus said it Himself.

BTT allows one to see that the Gospel of Jesus Christ divinely united the Jews and the Gentiles (everyone that was not a Jew) of the 1st Century under one Gospel. Specifically, the Bible states, "*There is neither Jew nor Greek, there is neither slave nor free, there is neither male nor female; for you are all one in Christ Jesus*" (Galatians 3:28). This Gospel produces "Christians" and the Bible documents for all non-Jews, we were "*...once Gentiles in the flesh—who are called Uncircumcision by what is called the Circumcision made in the flesh by hands—that at that time you were without Christ, being aliens from the commonwealth of Israel and strangers from the covenants of promise, having no hope and without God in the world. But now in Christ Jesus you who once were far off have been brought near by the blood of Christ*" (Ephesians 2:11-13). However, the negative forces influence religious names other than the name "Christian". BTT allows one to see that the name "Christian" was divinely prophesized in Isaiah 62:1-2, came into being in Acts 11:26, and deemed a worthy name according to James 2:7. In fact, on the spiritual battlefield today, the negative forces are using the religious community to separate the very people that God's Word seeks to unite by using denominational and nondenominational names. Where God provides the world a single unifying name and doctrine to bring His people together in one church established by Christ, ***false*** teachers have created other religious names to confuse and separate immeasurable numbers of people. These religious leaders violate Jesus' prayer to God when He prayed, "*I do not pray for these alone, but also for those who will believe in Me through their word; that they all may be one, as You, Father, are in Me, and I in You; that they also may be one in Us, that the world may believe that You sent Me*" (John 17:20-21). Throughout the Bible, the prophets and Gospel writers of the Biblical record documented the presence of the ***false*** teachers. One must understand that to lay claim to a name other than "Christian" is to form an allegiance to something that is not from God. Paul addressed this truth when he wrote, "*Now I plead with you, brethren, by the name of our Lord Jesus Christ, that you all speak the same thing, and that there be no divisions among you, but that you be perfectly joined together in the same mind and in the same judgment*" (1 Corinthians 1:10). Further, he provided an example when he stated, "*For it has been declared to me concerning you, my brethren, by those of Chloe's household, that there are contentions among you. Now I say this, that each of you says, "I am of Paul," or "I am of Apollos," or "I am of Cephas," or "I am of Christ." Is Christ divided? Was Paul crucified for you? Or were you baptized in the name of Paul?*" (1 Corinthians 1:11-13). He addressed it again with the church in Ephesus when he wrote, "*I, therefore, the prisoner of the Lord, beseech you to walk worthy of the calling with which you were called, with all lowliness and gentleness, with longsuffering, bearing with one another in love, endeavoring to keep the unity of the Spirit in the bond of peace. There is one body and one Spirit, just as you were called in one hope of your calling; one Lord, one **faith**, one baptism; one God and Father of all, who is above all, and through all, and in you all*" (Ephesians 4:1-6). Any other names or doctrines that take one away from the name Christian (Acts 11:26) is divisive and originates from a strategy of the negative forces of the war campaign.

As it pertains to Christ's church, the practice of division inhibits one from growing spiritually. Everyone involved in division, to include separation from the worship that the one

True God calls for, will remain a babe in Christ and lost in the war of the campaign. Paul wrote, *"...I, brethren, could not speak to you as to spiritual people but as to carnal, as to babes in Christ. I fed you with milk and not with solid food; for until now you were not able to receive it, and even now you are still not able; for you are still carnal. For where there are **envy**, strife, and divisions among you, are you not carnal and behaving like mere men? For when one says, "I am of Paul," and another, "I am of Apollos," are you not carnal?"* (1 Corinthians 3:1-4). God wants one's attention on this matter and calamity is occurring in Christ's church and the religious communities around the world today to get that attention. BTT allows one to see this truth and the unseen forces at work. The real division is the spiritual war that is raging within the inner spirits of people themselves. Past and present leaders and teachers have forsaken their responsibility for, *"...rightly dividing the word of truth"* (2 Timothy 2:15). They either deny this truth or are ignorant of its meaning. Additionally, there are people within the body of Christ who have allowed the influences of the negative attributes by refusing to submit to church leadership; i.e. the eldership. The requirement to, *"Obey those who rule over you, and be submissive, for they watch out for your souls, as those who must give account. Let them do so with joy and not with grief, for that would be unprofitable for you"* (Hebrews 13:17) is stubbornly trampled as **envious** and **self-seeking** men and women enter the body of Christ (James 3:16). The results are the maintenance of the fog of the war campaign, the fueling of world strife, and the advancement of the negative forces.

One must get back to God's Word if one desires to be saved from this **wicked** and **perverse** generation (Acts 2:40; Philippians 2:15). One must seek a church where Christians meet who are dedicated to keeping the pattern that God established after the Day of Pentecost. These congregations may be small, but they are extremely powerful on the spiritual battlefield. These churches do exist, and one needs only to know what to look for outside of the worldly creations of men. BTT allows one to see that a collective body of the **righteous** people can impact the war campaign in supernatural ways. Remember, James informed us that *"...The effective, fervent prayer of a **righteous** man avails much"* (James 5:16).

There are many counterfeit churches and religious groups claiming Christ on the spiritual battlefield today. These organizations are simply aiding the advancement of the negative attributes in the war campaign. BTT is necessary to see that any person, religious group, belief, or doctrine that claims to follow Christ, but modifies His word for their convenience, is counterfeit and invites God's calamity to purge them as He did during the time of the Israelites. Remember, the Biblical record documented of God's people then, *"...with most of them God was not well pleased, for their bodies were scattered in the wilderness"* (1 Corinthians 10:5). The Biblical record, the very Book used to teach Christ's doctrine, documents this:

- *"You shall not add to the word which I command you, nor take from it, that you may keep the commandments of the Lord your God which I command you"* (Deuteronomy 4:2)

- *"The entirety of Your word is truth, and every one of Your **righteous** judgments endures forever"* (Psalms 119:160)

- *"Every word of God is pure; He is a shield to those who put their trust in Him. Do not add to His words, lest He rebuke you, and you be found a **liar**"* (Proverbs 30:5-6)

- *"For I testify to everyone who hears the words of the prophecy of this book: If anyone adds to these things, God will add to him the plagues that are written in this book; and if anyone takes away from the words of the book of this prophecy, God shall take away his part from the Book of Life, from the holy city, and from the things which are written in this book"* (Revelation 22:18-19)

With these scriptural references in mind, understand that **false** teachers are contributing to the degradation of society. They are **perverting** God's Word and the very conduct that God demands of His people who claim His Son Jesus Christ. Jesus stated, *"You shall love the Lord your God with all your heart, with all your soul, and with all your mind.' This is the first and great commandment. And the second is like it: 'You shall love your neighbor as yourself.' On these two commandments hang all the Law and the Prophets"* (Matthew 22:37-40) and *"…There is no other commandment greater than these"* (Mark 12:32). From Jesus' own Word, he did not provide room for deviation. Further, He stated, *"…whatever you want men to do to you, do also to them, for this is the Law and the Prophets"* (Matthew 7:12). A congregation of people who practices otherwise, or allow preaching and teaching different from Jesus' Word stated here, has **perverted** Christ's Gospel. Even a scribe talking to Jesus understood this simple message. The Biblical record documented, *"So the scribe said to Him, "Well said, Teacher. You have spoken the truth, for there is one God, and there is no other but He. And to love Him with all the heart, with all the understanding, with all the soul, and with all the strength, and to love one's neighbor as oneself, is more than all the whole burnt offerings and sacrifices." Now when Jesus saw that he answered **wisely**, He said to him, "You are not far from the kingdom of God"* (Mark 12:32-34). Further, Jesus told the scribe, *"You have answered **rightly**; do this and you will live"* (Luke 10:26-28). If one allows the **perverse** attribute to sway one from Jesus' Truth, one will hear Jesus declare, *"…I never knew you; depart from Me, you who practice lawlessness!"* (Matthew 7:23). No one should desire to be part of a congregation that God will reject at the end of time. Unfortunately, many people are **deceived** by people influenced by the negative forces preying on those seeking God. Thus, God's calamity will continue until Jesus returns.

Another sign of the **perverse**, **immoral**, and **ungodly** attributes working in religious communities today are the practices of mutilating or scarring one's flesh, shaming, abusing (as in hazing), or psychologically controlling church members in any way in the name of Christ. Nowhere in God's Word or Jesus's teachings are any practices of this nature found or authorized. These same activities give way to the private molestation of children. Any religious leadership that condones any practices of this nature has become heavily influenced by the negative attributes. Followers of these leaders and their **immoral**, **ungodly**, or **perverted** practices will fall in the same pit of condemnation. Moreover, the progeny of these followers may be scarred for the rest of their lives.

Finally, all of the **false** teaching has led to an unprecedented arrogance perpetrated by **false** teachers of God's Word. This arrogance has risen to such an epic level that **false** teachers teach, and people believe, they can defeat Satan by their own resources. ***False*** teachers say things like, "We're going to stomp on Satan's head" or "We're going to put Satan under our feet" and other such <u>arrogant</u> things. BTT allows one to see that this form of speech openly challenges Satan. It is unscriptural and unwise. Moreover, adding words of this nature to song and teaching generations to think they have some form of authority and power over Satan through their own resources sets them up for a complete failure in life. The Holy Spirit led Jude to document, "*...dreamers defile the flesh, reject authority, and **speak evil** of dignitaries. Yet Michael the archangel, in contending with the <u>devil</u>, when he disputed about the body of Moses, <u>dared not bring against him a reviling accusation</u>, but said, "The Lord rebuke you!" But these **speak evil** of whatever they do not know; and whatever they know naturally, like brute beasts, in these things they corrupt themselves*" (Jude 8-10). Likewise, Peter wrote, "*...They are presumptuous, self-willed. They are not afraid to **speak evil** of dignitaries, whereas angels, who are greater in power and might, do not bring a reviling accusation against them before the Lord*" (2 Peter 2:10-11). Even Jesus, as He dealt with Satan directly, simply used God's Word to rebuke him according to Luke 4:1-13. Satan is an ancient and powerful deity. Only God controls Satan and He has given us His tools to deal with him. Anything else is ***foolishness*** and invites God's <u>calamity</u> on religious organizations and people teaching this ***false*** belief on the spiritual battlefield. In spiritual warfare, to challenge Satan invites *him* to show up. Do not be ***deceived***.

The point to all of this is: God said to listen to His Son Jesus Christ. Jesus gave us His Word, by men whom He chose (Luke 6:13), who were later inspired by the Holy Spirit (John 14:26), and who documented our New Testament. So, if God would not even recognize His angels with this responsibility (Hebrews 1:4-14), which are greater than human beings (Psalms 8:4-5; Hebrews 2:6-8); then why would anyone entrust themselves with the words of men, women, spiritualist, the enlightened, religious, or even a religious hierarchy over Jesus's Word. One can freely read Jesus' Word for one's self. Actually, reading God's Word for oneself will eliminate a majority of the ***false*** teachers traversing the spiritual battlefield. Placing hope in the word of ***false*** teachers is worse than gambling. In gambling, one at least has a chance for having a favorable outcome. However, listening to ***false*** teachers offers no hope; the odds of a favorable outcome is zero. For the Bible unforgivingly documents, "*Truly, these times of ignorance God overlooked, but now commands all men everywhere to repent, because He has appointed a day on which He will judge the world in righteousness by the Man whom He has ordained. He has given assurance of this to all by raising Him from the dead*" (Acts 17:30-31). This man is Jesus and no <u>grace</u> will override this fact stated in Acts 17.

I believe the second critical reason for God's <u>calamity</u> today is because of the religious community's ***false*** representation of the numbers of Christians in the world. This reason has ties to the first reason presented above but its impact is far greater. Please meditate on this: Christians are different from people who claim to be religious or spiritual. The religious and spiritual do not adhere to the full teachings of Jesus Christ because they view His Word as a guideline to follow. However, to be a Christian, one sees the Word of Christ as a command that one must adhere to to be saved. Man's efforts to tolerate Christian, religious, and spiritual beliefs under the same roof means Christ's teachings must be modified to ensure unity and keep the numbers. God is not happy with this for He provided one standard according to Ephesians 4:4-6. Christians are to teach God's Truth with patience to the religious, spiritual, and secular communities to convert them to the one Christ; not modify or compromise His Word to satisfy any of them. This is why the Holy Spirit revealed to Paul and he documented, "*So then neither he who plants is anything, nor he who waters, but God who gives the increase*" (1 Corinthians 3:7). If God does not give the increase, then man should not create it for the purpose of having large numbers. BTT allows one to see that even as far back as the children of Israel, God told the Israelites that their numbers were not important. The Biblical record documented that Moses told them, "*The Lord did not set His love on you <u>nor choose you because you were more in number than any other people</u>, for <u>you were the least of all peoples</u>; but because the Lord loves you, and because He would keep the oath which He swore to your fathers ...*" (Deuteronomy 7:7-8).

BTT allows one to see that the inflation of the size of the Christian community goes back to the beginning of Christ's church and the struggle between the Jews and the Christians. When the Jewish leadership realized they could not stop Christ or the establishment of His church, they sought ways to infiltrate it and make it like Judaism. In one of many instances, Paul would document, "*I marvel that you are turning away so soon from Him who called you in the <u>grace</u> of Christ, to a different gospel, which is not another; but there are some who trouble you and want to **pervert** the gospel of Christ. But even if we, or an angel from heaven, preach any other gospel to you than what we have preached to you, let him be accursed. As we have said before, so now I say again, if anyone preaches any other gospel to you than what you have received, let him be accursed*" (Galatians 1:6-9). The infiltration of Christ's church in this instance was a strategy of the negative forces in spiritual warfare. The negative forces tried to piggyback on Christianity to spread a ***false*** gospel laced with ***deceit***. Congregations, like the Galatian church, were practicing a ***perverted*** gospel. Paul stepped in and chastised their behavior and even corrected division based on race and status that was forming in Christ's church. He stated, "*There is neither Jew nor Greek, there is neither slave nor free, there is neither male nor female; for you are all one in Christ Jesus*" (Galatians 3:28) and, "*...there is neither Greek nor Jew, circumcised nor uncircumcised, barbarian, Scythian, slave nor free, but Christ is all and in all*" (Colossians 3:11). The negative forces used division to give rise to corrupt leaders who were high jacking the church. These leaders would mix in pagan practices, traditions, and beliefs to grow the churches and "*satisfy itching ears*" according to 2 Timothy 4:3. Why? Because the numbers brought profit to those in control. There is more on this subject later. But for now, understand that these leaders altered the teachings of the apostles and did as the Jews attempted to do who had "*... a zeal for God, but not according to knowledge. For they being ignorant of God's **righteousness**, and seeking to establish their own **righteousness**, have not submitted to the **righteousness** of God*" (Romans 10:2-3). Moreover, one must understand that congregations that mix in Old Testament practices with Christ's Gospel, both then and today, are not part of God's people. The Bible clearly documents, "*You have become estranged from Christ, you who attempt to be justified by law; you have fallen from <u>grace</u>*" (Galatians 5:4). The fog, generated by the negative forces in spiritual warfare, blinds religious leaders and followers to this very critical point.

BTT allows one to see that after the Day of Pentecost, the attacks on Christ's churches were relentless. The attacks from the negative forces were designed to destroy God's plan. For this reason, Jude documented that certain men would creep into some of Christ's churches unnoticed. He documented that these men, "*...who long ago were marked out for this condemnation, **ungodly** men, who turn the grace of our God into **lewdness** and deny the only Lord God and our Lord Jesus Christ*" (Jude 1:4), would skew the teachings within some of Christ's churches. Once again, one had to diligently seek the truth to find the true church of Christ. If not, one could easily become lost in a counterfeit group waving a flag of Christianity on the spiritual battlefield.

The practice of Jude 1:4 has severely increased today under a new header of diversity, inclusion, and tolerance. This new header allows people with separate religious beliefs to come together and worship the one True God without compliance to His divine standard of, "*There is one body and one Spirit, just as you were called in one hope of your calling; one Lord, one **faith**, one baptism; one God and Father of all, who is above all, and through all, and in you all*" (Ephesians 4:4-6). "One **faith**" does not leave room for multiple **faiths** with the "one Lord." However, this Biblical principle is unacceptable to religious leaders who desire to "*...establish their own **righteousness***" without submitting "*...to the **righteousness** of God*" according to Romans 10:3. This same verse tells one that these same people are "*...ignorant of God's **righteousness**...*" Many unintended consequences are created by their ignorance. First, their ignorance creates fertile ground for the negative attributes to breed. How? When different groups and organizations that claim Christ while teaching a variety of doctrines from the "same" Bible assemble, the purity demanded by Christ is lost. Moreover, poor behavior by anyone in this assembly taints everyone involved. This includes the espousal of non-Biblical views and physically altercations that occur over differing opinions. Satan loves this non-Biblical confederation and the opportunities it presents. But the Holy Spirit inspired James to write, "*Does a spring send forth fresh water and bitter from the same opening? Can a fig tree, my brethren, bear olives, or a grapevine bear figs? Thus no spring yields both salt water and fresh*" (James 3:11-12). The Biblical principle espoused here documents spiritually that God's Truth cannot physically coexist with anything else. However, many people in the religious community have decided to ignore the Biblical teachings on this doctrine. **False** teachers are teaching that all beliefs can come together in the name of God and retain their separate practices, conventions, and traditions under one roof. This ***false*** practice is presented as "Coexistence," as seen in **Figure 33.** This is a subversive strategy of the negative attribute using spiritual warfare to confuse younger generations of people against the "One Faith" of Ephesians 4:4-6 under the pretext of diversity, inclusion, tolerance, and equality. Please do not be ***deceived***. **False** teachers of this blasphemous concept will incur the wrath of God for the Biblical record documents, "*...whoever causes one of these little ones who believe in Me to stumble, it would be better for him if a millstone were hung around his neck, and he were thrown into the sea*" (Mark 9:42). Even in the Old Testament, the children of Israel were told "*You shall not go after other gods, the gods of the peoples who are all around you (for the Lord* *your God is a jealous God among you), lest the anger of the Lord your God be aroused against you and destroy you from the face of the earth"* (Deuteronomy 6:14-16), and *"They provoked Him to jealousy with foreign gods; with abominations they provoked Him to anger"* (Deuteronomy 32:16). In the Book of 1st Samuel the author declared, *"Therefore You are great, O Lord God. For there is none like You, nor is there any God besides You, according to all that we have heard with our ears"* (2 Samuel 7:22). Later in the Book of Isaiah, the nation of Israel

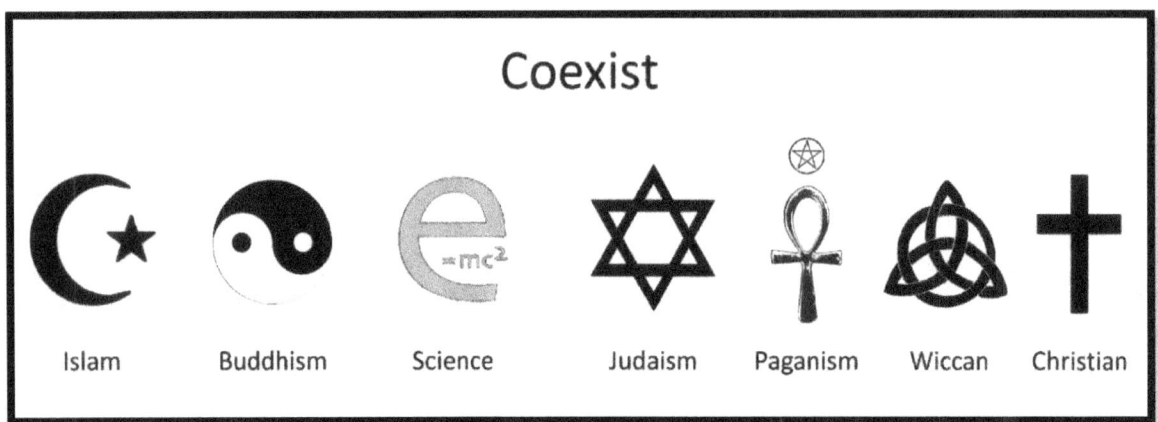

Figure 33: The Unscriptural Movement of Coexistence

was told, *"I, even I, am the Lord, and besides Me there is no savior. I have declared and saved, I have proclaimed, and there was no foreign god among you; therefore you are My witnesses,"* Says the Lord, *"that I am God"* (Isaiah 43:11-12). Even Solomon prayed *"...that all the peoples of the earth may know that the Lord is God; there is no other"* (1 Kings 8:60). This knowledge has been compromised through spiritual warfare as ***false*** ministers, teachers, and scholars traverse the battlefield spewing ***false*** doctrine.

Paul documented *"...your **faith** should not be in the wisdom of men but in the power of God"* (1 Corinthians 2:5). Further he wrote, *"Beware lest anyone cheat you through philosophy and empty **deceit**, according to the tradition of men, according to the basic principles of the world, and not according to Christ"* (Colossians 2:8). And even the Proverbs documented, *"There is a way that seems right to a man, but its end is the way of death"* (Proverbs 14:12). Coexistence is simply another path to spiritual death orchestrated by the influences of the negative attributes. This consolidation of "faiths" in a "church," while allowing each person to preserve their different doctrines or beliefs under the name "Christian" is an abomination to God. The strategy behind this abomination is an attempt to nullify God's Word. As for these organizations themselves, Jesus stated, *"...if anyone says to you, 'Look, here is the Christ!' or 'There!' do not believe it. For **false** christs and **false** prophets will rise and show great signs and wonders to **deceive**, if possible, even the elect. See, I have told you beforehand"* (Matthew 24:23-25). Jesus gave this strict warning for a reason. There is only one Christ in the one Gospel that everyone claiming the name Jesus Christ is to follow. But one must invest the time in seeking this Truth. Here are some infallible Truths from Jesus for all Christians. Jesus said Himself:

- *"...whoever confesses Me before men, him I will also confess before My Father who is in heaven. But whoever denies Me before men, him I will also deny before My Father who is in heaven"* (Matthew 10:32-33)

- *"He who has the Son has life; he who does not have the Son of God does not have life"* (1 John 5:12)

- *"I am the bread of life. He who comes to Me shall never hunger, and he who believes in Me shall never thirst"* (John 6:35)

- *"I am the light of the world. He who follows Me shall not walk in darkness, but have the light of life"* (John 8:12)

- *"I am the resurrection and the life. He who believes in Me, though he may die, he shall live"* (John 11:25)

- *"I am the way, the truth, and the life. No one comes to the Father except through Me"* (John 14:6)

The negative forces' strategy uses **false** teachers, ministers, and social media, to blanket the world with different doctrines about Christ and His teachings under the same umbrella call "Christianity". This is one of the most successful strategies employed in the war campaign. It dilutes God's Word and He is not happy with this. Anyone who denies the Truth above has made their home with the negative forces of the war campaign. Anyone desiring to be saved when their part ends in the war campaign must not be found among congregations of **false** teachers or anyone denying this Truth on their own accord. Please do not be **deceived**.

BTT allows one to see that the religious community's reporting of huge numbers of Christians in the world is **false**. This numbering scheme is motivated by a sinister strategy of the negative forces to drive financial <u>gain</u>. The religious community **falsely** espouses that every religious organization that names the name of Christ, regardless of their doctrine, is Christian. This successful strategy confuses the average believer who become captivated by the size of his or her accepted community. In reality, these believers have accepted a **false** paradigm that is no more than the equivalent of a white collar crime in the secular society in which resources are moved around the battlefield. Paul warned Timothy about men who would practice this form of crime when he stated, *"If anyone teaches otherwise and does not consent to wholesome words, even the words of our Lord Jesus Christ, and to the doctrine which accords with* **godliness***, he is* **proud***, knowing nothing, but is obsessed with disputes and arguments over words, from which come* **envy***,* <u>strife</u>*,* **reviling***,* **evil** *suspicions, useless wranglings of men of corrupt minds and destitute of the truth, who suppose that* **godliness** *is a means of* <u>gain</u>*. From such withdraw yourself"* (1 Timothy 6: 3-5). Titus documented this same thought when he wrote, *"For there are many insubordinate, both* **idle** *talkers and* **deceivers***, especially those of the circumcision, whose mouths must be stopped, who* **subvert** *whole households, teaching things which they ought not, for the sake of* <u>dishonest</u> <u>gain</u>*"* (Titus 1:10-12). The negative forces use this **false** premise to dilute Christ's church, His doctrine and teaching, and most importantly His Truth. One must remember that to accommodate every religious group that claims Christ, one must make compromises in God's Word to keep the peace. Does God give one this authority? BTT allows one to see, from the history of the Biblical record, that the answer to this question is "No." God does not allow the compromise of His Word. The Proverbs documents for the one who pursues this strategy has his or her inner spiritual heart hardened and, "...*he who hardens his heart will fall into calamity*" (Proverbs 28:14).

Inflating the number of people in the Christian community by using religious groups that claim Christ creates the ***false*** belief that everyone in that community, regardless of their beliefs, will be saved. This book documents that this teaching and belief is completely ***false***. One's salvation depends on his or her obedience to God's Word, repentance, striving for ***righteousness***, and God's grace. God's grace covers one who is actively striving to do His will. For the Biblical record plainly documents, "...*for all have sinned and fall short of the glory of God, being justified freely by His grace through the redemption that is in Christ Jesus...*" (Romans 3:23-24). However, ***false*** teachers and ministers belittle this truth by their teachings. But God's calamity makes ***fools*** of people who teach otherwise and upholds those who hold fast to teaching His Truth. The truth is, the positive force's numbers in the war campaign are small because a lot rides on the back of true believers during the course of the war. The burden is so heavy in a world that, "...*lies under the sway of the **wicked** one*" (1 John 5:19), that most people cannot carry the load. Hence, the Biblical record provides evidence of the small numbers of the positive forces of the war campaign through numerous examples. Examples include that of Gideon in the Book of Judges in Chapter 7:1-26. In this example, Gideon and three hundred men, destroyed the armies of the, "...*Midianites and Amalekites, all the people of the East, were lying in the valley as numerous as locusts; and their camels were without number, as the sand by the seashore in multitude*" (Judges 7:12). Gideon had all the positive attributes. Another example is in the Book of 1 Kings 18:22 in which Elijah said to the people "*I alone am left a prophet of the Lord; but Baal's prophets are four hundred and fifty men.*" Elijah stood against a large population that was influenced by the negative attributes. The numbers documented of the prophet and the people illustrated a ratio similar to the positive and negative forces in the war campaign. One can also consider Lot and his family in the city of Sodom. Abraham pleaded with the Lord to save Sodom and Gomorrah if just ten ***righteous*** souls were found. Sodom and the cities on the plain, a large but undocumented number of people, were destroyed. Only four souls were found and escaped the destruction (Genesis 18:16-33; 19:1-30). Unfortunately, Lot's wife died when she looked back at the destruction. But the truth is, she died because she disobeyed God's Word not to look back. Did one of the negative attributes influence her to ignore God's command? By now, one should be able to answer this question with a resounding "Yes"!

In addition, for Noah and his family, only eight souls were numbered with the positive forces against everyone else on earth at that time who were influenced by ***wickedness*** according to Genesis Chapters 6, 7, and 8. And even in the New Testament, one can consider Jesus and His disciples against millions of Jews. Or even Paul, Luke, and Aristarchus on a ship destroyed in a storm in Acts 27:41-44. Paul, Luke, and Aristarchus's presence onboard that ship saved the lives of the unbelievers aboard who were lost in the fog of the negative forces of the campaign. The Biblical record documented that God spared, "...*two hundred and seventy-six persons on the ship*" (Acts 27:37). Think about it. Even among God's people, a ratio is found.

For John wrote, "*I rejoiced greatly that I have found <u>some of your children walking in truth</u>, as we received commandment from the Father*" (2 John 1:4). Everyone in a Christian's family may not be obedient to Christ. This confirms that the Christian population in this world is always going to be small, because God desires true worshipers who "*...will worship the Father in spirit and truth; for the Father is seeking such to worship Him*" (John 4:23), and who understand that "*God is Spirit, and those who worship Him must worship in spirit and truth*" (John 4:24). Some families will split apart or leave the church because pursing the Truth will be too hard for some that are enraptured with the world. **False** teachers and ministers prey on this departure from the Truth and their influences continue to invite God's *calamity* at increasing levels of severity. When one acknowledges this fact, then it calls into question all of the counterfeit religious bodies that claim the name of Christ. BTT allows one to see these counterfeit religious bodies can only be eliminated when the people in them wake up to the Truth of the Gospel. Peter wrote, "*Therefore, laying aside all **malice**, **all deceit**, hypocrisy, **envy**, and all **evil speaking**, as newborn babes, <u>desire the pure milk of the word, that you may grow thereby</u>, if indeed you have tasted that the Lord is gracious*" (1 Peter 2:1-3). If the people fail to wake up, the negative forces will continue to advance in the war campaign and God's *calamity* may become even greater.

As encouragement and confirmation of the truth and power of God's Word, consider these three Scriptural references from the Biblical record. For the positive forces of the war campaign fighting the negative forces, the Biblical record documents:

- "*How could one chase a thousand, and two put ten thousand to flight, unless their Rock had sold them, and the Lord had surrendered them? For their rock is not like our Rock, even our enemies themselves being judges. For their vine is of the vine of Sodom and of the fields of Gomorrah; their grapes are grapes of gall, their clusters are bitter. Their wine is the poison of serpents, and the cruel venom of cobras.*" (Deuteronomy 32:30-33)

- "*Five of you shall chase a hundred, and a hundred of you shall put ten thousand to flight; your enemies shall fall by the sword before you*" (Leviticus 26:8)

- "*One man of you shall chase a thousand, for the Lord your God is He who fights for you, as He promised you*" (Joshua 23:10)

The small numbers of true and ***faithful*** Christians have the strength of the Almighty God leading them into battle in spiritual warfare. His army, comprised of the positive forces of the war campaign, will overcome in the end. The positive forces have nothing to *fear* from the negative forces in spiritual warfare. They simply need to stay in Christ's teachings, mature, be obedient to His word, and keep on their spiritual armor to contend with the negative forces of the war.

I believe the third critical reason for God's *calamity* today is because of the senseless division within the Lord's churches over race, politics, and personal opinions. This division should not be with all the obstacles confronting Christ's church; but it is. Churches of Christ world-wide, the last ark of safety, are becoming fragmented over men's opinions. Differences between how communion is conducted, the use of race as a criterion for selecting a preacher and elders, styles of singing, preaching, praying, and even the use of technology in a church, all provide evidence of spiritual warfare's advancement among the brethren. BTT allows one to see the broader application of Paul statement in Romans 14:10-13 beyond just eating and drinking. When Paul stated, "*But why do you judge your brother? Or why do you show contempt for your brother? For we shall all stand before the judgment seat of Christ. For it is written: "As I live, says the Lord, every knee shall bow to Me, and every tongue shall confess to God." So then each of us shall give account of himself to God. Therefore let us not judge one another anymore, but rather resolve this, not to put a stumbling block or a cause to fall in our brother's way*" (Romans 14:10-13), his greater point was about putting "*a stumbling block or a cause to fall in our brother's way*". The negative attributes are now causing Christians to miss the greater point.

As it pertained to people of different races in Christ's church, BTT allows one to see that after Peter's powerful sermon on the Day of Pentecost, Christ's church started with, "*those who gladly received his word were baptized; and that day about three thousand souls were added to them*" (Acts 2:41). A closer look reveals that the first congregation was composed of Galileans, Parthians, Medes, Elamites, people dwelling in Mesopotamia, Judea and Cappadocia, Pontus and Asia, Phrygia and Pamphylia, Egypt and the parts of Libya adjoining Cyrene, visitors from Rome, both Jews and proselytes, and Cretans and Arabs according to Acts 2:7-11. This racial make-up of Christ's church established the true pattern of His church on the spiritual battlefield. It even extended to other races among the Gentiles (us) when Cornelius and his whole household were _baptized_ into Christ. Peter, who would _baptize_ these Gentiles stated, "*In truth I perceive that God shows no partiality. But in every nation whoever fears Him and works* **righteousness** *is accepted by Him*" (Acts 10: 34-35). This is the expected pattern to be replicated to this very day. This racial make-up not only served as an example for future congregations, but it provided perspectives on spiritual matters necessary for strengthening Christ's church in its future role on the spiritual battlefield. Without this mix of different peoples and backgrounds, homogeneous views would have isolated Christ's church in the hands of a few. A cursory review of church history confirms the spin-off of this type of thinking. Over time and circumstances, the negative attributes influenced people to have _prejudicial_ attitudes toward their fellow brothers and sisters in Christ. These attitudes are segregating churches and people on the spiritual battlefield by race and political views. _Prejudice_ resonates in people with **unclean spirits** influencing them to rejected the Holy Spirit's proclamation through Paul that God, "*…has made from one blood every nation of men to dwell on all the face of the earth, and has determined their preappointed times and the boundaries of their dwellings…*" (Acts 17:26).

Today, this should not be so. God's people must overcome _prejudices_ and _favoritism_. If not, how can every potential soul be a candidate for hearing the Gospel. True Christians know this. Thus, I believe God brings _calamity_ on His congregations who actively practice _segregation_, _prejudice_, or _favoritism_ towards any other race. Church leadership that sanctions, turns a blind eye, or ignores issues in these areas are complicit in the congregation's behavior and will be held accountable by God in the worst possible way. When the Holy Spirit led Paul to document, "*Be kindly affectionate to one another with brotherly love, in* **honor** *giving preference to one another…*" (Romans 12:10), and "*Bear one another's burdens, and so fulfill* *the law of Christ*"(Galatians 6:2), the Scriptures were not documented for maintaining a homogeneous racial state. Jesus said, and His apostles taught, "*If anyone <u>loves</u> Me, he will keep My word; and My Father will <u>love</u> him, and We will come to him and make Our home with him*" (John 14:23). God and His Son are not among people who keep division alive regardless of what they or anyone else preaches. Unfortunately, the fog of spiritual warfare even blinds a lot of **good** people today who keep silent on these spiritual infractions.

BTT allows one to see that when diverse races and ethnicities of people in the 1st Century church came together, they overcame stereotypes and **evil** thoughts about each other. Their behavior shaped the community in which they lived. Not the other way around. The Biblical record informs one that they continued, "*...daily with one accord in the temple, and breaking bread from house to house, they ate their food with gladness and simplicity of heart, praising God and having favor with <u>all the people</u>. And <u>the Lord added to the church daily those who were being saved</u>*" (Acts 2:46-47). To be saved, these three thousand plus Christians had to put aside their differences and the influence of any negative attributes that hindered them.

One must understand that the negative forces exploit race and politics to divide Christ's church. This exploitation seeks to destroy His examples of unity and <u>peace</u> from among God's creation. Peter recognized this fact when he documented, "*...In truth I perceive that God shows <u>no partiality</u>*" (Acts 10:34). For Christians, this means that holding views of <u>prejudice</u>, especially concerning skin color, is sinful. This truth applies to any scenario that one can conceive. In fact, <u>partiality</u>, <u>discrimination</u>, and <u>prejudice</u> begins with the influence of the **unjust** attribute in spiritual warfare and ends with other unclean behaviors, attitudes, and thoughts from the **hater** to the **bloodthirsty** attributes. BTT allows one to see, for unity and peace to <u>exist</u>, positive attributes which start from examples set in Christ's church and the home must be present. The Biblical record documents that God, "*...made from one blood every nation of men to dwell on all the face of the earth, and has determined their preappointed times and the boundaries of their dwellings, so that they should seek the Lord, in the <u>hope</u> that they might grope for Him and find Him, though He is not far from each one of us; for in Him we live and move and have our being...*" (Acts 17:26-28).

For issues of politics, the Biblical record is very clear on how God expects His people to behave. God's command for Christians, the people of Christ's church, to place their focus squarely on Him. If one is in Christ's church, one should understand, "*...our <u>citizenship</u> is in heaven, from which we also eagerly wait for the Savior, the Lord Jesus Christ, who will transform our lowly body that it may be conformed to His glorious body, according to the working by which He is able even to subdue all things to Himself*" (Philippians 3:19-21). Further Paul documented, "*Now, therefore, you are no longer strangers and foreigners, but <u>fellow citizens with the saints and members of the household of God</u>...*" (Ephesians 2:19). This means, that one's citizenship is in another kingdom and with another nation of people and one cannot get caught up in the politics of this world as Christ's "*...sojourners and pilgrims...*" (1 Peter 2:11). Now this is not to say that one should not exercise his or her liberty to participate in the political process of democracy or vote in a secular election process to support <u>peace</u> for all men. As Christians, we must follow the laws of the land as long as they do not contradict God's laws.

However, when people who claim Christ fail to understand where their citizenship is, they get lost in the fog of the war campaign. The prophet Isaiah told the nation of Israel long ago, "*...for the Lord is our Judge, the Lord is our Lawgiver, the Lord is our King; He will save us...*" (Isaiah 33:22). Man, nor his politics, can save a single soul; only God can. Christians, the sojourners and pilgrims of the earth, are to focus on obedience, **godly** works, and teaching God's way through evangelism. It is the universal Christian nation of today among the body of Christ that the Psalmist words applies in which he stated, "*Blessed is the nation whose God is the Lord, the people He has chosen as His own inheritance*" (Psalm 33:12).

God provides two directives when it comes to the politics of this world. The directives are:

- "*Let every soul be subject to the governing authorities. For there is no authority except from God, and the authorities that exist are appointed by God. Therefore whoever resists the authority resists the ordinance of God, and those who resist will bring judgment on themselves*" (Romans 13:1-2)

- "*Therefore submit yourselves to every ordinance of man for the Lord's sake, whether to the king as supreme, or to governors, as to those who are sent by him for the punishment of **evildoers** and for the praise of those who do **good**. <u>For this is the will of God</u>, that by doing **good** you may put to silence the ignorance of **foolish** men— as free, yet not using liberty as a cloak for vice, but as bondservants of God. **Honor** all people. <u>Love</u> the brotherhood. <u>Fear</u> God. **Honor** the king*" (1 Peter 2:13-17)

When Christians place issues of politics above God's Word, they become compromised. The truth is this: Jesus- "*... gave Himself for us, that He might redeem us from every lawless deed and purify for Himself His own special people, zealous for **good** works*" (Titus 2:14). **False** teachers around the world, on the spiritual battlefield, **rob** their audiences of God's sound messages on this subject. Politics has no place among the body of Christ; only His Word that unites. Moreover, if Christians take the true Word of God to everyone who will hear, including politicians, positive change will occur. This effort requires personal work in which one takes the gospel to the homes of the lost. Even the politician's soul is precious to the Lord.

Lastly, personal opinions are compromising Christ's church on the spiritual battlefield in alarming numbers. This tide stems from men and women who refuse to submit to leadership selected in Christ's churches who serve as "*...overseers, to shepherd the church of God which He purchased with His own blood*" (Acts 20:28). In fact, many churches have compromised the term "overseer". This is discussed in detail in Chapter VII of this book. For now, one needs to understand that his or her personal opinion is just that – personal opinion. It has no value in Christ's church where Jesus's Word is the law. Jesus' Word and His teachings to His apostles guide His church. These teaching include the selection of elders, "*...**faithful** men who will be able to teach others...*" (2 Timothy 2:2). However, when personal opinion, politics and race get involved, qualified men of different races capable of serving as elders are overlooked due to the congregation's lack of <u>discernment</u>. Hence, the rich knowledge of a diverse leadership is lost and the church's ability to serve its members and their community on the spiritual battlefield is compromised. Christians are to be above this nonsense. Moreover, when negative attributes find a niche into Christ's church through the inner spirit of immature Christians and is not corrected, the condition eventually leaves the entire congregation facing God's strongest judgement of, "*...I never knew you; depart from Me, you who practice **lawlessness**!*" (Matthew 7:23). Incidents of this nature have succeeded in fragmenting many congregations of Christ's churches in local communities on the spiritual battlefield worldwide. This fragmentation has created smaller congregations, sometimes *"just down the road"* from another congregation. Because of the membership's size, external obligations such as work and travel, and the relentless attack of the negative attributes, many of these smaller congregations find themselves ill-equipped to carry out Christ's mission. In many cases, these churches are in survival mode in their location on the battlefield. They are ill-equipped because God's resources from the **harvest** of people within them, the physical resources and support to the campaign, are diluted. Remember, the resources of the **harvest** include manpower, finances, logistics, maintenance, guidance and instruction, and consistent leadership. When fragmentation occurs, which is often over cultural issues or opinions unimportant to God and never sanctioned by His Word, these smaller churches of Christ are weakened in battle. BTT allows one to see that if these congregations would combine and achieve unity as one body, the full power of Christ's church could be brought to bear in that location. Paul pleaded, *"Therefore if there is any consolation in Christ, if any comfort of love, if any fellowship of the Spirit, if any affection and **mercy**, fulfill my joy by being like-minded, having the same love, being of one accord, of one mind"* (Philippians 2:1-2). This was a plea to the one body of Christ. One cannot allow spiritual warfare to blind him or her to this truth. If one does while claiming to follow Christ, God's calamity will bring the truth out.

I believe the fourth critical reason for God's calamity today is because the negative forces have significantly advanced on the spiritual battlefield by altering God's divine plan for His male and female creation. As difficult as this subject may be, it must be addressed. Today, this is possibly the biggest spiritual issue facing humanity next to apostasy. When the ***perverse*** and ***immoral*** attribute's combine, their influences produce an array of negative behaviors that are unacceptable to God. One of the behaviors is *"vile passions"* as documented by Paul by inspiration of the Holy Spirit. The Biblical record documented, *"For even their women exchanged the natural use for what is against nature. Likewise also the men, leaving the natural use of the woman, burned in their lust for one another, men with men committing what is **shameful**..."* (Romans 1:26-27). BTT allows one to see that this was the same type of behavior, influenced by the ***perverse*** and ***immoral*** attributes, that cost millions of people their lives during the time of Sodom and Gomorrah in Genesis 19 and the lives of the men of Gibeah in Judges 19:22. But it is not the people that are the real issue. Its ***unclean spirits*** influencing their behavior that is the issue. Why? Because the ***unclean spirits*** behind the behavior corrupted their inner spirits and led them to ***sexually immoral*** activities. These ancient spirits know how to spread like a cancer to one's inner spirit and use other negative attributes, such as the ***seducer***, ***evil***, and ***adulterer*** attributes to destroy ***good*** people throughout the spiritual battlefield. The combination of the ***perverse*** and ***immoral*** attributes even corrupts the innocent minds of children and young adults who experiment with sexual activities out of ignorance. This includes children who become **witnesses** of or are forced to participate in unwanted sexual activity. This also includes children who gain access to free images of sexual behavior through social media. All of these initial events embed negative thoughts in the carnal mind that leads to negative behaviors that are hard to erase. Only God's Word contains the balm to cleanse these images from the carnal mind through his or her inner spirit. God placed the responsibility to teach *godly* behavior and set *godly* examples on the shoulders of parents. Hence, parents have the responsibility of shaping *godly* behavior in their children. When parents or adults engage in *ungodly* behavior or when parents allow their children or young adults to acts of *perversion* or *immorality*, God is not happy.

In fact, when man puts in place earthly laws to invalidate, nullify, or make illegal the divine laws of God, His <u>*calamity*</u> is initiated. Moreover, when religious leaders and people who claim the name of Christ supports *ungodly* principles, rules, activities, or the people who clearly contradict God's Word, they invite God's <u>*calamity*</u>. His <u>*calamity*</u> is impacting people in Christ's church who refuse to put on their spiritual armor or begin supporting *false* rhetoric for *homosexual*, *lesbian*, *pedophilic*, and the like, lifestyles. Once again, the Biblical record warned, *"For the time has come for judgment to begin at the house of God; and if it begins with us first, what will be the end of those who do not obey the gospel of God?"* (1 Peter 4:17). Do not be *deceived*.

Figure 34: God's Plan vs. Man's Additions

Figure 34 illustrates the changes to God's initial plan for man and woman. Today, God's <u>*calamity*</u> is occurring in the world because the negative attributes have influenced congregations to support altering God's plan for His male and female creation. Religious men and women, educated in worldly theologies, philosophies, and divinity are preaching God's Word from pulpits worldwide to gain secular acceptance. BTT allows one to see that this should not be so. Their very behavior contradicts God's Word as documented in the Bible. Nevertheless, *false* teachers are pushing *ungodly*, *immoral*, and *perverse* ideologies across the spiritual battlefield. These very ideologies are used to justify both women and homosexual preachers in church pulpits worldwide. One must consider that the Holy Spirit, working through Paul, documented, *"And even as they did not like to retain God in their knowledge, God gave them over to a debased mind, to do those things which are not fitting; being filled with all **unrighteousness, sexual***

immorality, wickedness, covetousness, maliciousness; full of envy, murder, <u>*strife*</u>*, deceit, evil-mindedness; they are whisperers, backbiters, haters of God, violent, proud, boasters, inventors of evil things, disobedient to parents,* <u>*undiscerning*</u>*,* **untrustworthy, unloving, unforgiving, unmerciful**; who, knowing the **righteous** judgment of God, that those who practice such things are deserving of death, <u>not only do the same but also approve of those who practice them</u>" (Romans 1: 28-32). Paul's message was to Christians first and then to the religious world. He followed it up with this warning: "*Therefore you are inexcusable, O man, whoever you are who judge, for in whatever you judge another you condemn yourself; for you who judge practice the same things. But we know that the judgment of God is according to truth against those who practice such things. And do you think this, O man, you who judge those practicing such things, and doing the same, that you will escape the judgment of God?*" (Romans 2:1-3).

One need only to consider the increasing number of **perverse** acts growing in every nation. The number of missing persons, especially children, are staggering. **Sexual immorality** is rampant and destroying people spiritually, emotionally, psychologically. Moreover, there is an increasing number of parents and institutions who refuse to recognize the male and female gender which furthers contributes to society's confusion and degradation. Parents who chose to allow a child to select their gender when the child <u>is ready to decide</u> are engaged in sin. This behavior is an abdication of parental responsibility and contributes to a societal abomination that God destroyed Sodom, Gomorrah, and the cities on the plains for. If God's people and the religious world do not speak out on this matter, His <u>calamity</u> will only increase until the final day of judgement. God will not be **mocked**.

I believe the fifth critical reason for God's <u>calamity</u> today is because the negative forces have **deceived** incredible numbers of religious leaders and followers to ignore and deny God's requirement for water <u>baptism</u>. The rejection of, and **false** teaching on, this subject as prescribed by God's Word has placed enmity between God and man in the war campaign. There are several terms/words in the Greek language for getting oneself wet. However, "<u>baptize</u>" comes from the Greek transliterated word "<u>baptizō</u>[2]" which means to immerse. This term in context is used 81 times in the New King James New Testament of the Biblical record. "*Katachéō* or *cheno*[3]" are Greek transliterated words for pouring and "*rhantízō*[4]" is the Greek transliterated word for sprinkling according to several Greek/English lexicons. Christians "<u>baptizo</u>"; there is no other authorized substitute given from God.

Hence, the act of <u>baptism</u> by immersion is the most attacked teaching of Jesus Christ by the negative attributes today. The reason for this is simple and goes back to what Paul explained

---

[2] Strong's #907- βαπτίζω - Old & New Testament Greek Lexicon. (n.d.). Retrieved from https://www.studylight.org/lexicons/greek/907.html. Accessed 18 February 2019

[3] Strong's # 2708 - καταχέω - Old & New Testament Greek Lexicon. (n.d.). Retrieved from https://www.studylight.org/lexicons/greek/2708.html. Accessed 18 February 2019

[4] Strong's # 4472 - ῥαντίζω - Old & New Testament Greek Lexicon. (n.d.). Retrieved from https://www.studylight.org/lexicons/greek/4472.html. Accessed 18 February 2019

to the Jews. He said, "*Brethren, my heart's desire and prayer to God for Israel is that they may be saved. For I bear them* **witness** *that they have a zeal for God, but not according to knowledge. For they being ignorant of God's* **righteousness**, *and seeking to establish their own* **righteousness**, *have not submitted to the* **righteousness** *of God. For Christ is the end of the law for* **righteousness** *to everyone who believes*" (Romans 10:1-4). To submit to the **righteousness** of God is to submit to the <u>baptism</u> established by God. Even Jesus understood this and submitted to <u>baptism</u>. The Bible documents that Jesus told John, who tried to stop Him from being <u>baptized</u>, "*Permit it to be so now, for thus it is fitting for us to fulfill all* **righteousness**.*" Then he allowed Him*" (Matthew 3:15). This physical act places one in a state for spiritual salvation, operationalizes BTT, and strengthens one's maturity for <u>discernment</u>. This means that one's <u>discernment</u> between **right** and **wrong** is at its clearest moment in time *if* the act of <u>baptism</u> is sincere. Directly after <u>baptism</u> is the most opportune time to feed the spirit with more Truth from the Word of God. For people influenced by the negative attributes will launch a full spiritual assault to discourage one from his or her new walk. Jesus addresses these assaults in His parable of the sower and the Seed. It is during <u>baptism</u> that a new Christian makes his or her first stand against Satan. This is why *churches* of Christ teach <u>baptism</u> by immersion and not the prevailing unscriptural view of "ask Jesus to come into one's heart" or "say the sinner's prayer." The Biblical record is void of these two practices. The influences of the negative attributes have **deceived** many. BTT allows one to see that when Jesus talked to Nicodemus about water <u>baptism</u>, He shut down all discussions on alternate practices for salvation. Jesus told Nicodemus, "…*Most assuredly, I say to you, unless one is born again, he cannot see the kingdom of God." Nicodemus said to Him, "How can a man be born when he is old? Can he enter a second time into his mother's womb and be born?" Jesus answered, "Most assuredly, I say to you, unless one is born of water and the Spirit, he cannot enter the kingdom of God. That which is born of the flesh is flesh, and that which is born of the Spirit is spirit. Do not marvel that I said to you, 'You must be born again'*" (John 3:3-7). In the context of Jesus' statement, He clearly states that water <u>baptism</u> is required to see the kingdom of God. For it is this <u>baptism</u> that brings one in contact with the spiritual blood of Christ that cleanses one of sin. Jesus defines the standard for Salvation; not man. The Holy Spirit inspired Peter to write, "*There is also an antitype which now saves us—*<u>baptism</u> *(not the removal of the filth of the flesh, but the answer of a good conscience toward God), through the resurrection of Jesus Christ, who has gone into heaven and is at the right hand of God, angels and authorities and powers having been made subject to Him*" (1 Peter 3:21-22). In other words, <u>baptism</u> is the divine method God chose to put one in a state that would allow Jesus to enter one's inner spirit which creates an opportunity for heaven. Based on the Biblical record, this is the only authorized method God has for one to put on Christ and for Christ to dwell spiritually in one's spirit. <u>Baptism</u> opens the spiritual gate to salvation. Moreover, there is only one gate and Jesus stated, "*Strive to enter through the narrow gate, for many, I say to you, will seek to enter and will not be able*" (Luke 13:24). People will not be able to enter the gate to heaven due to their disobedience to God's Word and their beliefs in alternative paths.

As one looks further into this, BTT allows one to see something divine. The act of <u>baptism</u>, which is the physical act of being submerged under water and brought out again, is designed to spiritually refresh one's inner spirit and physical life. The act mimics Jesus' burial and resurrection; His death and return to life. No one can fully explain the things that occur from this act of submission to God's Word, but one can know this physical act does something for us in both the physical and spiritual realms. <u>Baptism</u> is foreign to man's wisdom and as Peter documented, "*...some things hard to understand, which untaught and **unstable** people twist to their own destruction, as they do also the rest of the Scriptures*" (2 Peter 3:16). God established <u>baptism</u>; not man. Remember, the Biblical record documented from the Lord, "*For My thoughts are not your thoughts, nor are your ways My ways," says the Lord. For as the heavens are higher than the earth, so are My ways higher than your ways, and My thoughts than your thoughts*" (Isaiah 55:8-9). To refuses this Truth, the Spirit of wisdom reminds all that, "*Because you disdained all my **counsel**, and would have none of my rebuke, I also will laugh at your <u>calamity</u>; I will **mock** when your <u>terror</u> comes, when your <u>terror</u> comes like a <u>storm</u>, and your destruction comes like a <u>whirlwind</u>, when <u>distress and anguish</u> come upon you*" (Proverbs 1:25-27). The religious community is experiencing God's <u>calamity</u> for rejection of His water <u>baptism</u> as they move worldwide teaching doctrines of demons (1 Timothy 4:1) across the spiritual battlefield. One should always keep in mind that to become a Christian the right way is the most important decision one will ever make in his or her lifetime. If not done right, one's efforts to be saved in this life becomes a waste of time. Peter stated, "*Therefore, brethren, be even more diligent to make your call and election sure...*" (2 Peter 1:10).

Here is what one needs to know about <u>baptism</u>. <u>Baptism</u> places one in Christ. This means that one gains Christ dwelling in one's inner spirit by submitting to the act of <u>baptism</u>. <u>Baptism</u> is a logical step when one believes God's Word, repents from sin, confess His Holy name, and desires to live obediently to His Word. The Holy Spirit inspired the apostles to document that to be in Christ means a unique spiritual phenomenon occurs between God and His human creation. This spiritual phenomenon provides God's creation unique benefits acquired no other way. David even documented, "*Blessed be the Lord, Who daily loads us with benefits, the God of our salvation!*" (Psalms 68:19). Thus, one must understand that these unique benefits are only provided when a person comes to God His way; that is "*...as many of you as were <u>baptized into Christ have put on Christ</u>*" *(Galatians 3:27)*. The unique benefits that come with being <u>in Christ</u> are:

To Be In Jesus Christ Offers	**What Is Documented**
Redemption	"<u>In Him</u> we have <u>redemption</u> through His blood, the forgiveness of sins, according to the riches of His <u>grace</u>..." (Ephesians 1:7)
	"...being <u>justified</u> freely by His <u>grace</u> through the <u>redemption</u> that <u>is in Christ Jesus</u>..." (Romans 3:24)
Justification	"...knowing that a man is not justified by the works of the law but by **faith** in Jesus Christ, even we have believed in Christ Jesus, that we might be <u>justified</u> by **faith** <u>in Christ</u> and not by the works of the law; for by the works of the law no flesh shall be justified" (Galatians 2:16)
Life with God	"Likewise you also, reckon yourselves to be dead indeed to sin, but <u>alive to God in Christ Jesus</u> our Lord" (Romans 6:11)
	"For as in Adam all die, even so <u>in Christ</u> <u>all shall be made alive</u>" (1 Corinthians 15:22)

	"Paul, an apostle of Jesus Christ by the will of God, according to the _promise of life_ which is _in Christ Jesus_..." (2 Timothy 1:1)
Eternal life	"For the wages of sin is death, but the gift of God is _eternal life_ _in Christ Jesus_ our Lord" (Romans 6:23)
	"...whoever believes _in Him_ should not perish but have _eternal life_" (John 3:15)
	"For God so _loved_ the world that He gave His only begotten Son, that whoever believes _in Him_ should not perish but have _everlasting life_" (John 3:16)
	"Most assuredly, I say to you, he who hears My word and believes _in Him_ who sent Me has _everlasting life_, and shall not come into judgment, but has passed from death into life" (John 5:24)
No condemnation	"There is therefore now _no condemnation_ to those who are _in Christ Jesus_, who do not walk according to the flesh, but according to the Spirit" (Romans 8:1)
	"He who believes _in Him_ is _not condemned_; but he who does not believe _is condemned_ already, because he has not believed in the name of the only begotten Son of God" (John 3:18)
Triumph	"Now thanks be to God who always _leads us in triumph_ _in Christ_, and through us diffuses the fragrance of His knowledge in every place" (2 Corinthians 2:14)
Liberty	"And this occurred because of **false** brethren secretly brought in (who came in by stealth to spy out our _liberty_ which we have _in Christ Jesus_, that they might bring us into bondage)..." (Galatians 2:4)
Simplicity	"But I fear, lest somehow, as the serpent **deceived** Eve by his craftiness, so your minds may be corrupted from the _simplicity_ that is _in Christ_" (2 Corinthians 11:3)
A different way of thinking	"Therefore if there is any consolation _in Christ_, if any comfort of _love_, if any fellowship of the Spirit, if any affection and **mercy**, fulfill my joy by being like-minded, having the same _love_, being of one accord, of one mind. Let nothing be done through **selfish ambition** or **conceit**, but in lowliness of mind let each esteem others better than himself. Let each of you look out not only for his own interests, but also for the interests of others. Let _this mind be in you_ which was also _in Christ Jesus_..." (Philippians 2:1-5)
God's abundant _grace_, **faith** and _love_	"And the _grace_ of our Lord was exceedingly abundant, with _faith and love_ which are _in Christ Jesus_" (1 Timothy 1:14)
	"Hold fast the pattern of sound words which you have heard from me, in _faith and love_ which are _in Christ Jesus_" (2 Timothy 1:13)
A **Good** standing and boldness in the **faith**	"For those who have served well as _deacons obtain for themselves a **good** standing and great boldness in the **faith** which is in Christ Jesus_" (1 Timothy 3:13)
Grace	"You therefore, my son, be strong in the _grace_ that is _in Christ Jesus_" (2 Timothy 2:1)
Salvation	"Therefore I endure all things for the sake of the elect, that they also may obtain the _salvation_ which is _in Christ Jesus_ with eternal glory" (2 Timothy 2:10)

Perfection	"*Him we preach, warning every man and teaching every man in all wisdom, that we may <u>present every man perfect</u> <u>in Christ Jesus</u>*" (Colossians 1:28)
	"*For <u>in Him</u> dwells all the fullness of the Godhead bodily; and <u>you are complete</u> <u>in Him</u>, who is the head of all principality and power. <u>In Him</u> you were also circumcised with the circumcision made without hands, by putting off the body of the sins of the flesh, by the circumcision of Christ, buried with Him in <u>baptism</u>, in which you also were raised with Him through **faith** in the working of God, who raised Him from the dead*" (Colossians 2:9-12)
	"*But whoever keeps His word, truly the <u>love</u> of God is <u>perfected</u> in him. By this we know that we are <u>in Him</u>. He who says he abides <u>in Him</u> ought himself also to walk just as He walked*" (1 John 2:5-6)
Purity	"*…everyone who has this hope <u>in Him</u> <u>purifies</u> himself, just as He is pure*" (1 John 3:3)
Confidence	"*Now this is the <u>confidence</u> that we have <u>in Him</u>, that if we ask anything according to His will, He hears us*" (1 John 5:14)
The <u>Love</u> of God	"*…neither death nor life, nor angels nor principalities nor powers, nor things present nor things to come, nor height nor depth, nor any other created thing, shall be able to separate us from the <u>love of God</u> which is <u>in Christ Jesus</u> our Lord*" (Romans 8:23-39)
A future inheritance	"*<u>In Him</u> also we have obtained an <u>inheritance</u>, being predestined according to the purpose of Him who works all things according to the **counsel** of His will…*" (Ephesians 1:11)

Table 156: Unique Benefits of Being in Christ

When one can mentally grasp the unique benefits of being in Christ, <u>baptism</u> allows him or her to reach a higher level of BTT beyond earthly critical thinking. BTT and <u>discernment</u> lifts one above the fog created by the negative attributes. The rejection of <u>baptism</u> is sin; sin stops the progression and maturing of BTT. Satan, using the influences of the negative attributes, convinces many souls that <u>baptism</u> is unnecessary. The Holy Spirit warned Paul about this. He documented, "*The coming of the lawless one is according to the working of Satan, with all power, signs, and **lying** wonders, and with all **unrighteous deception** among those who perish, <u>because they did not receive the love of the truth, that they might be saved</u>. And <u>for this reason God will send them</u> **strong delusion**, <u>that they should believe the</u> **lie**, <u>that they all may be condemned who did not believe the truth</u> but had pleasure in **unrighteousness**" (2 Thessalonians 2:9-12). <u>Baptism</u> has the power to save one's soul and it opens the connection between God and the inner spirit of man. <u>Baptism</u> also establishes a clean path for BTT to mature. Only one's choice to not feed and discipline his or her inner spirit with God's Word will stop BTT from maturing. Now there are other reasons for God's <u>calamity</u> on the world over the issue of <u>baptism</u>.

Today, **false** teachers in religious communities are promoting a united doctrine that places Judaism and Christianity on an equal plain. This is a strategy of compromise generated by the influence of the negative forces of the war campaign. Peter told the Jews, "*…Repent, and let every one of you be <u>baptized</u> in the name of Jesus Christ for the remission of sins; and you shall receive the gift of the Holy Spirit*" (Acts 2:38). To accept what Peter preached meant that the Jews had to submit to the whole truth of the Biblical record. This included seeing the closure of their prophesies. God did not authorize either community to take parts of the Old and New Covenants and combine them for salvation. Paul provided the example of this Truth. When Ananias explained the Gospel and _baptism_ to Paul, Ananias said, "*And now why are you waiting? Arise and be _baptized_, and wash away your sins, calling on the name of the Lord.*" (Acts 22:16). Paul arose and was _baptized_ into Christ. He put away the teaching of Judaism. In effect, _baptism_ opened Paul's mind and inner spirit to God's complete Truth through his transformed mind. The Holy Spirit helped Paul see the Truth about life and salvation. His maturing inner spirit allowed him to make sense of spiritual warfare. He then provided clarity into the influences of the positive and negative attributes for everyone to read about. He put on Christ through _baptism_, left Judaism behind, and became a Christian. Through his transformation, Paul began to understand that "*the law was our tutor to bring us to Christ, that we might be justified by **faith**. But after **faith** has come, we are no longer under a tutor*" (Galatians 3:24-25). Christ lived in Paul's inner spirit as a Christian; not as a Jew. For **false** teachers today, who insist that the practicing aspects of the Mosaic Laws or Judaism are acceptable to God, Paul documented six important points on this subject.

1. "*It was necessary that the word of God should be spoken to you first; but since you reject it, and judge yourselves unworthy of everlasting life, behold, we turn to the Gentiles*" (Acts 13:46)

2. "*For the hearts of this people have grown dull. Their ears are hard of hearing, and their eyes they have closed, lest they should see with their eyes and hear with their ears, lest they should understand with their hearts and turn, so that I should heal them*" (Acts 28:27-28)

3. "*...their minds were blinded. For until this day the same veil remains unlifted in the reading of the Old Testament, because the veil is taken away _in Christ_*" (2 Corinthians 3:14)

4. "*For by one Spirit we were all _baptized_ into one body—whether Jews or Greeks, whether slaves or free—and have all been made to drink _into one Spirit_*" (1 Corinthians 12:13)

5. "*Do not **lie** to one another, since you have put off the old man with his deeds, and have put on the new man who is renewed in knowledge according to the image of Him who created him, where there is neither Greek nor Jew, circumcised nor uncircumcised, barbarian, Scythian, slave nor free, but _Christ is all and in all_*" (Colossians 3:9-11)

6. For the non-Jews (Gentiles) he documented, "*...that the blessing of Abraham might come upon the Gentiles _in Christ Jesus_, that we might receive the promise of the Spirit through **faith***" (Galatians 3:14), and

    o "*...that the Gentiles should be fellow heirs, _of the same body_, and partakers of His promise _in Christ_ through the gospel...*" (Ephesians 3:6) with Jews and everyone else who converts to Christianity, and

- o "*Stand fast therefore in the liberty by which Christ has made us free, and do not be entangled again with a yoke of bondage. Indeed I, Paul, say to you that if you become circumcised, Christ will profit you nothing. And I testify again to every man who becomes circumcised that he is a debtor to keep the whole law. You have become estranged from Christ, you who <u>attempt to be justified by law</u>; you have fallen from <u>grace</u>. For we through the Spirit eagerly wait for the hope of **righteousness** by **faith**. For <u>in Christ Jesus</u> neither circumcision nor uncircumcision avails anything, but **faith** working through <u>love</u>*" (Galatians 5:1-6)

Yet, for all of Paul's teaching, ***false*** teachers today are attempting to discredit Paul, his writings, and even the fact that he was a Jew of great stature prior to his conversion to Christianity. But the Biblical record need only be read to understand that Paul documented:

- "*I am indeed a Jew, born in Tarsus of Cilicia, but brought up in this city at the feet of Gamaliel, taught according to the strictness of our fathers' law, and was zealous toward God as you all are today. I persecuted this Way to the death, binding and delivering into prisons both men and women, as also the high priest bears me witness, and all the council of the elders, from whom I also received letters to the brethren, and went to Damascus to bring in chains even those who were there to Jerusalem to be punished*" (Acts 22:3-5)

  - o "*As for Saul* **[his name prior to his conversion to Christianity]**, *he made havoc of the church, entering every house, and dragging off men and women, committing them to prison*" (Acts 8:3)

- "*For you have heard of my former conduct in Judaism, how I persecuted the church of God beyond measure and tried to destroy it. And I advanced in Judaism beyond many of my contemporaries in my own nation, being more exceedingly zealous for the traditions of my fathers*" (Galatians 1:13-14)

- "*…If anyone else thinks he may have confidence in the flesh, I more so: circumcised the eighth day, of the stock of Israel, of the tribe of Benjamin, a Hebrew of the Hebrews; concerning the law, a Pharisee; concerning zeal, persecuting the church; concerning the* **righteousness** *which is in the law,* **blameless**" (Philippians 3:4-6)

Paul left the practices of Judaism after he met Jesus and complied with the requirements to become a Christian. The Bible documented that Paul, known as Saul, stated, "*And when we all had fallen to the ground, I heard a voice speaking to me and saying in the Hebrew language, 'Saul, Saul, why are you persecuting Me? It is hard for you to kick against the goads.' So I said, 'Who are You, Lord?' And He said, 'I am Jesus, whom you are persecuting. But rise and stand on your feet; for I have appeared to you for this purpose, to make you a minister and a witness both of the things which you have seen and of the things which I will yet reveal to you. I will deliver you from the Jewish people, as well as from the Gentiles, to whom I now send you, to open their eyes, in order to turn them from darkness to light, and from the power of Satan to God, that they may receive forgiveness of sins and an inheritance among those who are sanctified by faith in Me.'*" (Acts 26:14-18). After this encounter, the

Biblical record firmly documented that Paul was <u>*baptized*</u> into Christ (Acts 9:18) and he put Judaism away and became a Christian.

Now just to make sure one understands what is happening in the fog in the war campaign, one must accept that God Himself found fault with the covenant the nation of Israel had. The Biblical record documented, *"Because finding fault with them, He says: "Behold, the days are coming, says the Lord, when I will make a new covenant with the house of Israel and with the house of Judah—"* (Hebrews 8:8). The Bible further records that God, *"...says, "A new covenant," He has made the first obsolete. Now what is becoming obsolete and growing old is ready to vanish away"* (Hebrews 8:13). Israel's covenant vanished with Jesus's death and resurrection. The Bible documents, *"For He Himself is our peace, who has made both one, and has broken down the middle wall of separation, having abolished in His flesh the enmity, that is, the law of commandments contained in ordinances, so as to create in Himself one new man from the two, thus making peace, and that He might reconcile them both to God in one body through the cross, thereby putting to death the enmity"* (Ephesians 2:14-16). Simply put, Christ's Word overrides the Mosaic Law of the Jews and combines Jews and Gentiles (us) under one new covenant. Consider several things one gains from Christ's new covenantal relationship. First, the Bible documents *"But now we have been delivered from the law, having died to what we were held by, so that we should serve in the newness of the Spirit and not in the oldness of the letter"* (Romans 7:6). One learns from BTT and <u>discernment</u> that, *"...the blood of Christ, who through the eternal Spirit offered Himself without spot to God, cleanse your conscience from dead works to serve the living God? And for this reason He is the Mediator of the new covenant, by means of death, for the redemption of the transgressions under the first covenant, that those who are called may receive the promise of the eternal inheritance"* (Hebrews 9:14-15). Jesus is *"...the Mediator of the new covenant, and to the blood of sprinkling that speaks better things than that of Abel"* (Hebrews 12:24) for Christians. Thus, a Christian gains a fresh start at life regardless of one's past. Think about Paul. Moreover, Christians gain:

Gained	What Is Documented
The Remission of Sins by Jesus' Blood	*"For this is My blood of the new covenant, which is shed for many for <u>the remission of sins</u>"* (Matthew 26:28)
	"And He said to them, "This is <u>My blood of the new covenant</u>, which is shed for many" (Mark 14:24)
	"Likewise He also took the cup after supper, saying, "This cup is <u>the new covenant in My blood</u>, which is shed for you" (Luke 22:20)
	"In the same manner He also took the cup after supper, saying, "This cup <u>is the new covenant in My blood</u>. This do, as often as you drink it, in remembrance of Me."" (1 Corinthians 11:25)
A New Commandment	*"<u>A new commandment</u> I give to you, that you love one another; as I have loved you, that you also love one another"* (John 13:34)
	"Again, <u>a new commandment</u> I write to you, which thing is true in Him and in you, because the darkness is passing away, and the true light is already shining. He who says he is in the light, and hates his brother, is in darkness until now" (1 John 8-9)

A New Doctrine	"And they took him **[Paul]** and brought him to the Areopagus, saying, "May we know what this <u>new doctrine</u> is of which you speak?" (Acts 17:19)
Newness of Life through Baptism	"Therefore we were buried with Him through baptism into death, that just as Christ was raised from the dead by the glory of the Father, even so we also should walk in <u>newness of life</u>" (Romans 6:4)
	"Therefore purge out the old leaven, that <u>you may be a new lump</u>, since you truly are unleavened. For indeed Christ, our Passover, was sacrificed for us" (1 Corinthians 5:7)
	"Therefore, if anyone is in Christ, he is <u>a new creation</u>; old things have passed away; behold, all things have become new" (2 Corinthians 5:17)
	"For not even those who are circumcised keep the law, but they desire to have you circumcised that they may boast in your flesh. But God forbid that I should boast except in the cross of our Lord Jesus Christ, by whom the world has been crucified to me, and I to the world. For in Christ Jesus neither circumcision nor uncircumcision avails anything, but <u>a new creation</u>" (Galatians 6:13-15)
A New Persona	"But you have not so learned Christ, if indeed you have heard Him and have been taught by Him, as the truth is in Jesus: that you put off, concerning your former conduct, the old man which grows corrupt according to the deceitful lusts, and be <u>renewed in the spirit of your mind</u>, and that <u>you put on the new man</u> which was <u>created according to God</u>, in <u>true righteousness and holiness</u>" (Ephesians 4:20-24)
	"…and have <u>put on the new man</u> who is <u>renewed in knowledge according to the image of Him who created him</u>" (Colossians 3:10)
A New and Living Way	"Therefore, brethren, having boldness to enter the Holiest by the blood of Jesus, by <u>a new and living way</u> which He consecrated for us, through the veil, that is, His flesh, and having a High Priest over the house of God, let us draw near with a true heart in full assurance of faith, having our hearts sprinkled from an evil conscience and our bodies washed with pure water. Let us hold fast the confession of our hope without wavering, for He who promised is faithful. And let us consider one another in order to stir up love and good works, not forsaking the assembling of ourselves together, as is the manner of some, but exhorting one another, and so much the more as you see the Day approaching" (Hebrews 10:19-25)
A New Name	"He who has an ear, let him hear what the Spirit says to the churches. To him who overcomes I will give some of the hidden manna to eat. And I will give him a white stone, and <u>on the stone a new name</u> written which no one knows except him who receives it" (Revelation 2:17; Revelation 3:12)

Table 157: Benefits of Christ's Covenantal Relationship

When Christ died on the cross, he ushered in a new covenant completely different from the old covenant of the nation of Israel. Jesus discussed this concept using examples of fabric and wineskins. These examples are important to understanding conceptually the old and new covenants. Jesus said, *"No one puts a piece of unshrunk cloth on an old garment; for the patch pulls away from the garment, and the tear is made worse. Nor do they put new wine into old wineskins, or else the wineskins break, the wine is spilled, and the wineskins are ruined. But they put new wine into new wineskins, and both are preserved"* (Matthew 9:16-17; Mark 2:21-22; Luke 5:36-39). For the old garment, the major point was not about patching a hole with a new patch of cloth. The major point was the hole would eventually become worse than the original. The same is true of placing new wine and old wineskins. It is not about the wine or skins. It is what happens over time with their contact with each other. These examples highlighted the interaction and difficulty between Christianity and Judaism. Jesus even expressed this point when He spoke about the wine and wineskins and said, *"And no one, having drunk old wine, immediately desires new; for he says, 'The old is better.'"* (Luke 5:39). The same remains true when it comes to Christ and obedience to His Word for the Jews, nonbelievers, and the religious community. The old way always seems better.

Please consider these final pearls of wisdom that Paul and the other apostles documented about being *in Christ*:

Jesus said to them, *"This is the work of God, that you believe in Him whom He sent"* (John 6:29)	*"For as many of you as were baptized into Christ have put on Christ"* (Galatians 3:27)	*"...so we, being many, are one body in Christ, and individually members of one another"* (Romans 12:5)
"Or do you not know that as many of us as were baptized into Christ Jesus were baptized into His death?" (Romans 6:3)	*"But now in Christ Jesus you who once were far off have been brought near by the blood of Christ"* (Ephesians 2:13)	*"For in Christ Jesus neither circumcision nor uncircumcision avails anything, but a new creation"* (Galatians 6:15)
"Rejoice always, pray without ceasing, in everything give thanks; for this is the will of God in Christ Jesus for you" (1 Thessalonians 5:16-18)	*"There is neither Jew nor Greek, there is neither slave nor free, there is neither male nor female; for you are all one in Christ Jesus"* (Galatians 3:28)	*"...having a **good conscience**, that when they defame you as **evildoers**, those who r**evil**e your **good conduct** in Christ may be ashamed"* (1 Peter 3:16)
"Therefore, if anyone is in Christ, he is a new creation; old things have passed away; behold, all things have become new" (2 Corinthians 5:17)		*"...be kind to one another, tenderhearted, forgiving one another, even as God in Christ forgave you"* (Ephesians 4:32)
*"Yes, and all who desire to live **godly** in Christ Jesus will suffer persecution"* (2 Timothy 3:12)	*"...He is before all things, and in Him all things consist"* (Colossians 1:17)	*"Greet every saint in Christ Jesus..."* (Philippians 4:21)
"I am the vine, you are the branches. He who abides in Me, and I in him, bears much fruit; for without Me	*"To Him all the prophets witness that, through His name, whoever believes in*	*"...now, little children, abide in Him, that when He appears, we may have confidence and not be*

you can do nothing" (John 15:5)	<u>Him</u> will receive remission of sins" (Acts 10:43)	ashamed before Him at His coming" (1 John 2:28)
"For though you might have ten thousand instructors <u>in Christ</u>, yet you do not have many fathers; for <u>in Christ Jesus</u> I have begotten you through the gospel" (1 Corinthians 4:15)	"...you know that He was manifested to take away our sins, and <u>in Him</u> there is no sin. Whoever abides <u>in Him</u> does not sin. Whoever sins has neither seen Him nor known Him" (1 John 3:5-6)	"As you therefore have received Christ Jesus the Lord, so walk <u>in Him</u>, rooted and built up in Him and established in the faith, as you have been taught, abounding in it with thanksgiving" (Colossians 2:6)
"All things were made through Him, and without Him nothing was made that was made. <u>In Him</u> was life, and the life was the light of men. And the light shines in the darkness, and the darkness did not comprehend it" (John 1:3-5)	"...that the name of our Lord Jesus Christ may be glorified in you, and you <u>in Him</u>, according to the <u>grace</u> of our God and the Lord Jesus Christ" (2 Thessalonians 1:12)	"Now he who keeps His commandments abides <u>in Him</u>, and He in him. And by this we know that <u>He abides in us</u>, by the Spirit whom He has given us" (1 John 3:24)

Table 158: Pearls of Wisdom Dedicated to Being in Christ

<u>Baptism</u> is vital to BTT. The Book of Acts documents <u>baptism</u> by submersion in water to show readers what God commands through His inspired examples. The influences of the negative attributes silence many religious teachers on God's command or they cause ***false*** teachers to reject what the Biblical record documents. In both cases, entire congregations are led through the wide gate. Table 158 reveals what the Book of Acts documented.

Where Documented	Who Heard God's Word	How Many <u>Baptized</u>
Acts 2:36-41	People from many nations	About 3,000
Acts 2:46, 47	Many Jews	An unknown number; people were <u>baptized</u> daily
Acts 8: 5-16	Many Samaritans and Simon the Sorcerer	An unknown number in Samaria and Simon
Acts 8: 26-38	An Ethiopian Eunuch	The Eunuch
Acts 9:1-18; 22:6-18	Saul renamed Paul	Paul
Acts 9:36-43	People in the city of Joppa	An unknown number in Joppa*
Acts 10: 30-48	Cornelius and his household	Cornelius and his household
Acts 13:6-12	Proconsul Sergius Paulus	Proconsul Sergius Paulus*
Acts 13:47, 48	Many Gentiles in Antioch	Many Gentiles*
Acts 16:13-15	Lydia and her household	Lydia and her household
Acts 16:26-33	A Philippian jailer and his household	The jailer and his household
Acts 17:34	Dionysius, Damaris and others	An unknown number in Athens

Acts 18:8	Crispus, his household, and many others	An unknown number in Corinth including Crispus and his household
Acts 18: 24-26	Apollos of Alexandria	Apollos*
Acts 19:1-6	Some of John's disciples	12 disciples
		* =_Baptism_ is implied based on context of the scriptures

Table 159: Examples of _Baptism_ Documented in the Biblical Record

Baptism is a physical, mental, and spiritual contract between oneself and God. The physical part of the contract is one's submersion in physical water just as the Biblical record documents. There is no substitute. The mental part of the contract represents one's complete submission to God's will and one's surrender to His authority. Jesus told His disciples to "*Go therefore and make disciples of all the nations, baptizing them in the name of the Father and of the Son and of the Holy Spirit, teaching them to observe all things that I have commanded you...*" (Matthew 28:19-20). No man on earth has the authority to undo this command. One must be obedient to Jesus' authority if they claim the name of Christ.

The spiritual portion of the contract occurs when one's inner spirit connects with the spiritual Source through _baptism_. Spiritually, when one encounters the blood of Jesus Christ, one's inner spirit connects with the spiritual realm. For a moment, this connection allows one to become a, "*...new creation; old things have passed away; behold, all things have become new*" (2 Corinthians 5:17) in Christ. When one truly believes and is _baptized into Christ_, one puts all the things that defiles the inner spirit to death ("*...from within, out of the heart of men,* **proceed evil thoughts, adulteries, fornications, murders, thefts, covetousness, wickedness, deceit, lewdness, an evil eye, blasphemy, pride, foolishness**. *All these* **evil** *things come from within and defile a man*" (Mark 7:21-23) and then one's inner spirit rises out of the water anew. Paul asked, "*...do you not know that as many of us as were baptized into Christ Jesus were baptized into His death?*" (Romans 6:3). This is the same _baptism_ that Peter and the apostles told the Jews about in Acts 2:38 when about three thousand souls were added to Christ's church according to Acts 2:41. This is the _baptism_ that Ananias told Saul about when he said to him, "*...why are you waiting? Arise and be baptized, and wash away your sins, calling on the name of the Lord*" (Acts 22:16). Saul was converted and was known thereafter as Paul. Improper teaching and the execution of _baptism_ leaves one's soul in a lost state of existence. One must be both physically old enough and spiritually mature enough to understand this Truth. Hence, infant _baptism_ is born out of a strategy of spiritual warfare. Babies do not sin nor do they have a reason to repent. Babies cannot comprehend God's Truth. However, for young adults and up, one must have a correct understanding of _baptism_ to be _baptized_ correctly. One cannot be taught wrong and _baptized_ right. This also means that one cannot be _baptized_ under **false** doctrines, live their life religiously or spiritually, and then expect God's _grace_ to get one into heaven. God's Truth is present in the world. When one chooses to ignore or be obedient to it, this is his or her choice. For one to receive Christ, one must do things His way. This is why John ably wrote, "*But as many as received Him, to them He gave the right to become children of God, to those who believe in His name: who were born, not of blood, nor of the will of the flesh, nor of the will of man, but of God*" (John 1:12-13).

There is only "**one**" sin that will not be forgiven that is identified in the Bible. Jesus said, "*And anyone who speaks a word against the Son of Man, it will be forgiven him; but to him who blasphemes against the Holy Spirit, it will not be forgiven*" (Luke 12:10). Blaspheming the Holy Spirit possibly places one directly in the middle of spiritual warfare in a way that makes him or her an abomination to God. Every other sin is forgivable when one is properly <u>baptized into Christ</u>. This means **ALL** sin. For the Bible securely documents, "*But the Holy Spirit also witnesses to us; for after He had said before, "This is the covenant that I will make with them after those days, says the Lord: I will put My laws into their hearts, and in their minds I will write them," then He adds, "Their sins and their lawless deeds I will remember no more." Now where there is <u>remission</u> of these, there is no longer an offering for sin. Therefore, brethren, having boldness to enter the Holiest by the blood of Jesus, by a new and living way which He consecrated for us, through the veil, that is, His flesh, and having a High Priest over the house of God, let us draw near with a true heart in full assurance of **faith**, having our hearts sprinkled from an **evil** conscience and our bodies washed with pure water*" (Hebrews 10:15-22). Please be careful, even in Christ's church, when men add beyond the sin of blasphemy which contradicts the power of the blood of Christ in <u>*baptism*</u>.

When one understands <u>*baptism*</u> and believes that God has specified this physical act for a spiritual purpose, then a spiritual connection with God can occur. When one's body contacts the physical water, his or her inner spirit connects with the blood of Christ. Once again, this is a spiritual transaction that cannot be rationalized by human science or logic. Peter documented that this "*...is also an antitype which now saves us—<u>baptism</u> (not the removal of the filth of the flesh, but the answer of a good conscience toward God), through the resurrection of Jesus Christ...*" (1 Peter 3:21). As one emerges from the water, Paul documented in Ephesians 2: 1-10,

> "*...you He made alive, who were dead in trespasses and sins, in which you once walked according to the course of this world, according to the prince of the power of the air, the spirit who now works in the sons of disobedience, among whom also we all once conducted ourselves in the **lusts of our flesh**, fulfilling the **desires of the flesh and of the mind**, and were by nature children of **wrath**, just as the others. But God, who is rich in **mercy**, because of His great <u>love</u> with which He <u>loved</u> us, even when we were dead in trespasses, made us alive together with Christ (by <u>grace</u> you have been saved), and raised us up together, and made us sit together in the heavenly places <u>in Christ Jesus</u>, that in the ages to come He might show the exceeding riches of His <u>grace</u> in His kindness toward us <u>in Christ Jesus</u>. For by <u>grace</u> you have been saved through **faith**, and that not of yourselves; it is the gift of God, not of works, lest anyone should **boast**. For we are His workmanship, created <u>in Christ Jesus</u> for **good** works, which God prepared beforehand that we should walk in them*"

Further Paul documented in Hebrews 10:19-23, one now gains the privilege with,

> "*...boldness to enter the Holiest by the blood of Jesus, by a new and living way which He consecrated for us, through the veil, that is, His flesh, and having a High Priest over the house of God, let us draw near with a true heart in full assurance of **faith**, having our hearts sprinkled from an **evil***

conscience *and our bodies washed with pure water. Let us hold fast the confession of our hope without wavering, for He who promised is **faithful***"

This singular way to God renders the teachings that "<u>baptism</u> is a work", "ask God into your heart to be saved", and "pray the sinner prayer" all ***false*** strategies generated by the negative forces of the war campaign. BTT allows one to see that it is much easier to make a statement than it is to execute a God-given task. Consider the example from Peter who boldly stated, "*Even if I have to die with You, I will not deny You!*" (Matthew 26:35). But when Jesus was arrested, the Bible documented, "*...But Peter followed at a distance*" (Luke 22:54) and he denied Jesus three times according to John 18:15-27. Or consider the **rich** young ruler who was on the right track to salvation. The Bible documented that he told Jesus of all the **good** things he lived by and had done in his life in Matthew 19:16, Mark 10:17, and Luke 18:18. Jesus confirmed that this young ruler spoke the truth. However, when the young ruler asked Jesus what else he needed to do to inherit eternal life, Jesus responded, and the Bible documented, "*...he was sad at this word, and went away sorrowful, for he had great possessions....*" (Mark 10:22). BTT allows one to see that words are easy, but obedience to God's Word is much harder. The strategies of "<u>baptism</u> is a work," "ask God into your heart to be saved," and "praying the sinner prayer" are all designed to keep as many people as possible away from God.

Teaching these strategies contradict Christ's word and prevent BTT from taking place. When one comes up out of the water, one signs a spiritual contract of commitment between one's self and God. One should not be surprised at this idea. One should also consider that a contract is required in every significant line of work. To purchase anything of importance or worth, a contract is required. A contract is required even to enter into marriage. Yet, when it comes to committing one's life to the Almighty God, suddenly, the idea of a contract becomes inconceivable, but a verbal commitment is enough. Why? Because the negative forces influenced religious leaders long ago to deny the truth of a spiritual contract. The force's influences continue today and are causing massive confusion among the positive forces of the campaign and effectively aiding the negative forces with a ***lie***. Please do not be ***deceived***.

<u>Baptism</u> is the ultimate commitment of commitments. Walking away from this spiritual contract has far greater consequences than any human contract ever signed. One will forfeit eternal life when the spiritual contract is not spiritually signed or broken. Many people chose to worship in places without the requirement of <u>baptism</u>. Some people believe that this practice is archaic or completely unnecessary. One should always consider that Jesus' teachings trump man's teachings. Unfortunately, the negative attributes have influenced congregations by **deceit**, **pride**, and sin to remain in their sinful state worldwide. When Jesus stated, "*I am the way, the truth, and the life. No one comes to the Father except through Me*" (John 14:6), He provided the only path to salvation. <u>Baptism</u> is God's choice and He decided that it is the path through Christ, to *Him*.

For those who feel a contract is absurd, a cursory review of the Bible allows one to see that the idea of a contract between God and man has been around for a long time. The Biblical record referred to the contracts of old as "<u>covenants</u>." If one uses the New King Version of the Bible, one will see that the term covenant is used three hundred and fifteen (315) times. A few examples of a <u>covenant</u> between God and man include:

- Between God and Noah: "*But I will establish My <u>covenant</u> with you; and you shall go into the ark—you, your sons, your wife, and your sons' wives with you*" (Genesis 6:18)

- Between God and the earth: "*I set My rainbow in the cloud, and it shall be for the sign of the <u>covenant</u> between Me and the earth*" (Genesis 9:13)

- Between God and Abraham: "*On the same day the Lord made a <u>covenant</u> with Abram, saying: "To your descendants I have given this land, from the river of Egypt to the great river, the River Euphrates—*" (Genesis 15:18)

- Between God and the children of Israel: "*Now therefore, if you will indeed obey My voice and keep My <u>covenant</u>, then you shall be a special treasure to Me above all people; for all the earth is Mine*" (Exodus 19:5)

- The Ten Commandments were a <u>covenant</u>: "*And it came to pass, at the end of forty days and forty nights, that the Lord gave me the two tablets of stone, the tablets of the <u>covenant</u>*" (Deuteronomy 9:11)

- God made a new <u>covenant</u> with Israel: "*And He said: "Behold, I make a <u>covenant</u>. Before all your people I will do marvels such as have not been done in all the earth, nor in any nation; and all the people among whom you are shall see the work of the Lord. For it is an awesome thing that I will do with you*" (Exodus 34:10)

But one of the most important <u>covenants</u> by God to man came by way of a prophesy documented in the Books of Jeremiah and Isaiah. This <u>covenant</u> came to fruition and is in force today. Jeremiah documented "*Behold, the days are coming, says the Lord, when I will make a new <u>covenant</u> with the house of Israel and with the house of Judah— not according to the <u>covenant</u> that I made with their fathers in the day that I took them by the hand to lead them out of the land of Egypt, My <u>covenant</u> **which they broke**, though I was a husband to them, says the Lord. But this is the <u>covenant</u> that I will make with the house of Israel after those days, says the Lord: I will put My law in their minds, and write it on their hearts; and I will be their God, and they shall be My people*" (Jeremiah 31:31-33). The prophet Isaiah documented, "*For Zion's sake I will not hold My peace, and for Jerusalem's sake I will not rest, until her **righteousness** goes forth as brightness, and her salvation as a lamp that burns. The Gentiles shall see your **righteousness**, and all kings your glory. You shall be called by a new name, which the mouth of the Lord will name. You shall also be a crown of glory in the hand of the Lord, and a royal diadem in the hand of your God*" (Isaiah 62:1-3). The fulfillment of these prophesies came with the new name given as "Christian" under a new <u>covenant</u> (contract). This new contract is enforced today. Moreover, one should keep in mind that the Biblical record documents, "*...know that the Lord your God, He is God, the faithful God who keeps <u>covenant</u> and **mercy** for a thousand generations with those who love Him and keep His commandments; and He repays those who **hate** Him to their face, to destroy them. He will not be slack with him who **hates** Him; He will repay him to his face*" (Deuteronomy 7:9-10). Yes, when God makes a <u>contract</u> with man based on His Word, He will **honor** it forever. Man, on the other hand, will easily break a contract when influenced by the negative attributes. The Bible contains many examples; and yes, one has the right to break their contract with God and walk away just as the nation of Israel did. God gives everyone that right to choose. And yes, because two parties agreed to the terms of the contract, if one breaks it, a penalty is justified. A penalty keeps all the participants involved _honest_. God is always **honest**. So, it is man that must live up to the standard. BTT allows one to see that a penalty does not mean that God does not _love_ a person who spiritually signed and then broke His contract. No! It is because of His great _love_ that there is a penalty and He always enforces it to remain a **_just_** God – one without _partiality_. Hence, with this knowledge, one can see why the spiritual contract of _baptism_ is necessary. Consider this:

The Spiritual Contract	Why It Is Necessary
① If one never signs God's spiritual contract, under His terms as specified in the Bible, then one commits his or her soul to eternal death by one's own choice. There is no Biblical basis for asking God to simply come into one's heart or praying a sinner's prayer.	BTT never begins!
② If one attempts to sign God's spiritual contract but does not executed it according to His instructions as specified by His word, then no spiritual contract is executed. One remains in the same condition as person ① above. The sprinkling of water for _baptism_ falls in this category.	BTT ceases!
③ If one signs God's spiritual contract through _baptism_, under **_false_** pretenses, i.e. to please family, for show, etc..., one simply gets wet and will remain in the condition as ① above. Why? God knows one's heart and man can see non-penitent behavior and attitudes. The Psalmist documented, "_Would not God search this out? For He knows the secrets of the heart_" (Psalm 44:21).	BTT stops!
④ If one signs God's spiritual contract through _baptism_ and then breaks it by walking away from it by choice, then one returns to the condition as person ① above. Why? Because "..._they crucify to themselves the Son of God afresh, and put him to an open shame_" (Hebrew 6:6). One is not "Always saved."	BTT stops!
⑤ Infant _baptism_ is made up. It is not found in God's Word. Its use is void. Those who practice it and those who accept it as God's way remain in the fog of the war campaign and the same condition as person ① above.	BTT never began!
⑥ However, if one signs God's spiritual contract through _baptism_ the correct way based on His Word (Luke 8:15) and strives to walk in His way according to the Gospel, then one prepares his or her soul for eternal life. One makes this commitment through personal choice.	BTT begins and matures.

Table 160: _Baptism_ and BTT

The negative forces of the war campaign are committed to keeping the truths documented above hidden from people who desire to understand eternal life. But as BTT matures, the truths above can be clear through God's Word. One must remember, by inspiration of the Holy Spirit, Paul documented that there are people who, "..._did not like to retain God in_ *their knowledge, God gave them over to a debased mind...*" (Romans 1:28-32). After listing what constitutes a debased mind, Paul wrote that these same people knew "*... the **righteous** judgment of God, that those who practice such things are deserving of death, <u>not only do the same but also approve of those who practice them</u>*" (Romans 1:32). BTT allows one to see that Paul was also stating that these same people hide the knowledge of God. This thought still applies today. However, one should now understand that behind their behavior is a driver toward a greater end; to gain support for the negative forces. Their behaviors are manifested by the influence of the negative attributes.

BTT allows one to see a final important point concerning <u>baptism</u> and all its spiritual benefits. This may be the hardest of all concepts to understand and to accept as God's <u>calamity</u> weighs heavy on people who claim Christ and yet have not come to Him His way. BTT, based on everything documented above, allows one to see that <u>baptism</u> justifies and validates one's privilege to come to God in prayer. Paul documented for Christians, "*Be anxious for nothing, but in everything by prayer and supplication, with thanksgiving, let your requests be made known to God...*" (Philippians 4:6). But God will not support people who are not His or those who refuse to obey His word even if they come to Him in prayer. Their efforts are in vain. God's action is not because He cannot hear their prayers. No, He chooses not to listen to people who refuse to repent of sin and who insist on praying to Him by their standards. People, especially those who claim to be religious, who resist the clear teachings of God's Word have no part with Him. One cannot live in sin and pray to God when His <u>calamity</u> comes and expect Him to respond. God will not spare the sinner in His wrath for the Biblical record documents, "*For we know Him who said, "Vengeance is Mine, I will repay," says the Lord. And again, "The Lord will judge His people"* (Hebrews 10:30). The Biblical record documented such things done in vain as:

- Prayer: "*And when you pray, do not use <u>vain</u> repetitions as the heathen do. For they think that they will be heard for their many words*" (Matthew 6:7)

- Worship: "*And in <u>vain</u> they worship Me, teaching as doctrines the commandments of men*" (Matthew 15:9; Mark 7:7)

- Labor: "*Therefore, my be<u>loved</u> brethren, be steadfast, immovable, always abounding in the work of the Lord, knowing that your labor is not in <u>vain</u> in the Lord*" (1 Corinthians 15:58)

The prayers, worship, and labor of compromised religious leaders or leadership produces a compromised congregation. This removes the opportunity of God to hear their prayers. This sounds harsh, but in reality, the influence of the negative forces has **deceived** people in believing that their prayers, worship, and labor are reaching God. Satan, "*...the god of this age...*" (2 Corinthians 4:4), has blinded the minds of many people by answering their prayers and desires to mimic God's response. Only BTT and <u>discernment</u> can help one see this Truth. Unfortunately, the Biblical record documents that these people are lost in the fog of spiritual warfare. They are causalities of the war campaign because they willfully listen to the **deceit** of the negative forces. Their prayers, worship, and labor does not help the positive forces of the war campaign in any way. Sadder, because of their religious beliefs and traditions, the people themselves are of no threat to the negative forces. Hence, their lives seem well but in reality they are spiritually lost. On the spiritual battlefield, *strife* continues to grow and consumed these and all non-believers because their communities have no defense against the negative forces. Moreover, these people compromise others who are legitimately seeking God's Word. Through ***false*** evangelism, and ***counsel***, they add unsuspecting souls to the negative forces. I know this is tough to swallow but that is why BTT is so important. BTT allows one to see the difficult concepts and understand the complexity of spiritual warfare and the war campaign.

      To close out this portion for my book for God's *calamity*, I offer **Figures 35 and 36** to help one see how *baptism*, which puts on Christ, allows Christ to dwell in one's inner spirit. **Figure 35** illustrates how one leaves worldliness to begin a new life and walk on earth. It shows the correlation between a Christian, Christ's church, and one's new "citizenship" on the spiritual battlefield. This new citizenship cannot be overlooked nor taken lightly as so many in the religious community do. It is a status that places one above politics, social affiliation, ***hatred***, *prejudice*, and ***pride*** so all decisions and one's walk are Christ-like. The truth established in **Figures 35 and 36** should help one understand why the world continues to grow more corrupt and ***violent*** each day instead of improving. It documents that there are only two sides for people in the world today. That is a side of ***good*** with Jesus or a side of ***evil*** with Satan. Jesus said, "*He who is not with Me is against Me, and he who does not gather with Me scatters abroad*" (Matthew 12:30; Luke 11:23). Hence, when one becomes a Christian, the Bible informs us "*…that we should no longer be children, tossed to and fro and carried about with every wind of doctrine, by the trickery of men, in the cunning craftiness of **deceitful** plotting, but, speaking the truth in love, may grow up in all things into Him who is the head—Christ…*" (Ephesians 4:14-15). Moreover, the very document informs every Christian that has put on Christ in *baptism*, "*As you therefore have received Christ Jesus the Lord, so walk in Him, rooted and built up in Him and established in the **faith**, as you have been taught, abounding in it with thanksgiving. Beware lest anyone cheat you through philosophy and empty **deceit**, according to the tradition of men, according to the basic principles of the world, and not according to Christ. For in Him dwells all the fullness of the Godhead bodily; and you are complete in Him, who is the head of all principality and power*" (Colossians 2:6-10).

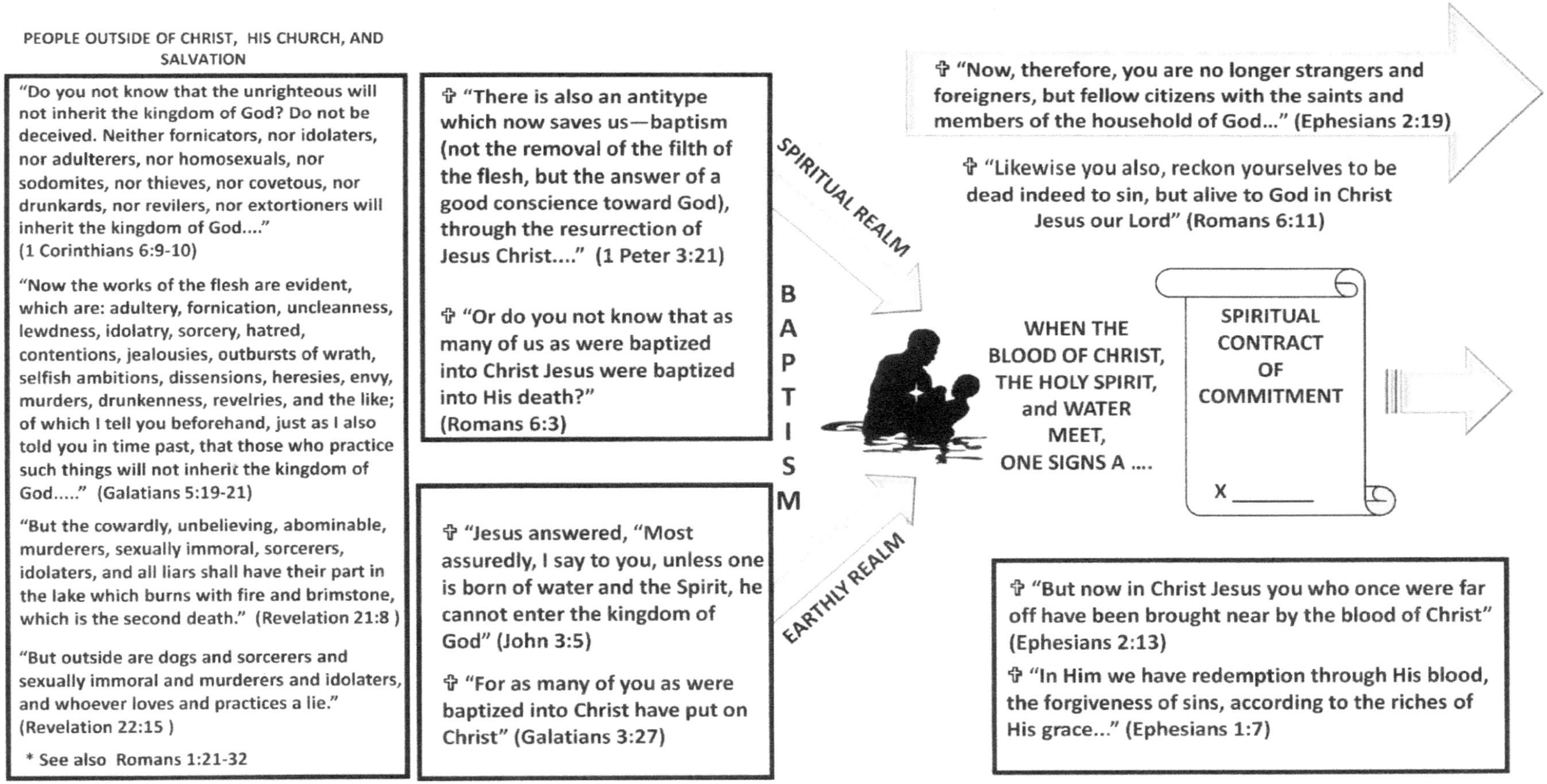

PEOPLE OUTSIDE OF CHRIST, HIS CHURCH, AND SALVATION

"Do you not know that the unrighteous will not inherit the kingdom of God? Do not be deceived. Neither fornicators, nor idolaters, nor adulterers, nor homosexuals, nor sodomites, nor thieves, nor covetous, nor drunkards, nor revilers, nor extortioners will inherit the kingdom of God....." (1 Corinthians 6:9-10)

"Now the works of the flesh are evident, which are: adultery, fornication, uncleanness, lewdness, idolatry, sorcery, hatred, contentions, jealousies, outbursts of wrath, selfish ambitions, dissensions, heresies, envy, murders, drunkenness, revelries, and the like; of which I tell you beforehand, just as I also told you in time past, that those who practice such things will not inherit the kingdom of God....." (Galatians 5:19-21)

"But the cowardly, unbelieving, abominable, murderers, sexually immoral, sorcerers, idolaters, and all liars shall have their part in the lake which burns with fire and brimstone, which is the second death." (Revelation 21:8)

"But outside are dogs and sorcerers and sexually immoral and murderers and idolaters, and whoever loves and practices a lie." (Revelation 22:15)

* See also Romans 1:21-32

BAPTISM

✠ "There is also an antitype which now saves us—baptism (not the removal of the filth of the flesh, but the answer of a good conscience toward God), through the resurrection of Jesus Christ...." (1 Peter 3:21)

✠ "Or do you not know that as many of us as were baptized into Christ Jesus were baptized into His death?" (Romans 6:3)

✠ Jesus answered, "Most assuredly, I say to you, unless one is born of water and the Spirit, he cannot enter the kingdom of God" (John 3:5)

✠ "For as many of you as were baptized into Christ have put on Christ" (Galatians 3:27)

EARTHLY REALM ← → **SPIRITUAL REALM**

WHEN THE BLOOD OF CHRIST, THE HOLY SPIRIT, and WATER MEET, ONE SIGNS A ....

SPIRITUAL CONTRACT OF COMMITMENT

X_____

✠ "Now, therefore, you are no longer strangers and foreigners, but fellow citizens with the saints and members of the household of God...." (Ephesians 2:19)

✠ "Likewise you also, reckon yourselves to be dead indeed to sin, but alive to God in Christ Jesus our Lord" (Romans 6:11)

✠ "But now in Christ Jesus you who once were far off have been brought near by the blood of Christ" (Ephesians 2:13)

✠ "In Him we have redemption through His blood, the forgiveness of sins, according to the riches of His grace..." (Ephesians 1:7)

Figure 35: The Divine Construct of Baptism Part I

✢ "...our citizenship is in heaven, from which we also eagerly wait for the Savior, the Lord Jesus Christ, who will transform our lowly body that it may be conformed to His glorious body..." (Philippians 3:19-21)

✢ "Therefore, if anyone is in Christ, he is a new creation; old things have passed away; behold, all things have become new" (2 Corinthians 5:17)

NEW CREATION IN CHRIST

CHRIST IN YOU

✢ "Therefore, laying aside all malice, all deceit, hypocrisy, envy, and all evil speaking, as newborn babes, desire the pure milk of the word, that you may grow thereby, if indeed you have tasted that the Lord is gracious." (1 Peter 2:1-3)

✢ "Now you are the body of Christ, and members individually" (1 Corinthians 12:27)

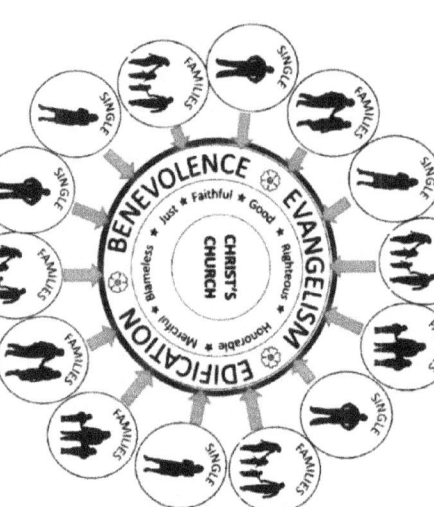

✢ "And let us consider one another in order to stir up love and good works, not forsaking the assembling of ourselves together, as is the manner of some, but exhorting one another, and so much the more as you see the Day approaching" (Hebrews 10:24-25)

THE BODY OF CHRIST
(Made up of thousands of single people and families world-wide)

✢ "...so we, being many, are one body in Christ, and individually members of one another" (Romans 12:5)

✢ "There is neither Jew nor Greek, there is neither slave nor free, there is neither male nor female; for you are all one in Christ Jesus" (Galatians 3:28)

✢ "...endeavoring to keep the unity of the Spirit in the bond of peace. There is one body and one Spirit, just as you were called in one hope of your calling; one Lord, one faith, one baptism; one God and Father of all, who is above all, and through all, and in you all" (Ephesians 4:3-6)

✢ "For as the body is one and has many members, but all the members of that one body, being many, are one body, so also is Christ. For by one Spirit we were all baptized into one body—whether Jews or Greeks, whether slaves or free—and have all been made to drink into one Spirit. For in fact the body is not one member but many" (1 Corinthians 12:12-14)

Figure 36: The Divine Construct of Baptism Part II

 I believe the sixth critical reason for God's <u>calamity</u> today is because of the increasing number of people abiding in Christ's church who refuse to partake in evangelism. Their reasons vary. However, none of them are acceptable. For all Christians that understand that we are living in the last days need to act like it. This begins by telling others about Christ so that they can have the same opportunity to be saved too. This is vital to the efforts of the positive forces in the war campaign; but most importantly, Christ demands it. The primary reasons people refuse to engage in evangelism are <u>complacency</u>, <u>fear,</u> and outright disobedience to God's Word. However, BTT allows one to see that these reasons amount to excuses and do not negate Jesus' command to "*Go therefore and make disciples of all the nations, <u>baptizing</u> them in the name of the Father and of the Son and of the Holy Spirit, teaching them to observe all things that I have commanded you; and lo, I am with you always, even to the end of the age." Amen*" (Matthew: 28:19-20). Yes, deteriorating social conditions worldwide have caused the element of <u>fear</u> to run rampant among the Christian community. However, evangelism is a requirement of submission to Christ's teachings. Personal discipline, self-sacrifice, and overcoming one's <u>fear</u> goes hand-in-hand with this requirement. These three items apply in real warfare where an enemy can be seen. But more importantly, they are just as applicable where the enemy is hidden. Evangelism reflects the positive attribute's influence on people who do as Christ commands. Although purely Bible-based messages from God's Word are unpopular on the spiritual battlefield and can bring possible harm to those simply delivering them, the need remains. This reality, borne from the history of the prophets and Jesus' disciples, has never abated. Jesus provided insights into the behavior of people who allowed the influence of the **hater** attribute, both then and now, toward people delivering His message when He said to His disciples:

- "*The world cannot **hate** you, but it **hates** Me because I testify of it that its works are **evil***" (John 7:7)

- "*If the world **hates** you, you know that it **hated** Me before it **hated** you*" (John 15:18)

- "*If you were of the world, the world would <u>love</u> its own. Yet because you are not of the world, but I chose you out of the world, therefore the world **hates** you*" (John 15:19)

- "*Do not marvel, my brethren, if the world **hates** you*" (1 John 3:13)

Regardless of the unpopularity of the message or the actions of the people influenced by the **hater** attribute, or any of the other negative forces, the requirement to evangelize remains. In fact, Jesus laid the foundation for a Christian's behavior concerning people influenced by the **hater**, **evil**, and **unjust** attributes when He said,

- "*But I say to you, <u>love</u> your enemies, bless those who curse you, do **good** to those who **hate** you, and pray for those who spitefully use you and persecute you, that you may be sons of your Father in heaven; for He makes His sun rise on the **evil** and on the **good**, and sends rain on the **just** and on the **unjust***" (Matthew 5:44-45)

- "*But I say to you who hear: <u>Love</u> your enemies, do **good** to those who **hate** you...*" (Luke 6:27)
- "*Blessed are you when men **hate** you, and when they exclude you, and revile you, and cast out your name as **evil**, for the Son of Man's sake*" (Luke 6:22)

Jesus' Word alone provides the direction and strength to take His message out to a lost and dying world and it must be followed. However, part of the grand strategy of the negative forces is to inject the element of <u>confusion</u>, which is also synonymous with fog in spiritual warfare. <u>Confusion</u> breeds <u>*fear*</u>. But Paul, as he wrote about spiritual warfare, documented that "*...God is not the author of <u>confusion</u> but of <u>peace</u>, as in all the churches of the saints*" (1 Corinthians 14:33). Still further he documented, "*...God has not given us a spirit of <u>fear</u>, but of power and of <u>love</u> and of a sound mind*" (2 Timothy 1:7). He knew that within Christ's church, with the proper teaching of the Gospel, one would gain the necessary tools to overcome <u>*fear*</u> and evangelize to others. BTT allows one to see that teaching the truth about God's perfect <u>*love*</u> is the key to overcoming <u>*fear*</u>. Moreover, Christians evangelize because they <u>*love*</u> people and desire them to know the Truth about salvation. The Holy Spirit led John to document, "*There is no <u>fear</u> in <u>love</u>; but perfect <u>love</u> casts out <u>fear</u>, because fear involves torment. But he who <u>fears</u> has not been made perfect in <u>love</u>*" (1 John 4:18). This statement holds the key to understand what the element of <u>*fear*</u> does in the world. This element causes torment in one's inner spirit which means that the person has not been made perfect by the element of <u>*love*</u>. To be perfect in this sense is to be a mature Christian. God's Word overcomes the element of <u>*fear*</u> and allows His Gospel to spread to everyone.

When evangelism occurs, people do respond. Unfortunately, some people find themselves in religious organizations that mimic the world they left. This situation provides a ***false*** sense of comfort and security. These organizations claim the name of Christ but are hollow and serve only to enslave people in ***false*** teachings. This is part of the negative force's strategy. These same people unknowingly assist the negative forces through traditions and practices of men that are not authorized by God. But there is also a greater hidden strategy inspired by the negative forces that occur in Christ's church.

Within many of Christ's *churches* on the spiritual battlefield, the element of <u>*fear*</u> has gripped too many members. Outside these congregations, the same conditions have had an opposite effect on human behavior. For many people who have heard of the Bible or are vaguely familiar with it, the element of <u>*fear*</u> causes them to flock to religious organizations each year after a major <u>calamity</u> from God occurs. Unfortunately, their <u>*fear*</u> only last for a season because they are not sincere in their search. Most of the people return to the world disillusioned by what they found. This too is part of the strategy of the negative attributes. For once these people can claim they sought Christ and were disenfranchised with their search, it becomes twice as hard to gain their confidence again for a second look at the truth. Just as the Books of Matthew, Mark, and Luke documented, the ***wicked*** one incapacitates the inner spirits of people on the wayside, in stony places, and among the thorns based on the parable of the "*Sower and the seed.*" Jesus was speaking to both initial hearers of His Word and new converts to Christianity.

Moreover, for the people within Christ's church who have allowed complacency and immaturity to prevent them from maturing in the Gospel, they lose out on the opportunity to help seekers and new converts understand God's Way. These immature Christians cannot even evangelize those brought to their doorstep. Paul scolded immature Christian's about this when he said, *"For though by this time you ought to be teachers, you need someone to teach you again the first principles of the oracles of God; and you have come to need milk and not solid food"* (Hebrews 5:12). Sadly, these Christians, who refuse to carry out Jesus' commission to evangelize, are unknowingly assisting the negative forces. Nevertheless, there is an even greater hidden strategy inspired by the negative forces that occur in Christ's *church* that one must also consider.

BTT allows one to see, when God's _calamities_ cause people to seek Him out of the fog of the war campaign, new challenges come to Christ's *churches*. **Figure 37** graphically illustrates the challenges for His church on the spiritual battlefield.

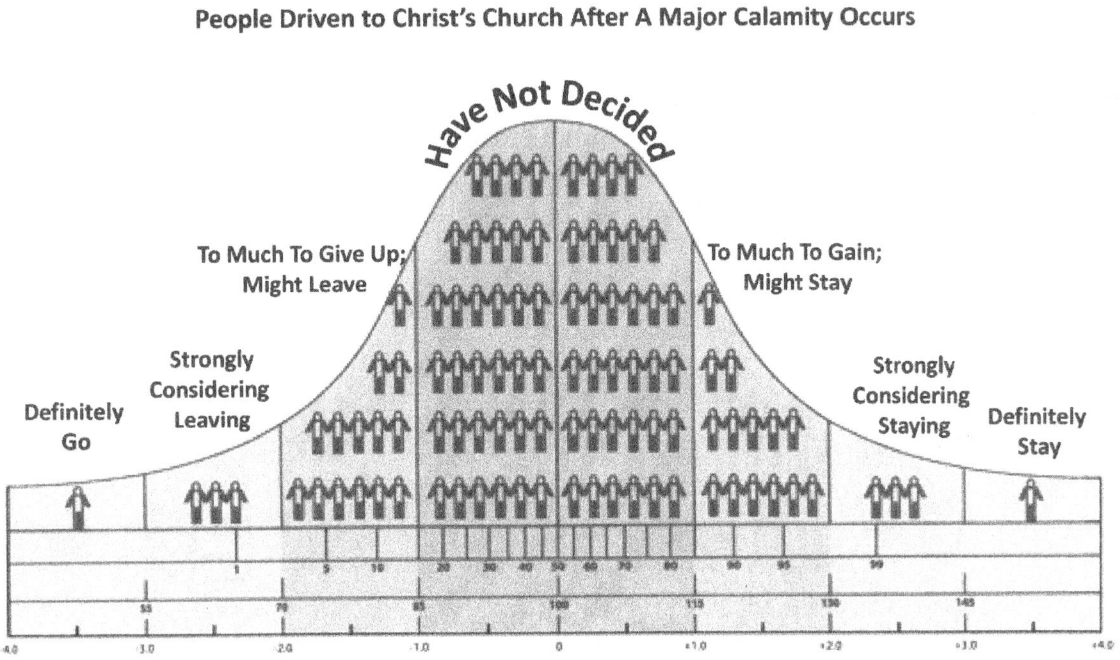

People Driven to Christ's Church After A Major Calamity Occurs

Figure 37: Worldly Reaction to God's Calamity Verses Commitment to His Church

On one end of the spectrum, there will be people who will hear the Gospel and stay in Christ's church. In most cases, these are people on ***good*** ground and they will be converted from the world. These are the people who desire to know the Truth about God as a benefit versus a sacrifice. Conversely, on the opposite far end of the spectrum are people who hear the same Gospel message and walk away from it. They leave because the call of worldly life is strong. These are the people who look at life in Christ in terms of what they must give up instead of what they gain. Next, there is this massive middle group of people who contemplate their decisions to go or stay while attempting to retain or slowly let go of their worldly behaviors, beliefs, and attitudes. They struggle to fully commit to Christ, yet they find relief in being around people who express _love_, concern, _compassion_, and spiritual discipline. But their patience teeters to the right or left depending on their physical or emotional experience within the assembly. This group tends to be made up of "takers" and "receivers" within the assembly who make little to no contribution. They complain of not getting anything out of the church service and fail to spiritually mature. This group presents a greater challenge in that while they contemplate their decision to commit to Christ, their spiritual hearts struggle to transform. When the negative attributes find opportunity to influence them, this group begins to poison the spiritually weak and those influenced by the **simple** attribute within the *church*. If an eldership or minister is not attentive, a cancer develops out of this group that retards the learning of the spiritually weak and the **simple**. As friendships develop, the spiritually weak and **simple** become blind to the fact that this group came into Christ's *church* out of *fear* and may have never committed to Christ. The spiritually weak and **simple** begin to mistakenly accept this as growth in Christ's *church* or God's way of replenishing His church without evangelism. This is ***false*** growth. As they become complacent in their friendships, opportunities to evangelize dissipates. The negative forces exploit this opportunity and further weakens them and the *church* overall. Hence, when the *church* elders, God's authorized disciplinarians (Titus 1:10-16) execute discipline, *strife* occurs within the *church*. This is a hard concept to understand but it is a real strategy of both spiritual and physical warfare – the weakening of one's opponent from within. For this reason, BTT allows one to see that the Holy Spirits provided a standard for Christ's *churches* to operate by. Paul documented this standard when he wrote, "*...fulfill my joy by being like-minded, having the same love, being of one accord, of one mind*" (Philippians 2:2). One cannot be like-minded without a full commitment to Christ. Collectively, if the behavior of this middle group, the spiritually weak, and the **simple** is left uncorrected, the internal *strife* that develops from the cancer will either cause dysfunction in Christ's *church* or destroy it. God's requirement for things to be accomplished decently and in order (1 Corinthians 14:40) will fail when the middle group's cancer is not removed.

BTT allows one to see that there is another challenge caused by the cancer of the middle group. This is the cancer that convinces weaker Christians that there is no need to evangelize since people will come to the church because of worldly conditions. This causes *complacency* which comes from the influence of the ***lazy*** attribute. This attribute's influence will cause Christians to abdicate their responsibilities to Christ. The two primary responsibilities abdicated are identified by Jesus himself. They are:

- "*Go therefore and make disciples of all the nations, baptizing them in the name of the Father and of the Son and of the Holy Spirit...*" (Matthew 28:19), and

- "*If anyone desires to come after Me, let him deny himself, and take up his cross daily, and follow Me*" (Luke 9:23; Mark 8:34; Matthew 16:24)

These two responsibilities came with one's signing of the spiritual contract of commitment during *baptism*. There is no fine print. Yes, over time battle fatigue can set in from the daily struggles of the war campaign. The work, *persecution*, and even loss of friends and family causes spiritual battle fatigue. Paul documented, "*Yes, and all who desire to live **godly** in Christ Jesus will suffer persecution*" (2 Timothy 3:12). Within the chosen lifestyle of ***godly*** living, spiritual battle fatigue is a natural part of the war. However, evangelizing remains an equal part of the requirement for **godly** living. As for the persecution, God's Word provides one comfort in that the Bible documents, "...*it is a **righteous** thing with God to repay with tribulation those who trouble you, and to give you who are troubled rest with us when the Lord Jesus is revealed from heaven with His mighty angels, in flaming fire taking vengeance on those who do not know God, and on those who do not obey the gospel of our Lord Jesus Christ. These shall be punished with everlasting destruction from the presence of the Lord and from the glory of His power...*" (2 Thessalonians 1:6-10). One should not be concerned with people influenced by the negative attributes who bring persecution while carrying out God's will through evangelism. If one does, one invites God's calamity in one's own life.

Another reason God's calamity comes to Christians who refused to evangelize is because the four variables identified in (Matthew 13:22; Mark 4:18, 19; and Luke 8:14) take precedence in their lives. The four variables are:

Variable	Where
The cares of this world	Matthew 13:22; Mark 4:19; Luke 8:14
The **deceitfulness** of riches	Matthew 13:22; Mark 4:19; Luke 8:14
The desires for other things	Mark 4:19
The pleasures of life	Luke 8:14

Table 161: Four Distractors in Spiritual Warfare

These variables distract Christians from the mission Christ gave and allows the negative forces to make major advances on the battlefield. In fact, within the same Scriptures that identify these variables, the Christians became unfruitful (Matthew 13:22), had God's Word choked out of them (Mark 4:19), and brought no fruit to maturity (Luke 8:14). For these people, Jesus' Word applies that state, "...*he who does not take his cross and follow after Me is not worthy of Me*" (Matthew 10:38). Unfortunately today, many people on the spiritual battlefield claiming Christ are not worthy of Christ. They have allowed the negative attributes to influence their behavior and they hinder growth in Christ's *church* by refusing to fulfill their responsibilities to include - evangelizing. They become unfruitful (Matthew 13:22; Mark 4:19; Titus 3:14; 2 Peter 1:8). God is not happy with this.

The reductants to evangelize have set many of Christ's *churches* on a path to die out on the spiritual battlefield. Even worse, some of Christ's *churches* on the spiritual battlefield have dropped His name from their banner, added a few worldly modifications, relaxed His teachings and doctrine, and identify as community churches to attract growth and money. But for Christ's *churches* that stay true to the original pattern of the 1st Century *church*, God will increase His *church* through evangelism to keep it refreshed "*some thirtyfold, some sixtyfold, some hundredfold*" (Matthew 13:23; Mark 4:20) on the spiritual battlefield. When the leadership of Christ's *church* fails to implement strategies to keep members of the body actively engaged in evangelism, or when members of the body refuse to engage in evangelism themselves, both are guilty of sin.

Today, there are many Christians, armed with the Truth of the Gospel who choose to stay silent on the spiritual battlefield. Moreover, many forsake "...*the assembling of ourselves together...*" (Hebrews 10:25), and even leave Christ's *church* to avoid the responsibility of evangelizing or even hearing the Truth. These are the same Christians who cannot "...*endure sound doctrine, but according to their own desires, because they have itching ears, they will heap up for themselves teachers; and they will turn their ears away from the truth, and be turned aside to fables*" (2 Timothy 4:3-4). In addition to this folly, they are the same Christians who invite God's _calamity_ and are eventually purged from His house. They violate the terms of the spiritual contract of commitment that they freely made with God to walk in error. They unknowingly are influenced by the **wicked** attribute and fail to understand, "*...what makes them stumble*" (Proverbs 4:19). All the while, by their behavior they aide the negative force's advancement on the spiritual battlefield. Christians are required to commit to a local body of Christ. They cannot float from *church* to *church*. With all the work to be done on the battlefield, floaters do no one any good; neither their own spiritual growth nor the congregation's need for dedicated workers. Commitment in Christ's *church* creates growth and allows the congregation to respond to the needs of the community it supports. Every member has a role in Christ's *church*. In spiritual warfare, Christian floater's place their souls in sin when they forgo their commitment to a local body of Christ. Their lack of commitment and unsteady attendance aids the negative forces of the war campaign.

Finally, as it pertains to evangelism, as one's mind is spiritually transformed and one becomes a Christian, his or her eyes are opened to the reality of mortality's brevity. Like the Psalmist, Christians pray that the Lord will "*...teach us to number our days, that we may gain a heart of wisdom*" (Psalm 90:12). For they know without God's wisdom during their brief time on earth, there is no _hope_ to survive the war campaign. True Christians come to the understanding of two very important things about mortality's brevity that makes their mission to proclaim the Gospel of Jesus Christ so expedient. From the Old Testament to the New, Christians know from God, "*Indeed, You have made my days as handbreadths, and my age is as nothing before You; certainly every man at his best state is but vapor...*" (Psalm 39:5), and "*...whereas you do not know what will happen tomorrow. For what is your life? It is even a vapor that appears for a little time and then vanishes away*" (James 4:14). These two Scriptures convey the motivation behind a Christian's expediency to proclaim Christ to a world under the sway of Satan according to 1 John 5:19. Hence, Paul wrote to all Christians, "*I beseech you therefore, brethren, by the **mercies** of God, that you present your bodies a living sacrifice, holy, acceptable to God, which is your reasonable service*" (Romans 12:1). In the war campaign, the investment of one's time spent evangelizing comes with being a "*living sacrifice, holy, acceptable to God*". Thus, this requirement is part of the Christian's reasonable service.

I believe the seventh critical reason for God's _calamity_ today is because of the large number of _men_ who have abdicated their role as _men_, as spiritual leaders of their homes, and families, and their duty to God. Regardless of what the world teaches or preaches, the Biblical record documented that God made _man_ first and then woman. BTT allows one to see that this sequence of events had significance and obligations built into the construct. Consider what the Biblical record documented for a moment. At the macro-level, the Bible documented that God said, "*Let Us make _man_ in Our image, according to Our likeness; let them have dominion over the fish of the sea, over the birds of the air, and over the cattle, over all the earth and over every creeping thing that creeps on the earth." So God created _man_ in _His_ own image...*" (Genesis 1:26-27).

This piece of the Biblical record documented that _man_ was created first and given a leadership role "*over all the earth*". To deny this truth is to deny God. Then at the micro-level, as _man_ began to perform the responsibilities God gave _him_, the Bible reveals that God decided "*It is not **good** that _man_ should be alone; I will make _him_ a helper comparable to _him_*" (Genesis 2:18), and "*He took one of _his_ ribs, and closed up the flesh in its place. Then the rib which the Lord God had taken from _man_ He made into a woman, and He brought her to the _man_*" (Genesis 2:21-22). This order, established by God, placed leadership responsibility on the _man_ for the things that God defined for _him_ with the woman as _his_ helper. Nothing else. Before one becomes lost in the fog over the initial parts of these statements, understand that God did not place

Figure 38: Man's Responsibility to His Family

man in a leadership role to dominate woman, to make her subservient, or give _man_ the right to abuse her in any way. These negative behaviors were conceived in strategies generated by the negative attributes simply to destroy the relationship God intended for the _man_ and the woman. These strategies, and _man's_ weakness, gave rise to a feminist ideology that began long ago before it was defined in name or called a movement.

Throughout the Biblical record, _man_ was given the lead role for spiritual matters and providing for _his_ family. Thus, when a single or married _man_ avoids God, or when a _man_ marries and refuses to carry out God's task for _him_; or if a _man_ marries and then walks away from _his_ responsibilities altogether, God's _calamity_ is ever present. God gave _man_ the responsibility for caring for _his_ family's wellbeing, protecting the family from harm, and preparing them to navigate spiritual warfare. **Figure 38** shows the relationship. One can see the application of Ephesians 2:10 here. Paul wrote, "*For we are His workmanship, created in Christ Jesus for **good** works, which God prepared beforehand that we should walk in them*" (Ephesians 2:10). These responsibilities are imprinted on _man's_ inner spirit by God's hand and sealed with the element of _love_. This imprint explains why young _men_ feel compelled to step up in a home when a _father_ is missing in action for whatever the reason. God's Holy Word is the key for understanding the imprint that is so tightly woven within a _man_, _his_ inner spirit, and the spiritual realm that impacts _him_. Without God's Word, both _strife_ and _calamity_ reign in a _man's_ life as _he_ is influenced by the negative attributes.

Here is a concept worthy of consideration. Based on conflicts recorded in both the Biblical and historical records, a large portion of the male population is removed from the earth by physical war. Another large portion dies in the spiritual warfare as they are overcome by the negative attributes. This war accounts for the _men_ who are incarcerated or have chosen a life style foreign to God's design. The sum of these populations leave a small number of _men_ with the positive attributes to fight spiritual warfare and set proper examples for each generation.

But they do exist in every society. However, when their strength begins to fail, then God's _calamity_ occurs to support His way. BTT allows one to see that the demands placed on this small population are the chief reasons for their failure. But God ensures examples can always be found in those who follow Christ's example. These are the _men_ who fully accept the challenge from Christ of: "*If anyone desires to come after Me, let _him_ deny _himself_, and take up _his_ cross daily, and follow Me*" (Luke 9:23; Mark 8:34; Matthew 16:24). These are the spiritual warriors on the spiritual battlefield. Moreover, one can find _men_ of all races serving as examples in Christ's _church_, and where this truth is denied, that _church_ is a counterfeit.

God has an expectation for the _man_ He created. That expectation was, and still is, for _him_ to be a _man_ first, then a _husband_, and finally a _father_, in that order. With this order, the Biblical record documented a vast amount of wisdom to support God's expectation and the great responsibility that goes along with it. One can conclude, from the wisdom contained in this book, that spiritual warfare is playing a major role in the direction _man_ is taking each day. Let us consider God's expectations for _man_ and the consequences of distorting the order of God's design.

Beginning with the expectation for the _man_, the Biblical record makes it painfully clear that the rearing, teaching, and preparation of a _man_ for the world belongs to two parents; a male and a female. Everything begins with the two-parent model to include the most important responsibility of all: to teach the _man_ about God and _his_ divine relationship with God. The Biblical record documented that parents are responsible to, "*Train up a child in the way _he_ should go, and when _he_ is old _he_ will not depart from it*" (Proverbs 22:6). The _man_ has the responsibly for modeling the **godly** example of a future _man_ to a _male_ child and the same is true for a woman and her daughter. This divinely designed combination of parenting prepares a _man_ for _his_ journey in life and provides _him_ the best chance for surviving the spiritual war awaiting _him_. For the Bible makes it clear that the _man_ must leave _his_ parents. It documented, "*Therefore a _man_ shall leave _his father_ and mother and be joined to _his_ wife, and they shall become one flesh*" (Genesis 2:24). The emphasis here is on the fact that there is a point where the adult _man_ "leaves" _his_ parents to begin _his_ cycle of life for _himself_ on the spiritual battlefield. _He_ will put to test the rearing, teaching, and preparation _he_ received from _his_ parent. What is important to understand is that from the time the _man_ leaves _his_ home, God gives _him_ a limited time to use what _he_ has learned from _his_ parents. The Psalmist documented, "*Indeed, You have made my days as handbreadths, and my age is as nothing before You; certainly every _man_ at _his_ best state is but vapor*" (Psalm 39:5) and "*Surely every _man_ walks about like a shadow...*" (Psalm 39:6). The Psalmist concluded on the matter, "*_Man_ is like a breath; _his_ days are like a passing shadow*" (Psalm 144:4) and he prayed to God, "*So teach us to number our days, that we may gain a heart of wisdom*" (Psalm 90:12).

BTT allows one to see that when it comes to the _man_ that God created in _his_ own image, the expectation for the _man_ is that _he_ follows God and do _His_ will. Yes, this same ideal applies to women, too. But it applies to the _man_ first by the Biblical standard with the understanding that if the _man_ gets it right, so will the woman who is charged to be "*...a helper comparable to _him_*" (Genesis 2:18) and "*...bone of my bones and flesh of my flesh...because she was taken out of _Man_*" (Genesis 2:23). God gave _man_ a helper because _his_ way is difficult. God foreknew that the _man_ would need help, and _he_ still needs help. One can know this because of some critical verses in the Biblical record that emphasized this fact. The Bible documented:

- *"The Lord knows the thoughts of _man_, that they are futile"* (Psalm 94:11)

- *"…the ways of _man_ are before the eyes of the Lord, and _He_ ponders all _his_ paths"* (Proverbs 5:21)

- *"There is a way that seems right to a _man_, but its end is the way of death"* (Proverbs 14:12; 16:25)

- *"All the ways of a _man_ are pure in _his_ own eyes, but the Lord weighs the spirits"* (Proverbs 16:2)

- *"Every way of a _man_ is right in _his_ own eyes, but the Lord weighs the hearts"* (Proverbs 21:2)

- *"A _man_ who wanders from the way of understanding will rest in the assembly of the dead"* (Proverbs 21:16)

- *"The preparations of the heart belong to _man_, but the answer of the tongue is from the Lord"* (Proverbs 16:1)

- *"A _man's_ heart plans _his_ way, but the Lord directs _his_ steps"* (Proverbs 16:9)

- *"There are many plans in a _man's_ heart, nevertheless the Lord's **counsel**—that will stand"* (Proverbs 19:21)

- *"Truly, this only I have found: That God made _man_ **upright**, but they have sought out many schemes"* (Ecclesiastes 7:29)

- *"O Lord, I know the way of _man_ is not in _himself_; it is not in _man_ who walks to direct _his_ own steps"* (Jeremiah 10:23)

- *"I, the Lord, search the heart, I test the mind, even to give every _man_ according to _his_ ways, according to the fruit of _his_ doings"* (Jeremiah 17:10)

Thus, based on the Scriptures documented above, one can legitimately ask if, *"A _man's_ steps are of the Lord; how then can a _man_ understand _his_ own way?"* (Proverbs 20:24). The answer: God's Word provides everything one needs. God's Word gives a _man_ *"…all things that pertain to life and **godliness**, through the knowledge of Him who called us by glory and virtue…"* (2 Peter 1:3). Through God's Word, the positive attributes can mature a _man_ and influence _him_ in the path of **godliness** and save _him_ as _he_ strives for **righteousness**. Paul aptly wrote, *"When I was a child, I spoke as a child, I understood as a child, I thought as a child; but when I became a _man_, I put away childish things"* (1 Corinthians 13:11). As a _man_ begins to understand _his_ way and matures in God's Word, _he_ will automatically begin to put childish things away. As _he_ does, then BTT allows _him_ to _discern_ between the positive and negative attributes influencing behaviors, words, and attitudes. Consider the numerous pearls of wisdom surrounding this truth for a _man_ to fulfill God's expectation. The Bible documents:

"Who is the _man_ that _fears_ the Lord? _Him_ shall He teach in the way He chooses" (Psalm 25:12)	"A little that a **righteous** _man_ has is better than the riches of many **wicked**" (Psalm 37:16)	"A **righteous** _man_ regards the life of _his_ animal..." (Proverbs 12:10)
"Mark the **blameless** _man_, and observe the **upright**; for the future of that _man_ is peace" (Psalm 37:37)	"A **good** _man_ deals graciously and lends; He will guide _his_ affairs with discretion" (Psalm 112:5)	"A **wise** _man_ will hear and increase learning, and a _man_ of understanding will attain **wise counsel**..." (Proverbs 1:5, 6)
"Every **prudent** _man_ acts with knowledge..." (Proverbs 13:16)	"...a **prudent** _man_ covers shame" (Proverbs 12:16)	"...a _man_ of understanding has wisdom" (Proverbs 10:23)
"...a **good** _man_ will be satisfied from above" (Proverbs 14:14)	"A **righteous** _man_ **hates lying**..." (Proverbs 13:5)	"A **good** _man_ obtains favor from the Lord..." (Proverbs 12:2)
"Happy is the _man_ who finds wisdom, and the _man_ who gains understanding; for her proceeds are better than the profits of silver, and her gain than fine gold" (Proverbs 3:13-14)	"A _man's_ stomach shall be satisfied from the fruit of _his_ mouth; from the produce of _his_ lips he shall be filled" (Proverbs 18:20)	"A _man_ will be satisfied with **good** by the fruit of _his_ mouth, and the recompense of a _man's_ hands will be rendered to _him_" (Proverbs 12:14)
"A _man_ will be commended according to _his_ wisdom..." (Proverbs 12:8)	"A _man_ shall eat well by the fruit of _his_ mouth..." (Proverbs 13:2)	"The **merciful** _man_ does **good** for _his_ own soul..." (Proverbs 11:17)
"It is **honorable** for a _man_ to stop striving, since any **fool** can start a quarrel" (Proverbs 20:3)	"A **good** _man_ leaves an inheritance to _his_ children's children..." (Proverbs 13:22)	"...a _man_ of understanding holds _his_ peace" (Proverbs 11:12)
"A **wise** _man_ fears and departs from **evil**..." (Proverbs 14:16)	"...a _man_ of understanding is of a calm spirit" (Proverbs 17:27)	"A _man_ has joy by the answer of _his_ mouth..." (Proverbs 15:23)
"A _man_ who has friends must _himself_ be friendly..." (Proverbs 18:24)	"...a _man_ of understanding walks **uprightly**" (Proverbs 15:21)	"A _man's_ gift makes room for _him_, and brings _him_ before great _men_" (Proverbs 18:16)
"The steps of a **good** _man_ are ordered by the Lord, and He delights in _his_ way" (Psalm 37:23)	"When a _man's_ ways please the Lord, He makes even _his_ enemies to be at peace with _him_" (Proverbs 16:7)	"The discretion of a _man_ makes _him_ slow to **anger**, and _his_ glory is to overlook a transgression" (Proverbs 19:11)
"What is desired in a _man_ is _kindness_, and a **poor** _man_ is better than a **liar**" (Proverbs 19:22)	"Let not **mercy** and truth forsake you...and so find favor and high esteem in the sight of God and _man_" (Proverbs 3:3-4)	

"A **wise** man scales the city of the mighty, and brings down the trusted stronghold" (Proverbs 21:22)	"The **righteous** man walks in his **integrity**; his children are blessed after him" (Proverbs 20:7)	"Do you see a man who excels in his work? He will stand before kings; he will not stand before unknown men" (Proverbs 22:29)
"A **wise** man is strong, yes, a man of knowledge increases strength…" (Proverbs 24:5)	"For a **righteous** man may fall seven times and rise again…" (Proverbs 24:16)	"A **prudent** man foresees **evil** and hides himself…" (Proverbs 22:3; 27:12)
"Let another man praise you, and not your own mouth; a stranger, and not your own lips" (Proverbs 27:2)	"A **righteous** man who falters before the **wicked** is like a murky spring and a polluted well" (Proverbs 25:26)	"Happy is the man who is always reverent, but he who hardens his heart will fall into calamity" (Proverbs 28:14)
"As iron sharpens iron, so a man sharpens the countenance of his friend" (Proverbs 27:17)	"A **faithful** man will abound with blessings…" (Proverbs 28:20)	"…a **wise** man's heart discerns both time and judgment…" (Ecclesiastes 8:5)
"…a **generous** man devises generous things, and by **generosity** he shall stand" (Isaiah 32:8)	"A **good** man out of the **good** treasure of his heart brings forth **good** things…" (Matthew 12:35; Luke 6:45)	

Table 162: Pearls of Wisdom Concerning Man when Influenced by the Positive Attributes

To this end, the Biblical record documented the blessings God's has for man. The Bible documents:

- "Blessed is the man who walks not in the **counsel** of the **ungodly**, nor stands in the path of sinners, nor sits in the seat of the **scornful**; but his delight is in the law of the Lord, and in His law he meditates day and night" (Psalm 1:1-2)

- "Blessed is the man to whom the Lord does not impute iniquity, and in whose spirit there is no **deceit**" (Psalm 32:2)

- "Oh, taste and see that the Lord is **good**; blessed is the man who trusts in Him!" (Psalm 34:8)

- "Blessed is that man who makes the Lord his trust, and does not respect the **proud**, nor such as turn aside to **lies**" (Psalm 40:4)

- "Blessed is the man You choose, and cause to approach You, that he may dwell in Your courts. We shall be satisfied with the **goodness** of Your house, Of Your holy temple" (Psalm 65:4)

- "Blessed is the man whose strength is in You, whose heart is set on pilgrimage" (Psalm 84:5)

- "O Lord of hosts, blessed is the <u>man</u> who trusts in You!" (Psalm 84:12)

- "Blessed is the <u>man</u> whom You instruct, O Lord, and teach out of Your law, that You may give <u>him</u> rest from the days of adversity, until the pit is dug for the **wicked**" (Psalm 94:12)

- "Praise the Lord! Blessed is the <u>man</u> who <u>fears</u> the Lord, who delights greatly in <u>His</u> commandments" (Psalm 112:1)

- "Behold, thus shall the <u>man</u> be blessed who <u>fears</u> the Lord" (Psalm 128:4)

- The Spirit of Wisdom said: "Blessed is the <u>man</u> who listens to me, watching daily at my gates, waiting at the posts of my doors" (Proverbs 8:34)

- "Blessed is the <u>man</u> who trusts in the Lord, and whose <u>hope</u> is the Lord" (Jeremiah 17:7)

- "Blessed is the <u>man</u> to whom the Lord shall not impute sin" (Romans 4:8)

- "Blessed is the <u>man</u> who endures <u>temptation</u>; for when <u>he</u> has been approved, <u>he</u> will receive the crown of life which the Lord has promised to those who <u>love</u> Him" (James 1:12)

Unfortunately, because of choice, <u>man</u> allows the influences of the negative attributes to influence <u>his</u> behavior more times than not. Perhaps because God gave <u>man</u>, "...*dominion over the fish of the sea, over the birds of the air, and over the cattle, over all the earth and over every creeping thing that creeps on the earth*" (Genesis 1:26), the negative attributes use this initial imprint to exploit <u>man's</u> inner spirit. Once the influences of the negative attributes gain a foothold and begin impacting <u>man's</u> behavior, the Biblical truth that "*Hell and destruction are never full; so the eyes of <u>man</u> are never satisfied*" (Proverbs 27:20) gains greater meaning in both spiritual and physical warfare. When the negative attributes influence any <u>man</u>, <u>his</u> behavior will not allow <u>him</u> to fulfill God's expectation. This <u>man</u> is separated from God until <u>he</u> comes "*...to the knowledge of the truth*" (1 Timothy 2:4) to be saved as God desires. Consider some of the numerous pearls of wisdom surrounding this truth for the <u>man</u> who fails to fulfill God's expectation because of the influences of the negative attributes. The Bible documents:

"...The Lord abhors the **bloodthirsty** and **deceitful** <u>man</u>" (Psalm 5:6)	"The way of the **lazy** <u>man</u> is like a hedge of thorns..." (Proverbs 15:19)	"A worthless person, a **wicked** <u>man</u>, walks with a **perverse** mouth..." (Proverbs 6:12)
"<u>His</u> own iniquities entrap the **wicked** <u>man</u>, and <u>he</u> is caught in the cords of <u>his</u> sin" (Proverbs 5:22)	"For by means of a **harlot** a <u>man</u> is reduced to a crust of bread; and an **adulteress** will prey upon <u>his</u> precious life" (Proverbs 6:26)	"The hand of the diligent will rule, but the **lazy** <u>man</u> will be put to forced labor" (Proverbs 12:24)

"...a **wicked** man is loathsome and comes to shame" (Proverbs 13:5)	"The **wicked** man does **deceptive** work..." (Proverbs 11:18)	"...a man of **wicked** intentions He will condemn" (Proverbs 12:2)
"A man is not established by **wickedness**..." (Proverbs 12:3)	"A **prudent** man conceals knowledge..." (Proverbs 12:23)	"The **rich** man's wealth is his strong city..." (Proverbs 10:15)
"The soul of a **lazy** man desires, and has nothing; but the soul of the diligent shall be made rich" (Proverbs 13:4)	"The **lazy** man does not roast what he took in hunting, but diligence is man's precious possession" (Proverbs 12:27)	"When a **wicked** man dies, his expectation will perish, and the hope of the unjust perishes" (Proverbs 11:7)
"An **evil** man seeks only rebellion..." (Proverbs 17:11)	"He who **loves** pleasure will be a **poor** man..." (Proverbs 21:17)	"A **wrathful** man stirs up strife..." (Proverbs 15:18)
"A **perverse** man sows strife..." (Proverbs 16:28)	"...a **foolish** man despises his mother" (Proverbs 15:20)	"An **ungodly** man digs up **evil** ..." (Proverbs 16:27)
"A man who is in **honor**, yet does not understand, is like the beasts that perish" (Psalm 49:20)	"A **violent** man entices his **neighbor**, and leads him in a way that is not **good**" (Proverbs 16:29)	"A **quick-tempered** man acts **foolishly**, and a man of **wicked** intentions is **hated**" (Proverbs 14:17)
"A **proud** and **haughty** man— "**Scoffer**" is his name; He acts with **arrogant pride**" (Proverbs 21:24)	"A **wicked** man accepts a bribe behind the back to **pervert** the ways of justice" (Proverbs 17:23)	"A man who isolates himself seeks his own desire; he rages against all **wise** judgment" (Proverbs 18:1)
"The **rich** man's wealth is his strong city, and like a high wall in his own esteem" (Proverbs 18:11)	"Bread gained by **deceit** is sweet to a man, but afterward his mouth will be filled with gravel" (Proverbs 20:17)	"The **foolishness** of a man twists his way, and his heart frets against the Lord" (Proverbs 19:3)
"A man of great wrath will suffer punishment; for if you rescue him, you will have to do it again" (Proverbs 19:19)	"A **lazy** man buries his hand in the bowl, and will not so much as bring it to his mouth again" (Proverbs 19:24)	"The **lazy** man will not plow because of winter; he will beg during harvest and have nothing" (Proverbs 20:4)
"Before destruction the heart of a man is haughty..." (Proverbs 18:12)	"The **rich** man is **wise** in his own eyes..." (Proverbs 28:11)	"The way of a guilty man is **perverse**..." (Proverbs 21:8)
"The **poor** man is hated even by his own **neighbor**..." (Proverbs 14:20)	"A man devoid of understanding shakes hands in a pledge..." (Proverbs 17:18)	"The desire of the **lazy** man kills him, for his hands refuse to labor" (Proverbs 21:25)
"For there will be no prospect for the **evil** man..." (Proverbs 24:20)	"And put a knife to your throat If you are a man given to appetite" (Proverbs 23:2)	"The **lazy** man says, "There is a lion outside! I shall be slain in the streets!" (Proverbs 22:13)
"Make no friendship with an **angry** man, and with a **furious** man do not go, lest	"Do not lie in wait, O **wicked** man, against the dwelling of the **righteous**;	"For the drunkard and the glutton will come to **poverty**, and drowsiness

you learn his ways and set a snare for your soul" (Proverbs 22:24-25)	*do not plunder his resting place..."* (Proverbs 24:15)	*will clothe a man with rags"* (Proverbs 23:21)
*"Do you see a man hasty in his words? There is more hope for a **fool** than for him"* (Proverbs 29:20)	*"A **false** witness shall perish, but the man who hears him will speak endlessly"* (Proverbs 21:28)	*"A man who bears **false witness** against his **neighbor** is like a club, a sword, and a sharp arrow"* (Proverbs 25:18)
*"Confidence in an **unfaithful** man in time of trouble is like a bad tooth and a foot out of joint"* (Proverbs 25:19)	*"Do you see a man **wise** in his own eyes? There is more hope for a **fool** than for him"* (Proverbs 26:12)	*"As a door turns on its hinges, so does the **lazy** man on his bed"* (Proverbs 26:14)
*"The **lazy** man buries his hand in the bowl; it wearies him to bring it back to his mouth"* (Proverbs 26:15)	*"The **lazy** man is wiser in his own eyes than seven men who can answer sensibly"* (Proverbs 26:16)	*"A man burdened with **bloodshed** will flee into a pit; let no one help him"* (Proverbs 28:17)
*"...when a **wicked** man rules, the people groan"* (Proverbs 29:2)	*"...he who hastens to be **rich** will not go unpunished"* (Proverbs 28:20)	*"An **angry** man stirs up **strife**, and a **furious** man abounds in transgression"* (Proverbs 29:22)
*"A **fool** vents all his feelings, but a **wise** man holds them back"* (Proverbs 29:11)	*"A **poor** man who **oppresses** the **poor** is like a driving rain which leaves no food"* (Proverbs 28:3)	*"A man who flatters his **neighbor** spreads a net for his feet"* (Proverbs 29:5)
*"A man with an **evil** eye hastens after **riches**, and does not consider that poverty will come upon him"* (Proverbs 28:22)	*"As charcoal is to burning coals, and wood to fire, so is a contentious man to kindle strife"* (Proverbs 26:21)	*"To show **partiality** is not **good**, because for a piece of bread a man will transgress"* (Proverbs 28:21)
*"By transgression an **evil** man is snared..."* (Proverbs 29:6)	*"A man's **pride** will bring him low..."* (Proverbs 29:23)	*"A **wicked** man hardens his face..."* (Proverbs 21:29)
"It is a snare for a man to devote rashly something as holy, and afterward to reconsider his vows" (Proverbs 20:25)	*"Like a **madman** who throws firebrands, arrows, and death, is the man who **deceives** his **neighbor**, and says, "I was only joking!"* (Proverbs 26:18, 19)	*"An **unjust** man is an abomination to the **righteous**, and he who is **upright** in the way is an abomination to the **wicked**"* (Proverbs 29:27)
*"For from within, out of the heart of men, proceed **evil** thoughts, **adulteries, fornications, murders, thefts, covetousness, wickedness, deceit, lewdness, an evil eye, blasphemy, pride, foolishness**. All these **evil** things come from within*	*"...an **evil** man out of the **evil** treasure of his heart brings forth **evil**. For out of the abundance of the heart his mouth speaks"* (Luke 6:45; Matthew 12:35)	*"...Cursed is the man who trusts in man and makes flesh his strength, whose heart departs from the Lord"* (Jeremiah 17:5)

and defile a <u>man</u>" (Mark 7:21-23) and "***false witness***" (Matthew 15:19-20)		

Table 163: Pearls of Wisdom Concerning the <u>Man</u> Influenced by the Negative Attributes

As a <u>man</u> gains an appreciation for <u>his</u> role as a <u>man</u>, <u>he</u> can then move to the next phase of <u>manhood</u> to become a <u>husband</u>. The Biblical record documented, "*Therefore a <u>man</u> shall leave <u>his father</u> and mother and be joined to <u>his</u> wife, and they shall become one flesh*" (Genesis 2:24). Thus, marriage serves a divine purpose. However, there is one exception. There are <u>men</u> who have no desire to marry. These are <u>men</u> in their own category of life, but they are still <u>men</u>. Jesus talked about this to *His* disciples. *He* said, "*All cannot accept this saying, but only those to whom it has been given: For there are eunuchs who were born thus from their mother's womb, and there are eunuchs who were made eunuchs by <u>men</u>, and there are eunuchs who have made themselves eunuchs for the kingdom of heaven's sake. <u>He</u> who is able to accept it, let <u>him</u> accept it*" (Matthew 19:11-12). Therefore, there are <u>men</u> who may never marry, but nowhere in the translation does God authorize, sanction, or make accommodations for them to practice fornication or co-habitation. Paul wrote that one must "*Abstain from every form of* ***evil***" (1 Thessalonians 5:22). God considers the practice of fornication and co-habitation to be ***sexually immoral*** because these practices are against God's plan for both <u>men</u> and women. In fact, the Holy Spirit revealed through Paul, that one must, "*Flee **sexually immorality**. Every sin that a <u>man</u> does is outside the body, but <u>he</u> who commits **sexually immorality** sins against <u>his</u> own body*" (1 Corinthians 6:18). Moreover, the Holy Spirit inspired Paul to write, "*Nevertheless, because of **sexually immorality**, let each <u>man</u> have <u>his</u> own wife, and let each woman have her own <u>husband</u>*" (1 Corinthians 7:2).

The truth of God's Word becomes bitter to <u>men</u> because of several factors. These factors include <u>man's</u>:

- Failure to live up to God's expectation,
- Ignorance of <u>his</u> role and sound examples to follow,
- Lack the knowledge in sustaining a healthy relationship with a woman,
- Desires to pursue multiple women or other flesh

Because of these factors, in many corners of the world God's Word is no longer taught as it pertains to the role of a <u>man</u> or a <u>husband</u> in the home. But the Biblical record documents "*Do not be **deceived**, God is not **mocked**; for whatever a <u>man</u> sows, that <u>he</u> will also reap*" (Galatians 6:7). <u>Men</u> who chose to marry but refuse to take on the full responsibility of being a <u>husband</u>, especially when children come along, face the wrath of God daily. This is an area too where God's Word applies that states, "*So shall My word be that goes forth from My mouth; it shall not return to Me void, but it shall accomplish what I please, and it shall prosper in the thing for which I sent it*" (Isaiah 55:11). Not even the negative forces of the war campaign can void God's Word. Thus, consider what the Biblical record documents for a <u>husband</u>.

Throughout the Biblical record, the evidence shows that God established the home with a patriarchal structure; not matriarchal. <u>Man</u> altered God's structure when <u>he</u> abdicated <u>his</u> responsibilities through ignorance, neglect, and absence from the home. But none of these factors changed what God designed. God still holds <u>man</u> accountable. God placed the <u>man</u> in charge of the home, and this includes the woman who consents to marry <u>him</u> despite how distasteful this sounds in a modern politically correct world. This occurred when God Himself said to the woman "*...I will greatly multiply your sorrow and your conception; in pain you shall bring forth children; your desire shall be for your <u>husband</u>, and <u>he shall rule over you</u>*" (Genesis 3:16). Why did God make this seemingly harsh command? The answer may be due to the fact that the woman stumbled in the Garden of Eden at the first encounter with the negative forces' ***deceit***. Using a serpent (Genesis 3:1), the negative forces convinced the women to ignore God's command. She clearly knew God's command because the Biblical record documented, "*...the woman said to the serpent, "We may eat the fruit of the trees of the garden; but of the fruit of the tree which is in the midst of the garden, <u>God has said, 'You shall not eat it, nor shall you touch it, lest you die</u>*'" (Genesis 3:2-3). However, the Bible goes on to document, "*...when the woman saw that the tree was **good** for food, that it was pleasant to the eyes, and a tree desirable to make one wise, <u>she took of its fruit and ate</u>. She also gave to her <u>husband</u> with her, and <u>he</u> ate*" (Genesis 3:6). For a moment, the <u>man</u> abdicated <u>his</u> authority and followed the woman's lead against God's command. Before she was created, the Biblical record documented that, "*...the Lord God took the <u>man</u> and put <u>him</u> in the garden of Eden to tend and keep it. And the Lord God commanded the <u>man</u>, saying, "Of every tree of the garden you may freely eat; but of the tree of the knowledge of **good** and **evil** you shall not eat, for in the day that you eat of it you shall surely die.*" (Genesis 2: 15-17). The <u>man</u> clearly knew God's command too. Thus, for <u>his</u> role in this grave sin, the Bible documented that God punished <u>him</u> too. God said to the <u>man</u>, "*Because you have heeded the voice of your wife, and have eaten from the tree of which I commanded you, saying, 'You shall not eat of it': "Cursed is the ground for your sake; in toil you shall eat of it all the days of your life. Both thorns and thistles it shall bring forth for you, and you shall eat the herb of the field. In the sweat of your face you shall eat bread till you return to the ground, for out of it you were taken; for dust you are, and to dust you shall return*" (Genesis 3:17-19). God's pronounced judgement, captured in the Biblical record in Genesis 3:14-19, not only cemented the pattern for the <u>male</u> and female relationship in the home, but it also reprimanded the <u>man</u> for listening to <u>his</u> wife over God. Hence, BTT allows one to see that in God's punishment of the <u>man</u>, God specifically said to <u>him</u>, "*Because you have heeded the voice of your wife...*" (with "over My command implied"), God established a judgement of precedence for the <u>man</u> to lead in spiritual matters. The Biblical record thoroughly documented this fact. However, the negative attributes **hate** God's decision and continue to use His decision as a source of division through spiritual warfare. This order does not apply to business, government, or any other leadership role. This order deals with spiritual leadership and God's supreme decision because of sin. Thus, in God's order, "*the head of every <u>man</u> is Christ, the head of woman is <u>man</u>, and the head of Christ is God*" (1 Corinthians 11:3). One's obedience to this order in spiritual matters is required. In fact, when the Holy Spirit inspired Paul to write to women "*...if they want to learn something, let them ask their own husbands at home; for it is shameful for women to speak in church*" (1 Corinthians 14:35), the onus was actually on the _husband_ to perform _his_ spiritual duty of teaching. This was never said to denigrate women. But spiritual warfare has **perverted** God's Word. For women without _husbands_, God holds the _male_ leaders of His _church_ responsible and accountable for their spiritual welfare in His _church_.

Some of the many pearls of wisdom that concern the _man_ fulfilling _his_ responsibilities as a _husband_ in the home include:

"_Husbands_, _love_ your wives and do not be bitter toward them" (Colossians 3:19)	"The heart of her _husband_ safely trusts her; so _he_ will have no lack of gain" (Proverbs 31:11)	"Her children rise up and call her blessed; her _husband_ also, and _he_ praises her…" (Proverbs 31:28)
"…because of **sexually immorality**, let each _man_ have _his_ own wife, and let each woman have her own _husband_" (1 Corinthians 7:2)	"Let the _husband_ render to _his_ wife the affection due her, and likewise also the wife to her _husband_" (1 Corinthians 7:3)	"For **jealousy** is a _husband's_ **fury**; therefore _he_ will not spare in the day of vengeance" (Proverbs 6:34)
"For the _husband_ is head of the wife, as also Christ is head of the church; and _He_ is the Savior of the body" (Ephesians 5:23)	"_Husbands_, _love_ your wives, just as Christ also _loved_ the church and gave _Himself_ for her…" (Ephesians 5:25)	"So _husbands_ ought to _love_ their own wives as their own bodies; _he_ who _loves_ _his_ wife _loves himself_" (Ephesians 5:28)
"…let each one of you in particular so _love_ _his_ own wife as _himself_, and let the wife see that she respects her _husband_" (Ephesians 5:33)	"The wife does not have authority over her own body, but the _husband_ does. And likewise the _husband_ does not have authority over _his_ own body, but the wife does" (1 Corinthians 7:4)	"_Husbands_, likewise, dwell with them with understanding, giving **honor** to the wife, as to the weaker vessel, and as being heirs together of the _grace_ of life, that your prayers may not be hindered" (1 Peter 3:7)

Table 164: Pearls of Wisdom for the _Man_ as a _Husband_

BTT allows one to see that marriage is a divine partnership and not for one to enter haphazardly. The marriage agreement before the eyes of God is permanent. This nullifies the worldly practice of short marriages for fornication sake. God's expectation is for both the _man_ and woman to understand the commitment prior to making the commitment. Taking one's time before making a decision to marry goes a long way and allows both people to get to know each other. Fornication before marriage creates a spiritual impediment prior to a marriage contract that is often hard to overcome. Fornication provides an easily exploitable spiritual gap for the negative attributes to use in spiritual warfare. The exploitable gap comes through both participant's cognitive emotions from the element of _lust_. Spiritual warfare during acts of fornication is extremely strong. The responsibility to teach and set the example for marriage lies with both parents of a new prospective _husband_ and wife. However, sound teaching and examples are disappearing on the spiritual battlefield because of the negative force's superior use of fog. Acts of **adultery** and divorce gain quick and widespread attention over strong, stable, and long-lasting marriages. However, God's requirement remains and the failure of parents to teach the truth about marriage simply aids the negative forces of the war campaign. So, one can clearly understand God's intent for both a _man_ and a woman who enters into a marriage contract, please consider Table 165.

The _Husband_	The _Wife_
"...whoever divorces _his_ wife for any reason except **sexually immorality** causes her to commit **adultery**..." (Matthew 5:31-32)	"...whoever marries a woman who is divorced commits **adultery**" (Matthew 5:31-32)
"...whoever divorces _his_ wife, except for **sexually immorality**, and marries another, commits **adultery**..." (Matthew 19:8-9)	"...whoever marries her who is divorced commits **adultery**" (Matthew 19:8-9)
"...Whoever divorces _his_ wife and marries another commits **adultery** against her..." (Mark 10:11-12)	"...And if a woman divorces her _husband_ and marries another, she commits **adultery**" (Mark 10:11-12)
"Whoever divorces _his_ wife and marries another commits **adultery** ..." (Luke 16:18)	"...and whoever marries her who is divorced from her _husband_ commits **adultery**" (Luke 16:18)
"But if the _husband_ dies, she is released from the law of her _husband_. So then if, while her _husband_ lives, she marries another _man_, she will be called an **adulteress**; but if her _husband_ dies, she is free from that law, so that she is no **adulteress**..." (Romans 7:2-3)	For the woman who has a _husband_ is bound by the law to her _husband_ as long as _he_ lives. But if the _husband_ dies, she is released from the law of her _husband_. So then if, while her _husband_ lives, she marries another _man_, she will be called an **adulteress**; but if her _husband_ dies, she is free from that law, so that she is no **adulteress**, though she has married another _man_" (Romans 7:2-3)
"...because of **sexually immorality**, let each _man_ have _his_ own wife..." (1 Corinthians 7:2)	"...because of **sexually immorality**, ...let each woman have her own _husband_" (1 Corinthians 7:2)
"Let the _husband_ render to _his_ wife the affection due her, and likewise also the wife to her _husband_. (1 Corinthians 7:3)	"Let the _husband_ render to _his_ wife the affection due her, and likewise also the wife to her _husband_. (1 Corinthians 7:3)
"...likewise the _husband_ does not have authority over _his_ own body, but the wife does" (1 Corinthians 7:4)	"The wife does not have authority over her own body, but the _husband_ does..." (1 Corinthians 7:4)
"...And a _husband_ is not to divorce _his_ wife" (1 Corinthians 7:11)	"Now to the married I command, yet not I but the Lord: A wife is not to depart from her _husband_. But even if she does depart, let her remain unmarried or be reconciled to her _husband_" (1 Corinthians 7:10-11)
"But to the rest I, not the Lord, say: If any _brother_ has a wife who does not believe, and she is willing to live with _him_, let _him_ not divorce her" (1 Corinthians 7:12)	"And a woman who has a _husband_ who does not believe, if _he_ is willing to live with her, let her not divorce _him_" (1 Corinthians 7:13)
"For the unbelieving _husband_ is sanctified by the wife...; otherwise your children	"...the unbelieving wife is sanctified by the _husband_; otherwise your children would be

would be unclean, but now they are holy" (1 Corinthians 7:14)	unclean, but now they are holy" (1 Corinthians 7:14)
"But if the unbeliever departs, let _him_ depart; a brother or a sister is not under bondage in such cases. But God has called us to peace" (1 Corinthians 7:15)	"But if the unbeliever departs, let _him_ depart; a brother or a sister is not under bondage in such cases. But God has called us to peace" (1 Corinthians 7:15)
"...how do you know, O _husband_, whether you will save your wife?" (1 Corinthians 7:16)	"For how do you know, O wife, whether you will save your _husband_? ..." (1 Corinthians 7:16)
"Are you bound to a wife? Do not seek to be loosed. Are you loosed from a wife? Do not seek a wife" (1 Corinthians 7:27)	
"..._he_ who is married cares about the things of the world—how _he_ may _please_ _his_ wife" (1 Corinthians 7:33)	"...she who is married cares about the things of the world—how she may please her _husband_" (1 Corinthians 7:34)
"...if her _husband_ dies, she is at liberty to be married to whom she wishes, only in the Lord" (1 Corinthians 7:39)	"A wife is bound by law as long as her _husband_ lives; but if her _husband_ dies, she is at liberty to be married to whom she wishes, only in the Lord" (1 Corinthians 7:39)
	"Wives, submit to your own _husbands_, as to the Lord" (Ephesians 5:22)
"For the _husband_ is head of the wife, as also Christ is head of the church; and _He_ is the Savior of the body" (Ephesians 5:23)	"Therefore, just as the church is subject to Christ, so let the wives be to their own _husbands_ in everything" (Ephesians 5:24)
"_Husbands_, _love_ your wives, just as Christ also _loved_ the church and gave Himself for her..." (Ephesians 5:25)	
"So _husbands_ ought to _love_ their own wives as their own bodies; _he_ who _loves_ _his_ wife _loves_ _himself_" (Ephesians 5:28)	
"For this reason a _man_ shall leave _his_ father and mother and be joined to _his_ wife, and the two shall become one flesh" (Ephesians 5:31)	
"Nevertheless let each one of you in particular so _love_ _his_ own wife as _himself_..." (Ephesians 5:33)	"...let the wife see that she respects her _husband_" (Ephesians 5:33)
"_Husbands_, _love_ your wives and do not be bitter toward them" (Colossians 3:19)	"Wives, submit to your own _husbands_, as is fitting in the Lord" (Colossians 3:18)
"_Husbands_, likewise, dwell with them with understanding, giving **honor** to the wife, as to the weaker vessel, and as being heirs together of the _grace_ of life, that your prayers may not be hindered" (1 Peter 3:7)	"Wives, likewise, be submissive to your own _husbands_, that even if some do not obey the word, they, without a word, may be won by the conduct of their wives when they observe your chaste conduct accompanied by _fear_" (1 Peter 3:1-2)
	"For in this manner, in former times, the holy women who trusted in God also adorned themselves, being submissive to their own _husbands_..." (1 Peter 3:5)

| | "...*older* women ...*admonish the young women to* <u>*love*</u> *their* <u>*husbands*</u>*, to* <u>*love*</u> *their children, to be discreet, chaste, homemakers,* ***good****, obedient to their own* <u>*husbands*</u>*, that the word of God may not be blasphemed*" (Titus 2:3-5) |

Table 165: The Divine Rules of the Marriage Contract

Clearly from Table 165, the woman accepts a major responsibility in a marriage. Her greatest responsibility and challenge is that she must yield in submission to the <u>man</u> as God commanded. The Biblical record documented, "*An excellent wife is the crown of her* <u>*husband*</u>*, but she who causes shame is like rottenness in* <u>*his*</u> *bones*" (Proverbs 12:4). Shame comes on both parties when both fail to take care of their responsibilities in the marriage. Biblical submission to the <u>man</u> is difficult due to the influences of spiritual warfare, however, it is still part of the agreement.

A woman's submission to the <u>man</u> is first an act of obedience to God's Word, and then a matter of personal discipline and strength. BTT allows one to see that the negative attributes, using spiritual warfare, have strategically convinced many women that submission is an act of weakness. These attributes are successful when a <u>man</u> does not know or fails to carry the weight of responsibility God placed on <u>him</u>. <u>Man</u> becomes weak by <u>his</u> own choices when <u>he</u> fails to be obedient to God. This leads to the issues of divorce, separation, and **adultery**.

Divorce and separation causes a <u>husband</u> to abdicate <u>his</u> family responsibilities which leads to God's <u>calamity</u>. For **adultery**, Wisdom told Solomon "*Like a bird that wanders from its nest is a* <u>*man*</u> *who wanders from* <u>*his*</u> *place*" (Proverbs 27:8). From this Proverb, BTT allows one to see that both the bird and the <u>man</u> are lost. In the world today, acts of divorce, separation and **adultery** are rampant. Instead of writing another book on these subjects, I will simply provide one with some of the pearls of wisdom from the Biblical record. One can pursue these subjects in his or her own study. However, one should start with the knowledge that the Biblical record documented that God "...<u>*hates*</u> *divorce, for it covers one's garment with* ***violence****,*" *says the Lord of hosts. "Therefore take heed to your spirit, that you do not deal* ***treacherously***"" (Malachi 2:16). If one accepts that the prophet Malachi got this directly from God, then one needs to pay attention to the fact that God <u>hates</u> the behavior and a dangerous negative attribute and treachery may be involved. Further, Jesus stated <u>himself</u>, "*Have you not read that He who made them at the beginning 'made them* <u>*male*</u> *and female,' and said, 'For this reason a* <u>*man*</u> *shall leave* <u>*his father*</u> *and mother and be joined to* <u>*his*</u> *wife, and the two shall become one flesh'? So then, they are no longer two but one flesh. Therefore what God has joined together, let not* <u>*man*</u> *separate*" (Matthew 19:4-6). As Jesus was further pressed on the matter, He stated with clarity, "*Moses, because of the hardness of your hearts, permitted you to divorce your wives, but from the beginning it was not so. And I say to you, whoever divorces* <u>*his*</u> *wife, except for* ***sexually immorality****, and marries another, commits* ***adultery****; and whoever marries her who is divorced commits* ***adultery***" (Matthew 19:8-9). From this scripture, one can see the reason for the first Biblical divorce; the negative attributes were involved. Hence, the act was not from or approved by God. Moses allowed it because the people were <u>stubborn</u> and would not obey God's Word. Based on Jesus' teaching to His apostles, they further documented the following pearls of wisdom specifically concerning divorce for one's learning and spiritual journey:

"...if a woman **divorces** her <u>husband</u> and marries another, she commits **adultery**" (Mark 10:12)	"Whoever **divorces** <u>his</u> wife and marries another commits **adultery**; and whoever marries her who is **divorced** from her <u>husband</u> commits **adultery**" (Luke 16:18)	"For the woman who has a <u>husband</u> is bound by the law to her <u>husband</u> as long as <u>he</u> lives. But if the <u>husband</u> dies, she is released from the law of her <u>husband</u>" (Romans 7:2)
"And a woman who has a <u>husband</u> who does not believe, if <u>he</u> is willing to live with her, let her not **divorce** <u>him</u>" (1 Corinthians 7:13)	"Now to the married I command, yet not I but the Lord: A wife is not to depart from her <u>husband</u>" (1 Corinthians 7:10)	"But even if she does depart, let her remain unmarried or be reconciled to her <u>husband</u>. And a <u>husband</u> is not to **divorce** <u>his</u> wife" (1 Corinthians 7:11)
"So then if, while her <u>husband</u> lives, she marries another <u>man</u>, she will be called an **adulteress**; but if her <u>husband</u> dies, she is free from that law, so that she is no **adulteress**, though she has married another <u>man</u>" (Romans 7:3)	"For the unbelieving <u>husband</u> is sanctified by the wife, and the unbelieving wife is sanctified by the <u>husband</u>; otherwise your children would be unclean, but now they are holy" (1 Corinthians 7:14)	"For how do you know, O wife, whether you will save your <u>husband</u>? Or how do you know, O <u>husband</u>, whether you will save your wife?" (1 Corinthians 7:16)

Table 166: Pearls of Wisdom Concerning the Marriage Relationship

Table 166 emphasizes the point that God <u>hates</u> divorce. His Word in the Biblical record is clear about divorce and remarriage. Confusion occurs as the influence of the negative attributes escalates <u>strife</u> with physical and verbal abuse. In these cases, one must apply <u>discernment</u>. For physical and verbal abuse that **oppresses** one's inner spirit (reread the **oppressor** attribute if necessary) and leads to **violence**, the **bloodthirsty** attributes can create a relationship that has a form of **immorality**. **Counseling** is necessary before the spilling of **innocent blood** occurs. In these cases, divorce or separation becomes necessary. But, one cannot expect *false* teachers to teach God's truth about divorce when many of them have illegitimately divorced. They lack the understanding necessary to teach on this spiritual subject. BTT allows one to see that God's <u>calamity</u> is occurring on the religious world today for its inappropriate teachings on this spiritual subject. For the very act is disqualifying <u>men</u> worldwide from God's service as **faithful**, **honorable**, and **blameless** examples of **good** conduct. This is why within Christ's church, God requires His elders, deacons, and ministers, to set the example in this area. The Biblical record documents for elders, bishops, overseers or other synonymous terms, "...*set in order the things that are lacking, and appoint elders in every city as I commanded you— if a <u>man</u> is **blameless**, the <u>husband</u> of one wife, having **faithful** children not accused of dissipation or insubordination*" (Titus 1:5, 6) and "*A bishop then must be **blameless**, the <u>husband</u> of one wife, temperate, sober-minded, of **good** behavior, hospitable, able to teach...*" (1 Timothy 3:2). For the deacon, the Biblical record documents, "*Let deacons be the <u>husbands</u> of one wife, ruling their children and their own houses well*" (1 Timothy 3:12). <u>Man</u> places Christ's church in jeopardy when these requirements are ignored. God's <u>calamity</u> will eventually purge the sin from the church or the church itself will cease to be Christ's church and become a casualty of the war campaign.

This brings us to the third and most critical responsibility placed on the <u>man</u>. Once <u>he</u> understands <u>his</u> responsibilities to God, leaves <u>his</u> mother and <u>father</u> and marries a wife to start <u>his</u> own family, then begins the responsibility of <u>fatherhood</u>. If a marriage is appropriately committed in God's eyes by both the <u>man</u> and woman, over time children will come whether by birth or adoption. However, when that time comes, the <u>man</u> incurs the responsibility to, "*Train up a child in the way <u>he</u> should go, and when <u>he</u> is old <u>he</u> will not depart from it*" (Proverbs 22:6) and more specifically, not to "*...provoke your children to <u>wrath</u>, but bring them up in the training and admonition of the Lord*" (Ephesians 6:4). There is no release from this duty. Yes, the <u>man</u> can simply walk away from <u>his</u> responsibilities; but walking away does not release <u>him</u> from this God given duty. Walking away from the duty is sin. Yes, the woman shares in this responsibility, but a greater portion falls to the <u>man</u> that is difficult to put in worldly terms. The reason can be found in the fact that there is a spiritual element involved. The <u>man</u> bares the primary duty for preparing the child for spiritual warfare. The <u>man's</u> inherent responsibility is <u>his</u> whether <u>he</u> received fair treatment from <u>his</u> parents or not. Table 167 below, depicts an interesting parallel between the inherent responsibilities of <u>fathers</u> and the influence of the negative attributes on their children. Please understand that once children reach an age of accountability, they become accountable for their own responses to the influences of the positive or negative attributes. But until then, a <u>father</u> is held accountable. <u>His</u> response to negative attributes does not excuse <u>him</u> from performing <u>his</u> duties to <u>his</u> children in their early stages of life. For a <u>father</u>'s behavior can afford a child the necessary examples and tools to navigate spiritual warfare as they mature. Without the <u>father's</u> involvement, a household and the children risk becoming like Eli and his sons of whom the prophet Samuel stated from the Lord, "*For I have told him that I will judge his house forever for the iniquity which he knows, because his sons made themselves vile, and he did not restrain them. And therefore I have sworn to the house of Eli that the iniquity of Eli's house shall not be atoned for by sacrifice or offering forever*" (1 Samuel 3:13-14).

Now consider some parallels and conclusions that can be drawn from examples of <u>fathers'</u> behaviors and their children in the following Table:

<u>Fathers</u> Are To:	If Not, the Negative Attributes Can Exploit Their Children and Lead to:
Be Sober	**Foolishness**: "*...Ham, the <u>father</u> of Canaan, saw the nakedness of <u>his</u> father, and told <u>his</u> two brothers outside*" (Genesis 9:22)
	Immorality: Lot's daughters said to each other, "*Come, let us make our <u>father</u> drink wine, and we will lie with <u>him</u>, that we may preserve the lineage of our <u>father</u>*" (Genesis 19:32). Their sins produced the <u>fathers</u> of the Moabites (Genesis 19:37) and the people of Ammon (Genesis 19:38)
Be **honest**	**Deceit**: Jacob told Rachel, "*...your <u>father</u> has **deceived** me and changed my wages ten times, but God did not allow <u>him</u> to hurt me*" (Genesis 31:7)

	Deceit: Rachel learned from her <u>father</u>'s way: "*Now Laban had gone to shear <u>his</u> sheep, and Rachel had **stolen** the household idols that were her <u>father</u>'s*" (Genesis 31:19)
Provide **wise counsel** and **advice**	Ignorance in management: As Moses tried to manage all the children of Israel <u>himself</u>, Moses' <u>father</u>-in-law told <u>him</u>, "*…The thing that you do is not **good***" (Exodus 18:17). <u>He</u> gave <u>him</u> **good counsel** and **advise**, and the Bible documented, "*So Moses heeded the voice of <u>his</u> <u>father</u>-in-law and did all that <u>he</u> had said*" (Exodus 18:24) which relived a lot of the weight of leadership from Moses' shoulders.
	"*Remember the days of old, consider the years of many generations. Ask your <u>father</u>, and <u>he</u> will show you; your elders, and they will tell you…*" (Deuteronomy 32:7)
Be **honored**	Shortened life: God said, "***Honor*** *your <u>father</u> and your mother, that your days may be long upon the land which the Lord your God is giving you*" (Exodus 20:12; Deuteronomy 5:16)
	Violence: "*And <u>he</u> who strikes <u>his father</u> or <u>his</u> mother shall surely be put to death*" (Exodus 21:15)
	Inappropriate language choices: "*And <u>he</u> who curses <u>his father</u> or <u>his</u> mother shall surely be put to death*" (Exodus 21:17)
	Discouragement: "***Honor*** *your <u>father</u> and mother," which is the first commandment with promise: that it may be well with you and you may live long on the earth*" (Ephesians 6:2-3)
	Rejection of God: "*And you have done worse than your <u>fathers</u>, for behold, each one follows the dictates of <u>his</u> own **evil** heart, so that no one listens to Me*" (Jeremiah 16:12)
Be <u>respected</u> and teach <u>humility</u>	"*Every one of you shall revere <u>his</u> mother and <u>his father</u>, and keep My Sabbaths: I am the Lord your God*" (Leviticus 19:3)
	Immorality: "*The nakedness of your <u>father</u> or the nakedness of your mother you shall not uncover. She is your mother; you shall not uncover her nakedness*" (Leviticus 18:7)
	Immorality: "*The nakedness of your <u>father</u>'s wife you shall not uncover; it is your <u>father</u>'s nakedness*" (Leviticus 18:8)
	Immorality: "*The nakedness of your sister, the daughter of your <u>father</u>, or the daughter of your mother, whether born at home or elsewhere, their nakedness you shall not uncover*" (Leviticus 18:9 and Leviticus 18:11)
	Immorality: "*You shall not uncover the nakedness of your <u>father</u>'s sister; she is near of kin to your <u>father</u>*" (Leviticus 18:12)
	Immorality: "*You shall not uncover the nakedness of your <u>father</u>'s brother. You shall not approach <u>his</u> wife; she is your aunt*" (Leviticus 18:14)
	Inappropriate language choices: "*For everyone who curses <u>his father</u> or <u>his</u> mother shall surely be put to death. <u>He</u> has cursed <u>his father</u> or <u>his</u> mother. <u>His</u> blood shall be upon <u>him</u>*" (Leviticus 20:9)
	Contempt: "*Cursed is the one who treats <u>his father</u> or <u>his</u> mother with contempt.' "And all the people shall say, 'Amen!'*" (Deuteronomy 27:16)
	Disrespect: "*Do not rebuke an older <u>man</u>, but exhort <u>him</u> as a <u>father</u>, younger <u>men</u> as brothers…*" (1 Timothy 5:1)

	Perversion: "*They pant after the dust of the earth which is on the head of the **poor**, and **pervert** the way of the humble. A man and his father go in to the same girl, to defile My holy name*" (Amos 2:7)
Manage and care for their children with *love* and understanding	Strife and conflict: "*...if a woman makes a vow to the Lord, and binds herself by some agreement while in her father's house in her youth, and her father hears her vow and the agreement by which she has bound herself, and her father holds his peace, then all her vows shall stand, and every agreement with which she has bound herself shall stand. But if her father overrules her on the day that he hears, then none of her vows nor her agreements by which she has bound herself shall stand; and the Lord will release her, because her father overruled her*" (Numbers 30:3-5)
	Stubbornness and rebellion: "*If a man has a stubborn and rebellious son who will not obey the voice of his father or the voice of his mother, and who, when they have chastened him, will not heed them, then his father and his mother shall take hold of him and bring him out to the elders of his city, to the gate of his city...*" (Deuteronomy 21:18) for appropriate action.
Protect their homes	Spiritual ignorance: "*They sacrificed to demons, not to God, to gods they did not know, to new gods, new arrivals that your fathers did not fear*" (Deuteronomy 32:17)
	Distrust and rebellion: "*Do not trust in a friend; do not put your confidence in a companion; guard the doors of your mouth from her who **lies** in your bosom. For son **dishonors** father, daughter rises against her mother, daughter-in-law against her mother-in-law; a man's enemies are the men of his own household. Therefore I will look to the Lord; I will wait for the God of my salvation; my God will hear me*" (Micah 7:5-6)

Table 167: Pearls of Wisdom for the Man as a *Father*

When a *father* fails to carry out *his* responsibilities as a *father* in the home, the impact on *his* children and the generations after *him* can be devastating. Consider some more Old Testament examples. Remember, Paul documented by inspiration of the Holy Spirit, "*For whatever things were written before were written for our learning, that we through the patience and comfort of the Scriptures might have hope*" (Romans 15:4). Therefore, the Biblical record documented:

Who Sinned	**What Is Documented**
The *fathers* Judah	"*Now Judah did **evil** in the sight of the Lord, and they provoked Him to **jealousy** with their sins which they committed, more than all that their fathers had done*" (1 Kings 14:22)
Abijam, son of Rehoboam	"*...he walked in all the sins of his father, which he had done before him; his heart was not loyal to the Lord his God, as was the heart of his father David*" (1 Kings 15:3)
Nadab, son of Jeroboam	"*...he did **evil** in the sight of the Lord, and walked in the way of his father, and in his sin by which he had made Israel sin*" (1 Kings 15:26)

Zechariah the son of Jeroboam	"And _he_ did **evil** in the sight of the Lord, _as his fathers had done;_ _he_ did not depart from the sins of Jeroboam the son of Nebat, who had made Israel sin" (2 Kings 15:9)
Ahaziah the son of Ahab	"_He_ did **evil** in the sight of the Lord, and _walked in the way of his father_ and in the way of _his_ mother and in the way of Jeroboam the son of Nebat, who had made Israel sin, for _he_ **served Baal and worshiped** _him_, and provoked the Lord God of Israel to **anger**, according to all that _his father_ had done" (1 Kings 22:52-53)
Jehoram the son of Ahab	"And _he_ did **evil** in the sight of the Lord, but not like _his father_ and mother; for _he_ put away the **sacred pillar of Baal** that _his father_ had made" (2 Kings 3:2)
	"Now when Jehoram was established over the kingdom of _his father_, _he_ strengthened _himself_ and **killed** all _his_ brothers with the sword, and also others of the princes of Israel" (2 Chronicles 21:4)
Amon the son of Manasseh	"And _he_ did **evil** in the sight of the Lord, _as his father Manasseh had done_. So _he_ walked in all the ways that _his father_ had walked; and _he_ **served the idols** that _his father_ had served, and worshiped them" (2 Kings 21:20, 21)
Jehoahaz the son of Josiah	"And _he_ did **evil** in the sight of the Lord, _according to all that his fathers had done_" (2 Kings 23:32)
Eliakim the son of Josiah	Pharaoh Necho made _him_ king and changed _his_ name to Jehoiakim (2 Kings 23:34) "And _he_ did **evil** in the sight of the Lord, _according to all that his fathers had done_" (2 Kings 23:37)
Jehoiachin son of Jehoiakim	"..._he_ did **evil** in the sight of the Lord, _according to all that his father had done_" (2 Kings 24:9)
Reuben, son of Jacob	"Now the sons of Reuben the firstborn of Israel—_he_ was indeed the firstborn, but because _he_ _defiled his father's bed_, _his_ birthright was given to the sons of Joseph, the son of Israel, so that the genealogy is not listed according to the birthright..." (1 Chronicles 5:1)

Table 168: Examples of _Fathers_ Influenced by the Negative Attributes and Their Legacies to Their Children

There are other sinful activities and behaviors that one can expect to see when _fathers_ fail to take care of their responsibilities to their children. The children will turn to other people or things to fulfill their needs. BTT allows one to see that the negative forces of the war campaign are free to corrupt the children. Consider some things documented in the Old Testament concerning **idolatry**:

- "As the **thief** is ashamed when _he_ is found out, so is the house of Israel ashamed; they and their kings and their princes, and their priests and their prophets, _saying to a tree, 'You are my father,' and to a stone, 'You gave birth to me.'_ For they have turned their back to Me, and not their face. But in the time of their trouble they will say, 'Arise and save us.'" (Jeremiah 2:27)

- "_The children gather wood, the fathers kindle the fire_, and the women _knead dough, to make cakes for the queen of heaven_; and they pour out drink offerings _to other gods_, that they may provoke Me to **anger**" (Jeremiah 7:18)

- "...*then you shall say to them, 'Because your <u>fathers</u> have forsaken Me,' says the Lord; 'they have <u>walked after other gods and have served them and worshiped them</u>, and have forsaken Me and not kept My law. And you have done worse than your <u>fathers</u>, for behold, each one follows the dictates of <u>his</u> own **evil** heart, so that no one listens to Me*" (Jeremiah 16:11-12)

Just so one understands, the Biblical record documents a variety of pearls of wisdom identifying the impact of the positive or negative attribute's influence on children when <u>fathers</u> are present, absent, negligent, or fails to set the proper example. The pearls of wisdom are too numerous to cover in detail. However, they are worth one's knowledge and consideration. Without the knowledge of them, the negative attributes will **deceive** one into believing that God left gaps for one to operate in outside of <u>His</u> purview. This is a **lie** from the **liar** attribute itself and a strategy used by the negative forces to entangle <u>man</u> in sin. Below are just a few pearls of wisdom from the Biblical writers about <u>fathers</u>, their responsibilities, and a few correlating actions from their children as they became influenced by either the positive or negative attributes. The Bible documents:

"*I was a <u>father</u> to the **poor**, and I searched out the case that I did not know*" (Job 29:16)	"*Our <u>fathers</u> trusted in You; they trusted, and You delivered them*" (Psalm 22:4)	"*As a <u>father</u> pities <u>his</u> children, so the Lord pities those who <u>fear</u> <u>Him</u>*" (Psalm 103:13)
"*When my <u>father</u> and my mother forsake me, then the Lord will take care of me*" (Psalm 27:10)	"*My son, hear the instruction of your <u>father</u>, and do not forsake the law of your mother...*" (Proverbs 1:8)	"*For whom the Lord <u>loves</u> <u>He</u> corrects, just as a <u>father</u> the son in whom <u>he</u> delights*" (Proverbs 3:12)
"*Hear, my children, the instruction of a <u>father</u>, and give attention to know understanding...*" (Proverbs 4:1)	"*My son, keep your <u>father's</u> command, and do not forsake the law of your mother*" (Proverbs 6:20)	"*...A **wise** son makes a glad <u>father</u>, but a **foolish** son is the **grief** of <u>his</u> mother*" (Proverbs 10:1)
"*A **wise** son heeds <u>his</u> <u>father's</u> instruction, but a **scoffer** does not listen to rebuke*" (Proverbs 13:1)	"*A **fool** despises <u>his father's</u> instruction, but <u>he</u> who receives correction is **prudent**" (Proverbs 15:5)	"*He who begets a **scoffer** does so to <u>his</u> sorrow, and the <u>father</u> of a **fool** has no joy*" (Proverbs 17:21)
"*Do not remove the ancient landmark which your <u>fathers</u> have set*" (Proverbs 22:28)	"*A **wise** son makes a <u>father</u> glad, but a **foolish** <u>man</u> despises <u>his</u> mother*" (Proverbs 15:20)	"*A **foolish** son is a grief to <u>his father</u>, and **bitterness** to her who bore <u>him</u>*" (Proverbs 17:25)
"*A **foolish** son is the ruin of <u>his father</u>, and the <u>contentions</u> of a wife are a continual dripping*" (Proverbs 19:13)	"*Houses and riches are an inheritance from <u>fathers</u>, but a **prudent** wife is from the Lord*" (Proverbs 19:14)	"*Whoever keeps the law is a <u>discerning</u> son, but a companion of gluttons shames <u>his father</u>*" (Proverbs 28:7)
"*Whoever curses <u>his father</u> or <u>his</u> mother, <u>his</u> lamp will be put out in deep darkness*" (Proverbs 20:20)	"*Children's children are the crown of old <u>men</u>, and the glory of children is their <u>father</u>*" (Proverbs 17:6)	"*Let your <u>father</u> and your mother be glad, and let her who bore you rejoice*" (Proverbs 23:25)

"Listen to your _father_ who begot you, and do not despise your mother when she is old" (Proverbs 23:22)	"The _father_ of the **righteous** will greatly rejoice, and _he_ who begets a **wise** child will delight in _him_" (Proverbs 23:24)	"There is a generation that curses its _father_, and does not bless its mother" (Proverbs 30:11)
"_He_ who mistreats _his father_ and chases away _his_ mother is a son who causes shame and brings reproach" (Proverbs 19:26)	"Whoever **robs** _his father_ or _his_ mother, and says, 'It is no transgression,' the same is companion to a **destroyer**" (Proverbs 28:24)	"The living, the living _man_, _he_ shall praise You, as I do this day; the _father_ shall make known Your truth to the children" (Isaiah 38:19)
"Woe to _him_ who says to _his father_, 'What are you begetting?' Or to the woman, 'What have you brought forth?'" (Isaiah 45:10)	"Behold, all souls are Mine; the soul of the _father_ as well as the soul of the son is Mine; the soul who sins shall die" (Ezekiel 18:4)	"Whoever _loves_ wisdom makes _his father_ rejoice, but a companion of **harlots** wastes _his_ wealth" (Proverbs 29:3)
"If you endure chastening, God deals with you as with sons; for what son is there whom a _father_ does not chasten?" (Hebrews 12:7)	"The eye that **mocks** _his father_, and **scorns** obedience to _his_ mother, the ravens of the valley will pick it out, and the young eagles will eat it" (Proverbs 30:17)	For a _father_ that sins, "...because _he_ cruelly **oppressed**, **robbed** _his_ brother by **violence**, and did what is not **good** among _his_ people, behold, _he_ shall die for _his_ iniquity" (Ezekiel 18:18)

Table 169: More Pearls of Wisdom Concerning _Fathers_

Finally, with the negative attributes successfully influencing _men_ to abdicate their responsibilities to God and their families, another category of people arise due to the error of this behavior. This category is called the "_fatherless_." Although physical war and natural death throughout history have always supplied people to this category, an untold number of children come from _men_ who abandon their marriage or produce them out of wedlock. God is not happy with this. God's _calamity_ pours out on His creation as this practice becomes more acceptable in societies. Since the beginning of the war campaign in human history, the negative forces have made a **mockery** of God's creation as _man_ failed to heed God's Word. Many homes have become causalities of the negative forces' strategy as children are forced to live in the streets or rear themselves as the woman struggles to raise her children, work, and provide on her own. When a _father_ abdicates _his_ responsibility to _his_ children, the children become targets of the **wicked** because of their innocence and vulnerability. The results are astonishing. Here is what the Biblical record documents of people influenced by the **wicked** attribute. They,

- "...slay the widow and the stranger, and **murder** the _fatherless_" (Psalm 94:6)

- "They have grown fat, they are sleek; yes, they surpass the deeds of the **wicked**; they do not plead the cause, the cause of the _fatherless_; yet they prosper, and the right of the **needy** they do not defend" (Jeremiah 5:28)

- Write **unrighteous** decrees (Isaiah 10:1) "*To **rob** the **needy** of justice, and to **take** what is **right** from the **poor** of My people, that widows may be their prey, and that they may **rob** the <u>fatherless</u>*" (Isaiah 10:2)

Like the city of Jerusalem, other cities have followed its direction in the **oppressive** practices toward the <u>fatherless</u>. The Biblical record documented of Jerusalem, "*In you they have made light of <u>father</u> and mother; in your midst they have **oppressed** the stranger; in you they have mistreated the <u>fatherless</u> and the widow*" (Ezekiel 22:7). The Bible also documented of their leaders: "*Your princes are rebellious, and companions of **thieves**; everyone <u>loves</u> <u>bribes</u>, and follows after rewards. They do not defend the <u>fatherless</u>, nor does the cause of the widow come before them*" (Isaiah 1:23). One can see the hopelessness experienced by the <u>fatherless</u>. But God and His written Word says:

- "*You shall not afflict any widow or <u>fatherless</u> child*" (Exodus 22:22)

- "*He administers justice for the <u>fatherless</u> and the widow, and <u>loves</u> the stranger, giving <u>him</u> food and clothing*" (Deuteronomy 10:18)

- "*You shall not **pervert** justice due the stranger or the <u>fatherless</u>, nor take a widow's garment as a pledge*" (Deuteronomy 24:17)

- "*Cursed is the one who **perverts** the justice due the stranger, the <u>fatherless</u>, and widow.' "And all the people shall say, 'Amen!'*" (Deuteronomy 27:19)

- "*Defend the **poor** and <u>fatherless</u>; do justice to the afflicted and **needy***" (Psalm 82:3)

- "*Do not remove the ancient landmark, nor enter the fields of the <u>fatherless</u>...*" (Proverbs 23:10)

- "*Learn to do **good**; seek justice, rebuke the **oppressor**; defend the <u>fatherless</u>, plead for the widow*" (Isaiah 1:17)

- "*Thus says the Lord: "Execute judgment and **righteousness**, and deliver the plundered out of the hand of the **oppressor**. Do no wrong and do no **violence** to the stranger, the <u>fatherless</u>, or the widow, nor **shed innocent blood** in this place*" (Jeremiah 22:3)

- "*Do not **oppress** the widow or the <u>fatherless</u>, the alien or the **poor**. Let none of you plan **evil** in <u>his</u> heart against <u>his</u> brother*" (Zechariah 7:10)

How does God accomplish His will with <u>man</u>? He does it through you, me, and His providence. The Biblical record documented for one's example:

- "*When you reap your harvest in your field, and forget a sheaf in the field, you shall not go back to get it; it shall be for the stranger, the <u>fatherless</u>, and the widow, that the Lord your God may bless you in all the work of your hands*" (Deuteronomy 24:19)

- "When you beat your olive trees, you shall not go over the boughs again; it shall be for the stranger, the _fatherless_, and the widow" (Deuteronomy 24:20)

- "When you gather the grapes of your vineyard, you shall not glean it afterward; it shall be for the stranger, the _fatherless_, and the widow" (Deuteronomy 24:21)

- " When you have finished laying aside all the tithe of your increase in the third year—the year of tithing—and have given it to the Levite, the stranger, the _fatherless_, and the widow, so that they may eat within your gates and be filled, then you shall say before the Lord your God: 'I have removed the holy tithe from my house, and also have given them to the Levite, the stranger, the _fatherless_, and the widow, according to all Your commandments which You have commanded me; I have not transgressed Your commandments, nor have I forgotten them" (Deuteronomy 26:12-13)

In other words, one's responsibility is to help the _fatherless_ as one is able through _his_ or her prosperity, capabilities, or skills. Job provided an example for everyone to follow. _He_ stated to _his_ three tormenting friends, "When the ear heard, then it blessed me, and when the eye saw, then it approved me; because I delivered the **poor** who cried out, the _fatherless_ and the one who had no helper. The blessing of a perishing _man_ came upon me, and I caused the widow's heart to sing for joy. I put on **righteousness**, and it clothed me; my justice was like a robe and a turban" (Job 29:11-14). This is the same pattern that one is to follow in _his_ or her pursuit of the **righteous** attribute.

BTT allows one to see that God will defend the _fatherless_. God's wrath turns toward the people who create or abuse the _fatherless_. The Biblical record documents:

- "But You have seen, for You observe trouble and grief, to repay it by Your hand. The helpless commits _himself_ to You; You are the helper of the _fatherless_" (Psalm 10:14)

- "A _father_ of the _fatherless_, a defender of widows, is God in His holy habitation" (Psalm 68:5)

- "The Lord watches over the strangers; He relieves the _fatherless_ and widow; but the way of the **wicked** _He_ turns upside down" (Psalm 146:9)

One must pay attention to what is occurring worldwide where it concerns the growing numbers of _fatherless_ children. This growing catastrophe invites God's _calamity_ and requires sound preaching and teaching from God's people.

Before I close this section on _calamity_, allow me to address two misunderstood Scriptural references concerning _fathers_. The negative attributes are exploiting these references today through spiritual warfare. The first concerns Jesus' statements, "For I have come to 'set a _man_ against _his father_, a daughter against her mother, and a daughter-in-law against her mother-in-law'; and 'a _man's_ enemies will be those of _his_ own household. _He_ who _loves father_ or mother more than Me is not worthy of Me. And _he_ who _loves_ son or daughter more than Me is not worthy of Me" (Matthew 10:35-37) and "If anyone comes to Me and does not **hate** _his father_ and mother, wife and children, brothers and sisters, yes, and _his_ own life also, _he_ cannot be My disciple" (Luke 14:26). Jesus' statements concerned His bringing the true Gospel from God to the world. Because of Jesus' Truth, families often split apart. This occurs because spiritual warfare ensues between family members. Some members accept Jesus and His Truth, while others reject Him. BTT allows one to see the application of a spiritual principle that Jesus taught. He said, "*...if a house is divided against itself, that house cannot stand*" (Mark 3:25). When members of households hear the True Gospel, they are compelled to examine the teachings and traditions that sustained them against this new knowledge. This examination and the acceptance of Jesus and His Word can split households. BTT allows one to see that the religious community will allow alternative beliefs to be mixed with the Gospel if the combination will retain the family. But the reality is that God's Word got diluted. When the Word is diluted, its power is voided and family members remain in their same lost state. The household may retain their unity with mixed beliefs and views about Christianity, but they all may fall in battle on the spiritual battlefield. This strategy may allow the religious organization to coopt the entire household into their fold, but it decreases each family member's chance to be saved. In the end, this strategy only provided numbers, resources, and financial support to the religious group that did not desire to "step on toes" with the Truth. On the spiritual battlefield, these households simply helped maintain the jobs of ***false*** teachers, the spread of ***false*** doctrine, and added more weight on the shoulders of the positive forces fighting the ***good*** fight. God is not happy with these sustained and growing practices and He is pouring out His <u>calamity</u> on the world today because of it. In fact, one can see a broad application of Jesus's principle when He stated, "*...Every kingdom divided against itself is brought to desolation, and every city or house divided against itself will not stand*" (Matthew 12:25). The bottom line is this: If anyone teaches that Jesus came to earth to turn family members against each other, his or her teaching is a ***lie***. This person is a ***false*** teacher. Their literal view would mean that the negative forces were influencing Jesus. This twisting of Matthew 10:35-37 and Luke 14:26 comes from "***deceiving*** spirits and doctrines of demons" (1 Timothy 4:1).

  The second ***false*** teachings concerns the term "<u>father</u>" from Jesus' statement, "*Do not call anyone on earth your **father**; for One is your **Father**, He who is in heaven*" (Matthew 23:9). Jesus' statement concerned calling a <u>man</u> of flesh and blood a "spiritual" ***Father***. Jesus forbids this behavior. No <u>man</u> on earth is authorized this status. This status exclusively belongs to God. This statement upsets many people today. Nevertheless, this is the Gospel from God and ***false*** teachings about it accounts for His <u>calamity</u> today; ***false*** teachers and unlearned people teach otherwise. This goes back to understanding Paul statement that, "*These things we also speak, not in words which <u>man's</u> wisdom teaches but which the Holy Spirit teaches, comparing spiritual things with spiritual. But the natural <u>man</u> does not receive the things of the Spirit of God, for they are **foolishness** to <u>him</u>; nor can <u>he</u> know them, because they are spiritually <u>discerned</u>. But <u>he</u> who is spiritual judges all things, yet <u>he</u> <u>himself</u> is rightly judged by no one*" (1 Corinthians 2:13-15). Calling a <u>man</u> one's spiritual ***father*** contradicts Jesus' Word documented in Matthew 23:9 above. BTT allows one to see that we have our earthly <u>fathers</u>, <u>stepfathers</u>, <u>grandfathers</u>, and <u>fathers</u>-in-law; but, we have only one spiritual ***Father***, and that is God. Do not be ***deceived*** by the negative force's influences to call anyone one's spiritual ***father***. To do so, one will become a causality of the war campaign.

  To be fair, it seems that everything discussed so far under this <u>calamity</u> places a lot of responsibility on <u>man's</u> shoulders. It may seem like a lot, but it really is not. God desires a <u>man</u>

today to be like Joshua of old. For Joshua said, *"And if it seems **evil** to you to serve the Lord, choose for yourselves this day whom you will serve, whether the gods which your fathers served that were on the other side of the River, or the gods of the Amorites, in whose land you dwell. But as for me and my house, we will serve the Lord"* (Joshua 24:15). God desires man to commit to a spiritual lifestyle; a lifestyle that occurs when fathers trains both their sons and daughters generation after generation in God's Word. The Spirit of wisdom revealed to Solomon, *"As iron sharpens iron, so a man sharpens the countenance of his friend"* (Proverbs 27:17). In today's case, a man must sharpen his children with God's Truth. With each generation, **godly** men must take up this mantle. To do this, each man must first accept that *"...God created man in His own image; in the image of God He created him; male and female He created them"* (Genesis 1:27). With this acceptance, then man can be about the business of getting his own image in order, so he can take care of his responsibilities to others. This requires discipline, commitment, and focus. God desires a man's full engagement and his understanding of his role on earth. To gain an appreciation for the commitment that God desires of a man, the Table below may help. This Table is a composite of the spiritual man that God desires. Yes, many of the Scriptures apply to women too, but my focus is on fixing man's issues; then man's helpmate will follow. My point is not sexist, it simply exposes what spiritual warfare has hidden for centuries. The entire Biblical record documents:

Bodily Commitment	**What Is documented**
The Head and Neck	For one to hear one's father's instruction, and not forsake the law of one's mother and allow these to be *"...a graceful ornament on your head, and chains about your neck"* (Proverbs 1:8-9)
	For one to *"keep your father's command, and do not forsake the law of your mother. Bind them continually upon your heart; tie them around your neck"* (Proverbs 6:20-21)
	Not to hardens one's neck for, *"He who is often rebuked, and hardens his neck, will suddenly be destroyed, and that without remedy"* (Proverbs 29:1)
The Thoughts	*"Commit your works to the Lord, and your thoughts will be established"* (Proverbs 16:3)
	To understand that the **ungodliness** and **unrighteousness,** *"become futile in their thoughts, and their **foolish** hearts are darkened"* (Romans 1:18-21)
	"...to be carnally minded is death, but to be spiritually minded is life and peace. Because the carnal mind is enmity against God; for it is not subject to the law of God, nor indeed can be" (Romans 8:5-7)
	*"Do not be **wise** in your own eyes; fear the LORD and depart from **evil**. It will be health to your flesh, and strength to your bones"* (Proverbs 3:7-8)
	"All the ways of a man are pure in his own eyes, but the Lord weighs the spirits" (Proverbs 16:2)
	*"You have heard that it was said, 'You shall love your **neighbor** and **hate** your enemy.' But I say to you, love your enemies, bless those who curse you, do **good** to those who **hate** you, and pray for those who spitefully*

	use you and persecute you, that you may be sons of your Father in heaven; for He makes His sun rise on the **evil** and on the **good**, and sends rain on the **just** and on the **unjust**" (Matthew 5:43-45)
The Eyes	*"The light of the eyes rejoices the heart…"* (Proverbs 15:30)
	"Let your eyes look straight ahead, and your eyelids look right before you" (Proverbs 4:25)
	"Hell and Destruction are never full; so the eyes of <u>man</u> are never satisfied" (Proverbs 27:20)
	*"A <u>man</u> with an **evil** eye hastens after riches, and does not consider that <u>poverty</u> will come upon <u>him</u>"* (Proverbs 28:22)
	*"Do not overwork to be **rich**; because of your own understanding, cease! Will you set your eyes on that which is not? For <u>riches</u> certainly make themselves wings; they fly away like an eagle toward heaven"* (Proverbs 23:4-5)
	"Open your eyes, and you will be satisfied with bread." (Proverbs 20:13)
	*"Who has woe? Who has sorrow? Who has <u>contentions</u>? Who has complaints? Who has wounds without cause? Who has redness of eyes? Those who linger long at the wine, those who go in search of mixed wine. Do not look on the wine when it is red, when it sparkles in the cup, when it swirls around smoothly; At the last it bites like a serpent, and stings like a viper. Your eyes will see strange things, and your heart will utter perverse things. Yes, you will be like one who lies down in the midst of the sea, or like one who **lies** at the top of the mast, saying: "They have struck me, but I was not hurt; they have beaten me, but I did not feel it. When shall I awake, that I may seek another drink?"* (Proverbs 23:29-34)
	*"Do not <u>love</u> the world or the things in the world. If anyone <u>love</u>s the world, the <u>love</u> of the Father is not in <u>him</u>. For all that is in the world— the <u>lust</u> of the flesh, the <u>lust</u> of the eyes, and the **pride** of life—is not of the <u>Father</u> but is of the world. And the world is passing away, and the <u>lust</u> of it; but <u>he</u> who does the will of God abides forever"* (1 John 2:15-17)
	Jesus said, *"But I say to you that whoever looks at a woman to <u>lust</u> for her has already committed **adultery** with her in <u>his</u> heart"* (Matthew 5:28)
	"The lamp of the body is the eye. If therefore your eye is good, your whole body will be full of light. But if your eye is bad, your whole body will be full of darkness. If therefore the light that is in you is darkness, how great is that darkness!" (Matthew 6:22-23)
The Mouth	*"Death and life are in the power of the tongue, and those who <u>love</u> it will eat its fruit"* (Proverbs 18:21)
	*"A <u>man</u> will be satisfied with **good** by the fruit of <u>his</u> mouth, and the recompense of a <u>man's</u> hands will be rendered to <u>him</u>"* (Proverbs 12:14)
	"A <u>man</u> shall eat well by the fruit of <u>his</u> mouth…" (Proverbs 13:2)
	*"Put away from you a **deceitful** mouth, and put **perverse** lips far from you"* (Proverbs 4:24)
	"…pay attention to my wisdom; lend your ear to my understanding, that you may preserve discretion, and your lips may keep knowledge" (Proverbs 5:1-2)

The Mouth ~continued~	"_He who guards his mouth preserves his life, but he who opens wide his lips shall have destruction_" (Proverbs 13:3)
	"_A wholesome tongue is a tree of life, but **perverseness** in it breaks the spirit._" (Proverbs 15:4)
	"_Let another man praise you, and not your own mouth; a stranger, and not your own lips_" (Proverbs 27:2)
	"_Wisdom is found on the lips of him who has understanding..._" (Proverbs 10:13)
	"_In the multitude of words sin is not lacking, but he who restrains his lips is **wise**_" (Proverbs 10:19)
	"_**Righteous** lips are the delight of kings, and they love him who speaks what is **right**_" (Proverbs 16:13)
	"_He who **hates**, **disguises** it with his lips..._" (Proverbs 26:24)
	"_Whoever hides **hatred** has **lying** lips, and whoever spreads **slander** is a **fool**_" (Proverbs 10:18)
	"_**Lying** lips are an abomination to the LORD..._" (Proverbs 12:22)
	"_An **ungodly** man digs up **evil**, and it is on his lips like a burning fire_" (Proverbs 16:27)
	"_Do not be **envious** of **evil** men, nor desire to be with them; for their heart **devises violence**, and their lips talk of troublemaking_" (Proverbs 24:1-2)
	"_The tongue of the **wise** uses knowledge rightly but the mouth of **fools** pours forth **foolishness**_" (Proverbs 15:2)
	"_Whoever guards his mouth and tongue, keeps his soul from troubles_" (Proverbs 21:23)
	"_...the tongue of the **wise** promotes health_" (Proverbs 12:18)
	"_...a gentle tongue breaks a bone_" (Proverbs 25:15)
	"_A word **fitly** spoken is like apples of gold in settings of silver_" (Proverbs 25:11)
	"_A soft answer turns away wrath, but a harsh word stirs up **anger**_" (Proverbs 15:1)
	"_He who answers a matter before he hears it, it is **folly** and shame to him._" (Proverbs 18:13)
	"_Let another man praise you, and not your own mouth; a stranger, and not your own lips_" (Proverbs 27:2)
	"_Do not boast about tomorrow, for you do not know what a day may bring forth_" (Proverbs 27:1)
	"_Whoever **falsely** boasts of giving is like clouds and wind without rain_" (Proverbs 25:14)
	"_He who blesses his friend with a loud voice, rising early in the morning, it will be counted a curse to him_" (Proverbs 27:14)
	"_He who rebukes a man will find more favor afterward than he who flatters with the tongue_" (Proverbs 28:23)
	"_Getting treasures by a **lying** tongue is the fleeting fantasy of those who seek death_" (Proverbs 21:6)
	"_He who has a **deceitful** heart finds no **good**, and he who has a **perverse** tongue falls into **evil**_" (Proverbs 17:20)

The Mouth ~ continued ~	"The truthful lip shall be established forever but a **lying** tongue is but for a moment." (Proverbs 12:19)
	"An **evildoer** gives heed to **false** lips; a **liar** listens eagerly to a spiteful tongue" (Proverbs 17:4)
	"He who **mocks** the **poor** reproaches his Maker; he who is glad at calamity will not go unpunished" (Proverbs 17:5)
	"A man's stomach shall be satisfied from the fruit of his mouth; from the produce of his lips he shall be filled. Death and life are in the power of the tongue, and those who love it will eat its fruit" (Proverbs 18:20-21)
	"He who has knowledge spares his words, and a man of understanding is of a calm spirit" (Proverbs 17:27)
	"Do you see a man hasty in his words? There is more hope for a **fool** than for him" (Proverbs 29:20)
	Jesus said, "...But I say to you, do not **swear** at all: neither by heaven, for it is God's throne; nor by the earth, for it is His footstool; nor by Jerusalem, for it is the city of the great King" (Matthew 5:34-35)
	"But let your 'Yes' be 'Yes,' and your 'No,' 'No.' For whatever is more than these is from the **evil** one" (Matthew 5:37)
	"But I say to you that for every **idle** word men may speak, they will give account of it in the day of judgment" (Matthew 12:36)
	"Do you not yet understand that whatever enters the mouth goes into the stomach and is eliminated? But those things which proceed out of the mouth come from the heart, and they defile a man. For out of the heart proceed **evil thoughts, murders, adulteries, fornications, thefts, false** witness, **blasphemies**. These are the things which defile a man, but to eat with unwashed hands does not defile a man" (Matthew 15:17-20)
	"A **good** man out of the **good** treasure of his heart brings forth **good**; and an **evil** man out of the **evil** treasure of his heart brings forth **evil**. For out of the abundance of the heart his mouth speaks" (Luke 6:45)
	"Let no **corrupt** word proceed out of your mouth, but what is **good** for necessary edification, that it may impart grace to the hearers" (Ephesians 4:29)
	"For he who would love life and see **good** days, let him refrain his tongue from **evil**, and his lips from speaking **deceit**" (1 Peter 3:10)
	"If anyone among you thinks he is religious, and does not bridle his tongue but **deceives** his own heart, this one's religion is useless." (James 1:26-27)
	"...the tongue is a little member and boasts great things. See how great a forest a little fire kindles! And the tongue is a fire, a world of iniquity. The tongue is so set among our members that it defiles the whole body, and sets on fire the course of nature; and it is set on fire by hell. For every kind of beast and bird, of reptile and creature of the sea, is tamed and has been tamed by mankind. But no man can tame the tongue. It is an unruly **evil**, full of deadly poison. With it we bless our God and Father, and with it we curse men, who have been made in the similitude of God. Out of the same mouth proceed blessing and cursing. My brethren, these things ought not to be so." (James 3:5-12)

		"Walk in wisdom toward those who are outside, redeeming the time. Let your speech always be with <u>grace</u>, seasoned with salt, that you may know how you ought to answer each one." (Colossians 5:5-6)
	The Ears	"...hear the instruction of your <u>father</u>, and do not forsake the law of your mother" (Proverbs 1:8)
		"*Hear and be* **wise**; *and guide your heart in the way.*" (Proverbs 23:19)
		"*Cease listening to instruction, my son, and you will stray from the words of knowledge*" (Proverbs 19:27)
		"*My son, pay attention to my wisdom; lend your ear to my understanding...*" (Proverbs 5:1)
		"*The ear that hears the rebukes of life will abide among the* **wise**" (Proverbs 15:31)
		"*One who turns away <u>his</u> ear from hearing the law, even <u>his</u> prayer is an abomination*" (Proverbs 28:9)
		"*Whoever shuts <u>his</u> ears to the cry of the* **poor** *will also cry <u>himself</u> and not be heard*" (Proverbs 21:13)
		God said of Jesus, "*...This is My be<u>loved</u> Son, in whom I am well pleased. Hear <u>Him</u>!" And when the disciples heard it, they fell on their faces and were greatly afraid.*" (Matthew 17:5-6)
		Jesus said, "*Therefore whoever hears these sayings of Mine, and does them, I will liken <u>him</u> to a* **wise** *man who built <u>his</u> house on the rock: and the rain descended, the floods came, and the winds blew and beat on that house; and it did not fall, for it was founded on the rock.* "*But everyone who hears these sayings of Mine, and does not do them, will be like a* **foolish** *man who built <u>his</u> house on the sand: and the rain descended, the floods came, and the winds blew and beat on that house; and it fell. And great was its fall.*" (Matthew 7:24-27)
		"*Take heed what you hear. With the same measure you use, it will be measured to you; and to you who hear, more will be given. For whoever has, to <u>him</u> more will be given; but whoever does not have, even what <u>he</u> has will be taken away from <u>him</u>*" (Mark 4:23-25)
		Jesus said, "*Most assuredly, I say to you, <u>he</u> who hears My word and believes in Him who sent Me has everlasting life, and shall not come into judgment, but has passed from death into life. Most assuredly, I say to you, the hour is coming, and now is, when the dead will hear the voice of the Son of God; and those who hear will live. For as the Father has life in Himself, so He has granted the Son to have life in Himself...*" (John 5:24-26)
		"*<u>He</u> who is of God hears God's Words; therefore you do not hear, because you are not of God*" (John 8:47)
		"*Now we know that God does not hear sinners; but if anyone is a worshiper of God and does His will, He hears <u>him</u>.*" (John 9:31)
		I have come as a light into the world, that whoever believes in Me should not abide in darkness. And if anyone hears My words and does not believe, I do not judge <u>him</u>; for I did not come to judge the world but to save the world. <u>He</u> who rejects Me, and does not receive My words, has that which judges <u>him</u>—the word <u>that I have spoken will judge</u> <u>him</u> in the last day. (John 12:46-48)

The Ears *~continued~*	*If anyone loves Me, he will keep My word; and My Father will love him, and We will come to him and make Our home with him. He who does not love Me does not keep My words; and the word which you hear is not Mine but the Father who sent Me"* (John 14:23-24)
	*"You say rightly that I am a king. For this cause I was born, and for this cause I have come into the world, that I should bear **witness** to the truth. Everyone who is of the truth hears My voice"* (John 18:37)
	*"So then, my beloved brethren, let every man be swift to hear, slow to speak, slow to wrath; for the wrath of man does not produce the **righteousness** of God"* (James 1:19-20)
	*"…**faith** comes by hearing, and hearing by the word of God."* (Romans 10:17)
	*"lay aside all **filthiness** and overflow of **wickedness**, and receive with meekness the implanted word, which is able to save your souls. But be doers of the word, and not hearers only, **deceiving** yourselves. For if anyone is a hearer of the word and not a doer, he is like a man observing his natural face in a mirror; for he observes himself, goes away, and immediately forgets what kind of man he was. But he who looks into the perfect law of liberty and continues in it, and is not a forgetful hearer but a doer of the work, this one will be blessed in what he does"* (James 1:21-25)
The Heart	*"The spirit of a man is the lamp of the LORD searching all the inner depths of his heart"* (Proverbs 20:27)
	"Trust in the LORD with all your heart, and lean not on your own understanding; In all your ways acknowledge Him, and He shall direct your paths" (Proverbs 3:5-6)
	Solomon taught his children to apply their hearts to understanding (Proverbs 2:1-2), instruction, (Proverbs 23:12), let their hearts keep his commands (Proverbs 3:1), bind his command and mother's law continually upon your hearts (Proverbs 6:20-21), write **mercy** and truth on the tablet of their hearts, and so find favor and high esteem in the sight of God and man (Proverbs 3:3-4).
	Additionally, he taught them to give attention to his words keeping them in the midst of their heart for the words are life to those who find them, and health to all their flesh (Proverbs 4:20-22). Further, he told them to keep their heart with all diligence; for out of it spring the issues of life (Proverbs 4:23). He even asked his son to give him his heart, and let his eyes observe his ways (Proverbs 23:26). Thus, Solomon taught one should chasten his or her son while there is hope, and not to set one's heart on his destruction (Proverbs 19:18). Solomon understood that **foolishness** existed in a child's heart and the rod of correction would drive it away (Proverbs 22:15). Thus, he said hear, my son, and be **wise**; and guide your heart in the way (Proverbs 23:19).
	"A man's heart plans his way, but the LORD directs his steps" (Proverbs 16:9)
	*"There are many plans in a man's heart, nevertheless, the LORD's **counsel** will stand"* (Proverbs 19:21)
	"The preparations of the heart belong to man, but the answer of the tongue is from the LORD" (Proverbs 16:1)

The Heart ~continued~	The Spirit reveals that "*a **haughty** look, a **proud** heart, and the plowing of the **wicked** are sin*" (Proverbs 21:4)
	Those of a **proud** heart stir up <u>strife</u>, (Proverbs 28:25) and are an abomination to the LORD (Proverbs 16:5)
	The Spirit reveals that those who are of a **perverse** heart are an abomination to the LORD (Proverbs 11:20), and are despised (Proverbs 12:8)
	A worthless person, a **wicked** <u>man</u>, has **perversity** in <u>his</u> heart and devises **evil** continually and <u>he</u> sows discord (Proverbs 6:12-14)
	The Spirit also reveals that "***deceit** is in the heart of those who devise **evil***" (Proverbs 12:20) and "*<u>he</u> who has a **deceitful** heart finds no **good**, and <u>he</u> who has a **perverse** tongue falls into **evil***" (Proverbs 17:20)
	Six things the LORD <u>hates</u>, and seven are an abomination to <u>Him</u>, one is "*a heart that devises **wicked** plans*" (Proverbs 6:16-18)
	"*The heart of the **wicked** is worth little*" (Proverbs 10:20)
	"*For these people **disguise** their **hatred** with their lips, and lays up **deceit** within themselves; when they speak kindly you are not to believe them for there are seven abominations in their heart. Though <u>his</u> **hatred** is covered by **deceit**, their **wickedness** will be revealed before the assembly*" (Proverbs 26:24-26)
	"*Those things which proceed out of the mouth come from the heart and they defile a <u>man</u>. For out of the heart proceed **evil** <u>thoughts</u>, **murders**, **adulteries**, <u>fornications</u>, **thefts**, **false** witness, blasphemies, <u>covetousness</u>, **wickedness**, **deceit**, **lewdness**, an **evil** eye, **pride**, **foolishness**. These are the things which defile a <u>man</u>, but to eat with unwashed hands does not defile a <u>man</u>.*" (Matthew 15:18-20 and Mark 7:20-22)
	"*But take heed to yourselves, lest your hearts be weighed down with <u>carousing</u>, <u>drunkenness</u>, and <u>cares of this life</u>, and that Day come on you unexpectedly. For it will come as a snare on all those who dwell on the face of the whole earth*" (Luke 21:34-35)
	"*One who trusts in <u>his</u> own heart is a **fool**, but whoever walks **wisely** will be delivered*" (Proverbs 28:26)
	"*The **wise** in heart will receive commands but a prating **fool** will fall*" (Proverbs 10:8)
	"*...the **fool**'s heart proclaims **foolishness***" (Proverbs 12:23) and "*The **foolishness** of a <u>man</u> twists <u>his</u> way, and <u>his</u> heart frets against the LORD*" (Proverbs 19:3)
	"*...what is in <u>his</u> heart is made known*" (Proverbs 14:33)
	"*...the heart of the **fool** does not disperse knowledge*" (Proverbs 15:7)
	"*The heart of <u>him</u> who has understanding seeks knowledge...*" (Proverbs 15:14) while "*The heart of the **righteous** studies how to answer...*" (Proverbs 15:28)
	"*The **wise** in heart will be called **prudent** and sweetness of the lips increases learning*" (Proverbs 16:21)
	"*The refining pot is for silver and the furnace for gold, but the LORD tests the hearts.*" (Proverbs 17:3)

The Heart ~ continued ~	"And as strict chastening cleanse away **evil** so does stripes cleanse the inner depths of the heart" (Proverbs 20:30)
	"As in water face reflects face, so a <u>man's</u> heart reveals the <u>man</u>." (Proverbs 27:19)
	"Do not eat the bread of a miser, nor desire <u>his</u> delicacies; for as <u>he</u> thinks in <u>his</u> heart, so is <u>he</u>. "Eat and drink!" <u>he</u> says to you, but <u>his</u> heart is not with you. The morsel you have eaten, you will vomit up, and waste your pleasant words" (Proverbs 23:6-8)
	"Do not let your heart **envy** sinners, but be zealous for the fear of the LORD all the day; for surely there is a hereafter, and your hope will not be cut off" (Proverbs 23:17-18)
	"Do not be **envious** of **evil** <u>men</u>, nor desire to be with them; for their heart devises **violence**, and their lips talk of troublemaking" (Proverbs 24:1-2)
	"Do not rejoice when your enemy falls, and do not let your heart be glad when <u>he</u> stumbles; lest the LORD see it, and it displease <u>Him</u>, and <u>He</u> turn away <u>His</u> wrath from <u>him</u>" (Proverbs 24:17-18)
	"The light of the eyes rejoices the heart" (Proverbs 15:30)
	"A sound heart is life to the body…" (Proverbs 14:30)
	"A merry heart does **good**…" (Proverbs 17:22)
	"All the days of the afflicted are **evil**, but <u>he</u> who is of a merry heart has a continual feast" (Proverbs 15:15)
	"A merry heart makes a cheerful countenance, but by sorrow of the heart the spirit is broken" (Proverbs 15:13)
	"<u>He</u> who <u>loves</u> purity of heart and has <u>grace</u> on <u>his</u> lips, the king will be <u>his</u> friend" (Proverbs 22:11)
	"Hope deferred makes the heart sick, but when the desire comes, it is a tree of life" Proverbs 13:12)
	"Anxiety in the heart of <u>man</u> causes **depression**, but a **good** word makes it glad" (Proverbs 12:25)
	"The heart knows its own **bitterness**…" (Proverbs 14:10)
	"…<u>he</u> who hardens <u>his</u> heart will fall into <u>calamity</u>" (Proverbs 28:14)
	Jesus states, "Blessed are the pure in heart, for they shall see God." (Matthew 5:8)
	"…it is **good** that the heart be established by <u>grace</u>, and not with foods which have not profited those who have been occupied with them" (Hebrews 13:8-9)
	To understand that, "…where their treasure is, there their heart will be also" (Matthew 6:19-21)
	"…out of the heart proceed **evil** thoughts, **murders, adulteries, fornications, thefts, false** witness, <u>blasphemies</u>. These are the things which defile a <u>man</u>, but to eat with unwashed hands does not defile a <u>man</u>" (Matthew 15:19-20)
	"Beware, brethren, lest there be in any of you an **evil** heart of unbelief in departing from the living God; but exhort one another daily, while it is called "Today," lest any of you be hardened through the **deceitfulness of sin**" (Hebrews 3:12-13)

The Heart ~ continued ~	Do not be like those who are <u>lovers</u> of money and justify themselves before <u>men</u>. "*For God knows the heart; and what is highly esteemed among <u>men</u> is an abomination in the sight of God*" (Luke 16:14-15)
	"*Brood of vipers! How can you, being **evil**, speak **good** things? For out of the abundance of the heart the mouth speaks. A **good** <u>man</u> out of the **good** treasure of <u>his</u> heart brings forth **good** things, and an **evil** <u>man</u> out of the **evil** treasure brings forth **evil** things*" (Matthew 12: 34-35)
	"*And by this we know that we are of the truth, and shall assure our hearts before <u>Him</u>. For if our heart condemns us, God is greater than our heart, and knows all things. Beloved, if our heart does not condemn us, we have confidence toward God*" (1 John 3:19-21)
	For the **ungodly** and **unrighteous**, God gives "*...them up to **uncleanness**, in the <u>lusts</u> of their hearts, to **dishonor** their bodies among themselves, who exchanged the truth of God for the **lie**, and worshiped and served the creature rather than the Creator, who is blessed forever.*" Amen. (Romans 1:24-25)
	"*...if you have bitter **envy** and self-seeking in your hearts, do not <u>boast</u> and **lie** against the truth. This <u>wisdom</u> does not descend from above, but is earthly, sensual, demonic*" (James 3:14-15)
	"*Be anxious for nothing, but in everything by prayer and supplication, with thanksgiving, let your requests be made known to God; and the peace of God, which surpasses all understanding, will guard your hearts and minds through Christ Jesus*" (Ephesians 4:6-7)
	"*A <u>man</u> will be satisfied with **good** by the fruit of <u>his</u> mouth, and the recompense of a <u>man's</u> hands will be rendered to <u>him</u>.*" (Proverbs 12:14)
The Hands	"*A <u>man</u> devoid of understanding shakes hands in a pledge, and becomes surety for <u>his</u> friend*" (Proverbs 17:18)
	"*My son, if you become surety for your friend, if you have shaken hands in pledge for a stranger, you are snared by the words of your mouth; you are taken by the words of your mouth. So do this, my son, and deliver yourself; for you have come into the hand of your friend: Go and humble yourself; plead with your friend. Give no sleep to your eyes, nor slumber to your eyelids. Deliver yourself like a gazelle from the hand of the hunter, and like a bird from the hand of the fowler*" (Proverbs 6:1-5)
	"*Do not be one of those who shakes hands in a pledge, one of those who is surety for debts; If you have nothing with which to pay, why should <u>he</u> take away your bed from under you?*" (Proverbs 22:26-27)
	"*The desire of the **lazy** <u>man</u> kills <u>him</u>, for <u>his</u> hands refuse to labor. <u>He</u> <u>covets</u> <u>greedily</u> all day long, but the **righteous** gives and does not spare.*" (Proverbs 21:25-26)
	"*The **lazy** <u>man</u> buries <u>his</u> hand in the bowl; it wearies <u>him</u> to bring it back to <u>his</u> mouth.*" (Proverbs 26:15)
	"*Hands that **shed innocent blood** are one of the six things the LORD hates, yes, seven are an abomination to Him*" (Proverbs 6:16)
	"*Put your hand on your mouth if you have been **foolish** in exalting yourself, or if you have devised **evil**" (Proverbs 30:32)
	"*<u>He</u> who sends a message by the hand of a **fool** cuts off <u>his</u> own feet and drinks violence*" (Proverbs 26:6)

The Hands ~ **continued** ~	*"My son, keep my words, and treasure my commands within you. Keep my commands and live, and my law as the apple of your eye. Bind them on your fingers..."* (Proverbs 7:1-3)
	"If your hand or foot causes you to sin, cut it off and cast it from you. It is better for you to enter into life lame or maimed, rather than having two hands or two feet, to be cast into the everlasting fire." (Matthew 18:7-8)
	*"...nor give place to the devil. Let <u>him</u> who **stole steal** no longer, but rather let <u>him</u> labor, working with <u>his</u> hands what is **good**, that <u>he</u> may have something to give <u>him</u> who has need"* (Ephesians 4:27-28)
	"...that you also aspire to lead a quiet life, to mind your own business, and to work with your own hands, as we commanded you, that you may walk properly toward those who are outside, and that you may lack nothing" (1 Thessalonians 4:11-12)
	"Do not lay hands on anyone hastily, nor share in other people's sins; keep yourself pure" (1 Timothy 5:22)
	"Therefore submit to God. Resist the devil and <u>he</u> will flee from you. Draw near to God and <u>He</u> will draw near to you. Cleanse your hands, you sinners; and purify your hearts, you double-minded" (James 4:7-8)
The Feet	*"<u>He</u> stores up sound wisdom for the **upright**; <u>He</u> is a shield to those who walk **uprightly**; He guards the paths of justice, and preserves the way of His saints"* (Proverbs 2:7-8)
	Understand that the *"feet that are swift in running to **evil**"* (Proverbs 6:18), are among *"six things the Lord <u>hates</u>, yes, seven are an abomination to Him"* (Proverbs 6:16-19)
	*"Also it is not **good** for a soul to be without knowledge and <u>he</u> sins who hastens with <u>his</u> feet."* (Proverbs 19:2)
	*"Do not be afraid of sudden terror, nor of trouble from the **wicked** when it comes; for the Lord will be your confidence, and will keep your foot from being caught"* (Proverbs 3:25-26)
	*"Ponder the path of your feet, and let all your ways be established. Do not turn to the right or the left; remove your foot from **evil**"* (Proverbs 4:26-27)
	*"Do not walk in the way with sinners who try to entice you, want to **steal** and **shed blood**. Keep your foot from their path; for their feet run to **evil**, and they make haste to **shed blood**"* (Proverbs 1:10-19)
	*"A worthless person, a **wicked** <u>man</u>, who walks with a **perverse** mouth. <u>He</u> winks with <u>his</u> eyes, shuffles <u>his</u> feet, and points with <u>his</u> fingers. **Perversity** is in <u>his</u> heart, <u>he</u> devises **evil** continually, and <u>he</u> sows discord"* (Proverbs 6:12-14)
	*"Seldom set foot in your **neighbor's** house, lest <u>he</u> become weary of you and **hate** you"* (Proverbs 25:17)
	*"A <u>man</u> who <u>flatters</u> <u>his</u> **neighbor** spreads a net for <u>his</u> feet"* (Proverbs 29:5)
	*"...whoever walks **wisely** will be delivered"* (Proverbs 28:26)
	"If your hand or foot causes you to sin, cut it off and cast it from you. It is better for you to enter into life lame or maimed, rather than having

	two hands or two feet, to be cast into the everlasting fire" (Matthew 18:7-9 and Mark 9:45)
	*"How beautiful are the feet of those who preach the gospel of <u>peace</u>, who bring glad tidings of **good** things!"* (Romans 10:14-16)
The Body	*"...**envy** is rottenness to the bones"* (Proverbs 14:30)
	"...a broken spirit dries the bones" (Proverbs 17:22)
	*"Do not be **wise** in your own eyes; fear the LORD and depart from **evil**. It will be health to your flesh and strength to your bones.* (Proverbs 3:7-8)
	*"The light of the eyes rejoices the heart, and a **good** report makes the bones healthy"* (Proverbs 15:30)
	"Pleasant words are like a honeycomb, sweetness to the soul and health to the bones." (Proverbs 16:24)
	"An excellent wife is the crown of her <u>husband</u>, but she who causes shame is like rottenness in <u>his</u> bones" (Proverbs 12:4)
	"My son, give attention to my words; incline your ear to my sayings. Do not let them depart from your eyes; keep them in the midst of your heart; for they are life to those who find them, and health to all their flesh" (Proverbs 4:20-22)
	"For those who live according to the flesh set their minds on the things of the flesh, but those who live according to the Spirit, the things of the Spirit. For to be carnally minded is death, but to be spiritually minded is life and <u>peace</u>. Because the carnal mind is enmity against God; for it is not subject to the law of God, nor indeed can be" (Romans 8:5-7)
	"I say then: Walk in the Spirit, and you shall not fulfill the <u>lust</u> of the flesh. For the flesh <u>lusts</u> against the Spirit, and the Spirit against the flesh; and these are contrary to one another, so that you do not do the things that you wish." (Galatians 5:16-17)
	"Or do you not know that your body is the temple of the Holy Spirit who is in you, whom you have from God, and you are not your own?" (1 Corinthians 6:19)
One's Conduct	*"The **wicked** have drawn the sword and have bent their bow, to cast down the **poor** and **needy**, to slay those who are of upright <u>conduct</u>"* (Psalm 37:14)
	"Whoever offers praise glorifies Me; and to <u>him</u> who orders <u>his</u> <u>conduct</u> aright I will show the salvation of God" (Psalm 50:23)
	"Moreover if your brother sins against you, go and tell <u>him</u> his fault between you and <u>him</u> alone. If he hears you, you have gained your brother" (Matthew 18:15)
	*"But you have not so learned Christ, if indeed you have heard Him and have been taught by Him, as the truth is in Jesus: that you put off, concerning your former <u>conduct</u>, the old <u>man</u> which grows corrupt according to the **deceitful** <u>lusts</u>, and be renewed in the spirit of your mind, and that you put on the new <u>man</u> which was created according to God, in true **righteousness** and holiness."* (Ephesians 4:20-24)
	"For you have heard of my former <u>conduct</u> in Judaism, how I persecuted the church of God beyond measure and tried to destroy it" (Galatians 1:13)

	*"Let no one despise your youth, but be an example to the believers in word, in <u>conduct</u>, in <u>love</u>, in spirit, in **faith**, in purity"* (1 Timothy 4:12)
	*"...having a **good** conscience, that when they defame you as **evildoers**, those who revile your **good** <u>conduct</u> in Christ may be ashamed"* (1 Peter 3:16)
	*"Only let your <u>conduct</u> be worthy of the gospel of Christ, so that whether I come and see you or am absent, I may hear of your affairs, that you stand fast in one spirit, with one mind striving together for the **faith** of the gospel..."* (Philippians 1:27)
	"...but if I am delayed, I write so that you may know how you ought to <u>conduct</u> yourself in the house of God, which is the church of the living God, the pillar and ground of the truth" (1 Timothy 3:15)
	"...among whom also we all once <u>conducted</u> ourselves in the <u>lusts</u> of our flesh, fulfilling the desires of the flesh and of the mind, and were by nature children of <u>wrath</u>, just as the others" (Ephesians 2:3)
	"Let your <u>conduct</u> be without <u>covetousness</u>; be content with such things as you have. For He Himself has said, "I will never leave you nor forsake you" (Hebrews 13:5)
One's Conduct ~ continued ~	*"Remember those who rule over you, who have spoken the word of God to you, whose **faith** follow, considering the outcome of their <u>conduct</u>"* (Hebrews 13:7)
	*"Who is **wise** and understanding among you? Let <u>him</u> show by **good** <u>conduct</u> that <u>his</u> works are done in the meekness of wisdom"* (James 3:13)
	"...but as He who called you is holy, you also be holy in all your <u>conduct</u>, because it is written, "Be holy, for I am holy." (1 Peter 1:15-16)
	*"...and delivered **righteous** Lot, who was **oppressed** by the **filthy** <u>conduct</u> of the **wicked**..."* (2 Peter 2:7)
	*"Therefore, since all these things will be dissolved, what manner of persons ought you to be in holy <u>conduct</u> and **godliness**..."* (2 Peter 3:11)
	*"For our boasting is this: the testimony of our conscience that we <u>conducted</u> ourselves in the world in simplicity and **godly** sincerity, not with fleshly wisdom but by the <u>grace</u> of God, and more abundantly toward you"* (2 Corinthians 1:12)
	"And if you call on the Father, who without <u>partiality</u> judges according to each one's work, <u>conduct</u> yourselves throughout the time of your stay here in <u>fear</u>; knowing that you were not redeemed with corruptible things, like silver or gold, from your aimless <u>conduct</u> received by tradition from your <u>fathers</u>..." (1 Peter 1:17-18)
	*"...having your <u>conduct</u> **honorable** among the Gentiles, that when they speak against you as **evildoers**, they may, by your **good** works which they observe, glorify God in the day of visitation"* (1 Peter 2:12)
One's Life	Then Jesus spoke to them again, saying, *"I am the light of the world. He who follows Me shall not walk in darkness, but have the light of life"* (John 8:11-13)
	Jesus said to <u>him</u>, *"I am the way, the truth, and the life. No one comes to the Father except through Me* (John 14:7)
	*"<u>He</u> who believes in the Son of God has the **witness** in <u>himself</u>; <u>he</u> who does not believe God has made Him a **liar**, because <u>he</u> has not believed

One's Life ~continued~	*the testimony that God has given of His Son. And this is the testimony: that God has given us eternal life, and this life is in His Son. <u>He</u> who has the Son has life; <u>he</u> who does not have the Son of God does not have life. These things I have written to you who believe in the name of the Son of God, that you may know that you have eternal life, and that you may continue to believe in the name of the Son of God."* (1 John 5:10-13)
	Jesus said, *"...do not worry about your life, what you will eat or what you will drink; nor about your body, what you will put on. Is not life more than food and the body more than clothing?"* (Matthew 6:25)
	"Take heed and beware of <u>covetousness</u> for one's life does not consist in the abundance of the things <u>he</u> possesses" (Luke 12:15)
	"So are the ways of everyone who is <u>greedy</u> for <u>gain</u>; it takes away the life of its owners" (Proverbs 1:19)

Table 170: God Desires <u>Man's</u> Complete Commitment

Total commitment affects the quality and quantity of work a <u>man</u> does for the Lord. Now this does not mean a <u>man</u> is justified by <u>his</u> works in the eyes of God. However, James eloquently explain how works and **faith** together please God in James 2: 14-24. Total commitment demonstrates one's **faith** in God. It is by this commitment, one appreciates Paul's word of, *"...whatever you do in word or deed, do all in the name of the Lord Jesus, giving thanks to God the Father through Him"* (Colossians 3:17). When a <u>man</u> is committed to God and is obedient to His will, <u>he</u> can *"...Walk in the Spirit, and you shall not fulfill the **lust** of the flesh"* (Galatians 5:16) and avoid God's <u>calamity</u>.

Finally, can a <u>man</u> or women know the will of God? Sure, they can. The Biblical record documents:

God's Will Is For You To:	What Is Documented
Be <u>Baptized</u>	*"And when all the people heard <u>Him</u>, even the tax collectors justified God, having been <u>baptized</u> with the <u>baptism</u> of John. But the Pharisees and lawyers <u>rejected the will of God</u> for themselves, not having been <u>baptized</u> by <u>him</u>"* (Luke 7:29-30)
Transform your way of thinking	*"And do not be conformed to this world, but be transformed by the renewing of your mind, that you may prove what is <u>that good and acceptable and perfect will of God</u>"* (Romans 12:2)
Be sanctified	*"For <u>this is the will of God</u>, your sanctification: that you should abstain from **sexual immorality**; that each of you should know how to possess <u>his</u> own vessel in sanctification and **honor**, not in passion of <u>lust</u>, like the Gentiles who do not know God; that no one should take advantage of and **defraud** <u>his</u> brother in this matter, because the Lord is the avenger of all such, as we also forewarned you and testified. For God did not call us to **uncleanness**, but in **holiness**. Therefore <u>he</u> who rejects <u>this</u> does not reject <u>man</u>, but God, who has also given us His Holy Spirit"* (1 Thessalonians 4:3-8)
Rejoice, pray, and give thanks	*"Rejoice always, pray without ceasing, in everything give thanks; <u>for this is the will of God</u> in Christ Jesus for you. Do not quench the Spirit. Do not*

	*despise prophecies. Test all things; hold fast what is **good**. Abstain from every form of **evil**"* (1 Thessalonians 5:16-22)
Submit and do **good**	"Therefore submit yourselves to every ordinance of <u>man</u> for the Lord's sake, whether to the king as supreme, or to governors, as to those who are sent by <u>him</u> for the punishment of **evildoers** and for the praise of those who do good. For <u>this is the will of God</u>, that by doing **good** you may put to silence the ignorance of **foolish** <u>men</u>— as free, yet not using liberty as a cloak for vice, but as bondservants of God. **Honor** all people. <u>Love</u> the brotherhood. <u>Fear</u> God. **Honor** the king"(1 Peter 2:15)
	"<u>For it is better, if it is the will of God</u>, to suffer for doing good than for doing **evil**" (1 Peter 3:17)
	"Therefore let those who suffer <u>according to the will of God</u> commit their souls to Him in doing **good**, as to a **faithful** Creator" (1 Peter 4:19)

Table 171: God's Will

Thus, to close this chapter, here are the rest of the facts from the Bible for one who desires to know God's will:

1. We must understand and embrace the fact that Jesus said, "*For <u>whoever does the will of God</u> is My brother and My sister and mother*" (Mark 3:35)

2. Jesus suffered and died for this cause: "*Therefore, since Christ suffered for us in the flesh, arm yourselves also with the same mind, for <u>he</u> who has suffered in the flesh has ceased from sin, that <u>he</u> no longer should live the rest of <u>his</u> time in the flesh for the <u>lusts</u> of <u>men</u>, but for <u>the will of God</u>. For we have spent enough of our past lifetime in doing the will of the Gentiles—when we walked in <u>lewdness</u>, <u>lusts</u>, <u>drunkenness</u>, <u>revelries</u>, <u>drinking parties</u>, and <u>abominable</u> **idolatries***" (1 Peter 4:1-3)

3. Jesus helps those who embrace Him and makes intercessions to God on their behalf as they try to be obedient to His Word. The Bible 'documents, "*Now He who searches the hearts knows what the mind of the Spirit is, because He makes intercession for the saints <u>according to the will of God</u>*" (Romans 8:27)

4. When we commit to Christ, we become His bondservants to <u>do God's will</u>. The Bible documents, "*Bondservants, be obedient to those who are your masters according to the flesh, with fear and trembling, in sincerity of heart, as to Christ; not with eyeservice, as <u>men</u>-pleasers, but as <u>bondservants of Christ, doing the will of God from the heart</u>, with **goodwill** doing service, as to the Lord, and not to <u>men</u>, knowing that whatever **good** anyone does, <u>he</u> will receive the same from the Lord, whether <u>he</u> is a slave or free*" (Ephesians 6:6)

5. If we endure in this lifetime, God will reward us in the life to come. The Bible documents:

    - "*Therefore do not cast away your confidence, which has great reward. For you have need of endurance, so that <u>after you have done the will of God</u>, you may receive the promise...*" (Hebrews 10:35-36)

"*And the world is passing away, and the <u>lust</u> of it; but <u>he who does the will of God abides forever</u>*" (1 John 2:17)

CHAPTER XI: A View of the Spiritual Battlefield and the Complicated Nature of Spiritual Warfare

"Woe to the world because of offenses! For offenses must come, but woe to that man by whom the offense comes!"

~ Matthew 18:7 ~

BTT allows one to visualize the greatest war campaign ever conceived. It is taking place before our very eyes. Unfortunately, because of the mass rejection of God, the Bible, and spiritual warfare's growth, very few people can *discern* the elements of this war. Religious communities are spiritually lost in the fog of the negative attributes generated from the dawn of creation. This fog has stripped these communities of *discernment* and is now bleeding into many of Christ's *churches* today. Because this war is spiritual, many people ignorantly offer their souls to Satan as bounty. They do not understand that they are active participants in a war governed by spiritual forces that can influence their behaviors, attitudes, and words. Because of spiritual blindness, people become collateral damage and are lost by their own rejection of God's complete revelation.

In the beginning of this book, I stated that in every corner of the world, heinous and incomprehensible acts of **wickedness, evil, perversion**, and corruption are being conceived, in progress, or being completed. I emphasized that taking a human life for some people is no different from killing an animal for sport. I stated, that there are others who lack respect for any form of flesh and their behavior and attitude defy both reason and understanding. I stated that there are random acts of kindness from time to time, but I emphasized that people influenced by the **wicked**, **evil**, and **perverse** attributes dominate and disrupt the sanctity of the home as whole communities unravel. I also talked about corruption in the legal system by judges and lawyers influenced by the negative attributes and their roles in the war campaign through. Two Biblical examples from the Old Testament documents their impact today:

- *"Because the sentence against an **evil** work is not executed speedily, therefore the heart of the sons of men is fully set in them to do **evil**. Though a sinner does **evil** a hundred times, and his days are prolonged, yet I surely know that it will be well with those who fear God, who fear before Him. But it will not be well with the **wicked**; nor will he prolong his days, which are as a shadow, because he does not fear before God"* (Ecclesiastes 8:11-13)

- *"That they may successfully do **evil** with both hands— The prince asks for gifts, the judge seeks a bribe, and the great man utters his **evil** desire; so they scheme together"* (Micah 7:3)

I have discussed the impact that these things have on the world's most precious population - our children. Children exposed to despicable adult behavior are corrupted and their visions of a hopeful future destroyed. The things that served as cornerstones of truth, nobility, justice, purity, love, **good** reporting, virtuosity, and praiseworthiness have been twisted to appear bad or *false*. The Biblical record documented that this would happen when the Lord told Isaiah, *"Woe to those who call **evil good**, and **good evil**; who put darkness for light, and light for darkness; who put bitter for sweet, and sweet for bitter!"* (Isaiah 5:20). This Scripture helps one to put in perspective what Wisdom revealed to Solomon about, *"...a generation that curses its father, and does not bless its mother. There is a generation that is pure in its own eyes, yet is not washed from its **filthiness**. There is a generation—oh, how **lofty** are their eyes! And their eyelids are lifted up. There is a generation whose teeth are like swords, and whose fangs are like knives, to devour the **poor** from off the earth, and the **needy** from among men"* (Proverbs 30:11-14). BTT allows one to see that when children become corrupt at a young age, one can know what the future will hold as they get older and are placed in charge. Do not be ***deceived*** by the strategies of the negative attributes and spiritual warfare.

I also stated that **counselors**, psychologist, psychiatrist, and mental wellness professionals have proven themselves powerless in this world of deteriorating human conditions. Their ignorance and or dismissal of how God designed mankind along with the interaction of the human mind, blood, inner spirit, and soul, simply aids the advancement of the negative forces. More importantly, the greatest fault lies at the door of the religious community. The world's ignorance of the greatest war campaign ever conceived lies with people who have ***falsely*** proclaimed and misused God's Word. Remember, the negative attributes love to influence people blessed with leadership skills. Religious leaders with leadership skills, charisma, and knowledge who give in to the negative attributes, aid in the perpetuation of the war campaign. They establish thousands of religious organizations with diverse messages supposedly from the one Biblical source. Some *false* religious leaders even write their own Bibles. There *lies* not only dilute God's Truth to humanity, but they ***deceive*** and divide people generation after generation. Generations of people come to believe that they are in charge of life and they are not accountable to God. This ***ungodly*** belief results in a leadership void with followers completely estranged from God. These *false* religious leaders become teachers who conveniently exploit humanity through social media outlets that broadcast error simultaneously and continuously. This scandalous practice has bolstered spiritual warfare to unfathomable levels. Today, as it was in the past, *false* teachers are peddling *false*, confused, and twisted messages from the Gospel through spiritual warfare. Paul spoke of these people to the church in Corinth when he stated, *"For we are not, as so many, peddling the word of God..."* (2 Corinthians 2:17).

BTT allows one to see that without the correct teaching of God's Word, there can be no <u>peace</u> in the world. Without God's Word, <u>peace</u> will always remain an elusive conundrum while <u>strife</u>, chaos, ***oppression***, and ***violence*** dominate the world scene. The god of this age (2 Corinthians 4:4) pushes topics like racial injustice, politics, financial iniquities, sexual and gender identity, judicial paralysis, and the like over the teachings of God's Word. Drug and alcohol abuse escalates as ***immorality*** of all kinds proportionally destroys homes and families. Moreover, prison and jail construction increases as the compromised legal system quenches the appetites of people influenced by the ***wicked***, ***evil***, ***perverse***, and ***haters*** attributes. BTT allows one to see the truth behind all of these things when one opens God's Word and investigates the Creator of the universe's handiwork and His design to preempt man's ***perversion***. Until then, these Biblical Truths will stand on their own merit :

- *"For the time will come when they will not endure sound doctrine, but according to their own desires, because they have itching ears, they will heap up for themselves teachers; and they will turn their ears away from the truth, and be turned aside to fables"* (2 Timothy 4:3-4)

- *"...Jesus Christ, who gave Himself for our sins, that He might deliver us from this present **evil** age, according to the will of our God and Father..."* (Galatians 1:4)

- *"...take up the whole armor of God, that you may be able to withstand in the **evil** day, and having done all, to stand"* (Ephesians 6:13)

- *"...not all have **faith**. But the Lord is **faithful**, who will establish you and guard you from the **evil** one..."* (2 Thessalonians 3:1-4)

- *"Woe to you lawyers! For you have taken away the key of knowledge. You did not enter in yourselves, and those who were entering in you hindered"* (Luke 11:52)

- *"...many walk, of whom I have told you often, and now tell you even weeping, that they are the enemies of the cross of Christ: whose end is destruction, whose god is their belly, and whose glory is in their shame—who set their mind on earthly things"* (Philippians 3:18-19)

- *"...many deceivers have gone out into the world who do not confess Jesus Christ as coming in the flesh. This is a deceiver and an antichrist. Look to yourselves, that we do not lose those things we worked for, but that we may receive a full reward. Whoever transgresses and does not abide in the doctrine of Christ does not have God. He who abides in the doctrine of Christ has both the Father and the Son. If anyone comes to you and does not bring this doctrine, do not receive him into your house nor greet him; for he who greets him shares in his **evil** deeds"* (2 John 1:7-11)

BTT helps one to understand that the times are **evil** according to Galatians 1:4. However, God is ***faithful*** and still desires, *"...a chosen generation, a royal priesthood, a holy nation, His own special people, that you may proclaim the praises of Him who called you out of darkness into His marvelous light..."* (1 Peter 2:9). God's people are to be different from the world's people in behavior, speech, appearance, actions, and priorities. God's people are to exemplify what is ***good*** so that people caught up in sin have examples to see when they desire to change their lives. How can a person know what to look for if everyone's behavior around them resembles their own? Moreover, how can one know there is a ***godly*** standard if a Christian behaves, walks, talks, and looks just like the people in sin? BTT allows one to see that Satan's people are tied down by the negative attributes and *"...lies under the sway..."* (1 John 5:19) of him. Satan's forces are massive in number because religious organizations on the spiritual battlefield are running assembly lines that convert people to the negative side of the war with entertainment, promises of prosperity (primarily money), and motivational speaking activities sprinkled with God's Word.

With all of this said, society is left hemorrhaging through corruption and **violence** perpetrated by the influence of the negative forces at the highest levels of religious enterprise and governments in every nation. However, one can slow down and possibly stop the hemorrhage in some locations. I say some locations because some religious practices will keep some locations closed to God's Truth. No human can stop the war campaign itself because the Biblical record declares, "*...the whole world lies under the sway of the **wicked** one*" (1 John 5:19). This part is absolute. However, one can come out from under the "*sway*". Defensive pockets on the spiritual battlefield can have major impacts on the outcome of the campaign for the souls of many combatants. These defensive pockets are pockets of Truth that contain people equipped with God's True Word and are dedicated to advancing the True Gospel on the battlefield. These are the people who strive to maintain the balance of the spiritual war by keeping it from tilting completely in the favor of the negative forces. Consider the next series of graphics specifically developed to help one see the entire spiritual war campaign and the solution for ensuring one's safety and salvation.

To begin with, consider this familiar graphic – **Figure 39**. The war campaign operates around a person's life starting from birth. This does not mean or imply a baby, toddler, or a child sins. A baby, toddler, or a child may do things that one may perceive as right or wrong, but until they are able to understand cognitively the difference between right and wrong, they simply react to positive or negative stimuli from the environment. This is where two parents play a vital role in God's plan. He **requires** parents united guidance for nurturing and shaping the growth, development, and personality of a baby, toddler, and a child. In time, as the child

Figure 39: Man and Woman in the Home

grows, he or she will reach an age of accountability; a time when he or she can understand right from wrong based on the teaching of the parents or others that have come into their lives. Parents are the first line of defense in the war campaign. They have the **godly** responsibility to teach and "*Train up a child in the way he should go, and when he is old he will not depart from it*" (Proverbs 22:6). This includes discipline. The Spirit of wisdom revealed to Solomon numerous pearls of wisdom about discipline in the home and the outcome when discipline is not applied. Here are a variety of those pearls for one to consider through the lens of spiritual warfare:

"*...keep your father's command, and do not forsake the law of your mother*" (Proverbs 6:20)	"*...A **wise** son makes a glad father, but a **foolish** son is the grief of his mother*" (Proverbs 10:1)	"*A **wise** son heeds his father's instruction, but a **scoffer** does not listen to rebuke*" (Proverbs 13:1)
"*A **fool** despises his father's instruction, but he who receives correction is **prudent***" (Proverbs 15:5)	"***Foolishness** is bound up in the heart of a child; the rod of correction will drive it far from him*" (Proverbs 22:15)	"*Listen to your father who begot you, and **do not despise** your mother when she is old*" (Proverbs 23:22)

"A **foolish** son is a grief to his father, and bitterness to her who bore him" (Proverbs 17:25)	"A **foolish** son is the ruin of his father…" (Proverbs 19:13)	"Even a child is known by his deeds, whether what he does is pure and right" (Proverbs 20:11)
"Do not withhold correction from a child, for if you beat him with a rod, he will not die" (Proverbs 23:13)	"The **righteous** man walks in his integrity; his children are blessed after him" (Proverbs 20:7)	"Whoever curses his father or his mother, his lamp will be put out in deep darkness" (Proverbs 20:20)
"A **wise** son makes a father glad, but a **foolish** man despises his mother" (Proverbs 15:20)	"There is a generation that **curses** its father, and does not bless its mother" (Proverbs 30:11)	"He who begets a **scoffer** does so to his sorrow, and the father of a **fool** has no joy" (Proverbs 17:21)
"The father of the **righteous** will greatly rejoice, and he who begets a **wise** child will delight in him" (Proverbs 23:24)	"Let your father and your mother be glad, and let her who bore you rejoice" (Proverbs 23:25)	"Whoever keeps the law is a discerning son, but a companion of gluttons shames his father" (Proverbs 28:7)
	"Whoever loves wisdom makes his father rejoice, but a companion of **harlots** wastes his wealth" (Proverbs 29:3)	"The rod and rebuke give wisdom, but a child left to himself brings shame to his mother" (Proverbs 29:15)
"Whoever **robs** his father or his mother, and says, 'It is no transgression,' the same is companion to a **destroyer**" (Proverbs 28:24)	"The eye that **mocks** his father, and **scorns** obedience to his mother, the ravens of the valley will pick it out, and the young eagles will eat it" (Proverbs 30:17)	"He who mistreats his father and chases away his mother is a son who causes shame and brings reproach" (Proverbs 19:26)

Table 172: Pearls of Wisdom Concerning the Home and Spiritual Warfare

The greatest positive influence on a child is a home that provides a secure, loving, and **godly** environment. This is exactly why Moses commanded the children of Israel from the Lord to, *"Hear, O Israel: The Lord our God, the Lord is one! You shall love the Lord your God with all your heart, with all your soul, and with all your strength. "And these words which I command you today shall be in your heart. You shall teach them diligently to your children, and shall talk of them when you sit in your house, when you walk by the way, when you lie down, and when you rise up. You shall bind them as a sign on your hand, and they shall be as frontlets between your eyes. You shall write them on the doorposts of your house and on your gates"* (Deuteronomy 6:4-9). Parents today must take a similar approach with God's Word to prepare their children for spiritual warfare and the war campaign itself. For if the home is dysfunctional, the war campaign begins around the child and the negative attribute's influence through the parents will shape the child's behavior, attitude, and personality. As a child comes in contact with family members, friends, other authority figures, and social media (including games, television, and radio), the positive or negative influences on that child becomes profound. Thus, **Figure 40** documents a family's spiritual journey at the macro level as

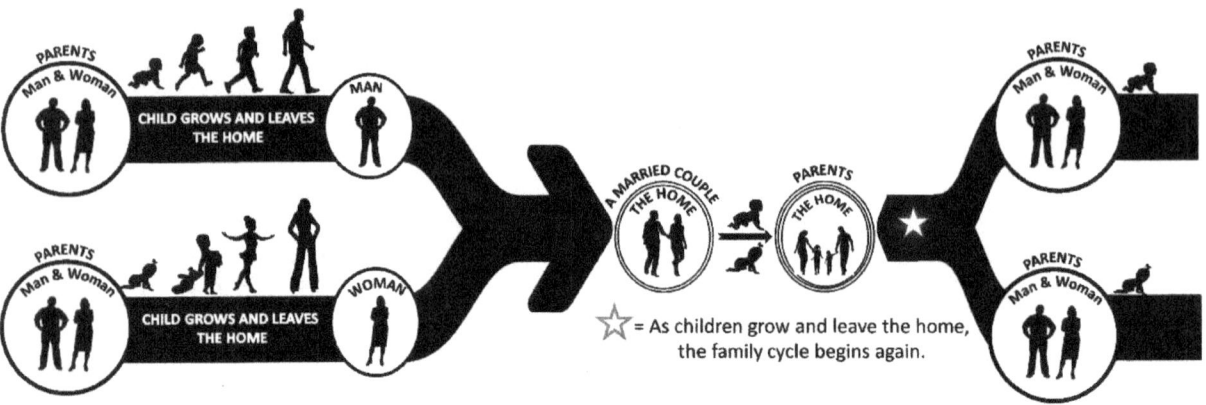

Figure 40: Parents: The Beginning of the Spiritual Journey

children are born and start the cycle of the home again. BTT allows one to see how everything starts in the home. Here is an important point I do not want one to miss. When a man and woman come together, whether they marry or not, **IF** they produce a child, they are accountable for that child together. They both have the responsibility to teach that child in the way he or she should go according to Proverbs 22:6 and Ephesians 6:4. The Biblical record never gives a parent the authority to abdicate this responsibility. When one does, the parent that abdicates his or her responsibility, regardless of the situation, remain in sin until they complete their responsibilities. In fact, the Biblical record documents, *"But if anyone does not provide for his own, and especially for those of his household, he has denied the **faith** and is worse than an unbeliever"* (1 Timothy 5:8)". The King James Version of the Bible calls this unbeliever an "infidel." I strongly agree. One's abdication of his or her responsibilities to a child places the child in the crosshairs of the negative forces. Moreover, abdication of responsibility almost guarantees the child's deferment to the negative forces of the war campaign as he or she comes of age. Jesus strictly warned parents, and all who may have a part of that child's life, *"...whoever causes one of these little ones who believe in Me to stumble, it would be better for him if a millstone were hung around his neck, and he were thrown into the sea"* (Matthew 18:6; Mark 9:42; Luke 17:2). For as children reach an age of accountability, they begin the full struggle against the negative forces of the war campaign with whatever measure of preparation they received from within the home.

When a man and a woman come together, regardless of having children or not, their involvement in the war campaign has already begun. Remember, when the Biblical record documented that God said, *"...a man shall leave his father and mother and be joined to his wife, and they shall become one flesh"* (Genesis 2:24), something spiritual begins when they unite in marriage. Marriage itself is more than just two fleshly bodies coming together. Something else occurs that is beyond human comprehension which involves the inner spirits of both people. BTT allows one to see the strong application of Solomon's wisdom where he stated, *"Two are better than one, because they have a good reward for their labor. For if they fall, one will lift up his companion. But woe to him who is alone when he falls, for he has no one to help him up"* (Ecclesiastes 4:9-10). However, this union also brings more attacks from spiritual warfare because the negative attributes do not want the union of the couple's inner spirits to succeed. Their choices in life become even more critical because they must take into consideration each other's needs. The best start that a couple can ever have when facing spiritual warfare is to have their inner spirits fortified with God's Word prior to marriage. Why? Because the negative attributes will make a special effort to divide and destroy what God desires to be together. If Satan destroys the family through divorce, separation, child neglect, finances, drugs and alcohol abuse, and on and on, then winning in spiritual warfare becomes easier. Convincing families there is not a God, or there is no reason to believe His Word, or even to confuse families in what they believe, guarantees Satan a win.

Figure 41 illustrates that the negative attribute surrounds the parents, as well as the children, both within the home and once any of them leave the home. The negative attributes attempt to influence and pick off someone every day to destroy the home. One's day-to-day interactions with other people, social media, and time and circumstance, provides opportunities to bombard the home with negative attributes.

Generally, the average person is totally unaware of the negative attribute's influence. Most people believe that bad things just happen. This belief is far from true. The reality is, the day-to-day operations of people's

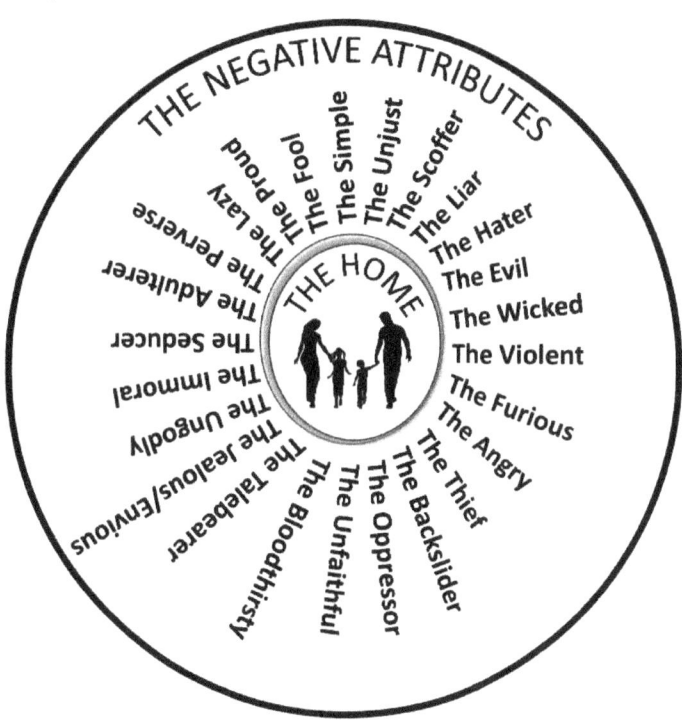

Figure 41: Some of the Negative Attributes Attacking the Home

lives consume them while they perceive they are in control of the choices they make. This perception thrives from the time one wakes up until one lies down. However, the truth is that every time a person encounters another human being, he or she is actually exposed to whatever positive or negative attributes are influencing that person's behavior, attitude, or words upon contact. Let this sink in for a minute. Consider **Figure 42**.

In **Figure 42**, the male and female silhouettes are unimportant. They can represent anyone. The focus is on the interaction of a person when contact is made with another person and the positive or negative attributes' influences at the time of contact with another person.

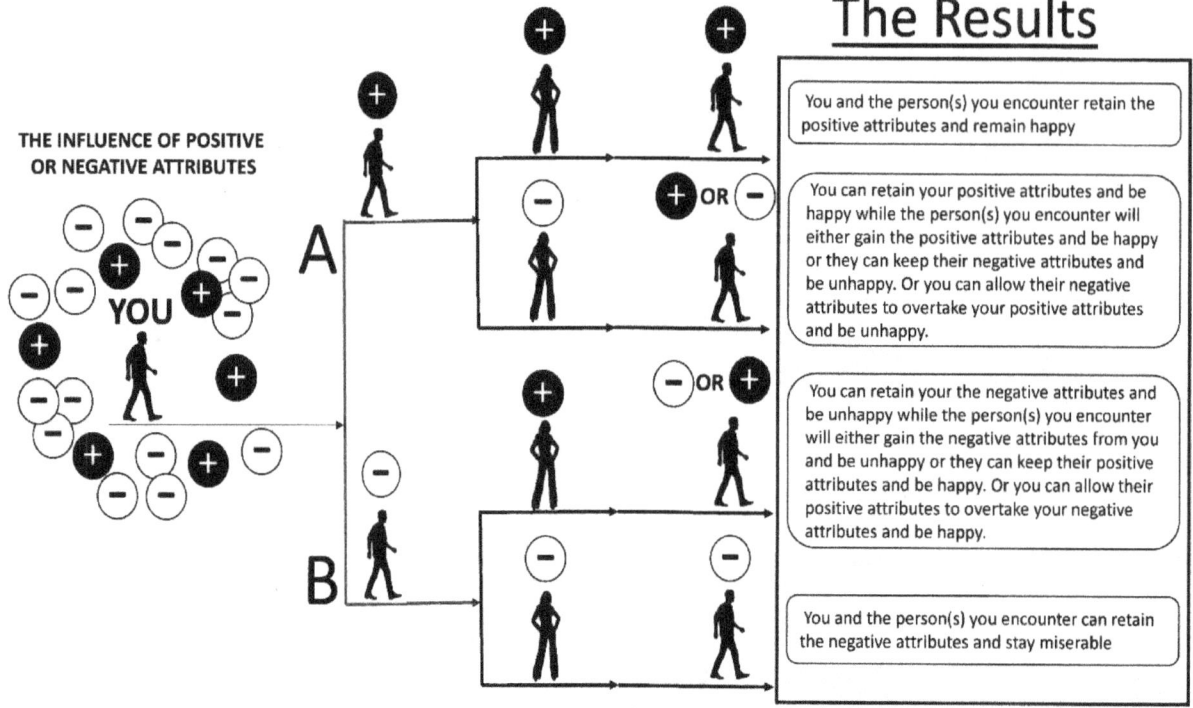

Figure 42: The Daily Interaction of the Influence of the Positive or Negative Attributes

When contact is broken, each person carries their same or a changed behavior to the next new encounter. This reality gets even more complicated than **Figure 41** depicts when groups of people are involved. Moreover, the Gospel writers documented a greater number of things on the negative path of life to cause people to stumble. **Figure 43** documents this.

Figure 43 illustrates that a person, and even the family, is under constant spiritual assault. This assault comes from spiritual warfare and is why BTT and _discernment_ are paramount. When Paul documented that one must, "..._not be conformed to this world, but be transformed by the renewing of your mind, that you may prove what is that **good** and acceptable and perfect will of God_" (Romans 12:2), he was talking about a spiritual transformation that opens one's eyes to the truth of the Gospel and all that it contains, including spiritual warfare, earthly chaos, and the masquerading of **_false_** teacher's works and deeds. Hence, the Biblical record contains God's answer for seeing the present world as it truly is and saving one's soul from condemnation. In addition to all the items depicted in **Figure 43**, there are two other elements that play a significant role in the spiritual war campaign. People often misunderstand the impact of _strife_ and _calamity_. In fact, secular **counselors**, psychologists, psychiatrists, and academics only inflame the spiritual situation occurring in the home when they try to resolve issues without God's Word. Remember, many of the negative attributes cause _strife_. This element by itself can destroy families, churches, and communities. God Himself uses _calamity_, on the other hand, to get one's attention. There are levels of **wickedness** and **evil**

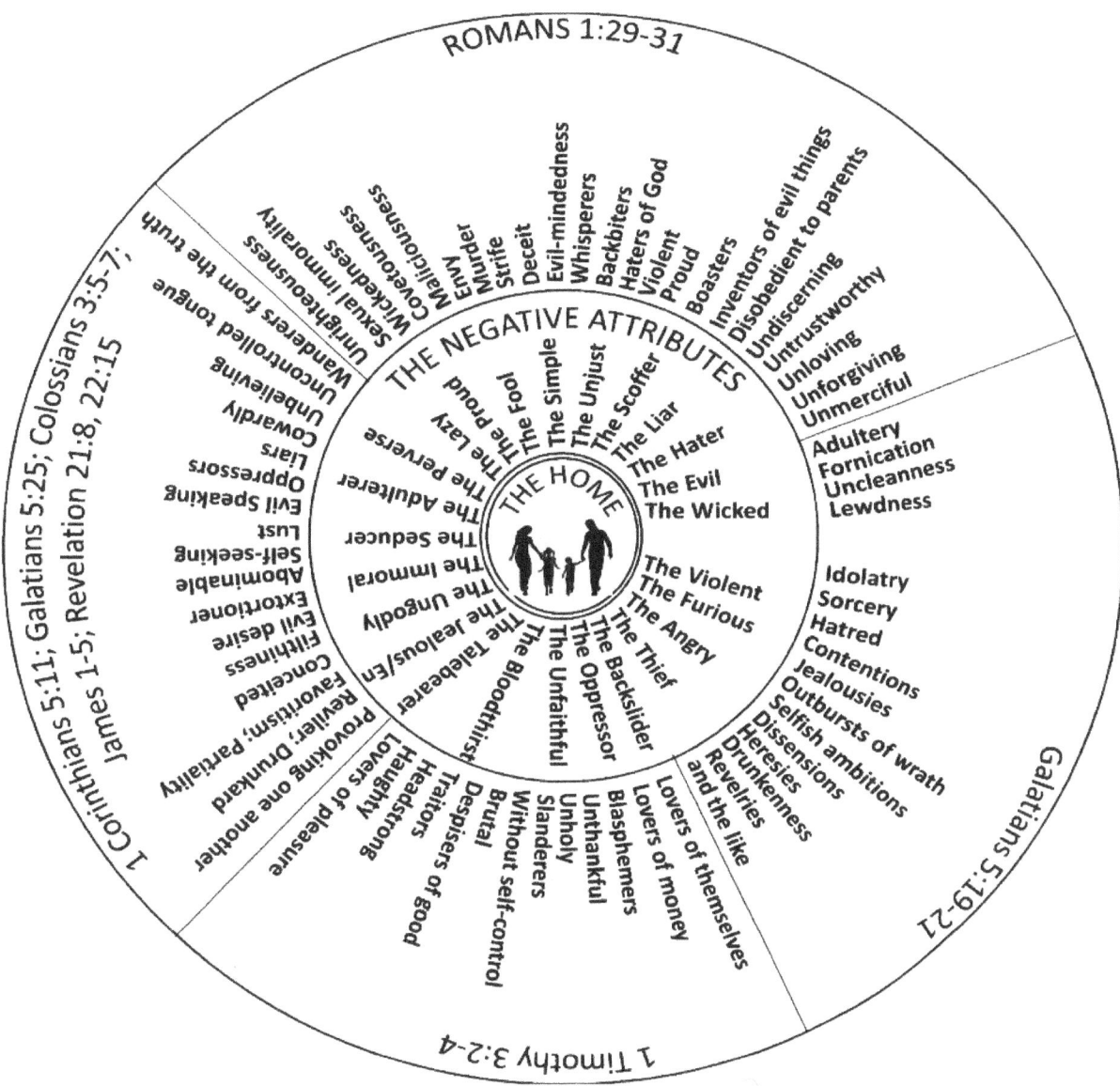

Figure 43: All the Negative Influences from the Biblical Record Against the Home

that tilt the war campaign in favor of the negative forces. When this happens, I believe God acts to bring the world's spiritual scale back into balance simply because He decides it is not the time to completely destroy the world and bring an end to the war campaign. This thought is based on Jesus' own statement of "...*that day and hour no one knows, not even the angels of heaven, but My Father only*" (Matthew 24:36; Mark 13:32). BTT is necessary to understand and <u>*discern*</u> the interactions between the spiritual and physical realms. **Figure 44** depicts everything stated thus far. BTT allows one to see that there is no real boundary between the home and a nation when it comes to the attributes influence.

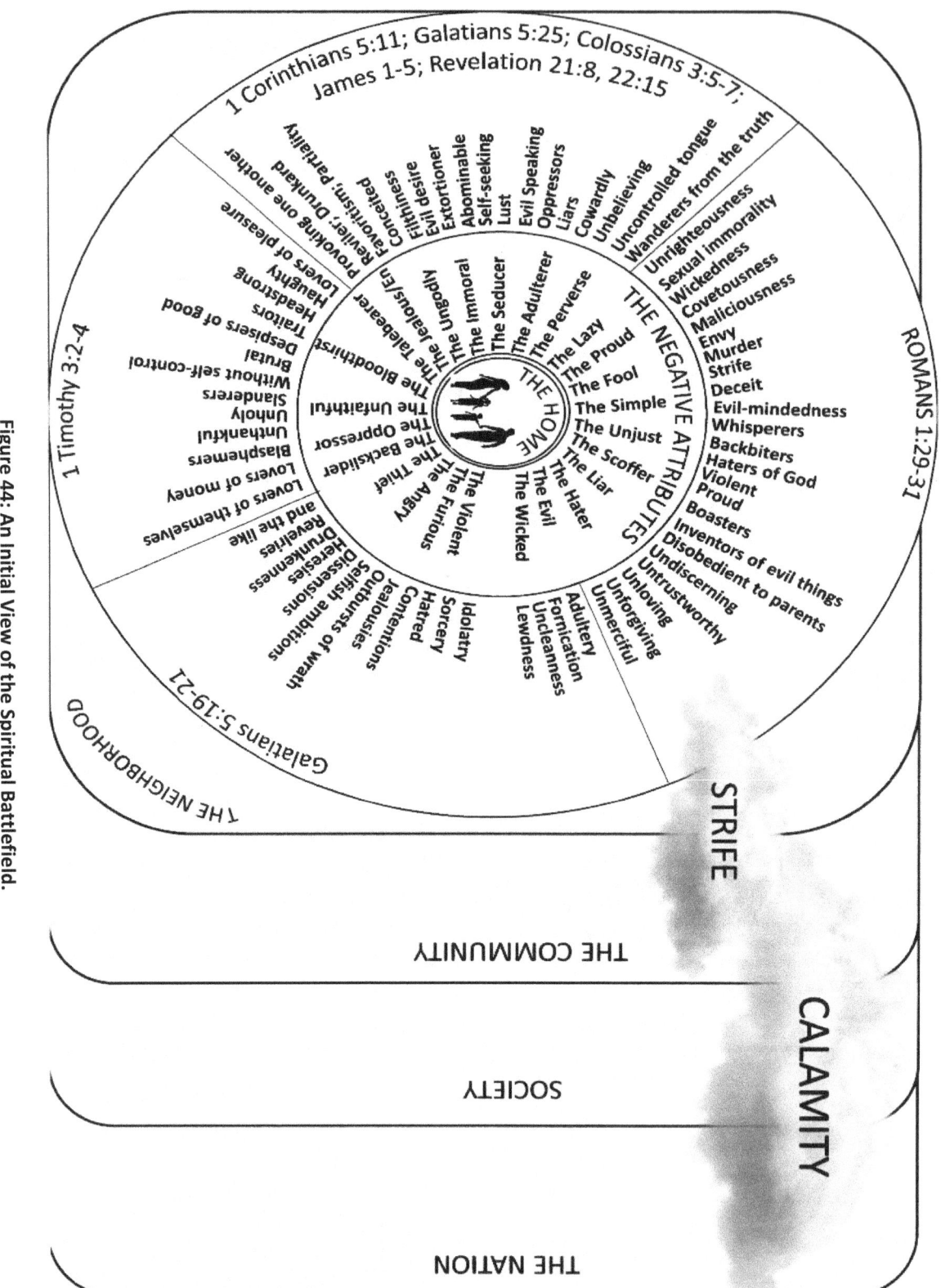

Figure 44: An Initial View of the Spiritual Battlefield.

With this big picture in mind, now consider that God in His infinite wisdom placed an entity on earth designed to disrupt the war campaign. For this entity to function properly, it must follow a pattern that He established. God's Son, Jesus Christ, established the church on earth which provides people a place to come to worship Him, learn "*...all things that pertain to life and godliness*" (2 Peter 1:3), and be saved. This is the very entity of which Jesus said, "*I will build My church, and the gates of Hades shall not prevail against it*" (Matthew 16:18). **Figure 45** depicts the Lord's church in its simplest form. Chapter XII explains Christ's church in more detail. For now, know that when it is functioning correctly, families are taught the Gospel which contains wisdom about God, His Son, the

Figure 45: The Lord's Church on the Spiritual Battlefield

Holy Spirit, the Biblical record, spiritual warfare, and salvation. From the church, the Gospel also teaches one how to withstand the negative attribute's assaults on both one's physical person and the family. This church is unique in that it serves as "*...the house of God, which is the church of the living God, the pillar and ground of the truth*" (1 Timothy 3:15). It serves a community of people who submit to the pattern provided in the New Testament by God's Holy Word. The church dedicates itself not only to the Truth about salvation, but also to the training and preparation of individuals and families for the war campaign in their local area of the spiritual battlefield. This is a very important point to understand. The religious community has failed in this area by teaching the doctrines of men (Matthew 15:9; Mark 7:7; Ephesians 4:14; Colossians 2:22) and their own traditions (Matthew 15:3; 15:6; Mark 7:8-9; 7:13; Colossians 2:8; 1 Peter 1:18) over God's Word. ***False*** teachers "*...seeking to establish their own **righteousness**, have not submitted to the **righteousness** of God*" (Roman 10:3). Paul warned Timothy, "*...the things that you have heard from me among many **witnesses**, commit these to **faithful** men who will be able to teach others also*" (2 Timothy 2:2). Paul understood spiritual warfare and the battlefield where the war rages. To understand the interaction of the Lord's church, **Figure 46** depicts the church on the spiritual battlefield interacting with people who are **added to** it according to Acts 2:41. The ratio of families and single people in the Lord's church is unknown and is not important. What is important is the fact that there are hundreds of His churches worldwide on the spiritual battlefield that are staying true to the original pattern of Christ's church established in the Book of Acts. These are people influenced by the ***faithful*** attribute who teach "*...wholesome words, even the words of our Lord Jesus Christ, and to the doctrine

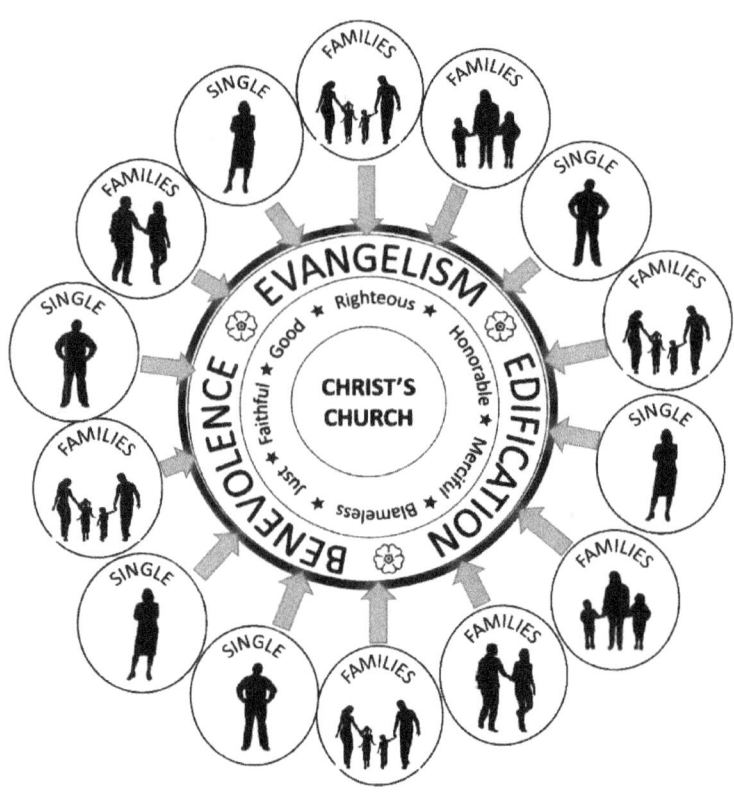

Figure 46: People Added to Christ's Church

which accords with godliness..." (1 Timothy 6:3). Moreover, these are the remnant of people who fully embrace Paul's inspired word from the Holy Spirit that they "*..are no longer strangers and foreigners, but fellow citizens with the saints and members of the household of God, having been built on the foundation of the apostles and prophets, Jesus Christ Himself being the chief cornerstone, in whom the whole building, being fitted together, grows into a holy temple in the Lord, in whom you also are being built together for a dwelling place of God in the Spirit*" (Ephesians 2:19-22). No race or nationally is excluded from Christ's church.

Hence, the importance of the Lord's church in the community cannot be understated. These pillars of Truth are supported by the power of God, and they train and prepare saints who pray regularly to combat all who "*...judge **unjustly**, and show partiality to the **wicked**...They do not know, nor do they understand; they walk about in **darkness**; all the foundations of the earth are unstable*" (Psalm 82:1-5). These saints know that, "*...The effective, fervent prayer of a **righteous** man avails much*" (James 5:16). The power of their prayers defy science and logic and helps to stabilize the foundations of the earth until Jesus returns.

The Lord's church follows an organizational pattern. The pattern consists of elders, deacons, teachers and a minister to preach the word of God. When members of the body are working, learning, maturing, and applying God's Word, then the dynamics of the war campaign are significantly impacted. As a collective body, the church prepares people to go out and fight the **good** spiritual fight with the proper spiritual equipment as outlined in Ephesians 6:10-18 and the proper mental attitude as outlined in Philippians 4:8-9. These people do not blend into the community; they stand out! Churches that blend into the community and look and sound like the secular community surrounding them, cannot offer any hope to the people they are trying to change to a **godly** standard. Jesus said, "*Do not love the world or the things in the world. If anyone loves the world, the love of the Father is not in him. For all that is in the world—the lust of the flesh, the lust of the eyes, and the pride of life—is not of the Father but is of the world*" (1 John 2:15-16). BTT allows one to see that God's way is different. The negative attributes have **deceived** many people by espousing a strategy that has churches mirroring the communities so much that the behavior and attitudes within the church are identical to the community they serve. These churches belong to the men and women that built them. These are not the Lord's *churches* found in His Holy Word. God's people are set apart, *"...a chosen generation, a royal priesthood, a holy nation, His own special people, that you may proclaim the praises of Him who called you out of darkness into His marvelous light..."* (1 Peter 2:9) and are not to be, *"...conformed to this world, but be transformed by the renewing of your mind, that you may prove what is that **good** and acceptable and perfect will of God"* (Romans 12:2). Religious organizations and churches that desire to reflect the physical community in which they operate, fail to understand spiritual warfare and *discernment*. **God never, anywhere in His Word, ever told anyone or any of His *churches* to mimic the world to gain followers for Him**. BTT allows one to see that religious leaders that take their congregations in this direction are serving the negative forces of the campaign. The congregants that support these establishments have no ability to transform their minds as God commands. Peter documented, *"but as He who called you is holy, you also be holy in all your conduct, because it is written, "Be holy, for I am holy"* (1 Peter 1:15-16). Christians are to be holy. This means Christ's *church* is to be holy. And if the *church* is to be holy, then it cannot conform to the standards of the world just to lure people inside under the pretext of teaching the Truth. Do not be ***deceived*** by this strategy employed by the negative forces. **Figure 47** depicts Christ's *church* and its standout mission on the spiritual battlefield. Chapter XIII will cover this mission in detail.

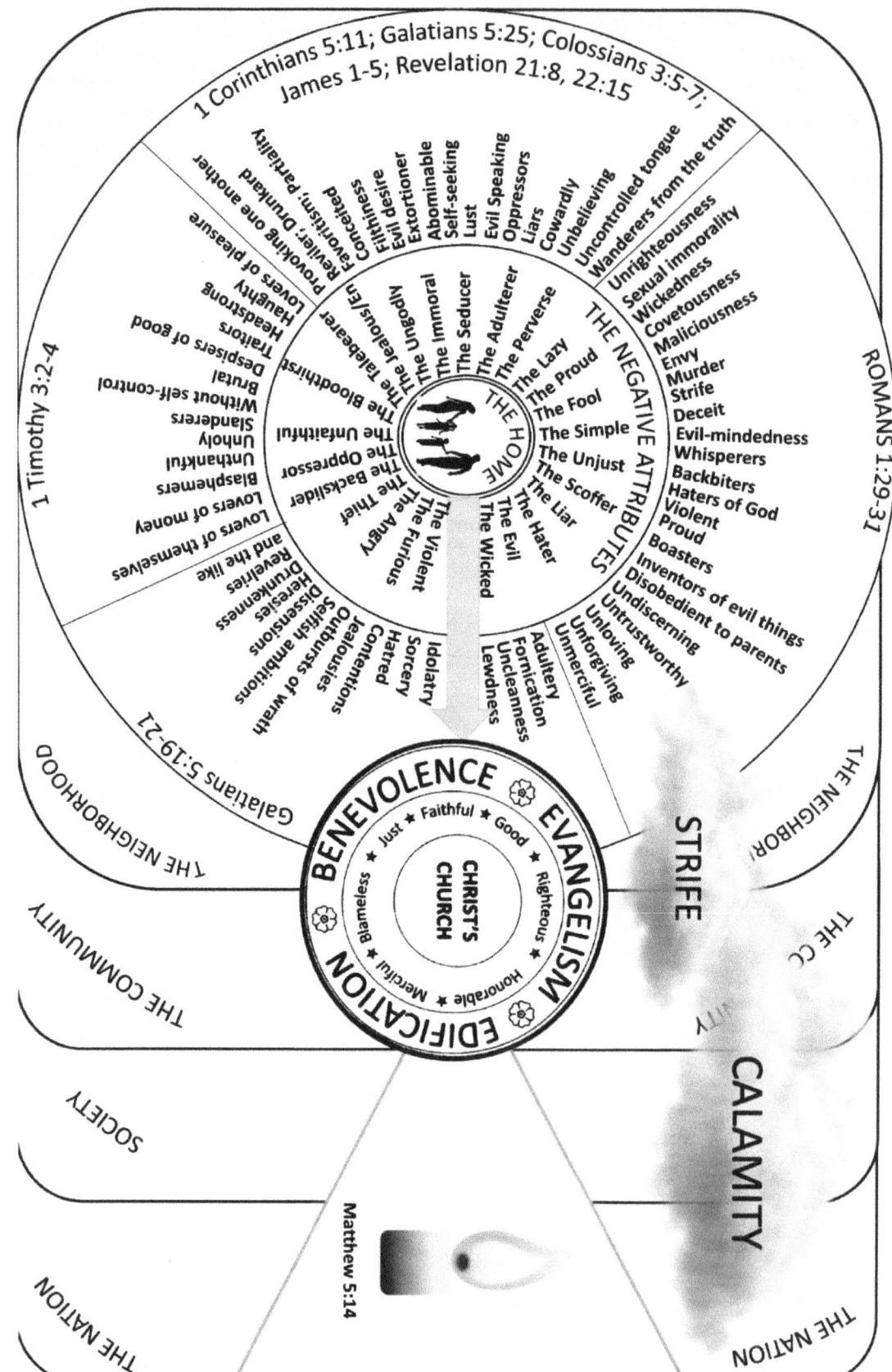

Figure 47: The Spiritual Battlefield with the Lord's Church

Why are there so many ***deceptive*** churches and religious man-made organizations in operation today calling themselves places of worship for the One True God? It is because of the influences of the negative attributes and their ancient ***deception*** strategies. In particular, the influence of the ***lazy*** attribute along with the fog of the war campaign has kept many people from seeking the proper teaching of God's Word. This is in spite of the fact that the providence of God often provides opportunities for people to hear and see the truth as they read the Bible and hear the contradictions orchestrated by their organization's preaching, behavior, and doctrine. The Biblical record documented twice for one's learning:

- *"For the leaders of this people cause them to err, and those who are led by them are destroyed"* (Isaiah 9:16)

- *"My people are destroyed for lack of knowledge. Because you have rejected knowledge, I also will reject you from being priest for Me; because you have forgotten the law of your God, I also will forget your children"* (Hosea 4:6)

For the people described above, God is not present in their lives as evidenced by the growing levels of ***violence*** in the world, and their ambivalence or participation in ***ungodly*** acts. These religious organizations validate the Old Testament Scripture that states, *"Were they ashamed when they had committed abomination? No! They were not at all ashamed; nor did they know how to blush. Therefore they shall fall among those who fall; at the time I punish them, they shall be cast down," says the Lord"* (Jeremiah 6:15; 8:12). Religious people seeking salvation today need the true Christ and His <u>church</u>. To see beyond the fog of spiritual warfare and overcome the influences of the negative attributes, one must come to Christ His way. Then and only then can one be armed with the spiritual armor of Ephesians 6:10-18 and filled with the fruit of the Spirit which is *"...<u>love</u>, <u>joy</u>, <u>peace</u>, <u>longsuffering</u>, <u>kindness</u>, **goodness**, **faithfulness**, <u>gentleness</u>, <u>self-control</u>..."* (Galatians 5:22-24). The spiritual armor and the fruit of the Spirit allow one to *"...Walk in the Spirit, and you shall not fulfill the <u>lust</u> of the flesh. For the flesh <u>lusts</u> against the Spirit, and the Spirit against the flesh; and these are contrary to one another, so that you do not do the things that you wish"* (Galatians 5: 16-17).

Figure 48 depicts another view of the entire spiritual battlefield. It depicts what should be communicated in Christ's <u>church</u> as families and individuals come out of the world and are added to His <u>church</u>. These are the people charged with making a real difference on the spiritual battlefield by their behavior, words, and deeds. From the illustration, one can see who is outside of Christ's <u>church</u> and attacking it at every moment. Moreover, BTT allows one to see that neither the positive nor the negative attributes have boundaries. Therefore, all the attributes move freely world-wide influencing those that listen. Hence, God's <u>calamity</u> and <u>strife</u> remain constant as the fog of the war campaign thickens from the ***deceit*** of ***false*** teachers who attempt to unbalance God's plan. BTT allows one to see that one can only be saved by the proper teaching of the Gospel and obedience to Christ's Word on this battlefield. Members of Christ's <u>church</u> are required to spread the Gospel of Jesus Christ across the spiritual battlefield in every nation. They are armed with the Gospel, teach His Truth, and strive to convert all who will freely come to Christ and the positive side of the spiritual war.

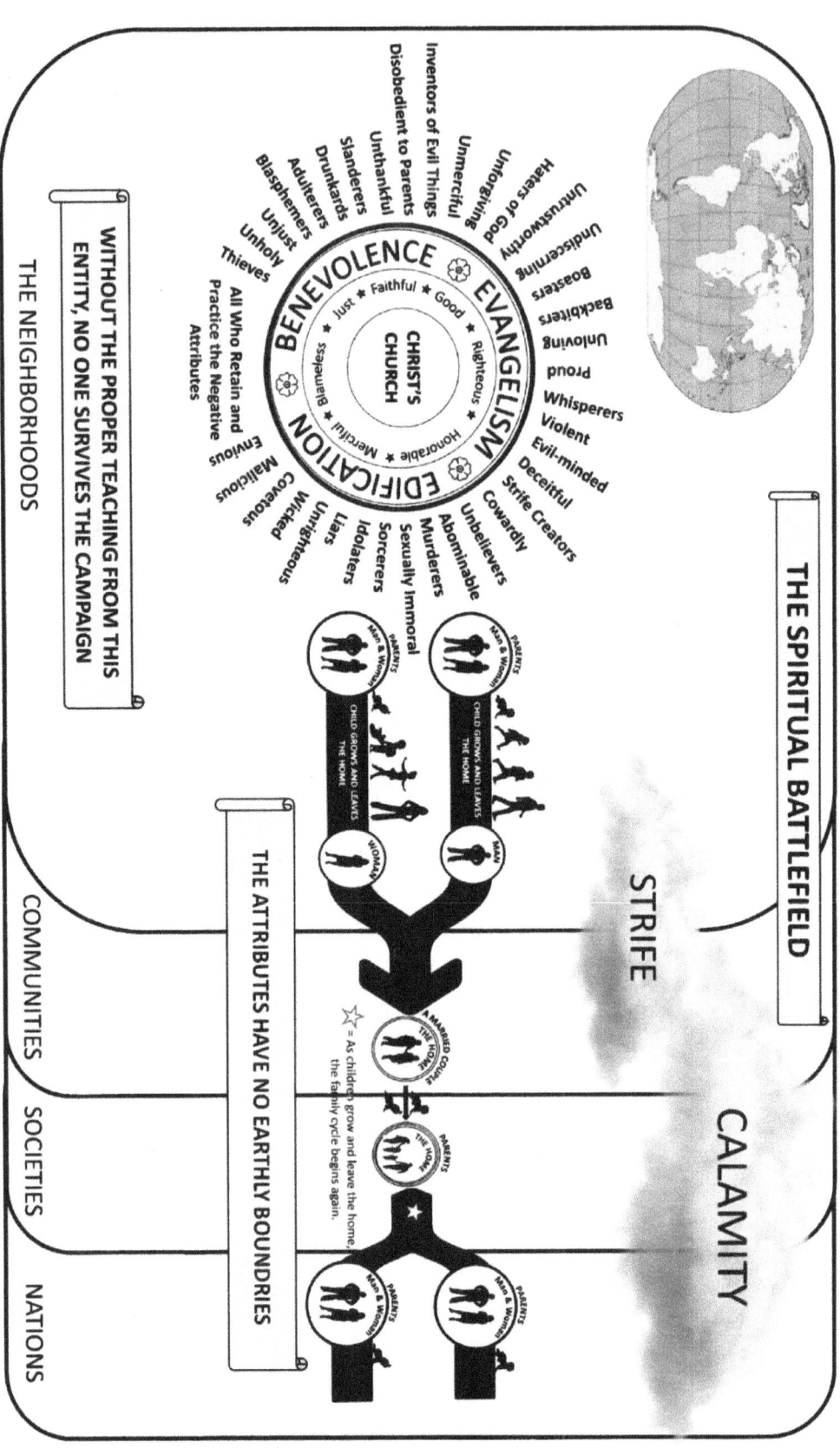

Figure 48: The Complete View of the Spiritual Battlefield

seen with the naked eye has common spiritual attributes driving them. The Holy Spirit's revelation to us through Paul that, "...*we do not wrestle against flesh and blood, but against principalities, against powers, against the rulers of the darkness of this age, against spiritual hosts of **wickedness** in the heavenly places*" (Ephesians 6:12), is the key for understanding spiritual warfare. BTT and <u>discernment</u> provides this realization. When one feeds his or her inner spirit with the Truth of the Gospel, <u>discernment</u> is possible, and it provides the solution to today's <u>strife</u> and <u>calamity</u>. The tug of war between **good** and **evil** as illustrated in **Figure 49** is real. Do not be **deceived**.

Finally, Paul's prayer to His Ephesian brothers is what I pray for all readers of this book. That is, I pray that the great God of heaven, "...*grant you, according to the riches of His glory, to be strengthened with might through His Spirit in the inner man, that Christ may dwell in your hearts through **faith**; that you, being rooted and grounded in love, may be able to comprehend with all the saints what is the width and length and depth and height— to know the love of Christ which passes knowledge; that you may be filled with all the fullness of God*" (Ephesians 3:16-19). I pray for all my family and friends, and the readers of this book, that they come to know the Truth and understand the spiritual war campaign as I have.

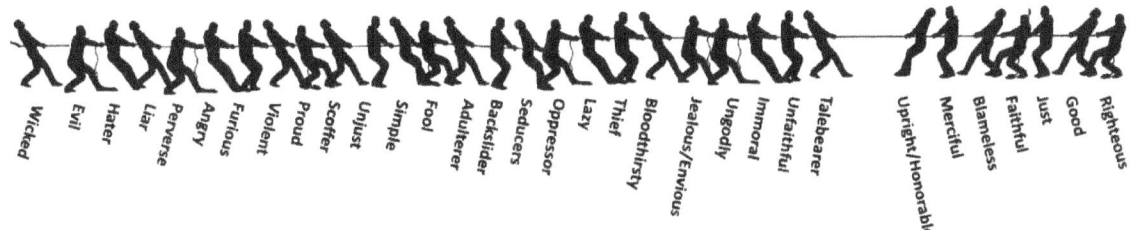

Figure 49: The Struggle between the Positive and Negative Forces of the War Campaign

CHAPTER XII: Understanding Christ's <u>Church</u> and Its Critical Role on the Spiritual Battlefield

"He is the head of the body, the <u>church</u>, who is the beginning, the firstborn from the dead, that in all things He may have the preeminence. For it pleased the Father that in Him all the fullness should dwell, and by Him to reconcile all things to Himself, by Him, whether things on earth or things in heaven, having made peace through the blood of His cross"

~ Colossians 1:18-20 ~

As I have stated in the previous chapter, God in His infinite wisdom, placed an entity physically on this earth to counteract the negative forces of the war campaign. This physical entity appears as His <u>church</u> and is made up of people who follow Christ's written Word exclusively. This chapter will explain Christ's <u>church</u> and the physical structure where Christians assemble together to worship God. The assembly is similar across the spiritual battlefield and looks like what is illustrated in **Figure 50**.

Now before we get into this chapter, it is imperative that one understands that God only placed one entity on this earth called the <u>church</u>. The Holy Spirit confirmed this through Paul. When Paul documented, *"There is <u>one body</u> and one Spirit, just as you were called in one hope of your calling; one Lord, one faith, one baptism; one God and Father of all, who is above all, and through all, and in you all"* (Ephesians 4:4-6), the one body he referred to was Christ's <u>church</u>. This <u>one body</u>, or <u>church</u> of Christ as it is commonly called, represented Jesus Christ's physical presence on earth to combat spiritual warfare. BTT allows one to see this in Paul's writings that plainly states that God, *"...put all things under His feet, and gave Him to be head over all things to the <u>church</u>, **which is His body**, the fullness of Him who fills all in all"* (Ephesians 1:22-23). Paul made the same correlation between Christ and His <u>church</u> in his letter to the <u>church</u> in Colosse in Colossians 1:24. When people are added to Christ's <u>church</u> through <u>baptism</u> and serve Him, they become the physical manifestation of Christ on the battlefield. Paul explained this when he documented, *"For we are members of His body, of His flesh and of His bones"* (Ephesians 5:30). Two other confirming Scriptures for this are:

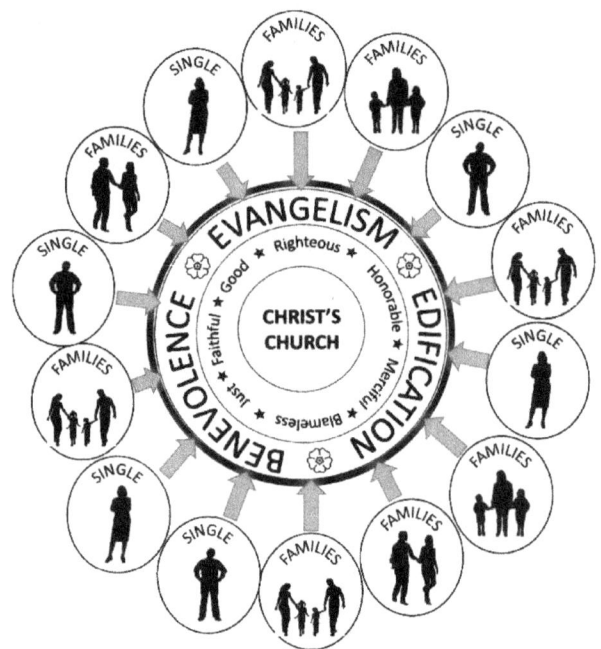

Figure 50: The Church God Established on Earth through His Son Jesus Christ

- "*For as we have many members in <u>one body</u>, but all the members do not have the same function, so we, being many, <u>are one body in Christ</u>, and individually members of one another*" (Romans 12:4-5)
- "*For <u>as the body is one</u> and has many members, but all the members of that one body, being many, <u>are one body</u>, so also is Christ. For by one Spirit we were all <u>baptized</u> into one body—whether Jews or Greeks, whether slaves or free—and have all been made to drink into one Spirit. For in fact <u>the body is not one member but many</u>*" (1 Corinthians 12:12-14)

Hence, God only placed one <u>church</u> on the spiritual battlefield in name to serve communities in different locations on the spiritual battlefield. On the other hand, the negative forces placed thousands of counterfeit churches with all sorts of names across the battlefield to confuse the world of God's Truth. This use of counterfeits, ruse operations, and **deceit** are consistent with acts even in physical warfare. However, when the right questions are asked, the Truth can be ascertained. For Jesus said, "*Ask, and it will be given to you; seek, and you will find; knock, and it will be opened to you. For everyone who asks receives, and he who seeks finds, and to him who knocks it will be opened*" (Matthew 7:7-8; Luke 11:9-10). Please do not be **deceived**.

Now to understand the simple, but often confused nature of the physical <u>church</u> that Christ established on earth, one must turn to the Old Testament of the Biblical record. It is here that one first learns that the entity called the "<u>church</u>" and "<u>kingdom</u>" are synonymous terms. The only difference is, where the term <u>church</u> represents a place of assembly of Christians in a given location, the term <u>Kingdom</u> represents the collective body of his <u>churches</u> dispersed across the spiritual battlefield. But both terms still represent his <u>one body</u>. Hence, a <u>church/kingdom</u> is established on earth today as one entity to combat the negative attributes in spiritual warfare. The fog of the negative forces and **false** teachers have caused much confusion on this point. Be that as it may, the <u>church/kingdom</u> was prophesized in the Biblical record by the prophets. Some of the prophecies included:

Daniel 2:44	"*And in the days of these kings the God of heaven will set up a <u>kingdom</u> which shall never be destroyed; and the <u>kingdom</u> shall not be left to other people; it shall break in pieces and consume all these kingdoms, and it shall stand forever*"
Daniel 7:13-14	"*I was watching in the night visions, and behold, One like the Son of Man, coming with the clouds of heaven! He came to the Ancient of Days, and they brought Him near before Him. Then to Him was given dominion and glory and a <u>kingdom</u>, that all peoples, nations, and languages should serve Him. His dominion is an everlasting dominion, which shall not pass away, and His <u>kingdom</u> the one which shall not be destroyed*"
Joel 2:28-32	"*And it shall come to pass afterward that I will pour out My Spirit on all flesh; your sons and your daughters shall prophesy, your old men shall*

	dream dreams, your young men shall see visions. And also on My menservants and on My maidservants I will pour out My Spirit in those days...And it shall come to pass that whoever calls on the name of the Lord shall be saved. For in Mount Zion and in Jerusalem there shall be deliverance, as the Lord has said, among the remnant whom the Lord calls"
Isaiah 2:2-3	*"Now it shall come to pass in the latter days that the mountain of the Lord's house shall be established on the top of the mountains, and shall be exalted above the hills; and all nations shall flow to it. Many people shall come and say, "Come, and let us go up to the mountain of the Lord, to <u>the house of the God</u> of Jacob; He will teach us His ways, and we shall walk in His paths." For out of Zion shall go forth the law, and the word of the Lord from Jerusalem"*

Table 173: Prophesies of Christ's Church/Christ's Kingdom in the Old Testament

Mark documented that Jesus told the His disciples, *"Assuredly, I say to you that there are some standing here who will not taste death till they see the <u>kingdom of God</u> present with power"* (Mark 9:1). This meant that some of the disciples would see the establishment of the <u>church/kingdom</u> as it came to earth with a display of power. John further documented a discussion between Jesus and Nicodemus about the <u>church/kingdom</u>. Jesus told Nicodemus, *"Most assuredly, I say to you, unless one is born of water and the Spirit, he cannot enter the <u>kingdom of God</u>"* (John 3:5). Thus, Jesus told Nicodemus what the entrance criteria would be for the <u>church/kingdom</u>. This is water <u>baptism</u>. Later, Jesus told Peter, *"...I also say to you that you are Peter, and on this rock I will build My <u>church</u>, and the gates of Hades shall not prevail against it. And I will give you the keys of the <u>kingdom</u> of heaven, and whatever you bind on earth will be bound in heaven, and whatever you loose on earth will be loosed in heaven"* (Matthew 16:18-19). So when Jesus left the earth, the <u>church/kingdom</u> was physically established on earth with a display of power (Act 2) and people used the criteria that Jesus told Nicodemus of to become part of this entity (Acts 2:40-41). BTT allows one to see that the Holy Spirit spoke through Peter on the Day of Pentecost. Through Peter's sermon (Acts 2:14-40), the pattern of Christ's <u>church</u> was bound on earth.

Now there are people across the spiritual battlefield that believe that Peter, a man, created the first <u>church</u> for God. For his role, they even label him as the first "pope." This teaching is patently ***false*** and a product of spiritual warfare. The Biblical record documents that, *"...when Jesus looked at him, He said, "You are Simon the son of Jonah. You shall be called Cephas" (which is translated, A Stone)"* (John 1:42). This new name that Jesus gave to Peter was an indication that Jesus knew that there was something in Peter's inner spirit that He would use in the future that pertained to the establishment of His <u>church</u>. Thus, a time came during Jesus' preparation of the disciples when He asked them two life changing questions. These questions demonstrated their knowledge between the worldly and spiritual nexus of the war campaign. To ensure they understood whom the religious and secular community thought He was, Jesus asked them, *"Who do men say that I, the Son of Man, am?"* (Matthew 16:13). They responded by naming reincarnations of worldly figures the Jew's knew according to Matthew 16:14. But then He asked them more directly, *"But who do you say that I am?"*

(Matthew 16:15). Of all the disciples, it was Peter who responded with the correct answer. The Bible documented that it was Peter who said, "*You are the Christ, the Son of the living God*" (Matthew 16:16). Because of this answer, Jesus then said to Peter, "*Blessed are you, Simon Bar-Jonah, for flesh and blood has not revealed this to you, but My Father who is in heaven. And I also say to you that you are Peter, and on this rock I will build My church, and the gates of Hades shall not prevail against it*" (Matthew 16:17-18). Jesus, addressing Peter directly and all the other disciples jointly, told them that Peter (who name is translated "a stone" in John 1:42, which is a rock) would have a role in the establishment of His church when the time came. This statement did not take anything away from the other disciples nor did it lessen their roles or responsibilities as some in the religious community teach. In fact, the Biblical record documents when the time came for Peter to fulfill this one specific role in the Book of Acts. After Jesus ascended to heaven, He sent the Holy Spirit back to earth (John 16:7) to guide the disciples in all "Truth" according to John 16:13. After the Holy Spirit returned (Acts 2:1-4) with representatives of many different nations **witnessing** the event (Acts 2:5-13), it was Peter who took the lead to preach to the first 3,000 people who would make up Christ's church according to Acts 2:14-41. But Peter was not a one-man operation. He was not in charge of anything. The Bible clearly documented that the people, "*continued steadfastly in the apostles' doctrine and fellowship, in the breaking of bread, and in prayers*" (Acts 2:42). All of the apostles were involved with the assembly that constituted the first church.

Here's the point and facts. Peter simply preached a sermon on the Truth that the Holy Spirit led him to preach. Based on the Word preached, the Spirit convicted the spiritual hearts (Acts 2:37) of everyone that "*gladly received his word* **[and]** *were baptized*" (Acts 2:41). Peter on his own had no special power or authority. He did not establish God's church. The Holy Spirit working through a human vessel, which happened to be Peter, established the church that belonged to Christ; not Peter. Because of spiritual warfare, the religious community seized on the fact that Peter was the human vessel and began teaching that he was responsible for the actual creation of Christ's church by himself. This is both religious and spiritual error. This belief comes from a greater strategy perpetrated by the influence of the negative forces of the war campaign to give glory to man over God. This strategy continues to grow worldwide through men and women who use it to start up their own churches based on their own brand of religion outside of God's Word while using the Bible as a reference. Do not be ***deceived***.

Thus, the first true physical church in Jerusalem after the Day of Pentecost was called by Christ's name both spiritually and physically. Christ's Church was easily identifiable from every other religious organization from that day forward. This first church or "place of assembly" served as a meeting place where the followers of Christ, Christians by name, came together to worship God in spirit and Truth (John 4:24) and to be educated about the true Gospel. This same purpose and assembling remains unchanged. Thus, true churches of Christ can be identified on the spiritual battlefield in a local area accomplishing these three key functions:

- **Evangelism:** Preaching the gospel to the lost according to 1 Thessalonians 1:8

- **Edification:** Strengthening the members of the body according to Hebrews 10:24-25

- **Benevolence:** Taking care of the poor and needy of the <u>church</u> according to Acts 6:1-6 and Romans 15:25-27. Also, supporting the needs of each other according to Romans 12:13; 12:18; 1 Corinthians 12:25

All these functions can be seen by example in the first <u>church</u> of Christ on the days following Pentecost. **Figure 51** depicts the <u>church</u> and its unique function serving as the pillar of truth for people who submit to the pattern of the <u>church</u> God provided on the battlefield. BTT allows one to see that there are no perfect <u>churches</u> as long as people are involved and the influences of the negative attributes exist. There will always be people attempting to prevent one of Christ's <u>churches</u> from reaching perfection. However, their actions do not stop the rest of the people assembling from striving to reach perfection.

Hence, the Holy Spirit led Paul to write Timothy, "...*I write so that you may know how you ought to conduct yourself in the house of God, which is the <u>church</u> of the living God, the pillar and ground of the truth*" (1 Timothy 3:15). Consider a few more important pearls of wisdom about the relationship between Christ and the <u>church</u>; the <u>church</u> He established on earth. The Bible documents:

Figure 51: The Operation of the Church on the Spiritual Battlefield

- "*For the husband is head of the wife, as also Christ is head of the <u>church</u>; and He is the Savior of the body*" (Ephesians 5:23)

- "*And He is the head of the body, the <u>church</u>, who is the beginning, the firstborn from the dead, that in all things He may have the preeminence*" (Colossians 1:18)

- Paul said, "*I now rejoice in my sufferings for you, and fill up in my flesh what is lacking in the afflictions of Christ, for the sake of His body, which is the <u>church</u>...*" (Colossians 1:24)

- "*...to the general assembly and <u>church</u> of the firstborn who are <u>registered in heaven</u>, to God the Judge of all, to the spirits of **just** men made perfect...*" (Hebrews 12:23)

- "*He who has an ear, let him hear what the Spirit says to the <u>churches</u>. To him who overcomes I will give to eat from the tree of life, which is in the midst of the Paradise of God*" (Revelation 2:7)

Here is the most important take-away from the items listed above. Jesus Christ purchased His <u>church</u> "*...with His own blood*" (Acts 20:28). Therefore, no man has the right to claim Christ's <u>church</u> as his own. A person can claim any religious operation they create as their own; and many do, but not Christ's <u>church</u>. Christ "*...gave Himself for us, that He might redeem us from every lawless deed and purify for Himself His own special people, zealous for good works*" (Titus 2:14). No preacher or earthly leader can make this claim. If they do, run! Further, the Biblical record documents "*...Christ was offered once to bear the sins of many. To those who eagerly wait for Him He will appear a second time, apart from sin, for salvation*" (Hebrews 9:28). Thus, finding the right place to worship Him is vitally important for one's soul, spiritual maturity, and protection during spiritual warfare.

Christ's <u>church</u> first mission is to seek and save the lost. This mission was established by Christ's example. In fact, Jesus stated Himself, "*...for the Son of Man has come to seek and to save that which was lost*" (Luke 19:10). For every Christian, Jesus gave the same mission when He said, "*All authority has been given to Me in heaven and on earth. <u>Go therefore and make disciples of all the nations</u>, <u>baptizing them in the name of the Father and of the Son and of the Holy Spirit</u>, <u>teaching them to observe all things that I have commanded you</u>; and lo, I am with you always, even to the end of the age*" (Matthew 28:18-20). Thus, Christians are charged to teach people outside the <u>church</u> the Truth and train and prepare them for spiritual warfare. **Figure 52** illustrates what is outside the <u>church</u> and explains why Christ's church is under constant assault. Moreover, these also represent people who were once lost but came into the <u>church</u> and allowed their minds to be transformed. Paul confirmed this when he told the <u>church</u> in Corinth, "*...such were some of you. But you were washed, but you were sanctified, but you were justified in the name of the Lord Jesus and by the Spirit of our God*" (1 Corinthians 6:9-11).

Hence, strong and, "*...**faithful** men who will be able to teach others...*" (2 Timothy 2:2) are required within Christ's <u>church</u> to maintain Christ's pattern for His <u>church</u>. This is the Gospel which contains wisdom about God, His son, the Holy Spirit, the Biblical record, spiritual warfare, and salvation. It is within this pattern that the Gospel of Jesus Christ stays vibrant and active on the spiritual battlefield. The pattern Christ provided must be maintained because "*...the message of the cross is **foolishness** to those who are perishing, but to us who are being saved it is the power of God*" (1 Corinthians 1:18). Hence, the mission of the <u>church</u> is critical to humanity because the Biblical record documents that there will be an end to all living things one day. When this day comes, the Bible documents, "*...it is written: "As I live, says the LORD, every knee shall bow to Me, and every tongue shall confess to God"*" (Roman 14:11). With this said, consider a closer look at Christ's <u>church</u>, its design, organization, and function in the war campaign.

Now before I go further, one must understand that the negative forces of the war campaign launched an effective strategy to confuse the religious world over the very concept of a church. Was Christ's _church_ established as a building? Certainly not. When Paul asked, "*Do you not know that you are the temple of God and that the Spirit of God dwells in you?*" (1 Corinthians 3:16), he said this to clarify that each person that comes to Christ through _baptism_ has the _church_ in him or her through Christ. Those who have accepted Christ then have a responsibility, based on the Biblical record, to assemble with other Christians to worship God and strengthen each other. This assembling (Hebrews 10:25) can necessitate the purchase or renting of a facility to support those who have come together in a given place. Depending on the number of people, the facility can be one's home or a building. Nevertheless, the important take away is the fact that Christ's _church_ has less to do with a building and more to do with like-minded Christians assembling to grow and mature together. However, the negative attributes have **deceived** people into believing that investments in architectural structures laced with worldly adornments alone are the dwelling places of God. This is just not so. Paul even addressed this point while he was in Athens when he stated, "*…God, who made the world and everything in it, since He is Lord of heaven and earth, does not dwell in temples made with hands*" (Acts 17:24). In physical warfare, structures are simply targets to attack. This same rule applies in spiritual warfare and especially when the idea behind the structure is not from God. With this said, consider a closer look at Christ's _church_ in the war campaign.

Figure 52: People outside of Christ's Church

After the Day of Pentecost, as documented in the Book of Acts, BTT allows one to see the beginning of Christ's _church_ recorded in Acts 2:40-47. The Bible documented that the people who followed Christ and were part of His _church_ and were, "*first called Christians in Antioch*" (Acts 11:26). Today, everyone who is added to Christ's church through _baptism_ and remains obedient to Him and His pattern established at Pentecost, share in the same legacy as the first Christians. Then and now, Christians are the people of Christ who are "*...as living stones, are being built up a spiritual house, a holy priesthood, to offer up spiritual sacrifices acceptable to God through Jesus Christ*" (1 Peter 2:5). Further, Christians are "*...a chosen generation, a royal priesthood, a holy nation, His own special people, that you may proclaim the praises of Him who called you out of darkness into His marvelous light; who once were not a people but are now the people of God, who had not obtained* **mercy** *but now have obtained* **mercy**" (1 Peter 2:9-10).

In Jerusalem, the <u>church</u> began and grew until God used His <u>calamity</u> to scatter the people across the spiritual battlefield to spread the Gospel. Literally, the replication of Christ's <u>church</u> occurred across the spiritual battlefield and the balance in the war campaign began to tilt towards the positive forces. In fact, the Biblical record documented <u>churches</u> in:

Jerusalem: Acts 2:47; Acts 11:22	Cenchrea: Romans 16:1	Antioch: Acts 11:26; Acts 13:1
Asia: 1 Corinthians 16:19	Syria and Cilicia: Acts 15:41	Caesarea: Acts 18:22
Apphia and Archippus house: Philemon 1:2	Throughout the regions of Judea, Samaria, and Galilee: Acts 8:1; Acts 9:31	Priscilla and Aquila's house: Romans 16:3-5; 1 Corinthians 16:19
Corinth: 1 Corinthians 1:2; 2 Corinthians 1:1	Galatia: 1 Corinthians 16:1; Galatians 1:2	Saints who are in all Achaia: 2 Corinthians 1:1
the Gentiles in Phoenicia and Samaria: Acts 15:3	Macedonia: 2 Corinthians 8:1	Nymphas house in Laodicea: Colossians 4:15
The Laodicea: Colossians 4:16	Thessalonica: 1 Thessalonians 1:1	Ephesus: Acts 20:17

Table 174: Christ's <u>Church</u> and Where They Were Located

All of these <u>churches</u> initially followed the same pattern established by Christ and taught to His apostles. However, at some point in the campaign, Satan began to regain territory as, "*...certain men have crept in unnoticed, who long ago were marked out for this condemnation,* **ungodly** *men, who turn the grace of our God into* **lewdness** *and deny the only Lord God and our Lord Jesus Christ*" (Jude 1:4). The results are seen in the image of the seven <u>churches</u> which are in Asia: to Ephesus, to Smyrna, to Pergamos, to Thyatira, to Sardis, to Philadelphia, and to Laodicea in Revelation 1:11. As long as the religious world refuses to accept Christ on His terms and continues "*...seeking to establish their own* **righteousness***, have not submitted to the* **righteousness** *of God*" (Romans 10:3) out of ignorance, Satan will maintain his dominance on earth as the ruler of the world according to John 14:30. This includes ruling over religious communities.

Nevertheless, Christ's <u>church</u> does exist. Remember, it was Jesus Himself Who said, "*I will build My <u>church</u>, and the gates of Hades shall not prevail against it*" (Matthew 16:18). If hell cannot destroy it, then the <u>church</u> Jesus built still exists today. It is still training, preparing soldiers, and fighting spiritual warfare on the spiritual battlefield. After seeking this entity for years, after the Gulf War of Desert Shield and Desert Storm, I found that entity that strives to follow that same pattern of the 1st Century <u>church</u>; that is to say, Christ's <u>church</u>. That <u>church</u> is called the <u>church</u> of Christ and the people are identified simply as "Christians". The place these Christians meet is not called by any other name nor is it identified by the name of the preacher in the pulpit as is the practice of the religious community. These Christians are from all races, backgrounds, and nationalities. They come to a building to worship God in spirit and truth. They are *"no longer strangers and foreigners, but fellow citizens with the saints and members of the <u>household of God</u>, having been built on the foundation of the apostles and prophets, Jesus Christ Himself being the chief cornerstone, in whom the whole building, being fitted together, grows into a holy temple in the Lord, in whom you also are being built together for a dwelling place of God in the Spirit"* (Ephesians 2:19-22). Now BTT and <u>*discernment*</u> allows one to see that the Christian's of Christ's <u>churches</u> are susceptible to the same influences of the positive and negative attributes as everyone else. For this reason, some of Christ's <u>churches</u> have entered into apostasy and fallen away from the original pattern. Where Jude 4 documented the actions of "**ungodly** <u>men</u>", it referred to some <u>men</u> in Christ's <u>church</u> who "*crept in unnoticed.*" This still happens today. Moreover, the Bible documented apostasy would happen because the negative attributes know the inner spirits of people and prey on human desires, emotions, and thoughts. The negative attributes employ strategies to bring satisfaction to people who lack <u>*discernment*</u> between worldly and spiritual things. The Bible even documents, *"For the time will come when they will not endure sound doctrine, but according to their own desires, because they have itching ears, they will heap up for themselves teachers; and they will turn their ears away from the truth, and be turned aside to fables"* (2 Timothy 4:3-4). What is scary about this Scripture is that it came from Paul to young Timothy to warn about some people in Christ's <u>church</u>. In 2 Timothy 4, the people within Christ's <u>church</u> itself sought **ungodly** men to bring in doctrines, practices, and traditions to satisfy their own desires. Today, some of these same church leaders mix Old Testament doctrines with the Gospel while others introduce ultraconservative views that strangle Christ's examples of <u>love</u>, <u>compassion</u>, and **mercy**.

Even with all of this said, there are still enough sound <u>churches</u> of Christ containing God's remnant on the battlefield. BTT and <u>*discernment*</u> allows one's inner spirit to distinguish the truth behind these views. The <u>church</u> of Christ is the closest entity that I have found that earnestly strives to follow the original pattern of authority that Christ gave to His apostles. Moreover, the Bible confirms, *"Nevertheless the solid foundation of God stands, having this seal: "The Lord knows those who are His," and, "Let everyone who names the name of Christ depart from iniquity"* (2 Timothy 2: 19). As for people who once identified with Christ's <u>church</u> but fell into apostasy, the Bible goes on the document, *"But in a great house there are not only vessels of gold and silver, but also of wood and clay, some for **honor** and some for **dishonor**. Therefore if anyone cleanses himself from the latter, he will be a vessel for **honor**, sanctified and useful for the Master, prepared for every **good** work"* (2 Timothy 2: 20-21).

Christ taught His apostles His pattern so people could distinguish His <u>church</u> from counterfeits. This pattern included the organization of the <u>church</u> and the proper way to worship His Father. Jesus' authority in these areas take precedence over any religious leader's beliefs, ideals, or tradition. In fact, Jesus said Himself *"And if anyone hears My words and does not believe, I do not judge him; for I did not come to judge the world but to save the world. He who rejects Me, and does not receive My words, has that which judges him—the word that I have spoken will judge him in the last day"* (John 12:47-48). The Bible documents Jesus' Word for everyone living today to read for themselves. However, this is where the negative forces increase their assault on humanity through their generated fog. It is in this vein that I offer two important thoughts about the _church_ of Christ in relation to BTT and spiritual warfare.

First, God the Master Strategist created His _church_ so that it would prevail during spiritual and physical warfare. Jesus told His disciples this early in His ministry when He said to Peter, "..._and the gates of Hades shall not prevail against it_" (Matthew 16:18). The twisting of Jesus' pronouncement of the establishment of His _church_ remains a focus of the negative attributes' influence on religious leaders. The focus began when Jesus first made His pronouncement to Peter about the _church_. BTT allows one to see that Jesus established His _church_ by His Word. Peter and the rest of the apostles took Jesus' Word, (think back to the parable of the Sower and the seed and specifically what was said in Matthew 13:19, Mark 4:14, and Luke 8:12), and established congregations of people practicing specifically what Jesus had taught them. From this statement, one can see Paul's application of 1 Corinthians 1:10 when he pleaded with members of Christ's church "_Now I plead with you, brethren, by the name of our Lord Jesus Christ, that you all speak the same thing, and that there be no divisions among you, but that you be perfectly joined together in the same mind and in the same judgment_". If Paul's plea were applied to the religious world, most of the denominational and nondenominational separate church organizations would disappear. All of them would be following the same Word of Christ and ascribed to the same _church_ pattern identified by the apostles. God's divine strategy confirms that "_...there is one God and one Mediator between God and men, the Man Christ Jesus, who gave Himself a ransom for all, to be testified in due time..._" (1 Timothy 2:5-6). God's way assures Christians that no man, hierarchy, or governing body of people are required to operate between Him and His _church_ except for Jesus Christ. In fact, Jesus declared, "_All authority has been given to Me in heaven and on earth_" (Matthew 28:18). The Ephesians writer declared that God "_...put all things under His feet, and gave Him to be head over all things to the _church_, which is His body, the fullness of Him who fills all in all_" (Ephesians 1:22-23). Of course, this verse speaks of Jesus Christ. Paul also wrote, "_... God also has highly exalted Him and given Him the name which is above every name, that at the name of Jesus every knee should bow, of those in heaven, and of those on earth, and of those under the earth, and that every tongue should confess that Jesus Christ is Lord, to the glory of God the Father_" (Philippians 2:9-11). No man, hierarchy, or governing body of people will ever have this **honor**; only Christ. **Figure 53** below illustrates what God put in place through His Son to contend with the negative forces of the war campaign. Christ gave His Word in the form of the Biblical record to govern His _church_ and He sits as the mediator between the people who follow His Word in His _church_. God's divine arrangement is simple, beautiful, and effective for combating the negative forces of the war campaign.

For this reason, Christ's _church_ was never meant to be a place of entertainment; there is too much at stake in the war campaign. This includes hosting manmade holidays and worship enhancements (i.e., plays, recitals, praise dance, and the like). _Discernment_ allows one to see that similar practices were used by the Jews of the Old Testament; that portion of the Bible was written for our learning (see Romans 15:4). However, these practices ceased for Christians under the new covenant of Christ. Unfortunately, these practices have made a resurgence on the spiritual battlefield by unlearned and/or **false** teachers and people with itching ears. Read closely what the Lord told Judah and Jerusalem in the Book of Isaiah Chapter One with

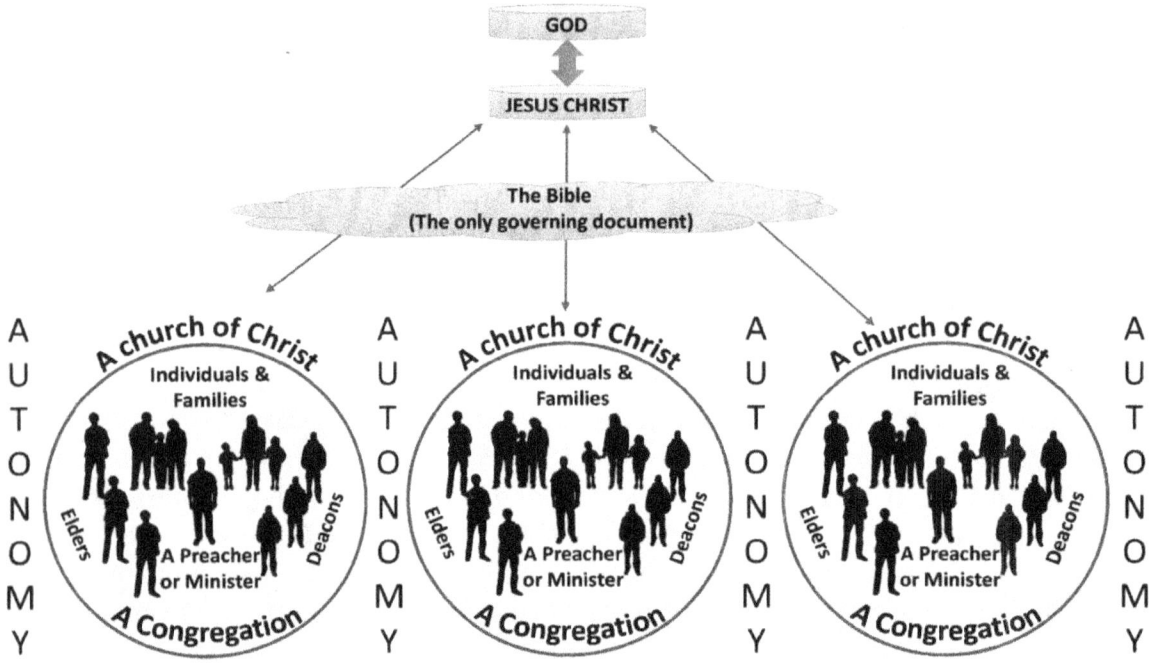

Figure 53: *Churches* of Christ on the Spiritual Battlefield

emphasis on verses 13 and 14. One should also note that the Lord likened these two nations' behaviors to that of Sodom and Gomorrah in verses 9 and 10. This is why the sole purpose of the *church* is to provide a place where people can come to learn how to save their souls. The by-product is preparation and education for fighting the spiritual battle placed before them. This is serious business and there is no room for any other distractors.

Within Christ's *church*, and God's divine design, BTT allows one to see the simplicity of the *church* structure. As one looks at **Figure 53**, one should first notice that there is no council or other governing body between the *church* and God. The negative forces of the war campaign have influenced religious leaders to manufacture organizational hierarchies where none exists in the Biblical record. These religious leaders ignore Paul's statement that "...*there is one God and one Mediator between God and men, the Man Christ Jesus...*" (1 Timothy 2:5). This occurs when human control is more important than what the Lord has said.

Next, one can see that the *church* itself has very few components. One should think about their own religious organization and compare it to what the Biblical record actually documents. To begin with, Christ's *church* is composed of individuals and families. BTT allows one to see that all of the adults who make up Christ's *church* have a role to play in it. God's divine strategy excludes no adult in Christ's *church* from doing His work. There is work for everyone; for serving beside the positive forces in the war campaign, requires everyone's effort, attention, and skills. Warming a seat in His structure is sinful. This behavior demonstrates a lack of spiritual maturity and the influences of the negative attributes are behind the behavior. Moreover, this behavior does not set the proper example for the children of the body; the future generation of Christ's *church*. The Biblical record documents:

- *"For as we have many members in one body, but all the members do not have the same function so we, being many, are one body in Christ, and individually members of one another"* (Romans 12:4-5)

- *"For as the body is one and has many members, but all the members of that one body, being many, are one body, so also is Christ"* (1 Corinthians 12:12)

- *"But now God has set the members, each one of them, in the body just as He pleased"* (1 Corinthians 12:18)

- *"But now indeed there are many members, yet one body"* (1 Corinthians 12:20)

- *"...from whom the whole body, joined and knit together by what every joint supplies, according to the effective working by which every part does its share, causes growth of the body for the edifying of itself in love"* (Ephesians 4:16)

- *"...those members of the body which seem to be weaker are necessary. And those members of the body which we think to be less **honorable**, on these we bestow greater **honor**; and our unpresentable parts have greater modesty, but our presentable parts have no need. But God composed the body, having given greater **honor** to that part which lacks it, that there should be no schism in the body, but that the members should have the same care for one another. And if one member suffers, all the members suffer with it; or if one member is **honored**, all the members rejoice with it. Now you are the body of Christ, and members individually"* (1 Corinthians 12:22-27)

Christ's physical <u>church</u> on the battlefield fails when individual people stop doing what the Lord commands. There is no Biblical sabbatical or holiday for members of the body of Christ. There is steady work to be done every day by every adult Christian. When one thinks otherwise and simply attends <u>church</u> but refuses to participate, he or she sets a dangerous precedence. These are the same people with behavior similar to all congregations across the battlefield who open the door for the **lazy** attribute to enter an assembly by their example. Still others move between congregations seeking personal satisfaction over the needs of their fellow brother or sister in Christ. In this case, they fail to understand *"Let nothing be done through selfish ambition or conceit, but in lowliness of mind let each esteem others better than himself. Let each of you look out not only for his own interests, but also for the interests of others"* (Philippians 2:3-5). Until they gain this understanding, their spiritual maturity will remain hindered. BTT allows one to see that God will not accept a plea of ignorance on these matters. Members of Christ's <u>church</u> will be held accountable for their actions as well as their inaction.

Another component of Christ's <u>church</u> is a preacher. The terms preacher, minister, and evangelist are synonymously used to describe the person who actively preaches God's Word to an assembly of God's people. Christ's <u>church</u> should always strive to have a dedicated preacher or preachers. Congregational finances determine this area. This component of the <u>church</u> is a <u>male</u> specific position. BTT allows one to see that based on everything one read in Chapter X of this book and the Lord's decision for man's responsibility in spiritual matters in the Book of Genesis, a man exclusively fills the role of a preacher in Christ's <u>church</u>. Paul confirmed this idea by inspiration of the Holy Spirit when he wrote, "*Let your women keep silent in the churches, for they are not permitted to speak; but they are to be submissive, as the law also says...*" (1 Corinthians 14:34). Yes, spiritual warfare automatically influences one to take Paul's statement out of context to be degrading to women. But do not allow yourself to be **deceived**. Religious organizations are free to do what they want, but in Christ's church, this is not the case. Further, nowhere in God's Word or His church is there a position for a "first lady" of the church as some organizations practice. This practice is borne out of a strategy from the negative forces to elevate a woman to eventually give her the authority to preach in a mixed assembly. Paul viewed this as an attempt to usurp authority in God's pattern and he told Timothy "*...I do not permit a woman to teach or to have authority over a man, but to be in silence. For Adam was formed first, then Eve. And Adam was not deceived, but the woman being deceived, fell into transgression*" (1 Timothy 2:12-14). In other words, the practice of having a "first lady" or other such titles have no Biblical basis or authority from God. One can either accept that Paul had authority from the Holy Spirit to make this statement or one can trust themselves and the influence of spiritual warfare's fog. For a preacher's primary role is to teach the Gospel correctly to the entire assembly. Paul wrote, "*How then shall they call on Him in whom they have not believed? And how shall they believe in Him of whom they have not heard? And how shall they hear without a preacher?*" (Romans 10:14). By inspiration of the Holy Spirit, Paul trained Timothy in the role of a preacher. The Bible documented that Paul instructed Timothy in 2 Timothy 3:14-17; 4:1-5:

> "*But you must continue in the things which you have learned and been assured of, knowing from whom you have learned them, and that from childhood you have known the Holy Scriptures, which are able to make you wise for salvation through faith which is in Christ Jesus. All Scripture is given by inspiration of God, and is profitable for doctrine, for reproof, for correction, for instruction in righteousness, that the man of God may be complete, thoroughly equipped for every good work. I charge you therefore before God and the Lord Jesus Christ, who will judge the living and the dead at His appearing and His kingdom: Preach the word! Be ready in season and out of season. Convince, rebuke, exhort, with all longsuffering and teaching. For the time will come when they will not endure sound doctrine, but according to their own desires, because they have itching ears, they will heap up for themselves teachers; and they will turn their ears away from the truth, and be turned aside to fables. But you be watchful in all things, endure afflictions, do the work of an evangelist, fulfill your ministry.*"

The preacher does not have the responsibility for running the business of the church. Correctly preaching and teaching God's Word is a full-time responsibility by itself. This is not to say that the preacher does not fulfill other duties such as **counseling** and visitation. He does but these roles are within the duties of elders and the members too. However, when a preacher is responsible for running the business of the church, focused, well developed, and comprehensive studies of God's complete Word suffers. The handling of God's Word takes time, preparation, and meditation. One must respect a preacher's time and a good eldership will ensure that a preacher has both the time and resources to accomplish his monumental task. Hence, Paul would tell Timothy, "*I charge you therefore before God and the Lord Jesus Christ, who will judge the living and the dead at His appearing and His kingdom: Preach the word! Be ready in season and out of season. Convince, rebuke, exhort, with all longsuffering and teaching*" (2 Timothy 4:1-2). To get to this state, Timothy required time to devote himself to the study and preparation in God's Word. All preachers deserve and must have this opportunity. For on their shoulders they carry the weight of precious souls.

BTT allows one to see that a preacher's role is difficult. He bears the responsibility for correctly teaching God's Word and preparing the assembly for spiritual warfare. The Bible documents many examples of the men who took on this task. For instance:

Preacher	What is Documented
Solomon	"*The words of the Preacher, the son of David, king in Jerusalem*" (*Ecclesiastes 1:1*) and "*I, the Preacher, was king over Israel in Jerusalem*" (Ecclesiastes 1:12).
	"*And moreover, because the Preacher was wise, he still taught the people knowledge; yes, he pondered and sought out and set in order many proverbs*" (Ecclesiastes 12:9)
	"*The Preacher sought to find acceptable words; and what was written was upright—words of truth*" (Ecclesiastes 12:10)
Isaiah	"*The Spirit of the Lord God is upon Me, Because the Lord has anointed Me to preach good tidings to the poor; He has sent Me to heal the brokenhearted, to proclaim liberty to the captives, And the opening of the prison to those who are bound; To proclaim the acceptable year of the Lord, and the day of vengeance of our God; to comfort all who mourn, to console those who mourn in Zion, to give them beauty for ashes, the oil of joy for mourning, the garment of praise for the spirit of heaviness; that they may be called trees of righteousness, the planting of the Lord, that He may be glorified*" (Isaiah 61:1)
Ezekiel	"*Son of man, set your face toward the south; preach against the south and prophesy against the forest land, the South, and say to the forest of the South, 'Hear the word of the Lord! ...*" (Ezekiel 20:46-47)
	"*Son of man, set your face toward Jerusalem, preach against the holy places, and prophesy against the land of Israel; and say to the land of Israel, 'Thus says the Lord: "Behold, I am against you, and I will draw My sword out of its sheath and cut off both righteous and wicked from you*" (Ezekiel 21:2)
Jonah	God told him, "*Arise, go to Nineveh, that great city, and preach to it the message that I tell you*" (Jonah 3:2)
	Jesus said, "*The men of Nineveh will rise up in the judgment with this generation and condemn it, because they repented at the preaching of Jonah; and indeed a greater than Jonah is here*" (Matthew 12:41; Luke 11:32)
Noah	The Bible documents that God "*...did not spare the ancient world, but saved Noah, one of eight people, a preacher of righteousness, bringing in the flood on the world of the ungodly...*" (2 Peter 2:5)
All of God's Prophets	"*Do not be like your fathers, to whom the former prophets preached, saying, 'Thus says the Lord of hosts: "Turn now from your evil ways and your evil deeds."' But they did not hear nor heed Me," says the Lord*" (Zechariah 1:4)

	"Of this salvation the prophets have inquired and searched carefully, who prophesied of the grace that would come to you, searching what, or what manner of time, the Spirit of Christ who was in them was indicating when He testified beforehand the sufferings of Christ and the glories that would follow. To them it was revealed that, not to themselves, but to us they were ministering the things which now have been reported to you through those who have preached the gospel to you by the Holy Spirit sent from heaven—things which angels desire to look into" (1 Peter 1:10-12)
John the Baptist	*"In those days John the Baptist came preaching in the wilderness of Judea..."* (Matthew 3:1)
	Jesus said, *"John came baptizing in the wilderness and preaching a baptism of repentance for the remission of sins"* (Mark 1:4), and *"And he went into all the region around the Jordan, preaching a baptism of repentance for the remission of sins..."* (Luke 3:3). Also see Mark 1:7; Luke 3:18
Jesus	*"...went about all Galilee, teaching in their synagogues, preaching the gospel of the kingdom, and healing all kinds of sickness and all kinds of disease among the people"* (Matthew 4:23; Matthew 9:35; Mark 1:39; Luke 4:44)
	"But He said to them, "Let us go into the next towns, that I may preach there also, because for this purpose I have come forth" (Mark 1:38; Luke 4:43)
	"Now it came to pass, when Jesus finished commanding His twelve disciples, that He departed from there to teach and to preach in their cities" (Matthew 11:1). See also Mark 1:14; Mark 2:2; Luke 7:22; Luke 8:1; Ephesians 2:17
Jesus' Disciples	Jesus told them to go, *"...to the lost sheep of the house of Israel. And as you go, preach, saying, 'The kingdom of heaven is at hand.' Heal the sick, cleanse the lepers, raise the dead, cast out demons. Freely you have received, freely give"* (Matthew 10:6-8)
	"Whatever I tell you in the dark, speak in the light; and what you hear in the ear, preach on the housetops" (Matthew 10:27)
	"So they went out and preached that people should repent" (Mark 6:12)
	"And they went out and preached everywhere, the Lord working with them and confirming the word through the accompanying signs. Amen" (Mark 16:20). See also Mark 16:15; Luke 9:2; Luke 9:6
Then His Apostles	*"And daily in the temple, and in every house, they did not cease teaching and preaching Jesus as the Christ"* (Acts 5:42)
	Jesus *"...commanded us to preach to the people, and to testify that it is He who was ordained by God to be Judge of the living and the dead"* (Acts 10:42)
Peter	*"...standing up with the eleven, raised his voice and said to them, "Men of Judea and all who dwell in Jerusalem, let this be known to you, and heed my words"* (Acts 2:14; Also Acts 10:34)
Peter and John	*"So when they had testified and preached the word of the Lord, they returned to Jerusalem, preaching the gospel in many villages of the Samaritans"* (Acts 8:25)
Philip	He *"...went down to the city of Samaria and preached Christ to them"* (Acts 8:5) and *"when they believed Philip as he preached the things concerning the kingdom of God and the name of Jesus Christ, both men and women were baptized"* (Acts 8:12)
	An angel of the Lord sent him to preached to an Ethiopian (Acts 8:26) and the Bible documented, *"Philip opened his mouth, and beginning at this Scripture, preached Jesus to him"* (Acts 8:35). After the Ethiopian was baptized, the Bible

	documents, "...*Philip was found at Azotus. And passing through, he preached in all the cities till he came to Caesarea*" (Acts 8:40)
Men from Cyprus and Cyrene	"*But some of them were men from Cyprus and Cyrene, who, when they had come to Antioch, spoke to the Hellenists, preaching the Lord Jesus. And the hand of the Lord was with them, and a great number believed and turned to the Lord*" (Acts 11:20-21)
Paul	After he met Jesus and was baptized, "*Immediately he preached the Christ in the synagogues, that He is the Son of God*" (Acts 9:20)
	He stated, "*...I make known to you, brethren, that the gospel which was preached by me is not according to man*" (Galatians 1:11). See also Acts 17:13; Acts 19:13; Romans 1:15; Romans 15:19; 1 Corinthians 9:16; Colossians 1:21-23; 1 Timothy 2:7; 2 Timothy 1:11; Galatians 2:2; 2 Timothy 4:17.
Barnabas and Paul	"*So, being sent out by the Holy Spirit, they went down to Seleucia, and from there they sailed to Cyprus. And when they arrived in Salamis, they preached the word of God in the synagogues of the Jews. They also had John as their assistant*" (Acts 13:4-5). See also Acts 14:8-15; Acts 14:21; Acts 15:35.

Table 175: Examples of Preachers in the Biblical Record

Based on the examples in Table 175, one should clearly see that God's Word is manifested through the practice of preaching. Paul told Titus that God, "*...has in due time manifested His word through preaching...*" (Titus 1:3). To this end, Matthews documented that the poor of Israel had, "*... the gospel preached to them*" (Matthew 11:5), and Jesus said, "*...this gospel of the kingdom will be preached in all the world as a* **witness** *to all the nations, and then the end will come*" (Matthew 24:14). One must also try to understand that the Bible, the consolidation of Scriptures – is preaching in and off itself. Paul even documented that, "*...the Scripture, foreseeing that God would justify the Gentiles by **faith**, preached the gospel to Abraham beforehand, saying, "In you all the nations shall be blessed."*" (Galatians 3:8). This thought may be difficult to understand because of pervasive spiritual warfare. But it follows a principle that Paul stated when he wrote, "*For indeed the gospel was preached to us as well as to them; but the word which they heard did not profit them, not being mixed with **faith** in those who heard it*" (Hebrews 4:2). Hence, BTT allows one to see that one of the scariest things of all about selecting a ***good*** preacher in spiritual warfare is the fact that both sides of the campaign employ them. So, what should one expect to hear from a preacher that takes on the responsibility of preaching the Gospel of Jesus Christ? Some clues from the Bible indicate:

- "*Therefore let it be known to you, brethren, that through this Man is preached to you the forgiveness of sins...*" (Acts 13:38)

- "*...explaining and demonstrating that the Christ had to suffer and rise again from the dead, and saying, "This Jesus whom I preach to you is the Christ*" (Acts 17:3)

- "*... Jesus and the resurrection*" (Acts 17:18)
    - "*Now if Christ is preached that He has been raised from the dead, how do some among you say that there is no resurrection of the dead?*" (1 Corinthians 15:12)

- And, *"...if Christ is not risen, then our preaching is empty and your faith is also empty. Yes, and we are found false witnesses of God, because we have testified of God that He raised up Christ, whom He did not raise up—if in fact the dead do not rise. For if the dead do not rise, then Christ is not risen. And if Christ is not risen, your faith is futile; you are still in your sins! Then also those who have fallen asleep in Christ have perished. If in this life only we have hope in Christ, we are of all men the most pitiable"* (1 Corinthians 15:14-19)

- *"...the kingdom of God and teaching the things which concern the Lord Jesus Christ ..."* (Acts 20:25; Acts 28:30-31)

- The difference between right and wrong – *"You, therefore, who teach another, do you not teach yourself? You who preach that a man should not steal, do you steal?"* (Romans 2:21)

- Paul stated, *"...I have made it my aim to preach the gospel, not where Christ was named, lest I should build on another man's foundation, but as it is written: "To whom He was not announced, they shall see; and those who have not heard shall understand.""* (Romans 15:20-21)

- *"...to preach the gospel, not with wisdom of words, lest the cross of Christ should be made of no effect"* (1 Corinthians 1:17)

- *"For since, in the wisdom of God, the world through wisdom did not know God, it pleased God through the foolishness of the message preached to save those who believe"* (1 Corinthians 1:21)

- *"...preach Christ crucified, to the Jews a stumbling block and to the Greeks foolishness..."* (1 Corinthians 1:23)

- Preaching, *"...not with persuasive words of human wisdom, but in demonstration of the Spirit and of power, that your faith should not be in the wisdom of men but in the power of God"* (1 Corinthians 2:4-5)

- *"...the Lord has commanded that those who preach the gospel should live from the gospel"* (1 Corinthians 9:14)

- *"But I fear, lest somehow, as the serpent deceived Eve by his craftiness, so your minds may be corrupted from the simplicity that is in Christ. For if he who comes preaches another Jesus whom we have not preached, or if you receive a different spirit which you have not received, or a different gospel which you have not accepted—you may well put up with it!"* (2 Corinthians 11:3-4)

- *"But even if we, or an angel from heaven, preach any other gospel to you than what we have preached to you, let him be accursed. As we have said before, so now I say again, if anyone preaches any other gospel to you than what you have received, let him be accursed"* (Galatians 1:8-9)

- *"...the unsearchable riches of Christ, and to make all see what is the fellowship of the mystery, which from the beginning of the ages has been hidden in God who created all things through Jesus Christ; to the intent that now the manifold wisdom of God might be made known by the church to the principalities and powers in the heavenly places, according to the eternal purpose which He accomplished in Christ Jesus our Lord..."* (Ephesians 3:8-11)

- *"...without controversy great is the mystery of godliness: God was manifested in the flesh, justified in the Spirit, seen by angels, preached among the Gentiles, believed on in the world, received up in glory"* (1 Timothy 3:16)

- *"...we preached to you the gospel of God"* (1 Thessalonians 2:9)

- *"Him [Jesus] we preach, warning every man and teaching every man in all wisdom, that we may present every man perfect in Christ Jesus"* (Colossians 1:28)

- *"Now, brothers and sisters, I want to remind you of the gospel I preached to you, which you received and on which you have taken your stand. By this gospel you are saved, if you hold firmly to the word I preached to you. Otherwise, you have believed in vain. For what I received I passed on to you as of first importance: that Christ died for our sins according to the Scriptures, that he was buried, that he was raised on the third day according to the Scriptures..."* (1 Corinthians 15:1-4)

Another component of Christ's church is an eldership. Once again, based on the same references cited above for the preacher, this component consists of men that willingly accept God's Word and enforce it within His church. Elders have the inherent responsibility of feeding the flock. Examples of this include strong classes in which only God's Word is taught and ensuring the church has a minister that does not stray from the Word. Inherent to this responsibility is the preparation of the flock for spiritual warfare. These are the men responsible for the business of the church, which includes teaching, preaching, and the administration of the body of Christ. The term "elders" is always plural, always men, and is synonymous with the terms "*bishop*" (1 Timothy 3:1), "*overseer*" (Acts 20:28), "*pastor/shepherd*" (Ephesians 4:11), and "*presbytery*" (1 Timothy 4:14). In the Greek language, all of these names identify the different purposes of elders. Greek terminology can be complicated. The Biblical record documented that Paul and Barnabas appointed "elders" in every church. The Greek word translated elders in Acts 14:23 as "*presbýteros*[5]" identifies "*one who is of sufficient maturity to hold the office of an elder*". The two terms, "*bishop*" and "*overseer*" is a transliteration of the term "*epískopos*[6]" which is a Greek word that refers to a man who watches out for the souls in a local congregation and oversees the work of that congregation to ensure that all things are done decently and in order. The next two terms, "pastor" and "shepherd", are transliterations

---

[5] Strong's #4245 - πρεσβύτερος - Old & New Testament Greek Lexicon. (n.d.). Retrieved from https://www.studylight.org/lexicons/greek/4245.html. Accessed 18 February 2019

[6] Strong's #1985 - ἐπίσκοπος - Old & New Testament Greek Lexicon. (n.d.). Retrieved from https://www.studylight.org/lexicons/greek/1985.html. Accessed 18 February 2019

of the term "*poimén*[7]", which is a Greek word that refers to one who tends a local flock, provides sound doctrine, and guards against **false** doctrine. And the last term, "*presbytery*" is a transliteration of the term "*presbytérion*[8]" which is a Greek word that refers to a plurality or body of elders and can be translated "eldership". BTT allows one to see that God's design for Christ's <u>church</u> never included these identities for a full-time preacher's position. A preacher has his own inherent and significant responsibilities to the <u>church</u>.

Elders must meet strict qualifications to serve as defenders of Christ's <u>church</u> as set by the Holy Spirit. Neither, requirements for elders, nor the qualifications are optional. Therefore, a congregation must be wise about their support for a man put forward for this great responsibility. For these men are to stand before the congregation as examples to the flock. The negative forces have **deceived** the religious community, and even some members of Christ's <u>church</u>, concerning the written standard for elders. However, a fully functioning body of Christ <u>must</u> strive to have elders. Hence, a preacher can serve as an elder for expediency. But this should always be temporary and never permanent. Why? Because Satan always seeks an opportunity to exploit, and where <u>church</u> administration and money are involved, he will find a hole to exploit even if by perception. The Bible documented the requirement for elders in the early <u>church</u> well. BTT allows one to see that the position of elders as protectors of their communities has been part of God's strategy in the war campaign since the flood of Noah's day. In the New Testament, elders serve in a plurality and are required to provide the security against the negative forces in Christ's <u>church</u>. Some examples that illustrated the placement of elders in Christ's <u>church</u> include:

- *"So when they had appointed elders in every <u>church</u>, and prayed with fasting, they commended them to the Lord in whom they had believed"* (Acts 14:23)

- *"Therefore take heed to yourselves and to all the flock, among which the Holy Spirit has made you overseers, to shepherd the <u>church</u> of God which He purchased with His own blood"* (Acts 20:28)

- *"Let the elders who rule well be counted worthy of double **honor**, especially those who labor in the word and doctrine. For the Scripture says, "You shall not muzzle an ox while it treads out the grain," and, "The laborer is worthy of his wages." Do not receive an accusation against an elder except from two or three **witnesses**. Those who are sinning rebuke in the presence of all, that the rest also may <u>fear</u>"* (1 Timothy 5:17-20)

- *"...holding fast the **faithful** word as he has been taught, that he may be able, by sound doctrine, both to exhort and convict those who contradict. For there are many insubordinate, both **idle** talkers and **deceivers**, especially those of the circumcision,*

---

[7] Strong's #4166 - ποιμήν - Old & New Testament Greek Lexicon. (n.d.). Retrieved from https://www.studylight.org/lexicons/greek/4166.html. Accessed 18 February 2019

[8] Strong's #4244 - πρεσβυτέριον - Old & New Testament Greek Lexicon. (n.d.). Retrieved from https://www.studylight.org/lexicons/greek/4244.html. Accessed 18 February 2019

*whose mouths must be stopped, who subvert whole households, teaching things which they ought not, for the sake of **dishonest** gain."* (Titus 1:9-11)

- *"Shepherd the flock of God which is among you, serving as overseers, not by compulsion but willingly, not for **dishonest** gain but eagerly; nor as being lords over those entrusted to you, but being examples to the flock; and when the Chief Shepherd appears, you will receive the crown of glory that does not fade away"* (1 Peter 5:2-4)

God's design for having elders serve in plurality demonstrates His wisdom that together they are harder to compromise under the weight of spiritual warfare. Yes, God recognizes that compromise sometimes happens because of spiritual immaturity. Spiritual immaturity among an eldership will lead to a <u>church's</u> compromise. Thus, all men desiring to serve as elders in Christ's <u>church</u> must meet the qualifications identified in 1 Timothy 3:1-7 and Titus 1:3-9. Although the qualifications seem tough, they are achievable and divinely necessary. For Paul documented the weight these men bear when he wrote, *"Obey those who rule over you, and be submissive, for they watch out for your souls, as those who must give account. Let them do so with <u>joy</u> and not with <u>grief</u>, for that would be unprofitable for you"* (Hebrews 13:17). Elders are held accountable for the role they play in Christ's <u>church</u>. Therefore, they must be capable of handling the <u>authorized</u> things of Christ's <u>church</u> while stopping the <u>unauthorized</u> things. Until elders are appointed, sound men in the Gospel, must lead the congregation. The qualifications documented in the Biblical record are:

1 Timothy 3:1-7	Titus 1:5-9
*"This is a **faithful** saying: If a man desires the position of a bishop, he desires a **good** work. A bishop then must be **blameless**, the husband of one wife, <u>temperate</u>, <u>sober-minded</u>, of **good** behavior, hospitable, able to teach; not given to wine, not **violent**, not <u>greedy</u> for money, but gentle, not <u>quarrelsome</u>, not <u>covetous</u>; one who rules his own house well, having his children in submission with all reverence (for if a man does not know how to rule his own house, how will he take care of the <u>church</u> of God?); not a novice, lest being <u>puffed up</u> with **pride** he fall into the same condemnation as the devil. Moreover he must have a **good** testimony among those who are outside, lest he fall into reproach and the snare of the devil"*	*"...set in order the things that are lacking, and appoint elders in every city as I commanded you— if a man is **blameless**, the husband of one wife, having **faithful** children not accused of dissipation or insubordination. For a bishop must be **blameless**, as a steward of God, not <u>self-willed</u>, not <u>quick-tempered</u>, not given to wine, not **violent**, not <u>greedy</u> for money, but hospitable, a lover of what is **good**, sober-minded, **just**, **holy**, <u>self-controlled</u>, holding fast the **faithful** word as he has been taught, that he may be able, by sound doctrine, both to exhort and convict those who contradict"*

Table 176: Qualifications for <u>Church</u> Elders

One should also take notice of the positive attributes required for the men of an eldership. Based on these qualifications, the eldership is required to protect the <u>church</u> from negative influences from both inside and outside the body of Christ. This protection includes from preachers who attempt to bring in ***false*** doctrine. Hence, in the religious community and unfortunately some _churches_ of Christ, the preacher or the congregation itself resists having an eldership. This is especially true where a preacher or members of the congregation are strong-willed and do not want to be held accountable. One must remember, in spiritual warfare as in physical warfare, **deception** is a strategy of the negative forces. Preachers are just as susceptible to negative influences as is any other member of a congregation.

Another primary role covered later in this book on the eldership concerns "autonomy" of Christ's _Church_. For now, understand that Paul documented that elders are to, "*Shepherd the flock of God <u>which is among you</u>, serving as overseers, not by compulsion but willingly, not for **dishonest** gain but eagerly; nor as being lords <u>over those entrusted to you</u>, but being examples to the flock...*" (1 Peter 5:2-3). Shepherding the <u>local</u> congregation involves both preparing and protecting that local body of Christ in spiritual warfare; not other congregations located somewhere else on the spiritual battlefield. Here is the bottom line when it comes to _church_ elders: These men can only lead people who want to be led. Today, even in Christ's _church_, there are many who still "*walk according to the flesh in the <u>lust</u> of uncleanness and despise authority. They are presumptuous, self-willed*" (2 Peter 2-10), who bring grief (Hebrews 13:17), and circumvent the work of existing elder's in Christ's _church_. Their actions in spiritual warfare erode the position and authority of the eldership. In the end, God will punish these men and women who grieve the eldership and refuse to submit to their authority.

The fourth component of Christ's _church_ is the deacon. Christ's _church_ <u>can</u> have deacons but the position is not mandatory. Deacons are not authorized as a substitute for an eldership. BTT allows one to see that the function of deacons exist to aid the eldership in carrying out specific functions of Christ's _church_. When the function goes away, so does the deacon selected to serve in that specific function. Unless, the elders assign another responsibility to that deacon based on the _church's_ needs, that deacon returns to their normal service with the rest of the assembly. The negative attributes and spiritual warfare have influenced some organizations to use deacons in non-Biblical and permanent roles. Elders must not allow this. It circumvents Christ's design for His _church_. The Biblical record documents the qualifications for deacons and their wives. Notice once again, just like the position for the preacher and elders, this position is also filled by married <u>men</u>. The Bible documents:

1 Timothy 3:8-10, 12-13 (Men)	1 Timothy 3:11 (Wives)
"*Likewise deacons must be <u>reverent</u>, not double-tongued, not given to much wine, not <u>greedy</u> for money, holding the mystery of the **faith** with a pure conscience. But let these also first be tested; then let them serve as deacons, being found **blameless**...Let deacons be the husbands of one wife, ruling their children and their own houses well. For those who have served well as deacons obtain for themselves a **good** standing and great boldness in the **faith** which is in Christ Jesus*"	"*Likewise, their wives must be reverent, not <u>slanderers</u>, <u>temperate</u>, **faithful** in all things*"

Table 177: Qualifications for _Church_ Deacons

Figure 53 on page 692 is the only authorized structure found in the Biblical record for God's divinely creation of Christ's <u>church</u>. BTT allows one to see that this structure is available for anyone to see. Unfortunately, the negative attributes generate fog on the battlefield to influence people to add all types of positions and titles to their organization. Sadly, this has happened in some of Christ's <u>churches</u> who have strayed from His original design. Do not be **deceived**. God does not direct these additions. Now one might ask where are the teachers in the design of **Figure 53**? Teachers are not standalone positions. All four of the authorized positions are teacher positions. Moreover, this requirement falls to every responsible adult members of Christ's <u>church</u>. In this role, women perform this vital function for the health of the <u>church</u>. Whether teaching formally, as Paul mentioned in Hebrews 5:12, or just providing Biblical guidance to the younger generations mentioned in Titus 2:1-8, all adults in the body of Christ have a responsibility to teach in some way. In this role, women are involved with other women, youth, and children in the congregation. There are other roles women fill in teaching with both men and women on secular topics based on their skills. But this should never be confused with serving in the positions of the elders, deacons, or preachers. For example, women doctors or nurses may be called upon to teach Cardiopulmonary Resuscitation (CPR) or defibrillator classes. Educators in the school systems may be called upon to teach a teacher's development seminar...etc. Christ's <u>church</u>, when functioning properly, requires a wealth of talent and task from both men and women to keep it spiritually fit. Elders are responsible and accountable in Christ's <u>church</u> to ensure God's Word is not violated. For example, when leadership in Christ's <u>church</u> teach that women cannot teach other men at all and begin citing views beyond what the Lord has documented in His Word, **false** teaching and the negative attributes have crept in the <u>church</u>. BTT, <u>discernment</u>, and discretion must be applied based on any given situations. The elderships is responsibility and accountable for the decisions made.

Within the topic of teachers, one can see where the negative attributes sharpen their use of spiritual warfare in Christ's <u>church</u>. Many qualified men and women are refusing to teach because of internal struggles within the body of Christ. Paul addressed this issue among a list of other works of the flesh that were evident when he wrote about "...<u>contentions</u>, **jealousies**, outbursts of <u>wrath</u>, <u>selfish ambitions</u>, <u>dissensions</u>, <u>heresies</u>..." (Galatians 5:20). Peter also addressed the issue when he said, "...*there will be* **false** *teachers among you, who will secretly bring in destructive heresies*..." (2 Peter 2:1). The issue is "heresy" and the people who cause it are known as "heretics." They often exist in the body of Christ constantly trying to denigrate teachers who strive to teach God's Word. In physical warfare, these are the people known as sharpshooters. Their job is to disrupt the opposing side from a place of stealth. Their weapons are specially designed to ensure accuracy, stealth, and maximum effectiveness at incredible distances. The sharpshooter's sole goal in physical warfare is to neutralize a target; that is to **kill** whomever their mission dictates. Conversely, in spiritual warfare, the sharpshooters are known as heretics and do the same thing as the sharpshooter of physical warfare. However, instead of using weapons to physically **kill**, the heretic uses his or her tongue (James 3:5-6) to openly contradict teachers or sublimely plant seeds of <u>doubt</u> in an open forum to spiritually **kill**. The heretic's slick but open assault on teachers has the effect of calling the credibility of a teacher into question. Even if the heretic is handled appropriately in class, their words kindle unseen dangers among the weaker members of the body. Future teacher prospects hold back from teaching out of _fear_ and embarrassment from the antics of the heretic. This should not be so. Over time, a body of Christ succumbs from the inability to convince qualified teachers to teach even though the congregation is blessed with a generous population of members. The heretic's subversive behavior can begin a cycle that often takes time to notice until it is too late. Over time, the <u>church</u> slowly succumbs to the inability to maintain qualified teachers. Those who regularly volunteer become fatigued, quit, or attrite for other reasons. Families eventually leave because there are not enough teachers available to satisfy their needs (human thinking). As things begin to unravel, the heretic simply moves on believing it was "the <u>church</u>" and not "them" who caused the <u>church's</u> demise.

    Now just in case the negative attributes are attempting to influence you to close this book over the topic of <u>male</u> and female specific roles in Christ's <u>church</u>, remember the spiritual battlefield is a complicated and filthy place filled with **deception** and **lies**. The negative forces have strategically sought to destroy Christ's <u>church</u> by teaching error through religious teaching. One can be assured of this truth based on everything one has read. Meditate on the examples, wording, and authorized qualifications of positions in Christ's <u>church</u>. For the war campaign that I have painstakingly laid out in this book, this next point is critical and I must repeat it. One must always remember that when God made man first, God gave him divine responsibilities for spiritual matters. When the man heeded the voice of his wife over God according to Genesis 3:17, the situation was an affront to God. This situation was such an affront to God that He placed <u>man</u> over the woman in spiritual matters (Genesis 3:16). The Holy Spirit confirmed the order through Paul as he documented:

- *"But I want you to know that the head of every man is Christ, the head of woman is man, and the head of Christ is God"* (1 Corinthians 11:3)

- *"Let your women keep silent in the <u>churches</u>, for they are not permitted to speak; but they are to be submissive, as the law also says"* (1 Corinthians 14:34)

    BTT allows one to see that this directive by God, confirmed by the Holy Spirit, is not debatable, as the negative attributes have influenced some to do. This is why spiritual warfare continues. The positions in Christ's <u>church</u>, elders (1 Timothy 3:1-7, and Titus 1:5-9), deacons (1 Timothy 3:8-11), and the preacher are <u>male</u>-only positions. This has no bearing on leadership positions in any other profession including business, government, or other secular leadership roles. This only has to do with Christ's <u>church</u>. God is pouring out His <u>wrath</u> on men worldwide who defer to women in this single area and violate His will in this divine area of responsibility.

    Now the negative forces have influenced religious leaders today to use the case of Deborah in the Book of Judges against God's design. One must consider that the Biblical record documents that she was a prophetess, a wife, and a judge according to Judges 4:4. A careful read of the text indicates her primary role was judging issues of sin based on the Mosaic Law. Even when she called Barak to attack the army of Sisera in Judges 4:6-7, the Bible indicates that God had already told Barak what to do but he was hesitating. Deborah, as the judge of Israel told Barak, *"Has not the Lord God of Israel commanded, 'Go and deploy troops at Mount Tabor; take with you ten thousand men of the sons of Naphtali and of the sons of Zebulun..."*

(Judges 4:6). The point is that even in this example, God dealt with the man; Deborah was the authority figure to enforce God's command. Thus, the religious community's erroneous teaching only furthers the advancement of the negative forces on the spiritual battlefield.

If the organizational structure and teaching is correct, one should be able to find Christ's _church_ following the same pattern anywhere on the spiritual battlefield. The consistent pattern based on the pattern of the 1st Century _church_ taught and enforced by the eldership every Sunday will include:

The Pattern	What Is Documented
Prayer	"And they continued steadfastly in the apostles' doctrine and fellowship, in the breaking of bread, and in prayers" (Acts 2:42)
Singing (Acapella)	"...speaking to one another in psalms and _hymns and spiritual songs, singing_ and making melody in your heart to the Lord" (Ephesians 5:19)
The Lord's supper	"Now on the first day of the week, when the disciples came together to _break bread_, Paul, ready to depart the next day, spoke to them and continued his message until midnight" (Acts 20:7)
	"For I received from the Lord that which I also delivered to you: that the Lord Jesus on the same night in which He was betrayed took _bread_; and when He had given thanks, He broke it and said, "Take, eat; this is My body which is broken for you; do this in remembrance of Me." In the same manner He also took the _cup_ after supper, saying, "This cup is the new covenant in My blood. This do, as often as _you drink it_, in remembrance of Me." For as often as you _eat this bread and drink this cup_, you proclaim the Lord's death till He comes"(1 Corinthians 11:23-26)
Giving	"On the first day of the week let each one of you _lay something aside_, storing up _as he may prosper_, that there be no collections when I come" (1 Corinthians 16:2). **Note:** This is not the practice of tithes and offerings from the Old Testament as some religious communities teach. The requirement to tithe in the manner prescribed by the Mosaic Law ceased upon the establishment of the New Covenant. For people who preach or practice the Mosaic Law (Leviticus 27:30), they must follow the whole law. That is a percent of their acquired animals (Leviticus 27:32); heave offering (Numbers 18:26); grain, wine, and oil (Deuteronomy 12:17; 14:22-23; Nehemiah 13:5); produce (Deuteronomy 14:28); general items including oxen and sheep (2 Chronicles 31:5-6); and); and all manner of herbs (Matthew 23:23; Luke 11:42)
	"But this I say: He who sows sparingly will also reap sparingly, and he who sows bountifully will also reap bountifully. _So let each one give as he purposes in his heart_, not grudgingly or of necessity; for God loves a cheerful giver. And God is able to make all grace abound toward you, that you, always having all sufficiency in all things, may have an abundance for every good work" (2 Corinthians 9:6-8)
Preaching and Bible Study	"How then shall they call on Him in whom they have not believed? And how shall they believe in Him of whom they have not _heard_? And how shall they hear without a preacher?" (Romans 10:14)
	"..._Preach_ the word! Be ready in season and out of season. Convince, rebuke, exhort, with all longsuffering and teaching" (2 Tim 4:2)

	"...they received the word with all readiness, and <u>searched the Scriptures</u> daily to find out whether these things were so. (Acts 17:11)
An Invitation to come to Christ	"For He says: "In an acceptable time I have heard you, and in the day of salvation I have helped you." Behold, now is the accepted time; behold, now is the day of salvation" (2 Corinthians 6:2)
	"Therefore, brethren, be even more diligent to make your call and election sure, for if you do these things you will never stumble..." (2 Peter 1:10)
	"Jesus said to him, "I am the way, the truth, and the life. No one comes to the Father except through Me" (John 14:6)
	"Go therefore and make disciples of all the nations, baptizing them in the name of the Father and of the Son and of the Holy Spirit..." (Matthew 28:19)
	"And now why are you waiting? Arise and be baptized, and wash away your sins, calling on the name of the Lord.'" (Acts 22:16)

Table 178: The Consistent Pattern of Activity in Christ's <u>Church</u>

This pattern allows Christ's <u>church</u> to be consistently recognized anywhere on the spiritual battlefield worldwide. This pattern is effective for teaching and enforcing what Jesus taught his apostles for engaging in spiritual warfare without worldly distractions. This includes the use of A capella singing, which is an exercise in unity as well as discipline. From a warfighting perspective, instruments offer the opportunity for some people to avoid individual participation in Christ's requirement to fully serve Him. A capella singing demands the participation of every voice on the spiritual battlefield. When one refuses to sing, they challenge God's requirement by their lack of participation in His worship service. A capella singing within Christ's <u>church</u> is like the call of cadence for soldiers training for physical war; no musical instruments are required. This mental discipline keeps everyone together and in step. Individually and collectively, this discipline allows everyone to help their fellow brother and sister in Christ at the spiritual level. Paul wrote for the individual level, one should allow "*...the word of Christ dwell in you richly in all wisdom, teaching and admonishing one another in psalms and hymns and spiritual songs, singing with grace in your hearts to the Lord*" (Colossians 3:16). But this same verse also documents the collective level where "*teaching and admonishing one another*" occurs. One must remember, when the Holy Spirit inspired John to write, "*God is Spirit, and those who worship Him must worship in spirit and truth*" (John 4:24), it meant that one cannot serve God in carnally thinking ways. Christ's <u>church</u> in Corinth grappled with this same issue and Paul told them, "*...I, brethren, could not speak to you as to spiritual people but as to carnal, as to babes in Christ. I fed you with milk and not with solid food; for until now you were not able to receive it, and even now you are still not able; for you are still carnal. For where there are envy, strife, and divisions among you, are you not carnal and behaving like mere men?*" (1 Corinthians 3:1-3). Moreover, as one puts both spiritual and physical warfare into perspective, BTT allows one to see that the unique sounds of musical instruments are noticeable on a battlefield. In the 1st Century <u>church</u>, during Roman and Jewish <u>persecution</u>, Christ's <u>church</u> was already a target of **violence** and **hate**. Any military soldier knows that the unique sounds of musical instruments can be heard even during the sounds of battle. An instrument that is heard can be quickly targeted and destroyed. Hence, the human voice is used on the battlefield and not an instrument. For the 1st Century <u>church</u>, if musical instruments were divine requirements, congregations of people would automatically be isolated, identified, and slaughtered by their **oppressors**. Thus, Jesus never prescribed musical instruments for His <u>church</u> or worship to His Father. Further, the Bible confirms, "*Jesus Christ is the same yesterday, today, and forever*" (Hebrews 13:8). Hence, only congregations that follow His Word and divine pattern will survive on the spiritual battlefield.

Jesus provided the pattern for the people of His <u>*Church*</u> to follow and to offer ***faithful*** worship to His Father in heaven. This pattern is distinctive on the spiritual battlefield. In the corporate worship service, and even in one's personal prayer, praying is to God through His Son Jesus Christ according (John 16:23). No other intercessor is authorized to include angels, Jesus' mother Mary, or any manmade saint. Please do not be ***deceived*** by the negative attributes. Anything beyond His simple pattern creates vain worship. The Lord said this to the nation of Israel. The prophet Isaiah documented, "*Therefore the Lord said: Inasmuch as these people draw near with their mouths and* **honor** *Me with their lips, but have removed their hearts far from Me, and their <u>fear</u> toward Me is taught by the commandment of men...*" (Isaiah 29:13). A study of the Book of Isaiah easily reveals the man-made rules and traditions Jewish leaders imposed to circumvent God's sacred commands for worship to Him. Later, Jesus would say to the religious leaders of His day, "*Hypocrites! Well did Isaiah prophesy about you, saying: 'These people draw near to Me with their mouth, and* **honor** *Me with their lips, but their heart is far from Me. And in vain they worship Me, teaching as doctrines the commandments of men* " (Matthew 15:7-9) and Mark added, "*...For laying aside the commandment of God, you hold the tradition of men—the washing of pitchers and cups, and many other such things you do*" (Mark 7:6-8). So why do so many religious organizations worship God in vain today? Why are so many people lost in the fog generated by the negative attributes and vainly worshiping a God who chooses not to listen to them (John 9:31)? Why is the war campaign becoming more ***violent*** even in the very pulpits of the communities that claims to worship God? The reasons are simple and laid out in His Word. Here are just a few examples:

- "*Now we know that God does not hear sinners; but if anyone is a worshiper of God and does His will, He hears him*" (John 9:31)

- "*Whoever* **transgresses** *and does not abide in the doctrine of Christ does not have God. He who abides in the doctrine of Christ has both the Father and the Son. If anyone comes to you and does not bring this doctrine, do not receive him into your house nor greet him; for he who greets him shares in his* **evil** *deeds*" (2 John 9-11)

- "*For there are many insubordinate, both* **idle** *talkers and* **deceivers**, *especially those of the circumcision, whose mouths must be stopped, who <u>subvert</u> whole households, teaching things which they ought not, for the sake of <u>dishonest</u> <u>gain</u>*" (Titus 1:10-11)

- "*This testimony is true. Therefore rebuke them sharply, that they may be sound in the* **faith**, *not giving heed to Jewish fables and commandments of men who turn from the* *truth. To the pure all things are pure, but to those who are defiled and unbelieving nothing is pure; but even their mind and conscience are defiled. They profess to know God, but in works they deny Him, being abominable, disobedient, and disqualified for every **good** work"* (Titus 1:13-16)

- *"Therefore, if you died with Christ from the basic principles of the world, why, as though living in the world, do you subject yourselves to regulations— "Do not touch, do not taste, do not handle," which all concern things which perish with the using— according to the commandments and doctrines of men? These things indeed have an appearance of <u>wisdom</u> in self-imposed religion, **false** <u>humility</u>, and neglect of the body, but are of no value against the indulgence of the flesh"* (Colossians 2:20-23)

- *"For the time will come when they will not endure sound doctrine, but according to their own desires, because they have itching ears, they will heap up for themselves teachers; and they will turn their ears away from the truth, and be turned aside to fables"* (2 Timothy 4:3-4)

Jesus, the Son of God, ensured that His <u>church</u> would survive on the spiritual battlefield by defining a requirement for all who desired to be a part of His <u>church</u>. In other words, one cannot just walk in and take up residence in Christ's <u>church</u>. The influences and baggage of spiritual warfare, and the negative attributes' influences, must be cleansed. Hence, there is an entrance criterion. One must summit to Christ's entrance criteria on earth because it paves the way for a journey with Him on one's way toward heaven. This journey crosses the spiritual battlefield. Jesus said two extremely important things that cement the relationship and correlation between Himself and His <u>church</u> at the nexus of the earthly and spiritual realms of the battlefield. He said:

- *"I am the way, the truth, and the life. No one comes to the Father except through Me"* (John 14:6)

- *"Most assuredly, I say to you, he who does not enter the sheepfold by the door, but climbs up some other way, the same is a **thief** and a **robber**. But he who enters by the door is the shepherd of the sheep. To him the doorkeeper opens, and the sheep hear his voice; and he calls his own sheep by name and leads them out. And when he brings out his own sheep, he goes before them; and the sheep follow him, for they know his voice"* (John 10:1-4)

So, what is the entrance criteria for Christ's <u>church</u> according to the pattern established by Christ Himself and taught by His apostles to the 1st Century <u>church</u>? The criteria are as follows:

The Criteria	What Is Documented
One must Hear the Gospel	"Behold, I stand at the door and knock. If anyone <u>hears</u> My voice and opens the door, I will come in to him and dine with him, and he with Me" (Revelation 3:20)
	"So then faith comes by <u>hearing</u>, and hearing by the word of God" (Romans 10:17)
	"How then shall they call on Him in whom they have not believed? And how shall they believe in Him of whom they have not <u>heard</u>? And how shall they hear without a preacher?" (Romans 10:14)
	"Blessed is he who reads and those who <u>hear</u> the words of this prophecy, and keep those things which are written in it; for the time is near" (Revelation 1:3)
	"He who has an ear, let him <u>hear</u> what the Spirit says to the <u>churches</u>. To him who overcomes I will give to eat from the tree of life, which is in the midst of the Paradise of God" (Revelation 2:7)
	"He who has an ear, let him hear what the Spirit says to the <u>churches</u>. He who overcomes shall not be hurt by the second death" (Revelation 2:11)
	"He who has an ear, let him <u>hear</u> what the Spirit says to the <u>churches</u>. To him who overcomes I will give some of the hidden manna to eat. And I will give him a white stone, and on the stone a new name written which no one knows except him who receives it" (Revelation 2:17)
Believe it	"But without faith it is impossible to please Him, for he who comes to <u>God must believe</u> that He is, and that He is a rewarder of those who diligently seek Him" (Hebrews 11:6)
	"But as many as received Him, to them He gave the right to become children of God, to those who <u>believe</u> in His name..." (John 1:12)
	"He who <u>believes</u> and is baptized will be saved; but he who <u>does not believe</u> will be condemned" (Mark 16:16)
	"For I bear them witness that they have a zeal for God, but not according to knowledge. For they being ignorant of God's righteousness, and seeking to establish their own righteousness, have not submitted to the righteousness of God. For Christ is the end of the law for righteousness to everyone who <u>believes</u>" (Romans 10:2-4)
Repent of one's sins	"I tell you, no; but unless you <u>repent</u> you will all likewise perish" (Luke 13:3)
	"<u>Repent</u> therefore and be converted, that your sins may be blotted out, so that times of refreshing may come from the presence of the Lord..." (Acts 3:19)
	"Truly, these times of ignorance God overlooked, but now commands all men everywhere to <u>repent</u>, because He has appointed a day on which He will judge the world in righteousness by the Man whom He has ordained. He has given assurance of this to all by raising Him from the dead" (Acts 17:30-31)
	"Therefore whoever <u>confesses</u> Me before men, him I will also <u>confess</u> before My Father who is in heaven. But whoever denies Me before men, him I will also deny before My Father who is in heaven" (Matthew 10:32-33)

Confess Christ	"...that if you <u>confess</u> with your mouth the Lord Jesus and <u>believe</u> in your heart that God has raised Him from the dead, you will be saved. For with the heart one <u>believes</u> unto righteousness, and with the mouth <u>confession</u> is made unto salvation" (Romans 10:9-10)
	"Whoever <u>confesses</u> that Jesus is the Son of God, God abides in him, and he in God" (1 John 4:15)
	An Example: Philips and the Ethiopian eunuch: "Now as they went down the road, they came to some water. And the eunuch said, "See, here is water. What hinders me from being baptized?" Then Philip said, "If you believe with all your heart, you may." And he answered and said, "I believe that Jesus Christ is the Son of God" (Acts 8:36-37)
Be Baptized	Jesus said, "All authority has been given to Me in heaven and on earth. Go therefore and make disciples of all the nations, <u>baptizing</u> them in the name of the Father and of the Son and of the Holy Spirit, teaching them to observe all things that I have commanded you..." (Matthew 28:18-20)
	"...<u>Repent</u>, and let every one of you be <u>baptized</u> in the name of Jesus Christ for the remission of sins; and you shall receive the gift of the Holy Spirit" (Acts 2:38)
	"For you are all sons of God through faith in Christ Jesus. For as many of you as were <u>baptized</u> into Christ have put on Christ" (Galatians 3:26-27)
	"There is also an antitype which now saves us—<u>baptism</u> (not the removal of the filth of the flesh, but the answer of a good conscience toward God), through the resurrection of Jesus Christ, who has gone into heaven and is at the right hand of God, angels and authorities and powers having been made subject to Him" (1 Peter 3:21-22)
	An Example among many: Ananias said to Paul prior to his conversion, "And now why are you waiting? Arise and be <u>baptized</u>, and wash away your sins, calling on the name of the Lord.'" (Acts 22:16)
Once one becomes a Christian: **Live faithfully**	"...Be <u>faithful until death</u>, and I will give you the crown of life" (Revelations 2:10)
	"Blessed is the man who <u>endures temptation</u>; for when he has been approved, he will receive the crown of life which the Lord has promised to those who love Him" (James 1:12)
	"For we have become partakers of Christ if we <u>hold the beginning of our confidence steadfast to the end</u>, while it is said: "Today, if you will hear His voice, do not harden your hearts as in the rebellion" (Hebrews 3:14-15)
	The words one wants to hear for God: "Well done, good and faithful servant; you were faithful over a few things, I will make you ruler over many things. Enter into the joy of your lord" (Matthew 25:21)

Table 179: Becoming Part of Christ's <u>Church</u> Based on God's Biblical Pattern

BTT allows one to see that entry into Christ's <u>church</u> and beyond begins with hearing the Gospel. When one begins to read and hear the Word of God, and if one's inner spirit is open to what he or she hears, then a spiritual connection can occur. The Word of God speaks spiritually to one's inner spirit. This may sound strange but remember that there is more to a person than just flesh and blood as **Figure 54** illustrates. We are living beings of flesh, blood, soul, and a spirit; and God's Word is powerful within it. When one sincerely desires to know God, a spiritual opportunity opens which human instruments cannot detect. Jesus said, *"It is the Spirit who gives life; the flesh profits nothing. The words that I speak to you are spirit, and they are life"* (John 6:63). Jesus' Word contains life

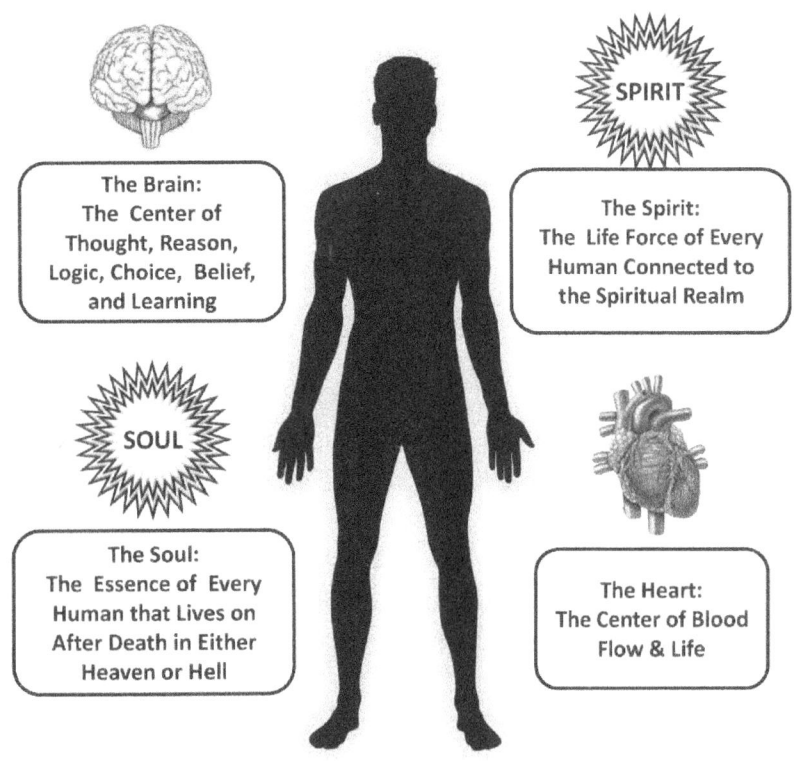

Figure 54: The Components of Man

itself. His Word speaks to our inner spirit, but only if we allow it. This is beyond human understanding, but it is true. When Jesus taught His apostles the same Word from God, as they passed the Word on to us, life stayed in the Word. We know this because Peter asked Jesus, *"Lord, to whom shall we go? You have the words of eternal life"* (John 6:68). In addition to this, an angel of the Lord, who freed the apostles from prison, told them, *"Go, stand in the temple and speak to the people all the words of this life"* (Acts 5:20). Paul, inspired by the Holy Spirit, communicated God's Word verbally and through letters to <u>churches</u>. Spiritual hearing occurs when one avails one's self to hearing it. If not, all one hears is static and the noise of the world. The positive and negative attributes, which are spirits, communicate with the inner spirit of man in this way. But unless one's inner man has developed <u>discernment</u>, then one's brain will always attempt to rationalize and override the spiritual with worldly things that the physical senses interpret. This is what causes the war in man. We know this is true because both Jesus and the Holy Spirit inspiring Paul provided us the information to validate it. Jesus said, *"Watch and pray, lest you enter into <u>temptation</u>. The spirit indeed is willing, but the flesh is weak"* (Matthew 26:41; Mark 14:38). Paul documented later, *"I say then: Walk in the Spirit, and you shall not fulfill the <u>lust</u> of the flesh. For the flesh <u>lusts</u> against the Spirit, and the Spirit against the flesh; and these are contrary to one another, so that you do not do the things that you wish"* (Galatians 5:16-17). Therefore, we know the fight between the carnal side of a person and the spiritual side is real. Paul even shared a personal example to help one see the spiritual war that occurs within each person. He stated in Romans 7:14-25:

*"For we know that the law is spiritual, but I am carnal, sold under sin. For what I am doing, I do not understand. For what I will to do, that I do not practice; but what I **hate**, that I do. If, then, I do what I will not to do, I agree with the law that it is **good**. But now, it is no longer I who do it, but sin that dwells in me. For I know that in me (that is, in my flesh) nothing **good** dwells; for to will is present with me, but how to perform what is **good** I do not find. For the **good** that I will to do, I do not do; but the **evil** I will not to do, that I practice. Now if I do what I will not to do, it is no longer I who do it, but sin that dwells in me. I find then a law, that **evil** is present with me, the one who wills to do **good**. For I delight in the law of God according to the inward man. But I see another law in my members, warring against the law of my mind, and bringing me into captivity to the law of sin which is in my members. O wretched man that I am! Who will deliver me from this body of death? I thank God—through Jesus Christ our Lord! So then, with the mind I myself serve the law of God, but with the flesh the law of sin"*

To rebuff the spiritual enemy actively engaging the carnal side of man, the spirit of man requires discipline, training, and education through the Word of God. The Biblical record documents that:

- *"The **spirit** of a man is the lamp of the LORD, searching all the inner depths of his heart"* (Proverbs 20:27)

- *"All the ways of a man are pure in his own eyes, but the LORD weighs the **spirits**"* (Proverbs 16:2)

- *"The **spirit** of a man will sustain him in sickness, but who can bear a broken **spirit**?"* (Proverbs 18:14)

- *"He who has knowledge spares his words, and a man of understanding is of a calm **spirit**"* (Proverbs 17:27)

- *"A man's **pride** will bring him low, but the <u>humble</u> in **spirit** will retain **honor**"* (Proverbs 29:23)

The Gospel of Jesus Christ has more meaning when one comes to grips with the fact that the inner spirit lives within one's body. Christ's Word provides the sustainment for the inner spirit and hearing Christ's Word is the first phase of BTT. When one begins to hear the Gospel, BTT begins to take place <u>at the spiritual level</u>. In addition, when one becomes a part of Christ's <u>church</u>, one takes up the mantle to support the rest of the positive forces of the war campaign and fight the spiritual fight until God calls one home.

With this said, now consider probably the greatest design of God's strategy for Christ's _church_ to survive on the spiritual battlefield. This is the implementation of "autonomy" among Christ's _churches_. All **good** military strategist understand that some of his or her fighting forces risk capture, compromise, or destruction during physical warfare. Thus, a **good** military strategist arrays his or her forces in such a way that plans for this possibility to allow for maximum strategic flexibility. This planning prevents the failing of all the strategist's forces from a single capture, compromise, or destruction of his forces. Well God, the Ultimate Strategist, designed Christ's _church_ on the same principle. Christ's _kingdom_ on earth is comprised of many _churches_ fighting the negative forces of the war campaign. Each of these _churches_ has its own localized areas of responsibilities on the spiritual battlefield. In God's divine plan, He foreknew that some of Christ's _churches_ would be compromised, captured, or destroyed in the course of spiritual warfare. Thus, one can see the beauty of God's design of autonomy in His masterful plan. BTT allows one to see that Christ's _church_ has the entire battle plan (the Bible), with full instructions for fighting the campaign. In military terms, the Bible documents the strategic war campaign plan. Christ, the General in Charge, has told us how to execute the plan. While preachers and evangelists preach and help people to understand God's plan, elders are the executers of the plan for the operation of His _church_. Nothing else is required outside of one's commitment and obedience to the plan. Each separate _church_, made up of congregations of Christians, have their marching orders on the spiritual battlefield and can independently execute the plan from their physical locations. Once again, the pattern looks like **Figure 55**.

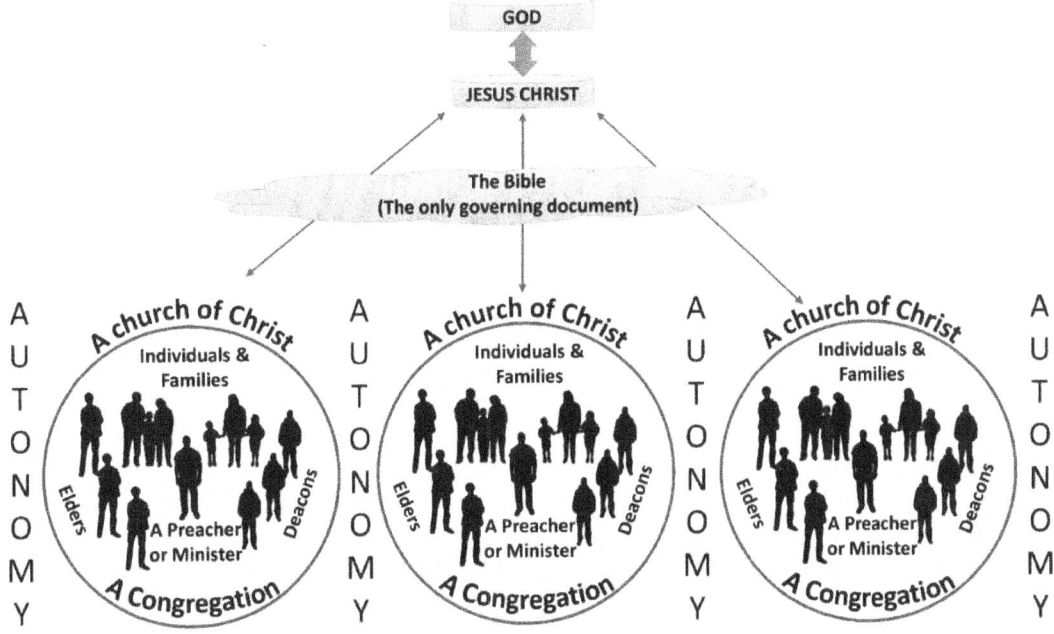

Figure 55: God's Pattern for His Church

God's design separates Christ's _churches_ to protect them from the negative forces' influence that can corrupt them all (see **Figure 56**). In addition, not having a fabricated hierarchy, counsel, or convention governing all of Christ's _churches_ ensures there is no chance that His _church_ and God's Word will be collectively compromised. Under God's strategic plan of autonomy, compromise, capture, or destruction of one of Christ's _churches_ does not impair the other arks of safety. In other words, the compromised church cannot take down the entire spiritual fighting force. In addition, autonomy between congregations prevents the eldership of one congregation from entering the compromised zone of another congregation to defend, fight, or save that congregation. Both Paul and Peter provided instruction on this from the Holy Spirit. Paul said, "*For I have not shunned to declare to you the whole counsel of God. Therefore take heed to yourselves and to all the flock, among which the Holy Spirit has made you overseers, to shepherd the _church_ of God which He purchased with His own blood. For I know this, that after my departure savage wolves will come in among you, not sparing the flock*" (Acts 20:27-29). Peter documented, "*Shepherd the flock of God which is among you, serving as overseers...*" (1 Peter 5:2). This is not cruel; this is God's design. BTT allows one to see that Satan's craftiness will cause well-intentioned members of Christ's _church_ to stumble in another congregation's **_folly_**. When one of Christ's _church_ fails, it fails by its own internal choices. One must understand that the influences of the negative forces not only compromised the congregation's leadership, the negative attributes also compromised the congregation. Therefore, each adult member must take the steps to make his or her "...*call and election sure, for if you do these things you will never stumble; for so an entrance will be supplied to you abundantly into the everlasting _kingdom_ of our Lord and Savior Jesus Christ*" (2 Peter 1:9-11). One cannot allow himself, herself, or one's family, to stay in a compromised church.

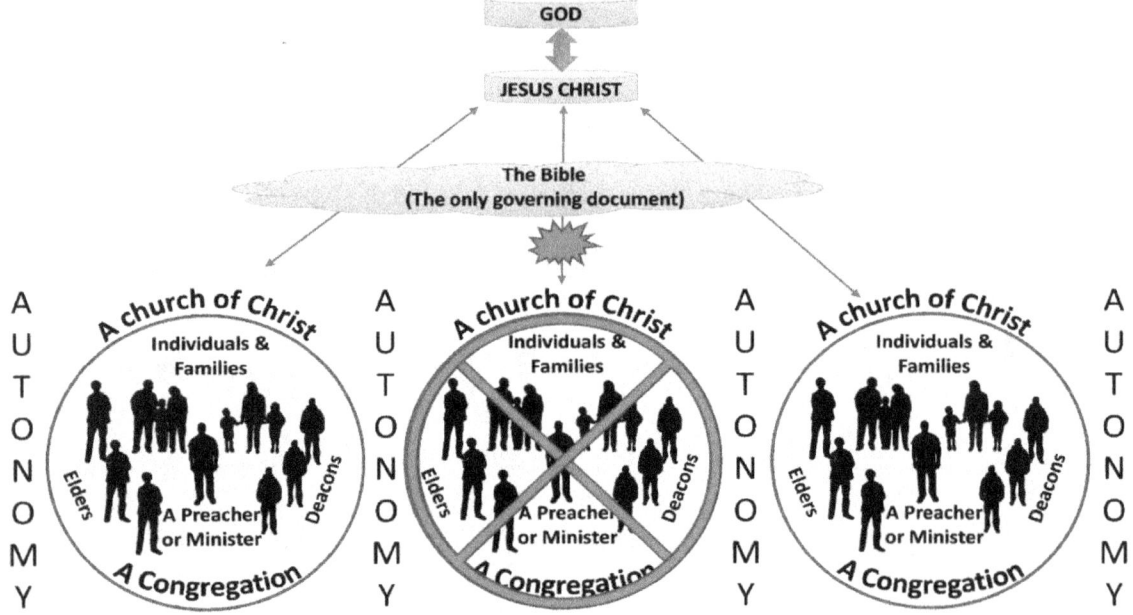

Figure 56: God's Divine use of Autonomy

An entire organization can ignorantly fall away and enter a state of apostasy when God's Truth is compromised. This also applies to the compromise of church elders or men acting in leadership roles. **Figure 56** captures this idea visually.

Once again, God's strategy is not harsh by any measure. It brings clarity to the need for autonomy and demonstrates why God is the Master Strategist. Autonomy allows Christ's _church_ to flourish on the spiritual battlefield even as a part of His body stumbles under the weight of the spiritual warfare. Members of the compromised church must use _discernment_ and leave a compromised church because the decision comes down to a choice between **good** or **evil**. A compromised church simply supports the negative forces of the war campaign. Further, one must remember that the Bible documents that a remnant will always survive. Somewhere in the world, there will always be a few dedicated Christians serving the Lord, through Christ His way, until He returns.

The negative forces set up their own operations to mimic Christ's _church_ by discarding God's pattern. These forces influence religious leaders who provide **false** doctrine to their occupied organizations. **Figure 57** illustrates the typical scenario found in many organizations

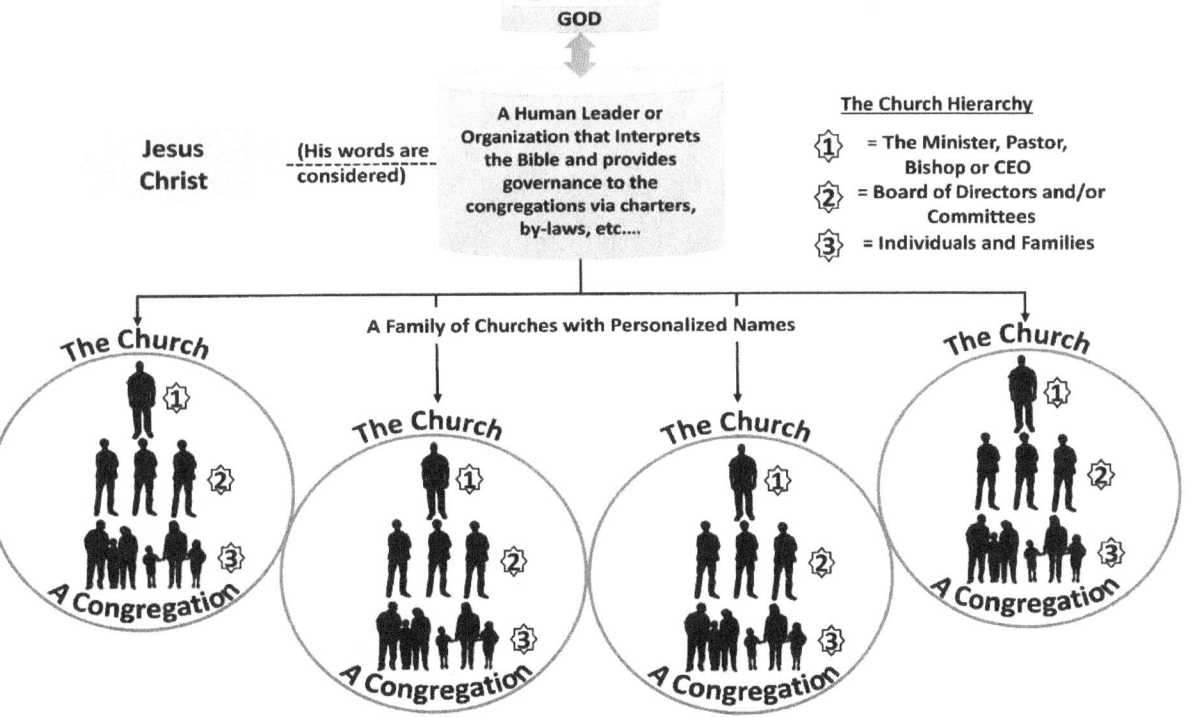

Figure 57: Typical Constructs of Man's Church Leadership Hierarchies

today.

When this construct is in place, the truth of the Gospel of Jesus Christ is filtered and then given to people for their understanding. Plain and simple, this hierarchy contradicts what God instituted. In fact, when Jesus is not the lead of His _church_, the whole hierarchy, its doctrine, its teachings, and its people's beliefs miss the mark. This also means that one cannot be taught wrong and _baptized_ right. Hence, when one desires to be added to the Lord's _church_, one is _baptized_ afresh to start a new walk with Christ even if _baptized_ previously. BTT allows one to see that in religious hierarchies, Christ's Word simply becomes a guideline. The hierarchy sets the rules while taking Jesus' Word into consideration. This directly violates God's command "..._This is My beloved Son, in whom I am well pleased. Hear Him!_" (Matthew 17:5; Mark 9:7; Luke 9:35). Therefore, these religious organizations are no more than outcasts on the spiritual battlefield. These are the people caught up in the negative force's fog generated in the war campaign. They believe they are in step with Christ but they are not. Jesus spoke about these people in Matthew 7: 21-29 when He said,

> "_Not everyone who says to Me, 'Lord, Lord,' shall enter the kingdom of heaven, but he who does the will of My Father in heaven. Many will say to Me in that day, 'Lord, Lord, have we not prophesied in Your name, cast out demons in Your name, and done many wonders in Your name?' And then I will declare to them, 'I never knew you; depart from Me, you who practice lawlessness!' "Therefore whoever hears these sayings of Mine, and does them, I will liken him to a wise man who built his house on the rock: and the rain descended, the floods came, and the winds blew and beat on that house; and it did not fall, for it was founded on the rock. "But everyone who hears these sayings of Mine, and does not do them, will be like a foolish man who built his house on the sand: and the rain descended, the floods came, and the winds blew and beat on that house; and it fell. And great was its fall." And so it was, when Jesus had ended these sayings, that the people were astonished at His teaching, for He taught them as one having authority, and not as the scribes._"

The knowledge of BTT and spiritual warfare arms one for the fight of the war campaign. This knowledge offers hope to a lost and dying world. Without this knowledge, _discernment_, and BTT, one will only see the results depicted in **Figure 58** below.

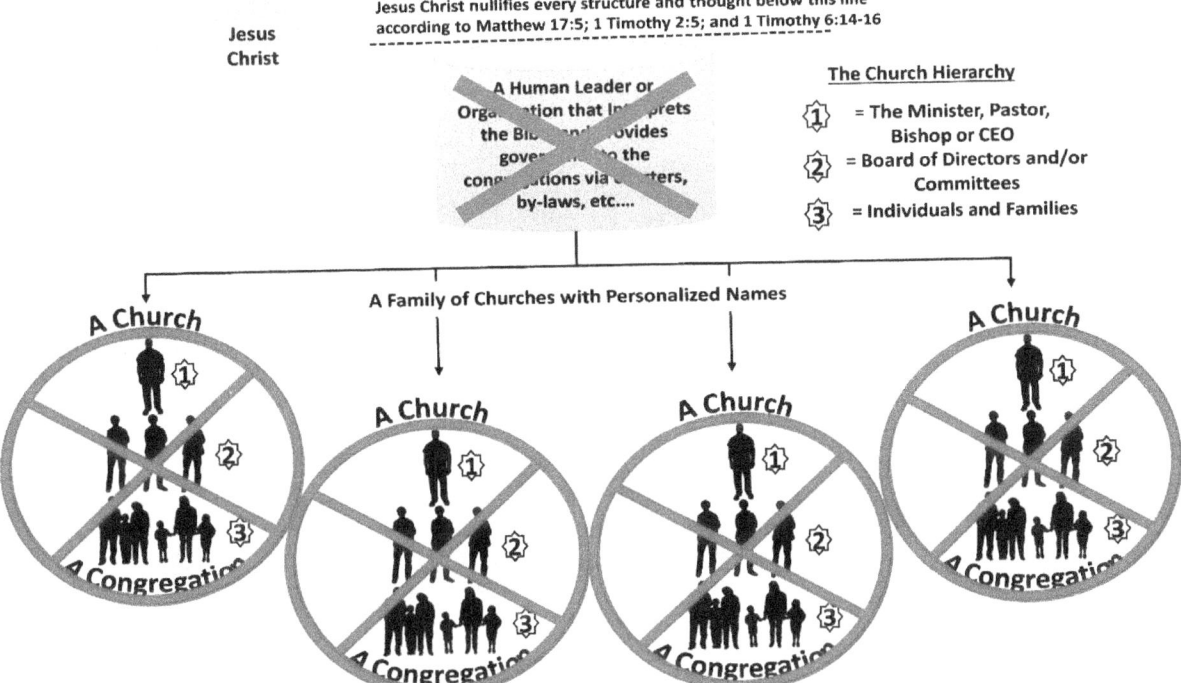

Figure 58: The Compromise of a Church

CHAPTER XIII: What Christ's <u>*Church*</u> Brings to the Positive Forces of the War Campaign

*"Finally, brethren, whatever things are true, whatever things are noble, whatever things are just, whatever things are pure, whatever things are lovely, whatever things are of **good** report, if there is any virtue and if there is anything praiseworthy—meditate on these things"*

~ Philippians 4:8 ~

What does Christ's *church* bring to the spiritual battlefield? In short, well-rounded Christians! Christians committed to God's Word who hold real solutions for resolving today's problems. Christians infused with the Gospel of Jesus Christ. Christians with the moral courage to defend the world from people consumed by the influences of the negative attributes. **Figure 59** illustrates the ***godly*** habits people in Christ's *church* are to have and the *church's* role on the spiritual battlefield in the war campaign. BTT allows one to see that the proper teaching of the Gospel inhibits the influences of the negative attributes. Inhibiting these attributes allow real and effective solutions to advance on the spiritual battlefield. Proper teaching of the Gospel

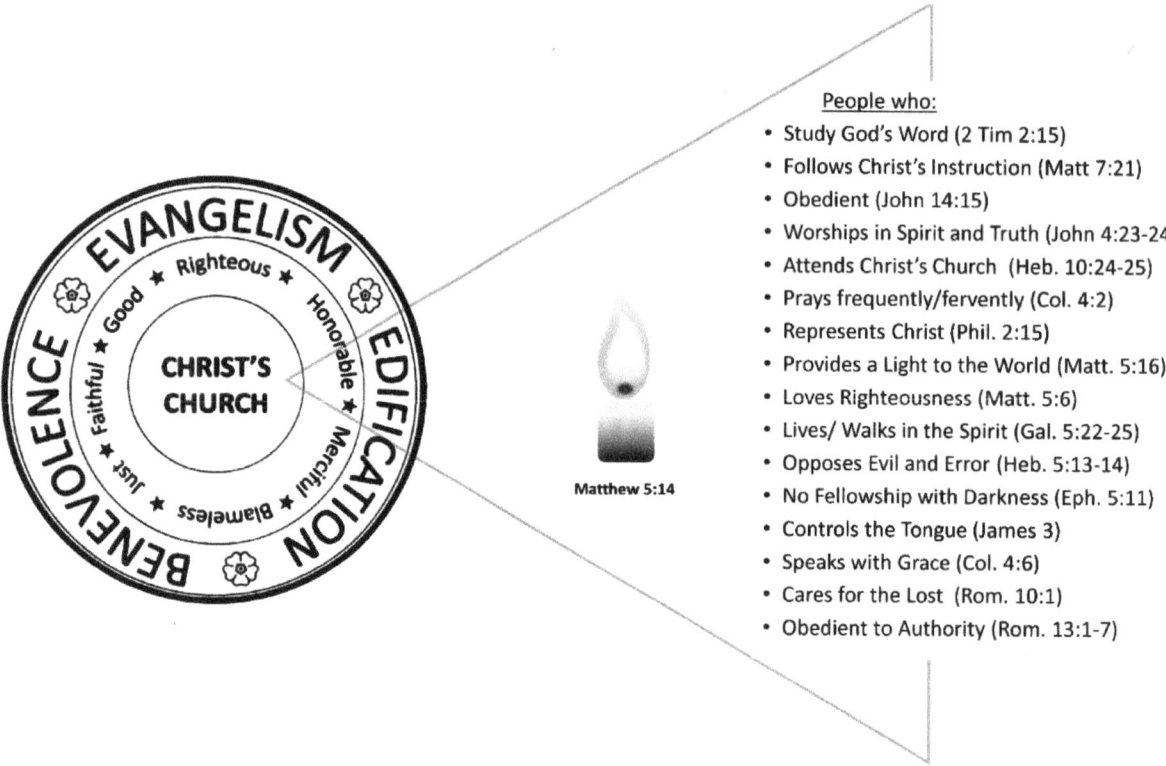

Figure 59: The Role of Christ's Church on the Spiritual Battlefield

provides people worldwide with the necessary tools for lifting up others from worldly depression by empowering their inner spirits with a sense of purpose, a willingness to achieve, and <u>*hope*</u>. The empowerment of a person's inner spirit with the Gospel of Jesus Christ allows them to be, "*the salt of the earth...*" and "*...light of the world. A city that is set on a hill cannot be hidden*" (Matthew 5:13-14). Conversely, BTT allows one to see that the negative attributes will always try to fill the spaces where God is not present. This happens when the negative attributes keep people distracted, ***false*** teachers teach, and Satan influences the lives of unsuspecting and nonbelieving people. Moreover, as each generation gets farther away from God's Truth, chaos, destruction, and lawlessness increases proportionally. From the Biblical history presented in this book, the facts are well documented and undeniable. So, let me show you God's solution.

When Christ's <u>churches</u> are fully functional and operating as God intended, His people are taught the Gospel correctly, armed with the full armor of God (Ephesians 6:10-18), and move out on the spiritual battlefield teaching the Gospel to everyone. No race, gender, nationality, or creed of people are excluded. Every person influenced by the negative attributes deserves the opportunity to hear the gospel. This includes those principalities and powers that Paul spoke of in the Book of Ephesians Chapter 6:12 where he declared, "*For we do not wrestle against flesh and blood, but against principalities, against powers, against the rulers of the darkness of this age, against spiritual hosts of **wickedness** in the heavenly places*." Christ's <u>church</u> has a very significant and strategic role. The role is documented in the same Book where Paul wrote, "*...to make all see what is the fellowship of the mystery, which from the beginning of the ages has been hidden in God who created all things through Jesus Christ; to the intent that now the manifold <u>wisdom</u> of God might be made known by the <u>church</u> to the principalities and powers in the heavenly places, according to the eternal purpose which He accomplished in Christ Jesus our Lord...*" (Ephesians 3:9-11). One can see that the <u>church</u> has the responsibility to make known the manifold <u>wisdom</u> of God to the principalities and powers even in heavenly places. This is accomplished as the gospel is taken to the principalities and powers by God's people. This wisdom speaks from the spiritual context of spiritual warfare; not physical warfare. For mankind cannot always see the impact of Christ's <u>church</u> on the battlefield when it operates and functions at full capacity. But God does!

Moreover, there is no reason to <u>*fear*</u> the principalities and powers, because God made them (John 1:3) and He knows how to handle them. The Bible even documents that, "*...by Him all things were created that are in heaven and that are on earth, visible and invisible, whether thrones or dominions or principalities or powers. All things were created through Him and for Him*" (Colossians 1:16). Then, when Jesus died on the cross, He disarmed them. The Biblical record documents, "*Having disarmed principalities and powers, He made a public spectacle of them, triumphing over them in it*" (Colossians 2:15). Thus, there is no reason to <u>*fear*</u> taking the Gospel to them, and carrying out the responsibilities of the <u>church</u>, for Paul wrote, "*Yet in all these things we are more than conquerors through Him who loved us. For I am persuaded that neither death nor life, nor angels nor principalities nor powers, nor things present nor things to come, nor height nor depth, nor any other created thing, shall be able to separate us from the love of God which is in Christ Jesus our Lord*" (Romans 8:37-39). We, as members of the body of Christ are conquerors in Christ through His <u>church</u>.

Now the Bible never claimed that the mission God gives to every Christian is easy. God knows what every Christian is up against. However, when a Christian is armed with the fruit of God's Spirit and teaches His Word, environments within the spiritual battlefield can be positively changed. Paul documented this fruit when he wrote, "...*the fruit of the Spirit is <u>love</u>, <u>joy</u>, <u>peace</u>, <u>longsuffering</u>, <u>kindness</u>, **goodness**, **faithfulnes**s, <u>gentleness</u>, <u>self-control</u>. Against such there is no law*" (Galatians 5:22-23). **Figure 60** depicts this truth as it should be.

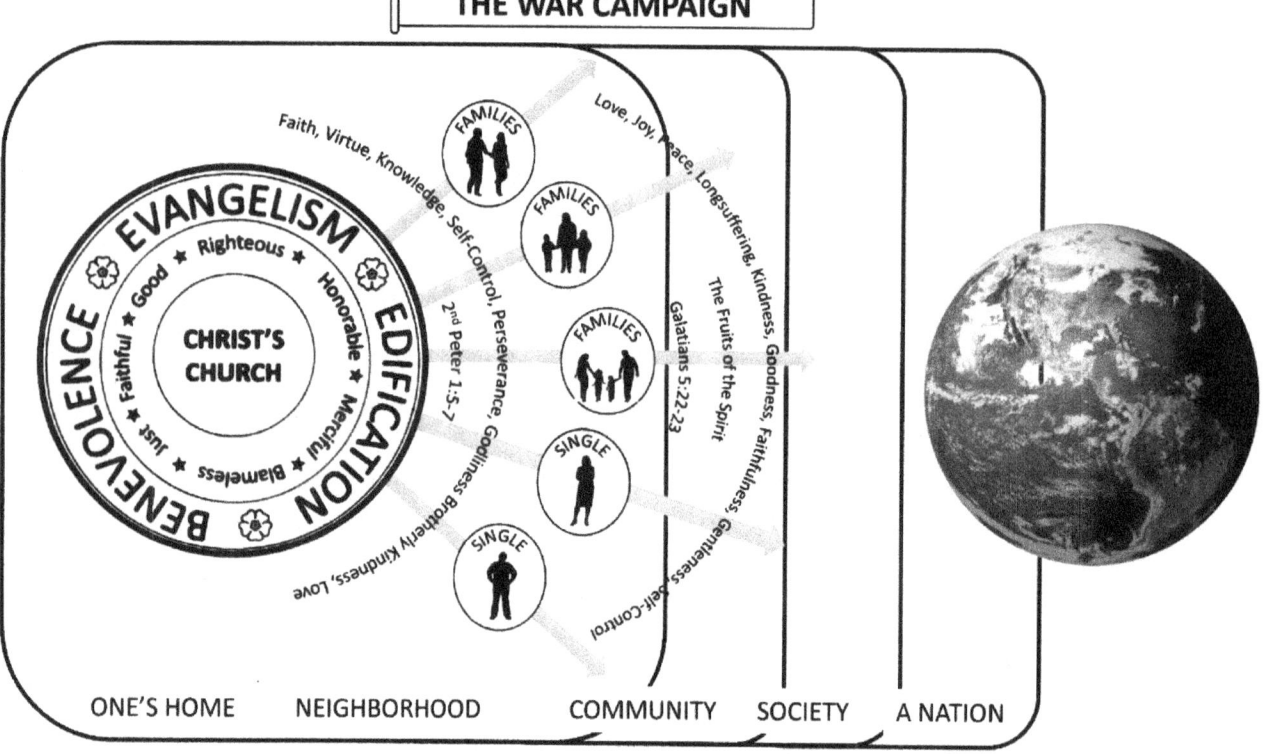

Figure 60: Church of Christ on the Spiritual Battlefield

Based on the text above, one can see that Paul identified nine Spiritual fruit. However, for the brevity of this book, I will concentrate on just three of them. I will focus on <u>peace</u>, <u>joy</u>, and <u>love</u> which are all spiritual elements; not manmade. However, BTT allows one to see that all of these spiritual elements can exist in one's inner spirit. No law or amount of human force can produce them. As for the environment effected by this fruit, the Book of Acts documents a **good** example. The Bible recorded *"Then the <u>churches</u> throughout all Judea, Galilee, and Samaria had <u>peace</u> and were edified. And walking in the <u>fear</u> of the Lord and in the <u>comfort</u> of the Holy Spirit, they were multiplied"* (Acts 9:31). One must consider that the creation of the environment came after the Gospel was properly taught:

- Among the first 3000 souls baptized into Christ in Jerusalem, the Bible documented, *"...they continued steadfastly in the apostles' doctrine and fellowship, in the breaking of bread, and in prayers. Then <u>fear</u> came upon every soul, and many wonders and signs were done through the apostles. Now all who believed were together, and had all things in common, and sold their possessions and goods, and divided them among all, as anyone had need. So continuing daily with one accord in the temple, and breaking bread from house to house, they ate their food with gladness and simplicity of heart, praising God and having favor with all the people. And the Lord added to the <u>church</u> daily those who were being saved"* (Acts 2:42-47)

- As the <u>church</u> continued to grow, "...*the multitude of those who believed were of one heart and one soul; neither did anyone say that any of the things he possessed was his own, but they had all things in common. And with great power the apostles gave* **witness** *to the resurrection of the Lord Jesus. And great <u>grace</u> was upon them all. Nor was there anyone among them who lacked; for all who were possessors of lands or houses sold them, and brought the proceeds of the things that were sold, and laid them at the apostles' feet; and they distributed to each as anyone had* **need**" (Acts 4:32-35)

- Further, "...*believers were increasingly <u>added to the Lord</u>, multitudes of both men and women, so that they brought the sick out into the streets and laid them on beds and couches, that at least the shadow of Peter passing by might fall on some of them. Also a multitude gathered from the surrounding cities to Jerusalem, bringing sick people and those who were tormented by* **unclean spirits**, *and they were all healed*" (Acts 5:14-16)

- And, "...*in those days, when the number of the disciples was multiplying, there arose a complaint against the Hebrews by the Hellenists, because their widows were neglected in the daily distribution. Then the twelve summoned the multitude of the disciples and said, "It is not desirable that we should leave the word of God and serve tables. Therefore, brethren, seek out from among you seven men of* **good** *reputation, full of the Holy Spirit and <u>wisdom</u>, whom we may appoint over this business; but we will give ourselves continually to prayer and to the ministry of the word*" (Acts 6:1-4)

- The result: "*Then the word of God spread, and the number of the disciples multiplied greatly in Jerusalem, and a great many of the priests were obedient to the* **faith**" (Acts 6:7)

BTT allows one to see that because of the Christ's <u>church</u> and the proper teaching of the Gospel, the fruit of the Spirit (<u>*peace*</u>, <u>*joy*</u>, and <u>*love*</u>) flourished and altered the balance of the spiritual battlefield. So, let us examine these three fruit a little more closely.

Beginning with the element of <u>*peace*</u>, no earthly organization can create and sustain this fruit without Christ. This element of <u>*peace*</u> comes from Christ and is not the kind of peace that man attempts to create. The Bible confirms this as Jesus told His disciples, "<u>*Peace*</u> *I leave with you,* **My** <u>*peace*</u> *I give to you; <u>not as the world gives</u> do I give to you. Let not your heart be troubled, neither let it be afraid*" (John 14:27). The unique design of Christ's <u>church</u> enables it to teach about <u>*peace*</u> from the author of <u>*peace*</u> Himself. God gave this non-negotiable responsibility for teaching on <u>*peace*</u> to His ministers and elders because <u>*peace*</u> comes from Jesus Christ. Paul documented for Christ's ministers, "*And how shall they <u>preach</u> unless they are sent? As it is written: "How beautiful are the feet of those who <u>preach the gospel of peace</u>, who bring glad tidings of* **good** *things!*" (Romans 10:15). He also documented for elders, "*And we urge you, brethren, to recognize those who labor among you, and <u>are over you in the Lord</u> and admonish you, and to esteem them very highly in <u>love</u> for their work's sake. Be at <u>peace</u> among yourselves*" (1 Thessalonians 5:12-13). When one truly recognizes the responsibility and role of the minister and the elders, one can see the application of Jesus' teaching when He said, "*Blessed are the <u>peacemakers</u>, for they shall be called sons of God*" (Matthew 5:9). These are the "initial" _peacemakers_ on the spiritual battlefield charged with bringing true and lasting _peace_ to the world with the Word of God. I say "initial" because once members of the body of Christ are prepared for the spiritual fight, they share in this responsibility too. Hence, Paul told the _church_ in Colossae, "... *let the peace of God rule in your hearts, to which also you were called in one body; and be thankful*" (Colossians 3:15).

Unfortunately, mankind has substituted politicians, ambassadors, military forces, and even police officers in the role _peacemakers_ armed only with worldly wisdom. This strategy came from _man_; not God. The _peacemaker_ of God's design follows His Word and offers **counsel** and **advice** based on ***godly*** wisdom and principles. BTT allows one to see that Christ's _church_ inherently has the tenants for _peace_. In this entity on the spiritual battlefield, the preacher serves as a _peacemaker_ by providing spiritual knowledge to the congregation. Elders are responsible for ensuring there are opportunities for the congregation to grow spiritually and mature through sound preaching. When _peacemakers_ perform their roles properly, _peace_ spreads throughout the community and the spiritual battlefield. Conversely, when people learn and embrace the element of _peace_, their homes, communities, and their societies transform as the strongholds of the negative attributes crumble. BTT allows one to see that true _peacemakers_ cause major shifts in the war campaign. They cause negative behaviors and attitudes to cease when the Gospel of _peace_ is taught correctly. Real _peace_ in spiritual warfare requires one to speak Jesus' name. Rejecting Jesus' name makes _peace_ unachievable and brings rebellion. Paul wrote to the _church_ in Colosse, "...*whatever you do in word or deed, do all in the name of the Lord Jesus, giving thanks to God the Father through Him*" (Colossians 3:17). The religious community nullifies _peace_ by rejecting Christ and replacing God's Word with their own ideas. In reality, as they preach words of _peace_ without Christ, they spread division because of their misuse of His Word.

God's _peacemakers_ are not to conform to the patterns or standards of the world. Their behavior and lifestyle are different so the world can distinguish right from wrong. Ministers and elders have the collective responsibility for ensuring that their congregations understand their examples as _peacemakers_. For every person that accepts the name of Christ also serves as a _peacemaker_ on the battlefield of the war campaign. Hence, when Peter documented, "...*you are a chosen generation, a royal priesthood, a holy nation, His own special people, that you may proclaim the praises of Him who called you out of darkness into His marvelous light...*" (1 Peter 2:9), the inherent responsibility contains the fruit of the Spirit of _peace_ within it. Christians are to represent light among a crooked and perverse generation (Philippians 2:15) by sharing the Gospel which brings _peace_ to people's inner spirits. Hence, the Bible documents:

- "...*do not be conformed to this world, but be transformed by the renewing of your mind, that you may prove what is that **good** and acceptable and perfect will of God*" (Romans 12:2)

- "*If you were of the world, the world would _love_ its own. Yet because you are not of the world, but I chose you out of the world, therefore the world **hates** you*" (John 15:19)

- "*Whoever transgresses and does not abide in the doctrine of Christ does not have God. He who abides in the doctrine of Christ has both the Father and the Son. If anyone comes to you and does not bring this doctrine, do not receive him into your house nor greet him...*" (2 John 9-10)

The _peacemaker's_ role is not easy. The more one teaches the truth, the more the negative forces retaliate in spiritual warfare. When Jesus stated, "*Do not think that I came to bring _peace_ on earth. I did not come to bring _peace_ but a sword*" (Matthew 10:34). He was not saying that He came to start a physical war with a weapon or tools of the world. No! Jesus' sword is the word of God which is, "*...living and powerful, and sharper than any two-edged sword, piercing even to the division of soul and spirit, and of joints and marrow, and is a _discerner_ of the thoughts and intents of the heart*" (Hebrews 4:12). When Jesus spoke, he brought out the effects of the sword and divided **right** from **wrong** and **good** from **evil**. His word, which is God's Word, brings spiritual _peace_ to every soul that will accept it. Inherently, some will reject His word to their own peril. Their rejection does not make God's Word untrue. The rejection just adds to division, conflict, and spiritual war. Now just so one understands Jesus, He had the power to physically defend Himself. He spoke and people "*fell to the ground*" (John 18:6) and if needed, He could command a response from, "*twelve legions of angels*" (Matthew 26:53). In addition to all this, He had control of the natural elements. The Biblical record documented that Jesus "*...arose and rebuked the wind, and said to the sea, "_Peace_, be still!" And the wind ceased and there was _a great calm_*" (Mark 4:39) which lead His disciples to exclaim, "*Who can this be, that even the wind and the sea obey Him!*" (Mark 4:41). BTT helps one to understand that Jesus simply was saying in Matthew 10:34 that the Truth that He brings from God is going to be hard for many to accept and therefore, people will fight against the Truth. Paul expressed that Jesus' Word was a spiritual sword when he talked about the "*armor of God*" and described God's Word as "*...the sword of the Spirit, which is the word of God*" (Ephesians 6:17). Thus, God's Word is metaphorically like a sword, and spiritually it is a sword, that divides the believers from the nonbelievers of God's Word and even those mishandling the Truth. God's Word, when used properly, divides **good** from **evil**. This division allows _peace_ to prevail. Worldly _wisdom_, logic and science cannot explain God's way. God said, "*For as the heavens are higher than the earth, so are My ways higher than your ways, and My thoughts than your thoughts*" (Isaiah 55:9). Thus, when people in either the religious or Christian communities advocate the use of physical weapons for _peace_, the negative attributes are involved. Move away from these people. God's way is different.

BTT allows one to understand that the spiritual element of _peace_ comes from God. The Psalmist wrote, "*The Lord will give strength to His people; the Lord will bless His people with _peace_*" (Psalm 29:11). The Bible documented in Paul's farewell comments to the _church_ in Corinth, "*...Become complete. Be of **good** comfort, be of one mind, live in _peace_; and the God of _love_ and _peace_ will be with you*" (2 Corinthians 13:11). For those who belong to Christ, one can expect that the God who created _peace_ can give _peace_ to those who recognize Him. James further stated, "*...the _wisdom_ that is from above is first pure, then peaceable, gentle, willing to yield, full of **mercy** and **good** fruits, without _partiality_ and without hypocrisy*" (James 3:17). God, who is in heaven, is willing to give us His wisdom, which is _peaceable_.

When _peacemakers_ properly teach about the fruit of the Spirit of _peace_, it works in tandem with the fruit of _joy_ and _love_ for the spiritual wellness of every individual. Paul understood this as he dealt with the sinful conditions of both the Jews and Gentiles alike. Using a series of truths from the Old Testament, Paul, documented the following statement in Romans 3:10-18:

> "...There is none **righteous**, no, not one; there is none who understands; there is none who seeks after God. They have all turned aside; they have together become unprofitable; there is none who does **good**, no, not one." "Their throat is an open tomb; with their tongues they have practiced **deceit**"; "The poison of asps is under their lips"; "Whose mouth is full of cursing and bitterness." "Their feet are swift to **shed blood**; destruction and misery are in their ways; and the way of _peace_ they have not known." "There is no _fear_ of God before their eyes."

One should see that Paul understood that until the Jews and the Gentiles acknowledged Jesus Christ, they could not receive the fruit of _peace_. Moreover, the fruit of _joy_ and _love_ would remain elusive. Without the fruit of the Spirit, their inner spirits could not achieve spiritual wellness. Both the Jews and the Gentiles alike remained in turmoil and conflict then and today. Spiritual warfare is destroying the Jewish nation and the world because of the rejection of Jesus Christ's Gospel. Nevertheless, BTT allows one to see that Christ's Gospel brings _peace_. The next series of tables simplify what Christ's _church_ teaches its members about the fruit of _peace_, _joy_, and _love_. The first table documents what Christ's _church_ teaches, trains, and prepares its members with to engage in spiritual warfare as it pertains to the application of _peace_, _joy_, and _love_:

The Gospel Teaches	Scriptures
If you _love_ those who _love_ you only, there is no reward or profit for this behavior	Matthew 5:46; Luke 6:32
One's _love_ is misdirected when one _loves_ to pray standing in places of worship or on street corners to be seen by men	Matthew 6:5
One's _love_ is misdirected when one _loves_ his or her family members over Christ	Matthew 10:37
One's _love_ is misdirected when one _loves_ the best places at fellowship meals and the best seats in places of worship	Matthew 23:6
One's _love_ is misdirected when one desires religious-looking apparel and _love_ greetings in the marketplaces just to be seen	Mark 12:38
One must _love_ his or her enemies, to do **good**, and to lend hoping for nothing in return	Luke 6:35
One's _love_ is misdirected when one cheats in their offerings to God, act **unjustly**, nor demonstrate the _love_ of God	Luke 11:42-43
There is more _joy_ in heaven over one sinner who repents than over ninety-nine **just** persons who need no repentance	Luke 15:7
There is _joy_ in the presence of the angels of God over one sinner who repents	Luke 15:10
One's _love_ is misdirected when one _loves_ the praise of men more than the praise of God	John 12:43
One must _love_ one another as Jesus has _loved_ people	John 13:34; 15:12; 15:17

When people claim to _love_ Jesus, they will keep His Word. God will _love_ them and both Jesus and God will make their home with the ones who _love_ Jesus	John 14:23
There is no greater _love_ than to lay down one's life for his friends	John 15:13
To be spiritually minded is life and _peace_	Romans 8:6
There is glory, **honor**, and _peace_ to everyone who works what is **good**	Romans 2:10
One must _love_ without hypocrisy. Abhor what is **evil**. Cling to what is **good**. Be kindly affectionate to one another with brotherly _love_, in **honor** giving preference to one another…	Romans 12:9-10
That the kingdom of God is **righteousness** and _peace_ and _joy_ in the Holy Spirit	Romans 14:17
To have _hope_ through the _patience_ and _comfort_ of the Scriptures	Romans 15:4
An understanding and sensitivity for things offered to idols: We know that we all have knowledge. Knowledge puffs up, but _love_ edifies	1 Corinthians 8:1
If one gives all their goods to feed the **poor**; damages their body, but has not _love_, it profits them nothing. _Love_ suffers long and is kind; _love_ does not **envy**; _love_ does not parade itself, is not _puffed up_	1 Corinthians 13:1-4
One must abide in **faith**, _hope_, _love_, with _love_ being the greatest of the three	1 Corinthians 13:13
Everything one does must be done with _love_	1 Corinthians 16:14
One must forgive and _comfort_ others who were scripturally disciplined, so they are not swallowed up with too much sorrow	2 Corinthians 2:7
One should give as he has purposed in his heart, not grudgingly or of necessity and know that God _loves_ a cheerful giver	2 Corinthians 9:7
One must speak the truth in _love_	Ephesians 4:14-16
One must walk in _love_	Ephesians 5:2
One must meditate on things that are _lovely_	Philippians 4:8
One must put on tender **mercies**, _kindness_, _humility_, _meekness_, _longsuffering_; bearing with one another, and forgiving one another, if anyone has a complaint against another; even as Christ forgave you, so you also must do. But above all these things put on _love_, which is the bond of perfection	Colossians 3:12-14
One must lead a quiet and _peaceable_ life in all **godliness** and reverence	1 Timothy 2:1-2
One must understand that the _love_ of money is a root of all kinds of **evil**, for which some have strayed from the **faith** in their _greediness_, and pierced themselves through with many sorrows and that one should flee these things and pursue **righteousness**, **godliness**, **faith**, _love_, _patience_, _gentleness_	1 Timothy 6:10-11
One must understand that God does not give us a spirit of _fear_ but a spirit of power, _love_, and a sound mind	2 Timothy 1:7
One must flee youthful _lusts_ and pursue **righteousness**, **faith**, _love_, _peace_ with those who call on the Lord out of a pure heart	2 Timothy 2:22
One must consider one another in order to stir up _love_ and **good** works	Hebrews 10:24
One gains an understanding of various _trials_ in one's life and why they should be counted with _joy_	James 1:2
One learns that the fruit of **righteousness** is sown in _peace_ by those who make _peace_	James 3:18

One learns that he who <u>loves</u> life and see **good** days must refrain his tongue from **evil**, his lips from speaking **deceit**, turn away from **evil** and do **good**, and seek <u>peace</u> and pursue it	1 Peter 3:8-12
One learns that above all things, one must strive to have a fervent <u>love</u> for one another, for "<u>love</u> will cover a multitude of sins"	1 Peter 4:8
One learns to add to one's **faith** virtue, to virtue knowledge, to knowledge self-control, to self-control perseverance, to perseverance **godliness**, to **godliness** brotherly kindness, and to brotherly kindness <u>love</u>. For if these things abound, one will be neither barren nor unfruitful in the knowledge of our Lord Jesus Christ	2 Peter 1:5-8
One learns that one who <u>loves</u> his brother abides in the light, and there is no cause for stumbling in him	1 John 2:10
One learns that one must <u>love</u> in deed and in truth and not in word or in tongue	1 John 3:18
One learns this is the <u>love</u> of God - that we keep His commandments. His commandments are not burdensome	1 John 5:2-3

Table 180: Applying the Elements of Peace, Joy, and Love to One's Self

BTT allows one to see that all of the things above are possible when one is taught the Gospel of Jesus Christ correctly. Paul succinctly provided this wisdom when he spoke of outfitting oneself with the armor of God in the Book of Ephesians in chapter 6:13-18. In the full reading of this portion of the Gospel, Paul stated that one must, "...*shod your feet with the preparation of the gospel of <u>peace</u>*..." (Ephesians 6:15). God's Word helps one's inner spirit to have the <u>peace</u> necessary for him or her to support others in achieving that same inner <u>peace</u>. Moreover, when one's inner spirit achieves a state of <u>peace</u>, the other fruit of the Spirit are near. Once one understands the fruit of <u>peace</u>, <u>joy</u>, and <u>love</u>, one can then teach others about them. Concerning Christ's <u>church</u> and one's personal household, one learns:

The Gospel Teaches	**Scriptures**
If one's grieves his or her brother over food choices, one is not walking in <u>love</u>. Do not destroy another person whom Christ died for over your liberties or choices	Romans 14:15
That God has called us to <u>peace</u>	1 Corinthians 7:15
To have <u>comfort</u> in all <u>tribulations</u>. For with this <u>comfort</u>, one may be able to <u>comfort</u> those who are in any trouble by the <u>comfort</u> God provides	2 Corinthians 1:3-4
That husbands are to <u>love</u> their wives just as Christ <u>loved</u> the <u>church</u> and gave Himself for her	Ephesians 5:25
That husbands ought to <u>love</u> their own wives as their own bodies for he who <u>loves</u> his wife <u>loves</u> himself	Ephesians 5:28
That wives should respect their husbands	Ephesians 5:33
That wives are to submit to their own husbands, as is fitting in the Lord. That husbands <u>love</u> their wives and not be bitter toward them. That children are to obey their parents in all things for this is well pleasing to the Lord. That fathers are not to provoke their children lest they become <u>discouraged</u>	Colossians 3:18-21

That woman will be saved in childbearing if they continue in **faith**, _love_, and **holiness**, with _self-control_	1 Timothy 2:15
That older men are to be sober, reverent, _temperate_, and sound in **faith**, in _love_, in _patience_	Titus 2:2
That older women are to teach the younger women to _love_ their husbands and to _love_ their children	Titus 2:4
That discipline is not _joyful_ when applied but it yields the _peaceable_ fruit of **righteousness** to those who have been trained by it	Hebrews 12:11
To let brotherly _love_ continue	Hebrews 13:1
That elders have a role and one must obey and be submissive to them. For they watch out for souls as those who must give account. They must be able to perform their role with _joy_; not grief. Grief is unprofitable for the one causing it.	Hebrews 13:17

Table 181: Applying the Elements of Peace, Joy, and Love in One's Home

In Christ's _church_, as the members learns _peace_, _joy_, and _love_, they are required to engage their community, society, and nation. Here is what Christ's _church_ teaches on how to engage on the broader spiritual battlefield:

The Gospel Teaches	**Scriptures**
To _love_ your enemies. Bless those who curse you. Do **good** to those who **hate** you, and pray for those who spitefully use and persecute you	Matthew 5:43-44; Luke 6:27
To _love_ the Lord your God with all your heart, with all your soul, and with all your mind. To _love_ your **neighbor** as yourself	Matthew 22:37-40; Mark 12:28-34; Luke 10:25-28
Because lawlessness abounds, the _love_ of many will grow cold	Matthew 24:12
To have _peace_ with one another	Mark 9:50
That men _love_ darkness rather than light because their deeds are **evil**	John 3:19
That _joy_ comes when the Gospel is brought to cities	Acts 8:8; Acts 15:3
To live _peaceably_ with all men (If it is possible and as much as depends on you)	Romans 12:18
That one should owe no one anything except to _love_ one another. For he who _loves_ another has fulfilled the law	Romans 13:8
To _love_ your **neighbor** as yourself. For _love_ does no harm to a **neighbor** and it is the fulfillment of the law	Romans 13:9, 10
To pursue the things which make for _peace_ and the things by which one may edify another	Romans 14:19
That "_Love_ never fails"	1 Corinthians 13:8
To have _comfort_ in all _tribulations_. For with this _comfort_, one may be able to _comfort_ those who are in any trouble by the _comfort_ God provides	2 Corinthians 1:3-4
That God _comforts_ the downcast	2 Corinthians 7:6
Not to use one's liberty as an opportunity for the flesh, but through _love_, serve one another	Galatians 5:13
To be like-minded and have the same _love_ in one accord. To esteem others better than oneself. To look out not only for one's own interests, but for the interests of others.	Philippians 2:1-4

To _comfort_ each other and edify one another	1 Thessalonians 5:11
To warn those who are unruly, _comfort_ the fainthearted, uphold the weak and be patient with all	1 Thessalonians 5:14
To turn away from people who have these qualities: lovers of themselves, lovers of money, boasters, **proud**, blasphemers, disobedient to parents, unthankful, unholy, unloving, unforgiving, slanderers, without self-control, **brutal**, despisers of **good**, traitors, headstrong, haughty, lovers of pleasure rather than lovers of God, having a form of **godliness** but denying its power	2 Timothy 3:2-5
That elders are to be hospitable. A lover of what is **good**. Sober-minded, **just**, holy, and self-controlled	Titus 1:8
To not speak **evil** of others but to be _peaceable_, gentle, and showing all **humility** to all men	Titus 3:2
To pursue _peace_ and holiness with all people without which no one will see the Lord	Hebrews 12:14
To _care_ for others	James 2:16
To **honor** all people, to _love_ the brotherhood, to _fear_ God, and to **honor** leaders at the highest level	1 Peter 2:17
To be of one mind, to have _compassion_ for one another, to _love_ as brothers, to be tenderhearted, to be courteous; and not to return **evil** for **evil** or reviling for reviling	1 Peter 3:8-9
That whoever has this world's goods and sees his brother in need, and shuts up his heart from him, does not have the _love_ of God abiding in him	1 John 3:17
That anyone that _loves_ the world or the things in the world, does not have the _love_ of the Father in him	1 John 2:15
That one who does not _love_ his brother abides in death	1 John 3:14
That God is _love_, and he who abides in _love_ abides in God, and God in him	1 John 4:16-21
That, "... _If someone says, "I love God," and **hates** his brother, he is a **liar**; for he who does not love his brother whom he has seen, how can he love God whom he has not seen? And this commandment we have from Him: that he who loves God must love his brother also_"	1 John 4:16-21
That only those who keep Christ's word will see heaven; but outside are dogs and sorcerers and **sexually immoral** and **murderers and idolaters**, and whoever _loves_ and **practices a lie**	Revelation 22:15

Table 182: Applying the Elements of Peace, Joy and Love in One's Community, Society, and the Nation

BTT allows one to see with clarity that teaching the Gospel properly satisfies the inner spirit of man. Satisfaction of one's inner spirit allows the carnal side of man to maintain control of his or her inner spirit by the knowledge and discipline of the Gospel. _Peacemakers_, through Christ's _church_, bring the proper teaching of the Gospel to the spiritual battlefield and usher in the fruit of _peace_, _joy_, and _love_. Once again, the fruit renders the influences of the negative attributes powerless in one's home, community, and society. Any person or family committed and willing to stand for the Lord can make a difference in a world lost in the fog of the negative forces of the war campaign. When individuals and families take a stand for Jesus, the influences of the negative attributes can be broken, and the balance of spiritual warfare can shift to the positive side of the campaign. BTT and *discernment* provide the keys for moving forward in a positive direction on the spiritual battlefield.

Can an entire nation find *peace*, *joy*, and *love* when the principles of BTT and *discernment* are applied? The answer is yes! The first thing one must understand is, "*God reigns over the nations; God sits on His holy throne*" (Psalm 47:8). So, God is in control. If one can accept this, then one can also understand the following references documented in the Bible:

- "*He makes nations great, and destroys them; He enlarges nations, and guides them*" (Job 12:23)

- "***Righteousness*** *exalts a nation, but sin is a reproach to any people*" (Proverbs 14:34)

- "*Blessed is the nation whose God is the Lord, the people He has chosen as His own inheritance*" (Psalms 33:12)

- "*The **wicked** shall be turned into hell, and all the nations that forget God*" (Psalm 9:17)

The challenge lies in the will of the congregations of the *churches* of Christ to go out and teach this Truth. The religious community itself must repent, **humble** itself, and teach only the Bible. The Book of 2nd Chronicles provides a good example to study on this subject. The Biblical record documented God's way verses a nation in 2 Chronicles 15:1-6. It records:

> "*Now the Spirit of God came upon Azariah the son of Oded. And he went out to meet Asa, and said to him: "Hear me, Asa, and all Judah and Benjamin. The Lord is with you while you are with Him. If you seek Him, He will be found by you; but if you forsake Him, He will forsake you. For a long time Israel has been without the true God, without a teaching priest, and without law; but when in their trouble they turned to the Lord God of Israel, and sought Him, He was found by them. And in those times there was no peace to the one who went out, nor to the one who came in, but great turmoil was on all the inhabitants of the lands. So nation was destroyed by nation, and city by city, for God troubled them with every adversity. But you, be strong and do not let your hands be weak, for your work shall be rewarded!*"

One may recall that I indicted the religious community for the majority of the problems that exists on the spiritual battlefield. I stand behind this indictment. The entire premise of this book has established and documented the consequences of spiritual blindness according to the Biblical record. Spiritual blindness occurs when God's creation either willfully chooses to ignore God or when they become spiritually ignorant because of the long-term effects of ***false*** teaching. Generationally, the world has spiritually and physically moved away from God since the flood of Noah's day. The negative attributes continue to ***deceive*** mankind by their ancient knowledge and wisdom that predates Adam and Eve. People are ***deceived*** into believing that there are other paths to eternal life or that there is nothing after this life. Many even believe there is no God or that one is his or her own god. BTT allows one to see that the negative attribute's tricks were so prolific and convincing in the past that huge numbers of prophets and priest fell to their influence. Over time, their same **lies**, which were part of the "*...wiles of the devil*" (Ephesians 6:11), were accepted by the generations of today and continue to influence religious leaders across the spiritual battlefield.

Now please understand, God does not hear the prayers of people who do not know Him nor follow His commands. For the Bible documents, "*...we know that God does not hear sinners; but if anyone is a worshiper of God and does His will, He hears him*" (John 9:31). Hence, the world continues to spiral deeper into darkness and the fog of the war campaign grows thicker each day. BTT allows one to see that the majority of people praying to God for His help are not approaching Him on His terms. This means the numerous religious organizations stretched across the spiritual battlefield claiming the name of Christ on their terms are ineffective. Their prayers are just like the **profane** fire Nadab and Abihu attempted to bring to the Lord in the Book of Leviticus. The Biblical record documented, "*...Nadab and Abihu, the sons of Aaron, each took his censer and put fire in it, put incense on it, and offered* **profane** *fire before the Lord, <u>which He had not commanded them</u>. So fire went out from the Lord and devoured them, and they died before the Lord*" (Leviticus 10:1-2). The prayers of people in the religious community are **profane** to God and whole communities are dying physically and spiritually in the war campaign. BTT allows one to see this truth heavily documented in God's written Word. God is the creator and He set the rules for how one calls upon Him. This is precisely why Paul told Timothy, "*...charge some that they teach no other doctrine, nor give heed to fables and endless genealogies, which cause disputes rather than godly edification which is in* **faith**. *Now the purpose of the commandment is <u>love</u> from a pure heart, from a* **good** *conscience, and from sincere* **faith**, *from which some, having strayed, have turned aside to* **idle** *talk, desiring to be teachers of the law, understanding neither what they say nor the things which they affirm*" (1 Timothy 1:3-7).

In case my indictment sounds harsh and unfounded, I want everyone to see what the Biblical record actually documents about the consequences of religious error and sin on the part of those entrusted with teaching God's Word. These scriptures are specific for their time but are universal in their application in spiritual warfare. Man's nature has not changed and nor have the negative influences that are driving mankind's behavior. Solomon aptly documented, "*That which has been is what will be, that which is done is what will be done, and there is nothing new under the sun. Is there anything of which it may be said, "See, this is new"? It has already been in ancient times before us. There is no remembrance of former things, nor will there be any remembrance of things that are to come by those who will come after*" (Ecclesiastes 1:9-11). Consider the Biblical references below for my indictment. Try to understand the need for strengthening Christ's <u>church</u> on the spiritual battlefield today. These references also illustrate why BTT and <u>discernment</u> are so hard to achieve. The Bible documents:

Who	What Was Said
Isaiah	"*Now go, write it before them on a tablet, and note it on a scroll, that it may be for time to come, forever and ever: That this is a rebellious people,* **lying** *children, children who will not hear the law of the Lord; who say to the seers, "Do not see," and to the prophets, "Do not prophesy to us* **right things**; *speak to us smooth things, prophesy* **deceits**" (Isaiah 30:8-10)

Jeremiah	*"The priests did not say, 'Where is the Lord?' And those who handle the law did not know Me; the rulers also **transgressed** against Me; the prophets prophesied by Baal, and walked after things that do not profit"* (Jeremiah 2:8)
	"And the prophets become wind, for the word is not in them. Thus shall it be done to them" (Jeremiah 5:13)
	*"Because from the least of them even to the greatest of them, everyone is given to <u>covetousness</u>; and from the prophet even to the priest, everyone deals **falsely**"* (Jeremiah 6:13; Jeremiah 8:10)
Jeremiah	*"Then the Lord said to me, "Do not pray for this people, for their **good**. When they fast, I will not hear their cry; and when they offer burnt offering and grain offering, I will not accept them. But I will consume them by the sword, by the famine, and by the pestilence." Then I said, "Ah, Lord God! Behold, the prophets say to them, 'You shall not see the sword, nor shall you have famine, but I will give you assured <u>peace</u> in this place.'" And the Lord said to me, "The prophets prophesy **lies** in My name. I have not sent them, commanded them, nor spoken to them; they prophesy to you a **false** vision, divination, a worthless thing, and the **deceit** of their heart"* Jeremiah 14:11-14)
	*"Therefore thus says the Lord concerning the prophets who prophesy in My name, whom I did not send, and who say, 'Sword and famine shall not be in this land'—'By sword and famine those prophets shall be consumed! And the people to whom they prophesy shall be cast out in the streets of Jerusalem because of the famine and the sword; they will have no one to bury them—them nor their wives, their sons nor their daughters—for I will pour their **wickedness** on them.'"* (Jeremiah 14:15-16)
	*"My heart within me is broken because of the prophets; all my bones shake... For both prophet and priest are **profane**; yes, in My house I have found their **wickedness**,"* says the Lord. *"Therefore their way shall be to them like slippery ways; in the darkness they shall be driven on and fall in them; for <u>I will bring disaster</u> on them, the year of their punishment," says the Lord"* (Jeremiah 23:9-12)
	*"And I have seen **folly** in the prophets of Samaria: They prophesied by Baal and caused My people Israel to err. Also I have seen a horrible thing in the prophets of Jerusalem: They commit **adultery** and walk in **lies**; they also strengthen the hands of **evildoers**, so that no one turns back from his **wickedness**. All of them are like Sodom to Me, and her inhabitants like Gomorrah. "Therefore thus says the Lord of hosts concerning the prophets: 'Behold, I will feed them with wormwood, and make them drink the water of gall; for from the prophets of Jerusalem profaneness has gone out into all the land.'"* (Jeremiah 23:13-15)
	*Thus says the Lord of hosts: "Do not listen to the words of the prophets who prophesy to you. They make you worthless; they speak a vision of their own heart, not from the mouth of the Lord. They continually say to those who despise Me, 'The Lord has said, "You shall have <u>peace</u>"'; and to everyone who walks according to the dictates of his own heart, they say, 'No **evil** shall come upon you.'" For who has stood in the **counsel** of the Lord, and has perceived and heard His word? Who has marked His word and heard*

	*it? Behold, a <u>whirlwind</u> of the Lord has gone forth in fury—a **violent** <u>whirlwind</u>!"* (Jeremiah 23:16-20)
	*"I have not sent these prophets, yet they ran. I have not spoken to them, yet they prophesied. But if they had stood in My **counsel**, and had caused My people to hear My words, then they would have turned them from their **evil** way and from the **evil** of their doings.* (Jeremiah 23:21-22)
	*"I have heard what the prophets have said who prophesy **lies** in My name, saying, 'I have dreamed, I have dreamed!' How long will this be in the heart of the prophets who prophesy **lies**? Indeed they are prophets of the **deceit** of their own heart, who try to make My people forget My name by their dreams which everyone tells his **neighbor**, as their fathers forgot My name for Baal. "The prophet who has a dream, let him tell a dream; and he who has My word, let him speak My word **faithfully**..."* (Jeremiah 23:25-28)
	*"Therefore behold, I am against the prophets," says the Lord, "who steal My words every one from his **neighbor**. Behold, I am against the prophets," says the Lord, "who use their tongues and say, 'He says.' Behold, I am against those who prophesy **false** dreams," says the Lord, "and tell them, and cause My people to err by their **lies** and by their **recklessness**. Yet I did not send them or command them; therefore they shall not profit this people at all," says the Lord.* (Jeremiah 23:30-32)
	*"And as for the prophet and the priest and the people who say, 'The oracle of the Lord!' I will even punish that man and his house. Thus every one of you shall say to his **neighbor**, and every one to his brother, 'What has the Lord answered?' and, 'What has the Lord spoken?' And the oracle of the Lord you shall mention no more. For every man's word will be his oracle, for you have **perverted** the words of the living God, the Lord of hosts, our God"* (Jeremiah 23:34-36)
Lamentations	*"Your prophets have seen for you **false** and **deceptive** visions; they have not uncovered your iniquity, to bring back your captives, but have envisioned for you **false** prophecies and delusions"* (Lamentations 2:14)
	*"The kings of the earth, and all inhabitants of the world, would not have believed that the adversary and the enemy could enter the gates of Jerusalem—because of the sins of her prophets and the iniquities of her priests, who **shed** in her midst the **blood of the just**"* (Lamentations 4: 12-13)
Ezekiel	*"...Son of man, prophesy against the prophets of Israel who prophesy, and say to those who prophesy out of their own heart, 'Hear the word of the Lord!'" Thus says the Lord God: "Woe to the **foolish** prophets, who follow their own spirit and have seen nothing! O Israel, your prophets are like foxes in the deserts.* (Ezekiel 13:1-4)
	*They have envisioned **futility** and **false** divination, saying, 'Thus says the Lord!' But the Lord has not sent them; yet they hope that the word may be confirmed.* (Ezekiel 13:6)
	*"Therefore thus says the Lord God: "Because you have **spoken nonsense** and **envisioned lies**, therefore I am indeed against you," says the Lord God. "My hand will be against the prophets who **envision futility** and who **divine lies**; they shall not be in the assembly of My people, nor be written in the record of the house of Israel, nor shall they enter into the land of Israel. Then you shall know that I am the Lord God. "Because, indeed,*

	*because they have **seduced** My people, saying, 'Peace!' when there is no peace..."* (Ezekiel 13:8-10)
	*"...The conspiracy of her prophets in her midst is like a roaring lion tearing the prey; they have devoured people; they have taken treasure and precious things; they have made many widows in her midst. Her priests have violated My law and **profaned** My holy things; they have not distinguished between the **holy** and **unholy**, nor have they made known the difference between the **unclean** and the **clean**; and they have hidden their eyes from My Sabbaths, so that I am **profaned** among them"* (Ezekiel 22:25-26)
	*Her prophets plastered them with untempered mortar, seeing **false visions**, and **divining lies** for them, saying, 'Thus says the Lord God,' when the Lord had not spoken"* (Ezekiel 22:28)
Zephaniah	*"Her prophets are **insolent, treacherous** people; her priests have **polluted the sanctuary**, they have done **violence** to the law"* (Zephaniah 3:3-4)
Matthew	*"And Jesus answered and said to them: "Take heed that no one **deceives** you. For many will come in My name, saying, 'I am the Christ,' and will **deceive** many"* (Matthew 24:4-5)
Matthew, Mark	*"For **false** christs and **false** prophets will rise and show great signs and wonders to **deceive**, if possible, even the elect"* (Matthew 24:24; Mark 13:22)
Paul	On the island to Paphos, a certain sorcerer, a ***false*** prophet, a Jew whose name was Bar-Jesus, was there. *"This man called for Barnabas and Saul and sought to hear the word of God. But Elymas the sorcerer (for so his name is translated) withstood them, seeking to turn the proconsul away from the **faith**"* (Acts 13:6-8)
	"If anyone thinks himself to be a prophet or spiritual, let him acknowledge that the things which I write to you are the commandments of the Lord" (1 Corinthians 14:37)
	*"Now the Spirit expressly says that in latter times some will depart from the **faith**, giving heed to **deceiving spirits** and doctrines of demons, speaking **lies** in hypocrisy, having their own conscience seared with a hot iron, forbidding to marry, and commanding to abstain from foods which God created to be received with thanksgiving by those who believe and know the truth. For every creature of God is **good**, and nothing is to be refused if it is received with thanksgiving; for it is sanctified by the word of God and prayer"* (1 Timothy 4:1-5)
Peter	*"But there were also **false** prophets among the people, even as there will be **false** teachers among you, who will secretly bring in destructive heresies, even **denying** the Lord who bought them, and bring on themselves swift destruction. And many will follow their destructive ways, because of whom the way of truth will be blasphemed. By covetousness they will exploit you with **deceptive** words; for a long time their judgment has not been **idle**, and their destruction does not slumber"* (2 Peter 2:1-3)
	False Teachers *"...and especially those who walk according to the flesh in the lust of **uncleanness** and despise authority. They are presumptuous, self-willed. They are not afraid to speak **evil** of dignitaries, whereas angels, who are greater in power and might, do not bring a reviling accusation*

	*against them before the Lord. But these, like natural brute beasts made to be caught and destroyed, speak **evil** of the things they do not understand, and will utterly perish in their own corruption, and will receive the wages of **unrighteousness**, as those who count it pleasure to carouse in the daytime. They are spots and blemishes, carousing in their own **deceptions** while they feast with you, having eyes full of **adultery** and that cannot cease from sin, **enticing** unstable souls. They have a heart trained in <u>covetous</u> practices, and are accursed children. They have forsaken the **right** way and gone astray…"* (2 Peter 2:10-14)
	*"These are wells without water, clouds carried by a tempest, for whom is reserved the blackness of darkness forever. For when they speak great swelling words of emptiness, they allure through the <u>lusts</u> of the flesh, through **lewdness**, the ones who have actually escaped from those who live in error. While they promise them liberty, they themselves are slaves of corruption; for by whom a person is overcome, by him also he is brought into bondage"* (2 Peter 2:17-19)
John	*"Beloved, do not believe every spirit, but test the spirits, whether they are of God; because many **false** prophets have gone out into the world"* (1 John 4:1)
	*"And I saw three **unclean spirits** like frogs coming out of the mouth of the dragon, out of the mouth of the beast, and out of the mouth of the **false** prophet"* (Revelation 16:13)

Table 183: Why BTT and <u>Discernment</u> are so Hard to Achieve

The Bible rightly documents from the Lord that, *"My people are destroyed for lack of knowledge…"* (Hosea 4:6). This applies today for all who ignore the divine source of information from God. BTT allows one to see that the current state of negative affairs can change in committed locations of the spiritual battlefield where fervent prayer, positive behavior, and love for one's **neighbor** is dominant. Just as Solomon learned and understood God's conditions for His <u>love</u>; we must also. One must remember that God told Solomon, *"…walk in My ways, to keep My statutes and My commandments, as your father David walked, then I will lengthen your days"* (1 Kings 3:14). If we commit to God by His terms, we too, can be granted the time to fix the issues of our lifetime at least for our children. We must be obedient to God's Word and submit to the teachings found in His <u>church</u>. BTT provides the clarity for this and all the rewards that come afterwards.

I have done my best to explain BTT, <u>discernment</u>, and to clarify the unseen forces at work in the world today. I have defined spiritual warfare and laid out the war campaign that is currently consuming the world and stands at our doorstep. Conversely, I have laid out Biblically what is required to break the cycle of **violence**, <u>chaos</u>, and <u>strife</u> plaguing our souls and the generations to come. Now it is up to you to choose. The prophet Jeremiah documented, *"The prophets prophesy **falsely**, and the priests rule by their own power; and My people <u>love</u> to have it so. But what will **you** do in the end?"* (Jeremiah 5:31). Please do not allow the negative attributes and spiritual warfare to bury you in the fog of the spiritual battle. Meditate on all the documentation presented. Remember, Paul stated, *"For we do not wrestle against flesh and blood, but against principalities, against powers, against the rulers of the darkness of this age, against spiritual hosts of **wickedness** in the heavenly places"* (Ephesians 6:12). Paul provided clear insight into the spiritual battle between the positive and negative attributes by inspiration of the Holy Spirit. All one needs to do is believe what God has provided humanity – that is – the Bible; a complete battle plan.

CHAPTER XIV: Conclusion: A Call for Leaders

"...if we live, we live to the Lord; and if we die, we die to the Lord. Therefore, whether we live or die, we are the Lord's"

~ Romans 14:8 ~

The current path that humanity is on is destroying families, communities, and nations. The lack of civility, ***immoral*** behavior, and ***perversion*** of God's Word have reached epic levels. Clearly, the spiritual warfare identified in the Biblical record is real and the fight between the positive and negative forces of this war has intensified. As the world rejects God and His Word, proportionally the negative forces gain ground by destroying everything that one can meditate on that is <u>true, **noble**, **just**, pure, lovely, of **good** report, virtuous and praiseworthy</u> in accordance with Philippians 4:8. As the spirit of ***wickedness*** influences leaders of governments, businesses, and religions, the <u>strife</u> producing attributes (the ***scoffer***, ***talebearer***, ***proud***, ***hater***, ***liar***, ***angry***, ***furious***, and ***violent***) are taking chaos and ***violence*** to increasing levels of severity on the spiritual battlefield. Thus, as each day's battle intensifies, more and more people are lost to the fog generated by the negative attributes. Moreover, God's <u>calamity</u> continues to purge His <u>church</u> while He demonstrates His power to get the attention of religious and secular communities alike. God's <u>calamity</u>, in ways we cannot fathom, continues to maintain the balance of the war campaign until His Son, Jesus Christ, returns to permanently end the war.

Now one might ask why purge the <u>church</u>? There are two reasons for this. First, Jesus is coming back for His <u>church</u> and it must be in a holy and pure state. The Biblical record documents, *"...Christ also loved the <u>church</u> and gave Himself for her, that He might sanctify and cleanse her with the washing of water by the word, that He might present her to Himself a glorious <u>church</u>, not having spot or wrinkle or any such thing, but that she should be holy and without blemish"* (Ephesians 5:25-27). Second, until He returns, an ***unclean*** <u>church</u> cannot fight in spiritual warfare and be expected to defeat the negative attributes while influenced by ***unclean spirits***. That's like asking Satan to police his own actions.

The Lord has provided what one needs to know about spiritual warfare and the war campaign described in the Bible. The Psalmist wrote, *"Blessed is the man who walks not in the **counsel** of the **ungodly**, nor stands in the path of sinners, nor sits in the seat of the **scornful**; but his delight is in the law of the Lord, and in His law he meditates day and night"* (Psalm 1:1-2). While on earth, Jesus taught the wisdom of God to His apostles. The apostles, by the help of the Holy Spirit, documented and taught the same knowledge to the world. Someone will always say that there must be more to "it" than this. Well, that someone would be right from the standpoint that John wrote, *"...there are also many other things that Jesus did, which if they were written one by one, I suppose that even the world itself could not contain the books that would be written. Amen"* (John 21:25). However, this is where the ***faith*** attribute comes into play. For if one's ideas about what one thinks should be in the Bible did not make it into the Bible, then it is not necessary. The Holy Spirit working through Peter led him to write, *"...His divine power has given to us **all** things that pertain to <u>life</u> and **godliness**..."* (2 Peter 1:3). Thus, the Bible provides everything one needs for salvation and surviving spiritual warfare. In fact, Jesus even said, *"I spoke openly to the world. I always taught in synagogues and in the temple, where the Jews always meet, and in secret I have said nothing"* (John 18:20). I choose to believe the Son of God in this matter. Before Jesus left the earth, He told His disciples about the *"... Helper, the Holy Spirit, whom the Father will send in My name, He will teach you all things, and bring to your remembrance all things that I said to you"* (John 14:26). The Holy Spirit continues to help everyone who has come to Christ on His terms. For the Biblical record documented, *"...the Spirit also helps in our weaknesses. For we do not know what we should pray for as we ought, but the Spirit Himself makes intercession for us with groanings which cannot be uttered. Now He who searches the hearts knows what the mind of the Spirit is, because He makes intercession for the saints according to the <u>will of God</u>. And we know that all things work together for **good** to those who <u>love</u> God, to those who are the called according to His purpose"* (Romans 8:26-28). When Christians fully embrace this knowledge, congregations within Christ's <u>church</u> will have a major impact on the spiritual battlefield and the war campaign.

In spiritual warfare, the home is ground zero for the spiritual fight. Every man and woman must prepare themselves to survive the war campaign. This begins with understanding who the true enemy is and preparing oneself for the truth fight. Hence, one must seek the Source that provides the knowledge one needs. The Bible is the only Source for understanding this form of warfare. Moreover, within this Book one learns of the positive attributes **(Figure 61)** and gains the <u>wisdom</u> to fight the spiritual fight. Without the <u>wisdom</u> of the Source Book, the Spirit of wisdom explained to Solomon that *"The way of the **wicked** is like darkness; they do not know what makes them stumble"* (Proverb 4:19). The truth of this statement helps one put spiritual warfare in its proper perspective.

Figure 61 The Positive Attributes

Unfortunately, when **good** people lose their way in the fog, they do major damage on the spiritual battlefield by following their own self-righteous wisdom. They follow the path similar to Balaam who ran **greedily** in error for profit (Jude 1:11) and *"...loved the wages of **unrighteousness**"* (2 Peter 2:15). When corruption by the negative attributes influence leaders, most people following them will walk a similar path. Their environments eventually become toxic and a nesting place for the negative forces.

In order to affect the current destructive trajectory of the world's behavior, change must begin with the people going to churches across the spiritual battlefield and their choice of leadership in and outside the church. The world today needs leaders like Daniel of the Old Testament. The Biblical record documented, *"...this Daniel distinguished himself above the governors and satraps, because an* **excellent spirit** *was in him; and the king gave thought to setting him over the whole realm"* (Daniel 6:3). Leaders with an "**excellent spirit**" have a healthy *respect* and *fear* of God that enables them to change the direction of the war campaign toward a positive path. *Fear* and *respect* are two completely different spiritual elements that are poorly taught today. With *respect*, a leader **honors** the Almighty God and esteems His Word in such a way that it permeates his or her character and is reflected in his or her behavior. They obey what God's Word says. They treat all people equally with dignity and respect, and without *discrimination*, *prejudice*, and *partiality*. *Fear* on the other hand, keeps leaders from crossing the boundaries that the Almighty God has established by His Word. Leaders who *fear* the Lord understand, "*It is a fearful thing to fall into the hands of the living God*" (Hebrews 10:31) and appreciate James's comment that, "*You believe that there is one God. You do well. Even the demons believe—and tremble!*" (James 2:19). If demons believe and tremble, so should every leader that desires to do what is **right**. But sadly today, many leaders have no *fear* or *respect* for God and treat people accordingly. The leaders that God desires understand this and they desire to be God's warriors on the spiritual battlefield. These leaders understand Paul's statement given by inspiration of the Holy Spirit that says, "*...the things that you have heard from me among many witnesses, commit these to* **faithful** *men who will be able to teach others also. You therefore must endure hardship as a* **good** *soldier of Jesus Christ. No one engaged in warfare entangles himself with the affairs of this life, that he may please him who enlisted him as a soldier. And also if anyone competes in athletics, he is not crowned unless he competes according to the rules*" (2 Timothy 2:2-5).

Only leaders with the prerequisite of God's Holy Word are capable of leading the positive forces of the war campaign to make lasting changes necessary for *peace* and order on the spiritual battlefield. God's Word, through His *church*, can eliminate *strife* and soothe God's *calamity* plaguing the world. **Godly** *fear* of the Lord brings *respect* for His deity and authority. Moreover, the *fear* of the Lord provides the opportunity for the first measure of BTT to occur and eventually salvation **if** one's heart is sincere. Even in the physical warfare, *fear* and *respect* of one's enemy, mixed with discipline, helps one to survive the battles he or she faces. Why? Because these elements minimize mistakes on the battlefield by encouraging caution; not hasty actions or decisions. The enemy needs only one mistake from his or her foe to gain the advantage. Consider these critical pearls of wisdom. The *fear* of the Lord:

- "*...is the beginning of knowledge, but* **fools** *despise wisdom and instruction*" (Proverbs 1:7)

- "*...is the beginning of wisdom, and the knowledge of the Holy One is understanding*" (Proverbs 9:10)

- "*...prolongs days, but the years of the* **wicked** *will be shortened*" (Proverbs 10:27)

- "*...is a fountain of life, to turn one away from the snares of death*" (Proverbs 14:27)

- "*...is the instruction of wisdom, and before* **honor** *is* **humility**" (Proverbs 15:33)

- "*...leads to life, and he who has it will abide in satisfaction; he will not be visited with **evil***" (Proverbs 19:23)

The world needs leaders who want to actually help the human condition on a permanent basis. This requires an acknowledgement and development of the spiritual dimension of leadership. For it is in this dimension that one can come in contact with true spiritual <u>wisdom</u> that has the solutions for the human condition.

The world needs leaders armed with BTT and <u>discernment</u> who appreciate and depend on God for solutions. Leaders whose inner spirits can perceive the spiritual force behind the behaviors of the issues at hand. These leaders understand that, "*...the word of God is living and powerful, and sharper than any two-edged sword, piercing even to the division of soul and spirit, and of joints and marrow, and is a <u>discerner</u> of the thoughts and intents of the heart. And there is no creature hidden from His sight, but all things are naked and open to the eyes of Him to whom we must give account*" (Hebrews 4:12-13). Hence, they understand that the Word of God is the only spiritual tool available in the universe that is capable of fighting spiritual warfare.

The world needs leaders who are "active" watchmen. Leaders who are willing to standup for Truth. The Old Testament of the Bible provides one an understanding and example of the watchmen's behavior. It documents:

- "*But if the watchman sees the sword coming and does not blow the trumpet, and the people are not warned, and the sword comes and takes any person from among them, he is taken away in his iniquity; but his blood I will require at the watchman's hand*" (Ezekiel 33:6)

- "*Nevertheless if you warn the **wicked** to turn from his way, and he does not turn from his way, he shall die in his iniquity; but you have delivered your soul*" (Ezekiel 33:9)

- "*I have set watchmen on your walls, O Jerusalem; they shall never hold their peace day or night. You who make mention of the Lord, do not keep silent...*" (Isaiah 62:6)

Hence, the Holy Spirit identified a fully protective compliment of armor for leaders to engage the negative forces of the war. In fact, the Holy Spirit inspired Paul to document, "*For though we walk in the flesh, we do not war according to the flesh. For the weapons of our warfare are not carnal but mighty in God for pulling down strongholds, casting down arguments and every high thing that exalts itself against the knowledge of God, bringing every thought into captivity to the obedience of Christ, and being ready to punish all disobedience when your obedience is fulfilled*" (2 Corinthians 10:3-6). Leaders must be willing to put on the spiritual armor depicted in **Figure 62** as described by Paul in the Book of Ephesians. Paul wrote in Ephesians 6:10-18:

*"Finally, my brethren, be strong in the Lord and in the power of His might. Put on the whole armor of God, that you may be able to stand against the wiles of the devil. For we do not wrestle against flesh and blood, but <u>against principalities, against powers, against the rulers of the **darkness** of this age, against spiritual hosts of **wickedness** in the heavenly places</u>. Therefore take up the whole armor of God, that you may be able to withstand in the **evil** day, and having done all, to stand. Stand therefore, having girded your waist with truth, having put on the breastplate of **righteousness**, and having shod your feet with the preparation of the gospel of <u>peace</u>; above all, taking the shield of **faith** with which you will be able to quench all the fiery darts of the wicked one. And take the helmet of salvation, and the sword of the Spirit, which is the word of God; praying always with all prayer and supplication in the Spirit, being watchful to this end with all <u>perseverance</u> and supplication for all the saints…"*

Figure 62: The Tools for Spiritual Warfare

Leaders must understand that every piece of the spiritual armor provided by the Lord has a unique purpose and capability in spiritual warfare. Here are a few examples of what can be learned about the shield of ***faith*** from the Biblical record to whet one's appetite. For example the Bible documents:

Who Said	What is Documented
The Lord told Abram	*"Do not be <u>afraid</u>, Abram. I am your **shield**, your exceedingly great reward"* (Genesis 15:1)
David said	*"The God of my strength, in whom I will trust; my **shield** and the horn of my salvation, my stronghold and my refuge; my Savior, You save me from **violence**"* (2 Samuel 22:3)
	*"As for God, His way is perfect; The word of the Lord is proven; He is a **shield** to all who trust in Him"* (2 Samuel 22:31)
	*"But You, O Lord, are a **shield** for me, my glory and the One who lifts up my head"* (Psalm 3:3)
	*"For You, O Lord, will bless the **righteous**; with favor You will surround him as with a **shield**"* (Psalm 5:12)
	*"The Lord is my rock and my fortress and my deliverer; My God, my strength, in whom I will trust; my **shield** and the horn of my salvation, my stronghold"* (Psalm 18:2)
	*"As for God, His way is perfect; the word of the Lord is proven; He is a **shield** to all who trust in Him"* (Psalm 18:30)

	"You have also given me the **shield** of Your salvation; Your right hand has held me up, Your gentleness has made me great" (Psalm 18:35)
	*"The Lord is my strength and my **shield**; my heart trusted in Him, and I am helped; Therefore my heart greatly rejoices, and with my song I will praise Him"* (Psalm 28:7)
	*"Our soul waits for the Lord; He is our help and our **shield**"* (Psalm 33:20)
	*"For the Lord God is a sun and **shield**; the Lord will give <u>grace</u> and glory; no **good** thing will He withhold from those who walk **uprightly**"* (Psalm 84:11)
	*"You are my hiding place and my **shield**; I hope in Your word"* (Psalm 119:114)
	*"...my lovingkindness and my fortress, my high tower and my deliverer, my **shield** and the One in whom I take refuge, Who subdues my people under me"* (Psalm 144:2)
Solomon said	*"He stores up sound wisdom for the **upright**; He is a **shield** to those who walk **uprightly**..."* (Proverbs 2:7)
	*"Every word of God is pure; He is a **shield** to those who put their trust in Him"* (Proverbs 30:5)

Table 184: Wisdom about the Shield of Faith

The world needs leaders who understand BTT and two other important aspects of spiritual warfare. Paul first explained what the Spirit of Wisdom meant when she revealed to Solomon, *"The <u>fear</u> of man brings a snare, but whoever trusts in the Lord shall be safe"* (Proverbs 29:25). <u>Fearing</u> other people and allowing that <u>fear</u> to prevent one from doing God's will, only leads one into a trap sooner or later. God's Word is so much stronger and He provides safety for those who do His will. There is absolutely no need to <u>fear</u> man. Followers of Christ know that *"...God has not given us a spirit of <u>fear</u>, but of power and of love and of a sound mind"* (2 Timothy 1:7). Secondly, Paul understood Jesus' Word, *"...do not <u>fear</u> those who **kill** the body but cannot **kill** the soul. But rather <u>fear</u> Him who is able to destroy both soul and body in hell"* (Matthew 10:28). BTT allows one to see that life goes on after one's earthly journey is over. The flesh we have is only for this present life. Once death comes, a new era begins for one's spirit and soul. Therefore, one's walk on earth must reflect one's desire to spend eternity with God - if that is one's goal. Paul said, *"See then that you walk circumspectly, not as **fools** but as **wise**, redeeming the time, because the days are **evil**"* (Ephesians 5:15-16). The world needs Christians and leaders who understand the circumspect walk. Their life reflects that they know the Truth of Paul's words when he stated, *"Who shall separate us from the love of Christ? Shall tribulation, or distress, or persecution, or famine, or nakedness, or peril, or sword? Yet in all these things we are more than conquerors through Him who loved us"* (Romans 8:35-37). Please do not let the fog of the negative attributes **rob** you of this Truth.

God desires leaders who understand that His Word provides <u>discernment</u> between **right** and **wrong**. A leader who does not desire God will never know or receive an understanding of the spiritual fight consuming the world. Leaders that desire this truth are the ones who take the necessary steps to sign the spiritual contract through <u>baptism</u> and commit to the way of Jesus Christ. Then and only then, can one be empowered with the full measure of knowledge to deal with the issues of this life through obedience and discipline to God's Word. Paul wrote, "*Beware lest anyone cheat you through philosophy and empty **deceit**, according to the tradition of men, according to the basic principles of the world, and not according to Christ*" (Colossians 2:8). The influences of the negative attributes have caused many people to err from the time of Adam and Eve. Leaders must understand this simple fact in order to effectively engage the manifestations of the negative attributes in spiritual warfare. When in doubt, one need only look to God's Word documented in the Biblical record.

God's Word and Christian leaders can make a difference in the direction of the ongoing war campaign. Without strong leaders who are willing to stand up for God's Word and teach people correctly, <u>strife</u> and <u>calamity</u> will dominate the world scene. God desires, and the world needs Christian leaders and followers who can stand and boldly state like Job, "*But He knows the way that I take; when He has tested me, I shall come forth as gold. My foot has held fast to His steps; I have kept His way and not turned aside. I have not departed from the commandment of His lips; I have treasured the words of His mouth more than my necessary food*" (Job 23:10-12). These are the people who follow Christ with the same vigor. Christian leaders are needed to lead and here is the bottom line: The reality to everything that I have documented in this book is that the war campaign will end. The question then becomes, what side of the war will you be on when it ends for you?

- Solomon knew the war would end and stated, "*For God will bring every work into judgment, including every secret thing, whether **good** or **evil**"* (Ecclesiastes 12:14).

- Paul knew it and stated, "*For the Lord Himself will descend from heaven with a shout, with the voice of an archangel, and with the trumpet of God. And the dead in Christ will rise first. Then we who are alive and remain shall be caught up together with them in the clouds to meet the Lord in the air. And thus we shall always be with the Lord*" (1 Thessalonians 4:16-17) and "*...concerning the times and the seasons, brethren, you have no need that I should write to you. For you yourselves know perfectly that the day of the Lord so comes as a **thief** in the night. For when they say, "<u>Peace</u> and safety!" then sudden destruction comes upon them, as labor pains upon a pregnant woman. And they shall not escape. But you, brethren, are not in **darkness**, so that this Day should overtake you as a **thief***" (1 Thessalonians 5:1-4).

- Peter knew it and stated "*But the day of the Lord will come as a **thief** in the night, in which the heavens will pass away with a great noise, and the elements will melt with fervent heat; both the earth and the works that are in it will be burned up. Therefore, since all these things will be dissolved, <u>what manner of persons ought you to be</u> in holy conduct and **godliness**, looking for and hastening the coming of the day of God, because of which the heavens will be dissolved, being on fire, and the elements will melt with fervent heat? Nevertheless we, according to His promise, look for new heavens and a new earth in which **righteousness** dwells. Therefore, beloved, looking forward to these things, be diligent to be found by Him in <u>peace</u>, **without spot** and **blameless**; and consider that the longsuffering of our Lord is salvation—as also our* *beloved brother Paul, according to the wisdom given to him, has written to you..."* (2 Peter 3:10-15).

- John knew it and wrote, *"Then I saw a great white throne and Him who sat on it, from whose face the earth and the heaven fled away. And there was found no place for them. And I saw the dead, small and great, standing before God, and books were opened. And another book was opened, which is the Book of Life. And the dead were judged according to their works, by the things which were written in the books. The sea gave up the dead who were in it, and Death and Hades delivered up the dead who were in them. And they were judged, each one according to his works. Then Death and Hades were cast into the lake of fire. This is the second death. And anyone not found written in the Book of Life was cast into the lake of fire"* (Revelations 20:11-15).

But most important of all, Jesus knew it and shared with the world, *"But of that day and hour no one knows, not even the angels in heaven, nor the Son, but only the Father"* (Mark 13:32; Matthew 24:36). Thus, we can only prepare for that inevitable day when the war campaign will end and all things in this life will come into judgement by Jesus Christ. Preparation starts with God's Word and obedience to it. I only pray that this book brings some understanding of spiritual warfare and the greatest war campaign ever conceived.

In closing, one must remember there is a General in-charge and a Leader of the positive forces of the war campaign. His name is Jesus Christ and the Biblical record documents:

God said of Jesus Christ:

"This is My beloved Son, in whom I am well pleased. Hear Him!" (Matthew 17:5; Mark 9:7; Luke 9:35)

Jesus said:

"For I have not spoken on My own authority; but the Father who sent Me gave Me a command, what I should say and what I should speak" (John 12:49)

"... It is written, 'Man shall not live by bread alone, but by every word that proceeds from the mouth of God'" (Matthew 4:4)

*"You are the light of the world. A city that is set on a hill cannot be hidden. Let your light so shine before men, that they may see your **good** works and glorify your Father in heaven"* (Matthew 5:14-16)

"Are not five sparrows sold for two copper coins? And not one of them is forgotten before God. But the very hairs of your head are all numbered. Do not <u>fear</u> therefore; you are of more value than many sparrows" (Luke 12:6-7)

*"For everyone practicing **evil hates** the light and does not come to the light, lest his deeds should be exposed. But he who does the truth comes to the light, that his deeds may be clearly seen, that they have been done in God"* (John 3:20-21)

"I am the light of the world. He who follows Me shall not walk in darkness, but have the light of life"" (John 8:12)

"I am the resurrection and the life. He who believes in Me, though he may die, he shall live" (John 11:25)

"I am the way, the truth, and the life. No one comes to the Father except through Me" (John 14:6)

John documented for the followers of Christ:

"And we have seen and testify that the Father has sent the Son as Savior of the world" (1 John 4:14)

To all my Christian family and those who are of Christ's <u>church</u> worldwide, I want to encourage you to keep up the **good** fight. Remember, Paul told us, *"You therefore must endure hardship as a **good** soldier of Jesus Christ. No one engaged in warfare entangles himself with the affairs of this life, that he may please him who enlisted him as a soldier"* (2 Timothy 2:3-4). If we endure in this war and remain ***faithful***, we will please our True Commander and Chief and gain a crown in the end according to Revelation 2:10. A Christian leader's standard is God's Word and he or she knows that they *"Repay no one **evil** for **evil**. Have regard for **good** things in the sight of all men. If it is possible, as much as depends on you, live <u>peaceably</u> with all men. Beloved, do not avenge yourselves, but rather give place to wrath; for it is written, "Vengeance is Mine, I will repay," says the Lord. Therefore If your enemy is hungry, feed him; if he is thirsty, give him a drink; for in so doing you will heap coals of fire on his head. Do not be overcome by **evil**, but overcome **evil** with **good**"* (Romans 12:17-21).

From the Old Testament to the New, God desires leaders who will stand up for His Truth. Here are some of the basic tenants God desires for His leaders and watchmen to know and find encouragement until their part in the war campaign ends. Consider these final pearls of wisdom:

*"I will both lie down in <u>peace</u>, and sleep; for You alone, O Lord, make me dwell in **safety**"* (Psalm 4:8)	*"As for God, His way is perfect; the word of the Lord is proven; He is a shield to all who trust in Him"* (Psalm 18:30)	*"I have set the Lord always before me; because He is at my right hand I shall not be moved"* (Psalm 16:8)
*"A **good** man deals graciously and lends; he will guide his affairs with discretion"* (Psalm 112:5)	*"In God (I will praise His word), in God I have put my trust; I will not <u>fear</u>. What can flesh do to me?"* (Psalm 56:4)	*"The entrance of Your words gives light; it gives understanding to the simple"* (Psalm 119:130).
*"The <u>fear</u> of man brings a snare, but whoever trusts in the LORD shall be **safe**"* (Proverbs 29:25)	*"I have chosen the way of truth; Your judgments I have laid before me"* (Psalm 119:30)	*"I will never forget Your precepts, for by them You have given me life"* (Psalm 119:93)

"The entirety of Your word is truth, and every one of Your **righteous** judgments endures forever" (Psalm 119:160)	"The <u>fear</u> of the LORD is the beginning of wisdom, and the knowledge of the Holy One is understanding" (Proverbs 9:10)	"A man has joy by the answer of his mouth, and a word spoken in due season, how good it is!" (Proverbs 15:23)
"Wait on the Lord; be of **good** courage, and He shall strengthen your heart; wait, I say, on the Lord!" (Psalms 27:14)	"For you, brethren, have been called to liberty; only do not use liberty as an opportunity for the flesh, but through <u>love</u> serve one another" (Galatians 5:13)	"Who is **wise** and understanding among you? Let him show by **good** <u>conduct</u> that his works are done in the meekness of wisdom" (James 3:13)
"Or do you not know that your body is the temple of the Holy Spirit who is in you, whom you have from God, and you are not your own? For you were bought at a price; therefore glorify God in your body and in your spirit, which are God's" (1 Corinthians 6:19-20)	"Be sober, be vigilant; because your adversary the devil walks about like a roaring lion, seeking whom he may devour. Resist him, <u>steadfast</u> in the **faith**, knowing that the same <u>sufferings</u> are experienced by your brotherhood in the world" (1 Peter 5:8-9)	"Do not be **deceived**, God is not **mocked**; for whatever a man sows, that he will also reap. For he who sows to his flesh will of the flesh reap corruption, but he who sows to the Spirit will of the Spirit reap everlasting life" (Galatians 6:7-8)
"But "he who glories, let him glory in the Lord." For not he who commends himself is approved, but whom the Lord commends" (2 Corinthians 10:17-18)	"Brethren, if a man is overtaken in any trespass, you who are spiritual restore such a one in a spirit of gentleness, considering yourself lest you also be tempted" (Galatians 6:1)	"Ah, Lord God! Behold, You have made the heavens and the earth by Your great power and outstretched arm. There is nothing too hard for You" (Jeremiah 32:17)
"But the **mercy** of the Lord is from everlasting to everlasting on those who <u>fear</u> Him, and His **righteousness** to children's children, to such as keep His covenant, and to those who remember His commandments to do them" (Psalm 103:17-18)	"Wash yourselves, make yourselves clean; put away the **evil** of your doings from before My eyes. Cease to do **evil**, learn to do **good**; seek justice, rebuke the **oppressor**; defend the <u>fatherless</u>, plead for the <u>widow</u>" (Isaiah 1:16-17)	"For everyone practicing **evil hates** the light and does not come to the light, lest his deeds should be exposed. But he who does the truth comes to the light, that his deeds may be clearly seen, that they have been done in God" (John 3:20-21)
"Let no corrupt word proceed out of your mouth, but what is **good** for necessary edification, that it may impart <u>grace</u> to the hearers" (Ephesians 4:29)	"And whatever you do in word or deed, do all in the name of the Lord Jesus, giving thanks to God the Father through Him" (Colossians 3:17)	"But the Lord is **faithful**, who will establish you and guard you from the **evil** one" (2 Thessalonians 3:3)
"Let nothing be done through selfish ambition or conceit, but in lowliness of mind let each esteem others better than himself. Let each	"For the grace of God that brings salvation has appeared to all men, teaching us that, denying **ungodliness** and worldly	"For we know Him who said, "Vengeance is Mine, I will repay," says the Lord. And again, "The Lord will judge His people. It is a

of you look out not only for his own interests, but also for the interests of others" (Philippians 2:3-4)	*lusts*, we should live soberly, **righteously**, and **godly** in the present age..." (Titus 2:11-12)	*fearful* thing to fall into the hands of the living God" (Hebrews 10:30-31)
"And do not be conformed to this world, but be transformed by the renewing of your mind, that you may prove what is that **good** and acceptable and *perfect will of God*" (Romans 12:2)	"We then who are strong ought to bear with the scruples of the weak, and not to please ourselves. Let each of us please his **neighbor** for his **good**, leading to edification" (Romans 15:1-2)	"For this is the will of God, that by doing **good** you may put to silence the ignorance of **foolish** men—as free, yet not using liberty as a cloak for vice, but as bondservants of God" (1 Peter 2:15-16)
	"Walk in wisdom toward those who are outside, redeeming the time. Let your speech always be with *grace*, seasoned with salt, that you may know how you ought to answer each one" (Colossians 4:5-6)	"For God has not given us a spirit of *fear*, but of power and of *love* and of a sound mind" (2 Timothy 1:7)

Table 185: Pearls of Wisdom for Encouragement

Colonel (Retired) Joseph J. Frazier

J.J. is President and Founder of Mastering The Positive, LLC; a company dedicated to improving leader's effectiveness. He blends soft skills education with inspirational/motivational speaking techniques, tactics, and methodologies to improve productivity, morale, collaboration, and communication. He employs Socratic teaching methods and experiential learning techniques in courses such as "*Leader's Communication Skills*" and "*What is Effective Leadership?*"

Prior to establishing Mastering The Positive, LLC, J.J. supported Porter House, Inc. as a consultant. He served as Curriculum Co-Chair of LEADS Hampton Roads for Hampton Roads' Chamber of Commerce, and as a Board Member of the Future of Hampton Roads Board, Inc.

As a former U.S. Army Colonel, he led organizations to achieve award-winning results. In his last senior civilian and active duty assignments, he served as the Chief of Staff, Dean of Students, and twice as Interim President of the Joint Forces Staff College, National Defense University. During this assignment, he hosted over 300 senior foreign and domestic dignitaries, Ambassadors, congressional leaders and senior officers speaking or participating at the college. During this same period, Regent University's President recognized him for his superior community leadership.

J.J. has successfully served in numerous leadership roles mentoring both civilian and military men and women throughout his 30 year career. Such roles included Deputy Chief Information Officer in Europe whose organization supplied world-class IT support customers in 92 countries and the Director of Information Management of Fort Hood, Texas where he provided all Information Technology infrastructure and networks support to customers serving the largest military installation in the free world.

J.J. has served in command and staff positions in Germany, Belgium, Kuwait, Iraq, and the United States. He served in the prestigious Eisenhower Series College Program at the Army War College and as an instructor and curriculum developer at the Joint Forces Staff College in Norfolk, Virginia. He is a graduate of the U.S. Army War College with a Master of Science in Strategic Studies; Central Michigan University with a Master of Science in Administration; the University of Georgia with a Bachelor of Science in Education; and a graduate of the Defense Strategy Course and nationally renowned Dale Carnegie Leadership Course.

He has numerous military awards and decorations to include the Defense Superior Service Medal and the Bronze Star for his leadership role during Operation Desert Shield and Desert Storm.

J.J. served as an elder in a <u>church</u> of Christ, loves teaching the Bible, and enjoys mentoring and developing future leaders for the ongoing war campaign.

J.J. is married to the former Allegra Mosley. They have a daughter, a son, a spiritually adopted daughter, and two granddaughters.

www.ingramcontent.com/pod-product-compliance
Lightning Source LLC
Chambersburg PA
CBHW081140290426
44108CB00018B/2394